LIFE SAFETY
CODE® HANDBOOK

Fourth Edition

LIFE SAFETY CODE HANDBOOK

Fourth Edition

Based on the 1988 Edition of the
Life Safety Code®

Edited by

James K. Lathrop

National Fire Protection Association, Inc.
Quincy, Massachusetts

This *Handbook* has not been processed in accordance with NFPA Regulations Governing Committee Projects. Therefore, the commentary in it shall not be considered the official position of NFPA or any of its committees and shall not be considered to be, nor relied upon as, a Formal Interpretation of the meaning or intent of any specific provision or provisions of NFPA *101*®, *Life Safety Code*®.

NFPA AX-101-HB88
ISBN: 0-87765-343-7
Library of Congress No.: 88-060165
Printed in U.S.A.

Second Printing, February 1989

Contents

Foreword   xi

Preface   xiii

Revision and Use of the *Life Safety Code*   xvii

Acknowledgments   xix

Photograph Acknowledgments   xxi

Chapter 1   Administration   1
   Section   1-1   Title   1
   Section   1-2   Purpose   1
   Section   1-3   Scope   2
   Section   1-4   Application   3
   Section   1-5   Equivalency Concepts   10
   Section   1-6   Occupancy   12
   Section   1-7   Maintenance   14

Chapter 2   Fundamental Requirements   15

Chapter 3   Definitions   19
   Section   3-1   General   19
   Section   3-2   Definitions   19

Chapter 4   Classification of Occupancy and Hazard of Contents   29
   Section   4-1   Classification of Occupancy   29
   Section   4-2   Hazard of Contents   35

Chapter 5   Means of Egress   39
   Section   5-1   General   39
   Section   5-2   Means of Egress Components   55
   Section   5-3   Capacity of Means of Egress   144
   Section   5-4   Number of Means of Egress   151
   Section   5-5   Arrangement of Means of Egress   153
   Section   5-6   Measurement of Travel Distance to Exits   167
   Section   5-7   Discharge from Exits   173
   Section   5-8   Illumination of Means of Egress   178
   Section   5-9   Emergency Lighting   180
   Section   5-10   Marking of Means of Egress   188
   Section   5-11   Special Provisions for Occupancies with High Hazard
                  Contents   195

Chapter 6   Features of Fire Protection   199
   Section   6-1   General   199
   Section   6-2   Construction and Compartmentation   199
   Section   6-3   Smoke Barriers   233
   Section   6-4   Special Hazard Protection   239
   Section   6-5   Interior Finish   240

Chapter 7   Building Service and Fire Protection Equipment   259
Section   7-1   Utilities   259
Section   7-2   Heating, Ventilating, and Air Conditioning   260
Section   7-3   Smoke Control   261
Section   7-4   Elevators, Dumbwaiters, and Vertical Conveyors   262
Section   7-5   Rubbish Chutes, Incinerators, and Laundry Chutes   265
Section   7-6   Fire Detection, Alarm, and Communications Systems   266
Section   7-7   Automatic Sprinklers and Other Extinguishing Equipment   . .   279

Chapter 8   New Assembly Occupancies   287
Section   8-1   General Requirements   288
Section   8-2   Means of Egress Requirements   304
Section   8-3   Protection   337
Section   8-4   Special Provisions   353
Section   8-5   Building Services   363

Chapter 9   Existing Assembly Occupancies   365
Section   9-1   General Requirements   366
Section   9-2   Means of Egress Requirements   381
Section   9-3   Protection   414
Section   9-4   Special Provisions   428
Section   9-5   Building Services   435

Chapter 10   New Educational Occupancies   437
Section 10-1   General Requirements   437
Section 10-2   Means of Egress Requirements   443
Section 10-3   Protection   455
Section 10-4   Special Provisions   465
Section 10-5   Building Services   467
Section 10-6   Flexible Plan and Open Plan Buildings   467
Section 10-7   Day-Care Centers   469
Section 10-8   Group Day-Care Homes   486
Section 10-9   Family Day-Care Homes   491

Chapter 11   Existing Educational Occupancies   497
Section 11-1   General Requirements   497
Section 11-2   Means of Egress Requirements   503
Section 11-3   Protection   517
Section 11-4   Special Provisions   526
Section 11-5   Building Services   526
Section 11-6   Flexible Plan and Open Plan Buildings   527
Section 11-7   Day-Care Centers   529
Section 11-8   Group Day-Care Homes   545
Section 11-9   Family Day-Care Homes   550

Chapter 12   New Health Care Occupancies   555
Section 12-1   General Requirements   555
Section 12-2   Means of Egress Requirements   571
Section 12-3   Protection   593

Section 12-4 Special Provisions 620
Section 12-5 Building Services 620
Section 12-6 New Ambulatory Health Care Centers 623

Chapter 13   Existing Health Care Occupancies 637
Section 13-1 General Requirements 637
Section 13-2 Means of Egress Requirements 654
Section 13-3 Protection 671
Section 13-4 Special Provisions 695
Section 13-5 Building Services 695
Section 13-6 Existing Ambulatory Health Care Centers 697

Chapter 14   New Detention and Correctional Occupancies 711
Section 14-1 General Requirements 711
Section 14-2 Means of Egress Requirements 724
Section 14-3 Protection 736
Section 14-4 Special Provisions 749
Section 14-5 Building Services 749

Chapter 15   Existing Detention and Correctional Occupancies 751
Section 15-1 General Requirements 751
Section 15-2 Means of Egress Requirements 764
Section 15-3 Protection 775
Section 15-4 Special Provisions 790
Section 15-5 Building Services 790

Chapter 16   New Hotels and Dormitories 793
Section 16-1 General Requirements 794
Section 16-2 Means of Egress Requirements 797
Section 16-3 Protection 806
Section 16-4 Special Provisions 813
Section 16-5 Building Services 814

Chapter 17   Existing Hotels and Dormitories 817
Section 17-1 General Requirements 818
Section 17-2 Means of Egress Requirements 821
Section 17-3 Protection 829
Section 17-4 Special Provisions 837
Section 17-5 Building Services 838

Chapter 18   New Apartment Buildings 839
Section 18-1 General Requirements 840
Section 18-2 Means of Egress Requirements 843
Section 18-3 Protection 851
Section 18-4 Special Provisions 860
Section 18-5 Building Services 860

Chapter 19   Existing Apartment Buildings 865
Section 19-1 General Requirements 866

Section 19-2   Means of Egress Requirements 869
Section 19-3   Protection 878
Section 19-4   Special Provisions 886
Section 19-5   Building Services 886

Chapter 20   Lodging or Rooming Houses 889
Section 20-1   General Requirements 889
Section 20-2   Means of Escape 891
Section 20-3   Protection 896
Section 20-4   Special Provisions 898
Section 20-5   Building Services 898

Chapter 21   Residential Board and Care Occupancies 901
Section 21-1   General Requirements 901
Section 21-2   Small Facilities 908
Section 21-3   Large Facilities 923
Section 21-4   Suitability of an Apartment Building to House a Board and
                Care Occupancy 942

Chapter 22   One- and Two-Family Dwellings 945
Section 22-1   General Requirements 945
Section 22-2   Means of Escape Requirements 947
Section 22-3   Protection 957
Section 22-4   (Reserved) 958
Section 22-5   Building Services 958

Chapter 23   (Reserved) 958

Chapter 24   New Mercantile Occupancies 959
Section 24-1   General Requirements 959
Section 24-2   Means of Egress Requirements 972
Section 24-3   Protection 985
Section 24-4   Special Provisions 989
Section 24-5   Building Services 997

Chapter 25   Existing Mercantile Occupancies 999
Section 25-1   General Requirements 999
Section 25-2   Means of Egress Requirements 1012
Section 25-3   Protection 1026
Section 25-4   Special Provisions 1030
Section 25-5   Building Services 1037

Chapter 26   New Business Occupancies 1039
Section 26-1   General Requirements 1039
Section 26-2   Means of Egress Requirements 1044
Section 26-3   Protection 1054
Section 26-4   Special Provisions 1058
Section 26-5   Building Services 1063

viii

Chapter 27   Existing Business Occupancies 1065
Section 27-1   General Requirements 1065
Section 27-2   Means of Egress Requirements 1070
Section 27-3   Protection 1081
Section 27-4   Special Provisions 1084
Section 27-5   Building Services 1087

Chapter 28   Industrial Occupancies 1089
Section 28-1   General Requirements 1090
Section 28-2   Means of Egress Requirements 1097
Section 28-3   Protection 1108
Section 28-4   Special Provisions 1112
Section 28-5   Building Services 1112

Chapter 29   Storage Occupancies 1113
Section 29-1   General Requirements 1113
Section 29-2   Means of Egress Requirements 1115
Section 29-3   Protection 1121
Section 29-4   Special Provisions 1123
Section 29-5   Building Services 1123
Section 29-6   Special Provisions for Aircraft Hangars 1123
Section 29-7   Special Provisions for Grain or Other Bulk Storage Elevators   1124
Section 29-8   Special Provisions for Parking Garages 1126

Chapter 30   Special Structures and High Rise Buildings 1133
Section 30-1   General Requirements 1133
Section 30-2   Means of Egress Requirements 1137
Section 30-3   Protection 1142
Section 30-4   Special Provisions 1143
Section 30-5   Building Services 1144
Section 30-6   Special Provisions for Vehicles and Vessels 1144
Section 30-7   Special Provisions for Underground Structures and
                  Windowless Buildings 1144
Section 30-8   High Rise Buildings 1145

Chapter 31   Operating Features 1149
Section 31-1   General Requirements 1150
Section 31-2   Assembly Occupancies 1155
Section 31-3   Educational Occupancies 1158
Section 31-4   Health Care Occupancies 1162
Section 31-5   Detention and Correctional Occupancies 1169
Section 31-6   Residential Occupancies 1170
Section 31-7   Board and Care Homes 1173
Section 31-8   Mercantile Occupancies 1173
Section 31-9   Business Occupancies 1174

Chapter 32   Referenced Publications 1175

Appendix A 1179

Appendix B Referenced Publications 1181

Cross-Reference to 1985 Edition 1185

Index 1203

Foreword

For well over half a century, the National Fire Protection Association has been the publisher of the *Life Safety Code*. Formerly known as the *Building Exits Code*, the *Code* is prepared by the NFPA Committee on Safety to Life, one of the more than 175 technical committees operating within the framework of the NFPA's standards-making activities. The Committee on Safety to Life is made up of a group of highly qualified individuals who have demonstrated knowledge and competence in the design and construction of buildings and structures, in the manufacture and testing of building components and accessories, and in the enforcement of regulations pertaining to life safety from fire and other perils encountered in buildings and structures.

The *Life Safety Code* is a unique document; its contents addresses specific requirements that have a direct influence on safety to life in both new *and* existing structures and not just in new construction alone. Then, too, although the *Code*'s paramount concern is life safety and not protection of property per se, there is, by observance of *Code* requirements, ancillary benefit to property protection.

The impact that application of the *Code* may have on saving lives is difficult to measure; however, it is reasonable to assume that its influence is extremely significant. For example, of the many fatal building fires (other than in one- and two-family dwellings) investigated by the NFPA, invariably, one or more of the factors contributing to loss of life from fire were in violation of the requirements of the *Code*.

The NFPA recognizes that a code suitable for enforcement must, by the nature of its purpose, be concise and without explanatory text. In addition, a code cannot be written to cover every situation that will be encountered; thus, it must be applied with judgment and used with good sense and with an awareness of the rationale for the requirements that must be enforced. A little help and counsel along the way make the job a lot easier; hence the reason for this *Life Safety Code Handbook*.

This *Handbook* gives users of the *Life Safety Code* background information on the reasons for certain *Code* provisions, as recalled by several members of the Committee on Safety to Life and by NFPA staff members. It also provides some suggestions, through its text and illustrations, on how some *Code* requirements can be implemented intelligently. With the availability of this kind of information, it is hoped that users of the *Code* will have a better understanding of, and appreciation for, the requirements contained in the *Code*. The net result should be buildings and structures that are more firesafe than ever. The reader is cautioned, though, to look upon the commentary that appears in the *Handbook* only as the views expressed by the contributors to the *Handbook*. The commentary does not necessarily reflect the official position of NFPA or of the Committee on Safety to Life.

The editor welcomes critiques of the commentary on *Code* requirements appearing in this Fourth Edition as well as suggestions on which other *Code* provisions should be discussed. In the sense that the *Life Safety Code* reflects a synthesis of the best efforts of a representative committee, so should the *Life Safety Code Handbook* represent the best in thought by fire protection practitioners involved with the *Code* and its requirements. It is knowledge that must be shared.

ARTHUR E. COTE, P.E.
Assistant Vice President and Chief Engineer
National Fire Protection Association

Preface

The *Life Safety Code* had its origin in the work of the Committee on Safety to Life of the National Fire Protection Association, which was appointed in 1913. For the first few years of its existence the Committee devoted its attention to a study of notable fires involving loss of life and to analyzing the causes of this loss of life. This work led to the preparation of standards for the construction of stairways, fire escapes, etc., for fire drills in various occupancies and for the construction and arrangement of exit facilities for factories, schools, etc., which form the basis of the present *Code*. These reports were adopted by the National Fire Protection Association and published in pamphlet form as "Outside Stairs for Fire Exits" (1916) and "Safeguarding Factory Workers from Fire" (1918). A pamphlet, "Exit Drills in Factories, Schools, Department Stores and Theatres," which was published in 1912 following its presentation by the late Committee member Mr. R. H. Newbern at the 1911 Annual Meeting of the Association, although antedating the organization of the Committee, was considered to have the status of a Committee publication and had been used with the other pamphlets as a groundwork for the present *Code*. These pamphlets were widely circulated and put into general use.

In 1921 the Committee was enlarged to include representation of certain interested groups not previously participating, and work was started on the further development and integration of previous Committee publications to provide a comprehensive guide to exits and related features of life safety from fire in all classes of occupancy. Known as the *Building Exits Code*, various drafts were published, circulated, and discussed over a period of years, and the first edition of the *Building Exits Code* was published by the National Fire Protection Association in 1927. Thereafter, the Committee continued its deliberations, adding new material on features not originally covered and revising various details in light of fire experience and practical experience in the use of the *Code*. New editions published in 1929, 1934, 1936, 1938, 1939, 1942, and 1946 to incorporate the amendments adopted by the National Fire Protection Association.

The Cocoanut Grove Night Club fire in Boston in 1942, in which 492 lives were lost, focused national attention upon the importance of adequate exits and related firesafety features. Public attention to exit matters was further stimulated by the series of hotel fires in 1946 (the LaSalle, Chicago — 61 dead; the Canfield, Dubuque — 19 dead; and the Winecoff, Atlanta — 119 dead). Thereafter, the *Building Exits Code* was used to an increased extent for legal regulatory purposes. However, the *Code* was not in suitable form for adoption into law, as it had been drafted as a reference document containing many advisory provisions useful to designers of buildings, but not appropriate for legal use. This led to a decision by the Committee to re-edit the entire *Code*, limiting the body of the text to requirements suitable for mandatory application and placing advisory and explanatory material in notes. The re-editing also involved adding to the *Code* provisions for many features in order to produce a complete document. Preliminary work was carried on concurrently with development of the 1948, 1949, 1951 and 1952 Editions. The results were incorporated in the 1956 Edition and further refined in subsequent editions dated 1957, 1958, 1959, 1960, 1961, and 1963.

In 1955 separate documents, NFPA 101B and NFPA 101C, were published covering nursing homes and interior finish, respectively. NFPA 101C was revised in 1956. These publications have since been withdrawn.

In 1963 the Committee on Safety to Life was reconstructed. The Committee was decreased in size to include only those individuals having very broad knowledge in fire matters and representing all interested factions. The Committee served as a review and correlating committee for seven Sectional Committees whose personnel included members having a special knowledge and interest in various portions of the *Code*.

Under the revised structure, the Sectional Committees, through the Safety to Life Committee, prepared the 1966 Edition of the *Code*, which was a complete revision of the 1963 Edition. The *Code* title was changed from *Building Exits Code* to *"Code for Safety to Life from Fire in Buildings and Structures."* The text was put in "code language," and all explanatory notes were placed in an appendix. The contents of the *Code* was arranged in the same general order as the contents of model building codes because the *Code* is used primarily as a supplement to building codes.

The *Code* was placed on a three-year revision schedule, with new editions adopted in 1967, 1970, 1973, and 1976.

In 1977 the Committee on Safety to Life was reorganized as a Technical Committee with an Executive Committee and eleven standing subcommittees responsible for various chapters and sections. The 1981 Edition contained major editorial changes, including reorganization within the occupancy chapters to make them parallel to each other and separation of requirements for new and existing buildings into individual chapters. New chapters on Detention and Correctional Facilities were added as well as new requirements for Atriums, Apartments for the Elderly, and Ambulatory Health Care Centers. The 1985 Edition contained major editorial and technical changes in Section 5-2 on Means of Egress Components, a new Chapter 21 on Residential Board and Care Occupancies with related Appendices F and G, deletion of special provisions for housing for the elderly and dormitories, a new Appendix D on Alternative Calculations for Stair Width, and Appendix E, a Firesafety Evaluation System (FSES) for Detention and Correctional Facilities.

The 1988 edition contains a major change in the method of determining egress capacity as a result of the deletion of the traditional units of exit width and the substitution of a straight linear approach to calculating egress capacity. Also, revisions to the method of measuring travel distance, the establishment of a base minimum number of means of egress, and specific requirements for remoteness of exits, as well as new provisions for amusement buildings and exhibit halls have been made. Appendices C through G have been moved from NFPA 101 into a new document, NFPA 101M, *Manual on Alternative Approaches to Life Safety.*

In all of the work in developing the various sections of the *Code*, the groups particularly concerned have been consulted. All public proposals have been reviewed, and these proposals along with Committee proposals and the Committee's response to all proposals have been published by the NFPA for review by all concerned, and any comments received have been discussed and many have been adopted by the Committee or at meetings of the NFPA. Records of the discussions and action taken by the NFPA can be found in the *Technical Committee Reports* and the *Technical Committee Documentation*.

The Committee on Safety to Life welcomes comments and suggestions on the *Life Safety Code*. Any reader may file a request for consideration of changes to the *Code*. Such requests should be filed in writing, giving specific proposals and supporting data.

JAMES K. LATHROP, Editor
Chief Life Safety Engineer
National Fire Protection Association

Revision and Use of the *Life Safety Code*

The *Life Safety Code* is revised approximately every three years. During each cycle, the Secretary of the Committee on Safety to Life accepts revision proposals from the public until an established deadline. These proposals are referred to appropriate subcommittees.

When the subcommittees meet, each proposal is considered, and some form of action is taken. A proposal may be accepted, accepted-in-part, accepted-in-principle, or rejected. This work is reviewed by the Committee on Safety to Life. Proposals and Committee actions are published in the *Technical Committee Reports* (TCR), which are distributed on request.

Following the publication of the TCR, a comment period of approximately sixty days is established. During this time, the public has the opportunity to respond to both the proposals and the Committee action. Comments must address TCR contents only; new concerns are not considered at this point in the cycle. At the closing of the comment period, the subcommittees reconvene to act on the public comments. Action on comments is similar to action on proposals and is published in the *Technical Committee Documentation* (TCD), which is distributed on request.

The content of the TCR, as amended by the TCD, forms the Committee's report to the NFPA membership. The membership votes to adopt, amend, or return the report (in whole, or in part) to the Committee for further study. When the report is adopted, the new edition of the *Life Safety Code* is published.

During the revision cycle, *Tentative Interim Amendments* (TIAs) may be approved and released by NFPA's Standards Council. TIAs are not subject to the standards-making procedure until the next successive edition of the *Code* is acted upon. Nevertheless, a TIA has the force of a mandatory requirement, but only if the local authority having jurisdiction adopts it.

The 1988 Edition of the *Life Safety Code* was adopted by the National Fire Protection Association, Inc. on November 11, 1987 at its 1987 Fall Meeting in Portland, Oregon and was issued by the Standards Council on January 13, 1988 with an effective date of February 2, 1988.

Two of the most significant changes from the 1985 Edition of the *Code* are revisions to the method of determining egress capacity and revisions to the methods of measuring travel distance. The concept of unit of exit width has been eliminated and a straight linear function for egrees capacity has been established. Travel distance is now measured from the most remote point subject to occupancy without exception. Other major changes include: addition of a specific definition of common path of travel; recognition of stairs for small changes in levels of elevation; more recognition of other than side-hinged swinging doors and specific requirements for horizontal sliding doors; provisions for nonrated exterior walls of enclosed stairs; revised heights for handrails; establishment of a base minimum number egress paths based on occupant load; movement of the half-diagonal separation of exit paths from an appendix recommendation to a *Code* mandate; establishment of some initial minimum provisions for arrows on exit signs; more stringent requirements for textile materials that are put on walls or ceilings; new provisions for amusement buildings and for exhibits in exhibit halls; specific egress provisions for balconies or mezzanines in assembly occupancies; and total rewrite of the method of calculating seating and aisle capacity in assembly occupancies;

clarification of where and how to sprinkler assembly occupancies as well as a reduction in the number of exceptions for sprinklers in assembly occupancies; elimination of the category of residential-custodial care and supervisory care in Chapters 12 and 13 and the establishment of a new category of limited care in those chapters; reduction in the the building height that mandates use of sprinklers in new nursing home and new limited care facilities; reorganization of the corrridor provisions for health care; mandatory sprinkler requirements in new high rise educational, detention and correctional, hotels, dormitories and apartment buildings; revisions to Chapter 21 to bring it into similar format with the rest of the *Code* and eliminate reliance of references to other chapters such as 20 and 17; new controls on upholstered furniture in nonsprinklered health care occupancies; new reuquirements for emergency instructions for residents and guests of hotels and apartment buildings; and, lastly, the moving of Appendices C through G out of NFPA 101 and into NFPA 101M®. All significant changes and requirements have been identified by a vertical line in the margin. A cross-reference index between the 1985 and 1988 editions has been included to assist the user.

This 1988 edition has been approved by the American National Standards Institute.

The following comments are offered to assist in the use of the *Life Safety Code*.

The *Code* essentially consists of five major parts. The first part consists of Chapters 1 through 7; these are often referred to as the base chapters or fundamental chapters. The next part consists of Chapters 8 through 30, which are the occupancy chapters. The third part consists of Chapter 31 covering operating features. The fourth part is Chapter 32, which covers mandatory referenced publications, and the fifth and last part consists of Appendices A and B, which contain useful additional information.

A thorough understanding of Chapters 1 through 7 is necessary before using the *Code*, as these chapters provide the "building blocks" upon which the occupancy chapters have built their requirements. It should be noted that many of the provisions of Chapters 1 through 7 are mandatory for all occupancies. Some provisions are mandated only where referenced by a specific occupancy while others are exempted for specific occupancies. Often, in one of the base chapters, especially in Chapter 5, the term "where permitted by Chapters 8 through 30" appears. Where this does appear, that provision can be used only where specifically allowed by an occupancy chapter. For example, the provisions of 5-2.1.6 on special locking devices are allowed only where permitted by Chapters 8 through 30. Permission to use this special locking device is normally found in the "2.2" subsection of each occupancy chapter. For example, 8-2.2.2.4 specifically allows the use of these special locking arrangements in new assembly occupancies. If this permission is not found in an occupancy chapter, the special locking devices cannot be used. Similar types of restricted permission are found for such items as security grilles, double cylinder locks, special stairway reentry, revolving doors, atriums, etc. In other locations in the base chapters, the term "unless prohibited by Chapters 8 through 30" is used. In this case, the provision is allowed in all occupancies unless specifically prohibited by an occupancy chapter.

Metric units of measurement in this *Code* are in accordance with the modernized metric system known as the International System of Units (SI). The unit "liter," which is outside of but recognized by SI, is commonly used and is therefore used in this *Code*. In this *Code*, values for measurements are followed by an equivalent in SI units. The first stated value shall be regarded as the requirement, because the given equivalent value may be approximate.

Acknowledgments

As editor of the Fourth Edition of the *Life Safety Code Handbook*, I offer my sincere gratitude and appreciation to those who gave so generously of their time, support, and knowledge in the preparation of this *Handbook*. The following persons deserve special acknowledgment for their extensive work in researching, writing, and reviewing the materials contained herein:

John F. Behrens

Donald W. Belles

Wayne G. (Chip) Carson

George Flach

Charles (Chuck) Kime

William Koffel

Jake Pauls

Much of the material in this Fourth Edition is based on the First, Second, and Third Editions. Contributors to the First Edition include: Donald W. Belles, Michael Slifka, Calvin Yuill, James Thompson, Harold Clar, Orville (Bud) Slye, and John A. Sharry (editor of First Edition). Contributors to the Second Edition include: John A. Sharry, Donald W. Belles, Wayne G. (Chip) Carson, and David P. Demers. Contributors to the Third Edition include: John F. Behrens, Donald W. Belles, Wayne G. (Chip) Carson, Clifford S. Harvey, Alfred J. Longhitano, and John A. Sharry.

I sincerely appreciate the efforts of the NFPA staff members who attended to the countless details that went into the preparation of this *Handbook* and without whose efforts this book would never have gone to press. Included are:

Jennifer Evans, Project Manager

Pamela Nolan, Project Editor

Kathleen Barber, Composition

Donald McGonagle, Production

Special appreciation is extended to Pamela Nolan, Greg Kyte, and Ron Coté of the NFPA staff. Pamela's dedicated attention to detail in the proofreading and copy editing of the 1988 *Life Safety Code* contributed significantly to the quality of the document upon which this *Handbook* is based. Her tireless effort in editing and art coordination added to the high quality of this *Handbook*. Ron not only contributed to many chapters of this *Handbook*, but in his staff position as a Senior Life Safety Engineer, he, along with Greg Kyte, Life Safety Specialist, handled much of the day-to-day workload of the Life Safety Field Service during the period in which this book was being prepared.

Illustrations: Jerry Peterson; George Nichols
Cover Design: Barbara Quinn

JAMES K. LATHROP

Photograph Acknowledgments

Photograph, page 80, reproduced with permission of Won-Door Corp.

Photograph, page 108, reproduced with permission of Jake Pauls, Hughes Associates, Inc.

Photograph, pages 299 and 376, by Jake Pauls, NRC Canada. Reproduced with permission of Jake Pauls, Hughes Associates, Inc.

Photograph, pages 309 and 386, by L. Smith, NRC Canada. Reproduced with permission of Jake Pauls, Hughes Associates, Inc.

Photograph, pages 323 and 400, by Pauls/Swibold/Garsonnin. Reproduced from the documentary film "The Stair Event," with permission of Jake Pauls, Hughes Associates, Inc.

Photograph, pages 324 and 401, by L. Smith, NRC Canada. Reproduced with permission of Jake Pauls, Hughes Associates, Inc.

Photograph, pages 325 and 402, by Jake Pauls, NRC Canada. Reproduced with permission of Jake Pauls, Hughes Associates, Inc.

Photograph, pages 330 and 407, by E. Garsonnin. Reproduced with permission of Jake Pauls, Hughes Associates, Inc.

Photograph, pages 333 and 410, L. Smith, NRC Canada. Reproduced with permission of Jake Pauls, Hughes Associates, Inc.

Dedication

This fourth edition of the *Life Safety Code Handbook* is dedicated to the memory of the late Irwin A. Benjamin, who served on the NFPA Committee on Safety to Life for over 15 years.

He was very active in the affairs of the Association, particularly with regard to the *Life Safety Code,* where he served as Chairman of the Subcommittee on Residential Occupancies for many years. He was also one of the original memers of the NFPA Standards Council, serving from 1974 to 1979, and was a member of the NFPA Technical Committees on Smoke Management Systems, Air Conditioning, and Fire Tests.

Mr. Benjamin, a registered professional engineer and fellow of the Society of Fire Protection Engineers, had a long and distinguished career as a fire researcher at the National Bureau of Standards Center for Fire Research. During his tenure at the Bureau, he developed and instituted new test methods for the control of fire hazards, which eventually culminated in better codes for the built environment.

The Committee on Safety to Life and the NFPA staff, especially the staff of the Life Safety Field Services Department, will deeply miss our friend, Irwin Benjamin, who made such an immense contribution to the *Life Safety Code*, to the mission of the NFPA, and to the field of fire protection.

NOTE: The text and illustrations that make up the commentary on the various sections of the *Life Safety Code* are printed in color. The text of the *Code* itself is printed in black.

The Formal Interpretations included in this *Handbook* were issued as a result of questions raised on specific editions of the *Code*. They apply to all previous and subsequent editions in which the text remains substantially unchanged. Formal Interpretations are not part of the *Code* and therefore are printed in color to the full column width.

An asterisk (*) following a paragraph number indicates explanatory material on that paragraph in Appendix A. Material from Appendix A is integrated with the text and is identified by the letter A preceding the paragraph number to which it relates. Appendix A is not a part of the requirements of this NFPA *Code*, but is included for information purposes only.

Information on referenced publications can be found in Chapter 32 and Appendix B.

1 ADMINISTRATION

SECTION 1-1 TITLE

1-1.1 This *Code* shall be known as the *Life Safety Code*, may be cited as such, and is referred to herein as "this *Code*" or "the *Code*."

As discussed in the Preface to this *Life Safety Code Handbook*, the name of the *Code* was changed from the *Building Exits Code* to the *Life Safety Code* in 1966. What is significant is that the change in title expanded this document beyond a specification code for stairways, doors, and fire escapes (as the *Building Exits Code*) into a performance and specification code dealing with all factors that contribute to or center upon life safety in the event of fire.

SECTION 1-2 PURPOSE

1-2.1 The purpose of this *Code* is to establish minimum requirements that will provide a reasonable degree of safety from fire in buildings and structures.

The purpose of the *Code* is not directed to fire alone but also covers "similar emergencies," such as explosions, since those similar emergencies also involve being able to leave the structure safely. However, the primary motivating forces behind this document are the need to counter the effect of fire upon the occupants of a structure, the need for occupants to find safety, and the need to provide the structural elements that will ensure safety.

1-2.2 The *Code* endeavors to avoid requirements that might involve unreasonable hardships or unnecessary inconvenience or interference with the normal use and occupancy of a building, but insists upon compliance with a minimum standard for firesafety consistent with the public interest.

When a building or structure is built, there is normally a reason for its presence. The *Code* takes into consideration the normal occupancy of a building and tries not to interfere with the normal use of a building or set requirements that would cause unreasonable hardships or unnecessary inconvenience. Therefore, the *Life Safety Code* tends to be "occupancy oriented," but nevertheless, the *Code* still insists upon compliance with a minimum standard of firesafety that is necessary for the public interest.

SECTION 1-3   SCOPE

1-3.1* This *Code* addresses life safety from fire and similar emergencies.

A-1-3.1 Panic. The *Code* recognizes that panic in a burning building may be uncontrollable, but deals with the potential panic hazard through measures designed to prevent the development of panic. Experience indicates that panic seldom develops, even in the presence of potential danger, so long as occupants of buildings are moving toward exits that they can see within a reasonable distance with no obstructions or undue congestion in the path of travel. However, any uncertainty as to the location or adequacy of means of egress, the presence of smoke, or stoppage of exit travel, such as may occur when one person stumbles and falls on the stairs, may be conducive to panic. Panic danger is greatest when there are numbers of people in a confined area.

Recent studies focusing on human behavior under the duress of fire have re-examined the question of panic. It is now recognized that actions the outside observer might consider the result of panic are in fact a rational form of behavior on the part of an occupant confronted by a clear and present danger. Human behavior in a dangerous situation may follow one of many courses. The usual choices are: (1) investigate, (2) sound an alarm, (3) rescue, (4) seek help, and (5) flee. Any of these actions would be considered normal behavior, even when taken en masse. The objective uppermost in the minds of most people is to avoid direct contact with a fire in the course of action taken.

In studies of recent emergency situations supposedly involving "panic," it was found that the occupants performed well. Crowds of people have been found to move through smoke- and heat-contaminated corridors or exits with only slight difficulty or discomfort.

1-3.2 The *Code* addresses those construction, protection, and occupancy features necessary to minimize danger to life from fire, smoke, fumes, or panic.

There may not be a great deal of fire incident data or many statistics to justify the existence of some of the requirements of the *Code*. However, there is a factor that needs to be considered: certain building features innately present potential problems in a fire situation. Awareness of this has resulted in the limited presence of certain hazardous features and their subsequent limited presence in available fire statistics. This, in many cases, indicates that authorities having jurisdiction are doing their job.

1-3.3 The *Code* identifies the minimum criteria for the design of egress facilities so as to permit prompt escape of occupants from buildings or, where desirable, into safe areas within the building.

Evacuation into safe areas (areas of refuge) should not be overlooked as an important aspect in means of egress design. In some cases, it is not practical to consider total evacuation to the exterior. Evacuation to areas of refuge can also increase design flexibility.

1-3.4 The *Code* recognizes that life safety is more than a matter of egress and, accordingly, deals with other considerations that are essential to life safety.

There are numerous elements that impact on the ultimate level of life safety. The *Code* does address many of these items. There are, however, elements that are not dealt with. An example would be public education related to firesafety.

1-3.5 When in fixed locations and occupied as buildings, vehicles, vessels, or other mobile structures shall be treated as buildings.

It is not uncommon to find railroad cars being turned into lounges or restaurants; to find ships or barges turned into hotels, lounges, or restaurants; or to find the trailer units of tractor semitrailer combinations being used for storage or even assembly purposes. Where these types of vehicles, vessels, or other mobile structures are in a fixed location and are being occupied as a building, the *Code* intends that they be regulated as a building under the *Code*. The fact that there are tires on a trailer or that a ship is still floating does not automatically mean that they are not fixed locations and occupied as buildings. The authority having jurisdiction should ensure that the vehicle or vessel is being regulated by some other agency, such as the Coast Guard or Department of Transportation, before exempting it from the requirements of the *Code*.

1-3.6 The *Code* does not attempt to address those general fire prevention or building construction features that are normally a function of fire prevention and building codes.

1-3.7 The prevention of accidental personal injuries during the course of normal occupancy of buildings, personal injuries incurred by an individual's own negligence, and the preservation of property from loss by fire have not been considered as the basis for any of the provisions of this *Code*.

The scope of the *Code* indicates that the *Code* covers only those design elements that relate to life safety from fire; however, accident prevention and the preservation of property may result from adhering to the provisions of the *Code*.

The *Life Safety Code* is not a building code, a fact stated in 1-3.6. It is often used with a building code. Further, the *Code* clearly states that it cannot "save" everyone in an occupancy even if all the design and operational requirements of the *Code* are met. In particular, those people who accidentally or deliberately initiate a fire or who are close by the point of ignition are beyond the *Code's* capability to totally or, in some cases, partially protect.

SECTION 1-4 APPLICATION

1-4.1 The *Code* applies to both new construction and existing buildings. In various chapters there are specific provisions for existing buildings that may differ from those for new construction.

This concept is essential to understanding the intent of the *Code*, which is to achieve at least a minimal level of life safety in all structures and in all occupancies. To this end, there are provisions throughout the document that either specifically apply to existing buildings or that are specifically modified for existing buildings. This represents an attempt to limit the impact of provisions of the *Code* on existing buildings. If no special provisions are made for existing structures, then the provisions for new construction apply, an approach quite different from that of a building code. The following applies to the entire text: where life safety is involved, there is no reason for an existing structure not to conform to the *Code*. As a minimum, the *Code* will modify or will alter the "new" requirements as they are applied to "existing" buildings. Yet, in many instances, the *Code* will not alter a basic provision at the expense of life safety and will call for its application in both new and existing buildings. In recognition of the fact that the Life Safety *Code* is a general code that applies across the board to all structures and occupancies, the *Code* is designed to be flexible in the event of the extenuating circumstances that may exist in an individual case. Since only the individuals involved can properly assess these extenuating circumstances, the authority having jurisdiction is recognized as the best judge of the extent to which the *Code* may be further modified. However, the *Code* does establish the minimum provision so that reasonable life safety against the hazards of fire, explosion, and panic is provided and maintained.

Also see 1-4.2, 1-4.4, 1-4.6, Section 1-5, and 1-6.2.

1-4.2   A limited but reasonable time shall be allowed for compliance with any part of this *Code* for existing buildings, commensurate with the magnitude of expenditure, disruption of services, and degree of hazard.

In some cases, appreciable costs, in terms of actual monetary expenditures and disruption of daily activities, may be involved in bringing an existing occupancy into compliance with the requirements of the *Code*. Where this is true, it would be appropriate for the owner of the facility to formulate a schedule, approved by the authority having jurisdiction, that allows suitable periods of time for correcting various deficiencies and gives due consideration to the ability of the owner to secure the necessary funding. However, the degree of hazard is an important consideration here, and, if the degree of hazard is serious enough, it may be necessary to close the building while renovations are made to bring the building into compliance.

1-4.3   The authority having jurisdiction shall determine the adequacy of means of egress and other measures for life safety from fire in accordance with the provisions of this *Code*.

This paragraph gives the authority having jurisdiction the final determination of whether adequate life safety is or is not provided in the building. This paragraph, in conjunction with the fundamental requirements of Chapter 2, can be used by the authority having juridiction where that authority determines that the *Code* has not contemplated the specific situation encountered. Based upon this paragraph, the authority having jurisdiction could increase or decrease the requirements for the specific installation. This is an important paragraph since the *Code* cannot anticipate every type of building and occupancy configuration, and, therefore, the authority having jurisdiction is given the final power to determine whether life safety is or is not adequately provided.

1-4.4* The requirements for existing buildings may be modified if their application clearly would be impractical in the judgment of the authority having jurisdiction, but only where it is clearly evident that a reasonable degree of safety is provided.

A-1-4.4 In existing buildings it is not always practical to strictly apply the provisions of this *Code*. Physical limitations may require disproportionate effort or expense with little increase in life safety. In such cases the authority having jurisdiction shall be satisfied that reasonable life safety is assured.

In existing buildings it is intended that any condition that represents a serious threat to life be mitigated by application of appropriate safeguards. It is not intended to require modifications for conditions that do not represent a significant threat to life even though the circumstances are not literally in compliance with the *Code*.

This provides the authority having jurisdiction latitude where applying the *Code* to existing buildings. The *Code* recognizes that there may be situations where the requirements for existing buildings are not practical and gives the authority having jurisdiction the ability to modify those requirements, but re-emphasizes that a reasonable degree of safety still must be provided. In existing buildings, it is not always practical to strictly apply the provisions of this *Code*. Physical limitations may require disproportionate effort or expense with little increase in life safety. In such cases, the authority having jurisdiction should be satisfied that reasonable life safety is ensured. In existing buildings, it is intended that any condition that represents a serious threat to life be mitigated by application of appropriate safeguards. It is not intended to require modifications for conditions that do not represent a significant threat to life, even though the circumstances are not literally in compliance with the *Code*.

1-4.5 Additions. Additions shall conform to the provisions for new construction.

1-4.6* Modernization or Renovation. Any alteration, or any installations of new equipment, shall be accomplished as nearly as practical in conformance with the requirements for new construction. Alterations shall not diminish the level of life safety below that which exists prior to the alteration. In no case shall the resulting life safety be less than that required for existing buildings. Life safety features that do not meet the requirements for new buildings but exceed the requirements for existing buildings shall not be further diminished. Life safety features in excess of those required for new construction are not required to be maintained.

A-1-4.6   The following is an example of what is intended by 1-4.6. In a hospital that has 6-ft (183-cm) corridors, these corridors cannot be reduced in width even though the requirements for existing buildings do not require 6-ft (183-cm) wide corridors. However, if a hospital had 10-ft (3-m) wide corridors they may be reduced to 8 ft (244 cm), which is the requirement for new construction. If the hospital corridor was 3 ft (91 cm) wide it would have to be increased to 4 ft (122 cm). If alterations require replacement of a portion of a hospital corridor wall, this portion of the wall should be increased to 1-hour fire resistance in accordance with the requirements for new construction. However, it would not be required that the corridor width be increased to 8 ft (244 cm) unless it was practical to do so.

It should be recognized that all changes and alterations that are made must be in conformance with the minimum provisions of the *Code* for new construction. It may not be practical if the structure involved cannot accommodate the design provisions for new construction. For example, an existing hospital may have a corridor 6 ft (183 cm) wide that, if renovated, is required to be 8 ft (244 cm) wide. However, if the building's column spacing is 7 ft by 7 ft (213 cm by 213 cm) (a dimension common to fire-resistive multistory buildings), there is no way to achieve an 8-ft (244-cm) corridor width. Therefore, the authority having jurisdiction would have to decide if a 6-ft (1.8-m) wide or even a 7-ft (213-cm) wide corridor is adequate or if additional provisions may be required to accommodate a corridor less than 8 ft (244 cm) in width.

It is important to note here that the occupancy chapters on existing buildings deal essentially with existing conditions and that where renovations or alterations are being made they must comply with the requirements for new construction to the extent practical. For example, where installing new carpeting, it is very practical to install it within the requirements for new interior floor finish; or, where rebuilding a corridor wall, it may not be practical to move it to widen the corridor to the requirements for new corridor width, but most likely it will be practical to build it to the required fire resistance rating for new construction. Another example would be the installation of a new smoke barrier in an existing hospital. A smoke barrier can be made to meet all the requirements for a new smoke barrier; however, if the corridor through which the smoke barrier extends is not sufficiently wide to install two 44-in. (112-cm) doors, the requirement for two 44-in. (112-cm) doors would have to be modified by the authority having jurisdiction to a set of doors or possibly a single door of sufficient width that the corridor could accommodate. The "nearly as practical" provision may seem arbitrary but is necessary in order to allow evaluation on a case-by-case basis.

Paragraph 1-4.6 does not specify the degree or magnitude of a change or alteration at which conformance with the provisions of the *Code* becomes mandatory. Both minor and major alterations and changes must comply. The authority having jurisdiction may still modify the *Code's* requirements or accept equivalent design options based on the special circumstances and the technical documentation presented.

1-4.7 Mixed Occupancies. Where two or more classes of occupancy occur in the same building or structure, and are so intermingled that separate safeguards are impracticable, means of egress facilities, construction, protection, and other safeguards shall comply with the most restrictive life safety requirements of the occupancies involved.

Formal Interpretation 81-25
Reference: 1-4.7, 8-1.6, 24-4.3.1

Given that, per 8-1.6, a 3-story shopping mall with a food park (restaurant) on the third level is required to be of fire-resistive construction under the criteria for a Class A assembly occupancy above grade level:

Question 1: Is it possible to construct an anchor store of a different construction type from the mall building by separating it from the mall building by a 3-hour fire wall?

Question 2: Are 3-hour fire doors required for openings in this 3-hour wall between the mall and the anchor store?

Question 3: If the answer to Question 2 is no, is any type of opening protection required for openings between the mall and anchor store?

Answer: With only a few exceptions, the *Life Safety Code* sets no specific occupancy separation requirements. The authority having jurisdiction determines what separation is needed, if any, based on 1-4.7 and the 1.2 subsection of each occupancy chapter. The local building code or the model building codes may be consulted by the authority having jurisdiction in making this determination, keeping life safety rather than property protection in mind.

Issue Edition: 1981
Reference: 1-4.5, 8-1.6, 24-4.3.1
Date: October 1982

Note that the *Code* does not automatically require that separate occupancies be provided with a fire resistance rated separation, as is often required by building codes. Some of the occupancies do require a specific fire resistance rated separation, but, for the most part, the question of whether or not a fire resistance rated separation is needed and the extent to which it is needed is left to the authority having jurisdiction on a case-by-case basis. However, in the case where the occupancies are so intermingled that separate safeguards cannot be provided, the entire facility must meet the most restrictive life safety requirements for all the occupancies involved. It should also be noted that in many cases an occupancy requires a type of protection to be provided throughout the building, and this would be required throughout the structure regardless of fire separation, unless the structure was being built as "separate buildings." If the authority having jurisdiction accepts them as separate buildings, even though a single structure, the requirements could be applied to only the applicable side of the barrier. The authority having jurisdiction makes the determination whether separate buildings are or are not, in fact, involved.

A fairly simple example, although quite common, is illustrated in Figure 1-1. As shown, this is not a mixed occupancy. Several factors should be considered by the authority having jurisdiction in determining what fire resistance rating and other requirements should be established for the walls between occupancies. Some occupancies do establish a specific fire resistance rating for these walls; see the 1.4 subsection of each occupancy chapter (e.g., 12-1.4). If the occupancies involved do not require automatic sprinkler protection or fire alarm systems or do not involve sleeping or high hazards, the separation may be required to have little if any fire resistance (something one might find in older "strip shopping centers"). At the other end of the spectrum, if one of the occupancies involved requires automatic sprinkler protection or involves sleeping, then the authority may require a higher-rated fire barrier.

In any case, the *Code* will allow the facility to be a mixed occupancy with no separation as long as the entire facility complies with the most stringent requirements of the occupancies involved.

An example of common mixed occupancy arrangement is illustrated in Figure 1-2.

The commentary following 8-1.6 discusses in greater detail the problem of separating sprinklered and nonsprinklered occupancies. In general, for life safety purposes, nonsprinklered areas should not exist below sprinklered areas, regardless of separation. For example, an occupancy on the ground floor of a building with floors numbered B through 5 would require that at least floors B and 1 be sprinklered regardless of separation; a similar building with an occupancy that requires sprinkler protection on the top floor would result in the entire building being sprinklered. Again, 8-1.6 provides excellent guidance on this subject.

In some cases, an occupancy will require that the "building" be sprinklered throughout. Where this is required, the entire structure must be protected throughout regardless of the fire resistance of any separation. The model building codes do establish requirements for separate buildings and, if met, the authority having jurisdiction could (and should if the building code is mandated in addition to the *Life Safety Code*) rule that although one structure is involved, it does consist of separate buildings.

Lastly, as indicated above, where the *Life Safety Code* is being used in conjunction with a building code, the authority having jurisdiction enforcing the *Life Safety Code* should work in conjunction with the authority enforcing the building code, especially on matters such as this.

For further information on mixed occupancies see commentary on the 1.4 subsection of each occupancy chapter as well as commentary following 8-1.6 and 8-3.5.

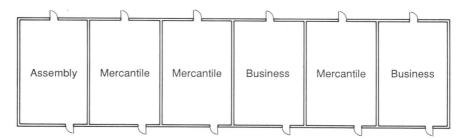

Figure 1-1. An Example of a Building That, Although it Has More Than One Occupancy in it, Is Not a Mixed Occupancy. Each occupancy can be treated separately with regard to egress, interior finish, corridors etc. Most occupancies do not establish specific fire resistance ratings for the wall between occupancies, and this would be determined by the authority having jurisdiction.

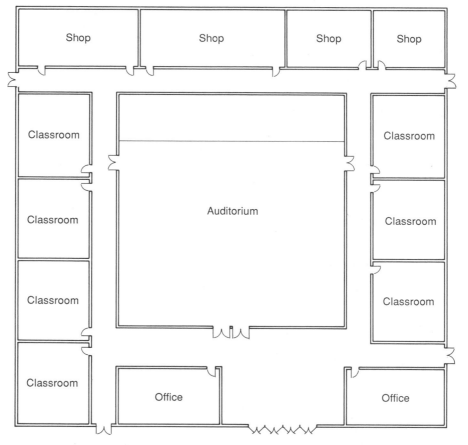

Figure 1-2. An Example of a Mixed Occupancy Building. Regardless of the fire separations provided, the egress system is mixed, and, therefore, the most stringent requirements of the occupancies involved must be met.

1-4.8   Where specific requirements contained in Chapters 8 through 30 differ from similar requirements contained in Chapters 1 through 7, the requirements of Chapters 8 through 30 shall govern.

> Paragraph 1-4.8 indicates the general arrangement of the *Life Safety Code*. The first seven chapters contain administrative provisions and fundamental requirements establishing minimum acceptable criteria for all types of occupancies. Chapters 8 through 30 of the *Code* establish criteria for life safety based upon specific occupancies. If conflicts between the general requirements and specific occupancy requirements occur, the requirements contained in the specific occupancy chapter apply.
>
> It is interesting to note that the Committee on Safety to Life prohibits occupancy subcommittees from establishing provisions less stringent than those in Chapters 1 through 7 without an exception in Chapters 1 through 7, but since "stringent," whether more or less, could be subject to interpretation, the *Code* establishes that the more specific provisions, i.e., the occupancy chapters, rule where questions develop during the enforcement of the *Code*.

1-4.9 Provisions in Excess of Code Requirements.   Nothing in this *Code* shall be construed to prohibit a better type of building construction, more exits, or otherwise safer conditions than the minimum requirements specified in this *Code*.

> Because the *Life Safety Code* is a minimum code, it never prohibits the use of a design that exceeds the provisions of the *Code*. In practice, however, economic considerations usually prevent the use of a design that exceeds the written provisions of the *Code*.
>
> However, there have been situations in which, by exceeding the *Code* provisions, money was saved or generated. A specific example is a hotel project that was not required to have complete automatic sprinkler protection. By including sprinklers, a stairway was eliminated due to allowable increases in travel distance, and many revenue-producing guest rooms were put in the vacated space.

SECTION 1-5   EQUIVALENCY CONCEPTS

> Section 1-5 helps to establish one of the most sensitive and the most critical design criteria found in the *Code*. It takes the *Life Safety Code* beyond the scope of a typical general specification code into that of a goal-oriented performance code, where state-of-the-art fire protection design is permissible and even desirable.

1-5.1*   Nothing in this *Code* is intended to prevent the use of systems, methods, or devices of equivalent or superior quality, strength, fire resistance, effectiveness, durability, and safety to those prescribed by this *Code*, provided technical documentation is submitted to the authority having jurisdiction to demonstrate equivalency and the system, method, or device is approved for the intended purpose.

A-1-5.1 It is the intent of the Committee on Safety to Life to recognize that future editions of this *Code* are a further refinement of this edition and earlier editions. The changes in future editions will reflect the continuing input of the fire protection/life safety community in its attempt to meet the goals stated in Chapter 2, Fundamental Requirements.

Paragraph 1-5.1 recognizes that a code can reflect only what is known and commonly practiced in fire protection design at the time it was written. Considering the rate at which technology advances, a major breakthrough or even a simple change in existing hardware can mean the creation of design capabilities not contemplated at the time that the current edition of the *Code* was written. In realization of the limitations of a written code, 1-5.1 permits the use of "systems, methods, or devices of equivalent or superior quality, strength, fire resistance, effectiveness, durability, and safety;" the stipulation is that technical documentation be submitted to the authority having jurisdiction, justifying the use of the new approach.

This paragraph is important for two reasons. First, it recognizes that the judgment of the authority having jurisdiction is instrumental in achieving the letter and intent of the *Code*. Second, it states that the intent of the *Code* is neither limited nor bound by the written provisions of the *Code*. Thus, it allows for the development of new technology, new systems, new devices, and new designs not recognized by or written into the *Code*. This permits the designer and the authority having jurisdiction to pursue the state-of-the-art in applying fire protection engineering for the purpose of achieving life safety. It also gives the *Code* a broader perspective than that of a specification code that concerns itself only with the construction details of individual items. In fact, there was little assurance that the elements found in a specification code would necessarily fit together into a design approach that achieved firesafety. The paragraph actually opts for an approach to design that goes beyond the individual elements of the *Code*, provided that technical documentation is available to support the design.

There is material available in NFPA 101M, *Manual on Alternative Approaches to Life Safety*,[1] that can be used to help determine equivalencies. These are tools, however, and in no way limit the authority having jurisdiction in granting or denying equivalent methodologies.

1-5.2 The specific requirements of this *Code* may be modified by the authority having jurisdiction to allow alternative arrangements that will secure as nearly equivalent safety to life from fire as practical, but in no case shall the modification afford less safety to life than, in the judgment of the authority having jurisdiction, that which would be provided by compliance with the corresponding provisions contained in this *Code*.

This is a further enhancement of 1-5.1. To further the flexibility of the *Code* requirements in instances where new technology can be effectively incorporated into structures, 1-5.2 allows the authority having jurisdiction to modify the requirements of the *Code*. These modifications must result in a level of safety equal to or greater than that attained by a strict compliance with those *Code* provisions that would normally apply.

Paragraph 1-5.2 also allows the authority having jurisdiction to exercise some flexibility in dealing with historically preserved buildings. These buildings may have numerous design defects, such as open stair shafts or highly combustible interior finishes. To attain an equivalent level of safety, the authority having jurisdiction may require the use of sprinkler systems, smoke detection systems, voice alarm systems for staged evacuation, smoke control systems, etc., to overcome the built-in design defects. This would be done in lieu of rebuilding the structure to the written *Code* requirements, which might mean totally destroying the historical character of the structure that is to be preserved. The design alternatives used in such an instance may actually raise the level of safety many times over that which is already found in the existing structure. They must, however, provide equivalent safety to life or greater safety to life than the written *Code* provisions.

1-5.3   Buildings with alternative fire protection features accepted by the authority having jurisdiction shall be considered as conforming with the *Code*.

This emphasizes the difference between accepted alternatives and waivers. When one presents an alternative appproach to life safety, and that alternative is accepted by the authority having jurisdiction, the building is considered in compliance. This is different from a waiver that allows a noncomplying building to continue in use.

SECTION 1-6   OCCUPANCY   (*See also Section 31-1.*)

1-6.1   No new construction or existing building shall be occupied in whole or in part in violation of the provisions of this *Code*.

From the enforcement standpoint, this paragraph is probably one of the most important in the *Code*, since it says that no building, whether it be new or existing, may be occupied when the building is in violation of the provisions of the *Code*.

1-6.2   Existing buildings that are occupied at the time of adoption of the *Code* may remain in use provided:

(a) The occupancy classification remains the same.

(b) No serious life safety hazard exists that would constitute an imminent threat.

Because the *Code* is to be applied retroactively, 1-6.1 prohibits the use of existing nonconforming facilities. However, 1-6.2 goes on to modify this by saying that the building may be continued in use provided that the occupancy classification remains the same and there is no serious life safety hazard that would constitute an imminent threat. It should be noted that this does not exempt the building from compliance with the *Code* but only states that it can be continued in use. A plan, as described under

1-4.2, for bringing the building into compliance with the *Code* to the extent deemed necessary by the authority having jurisdiction under 1-4.4 and 1-5.2, must be established and its provisions met.

1-6.3* Buildings or portions of buildings may be occupied during construction, repair, alterations, or additions only if all means of egress and all fire protection features are in place and continuously maintained for the part occupied.

A-1-6.3 Fatal fires have occurred when a required stairway has been closed for repairs or removed for rebuilding, when a required automatic sprinkler system has been shut off to change piping, etc.

Paragraph 1-6.3 helps to control a now common practice: the occupation of a partially completed structure (done usually to obtain rent revenue). The *Code* first requires that all exit facilities for the part occupied be complete. In many cases the exit facilities, although completed, may be blocked with supplies and equipment needed for the ongoing construction, or the exits may be locked to limit access to parts of the building still under construction. If any of these conditions are found, occupancy should be absolutely prohibited. One must bear in mind that the incidence of fire is more frequent, and therefore more likely, during construction, alterations, repairs, etc. Extra caution and concern must be exercised to ensure adequate exit capacity and arrangement during periods of construction in any occupied building. Secondly, all fire protection features must also be in place and continuously maintained for similar reasons.

1-6.4* Changes of Occupancy.   In any building or structure, whether necessitating a physical alteration or not, a change from one occupancy classification to another, or from one occupancy subclassification to another subclassification of the same occupancy may be made only if such building or structure conforms with the requirements of this *Code* applying to new construction for the proposed new use.

A-1-6.4 Examples of changes from one occupancy subclassification to another subclassification of the same occupancy could include a change from a Class C to a Class B assembly occupancy or a change from a Class B to a Class A mercantile occupancy. Hospitals and nursing homes are both health care occupancies and are defined separately but are not established as separate suboccupancies, thus a change from one to the other does not constitute a change of occupancy subclassification.

Hotels and apartments, although both are residential occupancies, are treated separately, and a change from one to the other constitutes a change of occupancy.

Formal Interpretation 81-12
Reference: 1-6

Question: A building was used as a hospital but has been closed for four years. It is again to be used as a hospital. Is the facility to be considered new or existing under the *Life Safety Code?*

Answer: As long as the building was not used as another occupancy during the time, it would be considered existing.

Issue Edition: 1981
Reference: 1-6
Date: January 1982

SECTION 1-7   MAINTENANCE   *(See also Section 31-1.)*

1-7 Maintenance.   Whenever or wherever any device, equipment, system, condition, arrangement, level of protection, or any other feature is required for compliance with the provisions of this *Code,* such device, equipment, system, condition, arrangement, level of protection, or other feature shall thereafter be permanently maintained unless the *Code* exempts such maintenance.

This paragraph is new to the 1988 *Code.* Although maintenance has been addressed to some extent in Chapter 31 of previous editions, Section 1-7 helps emphasize the importance of maintenance of items required by the *Code.* It is useless to have a door that will not open or a closer that does not close the door or a sprinkler system with no water. See Chapter 31 for additional maintenance provisions.

REFERENCE CITED IN COMMENTARY

[1]NFPA 101M®, *Manual on Alternative Approaches to Life Safety,* National Fire Protection Association, Quincy, MA, 1988.

2 FUNDAMENTAL REQUIREMENTS

The goals toward which the provisions of this *Code* are aimed are specified in Chapter 2. The achievement of these goals ensures a reasonable level of life safety in building design and arrangement. Simply stated they are:

1. To provide for adequate exits without dependence on any single safeguard,

2. To ensure that construction is sufficient to provide structural integrity during a fire while occupants are exiting,

3. To provide exits that have been designed to the size, shape, and nature of the occupancy,

4. To ensure that the exits are clear, unobstructed, and unlocked,

5. To ensure that the exits and routes of escape are clearly marked so that there is no confusion in reaching an exit,

6. To provide adequate lighting,

7. To ensure early warning of fire,

8. To provide for back-up or redundant exit arrangements,

9. To ensure the suitable enclosure of vertical openings, and

10. To make allowances for those design criteria that go beyond the *Code* provisions and are tailored to the normal use and needs of the occupancy in question.

2-1* Every building or structure, new or old, designed for human occupancy shall be provided with exits sufficient to permit the prompt escape of occupants in case of fire or other emergency. The design of exits and other safeguards shall be such that reliance for safety to life in case of fire or other emergency will not depend solely on any single safeguard; additional safeguards shall be provided for life safety in case any single safeguard is ineffective due to some human or mechanical failure.

A-2-1 It is not always necessary to completely evacuate the building or structure to escape from a fire or other emergency. An area of refuge formed by horizontal exits, smoke barriers, other floors, or like compartmentation often can serve as a place for the occupants to remain in relative safety until the emergency is over. In those occupancies where access to the exits is by way of enclosed corridors, particularly those occupancies with sleeping occupants, a single fire may block access to all exits, including horizontal exits and smoke barriers. In such cases, the occupants may achieve a greater degree of safety by remaining in their rooms.

2-2 Every building or structure shall be so constructed, arranged, equipped, maintained, and operated as to avoid undue danger to the lives and safety of its occupants from fire, smoke, fumes, or resulting panic during the period of time reasonably necessary for escape from the building or structure in case of fire or other emergency.

2-3 Every building or structure shall be provided with exits of kinds, numbers, location, and capacity appropriate to the individual building or structure, with due regard to the character of the occupancy, the number of persons exposed, the fire protection available, and the height and type of construction of the building or structure, to afford all occupants convenient facilities for escape.

2-4 In every building or structure, exits shall be so arranged and maintained as to provide free and unobstructed egress from all parts of the building or structure at all times when it is occupied. No lock or fastening shall be installed to prevent free escape from the inside of any building.

Exception: Locks shall be permitted in mental health, detention, or correctional facilities where supervisory personnel are continually on duty and effective provisions are made to remove occupants in case of fire or other emergency.

Problems with locking devices have consistently been a contributing factor in multiple-fatality fires in correctional facilities. Some of these problems include malfunction of locks, inability to locate keys in smoke or in the dark (frequently caused by smoke obscuration of lighting), locks jammed from toothpicks and chewing gum, and locks made inoperative due to pushing against the doors. All of these problems have shown up in the fire record. Many times, prior to a fire, it might have been assumed that in the event of an emergency, there would be effective provisions for unlocking locks and that personnel would be continually on duty. Extreme care must be exercised to ensure that locks can and will be unlocked or that alternate methods of providing life safety, other than total evacuation, are provided.[1,2]

2-5 Every exit shall be clearly visible, or the route to reach it shall be conspicuously indicated in such a manner that every occupant of every building or structure who is physically and mentally capable will readily know the direction of escape from any point. Each means of egress, in its entirety, shall be so arranged or marked that the way to a place of safety is indicated in a clear manner. Any doorway or passageway that is not an exit or a way to reach an exit, but is capable of being confused with an exit, shall be so arranged or marked to prevent occupant confusion with acceptable exits. Every effort shall be taken to avoid occupants mistakenly traveling into dead-end spaces in a fire emergency.

2-6 Where artificial illumination is required in a building or structure, exit facilities shall be included in the lighting design in an adequate and reliable manner.

2-7 In every building or structure of such size, arrangement, or occupancy that a fire itself may not provide adequate occupant warning, fire alarm facilities shall be provided where necessary to warn occupants of the existence of fire. Fire alarms will alert occupants to initiate escape. Fire alarms facilitate the orderly conduct of fire exit drills.

Several multiple-fatality fire incidents in recent years, especially in hotels, have shown that fire alarm sounding devices were inadequate to alert building occupants. This was because occupants either could not hear the alarm or did not recognize the alarm as a fire alarm signal. Confusion with telephones or alarm clocks has been reported. Authorities having jurisdiction must ensure that sounding devices can be heard over ambient noise levels and can be recognized as fire alarm signals.[3,4]

2-8   Two means of egress, as a minimum, shall be provided in every building or structure, section, or area where the size, occupancy, and arrangement endangers occupants attempting to use a single means of egress that is blocked by fire or smoke. The two means of egress shall be arranged to minimize the possibility that both may be impassable by the same fire or emergency condition.

2-9   Every vertical way of exit and other vertical opening between floors of a building shall be suitably enclosed or protected, as necessary, to afford reasonable safety to occupants while using exits, and to prevent spread of fire, smoke, or fumes through vertical openings from floor to floor before occupants have entered exits.

Unprotected or improperly protected vertical openings have consistently shown up in NFPA fire records as a major contributing factor to multiple-death fires. Some recent multiple-death fires in which unprotected vertical openings have been identified as a significant factor in the deaths are:

November 20, 1980, Las Vegas, NV	85 dead[5]
January 9, 1981, Keansburgh, NJ	31 dead[6]
March 14, 1981, Chicago, IL	19 dead[7]
October 28, 1982, Pittsburgh, PA	5 dead[8]
April 19, 1983, Worcester, MA	7 dead[9]
June 14, 1983, Fort Worth, TX	5 dead[10]
August 31, 1983, Gwinnett, GA	8 dead[11]
December 31, 1986, San Juan, PR	97 dead[12]

2-10*   Compliance with this *Code* shall not be construed as eliminating or reducing the necessity for other provisions for safety of persons using a structure under normal occupancy conditions. Also, no provision of the *Code* shall be construed as requiring or permitting any condition that may be hazardous under normal occupancy conditions.

A-2-10   The provisions of this *Code* will not necessarily provide a building suitable for use by physically handicapped people. Reference is made to ANSI A117.1, *Specifications for Making Buildings and Facilities Accessible to and Usable by the Physically Handicapped*. (*See Appendix B.*)

REFERENCES CITED IN COMMENTARY

[1]Best, Richard, "The Seminole County Jail Fire," *Fire Journal*, Vol. 70, No. 1, January 1976, pp. 5-10, 17.
[2]Demers, David P., "Fire in Prisons," *Fire Journal*, Vol. 72, No. 2, March 1978, pp. 29-42.

[3]_____, "Familiar Problems Cause 10 Deaths in Hotel Fire," *Fire Journal*, Vol. 74, No. 1, January 1980, pp. 52-56.

[4]_____, "Ten Die in Greece, New York Hotel Fire," *Fire Journal*, Vol. 73, No. 4, July 1979, pp. 25-30.

[5]_____, "Fire at the MGM Grand," *Fire Journal*, Vol. 76, No. 1, January 1982, pp. 19-37.

[6]_____, "Fires in Two Boarding Facilities Kill 34 Residents," *Fire Journal*, Vol. 76, No. 4, July 1982, pp. 44-57, 106.

[7]Hill, Steven, "19 Die in Chicago Hotel Fire," *Fire Journal*, Vol. 76, No. 2, March 1982, pp. 53-55, 60-61.

[8]Bell, James R., "Five Die in Pittsburgh Boarding Home Fire," *Fire Journal*, Vol. 77, No. 5, September 1983, pp. 68-71, 75.

[9]Best, Richard, "Fire in Community Home Causes Seven Deaths," *Fire Journal*, Vol. 78, No. 2, March 1984, pp. 19-23, 79-80.

[10]Cote', Ron; Klem, Thomas; and Walls, William P., "Five Die in Fire at Texas Ramada Inn," *Fire Journal*, Vol. 78, No. 2, March 1984, pp. 55-57, 60-70.

[11]Timoney, Tom, "Eight Mentally Handicapped Occupants Die in Georgia Fire," *Fire Journal*, Vol. 78, No. 3, May 1984, pp. 91-97, 134.

[12]Klem, Thomas J., Investigation Report on the Dupont Plaza Hotel Fire, *NFPA LS-11*, National Fire Protection Association, Quincy, MA 1987.

3 DEFINITIONS

SECTION 3-1   GENERAL

3-1.1   The following terms, for the purposes of this *Code*, shall have the meanings given in this chapter, if not otherwise modified for a specific occupancy.

3-1.2   Words used in the present tense include the future; words used in the masculine gender include the feminine and neuter; the singular number includes the plural and the plural the singular.

3-1.3   Where terms are not defined in this chapter, they shall have their ordinarily accepted meanings or such as the context may imply.

SECTION 3-2   DEFINITIONS

Addition.   An extension or increase in floor area or height of a building or structure.

Also see 1-4.5

Apartment Building.   *(See Section 18-1 or 19-1.)*

Approved.*   Means "acceptable to the authority having jurisdiction."

A-3-2   Approved.   The National Fire Protection Association does not approve, inspect or certify any installations, procedures, equipment or materials, nor does it approve or evaluate testing laboratories. In determining the acceptability of installations or procedures, equipment or materials, the authority having jurisdiction may base acceptance on compliance with NFPA or other appropriate standards. In the absence of such standards, said authority may require evidence of proper installation, procedure or use. The authority having jurisdiction may also refer to the listings or labeling practices of an organization concerned with product evaluations that is in a position to determine compliance with appropriate standards for the current production of listed items.

A common error is the assumption that "approved" means listed or labeled or similar designation. Although the authority having jurisdiction may use a listing or label to assist in approving an item, that does not mean that all approvals are based on listing or labeling and does not mean that listings and/or labels automatically mean approval.

Area.   See Floor Area.

Arena Stage.   A stage or platform open on at least three sides to audience seating. It may be with or without overhead scene handling facilities.

Assembly Occupancy.   *(See Section 4-1.)*

Atrium.   A floor opening or series of floor openings connecting two or more stories that is covered at the top of the series of openings and is used for purposes other than an enclosed stairway; elevator hoistway; escalator opening; or utility shaft used for plumbing, electrical, air conditioning, or communication facilities.

Also see 6-2.4.5.

Authority Having Jurisdiction.*   The "authority having jurisdiction" is the organization, office, or individual responsible for "approving" equipment, an installation, or a procedure.

A-3-2 Authority Having Jurisdiction.   The phrase "authority having jurisdiction" is used in NFPA documents in a broad manner since jurisdictions and "approval" agencies vary, as do their responsibilities. Where public safety is primary, the "authority having jurisdiction" may be a federal, state, local, or other regional department or individual such as a fire chief, fire marshal, chief of a fire prevention bureau, labor department, health department, building official, electrical inspector, or others having statutory authority. For insurance purposes, an insurance inspection department rating bureau or other insurance company representative may be the "authority having jurisdiction." In many circumstances, the property owner or his designated agent assumes the role of the "authority having jurisdiction"; at government installations, the commanding officer or departmental official may be the "authority having jurisdiction."

In the simplest terms the authority having jurisdiction (AHJ) is that person or office enforcing the *Code*. Commonly the AHJ is a fire marshal or building official where enforcement is mandatory. It can also be a safety office, insurance engineer, accreditation service, or other agency, especially where enforced on a nongovernmental level.

Automatic.   Providing a function without the necessity of human intervention.

Examples are an automatic sprinkler system or automatic fire detection system. An automatic-closing door is one that closes when necessary, usually by activation of a smoke detector, whereas a self-closing door closes each time it is opened.

Board and Care.   *(See Section 21-1.)*

Building.   Any structure used or intended for supporting or sheltering any use or occupancy. The term building shall be construed as if followed by the words "or portions thereof." *(See Structure.)*

Building, Existing.   Any structure erected prior to the adoption of this *Code* or for which a permit for construction has been issued.

Also see definition of Existing.

Business Occupancy.   (*See Section 4-1.*)

Combustible.   Capable of undergoing combustion.

Combustion.   A chemical process that involves oxidation sufficient to produce light or heat.

Common Atmosphere (Educational Occupancies).   (*See Section 10-1 or 11-1.*)

Common Path of Travel.   That portion of exit access that must be traversed before two separate and distinct paths of travel to two exits are available. Paths that merge are common paths of travel. Common path of travel is measured in the same manner as travel distance but terminates at that point where two separate and distinct routes become available.

See commentary on 5-5.1.2.

Complete Smoke Detection System.   (*See 7-6.2.7.*)

Correctional Occupancies.   (*See Section 4-1.*)

Court.   An open, uncovered, unoccupied space, unobstructed to the sky, bounded on three or more sides by exterior building walls.

Court, Enclosed.   A court bounded on all sides by the exterior walls of a building or exterior walls and lot lines on which walls are allowable.

Critical Radiant Flux.   The level of incident radiant heat energy on a floor covering system at the most distant flameout point as determined by the test procedure of NFPA 253, *Standard Method of Test for Critical Radiant Flux of Floor Covering Systems Using a Radiant Heat Energy Source.* The unit of measurement of critical radiant flux is watts per square centimeter (watts/cm^2).

Also see commentary in Section 6-5.

Day-Care Centers.   (*See Section 10-7 or 11-7.*)

Detention Occupancies.   (*See Section 4-1.*)

Dormitories.   (*See Section 16-1 or 17-1.*)

Draft Stop.   A continuous membrane to subdivide a concealed space to restrict the passage of smoke, heat, and flames.

Educational Occupancies.   *(See Section 10-1 or 11-1.)*

Existing.   That which is already in existence at the date when this *Code* goes into effect, as existing buildings, structures, or exit facilities.

Formal Interpretation 76-118
Reference: 3-2

Question 1: The definition of "existing" in Section 3-2 states "that which is already in existence at the date when this *Code* goes into effect...." If a building was designed and construction began before adoption of the *Code*, but the construction was not finished until after the adoption, should the building be inspected under the "new" or "existing" criteria?

Answer: Existing.

Question 2: If a building was designed before adoption of the *Code*, but construction was not started until after adoption of the *Code*, should the building be inspected under the "new" or "existing" criteria?

Answer: The key is not when the building was designed or when construction started, but rather the date of plan approval. If permission (approval) was given prior to adoption, inspection should be based on the *Code* in effect at the time of approval. Subsequently, "existing" sections of newly adopted editions would be used.

Issue Edition: 1976
Reference: 3-2
Date: October 1979

Exit.   That portion of a means of egress that is separated from all other spaces of the building or structure by construction or equipment as required in 5-1.3.1 to provide a protected way of travel to the exit discharge.

Exit Access.   That portion of a means of egress that leads to an entrance to an exit.

Exit Discharge.   That portion of a means of egress between the termination of an exit and a public way.

Family Day-Care Home.   *(See Section 10-9 or 11-9.)*

Fire Barrier.   A fire barrier is a continuous membrane, either vertical or horizontal, such as a wall or floor assembly, that is designed and constructed with a specified fire resistance rating to limit the spread of fire, and that will also restrict the movement of smoke. Such barriers may have protected openings. *(See 6-2.3.)*

Fire Compartment.*   A fire compartment is a space within a building that is enclosed by fire barriers on all sides, including the top and bottom. *(See 6-2.2.)*

A-3-2 Fire Compartment. In the provisions of fire compartments utilizing the outside walls of a building, it is not intended that the outside wall be specifically fire resistance rated unless required by other standards. Likewise it is not intended for outside windows or doors to be protected unless specifically required for exposure protection by another section of this *Code* or by other standards.

Fire Resistance Rating. The time, in minutes or hours, that materials or assemblies have withstood a fire exposure as established in accordance with the test procedures of NFPA 251, *Standard Methods of Fire Tests of Building Construction and Materials*.

Fire Window. A window assembly, including frame, wired glass, and hardware that under NFPA 257, *Standard for Fire Tests of Window Assemblies*, meets the fire protective requirements for the location in which it is to be used.

Flame Spread. The propagation of flame over a surface. (*See Section 6-5.*)

Flexible Plan Educational Buildings. (*See Section 10-1 or 11-1.*)

Floor Area, Gross. Gross floor area shall be the floor area within the inside perimeter of the outside walls of the building under consideration with no deduction for hallways, stairs, closets, thickness of interior walls, columns, or other features. Where the term area is used elsewhere in this *Code*, it shall be understood to be gross area unless otherwise specified.

Floor Area, Net. Net floor area shall be the actual occupied area, not including accessory unoccupied areas or thickness of walls.

The net area is arrived at after deductions have been made for the space that structural features and fixed fixtures occupy. Deductions could be made for hallways, stairs, closets, interior walls, columns, fixed counters and display racks, fixed tables and bars, and other fixed items that take up space that might otherwise have been used for human occupancy.

General Industrial Occupancies. (*See Section 28-1.*)

Group Day-Care Homes. (*See Section 10-8 or 11-8.*)

Guard. A vertical protective barrier erected along exposed edges of stairways, balconies, etc.

Handrail. A bar, pipe, or similar member designed to furnish persons with a handhold. (A handrail, if of suitable design, may also serve as part of a guard.)

Hazardous Areas. Areas of structures, buildings, or parts thereof having a degree of hazard greater than that normal to the general occupancy of the building or structure, such as storage or use of combustibles or flammables, toxic, noxious, or corrosive materials, or use of heat-producing appliances.

Health Care Occupancies.   (*See Section 4-1.*)

High Hazard Areas.   Areas of structures, buildings, or parts thereof used for purposes that involve highly combustible, highly flammable, or explosive products or materials that are likely to burn with extreme rapidity, or that may produce poisonous fumes or gases, including highly toxic or noxious alkalies, acids, or other liquids or chemicals that involve flame, fume, explosive, poisonous, or irritant hazards; also uses that cause division of material into fine particles or dust subject to explosion or spontaneous combustion, and uses that constitute a high fire hazard because of the form, character, or volume of the material used.

High Hazard Industrial Occupancy.   (*See Section 28-1.*)

High Rise Building.*   A building more than 75 ft (23 m) in height. Building height shall be measured from the lowest level of fire department vehicle access to the floor of the highest occupiable story.

A-3-2 High Rise Building.   It is the intent of this definition that in determining the level from which the highest occupiable floor is to be measured, the enforcing agency should exercise reasonable judgment, including consideration of overall accessibility to the building by fire department personnel and vehicular equipment. Where a building is situated on a sloping terrain and there is building access on more than one level, the enforcing agency may select the level which provides the most logical and adequate fire department access.

> This is a new definition for the 1988 Edition of the *Code*. Prior to this time, each occupancy set its own criteria. Business and health care used similar provisions, while the residential occupancies used six stories as the criteria. This establishes one definition so the *Code* can use the term consistently throughout. The definition has been accepted fairly well throughout the United States, but some jurisdictions set a lower height at which the definition applies due to local conditions. The Appendix note highlights the need for reasonable judgment in establishing the level from which to start the measurement.
>
> The "Airlie House" Report[1] is considered to be one of the principal founders of this definition. Although most admit that the definition has flaws, it is widely acknowledged as an acceptable method to determine if a building is high rise. One major flaw is the problem of lower height buildings that are set back over a large one-story section.
>
> High rise buildings have several problems:
>   1) Potential for significant stack effect
>   2) Difficulty in evacuation
>   3) Difficulty experienced by fire services in reaching fire.
> Also see definition of occupiable story.

Horizontal Exit.   (*See 5-1.2.5.*)

Hospital.   (*See Section 12-1 or 13-1.*)

Hotel.   *(See Section 16-1 or 17-1.)*

Industrial Occupancy.   *(See Section 4-1.)*

Interior Finish.   *(See Section 6-5.)*

Interior Floor Finish.   *(See Section 6-5.)*

Interior Room (Educational Occupancies).   *(See Section 10-1 or 11-1.)*

Limited Care Facility.   *(See Section 12-1 or 13-1.)*

Limited-Combustible.*   As applied to a building construction material, other than interior finish, means a material not complying with the definition of noncombustible material that, in the form in which it is used, has a potential heat value not exceeding 3500 Btu per lb (8.14 × 10^6 J/Kg), and complies with one of the following paragraphs (a) or (b).

Materials subject to increase in combustibility or flame spread rating beyond the limits herein established through the effects of age, moisture, or other atmospheric condition shall be considered combustible.

(a) Materials having a structural base of noncombustible material with a surfacing not exceeding a thickness of ⅛ in. (0.3 cm) that has a flame spread rating not greater than 50.

(b) Materials, in the form and thickness used, other than as described in (a), having neither a flame spread rating greater than 25 nor evidence of continued progressive combustion, and of such composition that surfaces that would be exposed by cutting through the material on any plane would have neither a flame spread rating greater than 25 nor evidence of continued progressive combustion.

A-3-2 Limited Combustible.   See NFPA 259, *Standard Test Method for Potential Heat of Building Materials* and NFPA 220, *Standard Types of Building Construction. (See Appendix B.)*

Load, Live.   The weight superimposed by the use and occupancy of the building, not including the wind load, earthquake load, or dead load.

Lodging Homes.   *(See Section 20-1.)*

Means of Egress.   *(See Section 5-1.)*

Means of Escape.   A way out of a building or structure that does not conform to the strict definition of means of egress but does provide an alternate way out.

Mercantile Occupancies.   *(See Section 4-1.)*

Mezzanine.   An intermediate level between the floor and the ceiling of any room or space and covering not more than one-third of the floor area of the room or space in which it is located.

Noncombustible.   A material that, in the form in which it is used and under the conditions anticipated, will not aid combustion or add appreciable heat to an ambient fire. Materials, where tested in accordance with ASTM E136, *Standard Test Method for Behavior of Materials in a Vertical Tube Furnace at 750°C,* and conforming to the criteria contained in Section 7 of the referenced standard shall be considered as noncombustible.

Nursing Homes.   *(See Section 12-1 or 13-1.)*

Occupancy.   The purpose for which a building or portion thereof is used or intended to be used.

Occupant Load.   The total number of persons that may occupy a building or portion thereof at any one time.

Occupiable Story.   A story occupied by people on a regular basis. Stories used exclusively for mechanical equipment rooms, elevator penthouses, and similar spaces are not occupiable stories.

Also see definition of High Rise.

One- and Two- Family Dwellings.   *(See Section 22-1.)*

Open Industrial Structures.   *(See Section 28-1.)*

Open Plan Educational Buildings.   *(See Section 10-1 or 11-1.)*

Outpatient (Ambulatory) Clinics.   *(See Section 12-1 or 13-1.)*

Outside Stairs.   Outside stairs include stairs in which at least one side is open to the outer air. *(See 5-2.2.)*

Partial Smoke Detection System.   *(See 7-6.2.8.)*

Place of Assembly.   *(See Assembly Occupancy in Section 4-1.)*

Platform.   *(See Section 8-1 or 9-1.)*

Plenum.   An air compartment or chamber to which one or more ducts are connected and that forms part of an air distribution system.

Proscenium Wall.   *(See Section 8-1 or 9-1.)*

Public Way.   Any street, alley, or other similar parcel of land essentially open to the outside air, deeded, dedicated, or otherwise permanently appropriated to the public for public use and having a clear width and height of not less than 10 ft (3 m).

Ramp.   An inclined floor surface. *(See 5-1.2.7 and 5-2.5.)*

Residential Occupancies.   *(See Section 4-1.)*

Residential Board and Care. *(See Section 21-1.)*

Room (Educational Occupancies). *(See Section 10-1 or 11-1.)*

Rooming House. *(See Section 20-1.)*

Self-Closing. Equipped with an approved device that will ensure closing after having been opened.

This is different from automatic-closing in that automatic-closing means equipped with a device that will ensure closing when needed, usually upon activation of a smoke detector and/or power failure.

Separate Atmosphere (Educational Occupancies). *(See Section 10-1 or 11-1.)*

Separate Means of Egress (Educational Occupancies). *(See Section 10-1 or 11-1.)*

Separated Exit Stair. *(See 5-1.3.1.)*

Separated Exit Ramp. *(See 5-1.3.1.)*

Smoke Barrier. A smoke barrier is a continuous membrane, either vertical or horizontal, such as a wall, floor, or ceiling assembly, that is designed and constructed to restrict the movement of smoke. A smoke barrier may or may not have a fire resistance rating. Such barriers may have protected openings. *(See Section 6-3.)*

Smoke Compartment.* A smoke compartment is a space within a building enclosed by smoke barriers on all sides, including the top and bottom. *(See Section 6-3.)*

A-3-2 Smoke Compartment. In the provision of smoke compartments utilizing the outside walls or the roof of a building, it is not intended that outside walls or roofs or any openings therein be capable of resisting the passage of smoke.

Smoke Detector. A device that senses visible or invisible particles of combustion.

Special Purpose Industrial Occupancies. *(See Section 28-1.)*

Special Structures. *(See Section 4-1.)*

Stage. *(See Section 8-1 or 9-1.)*

Storage Occupancy. *(See Section 4-1.)*

Stores. *(See Section 24-1 or 25-1.)*

Story. That portion of a building included between the upper surface of a floor and the upper surface of the floor or roof next above.

Street.   Any public thoroughfare (street, avenue, boulevard) 30 ft (9.1 m) or more in width that has been dedicated or deeded to the public for public use and is accessible for use by the fire department in fighting fire. Enclosed spaces and tunnels, even though used for vehicular and pedestrian traffic, are not considered as streets for the purposes of the *Code*.

Street Floor.   Any story or floor level accessible from the street or from outside the building at ground level with floor level at main entrance not more than three risers above or below ground level at these points, and so arranged and utilized as to qualify as the main floor. Where, due to differences in street levels, there are two or more stories accessible from the street, each is a street floor for the purposes of the *Code*. Where there is no floor level within the specified limits for a street floor above or below ground level, the building shall be considered as having no street floor.

Structure.   That which is built or constructed. The term structure shall be construed as if followed by the words "or portion thereof." (*See Building.*)

Thrust Stage.   (*See Section 8-1 or 9-1.*)

Vertical Opening.   An opening through a floor or roof.

Yard.   An open, unoccupied space other than a court, unobstructed from the ground to the sky, except where specifically provided by the *Code*, on the lot on which a building is situated.

REFERENCE CITED IN COMMENTARY

[1]_____ , Public Buildings Service International Conference on Firesafety in High-Rise Buildings, April 12-16, Airlie House, Warrenton, VA, U.S. Government Printing Office 2204-0005, Washington, D.C., May 1971.

4 CLASSIFICATION OF OCCUPANCY AND HAZARD OF CONTENTS

SECTION 4-1   CLASSIFICATION OF OCCUPANCY

The occupancy groupings found in Chapter 4 are based upon design features and occupancy patterns that are particular to certain types of occupancies, the main concern being to achieve a certain level of life safety for each. These groups are:

Assembly.   These occupancies generally house large groups of people who are unfamiliar with the space and therefore subject to indecision about the best means of egress should an emergency occur.

Educational.   Primarily, the *Code* is concerned with the large numbers of young people found in school buildings. In some cases (as with the day-care and preschool ages), they may even have to be carried out.

Health Care.   The overriding concern with these occupancies is that no matter how many exits are called for or provided, the occupants are not necessarily able or free to use them. They might be immobile, perhaps wired to monitoring equipment, debilitated, or recovering from surgery; or they might be in some way handicapped. The *Code*, in this instance, calls for a design that stresses horizontal movement and compartmentation. It recognizes that the occupants must be provided enough protection to enable them to survive the fire by staying in the structure, at least temporarily, during the fire.

Detention and Correctional.   Many of the concerns for life safety in detention and correctional facilities are similar to those in health care facilities; however, there are additional special problems. Among these problems are security, inmate population, ignition potential, and staff training.

The large number of multiple-fatality fires in correctional facilities during the mid-1970s led to the formation of a new subcommittee on correctional facilities, and in the 1981 Edition of the *Code*, new chapters for this type of occupancy were added.

Residential.   The main concern is that the occupants will be asleep for a portion (sometimes the major portion) of the time they occupy the building. Thus, they will be unaware of an incipient fire and may be trapped before actions to exit can be taken. In the 1985 Edition of the *Code*, a new chapter was added on residential board and care facilities. The poor fire record in these facilities has been well documented.[1]

Mercantile.   As with assembly occupancies, large numbers of people are gathered in a space relatively unfamiliar to them, sometimes in the presence of a sizable fuel load.

Business. A lower occupant density occurs here than in mercantile, and the occupants are generally more familiar with their surroundings. However, confusing and indirect egress patterns are often developed. The problems associated with high rise office occupancies have been recognized. Provisions contained in the *Code* are based on the fact that a rapid evacuation (and possibly any evacuation at all) may not be physically possible in multistory office buildings. As in health care occupancies, occupants may have to survive a fire while located within the structure.

Industrial. Because of the special circumstances involved, the *Code* relates the hazard of the occupancy to its incipient fuel load and considers the hazard of sizable industrial processes (including their unique or unusual features) where determining the requirements for exiting.

Storage. As in the case of industrial occupancies, fuel load and fuel arrangement, as well as a relatively low human population, are the basis for the *Code* provisions.

4-1.1 A building or structure shall be classified as follows, subject to the ruling of the authority having jurisdiction in case of question as to proper classification in any individual case.

This paragraph includes an important provision. If there is doubt about the proper occupancy classification the authority having jurisdiction makes the determination.

4-1.2* Assembly. (*For requirements see Chapters 8 and 9.*) Assembly occupancies include, but are not limited to, all buildings or portions of buildings used for gathering together 50 or more persons for such purposes as deliberation, worship, entertainment, eating, drinking, amusement, or awaiting transportation. Assembly occupancies include:

Armories
Assembly halls
Auditoriums
Bowling lanes
Churches
Club rooms
College and university
  classrooms, 50 persons
  and over
Conference rooms
Courtrooms
Dance halls
Drinking establishments
Exhibition halls

Gymnasiums
Libraries
Mortuary chapels
Motion picture theaters
Museums
Passenger stations and terminals of air,
  surface, underground, and marine public
  transportation facilities
Pool rooms
Recreation piers
Restaurants
Skating rinks
Theaters

Occupancy of any room or space for assembly purposes by less than 50 persons in a building of other occupancy and incidental to such other occupancy shall be classed as part of the other occupancy and subject to the provisions applicable thereto.

A-4-1.2 Such occupancies are characterized by the presence or potential presence of crowds with attendant panic hazard in case of fire or other emergency. They are generally open to the public, or may on occasion be open to the public, and the occupants, present voluntarily, are not ordinarily subject to discipline or control. Such buildings are ordinarily occupied by able-bodied persons and are not used for sleeping purposes. The need for alternate exit routes for small commercial places of assembly, such as restaurants, lounges, theaters, etc., with capacities of as few as 50 persons, is specially treated in this method of classification. Special conference rooms, snack areas, etc., incidental to and under the control of the management of other occupancies, such as offices, fall under the 50-person limitation.

Formal Interpretation 76-119
Reference: 4-1.2

Question 1: Is it the intent of the Committee that those facilities that are occupied by 49 persons or fewer are in fact not considered as assembly occupancies and are not subject to the requirements specified in Chapter 8 (Assembly Occupancies)?

Answer: Yes.

Question 2: If the answer to Question 1 is yes, under what occupancy classification would such an eating and drinking establishment be properly placed?

Answer: Mercantile.

Issue Edition: 1976
Reference: 4-1.2
Date: October 1979

4-1.3* Educational.   *(For requirements see Chapters 10 and 11).* Educational occupancies include all buildings or portions of buildings used for educational purposes through the twelfth grade by six or more persons for four or more hours per day or more than 12 hours per week. Educational occupancies include:

Academies	Nursery schools
Kindergartens	Schools

Educational occupancies also include day-care facilities of any occupant load. (*See Sections 10-7, 10-8, 10-9; 11-7, 11-8, 11-9.*)

Other occupancies associated with educational institutions shall be in accordance with the appropriate parts of this *Code.*

In cases where instruction is incidental to some other occupancy, the section of this *Code* governing such other occupancy shall apply.

A-4-1.3   Educational occupancy is distinguished from assembly in that the same occupants are regularly present and they are subject to discipline and control.

> Educational occupancies include buildings or portions of buildings used for educational purposes through the twelfth grade. College classroom buildings are considered Business Occupancies. See 10-1.1.3 for further information on requirements over the twelfth grade.

4-1.4 Health Care.   (*For requirements see Chapters 12 and 13.*) Health care occupancies are those used for purposes such as medical or other treatment or care of persons suffering from physical or mental illness, disease or infirmity; and for the care of infants, convalescents, or infirm aged persons. Health care occupancies provide sleeping facilities for four or more occupants and are occupied by persons who are mostly incapable of self-preservation because of age, physical or mental disability, or because of security measures not under the occupants' control.

Health care occupancies include:

(a) Hospitals

(b) Nursing homes

(c) Limited care facilities

Health care occupancies also include ambulatory health care centers. (*See Sections 12-6 and 13-6.*)

> Chapters 12 and 13 provide detailed definitions for the terms hospital, nursing home, limited care facility, and ambulatory care facility. Each of these definitions carries a requirement that the facility handle four or more persons (Chapter 22 allows up to three outsiders in a one- or two-family dwelling).

4-1.5 Detention and Correctional Occupancies.   (*For requirements see Chapters 14 and 15.*) Detention and correctional occupancies (also known as Residential-Restrained Care Institutions) are those used to house occupants under some degree of restraint or security. Detention and correctional occupancies are occupied by persons who are mostly incapable of self-preservation because of security measures not under the occupants' control.

Detention and correctional occupancies include:

Correctional institutions	Penal institutions
Detention centers	Prerelease centers
Houses of correction	Reformatories
Jails	Residential-restrained care

4-1.6 Residential.   (*For requirements see Chapters 16 through 23.*) Residential occupancies are those occupancies in which sleeping accommodations are provided for normal residential purposes and include all buildings designed to provide sleeping accommodations.

Exception: Those classified under Health Care or Detention and Correctional Occupancies.

Residential occupancies are treated separately in this *Code* in the following groups:

(a) Hotels (*Chapters 16 and 17*)
    Motels
    Dormitories

(b) Apartments (*Chapters 18 and 19*)

(c) Lodging or rooming houses (*Chapter 20*)

(d) Board and care facilities (*Chapter 21*)

(e) One- and two-family dwellings (*Chapter 22*)

Each of the occupancies is specifically defined within the chapters which govern them.

4-1.7* Mercantile. (*For requirements see Chapters 24 and 25.*) Mercantile occupancies include stores, markets, and other rooms, buildings, or structures for the display and sale of merchandise. Mercantile occupancies include:

Auction rooms	Shopping centers
Department stores	Supermarkets
Drugstores	

Minor merchandising operations in buildings predominantly of other occupancies, such as a newsstand in an office building, shall be subject to the exit requirements of the predominant occupancy.

A-4-1.7   Office, storage, and service facilities incidental to the sale of merchandise and located in the same building are included with mercantile occupancy.

4-1.8* Business. (*For requirements see Chapters 26 and 27.*) Business occupancies are those used for the transaction of business (other than that covered under Mercantile), for the keeping of accounts and records, and similar purposes. Business occupancies include:

City halls	Doctors' offices
College and university instructional buildings, classrooms under 50 persons, and instructional laboratories	General offices
	Laboratories for basic or applied research not including hazardous chemicals
Courthouses	Outpatient clinics, ambulatory
Dentists' offices	Town halls

Minor office occupancy incidental to operations in another occupancy shall be considered as a part of the predominating occupancy and shall be subject to the provisions of this *Code* applying to the predominating occupancy.

A-4-1.8   Doctors' and dentists' offices are included unless of such character as to be classified as hospitals. Service facilities usual to city office buildings such as newsstands, lunch counters serving less than 50 persons, barber shops, and beauty parlors are included in this occupancy group.

City halls, town halls, and court houses are included in this occupancy group insofar as their principal function is the transaction of public business and the keeping of books and records. Insofar as they are used for assembly purposes, they are classed as assembly occupancies.

4-1.9 Industrial.   *(For requirements see Chapter 28.)* Industrial occupancies include factories making products of all kinds and properties devoted to operations such as processing, assembling, mixing, packaging, finishing or decorating, and repairing. Industrial occupancies include:

Creameries	Laundries
Dry cleaning plants	Power plants
Factories of all kinds	Pumping stations
Gas plants	Refineries
Laboratories involving	Sawmills
hazardous chemicals	Smokehouses

4-1.10* Storage.   *(For requirements see Chapter 29.)* Storage occupancies include all buildings or structures utilized primarily for the storage or sheltering of goods, merchandise, products, vehicles, or animals. Storage occupancies include:

Barns	Parking garages
Bulk oil storage	Stables
Cold storage	Truck and marine
Freight terminals	terminals
Grain elevators	Warehouses
Hangars	

Minor storage incidental to another occupancy shall be treated as part of the other occupancy.

A-4-1.10   Storage properties are characterized by the presence of relatively small numbers of persons in proportion to the area; any new use that increases the number of occupants to a figure comparable with other classes of occupancy changes the classification of the building to that of the new use.

4-1.11 Special Structures.   Special structures that house occupancies include the occupancies from the preceding groups that are in special structures or buildings including, among others, the following:

Open structures	Vessels
Towers	Water surrounded structures
Underground structures	Windowless buildings
Vehicles	

Such special buildings and structures shall conform to the requirements of the specific occupancy Chapters 8 through 29 except as modified by Chapter 30.

In reality, special structures can be one of two types. The first type is a structure that houses an unusual occupancy, such as a railroad signal tower or forest fire tower. Another type is a structure that houses an occupancy regulated under one of the normal descriptions but in a special building, such as a restaurant on top of a tower, or an assembly or mercantile function on a pier. In either case, Chapter 30 should be referred to for specific requirements.

4-1.12 Mixed Occupancies (*see 1-4.7*).

SECTION 4-2   HAZARD OF CONTENTS

4-2.1 General.

4-2.1.1   The hazard of contents, for the purpose of this *Code*, shall be the relative danger of the start and spread of fire, the danger of smoke or gases generated, and the danger of explosion or other occurrence potentially endangering the lives and safety of the occupants of the building or structure.

To understand the purpose of Section 4-2, one must recognize that the classification of hazard is based on the potential threat to life the contents represent. A fuel load that might be considered as a "light" hazard in terms of its ease of extinguishment by a sprinkler system may, in fact, produce enough smoke and other toxic products of combustion to threaten the lives of the occupants; hence, the *Code* may classify the material as an "ordinary" hazard.

The *Code's* method of hazard classification is based on life safety. For this reason, its provisions are not readily incorporated into the design criteria of other codes where hazard classification is based on property preservation. Thus, for a material considered to be a high hazard by the *Life Safety Code*, there may be no constructive design or system arrangement to compensate for the potential threat to life short of total enclosure and isolation of the material involved. Further, many "light hazard" fuels (from an extinguishment point of view) may be treated as ordinary hazards under the *Life Safety Code*. For example, an office occupancy may have a "light" hazard classification under NFPA 13, *Standard for the Installation of Sprinkler Systems*[2], but is considered "ordinary" hazard under the *Life Safety Code*.

4-2.1.2   Hazard of contents shall be determined by the authority having jurisdiction on the basis of the character of the contents and the processes or operations conducted in the building or structure.

4-2.1.3*   Where different degrees of hazard of contents exist in different parts of a building or structure, the most hazardous shall govern the classification for the purpose of this *Code*.

Exception: Where hazardous areas are separated or protected, as specifed in Section 6-4 and the applicable sections of Chapters 8 through 30.

A-4-2.1.3   Under this provision, any violation of the requirements of Chapters 8 through 30 for separation or protection of hazardous operation or storage would inherently involve violation of the other sections of the *Code* unless additional exit facilities appropriate to high hazard contents were provided.

4-2.2 Classification of Hazard of Contents.

4-2.2.1*   The hazard of contents of any building or structure shall be classified as low, ordinary, or high in accordance with 4-2.2.2, 4-2.2.3, and 4-2.2.4.

A-4-2.2.1   These classifications do not apply to the application of sprinkler protection classifications. (*See NFPA 13, Installation of Sprinkler Systems.*) (*See Appendix B.*)

4-2.2.2* Low Hazard.   Low hazard contents shall be classified as those of such low combustibility that no self-propagating fire therein can occur.

A-4-2.2.2   Chapter 29, Storage Occupancies, recognizes storage of noncombustible materials as low hazard. In other occupancies it is assumed that even where the actual contents hazard may normally be low, there is sufficient likelihood that some combustible material or hazardous operations will be introduced in connection with building repair or maintenance, or that some psychological factor might create conditions conducive to panic, so that the exit facilities cannot safely be reduced below those specified for ordinary hazard contents.

It should be noted that very few occupancies qualify as having low hazard contents.

4-2.2.3* Ordinary Hazard.   Ordinary hazard contents shall be classified as those that are likely to burn with moderate rapidity or to give off a considerable volume of smoke.

A-4-2.2.3   This classification represents the conditions found in most buildings and is the basis for the general requirements of this *Code*.

The fear of poisonous fumes or explosions is necessarily a relative matter to be determined on a judgment basis. All smoke contains some toxic fire gases, but under conditions of ordinary hazard there should be no unduly dangerous exposure during the period necessary to escape from the fire area, assuming there are proper exits.

4-2.2.4* High Hazard.   High hazard contents shall be classified as those that are likely to burn with extreme rapidity or from which explosions are to be feared. (*For means of egress requirements see Section 5-11.*)

A-4-2.2.4   High hazard contents may include occupancies where gasoline and other flammable liquids are handled or used or are stored under conditions involving possible release of flammable vapors; where grain dust, wood flour or plastic dusts, aluminum or magnesium dust, or other explosive dusts may be produced; where hazardous chemicals or explosives are manufactured, stored, or handled; where cotton or other combustible fibers are processed or handled under conditions producing flammable flyings; and other situations of similar hazard.

Chapter 28, Industrial Occupancies, and Chapter 29, Storage Occupancies, include detailed provisions on high hazard contents.

As can be seen from the definitions, occupancies containing low hazard or high hazard contents are rare. As an aid to the user of the *Code* in deciding which hazard classification applies, it is suggested that the users ask themselves the following questions: Do the contents qualify for a low hazard classification? Do the contents qualify for a high hazard classification? If the answer to both of these questions is "no," then the hazard of contents must be in the "ordinary" classification.

REFERENCES CITED IN COMMENTARY

[1]NFPA SPP-76, *Firesafety in Boarding Homes*, National Fire Protection Association, Quincy, MA, 1982.

[2]NFPA 13, *Standard for the Installation of Sprinkler Systems*, National Fire Protection Association, Quincy, MA, 1987.

5
MEANS OF EGRESS

(See also Chapter 31.)

The purpose of this chapter is to establish minimum requirements for the means of egress, requirements that can be applied to all classifications of occupancy. Those instances in which these requirements are not specific enough for the needs of a particular situation are noted in the exceptions.

Means of egress is a term defined in 5-1.2.1 as including the exit, the exit access, and the exit discharge. This chapter covers the type, width, number, and arrangement of exits; their lighting and identification; as well as such key factors as travel distances and exit capacity. It also contains detailed requirements for the various components that may be included in the means of egress.

SECTION 5-1 GENERAL

5-1.1 Application.

Means of egress must comply with this chapter. The occupancy chapters, Chapters 8 through 30, may not contain provisions or requirements less stringent than those in Chapter 5 unless Chapter 5 expressly authorizes such difference. This provision was adopted to standardize, to the greatest extent possible, similar requirements as they apply to the various occupancies.

Since this was a shift in the prior organization of the *Code*, undetected discrepancies may arise, and therefore, for enforcement purposes, 1-4.8 continues to state that, where conflicts occur, the more specific requirements of the occupancy chapters prevail.

5-1.1.1* Means of egress for both new and existing buildings shall comply with this chapter. (*Also see Section 31-1.*)

A-5-1.1.1 Portable ladders, rope fire escapes, and similar emergency escape devices may have a useful function in facilitating escape from burning buildings lacking adequate exits of the stair or other standard type, but they are not the equivalent of standard exits, and their use is not in any way recognized by this *Code* as satisfying the requirements for means of egress. Furthermore, many such devices are of types quite unsuited to use by aged or infirm persons or by small children. Therefore, such devices may give a false sense of security and should not be made an excuse for not providing standard exit facilities.

These requirements apply to both new construction and to existing buildings. No change, either in the structure or the occupancy, that reduces the level of life safety is permitted. The objective is to provide an acceptable degree of safety in terms of not only the present but also the future use of a building.

5-1.1.2 Any alteration or addition that would reduce means of egress below the requirements of this *Code* is prohibited.

5-1.1.3 Any change of occupancy that would result in means of egress below the requirements of this *Code* is prohibited.

Whenever a building is renovated or when additions are made to it, care must be taken not to reduce the means of egress below the level required by the *Code*. Even though a new addition in itself may meet all requirements, it is prohibited to add to an existing building if, by doing so, the means of egress in the existing portion is reduced to a level below that specified by the *Code*. Similarly, any change in building occupancy or occupancy subclassification requires a review of the means of egress to ensure that the requirements specified for the new occupancy classification are met. (*See 1-4.6 for additional information regarding application to alterations and 1-6.4 regarding application to changes of occupancy or occupancy subclassification.*)

5-1.2 Definitions.

5-1.2.1 Means of Egress. A means of egress is a continuous and unobstructed way of exit travel from any point in a building or structure to a public way and consists of three separate and distinct parts: (a) the exit access, (b) the exit, and (c) the exit discharge. A means of egress comprises the vertical and horizontal travel and shall include intervening room spaces, doorways, hallways, corridors, passageways, balconies, ramps, stairs, enclosures, lobbies, escalators, horizontal exits, courts, and yards.

A means of egress, by definition, leads to a public way. This is the most succinct way the *Code* can express the need to get a building occupant to a safe place. In many instances, such as university campuses, military bases, resorts, and other large complexes, there are numerous places where a building occupant would be safe from a building fire before reaching an actual public way. It is the basic intent of the *Code* that occupants be able to get to a safe place.

From every location in a building, there must be a means of egress or path of travel over which a person can move to gain access to the outside or gain access to a place of safety or refuge should the need arise. Any person who gains entrance to a building has available that same route by which to exit. Yet, one important consideration makes exiting more than just reversing one's route of entry, especially if emergency conditions exist. This reverse route, or any other route chosen for exiting, may present features that, though they were not obstacles upon entrance, prove to be such upon exit. For example, a door hinged to swing in the direction of entry can become an obstacle when one attempts to leave the building in the opposite direction. The door swings against the flow of traffic — a flow that in an emergency situation is greatly increased as compared with the leisurely flow of people entering a building. The path of travel must be one that is easily traversable and recognizable.

A basic principle of the *Code* is that every component of a means of egress be operable by and under the control of the occupant seeking egress. Where the *Code* makes any exception to this basic concept, it does so only by imposing conditions deemed adequate to maintain the desired level of life safety.

The occupant of a building must be protected from obstacles to safe egress. To achieve this goal, the protection of each component in the exiting process must be considered individually. Clear and concise definitions are needed, definitions that help point to the special needs for that component.

The term "means of egress" has been used for many years in building codes, but it was not until the late 1950s that it took on a more meaningful definition, comprising three separate and distinct parts: (1) the exit access, (2) the exit, and (3) the exit discharge. Until the late 1950s, the term exit was used more often than not, a fact evidenced by the *Life Safety Code*'s original title — the *Building Exits Code*. At that time, the Sectional Committee on Means of Egress developed a proposed definition for "means of egress" and presented it for consideration to the NFPA Committee on Safety to Life. The original definition proposed contained the description of just two parts — an exit access and an exit. The Committee saw the need for a third part — the exit discharge. Now when reference is made to any of the three parts, there is a clear understanding of the part of a building being referenced and the function it serves in relation to the total means of egress.

Formal Interpretation 76-81
Reference: 5-1.2.1, 5-2.1.5.1

Question 1: Are doors which serve individual rooms, such as offices and classrooms, intended to be classified as a portion of a means of egress as defined in Paragraph 5-1.2.1?

Answer: Yes.

Question 2: If the answer to Question 1 is yes, are these doors then required to comply with Subparagraph 5-2.1.5.1, whereby locks requiring the use of a key from the side from which egress is to be made are prohibited?

Answer: Yes.

Issue Edition: 1976
Reference: 5-1.2.1
Date: September 1978

5-1.2.2 Exit Access.   Exit access is that portion of a means of egress that leads to an entrance to an exit.

The exit access includes the room or space in a building in which a person is located and the aisles, stairs, ramps, passageways, corridors, and doors that must be traversed on the way to an exit. Special protection may be required for corridor portions of the exit access beyond that which is normally required by building regulations for compartmentation within the building. (*See 5-1.3.4 and the applicable occupancy chapters.*) For maximum travel distances, see Section 5-6 and the occupancy chapters, Chapters 8 through 30. Some variations in arrangement of exit access are shown in Figure 5-1.

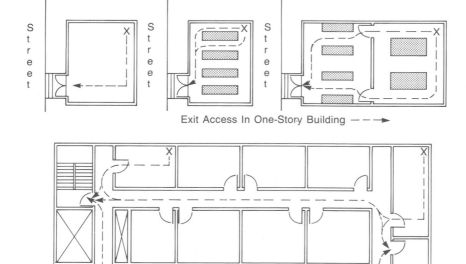

Exit Access In One-Story Building — — →

Exit Access On Upper Office Floor — — — →

Figure 5-1.   Variations of Exit Access.

5-1.2.3* Exit. Exit is that portion of a means of egress that is separated from all other spaces of the building or structure by construction or equipment as required in 5-1.3.1 to provide a protected way of travel to the exit discharge. Exits include exterior exit doors, exit passageways, horizontal exits, and separated exit stairs or ramps.

A-5-1.2.3 In the case of a stairway, the exit includes the door to the stairway enclosure, stairs and landings inside the enclosure, the door from the stairway enclosure to the street or open air, or any passageway and door necessary to provide a path of travel from the stairway enclosure to the street or open air. In the case of a door leading directly from the street floor to the street or open air, the exit comprises only the doorway.

Doors of small individual rooms, as in hotels, while constituting exit access from the room, are not referred to as exits except when they lead directly to the outside of the building or other place of safety.

> The exit is that portion of the means of egress that is separated from other building spaces by enclosing it within construction having the minimum degree of fire resistance as specified in 5-1.3.1, with limited openings through the enclosing construction, and protection of such openings. The exit may include parts of corridors, stairs, smokeproof enclosures, outside balconies, ramps, and doors. In each case, the exit component must conform to the specifications for fire protection and the maximum or minimum dimensions established by the *Code*. In its simplest form, an exit is simply a door leading to the outside. An example of this is the schoolroom having a door or doors opening directly to the exterior at grade.
>
> In the case of a stairway, the exit includes the stair enclosure, the door to the stairway enclosure, the stairs and landings inside the enclosure, the door from the enclosure to the street or open air, and any exit passageway necessary to provide a protected path of travel from the stairway enclosure to the street or open air.
>
> The entrance to an exit (part of the exit) is a fire door that provides a protected entrance into a protected area. A fire door, however, does not always signal an entrance to an exit. A door or fire door between a hotel room and a corridor, or a fire door across a corridor or lobby, is not part of an exit unless the corridor or lobby and all other openings into the corridor or lobby are separated and protected as required for an exit in accordance with 5-1.3.1.
>
> The important fact to remember is that an exit provides a protected path of travel within a building.
>
> A new last sentence has been added to 5-1.2.3 to specifically identify those building features that, when properly arranged and constructed, constitute an exit such as an exterior exit door, an exit passageway, a horizontal exit, and an enclosed exit stair or ramp.
>
> Several types of exits, as they may actually occur in some buildings, are shown in Figure 5-2. For detailed requirements for a horizontal exit, see 5-2.4.

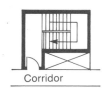

Corridor

Simple Exit Stair Enclosed In
Fire Rated Construction And
With Self-Closing Fire Door

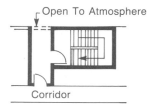

Open To Atmosphere

Corridor

Smokeproof Enclosure Enclosed In
Fire Rated Construction And With
Self-Closing Fire Doors And
Vestibule Open To The Outside

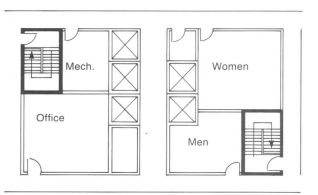

Core-Type Exits With Stairs Enclosed In Fire
Rated Construction And With Self-Closing
Fire Doors

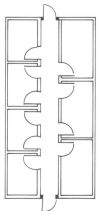

The Simplest of All
Exits, Doors Directly
To The Exterior

Figure 5-2.   Variations of Exits.

5-1.2.4 Exit Discharge.   Exit discharge is that portion of a means of egress between
the termination of an exit and a public way.

Not all exits discharge directly into a public way. In such cases there
remains some travel from the point where the occupant leaves the exit
enclosure to the public way or other equivalent safe place. This travel may
be inside the building, as permitted in 5-7.2, or outside. Where an exit
opens onto an alley, court, or yard, a safe passageway must be provided to
a public way or some equivalent safe area. In each case, this portion of the
means of egress is the exit discharge. (*See also* 5-7.1.)

Typical plans of various forms of the exit discharge are shown in
Figures 5-3, 5-4, and 5-5.

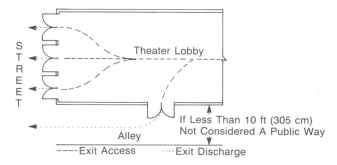

Figure 5-3. Examples of Exit Discharge. If the alley is less than 10 ft (305 cm) wide, it will not meet the definition of a public way; thus, the exit discharge continues to the street.

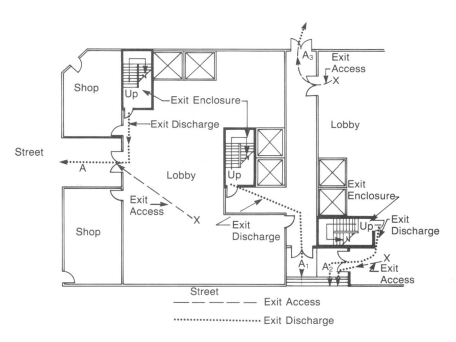

Figure 5-4. Examples of Exit Discharge in a Multistory Building. To the occupants of the building at the discharge level, the doors at A, A_1, A_2, and A_3 are exits, and the path denoted by long dash lines (- - - -) is the exit access. To people emerging from the exit enclosure, the same doors and the paths denoted by dotted lines (. . . .) are the exit discharges. This arrangement must meet the requirements of 5-7.2.

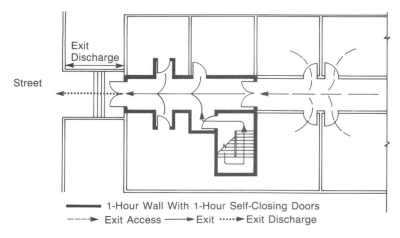

1-Hour Wall With 1-Hour Self-Closing Doors
----► Exit Access ──────► Exit ·····► Exit Discharge

Figure 5-5. Example of Exit Discharge from an Exit That Uses an Exit Passageway. The exit discharge from a building of this configuration, which includes an enclosed stair and exit passageway, extends from the exterior door to the public way (street).

5-1.2.5* Horizontal Exit.   A horizontal exit is a way of passage from one building to an area of refuge in another building on approximately the same level, or a way of passage through or around a fire barrier to an area of refuge on approximately the same level in the same building that affords safety from fire and smoke from the area of incidence and areas communicating therewith. (*See 5-2.4.*)

A-5-1.2.5   Horizontal exits should not be confused with egress through doors in smoke barriers. Doors in smoke barriers are designed only for temporary protection against smoke, whereas horizontal exits provide protection against serious fire for a relatively long period of time in addition to providing immediate protection from smoke.

A horizontal exit is a protected passage from one area of a building to another area in the same building or in an adjoining building on approximately the same level. Substantial fire separations are required since the area to which exit is made is to serve as an area of refuge. The horizontal exit may be a fire door in a 2-hour fire resistance rated wall separating a building into two areas, or it may be a bridge or balcony leading to an adjoining building. Examples of horizontal exits are shown in Figure 5-6.

Horizontal exits may be useful in any occupancy. They are particularly useful in health care occupancies. They make it possible to move bedridden patients horizontally to an area of refuge rather than vertically down stairs. Horizontal exits are very effective in the defend-in-place concept. With their use, total evacuation can often be avoided. For complete details of horizontal exits, see 5-2.4.

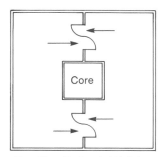

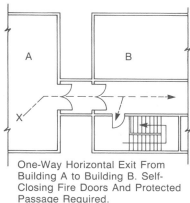

Two-Way Horizontal Exit In An Open Plan Building. Self-Closing Fire Doors Required In Fire Separation.

One-Way Horizontal Exit From Building A to Building B. Self-Closing Fire Doors And Protected Passage Required.

Figure 5-6. Types of Horizontal Exits. See 5-2.4 for more details on horizontal exits.

5-1.2.6 Common Path of Travel. That portion of exit access that must be traversed before two separate and distinct paths of travel to two exits are available. Paths that merge are common paths of travel. Common path of travel is measured the same as travel distance but terminates at that point where two separate and distinct routes become available.

A needed definition of common path of travel has been added to identify that part of the exit access to be considered in applying the common path provisions of certain occupancy chapters. For discussion of common path of travel, see 5-5.1.6.

5-1.2.7 Ramp. A ramp is a walking surface in an accessible space that has a running slope greater than 1 in 20.

For requirements for ramps used in a means of egress, see 5-2.5.

5-1.3 Separation of Means of Egress. *(See also Section 6-2.)*

5-1.3.1 Exits. Where an exit is required by this *Code* to be protected by separation from other parts of the building, the separating construction shall meet the requirements of Section 6-2 and the following requirements:

(a) The separation shall have at least a 1-hour fire resistance rating where the exit connects three stories or less. This applies whether the stories connected are above or below the story at which exit discharge begins.

Exception to (a): Existing apartment buildings in accordance with 19-2.2.1.2.

(b) The separation shall have at least a 2-hour fire resistance rating where the exit connects four or more stories, whether above or below the level of exit discharge. It shall be constructed of an assembly of noncombustible or limited-combustible materials and shall be supported by construction having at least a 2-hour fire resistance rating.

Exception to (b): Hotels in accordance with 16-2.2.1.2 and 17-2.2.1.2 and apartment buildings in accordance with 18-2.2.1.2 and 19-2.2.1.2.

(c) Any opening therein shall be protected by a fire door assembly equipped with a door closer complying with 5-2.1.8.

(d) Openings in exit enclosures shall be limited to those necessary for access to the enclosure from normally occupied spaces, from corridors, and for egress from the enclosure.

(e) Penetrations into and openings through an exit enclosure assembly are prohibited except for required exit doors; duct work and equipment necessary for independent stair pressurization; sprinkler piping; standpipes; and electrical conduit serving the stairway.

There shall be no penetrations or communicating openings between adjacent exit enclosures.

Exits must provide protection from fire throughout their entire length. This is accomplished by enclosure with construction having a designated degree of fire resistance, by the use of interior finish within the exit that meets the *Code*'s requirements related to flame spread and smoke development, and by careful control of openings into the exit enclosure itself. (*For the discussion of interior finish, see Section 6-5 and the occupancy chapters, Chapters 8 through 30.*) The only openings permitted in the enclosure walls between the exit and the building spaces are those needed to get into the exit from any normally occupied space and those needed to get out of the exit at the level of exit discharge; in other words, only openings necessary for an occupant to get into and out of the exit enclosure.

No opening through the enclosure walls is permitted from storage rooms, equipment spaces, utility rooms, electrical vaults or similar spaces that are not normally occupied. The *Code* also prohibits the use of an exit enclosure for any purpose that could possibly interfere with the exit's ability to function as a protected path of travel. Every measure must be taken to preserve the integrity of that portion of the means of egress.

The degree of fire resistance required is dependent upon the number of stories or floor levels that the individual exit connects and not the height of the building. It is possible to have stairs in a high rise building connecting only three stories. In such a case, the enclosing construction need not be more than 1-hour fire resistant. (*See Figures 5-7 and 5-8.*)

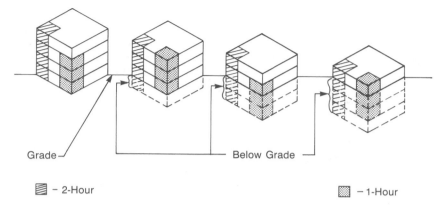

Grade

Below Grade

▨ – 2-Hour   ▦ – 1-Hour

Figure 5-7.   With Four Stories or More, Exit Stairs Must Be Enclosed in 2-Hour Noncombustible or Limited-Combustible Construction (Shaded Areas) and Supported by 2-Hour Construction.

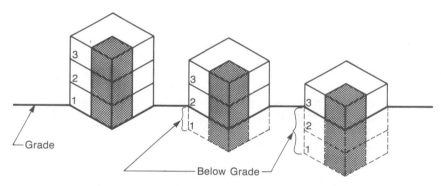

Grade

Below Grade

Figure 5-8.   With Three Stories or Less, Exit Stairs Must Be Enclosed in 1-Hour Construction (Shaded Areas).

The doors are to be 1-hour fire protection rated where used in 1-hour enclosures and 1½-hour fire protection rated where used in 2-hour enclosures. (*See 6-2.3.2.*)

If a pair of fire doors opening in the same direction without a mullion is to be used in an exit enclosure, the pair of doors should be listed for use without an astragal. The reason for this is the need for pairs of doors with an astragal to close in sequence. A coordinator is required to accomplish the sequential closing, and the record of coordinators functioning properly is poor.

Fire doors, if they are to function as intended, must not only be tightly closed, but also held closed with positive latching. To avoid the possibility of doors not properly closing, the use of pairs of doors with an astragal in an exit enclosure should be avoided. However, without an astragal, considerable smoke could pass between the doors into the exit; therefore the use of pairs of fire doors opening in the same direction into an exit enclosure is discouraged. Doors opening in opposite directions from each other, such as are often found in horizontal exits, are easily equipped with astragals, and as such, these doors and doors with mullions do not present this problem.

The only openings permitted into the exit enclosure are for the exiting of people at the point of entry from normally occupied spaces and at the exit discharge. These are required to be self-closing fire doors, as described in 5-2.1.8. Openings are not allowed, therefore, from storage rooms, closets, boiler rooms, electrical equipment rooms, maids' rooms, and similar areas. Openings for ductwork serving smokeproof enclosures may be permitted (*see 5-2.3*), but penetration by other ductwork is not allowed. Such openings to the exterior are permitted provided there is no potential fire exposure from an adjacent source. They need not be protected with fire protection rated assemblies since they are not separating the exit from other parts of the building. (*See 5-2.2.3.2.*)

Certain exit access corridors must also be separated from other building spaces in new construction. (*See 5-1.3.4.*) However, some of the occupancy chapters contain varying provisions.

5-1.3.2   The enclosing walls of exits shall be so arranged as to provide a continuous protected path of travel, including landings and passageways, to an exit discharge.

This extremely important paragraph emphasizes that exits, and the protection they afford the occupants, must be continuous. It is a fundamental premise that once an occupant has been provided the level of protection afforded by an exit, that level of protection shall not be thereafter reduced.

This paragraph prohibits a required exit stair or exit ramp design that requires a person to leave the exit enclosure, enter a floor, and then reenter the exit enclosure to continue down. Figure 5-9 shows an *unacceptable* arrangement.

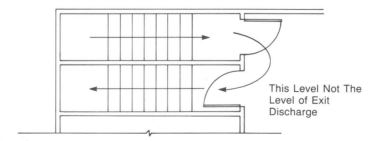

This Level Not The
Level of Exit
Discharge

Figure 5-9.   An Unacceptable Arrangement for Enclosing a Stairway Serving as a Required Exit.

5-1.3.3   No exit enclosure shall be used for any purpose that would interfere with its use as an exit, such as for storage or similar purposes. (*Also see 5-2.2.3.5.*)

Paragraph 5-1.3.3 prohibits the use of an exit for any purpose that might interfere with its use as an exit. For example, equipment rooms, closets, maids' rooms, wiring, vending machines, copying machines, and similar spaces or equipment are not permitted within an exit enclosure. Standpipes and emergency lighting that are part of the egress system are permitted, but only if arranged so as not to interfere with the passage of people. The paragraph also prohibits the use of an exit enclosure for storage or other similar purpose that may interfere with its use as an exit.

It should be noted that these prohibitions also apply to exit passageways, and horizontal exits, which are also exits.

Also see 5-1.3.1(d), which would prohibit such spaces from having doors into an exit enclosure, 5-1.7.3, 5-2.2.3.5 and 31-1.2.1.

5-1.3.4* Exit Access Corridors.   Corridors used as exit access and serving an area having an occupant load of more than 30 shall be separated from other parts of the building by construction having at least a 1-hour fire resistance rating. Openings in such separations shall be protected by an approved fire door assembly having a fire protection rating of at least 20 minutes when tested in accordance with NFPA 252, *Standard Methods of Fire Tests of Door Assemblies,* without the hose stream test. Such door shall be designed and installed to minimize smoke leakage.

Exception No. 1:   Existing buildings.

Exception No. 2:   Where requirements differ in Chapters 8 through 30.

A-5-1.3.4   The purpose of a tight-fitting door is to control the flow of smoke. The tight fit can be achieved by close attention to tolerances or by supplemental means. In no case should the "crack dimensions" exceed the maximum tolerances allowed in NFPA 80, *Standard for Fire Doors and Windows.* (*See Appendix B.*) (*Also see NFPA 105, Recommended Practice for the Installation of Smoke- and Draft-Control Door Assemblies.*)

Paragraph 5-1.3.4 establishes protection of certain exit access corridors in new buildings. It must be noted, however, that most of the occupancy chapters establish exit access corridor protection requirements that supersede these requirements. Also, many of the occupancy chapters establish corridor requirements for existing buildings. These special corridor provisions are usually in the —3.6 subsection of each occupancy chapter. For example, see 10-3.6 or 12-3.6. If no special requirements appear in subsection —3.6, then the provisions of 5-1.3.4 prevail.

Paragraph 5-1.3.4 does not require corridors, but does require that where corridors do exist and they serve an area having an occupant load of more than 30, they must be separated. Since openings must be protected by an assembly having a fire protection rating of at least 20 minutes, a closer and latch are required. (*See Figure 5-10.*)

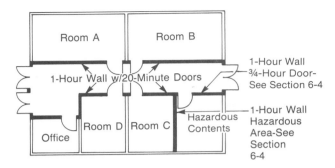

Figure 5-10.   Protection of Exit Access Corridors.   This plan shows an example of the requirement for protection of exit access corridors required by 5-1.3.4. Note the difference for the protection from the hazardous area.

5-1.4 Interior Finish in Exits.   The flame spread of interior finish on walls and ceilings shall be limited to Class A or Class B in exit enclosures. Chapters 8 through 30 governing individual occupancies may impose further limitations.

Except as provided in Chapters 8 through 30, the interior finish in exits is required to be Class A (0-25 flame spread rate, 0-450 smoke development) or Class B (26-75 flame spread rate, 0-450 smoke development) as defined in Section 6-5. Obviously, the effort is to minimize the possibility of fire spreading into and within the exit.

5-1.5 Headroom.   Means of egress shall be so designed and maintained as to provide adequate headroom as provided in other sections of this *Code* (*see 5-2.2.2.1*), but in no case shall the ceiling height be less than 7 ft 6 in. (229 cm) nor shall any projection from the ceiling be less than 6 ft 8 in. (203 cm) nominal height from the floor. Headroom on stairs is the vertical distance above a plane parallel to and tangent with the most forward projection of the stair tread.

Exception: In existing buildings, the ceiling height shall not be less than 7 ft (213 cm) from the floor with no projection below a 6 ft 8 in. (203 cm) nominal height from the floor.

The lowest projection of 6 ft 8 in. (203 cm) is now identified as nominal height. It is the intent to recognize and permit standard door height. Note that 5-2.2.2.1 allows the 6 ft 8 in. (203 cm) height on stairways also. (*See Figure 5-11.*)

5-1.6 Changes in Level in Means of Egress.

5-1.6 is a restatement, in more fundamental terms, of three separate requirements that were in previous editions of the *Code*. (These requirements were previously designated 5-1.6, 5-2.2.4.5, and 5-2.2.4.7). They dealt with both the elevation differences and the minimum number of

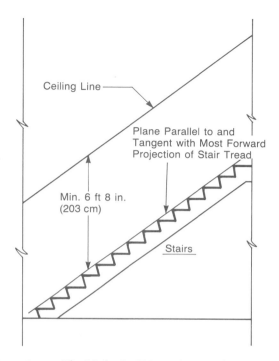

Figure 5-11.   The Method of Measuring Headroom on Stairs.

risers that could be used with stairs as opposed to ramps. These previous rules have not been well respected in actual practice, and a major problem remained to be solved with regard to a more basic approach to stairs traversing small elevation differences. Paragraph 5-1.6 now permits stairs to be used generally and to have fewer than three risers. However, it should be emphasized that such situations are not desirable, and if they are built, they must meet even more stringent requirements than those for other stairs because of the record of accidents on such limited-rise stairs. It should be made clear to designers that, as far as the *Code* (and, increasingly, litigation practice) is concerned, single risers and two-riser combinations are stairs and must meet all the requirements for stairs. Additionally, they must be designed more carefully, with particular attention to making their presence evident to all users and allowing for the larger walking stride that may occur in such situations [hence the requirement for a larger minimum tread size of 13 in. (33.0 cm)].

5-1.6.1   Changes in level in means of egress shall be by a ramp or a stair where the elevation difference is more than 21 in. (53.3 cm).

5-1.6.2*   Changes in level in means of egress not more than 21 in. (53.3 cm) shall be either by a ramp or by a stair complying with the requirements of 5-2.2. The minimum tread depth of such stair shall be 13 in. (33.0 cm) and the location of each step shall be readily apparent.

A-5-1.6.2   Aside from the problems created for persons with mobility disabilities, small changes of elevations of floors are best avoided because of the increased occurrence of missteps where the presence of single steps or a series of steps is not readily apparent. A contrasting marking stripe on each stepping surface may be provided at the nosing or leading edge such that the location of each step is readily apparent, especially when viewed in descent. Such stripes should be at least 1 in. (2.5 cm) but not more than 2 in. (5.0 cm) in width. Other methods could include lighting of each tread, contrasting colors, contrasting textures, a combination thereof, or other similar means. The construction or application of marking stripes should be such that slip resistance is consistent over the walking surface, and no tripping hazard is created. (*See also A-5-2.2.4.4.*) Depending on the distractions of the surroundings, the familiarity of users with a particular small change of level, and the number of people that might be in a group traversing the change of level (thereby reducing visibility of the level changes), additional warning measures might be needed to make sure that everyone's attention is drawn to such ramps, platforms, and steps, especially for descent. These measures include prominent handrails within reach of users, warning signs, highlighting each step by illumination.

Prior editions of the *Code* prohibited stairs where changes of elevation were less than 21 in. (53.3 cm). The Committee recognized a need to allow steps in these locations for functional reasons but noted that something needed to be done to avoid missteps. The minimum 13 in. tread (33.0 cm) was established to help reduce missteps. The Appendix note provides very useful information to further help reduce problems in these situations. (*Also see commentary following 5-1.6.*)

5-1.7 Workmanship, Impediments to Egress.

5-1.7.1   Doors, stairs, ramps, passageways, signs, and all other components of means of egress shall be of substantial, reliable construction and shall be built or installed in a workmanlike manner.

5-1.7.2   Any device or alarm installed to restrict the improper use of a means of egress shall be so designed and installed that it cannot, even in case of failure, impede or prevent emergency use of such means of egress. (*Also see 5-2.1.6.*)

Exception: In detention and correctional occupancies as provided in Chapters 14 and 15.

Formal Interpretation 76-83
Reference: 5-1.7.2

Question: Is it the intent of 5-1.7.2 to permit, under controlled conditions, the use of an electric locking device on an outside exit door equipped with panic hardware?

Answer: It is the intent of the Committee that the exits in a building be under the control of any individual occupant seeking egress.

Issue Edition: 1976
Reference: 5-1.6.2
Date: September 1978

5-1.7.3*   Means of egress shall be free of obstructions that would prevent its use.

A-5-1.7.3   Means of egress must permit unobstructed travel at all times. Any type barrier including, but not limited to, the accumulations of snow and ice in those climates subject to such accumulations is an impediment to free movement in the means of egress.

Paragraph 5-1.7.3 is intended to prevent the obstruction or partial obstruction of any portion of the means of egress by construction features, furniture, fixtures, accumulations of ice and snow, or by any other condition. This paragraph is not only a design requirement but also a maintenance requirement. It should be remembered that this provision applies to the entire means of egress, including the exit discharge that may include sidewalks leading to the public way.
(*Also see 5-1.3.3 and 31-1.2.1.*)

SECTION 5-2   MEANS OF EGRESS COMPONENTS

While moving along any means of egress, many different components of the building or structure are encountered — components that make up the features of the means of egress. These components are items such as the doors, stairs, ramps, horizontal exits, exit passageways, hardware, handrails, guardrails, balconies, and other features. Their composition, properties, use, limits, and function relative to the total means of egress must be understood.

Portable ladders, rope ladders, and similar devices are not recognized by the *Code* as providing any portion of the required capacity of a means of egress. Neither should they be considered as in any way upgrading an inadequate means of egress in an existing building where the means of egress system is below minimum requirements. While on occasion such devices have been used and have provided a way to safety, they most definitely should not be relied upon and can lead to a false sense of security. They are often unusable by small children, older people, the physically handicapped, or those who simply have not used them before.

The components of a means of egress must meet certain standards, be built in a prescribed manner, and perform at a level specified by the *Code*, depending upon whether they are part of the access to an exit, the exit itself, or the exit discharge. In some instances, the requirements are the same throughout the means of egress.

5-2.1 Doors.

5-2.1.1 General.

Doors serve three purposes related to the comfort and safety of building occupants. They provide protection from:

1. Weather, drafts, and noise and disturbance from adjoining areas;
2. Trespass by unauthorized persons; and,
3. Fire and smoke, with which this *Code* is concerned.

There are three broad categories of doors, each providing varying degrees of protection from fire. The first is the non-fire-rated door, such as is used in one- and two-family dwelling construction. While not fire-rated, such doors do, in fact, provide a limited degree of protection if closed. The second is the tested fire door that has passed the standard fire test for doors (NFPA 252, *Standard Methods of Fire Tests of Door Assemblies*).[1] These doors will withstand a severe fire and hose stream exposure for a definite period of time, as is required for various uses and occupancies. Finally, there is the smoke-stop door that is usually of lighter construction than the fire door. Its function is to provide a temporary barrier against the passage of heat, smoke, and gases.

None of these doors will perform satisfactorily if they are left open during a fire, thus allowing the entry of fire and combustion products into what should be a safer area. The history of fire is full of tragic examples of those who died because of an open door. There are also many examples of people saved because a door was closed. Less frequent, but nonetheless tragic, are those situations in which doors needed for escape were blocked or locked, resulting in dire consequences. *Code* requirements take these possibilities into consideration.

Some types of doors that are designed to prevent spread of fire through wall openings are not necessarily suitable for use in means of egress, and they pose the potential hazard of personal injury if they are so used. This category includes various rolling-shutter and sliding-door types.

5-2.1.1.1 A door assembly, including the doorway, frame, door, and necessary hardware, may be used as a component in a means of egress where it conforms to the general requirements of Section 5-1 and to the special requirements of this subsection. As such, the assembly is designated as a door.

Paragraph 5-2.1.1.1 is alerting the *Code* user to the fact that the *Code* uses the term "door" to mean door assembly. Thus, whenever the *Code* refers to a rated door or fire door, it is referring to the entire door assembly. If any single component is not properly provided, installed, and functioning, the assembly is not a fire protection rated assembly.

5-2.1.1.2 Every door and every principal entrance that is required to serve as an exit shall be so designed and constructed that the way of exit travel is obvious and direct. Windows that, because of their physical configuration or design and the materials used in their construction, could be mistaken for doors shall be made inaccessible to the occupants by barriers or railings conforming to the requirements of 5-2.2.6.

5-2.1.1.3   For the purpose of Section 5-2, unless otherwise provided by Chapters 8 through 30, a building is occupied at any time it is open to or accessible to the public or at any other time it is occupied by more than 10 persons.

There are many industrial, storage, and business buildings that are never open to or accessible to the public, and therefore, there are times or situations where the term "accessible to the public" should not be taken too literally but should be interpreted as "operating" or "functioning." Usually, the 10-person maximum will prevent abuse of this situation, but in smaller buildings or storage buildings, the authority having jurisdiction will have to broadly interpret "public." The intent of this provision is to allow small security or cleaning crews to be in a building and not have the building considered occupied. This will allow doors to be locked and lights turned off without violating the *Code*. The intent is that these people will use lights as they need them and turn them off, or in the case of security, carry their own lights and carry their own keys. [*See 5-2.1.5.1(d)*.] It is not the intent to allow people, no matter how few the number, to be locked in a building without a ready means of escape.

5-2.1.2 Egress Width.

5-2.1.2.1*   In determining the egress width for a doorway, only the clear width of the doorway when the door is in the full open position shall be measured. Clear width shall be the net, unobstructed width of the door opening without projections into such width.

Exception: In existing buildings, projections into the door opening by stops or by the hinge stile shall be permitted.

A-5-2.1.2.1   Figure A-5-2.1.2.1 illustrates the difference in measuring the width of doors in new and existing buildings.

In New Buildings the Actual Net Unobstructed Width of the Door Opening is Measured

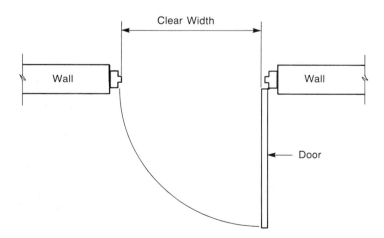

Door Stop and Hinge Stile Projections are Disregarded
in Determining Width in Existing Buildings.

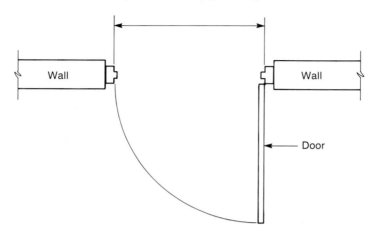

Figure A-5-2.1.2.1

5-2.1.3 Width and Floor Level.

5-2.1.3.1   No door opening in the means of egress shall be less than 32 in. (81 cm) in clear width. Where a pair of doors is provided, at least one of the doors shall provide a minimum 32 in. (81 cm) clear width opening.

Exception No. 1:   Exit access doors serving a room not greater than 70 sq ft (6.5 sq m) and not required to be accessible to the handicapped shall be not less than 24 in. (61 cm) wide.

Exception No. 2:   In existing buildings the minimum door width shall be not less than 28 in. (71 cm).

Exception No. 3:   In detention and correctional occupancies as provided in Chapters 14 and 15.

Exception No. 4:   Interior doors within dwelling units as provided in Chapter 22.

Generally, there are doors of varying types along the entire route of a means of egress, and each door opening must be wide enough to accommodate the number of people expected to move through that doorway during an emergency. This width is based on the occupant load served and on the capacity factors in 5-3.3.1. A doorway is a level egress component. Therefore, its capacity is based on that specified for level components. In general, no door opening may be less than 32 in. (81 cm) wide. Where another particular *Code* section specifies a width greater than 32 in. (81 cm), that greater width must be used. It is the intent of the *Code* that the doorway not create a bottleneck in the means of egress. At times, another portion of the means of egress may be larger than required, creating the illusion of a bottleneck. However, the door opening width is determined by the occupant load served, and this specified width will be sufficient. A door serving a hallway need not be as wide as the hallway since hallway width requirements are determined by other factors in addition to the occupant load. (*See Figure 5-12.*) An example is a health care facility, where corridor and doorway widths are much wider than the occupant load would seem to dictate. In this instance, the sizes of the corridor and door opening are governed by the necessity to move patients in their beds along the means of egress route; therefore, their widths are sized accordingly.

Exception No. 1 is new to the 1988 *Code.* The intent of this Exception is to allow a small room (probably occupied by only a couple of people) that is not required to be accessible to the handicapped to use what may be considered to be an absolute minimum size door.

Previous editions of the *Code* specified that no single door in a doorway be less than 28 in. (71 cm) wide; therefore, an Exception is provided for existing buildings. The new wider width permits the passage of wheelchairs. It should also be noted that the minimum width required may not be adequate for the normal usage of the doorway for purposes other than exiting.

For security and operations purposes, detention and correctional facilities are allowed to have doors of smaller width. (*See Chapters 14 and 15.*)

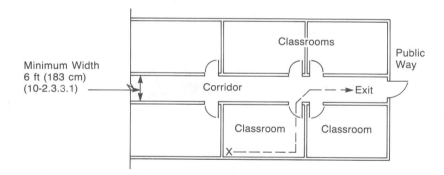

Figure 5-12.   Exit Door Need Not Be as Wide as the Corridor Is Required to Be, Because Operational Features of the Occupancy in Addition to the Occupant Load Are Used in Determining Required Corridor Width.   In this example of a school, the corridor is required to be 6 ft (180 cm) wide while the occupant load served would dictate the size of the exit door.

5-2.1.3.2   No single door in a doorway shall exceed 48 in. (122 cm) in width.

The *Code* places a maximum of 48 in. (122 cm) on any door leaf width. This requirement prevents the possible installation of doors of unwieldly size, a size that would make them difficult to handle, and thus not easily accommodate the occupant load to be served.

5-2.1.3.3   The floor on both sides of a doorway shall be substantially level and shall have the same elevation on both sides of the doorway, for a distance at least equal to the width of the widest leaf.

Exception: In one- and two-family dwellings and in existing buildings where the door discharges to the outside or to an exterior balcony, exterior exit, or exterior exit access, the floor level outside the door may be one step lower than the inside, but not more than 8 in. (20.3 cm) lower.

Previously the *Code* permitted the floor level outside exterior doors to be one step but not more than 8 in. (20.3 cm) lower than the floor level inside the door. The reason was to avoid blocking the outward swing of the door by a buildup of snow or ice. The Committee changed the paragraph to prohibit the one exterior step based on the possible tripping hazard. The Committee also noted that other provisions of the *Code* require that the means of egress be maintained free of obstructions or be protected from the weather, thus providing for the removal of snow or ice accumulations. Existing buildings and one- and two-family dwellings are permitted to use the one exterior step as noted in the exception.

5-2.1.4 Swing and Force to Open.

5-2.1.4.1*   Any door in a means of egress shall be of the side-hinged or pivoted swinging type. The door shall be so designed and installed that it shall be capable of swinging from any position to the full use of the opening in which it is installed. Doors shall swing in the direction of exit travel:

(a) Where used in an exit enclosure, or

(b) Where serving a high hazard area, or

(c) Where serving a room or area with an occupant load of 50 or more.

Exception No. 1: Sliding doors in detention and correctional occupancies as provided in Chapters 14 and 15, and doors for dwelling units as provided in Chapter 22.

Exception No. 2: Smoke barrier door swing in existing health care occupancies as provided in Chapter 13.

Exception No. 3: Where permitted by Chapters 8 through 30, horizontal sliding or vertical rolling security grilles or doors that are a part of the required means of egress shall conform to the following:

(a) They must remain secured in the full open position during the period of occupancy by the general public.

(b) On or adjacent to the door, there shall be a readily visible, durable sign stating THIS DOOR TO REMAIN OPEN WHEN THE BUILDING IS OCCUPIED. The sign shall be in letters not less than 1 in. (2.5 cm) high on a contrasting background.

(c) Doors or grilles shall not be brought to the closed position when the space is occupied.

(d) Doors or grilles shall be openable from within the space without the use of any special knowledge or effort.

(e) Where two or more means of egress are required, not more than half of the means of egress may be equipped with horizontal sliding or vertical rolling grilles or doors.

Exception No. 4: An elevator lobby that is not a part of the exit access system for the remainder of the story may be provided with an approved self-closing or automatic-closing horizontal sliding door. (See 5-2.1.12.)

Exception No. 5: An elevator lobby may be provided with a horizontal sliding door that conforms with the requirements of 5-2.1.14.

Exception No. 6: Where permitted by Chapters 8 through 30, any door in a means of egress serving an occupant load of less than 50 may be a horizontal sliding door that conforms to the requirements of 5-2.1.14.

Exception No. 7: Where permitted by Chapters 8 through 30, horizontal exits or smoke barriers may be provided with horizontal sliding doors that conform to the requirements of 5-2.1.14.

Exception No. 8: Doors to private garages and industrial and storage areas with an occupant load of not more than 10 need not be side-hinged swinging doors where such garages, industrial and storage areas contain low or ordinary hazard contents.

Exception No. 9: Revolving doors complying with 5-2.1.10.

A-5-2.1.4.1   Where doors are subject to two-way traffic, or where their opening may interfere with pedestrian traffic, an appropriately located vision panel can reduce the chance of accidents.

   Ideally, all doors in a means of egress would swing in the direction of exit travel. The *Code* requires that those doors that are in an exit enclosure itself shall swing in the direction of exit travel. Doors that occur in the exit access should be considered separately, since there are cases where swing in the direction of travel is not necessary or even desirable. An example is a classroom door that provides passage into a corridor that serves as an exit access for several other classrooms. It is felt that because a student is aware of and accustomed to a door opening into a room, it is better to let the door swing into the room. If the door opened into the corridor, it could open against another door or against the flow of people and possibly restrict or decrease the width of passage in that more critical element of the means of egress. The *Code* recognizes this danger and limits the occupant load of such a room to less than 50, thus limiting the number of people using a door that swings against traffic. The *Code* also recognizes similar constraints with regard to an exterior exit door, and even though it is an exit, does not require that it swing in direction of exit travel unless it serves 50 or more occupants. Of course, all doors serving a high hazard area shall swing in direction of exit travel regardless of occupant load. (*See Figure 5-13.*)
   Paragraph 5-2.1.4.1 requires that doors be the side-hinged, swinging type. This is the type of door most familiar to the general public, and its operation is readily understood.
   Some of the occupancy chapters provide exceptions to these requirements. For example, detention and correctional occupancies allow certain sliding doors. An exception is also allowed for horizontal sliding or vertical rolling security grilles or doors, provided the exception is

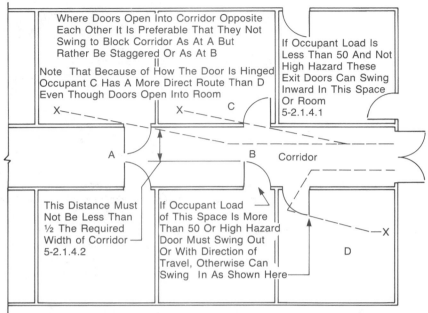

Where Doors Open Into Corridor Opposite Each Other It Is Preferable That They Not Swing to Block Corridor As At A But Rather Be Staggered Or As At B

Note That Because of How The Door Is Hinged Occupant C Has A More Direct Route Than D Even Though Doors Open Into Room

If Occupant Load Is Less Than 50 And Not High Hazard These Exit Doors Can Swing Inward In This Space Or Room
5-2.1.4.1

This Distance Must Not Be Less Than ½ The Required Width of Corridor
5-2.1.4.2

If Occupant Load of This Space Is More Than 50 Or High Hazard Door Must Swing Out Or With Direction of Travel, Otherwise Can Swing In As Shown Here

Corridor

Note: All Doors To Stairways Must Swing In Direction of Exit Travel (5-2.1.4.1)

Figure 5-13. Door Swing Considerations. A diagramatic representation of some of the considerations involved in evaluating the effect of various arrangements of door swing at entrances to corridors.

specifically allowed by the applicable occupancy chapter. This exception permits the security doors and grilles normally found in a covered shopping mall. It should be noted that there is a difference between items (a) and (c) in Exception No. 3. Item (a) requires that the door be fully open when the space is occupied by the public, while item (c) states that the door cannot be closed when the space is occupied. This allows the common practice of the door being partially closed during inventory, closing, and at other times when restricting entry by the general public is desired.

The following occupancies allow the use of the horizontal sliding or vertical rolling doors complying with Exception No. 3. Check the referenced paragraphs for additional restrictions that may be imposed by the occupancy chapter:

Assembly — 8-2.2.2.2, 9-2.2.2.2

Mercantile — 24-2.2.2.5, 25-2.2.2.5

Business — 26-2.2.2.5, 27-2.2.2.5

In addition, three new Exceptions from the side-hinged, swinging requirement that allow use of special horizontal sliding doors conforming with the new provisions of 5-2.1.14 have been added.

Note that both Exception No. 6 and Exception No. 7 require permission of the occupancy chapter whereas Exception No. 5 is allowed regardless of occupancy as it serves only the elevator lobby and not the rest of the building.

The following occupancies allow the use of Exceptions 6 or 7. Check the referenced paragraphs for additional restrictions that may be imposed by the occupancy chapter.

Health Care — 12-2.2.5, 13-2.2.5, 12-3.7.5, 13-3.7.7
Industrial — 28-2.2.2.3 and 28-2.2.2.4
Storage — 29-2.2.2.3, 29-2.2.2.4 and 29-8.2.2.2
Unusual — 30-2.2.2.2 and 30-2.2.2.3

5-2.1.4.2* During its swing, any door in a means of egress shall leave unobstructed at least one-half of the required width of an aisle, corridor, passageway, or landing. When fully open, the door shall not project more than 7 in. (17.8 cm) into the required width of an aisle, corridor, passageway, or landing.

Exception: In existing buildings, a door giving access to a stair shall neither reduce the unobstructed width of a stair or landing to less than 22 in. (55.9 cm), nor, when open, project more than 7 in. (17.8 cm) into the required width of a stair or landing.

A-5-2.1.4.2 This section is not intended to apply to the swing of cross corridor doors such as smoke barrier doors and horizontal exits.

Doors that open 180 degrees have a greater utility than those opening only 90 degrees. As shown in Figure 5-14, the former can open into a corridor without blocking the passageway. The 90 degree door, however, must either open into an unusually wide corridor or must be set into an alcove as shown, or otherwise recessed.

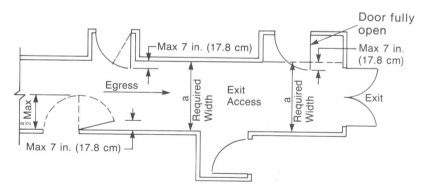

Figure 5-14. Door Swing into a Corridor. Doors that swing 180 degrees to come to rest against a wall provide the best arrangement for clear passage in an exit access corridor. A door swinging 90 degrees into the path of travel is considered to partially block an exit access if more than 7 in. (17.8 cm) of the required width of the corridor remains obstructed.

Doors serving as an entrance to an exit stairway should not unduly block the stair landing or the stairs. It is preferred that the door not reduce the required width either during its swing or at rest. However, the

Code does allow arrangements similar to Figure 5-15. An acceptable arrangement for a door opening onto a stair landing in an existing building is shown in Figure 5-16.

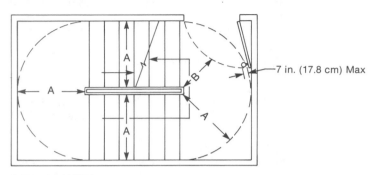

A-Required Width
B-At Least ½ A

Figure 5-15.   A Typical Interior Stairway Showing Clearances that Must Be Observed in New Buildings.   For example, if the stairway is required to be 66 in. (168 cm) in width, Dimension "B" must be at least 33 in. (84 cm).

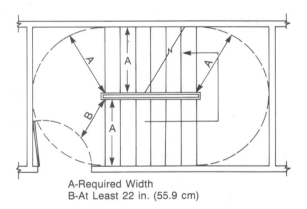

A-Required Width
B-At Least 22 in. (55.9 cm)

Figure 5-16.   A Typical Interior Stairway Showing Clearances that Must Be Observed in Existing Buildings. Stair widths and landing radii (A) are equal; clearance (B) between opening door and stair newel post must be at least 22 in. (55.9 cm).

5-2.1.4.3   The forces required to fully open any door manually in a means of egress shall not exceed a 15 lbf (67 N) to release the latch, a 30 lbf (133 N) to set the door in motion and a 15 lbf (67 N) to open the door to the minimum required width. These forces shall be applied at the latch stile.

Exception No. 1:   The opening force for doors in existing buildings shall not exceed 50 lbf (222 N) applied to the latch stile.

Exception No. 2: *In detention and correctional occupancies as provided in Chapters 14 and 15.*

Exception No. 3: *As otherwise provided in 5-2.1.9.*

The *Code* recognizes that in the operation of any door, there are several movements necessary and identifies each of the movements and its required force. As a result, the force required to unlatch the door is limited to 15 lbf (67 N); that necessary to start the door in motion, or to overcome its inertia, cannot exceed 30 lbf (133 N); and that to fully open the door can be no more than 15 lbf (67 N). The Committee concluded that many people may not be capable of exerting 50 lbf (222 N) horizontally under some rather common circumstances. (*Also see 5-2.1.9 for power-operated doors.*)

Care must be taken to ensure that the 30 lbf (133 N) to overcome the inertia of a door in a means of egress is not exceeded for doors opening into pressurized stairs. Many times the pressure necessary to protect the stair may be such that a 30 lbf (133 N) will not be sufficient to open the door. The use of barometric relief dampers or other pressure regulating methods may be required.

5-2.1.4.4 Screen and Storm Doors. No screen door or storm door used in an exit shall swing against the direction of exit travel where doors are required to swing in the direction of exit travel. (*See 5-2.1.4.1.*)

There are various methods by which the function of screen or storm doors may be provided without having any door swing against the exit travel. A screen or storm door may be used in the same doorway with an ordinary door by means of a vestibule of sufficient size as to permit the inner door to swing outwardly without interfering with the operation of the door at the other end of the vestibule. (See Figure 5-17.)

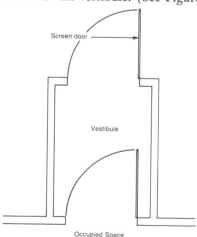

Screen door

Vestibule

Occupied Space

Figure 5-17. A Possible Arrangement of a Vestibule Leading to a Screen Door that Complies with 5-2.1.4.4.

A jalousie door, with a screen or storm sash panel, provides the function of both a regular door and screen or storm sash, all in a single unit.

5-2.1.5 Locks, Latches, Alarm Devices.

The increase in theft, molestations, and similar actions has led, in some instances, to the practice of providing extra security on exit doors and doors leading to them. Such practices, particularly involving the doors to exit stairs and exit discharges, are open invitations to tragedy in the event of fire or other emergency. Paragraph 5-2.1.5 is aimed at preventing locked doors in means of egress or any other unnecessary interference with the orderly movement of people in the event of fire. The Committee on Safety to Life has attempted to accomplish this objective while maintaining those features essential to security within the building.

Consistent with the concept that everything in the means of egress must be under the control of the occupant, doors must be easily openable from the egress side, even in complete darkness. This means no key locks or hard-to-use devices, such as door handles or latches covered with glass that has to be broken. Where panic hardware is used, no device that might interfere with its operation can be used; however, this does not prevent the use of alarm connections that will indicate that the door is in use.

Requirements for doors leading to exits apply also to doors opening to roofs where exit stairs terminate at a recognized roof exit and to exit discharge doors leading to the street or other public way.

5-2.1.5.1 Doors shall be arranged to be readily opened from the egress side whenever the building is occupied. Locks, if provided, shall not require the use of a key, tool, special knowledge or effort for operation from the inside of the building.

Exception No. 1: In health care occupancies as provided in Chapters 12 and 13, and in detention and correctional occupancies as provided in Chapters 14 and 15.

Exception No. 2: Exterior doors may have key operated locks from the egress side provided:

(a) That on the egress side, on or adjacent to the door, there is a readily visible, durable sign stating THIS DOOR TO REMAIN UNLOCKED WHEN THE BUILDING IS OCCUPIED. The sign shall be in letters not less than 1 in. (2.5 cm) high on a contrasting background, and

(b) The locking device is of a type that is readily distinguishable as locked, and

(c) This Exception is specifically permitted by Chapters 8 through 30 for the specific occupancy.

(d) A key shall be immediately available to any occupant inside the building when it is locked.

(e) This Exception may be revoked by the authority having jurisdiction for cause.

Exception No. 3: Where permitted by Chapters 8 through 30, key operation is allowed provided the key cannot be removed when the door is locked from the side from which egress is to be made.

Formal Interpretation 76-81
Reference: 5-1.2.1, 5-2.1.5.1

Question 1: Are doors which serve individual rooms, such as offices and classrooms, intended to be classified as a portion of a means of egress as defined in Paragraph 5-1.2.1?

Answer: Yes.

Question 2: If the answer to Question 1 is yes, are these doors then required to comply with Subparagraph 5-2.1.5.1, whereby locks requiring the use of a key from the side from which egress is to be made are prohibited?

Answer: Yes.

Issue Edition: 1976
Reference: 5-1.2.1
Date: September 1978

Paragraph 5-2.1.5.1 establishes the principle that doors must be readily openable from the side from which egress is to be made. It prohibits the installation of locks that require the use of a key to open the door from the inside. Paragraph 5-2.1.1.3 defines "occupied" for the purpose of this requirement. It should be noted that the *Code* prohibits the installation of such a lock as well as its use when the building is occupied.

Exception No. 2 is provided for key-operated locks under five conditions, one of which is that the appropriate occupancy chapter must specifically allow the exception. In permitting up to 10 persons in a locked building, the *Code* is not writing off those persons as unimportant. It is recognizing that there are instances where a building must be occupied by security personnel or by janitorial crews when it is locked. Such persons are generally familiar with the premises and the *Code* requires that they have keys available for egress when necessary. (*Also see commentary following 5-2.1.1.3.*) The following occupancies allow the use of the key-operated lock in Exception No. 2. Check the referenced paragraphs for additional restrictions that may be imposed by the occupancy chapter:

Assembly — 8-2.2.2.3 Exception No. 1, 9-2.2.2.3 Exception No. 1
Mercantile — 24-2.2.2.2, 25-2.2.2.2
Business — 26-2.2.2.2, 27-2.2.2.2

In addition, there is an exception to allow special provisions in the occupancy chapters for detention and correctional occupancies as well as special health care occupancies to override these requirements.

Exception No. 3, allowing the "captive key" hardware, has now been allowed in dwelling units in new and existing apartment buildings in 18-2.2.2.2 Exception No. 2 and 19-2.2.2.2 Exception No. 2 and in lodging and rooming houses in 20-2.8.

5-2.1.5.2* Every stairwell door shall allow reentry from the stairwell to the interior of the building, or an automatic release shall be provided to unlock all stairwell doors to allow reentry. Such automatic release shall be actuated with the initiation of the building fire alarm system.

Exception No. 1: Selected doors on stairwells may be equipped with hardware that prevents reentry into the interior of the building provided that:

(a) Such arrangement is specifically permitted by Chapters 8 through 30, and

(b) There are at least two levels where it is possible to leave the stairwell, and

(c) There shall be not more than four floors intervening between floors where it is possible to leave the stairwell, and

(d) Reentry is possible on the top or next to top floor permitting access to another exit, and

(e) Doors permitting reentry are identified as such on the stairwell side of the door.

Exception No. 2: In new health care occupancies as provided in Chapter 12, and in new detention and correctional occupancies as provided in Chapter 14.

Exception No. 3: Existing installations as permitted by Chapters 8 through 30.

A-5-2.1.5.2 This arrangement makes it possible to leave the stairway at such floor should the fire render the lower part of the stair unusable during egress or should the occupants seek refuge on another floor.

Every stairway door must be arranged to permit reentry into the building. However, the *Code* recognizes the need for varying degrees of security and does allow some equivalent alternatives. Stairway doors may be arranged to unlock automatically upon initiation of the fire alarm system. In addition, certain stairway doors may be arranged to prevent reentry where such arrangement is permitted by the appropriate occupancy chapter. In such instances, there must be at least two levels providing a way out of the stairway, one of which must be the top or next to top floor, and there may not be more than four floors between those levels providing a way out of the stairway. Any door providing a way out of the stairwell must be identified as such on the stairwell side.

5-2.1.5.3* A latch or other fastening device on a door shall be provided with a knob, handle, panic bar, or other simple type of releasing device having an obvious method of operation under all lighting conditions. Doors shall be openable with no more than one releasing operation.

Exception: Egress doors from individual living units and guest rooms of residential occupancies may be provided with devices that require not more than one additional releasing operation, such as a night latch, dead bolt, or security chain, provided such device is operable from the inside without the use of a key or tool and is mounted at a height not to exceed 48 in. (122 cm) above the finished floor. Existing security devices shall not exceed 60 in. (152 cm) in height above the finished floor and shall be permitted to have two additional releasing operations.

A-5-2.1.5.3 This requirement may be satisfied by the use of conventional types of hardware, whereby the door is released by the turning of a knob or handle, or pushing against a panic bar, but not by unfamiliar methods of operation such as a blow to break glass.

This paragraph requires that when a latch or other similar device is provided, its releasing device must be such that the method of operation is obvious even in the dark. This requires that the method be one that is familiar to the average person. Generally, a two-step release, such as a knob and an independent slide bolt, is not acceptable. In most occupancies, it is important that a single function unlatch the door. However, in living units and guest rooms, one additional device is permitted in new construction and two in existing situations.

This provision allows an existing situation to continue where a hotel room has hardware in which one operation releases the latch, another operation releases the lock, and a third operation releases the security device (chain or bar). However, in new installations, if a security device (chain or bar) is used, then one operation would have to release both the latch and lock.

5-2.1.5.4 Where pairs of doors are required in a means of egress, each leaf of the pair shall be provided with its own releasing device. Devices that depend upon the releasing of one door before the other shall not be used.

Exception: Where exit doors are used in pairs and approved automatic flush bolts are used, the door leaf having the automatic flush bolts shall have no doorknob or surface-mounted hardware. The unlatching of any leaf shall not require more than one operation.

This applies only to pairs of doors that are required for means of egress. If the second leaf is provided for other reasons and not for egress, the provision does not apply. In the situation where a second leaf is provided for reasons other than egress, the second leaf must be arranged so as not to be mistaken for the exit door.

5-2.1.5.5 No lock, padlock, hasp, bar, chain, or other device, or combination thereof, shall be installed or maintained at any time on or in connection with any door on which panic hardware or fire exit hardware is required by this *Code* if such device prevents or is intended to prevent the free use of the door for purposes of egress.

Exception: As otherwise provided in 5-2.1.6.

It is not the intent of 5-2.1.5.5 to require panic hardware. That requirement is made by the various occupancy chapters. It is the intent, however, that where panic hardware is installed, no device or arrangement interfere with its function.

5-2.1.6 Special Locking Arrangements.

5-2.1.6.1 In buildings protected throughout by an approved supervised automatic fire detection system or approved supervised automatic sprinkler system and where permitted by Chapters 8 through 30, doors in low and ordinary hazard areas, as defined by 4-2.2, may be equipped with approved, listed, locking devices that shall:

(a) Unlock upon actuation of an approved supervised automatic sprinkler system installed in accordance with Section 7-7, or upon the actuation of any heat detector or not more than two smoke detectors of an approved supervised automatic fire detection system in accordance with Section 7-6, and

(b) Unlock upon loss of power controlling the lock or locking mechanism, and

(c) Initiate an irreversible process that will release the lock within 15 seconds whenever a force of not more than 15 lbf (67 N) is continuously applied to the release device required in 5-2.1.5.3 for a period of not more than three seconds. Relocking of such doors shall be by manual means only. Operation of the release device shall activate a signal in the vicinity of the door to assure those attempting to exit that the system is functional.

Exception to (c): The authority having jurisdiction may approve a delay not to exceed 30 seconds provided that reasonable life safety is assured.

5-2.1.6.2* On the door adjacent to the release device, a sign shall be provided that reads:

PUSH UNTIL ALARM SOUNDS.
DOOR CAN BE OPENED IN 15 SECONDS.

Sign letters shall be at least 1 in. (2.5 cm) high and ⅛ in. (0.3 cm) wide stroke.

A-5-2.1.6.2 In the event that the authority having jurisdiction has allowed increased operation time, the sign should reflect the appropriate time.

5-2.1.6.3 Emergency lighting in accordance with Section 5-9 shall be provided at the door.

This special locking arrangement is allowed only where specifically permitted by the appropriate occupancy chapter. Paragraph 5-2.1.6.1 requires that the building be protected throughout with either a supervised automatic fire detection system or a supervised automatic sprinkler system, and item (a) requires that the locking devices unlock immediately upon activation of the system. Item (c) requires that once the release device is activated manually, the door unlock within 15 seconds. This action must be irreversible and cannot require that the user maintain pressure on the release device for more than 3 seconds. Once opened, the door may be relocked by manual means only.

It should be pointed out that the operations described do not automatically open the door. They simply unlock it, making it immediately openable by anyone seeking to exit. Security is not sacrificed. Of course, any exterior exit door may be locked against entry at any time.

The following occupancies allow the use of delay release hardware in accordance with 5-2.1.6. Check the referenced paragraphs for additional restrictions that may be imposed by the occupancy chapter:

Assembly — 8-2.2.2.4, 9-2.2.2.4

Educational — 10-2.2.2.3, 11-2.2.2.3

Health Care — 12-2.2.2.4 Exception No. 2, 13-2.2.2.4 Exception No. 2

Hotels — 16-2.2.2.2 Exception, 17-2.2.2.2 Exception

Apartment Buildings — 18-2.2.2.2 Exception No. 1, 19-2.2.2.2 Exception No. 1

Lodging and Rooming Houses — 20-2.7 Exception
Board and Care Facilities — 21-3.2.2.2
Mercantile — 24-2.2.2.4, 25-2.2.2.4
Business — 26-2.2.2.4, 27-2.2.2.4
Industrial — 28-2.2.2.2
Storage — 29-2.2.2.2, 29-8.2.2.2

5-2.1.7   Panic Hardware and Fire Exit Hardware.

The difference between panic hardware and fire exit hardware is that fire exit hardware is tested for use on fire-rated doors; panic hardware is not. See 5-2.1.7.1 and 5-2.1.7.3.

5-2.1.7.1   Panic hardware and fire exit hardware consist of a door latching assembly incorporating a device that releases the latch upon the application of a force in the direction of exit travel. Fire exit hardware additionally provides fire protection where used as part of a fire door assembly.

5-2.1.7.2   Where a door is required to be equipped with panic hardware or fire exit hardware by some other provision of this *Code*, such releasing device shall:

(a) Consist of bars or panels, the actuating portion of which shall extend across not less than one-half of the width of the door leaf, not less than 30 in. (76 cm) nor more than 44 in. (112 cm) above the floor, and

(b) Cause the door latch to release when a force not to exceed 15 lbf (67 N) is applied.

5-2.1.7.3   Only approved panic hardware shall be used on doors that are not fire doors. Only approved fire exit hardware shall be used on fire doors.

It is not the intent of this paragraph to require the use of panic hardware or fire exit hardware. The two requirements of this paragraph are (1) that only approved hardware is to be used, and (2) that where such devices are used on fire-rated doors, they must be tested for use on fire-rated doors. Panic hardware is not tested for use on fire-rated doors; fire exit hardware is tested for use on fire-rated doors.

5-2.1.7.4   Required panic hardware and fire exit hardware shall not be equipped with any locking device, set screw, or other arrangement that can be used to prevent the release of the latch when pressure is applied to the bar. Devices that hold the latch in the retracted position are prohibited on fire exit hardware unless listed and approved for such use.

Exception: In detention and correctional occupancies as provided in Chapters 14 and 15.

As the name implies, panic hardware and fire exit hardware should be designed for utility, serviceability, and reliability under conditions that range from the orderly evacuation of building spaces to the hurried egress that can accompany fast-moving fires; hence, the stress on ease of operation under extreme conditions.

Panic hardware and fire exit hardware, as specified in 5-2.1.7, must be able to be instantly and easily released. Panic hardware and fire exit hardware are to be located at a convenient height above the floor — 30 to 44 in. (76 to 112 cm) — and the actuating portion is to extend at least one-half the width of the door leaf. A force no greater than 15 lbf (67 N) shall be needed to operate the device. This is the force needed to release the latching device only. The force needed to open the door itself is governed by 5-2.1.4.3. Of course, nothing is permitted that could interfere with the proper operation of the panic hardware.

Note that 5-2.1.7 does not require panic hardware but sets the requirements for such hardware where called for by the applicable occupancy chapter.

The following occupancies require the use of panic hardware or fire exit hardware (check the referenced paragraphs for where such hardware is required):

Assembly — 8-2.2.2.3, 9-2.2.2.3

Educational — 10-2.2.2.2, 11-2.2.2.2

Although not required by the other occupancy chapters, panic hardware or fire exit hardware is often used either due to an assembly occupancy being located within another occupancy or as a means of complying with 5-2.1.5.3.

It is the intent of the *Code* to permit the use of the special locking arrangement permitted by 5-2.1.6 where panic hardware is required, if permitted by the occupancy chapters, Chapters 8 through 30.

5-2.1.8 Self-Closing Devices. A door designed to normally be kept closed in a means of egress, such as a door to a stair enclosure or horizontal exit, shall be a self-closing door and shall not at any time be secured in the open position.

Exception: In any building of low or ordinary hazard contents, as defined in 4-2.2.2 and 4-2.2.3, or where permitted by the authority having jurisdiction, doors may be automatic-closing where:

(a) Upon release of the hold-open mechanism, the door becomes self-closing; and

(b) The release device is so designed that the door may be instantly released manually and upon release become self-closing, or the door may be closed by some simple or readily obvious operation; and

(c) The automatic releasing mechanism or medium is activated by (1) the operation of an approved automatic smoke detection system installed to protect the entire building, so designed and installed as to provide for actuation of the system so promptly as to preclude the generation of heat or smoke sufficient to interfere with egress before the system operates, or (2) the operation of approved smoke detectors installed in such a way as to detect smoke on either side of the door opening, as detailed in NFPA 72E, Standard on Automatic Fire Detectors, Chapter 9. The above systems may be zoned as approved by the authority having jurisdiction; and

(d) Any fire detection system or smoke detector is provided with such supervision and safeguards as are necessary to assure complete reliability of operation in case of fire (see also Section 7-6); and

(e) Upon loss of power to the hold-open device, the hold-open mechanism is released and the door becomes self-closing; and

(f) The release by smoke detection of one door in a stair enclosure results in closing all doors serving that stair.

Doors in a means of egress route should be kept in the closed position, particularly those in the entrance to a stair enclosure, or in a horizontal exit; however, it is in these latter two locations that doors so often are blocked open by some type of door-stopping chock. The simple requirement that these doors be self-closing is not enough, since this feature works only when the door can move freely. Often a door is blocked open to aid in the free flow of normal traffic. This sets the stage for the easy and rapid spread of fire, smoke, and heat throughout the building — the very situation that the stringent design requirements for the exit enclosure are intended to prevent.

Realizing that tampering with the self-closing feature may occur, and in an effort to encourage the use of positive measures rather than the use of a printed prohibition unlikely to be followed, the *Code* makes an exception for doors located in buildings that house contents of low or ordinary hazard or where the authority having jurisdiction approves. There are some locations in the *Code* where automatic closing doors are required. The Exception to 5-2.1.8 allows for doors to be held open by an automatic releasing device. The triggering of the automatic release is done through the operation of an automatic smoke detection system protecting the entire building or through the operation of smoke detectors designed to detect smoke on either side of the door opening (*see NFPA 72E, Standard on Automatic Fire Detectors, Section 9-2*)[2]. Fusible links *are not* an acceptable trigger in this system because untenable smoke conditions could very easily render an exit enclosure unusable long before the heat has built up to a point high enough to operate the fusible link. Any detection system or detector is to be supervised to the extent necessary to ensure its reliability.

Note that the doors can be arranged to close throughout the building or only in the affected zones. Zoning is generally better. If protecting a room, that room may be considered a zone. If protecting a stair, the entire stair is a zone, and the signal to close one door in a stair must close all doors in that stair.

With the exception of certain hazardous areas where flash fires or explosions could occur, the use of automatic closers in accordance with these provisions is widely accepted and, in fact, encouraged to prevent doors from being blocked open.

5-2.1.9 Power-Operated Doors. Where required doors are operated by power, such as doors with a photoelectric-actuated mechanism to open the door upon the approach of a person or doors with power-assisted manual operation, the design shall be such that in event of power failure the door may be opened manually to permit exit travel or closed where necessary to safeguard means of egress. The forces required to open these doors manually shall not exceed those specified in 5-2.1.4.3 except that the force to set the door in motion shall not exceed 50 lbf (222 N). The door shall be so designed and installed that when a force is applied to the door on the side from which egress is made, it shall be capable of swinging from any position to the full use of the required width of the opening in which it is installed. (*See 5-2.1.4.*)

Exception No. 1:   Doors complying with 5-2.1.14.

Exception No. 2:   In detention and correctional occupancies as provided in Chapters 14 and 15.

Power-operated sliding doors activated by some automatic mechanism are permitted, provided their movement can be manually overpowered and the door made to swing in the direction of travel, still providing the capacity exit for which it has been given credit. The feature for manual operation must work at all times, even when other features of the door's mechanism (such as the treadle, an electric eye, or sliding rail) have failed. Such door must be arranged so that it can be made to swing manually from any position, fully closed or partially closed. Care must be taken to ensure that enclosing construction of any door pocket does not defeat its ability to swing. Note that the breakaway feature cannot require a force in excess of 50 lbf (222 N).

5-2.1.10 Revolving Doors.

5-2.1.10.1   All revolving doors shall comply with the following:

(a) Revolving doors shall be capable of being collapsed into a book-fold position.

Exception to (a): Existing revolving doors where approved by the authority having jurisdiction.

(b) When in the book-fold position, the parallel egress paths formed shall provide an aggregate width of 36 in. (91 cm).

Exception to (b): Existing revolving doors where approved by the authority having jurisdiction.

(c) Revolving doors shall not be used within 10 ft (3 m) of the foot of or top of stairs or escalators. Under all conditions there shall be a dispersal area acceptable to the authority having jurisdiction between the stairs or escalators and the revolving door.

(d) The revolutions per minute (RPM) of revolving doors shall not exceed the following:

Inside Diameter	Power Driven-type Speed Control (RPM)	Manual-type Speed Control (RPM)
6 ft 6 in. (198 cm)	11	12
7 ft 0 in. (213 cm)	10	11
7 ft 6 in. (229 cm)	9	11
8 ft 0 in. (244 cm)	9	10
8 ft 6 in. (259 cm)	8	9
9 ft 0 in. (274 cm)	8	9
9 ft 6 in. (290 cm)	7	8
10 ft 0 in. (305 cm)	7	8

(e) Each revolving door shall have a conforming side-hinged swinging door in the same wall as the revolving door and within 10 ft (3 m).

Exception No. 1 to (e): Revolving doors may be used without adjacent swinging doors for street floor elevator lobbies if no stairways or doors from other parts of the building discharge through the lobby and the lobby has no occupancy other than as a means of travel between elevators and street.

Exception No. 2 to (e): Existing revolving doors where the number of revolving doors does not exceed the number of swing doors within 20 ft (6.1 m).

These regulations governing revolving doors were completely rewritten for the 1985 *Code*. Before then, definitive requirements were lacking. With the assistance of the revolving door industry, specifications were developed to assist the designer and the authority having jurisdiction in determining what has been meant by an "approved" revolving door. These *Code* provisions deal with collapsibility, width of egress path, location, speed of rotation, credit for required egress capacity, and force to collapse.

5-2.1.10.2   Where permitted by Chapters 8 through 30, revolving doors may be used as a component in a means of egress under the following conditions:

(a) Revolving doors shall not be given credit for more than 50 percent of the required exit capacity.

(b) Each revolving door shall be credited with no more than 50 persons capacity.

(c) Revolving doors shall be capable of being collapsed into a book-fold position when a force of not more than 130 lbf (578 N) is applied to wings within 3 in. (7.6 cm) of the outer edge.

The following occupancies allow the use of a revolving door in a means of egress. Check the referenced paragraphs for additional restrictions that may be imposed by the occupancy chapter:
Assembly — 8-2.2.2.5, 9-2.2.2.5
Hotels — 16-2.2.2.4, 17-2.2.2.4
Apartments — 18-2.2.2.3, 19-2.2.2.3
Board and Care Facilities — 21-3.2.2.2
Mercantile — 24-2.2.2.7, 25-2.2.2.7
Business — 26-2.2.2.6, 27-2.2.2.6
Anyone who has used a revolving door can easily understand the problems encountered when too many people try to use it in too short a period of time. The congestion created is one reason why their use is prohibited at the foot or top of stairs. Because of the potential danger such doors present, they are not permitted to be used in numbers that would have them providing more than 50 percent of the required exit capacity. Where they are used, they each receive credit for a maximum of 50 persons, no matter what the width of the revolving panel.
Satisfying the 50-percent credit provision in item 5-2.1.10.2(a) does not automatically satisfy the 50-person maximum limit in (b) and vice versa.

5-2.1.10.3   Revolving doors not used as a component of a means of egress shall have a collapsing force of not more than 180 lbf (800 N).

Exception: Revolving doors may have a collapsing force set in excess of 180 lbf (800 N) if the collapsing force is reduced to not more than 130 lbf (578 N) when:

(a) There is a power failure or power is removed to the device holding the wings in position.

(b) There is an actuation of the automatic sprinkler system where such system is provided.

(c) There is actuation of a smoke detection system that is installed to provide coverage in all areas within the building that are within 75 ft (23 m) of the revolving doors.

(d) There is the actuation of a manual control switch that reduces the holding force to below the 130 lbf (578 N) level. Such switch shall be in an approved location and shall be clearly identified.

Note that 5-2.1.10.1 and 5-2.1.10.3 apply even if the door is not part of the required means of egress. The exception to 5-2.1.10.3 does not have to be complied with unless the collapsing force is otherwise in excess of 180 lbf (800 N).

5-2.1.11 Turnstiles.

The intent of 5-2.1.11 is to give as much guidance as possible on how best to place turnstiles in a building, and to describe the circumstances under which they are permitted, with the intent that this will reduce the probability of their improper use during an emergency.

5-2.1.11.1   No turnstile or similar device to restrict travel to one direction or to collect fares or admission charges shall be so placed as to obstruct any required means of egress.

Exception No. 1:   Approved turnstiles not over 39 in. (99 cm) high that turn freely in the direction of exit travel may be used in any occupancy where revolving doors are permitted by Chapters 8 through 30.

Exception No. 2:   Where permitted by the authority having jurisdiction and Chapters 8 through 30, turnstiles may be used for exiting and each turnstile credited for 50 persons capacity provided such turnstiles:

(a) Freewheel in the exit direction when primary power is lost, and freewheel in the direction of exit travel upon the manual release by an employee assigned in the area, and

(b) Shall not be given credit for more than 50 percent of the required exit width, and

(c) Shall not be over 39 in. (99 cm) high nor have a clear width less than 16½ in. (41.9 cm).

5-2.1.11.2   Turnstiles over 39 in. (99 cm) high shall be subject to the requirements for revolving doors.

5-2.1.11.3   Turnstiles in or furnishing access to required exits shall be of such design as to provide at least 16½ in. (41.9 cm) clear width at and below a height of 39 in. (99 cm) and at least 22 in. (55.9 cm) clear width at heights above 39 in. (99 cm).

Generally, turnstiles are installed to prevent or control entry. As such, they are not always suitable for installation in a means of egress. Certain turnstiles are permitted where revolving doors are permitted, although they are used in some occupancies where revolving doors are generally not found. This is not meant to imply that there is a relationship between revolving doors and turnstiles insofar as their purpose is concerned. The revolving door is not meant to restrict traffic in either direction, while the turnstile is often used to do just that, with the restriction or obstruction to traffic movement usually in the direction of entry. Yet, if a turnstile does not restrict egress, it may be looked upon the same as a revolving door.

While some turnstiles will not turn in the direction of entry until coin operated, there are those that are used simply to count numbers of people. Perhaps the most dangerous are those that do not bar entry but specifically bar egress. An example would be in the large stores where turnstiles turn freely for entering, but will not turn in the direction of egress, thereby causing patrons to go through a checkout slot. It is possible that the patrons of places using one-way turnstiles are quite aware of this limitation and will know the correct path to be taken in order to leave; however, this cannot be relied on, especially if the turnstiles are placed near the exit doors. In emergencies people do not always stop to think clearly, and could head for what appears to be the shortest means of escape, only to find the way blocked by a "wrong way" turnstile.

In some locations of certain occupancies, an approved turnstile is acceptable for providing a portion of the required exit capacity. Therefore, where the occupancy chapter specifically allows turnstiles, they may be installed provided they are in strict compliance with the dimensional criteria and performance requirements of 5-2.1.11.1 Exception No. 2. In no case may turnstiles be allowed to provide more than 50 percent of the required exit capacity, and no single turnstile can be rated at more than 50 persons.

Turnstiles not over 39 in. (99 cm) in height that allow free egress can be used anywhere a revolving door is allowed, subject to 5-2.1.11.3, and all turnstiles over 39 in. (99 cm) in height must meet all requirements for revolving doors.

5-2.1.12 Doors in Folding Partitions. Where permanently mounted folding or movable partitions are used to divide a room into smaller spaces, a swinging door or open doorway shall be provided as an exit access from each such space.

Exception No. 1: Under the following conditions the swinging door may be omitted and the partition may be used to enclose the space completely:

(a) The subdivided space shall not be used by more than 20 persons at any time.

(b) The use of the space shall be under adult supervision.

(c) The partitions shall be so arranged that they do not extend across any aisle or corridor used as an exit access to the required exits from the floor.

(d) The partitions shall conform to the interior finish and other applicable requirements of this Code.

(e) The partitions shall be an approved type, shall have a simple method of release, and shall be capable of being opened quickly and easily by inexperienced persons in case of emergency.

Exception No. 2:   Where a subdivided space is provided with at least two means of egress the swinging door in the folding partition may be omitted, and one such means of egress may be equipped with a horizontal sliding door complying with 5-2.1.14.

Although item (c) to Exception No. 1 may appear to be contradictory to the intent of the exception, it is referring to exit access for the rest of the floor, not the exit access for the small space created by the closing of the partition.

5-2.1.13 Balanced Doors.   If balanced doors are used and panic hardware is required, the panic hardware shall be of the pushpad type, and the pad shall not extend more than approximately one-half the width of the door measured from the latch side.

In the case of balanced doors, where the hinge or pivot point is set in from the edge of the door leaf, care must be taken to position the panic hardware device to the latch side of the pivot point; otherwise, pushing on the bar may actually hold the door closed. Figure 5-18 illustrates a balanced door and Figure 5-19 illustrates the difference between traditional panic hardware and pushpad panic hardware.

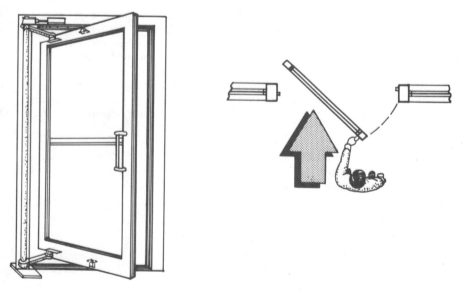

Figure 5-18   Balanced Door.   Balanced doors do not have side hinges but have a pivot point set in a small distance to reduce opening force.

Figure 5-19. Pushpad Panic Hardware. This figure illustrates the difference between "traditional" panic hardware (on the left) and "pushpad" panic hardware (on the right).

5-2.1.14 Horizontal Sliding Doors.

Provisions have been added that set forth the installation, operating, and fire protection rating requirements for horizontal sliding doors. Where permitted by other sections of the *Code*, horizontal sliding doors must comply with these requirements.

The provisions for the installation of horizontal sliding doors include typical door requirements for simple method of operation, from either side, without special knowledge or effort; for forces necessary to operate the door; for fire protection ratings applicable to their location and use; and for self-closing or automatic-closing by smoke detection installation.

Check the references for those locations where horizontal sliding doors complying with the paragraph might be used, and for additional restrictions that may be imposed by the occupancy chapter:

5-2.1.4.1, Exceptions No. 5, 6, and 7

5-2.1.9, Exception No. 1

5-2.1.12, Exception No. 2

Health Care — 12-2.2.5, 12-3.7.5, 13-2.2.5, 13-3.7.7

Industrial — 28-2.2.2.3, 28-2.2.2.4

Storage — 29-2.2.2.3, 29-2.2.2.4, 29-8.2.2.2

Unusual — 30-2.2.2.2, 30-2.2.2.3

Note particularly those instances where specific authorization to use horizontal sliding doors must be given by the particular occupancy chapter.

5-2.1.14.1   Horizontal sliding doors shall comply with the following:

(a) The door shall be operable by a simple method from either side without special knowledge or effort, and

(b) The force required to operate the door shall not exceed 30 lbf (133 N) to set the door in motion, and a 15 lbf (67 N) to close the door or open it to the minimum required width, and

(c) The door shall be operable with a force not to exceed 50 lbf (222 N) when a force of 250 lbf (1,110 N) is applied perpendicularly to the door adjacent to the operating device, and

(d) The door assembly shall comply with the applicable fire protection rating and, when rated, shall be self-closing or automatic-closing by smoke detection in accordance with 5-2.1.8 and shall be installed in accordance with NFPA 80, *Standard for Fire Doors and Windows.*

An example of the types of doors being discussed in 5-2.1.14 is shown in Figure 5-20.

Photo courtesy of Won-Door Corp.

Figure 5-20. Photograph of Horizontal Sliding Door. These illustrate the horizontal sliding doors permitted by 5-2.1.14.

5-2.2 Stairs.

Stairs, whether interior or outside, serve three functions: they are a means of normal circulation between the floors and different levels of a building; they serve as an emergency exit in case of fire; and they are essential for the rescue and fire-control operations conducted by fire fighters.

Stairs are part of the most critical component of a means of egress system — the exit. In addition, they are one of the most commonly used elements of buildings on a day-to-day, nonemergency basis. Stairs have also been identified by extensive statistics as one of the most common scenes of accidents costing hundreds of millions of dollars annually, not to mention personal suffering. For all of these reasons, it is of the utmost importance that extremely careful attention be given to the design, construction, and maintenance of stairs. In this edition of the *Code*, both interior and outside stairs are covered under "Stairs." Some requirements specifically apply to only one or the other.

5-2.2.1 General.   A stairway, either interior or outside, may be used as a component in a means of egress where it conforms to the general requirements of Section 5-1 and to the special requirements of this subsection.

Exception No. 1:   Aisle steps in assembly occupancies as provided in Chapters 8 and 9.

Aisle steps are detailed in 8-2.5.6.9 and 9-2.5.6.9.

Exception No. 2:   Existing noncomplying stairs may be continued in use subject to the approval of the authority having jurisdiction.

Stairs can be any one of the three means of egress components. They are most often thought of as an exit, but to be considered an exit they must be enclosed in accordance with 5-1.3.1. (Outside stairs need to be separated from the building in accordance with 5-2.2.3.3.) Open stairs are normally exit access rather than exits. (*See* 5-6.4.) Where an interior stairway connects two or more stories, it is a vertical opening and must comply with the requirements for vertical openings regardless of its egress status.

It is sometimes more difficult to determine whether outside stairs are exit access, exit, or exit discharge. If they are protected in accordance with 5-2.2.3.3, the stairway would normally be considered an exit. Outside stairs adjacent to the building and not protected would normally be considered part of the exit access with the exit being the discharge of the stairs. (*See* 5-6.6.) The *Code* is not clear with regard to where a stairway is part of an exit discharge. Where a set of stairs occurs in a sidewalk that connects an exit door to a public way, there is some unspecified distance away from the building where the stairs are no longer considered an exit but part of the exit discharge. Where the stairway is more than 10 ft (3 m) (*see* 5-6.6 *or* 5-2.2.3.2) from the building, it may easily be considered exit discharge. Distances shorter than 10 ft (3 m) require considerable judgment on the part of the authority having jurisdiction.

5-2.2.2 Types of Stairs.

5-2.2.2.1* Dimensional Criteria.   Stairs shall be in accordance with the following table:

New Stairs

Minimum width clear of all obstructions, except projections not exceeding 3½ in. (8.9 cm) at and below handrail height on each side	44 in. (112 cm) 36 in. (91 cm), where total occupant load of all floors served by stairways is less than 50.
Maximum height of risers	7 in. (17.8 cm)
Minimum height of risers	4 in. (10.2 cm)
Minimum tread depth	11 in. (27.9 cm)
Minimum headroom	6 ft 8 in. (203 cm)
Maximum height between landings	12 ft (3.7 m)
Doors opening immediately on stairs, without landing at least width of door	No

Exception: Existing stairs in existing buildings may remain in use or be rebuilt if they meet the requirements shown in the table for existing stairs.

Existing Stairs

	Class A	Class B
Minimum width clear of all obstructions, except projections not exceeding 3½ in. (8.9 cm) at and below handrail height on each side	44 in. (112 cm) 36 in. (91 cm), where total occupant load of all floors served by stairways is less than 50.	44 in. (112 cm)
Maximum height of risers	7½ in. (19.1 cm)	8 in. (20.3 cm)
Minimum tread depth	10 in. (24.4 cm)	9 in. (22.9 cm)
Minimum headroom	6 ft 8 in. (203 cm)	6 ft 8 in. (203 cm)
Maximum height between landings	12 ft (3.7 m)	12 ft (3.7 m)
Doors opening immediately on stairs, without landing at least width of door	No	No

A-5-2.2.2.1   It is the intent of 5-2.2.2.1 to use the table "Existing Stairs" in existing buildings even when there is a change in occupancy per 1-6.4.

Paragraph 5-2.2.2.1 presents complete information on required stair geometry for both new and existing stairs. The *Code* requires that all new stairs comply with the first table.

In editions of the *Code* prior to 1981, there was a requirement that "The height of every riser and the width of every tread shall be so proportioned that the sum of two risers and a tread, exclusive of its nosing or projection, is not less than 24 in. (61 cm) nor more than 25 in. (64 cm)". This requirement was deleted since it was based on a 300-year-old French formula in which the inch was a slightly larger unit of measure. Moreover, people's feet and stride length — the basis for the rule — were somewhat smaller at that time, and the rule was originally intended only for stairs of moderate steepness or pitch. For these reasons, research suggests that this rule not be used. Its use does not guarantee a good step geometry.

Due to the potential impact of these dimensions, the *Code* permits existing stairs in existing buildings to comply with previous requirements. It also allows existing stairs to be rebuilt to previous requirements since a new stairway may not fit in an existing stairwell. Therefore, existing stairs are divided into two classes: Class A and Class B. Actually, there is little difference between the two. As shown in Figure 5-21, the difference lies in the tread depth and riser height. If the total occupant load of all floors served is less than 50, the minimum width can be reduced from 44 in. (112 cm) to 36 in. (91 cm). The occupancy chapters specify which class of stair may be used. Also note that a change of occupancy does not require that stairways be rebuilt to meet the requirements for new construction.

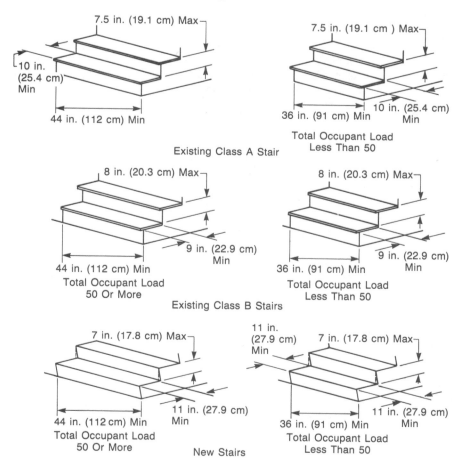

Figure 5-21. Stair Specifications. Stair specifications are illustrated for both new and existing stairs. Note existing Class A and B stairs showing maximum and minimum dimensions for each class.

5-2.2.2.2* Tread Slope.   Treads may slope a maximum of ¼ in. per ft (2.1 cm per meter) (1 in 48).

A-5-2.2.2.2   A small drainage slope for stair treads subject to wetting may improve tread slip resistance. (*See also A-5-2.2.4.4.*) A consistent slope to a side of the stair, where drainage is possible, may be preferable to a front-to-back slope of the treads.

Sloping treads are traditionally used in order to shed water. They might also occur, without planning, when the treads erode unevenly through usage or when differential settlement occurs. Limiting permitted tread slope is new to the *Code*. The limit is appropriate to reduce dimensional nonuniformity of the effective riser heights and to reduce the chance of slipping on sloping treads.

5-2.2.2.3* Riser Height and Tread Depth.   Riser height shall be measured as the vertical distance between tread nosings. Tread depth shall be measured horizontally between the vertical planes of the foremost projection of adjacent treads and at a right angle to the tread's leading edge but shall not include bevelled or rounded tread surfaces that slope more than 20 degrees (a slope of 1 in 2.75). At tread nosings such bevelling or rounding shall not exceed ½ in. (1.3 cm) in horizontal dimension.

A-5-2.2.2.3   Figures A-5-2.2.2.3(a), (b), (c), and (d) illustrate the method for measuring riser height and tread depth. Stairs that will be covered with resilient floor coverings may need additional tread depth beyond the minimum specified in the *Code*. Any horizontal projection of resilient covering materials, such as carpet and underlayment, beyond the tread nosing and riser, can interfere with users' feet and thereby reduces usable tread depth. At the tread nosing, such resilient covering materials may not be capable of providing stable support for users' feet. Generally, effective tread depth is reduced by the uncompressed thickness of such resilient coverings and might be further reduced, over time, if coverings are not well secured and move forward at the nosings. [*See Figure A-5-2.2.2.3(e).*]

RISER MEASUREMENTS:

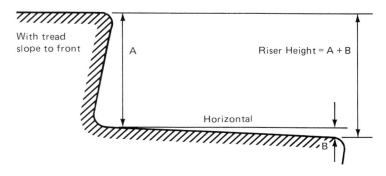

Figure A-5-2.2.2.3(a)

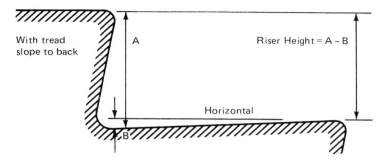

Figure A-5-2.2.2.3(b)

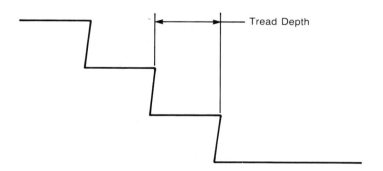

Figure A-5-2.2.2.3(c)

TREAD MEASUREMENTS:

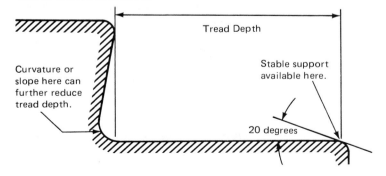

Figure A-5-2.2.2.3(d)

CARPETED STAIR:

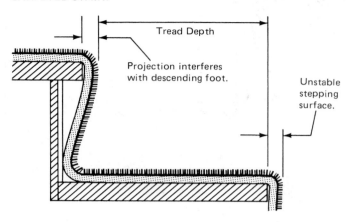

Figure A-5-2.2.2.3(e)

It will be noted that the (newly introduced) increased detail on measurement of riser and tread dimensions specifies that the measurement be consistent with how people actually experience the dimensions when walking up or down the stairs. Moreover, the tread dimension does not include any part of the tread that is not functional for normal foot placement, especially where the tread slopes mores than 20 degrees from the horizontal. Normal foot placement, when stepping down onto the step nosing, results in an initial contact angle of less than 20 degrees. Therefore, any part of the nosing sloping more than this angle is simply not effective, and furthermore, it might create a tripping hazard. Related to this is the limitation of ½-in. (1.3-cm) horizontal dimension for bevelling or rounding of the step nosings. Keeping the nosing bevelling or rounding under this limit will also reduce the chance of a slip occurring when the foot initially contacts the nosing in descent of a stair. By following this rule, the designer will also achieve acceptable step dimensions while keeping the space used for the stair to a minimum.

Stair designers should keep in mind the possibility that a stair, originally designed without a resilient covering, may someday be carpeted, thereby possibly significantly reducing the effective tread depth of the steps. Designing such stairs to provide slightly more than the minimum required tread depths is especially prudent in these cases. In addition, those responsible for maintaining stairs should keep in mind that the addition of resilient coverings may reduce the steps' tread dimensions to below the standard, and this will be made worse still if the coverings are not installed and maintained to be tight to the underlying steps.

5-2.2.2.4   There shall be no variation exceeding ³⁄₁₆ in. (.5 cm) in the depth of adjacent treads or in the height of adjacent risers, and the tolerance between the largest and smallest riser or between the largest and smallest tread shall not exceed ⅜ in. (1.0 cm) in any flight.

Exception: Where the bottom riser adjoins a sloping public way, walk, or driveway having an established grade and serving as a landing, a variation in height of the bottom riser of not more than 3 in. (7.6 cm) in every 3 ft (91 cm) of stairway width is permitted.

Many accidents have resulted from irregularities in stairs. There should be no design irregularities. Variations due to construction are permitted provided the variation between adjacent treads or adjacent risers does not exceed ³⁄₁₆ in. (.5 cm) and that the difference between the largest and smallest riser, as well as the largest and smallest tread, in any flight of stairs does not exceed ⅜ in. (1.0 cm). (*See Figure 5-22.*)

Figure 5-22 illustrates a stair that has various nonuniformities or irregularities. Note that the treads are not all uniformly horizontal and the risers are not all vertical. This situation, illustrating construction errors, is sometimes encountered with cast-in-place concrete stairs. Here there are unacceptable nonuniformities of the dimensions measured in accordance with 5-2.2.2.3. The nonuniformities measured at the backs of the treads and along the risers (that is, not the effective dimensions referred to in 5-2.2.2.3) might be greater or smaller depending on how the treads and risers slope.

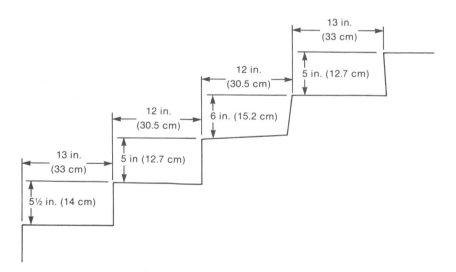

Figure 5-22.   Variations in Tread and Riser Dimensions Invite Accidents.   In this arrangement the variations are excessive and are prohibited.

Where a stair lands on sloping public property, such as a public sidewalk, the building owner has no right to alter the public property. Therefore, the *Code* accepts a certain minimum across-the-stair slope not in excess of 1 in 12. If reasonably possible, any such variation in riser height should be avoided. Figure 5-23 illustrates the Exception.

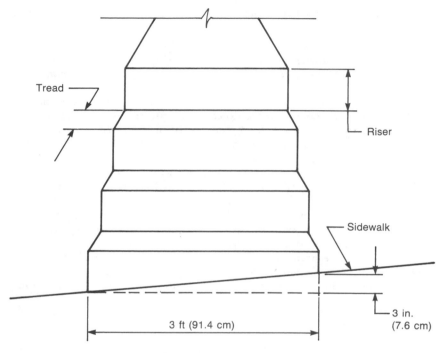

Figure 5-23.   Exception.

5-2.2.2.5 Monumental Stairs.   Monumental stairs, either inside or outside, may be used as a component in a means of egress if in compliance with all the requirements for stairs.

5-2.2.2.6 Curved Stairs.   Curved stairs may be used as a component in a means of egress provided the minimum depth of tread is 11 in. (27.9 cm) measured 12 in. (30.5 cm) from the narrower end of the tread, and the smallest radius is not less than twice the stair width.

Exception: Existing curved stairs may be continued in use provided the minimum depth of tread is 10 in. (25.4 cm) and the smallest radius is not less than twice the stair width.

Paragraph 5-2.2.2.6 relates the degree of curvature to the width of the stair, as shown in Figure 5-24. This relationship of least radius to stair width should be based on the actual width of the stair rather than just the required width. Otherwise, some rather unsafe conditions could be created toward the outside of wide curved stairs. The 11-in. (27.9-cm) tread depth is measured at the so-called "inner walking line" where feet land when walking on the inner part of the stair.

The *Code* now specifies the measurement method for curved stairs in a manner that is more closely related to how such stairs are used — with reference to a minimum 11-in. (27.9-cm) tread depth at the so-called "inner walking line." This is a concept that has been employed in the *Code's* requirement for winders for some time. With the minimum tread depth stated as a dimension similar to that of other stairs usable as a required means of egress, it is more evident that curved stairs are acceptable as a component in a required means of egress, without restriction of occupancy.

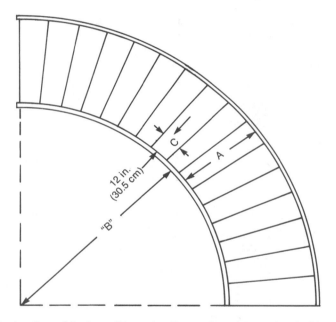

Figure 5-24. Curved Stairs. Dimension B must be at least twice A. Dimension C must be at least 11 in. (27.9 cm).

5-2.2.2.7 Spiral Stairs. Where permitted for individual occupancies by Chapters 8 through 30, spiral stairs may be used as a component in a means of egress provided:

(a) The clear width of the stairs is not less than 26 in. (66 cm).

(b) The height of risers shall not exceed 9½ in. (24.1 cm).

(c) Headroom shall be not less than 6 ft 6 in. (198 cm).

(d) Treads shall have a minimum depth of 7½ in. (19.1 cm) at a point 12 in. (30.5 cm) from the narrower edge.

(e) All treads shall be identical.

(f) The occupant load served is not more than 5.

In addition to setting the specifications for spiral stairs, 5-2.2.2.7 states that they may serve as required means of egress for an occupant load of not more than five. However, they can be used only where expressly allowed by the appropriate occupancy chapter. (*See Figure 5-25.*)

These applications make it very unlikely that there will be simultaneous use of the stair by a person ascending and another descending. A single user, descending the spiral stair, is able to use the best part of the small treads — the part closer to the outside of the stair.

The following occupancies allow the use of spiral stairs (check the referenced paragraphs for additional requirements that may be imposed by the occupancy chapter):

Detention and Correctional — 14-2.2.3.2, 15-2.2.3.2
Apartments — 18-2.2.3.3, 19-2.2.3.3
One and Two-Family Dwellings — 22-2.4.1
Mercantile — 24-2.2.3.2, 25-2.2.3.2
Business — 26-2.2.3.2, 27-2.2.3.2
Industrial — 28-2.2.3.2
Storage — 29-2.2.3.2
Unusual Occupancies — 30-2.2.3.2

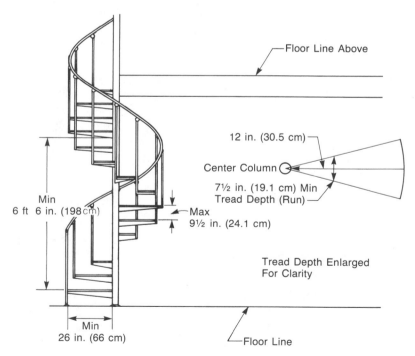

Figure 5-25.   Spiral Stairs.   Minimum and maximum dimensions for spiral stairs as given in 5-2.2.2.7. All treads must be identical, and the stair can serve a maximum occupant load of five.

5-2.2.2.8 Winders. Where permitted for individual occupancies by Chapters 8 through 30, winders are allowed in stairs. Such winders shall have a minimum depth of tread of 6 in. (15.2 cm), and a minimum depth of tread of 9 in. (22.9 cm) at a point 12 in. (30.5 cm) from the narrowest edge.

A winder is a tapered tread used to change the direction of the stairway. Because they introduce a variation in the stair geometry, and their effective tread dimensions are less than 11 in. (27.9 cm), winder stairs are suited to limited applications. These applications make it very unlikely that there will be simultaneous use of the stair by a person ascending and another descending. A single person descending the winders is able to use the best part of the treads — the part closer to the outside of the turn. At one time, the *Code* prohibited winders. Chapter 5 now sets criteria for winders if the appropriate occupancy chapter permits their use. (*See Figure 5-26.*)

The following occupancies allow the use of winders (check the referenced paragraphs for additional requirements that may be imposed by the occupancy chapter):

Apartments — 18-2.2.3.4
Existing Apartment Buildings — 19-2.3.4
Lodging and Rooming Houses — 20-2.6
Board and Care Facilities — 21-2.2.7
One- and Two-Family Dwellings — 22-2.4.1
Existing Mercantile — 25-2.2.3.3
Existing Business — 27-2.2.3.3
Existing Industrial — 28-2.2.3.3
Existing Storage — 29-2.2.3.3 and 29-8.2.2.3
Existing Unusual Structures — 30-2.2.3.3

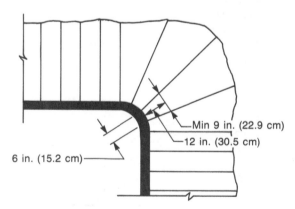

Figure 5-26. Acceptable Winders. Where allowed by the occupancy chapter, winders that comply with 5-2.2.2.8 are acceptable in a required means of egress.

5-2.2.3 Enclosures and Protection.

5-2.2.3.1 Enclosures.   All interior stairs serving as an exit or exit component shall be enclosed in accordance with 5-1.3.1. All other interior stairs shall be protected in accordance with 6-2.4.

> Paragraph 5-2.2.3.1 was rewritten for the 1985 Edition of the *Code* to emphasize the two different features of interior stairs that the *Code* is addressing: protection of vertical openings and enclosure of exits. Most interior stairs serve as exits and are vertical openings; they therefore must meet 5-1.3.1 and, as vertical openings, must comply with 6-2.4. Stairs that are not being used as exits but are vertical openings must be protected in accordance with 6-2.4. This is an important distinction since it is possible to comply with 6-2.4 and not comply with 5-1.3.1.

5-2.2.3.2*   Where nonrated walls or unprotected openings are used to enclose the exterior of a stairway, and the walls or openings are exposed by other parts of the building at an angle of less than 180 degrees, the building enclosure walls within 10 ft (3 m) horizontally of the nonrated wall or unprotected opening shall be constructed as required for stairway enclosures including opening protectives, but need not exceed 1-hour fire resistance rating with 45-minute fire protection rated opening protectives. This construction shall extend vertically from the ground to a point 10 ft (3 m) above the topmost landing of the stairway or to the roof line, whichever is lower.

A-5-2.2.3.2   The purpose of this *Code* section is to protect the exterior wall of a stairway from fires in other portions of the building. If the exterior wall of the stair is flush with the building exterior wall, the fire would need to travel around 180 degrees in order to impact the stair. This has not been a problem in existing buildings, so no protection is required. However, if the angle of exposure is less than 180 degrees, protection of either the stair wall or building wall is required.

The following diagrams illustrate the requirement (assuming nonrated glass on exterior wall of stair).

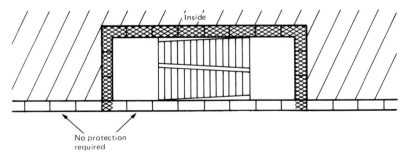

Figure A-5-2.2.3.2(a)

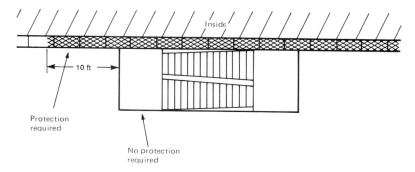

Figure A-5-2.2.3.2(b)

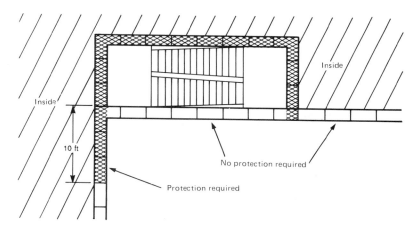

Figure A-5-2.2.3.2(c)

5-2.2.3.3 Separation and Protection of Outside Stairs. Outside stairs shall be separated from the interior of the building by walls with the fire resistance rating with fixed or self-closing opening protectives, as required for enclosed stairs. This construction shall extend vertically from the ground to a point 10 ft (3 m) above the topmost landing of the stairway or to the roofline, whichever is lower, and at least 10 ft (3 m) horizontally.

Exception No. 1: Outside stairways may be unprotected where serving an exterior exit access balcony that has two remote outside stairways or ramps.

Exception No. 2: Outside stairways may be unprotected where serving a two-story building where there is a remote second exit.

Exception No. 3: The fire resistance rating of the portion of the separation extending 10 ft (3 m) from the stairs need not exceed 1 hour with openings protected by ¾-hour fire protection rated assemblies.

Most important in the consideration of outside stairs is their proximity to openings in the wall of the building, openings through which fire emerging from the building could render stairs useless as a means of egress. Protection against this kind of occurrence takes two forms: (1) protection from openings, which is accomplished by distance separation; and (2) protection of openings, which must be done if the openings occur or are placed in a wall in such a way that the separation distances are less than required. The example of the old fire escape arrangement, in which a window access immediately below the fire escape landing leads to fire exposure of the fire escape, is the type of situation that must be avoided. By studying Figures 5-27 to 5-29, the enclosure provisions in 5-2.2.3.3 (outside stairs) can more easily be understood.

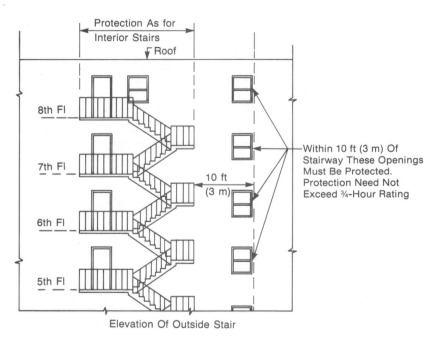

Figure 5-27. Protection of Openings for Outside Stairs — Example 1. If openings are within 10 ft (3 cm) of the outside stairs, they must be protected. (*See* 5-2.2.3.3.*) However, the fire resistance ratings in the 10-ft (3-m) "extension" need not exceed 1 hour, and opening fire protection rating need not exceed ¾ hour.

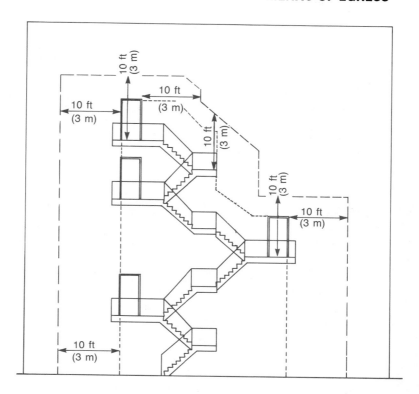

——————— Openings Within This Area Must Be 1-Hour Protected
———————— Openings Within This Area Must Be Protected For
   1 Hour If ≤3 Stories Served
   1½ Hour If >3 Stories Served

Figure 5-28.   Protection of Outside Stairs — Example 2.

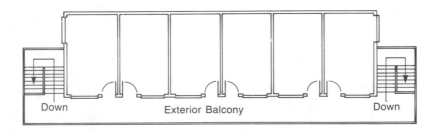

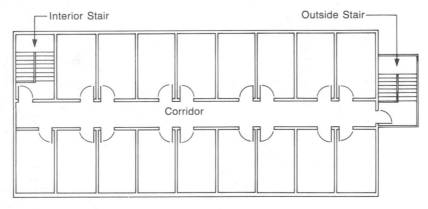

Figures 5-29a and b.   Protection of Openings for Outside Stairs — Examples 3 and 4. Exception No. 1 to 5-2.2.3.3 is illustrated in the top figure. Exception No. 2, which is restricted to two-story buildings, is illustrated in the bottom figure.

5-2.2.3.4   All openings below an outside stair shall be protected:

(a) Where located in a court, the least dimension of which is less than one-third its height, or

(b) Where located in an alcove having a width less than one-third its height and a depth greater than one-fourth its height.

Figure 5-30 illustrates the provisions of 5-2.2.3.4.

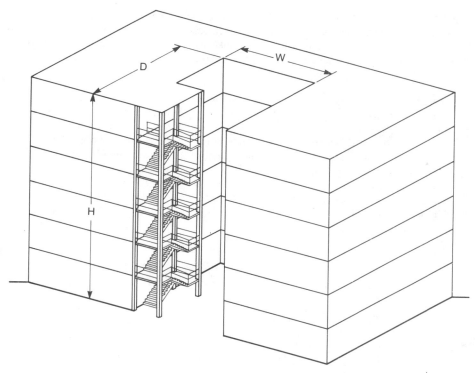

Figure 5-30. The Basis for Required Protection of Openings Below Open, Outside Stairs Discharging to a Courtyard.
1. If D or W is less than one-third of H, all openings within the courtyard below the open, outside stairs must be protected.
2. If D is greater than one-fourth of H and W is less than one-third of H, protection is required at openings.

Example 1
H = 60 ft (18.3 m)
D or W < 20 ft (610 cm)
Special Protection Required

Example 2
H = 60 ft (18.3 m)
D > 15 ft (457.2 cm) *and*
W < 20 ft (610 cm)
Special Protection Required

5-2.2.3.5   There shall be no enclosed usable space within an exit enclosure, including under stairs, nor shall any open space within the enclosure, including stairs and landings, be used for any purpose such as storage or similar use that could interfere with egress. Where there is enclosed usable space under stairs, the walls and soffits of the enclosed space shall be protected the same as the stair enclosure. (*Also see 5-1.3.3.*)

Although this paragraph may, at first, seem to contradict itself, it does not. First, the paragraph states that within an exit enclosure there shall be no enclosed usable space, nor shall any open space be used for any purpose that could interfere with the use of the exit enclosure. An enclosed usable space under a stair can be considered to be outside the exit enclosure if the walls and soffits of the enclosed space are protected the same as required for the stair enclosure, thereby separating the space from the exit enclosure. The door to the space cannot open into the exit enclosure, per 5-1.3.1(d). (*See Figure 5-31.*) (Also see 5-1.3.2 and 31-1.2.1.)

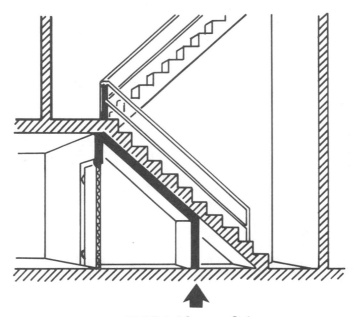

Wall Rated Same as Stairway

Figure 5-31.   Enclosed Usable Space Under Last Flight of Stairs.

5-2.2.3.6 Signs.   In buildings four or more stories in height, a sign shall be provided at each floor level landing. The sign shall indicate the floor level, the terminus of the top and bottom of the stair enclosure, and the identification of the stair. The sign shall also state the floor level of, and the direction to, exit discharge. The sign shall be located approximately 5 ft (152 cm) above the floor landing in a position that is readily visible when the door is in the open or closed position.

This provision, added in the 1985 *Code* and revised for this edition, requires the posting of important information at each floor landing in each stairwell in buildings four or more stories in height. The sign shall identify the stair, indicate the floor level of the landing and where the stairwell terminates at top and bottom, and show the direction to the exit discharge. While primarily intended as advice for fire fighting personnel in an emergency, the information is often useful to other building users.

5-2.2.4 Stair Details.

5-2.2.4.1   All stairs serving as required means of egress shall be of permanent fixed construction.

5-2.2.4.2   Each new stair and platform, landing, etc., used in conjunction therewith in buildings more than three stories in height and in new buildings required by this *Code* to be of fire-resistive construction, shall be of noncombustible material throughout.

Exception: Handrails are exempted from this requirement.

Paragraph 5-2.2.4.2 covers the combustibility of materials used in the construction of stairs. Stairs serving up to and including three stories may be of combustible construction unless the structure is otherwise required to be of fire-resistive construction (Type I) as described in NFPA 220, *Standard on Types of Building Construction.*[3] In the latter case, the materials used for the stair construction must be noncombustible. In all buildings of more than three stories, the stairway construction must be of noncombustible materials.

5-2.2.4.3   Stairways and intermediate landings shall continue with no decrease in width along the direction of exit travel. In new buildings every landing shall have a dimension, measured in direction of travel, equal to the width of the stair. Such dimension need not exceed 4 ft (122 cm) where the stair has a straight run.

5-2.2.4.4*   Stair treads shall be uniformly slip resistant and shall be free of projections or lips that could trip stair users.

A-5-2.2.4.4   The tripping hazard referred to in 5-2.2.4.4 occurs especially during descent where the tread walking surface has projections such as strips of high friction materials or lips from metal pan stairs that are not completely filled with concrete or other material. Tread nosings that project over adjacent treads can also be a tripping hazard. ANSI A117.1 (*see Appendix B*) illustrates projecting nosing configurations that minimize the hazard.

Regarding the slip resistance of treads, it should be recognized that when walking up or down stairs a person's foot exerts a smaller horizontal force against treads than achieved when walking on level floors. Therefore, materials that are acceptable as slip resistant used for floors (as described by ASTM) provide adequate slip resistance where used for stair treads, including the important leading edges of treads — the part of the tread that the foot first contacts during descent, the most critical direction of travel. If stair treads are wet there may be an increased danger of slipping, just as there may be an increased danger of slipping on wet floors of similar materials. A small wash or drainage slope on exterior stair treads is therefore recommended to shed water. [*See NBS BSS 120 (see Appendix B), p. 33.*] Where environmental conditions (such as illumination levels and directionality or a complex visual field drawing a person's attention away from stair treads) lead to a hazardous reduction in one's ability to perceive stair treads, they should be made of a material that permits ready discrimination of the number and position of treads. In all cases, the leading edges of all treads should be readily visible during both ascent and descent. A major factor in injury-producing stair accidents and in the ability to use stairs efficiently in conditions such as egress is the clarity of the stair treads as separate stepping surfaces.

Relatively little information is available on slip resistance. There is an ASTM Committee E-17 on Skid Resistance that published results of a symposium STP 649 "Walking Surfaces: Measurement of Skid Resistance," a symposium sponsored by ASTM Subcommittee E17.26, Denver, Colorado, June 30, 1977, published 1978.

5-2.2.4.5   Treads of stairs and landing floors shall be solid.

At this location, previous editions of the *Code* prohibited stairs with less than three risers. See 5-1.6 for special requirements where changes in elevation involve fewer than three risers.

5-2.2.4.6   Stairs and other exits shall be so arranged as to make clear the direction of egress to the street. Exit stairs that continue beyond the floor of discharge shall be interrupted at the floor of discharge by partitions, doors, or other effective means.

Exception: Exit stairs that continue one-half story beyond the level of exit discharge need not be interrupted by physical barriers where the exit discharge is clearly obvious.

Figure 5-32 illustrates an important stair detail (*see 5-2.2.4.6*) designed to minimize the possibility of a person inadvertently passing through the exit discharge level into a basement or some level below that of the exit discharge. This can be accomplished by the use of a partition, or other physical barrier, that effectively interrupts the flow of travel, causing a person to perform a conscious act to overcome the barrier. The use of railings, gates, or grilles to create this barrier is acceptable. (*Also see 5-2.2.3.6 and 5-7.3.*)

5-2.2.5 Special Provisions for Outside Stairs.

5-2.2.5.1 Balconies.   Balconies to which access doors lead shall be approximately level with the floor of the building.

Exception: In existing buildings in climates where balconies may be subject to accumulation of snow or ice, one step, not to exceed 8 in. (20.3 cm), may be permitted below the level of the inside floor.

Where snow and ice are a possibility, protection must be provided against accumulations that could block the free swing of the access doors

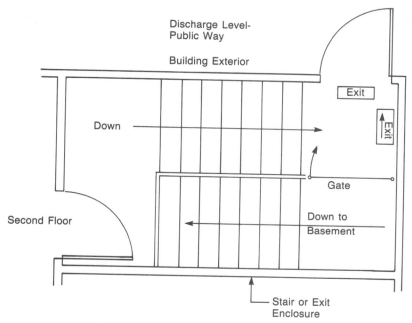

Figure 5-32. Interruption of Exit Stair at Level of Exit Discharge. This can be done by placing a physical barrier to prevent continuation below the level of exit discharge into the basement. This helps to warn occupants in the stair enclosure that they are on the level of exit discharge.

leading to balconies or prevent full use of the stairs. (See 5-1.7.3.) The 8-in. (20.3-cm) clearance provided in the Exception to 5-2.2.5.1 gives some of that protection; however, protection of the walking surfaces is also required.

5-2.2.5.2* Visual Protection. Outside stairs shall be so arranged as to avoid any handicap to the use of the stairs by persons having a fear of high places. For stairs more than three stories in height, any arrangement intended to meet this requirement shall be at least 4 ft (122 cm) in height.

A-5-2.2.5.2 The guards that are required by 5-2.2.6 will usually meet this requirement where the stair is not more than three stories high. Special architectural treatment, including application of such devices as metal or masonry screens and grilles, will usually be necessary to comply with the intent of the requirements for stairs over three stories in height.

Outside stairs frequently have an open side that must be protected by a railing or guard. On high buildings, the fear of height may interfere with use of such stairs, and so 5-2.2.5.2 calls for a 4-ft high (122-cm high) guard construction to protect against this possibility.

5-2.2.5.3   Subject to the approval of the authority having jurisdiction, outside stairs may be accepted where leading to roofs of other sections of the building or adjoining building, where the construction is fire resistive, where there is a continuous and safe means of exit from the roof, and where all other reasonable requirements for life safety are maintained. (*Also see 5-7.5.*)

Outside stairs leading to the roofs of other sections of the building or onto the roofs of adjoining buildings are acceptable as part of the means of egress, but only upon approval of the authority having jurisdiction. The conditions and settings of such paths of travel are likely to be so varied that it is virtually impossible to cover them by written provisions. Each situation is best judged individually by the authority having jurisdiction. (*Also see 5-7.5.*)

5-2.2.6 Guards and Handrails.

5-2.2.6.1 Guards.   Means of egress such as landings, balconies, corridors, passage-ways, floor or roof openings, ramps, aisles, porches, or mezzanines that are more than 30 in. (76 cm) above the floor or grade below shall be provided with guards to prevent falls over the open side. Stairs that are provided with handrails as specified in 5-2.2.6.5 need not be provided with guards.

5-2.2.6.2* Handrails.   Each new stair and each new ramp with a slope exceeding 1 in 15 shall have handrails on both sides. In addition, handrails shall be provided within 30 in. (76 cm) of all portions of the required egress width of stairs. The required egress width shall be along the natural path of travel. Existing stairs and stairs within dwelling units and within guest rooms shall have a handrail on at least one side. (*See also 5-2.2.6.5.*)

Exception: On existing stairs, handrails shall be provided within 44 in. (112 cm) of all portions of the required egress width of stairs.

A-5-2.2.6.2   The intent of this provision is to place handrails for the required exit width of stairs only regardless of the actual width of the stairs. The required exit width is along the natural path of travel to and from the building. Examples of this requirement are shown in Figure A-5-2.2.6.2. A reduced intermediate handrail spacing of approximately 60 in. (152 cm), along with a handrail height at the upper limit of permissible heights, is recommended in public assembly, educational and similar occupancies where crowds of people must simultaneously use a stair for normal access and egress as well as for emergency egress. This permits everyone to reach and grasp one handrail. Except as noted in 5-2.2.6.3 and 5-2.2.6.5, handrails are not required on stair landings.

Handrails are required on each side of new stairs and ramps, but they are not required on landings except as noted in 5-2.2.6.3 and 5-2.2.6.5. They provide support for people using stairs and can serve as a guide when, as sometimes happens, smoke enters the stairway in a quantity sufficient to interfere with one's vision or when the stair lighting system fails. Thus, it is important to have railings within reach of each file of people.

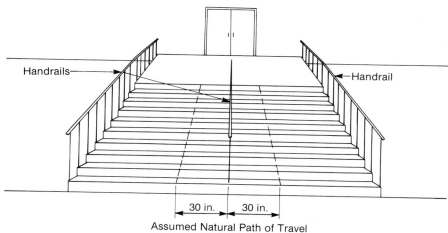

Building or Structure
Required Egress ≤ 60 in.

Handrails

Handrail

30 in. | 30 in.

Assumed Natural Path of Travel
Monumental Stairs

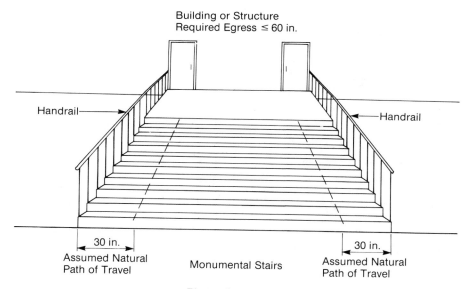

Building or Structure
Required Egress ≤ 60 in.

Handrail

Handrail

30 in.

Assumed Natural
Path of Travel

Monumental Stairs

30 in.

Assumed Natural
Path of Travel

Figure A-5-2.2.6.2

See additonal figure and commentary on next page.

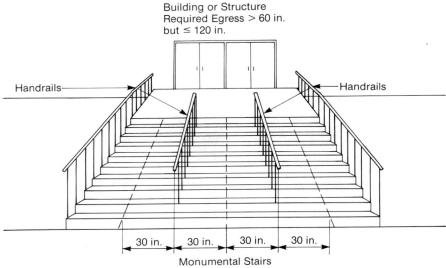

Conversion: 1 in. = 2.54 cm.

Figure A-5-2.2.6.2

Superficially, the design details for guards and handrails may appear to be relatively unimportant. Yet even in normal use, poorly designed and constructed guards and handrails can cause accidents. Lack of guards and handrails on stairs, ramps, landings, and balconies can be even more hazardous.

On monumental stairs the required handrails should be located along the normal path of travel to and from the building.

Figure A-5-2.2.6.2 illustrates the required provision of handrails on wide, monumental stairs. Handrails are provided along the natural paths of travel from the exit doors. (Note that where the doors are separated and are close to the two sides of the wide stair, the maximum stair egress width includes two of the 3½ in. (8.9 cm) projections permitted by 5-3.2.1, and thus the maximum width is actually 67 in. (170 cm), not 60 in. (152 cm). This does not occur with the handrails that are used by people on both sides.

The 30-in. (76-cm) figure, applying to stairs, is a significant change from previous Codes. It comes from the realization that people can only reach about 24 in. (60 cm) to the side to grasp a handrail. The 6 in. (15 cm) added to this reach distance accounts for the overlapping configuration of people in a crowd as illustrated in Figure 5-33. The arrangement of stair and people, seen in overhead plan view, is typical of what is observed in evacuation conditions where movement, speed, density, and flow are near optimum for safe, comfortable crowd movement.

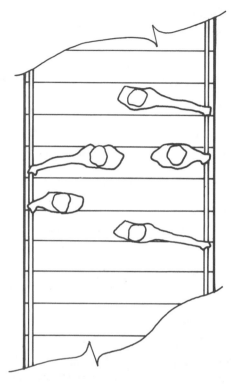

Figure 5-33. Overhead, Plan View of Stair with Handrails at the Maximum 60-in. (152-cm) Spacing Permitted by the *Code* for New Stairs. Crowd configuration shown is near optimum for efficient, safe and comfortable movement.

5-2.2.6.3   Required guards and handrails shall continue for the full length of each flight of stairs. At turns of stairs, inside handrails shall be continuous between flights at landings.

Exception: On existing stairs, the handrails are not required to be continuous between flights of stairs at landings.

It is not the intent of this *Code* to require handrails on stair landings. However, the interior handrail on stairs that change direction at a landing shall be continuous. [*See Figure A-5-2.2.6.5(e).*]

5-2.2.6.4   The design of guards and handrails and the hardware for attaching handrails to guards, balusters, or masonry walls shall be such that there are no projecting lugs on attachment devices or nonprojecting corners or members of grilles or panels that may engage loose clothing. Openings in guards shall be designed to prevent loose clothing from becoming wedged in such openings.

5-2.2.6.5* Handrail Details.

A-5-2.2.6.5   Aisle stairs forming part of a required means of egress should be provided with handrails located along the centerline of such aisles or at one side of such aisle. Center aisle handrails may be made up of short sections, with returns to the stair, and with the resulting gaps not greater than 36 in. (91 cm) measured horizontally.

See 8-2.5.6.9(f) for new requirements for handrails on aisle stairs.

(a) Handrails on stairs shall be not less than 34 in. (86 cm) nor more than 38 in. (97 cm) above the surface of the tread, measured vertically to the top of the rail from the tread at the leading edge.

Exception No. 1 to (a): Existing handrails shall not be less than 30 in. (76 cm) nor more than 38 in. (97 cm) above the upper surface of the tread, measured vertically to the top of the leading edge.

Exception No. 2 to (a): *Additional handrails may be provided lower or higher than the main handrail.*

A-5-2.2.6.5(a) Exception No. 2   On stairs that will be used extensively by children 5 years of age or younger, additional handrails at a height of approximately 24 in. (61 cm) are recommended.

Provision of the higher handrail height was the subject of extensive research by the National Research Council of Canada.

Very high handrails have been tested in field and laboratory conditions. Heights up to about 42 in. (107 cm) are very effective in helping people to stabilize themselves in order to help arrest a fall. Therefore, a guard-height railing that also meets the graspability criteria for handrails [5-2.2.6.5(c)] should serve well as a handrail also.

Three different types of studies of handrail height for stairs all led to the same conclusion: handrail heights previously required by the *Code* were suboptimum. The studies included anthropometric analyses (such as illustrated in Figure 5-34), field studies of the use of various handrails, and laboratory studies where functional capability of users to grasp a handrail as if arresting a fall could be accurately measured and compared for a range of handrail conditions. These studies included a wide range of ages and sizes of people, from young children to those in their seventies. Most functional heights, even for elderly persons tested, were in the range of 36 in. (91 cm) to 38 in. (97 cm), and the average height most preferred by elderly persons tested was about 37 in. (94 cm). (These studies were reported in the scientific journal, Ergonomics, Vol. 28, No. 7, 1985, pp. 999-1010; Review of stair-safety research with an emphasis on Canadian studies, by Jake Pauls.)

The recommendation for lower handrails for young children is particularly important for family dwellings and for children's day-care facilities.

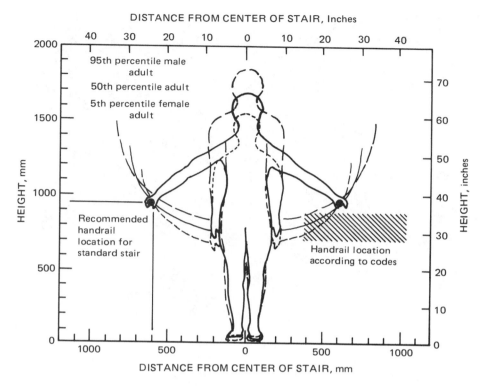

Figure 5-34. One of the Studies Leading to the *Code*'s Requirement for Higher Handrails and Closer Lateral Spacing Included this Anthropometric Analysis of User's Capability to Reach a Handrail to the Side. On the left side is shown the recommended height and spacing of handrails; on the right is the location of handrails formerly permitted by the *Code* for new stairs. It is evident that people in the middle of a wide stair will be unable to reach the lower, more distant handrails; therefore this condition is not desirable when a stair is crowded, as in an egress situation.

Photo Courtesy of J.L. Pauls
Figure 5-35.   Field Testing of an Adjustable-Height Handrail.

This frame from the documentary film, "The Stair Event," shows field testing of an adjustable-height handrail in an aisle stair in the Edmonton's Commonwealth Stadium. Evidence from such field testing, from anthropometric analyses, and from laboratory testing with a range of younger and older adults, has led to the higher handrail heights introduced in the 1988 Code. The upper handrail is located 37 in. (94 cm) above tread nosings — which, in the laboratory testing, was the average perferred height for elderly people and an especially effective height for arresting a fall in descent. The lower railing, provided for children, is approximately 24 in. (60 cm) above the tread nosings. Note that even in this case of ascent, one of the children has chosen to use the higher railing, located at about his shoulder height, in preference to the lower one. Such a lower railing is required for aisle handrails and is generally recommended for stairs that will be extensively used by children five years or less in age. (This is referred to in Appendix notes for Chapters 10 and 11.)

(b)* New handrails shall provide a clearance of at least 1½ in. (3.8 cm) between handrail and wall to which fastened.

A-5-2.2.6.5(b)   This 1½-in. (3.8-cm) clearance assumes that the wall adjacent to the handrail is a smooth surface. Where rough wall surfaces are used, greater clearances are recommended.

(c)* Handrails shall have a circular cross-section with an outside diameter of at least 1.25 in. (3.2 cm) and not greater than 2.0 in. (5 cm). New handrails shall be continuously graspable along the entire length.

Exception to (c):   Any other shape with a perimeter dimension of at least 4 in. (10.2 cm), but not greater than 6.25 in. (15.9 cm), and with the largest cross-sectional dimension not exceeding 2.25 in. (5.7 cm).

A-5-2.2.6.5(c)   Handrails should be designed so that they can be grasped firmly with a comfortable grip, and so that the hand can be slid along the rail without encountering obstructions. The profile of the rail should comfortably match the hand grips. For example, a round profile such as is provided by the simplest round tubing or pipe having an outside diameter of 1½ to 2 in. (3.8 to 5 cm) provides good graspability for adults. Factors such as the use of a handrail by small children and the wall-fixing details should be taken into account in assessing handrail graspability. The most functional as well as the most preferred handrail shape and size is circular with a 1.5 in. (3.8 cm) outside diameter (according to research with adults). Handrails used predominantly by children should be designed at the lower end of the permitted dimensional range.

It should be noted that handrails are one of the most important components of a stair; therefore, design excesses such as oversized wood handrail sections should be avoided unless there is a readily perceived and easily grasped handhold provided. At all times in handrail design it is useful to remember the effectiveness of a simple round profile that permits some locking action by fingers as they curl around the handrail.

Item (c) introduces a subtle but important requirement for handrails, that of graspability. People are incapable of exerting sufficient finger pressure to adequately grasp a handrail using only a "pinch grip" as opposed to a "power grip" when fingers curl around and under a properly shaped and sized railing. This would prohibit the use of rectangular lumber for handrails. Figure 5-36 shows examples of acceptable and unacceptable handrails. It also shows how an unacceptable rail can be retrofitted to make a *Code*-complying handrail.

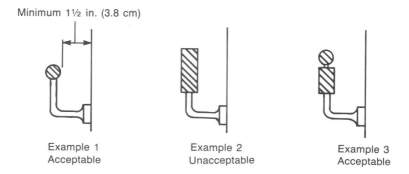

Minimum 1½ in. (3.8 cm)

| Example 1 | Example 2 | Example 3 |
| Acceptable | Unacceptable | Acceptable |

Figure 5-36.   Handrails.   Example 1 shows a typical handrail that is acceptable for graspability. Example 2 shows a handrail not acceptable from a graspability standpoint. Example 3 shows how to modify the handrail in Example 2 to comply with the graspability criteria and also increase the handrail height.

Figure 5-37 illustrates acceptable, unacceptable, and marginal handrail shapes and sizes based on a Canadian study, with younger and older adults, testing functional capability as well as user preference. The traditional residential handrail section, shown at the bottom center, did not perform well in the functional testing, and it was not a comfortable shape to grasp in comparison with other sections. A key difference between the acceptable and unacceptable handrail sections is the ability to wrap one's fingers completely around the handrail to achieve a "power grip." Unacceptable sections permit only a "pinch grip," which provides for little opportunity to help arrest a fall, even for people with ordinary hand dexterity and strength. Figure 5-36 shows how an ungraspable, oversized railing can be easily retrofitted with a proper handrail section on top of the railing to improve graspability as well as to bring the handrail into closer conformity with new height requirements.

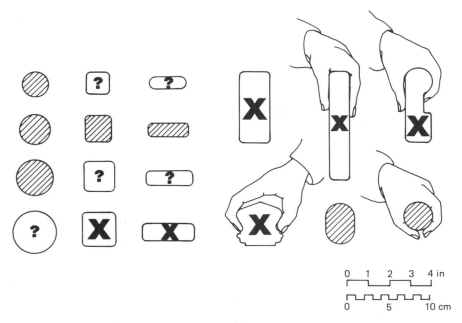

Figure 5-37.   Acceptable, Unacceptable, and Marginal Handrail Sections.

(d) New handrail ends shall be returned to the wall or floor or shall terminate at newel posts.

(e)* New handrails that are not continuous between flights shall be extended horizontally a minimum of 12 in. (30.5 cm) at the required height at landings where a guard or wall exists.

A-5-2.2.6.5(e)   Figure A-5-2.2.6.5(e) illustrates some of the requirements of 5-2.2.6.5.

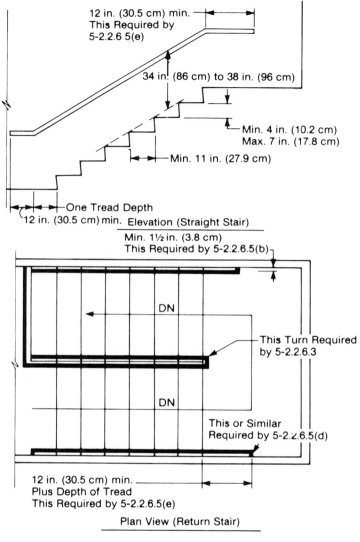

12 in. (30.5 cm) min.
This Required by
5-2.2.6 5(e)

34 in. (86 cm) to 38 in. (96 cm)

Min. 4 in. (10.2 cm)
Max. 7 in. (17.8 cm)

Min. 11 in. (27.9 cm)

One Tread Depth
12 in. (30.5 cm) min.   Elevation (Straight Stair)

Min. 1½ in. (3.8 cm)
This Required by 5-2.2.6.5(b)

DN

This Turn Required
by 5-2.2.6.3

DN

This or Similar
Required by 5-2.2.6.5(d)

12 in. (30.5 cm) min.
Plus Depth of Tread
This Required by 5-2.2.6.5(e)

Plan View (Return Stair)

Figure A-5-2.2.6.5(e)

(f) New handrails on open sides of stairs shall have intermediate rails or an ornamental pattern such that a sphere 6 in. (15.2 cm) in diameter cannot pass through any openings in such handrail.

Exception to (f): In detention and correctional occupancies as provided in Chapters 14 and 15, in industrial occupancies as provided in Chapter 28, and in storage occupancies as provided in Chapter 29.

In order to prevent small children from falling through guards or handrails and to prevent them from being caught in openings, the configuration and construction of a guard or handrail must meet certain minimum requirements. Rather than detailed specifications for intermediate rails, the *Code* sets a performance criterion that allows alternative solutions.

5-2.2.6.6 Guard Details.

(a) The height of guards required by 5-2.2.6.1 shall be measured vertically to the top of the guard from the surface adjacent thereto.

(b) Guards shall be not less than 42 in. (107 cm) high.

Exception No. 1 to (b): Guards within dwelling units may be 36 in. (91 cm) high.

Exception No. 2 to (b): In assembly occupancies as provided in Chapters 8 and 9.

(c) Open guards shall have intermediate rails or an ornamental pattern such that a sphere 6 in. (15.2 cm) in diameter cannot pass through any opening.

Exception No. 1 to (c): In detention and correctional occupancies, in industrial occupancies, and in storage occupancies, the clear distance between intermediate rails measured at right angles to the rails shall not exceed 21 in. (53.3 cm).

Exception No. 2 to (c): Approved existing open guards.

5-2.3 Smokeproof Enclosures.

5-2.3.1   Where smokeproof enclosures are required by other sections of this *Code*, they shall comply with 5-2.3.

Exception: Existing smokeproof enclosures subject to the approval of the authority having jurisdiction.

A smokeproof enclosure is a stair enclosure designed to limit the infiltration of heat, smoke, and fire gases from a fire in any part of a building. It is designed to provide improved protection against the products of combustion entering the actual stairway enclosure.

5-2.3.2*   A smokeproof enclosure shall be a stair enclosure so designed that the movement into the smokeproof enclosure of products of combustion produced by a fire occurring in any part of the building shall be limited.

A-5-2.3.2   For further guidance see:

(1) ASHRAE *Handbook of Fundamentals* (see *Appendix B*).

(2) Design of Smoke Control Systems for Buildings, by Klote and Fothergill. (*See Appendix B.*)

(3) NFPA 105, *Recommended Practice for the Installation of Smoke- and Draft-Control Door Assemblies. (See Appendix B.)*

See Figure 5-38a for examples of smokeproof enclosures that meet *Code* criteria.

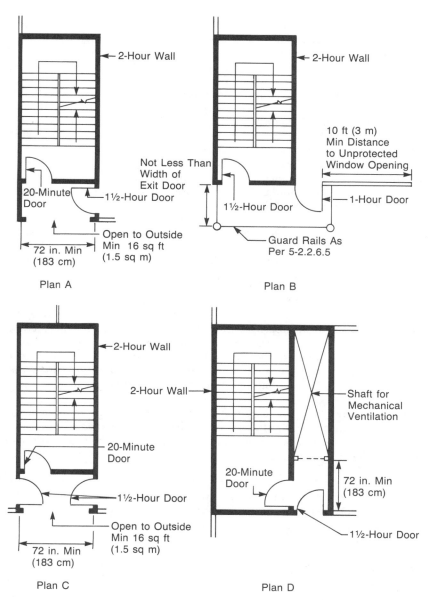

Figure 5-38a. Four Variations of Smokeproof Enclosures Conforming to *Code* Criteria.   Plan A utilizes an open air vestibule. Plan B shows an entrance by way of an outside balcony. Plan C could provide a stair enclosure entrance common to two buildings. In Plan D, smoke and gases entering the vestibule would be exhausted by mechanical ventilation. In each case, a double entrance to the stair enclosure with at least one side open or vented is characteristic of this type of construction. Pressurization of the stair enclosure in the event of fire provides an attractive alternate for sprinklered buildings and is a means of eliminating the entrance vestibule.

5-2.3.3   The appropriate design method shall be any system that meets the performance level stipulated in 5-2.3.2 above. The smokeproof enclosure may be accomplished by using natural ventilation, by using mechanical ventilation incorporating a vestibule, or by pressurizing the stair enclosure.

Paragraph 5-2.3.3 requires that smokeproof enclosures meet the "performance criteria" of 5-2.3.2. It goes on to specify three different types of smokeproof enclosures: (1) by using natural ventilation as detailed in 5-2.3.7; (2) by mechanical ventilation in accordance with 5-2.3.8; and (3) by pressurizing the stair enclosure as provided in 5-2.3.9, but the *Code* does not limit one to these if the design meets 5-2.3.2 and is acceptable to the authority having jurisdiction. This is especially important for existing smokeproof enclosures since they often do not meet all the specifications that follow.

5-2.3.4 Enclosure.   A smokeproof enclosure shall consist of a continuous stair enclosed from the highest point to the lowest point by fire barriers having a 2-hour fire resistance rating. Where a vestibule is used, it shall be within the 2-hour enclosure and is part of the smokeproof enclosure.

Paragraph 5-2.3.4 requires that the smokeproof enclosure and all of its components be within the required 2-hour fire-resistant enclosure with openings therein protected by a door having a 1½-hour fire protection rating. This enclosure protects the smokeproof enclosure from the direct attack of fire. However, the door from the vestibule into the actual stairway need have only a 20-minute fire protection rating since the purpose at this point is to minimize air or smoke leakage.

5-2.3.5 Discharge.   Every smokeproof enclosure shall discharge into a public way, into a yard or court having direct access to a public way, or into an exit passageway. Such exit passageways shall be without other openings and shall be separated from the remainder of the building by fire barriers having a 2-hour fire resistance rating.

Note that 5-2.3.5 prohibits smokeproof enclosures from discharging through the level of exit discharge. It emphasizes the need for continuity to a public way, the exit discharge, or an exit passageway. As an exit, such exit passageway may have only those openings required for exiting building occupants.

5-2.3.6 Access.   Access to the stair shall be by way of a vestibule or by way of an exterior balcony.

Exception: Smokeproof enclosures consisting of a pressurized stair enclosure complying with 5-2.3.9.

5-2.3.7 Natural Ventilation.   Smokeproof enclosures by natural ventilation shall comply with all the following:

(a) Where a vestibule is provided, the doorway into the vestibule shall be protected with an approved fire door assembly having a 1½-hour fire protection rating, and the fire door assembly from the vestibule to the stair shall have not less than a 20-minute fire protection rating. Doors shall be designed to minimize air leakage and shall be self-closing or shall be automatic-closing by actuation of a smoke detector within 10 ft (3 m) of the vestibule door. Where access to the stair is by means of an open exterior balcony, the door assembly to the stair shall have a 1½-hour fire protection rating and shall be self-closing or shall be automatic-closing by actuation of a smoke detector. Openings adjacent to such exterior balconies shall be protected as required in 5-2.2.3.3.

(b) Every vestibule shall have a minimum net area of 16 sq ft (1.5 sq m) of opening in an exterior wall facing an exterior court, yard, or public space at least 20 ft (6.1 m) in width.

(c) Every vestibule shall have a minimum dimension not less than the required width of the corridor leading to it and a minimum dimension of 72 in. (183 cm) in the direction of travel.

5-2.3.8 Mechanical Ventilation.

Smokeproof enclosures by mechanical ventilation shall comply with all of the following:

(a) The door assembly from the building into the vestibule shall have a 1½-hour fire protection rating, and the door assembly from the vestibule to the stairway shall have not less than a 20-minute fire protection rating. The door to the stairway shall be designed and installed to minimize air leakage. The doors shall be self-closing or shall be automatic-closing by actuation of a smoke detector located within 10 ft (3 m) of the vestibule door.

(b) Vestibules shall have a minimum dimension of 44 in. (112 cm) in width and 72 in. (183 cm) in direction of exit travel.

(c) The vestibule shall be provided with not less than one air change per minute, and the exhaust shall be 150 percent of the supply. Supply air shall enter and exhaust air shall discharge from the vestibule through separate tightly constructed ducts used only for that purpose. Supply air shall enter the vestibule within 6 in. (15.2 cm) of the floor level. The top of the exhaust register shall be located not more than 6 in. (15.2 cm) down from the top of the trap and shall be entirely within the smoke trap area. Doors, when in the open position, shall not obstruct duct openings. Duct openings may be provided with controlling dampers if needed to meet the design requirements but are not otherwise required.

(d) To serve as a smoke and heat trap and to provide an upward moving air column, the vestibule ceiling shall be at least 20 in. (50.8 cm) higher than the door opening into the vestibule. The height may be decreased where justified by engineering design and field testing.

(e) The stair shall be provided with a dampered relief opening at the top and supplied mechanically with sufficient air to discharge a minimum of 2500 cu ft/min (70.8 cu m/min) through the relief opening while maintaining a minimum positive pressure of 0.10 in. water column (25 Pa) in the stair relative to the vestibule with all doors closed.

Figure 5-38b illustrates an elevation view of a vestibule using mechanical ventilation.

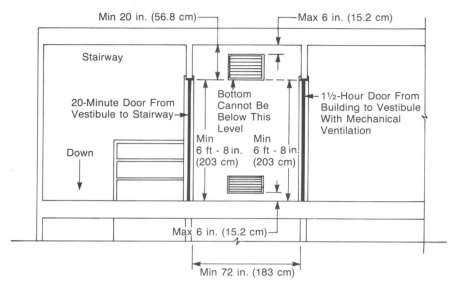

Figure 5-38b.   Elevation View of Vestibule Using Mechanical Ventilation.

5-2.3.9 Stair Pressurization.

5-2.3.9.1   Smokeproof enclosures by stair pressurization shall comply with all of the following:

(a) The building shall be protected throughout by an approved supervised automatic sprinkler system in accordance with Section 7-7.

(b) There shall be an engineered system to pressurize the stair enclosure capable of developing 0.05 in. water column (12.5 Pa) in addition to the maximum anticipated stack pressure relative to other parts of the building measured with all the enclosure doors closed. The combined positive pressure shall not exceed 0.35 in. water column (87.5 Pa).

5-2.3.9.2   Equipment and ductwork for stair pressurization shall be located:

(a) Exterior to the building and be directly connected to the stairway by ductwork enclosed in noncombustible construction, or

(b) Within the stair enclosure with intake and exhaust air directly to the outside or through ductwork enclosed in 2-hour construction, or

(c) Within the building if separated from the remainder of the building, including other mechanical equipment, with 2-hour construction.

In each case, openings into the required 2-hour construction shall be limited to those needed for maintenance and operation and shall be protected by self-closing 1½-hour fire protection rated devices.

Exception to (c): Where the building, including the stairway enclosure, is protected throughout by an approved supervised automatic sprinkler system in accordance with Section 7-7, fire-rated construction may be reduced to 1-hour construction.

Note that to accept pressurized stairs as smokeproof enclosures, the building must be sprinklered. Figure 5-39 illustrates some potential arrangements complying with 5-2.3.9.2.

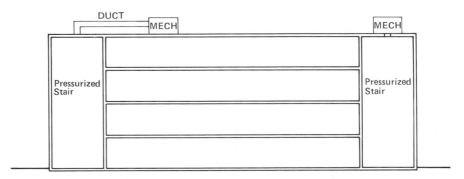

Figure 5-39(a).   Mechanical Equipment and Ductwork Complying with 5-2.3.9.2(a).

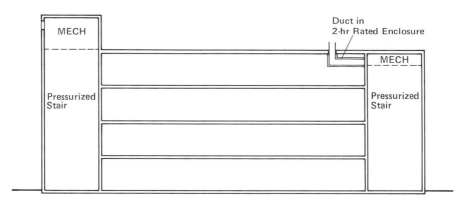

Figure 5-39(b).   Mechanical Equipment and Ductwork Complying with 5-2.3.9.2(b).

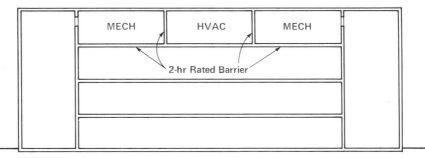

Figure 5-39(c).   Mechanical Equipment and Ductwork Complying with 5-2.3.9.2(c).

5-2.3.10 Activation of Mechanical Ventilation Systems.

5-2.3.10.1   For both mechanical ventilation and pressurized stair enclosure systems, the activation of the systems shall be initiated by a smoke detector installed in an approved location within 10 ft (3 m) of the entrance to the smokeproof enclosure.

5-2.3.10.2   The required mechanical systems shall operate at the activation of the smoke detectors in 5-2.3.10.1 and by manual controls accessible to the fire department. The required system shall also be initiated by the following, if provided:

(a) Waterflow signal from a complete automatic sprinkler system.

(b) General evacuation alarm signal. (*See 7-6.3.5.*)

5-2.3.11 Door Closers.   The activation of an automatic closing device on any door in the smokeproof enclosure shall activate all other automatic closing devices on doors in the smokeproof enclosure.

5-2.3.12 Standby Power.   Standby power for mechanical ventilation equipment shall be provided by an approved self-contained generator set to operate whenever there is a loss of power in the normal house current. The generator shall be in a separate room having a minimum 1-hour fire-resistive occupancy separation and shall have a minimum fuel supply adequate to operate the equipment for 2 hours.

5-2.3.13 Testing.   Before the mechanical equipment is accepted by the authority having jurisdiction, it shall be tested to confirm that the mechanical equipment is operating in compliance with these requirements.

5-2.3.14 Emergency Lighting.   The stair shaft and vestibule shall be provided with emergency lighting. A standby generator that is installed for the smokeproof enclosure mechanical ventilation equipment may be used for such stair shaft and vestibule power supply.

5-2.4 Horizontal Exits.

5-2.4.1* Application.   Horizontal exits may be substituted for other exits to an extent that the total exit capacity of the other exits (stairs, ramps, doors leading outside the building) will not be reduced below half that required for the entire area of the building or connected buildings if there were no horizontal exits.

Exception: In health care occupancies as provided in Chapters 12 and 13, and in detention and correctional occupancies as provided in Chapters 14 and 15.

A-5-2.4.1 Example: One way to provide the required exit capacity from the upper floor of a department store building 350 ft by 200 ft (107 m by 60 m) (occupant load 1166 per floor) would be to furnish eight 44-in. (112-cm) stairs. [*See Figure A-5-2.4.1(a).*]

Assume now that this building is divided into two sections by a fire wall meeting the requirements for a horizontal exit, one 130 ft by 200 ft (40 m by 60 m) and the other 220 ft by 200 ft (67 m by 60 m), with two pairs of 44-in. (112-cm) double egress doors, with each door providing 44 in. (112-cm) of egress width [*see Figure A-5-2.4.1(b)*]. The smaller section, considered separately, will require the equivalent of three 44-in. (112-cm) stairs and the larger section will require five such exits. The horizontal exits will serve as one of the three exits required for the smaller section and two of the five exits required for the larger section. Therefore, only two 44-in. (112-cm) stairs from the smaller section and three 44-in. (112-cm) stairs from the larger section will be required, if the exits can be arranged to meet the requirements for the 150-ft (45-m) travel distance allowed from any point in a sprinklered building. Thus, the total number of stairs required for the building will be five, as compared with eight if no horizontal exit had been provided.

Another option would be the use of two 56-in. (142-cm) stairs from the larger section, which would reduce the total number of stairways required from the floor to four [see *Figure A-5-2.4.1(c)*]. However, if the building were further subdivided by a second fire wall meeting the requirements for a horizontal exit, no further reduction in stairways would be permitted in order not to exceed the maximum one-half of exiting via horizontal exits.

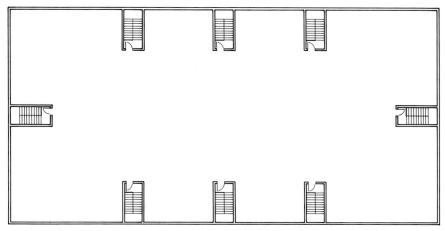

Figure A-5-2.4.1(a) Eight Exits, None Via Horizontal Exit, Required to Provide the Necessary Egress Capacity.

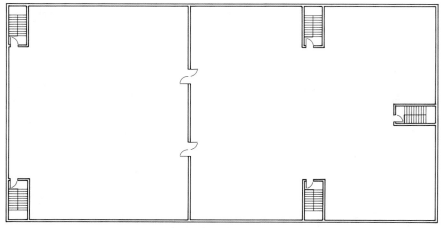

Figure A-5-2.4.1(b) Number of Stairs Reduced by Three Through Use of Two Horizontal Exits; Same Egress Capacity Provided.

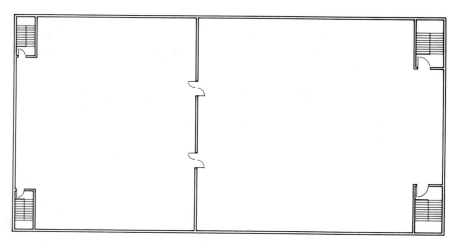

Figure A-5-2.4.1(c)   Number of Stairs Further Reduced, by Widening Stairs in Larger Compartment, but Not to Less Than One-Half the Required Number and Capacity of Exits from that Compartment.

A horizontal exit is a passage from one building area into another building area, each separated from the other by a fire barrier, space, or other form of protection of such a character that it enables each area to serve as an area of refuge from a fire in the other area. A horizontal exit, however, need not be confined to one building. It can be a bridge from one building to another. Just as with other types of exits, the horizontal exit has components consisting of doors and enclosure walls and often includes structural features, such as bridges and balconies, used in the passage from one area to the other. Because the horizontal exit is usually located on the same level as the area from which escape is desired, there are no stairs or ramps involved.

Although horizontal exits can provide as fast and as safe a means of reaching an area of refuge as any other exit, they cannot be given credit for providing more than one-half the required exits or exit capacity of the building or buildings connected, except in health care and detention and correctional occupancies where special exceptions apply.

Before any space can be used as an area of refuge in a horizontal exit, it must itself satisfy certain criteria. Such space, although separated with 2-hour fire barriers, cannot be used as an area of refuge unless there is at least one standard type of exit leading from it (not another horizontal exit) and unless the space is large enough to accommodate the occupants of both the fire area and area of refuge, allowing 3 sq ft (.28 sq m) of floor space per person. This area figure is modified in health care occupancies and in detention and correctional occupancies. The nature of a horizontal exit is such that the psychological feeling of being in another area or building, away from the fire, can do much to protect the occupants and prevent the disorderly movement of people.

Figure 5-40 illustrates how to apply the requirement allowing the substitution of horizontal exits for other exits. Figure 5-41 illustrates how that requirement is violated.

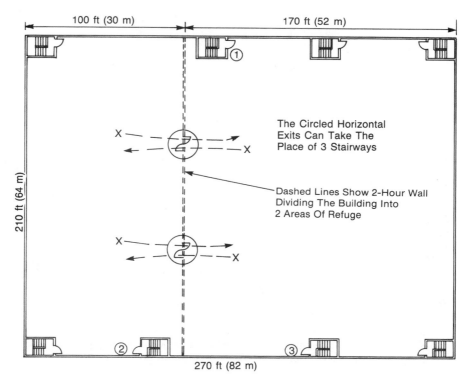

Figure 5-40.   An Example of Substituting Horizontal Exits for Other Exits. Note that the horizontal exits (circled) take the place of stair enclosures as paths of escape for the occupants on either side of the 2-hour wall (shown as a dashed line) dividing the area into two sections. This would permit the elimination of the three stair enclosures closest to the horizontal exits, stair enclosures that would be required if the entire area were to be considered as one.

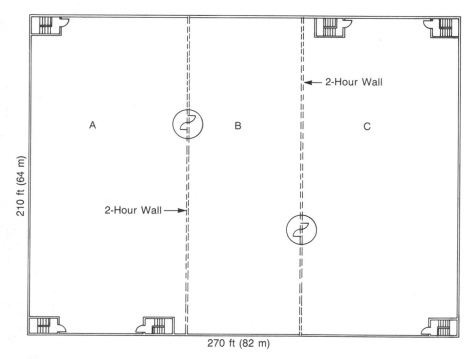

Figure 5-41.   An Example of How Horizontal Exits (Circled) Cannot Be Used. The two horizontal exits from area B violate 5-2.4.1 in that at least one-half of the required exits and exit capacity must be other than horizontal exits. Area B also does not provide a continuous path of travel by stairway or other type of exit for occupants evacuating either area A or C as required by 5-2.4.2.

5-2.4.2 Area of Refuge.

5-2.4.2.1   Every fire compartment for which credit is allowed in connection with a horizontal exit shall have, in addition to the horizontal exit or exits, at least one stairway or doorway leading outside or other exit that is not a horizontal exit. Any fire compartment not having a stairway or doorway leading outside shall be considered as part of an adjoining compartment with stairway.

Exception: In detention and correctional occupancies as provided in Chapters 14 and 15.

5-2.4.2.2   Every horizontal exit for which credit is given shall be so arranged that there are continuously available paths of travel leading from each side of the exit to stairways or other means of egress leading to outside the building.

5-2.4.2.3   Whenever either side of the horizontal exit is occupied, the doors used in connection with the horizontal exit shall be unlocked from the egress side.

Exception: In health care occupancies as provided in Chapters 12 and 13, and in detention and correctional occupancies as provided in Chapters 14 and 15.

5-2.4.2.4   The floor area on either side of a horizontal exit shall be sufficient to hold the occupants of both floor areas, allowing not less than 3-sq ft (.28-sq m) clear floor area per person.

Exception: Special floor area requirements in health care occupancies as provided in Chapters 12 and 13, and in detention and correctional occupancies as provided in Chapters 14 and 15.

The design or incorporation of a horizontal exit into a building is not a complicated process. For proper arrangement of the total means of egress system, it is simply a matter of designing each separated portion, or compartment, as if it were a completely separate building. The point of passage through the horizontal exit is treated as if it were, in fact, an exterior exit door. In determining the required exit capacities from each separated portion, or compartment, the occupant loads are *not* to be combined.

It must be kept in mind that exiting is a dynamic process. While each compartment must contain sufficient available floor area, at a rate of 3 sq ft (.28 sq m) per person for the total occupant load of both compartments, exiting from the area of refuge continues through its "other" exits. The 2-hour fire resistant separation from the compartment of fire origin provides the additional time for exiting from the compartment of refuge.

5-2.4.3 Walls for Horizontal Exits.

5-2.4.3.1   Fire barriers separating buildings or areas between which there are horizontal exits shall be an assembly of noncombustible or limited-combustible material having a 2-hour fire resistance rating. They shall provide a separation continuous to ground. (*See also 6-2.3.*)

Exception: Where a fire barrier is used to provide a horizontal exit in any story of a building, such fire barrier may be omitted on other stories under the following conditions:

(a) The stories on which the fire barrier is omitted shall be separated from the story with the horizontal exit by 2-hour construction.

(b) Vertical openings between the story with the horizontal exit and the open fire area story shall be enclosed with 2-hour construction.

(c) All required exits, other than horizontal exits, shall discharge directly outside.

Figure 5-42 illustrates how separation walls can be eliminated from the lower floors of a multistory building and still conform to the basic requirements of 5-2.4.3.

5-2.4.3.2   Any opening in such fire barriers, whether or not such opening serves as an exit, shall be protected as provided in 6-2.3.2.

5-2.4.3.3*   Doors in horizontal exits shall comply with 5-2.1.4.

Exception: Sliding doors in industrial occupancies as provided in Chapter 28, and in storage occupancies as provided in Chapter 29.

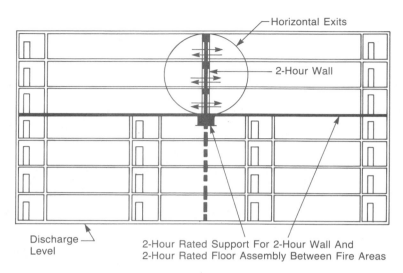

Figure 5-42.   A Multistory Building Showing How a 2-Hour Rated Division Wall for Horizontal Exits can Be Stopped at any Lower Floor Rather than Extending to the Ground Floor (as Shown by the Dashed Line), as Required by 5-2.4.3.1.   The same arrangement can be provided for basement areas.

A-5-2.4.3.3   Fusible link actuated automatic-closing doors do not qualify as horizontal exits under these provisions, as smoke might pass through the opening before there is sufficient time to release the hold open device.

Such doors are also subject to the objection that once closed they are difficult to open and would inhibit orderly egress.

> An Exception is provided in Chapters 28 and 29 for industrial and storage occupancies for those locations where a fire rated door may be required for insurance or building code reasons on both sides of the wall. (*See 28-2.2.5.2 and 29-2.2.5.2.*)

5-2.4.3.4   Where swinging fire doors are used in horizontal exits, they shall comply with the following:

(a) They shall swing in the direction of exit travel, and

(b) Where a horizontal exit serves areas on both sides of a fire barrier, there shall be adjacent openings with swinging doors at each, opening in opposite directions, with signs on each side of the fire barrier indicating the door that swings with the travel from that side, or

Exception to (b): Sleeping room areas in detention and correctional occupancies are exempt from the sign requirement.

(c) They shall be of other approved arrangement provided that doors always swing with any possible exit travel.

Exception: Door swing in existing health care occupancies as provided in Chapter 13.

5-2.4.3.5* Doors in horizontal exits shall be designed and installed to minimize air leakage.

A-5-2.4.3.5 For further information see NFPA 105, *Recommended Practice for the Installation of Smoke- and Draft-Control Door Assemblies.*

5-2.4.3.6 All fire doors in horizontal exits shall be self-closing or automatic-closing in accordance with 5-2.1.8. All opening protectives in horizontal exits are to be consistent with the fire resistance rating of the wall. Horizontal exit doors located across a corridor shall be automatic-closing in accordance with 5-2.1.8.

Exception: Where approved by the authority having jurisdiction, existing doors in horizontal exits may be self-closing.

5-2.4.4 Bridges and Balconies.

5-2.4.4.1 Each bridge or balcony utilized in conjunction with horizontal exits shall comply with the structural requirements for outside stairs and shall have guards and handrails in general conformity with the requirements of 5-2.2 for stairs and 5-2.3 for smokeproof enclosures.

5-2.4.4.2 Every bridge or balcony shall be at least as wide as the door leading to it and not less than 44 in. (112 cm) for new construction.

5-2.4.4.3 Every door leading to a bridge or balcony serving as a horizontal exit shall swing in the direction of exit travel.

Exception: In existing health care occupancies as provided in Chapter 13.

5-2.4.4.4 Where the bridge or balcony serves as a horizontal exit in one direction, only the door leading from the bridge or balcony into the area of refuge shall swing in.

5-2.4.4.5 Where the bridge or balcony serves as a horizontal exit in both directions, doors shall be provided in pairs, swinging in opposite directions. Only the door swinging with the exit travel shall be counted in determination of exit width.

Exception No. 1: If the bridge or balcony has sufficient floor area to accommodate the occupant load of either connected building or fire area on the basis of 3 sq ft (.28 sq m) per person.

Exception No. 2: In existing buildings, doors on both ends of the bridge or balcony may swing out from the building subject to the approval of the authority having jurisdiction.

5-2.4.4.6 The bridge or balcony floor shall be approximately level with the building floor and, in climates subject to the accumulation of snow and ice, shall be protected to prevent the accumulation of snow and ice.

Exception: In existing buildings in climates where balconies may be subject to the accumulation of snow or ice, one step, not to exceed 8 in. (20.3 cm), may be permitted below the level of the inside floor.

5-2.4.4.7   All wall openings, in both of the connected buildings or fire areas, any part of which is within 10 ft (3 m) of any bridge or balcony as measured horizontally or below, shall be protected with fire doors or fixed fire window assemblies.

Exception: Where bridges have solid sides not less than 6 ft (183 cm) in height, such protection of wall openings may be omitted.

5-2.5 Ramps.

Ramps are permitted as a part of a means of egress and, in fact, under some circumstances are to be preferred over stairs. Quoting from an earlier reference: "One can consider ramps and steps simply as prosthetic devices for assisting the human organism in climbing from floor to floor..."; and again: "When one must consider the energy cost of both horizontal and vertical movement, one finds that a ramp with a gradient of less than about eight degrees is more economical than any stairway that is likely to be encountered in normal activity."[4] The National Bureau of Standards study states in part: "For certain occupancies, such as schools and institutions, they (ramps) are believed to be more satisfactory and their use in these buildings is recommended"; and again: "...ramps have a rate of discharge between that of stairways and level passageways."[5]

The National Safety Council[6] has suggested the following criteria as a basis for the selection of a straight run of steps, a combination of steps and landings, or ramps:

Grade	Preference
20°-50°	Stairway
7°-20°	Stairway and landings
under 7°	Ramps

5-2.5.1 General.   A ramp, either interior or outside, may be used as a component in a means of egress where it conforms to the general requirements of Section 5-1 and to the special requirements of this subsection.

5-2.5.2 Classification.   A ramp shall be designated as Class A or Class B in accordance with the following table:

	Class A	Class B
Minimum width	44 in. (112 cm)	30 in. (76 cm)
Maximum slope	1 in 10	1 in 8
Maximum height between landings	12 ft (3.7 m)	12 ft (3.7 m)

Exception No. 1:   Existing Class B ramps with slopes of 1³/₁₆ to 2 in 12 (10 to 17 cm in 1 m) are permitted subject to the approval of the authority having jurisdiction.

Exception No. 2:   All existing Class A ramps and new ramps not exceeding a slope of 1 in 15 need not be provided with landings.

Paragraph 5-2.5.2 establishes two classes of ramps: Class A and Class B. Class A ramps are required to be at least 44 in. (112 cm) wide with a maximum slope of 1 in 10. Certain health care occupancies are permitted to use these ramps, and their utility for the movement of wheelchairs and beds is obvious. Class B ramps are to be at least 30 in. (76 cm) wide, with a maximum slope of 1 in 8. Considerable latitude is given the authority having jurisdiction with regard to the use of Class B ramps in existing buildings.

5-2.5.3 Enclosure and Protection.

Most of the commentary provided for the enclosure and protection of stairs applies to ramps. (*See commentary on stairs for additional information.*)

5-2.5.3.1   Where a ramp inside a building is used as an exit or exit component, it shall be protected by separation from other parts of the building, as specified in 5-1.3.

5-2.5.3.2   Fixed fire window assemblies may be installed in such a separation in a fully sprinklered building.

5-2.5.3.3 Separation and Protection of Outside Ramps.   Outside ramps shall be

separated from the interior of the building by walls with the fire resistance rating with fixed or self-closing opening protectives, as required for enclosed stairs. This protection shall extend at least 10 ft (3 m) upward or to the roofline, whichever is lower, and at least 10 ft (3 m) horizontally and downward to ground level.

Exception No. 1:   Outside ramps may be unprotected where serving an exterior exit access balcony that has two remote outside stairways or ramps.

Exception No. 2:   Outside ramps may be unprotected where serving a two-story building where there is a remote second exit.

Exception No. 3:   The fire resistance rating of the portion of the separation extending 10 ft (3 m) from the ramp need not exceed 1 hour.

Exception No. 4:   All openings below an outside ramp shall be protected:

(a) Where in a court, the least dimension of which is less than one-third of its height, or

(b) Where in an alcove having a width less than one-third of its height and a depth greater than one-fourth of its height.

Outside ramps may serve as part of a means of egress, subject to the regulations governing exits, exit access, and exit discharge. Where used as exits, ramps must afford the occupant a protected passage from the point of entrance to the point of discharge. This applies to outside ramps as well as inside ramps. In fact, the same regulations apply here as apply to outside stairs, including the requirements governing their location in a court or alcove.

5-2.5.3.4*   There shall be no enclosed usable space under ramps within an exit enclosure nor shall the open space under such ramps be used for any purpose. Where there is enclosed usable space under ramps, the walls and soffits of the enclosed space shall be protected the same as the ramp enclosure.

A-5-2.5.3.4   This is to prohibit closets and similar spaces under ramps within the enclosure. It is not to be interpreted to prohibit an enclosed ramp beneath another flight.

> Although this paragraph may at first seem to contradict itself, it does not. First, the paragraph states that within an exit enclosure there shall be no enclosed usable space, nor shall any open space be used for any purpose that could interfere with the use of the exit enclosure. An enclosed usable space under a ramp can be considered to be outside the exit enclosure if the walls and soffits over the enclosed space are protected the same as required for the ramp enclosure, thereby separating the space and the exit enclosure. The door to the space cannot open into the exit enclosure per 5-1.3.1(d).

5-2.5.3.5* Visual Protection.   Outside ramps shall be so arranged as to avoid any handicap to their use by persons having a fear of high places. For ramps more than three stories in height, any arrangement intended to meet this requirement shall be at least 4 ft (122 cm) in height.

A-5-2.5.3.5   The guards required by 5-2.2.6 for the unenclosed sides of ramps will usually meet this requirement where the ramp is not more than three stories high. Special architectural treatment, including application of such devices as metal or masonry screens and grilles, will usually be necessary to comply with the intent of the requirements for ramps over three stories in height.

5-2.5.4 Ramp Details.

5-2.5.4.1   All ramps serving as required means of egress shall be of permanent fixed construction.

5-2.5.4.2   A ramp used as a means of egress in a building more than three stories in height or in a building of any height of noncombustible or fire-resistive construction shall be constructed of an assembly of noncombustible or limited-combustible material. The ramp floor and landings shall be solid and without perforations.

5-2.5.4.3   A ramp shall have a slip-resistant surface.

5-2.5.4.4   The slope of a ramp shall not vary between landings. Landings shall be level, and changes in direction of travel, if any, shall be made only at landings.

5-2.5.4.5   Guards complying with 5-2.2.6 shall be provided for ramps. Handrails complying with 5-2.2.6 shall be provided for ramps with a slope exceeding 1 in 15.

5-2.5.4.6   Ramps and intermediate landings shall continue with no decrease in width along the direction of exit travel. Every landing shall have a dimension measured in the direction of travel equal to the width of the ramp. Such dimension need not exceed 4 ft (122 cm) where the ramp has a straight run.

5-2.5.5 Special Provision for Outside Ramps.

5-2.5.5.1   Balconies or landings to which doors lead shall be approximately level with the floor of the building.

Exception: In existing buildings in climates where balconies or landings may be subject to accumulation of snow or ice, one step, not to exceed 8 in. (20.3 cm), may be permitted below the level of the inside floor.

Paragraph 5-2.5.5 sets the same requirements for outside ramps as 5-2.2.5 does for outside stairs. (*See 5-2.2.5 for a discussion of the requirements for outside stairs.*)

5-2.6* Exit Passageways.

A-5-2.6   An exit passageway serves as a horizontal means of exit travel that is protected from fire in a manner similar to an enclosed interior exit stair. Where it is desired to offset exit stairs in a multistory building, an exit passageway can be used to preserve the continuity of the protected exit by connecting the bottom of one stair to the top of the other stair that continues to the street floor. Probably the most important use of an exit passageway is to satisfy the requirement that exit stairs shall discharge directly outside from multistory buildings. Thus, if it is impractical to locate the stair on an exterior wall, an exit passageway can be connected to the bottom of the stair to convey the occupants safely to an outside exit door. In buildings of extremely large area, such as shopping malls and some factories, the exit passageway can be used to advantage where the distance of travel to reach an exit would otherwise be excessive.

The fact that the word "exit" is used in the expression "exit passageway" signals that it is not just any passageway. It is a path of travel providing the same level of protection and safety that is required of any exit. It is a very versatile feature because it can be used to extend an exit, or, as is done in many cases, it can be used to bring an exit closer. As shown in Figure 5-43a, by simply extending the protecting enclosure as required for an exit passageway along what would otherwise be the corridor and then relocating the exit door, the exit is, in effect, extended. Since it is an exit, an exit passageway qualifies as an end point for measuring travel distance.

The proper use of an exit passageway can often solve what may seem to be insurmountable problems and very costly alternatives in the design of the means of egress. Figures 5-43a, b, and c illustrate some typical uses of exit passageways. While an exit passageway is a horizontal means of travel, it must be considered in light of the entire exit of which it is a part and have whatever protection is required for the number of stories that the overall exit serves. Paragraph 5-1.3 details separation requirements. A simple way to consider the protection requirements for exit passageways is that they are the same as for exit stairs.

Formal Interpretation 81-39
Reference: 5-2.6

Question: Is it the *Code*'s intent to allow an exit passageway in an apartment building that connects a discontinuous interior exit stair to serve as a corridor with apartment entrance doors penetrating the walls of the exit passageway if: (1) the exit passageway enclosure meets the applicable requirements of Chapter 5, including the separation requirements for exits of 5-1.3, and (2) the apartment door assemblies, complete with door closers, meet the required fire protection rating associated with the required fire resistance rated enclosures?

Answer: Yes.

Issue Edition: 1981
Reference: 5-2.7
Date: February 1984

5-2.6.1 General.   Any hallway, corridor, passage, tunnel, underfloor passageway, or overhead passageway shall be permitted as an exit passageway and as an exit or exit component where conforming to all other requirements of Section 5-1 as modified by the provisions of this section.

5-2.6.2 Enclosure.   An exit passageway shall be protected by separation from other parts of the building as specified in 5-1.3.1.

Exception: Fixed wired glass panels in steel sash may be installed in such a separation in a fully sprinklered building.

An important point here is not only the hourly fire resistance and fire protection ratings required by 5-1.3.1 but also the limitation on openings into the enclosure.

5-2.6.3 Width.   The width of an exit passageway shall be adequate to accommodate the aggregate capacity of all exits discharging through it.

5-2.6.4 Floor.   The floor shall be solid and without perforations.

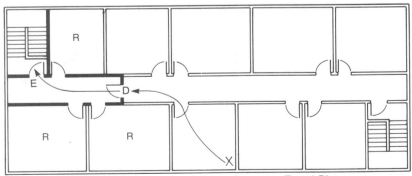

Exit Passageway Used to Eliminate Excessive Travel Distance
X→E >Permitted Travel Distance
X→D≤ Permitted Travel Distance

Figure 5-43a.

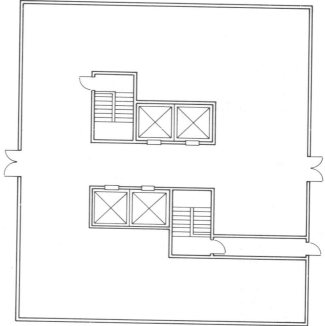

Exit Passageway To Connect Exit Stair To Exit Discharge
(Also See 5-7.2)

Figure 5-43b.

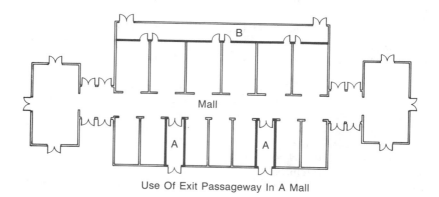

Use Of Exit Passageway In A Mall

Figure 5-43c.

Figures 5-34a, b, and c.   Typical Uses of Exit Passageways.   Note that in Figure 5-43a, rooms labeled "R" must be "normally occupied" spaces and cannot be storage rooms, boiler rooms, trash rooms, or similar spaces. In Figure 5-43c, the exit passageways are marked "A" and "B." Note that storage rooms cannot open directly into passageway "B" since it is an exit.

5-2.7 Escalators and Moving Walks.

5-2.7.1   Escalators and moving walks shall not constitute a part of the required means of egress.

Exception: Previously approved escalators and moving walks in existing buildings.

Prior editions of the *Code* allowed some credit for escalators serving as required exit capacity under certain circumstances. However, it has been determined that such devices should not be relied upon for required means of egress. Existing, previously approved escalators and moving walks may continue in use. Although not permitted as part of the required means of egress, escalators and moving walks, where installed, must comply with ANSI/ASME A17.1, *Safety Code for Elevators and Escalators.*[7] ANSI/ASME A17.1 is the source of generally accepted standards of safe engineering practice. Escalators should be designed according to provisions of that code.

It should be noted that even in existing buildings, escalators are acceptable as an egress component only in the following occupancies:

Existing Assembly — 9-2.2.8
Existing Hotels — 17-2.2.8
Existing Apartment Buildings — 19-2.2.8
Existing Mercantile — 25-2.2.8
Existing Business — 27-2.2.9.
Existing Industrial — 28-2.2.8
Existing Unusual Structures — 30-2.2.8

When evaluating escalators in existing buildings, the following should be considered:

1. The escalator should comply with the applicable requirements for stairs in 5-2.2.

It is assumed that where escalators serve as required means of egress, they will continue in operation in case of fire, but in case they stop due to electric current failure or other cause, they may be used as ordinary stairs.

2. Escalators constituting a means of egress should operate only in the direction of egress. Usually escalators are provided in pairs, with one separate stair moving up and another moving down; however, should the electricity fail and both stop, there would actually be two stairs available for downward movement. With this in mind, one might propose that both stairways be accepted as constituting a means of egress, with the idea that the current could intentionally be turned off. The problem is that in an emergency the current might not get turned off, and one stair would continue to move against traffic. For this reason, only those escalators moving in the direction of egress should be allowed to be part of a means of egress.

3. Escalators should be of the horizontal tread type and, with the exception of step tread surfaces, handrails, and step wheels, should be of noncombustible construction throughout.

4. A single escalator 32 in. (81 cm) wide should be given credit for 75 people. An escalator 48 in. (122 cm) wide should be given credit for

150 people. Even though a person does not have to exert any energy or do any moving while on an escalator, there are many people who are frightened by them and many who are extremely cautious in approaching them, factors that would contribute to a bottleneck. Thus, it is recognized that an escalator would have to be wider than a stair to effectively move the same number of people. Taking this into consideration, the permitted capacity of the escalator is kept the same as for other types of stairs by requiring a greater width.

5. There should be unobstructed spaces of at least 4 in. (10.2 cm) outside the handrail and above the handrail for the full length of the escalator.

6. No single escalator should have an uninterrupted vertical travel of more than one story.

It should be noted that, even in an existing building, an escalator cannot be counted as an exit unless it is enclosed as an exit in accordance with 5-1.3.1, something that is rarely seen.

Most of the same principles that apply to the design and operation of escalators also apply when evaluating existing moving walkways. The major difference is that the moving walkway — moving in the direction of exit travel — can be evaluated in terms of the usual exit capacities rather than the larger dimensions specified for escalators in item 4 above. (*See ANSI/ASME A17.1, Safety Code for Elevators and Escalators.*)[7]

5-2.8 Fire Escape Stairs.

Fire escape stairs and ladders have fallen into disfavor for a variety of reasons. These include:

1. Unsightly appearance;
2. Possible icing in winter weather;
3. Expense of maintenance (the metal is subject to corrosion);
4. Possibility of users being trapped by a fire below; and
5. Fear of height, and hence an objection to using them.

On the other hand, well-maintained fire escape stairs can and have saved many lives when smoke-filled exit stairs have become impassable. A classic example of this is the June 5, 1946 fire in the 22-story LaSalle Hotel in Chicago. "Hundreds" of people made their escape from the building on outside fire escape stairs.[8] Other similar examples could be quoted.

There are times when fire fighters have been able to use outside fire escape stairs to advantage. However, instances could be cited where rusted fire escapes have collapsed or where people have been fatally burned because fire broke out of windows or doors at a lower level. The Committee has consistently held that the goal of safety from fire can best be served by the proper internal design of means of egress and the gradual phasing out of fire escape stairs as new buildings replace old ones.

In summary, the provisions of 5-2.8 on fire escape stairs should be looked upon in this light: if fire escape stairs must be put on an existing building or are found on an existing building, they must adhere to provisions of the *Code* in order to provide as high a level of safety as possible.

5-2.8.1 General.

5-2.8.1.1   Fire escape stairs shall comply with the provisions of 5-2.8.

Exception: Existing noncomplying fire escape stairs may be continued in use subject to the approval of the authority having jurisdiction.

Fire escape stairs as specified in this section of the *Code* should not be confused with the outside stairs covered in 5-2.2.

At best, fire escape stairs are regarded as only an expedient in remedying the deficiencies in exits of existing buildings where it may not be practicable to provide outside stairs or additional inside stairways that are properly enclosed and conforming to all other provisions of this *Code*. Fire escape stairs, however, may greatly facilitate fire department rescue and fire fighting operations.

The fire escape stairs specified by this *Code* should not be confused with the inferior fire escapes that are commonly found on old buildings. These inadequate, flimsy, precipitous fire escapes, unshielded against fire in the structure to which they are attached, give an occupant a false sense of security. Such escape stairs are not recognized by this *Code*.

Even the fire escape stairs constructed in accordance with this *Code* have limitations that may prevent their effective use in time of fire. Even where window protection is provided, conditions may be such that fire (or the smoke from fire) on lower floors may render the stairs impassable before the occupants of the upper floors have had time to use them. Fire escape stairs may be blocked by snow, ice, or sleet at the time when they are most needed. People using fire escape stairs at a considerable height are likely to be timid and to descend the stairs, if at all, at a rate much slower than that used for inside stairs. This is true even when the solid tread stairs that are specified by the *Code* are used in place of the ordinary slatted-tread construction. Fire escape stairs are not a usual means of egress. Occupants of buildings will not so readily use them in case of fire as they will the usual means of exit, the inside stairway. Because they are an emergency device and not ordinarily used, their proper upkeep is often neglected.

5-2.8.1.2   Fire escape stairs shall not constitute any of the required means of egress in new buildings.

Fire escape stairs comprise an unfamiliar means of egress to most occupants of a building. Persons using fire escape stairs from a considerable height can be timid and seriously slow the rate of descent for themselves and people behind them. Since these stairs are used only in emergencies, maintenance is often neglected, and they should be inspected on a regular basis.

Fire escape stairs can, however, help correct serious means of egress deficiencies in existing buildings and are helpful to fire department rescue and fire fighting efforts.

Authorities having jurisdiction may wish to impose additional requirements because of climate. In conditions such as snow and ice, the effective use of fire escape stairs may be seriously impaired. In such a case, for example, exit capacity credit for the fire escape stairs could be reduced.

5-2.8.1.3 New fire escape stairs for existing buildings may be erected only where it has been determined that outside stairs (*see 5-2.2*) are not practical. New fire escape stairs shall not incorporate ladders or access windows regardless of occupancy classification or load.

In most cases, outside stairs complying with 5-2.2 must be used rather than fire escape stairs. However, the *Code* recognizes that there are situations in the case of some existing buildings that make stairs complying with 5-2.2 impractical. For example, a building may be too narrow to accommodate the space needed by a conforming stair, or it may be necessary to have the stair located over a sidewalk, alley, or similar space.

5-2.8.1.4 Fire escape stairs may be used in existing buildings as permitted in the applicable existing occupancy chapters but shall not constitute more than 50 percent of the required exit capacity.

The basic principles of the *Code* regarding fire escape stairs are contained in 5-2.8.1.1 to 5-2.8.1.4. Absolutely no recognition is given to the use of fire escape stairs in new buildings for any of the three parts of a means of egress. Only a token recognition of 50 percent is given for existing buildings, and this is simply because the fire escape stairs have already been installed or because they may be the only feasible manner of upgrading a means of egress in an existing building.

5-2.8.1.5 Fire escape stairs shall provide a continuous, unobstructed, safe path of travel to the exit discharge or a safe area of refuge.

5-2.8.1.6 Fire escape stairs of the return platform type with superimposed runs or the straight run type with platform and continuing in the same direction may be used.

5-2.8.1.7 Either type may be parallel to or at right angles to buildings. Either type may be attached to buildings or erected independently of buildings and connected by walkways.

5-2.8.2 Protection of Openings. Fire escape stairs shall be exposed to the smallest possible number of window and door openings. Each opening shall be protected with approved fire door or window assemblies where the opening or any portion of the opening is located as follows:

(a) *Horizontally.* If within 15 ft (4.5 m) of any balcony, platform, or stairway constituting a component of the fire escape stair.

(b) *Below.* If within three stories or 35 ft (10.7 m) of any balcony, platform, walkway, or stairway constituting a component of the fire escape stair or within two stories or 20 ft (6.1 m) of a platform or walkway leading from any story to the fire escape stair.

(c) *Above.* If within 10 ft (3 m) of any balcony, platform, or walkway as measured vertically or of any stair tread surface as measured vertically.

(d) *Top Story.* Protection for wall openings shall not be required where stairs do not lead to the roof.

(e) *Court.* Any wall facing a court served by a fire escape stair where the least dimension of the court is less than one-third of the height to the uppermost platform of the fire escape stair measured from the ground.

(f) *Alcove.* Any wall facing an alcove served by a fire escape stair where the width of the alcove is less than one-third or the depth greater than one-fourth of the height to the uppermost platform of the fire escape stair measured from the ground.

Exception: The provisions of 5-2.8.2 may be modified by the authority having jurisdiction in consideration of automatic sprinkler protection, low hazard occupancy, or other special conditions.

5-2.8.3 Access.

5-2.8.3.1   Access to fire escape stairs shall be in accordance with 5-2.8.4 and 5-5.1.2.

Exception: Where permitted by the existing occupancy chapters of this Code, access to fire escape stairs may be by way of windows. No screening or storm windows may be used if they impair free access to the fire escape stair. Windows shall be arranged and so maintained as to be easily opened with a minimum of physical effort.

5-2.8.3.2   Fire escape stairs shall extend to the roof in all cases where the roof is subject to occupancy or provides an area of safe refuge. In other cases, if the roof has a pitch of 1 to 6 or less, fire escape ladders in accordance with 5-2.9 shall be provided for access to the roof.

5-2.8.3.3   Access to a fire escape stair shall be directly to a balcony, landing, or platform. These shall be no higher than the floor or windowsill level and no lower than 8 in. (20.3 cm) below the floor level or 18 in. (45.7 cm) below the windowsill.

Figure 5-44 indicates the more critical measurements for windows opening onto fire escape stairs. (*See Table 5-2.8.4.*)

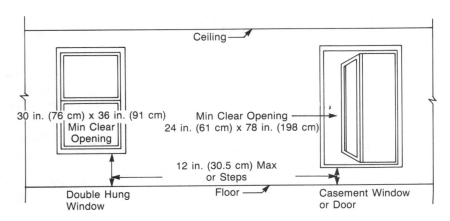

Figure 5-44.   Window Openings for Fire Escape Exits.

5-2.8.4 Stair Details. Fire escape stairs shall comply with the requirements of Table 5-2.8.4A and subsequent sections. Replacement of fire escape stairs shall comply with the requirements of Table 5-2.8.4B.

Table 5-2.8.4 A

	Fire Escape Stairs Serving more than 10 occupants	**Fire Escape Stairs** Serving 10 or fewer occupants
Minimum widths	22 in. (55.9 cm) clear between rails	18 in. (45.7 cm) clear between rails
Minimum horizontal dimension any landing or platform	22 in. (55.9 cm) clear	18 in. (45.7 cm) clear
Maximum riser height	9 in. (22.9 cm)	12 in. (30.5 cm)
Minimum tread, exclusive of nosing	9 in. (22.9 cm)	6 in. (15.3 cm)
Minimum nosing or projection	1 in. (2.5 cm)	No requirement
Tread construction	Solid, ½-in. (1.3-cm) dia. perforations permitted	Flat metal bars on edge or sq. bars secured against turning, spaced 1¼ in. (3.2 cm) max. on centers
Winders	None	Permitted subject to capacity penalty
Risers	None	No requirement
Spiral	None	Permitted subject to capacity penalty
Maximum height between landings	12 ft (3.7 m)	No requirement
Headroom, minimum	6 ft 8 in. (203 cm)	Same
Handrail height	42 in. (107 cm)	Same
Access to escape	Door or casement windows 24 in. × 6 ft 6 in. (61 cm × 198 cm) or double hung windows 30 in. × 36 in. (76 cm × 91 cm) clear opening	Windows
Level of access opening	Not over 12 in. (30.5 cm) above floor; steps if higher	Same
Discharge to ground	Swinging stair section permitted if approved by authority having jurisdiction	Swinging stair, or ladder if approved by authority having jurisdiction
Capacity, number of persons	45 per unit, if access by door; 20 if access by climbing over windowsill	10; if winders or ladder from bottom balcony, 5; if both, 1

Table 5-2.8.4 B

	Replacement Fire Escape Stairs Serving more than 10 occupants	**Replacement Fire Escape Stairs** Serving 10 or fewer occupants
Minimum widths	22 in. (55.9 cm) clear between rails	Same
Minimum horizontal dimension any landing or platform	22 in. (55.9 cm)	Same
Maximum riser height	9 in. (22.9 cm)	Same
Minimum tread, exclusive of nosing	10 in. (25.4 cm)	Same
Tread construction	Solid, ½-in. (1.3-cm) dia. perforations permitted	Same
Winders	None	Permitted subject to 5-2.2.2.8
Spiral	None	Permitted subject to 5-2.2.2.7
Risers	None	None
Maximum height between landings	12 ft (3.7 m)	Same
Headroom, minimum	6 ft 8 in. (203 cm)	Same
Access to escape	Door or casement windows 24 in. × 6 ft 6 in. (61 cm × 198 cm) or double hung windows 30 in. × 36 in. (76 cm × 91 cm) clear opening	Windows
Level of access opening	Not over 12 in. (30.5 cm) above floor; steps if higher	Same
Discharge to ground	Swinging stair section permitted if approved by authority having jurisdiction	Same
Capacity, number of persons	45 per unit, if access by door; 20 if access by climbing over windowsill	10 per unit

Generally, the requirements for fire escape stairs are similar to those specified for outside stairs. The major difference between the two types of stairways lies in the dimensions for fire escape stairs, as shown in Table 5-1. Also shown are the differences between the generally accepted fire escape stair of existing buildings and the lighter fire escape stair acceptable for existing "very small" buildings serving ten or fewer occupants.

The existing stair with a minimum width of 22 in. (55.9 cm) is a type that may be acceptable for buildings of small or moderate size. Depending upon local conditions, these existing fire escape stairs may generally be accepted.

The existing stair with a minimum width of 18 in. (45.7 cm) represents the absolute minimum that may be accepted in an existing fire escape stairway. Because of access over window sills, steep pitch, and a narrow width, travel down such stairs will necessarily be slow and may be dangerous. Stairs with spiral stair treads or stairs that terminate at a balcony above ground level with a fixed or movable ladder extending downward from that point are even worse. These stairs are suitable only in situations where a very small number of people is involved.

Table 5-1.   Differences Between Outside Stairs and Fire Escape Stairs.

Design Factor	New Outside Stair	Existing Outside Stair Class A	B	Fire Escape Stair Normal	Small Buildings
Accepted as Exit	Yes	Yes		Existing buildings	
Width	44 in.*	44 in.*	44 in.*	22 in.	18 in.
Maximum rise	7 in.	7½ in.	8 in.	9 in.	12 in.
Minimum tread	11 in.	10 in.	9 in.	9 in.	6 in.
Tread construction	solid	solid		solid	metal bars

Conversion: 1 in. = 2.54 cm

Note: The capacity of normal fire escape stairs is 45 persons for doors, and 20 for windows where a sill must be climbed over. On small buildings the capacity is 10 persons, 5 if winders or a ladder from bottom landing, 1 if both winders and a ladder from bottom landing.

*36 in. when serving occupant load of 50 or less.

5-2.8.5 Guards, Handrails, and Visual Enclosures.

5-2.8.5.1   All fire escape stairs shall have walls or guards and handrails on both sides in accordance with 5-2.2.6.

Exception: Existing handrails on existing fire escape stairs may continue to be used if the height does not exceed 42 in. (107 cm).

5-2.8.5.2   Replacement fire escape stairs in occupancies serving more than 10 occupants shall have visual enclosures to avoid any handicap to stair use by persons having a fear of high places. For stairs more than three stories in height, any arrangement intended to meet this requirement shall be at least 42 in. (107 cm) in height.

5-2.8.6 Materials and Strength.

5-2.8.6.1   Noncombustible materials shall be used for the construction of all components of fire escape stairs.

5-2.8.6.2   The authority having jurisdiction may approve any existing fire escape stair that has been shown by load test or other satisfactory evidence to have adequate strength.

5-2.8.7* Swinging Stairs.

A-5-2.8.7   Swinging stairs, although superior to fire escape ladders, are generally unsatisfactory for even emergency use. Although they are permitted by this *Code*, they should not be used where it is reasonably possible to terminate the fire escape stair at the ground.

5-2.8.7.1   A single swinging stair section shall be permitted to terminate fire escape stairs over sidewalks, alleys, or driveways where it is impractical to make the termination with fire escape stairs.

5-2.8.7.2   Swinging stair sections shall not be located over doors, over the path of travel from any other exit, or in any locations where there are likely to be obstructions.

5-2.8.7.3   Width of swinging stair sections shall be no less than that of the fire escape stairs above.

5-2.8.7.4   Pitch of swinging stair sections shall be no steeper than that of the fire escape stairs above.

5-2.8.7.5   Guards and handrails, in accordance with 5-2.2.6, shall be provided and shall be similar in height and construction to those used with the fire escape stairs above. Guards and handrails shall be designed to prevent any possibility of injury to persons where stairs swing downward. Minimum clearance between moving sections and any other portion of the stair system where hands might be caught shall be 4 in. (10.2 cm).

5-2.8.7.6   If the distance from the lowest platform to ground exceeds 12 ft (3.7 m), an intermediate balcony not more than 12 ft (3.7 m) from the ground or less than 7 ft (213 cm) in the clear underneath shall be provided with width not less than that of the stairs and length not less than 4 ft (122 cm).

5-2.8.7.7   Swinging stairs shall be counterbalanced about a pivot, and cables shall not be used. A weight of 150 lb (68 kg) one step from the pivot shall not start the swinging stairs downward, and a weight of 150 lb (68 kg) one-quarter of the length of the swinging stairs from the pivot will positively cause the stairs to swing down.

Where a fire escape stair would block a sidewalk or other public way, or provide ready access for intruders, the discharge may be counterweighted, and the unlocked swinging stair designed so that a 150-lb (68-kg) weight applied one-quarter of the length of the stair from the pivot point will cause the stair to drop into the usable position.

5-2.8.7.8   The pivot for swinging stairs shall be of a corrosion-resistant assembly or have clearances to prevent sticking due to corrosion.

5-2.8.7.9*   No device to lock a swinging stair section in the up position shall be installed.

A-5-2.8.7.9   A latch is desirable to hold swinging stairs down after they have swung to the ground.

5-2.8.8 Intervening Spaces.

5-2.8.8.1   Where approved by the authority having jurisdiction, fire escape stairs may lead to an adjoining roof that must be crossed before continuing downward travel. The direction of travel shall be clearly marked, and walkways with guards and handrails complying with 5-2.2.6 shall be provided.

5-2.8.8.2   Where approved by the authority having jurisdiction, fire escape stairs may be used in combination with interior or outside stairs complying with 5-2.2, provided a continuous safe path of travel is maintained.

5-2.9 Fire Escape Ladders.

5-2.9.1 General.   Fire escape ladders shall be permitted to be used only under the following conditions:

(a) To provide access to unoccupied roof spaces as permitted by 5-2.8.3.2;

(b) To provide a second means of escape from storage elevators as permitted by Chapter 29;

(c) To provide a means of egress from towers and elevated platforms around machinery or similar spaces subject to occupancy only by able-bodied adults, not more than three in number; or

(d) To provide a secondary means of egress from boiler rooms or similar spaces subject to occupancy only by able-bodied adults, not more than three in number; or

(e) To provide access to the ground from the lowest balcony or landing of a fire escape stair for very small buildings as permitted by 5-2.8.4 where approved by the authority having jurisdiction.

> Although the *Code* contains provisions for fire escape ladders, it does not recommend their use. These ladders are used because they are one of the only means of moving from one space to another along what might be a path of escape from spaces not normally occupied. The intent of the *Code* is not to encourage the use of ladders but to provide access to an exit from any regularly occupied area. The provisions of 5-2.9.1, and those contained in Chapters 29 and 30 for storage occupancies and unusual structures, constitute the very minimal recognition given fire escape ladders by this *Code*. The *Code* does specify requirements for ladder construction and installation to ensure their structural integrity and ease of use if they must be installed. (*Also see 5-2.11.*)

5-2.9.2 Construction and Installation.   Fire escape ladders shall comply with the requirements of ANSI A14.3, *Safety Code for Fixed Ladders*.

Exception No. 1: Existing ladders complying with this code in effect when the ladders were installed may continue to be used subject to the approval of the authority having jurisdiction.

Exception No. 2: Ladders installed with pitch less than 75 degrees shall not be permitted.

Exception No. 3: Combustible ladders shall not be permitted.

5-2.10 Slide Escapes.

5-2.10.1 General.

5-2.10.1.1   A slide escape may be used as a component in a means of egress where specifically authorized by Chapters 8 through 30.

5-2.10.1.2   Each slide escape shall be of an approved type.

5-2.10.1.3   Slide escapes used as exits shall comply with the applicable requirements of Chapter 5 for other types of exits subject to the approval of the authority having jurisdiction.

Slide escapes are permitted in limited locations as a component in a means of egress and even as exits. Customarily, one thinks of entering a slide escape through a window or special opening in an exterior wall, and from that point on, it functions as an exit discharge. Should the slide escape be entered from within the building, and thus be considered as an exit, it must be protected as an exit enclosure as required by 5-1.3; that is, until it passes through the exterior wall. It is the *Code*'s intent that slide escapes have the same separation or protection from openings in the exterior walls as do outside stairs and ramps.

Where provided, slide escapes should be regularly used in drills or for normal exit so that occupants are, through practice, familiar with their use.

A slide pole, of the type found in fire stations, is not considered as a slide escape.

Slide escapes are now permitted only in high hazard industrial occupancies (28-2.2) and where existing in storage occupancies (29-2.2).

5-2.10.2 Capacity.

5-2.10.2.1   Slide escapes, where permitted as required exits, shall be rated at a capacity of 60 persons.

5-2.10.2.2   Slide escapes shall not constitute more than 25 percent of the required exit capacity from any building or structure or any individual story or floor thereof.

Exception: As permitted for high hazard manufacturing buildings or structures.

The 25 percent limitation on slide escapes as a required exit prohibits designating a slide escape as one of two exits where two exits are required.

5-2.11* Alternating Tread Devices.

A-5-2.11   Special consideration should be given prior to the application of such devices where children, the elderly, or physically disabled persons may have to utilize such devices. These devices present obstacles in ascent and descent that differ from stairs and ladders.

Alternating tread device is the name given in the *Code* for a form of climbing implement that is intermediate between a ladder and a stair. Traditional forms of the device are varied; however, they have a steep succession of treads that alternate, one riser-height apart from the left side to the right side. A person using the device is constrained to place only one foot on each tread. This alternating tread design, now generally developed as a series of treads supported by a central spine, permits stair-like half treads to be used with ladder-like slopes. Use of such devices, while perhaps awkward at first or with infrequent usage, may be acceptable for some occupancy situations where the alternative means of changing levels are ladders or ships ladders; that is, devices that are generally in the range of 50 to 75 degrees in pitch. This is approximately twice the pitch of stairs permitted by the *Code*. A benefit claimed for the alternating tread devices is that one can descend with one's back to the device, unlike a ladder where one can only descend safely while facing the ladder because of the more limited surface area and depth of ladder rungs. A further benefit claimed for the device is that objects can be more easily carried while ascending or descending because the handrails provide support under the arms, which are left free. The *Code*, unlike some building codes and standards, limits the use of alternating tread devices to those situations where a ladder is acceptable.

5-2.11.1 Alternating tread devices complying with 5-2.11.2 may be used only as follows:

(a) To provide access to unoccupied roof spaces as permitted by 5-2.8.3.2;

(b) To provide a second means of egress from storage elevators as permitted by Chapter 29;

(c) To provide a means of egress from towers and elevated platforms around machinery or similar spaces subject to occupancy only by able-bodied adults, not more than three in number; or

(d) To provide a secondary means of egress from boiler rooms or similar spaces subject to occupancy only by able-bodied adults, not more than three in number.

5-2.11.2 Alternating tread devices shall comply with the following:

(a) Handrails, in accordance with 5-2.2.6.5, shall be provided on both sides of alternating tread devices; and

(b) The clear width between handrails shall be a minimum of 17 in. (43.2 cm) and shall not exceed 24 in. (61 cm); and

(c) Head room shall not be less than 6 ft 8 in. (203 cm); and

(d) The height of the riser shall not exceed 8 in. (20.3 cm); and

(e) Treads shall have a minimum projected tread depth of 9 in. (22.9 cm) measured in accordance with 5-2.2 with each tread providing 10½ in. (26.7 cm) of depth including tread overlap; and

(f) A minimum distance of 6 in. (15.2 cm) shall be provided between the stair handrail and any other object; and

(g) The initial tread of the stair shall begin at the same elevation as the platform, landing, or floor surface; and

(h) The alternating treads shall not be laterally separated by more than 2 in (5.0 cm); and

(i) The occupant load served shall not be more than three.

SECTION 5-3   CAPACITY OF MEANS OF EGRESS

5-3.1 Occupant Load.

5-3.1.1* The capacity of means of egress for any floor, balcony, tier, or other occupied space shall be sufficient for the occupant load thereof.

A-5-3.1.1 It is important that the distribution of exit capacity among the exits approximates the normal occupant load distribution when the building is occupied to its capacity.

It is a basic concept of the *Code* that a safe means of egress system be provided for all of the people occupying a building — whatever number that may be.

The geometry of a building, its occupancy and related occupant load, and the travel distance to exits, dictate in a large measure the appropriate location of exits, the number of exits, capacity of exits, and the access thereto. As a consequence, the exits themselves profoundly influence the plan and layout of the entire system of means of egress. The ability of the means of egress to accommodate a given volume of people is proportionately related to the ability of each component within it to accommodate that certain volume. It is beyond the scope of this chapter to do more than simply provide the basic stepping stones toward designing a safe and satisfactory system of means of egress from a building, while keeping economic considerations in mind at the same time.

The number of people or occupant load for which the means of egress must provide a path of travel must be determined first. This number is based on the maximum number of occupants that can be anticipated to be in the building rooms or spaces at any one given time, under all occasions or unusual circumstances. It must not be based only upon the normal occupancy. In no case may the means of egress system be based on an occupant load less than that specified in 5-3.1.2.

While occupant load distribution in buildings may vary, it is important that exit capacity distribution among the exits provided is not significantly unbalanced. The reason for requiring multiple exits is the assumption that in a fire event one of the exits will be obstructed by the fire and not available to the occupants. Even though the exit with the greatest share of the total required exit capacity may be the one nearest to the majority of the occupants, it may also be the one that is lost in the fire, and as a consequence, a disproportionate amount of the total exit capacity will be lost.

5-3.1.2* The occupant load permitted in any building or portion thereof shall not be assumed to be less than the number determined by dividing the floor area assigned to that use by the occupant load factor as specified in Chapters 8 through 30 for individual occupancies. Where both gross and net area figures are given for the same occupancy, calculations shall be made applying the gross area figure to the building as a whole and the net area figure to the net area of the specific use.

A-5-3.1.2   The occupant load is not necessarily a suitable criterion, as the greatest hazard may occur when an unusual crowd is present, a condition often difficult for authorities having jurisdiction to control by regulatory measures. The principle of this *Code* is to provide exits for the maximum probable number of occupants, rather than to attempt to limit the number of occupants to a figure commensurate with available exits; there are, however, limits of occupancy specified in certain special cases for other reasons.

The following table represents a compilation of the occupant load factors specified by the individual occupancies of Chapters 8 through 30.

These figures, based on counts of typical buildings, represent the average maximum density of occupancy.

Occupant Load Factors

Use	Sq Ft	Sq M
Assembly		
Less concentrated use without fixed seating	15 net	1.4
Concentrated use without fixed seating	7 net	.65
Waiting space	3 net	.28
Library — stack areas	100 gross	9.3
Library — reading areas	50 net	4.6
Mercantile		
Street floor and sales basement	30 gross	2.8
Multiple street floors — each	40 gross	3.7
Other floors	60 gross	5.6
Storage, shipping	300 gross	27.9
Malls	See 24-1.7.1	
Educational		
Classroom area	20 net	1.9
Shops and other vocational areas	50 net	4.6
Day-care centers	35 net	3.3
Business (offices), industrial	100 gross	9.3
Hotel and apartment	200 gross	18.6
Health care		
Sleeping departments	120 gross	11.1
Inpatient treatment departments	240 gross	22.3
Detention and correctional	120 gross	11.1

Occupant load is determined by the nature of the use of a building or space and the amount of space available for that use. Since different generic uses will be characterized by different occupant densities, the occupancy chapters have established appropriate density factors for each occupancy and use. The occupant load factor, being a density factor, tells us that we must assume at least one person present for the specified unit of area. The table under A-5-3.1.2 provides these occupant load factors, taken from the individual occupancy chapters, Chapters 8 through 30. Note that some values are for net area while others are based on gross area. The gross area figure applies to the building as a whole (the area within the exterior confines of the building), while the net area figure applies to actual occupied spaces, such as classroom spaces, and does not include the corridors, the area occupied by walls, or other unoccupied areas. None of the occupancy chapters gives values for both the net and gross areas of a building; however, there may be cases of mixed occupancy where, for example, a place of assembly having an occupant load based on net floor area may be located in an office or mercantile building, where the occupant load is based on gross area. In such instances, net and gross areas are used for the separate occupancies as appropriate.

Note, too, that 5-3.1 requires that exit capacity must be provided for at least the occupant load determined by dividing the area of the space (gross or net) by the appropriate occupant load factor.

The Table uses the term "use" rather than "occupancy" for an important reason, since the generic use of an area may be different from its occupancy classification. For example, a meeting room for fewer than 50 people in an office building is not an assembly occupancy, it is a business occupancy, but its occupant load is based on an assembly use. The same applies to a classroom in a university.

5-3.1.3 The occupant load permitted in any building or portion thereof may be increased from that number established for the given use as specified in 5-3.1.2 where all other requirements of this *Code* are also met, based on such modified number. The authority having jurisdiction may require an approved aisle, seating, or fixed equipment diagram to substantiate any increase in occupant load and may require that such diagram be posted in an approved location.

The concept of 5-3.1.3 is very important. The *Code* is not attempting to restrict the occupant load of a building on an area basis. An occupant load is established for later use in determining exit capacity, numbers of exits, aisle and corridor widths, and similar items. If all *Code* provisions are met using a higher occupant load, this higher occupant load may be permitted provided the authority having jurisdiction is satisfied that all corridors, aisles, stairs, and other means of egress components can accommodate the higher occupant load based on the specified criteria for each component.

For example, an office area of 20,000 sq ft (1,900 sq m) would be assigned a minimum occupant load of 200. However, that number may be increased if all provisions of the *Code* for aisles, corridors, exits, stairs, ramps, doors, exit capacity, discharge, and every means of egress component are met for the increased number.

Assembly occupancies have special but similar provisions for increasing occupant load.

Densities greater than one person for each 5 sq ft (.46 sq m) should be avoided since travel speeds are reduced to a crawl when an occupancy exceeds one person for each 3 sq ft (.65 m) density. This density is approaching the jam point.

5-3.1.4   Where exits serve more than one floor, only the occupant load of each floor considered individually need be used in computing the capacity of the exits at that floor, provided that exit capacity shall not be decreased in the direction of exit travel.

Paragraph 5-3.1.4 states another principle of the *Code*. This provides that once a maximum required exit capacity is determined, such required maximum capacity must be maintained throughout the remainder of the egress system.

Stair size is determined by the required exit capacity for each floor. It is not necessary to accumulate occupant loads from floor to floor to determine stair width. The reason for this is based on the theory of "staging"; that is, by the time the occupants of the fifth floor reach the fourth floor, the occupants from the fourth floor are already gone.

Each story or floor level is considered separately when calculating the occupant load to be served by the exits from that floor. The size or width of the exits at a floor level need be only that required to accommodate the floor served. However, in a multistory building, the floor requiring the greatest exit capacity dictates the minimum width of exits from that point on in the direction of exit travel. It is not permissible to reduce exit width for the floors below; that is, in the direction of exit travel. The exit must be capable of accommodating that number of people all along its path from the point where they had entered. Exits serving the stories above that critical floor may be equal or less in width as long as their occupant load does not require more capacity.

5-3.1.5   Where means of egress from floors above and below converge at an intermediate floor, the capacity of the means of egress from the point of convergence shall be not less than the sum of the two.

Figure 5-45 illustrates the intent of 5-3.1.5.

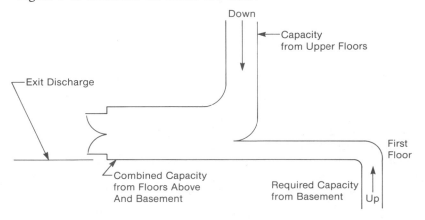

Figure 5-45.   Schematic Illustration of Requirements Contained in 5-3.1.5.

5-3.2* Measurement of Means of Egress.   Width of means of egress shall be measured in the clear at the narrowest point of the exit component under consideration.

Exception: Projections not to exceed 3½ in. (8.9 cm) on each side are permitted at and below handrail height.

A-5-3.2   For further information on stair capacity, see Chapter 2 of NFPA 101M, *Alternative Approaches to Life Safety.*

Projections at or below handrail height do not actually restrict the effective width of exits since the human body is usually widest at shoulder level. Other projections, however, may very well constitute obstructions and cause impediments to the free flow of pedestrian travel. The *Code*, therefore, bases the measurements of widths of means of egress on the clear, net, usable, available, unobstructed width. Only those projections specifically permitted may encroach on the required widths.

5-3.3 Egress Capacity.

5-3.3.1   Egress capacity for approved components of means of egress shall be based on the following:

Use	Stairways (inch per person) [cm per person]	Level Components and Class A Ramps (inch per person) [cm per person]
Board and Care	0.4 [1.0]	0.2 [0.5]
Detention & Correctional	0.3 [0.8]	0.2 [0.5]
Health Care Sprinklered	0.6 [1.5]	0.5 [1.3]
Health Care Nonsprinklered	1.0 [2.5]	0.7 [1.8]
High Hazard	0.7 [1.8]	0.4 [1.0]
All Others	0.3 [0.8]	0.2 [0.5]

For Class B ramps used for ascent, the width per person shall be increased by 10 percent beyond what is required for Class A ramps. Widths for Class B ramps used for descent shall be calculated the same as for Class A ramps.

A significant change in the calculation method has been introduced into the *Code*. The unit of exit width formerly widely used as a measure of egress capacity has been replaced by a system of smaller increments of egress width and capacity. For egress widths that were close to, and no smaller than the previously used units (22 in. [55.9 cm]) and half units (12 in. [30.5 cm]), there is little change in the egress capacities that are calculated. For other widths, as with doors and nonstandard stairs, the new method of small increments (approximating a linear formula) will provide significantly greater egress capacity. The following examples demonstrate this.

Example 1

The common combination of a 34-in. (86-cm) clear width doorway, giving access to a stair 44 in. wide with a 34-in. (86-cm) clear width discharge doorway, has always had its capacity based on the capacity of its least efficient element. Individual capacities of the elements are simply calculated by dividing the widths by the appropriate inch-per-person figure shown in 5-3.3.1. The doorways have a capacity of 36 divided by 0.2 = 180 persons. The stair has a capacity of 44 divided by 0.3 = 147 persons. The capacity of the exit is, therefore, 147. Under the previously used, unit width method, the capacities were 150 for the 1½-unit doorways and 150 for the 2-unit stair.

Example 2

If the entry doorway is 32 in. (81 cm) clear width, the discharge doorway 36 in. (91 cm) clear width, and the stair is 54 in. (137 cm), the individual capacities are, respectively:

32 in. divided by 0.2 = 160 persons for the entry doorway,

36 in. divided by 0.2 = 180 persons for the discharge doorway, and

54 in. divided by 0.3 = 180 persons for the stair.

Therefore, the capacity of the overall combination is the least of the three capacities, 160 persons. Under the previous unit width method, the capacities would have been as follows:

1 unit for the entry doorway times 100 = 100 persons,

1.5 units for the discharge doorway times 100 = 150 persons, and

2 units for the stair times 75 = 150 persons.

Therefore, the previously calculated capacity for the combination would be only 100 persons.

The small per person width figures specified in 5-3.3.1 are based on previously used values credited for full units. The chief difference is that small increments are now considered to add to capacity. Although relatively recent Canadian research studies, of egress movement in tall office buildings and in larger assembly occupancy buildings has demonstrated the validity of the small increment approach, there was evidence for this approach even in some significant early studies of egress and exit design. Excerpts from two very influential reports (dating from 1935 in the U.S.A.[5] and 1952 in Britain[9]) are provided in a discussion of the issue of exit unit size that was published in *Fire Technology*,[10] May 1984. These excerpts clearly show that this was an unsettled issue even in reports that were thought to support only the unit width method. The weight of more recent evidence relating egress facility width and crowd flow capacity, along with clear documentation that crowds do not move in regular files or lanes, especially on stairs where side-to-side body sway almost prevents people from walking shoulder to shoulder, has led to the change to the more linear, small increment method. Further information about the nature of crowd movement was published in the 1985 edition of the *Code* as Appendix D, which described an even more sophisticated approach to crediting egress capacity for stairs, the effective width method. The new methods, whether in the simplified form set out in 5-3.3.1 or the more-complex, alternative one set out for the effective width method (formerly Appendix D) now included in NFPA 101M, *Alternative Approaches to Life Safety*,[11] lead to more cost effective design of egress facilities with a better match of performance among different facilities.

The nominal performance to be expected when using the new methods, for most occupancies, is a flow time of about 3½ minutes, i.e., there will be sustained crowd flow past one point in the system (such as a doorway) for 3½ minutes when the width and egress population are related as set out in 5-3.3.1. Notably, the new methods are very useful in assessing the capacity of existing facilities that may fall slightly short of the integral unit width and half-unit width sizes credited under previous Codes.

The figures in 5-3.3.1 are simply derived from previously used combinations of egress component width and capacity, such as 75 persons per 22 in. (55.8 cm) unit of exit width for stairs; 22 divided by 75 is 0.293 which, when rounded off to the closest single digit value, is 0.3. Similarly, for level and ramped components, the derivation is simply 22 divided by 100, which is rounded off to 0.2.

The differences in the width figures specified in 5-3.3.1 arise from the following factors. Stairs entail a totally different type of movement, both individually and in crowds, than do level and moderately ramped components. These are differences in biomechanics as well as in the difficulty of seeing (or otherwise detecting) one's next stepping surface in order to avoid misstepping and suffering a serious fall with resulting injury. The approximate ratio of 3 to 2, relating the required widths of these respective components, is based on previous ratios and on empirical observations. The difference of 10 percent between Class A and Class B ramps reflects the decreased speed on steeper ramps along with greater concern that people in a crowd might have about the danger of misstepping or slipping.

The greater range of width requirements for different occupancies reflects two factors: the need for a much more rapid egress time in the case of high hazard occupancies, and the much-slower movement and greater need for assistance from others in evacuations in health care and related institutional and semi-institutional occupancies.

In summary, given the designer's knowledge of the occupancy, the occupant load of the floor level, and the type of egress component, the required minimum width for each component can be determined by simple division (that is, multiply the occupant load figure by the appropriate width per person figure given in the table in 5-3.3.1). These calculated minimum widths are then considered along with other *Code* requirements, including the matter of minimum widths based on other factors, to design a system in which performance will be closely matched from one part of the system to another.

5-3.3.2   The required capacity of a corridor is the occupant load utilizing the corridor for exit access divided by the required number of exits to which the corridor connects but shall not be less than the required capacity of the exit to which the corridor leads.

5-3.4 Minimum Width.

5-3.4.1   The minimum width of any exit access shall be as specified for individual occupancies by Chapters 8 through 30, but in no case shall such width be less than 36 in. (91 cm).

Exception No. 1: Doors as provided for in 5-2.1.3.

Exception No. 2:   In existing buildings the minimum width shall not be less than 28 in. (71 cm).

Exception No. 3:   Aisles in assembly occupancies as provided in Chapters 8 and 9.

5-3.4.2   Where a single exit access leads to an exit, its capacity in terms of width shall be at least equal to the required capacity of the exit to which it leads. Where more than one exit access leads to an exit, each shall have a width adequate for the number of persons it must accommodate.

The physical makeup of the ways of access to exits is dependent on the occupancy. The minimum width needed is given in the *Code* chapters for individual occupancies. The widths are based on experience and on observations of the manner in which people move along paths used for exit access purposes. The minimum width permitted for any passageway used as an exit access is 36 in. (91 cm), but most occupancies require more. Educational occupancies require a corridor width of not less than 6 ft (183 cm). Health care occupancies require a corridor width not less than 8 ft (244 cm), which reflects the need to be able to move bedridden patients along the path to an exit. Hotels, apartment buildings, business occupancies, and industrial occupancies generally require 44 in. (112 cm). Other occupancies rely on the provisions in Chapter 5, which set the following standard: where an exit has only a single way of access, the access width cannot be less than that of the exit itself. Under no circumstances, even in one- and two-family dwellings, is the exit access to be less than 36 in. (91 cm).

The exception for existing buildings is in recognition of the previous minimum of 28 in. (71 cm).

The thrust of 5-3.4.2 is to balance the flow of persons from the exit access to the exit to avoid a bottleneck and to assure that the occupants to be served by the exit can, in fact, reach it.

SECTION 5-4   NUMBER OF MEANS OF EGRESS

5-4.1 General.

5-4.1.1   The minimum number of means of egress from any story or portion thereof shall be two.

Exception: Where a single means of egress is permitted by Chapters 8 through 30.

In most occupancies, the principle of redundancy requires at least two means of egress. Some occupancies will identify minimal situations where only a single means of egress is needed. Where large numbers of occupants are to be served, additional means of egress must be provided as required in 5-4.1.2.

5-4.1.2   The minimum number of separate and remote means of egress from all floors or portions thereof shall be as follows:

Occupant load more than 500 but
   not more than 1,000:   3

Occupant load more than 1,000:   4

Exception: Existing buildings as permitted by Chapters 8 through 30.

In prior editions of the *Code*, the number of means of egress was established solely by the occupancy chapters. Chapter 5 now sets a minimum unless otherwise specified by the occupancy chapters. In most occupancies, by the time exit capacities and travel distances are complied with, the minimum numbers will automatically have been met. However, in assembly occupancies, educational occupancies, and mercantile occupancies this may require additional attention.

5-4.1.3   Where exits serve more than one story, only the occupant load of each story considered individually need be used in computing the number of exits at that story, provided that the required number of exits shall not be decreased in the direction of exit travel.

Similar to exit capacity (*see 5-3.1.4*), the number of exits is based on a floor by floor consideration rather than the accumulation of floors. However, the number of exits cannot decrease as one proceeds along the egress path. For example, if the sixth floor (800 people) requires three exits, and the seventh floor (700 people) requires three exits, only three exits are required, not six, regardless of the fact that the two floors together hold 1500 people. The three exits cannot be merged into two exits on the lower floors even though the lower floors may only require two exits. If a lower floor requires only two exits, one of the three exits could be left unaccessible (blind) on that floor. (*See Figure 5-46.*)

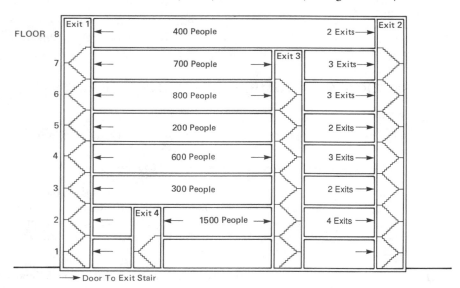

Figure 5-46 Illustrates Minimum Number of Exits Based on Capacity of Each Floor. The third, fifth, and eighth floors do not require access to the third exit, whereas the second floor requires four exits.

SECTION 5-5   ARRANGEMENT OF MEANS OF EGRESS

5-5.1 General.

5-5.1.1   Exits shall be so located and exit access shall be so arranged that exits are readily accessible at all times.

5-5.1.2*   Where exits are not immediately accessible from an open floor area, safe and continuous passageways, aisles, or corridors shall be maintained leading directly to every exit and shall be so arranged as to provide access for each occupant to at least two exits by separate ways of travel.

Exception No. 1:   Where a single exit is permitted by Chapters 8 through 30.

Exception No. 2:   Where common paths of travel are permitted for an occupancy by Chapters 8 through 30, such common path of travel shall be permitted but shall not exceed the limit specified.

A-5-5.1.2   See A-5-5.1.6.

5-5.1.3   Where more than one exit is required from a building or portion thereof, such exits shall be remote from each other and so arranged and constructed as to minimize any possibility that more than one may be blocked off by any one fire or other emergency condition.

It is a precept of life safety in buildings, repeated many times in the *Code*, that if multiple exits are required, they should be not only separate but also remote from one another. While the objective of this requirement is clear — if one exit is blocked by smoke or fire, the other will be available — the term "remote" cannot always be sharply defined.

Where exits are located at each end of a long corridor or at each end or side of a building, there is no problem of remotely located exits. However, core-type buildings with elevators, service shafts, and stairs in one central or side core introduce some challenging problems with respect to remote exits. Figure 5-47 shows two core-type buildings that illustrate the problem. The upper sketch shows the plan of the Rault Center Building in New Orleans where five women were trapped by fire on the fifteenth floor. Both exit stairways were blocked, and the women finally jumped to the roof of an adjacent eight-story building. Four of the five died.[12]

The lower sketch in Figure 5-47 shows the plan of the twentieth floor of a New York City office building. An incendiary device was evidently set off somewhere near the lobby reception area. One of fifteen people on the floor at the time made it to the stair exit, but the other fourteen were trapped and removed by fire fighters. One of the fourteen died.[13] In a sense, the exit stairs in each example might be described as being remote from each other, but with more attention given to life safety during the design stage, a much better solution might have been devised. Figure 5-48 was taken from a discussion of core-type building designs in the NFPA *Fire Journal*.[14] It illustrates how with a little thought and imagination and little, if any, added expense, a poor design can be greatly improved.

(See also discussion under 5-5.1.4.)

Rault Center Building - 15th Floor

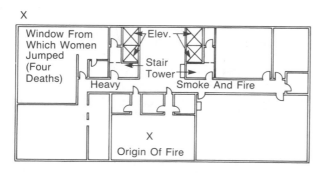

New York City Office Building - 20th floor

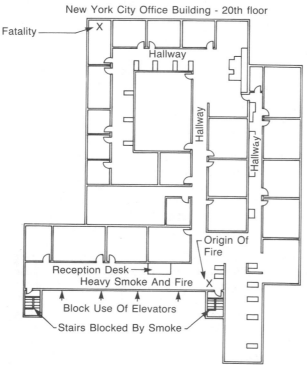

Figure 5-47. Plan Views of Upper Floors of Two Core-Type High-Rise Buildings where Fires Occurred. Exit stairs were located in the core areas, which became heavily involved in smoke and fire, blocking paths of escape.

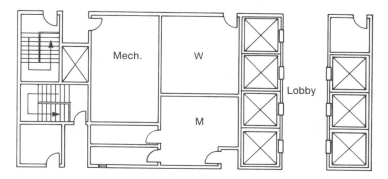

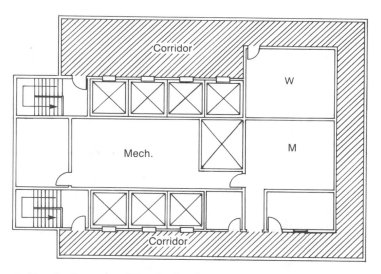

Figure 5-48.   An Example of Not-So-Good Planning and Good Planning of Exits in a Core-type Multitenanted Building.   In the upper plan view, the exit stairs are not as remote from each other as practicable; they are both on the same end of the core, a detriment when tenants, present and future, lay out their own partition arrangements to suit their needs. By removing the elevator lobby from the core, as shown in the lower plan, the designer can, by adding a corridor around three sides of the core, make sure that tenants will have access to two remote exits. This solution also assists in providing two ways out of each tenant space.

5-5.1.4*   In new construction, if two exits or exit access doors are required, they shall be placed a distance apart equal to not less than one-half the length of the maximum overall diagonal dimension of the building or area to be served, measured in a straight line between exits. Where exit enclosures are provided as the required exits and are interconnected by a corridor conforming to the requirements of 5-1.3.4, exit separation shall be permitted to be measured along the line of travel within the corridor.

In new construction where more than two exits or exit access doors are required, at least two of the required exits or exit access doors shall be so arranged to comply with the above. The other exits or exit access doors shall be so located that if one becomes blocked, the others will be available.

Exception: In buildings protected throughout by an approved automatic sprinkler system in accordance with Section 7-7, the minimum separation distance between two exits or exit access doors shall be not less than one-third the length of the maximum overall diagonal dimension of the building or area to be served, measured in a straight line between exits.

A-5-5.1.4   The following diagrams illustrate the method of measurement intended by 5-5.1.4.

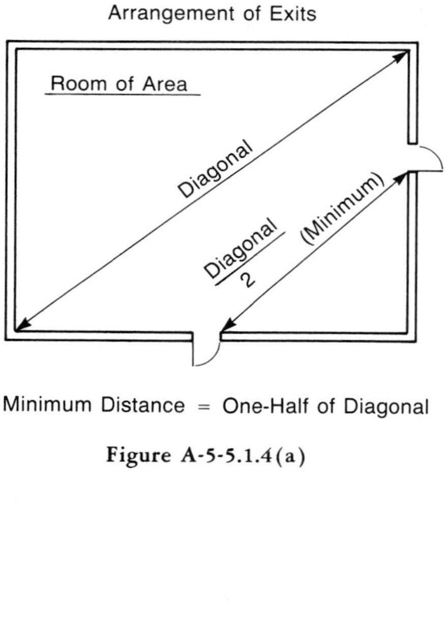

Arrangement of Exits

Minimum Distance = One-Half of Diagonal

Figure A-5-5.1.4(a)

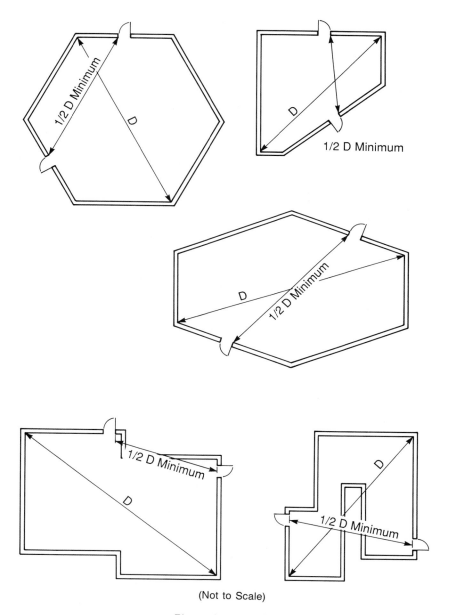

(Not to Scale)

Figure A-5-5.1.4(b)

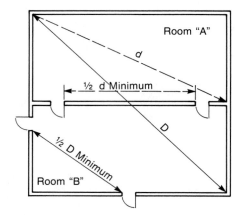

Figure A-5-5.1.4(c)

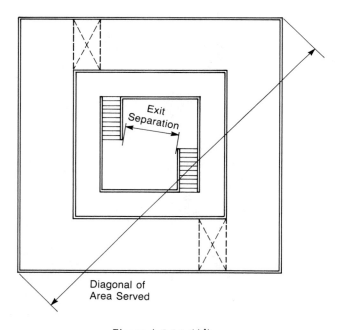

Figure A-5-5.1.4(d)

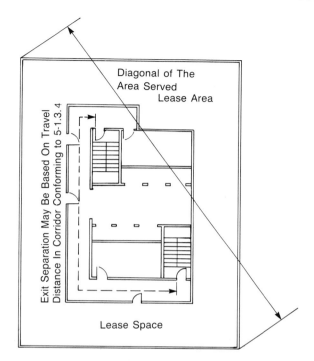

Figure A-5-5.1.4(e)

The Subcommittee on Means of Egress and the Committee on Safety to Life have concluded that it has become necessary to quantify remoteness in order to assure that exits are, in fact, sufficiently remote to reasonably assure that multiple exits will not be obstructed by the same fire incident. This need is demonstrated, in part, by the building configurations shown in Figure 5-47.

The 1988 *Code* contains a remoteness formula that has been used for years by the *Uniform Building Code.*[15] and has been more recently recommended by the *Board for the Coordination of the Model Codes (BCMC)* of the Council of American Building Officials (CABO).

The formula is referred to as the "one-half diagonal rule" and was contained in A-5-5.1.4 of the 1985 *Life Safety Code.* This rule is stated in full in the first paragraph of 5-5.1.4. Figures A-5-5.1.4(a) through (e) detail the application of the rule.

In adopting the rule, however, an amendment was added to allow the exit separation to be reduced to one-third the maximum overall diagonal in fully sprinklered buildings.

5-5.1.5* Interlocking or scissor stairs may be considered separate exits if enclosed in accordance with 5-1.3.1 and separated from each other by 2-hour fire resistance rated noncombustible construction. There shall be no penetrations or communicating openings, whether protected or not, between the stair enclosures.

A-5-5.1.5 Attention is called to the fact that it is difficult in actual practice to construct scissor stairs so that products of combustion having entered one stairway do not penetrate into the other. Use as separate required exits is discouraged. The term "limited-combustible" is intentionally not included in this paragraph. The user's attention is directed to the definitions in Chapter 3 of "noncombustible" and "limited-combustible."

Scissor-type stairs (*see Figure 5-49*) must be discussed since they are used and are a highly controversial subject. Some believe they are hazardous and should not be permitted; others believe just the opposite. Generally, the principal objection seems to be that they cannot be reliably built to present an absolute barrier to the passage of smoke and toxic gases. Even if they can be, there is still concern that building settlement or exposure to fire conditions might result in the cracking of the separating wall, which could permit smoke and gases to pass into one exit stairway from the other. On the other hand, those who feel the scissor stairs do not present these problems see advantages because they reduce construction costs and save space. The *Code* requires separating construction to be noncombustible and 2-hour fire resistance rated. Even though side by side, scissor stairs can be located with the entrances to the exits remote from one another and the exit discharges also remotely placed. It must be emphasized that the remoteness requirements are applicable to scissor stairs if they are to be considered as separate exits. Where not sufficiently remote, scissor stairs cannot be used as separate exits but can be used to increase the capacity of the single exit. These points can all be seen in the stairs illustrated in Figures 5-49 and 5-50.

5-5.1.6* Exit access shall be so arranged that there are no dead-end pockets, hallways, corridors, passageways, or courts.

Exception: Where dead ends are permitted for an occupancy by Chapters 8 through 30, such dead ends shall be permitted but shall not exceed the limit specified.

A-5-5.1.6 The terms dead end and common path of travel are commonly used interchangeably. While the concepts of each are similar in practice, they are two different concepts.

A common path of travel exists where a space is arranged so that occupants within that space are able to travel in only one direction to reach any of the exits or to reach the point at which the occupants have the choice of two paths of travel to remote exits. Figure A-5-5.1.6(a) is an example of a common path of travel.

While a dead end is similar, a dead end may occur where there is no path of travel from an occupied space, but where an occupant may enter a corridor or space thinking there is an exit at the end and, finding none, must retrace his or her path to again reach a choice of exits. Figure A-5-5.1.6(b) is an example of such a dead-end arrangement.

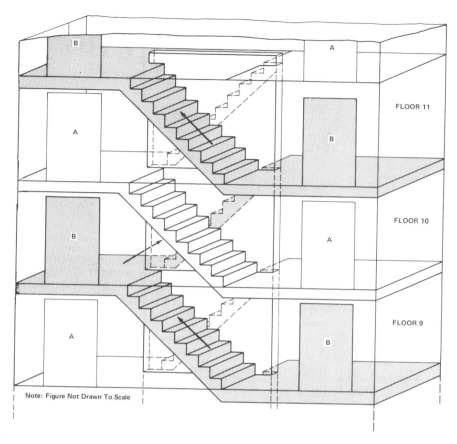

SCISSOR STAIR

Figure 5-49.   Scissor Stairs.   Two stairways in the same enclosure but completely separated from each other are called scissor stairs. This results in space saving — two stairways are provided in one enclosure. With this arrangement, two entirely independent escape paths are possible even though they may not qualify as separate exits. Note the continuity of all walls, providing a complete separation at all points. Follow arrows for path of travel.

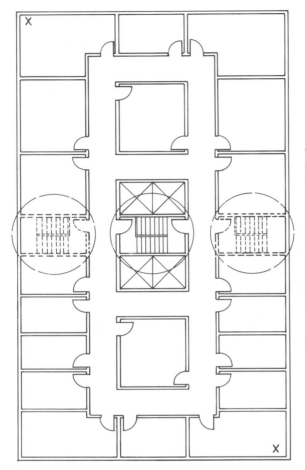

This set of scissor stairs provides the same degree of remote exit or extrance doors as the circled stairs shown by dotted lines—travel distance for all occupants is the same, even if the dotted exit stairs were located at opposite corners denoted by the cross mark. Space is saved, however, the integrity of the separation of the 2 scissored stairs may remain in question.

Figure 5-50.   Scissor Stairs Versus Conventional Exit Stairs — Advantages and Disadvantages.

Combining the two concepts, Figure A-5-5.1.6(c) is an example of a combined dead-end common path of travel problem.

Common paths of travel and dead-end travel are measured using the same principles used to measure travel distance as described in Section 5-6 of the *Code*. Starting in the room in Figure A-5-5.1.6(d), measurement is made 1 ft (30.5 cm) from the most remote point in the room along the natural path of travel, and through the doorway along the centerline of the corridor to Point C, located at the centerline of the corridor, which then provides the choice of two different paths to remote exits; this is common path of travel. The space between Point B and Point C is a dead end.

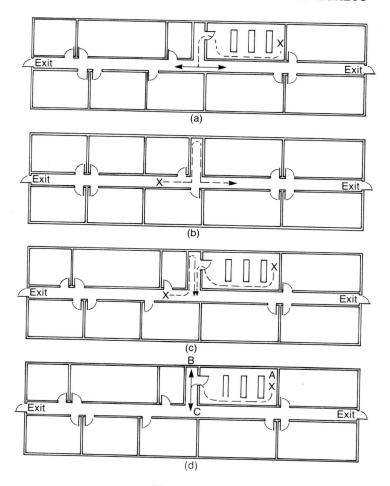

Figure A-5-5.1.6

A dead end occurs where a hallway or other space is so arranged that a person is able to travel in only one direction in order to reach any of the exits. Although relatively short dead ends are permitted by the *Code*, it is better practice to eliminate them as much as possible, for they increase the danger of people being trapped in case of fire. Compliance with the limits on dead ends does not necessarily mean that the requirements for remoteness of exits have been met. This is particularly true in small buildings or buildings with short public hallways.

Figure 5-51 gives examples of two types of dead-end corridors. The one serving the occupied rooms is far more dangerous than the one adjoining the bank of elevators or elevator lobby. The occupants of the rooms off the dead-end hall do not have a choice of two directions to an exit until they reach Point A. They could very easily be cut off altogether should a fire originate and break through a door such as at Point B. The elevator lobby, Point C, does not pose the same problem because there are no doors to occupied rooms from the lobby. However, people groping their way in a dark or smoke-filled corridor toward the exit stair could very easily turn into the dead-end corridors and become confused, as neither of the corridors leads to an exit. Sometimes it is very difficult to avoid dead ends, but there are some little-used spaces that can be conveniently located in a dead end without undue hazard to those who must frequent these spaces. A dead end is never a desirable feature.

In those limited situations where only one means of egress is required, travel in the opposite direction is not considered to be a dead end for that reason alone.

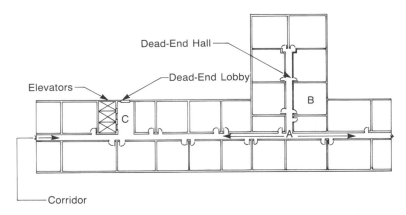

Figure 5-51   Examples of Two Types of Dead-End Corridors.   See commentary for 5-5.1.6.

5-5.1.7   Egress from rooms or spaces may open into adjoining or intervening rooms or areas, provided such adjoining rooms are accessory to the area served and provide a direct means of egress to an exit. Foyers, lobbies, and reception rooms constructed as required for corridors shall not be construed as intervening rooms. Exit access shall be so arranged that it will not be necessary to pass through any area identified under Protection from Hazards in Chapters 8 through 30.

Paragraph 5-5.1.7 prohibits the exit access from passing through any area identified under "Protection from Hazards" (generally in the -3.2 sections such as 18-3.2 or 24-3.2) in the appropriate occupancy chapter.

This carries through a fundamental principle regarding occupant safety. The principle is that, once an occupant is brought to a certain level of safety in the egress system, that level of safety is not to be reduced. Therefore, leading an occupant into an area of relatively greater hazard is prohibited.

5-5.2 Impediments to Egress. *(See also 5-1.7 and 5-2.1.5.)*

5-5.2.1   In no case shall access to an exit be through kitchens, storerooms, restrooms, workrooms, closets, bedrooms or similar spaces, or other rooms subject to locking.

Exception No. 1: Where the exit is required to serve only the bedroom or other room subject to locking, or adjoining rooms constituting part of the same dwelling or apartment used for single-family occupancy.

Exception No. 2: Exit access in detention and correctional occupancies may pass through rooms or spaces subject to locking as provided in Chapters 14 and 15.

Exception No. 3: Exit access in mercantile occupancies may pass through storerooms as provided in Chapters 24 and 25.

Paragraph 5-5.2.1 in combination with 5-5.1.7 prevents exit access from going through certain rooms due either to increased relative hazard, or to potential blockage or locking.

5-5.2.2*   Exit access and the doors to exits to which they lead shall be so designed and arranged as to be clearly recognizable. Hangings or draperies shall not be placed over exit doors or otherwise located so as to conceal or obscure any exit. Mirrors shall not be placed on exit doors. Mirrors shall not be placed in or adjacent to any exit in such a manner as to confuse the direction of exit.

A-5-5.2.2   Doors that lead through wall paneling and that harmonize in appearance with the rest of the wall so as to avoid detracting from some desired aesthetic or decorative effect are not acceptable, as casual occupants may not be aware of such exits even though actually visible.

Also see 31-1.2.

5-5.3 Exterior Ways of Exit Access.

These provisions are for exit access in the typical "motel" arrangement where exit access is provided via an open air exit access balcony to an open stair. This is also common for apartment buildings and office buildings in warm climates.

5-5.3.1   Exit access may be by means of any exterior balcony, porch, gallery, or roof that conforms to the requirements of this chapter.

5-5.3.2   Exterior exit access balconies shall be separated from the interior of the building by walls and opening protectives as required for corridors.

Exception: Where the exterior exit access balcony is served by at least two stairs and has no dead ends, or where dead ends occur, travel past an unprotected opening is not necessary to reach a stair.

This paragraph states that exterior exit access is to be protected the same as a corridor. However, the Exception is very important as in this case the Exception is more commonly used than is the requirement. Figure 5-52 illustrates different arrangements using the Exception to 5-5.3.2.

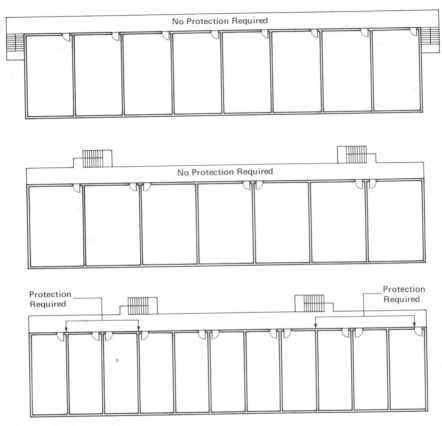

Figure 5-52. In Figure 5-52(a) and (b) no protection is required. Although a limited dead end occurs in (b), travel past an unprotected opening does not occur. In (c) protection is required, otherwise it would be necessary to travel past an unprotected opening.

5-5.3.3 A permanent, reasonably straight path of travel shall be maintained over the required exterior exit access.

5-5.3.4 There shall be no obstruction by railings, barriers, or gates that divide the open space into sections appurtenant to individual rooms, apartments, or other subdivisions.

5-5.3.5 An exterior exit access shall be so arranged that there are no dead ends in excess of 20 ft (6.1 m).

5-5.3.6 Any gallery, balcony, bridge, porch, or other exterior exit access that projects beyond the outside wall of the building shall comply with the requirements of this chapter as to width and arrangement.

5-5.3.7 Exterior exit access shall have smooth, solid, substantially level floors and shall have guards on the unenclosed sides at least equivalent to those specified in 5-2.2.6.

5-5.3.8 Where accumulation of snow or ice is likely because of the climate, the exterior exit access shall be protected by a roof.

The intent of the *Code* is to prevent the accumulation of ice and snow to the extent that they prevent the use of the exit access. Any method that accomplishes this goal and is acceptable to the local authority would be satisfactory. Examples of alternative methods are snow melting cables, pipes within the floor, or radiant heaters.

5-5.3.9 The materials of construction shall be as permitted for the building served.

SECTION 5-6   MEASUREMENT OF TRAVEL DISTANCE TO EXITS

The *Life Safety Code* specifies the maximum distance that a person should have to travel from his or her position in a building to the nearest exit. There is no formula by which this distance can be established.

The factors on which the Committee on Safety to Life bases maximum travel distances are:

1. The number, age, and physical condition of building occupants and the rate at which they can be expected to move;

2. The type and number of obstructions — display cases, seating, heavy machinery — that must be negotiated;

3. The number of people in any room or space and the distance from the farthest point in that room to the door;

4. The amount and nature of combustibles expected in a particular occupancy; and

5. The rapidity with which fire might spread — a function of the type of construction, the materials used, the degree of compartmentation, and the presence or absence of automatic fire detection and extinguishing systems.

It is obvious that travel distances will vary with the type and size of occupancy and the degree of hazard present. As given in Table A-5-6.1, maximum travel distances in unsprinklered buildings can vary from 75 ft (23 m) in high hazard locations to 200 ft (60 m). This figure may be increased by as much as 100 percent, in some cases, if complete sprinkler systems have been installed.

Having provided the occupant with at least two paths of travel to an exit, it becomes important that the time needed to travel those paths not be so long as to put the occupant in further danger. Many factors have been considered and weighed in establishing the maximum permitted travel distances. Because there are no formulae or exact criteria for determining these distances, they are the result of the observation of people in motion, good judgment, and many years of studying the results of fires in which the prefire conditions of a building were known.

5-6.1* The maximum travel distance in any occupied space to at least one exit, measured in accordance with the following requirements, shall not exceed the limits specified in 5-6.5.

It must be kept in mind that the maximum travel distance is that which must not be exceeded to reach the nearest exit as defined by 5-1.2.3.

A-5-6.1 Table A-5-6.1 is a compilation of the requirements of the individual occupancy chapters (Chapters 8 through 30) for length of dead-end corridors and permissible travel distance to at least one of the required exits.

A dead end occurs where a hallway or other space is so arranged that a person therein is able to travel in one direction only in order to reach any of the exits. Although relatively short dead ends are permitted by this *Code*, it is better practice to eliminate them wherever possible, as they increase the danger of persons being trapped in case of fire. Compliance with the dead-end limits does not necessarily mean that the requirements for remoteness of exits have been met. This is particularly true in small buildings or buildings with short public hallways. Adequate remoteness can be obtained in such cases by further reducing the length of dead ends.

**Table A-5-6.1   Exit Travel Distance and Dead-End Limits
(By Occupancy)**

Type of Occupancy	Dead-End Limit (ft)	Travel Limit to an Exit	
		Unsprinklered (ft)	Sprinklered (ft)
ASSEMBLY			
NEW	20[a] (6.1 m)	150 (45 m)	200 (60 m)
EXISTING	20[a] (6.1 m)	150 (45 m)	200 (60 m)
EDUCATIONAL			
NEW	20 (6.1 m)	150 (45 m)	200 (60 m)
EXISTING	20 (6.1 m)	150 (45 m)	200 (60 m)
NEW DAY-CARE CENTER	20 (6.1 m)	100[c] (30 m)	150[c] (45m)
EXISTING DAY-CARE CENTER	20 (6.1 m)	100[c] (30 m)	150[c] (45 m)
HEALTH CARE			
NEW	30 (9.1 m)	100[c] (30 m)	150[c] (45 m)
EXISTING	N.R.[b]	100[c] (30 m)	150[c] (45 m)
NEW AMBULATORY CENTER	20[d] (6.1 m)	100[c] (30 m)	150[c] (45 m)
EXISTING AMBULATORY CENTER	50 (15 m)	100[c] (30 m)	150[c] (45 m)
DETENTION AND CORRECTION			
NEW			
Use Conditions			
II, III, IV	50 (15 m)	100[c] (30 m)	150[c] (45 m)
V	20 (6.1 m)	100[c] (30 m)	150[c] (45 m)
EXISTING			
Use Conditions			
II, III, IV, V	N.R.[b]	100[c] (30 m)	150[c] (45 m)
RESIDENTIAL			
A. Hotels & Dormitories			
NEW	35[d] (10.7 m)	100[c,e] (30 m)	200[c,e] (60 m)
EXISTING	50 (15 m)	100[c,e] (30 m)	200[c,e] (60 m)
B. Apartments			
NEW	35[d] (10.7 m)	100[c,f] (30 m)	200[c,f] (60 m)
EXISTING	50 (15 m)	100[c,f] (30 m)	200[c,f] (60 m)
C. Board and Care	[g]	[g]	[g]
D. Lodging or Rooming Houses, 1- & 2-Family Dwellings	N.R.[b]	N.R.[b]	N.R.[b]
MERCANTILE			
Class A, B & C			
NEW	20[d] (6.1 m)	100 (30 m)	200 (60 m)
EXISTING	50 (15 m)	150 (45 m)	200 (60 m)
Open Air	0	N.R.[b]	N.R.[b]
Covered Mall			
NEW	20[d] (6.1 m)	100 (30 m)	400[h] (120 m)
EXISTING	50 (15 m)	150 (45 m)	400[h] (120 m)

(Table continued on next page.)

Table A-5-6.1   Exit Travel Distance and Dead-End Limits (By Occupancy) (Continued)

Type of Occupancy	Dead-End Limit (ft)	Travel Limit to an Exit	
		Unsprinklered (ft)	Sprinklered (ft)
BUSINESS			
NEW	20[d] (6.1 m)	200 (60 m)	300 (91 m)
EXISTING	50 (15 m)	200 (60 m)	300 (91 m)
INDUSTRIAL			
General	50 (15 m)	200 (60 m)	250[i] (75 m)
Special Purpose (Low or Ordinary Hazard)	50 (15 m)	300 (91 m)	400 (122 m)
High Hazard	0	75 (23 m)	75 (23 m)
Open Structures	N.R.[b]	N.R.[b]	N.R.[b]
STORAGE			
Low Hazard	N.R.[b]	N.R.[b]	N.R.[b]
Ordinary Hazard	50[j] (15 m)	200 (60 m)	400 (122 m)
High Hazard	0	75 (23 m)	100 (30 m)
Parking Garages, Open	50 (15 m)	200 (60 m)	300 (91 m)
Parking Garages, Enclosed	50 (15 m)	150 (45 m)	200 (60 m)
Aircraft Hangars, Ground Floor	50[j] (15 m)	Varies[i]	Varies[i]
Aircraft Hangars, Mezzanine Floor	50[j] (15 m)	75 (23 m)	75 (23 m)
Grain Elevators	[j]	200[j] (60 m)	400[j] (122 m)
Miscellaneous Occupancies, Towers, Piers & Water Surrounded Structures, Vehicles & Vessels & Emergency Shelters	50 (15 m)	100 (30 m)	150 (45 m)

[a] See chapters 8 & 9 for aisles.
[b] No requirement or not applicable.
[c] This dimension is from the room exit access door to the exit, for travel distance within the room or total travel distance see the appropriate occupancy chapter.
[d] In sprinklered facilities 50 ft (15 m).
[e] See Chapters 16 and 17 for exceptions.
[f] See Chapters 18 and 19 for exceptions.
[g] See Chapter 21.
[h] See Chapter 24 and 25 for exceptions and special considerations.
[i] See Chapter 28 for special considerations.
[j] See Chapter 29 for special considerations.

5-6.2* The travel distance to an exit shall be measured on the floor or other walking surface along the center line of the natural path of travel starting 1 ft (30.5 cm) from the most remote point, curving around any corners or obstructions with a 1-ft (30.5-cm) clearance therefrom, and ending at the center of the doorway or other point at which the exit begins. Where measurement includes stairs, the measurement shall be taken in the plane of the tread nosing.

Exception: Travel distance measurement may terminate at a smoke barrier in existing detention and correctional occupancies as provided in Chapter 15.

A-5-6.2 The natural exit access (path of travel) will be influenced by the contents and occupancy of the building. Furniture, fixtures, machinery, or storage may serve to increase the length of travel. It is good practice in building design to recognize this by spacing exits at closer intervals than would be needed for a completely open floor area, thus reducing the hazard of excessive travel distances due to introduction of furniture, fixtures, machinery, or storage, and minimizing the danger of violation of the travel distance requirements of this *Code*.

Figures 5-53a, b, and c illustrate the path along which travel distance to an exit is measured. Note that since maximum permitted travel distances have been increased by 50 ft, the Exception for excluding small rooms or spaces from the measurement of travel distance has been deleted. (*Also see* 5-6.3.)

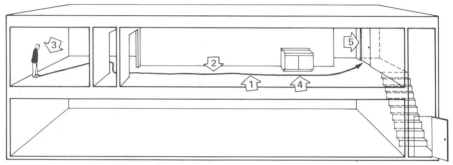

• Travel distance is measured:
1 - on the floor or other walking surface,
2 - along the center line of the natural path of travel,
3 - starting 1 foot from the most remote point,
4 - curving around corners/obstructions with a clearance of 1 foot,
5 - ending where exit begins

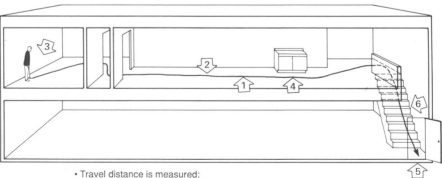

• Travel distance is measured:
1 - on the floor or other walking surface,
2 - along the center line of the natural path of travel,
3 - starting 1 foot from the most remote point,
4 - curving around corners/obstructions with a clearance of 1 foot,
5 - ending where exit begins
6 • Travel distance includes travel over open stairs and ramps; stairs
    are measured in the plane of the tread nosing

Figures 5-53a and b.   Measuring Travel Distance to an Exit. In 5-53a the stair is enclosed whereas in 5-53b the stair is not enclosed.

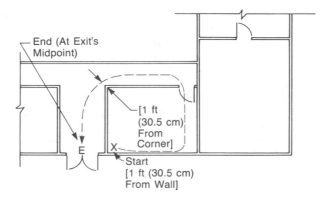

Figure 5-53c.   Measuring Travel Distance to an Exit.

Travel distance is that travel to an exterior exit door (as in Figure 5-53b), an enclosed stair (as in Figure 5-53a), an exit passageway, or a horizontal exit. It includes all travel within the occupied space and its atmosphere until an occupant reaches that level of protection afforded by an exit. Therefore, where stairs form part of an exit access rather than an exit, they are to be included in the travel distance (as in Figure 5-53b). The measurement, in such cases, would be taken in the plane of the tread nosings. (*See Figure 5-54.*)

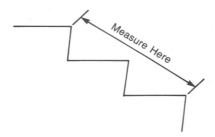

Figure 5-54   Method for Measuring Distance on Stairs.

5-6.3   Distance to exits shall be measured from the most remote point subject to occupancy.

Formerly the *Code* contained provisions to exempt rooms containing six or less people and having a travel distance within them of less than 50 ft (15 m) from being included in the overall travel distance measurement. Since this provision had little validity and was easily and often abused, it has been deleted from the *Code*. (*See Figure 5-53c.*) Most of the travel distances specified by the occupancy chapters have been increased to compensate for this change. Figure 5-53 illustrates the path along which travel distance to an exit is measured for both an enclosed stair (5-53a) and an open stair (5-53b). Since an open stair is exit access and not an exit, travel distance measurement must continue until an exit is reached.

5-6.4   Where open stairways or ramps are permitted as a path of travel to required exits, such as between mezzanines or balconies and the floor below, the distance shall include the travel on the stairway or ramp and the travel from the end of the stairway or ramp to reach an outside door or other exit in addition to the distance to reach the stairway or ramp.

5-6.5 Travel Distance Limitations.   Travel distance to at least one exit shall not exceed 200 ft (60 m) in buildings not sprinklered or exceed 250 ft (76 m) in buildings protected throughout by an approved supervised sprinkler system in accordance with Section 7-7.

Exception No. 1:   Where other travel distance limitations are specified in Chapters 8 through 30.

Exception No. 2:   Travel distance for areas having high hazard contents as specified in Section 5-11.

Although Chapter 5 establishes general travel distance limitations, all occupancy chapters establish their own limits, and therefore Exception No. 1 is very important.

5-6.6   Where any part of an exterior exit is within 10 ft (3 m) horizontal distance of any unprotected building opening, as permitted by 5-2.2.3.3 for outside stairs, the distance to the exit shall include the length of travel to ground level.

The intent of this paragraph is to clarify that, if the exterior stair is exposed by unprotected building openings, it is not considered as an exit but as an exit access, and the travel distance is measured down the stair. (*Also see commentary in 5-2.2.1.*)

SECTION 5-7   DISCHARGE FROM EXITS

5-7.1*   All exits shall terminate directly at a public way or at an exit discharge. Yards, courts, open spaces, or other portions of the exit discharge shall be of required width and size to provide all occupants with a safe access to a public way.

Exception No. 1:   As permitted by 5-7.2 and 5-7.5.

Exception No. 2:   Means of egress may terminate in an exterior area of refuge in detention and correctional occupancies as provided in Chapters 14 and 15.

A-5-7.1   An exit from the upper stories, in which the directon of exit travel is generally downward, should not be arranged so that it is necessary to change over to travel in an upward direction at any point before discharging to the outside. A similar prohibition of reversal of the vertical component of travel should be applied to exits from stories below the floor of exit discharge. However, an exception is permissible in the case of stairs used in connection with overhead or underfloor exit passageways that serve the street floor only.

It is important that ample roadways be available from buildings in which there are large numbers of occupants so that exits will not be blocked by persons already outside. Two or more avenues of departure should be available for all but very small places. Location of a larger theater, for example, on a narrow dead-end street, may properly be prohibited by the authority having jurisdiction under this rule unless some alternate way of travel to another street is available.

Formal Interpretation 81-33
Reference: 5-7.1

Question 1: In a health care occupancy, are sidewalks required between the exit door and the public way in order to qualify as an exit discharge as stated in Paragraph 5-7.1?

Answer: No.

Question 2: If the answer to Question 1 is "no," then is an open and unobstructed yard large enough to provide all occupants with a safe access to a public way acceptable as an exit discharge?

Answer: Yes, however, the path of safe access to the public way must also meet 5-1.6 with respect to changes in elevation and 5-1.7.3 with respect to maintaining the means of egress free of obstructions that would prevent its use, such as snow in some climates and the need for its removal.

Issue Edition: 1981
Reference: 5-7.1
Date: July 1983

The principle addressed in this section is that once a building occupant is brought into the protected portion of the means of egress, the level of protection cannot be reduced or eliminated. Therefore, except as noted, all exits must be continuous to a public way or other safe place or to an exit discharge that must, in turn, be continuous to the public way.

It is not enough to require that exits terminate at the outside of a building, because there may not be a space affording sufficient protection to provide safe movement away from the building involved. Also, the terminus cannot be to the outside in a closed court from which some sort of travel back through the building may be necessary in order to get away from the building. In such a case, an exit passageway at least as wide as the exit itself and constructed as specified for exits is required to provide travel from the courtyard to the safe place.

(*Also see commentary on exit passageways in 5-2.6.*)

5-7.2 A maximum of 50 percent of the required number of exits and 50 percent of the required exit capacity shall be permitted to discharge through areas on the level of discharge provided all of the following are met:

(a) Such exits discharge to a free and unobstructed way to the exterior of the building, which way is readily visible and identifiable from the point of discharge from the exit.

(b) The entire area on the level of discharge is separated from areas below by construction having a fire resistance rating not less than that for the exit enclosure.

(c) The level of discharge is protected throughout by an approved automatic sprinkler system, and any other portion of the level of discharge with access to the discharge area is protected throughout by an approved automatic sprinkler system or separated from it in accordance with the requirements for the enclosure of exits. (*See 5-1.3.1.*)

Exception to (c): The requirements of 5-7.2(c) may be waived if the discharge area is a vestibule or foyer meeting all of the following:

1. The depth from the exterior of the building is not greater than 10 ft (3 m) and the length is not greater than 30 ft (9.1 m).

2. The foyer is separated from the remainder of the level of discharge by construction providing protection at least the equivalent of wired glass in steel frames.

3. The foyer serves only for means of egress including exits directly to the outside.

Exception: One hundred percent of the exits may discharge through areas on the level of exit discharge in detention and correctional occupancies as provided in Chapters 14 and 15.

The intent of 5-7.2 is to provide an equivalent level of protection for exits discharging through the level of exit discharge. Probably the most often asked question concerning this section involves the requirements of item (c). The intent of item (c) is to require that the entire level of exit discharge and any area connected to the level of discharge with access to the discharge area be protected by automatic sprinkler protection. As an alternative, the sprinklered area must be separated from the rest of the level of discharge by construction as required for exits. (*See 5-1.3.1.*) An exception to the sprinkler requirement is the 10-ft (3-m) maximum by 30-ft (9.1-m) maximum wired glass foyer.

In prior editions of the *Code*, the use of the 50 percent rule for discharge through the level of exit discharge was an option of the respective occupancy chapters. Since all occupancies now allow the arrangement in 5-7.2, the subject is now specified here and has application to all occupancies.

Note, however, that Detention and Correctional Occupancies (14-2.7.2 and 15-2.7.2) and Mercantile Occupancies (24-2.7 and 25-2.7) have special requirements for discharging through the level of exit discharge.

Figures 5-55a and b illustrate alternate arrangements for the exit discharge required by 5-7.2.

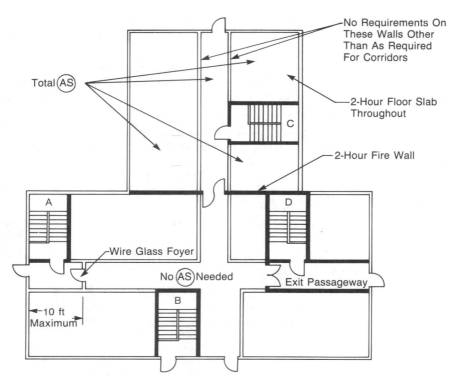

Figure 5-55a. Exit Discharge. The stairs provide four required exits for the upper floors. Two of these exits (B & D) exit directly outside (an exit passageway is part of the exit) and 50 percent discharge across the first floor (one using the wired glass foyer option).

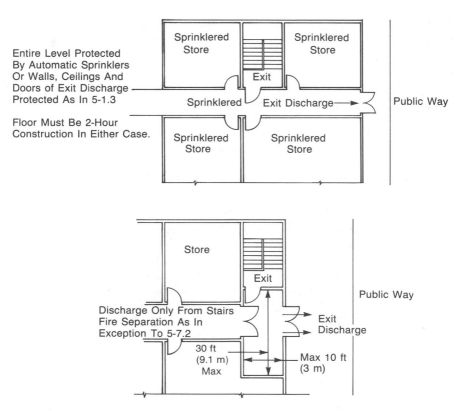

Figure 5-55b.   Alternate Arrangements for Exit Discharge. Two ways to comply with 5-7.2(c) are illustrated.

5-7.3   The exit discharge shall be so arranged and marked as to make clear the direction of egress to a public way. Exit stairs that continue beyond the level of discharge shall be interrupted at the level of discharge by partitions, doors, or other physical barriers.

Exception: Exit stairs that continue one-half story beyond the level of exit discharge need not be interrupted by physical barriers where the exit discharge is clearly obvious.

See also 5-2.2.4.9 on stair details.

The Exception to 5-7.3 is most commonly used in "garden-type" apartment buildings.

5-7.4   Stairs, ramps, bridges, balconies, escalators, moving walks, and other components of an exit discharge shall comply with the detailed requirements of this chapter for such components.

Section 5-2 details the requirements.

5-7.5   Subject to the approval of the authority having jurisdiction, exits may be accepted where:

(a) They discharge to the roof or other sections of the building or adjoining buildings, and

(b) The roof has a fire resistance rating at least the equivalent of that required for the exit enclosure, and

(c) There is a continuous and safe means of egress from the roof, and

(d) All other reasonable requirements for life safety are maintained.

An exit discharge to a roof is not acceptable unless there is another continuous and safe means of egress from the roof, and the roof construction affords protection against fire at least equivalent to that of the stair enclosure. Helicopter rescue from roofs is not dependable enough to be given credit as an exit; many factors are too unpredictable for this to be a consideration.

In addition, exits over roofs must be protected against the accumulation of snow or ice and other impediments to their free use as exits.

SECTION 5-8   ILLUMINATION OF MEANS OF EGRESS

When fire occurs in a building, the degree of visibility in corridors, stairs, and passageways may mean the difference between orderly evacuation and chaos — possibly between life and death. A brief glance at the history of fires reveals several famous fires in which the failure of normal or emergency lighting was a major factor in the casualties incurred. Here are a few:

Iroquois Theater, Chicago, 1903	602 died[16]
Cocoanut Grove Night Club, Boston, 1942	492 died[16]
Baltimore Oyster Roast, 1956	11 died[16]
Apartment House, Boston, 1971	8 died[17]
Summerland, Isle of Man, 1973	50 died[18]

5-8.1 General.

5-8.1.1   Illumination of means of egress shall be provided in accordance with this section for every building and structure where required in Chapters 8 through 30. For the purposes of this requirement, exit access shall include only designated stairs, aisles, corridors, ramps, escalators, and passageways leading to an exit.

The *Code* requires that there be at least 1 footcandle (10 lx) of illumination at floor level in all three elements of a means of egress — the exit access, the exit, and the exit discharge. For the purposes of this section only, the *Code* limits exit access to designated stairs, aisles, corridors, and passageways leading to an exit. Such components should include those portions of the exit access serving occupied spaces. It is not necessary to keep the lights on in all rooms if the rooms are not occupied. The stairs, aisles, and corridors should be designated by the authority having jurisdiction. While motion pictures, slides, and the like are being shown in theaters, auditoriums, and other assembly occupancies, the level of illumination can be reduced to one-fifth of a footcandle.

5-8.1.2 Illumination of means of egress shall be continuous during the time that the conditions of occupancy require that the means of egress be available for use. Artificial lighting shall be employed at such places and for such periods of time as required to maintain the illumination to the minimum footcandle [Lux (lx)] values herein specified.

Formal Interpretation 76-91
Reference: 5-8.1.2

Question 1: Is it the intent of 5-8.1.2 that all means of egress be continuously illuminated?

Answer: Yes, when occupied.

Question 2: Does 5-8.1.2 permit illumination of the means of egress to be shut off at times when the entire building is unoccupied?

Answer: Yes.

Question 3: Does 5-8.1.2 permit shutting off the illumination of the means of egress on an area-by-area basis, as the occupants of these areas leave the building?

Answer: Yes, as long as there are no required means of egress serving occupied areas through the nonilluminated areas.

Issue Edition: 1976
Reference: 5-8.1.2
Date: March 1979

5-8.1.3* The floors of means of egress shall be illuminated at all points including angles and intersections of corridors and passageways, stairways, landings of stairs, and exit doors to values of not less than 1 footcandle (10 lx) measured at the floor.

Exception: In assembly occupancies, the illumination of the floors of exit access may be reduced to values not less than ⅕ footcandle (2 lx) during periods of performances or projections involving directed light.

A-5-8.1.3   A desirable form of means of egress lighting is by lights recessed in walls about a foot (30.5 cm) above the floor. Such lights are not likely to be obscured by smoke.

5-8.1.4   Any required illumination shall be so arranged that the failure of any single lighting unit, such as the burning out of an electric bulb, will not leave any area in darkness.

In any case, the arrangement of lights, circuits, or auxiliary power must be such that continuity of egress lighting will be ensured. This can be accomplished in a number of ways: duplicate light bulbs in fixtures, overlapping light patterns, or overlapping dual circuits.

5-8.1.5   The equipment or units installed to meet the requirements of Section 5-10 shall be permitted also to serve the function of illumination of means of egress, provided that all applicable requirements of this section for such illumination are also met.

5-8.2 Sources of Illumination.

5-8.2.1   Illumination of means of egress shall be from a source of reasonably assured reliability, such as public utility electric service.

5-8.2.2   No battery-operated electric light nor any type of portable lamp or lantern shall be used for primary illumination of means of egress. Battery-operated electric lights shall be permitted to be used as an emergency source to the extent permitted under Section 5-9, Emergency Lighting.

Where batteries are used for emergency power, they shall be the type that will automatically be kept charged and shall perform at the specified levels for 1½ hours when needed.

SECTION 5-9   EMERGENCY LIGHTING

5-9.1 General.

5-9.1.1   Emergency lighting facilities for means of egress shall be provided in accordance with this section for every building or structure where required in Chapters 8 through 30.

Formal Interpretation 76-135
Reference: Section 5-9

Question: When an occupancy chapter requires emergency lighting, is it the intent of Section 5-9 to require emergency lighting in the exit discharge?

Answer: Yes. However, the authority having jurisdiction may modify this requirement if he believes that conditions are such that emergency lighting is not warranted based on other factors.

Issue Edition: 1976
Reference: Section 5-9
Date: May 1980

> Most occupancy chapters require emergency lighting in medium to large buildings. See the -2.9 subsection of each occupancy chapter. For example see 8-2.9 or 24-2.9.

5-9.1.2   Where maintenance of illumination depends upon changing from one energy source to another, there shall be no appreciable interruption of illumination during the changeover. Where emergency lighting is provided by a prime mover-operated electric generator, a delay of not more than 10 seconds shall be permitted.

> An on-site generator driven by a prime mover must be automatically started and capable of picking up the emergency lighting load within ten seconds. Where the generator set is not able to supply power within this time frame, an auxiliary power source must be provided.
>
> Some turbine driven emergency generators take longer than ten seconds to reach operating speed. A backup battery pack such as an Uninterruptible Power supply (UPS) capable of delivering emergency power for a few minutes must be used in conjunction with any on-site generator that cannot meet the ten second requirement.
>
> Section 700-5 of NFPA 70 the *National Electrical Code*®[19] allows use of an emergency generator for load shedding and peak load shaving provided that these loads can be disconnected when normal power to the emergency lighting system is lost.
>
> Although not required by the *National Electric Code*, the use of bypass-isolation transfer switches should be considered. These devices allow maintenance and repair of the transfer switch mechanism without interruption of power to the emergency loads. Bypass switches are interlocked to prevent simultaneous interconnection of the two power sources, and isolation of the transfer switch is usually accomplished by operation of a drawout handle. This type of construction should be used where continuity of electrical service to the emergency system is essential. (*See Figure 5-56.*)

5-9.2 Performance of System.

5-9.2.1   Emergency lighting facilities shall be arranged to maintain the specified degree of illumination throughout the means of egress, but not less than 1 footcandle (10 lx), for a period of 1½ hours in the event of failure of the normal lighting. The illumination may decline to 0.6 footcandle (6 lx) at the end of the emergency lighting time duration. (*See also 5-8.1.3.*)

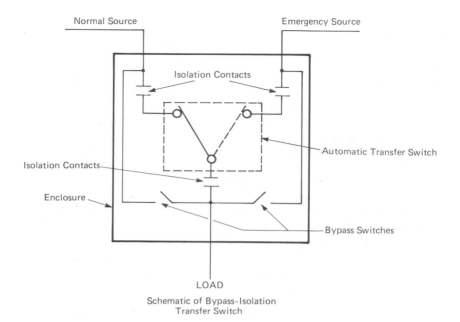

Figure 5-56.   Schematic of Bypass-Isolation Transfer Switch.

5-9.2.2*   Battery-operated emergency lights shall use only reliable types of rechargeable batteries provided with suitable facilities for maintaining them in properly charged condition. Batteries used in such lights or units shall be approved for their intended use and shall comply with NFPA 70, *National Electrical Code*®.

A-5-9.2.2   Automobile-type lead storage batteries are not suitable by reason of their relatively short life when not subject to frequent discharge and recharge as occurs in automobile operation.

For proper selection and maintenance of appropriate batteries, refer to NFPA 70, *National Electrical Code (see Appendix B)*.

The former prohibition against dry batteries has been removed provided they can meet performance criteria.

5-9.2.3*   The emergency lighting system shall be so arranged as to provide the required illumination automatically in the event of any interruption of normal lighting, such as any failure of public utility or other outside electrical power supply, opening of a circuit breaker or fuse, or any manual act(s), including accidental opening of a switch controlling normal lighting facilities.

A-5-9.2.3   Where approved by the authority having jurisdiction, this requirement may be met by means such as:

(a) Two separate electric lighting systems with independent wiring, each adequate alone to provide the specified lighting, one supplied from an outside source such as a public utility service and the other from an electric generator on the premises driven by an independent source of power, both sources of illumination being in regular simultaneous operation whenever the building is occupied during periods of darkness.

(b) An electric circuit or circuits used only for means of egress illumination, with two independent electric sources so arranged that on the failure of one the other will come automatically and immediately into operation. One such source shall be a connection from a public utility or similar outside power source and the other an approved storage battery with suitable provision to keep it automatically charged. Such battery shall also be so provided with automatic controls that after the battery comes into operation, due to failure of the primary power source or to turning off the primary electric source for the lights, it will be shut off after its specified period of operation and will be automatically recharged and ready for further service when the primary current source is again turned on.

(c) Electric battery-operated emergency lighting systems, where permitted, complying with the provisions of 5-9.2.2, and operating on a separate circuit and at a voltage different from that of the primary light. Refer to NFPA 70, *National Electrical Code. (See Appendix B.)*

These requirements are not intended to prohibit the connection of a feeder serving exit lighting and similar emergency functions ahead of the service disconnecting means, but such provision does not constitute an acceptable alternate source of power. It furnishes only supplementary protection for emergency electrical functions, particularly when intended to permit the fire department to open the main disconnect without hampering exit activities. Provision should be made to alert the fire department that certain power and lighting is fed by an emergency generator and will continue operation after the service disconnect is opened.

Formal Interpretation 76-94
Reference: Section 5-9

Question: Where emergency lighting is provided by automatic transfer between normal power service and an emergency diesel generator, does Section 5-9 permit installation of a single switch that can interrupt both energy sources for reasons of repair and maintenance?

Answer: No.

Issue Edition: 1976
Reference: Section 5-9
Date: March 1979

Formal Interpretation 76-50
Reference: 5-9.2.3

Question No. 1: Does a second "source of power" fed from a second substation (i.e., other than the normal feed), supplied by a second tie line fed by two public utilities, and requiring no automatic switch operation, if properly maintained, comply with the literal meaning of 5-9.2.3?

Answer: No.

Question No. 2: Does the design given in Question 1 comply with the intent of 5-9.2.3 regarding sources of emergency lighting system power?

Answer: No.

NOTE: Emergency lighting is to be designed to provide lighting for the emergency evacuation of building occupants regardless of the reason for power failure. However, it is not the intent of the *Code* that the emergency lighting system be capable of withstanding building structure damage as may be present in earthquakes or tornadoes.

Issue Edition: 1976
Reference: 5-9.2.3
Date: May 1978

Formal Interpretation 76-93
Reference: 5-9.2.3

Question: In a building with an independent emergency lighting system, is it the intent of 5-9.2.3 that the emergency lights automatically turn on when corridor lights are manually turned off during periods of adequate daylight, or when the building is unoccupied?

Answer: No.

Issue Edition: 1976
Reference: 5-9.2.3
Date: March 1979

Six methods of providing emergency power are recognized in NFPA 70, the *National Electrical Code*[19]; however, some of these sources do not meet the requirements for emergency lighting under NFPA 101, *Life Safety Code.*

Storage batteries are an acceptable emergency source and may be used to continuously supply required emergency lighting. For this arrangement, two separate lighting systems with independent wiring are employed. One system may be supplied from a public utility and the other from storage batteries. Either supply source must have sufficient capacity, and emergency lighting must be designed so that adequate light for a specified time is available should one system fail.

Instead of installing two separate wiring systems, a single emergency system connected to an automatic transfer switch is often used. The two sources of power — normal and emergency — are connected to the transfer switch, which automatically switches the emergency lighting load from the normal source to the emergency source upon loss of normal power. When normal power is restored, the emergency load is transferred to the normal source.

Batteries that are used for the emergency source must be suitable for the application. Automotive-type batteries are not acceptable.

Where an on-site generator is the emergency power source, it is generally controlled by a transfer switch. Upon loss of normal emergency power, a signal is sent to start the generator. When the generator is running at rated speed and its output voltage is correct, the emergency load is connected to this source by operation of the automatic transfer switch. This transfer must take place in ten seconds or less. (*See Figure 5-57.*)

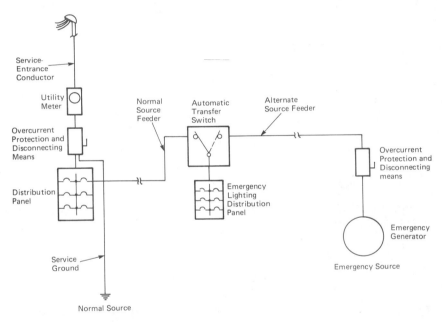

Figure 5-57.   Arrangement of Normal and Alternate Sources Where Emergency Power is Supplied from an On-Site Generator.

Figure 5-58 shows two methods of obtaining an emergency power supply by connection ahead of the service disconnecting means. Although not prohibited by NFPA 70, this method does not comply with the requirements for emergency lighting of NFPA *101* and may not be acceptable to the authority having jurisdiction. Before considering this method to supply emergency power for other than emergency lighting, the reliability of the utility system in the area must be evaluated, and the risk to occupants of the building must be carefully thought out. Since this arrangement only protects from electrical failures in the occupancy, such as blown fuses; tripped circuit breakers; a localized fire at the electric service, distribution panels, etc., availability of the emergency source is dependent on the reliability of the public utility.

Connecting the emergency lighting circuit to the main power line on the "live" side of the main disconnect has the advantage of service continuity should the main switch be thrown by employees or fire fighters as a precautionary measure. The *Code* does not prohibit this practice; however, it should be noted that this method does not meet the requirements for emergency lighting.

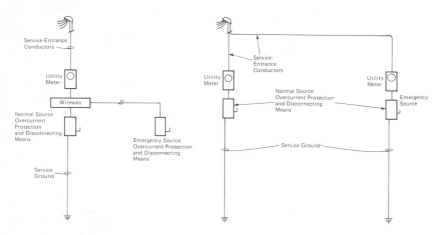

Figure 5-58. Two Methods of Obtaining an Emergency Source by Connection Ahead of the Service Disconnecting Means. (*See Section 700-12(e) of NFPA 70, National Electrical Code.*)

Two separate services — one for normal power and the other for emergency power — are also recognized by NFPA 70, the *National Electrical Code*[19], subject to approval by the authority having jurisdiction but again not acceptable by NFPA 101, *Life Safety Code*, for emergency lighting. Usually, this method provides a higher degree of reliability than the "connection ahead of the service disconnecting means" but does not satisfy the requirements in Section 5-9.2.3. However, underground loop systems in downtown areas of large cities are quite reliable. Many public utilities have not experienced an outage on their loop systems for many years, but there is no protection from any electrical failures that might occur outside of the occupancy. To reduce the possibility of simultaneous loss of both power sources, consideration should be given to the use of different voltages for the normal and emergency systems, taking power for each system from separate manholes, or other schemes that provide both electrical and physical separation between the normal and emergency source. (*See Figure 5-59.*)

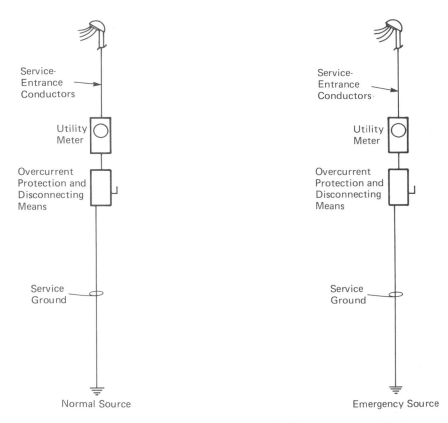

Figure 5-59.   Two Separate Services to the Same Building as Permitted by Section 700-12(d) of NFPA 70, *National Electrical Code.*

Individual battery operated lights can also be used for emergency lighting. Specific rules in NFPA 70, the *National Electrical Code*[19], govern installation. These products are referred to in the *National Electrical Code* as Unit Equipment.

To qualify for emergency lighting, each Unit Equipment must have a rechargeable battery, a battery charging means, provision for one or more lamps, and a relay to energize the lamps automatically upon failure of the normal supply. Unit Equipment must be connected to the same branch circuit that supplies normal lighting to the area in which it is located. Connection to this branch circuit must be ahead of, or on the line side of, any switches controlling the normal lighting. An Exception in the NEC allows connection of Unit Equipment directly to a branch circuit from a panelboard that also supplies a minimum of three normal lighting circuits to the area in which the Unit Equipment is installed. The overcurrent device protecting this Unit Equipment circuit must be provided with a lock-on feature that will prevent accidental disconnection.

5-9.2.4   The emergency lighting system shall be either continuously in operation or capable of repeated automatic operation without manual intervention.

5-9.3 Testing and Maintenance.   *(See Section 31-1.)*

SECTION 5-10   MARKING OF MEANS OF EGRESS

5-10.1 General.

5-10.1.1   Means of egress shall be marked in accordance with this section where required in Chapters 8 through 30.

5-10.1.2*   Exits shall be marked by an approved sign readily visible from any direction of exit access.

Exception: Main exterior exit doors that obviously and clearly are identifiable as exits.

A-5-10.1.2   Where a main entrance serves also as an exit, it will usually be sufficiently obvious to occupants so that no exit sign is needed.

The character of the occupancy has a practical effect upon the need for signs. In any place of assembly, hotel, department store, or other building subject to transient occupancy, the need for signs will be greater than in a building subject to permanent or semi-permanent occupancy by the same people, such as an apartment house where the residents may be presumed to be familiar with exit facilities by reason of regular use thereof. Even in a permanent residence type of building, however, there is need for signs to identify exit facilities such as outside stairs that are not subject to regular use during the normal occupancy of the building.

There are many types of situations where the actual need for signs may be debatable. In cases of doubt, however, it is desirable to be on the safe side by providing signs, particularly as the placing of signs does not ordinarily involve any material expense or inconvenience.

The requirement for the locations of exit signs visible from any direction of exit access may be illustrated as follows:

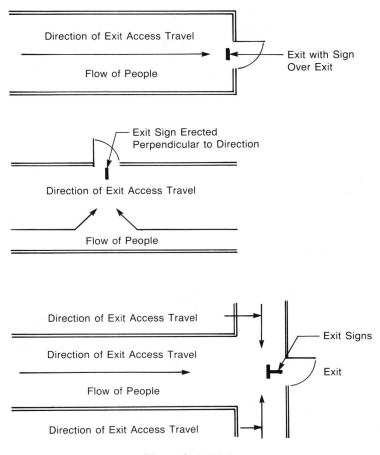

Figure A-5-10.1.2

5-10.1.3   Access to exits shall be marked by approved readily visible signs in all cases where the exit or way to reach it is not immediately visible to the occupants. Sign placement shall be such that no point in the exit access is more than 100 ft (30 m) from the nearest visible sign.

Exception: Signs in existing buildings need not meet the 100-ft (30-m) distance requirement.

The 100-ft (30-m) distance requirement is established since sign size and illumination levels are now based on visibility from 100 ft (30 m).

5-10.1.4*   Where low level exit signs are specifically required by Chapters 8 through 30, an approved luminescent, self-luminous, or self-illuminated sign shall be placed near the floor level below signs required for doors or in corridors by 5-10.1.2 and 5-10.1.3.

This sign shall have appropriate wording in plainly legible letters not less than 4½ in. (11.4 cm) nor more than 6 in. (15.2 cm) high with the principal strokes of letters not less than ¾ in. (1.9 cm) wide. The bottom of the sign shall be not less than 6 in. (15.2 cm) nor more than 8 in. (20.3 cm) above the floor. For exit doors, the sign shall be on the door or adjacent to the door with the closest edge of the sign within 4 in. (10.2 cm) of the door frame.

A-5-10.1.4   (See *A-5-10.2.*)

Since locations near the ceiling may be the first to become obstructed by smoke, this provision makes it possible for the occupancy chapters to specify low level signs to supplement the regular exit signs that are usually placed over the exits. Such supplemental signs may be approved luminescent, self-luminous, or self-illuminated types. They are not intended to replace standard exit signs but are designed as an extra asset to a building occupant seeking egress in a smoke-filled environment, at a location which is the last to become obscured.

The provisions of 5-10.1.3 can be used as guidance where it is desired to install low level signs even though they may not be required.

5-10.1.5*   Every sign required by Section 5-10 shall be so located and of such size, distinctive color, and design as to be readily visible and shall provide contrast with decorations, interior finish, or other signs. No decorations, furnishings, or equipment that impair visibility of an exit sign shall be permitted, nor shall there be any brightly illuminated sign (for other than exit purposes), display, or object in or near the line of vision to the required exit sign of such a character as to so detract attention from the exit sign.

A-5-10.1.5   In stores, for example, an otherwise adequate exit sign may be made inconspicuous by some high-intensity illuminated advertising sign in the immediate vicinity.

Red is the traditional color for exit signs and is required by law in many places. However, at an early stage in the development of the *Code*, a provision was made that green be the color for exit signs, following the idea of traffic lights where green indicates safety and red is the signal to stop. During the period when green signs were specified by the *Code*, many such signs were installed, but the traditional red signs also persisted. In 1949, the Fire Marshals Association of North America voted to request that red be restored as the required exit sign color, as they found that the provision for green involved difficulties in law enactment out of proportion to the importance of the subject. The 10th Edition of the *Code* accordingly specified red where not otherwise required by law. The present text avoids any specific requirement for color on the assumption that either red or green will be used in most cases, and that there may be some situations where some color other than red or green may actually provide better visibility.

In some locations, an otherwise adequate exit sign might be made inconspicuous by a high-intensity illuminated advertising sign in the immediate vicinity. For this reason, such distractions are not allowed near the line of vision to an exit sign.

The location of exit signs is not specified. Usually they are placed over the exit entrance or near the ceiling. There are those who argue, with reason, that smoke builds up more rapidly at higher levels and exit signs a foot or so above the floor would be visible for a much longer period in a fire situation. However, when several people are moving toward an exit, those in the back might not be able to see signs located at a low level. Also, in the absence of careful housekeeping, such signs might be damaged or blocked. Thus the *Code* simply states that exit signs be located as to be readily visible and provide contrast with the surroundings.

5-10.2* Size of Signs.   Every sign required by Section 5-10 shall have the word EXIT or other appropriate wording in plainly legible letters not less than 6 in. (15.2 cm) high with the principal strokes of letters not less than ¾ in. (1.9 cm) wide. The word "EXIT" shall have letters having a width not less than 2 in. (5 cm) except the letter "I," and the minimum spacing between letters shall be not less than ⅜ in. (1 cm). Signs larger than the minimum established in this paragraph shall have letter widths, strokes, and spacing in proportion to their height.

Exception No. 1:   Existing approved signs.

Exception No. 2:   Existing signs having the required wording in plainly legible letters not less than 4 in. (10.2 cm) high.

Exception No. 3:   Signs required by 5-10.1.4.

A-5-10.2   Where graphics are used, the symbols of NFPA 171, *Public Firesafety Symbols*, should be utilized. Such sign needs to provide equal visibility and illumination and comply with the other requirements of Section 5-10.

Traditionally, the letters in an exit sign have been required to be 6 in. (15.2 cm) in height with the principal strokes not less than ¾ in. (1.9 cm) wide. In an effort to increase visibility, the *Code* requires that the letters, other than the "I," be at least 2 in. (5 cm) wide and have a minimum spacing between letters of ⅜ in. (1.0 cm).

5-10.3 Illumination of Signs.

5-10.3.1*   Every sign required by 5-10.1.2 or 5-10.1.3 shall be suitably illuminated by a reliable light source. Externally and internally illuminated signs shall be visible in both the normal and emergency lighting mode.

A-5-10.3.1   It is not the intent of this paragraph to require emergency lighting but only to have the sign illuminated by emergency lighting if emergency lighting is required and provided.

Exit signs may be internally or externally illuminated. Internally illuminated signs are usually provided in occupancies where reduction of normal illumination is permitted, such as in motion picture theaters, but may be used anywhere.

Formal Interpretation 85-12
Reference: 5-10.3

Question 1: Is it the intent of 5-10-3 that all exit signs be continuously illuminated?

Answer: Yes, when occupied.

Question 2: Does 5-10.3 permit exit sign illumination to be shut off at times when the entire building is unoccupied?

Answer: Yes.

Question 3: Does 5-10.3 permit shutting off the illumination of exit signs on an area-by-area basis as the occupants of these areas leave the building?

Answer: Yes, as long as there are no required means of egress serving occupied areas through the nonilluminated areas.

Question 4: Is general area lighting subject to control by an ordinary, freely accessible light switch, permitted by 5-10.3 to serve as the required illumination of an externally illuminated exit sign?

Answer: No.

Question 5: Does 5-10.3 permit a freely accessible light switch to control the illumination of either an internally or externally illuminated exit sign?

Answer: No.

Issue Edition: 1985
Reference: 5-10.3
Date: September 1986

5-10.3.2* Externally illuminated signs shall be illuminated by not less than 5 footcandles (54 lx) and shall employ a contrast ratio of not less than 0.5.

A-5-10.3.2 Colors providing a good contrast are red or green letters on matte white background. Glossy background and glossy letter colors should be avoided.

5-10.3.3* The visibility of an internally illuminated sign shall be the equivalent of an externally illuminated sign that complies with 5-10.3.2.

Exception No. 1: Approved existing signs.

Exception No. 2*: Approved self-luminous or electroluminescent signs that operate in the 5,000 to 6,000 angstrom range that provide evenly illuminated letters may have a minimum luminance of 0.06 footlamberts (0.21 cd/sq m).

A-5-10.3.3 The average luminance of the letters and background shall each be measured in footlamberts. The contrast ratio shall be computed from these measurements by the formula:

$$\text{Contrast} = \frac{\text{Lg-Le}}{\text{Lg}}$$

Where Lg is the greater luminance and Le is the lesser luminance, either the variable Lg or Le may represent the letters and the remaining variable will represent the background. The average luminance of the letters and background may be computed by measuring the luminance at the positions indicated in the diagram by numbered spots.

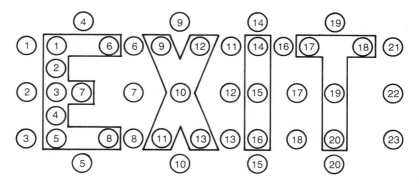

A-5-10.3.3 Exception No. 2 The luminance of these signs is determined by measuring the luminance of circular areas, no greater than ⅜ in. (1.0 cm) in diameter, at the positions indicated in the diagram by Xs.

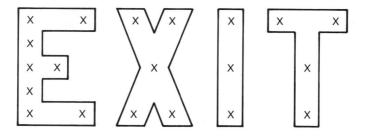

Self-luminous signs are illuminated by self-contained power sources and operate independently of external power sources. Batteries do not qualify as a self-contained power source under this definition.

The requirements for internally illuminated exit signs were greatly simplified in the 1985 Edition of the *Code*. The requirements are now stated on a performance basis. They must provide luminance and contrast ratios equivalent to an externally illuminated sign. Self-luminous and electroluminescent signs with evenly illuminated letters and a minimum luminance of 0.06 footlambert (0.21 cd/sq m) are permitted.

5-10.3.4   Every sign required by 5-10.1.4 shall provide evenly illuminated letters having a minimum luminance of 0.06 footlamberts (0.21 cd/sq m).

Exception: Signs complying with the requirements of 5-10.3.3 are acceptable.

5-10.3.5   Every sign required to be illuminated by 5-10.3 shall be continuously illuminated as required under the provisions of Section 5-8.

Exception*: Illumination for signs shall be permitted to flash on and off upon activation of the fire alarm system.

A-5-10.3.5 Exception   The flashing repetition rate should be approximately one cycle per second, and the duration of the off-time should not exceed one quarter second per cycle. During on-time, the illumination levels must be provided in accordance with 5-10.3.2 or 5-10.3.3. Flashing signs, when activated with the fire alarm system, may be of assistance.

5-10.3.6   Where emergency lighting facilities are required by the applicable provisions of Chapters 8 through 30 for individual occupancies, the exit signs, except approved self-luminous signs, shall be illuminated by the emergency lighting facilities. The level of illumination of the exit sign shall be at the levels provided in accordance with 5-10.3.2 or 5-10.3.3 for the required emergency lighting time duration as specified in 5-9.2.1 but shall be permitted to decline to 60 percent of the illumination level at the end of the emergency lighting time duration.

5-10.4 Specific Requirements.

5-10.4.1 Directional Signs.

5-10.4.1.1*   A sign complying with 5-10.2 reading EXIT or a similar designation with an arrow indicating the direction of travel shall be placed in every location where the direction of travel to reach the nearest exit is not immediately apparent.

A-5-10.4.1.1 Escalators, Moving Walks.   A sign complying with 5-10.4.1.1 indicating the direction of the nearest approved exit should be placed at the point of entrance to any escalator or moving walk. (*See A-5-10.2.*)

5-10.4.1.2 Arrow Designator.   The arrow shall be located outside of the EXIT legend, not less than ⅜ in. (1 cm) from any letter, and may be integral to or separate from the sign body. The arrow shall be of such size, character and location that it is plainly visible and identifiable as a directional arrow.

Exception: Existing approved signs.

The *Code*, for the first time, now specifies requirements for the arrow. There are two distinct requirements: 1) the arrow cannot be within the letters EXIT, 2) the arrow must be of such size, character and location to be identifiable as an arrow. Where symbols are used instead of "EXIT," the *Code* recommends use of NFPA 171, *Standard for Public Firesafety Symbols.*[20]

5-10.4.2* Special Signs.   Any door, passage, or stairway that is neither an exit nor a way of exit access and that is so located or arranged that it is likely to be mistaken for an exit shall be identified by a sign reading NO EXIT. Such sign shall have "NO" letters 2 in. (5 cm) high with stroke width of ⅜ in. (1 cm) and "EXIT" letters 1 in. (2.5 cm) high, with the word "EXIT" below "NO".

Exception: Approved existing signs.

A-5-10.4.2   The likelihood of mistaking for exit doors passageways or stairways that lead to dead-end spaces where occupants might be trapped depends upon the same considerations as govern the need for exit signs. Thus, such areas should be marked with a sign reading NO EXIT. Supplementary lettering indicating the character of the area such as TO BASEMENT, STOREROOM, LINEN CLOSET, or the like may be provided. (*See A-5-10.2.*)

The size of letters in the "NO EXIT" sign are now specified.

SECTION 5-11   SPECIAL PROVISIONS FOR OCCUPANCIES WITH HIGH HAZARD CONTENTS (*See Section 4-2.*)

Attention is called to the definition of High Hazard Areas in Chapter 3, which reads:

"High Hazard Areas. Areas of structures, buildings, or parts thereof used for purposes that involve highly combustible, highly flammable, or explosive products or materials that are likely to burn with extreme rapidity, or that may produce poisonous fumes or gases, including highly toxic or noxious alkalies, acids, or other liquids or chemicals that involve flame, fume, explosive, poisonous or irritant hazards; also uses that cause division of material into fine particles or dust subject to explosion or spontaneous combustion, and uses that constitute a high fire hazard because of the form, character, or volume of the material used."

Also note the definition of High Hazard Contents from 4-2.2.4, which reads:

"4-2.2.4 High hazard contents shall be classified as those that are likely to burn with extreme rapidity or from which explosions are to be feared. (*For means of egress requirements, see Section 5-11.*)"

5-11.1*   In all cases where the contents are classified as high hazard, exits shall be provided of such types and numbers and so arranged as to permit all occupants to escape from the building or structure or from the hazardous area thereof to the outside or to a place of safety with a travel distance of not over 75 ft (23 m), measured as specified in 5-6.2.

A-5-11.1 Seventy-five ft (23 m) can be traversed in approximately 10 to 15 seconds, even allowing for some momentary delay in decision as to which way to go, during which it may be assumed that a normal individual can hold his or her breath.

5-11.1 does not specify a 75-ft (23-m) travel distance, but 75 ft (23 m) to escape from the building or structure or from the hazardous area thereof.

5-11.2 Capacity of means of egress provided in accordance with 5-11.1 shall be as specified in the applicable section of Chapters 8 through 30 but not less than such as to provide 0.7 in. per person (1.8 cm/person) where exit is by inside or outside stairs or 0.4 in. per person (1.0 cm/person) where exit is by doors at grade level, by horizontal exits, or by Class A ramps.

5-11.3 At least two exits shall be provided from each building or hazardous area thereof.

Exception: Rooms or spaces not greater than 200 sq ft (18.6 sq m) and having an occupant load of not greater than three persons and having a maximum travel distance to the room door of 25 ft (7.6 m).

An exception has been added indicating that it is not always necessary or feasible to provide two ways out of a very small high hazard space.

5-11.4 Means of egress shall be so arranged that there are no dead-end pockets, hallways, corridors, passageways, or courts.

It is not the intent of the *Code* to apply the provisions of this section to hazardous areas as defined in each occupancy chapter, but to apply them to an area of high hazard contents. Small areas of high hazard are considered incidental to the main occupancy of the building. The decision as to when an area becomes sufficiently hazardous to warrant application of this section is left to the authority having jurisdiction.

REFERENCES CITED IN COMMENTARY

[1]NFPA 252, *Standard Methods of Fire Tests of Door Assemblies*, National Fire Protection Association, Quincy, MA, 1984.

[2]NFPA 72E, *Standard on Automatic Fire Detectors*, National Fire Protection Association, Quincy, MA, 1987.

[3]NFPA 220, *Standard on Types of Building Construction*, National Fire Protection Association, Boston, MA, 1985.

[4]Fitch, Templar, Corcoran, "The Dimensions of Stairs," Scientific American, October 1974.

[5]Design and Construction of Building Exits, Miscellaneous Publication M 51, October 10, 1935, National Bureau of Standards, Washington, DC (out of print).

[6]National Safety Council Safe Practices, Pamphlet No. 2, National Safety Council, 425 N. Michigan Avenue, Chicago, IL 60611, 1934.

[7]ANSI/ASME A17.1, *Safety Code for Elevators and Escalators*, American Society of Mechanical Engineers, 345 East 47th Street, New York, NY 10017, 1984.

[8]Paul Robert Lyons, *Fire in America*, NFPA SPP-33, National Fire Protection Association, Boston, 1976, p. 190.

[9]London Transit Board Research, "Second Report of the Operational Research Team on the Capacity of Footways," Research Report No. 95, London, August 1958.

[10]Pauls, Jake, *Fire Technology*, Vol. 20, No. 2, May, 1984, pp. 28-40.

[11]NFPA 101M, *Alternative Approaches to Life Safety*, National Fire Protection Association, Quincy, MA, 1988.

[12]Laurence D. Watrous, "High-Rise Fire in New Orleans," *Fire Journal*, Vol. 67, No. 3, May 1973, pp. 6-9.

[13]Robert F. Mendes, *Fighting High-Rise Building Fires — Tactics and Logistics*, NFPA FSP-44, National Fire Protection Association, Boston, 1975.

[14]Richard E. Stevens, "Exits in Core-Type Office Buildings," *Fire Journal*, Vol. 64, No. 3, May 1970, pp. 68-70.

[15]*Uniform Building Code*, International Conference of Building Officials, Whittier, CA

[16]R. S. Moulton, "Emergency Lighting for Fire Safety," *NFPA Quarterly*, Vol. 50, No. 2, October 1956, pp. 93-96.

[17]A. Elwood Willey, "Unsafe Existing Conditions! Apartment House Fire, Boston, Massachusetts," *Fire Journal*, Vol. 65, No. 4, July 1971, pp. 16-23.

[18]James K. Lathrop, "The Summerland Fire: 50 Die on Isle of Man," *Fire Journal*, Vol. 69, No. 2, March 1975, pp. 5-12.

[19]NFPA 70, *National Electrical Code*, National Fire Protection Association, Quincy, MA, 1987.

[20]NFPA 171, *Standard for Public Firesafety Symbols*, National Fire Protection Association, Quincy, MA, 1986.

6

FEATURES OF FIRE PROTECTION

SECTION 6-1   GENERAL

This chapter establishes basic requirements for features of fire protection, which include such items as construction, compartmentation through use of fire barriers, protection of vertical openings, protection of concealed spaces, subdivision of building space through use of smoke barriers, protection from hazards, and interior finish. For the most part, this chapter specifies a menu of protection options, which is then called into play by specific occupancy chapters. However, some of the provisions of this chapter apply as requirements to all occupancies.

6-1.1 Application.

6-1.1.1   The features of fire protection set forth in this chapter apply to both new construction and existing buildings.

Lack of compartmentation and rapid fire development have been found to be primary factors in numerous multiple-fatality fires, especially in residential occupancies. In many fire reports, the factors of unprotected vertical openings and highly combustible interior finish appear repeatedly, indicating the need to apply requirements to both new construction and existing buildings.

SECTION 6-2   CONSTRUCTION AND COMPARTMENTATION

The purpose of Section 6-2 is to set forth, in general terms, how those using exits and other "safe" areas in buildings are to be protected from fire in adjoining areas. Protection is achieved by providing wall, ceiling, and floor construction that will be reasonably free from penetration by fire and smoke for a safe period. Because requirements vary for different occupancies, specific details for construction and compartmentation are included in Chapters 8 through 30 of the *Code*.

To be consistent and to preserve the integrity of the "compartment" or safe area, all openings for doors, ducts, and building services, i.e., electric power, telephone, water supply, and waste lines, must also be effectively closed or fitted with automatic closures. Equally important, and sometimes overlooked, are concealed spaces, particularly those above suspended ceilings, that can be, and frequently have been, the means of spreading fire into otherwise protected areas.[1] In some instances, these interstitial spaces may be 8 ft (244 cm) or more in height; in others, they may serve as supply or return air plenum chambers for air conditioning systems. Proper protection of concealed spaces can include firestopping, draftstopping, automatic extinguishment, area limitations, and other limitations on the combustibility of contents, interior linings, and construction materials. For specific protection details, see 6-2.5.

In this section and throughout the *Code*, a distinction is made between smoke barriers and fire barriers. The function of the former is to restrict the passage of smoke, including fire gases. As such, a smoke barrier needs to be reasonably airtight even under an increase in air pressure on the fire side due to the expansion of the heated air. The fire barrier, on the other hand, must prevent passage of heat and flame for a designated period of time. In other words, it must be capable of withstanding direct impingement of the fire as determined by large-scale tests conducted in accordance with NFPA 251, *Standard Methods of Fire Tests of Building Construction and Materials*,[2] and NFPA 252, *Standard Methods of Fire Tests of Door Assemblies*.[3]

6-2.1* Construction.   Buildings or structures occupied or used according to the individual occupancy chapters (Chapters 8 through 30) shall meet the minimum construction requirements of those chapters. NFPA 220, *Standard on Types of Building Construction*, shall be used to determine the requirements for the construction classification.

A-6-2.1   Table A-6-2.1 on page 201 is a reprint of Table 3 from NFPA 220, *Standard on Types of Building Construction* (*see Appendix B*). This is included for the convenience of users of the *Life Safety Code*.

In general, the *Life Safety Code* is not a building code. However, in certain occupancies, minimum construction requirements are established to help maintain structural integrity for the time period needed for evacuation or, as in the case of health care occupancies where evacuation does not assure the safety of sick occupants, for an even longer period of time so as to establish a safe area of refuge within the building but away from the zone of fire origin.

Paragraph 6-2.1 does not set minimum construction requirements but rather provides the reference to the detailed NFPA 220, *Standard for Types of Building Construction*,[4] so that where construction types are specified in other sections of the *Code*, particularly in the occupancy Chapters 8 through 30, a shorthand notation, such as "Type I (332)," can be used without additional expansive detail. The user should then go to NFPA 220 for the necessary details.

The Appendix provides the user of the *Life Safety Code* with a reprint of Table 3 from NFPA 220. The table summarizes the verbiage of the document. Note that the shorthand notation, such as "Type I (332),"

**Table A-6-2.1 Fire Resistance Requirements
for Type I Through Type V Construction.**

	Type I		Type II			Type III		Type IV	Type V	
	443	332	222	111	000	211	200	2HH	111	000
EXTERIOR BEARING WALLS—										
Supporting more than one floor, columns or other bearing walls	4	3	2	1	0¹	2	2	2	1	0¹
Supporting one floor only	4	3	2	1	0¹	2	2	2	1	0¹
Supporting a roof only	4	3	1	1	0¹	2	2	2	1	0¹
INTERIOR BEARING WALLS—										
Supporting more than one floor, columns or other bearing walls	4	3	2	1	0	1	0	2	1	0
Supporting one floor only	3	2	2	1	0	1	0	1	1	0
Supporting a roof only	3	2	1	1	0	1	0	1	1	0
COLUMNS—										
Supporting more than one floor, bearing walls or other columns	4	3	2	1	0	1	0	H²	1	0
Supporting one floor only	3	2	2	1	0	1	0	H²	1	0
Supporting a roof only	3	2	1	1	0	1	0	H²	1	0
BEAMS, GIRDERS, TRUSSES & ARCHES—										
Supporting more than one floor, bearing walls or columns	4	3	2	1	0	1	0	H²	1	0
Supporting one floor only	3	2	2	1	0	1	0	H²	1	0
Supporting a roof only	3	2	1	1	0	1	0	H²	1	0
FLOOR CONSTRUCTION	3	2	2	1	0	1	0	H²	1	0
ROOF CONSTRUCTION	2	1½	1	1	0	1	0	H²	1	0
EXTERIOR NONBEARING WALLS	0¹	0¹	0¹	0¹	0¹	0¹	0¹	0¹	0¹	0¹

Those members listed that are permitted to be of approved combustible material.

[1] Requirements for fire resistance of exterior walls, the provision of spandrel wall sections, and the limitation or protection of wall openings are not related to construction type. They need to be specified in other standards and codes, where appropriate, and may be required in addition to the requirements of this Standard for the construction type.

[2] "H" indicates heavy timber members; see text for requirements.

provides the minimum hourly fire resistance ratings required to meet the definition of that construction type for only three components of the building: exterior bearing walls, structural frame/columns/girders, and floor construction. In order to meet the definition fully, other building components, such as roof construction and interior bearing walls, need to have certain minimum fire resistance ratings. Thus, the shorthand notation alone does not provide all the needed information. NFPA 220 should be consulted as necessary.

At times, the minimum construction requirements of other sections of the *Code* may establish criteria in addition to those of NFPA 220 for use in judging compliance with the definition of a specific building construction type. Chapter 12 for new health care, which provides an overall package of life safety to a population that is incapable of self-preservation and thus difficult to protect, requires that for a building to be classified as either Type I or Type II construction, it must meet the requirements of NFPA 220 and additionally have noncombustible or limited-combustible interior nonbearing walls. Interior nonbearing walls are not addressed by NFPA 220.

Table 6-1 matches the various NFPA 220 construction types with their approximate equivalent construction types as contained in the three major model building codes: the *Uniform Building Code* (UBC),[5] *National Building Code* (NBC),[6] and the *Standard Building Code* (SBC)[7]. For example, a building that NFPA 220 would consider Type I (332), the *Uniform Building Code* considers Type I FR, the *National Building Code* considers Type 1B, and the *Standard Building Code* considers Type II. When using the *Life Safety Code* in conjunction with one of these codes, the authority having jurisdiction may wish to consider (per Section 1-5) "equivalent" construction types by utilizing Table 6-1.

Table 6-1

NFPA 220	I (443)	I (332)	II (222)	II (111)	II (000)	III (211)	III (200)	IV (2HH)	V (111)	V (000)
UBC	—	I FR	II FR	II-1 hr	II N	III-1 hr	III N	IV HT	V 1-hr	V-N
NBC	1A	1B	2A	2B	2C	3A	3B	4	5A	5B
SBC	I	II	—	IV 1 hr	IV unp	V 1 hr	V unp	III	VI 1 hr	VI unp

6-2.2 Compartmentation.

6-2.2.1   Where required by Chapters 8 through 30, every building shall be divided into compartments to limit the spread of fire and restrict the movement of smoke.

6-2.2.2*   Fire compartments shall be formed with fire barriers that are continuous from outside wall to outside wall, from one fire barrier to another, or a combination thereof; including continuity through all concealed spaces, such as those found above a ceiling, including interstitial spaces.

Exception: A fire barrier required for an occupied space below an interstitial space is not required to extend through the interstitial space provided the construction assembly forming the bottom of the interstitial space has a fire resistance rating equal to that of the fire barrier.

A-6-2.2.2   To ensure that a fire barrier is continuous, it is necessary to completely seal all openings where the fire barrier abuts other fire barriers, exterior walls, the floor below, and the floor or ceiling above. In the Exception, the fire resistance rating of the bottom of the interstitial space must be provided by that membrane in and of itself. Ceilings of rated floor/ceiling and roof/ceiling assemblies do not necessarily provide the required fire resistance.

Interstitial spaces in some cases contain a considerable fuel load and are readily accessible by people. Over the life of a building, the possibility that an interstitial space will be used for storage cannot be overlooked. These factors must be considered to determine whether or not an interstitial space is in fact another floor.

Normally, ceilings are not tested alone but are tested as part of a floor/ceiling or roof/ceiling assembly. This test does not indicate the performance of the ceiling, but of the total assembly. For example, the ceiling of a 1-hour floor/ceiling assembly may fail after 20 minutes, but the overall assembly passes the 1-hour test. Often an architect or contractor will refer to a 1- or 2-hour ceiling and request to terminate a fire barrier at the ceiling, but in reality the ceiling is part of a 1-hour or 2-hour floor/ceiling or roof/ceiling assembly and therefore the fire barrier must extend from slab to slab. There are tests that indicate that, by using two layers of ⅝-in. (1.6-cm) fire-rated gypsum board properly installed as a ceiling, a fire barrier of approximately 1 hour can be obtained, and therefore termination of a 1-hour fire barrier at such a ceiling would be permitted by the exception.[8] (*See Figure 6-1.*)

Some occupancies do allow the fire barrier to terminate at the underside (i.e., ceiling) of a fire protection rated floor/ceiling assembly. However, caution must be exercised, since ceilings of these assemblies are often improperly installed or, once installed, have been violated during routine maintenance.

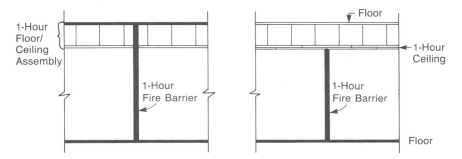

Figure 6-1.   Fire Barriers Must Extend Through Ceiling Spaces Unless the Ceiling Is Itself a Fire Barrier.

6-2.3 Fire Barriers.

6-2.3.1   Fire barriers used to provide enclosure of floor openings or used for subdivision of stories shall be classified in accordance with their fire resistance rating as follows:

(a) 2-hour fire resistance rating.

(b) 1-hour fire resistance rating.

(c) ¾-hour fire resistance rating.

(d) ½-hour fire resistance rating.

(e) 20-minute fire resistance rating.

The fire resistance of a fire barrier is determined by the test method described in NFPA 251, *Standard Methods of Fire Tests of Building Construction and Materials.*[2] The test is also commonly known by its ASTM designation, ASTM E119 (same title).[9] The NFPA 251 / ASTM E119 test standard provides for the construction of the particular assembly to be rated and the actual testing of the assembly in the test furnace. The test is conducted under very rigid conditions so that test results on the same assembly are reproducible and tests of different assemblies are comparable. Temperatures in the furnace are generated in strict accordance with the standard time-temperature curve and reach levels of 1000°F, 1300°F, 1550°F, 1700°F, and 1850°F (538°C, 704°C, 843°C, 927°C, and 1010°C) at time periods of 5, 10, 30, 60, and 120 minutes into the test. Temperatures both in the furnace and on the unexposed side of the assembly being tested are monitored closely at specified intervals and locations. During the course of the test, cotton waste is placed against the unexposed surface and observed for flaming. During the test, the assembly being tested is also loaded the same way that it would be expected to be loaded when in place in a building.

Acceptance criteria for an assembly to complete the fire test successfully for a specified time period include the following:

1. Cotton waste on unexposed side cannot ignite;

2. Temperature rise on the unexposed side cannot exceed 325°F (180°C) at any point or an average of 250°F (139°C);

3. The assembly must continue to support design loads.

The above criteria apply to floor, roof, wall, and partition assemblies. In addition, wall and partition assemblies to be rated at 1 hour or more are subjected to the hose stream test. A duplicate specimen of the assembly to be rated is tested in the furnace for one-half the time period indicated as the fire resistance rating in the fire endurance test. This specimen is then removed from the furnace and immediately subjected to the hose stream test. If there is any projection of water beyond the unexposed surface, the assembly is considered to have failed.

NFPA 251 testing is commonly done by testing laboratories, which normally issue a report of the test and then list the assembly. Listings of tested fire resistance rated assemblies may be found in any of the model building codes (*see commentary following A-6-2.1*) or in publications of the laboratories that conduct fire testing, such as the *Underwriters Laboratories Fire Resistance Directory*[10], or the *Factory Mutual Specification Tested Products Guide*.[11] It is important that the assembly in the field be the same as that listed. For example, if a floor/ceiling assembly calls for clips on the ceiling tiles, these must be installed and maintained. Another example is the special treatment often required for lights or air ducts in suspended ceilings. A common problem in walls is the installation of an untested material between the wallboard and the studs or the installation of recessed wall fixtures, which requires the removal of wallboard.

6-2.3.2* Every opening in a fire barrier shall be protected to limit the spread of fire and restrict the movement of smoke from one side of the fire barrier to the other. The fire protection rating for opening protectives shall be as follows:

(a) 2-hour fire barrier — 1½-hour fire protection rating.

(b) 1-hour fire barrier — 1-hour fire protection rating where used for vertical openings or ¾-hour fire protection rating where used for other than vertical openings.

Exception No. 1 to (b): Where a lesser fire protection rating is specified by Chapter 5 or Chapters 8 through 30.

Exception No. 2 to (b): Where the fire barrier is provided as a result of a requirement that corridor walls be of 1-hour fire resistance rated construction, the opening protectives shall have a fire protection rating of not less than 20 minutes when tested in accordance with NFPA 252, Standard Methods of Fire Tests of Door Assemblies, without the hose stream test.

Exception No. 3 to (b): Where special requirements for doors in 1-hour fire resistance rated corridor walls and 1-hour fire resistance rated smoke barriers are specified in Chapters 12 and 13.

(c) ¾-hour fire barrier — 20-minute fire protection rating.

(d) ½-hour fire barrier — 20-minute fire protection rating.

(e) 20-minute fire barrier — 20-minute fire protection rating.

A-6-2.3.2   Longer ratings may be required where doors are provided for property protection as well as life safety.

NFPA 80, *Standard for Fire Doors and Windows (see Appendix B)*, may be consulted for standard practice in the selection and installation of fire doors.

In existing installations only, a 1¾-in. (4.4-cm) solid bonded wood core door has been considered a satisfactory substitute for a door with a 20-minute fire protection rating.

Whereas 6-2.3.1 discussed the fire *resistance* rating of fire barriers, 6-2.3.2 addresses the fire *protection* rating of opening protectives. Fire barriers have fire resistance ratings; opening protectives, such as fire doors, have fire protection ratings. For a better understanding of the difference in test methods used for rating fire barriers and fire doors, compare the commentaries following 6-2.3.1 and 6-2.3.6.

In general, 1-hour fire barriers for vertical openings require doors with a 1-hour fire protection rating, and 1-hour fire barriers for other than vertical openings require doors with a ¾-hour fire protection rating.

Exception No. 1 to item (b) allows Chapter 5 and the occupancy chapters to alter this general rule. For the most part, though, this is usually done only in regard to the requirements that corridor walls be of a 1-hour fire resistance rating. Exception No. 2 to item (b) specifically deals with this subject.

Exception No. 3 to item (b) recognizes the special requirements contained in Chapters 12 and 13 for health care occupancies, which, for example, allow the omission of the self-closing device, which means that a true fire protection rated patient room door assembly is not required, in recognition of the functional needs of these facilities.

Note that the fire protection ratings of the opening protectives are, in some cases, allowed to be of a lower time rating than the fire resistance rating of the fire barrier whose openings are to be protected. For example, a 2-hour fire resistance rated fire barrier is allowed to have its openings protected by 1½-hour fire protection rated door assemblies. The perceived mismatch of ratings actually accomplishes a reasonable, practical match because:

1. The test procedures on which the ratings are based, i.e., NFPA 251 / ASTM E119 for fire barriers and NFPA 252 / ASTM E152 (*see commentary following 6-2.3.6*) for fire doors are different, and

2. It is thought that, whereas combustibles may be placed against a fire resistance rated wall and expose the wall to a considerable fire challenge, a fire protection rated door assembly will not have similar combustibles placed against it because the opening must be maintained clear to allow passage through the door. Such a scenario suggests that, if a door is not to be used and combustible storage is to be placed at the door opening, the door should be removed and the opening filled with material to restore the wall to its required fire resistance rating.

6-2.3.3   Fire door assemblies in fire barriers shall comply with the provisions of 5-2.1.

6-2.3.4 Penetrations and Miscellaneous Openings in Fire Barriers.

6-2.3.4.1*   Openings in fire barriers for air-handling ductwork or air movement shall be protected in accordance with 7-2.1.

A-6-2.3.4.1   In engineered smoke management systems, the designer should consider the use of high temperature links on fire dampers where air handling ductwork penetrates fire barriers.

Formal Interpretation 81-6
Reference: A-6-2.3.4.1

Question: Is it the intent of Paragraph A-6-2.3.4.1 of NFPA 101 to recommend to designers of engineered smoke control systems that they consider the use of high temperature fusible links that exceed the 285°F (141°C) maximum temperature for operation of all fire dampers required by UL555-1979, Fire Dampers and Ceiling Dampers, Conditions of Acceptance, Paragraph 7.15?

Answer: No, the intent of the Committee was to encourage the consideration of higher temperature fusible links, but not to exceed the maximums set in UL555.

Issue Edition: 1981
Reference: A-6.2.2.7
Date: April 1982

By referring the *Code* user to 7-2.1 for protection of openings in fire barriers for air-handling ductwork or air movement, the requirements of NFPA 90A, *Standard for the Installation of Air Conditioning and Ventilating Systems*[12], and not the usual *Life Safety Code* requirements with respect to opening protectives, i.e., 6-2.3.1, apply to HVAC penetrations of fire barriers. NFPA 90A requires that approved fire dampers be provided in all air transfer openings in partitions required to have a fire resistance rating. It requires that approved fire dampers be provided where ducts or air grilles penetrate partitions required to have a fire resistance rating of 2 hours or more. Thus, although any air transfer opening would have to be fire dampered in a required fire barrier of any rating, penetrations by ducts or air grilles would not have to be fire dampered if the required rating of the fire barrier is less than 2 hours. These requirements are depicted in Figure 6-2.

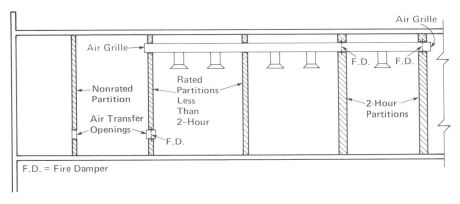

Figure 6-2.   Fire Damper Requirements of NFPA 90A for HVAC Penetrations of Partitions.

6-2.3.4.2   Pipes, conduits, bus ducts, cables, wires, air ducts, pneumatic tubes and ducts, and similar building service equipment that pass through fire barriers shall be protected as follows:

(a) The space between the penetrating item and the fire barrier shall:

1. Be filled with a material capable of maintaining the fire resistance of the fire barrier, or

2. Be protected by an approved device designed for the specific purpose.

(b) Where the penetrating item uses a sleeve to penetrate the fire barrier, the sleeve shall be solidly set in the fire barrier, and the space between the item and the sleeve shall:

1. Be filled with a material capable of maintaining the fire resistance of the fire barrier, or

2. Be protected by an approved device designed for the specific purpose.

(c)* Insulation and coverings for pipes and ducts shall not pass through the fire barrier unless:

1. The material is capable of maintaining the fire resistance of the fire barrier, or

2. Protected by an approved device designed for the specific purpose.

(d) Where designs take transmission of vibration into consideration, any vibration isolation shall:

1. Be made on either side of the fire barrier, or

2. Be made by an approved device designed for the specific purpose.

A-6-2.3.4.2(c)   See NFPA 90A, *Standard for the Installation of Air Conditioning and Ventilating Systems* (*see Appendix B*), for additional information on air handling duct work passing through fire barriers.

One source of information on tested materials, devices, and systems for protecting through-penetrations of fire resistance rated barriers is the Underwriters Laboratories *Building Materials Directory*[13] in the categories of Through-Penetration Firestop Devices and Through-Penetration Firestop Systems. Such devices and systems are designed to resist the spread of fire through openings made in fire resistance rated floor or wall barriers to accommodate penetrating items, such as electrical cables, cable trays, conduits, and pipes. Such devices and systems are classified by UL with respect to installation in a wall only, installation in a floor only, or suitability for installation in a wall or floor. The basic standard used by Underwriters Laboratories to investigate products in this category is UL 1479, *Fire Tests of Through-Penetration Firestops*.[14] A sampling of the currently classified devices includes the use of ceramic fibers, foamed silicones, mineral wool batts, intumescent sheets, sealing blankets and plugs, fittings and couplings, various caulks, putties and mastics, and even spring-loaded guillotine blades.

Over the life of a building, it is important to maintain the integrity of barriers to fire spread. Renovations or any changes to building utilities will tend to violate the compartmentation provided when a building is first occupied.

Figure 6-3 illustrates some of the typical fire barrier penetrations, which are covered in 6-2.3.1 through 6-2.3.4.

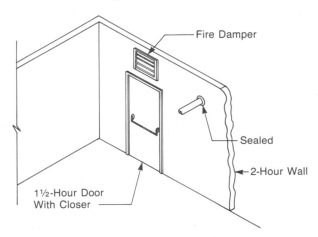

Figure 6-3.   Typical Penetrations of a Fire Barrier.

6-2.3.5   Floor-ceiling assemblies; bearing and nonbearing wall or partition assemblies used as fire barriers to form fire compartments; and columns, beams, girders, or trusses supporting such assemblies shall be of a design that has been tested to meet the conditions of acceptance of NFPA 251, *Standard Methods of Fire Tests of Building Construction and Materials.*

Not only is it necessary to provide the proper fire barriers, but the structural integrity of those barriers must be maintained. This aids not only in evacuation of occupants but helps to maintain safe areas of refuge, especially on the nonfire side of a horizontal exit. For additional information on NFPA 251, see the commentary following 6-2.3.1.

6-2.3.6   Door or window assemblies in fire barriers shall be of an approved type with appropriate rating for the location in which installed. Fire doors and windows shall be installed in accordance with NFPA 80, *Standard for Fire Doors and Windows.* Fire doors shall be of a design that has been tested to meet the conditions of acceptance of NFPA 252, *Standard Methods of Fire Tests of Door Assemblies.* Fire windows shall be of a design that has been tested to meet the conditions of acceptance of NFPA 257, *Standard for Fire Tests of Window Assemblies.*

Fire protection rated door assemblies are tested in accordance with NFPA 252, *Standard Methods of Fire Tests of Door Assemblies*, which is also commonly known as ASTM E152 (same title),[15] and must be installed in accordance with the requirements of NFPA 80, *Standard for Fire Doors and Windows.*[16] Where the *Life Safety Code* uses the term "door," it includes not only the door proper, but also the doorway, frame, and necessary hardware including hinges. Where describing a fire door, the applicable standards similarly define a fire protection rated assembly as including all of the above components as well as a listed door closer and positive latching.

Fire doors, if they are to do their job, must not only be closed but must also be held closed. Building fires are capable of generating pressures sufficient to force fire doors open if they are not held closed with positive latching, thereby rendering the doors incapable of protecting the opening in which they are installed.

The acceptance criteria for fire protection rated assemblies, such as fire doors, differ from those for fire resistance rated construction, such as a wall or floor/ceiling assembly. The limitation of temperature rise through the fire door is not normally a measure of acceptance, whereas it is for a fire resistance rated assembly. In addition, during the course of the fire test, fire doors will expand on the exposed side and, as a result, will warp, sometimes enough to come out of the door opening at the top of the door. This will, of course, result in some flaming through the top of the door openings. The test standard recognizes this phenomenon, and a certain amount of such flaming is permitted under the acceptance criteria. This does not adversely affect safety given that fire protection rated assemblies are intended to protect relatively small openings in larger fire resistance rated barriers. (*Also see the commentary following 6-2.3.1 and 6-2.3.2.*)

6-2.4 Vertical Openings.

6-2.4.1   Every floor that separates stories in a building shall be constructed as a smoke barrier to provide a basic degree of compartmentation. (*See Section 3-2 for definition of smoke barrier.*)

Exception No. 1:   As permitted by 6-2.4.4.

Exception No. 2:   As permitted by 6-2.4.5.

Exception No. 3:   As permitted by Chapters 8 through 30.

   Although the *Code* states that every floor should be constructed as a smoke barrier, the requirement is tempered to stress that it intends that a "basic degree" of compartmentation be provided. The reference to the Section 3-2 definition of smoke barrier provides the user with the statement that such barriers may have protected openings. Thus, it is not the *Code*'s intent that every floor must restrict the passage of smoke to the same degree as that of a required smoke barrier, in accordance with the provisions of Section 6-3. Even required smoke barriers, which are required to comply with Section 6-3, are afforded the use of 6-3.5.1 Exception No. 4, which allows smoke dampers to be omitted where ducts penetrate floors that serve as smoke barriers.

6-2.4.2*   Openings through floors, such as stairways, hoistways for elevators, dumbwaiters, inclined and vertical conveyors; shaftways used for light, ventilation, or building services; or expansion joints and seismic joints used to allow structural movements shall be enclosed with fire barriers (vertical), such as wall or partition assemblies. Such enclosures shall be continuous from floor to floor. Openings shall be protected as appropriate for the fire resistance rating of the barrier.

Exception No. 1:   As permitted by 6-2.4.4.

Exception No. 2:   As permitted by 6-2.4.5.

Exception No. 3:   As permitted by Chapters 8 through 30.

Exception No. 4:   Escalators and moving walks protected in accordance with 6-2.4.7.

Exception No. 5:   Expansion or seismic joints designed to prevent the penetration of fire for a time period not less than the required fire resistance rating of the floor.

   Based on lessons learned from the Las Vegas MGM Grand Hotel fire,[17] the above list of floor openings has been expanded to include expansion joints and seismic joints that allow structural movements. Exception No. 5 specifically recognizes the use of fire protection rated expansion or seismic joints, with a minimum rating not less than the required fire resistance rating of the floor, in lieu of full enclosure from floor to floor. Without appropriately rated joints, the enclosure requirements might be satisfied by an arrangement of walls and doors as shown in Figure 6-4.

A-6-2.4.2   Expansion joints are usually found only in large buildings [i.e., at least 200 ft (60 m) in length and/or width] of steel or concrete construction. They are provided to permit the separate portions of the structural frame to expand and contract with

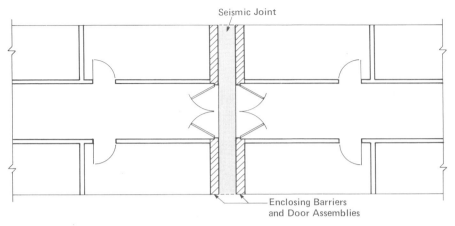

Figure 6-4. Enclosure of Seismic Joint Accomplished by Back-to-Back Fire Resistance Rated Barriers and Cross-Corridor Fire-Protection Rated Door Assemblies.

temperature and moisture changes without adversely affecting the building's structural integrity or serviceability. Expansion joints can usually be identified by the following characteristics: 1) a double row of columns; 2) a width of one to three inches (2.5 to 7.6 cm); and 3) a steel plate cover that is attached to the floor on one side of the joint and free to slide on the other side. Expansion joints should not be confused with control or construction joints.

Control joints are normally found in concrete or masonry walls and concrete slabs-on-grade. They are provided to: 1) prevent cracking of the wall or slab due to excessive tensile forces in the concrete or masonry caused by shrinkage upon drying; or 2) induce cracking due to excessive tensile forces caused by drying shrinkage to occur at a predetermined location, hence the term "control" joint.

Construction joints are used as a stopping and starting point for two successive concrete placements (pours) in walls, floors, and beams. Since a construction joint must be designed to transfer load across the joints, separation due to thermal or moisture induced movements is not anticipated.

Seismic joints may be found in buildings other than those that are rectangular in plan (e.g., L- and T-shaped buildings) in areas where the risk of an earthquake is moderate to high. Such joints in multi-story buildings can be as much as 12 in. (30.5 cm) in width. They are provided to allow the separated portions of the building to act independently of each other to undergo differential lateral displacements when an earthquake occurs.

With expansion or seismic joints, consideration should be given to the ability of the protecting system to remain in place and perform its intended function after repeated movements of the joint, and with the width of the joint varying from its maximum to minimum width. In the case of seismic joints, the protection system may be damaged during an earthquake that otherwise is not strong enough to cause major structural damage to the building. Therefore, it is necessary to conduct an inspection of those buildings after an earthquake.

Note that 6-2.4.1 and 6-2.4.2 apply to all occupancies unless the specific occupancy provides an exception. Protection of vertical openings is normally covered in the 3.1 subsection of each occupancy chapter.

Protection of vertical openings is of extreme importance if fire casualties are to be reduced. In report after report of fires involving fatalities, the major factors that contributed to loss of life included, again and again, unprotected vertical openings.

A correlation frequently exists between life loss from fire and monetary loss from fire, in that vertical fire spread is a major factor contributing to the extensive property damage characteristic of large loss building fires. This relates directly to the lack of protection for vertical openings, in that the principal structural weakness responsible for vertical spread of fire is the absence of the fire cutoffs at openings between floors.

Figure 6-5 illustrates some typical floor openings.

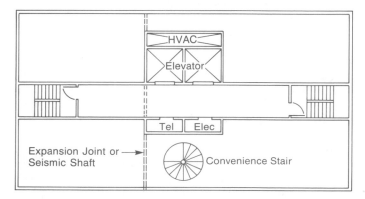

Figure 6-5. Typical Floor Openings in a Building that Result in Vertical Openings.

6-2.4.3*   The minimum fire resistance rating for the enclosure of floor openings shall be as follows (*see 5-1.3.1 for enclosure of exits*):

(a) Enclosures connecting four stories or more in new construction — 2-hour fire barriers.

(b) Other enclosures in new construction — 1-hour fire barriers.

(c) Enclosures in existing buildings — ½-hour fire barriers.

(d) As specified in Chapter 16 for new hotels, Chapter 18 for new apartment buildings, and in Chapter 20 for lodging and rooming houses.

An interior exit stair by definition (*see 5-1.2.3*), in order to be separated from other building spaces and to provide a protected way of travel to the exit discharge, must be enclosed. If not properly enclosed, it not only negates meeting the definition of an exit but also creates an unprotected vertical opening. Thus, an exit stair must meet both the requirements for enclosure of exits (*see 5-1.3.1*) and protection of vertical openings per this paragraph. Given that the requirements for enclosure of exits are more stringent than the requirements for protection of vertical openings, once the more stringent requirements are met, the other requirements are usually automatically met.

Paragraph 6-2.4.3(d) references the hotel, apartment, and lodging and rooming house occupancy chapters, which under certain conditions allow exceptions to the requirements of 6-2.4.3. In addition to occupancy chapters that use exceptions to be more lenient with respect to the enclosure of vertical openings than the basic Chapter 6 requirements, it is possible for a specific occupancy to be more stringent. For example, Chapter 12 for new health care occupancies, in recognition that the building occupants may be incapable of self-preservation and thus difficult to move, requires that vertical openings, regardless of number of communicating stories, be enclosed by construction having a 2-hour fire resistance rating. For specific exceptions to the stringent 2-hour requirement, see 12-3.1.1.

A-6-2.4.3   The application of the 2-hour rule, in buildings not divided into stories, may be based on the number of levels of platforms or walkways served by the stairs.

The key to understanding 6-2.4.3 is the fact that the *Code*'s concern is with the number of stories connected, not the height of the building. For example, if there is a vertical opening between the second, third, and fourth stories of an eight-story building, the enclosure of the opening must be of 1-hour and not 2-hour fire resistance rated construction.

Where addressing vertical openings, the *Code* does not use the height of buildings or a designated number of floors aboveground as the basis for its requirements. Rather, it refers to the total number of floors connected by the vertical opening. Where a vertical opening connects any total of four stories or more, whether they are all above the exit discharge level, all below the exit discharge level, or any combination thereof, the protection afforded must have at least a 2-hour fire resistance rating. (*See Figure 6-6.*) Where three stories or less are connected by the vertical opening, the rating must be at least 1-hour. (*See Figures 6-7, 6-8, and 6-9.*)

Experience shows that under some circumstances, each of the 1- and 2-hour rating levels provides a more-than-comfortable period of time for the occupants of a building to get out. On the other hand, there are times when the integrity of the construction will be taxed to its limit, e.g., during a situation in which a fire that has gone undetected for a long period generates heavy smoke and toxic gases, complicating evacuation by blocking the exit access. Further, allowance should be made for possible combinations of horizontal and vertical travel along the exit way.

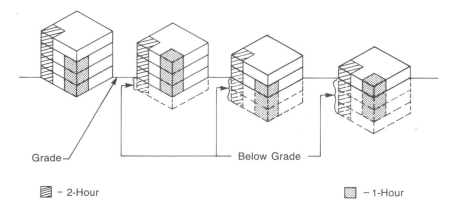

Grade   Below Grade

▨ – 2-Hour   ▦ – 1-Hour

Figure 6-6. Connecting Four Stories or More, Vertical Openings Must Be Enclosed in 2-Hour Construction.

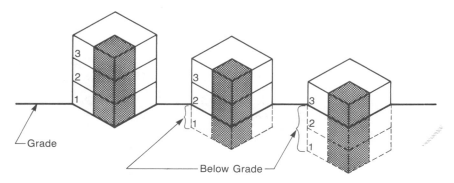

Grade

Below Grade

Figure 6-7. Connecting Three Stories or Less, Vertical Openings Must Be Enclosed in 1-Hour Construction (Shaded Areas).

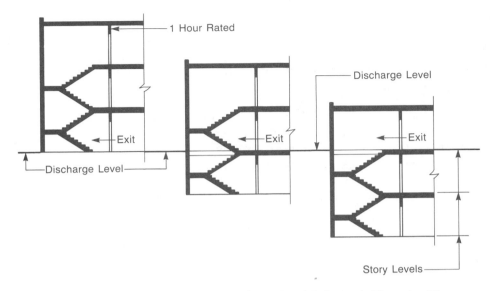

Figure 6-8. No Matter Where the Discharge Level Is Located, There Are Three Stories Connected in Each of the Arrangements Illustrated; Thus, the Enclosure Must Have at Least a 1-Hour Fire Resistance Rating. If more than three stories are involved, a 2-hour fire resistance rating is required.

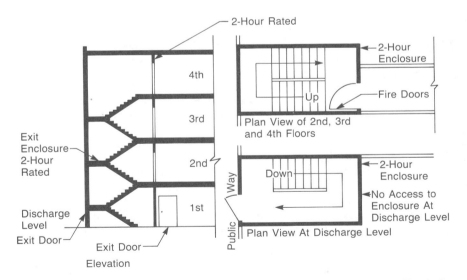

Figure 6-9. While the Stairway Serves Three Stories, the Stairway Is a Vertical Opening Among Four Stories; Thus, According to 6-2.4.3, the Enclosure Must Have at Least a 2-Hour Fire Resistance Rating.

6-2.4.4   Where permitted by Chapters 8 through 30, unenclosed floor openings forming a communicating space between floor levels are permitted, provided that the following conditions are met:

(a) The communicating space does not connect more than three contiguous stories.

(b) The lowest or next to lowest story within the communicating space is a street floor.

(c) The entire floor area of the communicating space is open and unobstructed such that a fire in any part of the space will be readily obvious to the occupants of the space prior to the time it becomes a hazard to them.

(d) The communicating space is separated from the remainder of the building by fire barriers with at least a 1-hour fire resistance rating.

Exception to (d): In buildings protected throughout by an approved automatic sprinkler system in accordance with Section 7-7, a smoke barrier in accordance with Section 6-3 may serve as the required separation.

(e) The communicating space has ordinary hazard contents protected throughout by an approved automatic sprinkler system in accordance with Section 7-6 or has only low hazard contents. (*See 4-2.2.*)

(f) Exit capacity is sufficient to provide to for all the occupants of all levels within the communicating space to simultaneously egress the communicating space by considering it as single floor area in determining the required exit capacity.

(g)* Each story within the communicating space, considered separately, has at least one-half of its individual required exit capacity provided by an exit or exits leading directly out of that story without occupants having to traverse another story within the communicating space.

A-6-2.4.4(g)   Given that a mezzanine, meeting the maximum ⅓ area definition of mezzanines per Chapter 3, is not a "story," it can therefore have 100 percent of its exit access within the communicating area back through the story below.

Paragraph 6-2.4.4 recognizes a vertical opening that is exempt from the normal enclosure requirements of 6-2.4.3 if such recognition is specifically permitted by the occupancy chapter for the occupancy type in question and if all the alternative protection provisions (a) through (g) of 6-2.4.4, as explained and illustrated below, are met:

(a) The vertical space cannot connect or communicate among more than three stories, and all connected stories are required to be contiguous to each other. The building itself, which houses the vertical opening in question, may be more than three stories in height. For example, the vertical opening might communicate among floors one through three of a six-story building. (*See Figure 6-10.*)

(b) The lowest of the maximum three communicating floor levels is at, or not more than one level below, the street level. In other words, the vertical opening can communicate among only the first, second, and third floors or among the basement, first, and second floors. (*See Figure 6-10.*) As mentioned above, additional building floor levels may be present either above or below the floors involving the vertical opening, but these additional floors cannot be left open to the vertical opening. If it is necessary or desirable either to have more than three levels open or to locate the communicating levels such that the lowest level does not meet the placement requirement with respect to street level, the more stringent set of provisions for atriums per 6-2.4.5 should be considered. Again, the occupancy chapter applicable to the occupancy in question must specifically recognize the use of the atrium provisions of 6-2.4.5.

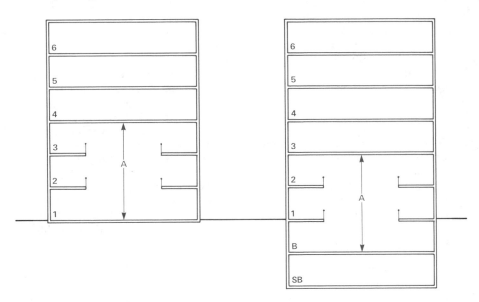

Figure 6-10.   Lowest Level of Maximum Three-Story Vertical Opening (A) Must Be At, or Not More Than, One Level Below, the Street Floor.

(c) The communicating space, meaning all areas within the vertical opening itself and all adjoining areas left open to the vertical opening, i.e., not separated by minimum 1-hour fire resistance rated barriers, must be open and unobstructed so as to allow awareness of fire and smoke conditions, which might emanate from any part of the communicating space, to occupants of the space prior to the time that such conditions become a hazard to them.

The provisions of 6-2.4.4 were written originally as an Exception to the enclosure requirements for vertical openings as a recognition of typical mercantile occupancy construction practices, which left partial, mezzanine-like floors open to the main street-level shopping floor below. Such arrangements were sufficiently open that when coupled with the other provisions of the Exception, they allowed for the necessary awareness of emergency conditions in sufficient time to make use of the egress system. It was not the intent to recognize use of the Exception for something like an unenclosed stairway. The small opening created by the unenclosed stairway is insufficient in size to allow for the needed degree of awareness.

Somewhere between the two extremes of vast amounts of openness, as in the case with the mezzanine-like floors described above, and little or no openness, as depicted above by the unenclosed stair, the problem of judging sufficient openness becomes difficult. Through use of the equivalency concept addressed in Section 1-5 of the *Code*, some authorities having jurisdiction have allowed complete automatic smoke detection systems with proper occupant notification features to be substituted for the openness and unobstructedness required by the *Code* for awareness and early warning purposes.

(d) The communicating space must be separated from the remainder of the building by fire barriers with minimum 1-hour fire resistance rating. Once the boundaries of the communicating space are established, for example based on determining how much area is open enough per requirement (c) above to allow for awareness and early warning, areas outside these boundaries must be separated from the communicating space associated with the vertical opening by barriers with a minimum 1-hour fire resistance rating. If the building is fully sprinklered, the barriers may be reduced to zero fire resistance rating but must resist the passage of smoke and meet the other smoke barrier requirements of Section 6-3. It is thought that the sprinkler system will control the fire and obviate the need for fire resistance rated barriers. The smoke barriers will control the limited smoke, under sprinklered conditions, and help maintain a tenable means of egress route.

In the case, for example, of a hotel building with fingerlike guest room wings fanning out from the vertical opening, it can be assumed that the guest room wing corridors will need separation from the vertical opening because persons in the corridor on the second or third floor will not be readily aware of a fire on the first floor before the fire becomes a hazard to them. The required 1-hour separation can be provided while the perception of openness is maintained by isolating the guest room wings from the vertical opening through the use of pairs of cross-corridor doors held open with automatic release devices. (*See Figure 6-11.*)

(e) If the communicating space, meaning the vertical opening itself and all adjoining areas open to it as described in (c) above, has ordinary hazard contents, per the definition of Section 4-2 of this *Code*, as opposed to the NFPA 13, *Standard for the Installation of Sprinkler Systems*,[18] definition of ordinary hazard occupancies, all areas within the confines of the communicating space must be sprinklered. If the contents are low hazard, again as defined by Section 4-2 of this *Code*, as opposed to the definition of light hazard occupancies from the sprinkler installation standard, no sprinklering is required by 6-2.4.4 itself. However, as stated and intended by Chapter 4, Classification of Occupancy and Hazard of Contents, of this *Code* most occupancies are ordinary hazard. Given that only low hazard and ordinary hazard contents are addressed in 6-2.4.4(e), high hazard contents therefore are prohibited from any vertical openings recognized by 6-2.4.4.

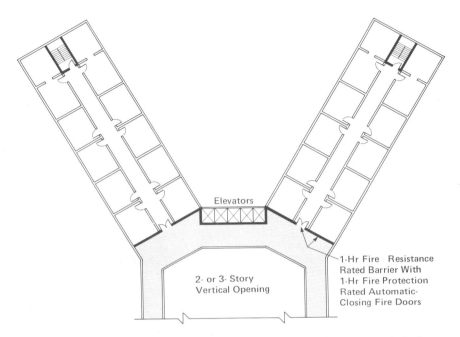

Figure 6-11.   With Cross-Corridor Fire Doors Held Open by Automatic Release Devices, Corridor Appears to Be Open to the Communicating Area of the Vertical Opening. Sprinkler protection must be provided for the vertical opening and the shaded adjoining areas up to the 1-hour barriers.

Although sprinklering is required with ordinary hazard contents, only the communicating area, as defined above, needs to be sprinklered by the provisions of 6-2.4.4. The sprinkler system should cover all areas within the boundaries established by the 1-hour fire barriers required by (d) above. (*See Figure 6-11.*)

(f) Because all occupants within the communicating area might be exposed within a short period of time to the effects of a fire within the area, simultaneous evacuation capability needs to be provided. Thus, the combined occupant load for all spaces, on all levels, within the boundaries of the communicating area needs to be used to size the means of egress for the communicating area. This represents an exception to the guidelines of 5-3.1.4, which normally exempt the accumulation of occupant loads from various floors.

(g) Each story of the building, for which any portion of that story is part of the communicating area associated with the vertical opening, must have at least one-half of that entire story's exit capacity provided by one or more exits (*see 5-1.2.3 definition*) that can be entered on that story and that then go to exit discharge without walking across any *other* level of the communicating space. Thus, for example, if there are two enclosed stairways from the upper floors associated with the communicating space, one must discharge directly outside and one can discharge through the street level of the communicating space in accordance with 5-7.2.

The above requirement also seems to intend that, as long as one-half of the exit capacity is provided so as not to require traversing some other level of the communicating area, one-half of the exit capacity may be arranged so as to force the traversing of some other level of the communicating space. This might, for some occupancies, involve traveling, for example, from floor two over an unenclosed, i.e., open, stair within the communicating area to and across floor one to the exit door to the outside. The path of travel, in this case, across the second floor, down the open stair, and across the first floor, is all exit access and must meet all *Code* requirements, such as maximum allowable travel distance. Not all occupancies would allow the vertical travel over the open stair as a means of reaching a required exit. For example, although Chapter 28 for industrial occupancies specifically allows use of the provisions of 6-2.4.4, it requires that a minimum of two exits be provided for every story and thus would not allow exit access travel to another story in order to reach either of the two required exits.

It is not the *Code*'s intent to prohibit any horizontal exit access travel through the communicating area as part of any or all egress routes serving any section of the building. Thus, exit access can be 100 percent via horizontal travel through the communicating area. (*See Figure 6-12.*)

The following occupancies permit the use of the provisions of 6-2.4.4. Check the referenced paragraphs for any limitations or additional requirements. For example, Chapters 10 and 11 for educational occupancies recognize 6-2.4.4 only if the entire building is protected by a supervised automatic sprinkler system.

Assembly — 8-3.1 Exception No. 1, 9-3.1 Exception No. 1
Educational — 10-3.1.1 Exception, 11-3.1.1 Exception
Detention and Correctional — 14-3.1.1 Exception No. 3, 15-3.1.1 Exception No. 3
Hotels — 16-3.1.1 Exception No. 1, 17-3.1.1 Exception No. 1
Apartments — 19-3.1.1 Exception No. 4
Residential Board and Care — 21-3.3.1.1 Exception No. 1
Mercantile — 24-3.1 Exception No. 1, 25-3.1 Exception No. 2
Business — 26-3.1.1 Exception No. 1, 27-3.1.1 Exception No. 1
Industrial — 28-3.1.1 Exception No. 1
Storage — 29-3.1.1 Exception No. 1

6-2.4.5* Atriums.   Where permitted by Chapters 8 through 30, an atrium may be utilized provided the following conditions are met:

(a)* No horizontal dimension between opposite edges of the floor opening is less than 20 ft (6.1 m), and the opening is a minimum of 1,000 sq ft (93 sq m).

(b) The exits are separately enclosed from the atrium in accordance with 6-2.4.3.

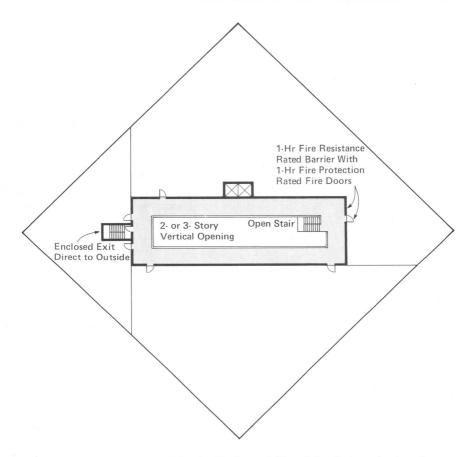

Figure 6-12. Access to Exit via Horizontal Travel in Communicating Space Permitted. Exit access over open stair allowed unless occupancy chapter requires two exits *on* each floor. Vertical opening and shaded areas require sprinklers.

Access to exits may be within the atrium. Exit discharge in accordance with 5-7.2 may be within the atrium.

(c) The occupancy within the space meets the specifications for classification as low or ordinary hazard contents. (*See 4-2.2.*)

(d) The entire building is protected throughout by an approved supervised automatic sprinkler system in accordance with Section 7-7.

Exception to (d): *Where the ceiling of the atrium is more than 55 ft (17 m) above the floor, the authority having jurisdiction may permit the omission of sprinklers at the top of the atrium.*

(e) In new construction, an engineered smoke control system acceptable to the authority having jurisdiction shall be provided. Factors such as means of egress and smoke control of adjacent spaces shall be considered.

Exception to (e): *In lieu of an engineered smoke control system, a smoke removal system acceptable to the authority having jurisdiction may be considered.*

(f)* In new construction, the required engineered smoke control system or smoke removal system shall be independently activated by each of the following:

1. Approved smoke detectors located to detect smoke above the highest floor level of the atrium and at return air intakes from the atrium, and

2. The required automatic sprinkler system, and

3. Manual controls that are readily accessible to the fire department.

(g) In new construction, atriums shall be separated from the adjacent spaces by fire barriers with at least a 1-hour fire resistance rating with opening protectives as for corridor walls. [See 6-2.3.2(b) Exception No. 2.]

Exception No. 1 to (g): *Any three levels of the building may open directly to the atrium without enclosure.*

*Exception No. 2 to (g):** *Glass walls may be used in lieu of the fire barriers where automatic sprinklers are spaced 6 ft (183 cm) apart or less along both sides of the glass wall, not more than 1 ft (30.5 cm) from the glass, and with the automatic sprinklers located so that the entire surface of the glass is wet upon operation of the sprinklers. The glass shall be tempered, wired, or laminated glass held in place by a gasket system that permits the glass framing system to deflect without breaking (loading) the glass before the sprinklers operate. Automatic sprinklers are not required on the atrium side of the glass wall where there is no walkway or other floor area on the atrium side above the main floor level. Doors in such walls may be glass or other material that will resist the passage of smoke. Doors shall be self-closing or automatic-closing upon detection of smoke.*

The allowance to omit the lines of closely spaced sprinklers on the atrium side of glass walls, used in lieu of 1-hour fire resistance rated barriers, is intended to apply to the floor levels above the atrium main floor level. In other words, if glass walls are used on the main floor level in lieu of 1-hour enclosure, sprinklers must be installed on both sides of the glass at that level because the atrium floor provides the possibility for combustibles to be placed on the atrium side of the glass at that level. (*See Figure 6-13.*)

A-6-2.4.5   Where atriums are used, there is an added degree of safety to occupants because of the large volume of space into which smoke can be dissipated. However, there is a need to ensure that dangerous concentrations of smoke are promptly removed from the atrium, and the exhaust system needs careful design.

A-6-2.4.5(a)   As some atriums may be of other than square or rectangular shape, the 20-ft (6.1-m) measurement obviously cannot be applied where the corners exist. This would necessitate that the designer and the authority having jurisdiction work out equivalent life safety.

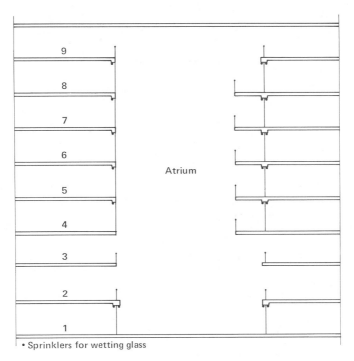

• Sprinklers for wetting glass

Figure 6-13. Levels 2, 3, and 9 Open to Atrium; Levels 1 and 4 Through 8 Enclosed by Glass Walls. Sprinklers required on non-atrium side of all glass walls, on atrium side at base of atrium, and on atrium side on other levels with walkways.

A-6-2.4.5(d) Exception Automatic sprinklers have been successfully tested at ceiling heights up to 50 ft (15 m). Permission is granted the authority having jurisdiction to omit sprinklers at higher ceiling heights, since it has not been demonstrated that sprinklers directly over the fire will effectively respond to the fire in a timely manner.

A-6-2.4.5(e) Exception The following information gives guidance for the smoke removal system, which may be used in lieu of an engineered smoke control system:

A mechanical exhaust system at the top of the atrium arranged so that the space does not become pressurized.

For additional information see: Butcher and Parnell, Smoke Control in Fire Safety Design (*see Appendix B*); and A-15-3.1.3.

Volume Determination. The volume of an atrium is determined by calculating all the space having a common atmosphere. The presence of a fire barrier with protected openings, whether developed by fire barriers or specially designed glass walls with special sprinkler protection, is intended to provide the limits of the common atmosphere.

A-6-2.4.5(f)   Activation of the ventilation system by manual fire alarms, extinguishing systems, and detection systems can cause unwanted operation of the system, and it is suggested that consideration be given to zoning of the activation functions so the ventilation system operates only when actually needed.

A-6-2.4.5 Exception No. 2 to (g)   The intent of the requirement for closely spaced sprinklers to wet the atrium glass wall is to ensure that the surface of the glass is wet upon operation of the sprinklers with a maximum spacing of sprinklers of 6 ft (183 cm) on centers. Provided that it can be shown that the glass can be wet by the sprinklers using a given discharge rate, and that the 6-ft (183-cm) spacing is not exceeded, then the intent of the requirement is met.

The concept of wetting the glass that is exposed to a fire, without specifying a water application rate, is similar to boiling water in a Pyrex® container over an open flame. As long as there is some water present to absorb the heat, the glass itself does not reach excessive temperatures that would cause failure. To assure that water will reach the surface of the glass, window blinds and draperies must not be placed between the line of closely spaced sprinklers and the glass. Careful design will allow for the sprinklers to be placed close enough to the glass to allow blinds and draperies to be installed within normal installation distances from the glass.

The following occupancies permit the use of atriums in accordance with 6-2.4.5. Check the referenced paragraphs for any additional limitations or restrictions:

Assembly — 8-3.1 Exception No. 2, 9-3.1 Exception No. 2

Health Care — 12-3.1.1 Exception No. 6, 13-3.1.1 Exception No. 4

Detention and Correctional — 14-3.1.1 Exception No. 4, 15-3.1.1 Exception No. 4

Hotels — 16-3.1.1 Exception No. 2, 17-3.1.1 Exception No. 2

Apartment Buildings — 18-3.1.1 Exception No. 2, 19-3.1.1 Exception No. 2

Residential Board and Care — 21-3.3.1.1 Exception No. 2

Mercantile — 24-3.1 Exception No. 3 (*also see* 24-4.5), 25-3.1 Exception No. 4 (*also see* 25-4.5)

Business — 26-3.1.1 Exception No. 3 (*also see* 26-4.3), 27-3.1.1 Exception No. 3 (*also see* 27-4.3)

Industrial — 28-3.1.1 Exception No. 2

Storage — 29-3.1.1 Exception No. 2

Figures 6-14a and b illustrate a typical atrium.

Plan View

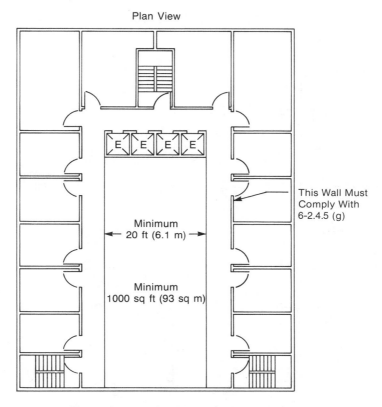

Figure 6-14a. Plan View of a Typical Atrium.

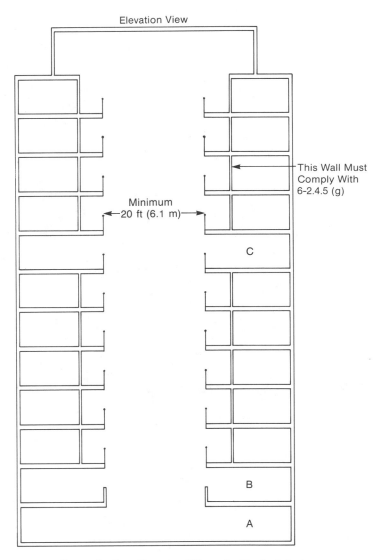

Figure 6-14b. Elevation View of a Typical Atrium.

It is not the *Code*'s intent that the provisions of 6-2.4.5 must be used in lieu of the provisions of 6-2.4.4 to protect an atrium that connects only two or three floor levels just because the vertical opening is called an atrium. Rather, use of the provisions of 6-2.4.4, if allowed by the specific occupancy, should adequately protect a two- or three-story atrium.

6-2.4.6 Any escalators or moving walks serving as a required exit in existing buildings shall be enclosed in the same manner as exit stairways. (*Also see 5-2.7.*)

Where used as an exit, an escalator must be completely enclosed with fire-rated construction, including entrance and discharge doors. It is rare to find an escalator enclosed in such a manner as to qualify as an exit. Note that 5-2.7 prohibits escalators from constituting any part of required means of egress in new buildings.

6-2.4.7 Escalators or moving walks not constituting an exit shall have their floor openings enclosed or protected as required for other vertical openings.

Exception No. 1: In lieu of such protection, in buildings protected throughout by an approved automatic sprinkler system in accordance with Section 7-7, escalator or moving walk openings may be protected in accordance with the method detailed in NFPA 13, Standard for the Installation of Sprinkler Systems, or in accordance with a method as approved by the authority having jurisdiction.

Exception No. 2: Escalators in large open areas such as atriums and enclosed shopping malls.

Exception No. 3: In lieu of such protection, in buildings protected throughout by an approved automatic sprinkler system in accordance with Section 7-7, escalators or moving walk openings may be protected by rolling steel shutters appropriate for the fire resistance rating of the vertical opening protected. The shutters shall close automatically by smoke detection and sprinkler operation, independently of each other. There shall be a manual means of operating and testing the operation of the shutter. The shutters shall be operated at least once a week to assure that they remain in proper operating condition. The shutters shall operate at a speed of not more than 30 ft per minute (.15 m/s) and shall be equipped with a sensitive leading edge. The leading edge shall arrest the progress of a moving shutter and cause it to retract a distance of approximately 6 in. (15.2 cm) upon the application of a force not in excess of 20 lbf (90 N) applied to the surface of the leading edge. The shutter, following this retraction, shall continue to close. The operating mechanism for the rolling shutter shall be provided with standby power complying with the provisions of NFPA 70, National Electrical Code.

A-6-2.4.7 Exception No. 1 The intent of the Exception is that a limitation be placed on the size of the opening to which the protection applies. The total floor opening should not exceed twice the projected area of the escalator or moving walk at the floor. Also, the arrangement of the opening is not intended to circumvent the requirements of 6-2.4.5.

As with any opening through a floor, the openings around the outer perimeter of the escalators should be considered as vertical openings. The sprinkler, draft stop installation is intended to provide adequate protection for these openings, provided that the criteria of NFPA 13, *Standard for the Installation of Sprinkler Systems*, as well as the area criteria described above are met.

An important exception contained in 6-2.4.7 provides that escalators not part of the means of egress need not be enclosed if certain provisions are met.

The sprinkler-draft curtain method is detailed in NFPA 13, *Standard for the Installation of Sprinkler Systems*. It consists of surrounding the escalator opening, in an otherwise fully sprinklered building, with an 18-in. (45.7-cm) deep draft stop located on the underside of the floor to which the escalator ascends. This would serve to delay the heat, smoke, and combustion gases developed in the early stages of a fire on that floor from entering into the escalator well. A row of closely spaced automatic sprinklers located outside of the draft stop also surrounds the escalator well. When activated by heat, the sprinklers provide a water curtain. A typical installation is shown in Figure 6-15. In combination with the sprinkler system in the building, this system should be effective in delaying fire spread and allowing time for evacuation.

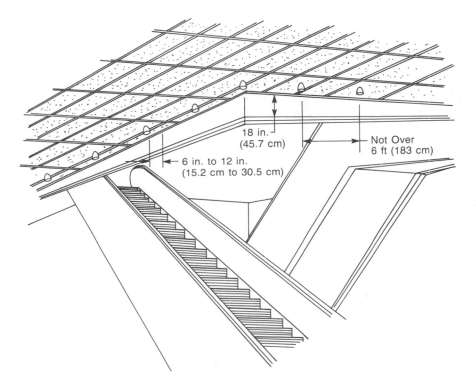

18 in. (45.7 cm)

Not Over 6 ft (183 cm)

6 in. to 12 in. (15.2 cm to 30.5 cm)

Figure 6-15.   Sprinklers Around an Escalator.

Several methods were detailed in prior editions of this *Code* to permit the use of unenclosed escalators in completely sprinklered buildings, where the escalators are not used as exits. The authority having jurisdiction may consider one of these methods in addition to the sprinkler-draft curtain or rolling shutter methods when evaluating existing buildings. These include:

(a) A sprinkler-vent method;

(b) A spray nozzle method; and

(c) A partial enclosure method.

The following discussion details these three methods.

(a) Sprinkler-Vent Method. Under the conditions specified, escalator or moving walk openings may be protected by the sprinkler-vent method, consisting of a combination of an automatic fire or smoke detection system, automatic exhaust system, and an automatic water curtain meeting the following requirements and of a design meeting the approval of the authority having jurisdiction:

1. The exhaust system should be of such capacity as to create a downdraft through the escalator or moving walk floor opening. The downdraft should have an average velocity of not less than 300 ft/min (1.5 m/s) under normal conditions for a period of not less than 30 minutes.

This requirement can be met by the provisions of an air intake from the outside of the building above the floor opening. The test of the system under "normal" conditions requires that the velocity of the downdraft be developed when windows or doors on the several stories normally used for ventilation are open. The size of the exhaust fan and exhaust ducts must be sufficient to meet such ventilation conditions. Experience indicates that fan capacity should be based on a rating of not less than 500 cfm/sq ft (8.3 cu m/s/sq m) of moving stairway opening to obtain the 300 ft/min (1.5 m/s) velocity required. If the building is provided with an air conditioning system, arranged to be automatically shut down in the event of fire, the test conditions should be met with the air conditioning system shut down. The 300 ft/min (1.5 m/s) downdraft through the opening provides for the testing of the exhaust system without requiring an expansion of air present under actual fire conditions.

2. Operation of the exhaust system for any floor opening should be initiated by an approved device in the story involved and should be one of the following means in addition to a manual means for operating and testing the system:

(i) Thermostats — fixed temperature, rate-of-rise, or a combination of both.

(ii) Water flow in the sprinkler system.

(iii) Approved supervised smoke detection. Smoke detection devices, if used, should be so located that the presence of smoke is detected before it enters the stairway.

3. Electric power supply to all parts of the exhaust system and its control devices should be designed and installed for maximum reliability. The electric power supply provisions of NFPA 20, *Standard for the Installation of Centrifugal Fire Pumps*,[20] may be referred to as a guide to design and installation features to assure maximum reliability.

4. Any fan or duct used in connection with an automatic exhaust system should be of the approved type and should be installed in accordance with the applicable standards listed in Chapter 32 and Appendix B.

5. Periodic tests, not less frequently than quarterly, should be made of the automatic exhaust system to maintain the system and the control devices in good working condition.

6. The water curtain should be formed by open sprinklers or spray nozzles so located and spaced as to form a complete and continuous barrier along all exposed sides of the floor opening and reaching from the ceiling to the floor. Water intensity for the water curtain should be not less than approximately 3 gal per min per lineal ft (0.6 L/sec/m) of water curtain, measured horizontally around the opening.

7. The water curtain should operate automatically from thermal-responsive elements of fixed temperature type so placed with respect to the ceiling (floor) opening that the water curtain comes into action upon the advance of heat toward the escalator or moving walk opening.

8. Every automatic exhaust system, including all motors, controls, and automatic water curtain system, should be supervised in an approved manner, similar to that specified for automatic sprinkler system supervision.

(b) Spray Nozzle Method. Under the conditions specified, escalator openings may be protected by the spray nozzle method, consisting of a combination of an automatic fire or smoke detection system and a system of high velocity water spray nozzles meeting the following requirements and of a design meeting the approval of the authority having jurisdiction.

1. Spray nozzles should be of the open type and should have a solid conical spray pattern with discharge angles between 45 and 90 degrees. The number of nozzles, their discharge angles, and their location should be such that the escalator or moving walk opening between the top of the wellway housing and the treadway will be completely filled with dense spray on operation of the system.

2. The number and size of nozzles and water supply should be sufficient to deliver a discharge of 2 gal of water/sq ft/min (1.4 L/sq m/sec) through the wellway, area to be figured perpendicularly to treadway. (*See Figure 6-16.*)

3. Spray nozzles should be so located as to effectively utilize the full advantage of the cooling and counterdraft effect. They should be so positioned that the center line of spray discharge is as closely in line as possible with the slope of the escalator or moving walk, not more than an angle of 30 degrees with the top slope of the wellway housing. Nozzles should also be positioned so that the center line of discharge is at an angle of not more than 30 degrees from the vertical sides of the wellway housing.

4. Spray nozzles should discharge at a minimum pressure of at least 25 lb/sq in. (172 kPa). Water supply piping may be taken from the sprinkler system, provided that in so doing an adequate supply of water will be available for the spray nozzles and the water pressure at the sprinkler farthest from the supply riser is not reduced beyond the required minimum. Supply taken from the sprinkler system is designed to provide protection to the wellway opening for life hazard during the exit period, but may not be relied upon to provide an effective floor cutoff.

5. Control valves should be readily accessible to minimize water damage.

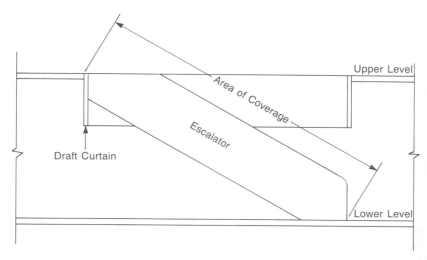

Figure 6-16. Area of Coverage for the Spray Nozzle Method of Protecting Vertical Openings.

6. A noncombustible or limited-combustible draft curtain should be provided extending at least 20 in. (50.8 cm) below and around the opening, and a solid noncombustible wellway housing at least 5 ft (152 cm) long, measured parallel to the handrail and extending from the top of the handrail enclosure to the soffit of the stairway or ceiling above, at each escalator floor opening should also be provided. When necessary, spray nozzles should be protected against mechanical injury or tampering that might interfere with proper discharge. (*See Figure 6-17.*)

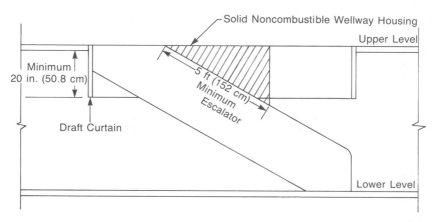

Figure 6-17. The Draft Curtain and Wellway Housing Method of Protecting Vertical Openings.

7. The spray nozzle system should operate automatically from thermal response elements of the fixed temperature type, so placed with respect to the ceiling (floor) opening that the spray nozzle system comes into action upon the advance of heat towards the escalator opening. Supervised smoke detection located in or near the escalator opening may be used to sound an alarm. The spray nozzle system should also be provided with manual means of operation. Smoke detection devices are not desirable for action of the spray nozzles as accidental discharge must be safeguarded against from both a panic hazard as well as a property damage standpoint.

8. Control valves for the spray nozzle system and approved smoke detection or thermostatic devices should be supervised in accordance with the applicable provisions of Section 7-6.

(c) Partial Enclosure Method. Under the conditions specified, escalator or moving walk openings may be protected by a partial enclosure, or so-called kiosk, so designed as to provide an effective barrier to the spread of smoke from floor to floor.

1. Partial enclosures should be of construction providing fire resistance equivalent to that specified for stairway enclosures in the same building, with openings therein protected by approved self-closing fire doors, or may be of approved wired glass and metal frame construction with wired glass panel doors.

2. Such doors may be equipped with an electric opening mechanism to open the door automatically upon the approach of a person. The mechanism should be such as to return the door to its closed position upon any interruption of electric current supply, and the adjustment should be such that the pressures generated by a fire will not cause opening of the door.

6-2.5 Concealed Spaces.

6-2.5.1* In new Type III, Type IV, or Type V construction, any concealed space in which materials having a flame-spread rating greater than Class A (as defined in Section 6-5) are exposed shall be effectively firestopped or draftstopped as provided below:

(a) Every exterior and interior wall and partition shall be firestopped at each floor level, at the top-story ceiling level, and at the level of support for roofs.

(b) Every unoccupied attic space shall be subdivided by draftstops into areas not to exceed 3,000 sq ft (280 sq m).

(c) Any concealed space between the ceiling and the floor or roof above shall be draftstopped for the full depth of the space along the line of support for the floor or roof structural members and, if necessary, at other locations to form areas not to exceed 1,000 sq ft (93 sq m) for any space between the ceiling and floor and 3,000 sq ft (280 sq m) for any space between the ceiling and roof.

Exception No. 1: If the space is protected throughout by an approved automatic sprinkler system in accordance with Section 7-7.

Exception No. 2: Concealed spaces serving as plenums. (See NFPA 90A, Standard for the Installation of Air Conditioning and Ventilating Systems.)

A-6-2.5.1 The area limitations are based on life safety considerations and are not intended to suggest that changes should be made in local building codes having similar or more restrictive requirements that are based on other reasons. Building codes generally contain detailed information on the proper selection and installation of firestopping materials.

The vertical spread of fire through shafts, chases, and hollow wall construction and the horizontal spread of fire through plenums and open attics are phenomena common to many serious fires. Where such spaces are protected with automatic sprinklers, the risk of unseen fires is minimized. Where this protection is not installed in new buildings of other than Type I or II construction, as defined by NFPA 220 and the commentary following 6-2.1, and the materials used have a flame spread rating of more than 25 (i.e., not Class A), certain additional precautions are required.

Draftstopping of attic spaces is particularly important in "one-story and attic" shopping centers and in two-story apartment buildings or row houses. Experience has shown that fires starting in one of these occupancy units frequently breaks into the attic space, spreads through the attic, and travels down into adjoining units.

Numerous fires in garden apartments have demonstrated two common weaknesses relating to the lack of adequate firestopping and draftstopping. The areas frequently not firestopped either are between the underside of the roof deck and the top of fire walls that do not extend above the roofline or are in the pipe chase that contains the plumbing vent stack. The vent stack is of particular concern because it frequently is between two mirror-image apartment units and interconnects all the floors of the apartment building. A fire that travels into this concealed space can spread to the attic and soon involve the entire structure.

Chapter 3 defines draft stop as follows: "A continuous membrane to subdivide a concealed space to restrict the passage of smoke, heat, and flames."

6-2.5.2   In every existing building, firestopping and draftstopping shall be provided as required by the provisions of Chapters 8 through 30.

An example of an occupancy chapter requiring firestopping appears in 13-1.6.5 for existing health care occupancies where firestopping is required between basement and first floor.

SECTION 6-3   SMOKE BARRIERS

6-3.1*   Where required by Chapters 8 through 30, smoke barriers shall be provided to subdivide building spaces for the purpose of restricting the movement of smoke.

A-6-3.1   Wherever smoke barriers and doors therein require a degree of fire resistance as may be specified by requirements in the various occupancy chapters (Chapters 8 through 30), the construction is more appropriately a fire barrier that has been defined: "to limit the spread of fire and restrict the movement of smoke." (*See 6-2.3.2 and 6-2.3.3.*)

It is a misnomer to refer to a "1-hour fire resistance rated smoke barrier." It is more correct to refer to a "smoke barrier which additionally has a 1-hour fire resistance rating." A barrier with only a fire resistance rating does not necessarily make an effective smoke barrier. For example, the fire barrier, if rated at less than 2 hours, would not be required to have either a fire damper or smoke damper where ductwork penetrates the barrier. A smoke barrier, in accordance with Section 6-3, would have ducted penetrations protected by smoke dampers per 6-3.5.1. For additional information on fire barrier testing, rating, and installation, see the commentaries following 6-2.3.1 and 6-2.3.4.

6-3.2* Smoke barriers required by this *Code* shall be continuous from outside wall to outside wall, from a floor to a floor, from a smoke barrier to a smoke barrier, or a combination thereof; including continuity through all concealed spaces such as those found above a ceiling, including interstitial spaces.

Exception: A smoke barrier required for an occupied space below an interstitial space is not required to extend through the interstitial space, provided the construction assembly forming the bottom of the interstitial space provides resistance to the passage of smoke equal to that provided by the smoke barrier.

A-6-3.2 To ensure that a smoke barrier is continuous, it is necessary to seal completely all openings where the smoke barrier abuts other smoke barriers, fire barriers, exterior walls, the floor below, and the floor or ceiling above.

It is not the intent to prohibit a smoke barrier from stopping at a fire barrier if the fire barrier meets the requirements of a smoke barrier (i.e., the fire barrier is a combination smoke barrier/fire barrier).

In occupancies where evacuation is a last resort or is expected to be otherwise delayed, smoke barriers and doors therein will require a degree of fire resistance as specified by the requirements found in the occupancy chapters (Chapters 8 through 30) of the *Code.*

Other openings in smoke and fire barriers must be protected as well. Heating, air conditioning, and ventilation ducts provide a ready path for smoke and fire to travel from one area to another unless carefully protected. Penetrations in walls and ceiling construction for utility lines and other building services must be firestopped to prevent fire spread. The hidden spaces behind suspended ceilings and attic spaces are out of sight and easily overlooked.

The Exception to 6-3.2 must be used with extreme care for several reasons. First, several chapters require the smoke barrier to have some fire resistance rating and therefore could only terminate at the ceiling if the ceiling could also obtain this rating. (*See commentary on 6-2.2.2.*) Also, even if no fire resistance were required, it is difficult to assure that a ceiling is smoketight unless it is of monolithic construction without air handling penetrations. However, this kind of construction is often found in apartment buildings, hotels, and dormitories, and consequently, the exception can be useful.

6-3.3   A fire barrier may also be used as a smoke barrier if it meets the requirements of 6-3.4 through 6-3.6.

6-3.4 Doors.

6-3.4.1*   Doors in smoke barriers shall close the opening with only a minimum clearance necessary for proper operation and shall be without undercuts, louvers, or grilles.

A-6-3.4.1   The clearance for proper operation of smoke doors has been defined as ⅛ in. (0.3 cm). For additional information on the installation of smoke-control door assemblies, see NFPA 105, *Recommended Practice for the Installation of Smoke- and Draft-Control Door Assemblies.*

> NFPA 105, *Recommended Practice for the Installation of Smoke- and Draft-Control Door Assemblies,*[20] acknowledges that a nationally recognized test specifically related to evaluating smoke-control doors does not exist. However, that document suggests that a test method developed for use in measuring the rate of air leakage through exterior doors may provide a reasonable measure of the leakage rate of smoke-laden ambient-temperature air and may be modified for also measuring the leakage of elevated temperature air. Thus, the test method described in ASTM E283, *Standard Test Method for Rate of Air Leakage through Exterior Windows, Curtain Walls, and Doors,*[21] should give satisfactory performance if, additionally, recognized design features are taken into account, such as close-fitting assemblies, limited deflections, and the use of gasketing and sealing materials. The document then provides performance criteria suggesting maximum air leakage rates expressed in air volume per time per area of door opening.

6-3.4.2*   Where a fire resistance rating for smoke barriers is specified elsewhere in the *Code*, the doors in the smoke barriers shall have a fire protection rating of at least 20 minutes. Vision panels in such doors shall be approved transparent wired glass.

Exception No. 1:   If a different fire protection rating for smoke barrier doors is specified by Chapters 8 through 30.

Exception No. 2:   Latching hardware is not required on doors in smoke barriers where so indicated by Chapters 8 through 30.

A-6-3.4.2   In existing installations only, a 1¾-in. (4.4-cm) solid bonded wood core door has been considered a satisfactory substitute for a door with a 20-minute fire protection rating.

> Doors in smoke barriers are not required to have a fire protection rating unless the occupancy chapter requires the smoke barrier to have a fire resistance rating. Therefore, any door that resists the passage of smoke, even a hollow core wood door or glass door, would be acceptable provided it is tight fitting. Stops at the head and sides of the door will help resist the passage of smoke. Where a pair of doors is used, it is

recommended (required in health care occupancies) that they open in opposite directions from each other so that rabbets, bevels, or astragals can be provided at the meeting edges without the use of coordinators. (*Also see 12-3.7.8.*)

Doors in smoke barriers, while not the equivalent of fire doors, and not completely smoketight, are effective in restricting the spread of smoke and reducing drafts, which might otherwise spread fire rapidly. Where the smoke barrier is required to have a fire resistance rating by an occupancy chapter, a 20-minute fire protection rated door assembly in a smoke partition has been accepted by the Committee on Safety to Life as a reasonable barrier. It has been shown by tests that the commonly used 1¾-in. (4.4-cm) solid wood core door assembly can be expected to fail in 22 to 24 minutes, and has performed well in actual fires when closed.[22] The use of the 20-minute designation replaces a specification standard with a performance standard. The same reference emphasizes that even fully rated fire doors will not keep out smoke because of the clearances needed to have the door work properly. Gasketing will help, but a tight-fitting door should keep out enough smoke so that orderly exiting may proceed.

6-3.4.3* Doors in smoke barriers shall be self-closing or automatic-closing and shall comply with the provisions of 5-2.1.

A-6-3.4.3 When, because of operational necessity, it is desired to have smoke barrier doors normally open, such doors should be provided with hold-open devices that are activated to close the doors by the operation of smoke detectors and other alarm functions.

Doors in a fire separation, horizontal exit, or smoke barrier should be closed at all times to impede the travel of smoke and fire gases. Functionally, however, this involves decreased efficiency and, for example, limits patient observation by the professional staff of a health care occupancy. To accommodate these necessities, it is practical to presume that the doors will be kept open even to the extent of employing wood chocks and other makeshift devices. When, because of operational necessity, it is desired to have smoke barrier doors normally open, such doors should be provided with hold-open devices that are activated to close the doors by the operation of smoke detectors. For additional information on the use of smoke detectors for releasing service, see the commentary associated with 7-6.3.2 Exceptions No. 3 and 4.

6-3.5 Smoke Dampers.

6-3.5.1 An approved damper designed to resist the passage of smoke shall be provided at each air-transfer opening or duct penetration of a required smoke barrier.

Exception No. 1: Smoke dampers may be omitted in ducts or air-transfer openings that are part of an engineered smoke control system in accordance with Section 7-3.

Exception No. 2: Smoke dampers may be omitted in ducts where the air continues to move and the air-handling system installed is arranged to prevent recirculation of exhaust or return air under fire emergency conditions.

Exception No. 3: Smoke dampers may be omitted where the air inlet or outlet openings in ducts are limited to a single smoke compartment.

Exception No. 4: Smoke dampers may be omitted where ducts penetrate floors that serve as smoke barriers.

Exception No. 5: Smoke dampers may be omitted where specifically permitted by Chapters 8 through 30.

Exception No. 1 to 6-3.5.1 addresses the omission of dampers in ducts that must remain open so that the smoke control system can operate. Exception No. 2 to 6-3.5.1 can be used only in very limited cases. It can be used only on small ventilation systems since NFPA 90A, *Standard for the Installation of Air Conditioning and Ventilating Systems,* requires that systems over 15,000 cfm (7.1 cu m/sec) that are not part of a smoke control system shut down upon detection of smoke. (*See NFPA 90A, Section 4-3.*) Even without the restriction of NFPA 90A, it is difficult to ensure that the air handling system will be in continuous operation. In this day of energy conservation, many systems are either cycled or shut down during parts of the day, or this feature could be added later without recognizing its potential detriment to building life safety. However, the exception can be useful for ductwork for small ventilation systems, such as for bathrooms or small suites.

Exception No. 3 to 6-3.5.1 covers situations where an "express" duct has no openings other than in a single smoke compartment. It can reasonably be extended to situations as illustrated in Figures 6-18a and b.

6-3.5.2   Required smoke dampers in ducts penetrating smoke barriers shall close upon detection of smoke by:

(a) Approved smoke detectors installed in accordance with Chapter 9 of NFPA 72E, *Standard on Automatic Fire Detectors,* or

(b) Approved local smoke detectors on either side of the smoke barrier door opening where ducts penetrate smoke barriers above the smoke barrier doors, or

(c) Approved smoke detectors located within the ducts in existing installations.

6-3.5.3   Required smoke dampers in air transfer openings shall close upon detection of smoke by approved smoke detectors installed in accordance with Chapter 9 of NFPA 72E, *Standard on Automatic Fire Detectors.*

Exception: Where a duct is provided on one side of the smoke barrier, the smoke detectors on the duct side shall be in accordance with 6-3.5.2.

NFPA 72E, *Standard on Automatic Fire Detectors,*[23] provides information on the installation of smoke detectors for closing smoke dampers. In addition, the *Code* continues to allow the damper to be closed by the same

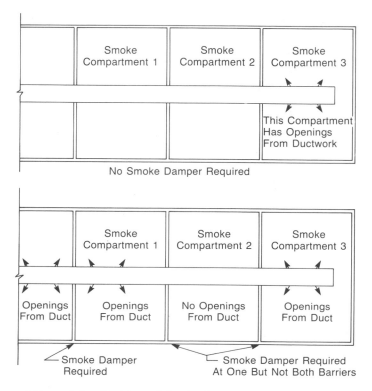

Figures 6-18a and b. Position of Smoke Dampers in Air-Handling Ductwork Utilizing Exception No. 3 to 6-3.5.1.

detector that closes the door in a smoke barrier if the duct penetrates the wall above the door. Existing installations of induct detectors, which may not be totally in compliance with NFPA 72E, continue to be recognized.

Item (c) does not prohibit the use of induct detectors in new construction provided that the installation complies with NFPA 72E as permitted in item (a).

6-3.6 Penetrations and Miscellaneous Openings in Floors and Smoke Barriers.

6-3.6.1   Pipes, conduits, bus ducts, cables, wires, air ducts, pneumatic tubes and ducts, and similar building service equipment that pass through floors and smoke barriers shall be protected as follows:

(a) The space between the penetrating item and the smoke barrier shall:

1. Be filled with a material capable of maintaining the smoke resistance of the smoke barrier, or

2. Be protected by an approved device designed for the specific purpose.

(b) Where the penetrating item uses a sleeve to penetrate the smoke barrier, the sleeve shall be solidly set in the smoke barrier, and the space between the item and the sleeve shall:

1. Be filled with a material capable of maintaining the smoke resistance of the smoke barrier, or

2. Be protected by an approved device designed for the specific purpose.

(c) Where designs take transmission of vibration into consideration, any vibration isolation shall:

1. Be made on either side of the smoke barrier, or

2. Be made by an approved device designed for the specific purpose.

6-3.6.2   Openings occurring at points where floors or smoke barriers meet the outside walls, other smoke barriers, or fire barriers of a building shall:

(a) Be filled with a material capable of maintaining the smoke resistance of the floor or smoke barrier, or

(b) Be protected by an approved device designed for the specific purpose.

As with fire barriers, it is important to maintain the integrity of smoke barriers over the life of a building.

Figure 6-19 illustrates some of the key items regarding smoke barrier penetrations discussed in 6-3.4 through 6-3.6.

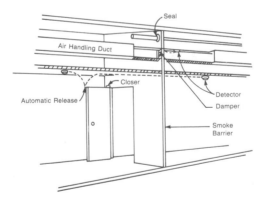

Figure 6-19.   Typical Penetrations of a Smoke Barrier.

SECTION 6-4   SPECIAL HAZARD PROTECTION

6-4.1 General.   Protection shall be provided from any area having a degree of hazard greater than that normal to the general occupancy of the building or structure, such as those areas used for storage of combustibles or flammables, areas housing heat-producing appliances, or areas used for maintenance purposes, as follows:

(a) Enclosure with construction in accordance with Section 6-2 with a fire resistance rating as specified by Chapters 8 through 30, but not less than 1 hour without windows and with doors of ¾-hour fire protection rating, or

(b) Protection with automatic extinguishing systems in accordance with Section 7-7 as required by Chapters 8 through 30, or

(c) Both (a) and (b) above where specified by Chapters 8 through 30.

Here, the *Code* attempts to minimize the effects of fire originating in hazardous areas and the need for evacuation by isolating those areas that have a high potential for fire or a high fuel load. The Committees responsible for the occupancy chapters identify the particular hazards against which protection is to be provided and generally address them in the 3.2 subsection of each occupancy chapter. The authority having jurisdiction is responsible for the final determination of what are and are not hazardous areas. This approach represents the fundamental fire protection step of either protecting against the known hazards via automatic extinguishment systems or isolating the known hazards by construction.

6-4.2* Explosion Protection.   Where hazardous processes or storage are of such a character as to introduce an explosion potential, explosion venting or an explosion suppression system specifically designed for the hazard involved shall be provided.

A-6-4.2   For details, see NFPA 68, *Guide for Venting of Deflagrations. (See Appendix B.)*

If the potential hazard is of an explosive nature, explosion venting or explosion suppression systems are required safeguards. NFPA 68, *Guide for Venting of Deflagrations,*[24] contains details of acceptable venting systems, and NFPA 69, *Standard on Explosion Prevention Systems,*[25] covers suppression systems. NFPA 654, *Standard for the Prevention of Dust Explosions in the Chemical, Dye, Pharmaceutical, and Plastics Industries,*[26] is useful where explosive dusts are encountered.

6-4.3 Flammable Liquids.   Flammable liquids shall be protected in accordance with NFPA 30, *Flammable and Combustible Liquids Code.*

6-4.4 Laboratories.   Laboratories that use chemicals shall comply with NFPA 45, *Standard on Fire Protection for Laboratories Using Chemicals,* unless otherwise modified by other provisions of this *Code.*

Exception: Laboratories in health care occupancies and medical and dental offices shall comply with NFPA 99, Standard for Health Care Facilities.

SECTION 6-5   INTERIOR FINISH

6-5.1 General.

6-5.1.1*   Interior finish includes interior wall and ceiling finish and interior floor finish.

A-6-5.1.1   The requirements pertaining to interior finish are intended to restrict the spread of fire over the continuous surface forming the interior portions of a building. Furnishings, which in some cases may be secured in place for functional reasons, should not be considered as interior finish.

The faster a fire develops, the greater a threat it represents to the occupants of a building and the more difficult it will be to control. Wall and ceiling surfaces of a building have a major influence on how fast a fire develops. In establishing restrictions for the use of interior finish materials, the intention is preferably to prevent entirely or, as a minimum, to limit the speed at which flame will travel across the interior surfaces of a building.

Any large fire within a building represents a threat to occupants. A successful fire protection strategy requires that fires be limited in size. Any interior finish that acts as a "fuse" to spread flame to involve objects remote from the point of origin or that contributes "fuel" to the early growth of a fire causing a fire to become large is considered undesirable. The restrictions found in the *Code* for wall and ceiling finishes vary as a function of occupancy characteristics. Where occupants are immobile or have security measures imposed that restrict freedom of movement (as in health care facilities or detention and correctional facilities), conservative interior finish limits are set. In contrast, more relaxed limits are imposed in industrial or storage occupancies where occupants are assumed to be alert and mobile.

Interior finishes are the interior surfaces of a building that are generally secured in place. Thus, wall, ceiling, and column coverings may be considered interior wall and ceiling finishes. The surfaces of movable walls or folding partitions would also be treated as interior wall and ceiling finishes. However, this section uses the expression "but not limited to," which allows the authority having jurisdiction to exercise judgment in determining what constitutes interior finish. For example, a tapestry would not normally be considered as interior finish. However, a large tapestry that is secured to and covers a major portion of a wall could promote the rapid growth of fire and may warrant regulation. (*See the commentary following A-6-5.3.1.*)

Furnishings, including high-backed, plastic-upholstered restaurant "booths," are not normally considered as interior finish even in the case where the furnishings are fixed in place. However, if the furnishings are judged to represent a hazard, they could be regulated as interior finish by the authority having jurisdiction. For example, the continuous expanse of plastic laminates and wood veneers created by the door surfaces of a wall of base cabinets and wall cabinets can be regulated as interior finish.

6-5.1.2   Interior wall and ceiling finish means the exposed interior surfaces of buildings including, but not limited to, fixed or movable walls and partitions, columns, and ceilings.

6-5.1.3   Interior floor finish means the exposed floor surfaces of buildings including coverings that may be applied over a normal finished floor or stair, including risers.

Interior floor finish includes both exposed surfaces of "structural" floor systems and decorative floor treatments, such as carpet or imitation wood flooring. Coverings on stair risers and treads are regulated as interior floor finish, even though risers involve vertical applications. This practice recognizes that floor coverings on risers and treads will perform similarly to other floor surfaces during a fire.

6-5.1.4 Classification of interior finish materials shall be in accordance with tests made under conditions simulating actual installations, provided that the authority having jurisdiction may by rule establish the classification of any material on which a rating by standard test is not available.

For proper evaluation and classification, assemblies of materials must be tested as they will actually be installed. For example, thermally thin coverings will have their performance altered by the nature of the substrate over which they are installed.[27] Adhesives may also be important. In the case of composites, such as textile wall coverings over gypsum board, the adhesive should be sufficient to maintain a bond between the "finish" and the substrate. However, excess adhesive may result in the adhesive contributing to the fire. Tests of textile wall coverings[28] have shown that changing adhesives, or simply changing the application rate for the same adhesive, may significantly alter product performance. Tests to qualify assemblies should use adhesives and application rates similar to actual installations.

Similarly, a product that is tested in intimate contact with a mineral board should be installed in contact with a mineral board or like substrate. In the case where products are tested in intimate contact with a substrate, performance may also be altered by installation of the product with air space behind the covering.

6-5.2* Use of Interior Finishes.

A-6-5.2 Table A-6-5.2 gives a compilation of the interior finish requirements of the occupancy chapters of the *Code*.

6-5.2.1 Requirements for interior wall and ceiling finish shall apply as specified elsewhere in this *Code* for specific occupancies. (*See Chapter 5 and the specific occupancy requirements of Chapters 8 through 30.*)

6-5.2.2* Requirements for interior floor finish shall apply only where (1) there is a floor finish of unusual hazard; or (2) where floor finish requirements are specified elsewhere in this *Code* for specific occupancies. (*See Chapters 8 through 30 for specific occupancy requirements.*)

A-6-5.2.2 This paragraph recognizes that traditional finish floors and floor coverings such as wood flooring and resilient floor coverings have not proved to present an unusual hazard.

Occupancy	Exits	Access to Exits	Other Spaces
Assembly — New			
Class A or B	A	A or B	A or B
Class C	A	A or B	A, B, or C
Assembly — Existing			
Class A or B	A	A or B	A or B
Class C	A	A or B	A, B, or C
Educational — New	A	A or B	A or B
			C on low partitions*
Educational — Existing	A	A or B	A, B, or C
Day-Care Centers—New	A	A	A or B
	I or II	I or II	
Day-Care Centers—Existing	A or B	A or B	A or B
Group Day-Care Homes	A or B	A, B, or C	A, B, or C
Family Day-Care Homes	A or B	A or B	A, B, or C
Health Care — New	A	A	A
		B lower portion of corridor wall*	B in small individual rooms*
	I	I	
Health Care — Existing	A or B	A or B	A or B
Detention & Correctional — New	A*	A*	A, B, or C
	I	I	
Detention & Correctional — Existing	A or B*	A or B*	A, B, or C
	I or II	I or II	
Residential, Hotels & Dormitories — New	A	A or B	A, B, or C
	I or II	I or II	
Residential, Hotels & Dormitories — Existing	A or B	A or B	A, B, or C
	I or II*	I or II*	
Residential, Apartment Buildings — New	A	A or B	A, B, or C
	I or II*	I or II*	

*See Chapters for details.

**See Section 30-1 for occupancy classification.

Notes:

    Class A Interior Wall and Ceiling Finish — flame spread 0-25, smoke developed 0-450.

    Class B Interior Wall and Ceiling Finish — flame spread 26-75, smoke developed 0-450.

    Class C Interior Wall and Ceiling Finish — flame spread 76-200, smoke developed 0-450.

    Class I Interior Floor Finish — minimum 0.45 watts per sq cm.

    Class II Interior Floor Finish — minimum 0.22 watts per sq cm.

    Automatic Sprinklers — where a complete standard system of automatic sprinklers is installed, interior wall and ceiling finish with flame spread rating not over Class C may be used in any location where Class B is required and with rating of Class B in any location where Class A is required; similarly, Class II interior floor finish may be used in any location where Class I is required and no critical radiant flux rating is required where Class II is required.

    Exposed portions of structural members complying with the requirements for heavy timber construction may be permitted.

(Table continued on next page.)

Occupancy	Exits	Access to Exits	Other Spaces
Residential, Apartment Buildings — Existing	A or B I or II*	A or B I or II*	A, B, or C
Residential, Board and Care — See Chapter 21			
Residential, 1- and 2-family, Lodging or Rooming Houses	A, B, or C	A, B, or C	A, B, or C
Mercantile — New	A or B	A or B	A or B
Mercantile — Existing Class A or B	A or B	A or B	ceilings — A or B existing on walls — A, B, or C
Mercantile — Existing Class C	A, B, or C	A, B, or C	A, B, or C
Office — New	A or B I or II	A or B I or II	A, B, or C
Office — Existing	A or B	A or B	A, B, or C
Industrial	A or B	A, B, or C	A, B, or C
Storage	A or B	A, B, or C	A, B, or C
Unusual Structures**	A or B	A, B, or C	A, B, or C

*See Chapters for details.
**See Section 30-1 for occupancy classification.
Notes:
Class A Interior Wall and Ceiling Finish — flame spread 0-25, smoke developed 0-450.
Class B Interior Wall and Ceiling Finish — flame spread 26-75, smoke developed 0-450.
Class C Interior Wall and Ceiling Finish — flame spread 76-200, smoke developed 0-450.
Class I Interior Floor Finish — minimum 0.45 watts per sq cm.
Class II Interior Floor Finish — minimum 0.22 watts per sq cm.
Automatic Sprinklers — where a complete standard system of automatic sprinklers is installed, interior wall and ceiling finish with flame spread rating not over Class C may be used in any location where Class B is required and with rating of Class B in any location where Class A is required; similarly, Class II interior floor finish may be used in any location where Class I is required and no critical radiant flux rating is required where Class II is required.
Exposed portions of structural members complying with the requirements for heavy timber construction may be permitted.

Experience has shown that traditional floor coverings, such as wood flooring and resilient tile, do not contribute to the early growth of fire. Paragraph 6-5.2.2 acknowledges the satisfactory performance of traditional floor coverings and exempts such materials from the restrictions that would otherwise be applicable. However, the authority having jurisdiction is empowered to require substantiation of the performance of any floor covering that may be of a type or nature with which he or she is not familiar. For example, "plastic" imitation wood floors, artificial turf, artificial surfaces of athletic fields, and carpeting are types of products that may merit substantiation. Where the authority having jurisdiction judges that a floor covering warrants testing and substantiation or where an occupancy chapter imposes restrictions — as is the case in Chapters 10 and 11, dealing with day-care centers; Chapters 12 and 13, dealing with health care occupancies; Chapters 14 and 15, dealing with detention and correctional occupancies; Chapters 16, 17, 18, and 19, dealing with residential occupancies; and others — the floor covering would be treated as interior floor finish and would be regulated on the basis of tests conducted with the Flooring Radiant Panel Test as required in 6-5.4.

6-5.2.3* Textile materials having a napped, tufted, looped, woven, nonwoven, or similar surface shall not be applied to walls or ceilings.

Exception No. 1: Such materials may be permitted on the basis of room/corner fire tests acceptable to the authority having jurisdiction that demonstrate that the product, using a product mounting system, including adhesive, representative of actual use, will not spread fire to the edges of the test sample or cause flashover in the test room.

Exception No. 2: Such materials having a Class A rating may be used in rooms or areas protected by an approved automatic sprinkler system.

Exception No. 3: Previously approved, existing, Class A installations.

A-6-5.2.3 Previous editions of the *Code* have regulated textile materials on walls and ceilings using NFPA 255, *Standard Method of Test for Surface Burning Characteristics of Building Materials*. Full scale room/corner fire test research has shown that flame spread indices produced by NFPA 255 may not reliably predict all aspects of the fire behavior of textile wall and ceiling coverings.

Textile materials should be evaluated using a reasonable sized ignition source to show the material will not spread fire to involve objects remote from the area of origin, nor should the textile product generate sufficient energy to cause the room of origin to flashover. Acceptance of textile wall covering materials should be contingent upon qualification tests in which a specific textile/adhesive pair has been evaluated. One means of testing has been developed at the University of California and involved a gas diffusion burner, creating a wastebasket-sized fire exposure (40 kW) for 5 minutes followed by an upholstered chair-sized fire exposure (150 kW) for an additional ten minutes. Results of the research at the University of California have been described in a report entitled, "Room Fire Experiments of Textile Wall Coverings."

Research is continuing to determine if correlation can be achieved between full scale tests and other test methods more suitable for regulatory purposes such as the cone calorimeter, the vertical flame spread apparatus (NBS), and the IMO flame spread test (NBS).

Prior to the 1988 edition of this *Code*, the danger of carpet-like textile coverings used on walls and ceilings was recognized and regulated by a requirement that only the best interior wall and ceiling finishes, i.e., Class A materials, be used, even in a sprinklered building, which normally would allow the use of the next lower class of material per 6-5.7.1. In 1981, a fire at the Las Vegas Hilton Hotel, which resulted in eight deaths, began in an elevator lobby and was fueled by carpet-like interior wall and ceiling finishes that did not meet the qualifications for Class A interior finish.[29] Other than the interior finish materials and a cushioned seat pad on a metal bench, there was little other combustible material to fuel the fire in the elevator lobby. Yet the lobby went to flashover; the fire broke out the windows and climbed to a nearly identical elevator lobby on the floor above; and the events repeated themselves in a leap frog fashion from the eighth floor through the twenty-fourth floor.

Research sponsored by the American Textile Manufacturers' Institute (ATMI), conducted by the Fire Research Laboratory of the University of California at Berkeley between March 1985 and January 1986, and described in the report "Room Fire Experiments of Textile Wall Coverings,"[28] has shown that consideration of only the flame spread rating, as measured by NFPA 255 (*see commentary following 6-5.3.1*), may not reliably predict the fire behavior of textile wall and ceiling coverings. Test results indicate that some Class A textile wall coverings can produce room flashover when subjected to an ignition source scenario which models a small fuel item, such as a wastebasket, igniting a chair or similar furnishing. Other Class A textile wall coverings did not produce room flashover when subjected to the same ignition source scenario. Thus, not all Class A textile wall coverings are alike with respect to potential for producing room flashover. Simply requiring textile wall coverings to be Class A interior wall and ceiling finishes does not assure the level of life safety intended by the *Code*. Exceptions No. 1 and 2 to 6-5.2.3 reflect new, more stringent requirements if textile wall coverings are to be used.

The testing at the University of California was conducted in an 8 × 12 × 8 ft (2.4 × 3.7 × 2.4 m) high room using a gas diffusion burner as an ignition source.[28] Products undergoing evaluation were applied to the walls of the room. The gas diffusion burner was placed in the corner of the room and provided with an ignition source by which various textile wall coverings were evaluated. Two of the sixteen products tested — one a tufted wall covering, the other a woven wall covering — were known to have flame spread ratings of 25 or less when tested in accordance with NFPA 255. When tested in the room/corner procedure these two products readily spread flame and caused the fire in the test room to grow quickly to large size, causing full room involvement — flashover. Concerns relative to performance of these low flame spread textile wall coverings led to the requirement for full scale room/corner testing to qualify products for use in nonsprinklered buildings.

Tests revealed the method of mounting, including adhesive and application rate, can be critically important. Changing the application rate of the same adhesive or changing the adhesive can cause a "safe" product to exhibit unsatisfactory performance.

The testing conducted at the University of California only included wall coverings. Caution should be exercised relative to the use of combinations of textile wall and ceiling coverings. Experience has shown combinations of textile wall/ceiling coverings may result in intense burning.[29] Research conducted at the Illinois Institute of Technology Research[30] has shown flame spread is more likely to occur with combinations of combustible wall and ceiling coverings than those situations involving only combustible wall coverings or only combustible ceiling coverings. Therefore, full scale room/corner testing, using an appropriately sized ignition source, should be conducted to substantiate the performance of textile wall and ceiling coverings.

In Exception No. 1, the authority having jurisdiction can accept test results on textile wall coverings tested by a room/corner fire test. Although there is no nationally recognized room/corner fire test specifically for textile wall coverings, the test protocol developed at the University of California at Berkeley for ATMI and described in the report referenced above is one test method worthy of consideration.

The protocol allows for a screening test to evaluate materials in a full scale environment without the need for lining the entire wall surface area of the room. The test results indicate that materials that produce a peak rate of heat release (RHR) of less than 300 kW and do not spread flame to the perimeter of the test material are not expected to lead to full room involvement, or flashover, when tested in a fully lined room. Materials producing a peak RHR in the 300 - 450 kW range may cause room flashover and thus need to be evaluated in a fully lined room in order to determine their firesafety. This is also true for materials that produce flaming droplets that fall to the floor and continue to burn. Materials that produce a peak RHR in excess of 450 kW during the screening test have a high probability of causing flashover when tested in a fully lined room.

In view of the fact that there is no recognized room/corner test for textile wall coverings, Exception No. 2 to 6-5.2.3 allows such materials if they are Class A *and* the areas in which they are installed are sprinklered. Exception No. 3 continues to recognize existing, previously approved Class A textile wall coverings without requiring sprinklering of the area, because prior to the 1988 edition of the *Code* this would have met the exception to the basic requirement of 6-5.2.3.

6-5.2.4*   Cellular or foamed plastic materials shall not be used as interior wall and ceiling finish.

Exception No. 1: Cellular or foamed plastic materials may be permitted on the basis of fire tests that substantiate on a reasonable basis their combustibility characteristics, for the use intended, in actual fire conditions.

Exception No. 2: Cellular or foamed plastic may be used for trim, not in excess of 10 percent of the wall or ceiling area, provided it is not less than 20 lb/cu ft (320 kg/m³) in density, is limited to ½ in. (1.3 cm) in thickness and 4 in. (10.2 cm) in width, and complies with the requirements for Class A or B interior wall and ceiling finish as described in 6-5.3; however, the smoke rating is not limited.

A-6-5.2.4   Cellular or foam plastic material means a heterogeneous system comprised of at least two phases, one of which is a continuous polymeric organic material, and a second of which is deliberately introduced for the purpose of distributing gas in voids throughout the material, and foamed and unfoamed polymeric or monomeric precursors (prepolymer, if used) plasticizers, fillers, extenders, catalysts, blowing agents, colorants, stabilizers, lubricants, surfactants, pigments, reaction control agents, processing aids and flame retardants.

This section sets forth the fundamental premise that exposed foamed plastics should not be used within buildings. This prohibition is based upon actual fire experience in which foamed plastics have contributed to very rapid fire development.[31] It is also acknowledged that tunnel testing (*per NFPA 255 / ASTM E84, see 6-5.3.1*) may not accurately assess the potential hazard of "plastics" in general. Therefore, if cellular or foamed plastics are to be used within a building, their use should be substantiated on the basis of full-scale fire tests or fire testing that simulates conditions of actual use.

Exception No. 2 addresses the limited use of plastics as a substitute for traditional wood trim. The exception suggests that foamed or cellular plastic materials may be used as trim assuming the performance under fire exposure will be comparable to that of wood. In establishing a minimum density of 20 lb/cu ft (320 kg/cu m), it is intended to prohibit the use of light [1 to 3 lb/cu ft (16 to 48 kg/cu m)] foamed plastics as trim. To control the "mass" of the material that can be used, limits have been established on width and thickness.

Limiting plastic trim to Class A or B materials, in combination with the 10 percent area limit of walls and ceilings, forms a more restrictive position than would be applicable to wood. This more restrictive position is established to ensure that the performance of the plastic trim will be equivalent to, or better than, that of traditional materials.

In establishing the 10 percent limit, it is intended that the trim will be used around doors and windows or at the junction of walls and ceilings. Therefore, the trim will be uniformly distributed throughout the room. There would be a significant difference in the probable performance if the 10 percent is concentrated in one area, and this exception intends to prohibit such a condition.

6-5.2.5   For requirements on decorations and furnishings not meeting the definition of interior finish, see 31-1.2 and 31-1.4.

6-5.3 Interior Wall and Ceiling Finish Classification.

6-5.3.1*   Interior wall and ceiling finish shall be classified in accordance with 6-5.3.2 based on test results from NFPA 255, *Standard Method of Test of Surface Burning Characteristics of Building Materials.*

Flame spread and smoke development are both recorded in the results of a test conducted in accordance with NFPA 255, *Method of Test of Surface Burning Characteristics of Building Materials,*[32] also known as ASTM E84, *Standard Test Method for Surface Burning Characteristics of Building Materials.*[33] Fuel contributed values are no longer recorded as a required portion of the test procedure. (*See A-6-5.3.2.*)

Interior wall and ceiling finish classifications, per 6-5.3.2, are based mainly on flame spread ratings with an additional requirement that smoke development not exceed a common value of 450 regardless of the class into which the material falls based on flame spread. Flame spread ratings offer a general indication of the speed with which fire may spread across the surface of a material. In assessing the hazard presented by a material on the basis of flame spread, it is assumed a person may be in close proximity to the fire and would thereby be directly exposed to the energy associated with the actual flames. Smoke developed ratings, on the other hand, address obscuration of the egress path by smoke. Given that the smoke development value is a cumulative measurement over the prescribed test duration, it considers both quantity and rate of smoke liberation. Thus, an interior wall and ceiling finish material with a low smoke development value should allow for better visibility in a given egress route than a material with a high smoke development value.

The *Code* requires the use of specific classes of interior wall and ceiling finish materials, which in effect are differentiated by their allowable flame spread rating, based on consideration of installed location within the building and its egress paths and on the occupancy in question. Different classes of interior finish materials are specified for an office area, for example, as compared to an exit stair enclosure or exit access corridor. The different classes recognize that, in escaping a building, people must move away from the flames while traveling through the means of egress toward an exit. The classes of interior finishes that are considered acceptable within an open office are, therefore, different from those that are required for exit enclosures. Similarly, occupancies characterized by occupants with evacuation difficulties have stricter interior finish requirements than occupancies with normal ambulatory occupants. For example, although both hospitals and hotels provide sleeping accommodations, the interior finish requirements are more severe for hospitals based on occupant incapability of self-preservation.

The same smoke developed limit is used for all three flame spread classifications. This limit recognizes that smoke generated during a fire may affect visibility both in the vicinity of and remote from the fire. Large building volumes can be quickly filled with smoke as a result of a fire. An upper limit has been established, therefore, that applies to interior finish materials irrespective of where the materials are located.

An exception is created for existing buildings. In existing buildings, interior finish materials are restricted only on the basis of flame spread. Editions of the *Life Safety Code* prior to 1976 did not regulate interior finish materials based upon smoke development. As a general rule, the replacement of existing materials that previously received approval on the basis only of flame spread is not warranted.

The smoke developed limit of 450 was developed on the basis of research conducted at Underwriters Laboratories Inc.[34] Smoke from the tunnel test chamber was distributed into a 5,000-cu ft (140-cu m) room. The room was equipped with illuminated exit signs. The time required to reach various stages of exit sign obscuration was recorded and compared to the smoke developed rating for the various materials involved. The report states "materials having smoke developed ratings above 325 showed 'good' to 'marginal' visibility (scale readings of 3—4.8) in a few cases; other materials produced conditions of 'marginal' to obscuration in the six minute period."

Considering both time and smoke levels, the 450 limit on smoke ratings as used in the *Code* is what has been judged to be a "reasonable" limit. In considering flame spread and smoke development, it should be emphasized that there is no direct relationship between the two. In the report referenced above, for example, one material had a flame spread rating of 490 and a smoke developed factor of 57, while another had a flame spread rating of 44 and a smoke developed factor of 1,387.

The 450 smoke developed limit is based solely on obscuration. Although not addressed by the requirements on interior finishes, other important factors in evaluations of materials based on smoke generation involve irritability and toxicity of gases. Smoke may also act as an irritant, further reducing visibility, and may in addition have a debilitating physiological effect on people attempting to escape from a building. These effects are not evaluated by the current smoke developed limit. Previous editions of the *Code* allowed the authority having jurisdiction to regulate products that present an "unreasonable life hazard due to the character of the products of decomposition." This provision was deleted in the 1988 Edition of the *Code* due to the unenforceable nature of the requirement. The adverse physiological effects on the human body resulting from exposure to heat and the effects from inhaling hot gases should also be considered as part of an overall hazard risk assessment separate from the Section 6-5 interior finish requirements.

A-6-5.3.1   It has been shown that the method of mounting interior finish materials may affect actual performance. Where materials are tested in intimate contact with a substrate to determine a classification, such materials should be installed in intimate contact with a similar substrate. Such details are especially important for "thermally thin" materials. For further information refer to NFPA 255, *Method of Test of Surface Burning Characteristics of Building Materials.*

Some interior wall and ceiling finish materials, such as fabrics not applied to a solid backing, may not lend themselves to a test made in accordance with NFPA 255, *Method of Test of Surface Burning Characteristics of Building Materials (see Appendix B)*. In these cases the large-scale test outlined in NFPA 701, *Standard Methods of Fire Tests for Flame-Resistant Textiles and Films (see Appendix B)*, may be used.

Samples are tested in accordance with NFPA 255, *Method of Test of Surface Burning Characteristics of Building Materials,*[32] with a noncombustible backing. Specimens are tested with adhesives, joints, and other conditions that would simulate the actual installation of a product in a building. NFPA 255 will provide a general indication of product performance only if the product is installed in a fashion similar to that which was tested. Data is available to show that the performance of interior finish materials varies on the basis of mounting conditions.[27] For example, a product installed over a combustible substrate will tend to propagate fire more readily than would be typical of the same product installed over a noncombustible substrate. Further, a wall covering installed with air space behind the covering would tend to spread flame more readily than one installed in contact with a noncombustible substrate. Mounting techniques, therefore, must be carefully considered in the evaluation of probable product performance.

In the case, for example, where decorative fabric is hung in front of a wall surface and covers a significant portion of that wall, the loosely hanging fabric creates a continuous surface that can spread flame and thus should be regulated under the subject of interior finish. Testing by NFPA 255, which reports a flame spread rating and smoke development value that can be used to classify the interior finish per 6-5.3.2, would not provide meaningful information for this specific use. Thus, Appendix note A-6-5.3.1 suggests that testing per NFPA 701, *Standard Methods of Fire Tests for Flame-Resistant Textiles and Films*,[35] may be of use to the authority having jurisdiction in judging the safety of hanging fabrics that constitute interior finish.

NFPA 701 describes two procedures, the small-scale and the large-scale test, which both apply a flame for a specified time period to a vertical sample. Upon removal of the flame-producing burner, the sample must self-extinguish and not have charred more than a specified distance in order to pass the test. Evidence of passing the NFPA 701 test should help in evaluating the installation even though a strict Class A, B, or C determination of interior finish classification, per 6-5.3.2, cannot be made.

6-5.3.2*   Interior wall and ceiling finishes shall be grouped in the following classes in accordance with their flame spread and smoke development:

Class A Interior Wall and Ceiling Finish.   Flame spread 0-25, smoke developed 0-450. Includes any material classified at 25 or less on the flame spread test scale and 450 or less on the smoke test scale described in 6-5.3.1. Any element thereof when so tested shall not continue to propagate fire.

Class B Interior Wall and Ceiling Finish.   Flame spread 26-75, smoke developed 0-450. Includes any material classified at more than 25 but not more than 75 on the flame spread test scale and 450 or less on the smoke test scale described in 6-5.3.1.

Class C Interior Wall and Ceiling Finish.   Flame spread 76-200, smoke developed 0-450. Includes any material classified at more than 75 but not more than 200 on the flame spread test scale and 450 or less on the smoke test scale described in 6-5.3.1.

Exception: Existing interior finishes complying with the above flame spread ratings only may be continued in use.

A-6-5.3.2   Prior to 1978, the test report described by NFPA 255, *Method of Tests of Surface Burning Characteristics of Building Materials*, included an evaluation of the fuel contribution as well as the flame spread rating and the smoke development value. However, it is now recognized that the measurement on which the fuel contribution is based does not provide a valid measure. Therefore, although the data are recorded during the test, the information is no longer normally reported. Classification of interior wall and ceiling finish thus relies only on flame spread index and smoke development value.

The Class A, B, or C designations used by the *Life Safety Code* and the *Standard Building Code* correlate directly with the Class I, II, or III designations used in the *National Building Code*[6] and the *Uniform Building Code*[5].

6-5.3.3   Wherever the use of Class C interior wall and ceiling finish is required, Class A or B shall be permitted. Where Class B interior wall and ceiling finish is required, Class A shall be permitted.

This section recognizes that the *Code* sets minimum criteria. One may always use an interior finish that performs better than that specifically prescribed by *Code*.

6-5.3.4   The classification of interior finish specified in 6-5.3.2 shall be that of the basic material used by itself or in combination with other materials.

Exception No. 1:   Subsequently applied paint or wall covering not exceeding $\frac{1}{28}$ in. (.09 cm) in thickness unless of such character or thickness or so applied as to affect materially the flame spread or smoke development characteristics.

Exception No. 2:   Exposed portions of structural members complying with the requirements for Type IV (2HH) construction per NFPA 220, Standard on Types of Building Construction.

Interior finish classifications apply to the basic materials used, such as wood, gypsum board, plaster, or any combination of the materials. Exception No. 1 notes that thin coverings — not exceeding $\frac{1}{28}$ in. (.09 cm) in thickness — will not significantly affect the performance of the basic wall or ceiling material. Thermally thin coverings, such as paint and wallpaper coverings, where secured to a noncombustible substrate will not significantly alter the performance of the substrate during a fire. However, thicker coverings, such as multiple layers of wallpaper, can and have contributed to rapid fire growth in actual fires. For example, multiple layers of wall coverings contributed to rapid fire growth in the multiple-death fire in the Holiday Inn in Cambridge, Ohio, which occurred on July 31, 1979.[36] Exception No. 1 would cause any wall or ceiling covering in excess of $\frac{1}{28}$ in. (.09 cm) in thickness to be treated as interior finish.

Exception No. 2 recognizes that exposed surfaces of heavy timber structural members, such as wood columns, beams, and girders, although they often have flame spread ratings in the 76 to 200 flame spread range and thus receive a Class C interior finish classification, can be safely used where Class A and B interior finish is required because the structural members occur on specific spacings and do not constitute a continuous surface to allow flame to spread, for example, across a ceiling.

6-5.4 Interior Floor Finish Classification.

Experience and full-scale fire test data have shown that floor coverings of modest resistance to flame spread are unlikely to become involved in the early growth of a fire. Regulation of flooring materials based upon flammability considerations should, therefore, only be undertaken where required by the *Code* or where a need is clearly recognized. Regulation of flooring materials in general use areas of a building, excepting those that are judged to represent an unusual hazard, is usually not warranted.

When the judgment is made to regulate floor coverings, the evaluation is to be made based upon tests conducted in accordance with NFPA 253, *Standard Method of Test for Critical Radiant Flux of Floor Covering Systems Using a Radiant Heat Energy Source,*[37] also known as ASTM E648, *Standard Test Method for Critical Radiant Flux of Floor-Covering Systems Using a Radiant Heat Energy Source.*[38] The Flooring Radiant Panel Test was specifically developed to evaluate the tendency of a floor covering material to propagate flame.

Fire tests have been conducted by the National Bureau of Standards (see NBSIR 76-1013, "Flame Spread of Carpet Systems Involved in Room Fires[39]") to demonstrate that carpet that passes the Federal Flammability Standard FF-1-70 "Pill Test"[40] is not likely to become involved in a fire until a room reaches or approaches flashover. Since all carpet manufactured for sale in the United States has been required since April 1971 to meet the "Pill Test," no further regulation is necessary for carpet located within rooms.

On the other hand, it has been shown that floor coverings may propagate flame under the influence of a sizable exposure fire. For example, it has been shown that carpet located in a corridor may spread flame when subjected to the energy emanating from the doorway of a room fully developed in fire. The fire discharges flame and hot gases into the corridor causing a radiant heat energy exposure to the floor. It has been shown that the level of energy radiating onto the floor is a significant determinant as to whether or not progressive flaming will occur. NFPA 253, *Standard Method of Test for Critical Radiant Flux of Floor Covering Systems Using a Radiant Heat Energy Source,* measures the minimum energy required in watts per square centimeter on the floor covering to sustain flame. This minimum value is termed the critical radiant flux. The Flooring Radiant Panel Test, therefore, provides a measure of a floor covering's tendency to spread flames when located in the corridor and exposed to the flame and hot gases from a room fire.

In summary, the Flooring Radiant Panel Test Method is to be used as a basis for estimating the fire performance of a floor covering installed in the building corridor or exit. Floor coverings in open building spaces and in rooms within buildings merit no further regulation provided the floor covering is at least as resistant to flame spread as a material that will meet the Federal Flammability Standard FF-1-70 "Pill Test."

Interior floor finishes should be tested as proposed for use. For example, where a carpet is to be used with a separate underlayment, the carpet should be evaluated with a separate underlayment. The Flooring Radiant Panel Test specifies a carpet may be tested using either the "standard" underlayment as defined in NFPA 253, *Standard Method of Test for Critical Radiant Flux of Floor Covering Systems Using a Radiant Heat Energy Source,* or the carpet may be tested over the actual underlayment proposed for use. Data generated using the "standard" underlayment is intended to allow the carpet tested to be used over any separate underlayment. Where assembly tests are conducted with an underlayment different from the standard underlayment, the results of such tests are valid only for the specific combination tested.

Floor coverings are not regulated on the basis of smoke generation. Smoke development limits are not believed to be practical or necessary. It is not necessary to establish smoke limits because, as indicated in the foregoing discussion, floor coverings generally will not contribute to a fire until the fire has grown to large proportions. Under the circumstances, the minimal benefits achieved by imposing smoke development limits does not generally warrant such regulation. Further, it is not considered practical to regulate on the basis of smoke, as no regulatory test method exists that has been shown capable of producing data that correlates with the performance of products in actual fires.

6-5.4.1* Interior floor finish shall be classified in accordance with 6-5.4.2 based on test results from NFPA 253, *Standard Method of Test for Critical Radiant Flux of Floor Covering Systems Using a Radiant Heat Energy Source.*

A-6-5.4.1   The flooring radiant panel provides a measure of a floor covering's tendency to spread flames when located in a corridor and exposed to the flame and hot gases from a room fire. The Flooring Radiant Panel Test method is to be used as a basis for estimating the fire performance of a floor covering installed in the building corridor. Floor coverings in open building spaces and in rooms within buildings merit no further regulation, providing it can be shown that the floor covering is at least as resistant to spread of flame as a material that will meet the federal flammability standard, FF1-70, Standard for the Surface Flammability of Carpets and Rugs (Pill Test). All carpeting sold in the U.S. since 1971 is required to meet this standard and therefore is not likely to become involved in a fire until a room reaches or approaches flashover. Therefore, no further regulations are necessary for carpet other than carpet in exitways and corridors.

It has not been found necessary or practical to regulate interior floor finishes on the basis of smoke development.

6-5.4.2   Interior floor finishes shall be grouped in the following classes in accordance with the critical radiant flux ratings:

Class I Interior Floor Finish.   Critical radiant flux, minimum of 0.45 watts per square centimeter as determined by the test described in 6-5.4.1.

Class II Interior Floor Finish.   Critical radiant flux, minimum of 0.22 watts per square centimeter as determined by the test described in 6-5.4.1.

Note that the greater the critical radiant flux value is, expressed in watts per square centimeter, the more resistant the floor finish is to flame propagation. Thus, a Class I interior floor finish, with a critical radiant flux of 0.45 watts per square centimeter or higher, should perform better under fire conditions than a Class II interior floor finish material with its lesser critical radiant flux value of 0.22 to less than 0.45 watts per square centimeter. Contrast that concept with the 6-5.3.2 classification of interior wall and ceiling interior finish materials for which higher flame spread ratings generally denote the poorer performers under fire conditions.

6-5.4.3 Wherever the use of Class II interior floor finish is required, Class I interior floor finish shall be permitted.

6-5.5 Trim and Incidental Finish. Interior wall and ceiling finish not in excess of 10 percent of the aggregate wall and ceiling areas of any room or space may be Class C materials in occupancies where interior wall and ceiling finish of Class A or Class B is required.

This paragraph is intended to allow the use of wood trim around doors and windows as a decoration or functional molding, as chair rails, and the like. Wood trim (*see 6-5.2.4, Exception No. 2 for restrictions applicable to plastic trim*) must meet the criteria for Class C materials. Where such trim is used in rooms or spaces requiring the use of Class A or B products, the trim may constitute not more than 10 percent of the aggregate wall or ceiling area. It is intended in establishing the 10 percent area limit that the trim will be more or less uniformly distributed throughout the room or space. If the trim is concentrated in one sizable continuous pattern, for example on one wall of a room, the materials could contribute to rapid fire growth, and application of this paragraph as substantiation for such a practice would be in error.

6-5.6 Fire Retardant Coatings.

6-5.6.1 The required flame spread or smoke developed classification of surfaces of walls, partitions, columns, and ceilings may be secured by applying approved fire retardant coatings to surfaces having higher flame spread ratings than permitted. Such treatments shall comply with the requirements of Chapter 3, NFPA 703, *Standard for Fire Retardant Impregnated Wood and Fire Retardant Coatings for Building Materials.*

6-5.6.2 Fire retardant coatings shall possess the desired degree of permanency and shall be maintained so as to retain the effectiveness of the treatment under the service conditions encountered in actual use.

Fire retardant paints, coatings, and penetrants are sometimes used to improve the flame spread ratings of materials or assemblies used as interior finishes within buildings. Fire retardant treatments may be used to satisfy the flame spread requirements for materials both in new construction and within existing buildings. Fire retardants are generally a surface treatment that, through intumescence or other chemical reaction, will delay ignition of a material and slow flame spread. The basic nature of the material, to which the treatment has been applied, is not changed. Fire exposures of sufficient duration or intensity can ultimately result in burning of a treated material. Therefore, as a fundamental premise, materials with favorable intrinsic performance characteristics are preferred over those that achieve a satisfactory level of performance via externally applied treatments. However, externally applied treatments properly applied and maintained can be effective in achieving reasonable fire performance.

Application of fire retardant paints, coatings, and penetrants must be performed strictly according to the manufacturer's instructions and in conformance with the specimens evaluated by fire tests. With most paints and coatings, this requires an application rate three to four times greater than that of ordinary paints. Application is usually by brush, spray, immersion, or pressure treatment. The treatment should be reapplied or renewed at periodic intervals. Treatments that may be removed by normal maintenance, washing, or cleaning procedures will require periodic examination and renewal to maintain the required level of performance.

The use of fire retardants can improve the performance of some Class C materials to a Class B category, and similarly, Class B materials can, in some cases, be upgraded to Class A. Likewise, materials having flame spread ratings in excess of 200 can sometimes be upgraded into the Class C category.

In approving fire retardant treatments, the authority having jurisdiction should give consideration to any increase in smoke generation that is likely to be produced by the treatment during a fire given that in reducing flame spread, some fire retardant treatments increase smoke generation of a material. In new construction, that material is required to have a smoke developed value of 450 or less.

6-5.7 Automatic Sprinklers.

6-5.7.1   Where an approved automatic sprinkler system is installed in accordance with Section 7-7, Class C interior wall and ceiling finish may be used in any location where Class B is required, and Class B interior wall and ceiling finish materials may be used in any location where Class A is required.

Exception: Unless specifically prohibited elsewhere in this Code.

Although Exception No. 3 to 6-5.2.3 does not specifically prohibit the use of 6-5.7.1, the intent of that Exception, which applies to previously approved, existing Class A installations of carpet-like textile materials used as interior wall and ceiling finishes, is to recognize only Class A and not to recognize Class B textile materials even if the area is sprinklered.

6-5.7.2   Where an approved automatic sprinkler system is installed in accordance with Section 7-7, Class II interior floor finish may be used in any location where Class I interior floor finish is required, and where Class II is required, no critical radiant flux rating is required.

Fire testing and actual fire experience have shown that automatic sprinklers are able to prevent flame spread across the surface of a wall, ceiling, or floor covering. Flame spread limits, applicable to interior wall and ceiling finishes, and critical radiant flux limits, applicable to interior floor finishes, are reduced in areas protected by an automatic sprinkler system. However, there is a value beyond which the potential for flame spread becomes unacceptably high. For example, for the occupancy types with the most lenient interior finish requirements, even in fully sprinklered buildings, interior wall and ceiling finishes must meet the criteria for Class C materials.

REFERENCES CITED IN COMMENTARY

[1]*Designing Buildings for Fire Safety*, NFPA SPP-24, National Fire Protection Association, Boston, 1975, pp. 72-74.

[2]NFPA 251, *Standard Methods of Fire Tests of Building Construction and Materials*, National Fire Protection Association, Quincy, MA, 1985.

[3]NFPA 252, *Standard Methods of Fire Tests of Door Assemblies*, National Fire Protection Association, Quincy, MA, 1984.

[4]NFPA 220, *Standard on Types of Building Construction*, National Fire Protection Association, Quincy, MA, 1985.

[5]*Uniform Building Code*, International Conference of Building Officials, Whittier, CA.

[6]*National Building Code*, Building Officials and Code Administrators International, Inc., Country Club Hills, IL.

[7]*Standard Building Code*, Southern Building Code Congress International, Inc., Birmingham, AL.

[8]*Fire Resistance Design Manual*, 11th Edition, Gypsum Association, Evanston, IL, 1983.

[9]ASTM E119-83, *Standard Methods of Fire Tests of Building Construction and Materials*, American Society for Testing and Materials, Philadelphia, PA.

[10]*UL Fire Resistance Directory*, Underwriters Laboratories, Northbrook, IL.

[11]*Factory Mutual Specification Tested Products Guide*, Factory Mutual Research Corp., Norwood, MA.

[12]NFPA 90A, *Standard for the Installation of Air Conditioning and Ventilating Systems*, National Fire Protection Association, Quincy, MA, 1985.

[13]*UL Building Materials Directory*, Underwriters Laboratories, Northbrook, IL.

[14]UL 1479-83 (Rev. 1985), *Fire Tests of Through-Penetration Firestops*, Underwriters Laboratories, Northbrook, IL.

[15]ASTM E152-81, *Standard Methods of Fire Tests of Door Assemblies*, American Society for Testing and Materials, Philadelphia, PA.

[16]NFPA 80, *Standard for Fire Doors and Windows*, National Fire Protection Association, Quincy, MA, 1986.

[17]Richard Best and David Demers, "Investigation Report on the MGM Grand Hotel Fire," National Fire Protection Association, Quincy, MA, 1980.

[18]NFPA 13, *Standard for the Installation of Sprinkler Systems*, National Fire Protection Association, Quincy, MA, 1987.

[19]NFPA 20, *Standard for the Installation of Centrifugal Fire Pumps*, National Fire Protection Association, Quincy, MA, 1987.

[20]NFPA 105, *Recommended Practice for the Installation of Smoke- and Draft-Control Door Assemblies*, National Fire Protection Association, Quincy, MA, 1985.

[21]ASTM E283-84, *Standard Test Method for Rate of Air Leakage through Exterior Windows, Curtain Walls, and Doors*, American Society for Testing and Materials, Philadelphia, PA.

[22]J. Degenkolb, "The 20-Minute Door and Other Considerations," *Building Standards*, Vol. XLV, No. 1, January-February 1976.

[23]NFPA 72E, *Standard on Automatic Fire Detectors*, National Fire Protection Association, Quincy, MA, 1987.

[24]NFPA 68, *Guide for Venting of Deflagrations*, National Fire Protection Association, Quincy, MA, 1988.

[25]NFPA 69, *Standard on Explosion Prevention Systems*, National Fire Protection Association, Quincy, MA, 1986.

[26]NFPA 654, *Standard for the Prevention of Dust Explosions in the Chemical, Dye, Pharmaceutical and Plastics Industries*, National Fire Protection Association, Quincy, MA, 1982.

[27]David Waksman and John B. Ferguson, "Fire Tests of Building Interior Covering Systems," *Fire Technology*, Vol. 10, No. 3, pp. 211-220.

[28]Fred Fisher, et al., "Room Fire Experiments of Textile Wall Coverings," Fire Research Laboratory, University of California, Berkeley, CA, March 1986.

[29]National Fire Protection Association, "Investigation Report of the Las Vegas Hilton Hotel Fire," *Fire Journal*, Vol. 76, No. 1, January 1982, pp. 52-63.

[30]W. J. Christian and T. E. Waterman, "Flame Spread in Corridors: Effects of Location and Area of Wall Finish," *Fire Journal*, Vol. 65, No. 4, July 1971, pp 25-32.

[31]John A. Sharry, "Foamed Plastic Fire: Fire Spreads 430 Feet in Eight Minutes," *Fire Journal*, Vol. 69, No. 1, January 1975, pp 5-6 and 56.

[32]NFPA 255, *Standard Method of Test of Surface Burning Characteristics of Building Materials*, National Fire Protection Association, Quincy, MA, 1984.

[33]ASTM E84-87, *Standard Test Method for Surface Burning Characteristics of Building Materials*, American Society for Testing and Materials, Philadelphia, PA.

[34]Underwriters Laboratories Inc., "Study of Smoke Ratings Developed in Standard Fire Tests in Relation to Visual Observations," *Bulletin of Research*, No. 56, April 1965.

[35]NFPA 701, *Standard Methods of Fire Tests for Flame-Resistant Textiles and Films*, National Fire Protection Association, Quincy, MA, 1977.

[36]David D. Demers, "Familiar Problems Cause 10 Deaths in Hotel Fire," *Fire Journal*, Vol. 74, No. 1, January 1980, pp. 52-56.

[37]NFPA 253, *Standard Method of Test for Critical Radiant Flux of Floor Covering Systems Using a Radiant Heat Energy Source*, National Fire Protection Association, Quincy, MA, 1984.

[38]ASTM E648-86, *Standard Test Method for Critical Radiant Flux of Floor-Covering Systems Using a Radiant Heat Energy Source*, American Society for Testing and Materials, Philadelphia, PA.

[39]King-Mon Tu and Sanford Davis, "Flame Spread of Carpet Systems Involved in Room Fires," NBSIR 76-1013, June 1976.

[40]Federal Flammability Standard FF-1-70, *Standard for the Surface Flammability of Carpets and Rugs (Pill Test)*.

7

BUILDING SERVICE AND FIRE PROTECTION EQUIPMENT

Primarily, Chapter 7 serves to provide the user of the *Code* with cross-references to other codes and standards that provide design guidance for building service equipment. The provisions of these various codes and standards must be followed in order for the facility to comply with the *Life Safety Code*. Referencing within the main body of the *Code* is meant to reinforce the fact that compliance with these codes is mandatory. Sections 7-6 and 7-7, which provide menus of the various options that can comprise detection, alarm, and communications systems or automatic extinguishing systems, are mandated only where referenced by another section of the *Code* such as a specific occupancy chapter.

SECTION 7-1 UTILITIES

7-1.1 Equipment utilizing gas and related gas piping shall be installed in accordance with NFPA 54, *National Fuel Gas Code*, or NFPA 58, *Standard for Storage and Handling of Liquefied Petroleum Gases.*

Exception: Existing installations may be continued in service, subject to approval by the authority having jurisdiction.

Although the referenced documents do not specify whether or not gas piping is allowed to pass through an exit enclosure, such as an enclosed stair, other provisions of the *Life Safety Code* apply. For example, see the commentary following 5-1.3.1, which stresses that the only openings permitted in the enclosure walls between an exit and the other building spaces are those needed to get into the exit from any normally occupied space and those needed to get out of the exit at the level of exit discharge; in other words, openings used only for an occupant to get into and out of the exit enclosure. The intent is that gas piping not pass through exit enclosure walls. Thus, the reference to some other document is not intended to negate related requirements of the *Life Safety Code*.

7-1.2 Electrical wiring and equipment installed shall be in accordance with NFPA 70, *National Electrical Code.*

Exception: Existing installations may be continued in service subject to approval by the authority having jurisdiction.

Because the installation of natural gas piping or electrical wiring may require a complicated system or array involving many specifications and design details, the *Life Safety Code* does not repeat them; rather, it provides a reference to the appropriate code or standard in which the necessary design and installation guidance can be found.

The *Life Safety Code* requirements applicable to emergency lighting, as addressed by Section 5-9 and in particular by 5-9.2.3 with respect to independence of the emergency lighting source and distribution network, go beyond the more general guidelines of NFPA 70, *National Electrical Code*,[1] on the subject. See the detailed commentary interspersed among the Section 5-9 emergency lighting requirements.

SECTION 7-2   HEATING, VENTILATING, AND AIR CONDITIONING

7-2.1   Air conditioning, heating, ventilating ductwork, and related equipment shall be installed in accordance with NFPA 90A, *Standard for the Installation of Air Conditioning and Ventilating Systems*, or NFPA 90B, *Standard for the Installation of Warm Air Heating and Air Conditioning Systems*, as applicable.

Exception: Existing installations may be continued in service, subject to approval by the authority having jurisdiction.

Paragraph 7-2.1 refers *Code* users to either NFPA 90A, *Standard for the Installation of Air Conditioning and Ventilating Systems*,[2] or, for occupancies with small overall volumes such as one- and two-family dwellings, NFPA 90B, *Standard for the Installation of Warm Air Heating and Air Conditioning Systems*,[3] for the proper installation of HVAC systems.

NFPA 90A addresses, for example, fire damper requirements for both ductwork and air transfer grilles that penetrate fire resistance rated barriers. NFPA 90A also prohibits means of egress corridors in health care, detention and correctional, and residential occupancies from being used as a portion of a supply, return, or exhaust air system serving adjoining areas.

7-2.2   Ventilating or heat-producing equipment shall be installed in accordance with: NFPA 91, *Standard for the Installation of Blower and Exhaust Systems*; NFPA 211, *Standard for Chimneys, Fireplaces, and Vents, and Solid Fuel Burning Appliances*; NFPA 31, *Standard for the Installation of Oil Burning Equipment*; NFPA 54, *National Fuel Gas Code*; NFPA 70, *National Electrical Code*, as applicable.

Exception: Existing installations may be continued in service, subject to approval by the authority having jurisdiction.

7-2.3   Commercial cooking equipment for use in occupancies shall be installed in accordance with NFPA 96, *Standard for the Installation of Equipment for the Removal of Smoke and Grease-Laden Vapors from Commercial Cooking Equipment*.

Exception: Existing installations may be continued in service, subject to approval by the authority having jurisdiction.

NFPA 96, *Standard for the Installation of Equipment for the Removal of Smoke and Grease-Laden Vapors from Commercial Cooking Equipment,*[4] by title and scope statement, is limited to commercial cooking equipment and should not automatically be applied to all food heating equipment just because the equipment is present in other than a residential dwelling unit. In determining if NFPA 96 protection is needed, consideration should first be given to the quantities of smoke and grease-laden vapors that will be produced by operation of the equipment in question.

It is not the *Code*'s intent, for example, to require NFPA 96 protection of a residential cook-top surface located in the snack preparation room on a hospital patient room floor, with the equipment used for heating foods or boiling water. Rather, the authority having jurisdiction, after assessing the situation, may determine that either no special protection is needed or that the food heating device creates a hazardous area requiring protection under the provisions of 12-3.2 or 13-3.2. If determined to be hazardous, the area may be isolated and protected by either automatic sprinkler protection or by one-hour fire resistance rated construction. In some cases, voluntary compliance with NFPA 96 may be judged by the authority having jurisdiction as a substitute for, and thus equivalent of, full sprinklering of the room in which the equipment is located.

NFPA 96 also provides design guidance on the safe arrangement of hoods, ducting, and exhaust systems.

SECTION 7-3   SMOKE CONTROL

7-3.1* Smoke control systems may be installed in lieu of other specific requirements in accordance with the provisions of Chapters 8 through 30. The design, installation, and testing shall be approved by the authority having jurisdiction.

A-7-3.1 For guidance on designing and installing engineered smoke control systems see:

(1) NFPA 90A, *Standard for the Installation of Air-Conditioning and Ventilating Systems. (See Appendix B.)*

(2) *Smoke Control in Fire Safety Design,* NFPA SPP-53, by Butcher and Parnell. (*See Appendix B.*)

(3) *Design of Smoke Control Systems for Buildings,* by Klote and Fothergill. (*See Appendix B.*)

(4) NFPA *Fire Protection Handbook* — Sixteenth Edition, Section 8, Chapter 4 including Bibliography. (*See Appendix B.*)

(5) *ASHRAE Handbook and Product Directory* - FUNDAMENTALS.

(6) In existing detention and correctional occupancies, also see A-15-3.1.3.

This provision does not require smoke control systems but highlights the fact that some *Code* requirements, such as those applicable to atriums, mandate smoke control systems or allow exceptions where smoke control is provided. Appendix references are provided to material that is presently available to assist in the design of smoke control systems.

Although not specifically referenced, NFPA 92A, *Recommended Practice for Smoke Control Systems*,[5] was adopted by the Association at the November 1987 Fall Meeting, during which this edition of the *Life Safety Code* also was adopted. NFPA 92A addresses smoke control utilizing barriers, airflows, and pressure differentials so as to confine the smoke of a fire to the zone of fire origin and thus maintain a tenable environment in other zones. The problem of maintaining tenable conditions within large zones of fire origin, such as atria and shopping malls, is not addressed by this document. This more difficult issue, in terms of the physics involved, will be addressed later in what is planned to be a separate document.

A recommended practice cannot be referenced mandatorily, but NFPA 92A should be used in the design, installation, testing, operation, and maintenance of smoke control systems covered by its limited scope.

SECTION 7-4   ELEVATORS, DUMBWAITERS, AND VERTICAL CONVEYORS

7-4.1* An elevator shall not be considered a component in a required means of egress.

A-7-4.1 Under certain limited conditions, elevators have been recognized as required exits by prior editions of this *Code*. No such credit is given in this edition due to some characteristics that make them unsuitable for emergency exit use.

The use of elevators for emergency evacuation purposes where operated by trained emergency service personnel (building personnel, fire personnel, etc.) should be utilized in the building evacuation program.

In high-rise buildings, towers, or in deep underground spaces where travel over considerable vertical distance on stairs may cause persons not capable of such physical effort to collapse before they reach the street exit, stairways may be used for initial escape from the immediate area of danger and elevators used to complete the travel to the street.

It may be reasonably assumed that in all buildings of sufficient height to indicate the need for elevators, they will be provided for normal use, and for this reason no requirements for mandatory installation of elevators are included in the *Code*.

For additional information on elevators, see ANSI/ASME A17.1, *Safety Code for Elevators and Escalators*, and ANSI/ASME A17.3, *Safety Code for Existing Elevators and Escalators*.

In the past, the exit capacity of elevators has been figured on the basis of three average elevators being roughly equivalent to the formerly used single unit of stairway exit width, and in this way, elevators have been accepted as required exits under certain limited conditions by prior editions of the *Code*. No such credit has been given since 1956 because of some inherent characteristics that may make elevators unsuitable for emergency exit use. These characteristics are accentuated in modern automatic elevators where no operator is available to exercise judgment in the control of the elevator in case of fire or other emergency. A summary of reasons why elevators are not credited as part of the required means of egress follows:

1. People seeking to escape from a fire by means of an elevator may have to wait at the elevator door for some time, during which they may be exposed to fire or smoke or become panicky.

2. Automatic elevators respond to the pressing of buttons in such a way that it is possible for an elevator being used to descend from floors above a fire to stop automatically at the floor of the fire, and for the doors to open automatically, thus exposing occupants to fire and smoke.

A further consideration is that an elevator shaft will act as a built-in "chimney" in a high rise building. Unless positively pressurized with respect to the fire floor, the shaft will carry heat and smoke from a fire and expose passengers to toxic levels of both, even if the elevator does not stop at the floor of the fire and continues to function.

3. Modern elevators will not operate until the doors are fully closed. In an emergency, a large number of people may try to crowd into an elevator, keeping the doors from closing and the elevator from operating.

4. Any power failure, such as the burnout of electric supply cables during a fire, may render the elevators inoperative or may cause people to become trapped in elevators stopped between floors. Under fire conditions, there might not be time to permit rescue of the trapped occupants through emergency escape hatches or doors.

Notwithstanding the dangers of using elevators for emergency exit purposes, they may serve an important function as a supplemental facility, particularly in occupancies such as hospitals, when under the controlled operation of trained emergency forces personnel. Elevators are also an important consideration in exiting from high rise buildings or from deep underground spaces, where travel over considerable vertical distance on stairs might cause people unaccustomed to such physical effort to collapse before they reach the street. In these instances, required exits, such as stairs or horizontal exits, may be used for the initial escape from the area of immediate fire and smoke danger, and the elevators, under fire department control, used to complete the travel to the level of exit discharge.

7-4.2   Except as modified herein, new elevators, escalators, dumbwaiters, and moving walks shall be installed in accordance with the requirements of ANSI/ASME A17.1, *Safety Code for Elevators and Escalators.*

7-4.3   Except as modified herein, existing elevators, escalators, dumbwaiters, and moving walks shall conform to the requirements of ANSI/ASME A17.3, *Safety Code for Existing Elevators and Escalators.*

The *Life Safety Code* references ANSI/ASME A17.1, *Safety Code for Elevators and Escalators*,[6] and ANSI/ASME A17.3, *Safety Code for Existing Elevators and Escalators*,[7] because of the automatic recall provisions and the fire fighters' override provisions that these documents contain. These provisions make possible the recall of elevators to the ground floor during a fire, thus taking them out of service, or permit fire fighters to override the controls manually and use the elevators as necessary.

For elevator installations, the *Life Safety Code* requires compliance with ANSI/ASME A17.1 or A17.3, and the *Code* additionally requires that a sprinkler system, if installed, meet the requirements of NFPA 13. Prior to the issuance of a recent ANSI/ASME A17.1 official interpretation, it appeared that the elevator code and the sprinkler installation standard were in conflict. ANSI/ASME A17.1 severely restricted the installation of sprinklers in elevator machine rooms, and NFPA 13 states that a complete automatic sprinkler system includes the installation of sprinklers in all rooms and spaces.

The ANSI/ASME A17.1 interpretation says that the intent of the elevator code, with respect to the sprinklering of machine rooms, is met if rate-of-rise/fixed temperature heat detectors, arranged to disconnect automatically the main line power supply, are provided in the elevator machine room and:

1. A detector is near each sprinkler;
2. The sprinkler rating exceeds the detector ratings; and
3. The detector is independent of the sprinkler system.

7-4.4   All elevators having a travel of 25 ft (7.6 m) or more above or below the level that best serves the needs of emergency personnel for fire fighting or rescue purposes shall conform to the requirements of ANSI/ASME A17.1, *Safety Code for Elevators and Escalators*, Rule 211.3, "Operation of Elevators Under Fire or Other Emergency Conditions."

Due to the extreme hazard of elevators going to a fire floor, either intentionally or unintentionally, the *Code* mandates that Rule 211.3 of ANSI/ASME A17.1 be complied with in both new and existing buildings. Rule 211.3a establishes elevator recall activated by smoke detection in each elevator lobby and in associated machine rooms. This recall function is controlled by a 3-position key-operated switch normally located in the main lobby at the elevators. Rule 211.3a mandates specific functions for the "on," "off," and "by-pass" positions of this switch. Rule 211.3c provides for "emergency in-car operations" or what is often referred to as fire fighters' service. This rule requires a 3-position key-operated switch in each elevator car. The functions of the "on," "off," and "hold" positions are specified in this rule. For specific details refer to ANSI/ASME A17.1. Commentary on this rule is available in the 1984 Edition of the *ASME Handbook A17.1*.[8]

7-4.5   Vertical conveyors, including dumbwaiters and pneumatic conveyors serving various stories in a building, shall be separately enclosed by walls or partitions in accordance with the provisions of Section 6-2. Service openings shall not open to an exit. Service openings, where required to be open on several stories at the same time for purposes of operation of the conveyor, shall be provided with closing devices that will close all service doors upon activation of smoke detectors that are located inside and outside the shaft enclosure in locations acceptable to the authority having jurisdiction.

Exception: Enclosure is not required for pneumatic tube conveyors protected in accordance with 6-2.3.4.2.

A pneumatic tube with characteristics similar to a pipe is exempted by the Exception from the enclosure requirements applicable to vertical conveyors if protected per 6-2.3.4.2, as is done for pipe penetrations of fire resistance rated barriers.

SECTION 7-5   RUBBISH CHUTES, INCINERATORS, AND LAUNDRY CHUTES

7-5.1   Each rubbish chute shall be separately enclosed by walls or partitions in accordance with the provisions of Section 6-2. Inlet openings serving chutes shall be protected in accordance with Section 6-2. Doors for such chutes shall open only to a separate room that is designed exclusively for that purpose. The room shall be separated from other spaces in accordance with Section 6-4.

Exception: Existing installations with properly enclosed service chutes and with properly installed and maintained service openings may open to a corridor or normally occupied room, subject to approval by the authority having jurisdiction.

According to the provisions of 7-5.1 and those of Chapter 6, rubbish chutes must be enclosed in fire-rated shafts and the openings to the chutes must be located in enclosed fire-rated room constructions as a back-up design feature. This redundant design prevents the possibility of an open incinerator chute directly exposing an exit access corridor to fire. Further, it prevents a fire in an incinerator chute from blocking exit access corridors with either smoke or flames before evacuation or corrective action can be taken. This arrangement also recognizes that occupants frequently pile rubbish in front of the incinerator door rather than put it into the chute.

Standard good practice for the installation and maintenance of incinerator flues is included in NFPA 82, *Standard on Incinerators, Waste and Linen Handling Systems and Equipment,*[9] referenced in 7-5.2, which also covers rubbish chutes and linen or laundry chutes, as the latter have hazards similar to those of rubbish chutes.

7-5.2   Rubbish chutes, laundry chutes, and incinerators shall be installed and maintained in accordance with NFPA 82, *Standard on Incinerators, Waste and Linen Handling Systems and Equipment.*

Exception: Existing installations may be continued in service, subject to approval by the authority having jurisdiction.

7-5.3   Laundry chutes shall be enclosed and any opening shall be protected as specified for rubbish chutes in 7-5.1.

Exception: Existing installations may be continued in service, subject to approval by the authority having jurisdiction.

SECTION 7-6   FIRE DETECTION, ALARM, AND COMMUNICATIONS SYSTEMS

7-6.1 General.

7-6.1.1   The provisions of Section 7-6 shall apply only where specifically required by another section of this *Code*.

> The intent of this section of the *Code* is to present a menu of a variety of general provisions related to protective signaling systems, not to indicate where any particular type is required. The actual requirements for providing detection, alarm, and communications systems appear in other parts of the *Code*, particularly in the various occupancy chapters. Thus, any or all of the signaling systems' menu of options, as presented but not mandated by Section 7-6, can be mandatorily called into play by other *Code* sections.

7-6.1.2*   The provisions of this section cover the basic functions of a complete protective signaling and control system including fire detection, alarm, and communication. These systems are primarily intended to provide the indication and warning of abnormal conditions, the summoning of appropriate aid, and the control of occupancy facilities to enhance protection of life.

A-7-6.1.2   Some of the provisions of this section are excerpted from NFPA 72A, *Standard for the Installation, Maintenance, and Use of Local Protective Signaling Systems for Guard's Tour, Fire Alarm, and Supervisory Service (see Appendix B)*. For purposes of this *Code*, some provisions of this section are more stringent than those of NFPA 72A. NFPA 72A should be consulted for additional details.

> The provision for early warning of fire, accompanied by notification of appropriate authorities, is a key element of a fire protection program. Where people are involved, protective signaling assumes even greater importance.
> A review of the "Fire Record," included in each issue of NFPA's *Fire Journal*, time and again emphasizes the need for such equipment and the sometimes tragic consequences in situations where it was lacking. Among the more common problems encountered have been:
> 1. Fire burned or smoldered for some time before discovery (the night watchman passed by "twenty minutes" before);
> 2. Fire was observed, but everyone assumed that someone else had turned in the alarm;
> 3. People didn't know who to notify, were confused, gave the wrong address;

4. People present were asleep, bedridden, or otherwise unable to act;

5. Worker attempted extinguishment rather than notify others and thus admit that a careless act had started the fire; or

6. Person in position of responsibility went or sent someone to investigate before sounding an alarm.

In educational, mercantile, and business occupancies there are usually enough people present, at least during a part of the day, to discover an incipient fire. Such circumstances are recognized by the *Code* by imposing less rigid requirements for protective signaling systems than would be mandated in some other occupancies. The installation of an automatic extinguishing system with an integral alarm can obviate the need for an independent signaling system.

Fire detection without warning is not enough. People must be alerted to the existence of an emergency in order to take appropriate action.

7-6.1.3* A fire alarm system required for life safety shall be installed, tested, and maintained in accordance with applicable requirements of the following:

NFPA 70, *National Electrical Code*;

NFPA 71, *Standard for the Installation, Maintenance, and Use of Signaling Systems for Central Station Service*;

NFPA 72A, *Standard for the Installation, Maintenance, and Use of Local Protective Signaling Systems for Guard's Tour, Fire Alarm, and Supervisory Service*;

NFPA 72B, *Standard for the Installation, Maintenance, and Use of Auxiliary Protective Signaling Systems for Fire Alarm Service*;

NFPA 72C, *Standard for the Installation, Maintenance, and Use of Remote Station Protective Signaling Systems*;

NFPA 72D, *Standard for the Installation, Maintenance, and Use of Proprietary Protective Signaling Systems*;

NFPA 72E, *Standard on Automatic Fire Detectors*;

NFPA 72F, *Standard for the Installation, Maintenance, and Use of Emergency Voice/Alarm Communications Systems*;

NFPA 74, *Standard for the Installation, Maintenance, and Use of Household Fire Warning Equipment*; and

NFPA 1221, *Standard for the Installation, Maintenance, and Use of Public Fire Service Communication Systems*.

Exception: Existing installations may be continued in use, subject to the approval of the authority having jurisdiction.

A-7-6.1.3 For additional information on the installation, testing, and maintenance of alarm systems, see NFPA 72G, *Guide for the Installation, Maintenance, and Use of Notification Appliances for Protective Signaling Systems*, and NFPA 72H, *Guide for Testing Procedures for Local, Auxiliary, Remote Station, and Proprietary Protective Signaling Systems*.

7-6.1.4 All systems and components shall be approved for the purpose for which installed.

Approval of both the system as a whole and of its components is required. Such approval is granted by the authority having jurisdiction. (*See the definition of "approved" in Section 3-2.*) Substantiating data could be in the form of test reports, listings in approval lists issued by such organizations as the Factory Mutual System or Underwriters Laboratories Inc., or testing or evaluation by another recognized source.

7-6.1.5   Fire alarm system installation wiring or other transmission paths shall be monitored for integrity in accordance with 7-6.1.3.

A broken or short-circuited wire between a fire alarm system initiating device, e.g., a smoke detector, and the central control equipment will render the device inoperative and yet allow an individual to believe that protection is still in service. By requiring monitoring of the system installation wiring, an audible trouble signal will indicate a circuit break or ground and allow for corrective action to be taken. It is not the intent of this paragraph to supersede or override the provisions for supervision in the standards referenced in 7-6.1.3 but only to highlight those requirements or to mandate them where the referenced standards may make such supervision optional.

7-6.1.6* Maintenance and Testing.   To assure operational integrity, the fire alarm system shall have an approved maintenance and testing program complying with the requirements of the applicable documents specified in 7-6.1.3.

A-7-6.1.6   Records of conducted maintenance and testing and a copy of the certificate of compliance should be maintained. For information in addition to the standards referenced in the body of the *Code*, see NFPA 72G, *Guide for the Installation, Maintenance, and Use of Notification Appliances for Protective Signaling Systems*, and NFPA 72H, *Guide for Testing Procedures for Local, Auxiliary, Remote Station, and Proprietary Protective Signaling Systems*.

7-6.1.7   For the purposes of this *Code*, a protective signaling and control system is used for initiation, notification, and control.

(a) *Initiation.*   The initiation function provides the input signal to the system.

Both automatic and manual signal initiation is considered. (*See 7-6.2.*)

(b) *Notification.*   The notification function is the means by which the system advises that human action is required in response to a particular condition.

This covers all forms of notification, whether audible or audible and visual. (*See 7-6.3.*) It includes both notification of occupants (*see 7-6.3*) and notification of the fire department (*see 7-6.4*) where required.

(c) *Control.*   The control function provides outputs to control building equipment to enhance protection of life.

This covers functions that the system may actuate to make the building safer, such as release of hold-open devices for self-closing doors or pressurization of stair enclosures. (*See 7-6.5.*)

7-6.2 Signal Initiation.

7-6.2.1   Where required by another section of this *Code*, actuation of the protective signaling and control system shall occur by any or all of the following means of initiation, but not limited thereto:

(a) Manual fire alarm initiation

(b) Automatic detection

(c) Extinguishing system operation.

The location of detector system components is of prime importance. If they are too close to a wall/ceiling intersection, particularly over a door, air currents may cause heat and smoke to bypass the unit completely. Likewise, location with respect to a dropped beam or other construction can have a similar nullifying effect. This can pose problems where partitions are moved without regard to the location of detector units. The problem is illustrated in Figure 7-1. NFPA 72E, *Standard on Automatic Fire Detectors*,[10] provides extensive guidance in this area.

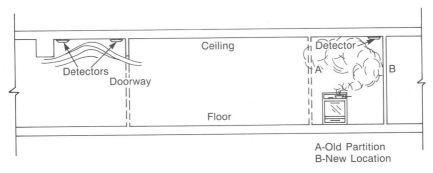

Figure 7-1.   Problems to Avoid in Detector Location.

Where both manual and automatic systems are in use, they should be complementary. If, due to poor maintenance, abuse, or mechanical failure, one system becomes inoperative, the second will provide backup support.

Any automatic fire detection system for life safety from fire should have a high degree of reliability. This indicates the need for such features as:

1. An electric current supply independent of the electric power source for the building;

2. Trouble signals to give warning in case of short circuits or breaks in wires, or other conditions that might interfere with the proper operation of the system;

3. Alarm indicating appliances located so as to ensure warning even to those sleeping; and

4. Above all, a regular maintenance program.

There is a very considerable diversity in the types of automatic fire detection and alarm equipment commercially available, and selection of types suitable for any given situation calls for the exercise of judgment based upon experience.

7-6.2.2   Manual fire alarm stations shall be approved for the particular application and shall be used only for fire protective signaling purposes. Combination fire alarm and guard's tour stations are acceptable.

7-6.2.3   A manual fire alarm station shall be provided in the natural path of escape near each required exit from an area, unless modified by another section of this *Code*.

Where manual fire alarm station boxes are required by Chapters 8 through 30 of the *Code*, they are required to be located near an exit, in the natural path of escape, and in a position of maximum visibility. The purpose is to expedite the occupant initiation of an alarm in a time of stress and to reduce the possibility of the person involved being caught by the fire between a remotely located alarm station and an exit. While the designer may not wish to detract from some special design effect at the end of a corridor, the advantage of proper placement, from the life safety point of view, is obvious, as shown in Figure 7-2.

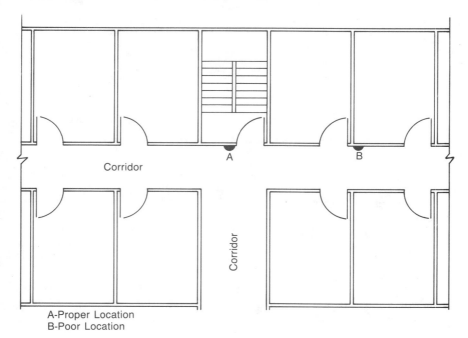

A-Proper Location
B-Poor Location

Figure 7-2.   Proper and Improper Location of a Manual Alarm Station.

7-6.2.4   Additional manual fire alarm stations shall be so located that, from any part of the building, not more than 200 ft (60 m) horizontal distance on the same floor shall be traversed in order to reach a manual fire alarm station.

7-6.2.5   Each manual fire alarm station on a system shall be accessible, unobstructed, visible, and of the same general type.

7-6.2.6   Where a sprinkler system provides automatic detection and alarm system initiation, it shall be provided with an approved alarm initiation device that will operate when the flow of water is equal to or greater than that from a single automatic sprinkler.

7-6.2.7   Where a "complete smoke detection system" is required by another section of this *Code*, automatic detection of smoke in accordance with NFPA 72E, *Standard on Automatic Fire Detectors*, shall be provided in all occupiable areas, common areas, and work spaces in those environments suitable for proper smoke detector operation.

7-6.2.8   Where a "partial smoke detection system" is required by another section of this *Code*, automatic detection of smoke in accordance with NFPA 72E, *Standard on Automatic Fire Detectors*, shall be provided in all common areas and work spaces, such as corridors, lobbies, equipment rooms, and other tenantless spaces in those environments suitable for proper smoke detector operation. Selective smoke detection unique to other sections of this *Code* shall be provided as required by those sections.

> Paragraphs 7-6.2.7 and 7-6.2.8 define the terms "complete smoke detection system" and "partial smoke detection system" so that some other *Code* paragraph can require either system with a reference to 7-6.2.7 or 7-6.2.8 but without further explanation. Selective smoke detection fits neither definition and relies on some other provision of the *Code* to detail what is intended. For example, new nursing homes are required to provide a corridor smoke detection system. The extent of such a system, which meets neither the definition of "complete" nor "partial" as addressed by 7-6.2.7 or 7-6.2.8 and is unique to new nursing homes, is explained in Chapter 12.

7-6.2.9*   Where required by another section of this *Code*, single station smoke detectors shall be installed in accordance with NFPA 74, *Standard for the Installation, Maintenance, and Use of Household Fire Warning Equipment*. In new construction, where two or more smoke detectors are required within a living unit, they shall be arranged so that the activation of any detector causes the operation of an alarm that shall be clearly audible throughout the living unit over background noise levels with all intervening doors closed. The detectors shall sound an alarm only within an individual living unit or similar area and shall not actuate the building protective signaling and control system. Remote annunciation shall be permitted.

Exception: Multiple station or system smoke detectors arranged to function in the same manner shall be permitted.

A-7-6.2.9   A living unit is that structure, area, room, or combination of rooms, including hotel rooms/suites, in which a family or individual lives. This is meant to cover living areas only and not common usage areas in multifamily buildings such as corridors, lobbies, basements, etc.

This provision allows the use of single station or multiple station smoke detectors that are not part of a fire alarm "system" to be used within a dwelling or living unit, such as within a one- or two-family dwelling, within an apartment, or within a hotel or dormitory room, provided that certain performance oriented criteria can be met. Audibility over background noises, such as running water, use of home appliances, and audio systems, with intervening doors closed between the occupants and the detector sounding device, is of key importance. In multistory or large-area living units, multiple detectors will probably need to be interconnected so that the sensing of smoke by one sounds the alarms of all detectors within that living unit.

The intent behind requiring smoke detection within an individual living unit without requiring connection to the overall building alarm system is to provide notification of a smoke condition within a living unit to occupants of that particular living unit. Once the occupants egress their unit to the building's common areas, they can use the manual pull stations to sound the building alarm to notify occupants of other living units of the emergency.

Mandatory interconnection of living unit smoke detectors to the building alarm system often results in numerous nuisance alarms due to the detection of cooking or bathroom shower vapors, which causes the initiation of an alarm. Nuisance alarms lead to the deliberate disabling of the system and the resulting lack of early warning. Thus, a complete *fire* detection (vs smoke detection) system usually includes system smoke detection within building common areas and system heat detection within individual living units. Single station smoke detectors are then still necessary within each living unit to afford to the occupants of that unit early warning of smoke conditions within that unit.

The term "single station" is often confused with the term "battery-operated." Single station means that the detector that senses smoke also sounds an integral sounding device and does not ring a general alarm. Multiple station means the interconnection of single station devices such that, when one sounds, all those interconnected sound. In neither case is the power source implied. The *Life Safety Code* allows battery-operated units only in existing one- and two-family dwellings, existing lodging and rooming houses, and under certain conditions in board and care facilities.

7-6.3 Occupant Notification.

7-6.3.1   Occupant notification shall provide signal notification to alert occupants of fire or other emergency as required by another section of this *Code*.

7-6.3.2*   Notification shall be a general audible alarm-type complying with 7-6.3.3 through 7-6.3.10.

Exception No. 1:   Except where prohibited by an occupancy chapter, a presignal system shall be permitted when the initial fire alarm signal is automatically transmitted without delay to a municipal fire department, a fire brigade, or a staff person trained to respond to a fire emergency. (See 7-6.1.3.)

A presignal system, rather than immediately and automatically sounding a general alarm throughout the building, delays the general alarm by sounding alarm devices initially in only an approved and constantly attended area, such as a fire brigade station, guard station, or similar location with trained staff who then investigate the signal's origin and may subsequently sound a general alarm. If a presignal system is not intentionally aborted within a predetermined period of time, an audible general building alarm is sounded.

Because the delay in sounding the general alarm, which is inherent in a presignal system, may do more harm than good in some occupancies with populations that are difficult to evacuate or protect, the *Code* allows occupancy chapters to prohibit their use specifically. Where used, a presignal system can delay only the general occupant notification but must, at time of initiation, immediately and automatically achieve emergency forces notification per the guidelines of 7-6.4.

Exception No. 2:*   Elevator lobby and associated machine room detectors used for elevator recall are not required to sound the building evacuation alarm if the power supply and installation wiring to these detectors are monitored by the building fire alarm system, and actuation of these detectors results in a supervisory alarm signal.

Exception No. 3:*   Duct detectors used for closing dampers or heating/ventilating/air conditioning system shutdown are not required to sound the building alarm.

Exception No. 4:*   Detectors at doors for the operation of automatic door release are not required to sound the building alarm.

A-7-6.3.2   Where coded stations are used and more than one station is operated, at least three complete rounds of a clear coded signal should be transmitted.

A-7-6.3.2 Exception No. 2:   The concept addressed by the Exception is that detectors used for "releasing service" for elevator recall need not sound the building evacuation alarm, provided that an alarm condition is indicated by an audible supervisory signal.

A-7-6.3.2 Exceptions No. 3 and 4   The concept addressed by the Exceptions is that detectors used for "releasing service," such as door or damper closing and fan shutdown, need not sound the building alarm.

Exceptions No. 3 and 4 reaffirm that not all detectors, simply because they are present, are required to sound the building alarm. Detectors used for "releasing service," such as for the release of an automatic door hold-open device so as to allow a door to be self-closing under the presence of smoke, need only perform their intended function. If area smoke detection, complete with occupant notification via the building alarm system, is needed to provide the *Code*'s intended level of life safety, a specific *Code* requirement will be present calling for either a complete or partial smoke detection system. Interconnection with the building alarm should not be mandated artificially simply because a detector may have been installed for another purpose, such as releasing service.

7-6.3.3   Where a standard evacuation signal is required by another section of this *Code*, the evacuation signal shall be the standard fire alarm evacuation signal described in NFPA 72A, *Standard for the Installation, Maintenance, and Use of Local Protective Signaling Systems for Guard's Tour, Fire Alarm, and Supervisory Service.*

See commentary following 7-6.3.7.

7-6.3.4   Notification signals for occupants to evacuate shall be by audible signals and, where deemed necessary by the authority having jurisdiction, shall also be by visible signals.

Visible alarm devices, in addition to the audible alarms, are desirable in buildings occupied by hearing-impaired persons.

7-6.3.5   The general evacuation alarm signal shall operate throughout the entire building.

Exception No. 1:   Where total evacuation of occupants is not practical due to building configuration, only the occupants in the affected zones shall be initially notified. Provisions shall be made to selectively notify occupants in other zones to afford orderly evacuation of the entire building.

Exception No. 2:   Where occupants are incapable of evacuating themselves because of age, physical/mental disabilities, or physical restraint, only the attendants and other personnel required to evacuate occupants from a zone, area, floor, or building are required to be notified. This notification shall include means to readily identify the zone, area, floor, or building in need of evacuation.

Exception No. 1 to 7-6.3.5 normally applies to high rise buildings. It makes provisions for zoned, staged evacuation. This exception anticipates that the portions of the building that do not receive the initial alarm are separated from the areas of immediate emergency, and initial evacuation by adequate fire resistance rated construction, such as the 2-hour fire separation that is usually provided between floors of high rise buildings. Exception No. 2 commonly applies to health care and detention and correctional occupancies. It is a common application in these occupancies to use coded chimes or a similar method of announcing throughout the facility the location of the fire emergency. This allows all members of the emergency response team, regardless of current location within what might be a sprawling facility, to respond to their assigned emergency duties. For example, an engineer who may be working on a plumbing problem in the facility's adjacent original building at the time the coded alarm is chimed throughout the facility will receive the proper notification to carry out the previously assigned task of checking the fire pump to assure that it is ready to operate if needed.

7-6.3.6 Audible alarm indicating appliances shall be of such character and so distributed as to be effectively heard above the average ambient sound level occurring under normal conditions of occupancy.

The authority having jurisdiction needs to review carefully the types and locations of alarm indicating appliances. Given that audibility above ambient sound level is of primary importance and that each additional sounding device adds cost to a system, a balance should be engineered so that excessive costs are not incurred while the installation of sufficient devices for adequate audibility is assured. This is extremely important in hotels and apartment buildings. Sounding devices located in corridors may not be audible within units, especially in new construction, due to increased levels of acoustical insulation.

7-6.3.7 Audible alarm indicating appliances shall produce signals that are distinctive from audible signals used for other purposes in the same building.

Where the provisions of Chapters 8 through 30 require an evacuation alarm signal, the standard fire alarm evacuation signal described in NFPA 72A, *Standard on Local Protective Signaling Systems*,[11] should be used.

The manner of sounding alarms should be standardized with a view to obtaining uniformity throughout as large a geographic area as practicable. In that way, people moving from one locality to another will not be misled and confused by differences in the manner of sounding alarms.

Two multiple-fatality fires in hotel occupancies that occurred in late 1978 and 1979 illustrate the need for standardized fire alarm signals with adequate audibility. In both incidents, which occurred in the middle of the night, many survivors reported not hearing any alarm device or mistaking the alarm for telephones or alarm clocks. An additional multiple-fatality fire in a hotel in 1978 illustrated the special problems with alarm notification when occupants' hearing is impaired. In this fire, several elderly occupants removed hearing aids before going to bed, thus challenging the adequacy of the audibility of the alarm.

7-6.3.8 Recorded or live voice evacuation or relocation instructions to occupants shall be permitted.

Rather than specify additional requirements for recorded or live voice evacuation or relocation instructions, the *Code*, via 7-6.1.3, mandatorily references NFPA 72F, *Standard for the Installation, Maintenance, and Use of Emergency Voice/Alarm Communications Systems*,[12] which contains the necessary requirements.

7-6.3.9 Audible and visible fire alarm indicating appliances shall be used only for fire alarm system or other emergency purposes.

Exception No. 1: Voice communication systems may be used for other purposes, subject to the approval of the authority having jurisdiction, if the fire alarm system takes precedence over all other signals.

Permitting a voice communication system to be used for some other purpose carries with it a requirement that approval of the authority having jurisdiction be secured for such use. The system designer or building operator and the authority having jurisdiction should determine how likely or susceptible the system is to deliberate tampering. For example, in a business occupancy where a combination emergency voice communication and day-to-day background music system is installed with a speaker located in the ceiling directly over an employee's desk, it should be predicted that the supposedly innocuous, but constant, background music may irritate the employee to the point that the speaker will be muffled or otherwise disabled. Even with the required feature under which the fire alarm system takes precedence over all other signals, a disabled speaker cannot deliver the required emergency message.

Exception No. 2: Where otherwise permitted by another section of this Code.

An example of this Exception's use by another section of the *Code* appears in 10-3.4.3.2 for educational occupancies where the fire alarm system is permitted to be used to designate class change provided that the fire alarm signal is distinctively different from the class change signal and overrides all other use.

7-6.3.10 Alarm notification signals shall take precedence over all other signals.

7-6.4* Emergency Forces Notification. Where required by another section of this *Code*, emergency forces notification shall be provided to alert the local fire brigade or municipal fire department of fire or other emergency.

Where fire department notification is required by another section of this *Code*, the fire alarm system shall be arranged to transmit the alarm automatically via any of the following means:

(a) An auxiliary alarm system in accordance with NFPA 72B, *Standard for the Installation, Maintenance, and Use of Auxiliary Protective Signaling Systems for Fire Alarm Service*, or

(b) A central station connection in accordance with NFPA 71, *Standard for the Installation, Maintenance, and Use of Signaling Systems for Central Station Service*, or

(c) A proprietary system in accordance with NFPA 72D, *Standard for the Installation, Maintenance, and Use of Proprietary Protective Signaling Systems*, or

(d) A remote station connection in accordance with NFPA 72C, *Standard for the Installation, Maintenance, and Use of Remote Station Protective Signaling Systems.*

Exception: Where none of the above means of notification is available, a plan for notification of the municipal fire department, acceptable to the authority having jurisdiction, shall be provided.

The following definitions are provided to help in differentiating among the above four alarm transmission methods for fire department notification:

Auxiliary Alarm System. A connection to the municipal fire alarm system to transmit an alarm of fire to the municipal communication center. Fire alarms from an auxiliary alarm system are received at the municipal communication center on the same equipment and by the same alerting methods as alarms transmitted from municipal fire alarm boxes located on streets.

Central Station. An office to which remote alarm and supervisory signaling devices are connected, and where personnel are in attendance at all times to supervise the circuits and investigate signals.

Central Station System. A system, or group of systems, in which the operations of circuits and devices are signaled automatically to, recorded in, maintained and supervised from an approved central station having competent and experienced observers and operators who shall, upon receipt of a signal, take such action as shall be required. Such systems shall be controlled and operated by a person, firm, or corporation whose principal business is the furnishing and maintaining of supervised signaling service.

Proprietary Protective Signaling System. An installation of protective signaling systems which serve contiguous and noncontiguous properties under one ownership from a central supervising station located at the protected property, where trained, competent personnel are in constant attendance. This includes the central supervising station, power supplies, signal-initiating devices, initiating device circuits, signal notification appliances, equipment for the automatic, permanent visual recording of signals, and equipment for the operation of emergency building control services.

Remote Station Protective Signaling System. An installation using supervised dedicated circuits to transmit alarm, supervisory, and trouble signals from one or more protected premises to a remote location at which appropriate action is taken.

A-7-6.4   The selection of the means of fire department notification should be the most reliable depending on local conditions and should be determined in consultation with the authority having jurisdiction.

Fire alarm equipment installed for the notification of occupants of a building, in localities under the protection of a regularly organized fire department or private fire brigade, can be arranged to give automatic transmission of alarms (either directly or through an approved central office) to the fire department or brigade upon operation of an alarm-sending station or system. Where no such connection is provided, a fire alarm box arranged to signal the fire department could be installed either at the main entrance to the building, at the telephone switchboard, or somewhere outside the building, plainly visible day or night and conveniently accessible from the main entrance. While this arrangement is desirable, it is not required by 7-6.4 unless the occupancy chapter specifically requires this feature.

7-6.5 Emergency Control.

7-6.5.1   A protective signaling and control system shall, where required by another section of this *Code*, be arranged to actuate automatically control functions necessary to make the protected premises safer for building occupants.

7-6.5.2   Where required by another section of this *Code*, the following functions shall be actuated by the protective signaling and control system:

(a) Release of hold-open devices for doors or other opening protectives

(b) Stairwell or elevator shaft pressurization

(c) Smoke management or smoke control systems

> Manual fire alarm pull stations should generally not be used to activate smoke control systems, other than stairtower pressurization systems, because of the likelihood of a person signaling an alarm from a station outside the smoke zone of fire origin.

(d) Emergency lighting control

(e) Unlocking of doors

7-6.5.3   The functions specified in 7-6.5.2 are permitted to be actuated by any protective signaling and control system where otherwise not required by this *Code*. Additionally, the protective signaling and control system may recall elevators, as required by 7-4.4, if the activation of the system for this purpose comes only from elevator lobby or associated machine room detectors, or if otherwise permitted by the authority having jurisdiction.

> The ANSI/ASME A17.1 *Safety Code for Elevators and Escalators*, which is referenced mandatorily for new elevators by 7-4.2, prohibits elevator recall from occurring by detection from anything but detectors installed in the elevator lobbies and associated elevator machine room. Recall by other detectors leads to numerous nuisance recalls under conditions where it would be safe to operate elevators. Rather than have elevators taken out of service every time any building system detector senses smoke, the recall feature is often deliberately disabled. In an attempt to keep the recall feature operational, ANSI/ASME A17.1 imposes the above limitation with respect to which detection devices can initiate elevator recall. Given that there may be situations under which elevator recall by additional detection devices would be desirable, paragraph 7-6.5.3 allows the authority having jurisdiction to permit such. The *Life Safety Code* reserves this right to differ from ANSI/ASME A17.1 via the introductory wording to 7-4.2, which reads: "Except as modified herein . . ."

7-6.5.4   The performance of emergency control functions shall not, in any way, impair the effective response of all required alarm notification functions.

7-6.5.5*   An auxiliary fire alarm relay used to control an emergency control device that provides any of the functions of 7-6.5.2 or elevator capture per 7-6.5.3, e.g., motor controller for HVAC system fan, shall be located within 3 ft (91 cm) of the emergency control device. The installation wiring between the protective signaling and control system panel and the auxiliary fire alarm relay shall be monitored for integrity.

A-7-6.5.5   Control devices that operate on loss of power to the actuator may be considered self-monitoring for integrity.

The concept of monitoring installation wiring for integrity is explained in the commentary following paragraph 7-6.1.5. The requirements of 7-6.5.5 explain that the monitoring needs to be done to within 3 ft (91 cm) of the actual device being controlled. The 3 ft (91 cm) dimension reasonably recognizes that different contractors are responsible for the building mechanical systems and the building protective signaling and control system. To require monitoring right to the device could create jurisdictional problems among the building trades, with the alarm contractor being asked to enter and modify the equipment installed by someone else.

7-6.6 Location of Controls.

7-6.6.1   Operator controls, visible alarm annunciators, and manual communications capability shall be installed in a control center at a convenient location acceptable to the authority having jurisdiction.

At times it is not practical physically nor from a security standpoint to locate control centers adjacent to an entrance. For example, control centers for proprietary protective signaling systems designed to NFPA 72D, *Standard for the Installation, Maintenance, and Use of Proprietary Signaling Systems*,[13] for reasons of security, often need to be located away from public areas. Thus, the *Code* no longer requires that control centers be located adjacent to an entrance but, because the controls are intended to be used by the fire department, they need to be located in a position approved by the authority having jurisdiction.

SECTION 7-7 AUTOMATIC SPRINKLERS AND OTHER EXTINGUISHING EQUIPMENT

7-7.1 Automatic Sprinklers.

7-7.1.1*   Each automatic sprinkler system required by another section of this *Code* shall be installed in accordance with NFPA 13, *Standard for the Installation of Sprinkler Systems*. Where partial sprinkler protection is permitted by another section of this *Code*, 4-1.2 of NFPA 13 shall apply.

Exception: NFPA 13D, Standard for the Installation of Sprinkler Systems in One- and Two-Family Dwellings and Mobile Homes, may be used as provided in Chapters 20, 21, and 22.

A-7-7.1.1   For a discussion of the effectiveness of automatic sprinklers as well as a general discussion on automatic sprinklers, see Section 18, Chapter 1, of the Sixteenth Edition of the NFPA *Fire Protection Handbook*. (*See Appendix B.*)

The requirements in the *Code* for automatic sprinklers have been carefully based on the sprinkler experience record, which shows that a sprinkler system is the most effective device, where installed properly, for protecting and safeguarding against loss of life and property. Occupants of a building who are aware of the presence of sprinkler protection can feel secure because they know that any fire will be detected and fought at its origin and that an alarm will be given; they know that it is probable that they will have time to evacuate a burning building before fire can cut off their escape.

There have been claims made by the uninformed that water in a sprinkler system can be heated to scalding temperatures and literally sprayed out onto occupants, thus causing injury and panic. Another fallacy is the belief that the mere spraying of large quantities of water will itself cause panic. As stated before, NFPA records of over a hundred thousand cases of sprinklers operating in building fires show no instances of this happening. The small quantity of water in the system piping over the fire that might be heated before the eutectic metal on the sprinkler melts and opens the flow will quickly be dissipated, and cool water will begin to flow. Other misconceptions about sprinkler systems, for example, that occupants of a room might be drowned, electrocuted, or scalded by steam, have not been shown by fire record data to exist and thus should be discounted.

NFPA 13, *Standard for the Installation of Sprinkler Systems*,[14] covers installation details for standard automatic sprinkler systems. It will generally be beneficial to provide a complete standard automatic sprinkler installation to protect the entire property, in the interest of both life safety from fire and the protection of property, even in situations where the *Code* requires sprinklers only for isolation and protection of hazardous areas.

NFPA 13, *Standard for the Installation of Sprinkler Systems*, is the so-called "bible" for sprinkler systems insofar as design, installation, and character and adequacy of water supply are concerned. Even though there are usually some areas in a building where fires are more likely to start than in others, it is impossible to predict where a fire might start and hence protect those areas only. Thus, it is recommended that, where sprinklers are installed, they be installed throughout a building. The basic requirements of NFPA 13 for spacing, location, and position of sprinklers are based on principles that include sprinkler installation throughout the building, including combustible concealed spaces.

NFPA 13, *Standard for the Installation of Sprinkler Systems*, provides for the installation of systems of various types appropriate for the individual building protected, subject to the approval of the authority having jurisdiction.

NFPA 13D, *Standard for the Installation of Sprinkler Systems in One- and Two-Family Dwellings and Mobile Homes*,[15] was developed after an extensive amount of research on the subject, including full-scale fire tests. It introduced the concept of a quick response sprinkler that, unlike its industrial standard spray sprinkler counterpart, which is inherently slow to fuse its relatively massive eutectic solder element, operates very quickly once its rated temperature is felt so as to begin controlling a fire early in its growth. In addition to being quick to respond, residential sprinklers, as mandated by NFPA 13D, have a specifically designed spray pattern that delivers water to nearly the full height of the walls of typical small rooms characteristic of residential occupancies.

NFPA 13A, *Recommended Practice for the Care and Maintenance of Sprinkler Systems*,[16] gives detailed information on maintenance procedures.

7-7.1.2 Sprinkler piping serving not more than six sprinklers for any isolated hazardous area may be connected directly to a domestic water supply system having a capacity sufficient to provide 0.15 gal per minute per sq ft (6.1 L/min/sq m) of floor area throughout the entire enclosed area. An indicating shut-off valve shall be installed in an accessible location between the sprinklers and the connection to the domestic water supply.

7-7.1.3* In areas protected by automatic sprinklers, automatic heat detection devices required by other sections of this *Code* may be deleted.

A-7-7.1.3 Properly designed automatic sprinkler systems provide the dual function of both automatic alarms and automatic extinguishment.

The preceding is not true in those cases where early detection of incipient fire and early notification of occupants are needed to initiate actions in behalf of life safety earlier than can be expected from heat-sensitive fire detectors.

> Properly designed automatic sprinkler systems provide the dual function of both automatic alarms and automatic extinguishment. Because the operation of an automatic sprinkler system is initiated by a heat sensing device and works on the same principle as an automatic heat detection and alarm system, the sprinkler system is judged to be capable of serving the same purpose. Even though some sprinkler systems may not give an alarm on activation, most properly designed systems do. Furthermore, while a particular sprinkler system may not give an alarm, it does begin immediate extinguishment, a feature that is equally as valuable, if not more so, as a system that sounds an alarm only.
>
> Detection of smoke, on the other hand, can be accomplished at the incipient stages of a fire and give rise to an earlier warning than that provided by heat detection, so it is considered in a somewhat different light. There are two schools of thought on the matter: some feel that a system that starts suppression of a fire immediately upon detection is better than one that simply detects the fire and gives an alarm, even though the latter is quicker in initiation of signal indication. Others believe, however, that an early alarm system is the more advantageous form. The first group is concerned with immediate arrest or containment of fire — it may take a considerable amount of time for fire fighters to arrive; the second group stresses immediate notification of occupants.

7-7.2 Supervision.

Supervision is not required by this subsection. Where a supervised automatic sprinkler system is specified by this *Code* or where required by the authority having jurisdiction for approval, the requirements of 7-7.2 apply.

7-7.2.1* Where supervised automatic sprinkler protection is required by another section of this *Code*, a distinct supervisory signal shall be provided to indicate a condition that will impair the satisfactory operation of the sprinkler system. This shall include, but not be limited to, monitoring of control valves, fire-pump power supplies and running conditions, water tank levels and temperatures, pressure of pressure tanks, and air pressure on dry-pipe valves.

A-7-7.2.1   NFPA 71, *Standard for the Installation, Maintenance, and Use of Signaling Systems for Central Station Service* (*see Appendix B*), gives details of standard practice in sprinkler supervision.

Subject to the approval of the authority having jurisdiction, sprinkler supervision may also be provided by direct connection to municipal fire departments or, in the case of very large establishments, to a private headquarters providing similar functions.

NFPA 72A, 72B, 72C, and 72D cover such matters. Where municipal fire alarm systems are involved, reference should also be made to NFPA 1221, *Public Fire Service Communications.* (*See Appendix B.*)

One reason why the automatic sprinkler system has attained a high level of satisfactory performance and response to fire conditions is that, through supervision, it can be kept in operative condition. Of course, keeping the system operative is dependent upon routine maintenance and the owner's willingness to repair the system when there are indications of some impairment. Features of the system can be automatically monitored, such as the opening and closing of water control valves, the power supplies for needed pumps, and water tank levels. If an undesirable situation develops, a signal is annunciated in the protected building or relayed to a central station.

A supervisory system will also indicate or activate a waterflow alarm that, in addition to being transmitted to proprietary or control stations, can be transmitted directly to the fire department. The signals for mechanical problems need not burden the fire department unnecessarily, whereas those indicating a fire can be received directly.

7-7.2.2   Supervisory signals for sprinkler systems shall terminate in a location within the protected building or premises that is constantly attended by qualified personnel in the employ of the owner or shall terminate in an approved remote receiving facility.

7-7.2.3   Where supervised automatic sprinkler protection is required by another section of this *Code*, waterflow alarms shall be transmitted to an approved proprietary alarm receiving facility, a remote station, a central station, or the fire department. Such connections shall be installed in accordance with 7-6.1.3.

7-7.3* Other Automatic Extinguishing Equipment.   In any occupancy where the character of the potential fuel for fire is such that extinguishment or control of fire may be more effectively accomplished by a type of automatic extinguishing system other than an automatic sprinkler system such as carbon dioxide, dry chemical, foam, Halon 1301, or water spray, a standard extinguishing system of other type may be installed in lieu of an automatic sprinkler system. Such systems shall be installed in accordance with appropriate NFPA standards.

A-7-7.3   Automatic extinguishing systems other than automatic sprinklers are covered by the following NFPA standards:

NFPA 11, *Standard for Low Expansion Foam and Combined Agent Systems.* (*See Appendix B.*)

NFPA 12, *Standard on Carbon Dioxide Extinguishing Systems.* (*See Appendix B.*)

NFPA 12A, *Standard on Halon 1301 Fire Extinguishing Systems.* (*See Appendix B.*)

NFPA 12B, *Standard on Halon 1211 Fire Extinguishing Systems.* (*See Appendix B.*)

NFPA 15, *Standard for Water Spray Fixed Systems for Fire Protection.* (*See Appendix B.*)

NFPA 17, *Standard for Dry Chemical Extinguishing Systems.* (*See Appendix B.*)

Use of special types of extinguishing systems is a matter of engineering judgment on the part of the designer, working in collaboration with the owner and the authorities concerned. Various NFPA standards are available to provide guidance in installation and maintenance procedures.

7-7.4 Manual Extinguishing Equipment.

7-7.4.1*   Where required by the provisions of another section of this *Code*, portable fire extinguishers shall be installed in accordance with NFPA 10, *Standard for the Installation of Portable Fire Extinguishers.*

A-7-7.4.1   For description of standard types of extinguishers and their installation, maintenance, and use, see NFPA 10, *Standard for the Installation of Portable Fire Extinguishers* (*see Appendix B*). The labels of recognized testing laboratories on extinguishers provide evidence of tests indicating reliability and suitability of the extinguisher for its intended use. Many unlabeled extinguishers are offered for sale that are substandard by reason of insufficient extinguishing capacity, questionable reliability, ineffective extinguishing agents for fires in ordinary combustible materials, or because they pose a personal hazard to the user.

7-7.4.2   Where required by the provisions of another section of this *Code*, standpipe and hose systems shall be provided in accordance with NFPA 14, *Standard for the Installation of Standpipe and Hose Systems.*

The *Code* has requirements for standpipes or extinguishers only in some of the individual occupancy chapters. For example, standpipes are required on stages of assembly occupancies and in detention and correctional occupancies. Portable extinguishers are required throughout health care, detention and correctional, mercantile, and business occupancies, but only in the hazardous areas of hotel, apartment, and board and care occupancies. Where the *Code* does require standpipes or extinguishers, the number, types, and locations required are beyond the scope of the *Code*; guidance can be found in NFPA 10, *Standard for Portable Fire Extinguishers,*[17] and NFPA 14, *Standard for the Installation of Standpipe and Hose Systems.*[18]

REFERENCES CITED IN COMMENTARY

[1]NFPA 70, *National Electrical Code*, National Fire Protection Association, Quincy, MA, 1987.

[2]NFPA 90A, *Standard for the Installation of Air Conditioning and Ventilating Systems*, National Fire Protection Association, Quincy, MA, 1985.

[3]NFPA 90B, *Standard for the Installation of Warm Air Heating and Air Conditioning Systems*, National Fire Protection Association, Quincy, MA, 1984.

[4]NFPA 96, *Standard for the Installation of Equipment for the Removal of Smoke and Grease-Laden Vapors from Commercial Cooking Equipment*, National Fire Protection Association, Quincy, MA, 1987.

[5]NFPA 92A, *Recommended Practice for Smoke Control Systems*, National Fire Protection Association, Quincy, MA, 1988.

[6]ANSI/ASME A17.1, *Safety Code for Elevators and Escalators*, American Society of Mechanical Engineers, 345 East 47th Street, New York, NY 10017, 1984.

[7]ANSI/ASME A17.3, *Safety Code for Existing Elevators and Escalators*, American Society of Mechanical Engineers, 345 East 47th Street, New York, NY 10017, 1986.

[8]*ASME Handbook A17.1*, American Society of Mechanical Engineers, 345 East 47th Street, New York, NY 10017, 1984.

[9]NFPA 82, *Standard on Incinerators, Waste and Linen Handling Systems and Equipment*, National Fire Protection Association, Quincy, MA, 1983.

[10]NFPA 72E, *Standard on Automatic Fire Detectors*, National Fire Protection Association, Quincy, MA, 1987.

[11]NFPA 72A, *Standard on Local Protective Signaling Systems*, National Fire Protection Association, Quincy, MA, 1987.

[12]NFPA 72F, *Standard for the Installation, Maintenance, and Use of Emergency Voice/Alarm Communications Systems*, National Fire Protection Association, Quincy, MA, 1985.

[13]NFPA 72D, *Standard for the Installation, Maintenance, and Use of Proprietary Signaling Systems*, National Fire Protection Association, Quincy, MA, 1986.

[14]NFPA 13, *Standard for the Installation of Sprinkler Systems*, National Fire Protection Association, Quincy, MA, 1987.

[15]NFPA 13D, *Standard for the Installation of Sprinkler Systems in One- and Two-Family Dwellings and Mobile Homes*, National Fire Protection Association, Quincy, MA, 1984.

[16]NFPA 13A, *Recommended Practice for the Care and Maintenance of Sprinkler Systems*, National Fire Protection Association, Quincy, MA, 1987.

[17]NFPA 10, *Standard for Portable Fire Extinguishers*, National Fire Protection Association, Quincy, MA, 1988.

[18]NFPA 14, *Standard for the Installation of Standpipe and Hose Systems*, National Fire Protection Association, Quincy, MA, 1986.

8

NEW ASSEMBLY OCCUPANCIES

(See also Chapter 31.)

Assembly occupancies include, but are not limited to, all buildings or portions of buildings used for gathering together 50 or more people for such purposes as deliberation, worship, entertainment, eating, drinking, amusement, or awaiting transportation. Assembly occupancies include, but are not limited to:

Armories	Discotheques
Assembly halls	Drinking establishments
Auditoriums	Exhibition halls
Bowling establishments	Gymnasiums
Churches	Libraries
Club rooms	Mortuary chapels
Conference rooms	Motion picture theaters
Courtrooms	Museums
Dance halls	Nightclubs

Passenger stations and terminals of air, surface, underground, and marine public transportation facilities. (If the jurisdiction enforcing the *Code* has adopted NFPA 130, *Standard for Fixed Guideway Transit Systems*,[1] there are some situations where transit stations would come under NFPA 130 rather than this *Code*. See NFPA 130 for additional details.)

Pool rooms	Skating rinks
Recreation piers	Theaters
Restaurants	

Also note that 10-1.1.3 requires university and college classrooms having a capacity of 50 or more persons to comply with the requirements of the assembly occupancy chapters.

Assembly occupancies with an occupant load of less than 50 are considered incidental to the predominate occupancy in which they are located. For example, a small conference room in an office area is considered part of the overall business occupancy. If it is a free standing occupancy or building, such as a small diner, normally a mercantile occupancy classification is assigned. In either case, the occupant load factors of 8-1.6 are used since it is still an assembly use.

Chapter 31 specifies the life safety requirements for the operation of assembly occupancies.

SECTION 8-1   GENERAL REQUIREMENTS

8-1.1 Application.   The requirements of this chapter apply to new assembly occupancies. (*See 8-1.3 for definition.*)

> Beginning with the 1981 Edition of the *Code*, new and existing occupancy requirements are in separate chapters. The provisions for existing assembly occupancies are found in Chapter 9.
>
> It should be noted that, if an existing building of some other occupancy were to change to an assembly occupancy classification, the portion of the building housing the assembly occupancy must comply with this chapter for new assembly occupancies, even though it is in an existing building. (*See 1-6.4.*) Also, should an existing assembly occupancy change occupancy subclassification, such as from a Class C to a Class B, it must meet the requirements for a new Class B assembly occupancy. (*See 1-6.4 and 9-1.1.*)

8-1.2 Mixed Occupancies.   (*See also 1-4.7.*)

8-1.2.1*   Any assembly occupancy and its access to exits in buildings of other occupancy, such as ballrooms in hotels, restaurants in stores, rooftop assembly occupancies, or assembly rooms in schools, shall be so located, separated, or protected as to avoid any undue danger to the occupants of the assembly occupancy from a fire originating in the other occupancy or smoke therefrom.

A-8-1.2.1   Depending upon the character of construction and the hazard of the occupancy, this will require some physical separation by walls of appropriate fire resistance, protection of the other occupancy by automatic sprinklers, or other appropriate measures. Where the building is of fire-resistive construction and the hazard of the other occupancy is low or ordinary, as in a school or hotel, no separation may be necessary.

> The intent of this provision is to protect the occupants of the assembly occupancy from the effects of a fire originating in the other occupancy. While this can be accomplished by several methods, two things must be considered in whichever method is chosen. First, consideration must be given to the protection of the means of egress of the assembly occupancy; second, the level of protection from the other occupancy that can be provided to the assembly occupancy itself must be considered. Methods that can be used to protect the assembly occupancy and its means of egress include construction of fire-rated partitions, use of independent exits, installation of automatic sprinklers, and careful analysis of the requirements of each occupancy when applying the provisions of 1-4.7 pertaining to mixed occupancies. (*Also see the discussion on 8-3.5.*)

8-1.2.2   Occupancy of any room or space for assembly purposes by fewer than 50 persons in a building of other occupancy and incidental to such other occupancy shall be classed as part of the other occupancy and subject to the provisions applicable thereto.

Fifty has traditionally been considered the minimum number of people assembled in one space for which the *Code* requires special provisions, such as requiring a door to swing in the direction of exit travel. (*See 5-2.1.4.1.*) Therefore, in Chapter 8, 50 people constitute a level of risk to life safety high enough to require classifying an occupancy as an assembly occupancy and, consequently, to subject the occupancy to the special design requirements found within this chapter. Since the space still contains an assembly use, the occupant load factors of 8-1.6 are still used even if the space is being regulated under another occupancy.

8-1.2.3   Assembly occupancies in buildings of other occupancy may use exits common to the assembly occupancy and the other occupancy provided that the assembly area and the other occupancy considered separately each have exits sufficient to meet the requirements of this *Code*.

Where applying this section, consideration must also be given to the provisions of 1-4.7 pertaining to mixed occupancies. Those provisions require that, in mixed occupancies, the more restrictive requirements of either occupancy be used for both occupancies.

8-1.2.4   Exits shall be sufficient for simultaneous occupancy of both the assembly occupancy and other parts of the building.

Exception*: Where the authority having jurisdiction determines that the conditions are such that simultaneous occupancy will not occur.

A-8-1.2.4 Exception Example: An assembly room for the inmates of a detention occupancy will not normally be subjected to simultaneous occupancy.

In 8-1.2.3 through 8-1.2.4, the *Code* requires that each occupancy, considered separately, have sufficient exits and that, where it is possible for simultaneous occupancy to occur, the exits be sufficient for the combined occupant load.

The Exception to 8-1.2.4 should be used judiciously. Consideration should be given to all possible uses before a decision is reached. A school gymnasium may normally be used only by the school occupants; however, several times a year, the gymnasium may be used by an outside group during school hours. A common example of this is the use of school gymnasiums as polling places on election day. Consideration should be given to all possible uses to provide the owner/occupant maximum flexibility in the use of the space.

8-1.3* Special Definitions.

Assembly Occupancies.   Include, but are not limited to, all buildings or portions of buildings used for gathering together 50 or more persons for such purposes as deliberation, worship, entertainment, dining, amusement, or awaiting transportation.

The definition for assembly occupancies indicates the need for alternate exit routes in small places of assembly, such as restaurants, lounges, or theaters, with capacities for as few as 50 people. (*Also see commentary at the beginning of this chapter.*)

Cyclorama.   The name generally applied to a neutral background that, with suitable lighting, can suggest the infinite space of the sky. It may be curved and may be painted to depict any required background.

The term "cyclorama" is used in the definition of "stage scenery." These definitions have been added to better clarify the terms used by the movie and theater industry.

Drop.   A large piece of scenic canvas that hangs vertically, usually across the stage area.

The definition of the term "drop" is intended to better clarify the *Code* with regard to stage productions.

Flow Time.   Flow time is the time during which there is crowd flow past a point in the means of egress system, and it is a component of total evacuation time.

The term "flow time" has been used in the technical literature on egress, and it is one worth understanding in relation to the *Code*'s requirements for the capacity of means of egress. Flow time is the time taken by a crowd to pass, for example, through a doorway during a mass egress situation. This egress time component, along with other egress time components for responding to an alarm (before beginning egress movement) and for traveling along the length of an egress route, contributes to the total time needed to evacuate an area after an emergency situation is detected and an alarm is sounded. In the case of large assembly buildings, the flow time is often the largest component of total evacuation time. Therefore, explicit information about flow time is now included in Chapters 8 and 9 of the *Code* to help improve understanding of the nominal performance expected where particular egress capacity requirements are satisfied.

Fly.   The space over the stage of a theater where scenery and equipment can be hung out of view. Also called lofts and rigging lofts.

Fly Gallery.   A narrow raised platform at the side of a legitimate stage from which the lines for flying scenery are manipulated.

Gridiron.   The arrangement of beams over a legitimate stage supporting the machinery for flying scenery and hanging battens from which lighting is hung.

Leg Drop.   A long narrow strip of fabric used for masking. Where used on either or both sides of the acting area, to provide entry to the stage by the actors, but also to mask. They may also be called "wings."

See commentary on the term "drop."

Life Safety Evaluation.   A life safety evaluation is a written review dealing with the adequacy of life safety features relative to fire, storm, collapse, crowd behavior, and other related safety considerations.

This definition has been added for use in conjunction with 8-2.3.2. See the appendix note and commentary dealing with 8-2.3.2. It is important to keep in mind that a Life Safety Evaluation deals with more than merely firesafety. The evaluation must consider all life safety hazards that could endanger occupants and require rapid egress or other measures to maintain safety. In some large assembly facilities, for example, fire might not be the most likely hazard; there might be more injuries and deaths due to incidents arising from the large number and high density of people in a limited space. This can happen in the course of normal occupancy conditions, such as where occupants are especially aroused about the event or where there is the possibility that occupants may have a strong desire to escape an area, e.g., when there is a sudden change of weather in the case of open facilities, or where there is a collapse of part of the structure. Such possibilities must be taken into account when doing a Life Safety Evaluation and, in some cases, special expertise will be required to properly assess and design or manage for social and behavioral factors in addition to factors of fire and structural safety. Generally, the evaluation must be based on a good understanding of the occupants — especially if they are crowded together — and the event that generates the assembly of people.

Multipurpose Assembly Occupancy.   An assembly room designed to accommodate temporarily any of several possible assembly uses.

This definition is needed to explain 8-3.5.1 Exception No. 2. The designer, user, and code enforcer need to evaluate the exit requirements and occupant loads for all potential uses of the multipurpose area. These requirements need to take into consideration simultaneous multiple use as well as any single purpose use.

Multipurpose assembly occupancies are often part of a school, office building, fellowship hall, or other occupancy. In these instances, the exiting and means of egress requirements must be considered, as they may affect or be affected by the use of the other occupancy.

Pinrail.   A beam at one side of a legitimate stage through which wooden or metal pins are driven, and to which lines from the flies are fastened.

Platform.*   That raised area within a building used for the presentation of music, plays, or other entertainment; the head tables for special guests; the raised area for lecturers and speakers; boxing and wrestling rings; theater-in-the-round; and similar purposes wherein there are no overhead drops, scenery, or stage effects other than lighting and a screening valance.

A-8-1.3 Definitions.

Platform.   It is not intended to prohibit the use of a curtain as a valance to screen or hide the electric conduit, lighting track or similar fixtures.

This is not intended to prohibit the use of curtains such as are used to obscure the back wall of the stage, curtain between the auditorium and the stage (grand or house curtain) and no more than four leg drops nor the use of a valance to screen light panels, plumbing and similar equipment from view.

The revised definition, along with the appendix note, is intended to bring the nontheatrical "stages" of many schools under the definition of platform. Hanging curtains commonly used on platforms are normally used to conceal lighting or to provide a more aesthetic appearance.

Platform, Temporary.   A platform erected within an area for not more than 30 days.

Platform, Permanent.   A platform erected within an area for more than 30 days.

Proscenium Wall.   The wall that separates the stage from the auditorium or house.

Smoke-Protected Assembly Seating.*   Seating served by means of egress that is not subject to blockage by smoke accumulation within or under a structure.

A-8-1.3 Definitions.

Smoke-Protected Assembly Seating.   An assembly area wherein the roof is not less than 15 ft (4.5 m) above the highest cross aisle or seat row, and having smoke-actuated venting facilities within that part of the roof sufficient to maintain the level of smoke at least 6 ft (183 cm) above the highest seating or walking level, is considered to be smoke-protected assembly seating.

Special Amusement Building.   Any building, temporary, permanent, or mobile, containing a device or system that conveys passengers or provides a walkway along, around, or over a course in any direction as a form of amusement so arranged that the egress path is not readily apparent due to visual or audio distractions or intentionally confounded egress path, or is not readily available due to the mode of conveyance through the building or structure. Included are such amusements as a "haunted house," a "roller coaster" type ride within a building, a "merry-go-round" within a building, a "submarine" ride, and similar amusements where the occupants are not in the open air.

This definition is needed for the new subsection 8-4.6, Special Provisions for Special Amusement Buildings. It is the intent of the Committee that this definition address the structure and the use of the structure. The structure may be a permanent building or may be a semi-truck trailer or other similar enclosure that is semi-permanent or mobile. Special amusement buildings are designed to provide a full enclosure for the patrons. Structures that are not fully enclosed, e.g., a merry-go-round with a roof and no sides, would not conform to this definition. This definition also includes special amusement buildings within a larger structure, such as an amusement building within a shopping mall. Theaters, movie houses, or similar public assembly occupancies used for amusement or entertainment are not defined as special amusement buildings.

Stage. An area within a building used for the purpose of entertainment, and utilizing drops or scenery or other stage effects and shall be classified as one of the following:

(a) *Stage, Legitimate.* A stage wherein scenery is retractable mechanically, either horizontally or vertically or suspended overhead.

(b) *Stage, Regular.* A stage wherein scenery is not retractable.

(c) *Stage, Thrust.* A platform extending beyond the proscenium arch and into the audience.

The new definition has been expanded to specifically include drops, scenery or other stage effects. The intent is to better differentiate between stages and platforms (*see the definition of platform*). The definition of legitimate, regular, and thrust stage remains the same. Temporary stage has been removed.

This revised definition of stage needs to be examined in conjunction with the revised definition of platform. The intent of these changes is to remove nontheatrical stages, such as those in many lower grade level schools, from the definition and call them platforms.

This definition of stage encompasses various types of stages, including arena stages (stages open to the audience on at least three sides).

The key point in the definition of a stage is the hanging of curtains, leg drops, and scenery. If none of these is present, then the arrangement is probably a platform. A potential problem is the arrangement commonly known as theater-in-the-round. For *Code* purposes, if the theater-in-the-round has scenery, leg drops, or curtains suspended on or above it, then it is a stage; if it has only lighting with a valance to hide the electrical fixtures, then it is a platform.

A typical example of a thrust stage is illustrated in Figure 8-1. The so-called "runway" at Atlantic City that is used annually for the Miss America Pageant is probably the most famous thrust stage.

Stage Properties. Furniture, carpet, and similar materials generally having an overall height of less than 5 ft (152 cm) and used to provide an appearance simulating a room or area.

The Committee felt this would better clarify the difference between the props used on a stage and the scenery used to dress the stage. The definition of "stage properties" and "stage scenery" is particularly important with regard to the flame-retardant requirements in 8-3.2.1.11.

Stage Scenery. Decorative materials such as flats, cycloramas, painted or photographic backings, and similar materials to "dress" the stage.

See commentary on stage properties.

A-8-1.3 Definitions. The following definitions may be useful to the enforcer of the *Code* although the terms are not used within the *Code*.

Accessory Rooms. The accessory rooms are dressing rooms, property master's

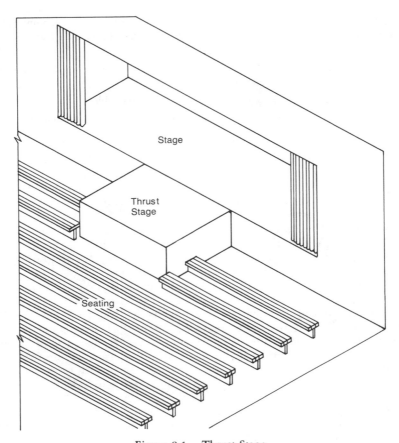

Figure 8-1.   Thrust Stage.

work and storage rooms, the carpenter's room, and similar rooms necessary for legitimate stage operations.

Batten.   In general a flown metal pipe or shape on which lights or scenery are fastened. While existing theater stages may still have wooden bars, they should not be used in new construction.

Scrim.   Finely woven fabric that can be translucent or opaque depending upon how it is used.

Theater-in-the-Round.   An acting area in the middle of a room with the audience sitting all around it.

8-1.4 Classification of Occupancy.   (See 4-1.2.)

8-1.4.1 Subclassification of Assembly Occupancies.   Each assembly occupancy shall be subclassified according to its occupant load as follows: Class A, occupant load greater than 1000 persons; Class B, occupant load greater than 300 but not greater than 1000 persons; Class C, occupant load of 50 or more but not greater than 300 persons.

Minor language changes were made for the 1988 Edition to make the language consistent with the rest of the *Code*.

As each increment of population is reached, the level of risk to life safety from exposure to fire rises. In view of this, the stringency of the requirements found in this chapter increases to counter each higher risk level.

8-1.5 Classification of Hazard of Contents.   Contents of assembly occupancies shall be classified in accordance with the provisions of Section 4-2.

8-1.6 Minimum Construction Requirements.   (*See 6-2.1.*) The location of an assembly occupancy shall be limited as follows:

Type of Construction	Below LED	LED	Number of Levels Above LED			
			1	2	3	4 & Above
I (443) I (332) II (222)	A†B†C† Any Number of Levels	ABC	ABC	ABC	ABC	A†B†C
II (111)	A†B†C† One Level Below LED	ABC	ABC	A†BC	B†C†	N.P.
III (211) IV (2HH) V (111)	A†B†C† One Level Below LED	ABC	ABC	A†B†C	B†C†	N.P.
II (000)	B†C† One Level Below LED	A†BC	C†	N.P.	N.P.	N.P.
III (200) V (000)	B†C† One Level Below LED	BC	C†	N.P.	N.P.	N.P.

†Permitted if all the following are protected throughout by an approved, supervised automatic sprinkler system in accordance with Section 7-7:

(a) The level of the assembly occupancy, and

(b) Any level below the level of the assembly occupancy, and

(c) In the case of an assembly occupancy located below the level of exit discharge, any level intervening between that level and the level of exit discharge, including the level of exit discharge.

N.P. — Not Permitted

LED — Level of Exit Discharge

It should be noted that the chart is arranged based on levels above the level of exit discharge (LED). Thus, in a normal building with the level of exit discharge at grade, the column "1" in the table refers to the second story of the building.

Since the Cocoanut Grove Night Club fire in Boston (1942), much emphasis has been placed by the Subcommittee on Assembly and Educational Occupancies on limiting the number of occupants in those assembly occupancies that provide only a minimum level of life safety because of the nature of the construction. The Cocoanut Grove fire illustrated the effect that a combustible structure (as well as combustible interior finish) and a multilevel location for an assembly occupancy can have on the severity of a fire and its high death count. More recently, the Beverly Hills Supper Club fire (1977) also illustrated these factors.

Paragraph 8-1.6 restricts the location of assembly occupancies. Type I and Type II (222) (fire-resistive) construction, with its "built-in-place" structural survivability (under fire attack), is acceptable for any assembly occupancy (hence, for any number of occupants) at the level of exit discharge and up to the fourth story. As the fire resistivity of the structure diminishes from Type II (111) (protected noncombustible) to Type V (000) (wood-frame) construction, the location of assembly occupancies (and the permitted number of occupants) is restricted. In addition, as the height of the building increases, so does the risk to the occupants; thus, the location of assembly occupancies is also restricted by height.

The table contained in 8-1.6 was revised in the 1985 Edition of the *Code*. The table presents a major provision of the *Code* for assembly occupancies and recognizes the value of automatic sprinklers as a life safety device. Note that the table deals with the location of the assembly occupancy in relation to the level of exit discharge. Thus, for example, if the building in question was a seven-story, Type I (fire-resistive) building with the level of exit discharge at the first floor, a Class A assembly occupancy could be located at the fourth floor without sprinkler protection. If the Class A assembly occupancy were located at the fifth floor, automatic sprinkler protection would be required for the fifth floor and all floors below the fifth floor, including any basement levels. (*See notes to table.*)

Any assembly occupancies located below the level of exit discharge require automatic sprinkler protection, as do all levels below the assembly occupancy and all levels intervening between the assembly level and the level of exit discharge.

The construction types given here are based on NFPA 220, *Standard on Types of Building Construction*.[2] (*See 6-2.1 and related appendix note.*)

Formal Interpretation 81-25
Reference: 1-4.7, 8-1.6, 24-4.3.1

Given that per 8-1.6, a 3-story shopping mall with a food park (restaurant) on the third level is required to be of fire-resistive construction under the criteria for a Class A place of assembly above grade level.

Question 1: Is it possible to construct an anchor store of a different construction type from the mall building by separating it from the mall building by a 3-hour fire wall?

Question 2: Are 3-hour fire doors required for openings in this 3-hour wall between the mall and the anchor store?

Question 3: If the answer to Question 2 is no, is any type of opening protection required for openings between the mall and anchor store?

Answer: With only a few exceptions, the *Life Safety Code* sets no specific occupancy separation requirements. The authority having jurisdiction determines what separation is needed, if any, based on 1-4.7 and the 1.2 subsection of each occupancy chapter. The local building code or the model building codes may be consulted by the authority having jurisdiction in making this determination, keeping life safety rather than property protection in mind.

Issue Edition: 1981
Reference: 1-4.5, 8-1.6, 24-4.3.1
Date: October 1982

Formal Interpretation 81-27
Reference: 8-1.6

Question: Taking guidance from 1-3.6 that states "the *Code* does not attempt to address those general fire prevention or building construction features that are normally a function of fire prevention and building codes," is it the intent of 8-1.6 to require fireproofing of the steel roof structure in Class A assembly areas, such as convention and exhibition centers, with ceiling heights greater than the 20-ft exemption point for fireproofing common to the model building codes?

Answer: The *Life Safety Code* establishes certain minimum construction types in some occupancies, such as assembly, but relies on NFPA 220, *Standard on Types of Building Construction*, to define the construction types. NFPA 220 does not provide an exception for roof protection similar to the exceptions found in some of the model building codes. It should be noted that Section 1-5 allows the authority having jurisdiction to determine equivalencies. If the authority having jurisdiction determines that, due to roof height, building use, sprinkler protection, or other features, roof protection is not needed, it is the authority's prerogative to do so.

Issue Edition: 1981
Reference: 8-1.6
Date: March 1983

8-1.7 Occupant Load.

8-1.7.1* The occupant load permitted in any assembly building, structure, or portion thereof shall be determined on the basis of the following occupant load factors:

For ease of using this handbook, A-8-1.7.1 appears following all discussion on 8-1.7.1.

(a)* An assembly area of concentrated use without fixed seats such as an auditorium, place of worship, dance floor, discotheque or lodge hall — one person per 7 net sq ft (0.65 sq m).

In the 1988 *Code*, the terminology "7 sq ft (0.65 sq m) per person" was changed to read "one person per 7 net sq ft (0.65 sq m)." The intent of the Committee was to clarify the meaning of the *Code*. The intent is that one person is assumed for each 7 sq ft (0.65 sq m) that is available to be used by occupants after deducting space occupied by permanently fixed counters, furnishings, etc.

The 7 sq ft (0.65 sq m) occupant load factor is based on open floor space with people standing in comfortable surroundings. This factor also can be used to estimate occupant load in a multipurpose room where portable chairs are placed in rows for meetings, film viewing, or lectures.

A-8-1.7.1(a)   This includes so-called "Festival Seating."

Festival seating is illustrated in Figure 8-2. This comfortable, low-density arrangement of people, providing them with the ability to sit directly on the ground or floor and to move relatively easily through and out of the area, likely evolved from festivals held in open areas. This concept has been abused where applied to indoor or outdoor events where the assembled spectators are not controllable in terms of their numbers, location, or behavior. Rock music concerts are examples of events where the "festival seating" concept might become decidedly unfestive due to unmanageable crowds of standing (not seated) people in front of the stage area and a complete loss of any maintained circulation routes through the assembled crowd. Injuries, due to crushing of bodies against bodies or portions of structure, are likely when this occurs. A description of a typical crush situation is found in a report titled, "Observations of crowd conditions at rock concert in Exhibition Stadium, Toronto, 16 July 1980," by J.L. Pauls. Because the number and arrangement of people here was not maintained throughout the event, there eventually were some thirty to forty thousand people distributed unevenly in an area of about 125,000 sq ft (10,600 sq m), resulting in an average density of about 1 person per 3.5 sq ft (.33 sq m). However, due to localized crowding at the stage area, several thousand people were at crushing densities of about 1 person per 2 sq ft (.19 sq m). Both normal access and emergency access into this congested area were all but impossible, and management efforts to have people move back toward less densely occupied areas proved futile. Incidents like this one have led to the area limitations shown in 8-1.7.2, which provides for increases of occupant load in some situations.

(b) An assembly area of less concentrated use, such as a conference room, dining room, drinking establishment, exhibit room, gymnasium, or lounge — one person per 15 net sq ft (1.4 sq m).

In the 1988 *Code*, the terminology "15 sq ft (1.4 sq m) per person" was changed to read "one person per 15 net sq ft (1.4 sq m)." The intent of the Committee was to clarify the meaning of the *Code*. The intent is that one person is assumed for each 15 sq ft (1.4 sq m) that is available to be used by occupants.

Photograph Courtesy of J. L. Pauls.

Figure 8-2.   Festival Seating at a Rock Music Concert Held in a Stadium.

The 15-sq ft (1.4-sq m) occupant load factor is based on a use that has a certain amount of space occupied by furniture or a use requiring a large amount of space per person to accomplish the use. Examples of these typical uses are spaces involving the use of tables and chairs as in restaurants or conference rooms. Gymnasiums are an example of a use that requires space for the occupants to perform their function (i.e., exercising or sport games).

(c) Bleachers, pews, and similar bench-type seating — one person for 18 linear in. (45.7 linear cm).

(d) *Fixed Seating.* The occupant load of an area having fixed seats shall be determined by the number of fixed seats installed. Required aisle space serving the fixed seats shall not be used to increase the occupant load.

(e) *Kitchens.*   One person per 100 gross sq ft (9.3 sq m).

This will clarify calculating the total occupant load in restaurants and cafeterias where a portion of the building is used as a kitchen, whether it is a separate room or only divided from the dining area by a serving counter. Note this occupant load is calculated by using "gross sq ft (sq m)." This takes into consideration that there will be stoves, sinks, cutting boards, counters, and other culinary machinery necessary to operate a kitchen.

(f) *Libraries.*   In stack areas—one person per 100 gross sq ft (9.3 sq m); in reading rooms — one person per 50 net sq ft (4.6 sq m).

The intent of the Committee is to clarify the meaning of the *Code*. In stack areas, the terminology was changed from "100 sq ft (9.3 sq m) per person" to "one person per 100 gross sq ft (9.3 sq m)." This takes into consideration that there will be bookshelves and permanent aisles. In reading areas, the terminology was changed from "50 sq ft (4.6 sq m) per person" to "one person per 50 net sq ft (4.6 sq m)." Reading rooms typically have large magazine racks, chairs, couches, and other furnishings that are arranged by librarians to make the area attractive to the user.

A-8-1.7.1   Suggested occupant load factors for components of large airport terminal buildings are given, however the authority having jurisdiction may elect to use different occupant load factors provided exit requirements herein are satisfied.

AIRPORT TERMINAL	SQ FT (GROSS)	SQ M (GROSS)
Concourse	100	[9.3]
Waiting Areas	15	[1.4]
Baggage Claim	20	[1.9]
Baggage Handling	300	[27.9]
Other	(See table in appendix A-5-3.1.2)	

The occupant load factors of 8-1.7.1 reflect the data developed from surveys of typical occupancies.

Consideration should be given to the actual use of a room or space. A multi-use room may have several occupant loads depending upon its function on a given day. This is especially true of multipurpose rooms in schools and hotels.

Figure 8-3a illustrates a 2500-sq ft (230-sq m) room with two 46-in. (117-cm) clear width doors. If the room were to be used as a banquet room with tables and chairs, its occupant load would be based on the 15-sq ft (1.4-sq m) factor, resulting in an occupant load of 167 occupants. If, however, the room were to be used for a stand-up cocktail party with essentially no furniture, then the occupant load would be based on the 7-sq ft (0.65-sq m) factor, resulting in an occupant load of 357 occupants. Thus, the room may have two occupant loads.

The exit capacity for the room is based on two 46-in. (117-cm) doors. Using only the criterion of exit capacity, the room can accommodate 460 occupants. Since either of the occupant loads calculated is less than the exit capacity, the situation is satisfactory.

As noted above, both criteria (exit capacity and occupant load) must be considered in establishing the permissible occupant load for a room or area. For example, the exit capacity of the room shown in Figure 8-3b is sufficient for an occupant load of 360 people. An occupant load calculated on the basis of the room size [3,600 sq ft (330 sq m) ÷ 7] would permit 514 people. Therefore, the exit capacity must be increased to 514 in accordance with Section 5-3 since exit capacity must be provided for the occupant load determined by application of the occupant load factor.

Many times there is controversy over where to use a 7-sq ft versus a

15-sq ft occupant load factor. It must be remembered that these factors are based on "concentrated" versus "less concentrated" use and choices are made strictly by means of judgment. Since the occupant load is used to establish exit capacity and subclassification (which establishes construction, alarm, and sprinkler requirements), it is usually safer to allow a larger occupant load (with related increased safety requirements) than to try, usually with great difficulty, to enforce a small occupant load limit. (*Also see 8-1.7.2.*)

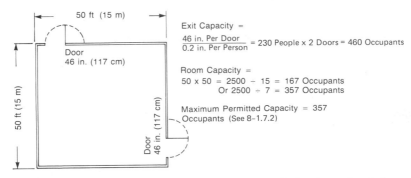

Figure 8-3a. Determination of Maximum Permitted Occupant Load for an Assembly Occupancy by Room Capacity.

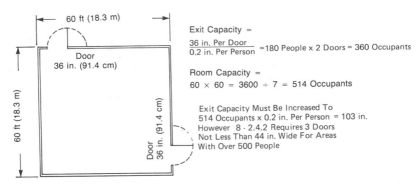

Figure 8-3b. Determination of Minimum Exit Capacity for an Assembly Occupancy.

8-1.7.2 The occupant load permitted in a building or portion thereof may be increased above that specified in 8-1.7.1 if the necessary aisles and exits are provided. To increase the occupant load, a diagram indicating placement of equipment, aisles, exits, and seating shall be provided to and approved by the authority having jurisdiction prior to any increase in occupant load. In areas not greater than 10,000 sq ft (930 sq m), the occupant load shall not exceed one person in 5 sq ft (.46 sq m); in areas greater than 10,000 sq ft (930 sq m), the occupant load shall not exceed one person in 7 sq ft (.65 sq m).

The accessibility of room exits is as important as the exit capacity. Therefore, where an increase is permitted over the occupant load established by 8-1.7.1, it must be demonstrated that adequate aisles and access ways leading to the room exits are provided. Spacing of tables must provide for occupied chairs plus an aisle. Consideration should be given to the probability that, when occupants leave during an emergency, they may not take time to move chairs out of the aisles. (*See 8-2.5.4.*)

Dining and drinking areas most frequently take advantage of the provision of 8-1.7.2. There have been large banquet layouts where the occupant load was successfully increased to reflect an occupant load factor of 11 sq ft (1 sq m) instead of the 15 sq ft (1.4 sq m) specified by 8-1.7.1(b). In all cases where an increase in the occupant load is permitted, the authority having jurisdiction should insist on complete fixture and furniture layouts and should strictly enforce adherence to approved layouts. As noted above, the same room may have several approved occupant loads depending on the various fixture and furniture layouts.

A major change in this paragraph from the 1985 Edition of the *Code* is a revision to the limit on the increased occupant load. This limit, which is based on an occupant load factor of 5 sq ft (0.46 sq m), was instituted for the 1985 Edition based on the Committee's concern for overcrowding, which affects the movement characteristics of the occupants. Due to problems with festival seating (*see 8-1.3*), the limit was modified in this edition so as to be restricted to facilities not larger than 10,000 sq ft (930 sq m).

It has been shown in research at the National Research Council in Canada and by the London Transport Board that if people are crowded into a space so that each person occupies less than 7 sq ft (0.65 sq m), then movement approaches a "shuffle"; when each person occupies less than 3 sq ft (0.28 sq m), "jam point" is approached, and all movement by the occupants is effectively stopped. Thus, the maximum occupant load factor of 5 sq ft (0.46 sq m) for areas less than or equal to 10,000 sq ft (930 sq m) was chosen by the Committee to prevent overcrowding and the attendant change in the movement characteristics of occupants.

See Figures 8-4a and 8-4b for two examples of increasing occupant load.

8-1.7.3 Waiting Spaces.   In theaters and other assembly occupancies where persons are admitted to the building at times when seats are not available to them, or when the permitted occupant load has been reached based on 8-1.7.1 or 8-1.7.2 and persons are allowed to wait in a lobby or similar space until seats or space are available, such use of lobby or similar space shall not encroach upon the required clear width of exits. Such waiting shall be restricted to areas other than the required means of egress. Exits shall be provided for such waiting spaces on the basis of one person for each 3 sq ft (0.28 sq m) of waiting space area. Such exits shall be in addition to the exits specified for the main auditorium area and shall conform in construction and arrangement to the general rules for exits given in this chapter.

This is most often used for theaters, motion picture theaters, and in some restaurants. This space cannot be in or interfere with the egress routes from the rest of the assembly occupancy.

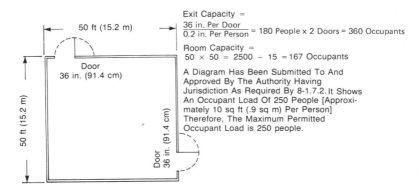

Exit Capacity =
$$\frac{36 \text{ in. Per Door}}{0.2 \text{ in. Per Person}} = 180 \text{ People} \times 2 \text{ Doors} = 360 \text{ Occupants}$$

Room Capacity =
50 × 50 = 2500 ÷ 15 = 167 Occupants

A Diagram Has Been Submitted To And Approved By The Authority Having Jurisdiction As Required By 8-1.7.2. It Shows An Occupant Load Of 250 People [Approximately 10 sq ft (.9 sq m) Per Person] Therefore, The Maximum Permitted Occupant Load is 250 people.

Figure 8-4a. Determination of Maximum Permitted Occupant Load for an Assembly Occupancy. Note that a practical upper limit for the room's population that will still ensure rapid and orderly movement to an exit may be 500 people (2,500 ÷ 5) based on 8-1.7.2. Since the exit capacity provides for 360 people, the authority having jurisdiction could conceivably allow a maximum permitted occupant load of 360.

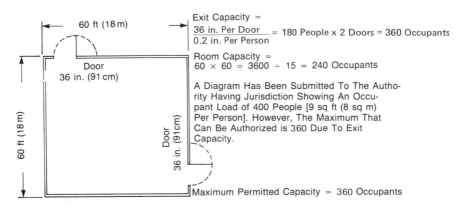

Exit Capacity =
$$\frac{36 \text{ in. Per Door}}{0.2 \text{ in. Per Person}} = 180 \text{ People} \times 2 \text{ Doors} = 360 \text{ Occupants}$$

Room Capacity =
60 × 60 = 3600 ÷ 15 = 240 Occupants

A Diagram Has Been Submitted To The Authority Having Jurisdiction Showing An Occupant Load of 400 People [9 sq ft (8 sq m) Per Person]. However, The Maximum That Can Be Authorized is 360 Due To Exit Capacity.

Maximum Permitted Capacity = 360 Occupants

Figure 8-4b. Determination of Maximum Permitted Occupant Load for an Assembly Occupancy by Exit Capacity. Note that a practical upper limit for the room's population that will still ensure rapid and orderly movement to an exit may be 720 people (3,600 ÷ 5) based on 8-1.7.2. However, the exit capacity of 360 must determine the maximum permitted occupant load.

SECTION 8-2   MEANS OF EGRESS REQUIREMENTS

8-2.1 General.   All means of egress shall be in accordance with Chapter 5 and this chapter.

8-2.2 Means of Egress Components.

Many of the provisions formerly found in 8-2.11 now appear in 8-2.2. The intent of the Committee is to bring all of the components of means of egress into this section and simplify the *Code* for the user.

8-2.2.1   Components of means of egress shall be limited to the types described in 8-2.2.2 through 8-2.2.7.

Slide escapes and elevators are not suited for rapid evacuation of the large numbers of people found in these occupancies. Further, elevators introduce other risk factors if used during a fire. (*See Section 7-4.*) Chapter 5 no longer allows escalators to be in the means of egress in new construction. It should be noted that these devices can be installed, but they cannot obstruct or interfere with the required means of egress.

8-2.2.2 Doors.

8-2.2.2.1   Doors shall comply with 5-2.1.

8-2.2.2.2   Class C assembly occupancies in covered malls (*see 24-4.4.1 Exception*) may have horizontal or vertical security grilles or doors complying with 5-2.1.4.1 Exception No. 3 on the main entrance/exits.

This provision allows small restaurants in malls to use the security grilles or doors as provided in 5-2.1.4.1 Exception No. 3.

8-2.2.2.3 Panic Hardware or Fire Exit Hardware.   Any door in a required means of egress from an area having an occupant load of 100 or more persons may be provided with a latch or lock only if it is panic hardware or fire exit hardware complying with 5-2.1.7.

Exception No. 1:   In assembly occupancies having an occupant load not greater than 500, where the main exit consists of a single door or single pair of doors, locking devices complying with 5-2.1.5.1 Exception No. 2 may be used on the main exit. Any latching device on this door(s) shall be released by panic hardware.

Exception No. 1 to 8-2.2.2.3 is in recognition of provisions for locking doors contained in Chapter 5, Means of Egress. These provisions recognize the need to lock doors for security purposes and provide limits on how this can be done. These provisions also recognize, in fact, that in order for the business to function, the main door must be open. If a latching device is used in addition to the lock, panic hardware is required to release the latch.

Exception No. 2: Special locking arrangements as permitted in 8-2.2.2.4.

8-2.2.2.4 Special locking arrangements complying with 5-2.1.6 are permitted on doors other than main entrance/exit doors.

> Paragraph 8-2.2.2.4 allows delayed release hardware meeting the requirements of 5-2.1.6 to be used on all but the main exit. In addition to other requirements, 5-2.1.6 requires that the building be protected throughout by either an approved automatic sprinkler system or an approved supervised automatic fire detection system.

8-2.2.2.5 Revolving doors complying with 5-2.1.10 are permitted.

8-2.2.2.6 Turnstiles. No turnstiles or other devices to restrict the movement of persons shall be installed in any assembly occupancy in such a manner as to interfere in any way with required means of egress facilities.

8-2.2.3 Stairs. Stairs shall comply with 5-2.2.

8-2.2.4 Smokeproof Enclosures. Smokeproof enclosures shall comply with 5-2.3.

8-2.2.5 Horizontal Exits. Horizontal exits shall comply with 5-2.4.

8-2.2.6 Ramps.

8-2.2.6.1 Ramps shall comply with 5-2.5.

8-2.2.6.2 Ramps in Class A assembly occupancies shall be Class A ramps.

8-2.2.7 Exit Passageways. Exit passageways shall comply with 5-2.6.

8-2.3 Capacity of Means of Egress.

8-2.3.1 The capacity of means of egress shall be in accordance with Section 5-3 or, in the case of means of egress serving theater-type seating or similar seating arranged in rows, in accordance with 8-2.3.2.

8-2.3.2* Minimum clear widths of aisles and other means of egress shall be in accordance with Table 8-2.3.2(a) or, for buildings providing Smoke-Protected Assembly Seating and for which an Approved Life Safety Evaluation is conducted, Table 8-2.3.2(b). For Table 8-2.3.2(b), the number of seats specified must be within a single assembly space and interpolation shall be permitted between the specific values shown. For both tables, the minimum clear widths shown shall be modified in accordance with all of the following:

(a) If risers exceed 7 in. (17.8 cm) in height, multiply the stair width in the tables by factor A, where $A = 1 + \dfrac{(\text{riser height} - 7.0 \text{ in.})}{}$

(b) Stairs not having a handrail within a 30-in. (76-cm) horizontal distance shall be 25 percent wider than otherwise calculated, i.e., multiply by B = 1.25.

(c) Ramps steeper than 1 in 10 slope, used in ascent, shall have their width increased by 10 percent, i.e., multiply by factor C = 1.10.

Table 8-2.3.2(a)
For Use Without Smoke-Protected Assembly Seating

| No. of Seats | Nominal Flow Time (sec.) | Inch of Clear Width Per Seat Served | |
		Stairs	Passageways, Ramps, and Doorways
Unlimited	200	0.300 AB	0.220 C

(1 in. = 2.54 cm)

Table 8-2.3.2(b)
For Use With Smoke-Protected Assembly Seating

| No. of Seats | Nominal Flow Time (sec.) | Inch of Clear Width Per Seat Served | |
		Stairs	Passageways, Ramps, and Doorways
2,000	200	0.300 AB	0.220 C
5,000	260	0.200 AB	0.150 C
10,000	360	0.130 AB	0.100 C
15,000	460	0.096 AB	0.070 C
20,000	560	0.076 AB	0.056 C
25,000 or more	660	0.060 AB	0.044 C

(1 in. = 2.54 cm)

A-8-2.3.2   Tables 8-2.3.2(a) and 8-2.3.2.(b) are based on a linear relationship between number of seats and nominal flow time, with a minimum of 200 seconds (3.3 minutes) for 2,000 seats plus 1 second for every additional 50 seats up to 25,000. Beyond 25,000 total seats, the nominal flow time is limited to 660 seconds (11 minutes). Nominal flow time refers to the flow time for the most-able group of patrons; some less-familiar, less-able groups might take longer to pass a point in the egress system. (Although three or more digits are noted in the tables, the resulting calculations should be assumed to provide only two significant figures of precision.)

A life safety evaluation is a written review dealing with the adequacy of life safety features relative to fire, storm, collapse, crowd behavior, and other related safety considerations. This review should be done by an approved person acceptable to the authority having jurisdiction. Such an evaluation includes, for example, a documented case that shows products of combustion in all conceivable fire scenarios will not significantly endanger occupants using means of egress in the facility (because of fire detection, automatic suppression, smoke control, large-volume space, management procedures, etc.). Moreover, means of egress facilities plus facility management capabilities should be adequate to cope with scenarios where certain egress routes are blocked for some reason.

In addition to making realistic assumptions about the capabilities of persons in the facility (e.g., an assembled crowd including many disabled persons or persons unfamiliar with the facility) the life safety evaluation should include a factor of safety of at least 2.0 in all calculations relating hazard development time and required egress time — the combination of flow time and other time needed to detect and assess an emergency condition, initiate egress, move along the egress routes, etc. This takes into account the possibility that half of the egress routes may not be used (or usable) in certain situations.

An example calculation may help describe the use of Table 8-2.3.2(b).

Within an arena providing Smoke-Protected Assembly Seating and having a total of 12,500 seats: for capacity purposes only, what should be the clear width of an aisle stair, with 8-in. (20.3-cm) risers and with a center handrail, providing means of egress for 340 seats? Interpolating between the width (0.13 and 0.096) respectively for 10,000 and 15,000 seat facilities, the required stair width, in inches, per seat served is 0.113 AB where A is 1.2 and B is 1.0. The aisle stair width, for capacity purposes, is the product of 340 (0.113) (1.2) (1.0) or 46.1 in. (117 cm). In this case a minimum width criterion of 48 in. (122 cm) (*see 8-2.5.6.7*) will govern its width. Previous editions of the *Code* credited this aisle stair with a capacity of only 150 persons.

Generally 8-2.3.2 takes account of the practice, with many intermediate-size facilities, such as arenas and stadiums, to design means of egress that are intermediate between the egress capacity requirements of previous editions of the *Code* and the less demanding egress capacity requirements that have been applied to large outdoor assembly facilities, such as those addressed by NFPA 102, *Assembly Seating, Tents, and Membrane Structures*[3]. Rather than merely giving a stamp of approval to this interpolation, the *Code* requires that extra caution be taken where reduced egress capacities are considered for a facility. In order to use the reduced egress capacities set out in Table 8-2.3.2(b), a case must first be made and accepted by the authority having jurisdiction showing that all life safety hazards have been considered and control measures provided to ensure that occupants evacuating the building will not be endangered by conditions developing faster than it takes for the means of egress to be cleared. This is described as a "Life Safety Evaluation," a process that should not be undertaken lightly or without special competence in a wide range of life safety issues including but not limited to firesafety.

The nominal flow time figures shown in Tables 8-2.3.2(a) and 8-2.3.2(b) are for reference and may be helpful to designers, consultants, managers, and others concerned with the expected performance of an egress system. Of course, if the facilities are to be used by groups of occupants who are unfamiliar with the facility or who are less able to move quickly and in dense groups than are younger individuals commonly found at athletic events, this will have to be taken into account, for example, when conducting the Life Safety Evaluation and in operating the facility. Alternatively, the capacity of means of egress should be increased so that a more rapid egress is possible without endangering or otherwise taxing the less able occupants. The need to consider the capabilities of occupants, in relation to circulation facility geometry, has led to the use of several correction factors in the tables' columns for clear width. In new facilities, there will be much emphasis on keeping the geometries as good as possible, and therefore, the correction factors will be 1.0 or very close to 1.0. With existing facilities, this might not be possible; however, it should be noted that handrails can be retrofitted on aisles and other means of egress to significantly improve occupant safety and comfort — an important factor in situations where efficient movement is needed. These factors are taken into account here and in other *Code* requirements for means of egress.

It should be noted that 8-2.3 addresses means of egress generally. The increased flexibility provided by Table 8-2.3.2(b) must be used with caution for proper balance between the relative capacities (and flow times) of each part of a means of egress system encountered by occupants as they leave the facility. Otherwise, with an unbalanced system, there will be queuing or waiting at some points other than the point of origin.

Attention should be given to the occupants' acceptance of the queue or the wait in their seats before proceeding out of the building; however, if a "downstream" component of the means of egress system is relatively underdesigned, even greater attention should be given to the actual and perceived conditions faced by occupants.

Figure 8-5 shows egress from a large stadium that provides egress performance that is perceived to be acceptable in terms of time and other factors. Occupants' acceptance of the longer egress flow times, permitted by the *Code* for larger assembly facilities, should be taken into account when doing a Life Safety Evaluation for the building. The photograph also shows a collection of people who can be expected to take somewhat longer to clear the building than is the case with football spectators [a reference group for the nominal flow time figures noted in Tables 8-2.3.2(a) and 8-2.3.2(b).]

8-2.3.3 Main Entrance/Exit.   Every assembly occupancy shall be provided with a main entrance/exit. The main entrance/exit shall be of sufficient width to accommodate one-half of the total occupant load but shall be not less than the total required width of all aisles, exit passageways, and stairways leading thereto and shall be at the level of exit discharge or shall connect to a stairway or ramp leading to a street. Each level of an assembly occupancy shall have access to the main entrance/exit, and such access shall have sufficient capacity to accommodate 50 percent of the occupant load of such levels.

Exception No. 1: A bowling establishment shall have a main entrance/exit of sufficient capacity to accommodate 50 percent of the total occupant load without regard to the number of aisles that it serves.

Exception No. 2: In assembly occupancies where there is no well defined main entrance/exit,

Photograph Courtesy of J. L. Pauls

Figure 8-5.   Crowd Egress from a Large Assembly Facility that Might be Eligible for Egress Capacity Provisions of Table 8-2.3.2(b).

such as stadiums, sports arenas, and passenger stations, exits may be distributed around the perimeter of the building provided the total exit width provides 116⅔ percent of the width needed to accommodate the permitted occupant load.

The term "Main Exit" has been replaced with the term "Main Entrance/Exit." The intent of the *Code* is to require that 50 percent of the occupants will be able to exit through the same door(s) they used to enter the building. It was brought to the Committee's attention that some building owners/managers did not want to designate the "main entrance" as the "main exit" as well. Therefore, this terminology clarifies the intent of the *Code* and will require that the "main entrance" to a public assembly occupancy also be designated as the "main exit."

The usual entrance to an assembly occupancy also generally serves as its main exit. As a rule, people desire to leave a building by way of their entrance to the structure. Therefore, the main exit needs to be sized to accommodate at least 50 percent of the occupants; however, it must not be less in width than the sum of the required widths of the aisles that it serves.

Bowling establishments usually have relatively few rows of seats for spectators, but are necessarily wide to accommodate the alleys. Due to the limitation of the number of seats in a row, many more aisles are required than in other types of assembly occupancies. Exception No. 1 to 8-2.3.3 modifies what would be the excessive main exit width required to accommodate the sum of the required aisle widths served by the exit.

Exception No. 2 clarifies the intent of the *Code* to provide the same 16⅔ percent *increase* in exit capacity in buildings having no main exits as in those with a main exit (50%+⅔=116⅔%). The intent is to distribute the extra width as equally as possible among all exits. (*Also see 8-2.3.4.*)

8-2.3.4 Other Exits.   Each level of an assembly occupancy shall have access to the main entrance/exit and shall be provided with additional exits of sufficient width to accommodate two-thirds of the total occupant load served by that level. Such exits shall discharge in accordance with 8-2.7. Such exits shall be located as far apart as practicable and as far from the main entrance/exit as practicable. Such exits shall be accessible from a cross aisle or a side aisle. (*See 8-2.3.3.*)

Exception No. 1:   Where only two exits are required, each exit shall be of sufficient width to accommodate not less than one-half the total occupant load.

Exception No. 2:   In assembly occupancies where there is no well defined main entrance/exit, such as stadiums, sports arenas, and passenger stations, exits may be distributed around the perimeter of the building provided the total exit width provides 116⅔ percent of the width needed to accommodate the permitted occupant load.

As an example of the requirements of 8-2.3.4, if an assembly occupancy had an occupant load of 900, the main exit would have to accommodate 450 people (50 percent). If there were two additional exits, together they would have to accommodate 600 people (two-thirds of the occupant load). Essentially, where more than two exits are required, the sum of the exit capacity must be at least one-sixth greater than (or 116⅔ percent of) the total required by the occupant load. Also, 8-2.4.2 requires that, in a Class B assembly occupancy with a capacity of more than 500 people, at least three exits must be provided and no exit may be less than 44 in. (112 cm) wide.

These requirements provide some relief from the congestion that would result if the main exit should become unusable during a fire.

8-2.4 Number of Exits.   (*See also Section 5-4.*)

8-2.4.1   Every Class A assembly occupancy shall have at least four separate means of egress as remote from each other as practicable.

8-2.4.2   Every Class B assembly occupancy shall have at least two separate means of egress as remote from each other as practicable and, if of a capacity of over 500, at least three separate means of egress, each not less than 44 inches (112 cm) wide.

8-2.4.3   Every Class C assembly occupancy shall have at least two means of egress consisting of separate exits or doors leading to a corridor or other spaces giving access to two separate and independent exits in different directions.

Formal Interpretation 81-28
Reference: 8-2.4

Question: Is it the intent of 8-2.4 and its subsections to require four exits from each level of a Class A assembly occupancy building where, individually, the floors have populations that fall in the range assigned to a Class B assembly occupancy?

Answer: No.

Issue Edition: 1981
Reference: 8-2.4
Date: January 1983

As the concentration or number of people increases in an assembly occupancy, the chance of a simultaneous exiting by a sizable group of occupants increases. Therefore, to reduce jamming at doorways (which leads to panic and disorder), more exits at a variety of locations are needed. Paragraphs 8-2.4.1 through 8-2.4.3 provide for this design requirement.

Since 8-1.2.2 specifies that assembly areas with individual occupant loads of fewer than 50 people in buildings of occupancies other than assembly shall be classed as part of the other occupancy, no criteria are given by 8-2.4 for the number and location of exits in such an occupancy.

8-2.4.4 Balconies or mezzanines having an occupant load not greater than 50 may be served by a single means of egress and such means of egress may lead to the floor below.

The intent of the Committee was to provide relief for small balconies and mezzanines, such as choir lofts that accommodate not greater than 50 people.

8-2.4.5 Balconies or mezzanines having an occupant load greater than 50 but not greater than 100 shall have at least two remote means of egress, but both such means of egress may lead to the floor below.

These balconies might typically be found in restaurants or small theaters. The Committee felt it was necessary to have two remote means of egress, but since the total number of people will be not greater than 100, it would be reasonable to let them exit onto the floor below.

8-2.4.6 Balconies or mezzanines having an occupant load greater than 100 shall have means of egress provided as for a floor.

The Committee felt that any balcony or mezzanine that could accommodate more than 100 people should be dealt with as a separate floor with regard to number of means of egress in order to avoid overloading the means of egress from the floor below and to protect people during egress from the mezzanine.

8-2.5 Arrangement of Means of Egress.   *(See also Section 5-5.)*

8-2.5.1   Exits shall be remote from each other and shall be arranged to minimize the possibility that they may be blocked by any emergency.

Exception No. 1:   A common path of travel may be permitted for the first 20 ft (6.1 m) from any point.

Exception No. 2:   As provided in 8-2.4.4.

Separation of exits as far as practicable cannot be overemphasized. Two or more exits that are located too close to each other can become unusable during the same incident. The fundamental principles of this *Code*, as expressed in Chapter 2, require remoteness of exits to the point that a single fire event will not simultaneously block both exits. This same concept applies to exit access doors. The remoteness requirements of Section 5-5 must be met.

Revolving rooftop places of assembly need special consideration; as the structure revolves, exit signs are often lost from view. To provide an unobstructed panoramic view, the exterior element revolves around a small stationary interior core in which the exits are often located. In many cases, the two exits are too close to each other to avoid both exits being involved in case of fire. Usually at least one stairway must transfer from its position in the stationary core to the normal location of the building stairways. This transfer, since it is a continuation of the stairway, must be made in an exit passageway possessing a fire resistance equal to that required for the stair enclosure.

8-2.5.2   Means of egress shall not be permitted through kitchens, storerooms, restrooms, closets, or hazardous areas as described in 8-3.2.

The purpose of this requirement is to make clear that exit access travel is not permitted to pass through areas subject to locking or areas possessing a hazard level higher than that normal for the occupancy.

8-2.5.3   Where the floor area of auditoriums and arenas is used for areas described by 8-1.7.1, at least 50 percent of the occupant load shall have means of egress provided independent of the means of egress for adjacent fixed seating areas.

8-2.5.4 Seating.

8-2.5.4.1   The spacing of rows of chairs shall provide a space of not less than 12 in. (30.5 cm) from the back of one chair to the front of the most forward projection of the chair immediately behind it. The rows of chairs shall be spaced not less than 33 in. (84 cm) back to back. Horizontal measurements shall be made between vertical planes. Where all chairs in a row have automatic or self-rising seats that comply with ASTM F851, *Test Method for Self-Rising Seat Mechanisms*, the measurement may be made with the seats in the up position. Where any chair in the row does not have an automatic or self-rising seat, the measurement shall be made with the seat in the down position.

The requirement for the spacing between rows of chairs is illustrated in Figure 8-6.

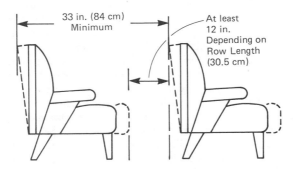

Figure 8-6. Correct Measurement of Minimum Spacing Between Rows of Chairs Without Self-Rising Seats.

8-2.5.4.2* For rows of chairs served by aisles or doorways at both ends, there shall be no more than 100 seats per row, and the minimum clear width between rows of 12 in. (30.5 cm) shall be increased by 0.3 in. (.76 cm) for every additional seat beyond 14, but need not exceed 22 in. (55.9 cm).

A-8-2.5.4.2 The system known as "continental seating" has one pair of egress doors provided for every five rows and located close to the ends of the rows. In previous editions of the *Code*, such egress doors were required to provide a minimum clear width of 66 in. (168 cm) discharging into a foyer, lobby, or to the exterior of the building. This continental seating arrangement can result in egress flow times that are approximately one-half as long as those resulting where side aisles lead to more remote doors (i.e., with nominal flow times of approximately 100 seconds rather than 200 seconds). Such superior egress flow time performance may be desirable in some situations; however, special attention should be given either to a comparably good egress capacity for other parts of the egress system or to sufficient space to accommodate queuing outside the seating space.

This is a major change in this edition of the *Code*. The new appendix note relates the expected egress flow time performance of "continental seating," as provided for in previous editions of the *Code*, to the egress flow time performance of the more flexible new requirements for egress width related to capacity. (*See 8-2.3.*) Additional design flexibility, built upon the continental seating principle of variable minimum seat row spacing and row length, is also introduced with this edition of the *Code*. The new requirement employs — as reference points for each end of the range — the previously employed requirements of 12 in. (30.5 cm) of clearance for rows up to 14 seats in length and 22 in. (55.9 cm) for rows over 45 seats in length. For example, under the new requirement, rows with 47 seats require a clearance of 21.9 in. (55.6 cm). This is calculated by subtracting 14 from 47 and multiplying the result, 33, by 0.3 in. to obtain 9.9 in., which is added to 12 in. to obtain the total required width clearance of 21.9 in. Rows with 48 to 100 seats require 22 in. (55.9 cm) of clear width.

The new flexibility, applying to all fixed seating arranged in rows, is based on the assumption that the egress time of a seating arrangement will be influenced more by the capacity of routes downstream from the rows of seating than by the rows' clear widths. Paragraph 8-2.3 provides a new standardized method for calculating the widths of those routes serving the seating space containing the seating. The combination of 8-2.3 and 8-2.5.4 offers designers of theaters, especially, much scope for laying out blocks of seating while still requiring a standard of egress flow time performance that is based on traditionally accepted egress performance (nominally about 200 seconds of flow time) resulting from very specific requirements on aisle and cross aisle design. For example, rows longer than 14 seats are permitted, and egress door locations can be more flexibly determined than permitted under continental seating rules contained in previous *Code* editions.

Figure 8-7a shows what is possible with a theater with 630 seats in one unbroken area with 21 rows ranging uniformly from 20 to 40 seats in length. The required minimum clear width between the front row (with 20 seats) and the one behind (with 21 seats) is 14.1 in. (35.8 cm). The required minimum clear width between the back row (with 40 seats) and the one in front of it (with 39 seats) is 19.8 in. (50.3 cm). The designer has the option of making all the clear widths uniform and at least 19.8 in., or progressively increasing them from front to back, from at least 14.1 in. to at least 19.8 in., as the row lengths increase.

The theater is a Class B assembly occupancy with over 500 seats; therefore, by 8-2.4.2, it requires at least three separate means of egress, each not less than 44 in. (112 cm) in width. A main set of doors, at the back of the seating and close to the main entrance/exit, has to provide at least one-half the egress capacity. In this case, it must serve at least 315 persons. According to 8-2.3.2, the minimum total clear width of these main doorways must be 70 in. (178 cm), and thus two doorways providing 35 in. (89 cm) clear width each would suffice for *Code* capacity purposes. However, 8-2.3.3 requires that the main entrance be as wide as all aisles leading to it, so the two 47-in. (119-cm) aisles require a 94-in. (239-cm) main entrance/exit. Two additional means of egress, providing total capacity for at least 420 seats (two-thirds of the 630 seats) according to 8-2.3.4, each need to have a minimum clear width of 47 in. (119 cm) (210 times 0.22 in.) according to 8-2.3.2 and not less than 44 in. (112 cm) according to 8-2.4.2. Minimum side aisle width, connecting the front and back egress doorways, would also have to be 47 in. (119 cm). Greater widths of aisle and doorways, especially those leading to the main entrance/exit, should be considered to help improve normal convenience and other aspects that go beyond the minimum *Code* requirements for means of egress.

In the example presented in Figure 8-7a, there is of course the option of doing a traditional layout with seats having no more than six intervening

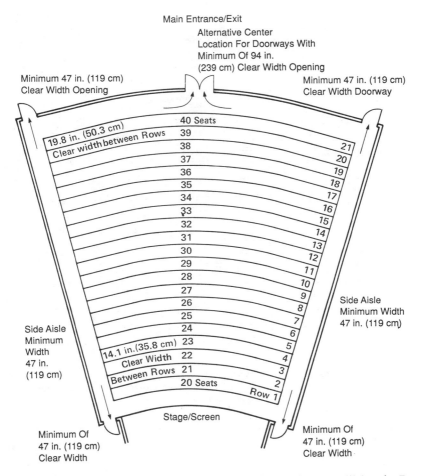

Figure 8-7a.   Minimum Means of Egress for a 630-Seat Theater Utilizing the Row
Spacing and Aisle Length Provisions of 8-2.5.4.2.

seats separating them from an aisle. This would require that more space
be devoted to aisles and cross aisles, but this space loss could be offset by
closer seat row spacings.

8-2.5.4.3   For rows of chairs served by an aisle or doorway at one end only, the
minimum clear width between rows of 12 in. (30.5 cm) shall be increased by 0.6 in. (1.5
cm) for every additional seat beyond 7, but need not exceed 22 in. (55.9 cm).

The incremental increase of 0.6 in. (1.5 cm) of required minimum clear
width between rows for each additional seat to be passed to reach an aisle
is the same here as in the case of the row served by aisles at each end
(8-2.5.4.2).

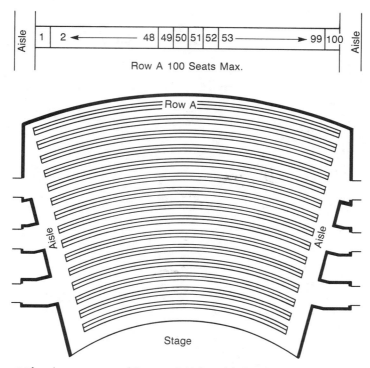

Figure 8-7b   Arrangement of Seats and Aisles with Continental Seating.   In prior editions of the *Code*, when more than 14 seats were in a row, this arrangement was required.   One hundred seats is the maximum number for one row.

8-2.5.4.4   For rows of chairs served by an aisle or doorway at one end only, the path of travel shall not exceed 30 ft (9.1 m) from any seat to a point where a person has a choice of two paths of travel to two exits.

The 30-ft (9.1-m) limit effectively means that only about 18 chairs can be put into a row served by an aisle at one end only, assuming that, when one reaches the aisle, it is possible to move in either of two directions to two exits. This requirement also influences the permitted maximum length of aisles providing a common path of travel to reach the two exits.

8-2.5.4.5   Chairs without dividing arms shall have their capacity determined by allowing 18 in. (45.7 cm) per person.

The fact that the *Code* uses the traditional 18-in. (45.7-cm) figure for seat width per person for determining maximum occupant load (and egress capacity) should not necessarily be taken as an endorsement for using the 18-in. (45.7-cm) figure as a basis for ticket sales. This is especially true where events are sold out and a specific seat is assigned on each ticket. Winter events, where spectators wear bulkier clothing, are examples of those for which a more generous seat spacing should be considered in the ticket sales policy. Generally, the 18-in. (45.7-cm) figure — applied to ticket sales — makes most sense with children and younger adults, under temperate weather conditions, and with a general admission policy when a full house is not expected. Otherwise, the space to be kept clear in aisles and other means of egress might be compromised.

8-2.5.4.6 Where bleacher or grandstand seating without backs is used indoors, rows of seats shall be spaced not less than 22 in. (55.9 cm) back to back.

Exception: Folding or telescopic seating shall comply with NFPA 102, Standard for Assembly Seating, Tents, and Membrane Structures, with a limit of dead ends in vertical aisles of 16 rows.

The elimination of backs allows the entire bleacher to be a path of exit access. Assuming they are fit and agile, people can simultaneously evacuate a bleacher upward or downward without using aisles. This compensates somewhat for the openness of bleacher-type structures, which can expose the entire population to a single fire either under or adjacent to the structure. The provisions of the *Code* concerning bleacher or grandstand seating and folding or telescopic seating have been modified to coordinate requirements with NFPA 102, *Standard for Assembly Seating, Tents, and Membrane Structures*[3]. It should be noted that, unless certain criteria are met (as set out in NFPA 102), aisles are required for bleachers, and such aisles must meet requirements comparable to those in the *Code*.

8-2.5.4.7* Fixed or loose chairs, tables, and similar furnishings or equipment shall be so arranged and maintained that a path of travel to an aisle or exit is provided. The path of travel shall not exceed 10 ft (3 m) from any point to an aisle or exit.

A-8-2.5.4.7 Figure A-8-2.5.4.7 illustrates the requirements of 8-2.5.4.7.

This provision, introduced in the 1985 Edition of the *Code*, attempts to clarify requirements for aisles in restaurants and similar assembly occupancies having tables, chairs, and other furnishings in cluster arrangements. The provision essentially establishes a cluster of tables where the travel distance from within the cluster to a well-defined and sized aisle is not to exceed 10 ft (3 m). The spacing between tables, chairs, and other furnishings within the cluster is not defined by the *Code* based on the assumption that use and service to the cluster will define adequate aisle space. When considering a restaurant with this arrangement, it is obvious that, in order to serve the tables, sufficient aisle space must be maintained for the restaurant staff. This space is considered adequate for means of egress purposes within the cluster. Note that the 10-ft (3-m) travel distance requirement within the cluster limits the occupants' exposure to these somewhat smaller aisle widths. (*See also 8-2.5.6.8 regarding aisle width.*)

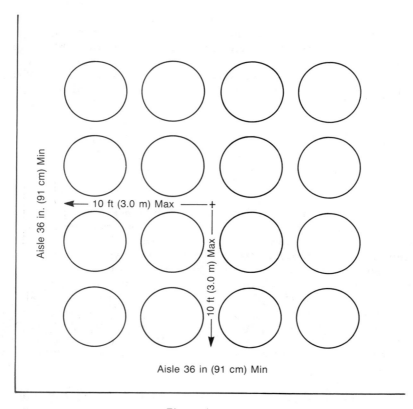

Figure A-8-2.5.4.7

8-2.5.4.8*   Rectangular banquet type tables used for drinking or dining, or purposes having similar seating configurations with the path of travel to an aisle exceeding 10 ft (3 m), shall be spaced not less than 54 in. (137 cm) apart where seating occurs back to back nor less than 36 in. (91 cm) where seating is on one side only. The path of travel to an aisle or exit shall not exceed 20 ft (6.1 m).

A-8-2.5.4.8   Figure A-8-2.5.4.8 illustrates the requirements of 8-2.5.4.8.

Note that the provisions of 8-2.5.4.7 apply to banquet tables if they form a cluster meeting the 10-ft (3-m) travel distance to a defined aisle. Where long rows of banquet tables are used and the 10-ft (3-m) travel distance is exceeded, the table spacing provisions of 8-2.5.4.8 apply.

8-2.5.5*   Tablet-Arm Chair Seating.

A-8-2.5.5   Tablet-arm chairs having a stored position have not been shown to require special regulation. Where an assembly occupancy is designed for dual purpose as instructional space and public purposes, management should require that the tablet arm be placed in the stored position when instruction is not the primary function.

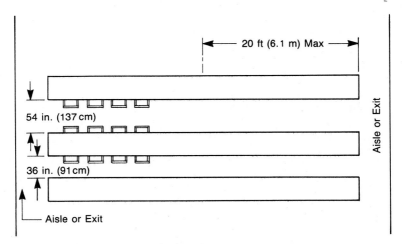

Figure A-8-2.5.4.8

8-2.5.5.1   Tablet-arm chairs shall not be permitted unless full compliance of row space requirements is provided when the tablet arm is in the usable position. Tablet-arm chairs that do not have a stored position for the tablet arm shall not be permitted unless the clearance required by 8-2.5.4 between rows of chairs is provided and maintained.

The Committee carefully examined the subject of tablet-arm chairs with storing provisions and determined that these chairs present little threat to life safety. Where the tablet arm is fixed in the use position, tablet-arm chairs must be arranged to meet the row spacing requirements found in 8-2.5.4.2 and 8-2.5.4.3. Figure 8-8 illustrates this provision. Note the exception to 8-2.5.5.2.

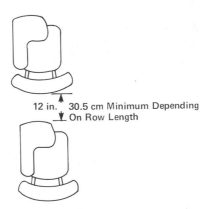

Figure 8-8.   Minimum Spacing Between Rows of Seats with Fixed Tablet Arms.   Measure with the tablet arm in the up (in-use) position. The clear space between the back of a seat and the leading edge of a tablet arm in normal seating is set by 8-2.5.4.2 and 8-2.5.4.3, depending on row length but not less than 12 in. (30.5 cm).

8-2.5.5.2   Where tablet-arm chairs are used, the clear width of rows of seats shall be measured with a tablet arm in the up or use position.

Exception: Tablet arms may be measured in stored position where the tablet arm automatically returns to the stored position when raised manually in one motion to a vertical position and falls to the stored position by force of gravity.

8-2.5.6 Aisles.

8-2.5.6.1   Aisle width shall provide sufficient egress capacity for the number of persons accommodated by the catchment areas served by the aisle. The catchment area served by an aisle is that portion of the total space that is naturally served by that section of the aisle. The establishment of catchment areas shall be based on a balanced use of all means of egress with the number of persons in proportion to egress capacity.

Figure 8-9 illustrates how catchment areas would be allotted in the case of a theater with four egress doorways having approximately similar egress capacity. Note that catchment areas for normal, nonemergency uses of only some of the available means of egress — especially those provided by the main entrance/exit — may be quite different from the catchment areas based on a balanced distribution of people in proportion to egress capacity of individual means of egress. Facility management procedures must take into account the difficulties of informing people about and directing them to all the available means of egress, especially when normally used, familiar routes become blocked in an emergency.

8-2.5.6.2   Where aisles converge to form a single path of egress travel, the required egress capacity of that path shall be not less than the combined required capacity of the converging aisles.

Note that the term "required capacity" is used here to make clear that the combined required width of the egress routes might be smaller than their combined actual widths, especially where the individual widths are made wider than required by the *Code* for egress capacity purposes. Such wider widths, beyond *Code* minimums, might be justified by considerations such as normal operating convenience.

8-2.5.6.3   Aisles shall terminate at a cross aisle, foyer, door, or vomitory giving access to an exit.

See 8-2.5.6.4 for an exception to this general rule for aisles.

8-2.5.6.4   Dead-end aisles shall not exceed 20 ft (6.1 m) in length.

Exception: A longer dead-end aisle is permitted where seats served by the dead-end aisle are not more than 24 seats from another aisle measured along a row of seats having a minimum clear width of 12 in. (30.5 cm) plus 0.6 in. (1.5 cm) for each additional seat above 7 in the row.

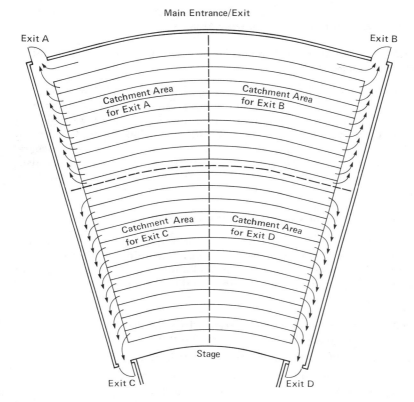

Figure 8-9   Plan of a Theater Showing how Catchment Areas for Means of Egress Are Based on a Balanced Use of all Means of Egress, in Proportion to Egress Capacity.

This exception to the traditional dead-end limit of 20 ft (6.1 m) is new in the 1988 Edition of the *Code.* The exception gives formal recognition to the inherent redundancy that exists where rows of seating are served by two or more aisles so that the blockage of any one aisle simply means that there is greater movement along rows to reach a somewhat more distant aisle. The exception recognizes that movement along rows, even with their constricted widths, provides many routes that permit faster movement to alternative aisles than would be possible with a dedicated cross aisle. As with the concept of wider clear spacings between rows where rows are longer (8-2.5.4.2), this exception gives additional credit for increased space to move along the rows to reach alternative aisles. At the row length limit of 24 seats, the required clear width spacing for use of this exception is 22.2 in. (56.4 cm). The exception may prove helpful in situations such as arenas and theaters where it is not easy to provide a cross aisle, doorway, etc., giving access to an exit, but where two or more aisles are relatively easy to reach when moving along rows.

8-2.5.6.5   In aisles where egress is possible in more than one direction, the aisles shall be uniform in required widths.

This requirement prohibits making some aisles wider at their ends (in an hourglass shape) simply because there are more people using them at their ends. A tapered aisle is acceptable and effective where there is only one direction of egress travel possible and the number of people served by the aisle increases in the direction of egress travel. In the more general case, where there are two directions of egress travel possible in the aisle, the width must be kept uniform to accommodate efficient egress travel that might have to reverse direction because of blockage at one end.

8-2.5.6.6   The width of aisles shall be sized in accordance with 8-2.3.1.

This refers to the capacity-related width requirements of 8-2.3.1. The capacity-related requirements must be considered along with other width requirements set out in 8-2.5.6.7. The final minimum width required by the *Code* is the larger of the widths established by the two sets of requirements.

8-2.5.6.7   In theater and similar type seating facilities, the minimum clear width of aisles shall be as determined by 8-2.3.2 but not less than:

(a) 48 in. (122 cm) for stairs having seating on each side.

(b) 36 in. (91 cm) for stairs having seating on only one side.

(c) 23 in. (58 cm) between a handrail or guardrail and seating where the aisle is subdivided by a handrail.

(d) 42 in. (107 cm) for level or ramped aisles having seating on both sides.

(e) 36 in. (91 cm) for level or ramped aisles having seating on only one side.

(f) 23 in. (58 cm) between a handrail and seating where aisle does not serve more than five rows on one side.

These requirements will often govern the final minimum widths of aisles, especially where a relatively limited amount of egress capacity is required by 8-2.3.1. The requirements of 8-2.5.6.7 take into account the width needed by individuals moving alone or with others, overtaking others, and moving in counterflow past others on aisles. Account is taken of the differing movement behavior and needs for handrails, for example, on various types of circulation facilities. Figures 8-10 and 8-11 illustrate how intensively a 48-in. (122-cm) aisle stair subdivided by a center handrail can be used. Figure 8-12 shows, in overhead plan view, a large male walking down one side of a similar aisle stair, 48 inches (122 cm) wide, subdivided by a handrail. Chair seating is shown adjoining the aisle in these photographs.

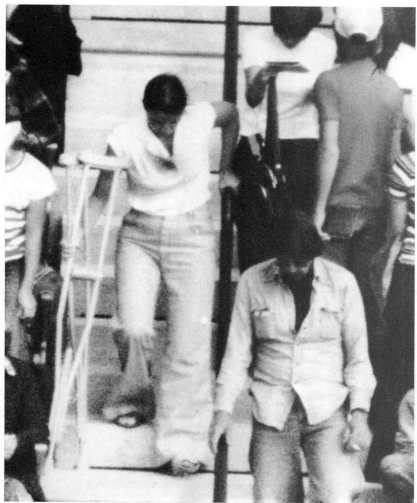

Photograph Courtesy of J. L. Pauls

Figure 8-10.   Intensive Use of Aisle Stair, 48 in. (122 cm) Wide with Central Handrail, in a Stadium.

Photograph Courtesy of J. L. Pauls

Figure 8-11.   Intensive Use of Handrail at Center of 48-in. (122-cm) Aisle Stair in a Stadium. The handrail height is approximately 34 in. (86.3 cm).

Photograph Courtesy of J. L. Pauls

Figure 8-12. Overhead Plan View of 48-in. (122-cm) Aisle Stair, with Center
Handrail, Used by a Large Male.

Paragraph 8-2.5.6.7(f) is based on the requirement for handrails in
aisle stairs, specifically the permission to extend such handrails down the
center of aisles for as much as five rows, leaving only about 23 in. (58 cm)
of nominal width clear to the side of the handrail. This width is readily
used by individuals moving in single or staggered file and can be used with
tolerable inconvenience where people must pass by each other on the same
side of the handrail. This provision of the *Code* might be helpful in cases
where a short stub aisle is needed to serve rows of seating immediately
beside a vomitory.

Generally, it might be noted that the effective width of aisles is often
somewhat wider than is the case for egress facilities that are bounded on
both sides by construction. One important exception to this generalization

occurs where many people are attempting to sit on undivided benches or bleachers served by an aisle. The 18-in. (45.7-cm) spacing usually provided for each person is often too small, and there is a natural tendency for people to have their legs (sometimes several inches of hips and shoulders) occupying a significant part of the aisle width. Therefore, it is prudent in designing for crowded, non-chair seating either to increase the width of seat per person or to increase the minimum aisle widths shown here by several inches on each side to facilitate normal circulation in the aisles.

8-2.5.6.8* In table and chair type seating facilities, the minimum clear width of aisles shall be as determined by 8-2.3.1 but not less than 36 in. (91 cm). Where loose seating occurs bordering on the aisle, the minimum aisle width is required plus an additional 19 in. (48 cm) for chairs on one side or an additional 38 in. (97 cm) for chairs on both sides of the aisle.

A-8-2.5.6.8

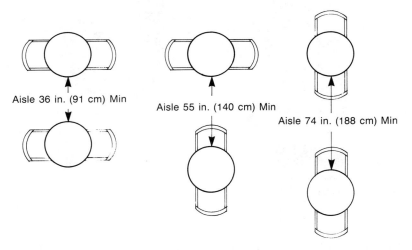

Aisle 36 in. (91 cm) Min

Aisle 55 in. (140 cm) Min

Aisle 74 in. (188 cm) Min

Figure A-8-2.5.6.8(a)

Figure A-8-2.5.6.8(a) illustrates the provisions of 8-2.5.6.8. This provides guidance on how aisles with movable chairs are to be measured, a subject that has often been questioned by enforcement officials.

Figure A-8-2.5.6.8(b) illustrates the aisle requirements for a banquet type arrangement. A reasonable space should be provided between tables for waitress or waiter access, otherwise the tables will gradually be pushed into the aisle width. This diagram illustrates aisle requirements only and would not be used to increase occupant load or approve layout, as it does not illustrate realistic layouts for servicing.

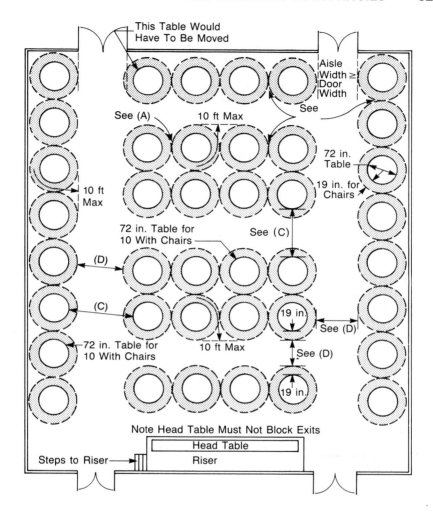

(A) A Small Aisle Would Normally Be Provided for Waiter/Waitress Access.

(B) No Aisle Requirement When Travel ≤ 10 ft

(C) Distance Between Table Must Be ≥ Required Aisle Width Plus 19 in. for Chairs on One or 38 in. for Chairs on Both Sides

(D) Aisle Must Be Sized in Accordance with 5-3.2 But Not Less Than 36 in.

Figure A-8-2.5.6.8(b)

Aisle widths surrounding the clusters described in 8-2.5.4.7 and aisle widths at the end of long rows of rectangular tables as described in 8-2.5.4.8 are required to be calculated per Chapter 5, Section 5-3, and per 8-2.3.1, with a minimum width of 36 in. (91 cm). Where loose chairs are used on aisles, the aisle width is to be increased by 19 in. (48.3 cm) for each side on which loose chairs are used, 19 in. (48.3 cm) being the most common front-to-rear measurement of chairs used for this purpose.

8-2.5.6.9 Aisle Stairs and Ramps.   Every aisle with a gradient 1 in 8 or less shall consist of a ramp. Every aisle with gradient exceeding 1 in 8 shall consist of a stair having treads, risers, and handrails complying with the following requirements:

Major changes relating to aisles were introduced in the 1985 Edition of the *Code*. The 1988 *Code* contains some minor changes that further underline the importance of design details for aisles. The changes in the previous and current editions address the need to design aisle stairs, for example, with all the attention and care required for stairs generally, supplemented by additional care because of unique design and use conditions encountered with aisles serving seating arranged in rows, especially where there are large elevation differences between the rows of seating. Paragraph 8-2.5.6.9 begins with a general requirement that divides aisles into two categories based on slope. Ideally, it would be preferable not to have to design aisles having about a 1 in 8 slope; however, sightlines might dictate such slopes in some situations. Ramps of this slope are relatively steep and problematic for people with walking difficulties. Stairs with a very small rise and long treads also present problems, notably trips and missteps because the presence of the low risers might not be evident, especially in a crowd situation. Generally, aisles also present unusual distractions for people because of their unusual lengths and the presence of other people in the aisles, and the presence of those entering the aisles from adjoining seating rows. Therefore, aisles of all slopes must be designed with considerable care and attention to human factors, both for the movement of individuals and the movement of crowds.

(a)* Tread depth shall be uniform in each aisle.

A-8-2.5.6.9(a)   Where nonuniformities occur due to construction tolerances, they should not exceed ³⁄₁₆ in. (0.5 cm) between adjacent treads.

Paragraph 8-2.5.6.9(a) contains a significant change from the previous edition of the *Code*. The provision of unequal-sized treads within aisle stairs, a traditional practice once believed to be useful in facilitating access to seat rows, is no longer permitted by the *Code*. Even with the increased minimum tread size requirement of the previous edition of the *Code*, the end result, i.e., larger treads at the seat row entry level and smaller intermediate treads between seat row levels, was not as good, from a stair safety point of view, as consistently sized treads. This is true even for uniformly sized treads as large as about 20 in. (50.8 cm) in depth (assuming a relatively low riser height). [Handrails, required by 8-2.5.6.9(f), help to compensate for the stretched but consistent stride length that may be needed in such long-tread aisle stairs.] It is preferable to keep treads uniform so that the risk of misstepping, particularly overstepping of relatively smaller treads, is reduced.

It cannot be overemphasized that special attention must be given to careful design detailing and construction practice in relation to the placement of treads in aisle stairs. Careful site supervision is recommended to avoid serious problems both in cast-in-place concrete construction and in precast concrete construction of aisle stairs. Field research studies of situations where aisle step dimensions are not consistent indicate that the incidence of missteps rises significantly where tolerances of tread uniformity are not respected.

(b)* Treads shall be a minimum of 11 in. (27.9 cm).

A-8-2.5.6.9(b)   Tread depth is more important to stair safety than is riser height. Therefore, in cases where seating area gradient is less than 5 in 11, it is recommended that the tread dimension be increased beyond 11 in. (27.9 cm) rather than reducing the riser height. Where seating area gradient exceeds 8 in 11, it is recommended that the riser height be increased while maintaining a tread depth of at least 11 in. (27.9 cm).

Figure 8-13 shows a side view of an aisle stair with 11-in. (28-cm) treads used by a person with footwear measuring 12 in. (30.5 cm) in length — a condition found with 5 percent of adults generally and a condition that might be somewhat more common in those assembly situations attracting a higher proportion of male adults.

It should also be noted, in relation to 8-2.5.6.9(a), that there is apparently no difficulty entering or leaving the aisles or when leaving or entering the seat row with the provision of the three equal-sized, 11-in. (17.9-cm) treads at each seat row shown in the photograph.

(c) Riser heights shall be a minimum of 4 in. (10.2 cm).

At the minimum slope limit set by the *Code* for aisle stairs (for slopes exceeding 1 in 8), there is a riser height of 4 in. (10.2 cm) where the seat platform is 32 in. (81.3 cm) deep. At such low riser heights, which present a tripping hazard if the risers are not detected by people, there is special value to the tread nosing marking requirement in 8-2.5.6.9(g).

(d) Riser heights shall not exceed 8 in. (20.3 cm).

Exception No. 1 to (d): Where the gradient of an aisle exceeds 8 in. (20.3 cm) in rise and 11 in. (27.9 cm) of run (to maintain necessary sight lines in the adjoining seating area), the rise height may exceed 8 in. (20.3 cm) but shall not exceed 9 in. (22.9 cm).

Exception No. 2 to (d): Folding and telescopic seating in accordance with NFPA 102, Standard for Assembly Seating, Tents, and Membrane Structures.

Photograph Courtesy of J. L. Pauls

Figure 8-13.   Side View of Aisle Stair, with 11-in. (17.9-cm) Treads in Stadium.

The 1988 Edition of the *Code* has reduced the maximum riser height permitted for new aisle stairs from 11 in. (27.9 cm) to 9 in. (22.9 cm). In addition to reducing movement safety, the unusually high risers of some aisle stairs reduce the speed and efficiency of movement, especially in the descending direction. This is taken into account in 8-2.3.2 where, for each additional inch of riser height above 7 in. (17.9 cm), an additional 20 percent must be added to the required capacity-related width of the aisle to satisfy *Code* requirements and achieve an acceptable egress flow time performance.

(e)* Riser heights shall be uniform within a flight.

Exception to (e): Riser height may be nonuniform, but only to the extent necessary due to changes in gradient within a seating area to maintain necessary sight lines. Where nonuniformities exceed ³⁄₁₆ in. (0.5 cm) between adjacent risers, the exact location of such nonuniformities shall be indicated by a distinctive marking stripe on each tread at the nosing or leading edge adjacent to the nonuniform risers.

A-8-2.5.6.9(e)   Nonuniformities arising from construction tolerances should not exceed ³⁄₁₆ in. (0.5 cm) in adjacent risers.

A special case is made here for especially nonuniform riser heights, beyond the usual ³⁄₁₆-in. (0.5-cm) tolerance, only for situations where there is a break in the slope of a seating deck to maintain adequate sightlines. The seating deck slope may change incrementally at each row or, more commonly, there may be a large change at one or more locations. At such locations, there is often a change on the row-to-row elevation that greatly exceeds the usual ³⁄₁₆-in. (0.5-cm) tolerance. Aisle step riser heights will, as a consequence, change radically at this point. It is the special duty of the designer and owner to warn people using the aisle of this unusual change in the riser dimensions. This warning might go well beyond the usual marking of all step nosings required by 8-2.5.6.9(g). A distinctive color or other standard hazard marking is needed on the step nosings. Additional warning techniques may have to be employed in some cases to help reduce the risk of stumbles and falls.

(f) Ramped aisles having a gradient exceeding 1 in 15, and aisle stairs, shall be provided with handrails at one side or along the center line.

Where there is seating on both sides of the aisle, the handrails shall be discontinuous with gaps or breaks at intervals not exceeding five rows to facilitate access to seating and to permit crossing from one side of the aisle to the other. These gaps or breaks shall have a clear width of at least 22 in. (55.9 cm) and not greater than 36 in. (91 cm) measured horizontally, and the handrail shall have rounded terminations or bends. Where handrails are provided in the middle of aisle stairs, there shall be an additional intermediate rail located approximately 12 in. (30 cm) below the main handrail.

Exception No 1 to (f): Handrails are not required for ramped aisles having a gradient not greater than 1 in 8 and having seating on both sides.

Exception No. 2 to (f): Handrails are not required if, at the side of the aisle, there is a guardrail that complies with the graspability requirements for handrails.

This edition of the *Code* and the previous edition contain significant changes regarding provision of handrails on aisles, especially aisle stairs. It should be noted that there is no longer an exception permitting aisle stairs in new construction without handrails where riser heights are less than 7 in. (17.9 cm). This is a result of growing experience with the provision and use of aisle handrails, as well as a general realization that aisles pose unique challenges to users that might go beyond those encountered on other ramps and stairs. Figures 8-10 and 8-11 on pages 323 and 324 illustrate the variety of use conditions in aisles and the extensive use of handrails. In field research studies, aisle stair handrail use has been shown to be used about twice as often as handrails provided to meet *Code* provisions for non-aisle stairs. When one considers the unusual lengths of aisles, the unusual step geometries, and the very complex use conditions (with people entering and leaving the aisle at many rows), this high level of use is not surprising. Aside from their value in increasing the safety and comfort of people using the aisles, the handrails also help to improve egress efficiency — a benefit that is taken into account in calculation of egress capacity. (*See 8-2.3.2.*)

The required gaps between sections of center-aisle handrails are illustrated in Figure 8-12 on page 325. Spacing such gaps as frequently as every three rows is recommended where there is extensive use of aisles during events. A greater spacing, up to five rows between gaps, might be acceptable where there is little use of the aisles during events and little counterflow at any time. Gap size should be kept at the lower end of the permitted range of 22 to 36 in. (55.9 cm to 91 cm) where the aisles are unusually steep and handrail use is especially valuable in reducing the risk of falls.

Exception No.2 takes into account the proven utility of handrails that are higher than those permitted even with the increased handrail height range introduced with the 1988 Edition of the *Code*. A guardrail, 42 in. (107 cm) high, such as at the side of an aisle where there is a vomitory, can be considered a usable handrail if it offers graspability as required for handrails. (*See 5-2.2.6.5.*)

(g)* A contrasting marking stripe shall be provided on each tread at the nosing or leading edge such that the location of such tread is readily apparent, particularly when viewed in descent. Such stripes shall be at least 1 in. (2.5 cm) wide and shall not exceed 2 in. (5 cm) wide.

Exception to (g): The marking stripe may be omitted where tread surfaces and environmental conditions in all conditions of use are such that the location of each tread is readily apparent, particularly when viewed in descent.

A-8-2.5.6.9(g)   Certain tread covering materials such as plush carpets, often used in theaters, produce an inherently well-marked tread nosing under most light conditions. On the other hand, concrete treads (with nosings having a sharp edge), especially under outdoor light conditions, are difficult to discriminate and therefore require an applied marking stripe. Slip resistance of such marking stripes should be similar to the rest of the treads and no tripping hazard should be created.

Figure 8-14 suggests some of the step visibility difficulties that are commonly encountered in outdoor facilities with concrete treads. Without the helpful shadows from the handrail posts, there would be little indication of the exact location of each tread nosing. This situation requires the applied nosing markings referred to in 8-2.5.6.9(g). The distractions of the playing field and the unusually long aisle add further justification for making the steps as obvious as possible. It should be stressed that each situation needs to be carefully evaluated (with mock-ups at the design stage and with inspection of actual conditions during use) to determine whether any improvements are warranted in marking and lighting of such aisles.

8-2.5.6.10   Where required by the authority having jurisdiction, plans drawn to scale showing the arrangement of furnishings or equipment shall be submitted to the authority by the building owner, manager, or authorized agent to substantiate conformance with the provisions of this section and shall constitute the only acceptable arrangement until revised or additional plans are submitted and approved.

Photograph Courtesy of J. L. Pauls

Figure 8-14. View Down Aisle Stair, Provided with Center Handrail, in a Stadium.

Exception: Temporary deviations from the specifics of the approved plans shall be permitted provided the occupant load is not increased and the intent of this section is maintained.

8-2.6 Travel Distance to Exits.   Exits shall be so arranged that the total length of travel from any point to reach an exit will not exceed 150 ft (45 m) in any assembly occupancy. (*See also Section 5-6.*)

Exception: The travel distance may be increased to 200 ft (60 m) in assembly occupancies protected throughout by an approved automatic sprinkler system.

Travel distance to exits from balconies or galleries that are served by unenclosed stairways must be measured to include the distance on the slope of the stair in the plane of the nosings and the distance from the bottom of the stair to the exit. Travel distance is measured as illustrated in Figure 8-15.

8-2.7 Discharge from Exits.

8-2.7.1   Exit discharge shall comply with Section 5-7.

8-2.7.2   The level of exit discharge shall be measured at the point of principal entrance to the building.

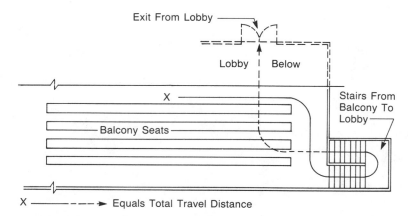

Exit From Lobby

Lobby | Below

X

Stairs From
Balcony To
Lobby

Balcony Seats

X — — — — ► Equals Total Travel Distance

Figure 8-15.   Measurement of Travel Distance to Exit Where Balconies Are
Served by Unenclosed Stairs.

8-2.7.3   Where the principal entrance to an assembly occupancy is via a terrace, either raised or depressed, such terrace may be considered to be the level of exit discharge for the purposes of 8-1.6 if:

(a) The terrace is at least as long (measured parallel to the building) as the total width of the exit(s) it serves, but not less than 5 ft (152 cm) long, and

(b) The terrace is at least as wide (measured perpendicularly to the building) as the exit(s) it serves, but not less than 10 ft (3 m) wide, and

(c) Required stairs leading from the terrace to grade are protected in accordance with 5-2.2.3.3 or are a minimum of 10 ft (3 m) from the building.

> The Committee determined that 10 ft (3 m) was the minimum distance necessary to allow people to exit the building in a depressed or raised area without causing a jamming effect at the exit. The same intent was used in requiring stairs to be at least 10 ft (3 m) from the face of the building unless they are protected as provided in Chapter 5.
>
> The requirements of 8-2.7.3 are illustrated in Figure 8-16.

8-2.8 Illumination of Means of Egress.   Means of egress shall be illuminated in accordance with Section 5-8.

8-2.9 Emergency Lighting.   Emergency lighting shall be provided in accordance with Section 5-9.

Formal Interpretation 76-72
Reference: 8-2.9, 9-2.9

Question: Where the *Code* states that all assembly occupancies and the means of egress shall be provided with emergency lighting, does this include Class C

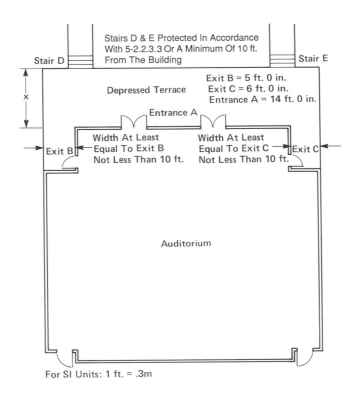

For SI Units: 1 ft. = .3m

Figure 8-16. Assembly Occupancy with Depressed Terrace as Principal Entrance. Assuming that Stair D serves Exit B plus ½ of Entrance A and that Stair E serves Exit C plus ½ of Entrance A, then X must be equal to or greater than the largest of the following: 10 ft (3 cm) per 8-2.7.3(b); 5 ft (1.5m) + ½ 14 ft (4.2 m) = 12 ft (3.6 m); or 6 ft (1.8 m) + ½ 14 ft (4.2 m) = 13 ft (3.9 m). Therefore, X ≥ 13 ft (3.9 m).

Assembly Occupancies, such as restaurants and drive-ins that have glass almost all around the dining area?

Answer: Yes. However, the authority having jurisdiction may modify the requirements if the authority feels adequate lighting is maintained from external sources.

Issue Edition: 1976
Reference: 8-2.10
Date: September 1978

8-2.10 Marking of Means of Egress.   Means of egress shall have signs in accordance with Section 5-10.

8-2.11 Special Features.

8-2.11.1 Railings.

(a) The fasciae of boxes, balconies, and galleries shall not rise less than 26 in. (66 cm) high above the adjacent floor or shall have substantial railings not less than 26 in. (66 cm) high above the adjacent floor.

(b) The height of the rail above footrests on the adjacent floor immediately in front of a row of seats shall be no less than 26 in. (66 cm). Railings at the ends of aisles shall not be less than 36 in. (91 cm) high for the full width of the aisle and shall be not less than 42 in. (107 cm) high for the width of the aisle where steps occur.

(c) Cross aisles shall be provided with railings not less than 26 in. (66 cm) high above the adjacent floor.

Exception: Where the backs of seats on the front of the aisle project 24 in. (61 cm) or more above the adjacent floor of the aisle.

Figure 8-17a illustrates the requirements of 8-2.11.1(a) and (b). Rail height at the fascia end of a sloping aisle must not be less than 36 in. (91 cm). However, where the aisle is not ramped but has steps, the rail height must be at least 42 in. (107 cm). There is greater danger of people tripping on steps than on a sloping surface with a maximum gradient of 1 ft (0.3 m) of rise to 8 ft (2.44 m) of run.

The *Code* requires a barrier along the downhill side of a cross aisle. [*See 8-2.11.1(c)*.] The barrier may be a rail or the backs of the seats that abut the downhill side of the aisle where the backs project 24 in. (60 cm) or more above the cross aisle. The difference between the 24-in. (60-cm) back height and the required 26-in. (66-cm) railing is not sufficient to require the railing. (*See Figure 8-17b.*)

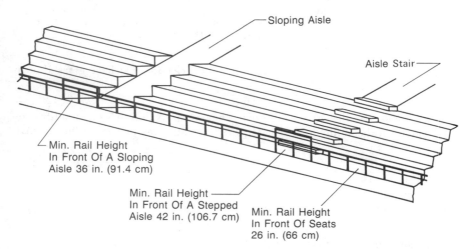

Figure 8-17a.   Railings Installed in Accordance with 8-2.11.1(a) and (b).

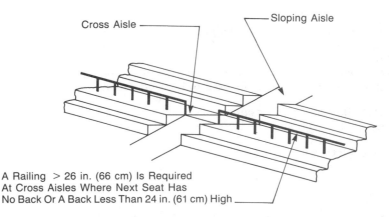

Cross Aisle ——

—— Sloping Aisle

A Railing > 26 in. (66 cm) Is Required
At Cross Aisles Where Next Seat Has
No Back Or A Back Less Than 24 in. (61 cm) High ——

Figure 8-17b.   Barrier for Cross Aisles in Accordance with 8-2.11.1(c). A railing [greater than 26 in. (66 cm)] is required unless the backs of seats in the row in front of the cross aisle are greater than 24 in. (60 cm) high above the cross aisle.

SECTION 8-3   PROTECTION

8-3.1 Protection of Vertical Openings.   All interior stairways and other vertical openings shall be enclosed and protected as provided in Section 6-2.

Exception No. 1:   Unprotected openings connecting not more than three floors may be permitted provided that they comply with 6-2.4.4.

Exception No. 2:   Atriums in accordance with 6-2.4.5 are permitted.

Exception No. 3:   Stairs may be open between balconies and main assembly floors in theaters, churches, or auditoriums where the travel distance is within the allowable limits. (See 8-2.6.)

Exceptions No. 1 and 2 permit the use of 6-2.4.4 and 6-2.4.5. (*See 6-2.4.4 and 6-2.4.5 for details. For egress requirements from off of balconies, see 8-2.4.4, 8-2.4.5 and 8-2.4.6.*)

8-3.2 Protection from Hazards.

8-3.2.1 Stages and Platforms.   (*See 8-1.3.*)

Modern stages pose problems that didn't exist in the past. Scenery may be shifted horizontally, vertically, or both ways. The use of thrust stages and arena stages creates other problems.

The classic stage of the past had great height above the proscenium opening to accommodate the rigid asbestos curtain. The high void was a natural place to house combustible scenery for a performance, along with the rigging necessary for handling scene changes. This vertical storage area represented both a high fuel load and a difficult space to reach in case of a fire. Many new theaters use a flexible noncombustible curtain that does not require much height to accommodate it. Scenery on these stages is moved horizontally, thus reducing the distance necessary for storage between the top of the proscenium opening and the stage ceiling. Most combustible scenery is now stored in areas adjacent to the stage. All rigging and lighting is condensed in less vertical space.

8-3.2.1.1 Materials and Design.   Materials used in the construction of platforms and stages shall conform to the applicable requirements of the local building code.

8-3.2.1.2 Platform Construction.   Temporary platforms may be constructed of any materials. The space between the floor and the platform above shall not be used for any purpose other than electrical wiring to platform equipment.

Permanent platforms shall be constructed of materials as required for the type of construction of the building in which the permanent platform is located. Where the space beneath the platform is used for storage or any purpose other than equipment wiring or plumbing, the floor construction shall be not less than 1-hour fire-resistive. Where the space beneath the platform is not used for any purpose other than equipment wiring or plumbing, the underside of the permanent platform need not be protected.

8-3.2.1.3 Stage Construction.   Regular stages and thrust stages shall be constructed of materials as required for the type of construction of the building in which they are located. In all cases the finish floor may be of wood.

Legitimate stages shall be constructed of materials required for Type I buildings, except that the area extending from the proscenium opening to the back wall of the stage, and for a distance of 6 ft (183 cm) beyond the proscenium opening on each side, may be constructed of steel or heavy timber covered with a wood floor not less than 1½ in. (3.8 cm) in actual thickness.

Openings through stage floors (traps) shall be equipped with tight-fitting trap doors of wood having an actual thickness of not less than 1½ in. (3.8 cm) with approved safety locks.

8-3.2.1.4 Accessory Rooms.   Dressing rooms, workshops, and storerooms accessory to stages shall be separated from each other and from the stage by not less than 1-hour fire-resistive construction, and openings within such separations shall be protected as required for corridors (20-minute fire door assemblies).

Exception: A separation is not required for stages having a floor area not exceeding 500 sq ft (46.5 sq m).

8-3.2.1.5 Vents.   Legitimate stages shall be provided with one or more vents constructed of noncombustible material. Ventilators shall be located near the center and above the highest part of the stage. They shall be raised above the stage roof and shall have a total ventilation area equal to at least 5 percent of the floor area of the stage.

Regular stages exceeding 1,000 sq ft (93 sq m) in area shall be provided with vents as required for legitimate stages or shall be provided with a mechanical vent installed in an exterior wall of the stage itself. Such vent shall be automatic upon operation of the sprinkler system and shall also be capable of manual operation. The capacity of the exhaust vent shall be approximately equivalent to that which would be provided for a legitimate stage.

Vents shall open by spring action or force of gravity sufficient to overcome the effects of neglect, rust, dirt, frost, snow, or expansion by heat or warping of the framework. Glass, if used in vents, must be protected against falling onto the stage. A wire screen, if used under the glass, must be so placed that, if clogged, it cannot reduce the required vent area or interfere with the operating mechanism or obstruct the distribution of water from an automatic sprinkler. Vents shall be arranged to open automatically by the use of fusible links. The fusible links and operating cable shall hold each door closed against the minimum 30 lb (133 N) counterforce, which may be exerted by springs or counterweights. This minimum counterforce shall be exerted on each door through its entire arc of travel and for a minimum of 115 degrees. A manual control shall also be provided.

Springs, where employed to actuate doors, shall be capable of maintaining full required tension. Springs shall not be stressed more than 50 percent of their rated capacity and shall not be located directly in the air stream nor exposed to the outside.

A fusible link shall be placed in the cable control system on the underside of the vents at or above the roofline or as approved by the authority having jurisdiction and shall be so located as not to be affected by the operation of a fire sprinkler system. Remote, manual, or electrical controls shall provide for both opening and closing of the vent doors for periodic testing and shall be located at a point on the stage designated by the authority having jurisdiction. Where remote control vents are electrical, power failure shall not affect their instant operation in the event of fire. Hand winches may be employed to facilitate operation of manually controlled vents.

> Small schools typically have multipurpose classrooms and classrooms separated by folding partitions. These schools commonly have stages that are greater than 500 sq ft (46.5 sq m) but less than 1000 sq ft (93 sq m). The Committee felt the venting requirements were too restrictive for facilities with small stages. Also note the new definition of stage and platform in 8-1.3.

8-3.2.1.6 Proscenium Walls.   Legitimate stages shall be completely separated from the seating area by a proscenium wall of not less than 2-hour fire-resistive noncombustible construction. The proscenium wall shall extend at least 4 ft (122 cm) above the roof of the auditorium.

Proscenium walls may have, in addition to the main proscenium opening, one opening at the orchestra pit level and not more than two openings into the auditorium at the legitimate stage floor level. Each such opening shall not be more than 25 sq ft (2.3 sq m) in area.

All openings in the proscenium wall of a legitimate stage shall be protected by a fire assembly having a 1½-hour fire protection rating, except that the main proscenium opening used for viewing performances shall be provided with an automatic-closing fire-resistive curtain as described below.

8-3.2.1.7 Proscenium Curtain.   The proscenium opening of every legitimate stage shall be provided with a curtain constructed and mounted so as to intercept hot gases, flames, and smoke and to guard against seeing flame from a fire on the stage from the auditorium side within a five-minute period where the curtain is of asbestos. Other materials may be used if they have passed a thirty-minute fire test in a small scale furnace, 3 ft (91 cm) by 3 ft (91 cm), with the sample mounted in the horizontal plane at the top of the furnace and subjected to the standard time-temperature curve.

The curtain shall be automatic-closing without the use of applied power.

Exception: *In lieu of the protection required herein, all the following may be provided:*

(a) A noncombustible opaque fabric curtain so arranged that it will close automatically, and

(b) An automatic fixed waterspray deluge system shall be located on the auditorium side of the proscenium opening and be so arranged that the entire face of the curtain will be wetted. The system shall be activated by a combination of rate-of-rise and fixed-temperature detectors located on the ceiling of the stage. Detectors shall be spaced in accordance with their listing. The water supply shall be controlled by a deluge valve and shall be sufficient to keep the curtain completely wet for 30 minutes or until the valve is closed by fire department personnel, and

(c) The curtain shall be automatically operated in case of fire by a combination of rate-of-rise and fixed-temperature detectors that also activate the deluge spray system. Stage sprinklers and vents shall be automatically operated in case of fire by fusible elements, and

(d) Operation of the stage sprinkler system or spray deluge valve shall automatically activate the emergency ventilating system and close the curtain, and

(e) The curtain, vents, and spray deluge system valve shall also be capable of manual operation.

Substitutes for asbestos have been a concern of environmentalists, school officials, and others. It was the intent of the Committee to provide guidelines for the use of materials other than asbestos. Although not specified by the *Code*, materials other than asbestos are expected to have a minimum weight of 2⅜ lbs per sq yard with a minimum warp and fill tensile strength of 400 lbs per inch reinforced with noncorrosive wire. A small-scale furnace test was considered appropriate by the Committee for this purpose.

If, instead of the fire resistant curtain specified in 8-3.2.1.7, a flexible proscenium curtain is used, the *Code* requires an automatic water spray system with nozzles on the auditorium side of the curtain. This system must be capable of completely wetting the curtain and of maintaining wetness for at least 30 minutes or until the deluge valve is closed by the fire department. Specifications for the installation of sprinkler systems in general are found in NFPA 13, *Standard for the Installation of Sprinkler Systems.*[4] Of course, for any sprinkler system to effectively minimize the hazards from fire to life safety or property, regular inspection and maintenance of the system is essential. NFPA 13A, *Recommended Practice for the Care and Maintenance of Sprinkler Systems,*[5] provides recommendations for ensuring that an extinguishing system will not fail in an emergency.

The spray nozzle system for the curtain is required to operate automatically by a combination of rate-of-rise and fixed temperature heat detectors. NFPA 72E, *Standard on Automatic Fire Detectors*,[6] and its appendix contain specifications and recommendations on the installation of heat detectors.

To complete the protection system, operation of the stage sprinklers or water spray system must also automatically close the proscenium curtain and activate the emergency ventilating system.

8-3.2.1.8 Gridirons, Fly Galleries, and Pinrails.   Gridirons, fly galleries, and pinrails shall be constructed of noncombustible materials.

8-3.2.1.9 Fire Protection.   Every stage (legitimate, regular, or thrust) larger than 500 sq ft (46.5 sq m) in area shall have a system of automatic sprinklers at the ceiling, in usable spaces under the stage, in auxiliary spaces and dressing rooms, storerooms, and workshops. Where there is a stage gridiron, 135°F (57°C) rated sidewall sprinklers with heat-baffle plates shall be installed around the perimeter of the stage, except above the proscenium opening, at points not more than 30 in. (76 cm) below the gridiron, and with sprinklers positioned 4 to 6 in. (10.2 to 15.2 cm) below the baffle plate.

Note the new definition for stage and platform in 8-1.3.

8-3.2.1.10 Special Exiting.   Each side of a legitimate stage shall be provided with at least one well marked exit providing not less than 32 in. (81 cm) clear width. Such exit shall open directly to a street, exit court, or exit passageway leading to a street.

Fly galleries shall be provided with a means of egress stair not less than 30 in. (76 cm) in width. Each tier of dressing rooms shall be provided with two means of egress meeting the requirements of the *Code.*

Stairways required by this subsection need not be enclosed.

8-3.2.1.11 Flame-Retardant Requirements.   Combustible scenery of cloth, film, vegetation (dry), and similar effects shall meet the requirements of NFPA 701, *Standard Methods of Fire Tests for Flame-Resistant Textiles and Films.* Foamed plastics (*see A-6-5.2.4*) may be used only by specific approval of the authority having jurisdiction. Scenery and stage properties on thrust stages shall be either noncombustible or limited-combustible materials.

It is the Committee's intent to reduce the amount of combustible material on stages. Foamed plastics as described in Chapter 6 (*see A-6-5.1.3*) have contributed to rapid fire spread in actual fire experience. Although 6-5.1.3 refers to interior finish, the Committee felt it to be an appropriate reference that could also be applied to the use of foamed plastics used on stage as props, furnishings, etc.

8-3.2.1.12 Standpipes.   Each legitimate or regular stage shall be equipped with a Class III standpipe located on each side of the stage, installed in accordance with 7-7.4.2.

There must be a standpipe located on each side of a stage to provide the stage hands and the responding fire department with a manual fire fighting capability at the area of a theater where a fire is most likely to occur. The installation of the standpipes must comply with NFPA 14, *Standard for the Installation of Standpipe and Hose Systems.*[7] NFPA 13E, *Recommendations for Fire Department Operations in Properties Protected by Sprinkler and Standpipe Systems,*[8] should also be consulted for a discussion of the necessity of a properly installed standpipe system. Standpipes are required whether or not the stage has automatic sprinkler protection.

8-3.2.2 Projection Booths.

8-3.2.2.1   Every assembly occupancy where an electric arc, Xenon, or other light source that generates hazardous gases, dust, or radiation is used shall have a projection room that complies with 8-3.2.2.2, from which the projection shall be made. Where cellulose nitrate film is used, the projection room shall comply with NFPA 40, *Standard for the Storage and Handling of Cellulose Nitrate Motion Picture Film. (See also Chapter 31.)*

The requirements for projection booths were developed jointly with those of NFPA 40, *Standard for the Storage and Handling of Cellulose Nitrate Motion Picture Film,*[9] and the motion picture industry at the height of movie popularity when cellulose nitrate film was still being used. Although only safety film is now used (except at film festivals or revivals) and the risk level has been reduced, the primary function of these requirements is to build a shelter around the projection booth, eliminating it as an exposure threat to the theater audience.

The intent of 8-3.2.2.1 is to protect the audience from the dangers associated with light sources, such as electric arc or Xenon. Where incandescent light is used, projection booths are not required in assembly occupancies. Note the booth is required based on the light source, not on the projection of film.

Paragraph 31-2.8 requires that, unless the construction of a projection booth complies with NFPA 40, *Standard for the Storage and Handling of Cellulose Nitrate Motion Picture Film*, a conspicuous sign must be posted on the door of the projection booth and also inside the booth. The sign must state: "Safety Film Only Permitted in This Room." The intent is to ensure that cellulose nitrate film is projected only with adequate safeguards.

8-3.2.2.2 Projection Rooms for Safety Film.   Projection rooms for safety film shall comply with 8-3.2.2.3 through 8-3.2.2.8.

It should be emphasized that 8-3.2.2.3 through 8-3.2.2.8 apply only to booths for the projection of cellulose acetate or other safety film. Although openings in the booth do not need to be protected, they must be provided with glass or other approved material that will completely close the opening and prevent gas, dust, or radiation from contaminating the audience or seating area.

8-3.2.2.3   Every projection room shall be of permanent construction consistent with the construction requirements for the type of building in which the projection room is located. Openings need not be protected. The room shall have a floor area of not less than 80 sq ft (7.4 sq m) for a single machine and at least 40 sq ft (3.7 sq m) for each additional machine. Each motion picture projector, floodlight, spotlight, or similar piece of equipment shall have a clear working space of not less than 30 in. (76 cm) on each side and at its rear, but only one such space shall be required between adjacent projectors.

The projection room and the rooms appurtenant thereto shall have a ceiling height of not less than 7 ft 6 in. (229 cm).

8-3.2.2.4   Each projection room shall have at least one out-swinging, self-closing door not less than 30 in. (76 cm) wide and 6 ft 8 in. (203 cm) high.

8-3.2.2.5   The aggregate of ports and openings for projection equipment shall not exceed 25 percent of the area of the wall between the projection room and the auditorium.

All openings shall be provided with glass or other approved material so as to completely close the opening.

8-3.2.2.6   Projection room ventilation shall be not less than the following:

(a) *Supply Air.* Each projection room shall be provided with adequate air supply inlets so arranged to provide well distributed air throughout the room. Air inlet ducts shall provide an amount of air equivalent to the amount of air being exhausted by projection equipment. Air may be taken from the outside; from adjacent spaces within the building provided the volume and infiltration rate is sufficient; or from the building air conditioning system, provided it is so arranged as to provide sufficient air whether or not other systems are in operation.

(b) *Exhaust Air.* Projection booths may be exhausted through the lamp exhaust system. The lamp exhaust system shall be positively interconnected with the lamp so that the lamp will not operate unless there is the airflow required for the lamp. Exhaust air ducts shall terminate at the exterior of the building in such a location that the exhaust air cannot be readily recirculated into any air supply system. The projection room ventilation system may also serve appurtenant rooms, such as the generator room and the rewind room.

New projection equipment in new theaters have a console that draws air in at the floor and up through the projection machine, thus eliminating the need to provide ducts 12 in. (30.5 cm) off the floor.

The requirements for the ventilation of a projection booth are designed to effectively "isolate" the booth from the theater so that any products of combustion created by a fire in a projection booth are not circulated into the theater. This is achieved by having an independent exhaust system for the booth, making certain that the exhaust outlet on the exterior of the building is located at a point where the air intake for the theater cannot recirculate the exhausted air.

If fresh air for the projection booth's ventilation system is supplied from the general system of the building, it is essential that the combined system be arranged to ensure the required air changes in the booth even when no air is supplied to the general system of the building.

8-3.2.2.7 Each projection machine shall be provided with an exhaust duct that will draw air from each lamp and exhaust it directly to the outside of the building. The lamp exhaust may serve to exhaust air from the projection room to provide room air circulation. Such ducts shall be of rigid materials, except for a flexible connector approved for the purpose. The projection lamp and projection room exhaust systems may be combined but shall not be interconnected with any other exhaust or return air system within the buildings.

(a) *Electric Arc Projection Equipment.* The exhaust capacity shall be 200 cfm (.09 cu m/s) for each lamp connected to the lamp exhaust system, or as recommended by the equipment manufacturer. Auxiliary air may be introduced into the system through a screened opening to stabilize the arc.

(b) *Xenon Projection Equipment.* The lamp exhaust system shall exhaust not less than 300 cfm (.14 cu m/s) per lamp, or not less than that exhaust volume required or recommended by the equipment manufacturer, whichever is the greater.

The *Code* sets forth the minimum capacity for the exhaust system of a projection machine; however, a greater capacity must be provided where recommended by the manufacturer of the projection equipment. This system must be independent of any other ventilation system in the building housing the theater; however, it can be combined with projection room ventilation.

8-3.2.2.8 Miscellaneous Equipment and Storage.

(a) Each projection room shall be provided with rewind and film storage facilities.

(b) A maximum of four containers for flammable liquids of not greater than 16 oz (.5 L) capacity and of a nonbreakable type may be permitted in each projection booth.

(c) Appurtenant electrical equipment, such as rheostats, transformers, and generators, may be located within the booth or in a separate room of equivalent construction.

The intent of the requirement for the storage and rewinding of film is to prevent these operations from occurring outside the projection booth at some less protected location where, if a fire occurred, the exposure to the theater would be significantly greater. All operations that relate to projection activities must be kept within the protected enclosure afforded by the projection booth.

8-3.2.3 Service Equipment, Hazardous Operations or Processes, and Storage Facilities.

8-3.2.3.1 Rooms containing high-pressure boilers, refrigerating machinery of other than domestic refrigerator type, large transformers, or other service equipment subject to possible explosion shall not be located directly under or adjacent to required exits. All such rooms shall be separated by a 1-hour fire barrier from other parts of the building.

The preservation of the integrity of exits in any building is one of the principal concerns of the *Code*. Therefore, hazardous areas, even if enclosed with the required fire resistant construction, must never be located where they might directly expose a required exit to fire.

8-3.2.3.2   All openings between the balance of the building and rooms or enclosures for hazardous operations or processes shall be protected by standard self-closing or smoke-actuated fire doors and shall be provided with adequate vents to the outer air, in accordance with Section 6-4 of this *Code*.

8-3.2.3.3   Rooms or spaces for the storage, processing, or use of the materials specified in this section shall be protected in accordance with the following:

(a) Rooms or spaces used for the storage of combustible supplies in quantities deemed hazardous by the authority having jurisdiction, hazardous materials in quantities deemed hazardous by recognized standards, or fuel shall be separated from the remainder of the building by construction having not less than a 1-hour fire resistance rating with all openings protected by self-closing or smoke-actuated fire doors, or such rooms or spaces may be protected by an automatic extinguishing system as set forth in Section 6-4.

(b) Rooms or spaces used for processing or use of combustible supplies in quantities considered hazardous by the authority having jurisdiction, hazardous materials, or flammable or combustible liquids in quantities deemed hazardous by recognized standards shall be separated from the remainder of the building by construction having not less than a 1-hour fire resistance rating with all openings protected by self-closing or smoke-actuated fire doors and shall also be protected by an automatic extinguishing system as set forth in Section 6-4.

(c) Boiler and furnace rooms, laundries, and maintenance shops, including woodworking and painting areas, shall be separated from the remainder of the building by construction having not less than a 1-hour fire resistance rating with all openings protected by self-closing or smoke-actuated fire doors.

Exception to (c): Rooms enclosing air-handling equipment.

(d)* Where automatic extinguishing systems are used to meet the requirements of this section, the rooms or spaces shall be separated from the remainder of the building by construction that resists the passage of smoke.

A-8-3.2.3.3(d)   It is not the intent of this provision to require a smoke barrier that meets the requirements of Section 6-3.

The intent of the Committee is to restrict the passage of smoke through the use of glass or other non-fire-rated material. This would not permit the use of wire or louvers but would not require all the components of a standard smoke barrier.

(e) Where automatic extinguishing is used to meet the requirements of this section, the protection may be in accordance with 7-7.1.2.

The Committee felt that the requirements identified in Chapter 7 for the use of six or fewer heads connected to the domestic system are adequate for these types of situations.

The intent of 8-3.2.3.3 is to specify the degree of protection necessary for certain hazardous areas. It has been divided into three sections based on the degree of hazard. The hazards noted in item (a) are required to be enclosed in 1-hour construction or protected by sprinklers. If the sprinkler option is chosen, an enclosure is still required; however, the enclosure need not be rated, but only form a membrane against the passage of smoke.

The hazards noted in item (b) must be enclosed in 1-hour construction and be protected by automatic sprinklers.

The hazards noted in item (c) are required to be enclosed in 1-hour construction with no option for a sprinkler equivalency for the enclosure. The exception to item (c) pertains to rooms housing air-handling equipment only. If the room is used for other purposes, then the provisions of item (a) or (b) apply.

Figure 8-18 illustrates the methods of protection specified by 8-3.2.3.3.

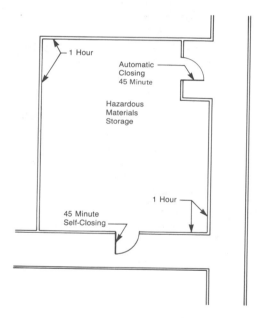

Figure 8-18(a). Protection of Hazardous Areas. Part (a) illustrates one method of complying with 8-3.2.3.3(a). (*See Figure 8-18(b) for the alternate method.*)

The three different types of protection of hazardous areas are illustrated in these figures. Parts (a) and (b) illustrate the two options for complying with 8-3.2.3.3(a). Part (c) illustrates the requirement of 8-3.2.3.3(b) that both fire-resistive separation and automatic protection be provided. Part (d) illustrates the special provisions for boiler rooms, furnace rooms, and similar areas contained in 8-3.2.3.3(c).

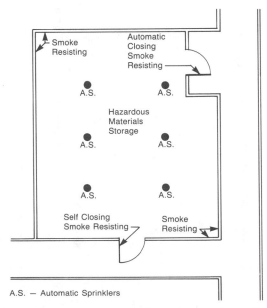

Figure 8-18(b). Protection of Hazardous Areas. Part (b) illustrates an alternate method of complying with 8-3.2.3.3(a). Part (a) illustrates another method of compliance.

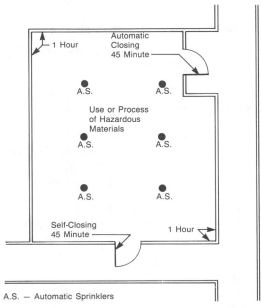

Figure 8-18(c). Protection of Hazardous Areas. Part (c) illustrates the requirements for complying with 8-3.2.3.3(b). Both one-hour separation and automatic sprinkler protection is required in this case.

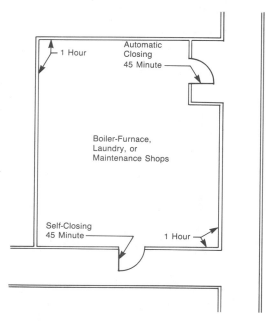

Figure 8-18(d). Protection of Hazardous Areas. Part (d) illustrates the requirements for complying with 8-3.2.3.3(c). Note that the automatic sprinkler option does not exist for these hazardous areas.

8-3.2.4 Special Provisions for Food Service Establishments.

8-3.2.4.1   All devices in connection with the preparation of food shall be so installed and operated as to avoid hazard to the safety of occupants.

8-3.2.4.2   All devices in connection with the preparation of food shall be of an approved type and shall be installed in an approved manner.

An "approved type" of device means that, from the standpoint of potential fire hazards, the unit is acceptable to the authority having jurisdiction. An "approved manner" of installation means installation in accordance with the requirements of the authority having jurisdiction.

8-3.2.4.3   Food preparation facilities shall be protected in accordance with 7-2.3 and are not required to have openings protected between food preparation areas and dining areas.

The intent of 8-3.2.4.3 is to provide some barrier between cooking areas and dining areas of restaurants. The intent of the barrier is to screen possible flash fires from the view of the patrons in an attempt to prevent panic. Openings in this barrier are not restricted and do not need to be protected. The *Code* is counting on the automatic extinguishing system to control any fire on the cooking surfaces, and thus no longer requires enclosure by rated construction. The degree of screening required, and thus the size of the barrier required, is left to the judgment of the authority having jurisdiction.

8-3.3 Interior Finish.

8-3.3.1   The interior finish requirements of this section shall be in accordance with Section 6-5.

8-3.3.2   Interior finish in all corridors and lobbies shall be Class A or B and, in enclosed stairways, Class A.

8-3.3.3   Interior finish in general assembly areas of Class A and B assembly occupancies shall be Class A or B. In Class C assembly occupancies it shall be Class A, B, or C.

Exception: In any assembly occupancy, exposed portions of structural members complying with the requirements for Type IV (2HH) construction may be permitted.

8-3.3.4   Screens on which pictures are projected shall comply with requirements of Class A or Class B interior finish.

8-3.4 Detection, Alarm, and Communication Systems.

8-3.4.1 General.   All Class A and all Class B assembly occupancies, and all theaters with more than one audience viewing room, shall be provided with an approved fire alarm system in accordance with this section.

Exception: Assembly occupancies that are a part of a mixed occupancy (see 1-4.7) may be served by a common fire alarm system provided the individual requirements of each occupancy are met.

The 1988 *Code* requires automatic sprinklers in all Class A and Class B assembly occupancies, with three exceptions. (*See 8-3.5.1.*) This language was changed to make the *Code* consistent. In the Exception, the Committee wanted to clarify that the intent of the alarm requirements was to meet the requirements of each occupancy in a mixed occupancy situation. This would allow an assembly occupancy in a school, hotel, hospital, mall, etc. to be served by the same fire alarm as in the predominate occupancy, provided it also met the requirements of the assembly occupancy.

8-3.4.2 Initiation.   Initiation of the required fire alarm system shall be by manual means in accordance with 7-6.2.1(a), which shall be provided with an emergency power source. The initiating device shall be capable of transmitting an alarm to a receiving station, located within the building, that is constantly attended when the assembly occupancy is occupied.

Exception No. 1:   Initiation may be by means of an approved automatic fire detection system, in accordance with 7-6.2.1(b), providing fire detection throughout the building.

Exception No. 2: Initiation may be by means of an approved automatic sprinkler system, in accordance with 7-6.2.1(c), providing fire detection and protection throughout the building.

For this edition of the *Code*, the Committee expanded this section to clarify the intent of "approved means" and to move into the body of the *Code* essentially what had previously been stated in the Appendix.

8-3.4.3 Notification.

8-3.4.3.1   The required fire alarm system shall sound an audible alarm in a constantly attended receiving station within the building for purposes of initiating emergency action.

8-3.4.3.2   Occupant notification shall be by means of either voice or prerecorded message announcement initiated by the person in the constantly attended receiving station.

8-3.4.3.3   The announcement shall be made via an approved voice communication or public address system, provided with an emergency power source, that is audible above the ambient noise level of the assembly occupancy.

8-3.4.3.4   Where the authority having jurisdiction determines that it is impractical to have a constantly attended location in an assembly occupancy other than a theater, a fire alarm system in accordance with Section 7-6 initiated by manual stations in accordance with 7-6.2.1(a) or other approved means of initiation, that automatically provides prerecorded evacuation instructions in accordance with 7-6.3.8, may be used.

The intent of the provisions of 8-3.4 is to provide an alarm system that will not produce a panic reaction from the occupants. Editions of the *Code* prior to 1981 required no alarm system. The intent of this section is to provide a system that will permit activation of the system by pull stations as required by 7-6.2.1, but that will not sound an audible alarm in the seating or audience areas of the assembly occupancy. In lieu of the audible alarm throughout the assembly occupancy, the system must sound an alarm in a constantly attended location. (Constantly attended, in this case, means that, during the time the assembly occupancy is in use, the alarm panel must be attended.) From that constantly attended location, voice messages that instruct the occupants can be issued via a public address system. This method allows for the orderly evacuation of the occupants and permits the issuance of proper instructions on how to evacuate rather than simply sounding an evacuation alarm, which may produce panic. A change in the 1985 Edition of the *Code* permits the use of prerecorded evacuation instructions that will automatically be played upon initiation of the system. This arrangement may be used in lieu of the attended station with the approval of the authority having jurisdiction.

8-3.5 Extinguishment Requirements.   *(See 8-1.6, 8-2.6, 8-3.2 and 8-3.6.)*

8-3.5.1   Buildings containing Class A or Class B assembly occupancies shall be protected by an approved supervised automatic sprinkler system installed in accordance with Section 7-7 as follows:

(a) Throughout the story containing the assembly occupancy, and

(b) Throughout any story below the story containing the assembly occupancy and

(c) In the case of an assembly occupancy located below the level of exit discharge, throughout any story intervening between that story and the level of exit discharge including the level of exit discharge.

Exception No. 1:   Assembly occupancies used primarily for worship with fixed seating.

Exception No. 2*:   Assembly occupancies consisting of a single multipurpose room less than 12,000 sq ft (1,100 sq m) and not used for exhibition or display.

A-8-3.5.1 Exception No. 2   A school gymnasium with egress independent of and separated from the school would be included in this exception as would a function hall attached to a church with a similar egress arrangement.

Exception No. 3:   Gymnasiums, skating rinks, swimming pools used exclusively for participant sports with no audience facilities for more than 300.

This requirement in the *Code* results from fires involving assembly occupancies, most notably the Beverly Hills Supper Club fire (1977) and the MGM Grand Hotel fire (1980). The exceptions to the general requirement are important in that they limit the areas or buildings needing the protection.

Two major changes were made for the 1988 *Code*. First, the Committee clarified the areas that need to be sprinklered. The concepts used in 8-1.6 were inserted here. If a five-story building has an assembly occupancy on the first floor, only the first floor and any basements need to be sprinklered; if on the fifth floor, then the entire building would have to be sprinklered.

The second major change involves the exceptions.

The exceptions for auditoriums with fixed seating, passenger terminals at or above grade, and Class B assembly occupancies used exclusively for restaurants have been eliminated in the 1988 *Code*. The Committee felt that these occupancies presented a sufficient life hazard to warrant automatic sprinkler protection where they had an occupant load greater than 300.

Exception No. 1 exempts places of worship with fixed seating. The life safety record is reasonably good in these occupancies.

Exception No. 2 exempts multipurpose assembly occupancies that are contained in one room and have an area of less than 12,000 sq ft (1100 sq m). If the multipurpose room is used as an exhibition hall or for a display room, the exception does not apply. Exhibit and display halls have been shown to be fire and life safety problems because of the high fuel load and potential for rapid fire spread.

Exception No. 3 combines Exceptions No. 4 and No. 5 in the 1985 *Code*. This exception exempts gymnasiums, skating rinks (including ice and roller), and swimming pools where there is an audience or spectator gallery having an occupant load of 300 or less. If the skating rink or swimming pool can be floored over and used for other purposes, then the multipurpose room requirements contained in Exception No. 2 apply. If the spectator gallery has an occupant load greater than 300, then an automatic system is required.

It should also be noted that automatic suppression systems may be required by 8-1.6 based on the location of the assembly occupancy, even though this paragraph would not normally require this protection.

Two major questions that arise on this provision deal with (1) mixed occupancies, especially assembly/educational, and (2) multiple assembly occupancies, especially religious halls with multipurpose rooms.

With regard to mixed occupancies, Chapter 1 (*see 1-4.7*) clearly states that if they *are* mixed, the more stringent requirements of the two must be met. Therefore, schools with assembly occupancies need to be sprinklered unless the assembly occupancy can be treated as a separate occupancy. This would normally require independent egress systems and fire separation. Also, many school multipurpose rooms could potentially utilize Exception No. 2. This exception emphasizes that the assembly occupancy is essentially a single room and thus could not be part of a mixed occupancy.

Exception No. 2 was originally intended for a typical fellowship hall, such as VFW, American Legion, Grange Hall, etc. The Committee recognizes that there will be some ancillary rooms, such as kitchens, restrooms, storage rooms, minor offices, etc., and it is not the intent of the Committee that these ancillary spaces disqualify a facility from using this exception, but it is the intent that the facility essentially consist of only one "major" room. Often a church or similar facility would like to use Exception No. 1 *and* Exception No. 2. This could only be done if each can be treated separately. In other words, the egress systems of each would have to be independent of each other and appropriate fire separation provided.

8-3.6 Corridors.

8-3.6.1   Interior corridors and lobbies shall be constructed in accordance with 5-1.3.4.

Exception No. 1: Corridor and lobby protection shall not be required where assembly rooms served by the corridor or lobby have at least 50 percent of their exit capacity discharging directly to the outside, independent of corridors and lobbies.

Exception No. 2: Corridor and lobby protection is not required in buildings protected throughout by an approved supervised automatic sprinkler system installed in accordance with Section 7-7.

Exception No. 3: Lobbies serving only one assembly area that meet the requirements for intervening rooms (see 5-5.1.6) need not have a fire resistance rating.

Subsection 8-3.6 is new to the 1988 *Code*. Prior to this Edition, the corridor provisions of Chapter 5 ruled in assembly occupancies. The Committee felt that it was important to specify the corridor protection needed in assembly occupancies. Exception No. 1 allows for corridor protection to be eliminated but requires 50 percent of the exit capacity of each assembly room to be direct to the outside, independent of corridors or lobbies. This allows theaters, for example, to eliminate panic hardware on doors leading into the lobby where they meet the other requirements of this section.

Exception No. 2 recognizes the excellent record of automatic sprinkler systems. However, this exception requires the entire building to be sprinklered, not just the assembly area.

Exception No. 3 recognizes the situation where the lobby serves only one assembly space and can, from a fire aspect, be considered part of that assembly area.

SECTION 8-4   SPECIAL PROVISIONS

8-4.1 Windowless or Underground Buildings.

8-4.1.1   Windowless or underground buildings shall comply with this chapter and Section 30-7.

8-4.1.2   Underground buildings or portions of buildings having a floor level more than 30 ft (9.1 m) below the level of exit discharge shall comply with the requirements contained in 8-4.1.3 through 8-4.1.5.

Exception No. 1: Areas within buildings used only for service to the building such as boiler/heater rooms, cable vaults, dead storage and the like.

Exception No. 2: Auditoriums without intervening occupiable levels complying with the requirements of Chapter 8.

The provisions of this chapter pertaining to subterranean buildings were totally revised for the 1985 Edition of the *Code*. In recognition of the potential hazard that underground buildings present, the *Code* now requires compliance with Section 30-7 and, in addition, requires compliance with the provisions of 8-4.1.3 through 8-4.1.5 if the underground building has an assembly occupancy more than 30 ft (9.1 m) below the level of exit discharge, or if an assembly building has a floor level more than 30 ft (9.1 m) below the level of exit discharge.

Two exceptions to the requirements are provided for areas used only for service functions, such as boiler rooms, heater rooms, etc., and for assembly occupancies where there is no occupiable intervening level between the assembly occupancy and the level of exit discharge.

8-4.1.3   Each level more than 30 ft (9.1 m) below the level of exit discharge shall be divided into not less than two smoke compartments by a smoke barrier complying with Section 6-3 and having a 1-hour fire resistance rating.

(a) Each smoke compartment shall have access to at least one exit without passing through the other required compartment. Any doors connecting required compartments shall be tight-fitting, 1-hour minimum fire doors designed and installed to minimize smoke leakage and to close and latch automatically upon detection of smoke.

(b) Each smoke compartment shall be provided with a mechanical means of moving people vertically, such as an elevator or escalator.

(c) Each smoke compartment shall have an independent air supply and exhaust system capable of smoke control or smoke exhaust functions and providing a minimum smoke exhaust rate of six air changes per hour.

(d) Each smoke compartment shall be provided with an automatic smoke detection system throughout. The system shall be designed such that the activation of any two detectors shall cause the smoke control system to operate and the building voice alarm to sound.

8-4.1.4   Any required smoke control or exhaust system shall be provided with a standby power system complying with Article 701 of NFPA 70, *National Electrical Code*.

8-4.1.5   The building shall be provided with an approved supervised voice alarm system in accordance with Section 7-6. The voice alarm system shall comply with 7-6.3.8. A prerecorded evacuation message shall be provided.

> The provisions for underground buildings or portions of assembly buildings with an occupiable floor more than 30 ft (9.1 m) below the level of exit discharge are designed to provide areas of refuge on the subterranean level. This, coupled with a smoke control or smoke exhaust system, will provide sufficient time to exit the building. Note that elevators or escalators are required in each compartment to help rapidly evacuate the area. It is felt these will not, themselves, create a life safety threat because of the other requirements of this section, including separate smoke compartments and smoke control or exhaust systems. It should also be recognized that the elevator or escalator is not being counted on as the required means of egress; normal exits are still required.
>
> In order to provide redundancy in the life safety provisions, standby power as defined in Article 701 of the *National Electrical Code*[10] is required for the smoke control or exhaust system.
>
> In order to permit orderly evacuation and to reduce the possibility of panic, this section requires the use of a supervised voice alarm system that will sound a prerecorded evacuation message.

8-4.2 High Rise Buildings.   High rise assembly occupancy buildings, and high rise mixed occupancy buildings that house assembly occupancies in the high rise portions of the building, shall comply with Section 30-8.

> A high rise public assembly occupancy has the same inherent life safety dangers that are found in other high rise buildings. Therefore, the Committee felt that protection provided for high rise buildings in general was appropriate and applicable to public assembly high rise occupancies and portions of high rise buildings that are used for public assembly.

8-4.3 Outdoor Assembly.

8-4.3.1 All assembly seating considered "smoke-protected assembly seating" as defined by NFPA 102, *Standard for Assembly Seating, Tents, and Membrane Structures,* outdoor assembly occupancies, tents, membrane structures, bleachers, grandstands, and stadiums shall comply with the requirements of NFPA 102, *Standard for Assembly Seating, Tents, and Membrane Structures.*

Exception: Smoke-protected assembly seating complying with 8-2.3.2 need not comply with 5-3.2 or NFPA 102, Standard for Assembly Seating, Tents, and Membrane Structures.

Where an outdoor assembly occupancy is created in an enclosed court so that exits can only be provided through a surrounding building, the requirements for exits, seating, and aisles must be the same as for an indoor assembly area.

8-4.4 Special Provisions for Exhibition Halls.

Exhibition halls have problems that differ from those of theaters, restaurants, or other assembly occupancies. They are large, multi-use facilities and have high ceilings appropriate to their size. Combustible materials are frequently displayed, and the containers in which the exhibits are shipped contribute to the fuel load. Due to the size of exhibition halls, most are required by 8-3.5 to be protected by automatic sprinklers.

This section has been expanded in the 1988 *Code* to provide more comprehensive guidance to the many people who are responsible for the different aspects of a trade show or exhibit. The authority having jurisdiction at the local level is often working with organizations that exhibit on a national basis and that are unaware of the local firesafety regulations. It is the Committee's intent that this *Code* provide more consistent and universal understanding of the firesafety regulations required in these occupancies and at the same time encourage more uniform enforcement practices.

The Committee learned that the trade show and exhibit hall regulations used by many jurisdictions were very similar; however, there was no nationally recognized model code that could be referenced. It was also recognized by the Committee that this lack of a model code presents a hardship as well as confusion between the local authority having jurisdiction and persons responsible for the various functions of the trade show or exhibit.

8-4.4.1 No display or exhibit shall be so installed or operated as to interfere in any way with access to any required exit or with visibility of any required exit or any required exit sign, nor shall any display block access to fire fighting equipment.

It is advisable to have prepared plans or diagrams to show the arrangement of displays or exhibits, including any that are to be suspended from the ceiling or an overhead structure. Displays or exhibits must never interfere in any way with access to any required exit, and they must not conceal exit signs. (*See Figure 8-19.*) A display should not block access to fire fighting equipment nor interfere with the normal operation of automatic extinguishing equipment or devices for smoke evacuation.

Rows of booths become exit accesses; therefore, booths and other temporary construction should be of minimal combustible construction or protected to avoid undue hazard of fire that might endanger occupants before they can reach available exits.

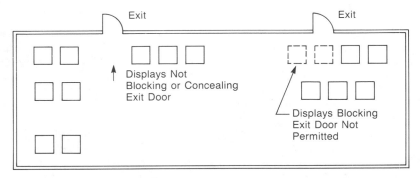

Figure 8-19. Arrangement of Displays in an Exhibition Hall.

8-4.4.2 A storage room having an enclosure with a smoke barrier having a fire resistance rating of 1 hour and protected by an automatic fire extinguishing system shall be provided for combustible materials not on display.

Displays or exhibits of combustible material must be limited in quantity in order to reduce the fuel load to an acceptable level. Excess combustible display material and all other combustible materials that are not in use should be kept in a separate storage room until needed. A separation with a fire resistance rating of 1 hour is required between such a storage room and all other parts of the building, and the room must be protected by an automatic sprinkler system.

8-4.4.3 Exhibits. Exhibits shall comply with the following:

(a) The travel distance within the exhibit booth or exhibit enclosure to an exit access aisle shall not be greater than 50 ft (15 m).

This requirement applies to standard exhibit booth arrangements, whether constructed of pipe and drape, or a large exhibit enclosure designed and built from other materials, which could include small booths, open displays, large board displays, etc. Also included in this requirement are exhibit enclosures that are created by the arrangement of products such as machinery or vehicles. The intent is to have a travel distance not greater than 50 ft (15 m) for occupants that are inside the enclosure, whether they are employees or patrons. Note that this is not travel distance to an exit, but only to an aisle.

(b) Exhibit booths shall be constructed of noncombustible or limited-combustible materials, pressure-treated fire retardant wood meeting the requirements of NFPA 703, *Standard for Fire Retardant Impregnated Wood and Fire Retardant Coatings for Building Materials*, or of flame-retardant materials complying with NFPA 701, *Standard Methods of Fire Tests for Flame-Resistant Textiles and Films*, both small and large scale tests. Textile wall coverings, such as carpeting having a napped, tufted, looped, or similar surface used as wall or ceiling finish, shall comply with 6-5.2.3. Plastic shall be limited to Class A or Class B interior wall and ceiling finish.

> This section is intended to provide direction to manufacturers of exhibit booths as well as decorators, exhibitors, and the authority having jurisdiction. The focus of this section is on the construction components of the ceilings, walls, and floors of an exhibit booth or display area, in addition to the finish treatment. It is the intent of the Committee to also include large signs and display boards. Small signs [approximately 2 ft by 3 ft (61 cm x 91 cm) or smaller] would not normally be considered part of the wall covering. However, this section does not apply to the goods or products that are being displayed.
>
> Plastics are limited to Class A and Class B for wall and ceiling finishes. It is the Committee's intent to prohibit the use of foamed plastics because of their inherent burning characteristics unless they meet the requirements of Section 6-5. Foamed plastics are found to be used in sign construction and display boards, and in some cases, the entire booth is constructed of foamed plastics.

(c) Curtains, drapes, and decorations shall comply with 31-1.4.

(d)* Acoustical and decorative material including, but not limited to, cotton, hay, paper, straw, moss, split bamboo, and wood chips shall be flame-retardant treated to the satisfaction of the authority having jurisdiction. Materials that cannot be treated for flame retardancy shall not be used.

A-8-4.4.3(d)   The authority having jurisdiction may use the field flame test contained in NFPA 701, *Standard Methods of Fire Tests for Flame-Resistant Textiles and Films*, as one method of determining flame retardancy.

> This paragraph only addresses materials used to decorate the booth or enhance its acoustics or aesthetics. This section does not cover products on display.

(e) Exhibit booths that are multilevel, consist of multiple rooms with ceilings, or are over 225 sq ft (20.9 sq m) with ceilings shall be protected by automatic sprinklers in buildings so protected.

Exception: Vehicles, boats, and similar exhibited products having over 100 sq ft (9.3 sq m) of roofed area shall be provided with smoke detectors acceptable to the authority having jurisdiction.

> Large booths and multistory booths present special problems in exhibit halls. A fire in these booths could grow to large enough proportions to have a significant negative impact on the performance of the building's

sprinkler system. It is the intent of the Committee to provide sprinkler protection in these booths by means of a temporary tap into the existing system. The Committee felt sprinklers would provide the protection necessary to extinguish a fire in its incipient stage, thus reducing the life hazard to occupants.

The Exception would exempt large vehicles, i.e., boats, mobile homes, recreational vehicles, from the sprinkler requirement but would require a smoke detector if the vehicle is greater than 100 sq ft (9.3 sq m) in area. The intent of the Committee was to provide early warning in the immediate area to allow for orderly evacuation. This provision could most probably be met by single station, battery operated smoke detectors.

(f) Open flame devices within exhibit booths shall comply with 31-2.3.

Open flame devices should be prohibited except for religious ceremonies and, where allowed, should be restricted to minimize the danger of igniting combustibles. Any use of open flames should only be allowed after approval by the authority having jurisdiction.

(g) Cooking and food warming devices in exhibit booths shall comply with 31-2.4 and the following:

1. Gas fired devices shall be installed in accordance with 7-1.1.

2. Devices shall be isolated from the public by at least 4 ft (122 cm) or a barrier between the device and the public.

3. Devices shall be limited to 288 sq in. (.19 sq m) of cooking surface area.

4. Devices shall be placed on noncombustible surface materials.

5. Devices used for cooking shall be separated from each other by a minimum distance of 2 ft (61 cm).

6. Devices shall be kept a minimum of 2 ft (61 cm) from any combustible materials.

7. Single well cooking equipment using combustible oils or solids shall have lids available for immediate use. Multi-vat cooking equipment using combustible oils or solids shall comply with 7-2.3.

8. A 20 BC fire extinguisher shall be provided within the booth for each device, or an approved automatic extinguishing system shall be provided.

The provisions of this section recognize the inherent dangers in cooking and warming devices where used in assembly occupancies that will be used for display purposes and are subject to large, transient crowds.

Item 1 requires that any gas fired device be installed in accordance with recognized standards.

Item 2 requires distance or a barrier between the public and the device. The purpose is to minimize the possibility of accidental spills of hot greases or foods and to minimize the potential for ignition of combustibles, especially clothing worn by patrons.

Item 3: The surface area was determined to be large enough to accommodate the average-sized deep-fat fryer. It was felt by the Committee that this would allow for exhibits that display deep-fat frying and at the same time provide reasonable safeguards.

Item 4: The bottom surface of many devices could be subject to heating to temperatures that could ignite combustible surfaces.

Item 5: The minimum separation distances are necessary to minimize the danger of a fire in one device extending into another device.

Item 6: The same principle that applies to Item 5 applies to Item 6, except the exposure is combustible decorations or other products as opposed to another cooking device.

Item 7: The object of the lid is to provide to the operator a ready method of smothering the fire. Multi-vat cooking equipment must comply with NFPA 96, *Standard for the Installation of Equipment for the Removal of Smoke and Grease-Laden Vapors from Commercial Cooking Equipment*[11].

Item 8 requires a 20-B:C extinguisher for each cooking device. The intent is to provide an extinguisher by each cooking device so the operator would be able to get to the extinguisher readily if the lid did not extinguish the fire or could not be applied. It was not the intent of the Committee to have all the extinguishers in one location.

(h) Combustible materials within exhibit booths shall be limited to a one day supply. Storage of combustible materials behind the booth is prohibited. (*See 8-4.4.2 and 31-2.6.2.*)

The intent of this section is to limit the amount of literature, brochures, boxes, give-aways, and other products that are kept in the booth. The amount necessary to constitute a one-day supply is obviously going to vary; however, the authority having jurisdiction should be able to make a judgment after reviewing the activity expected by the exhibitor. Additional supplies and combustible crates (used for shipping) should be kept in a separate storage area having a fire resistance rating of one hour and protected by an automatic sprinkler system.

(i) Plans, in a form acceptable to the authority having jurisdiction, shall be submitted to the authority having jurisdiction for approval prior to the move-in of any exhibit or trade show. The plan shall show all details of the proposed exhibit or show. No exhibit or trade show shall occupy any exhibit hall without approved plans.

The intent is to provide the authority having jurisdiction with a set of plans that shows aisle widths, travel distances, exits, booth locations, display area configurations, types of displays (e.g., cooking, machinery, drapery, crafts and arts, etc.), location of fire protection equipment (extinguishers, alarm pull stations, hose cabinets, etc.), lobby and registration area usage, etc. This is not a complete list, but it should provide some guidance in determining the plans that should be provided. The plan should also be drawn to scale. The scale used is not usually critical as long as it is indicated on the plan.

8-4.4.4 Vehicles.   Vehicles within an exhibit hall shall comply with the following:

The section on vehicles is intended to minimize the danger from both fuel and ignition sources.

(a) All fuel tank openings shall be locked and sealed in an approved manner to prevent the escape of vapors. Fuel tanks shall be not more than three-quarters nor less than one-eighth full.

It is important that fuel tank openings are locked to prevent tampering and accessibility to fuel. It is also important that the tank openings be taped to prevent the escape of flammable vapors. When the Committee reviewed the issue of amount of allowable fuel, it was found that some jurisdictions preferred empty tanks to eliminate fuel while others preferred full tanks to prevent vapors. It was determined that most exhibitors were unaware of the regulation until they arrived at the exhibit hall. After learning the specific rule (empty or full) they proceeded to make their adjustment in the adjacent parking area or some other unsuitable area. It is also difficult for the authority having jurisdiction to determine whether a tank is absolutely full or empty. The commmittee felt that this fueling and defueling by exhibitors outside the hall presented a greater danger than the level of fuel in the tanks, given that they are locked, sealed, and ignition sources are eliminated from the vehicle.

(b) At least one battery cable shall be removed from each set of batteries.

It is important that at least one of the battery cables is removed from each battery. Many vehicles have more than one battery. The intent is to eliminate the possibility of a spark from the battery that might ignite fuel or surrounding combustibles. It is usually suggested that battery cable connectors be thoroughly taped after they have been removed.

(c) Fueling or defueling of vehicles shall be prohibited.

Fueling and defueling in and around the exhibit hall is extremely dangerous. [*See comments on 8-4.4.4(a).*]

(d) Vehicles shall not be moved during show hours.

The movement of vehicles inside the exhibit hall compromises exiting and access to means of egress. Vehicles should be positioned prior to the hall being made accessible to the public to avoid compromising these exits. There is also a serious concern about the effects of carbon monoxide inside an exhibit hall that is occupied.

8-4.4.5   Compressed flammable gases, flammable or combustible liquids, hazardous chemicals or materials, Class II or greater lasers, blasting agents, and explosives shall be prohibited within exhibit halls.

Exception: The authority having jurisdiction may permit the limited use of any of the above items under special circumstances.

Compressed gases are subject to damage that could cause an explosion or create a serious threat to life safety under fire conditions. Flammable and combustible liquids compromise life safety by their inherent capability to contribute to rapid fire spread. Hazardous materials present a variety of hazards to life safety, from flammability to toxicity. Class II or greater lasers can cause tissue damage to humans, and blasting agents and explosives could cause a large loss of life or injury if handled improperly. Many exhibitors wish to display explosives or pesticides or a type of compressed gas container, etc.

These products can be effectively displayed by using empty containers without bringing the actual product into the hall.

The Exception gives the authority having jurisdiction the discretion to permit small amounts of otherwise prohibited materials under special circumstances. For example, an exhibit or trade show for collectors of small arms ammunition or a highly supervised and closed (to the public) vocational trade show can be allowed where special controls and professional supervision are provided.

8-4.5* Special Provisions for the Handicapped. Where assembly occupancies are required to be made accessible to the handicapped, the assembly area shall have accommodations for not less than two such persons.

A-8-4.5 Unless accommodations are specifically provided for the handicapped, the placement of handicapped persons may endanger the proper use of exits by others by blocking aisles and exits. Reference is made to ANSI A117.1, *American Standard Specifications for Making Buildings and Facilities Accessible to and Usable by the Physically Handicapped* (*see Appendix B*).

8-4.6 Special Provisions for Special Amusement Buildings.

8-4.6.1 Special amusement buildings shall meet the requirements for assembly occupancies in addition to the requirements of this subsection. Special amusement buildings with an occupant load not greater than 300 persons shall be considered Class C assembly occupancies.

It is important to note that any special amusement building is considered an assembly occupancy, even if the occupant load is not greater than 50. However, special amusement buildings do not include theaters, movie houses, and other similar types of public assembly occupancies.

8-4.6.2* Every special amusement building shall be protected throughout by an approved automatic sprinkler system installed and maintained in accordance with Section 7-7. Where the special amusement building is moveable or portable, sprinkler water supply may be by an approved temporary means.

A-8-4.6.2 It is the intent of the Committee to provide a suppression system that will act quickly to provide for life safety of the occupants.

It is felt that the residential or commercial quick-response heads would be appropriate in most cases. However, the design should be reviewed by competent automatic sprinkler designers and the authority having jurisdiction.

8-4.6.3   Where the nature of the special amusement building is such that it operates in reduced lighting levels, the building shall be protected throughout by an approved automatic smoke detection system in accordance with Section 7-6. Actuation of any smoke detection system device shall sound an alarm at a constantly attended location on the premises. Actuation of the automatic sprinkler system or actuation of a smoke detection system having an approved verification or cross zoning operation capability shall:

(a) Cause illumination in the means of egress to increase to that required by Section 5-8, and

(b) Stop any conflicting or confusing sounds and visuals.

It is the intent of the Committee to have the exits and means of egress well lighted upon the activation of a smoke detector or suppression system. It is also important that any conflicting or confusing sounds or visuals are also stopped and that, where a person's relative position to an exit is changed, additional exit signs may be needed.

8-4.6.4 Exit Marking.

8-4.6.4.1   Exit marking shall be in accordance with Section 5-10.

8-4.6.4.2   Exit marking in mobile special amusement buildings shall be of the luminescent, self-luminous, or electroluminescent type.

8-4.6.4.3   Low level exit signs shall be provided in accordance with 5-10.1.4.

The Committee recognizes that in special amusement buildings knowledge of exits and location of exit signs is a critical problem. Low level exit signs should provide patrons an additional advantage in finding their way out under emergency conditions. (*Also see commentary on 8-4.6.3.*)

8-4.6.4.4*   In special amusement buildings where mazes, mirrors, or other designs are used to confound the egress path, approved directional exit marking that will become apparent in an emergency shall be provided.

A-8-4.6.4.4   Consideration should be given to the provision of directional exit marking on or adjacent to the floor.

8-4.6.5 Interior Finish.   Interior finish shall be Class A throughout in accordance with Section 6-5.

8-4.7 Operating Features.   (*See Chapter 31.*)

SECTION 8-5   BUILDING SERVICES

8-5.1 Utilities.   Utilities shall comply with the provisions of Section 7-1.

8-5.2 Heating, Ventilating, and Air Conditioning Equipment.   Heating, ventilating, and air conditioning equipment shall comply with the provisions of Section 7-2.

8-5.3 Elevators, Dumbwaiters, and Vertical Conveyors.   Elevators, dumbwaiters, and vertical conveyors shall comply with the provisions of Section 7-4.

8-5.4 Rubbish Chutes, Incinerators, and Laundry Chutes.   Rubbish chutes, incinerators, and laundry chutes shall comply with the provisions of Section 7-5.

REFERENCES CITED IN COMMENTARY

[1]NFPA 130, *Standard for Fixed Guideway Transit Systems*, National Fire Protection Association, Quincy, MA, 1988.

[2]NFPA 220, *Standard on Types of Building Construction*, National Fire Protection Association, Boston, MA, 1985.

[3]NFPA 102, *Standard for Assembly Seating, Tents, and Membrane Structures*, National Fire Protection Association, Boston, MA, 1986.

[4]NFPA 13, *Standard for the Installation of Sprinkler Systems*, National Fire Protection Association, Quincy, MA, 1987.

[5]NFPA 13A, *Recommended Practice for the Care and Maintenance of Sprinkler Systems*, National Fire Protection Association, Quincy, MA, 1987.

[6]NFPA 72E, *Standard on Automatic Fire Detectors*, National Fire Protection Association, Quincy, MA, 1987.

[7]NFPA 14, *Standard for the Installation of Standpipe and Hose Systems*, National Fire Protection Association, Quincy, MA, 1986.

[8]NFPA 13E, *Recommendations for Fire Department Operations in Properties Protected by Sprinkler and Standpipe Systems*, National Fire Protection Association, Quincy, MA, 1984.

[9]NFPA 40, *Standard for the Storage and Handling of Cellulose Nitrate Motion Picture Film*, National Fire Protection Association, Quincy, MA, 1982.

[10]NFPA 70, *National Electrical Code*, National Fire Protection Association, Quincy, MA, 1987.

[11]NFPA 96, *Standard for the Installation of Equipment for the Removal of Smoke and Grease-Laden Vapors from Commercial Cooking Equipment*, National Fire Protection Association, Quincy, MA, 1987.

9 EXISTING ASSEMBLY OCCUPANCIES

(See also Chapter 31.)

Assembly occupancies include, but are not limited to, all buildings or portions of buildings used for gathering together 50 or more people for such purposes as deliberation, worship, entertainment, eating, drinking, amusement, or awaiting transportation. Assembly occupancies include, but are not limited to:

Armories	Discotheques
Assembly halls	Drinking establishments
Auditoriums	Exhibition halls
Bowling establishments	Gymnasiums
Churches	Libraries
Club rooms	Mortuary chapels
Conference rooms	Motion picture theaters
Courtrooms	Museums
Dance halls	Nightclubs

Passenger stations and terminals of air, surface, underground, and marine public transportation facilities. (If the jurisdiction enforcing the *Code* has adopted NFPA 130, *Standard for Fixed Guideway Transit Systems*,[1] there are some situations where transit stations would come under NFPA 130 rather than this *Code*. See NFPA 130 for additional details.)

Pool rooms	Skating rinks
Recreation piers	Theaters
Restaurants	

Also note that 11-1.1.3 requires university and college classrooms having a capacity of 50 or more persons to comply with the requirements of the assembly occupancy chapters.

Assembly occupancies with an occupant load of less than 50 are considered incidental to the predominate occupancy in which they are located. For example, a small conference room in an office area is considered part of the overall business occupancy. If it is a freestanding occupancy or building, such as a small diner, normally a mercantile occupancy classification is assigned. In either case, the occupant load factors of 9-1.6 are used since it is still an assembly use.

Chapter 31 specifies the life safety requirements for the operation of assembly occupancies.

365

SECTION 9-1   GENERAL REQUIREMENTS

9-1.1 Application.

9-1.1.1   The requirements of this chapter apply to existing assembly occupancies. (*See 9-1.3 for definition.*)

Exception: An existing building housing an assembly occupancy established prior to the effective date of this Code may have its use continued if it conforms to or is made to conform to the provisions of this Code to the extent that, in the opinion of the authority having jurisdiction, reasonable life safety against the hazards of fire, explosions, and panic is provided and maintained.

Beginning with the 1981 Edition of the *Code*, new and existing occupancy requirements are in separate chapters. The provisions for new assembly occupancies are found in Chapter 8.

It should be noted that, if an existing building of some other occupancy were to change to an assembly occupancy classification, the portion of the building housing the assembly occupancy must comply with Chapter 8 for new assembly occupancies, even though it is in an existing building. (*See 1-6.4.*)

Should an existing assembly occupancy change occupancy subclassification, such as from Class C to Class B, it must meet the requirements for a new Class B assembly occupancy. (*See 1-6.4, 9-1.1.2 and 9-1.1.3.*)

9-1.1.2   Additions to existing buildings shall conform to the requirements for new construction. Existing portions of the structure need not be modified provided that the new construction has not diminished the firesafety features of the facility.

Exception: Existing portions must be upgraded if the addition results in a change of assembly classification.

9-1.1.3   An assembly occupancy that has its occupant load increased resulting in a change of assembly classification shall meet the requirements for new assembly occupancies.

The provisions of 9-1.1.2 and 9-1.1.3 were new in the 1985 Edition of the *Code*. The provisions of 9-1.1.2 were necessary to make clear that the intent of the *Code* is to have additions to existing assembly occupancies meet the requirements for new construction. (*See 1-4.5.*) If, by constructing the addition, the classification of the assembly occupancy changes to a higher level (Class C to Class B, etc.), then the existing portion of the building must be modified to meet the requirements for new construction.

The provisions of 9-1.1.3 are similar to those of 9-1.1.2 in that, if for some reason the occupant load of an assembly occupancy changes, resulting in a higher classification (Class C to Class B, etc.), the existing building must be modified to comply with the requirements for new assembly occupancies. This may occur because of renovation of an existing building or because a higher occupant load is granted by the authority having jurisdiction under the provisions of 9-1.7.2.

9-1.2 Mixed Occupancies. (*See also 1-4.7.*)

9-1.2.1* Any assembly occupancy and its access to exits in buildings of other occupancy, such as ballrooms in hotels, restaurants in stores, rooftop assembly occupancies, or assembly rooms in schools, shall be so located, separated, or protected as to avoid any undue danger to the occupants of the assembly occupancy from a fire originating in the other occupancy or smoke therefrom.

A-9-1.2.1 Depending upon the character of construction and the hazard of the occupancy, this will require some physical separation by walls of appropriate fire resistance, protection of the other occupancy by automatic sprinklers, or other appropriate measures. Where the building is of fire-resistive construction and the hazard of the other occupancy is low or ordinary, as in a school or hotel, no separation may be necessary.

The intent of this provision is to protect the occupants of the assembly occupancy from the effects of a fire originating in the other occupancy. While this can be accomplished by several methods, two things must be considered in whichever method is chosen. First, consideration must be given to the protection of the means of egress of the assembly occupancy; second, the level of protection from the other occupancy that can be provided to the assembly occupancy itself must be considered. Methods that can be used to protect the assembly occupancy and its means of egress include construction of fire-rated partitions, use of independent exits, installation of automatic sprinklers, and careful analysis of the requirements of each occupancy where applying the provisions of 1-4.7 pertaining to mixed occupancies.

9-1.2.2 Occupancy of any room or space for assembly purposes by fewer than 50 persons in a building of other occupancy and incidental to such other occupancy shall be classed as part of the other occupancy and subject to the provisions applicable thereto.

Fifty has traditionally been considered the minimum number of people assembled in one space for which the *Code* requires special provisions, such as requiring a door to swing in the direction of exit travel. (*See 5-2.1.4.1.*) Therefore, in Chapter 9, 50 people constitute a level of risk to life safety high enough to require classifying an occupancy as an assembly occupancy and, consequently, to subject the occupancy to the special design requirements found within this chapter. Since the space still contains an assembly use, the occupant load factors of 9-1.6 are still used even if the space is being regulated under another occupancy.

9-1.2.3 Assembly occupancies in buildings of other occupancy may use exits common to the assembly occupancy and the other occupancy provided that the assembly area and the other occupancy considered separately each have exits sufficient to meet the requirements of this *Code*.

Where applying this section, consideration must also be given to the provisions of 1-4.7 pertaining to mixed occupancies. Those provisions require that, in mixed occupancies, the more restrictive requirements of either occupancy be used for both occupancies.

9-1.2.4   Exits shall be sufficient for simultaneous occupancy of both the assembly occupancy and other parts of the building.

Exception*:   Where the authority having jurisdiction determines that the conditions are such that simultaneous occupancy will not occur.

A-9-1.2.4 Exception Example: An assembly room for the inmates of a detention occupancy will not normally be subjected to simultaneous occupancy.

In 9-1.2.3 through 9-1.2.4, the *Code* requires that each occupancy, considered separately, have sufficient exits and that, where it is possible for simultaneous occupancy to occur, the exits be sufficient for the combined occupant load.

The Exception to 9-1.2.4 should be used judiciously. Consideration should be given to all possible uses before a decision is reached. A school gymnasium may normally be used only by the school occupants; however, several times a year, the gymnasium may be used by an outside group during school hours. A common example of this is the use of school gymnasiums as polling places on election day. Consideration should be given to all possible uses to provide the owner/occupant maximum flexibility in the use of the space.

9-1.3* Special Definitions.

Assembly Occupancies.   Include, but are not limited to, all buildings or portions of buildings used for gathering together 50 or more persons for such purpose as deliberation, worship, entertainment, dining, amusement, or awaiting transportation.

The definition for assembly occupancies indicates the need for alternate exit routes in small places of assembly, such as restaurants, lounges, or theaters, with capacities for as few as 50 people. (*Also see commentary at the beginning of this chapter.*)

Cyclorama.   The name generally applied to a neutral background that, with suitable lighting, can suggest the infinite space of the sky. It may be curved and may be painted to depict any required background.

The term "cyclorama" is used in the definition of "stage scenery." These definitions have been added to better clarify the terms used by the movie and theater industry.

Drop.   A large piece of scenic canvas that hangs vertically, usually across the stage area.

The definition of the term "drop" is intended to better clarify the *Code* with regard to stage productions.

Flow Time.   Flow time is the time during which there is crowd flow past a point in the means of egress system, and it is a component of total evacuation time.

The term "flow time" has been used in the technical literature on egress, and it is one worth understanding in relation to the *Code*'s requirements for the capacity of means of egress. Flow time is the time taken by a crowd to pass, for example, through a doorway during a mass egress situation. This egress time component, along with other egress time components for responding to an alarm (before beginning egress movement) and for traveling along the length of an egress route, contributes to the total time needed to evacuate an area after an emergency situation is detected and an alarm is sounded. In the case of large assembly buildings, the flow time is often the largest component of total evacuation time. Therefore, explicit information about flow time is now included in Chapters 8 and 9 of the *Code* to help improve understanding of the nominal performance expected where particular egress capacity requirements are satisfied.

Fly.   The space over the stage of a theater where scenery and equipment can be hung out of view. Also called lofts and rigging lofts.

Fly Gallery.   A narrow raised platform at the side of a legitimate stage from which the lines for flying scenery are manipulated.

Gridiron.   The arrangement of beams over a legitimate stage supporting the machinery for flying scenery and hanging battens from which lighting is hung.

Leg Drop.   A long narrow strip of fabric used for masking. Where used on either or both sides of the acting area, to provide entry to the stage by the actors, but also to mask. They may also be called "wings."

See commentary on the term "drop."

Life Safety Evaluation.   A life safety evaluation is a written review dealing with the adequacy of life safety features relative to fire, storm, collapse, crowd behavior, and other related safety considerations.

This definition has been added for use in conjunction with 9-2.3.2. (*See the appendix note and commentary dealing with 9-2.3.2.*) It is important to keep in mind that a Life Safety Evaluation deals with more than merely firesafety. The evaluation must consider all life safety hazards that could endanger occupants and require rapid egress or other measures to maintain safety. In some large assembly facilities, for example, fire might not be the most likely hazard; there might be more injuries and deaths due to incidents arising from the large number and high density of people in a limited space. This can happen in the course of normal occupancy conditions, such as where occupants are especially aroused about the event or where there is the possibility that occupants may have a strong desire to escape an area, e.g., when there is a sudden change of weather in the case of open facilities, or where there is a collapse of part of the structure. Such possibilities must be taken into account when doing a Life Safety Evaluation and, in some cases, special expertise will be required to properly assess and design or manage for social and behavioral factors in addition to factors of fire and structural safety. Generally, the evaluation must be based on a good understanding of the occupants — especially if they are crowded together — and the event that generates the assembly of people.

Pinrail.   A beam at one side of a legitimate stage through which wooden or metal pins are driven and to which lines from the flies are fastened.

Platform.*   That raised area within a building used for the presentation of music, plays, or other entertainment; the head tables for special guests; the raised area for lecturers and speakers; boxing and wrestling rings; theater-in-the-round; and similar purposes wherein there are no overhead drops, scenery, or stage effects other than lighting and a screening valance.

A-9-1.3 Definitions.

Platform.   It is not intended to prohibit the use of a curtain as a valance to screen or hide the electric conduit, lighting track or similar fixtures.

This is not intended to prohibit the use of curtains such as are used to obscure the back wall of the stage, curtain between the auditorium and the stage (grand or house curtain) and no more than four leg drops nor the use of a valance to screen light panels, plumbing and similar equipment from view.

> The revised definition, along with the appendix note, is introduced to bring nontheatrical "stages" of many schools under the definition of platform. Hanging curtains commonly used on platforms are normally used to conceal lighting or to provide a more aesthetic appearance.

Platform, Temporary.   A platform erected within an area for not more than 30 days.

Platform, Permanent.   A platform erected within an area for more than 30 days.

Proscenium Wall.   The wall that separates the stage from the auditorium or house.

Smoke-Protected Assembly Seating.*   Seating served by means of egress that is not subject to blockage by smoke accumulation within or under a structure.

A-9-1.3 Definitions.

Smoke-Protected Assembly Seating.   An assembly area wherein the roof is not less than 15 ft (4.5 m) above the highest cross aisle or seat row, and having smoke-actuated venting facilities within that part of the roof sufficient to maintain the level of smoke at least 6 ft (183 cm) above the highest seating or walking level, is considered to be smoke-protected assembly seating.

Stage. An area within a building used for the purpose of entertainment and utilizing drops or scenery or other stage effects and shall be classified as one of the following:

(a) *Stage, Legitimate.* A stage wherein scenery is retractable mechanically either horizontally or vertically, or suspended overhead.

(b) *Stage, Regular.* A stage wherein scenery is not retractable.

(c) *Stage, Thrust.* A platform extending beyond the proscenium arch and into the audience.

This revised definition of stage needs to be examined in conjunction with the revised definition of platform. The intent of these changes is to remove nontheatrical stages, such as those in many lower grade level schools, from this definition and call them platforms.

This definition of stage encompasses various types of stages, including arena stages (stages open to the audience on at least three sides).

The key point in the definition of a stage is the hanging of curtains, leg drops, and scenery. If none of these is present, then the arrangement is probably a platform. A potential problem is the arrangement commonly known as theater-in-the-round. For *Code* purposes, if the theater-in-the-round has scenery, leg drops, or curtains suspended on or above it, then it is a stage; if it has only lighting with a valance to hide the electrical fixtures, then it is a platform.

A typical example of a thrust stage is illustrated in Figure 9-1. The so-called "runway" at Atlantic City that is used annually for the Miss America Pageant is probably the most famous thrust stage.

Stage Properties. Furniture, carpet, and similar materials generally having an overall height of less than 5 ft (152 cm) and used to provide an appearance simulating a room or area.

The Committee felt this would better clarify the difference between the props used on a stage and the scenery used to dress the stage. The definition of "stage properties" and "stage scenery" is particularly important with regard to the flame-retardant requirements in 9-3.2.1.11.

Stage Scenery. Decorative materials such as flats, cycloramas, painted or photographic backings, and similar materials to "dress" the stage.

See commentary on stage properties.

A-9-1.3 Definitions. The following definitions may be useful to the enforcer of the *Code* although the terms are not used within the *Code*.

Accessory Rooms. The accessory rooms are dressing rooms, property master's work and storage rooms, the carpenter's room and similar rooms necessary for legitimate stage operations.

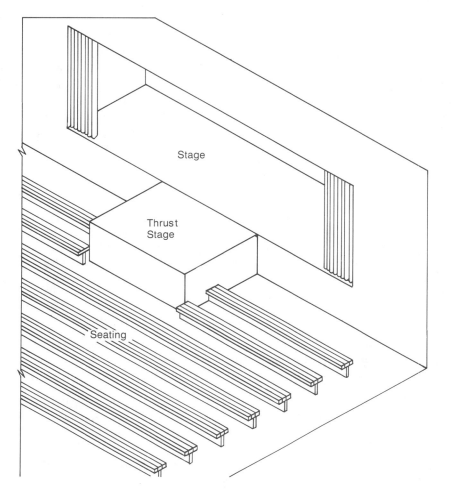

Figure 9-1.   Thrust Stage.

Batten.   In general a flown metal pipe or shape on which lights or scenery are fastened. While existing theater stages may still have wooden bars, they should not be used in new construction.

Scrim.   Finely woven fabric that can be translucent or opaque depending upon how it is used.

Theater-in-the-Round.   An acting area in the middle of a room with the audience sitting all around it.

9-1.4 Classification of Occupancy.   *(See 4-1.2.)*

9-1.4.1 Subclassification of Assembly Occupancies.   Each assembly occupancy shall be subclassified according to its occupant load, as follows: Class A, occupant load greater than 1000 persons; Class B, occupant load greater than 300 but not greater than 1000 persons; Class C, occupant load of 50 or more but not greater than 300 persons.

Minor language changes were made to make the language consistent with the rest of the *Code*.

As each increment of population is reached, the level of risk to life safety from exposure to fire rises. In view of this, the stringency of the requirements found in this chapter increases to counter each higher risk level.

9-1.5 Classification of Hazard of Contents. Contents of assembly occupancies shall be classified in accordance with the provisions of Section 4-2.

9-1.6 Minimum Construction Requirements. *(See 6-2.1.)* The location of an assembly occupancy shall be limited as follows:

Type of Construction	Below LED	LED	Number of Levels Above LED			
			1	2	3	4 & Above
I (443) I (332) II (222)	A†B†C† Any Number of Levels	ABC	ABC	ABC	ABC	A†BC
II (111)	A†B†C† One Level Below LED	ABC	ABC	A†BC	B†C†	N.P.
III (211) IV (2HH) V (111)	A†B†C† One Level Below LED	ABC	ABC	A†B†C	B†C†	N.P.
II (000)	B†C† One Level Below LED	A†BC	C†	N.P.	N.P.	N.P.
III (200) V (000)	B†C† One Level Below LED	A†BC	C†	N.P.	N.P.	N.P.

†Permitted if the level of the assembly occupancy and any story intervening between that level and the level of exit discharge are protected throughout by an approved automatic sprinkler system. If there are any openings between the level of exit discharge and the exits serving the place of assembly, the level of exit discharge shall also be protected throughout by an approved automatic sprinkler system (*see Section 7-7*).
N.P. — Not Permitted
LED — Level of Exit Discharge

It should be noted that the chart is arranged based on levels above the level of exit discharge (LED). Thus, in a normal building with the level of exit discharge at grade, the column "1" in the table refers to the second story of the building.

Since the Cocoanut Grove Night Club fire in Boston (1942), much emphasis has been placed by the Subcommittee on Assembly and Educational Occupancies on limiting the number of occupants in those assembly occupancies that provide only a minimum level of life safety because of the nature of the construction. The Cocoanut Grove fire illustrated the effect that a combustible structure (as well as combustible interior finish) and a multilevel location for an assembly occupancy can have on the severity of a fire and its high death count. More recently, the Beverly Hills Supper Club fire (1977) also illustrated these factors.

Paragraph 9-1.6 restricts the location of assembly occupancies. Type I and II (222) (fire-resistive) construction, with its "built-in-place" structural survivability (under fire attack), is acceptable for any assembly occupancy (hence, for any number of occupants) at the level of exit discharge and up to the fourth story. As the fire resistivity of the structure diminishes from Type II (111) (protected noncombustible) to Type V (000) (wood-frame) construction, the location of assembly occupancies (and the permitted number of occupants) is restricted. In addition, as the height of the building increases, so does the risk to the occupants; thus, the location of assembly occupancies is also restricted by height.

The table contained in 9-1.6 was revised in the 1985 Edition of the *Code*. The table presents a major provision of the *Code* for assembly occupancies and recognizes the value of automatic sprinklers as a life safety device. Note that the table deals with the location of the assembly occupancy in relation to the level of exit discharge. Thus, for example, if the building in question was a seven-story, Type I (fire-resistive) building with the level of exit discharge at the first floor, a Class A assembly occupancy could be located at the fourth floor without sprinkler protection. If the Class A assembly occupancy were located at the fifth floor, automatic sprinkler protection would be required for the fifth floor, as well as for the first through fourth floors. (*See notes to table.*) If the first floor of the building were so arranged that the exit stairs servicing the assembly floor were enclosed to the outside with no door openings into the first story or level of exit discharge, then sprinklers would not be required at that level.

Any assembly occupancy located below the level of exit discharge requires automatic sprinkler protection, as do all levels intervening between the assembly level and the level of exit discharge. The same rule concerning openings into the stair at the level of exit discharge applies.

The construction types given here are based on NFPA 220, *Standard on Types of Building Construction.*[2] (*See 6-2.1 and related appendix note.*)

9-1.7 Occupant Load.

9-1.7.1*   The occupant load permitted in any assembly building, structure, or portion thereof shall be determined on the basis of the following occupant load factors:

For ease of using this handbook, A-9-1.7.1 appears following all discussion on 9-1.7.1.

(a)* An assembly area of concentrated use without fixed seats, such as an auditorium, place of worship, dance floor, discotheque, or lodge hall — one person per 7 net sq ft (.65 sq m).

In the 1988 *Code*, the terminology "7 sq ft (0.65 sq m) per person" was changed to read "one person per 7 net sq ft (0.65 sq m)." The intent of the Committee was to clarify the meaning of the *Code*. The intent is that one person is assumed for each 7 sq ft (0.65 sq m) that is available to be used by occupants after deducting space occupied by permanently fixed counters, furnishings, etc.

The 7 sq ft (0.65 sq m) occupant load factor is based on open floor space with people standing in comfortable surroundings. This factor also can be used to estimate occupant load in a multipurpose room where portable chairs are placed in rows for meetings, film viewing, or lectures.

A-9-1.7.1(a)   This includes so-called "Festival Seating."

Festival seating is illustrated in Figure 9-2. This comfortable, low-density arrangement of people, providing them with the ability to sit directly on the ground or floor and to move relatively easily through and out of the area, likely evolved from festivals held in open areas. This concept has been abused where applied to indoor or outdoor events where the assembled spectators are not controllable in terms of their numbers, location, or behavior. Rock music concerts are examples of events where the "festive seating" concept might become decidedly unfestive due to unmanageable crowds of standing (not seated) people in front of the stage area and a complete loss of any maintained circulation routes through the assembled crowd. Injuries, due to crushing of bodies against bodies or portions of structure, are likely when this occurs. A description of a typical crush situation is found in a report titled, "Observations of crowd conditions at rock concert in Exhibition Stadium, Toronto, 16 July 1980," by J.L. Pauls. Because the number and arrangement of people here was not maintained throughout the event, there eventually were some thirty to forty thousand people distributed unevenly in an area of about 125,000 sq ft (10,600 sq m), resulting in an average density of about 1 person per 3.5 sq ft (.33 sq m). However, due to localized crowding at the stage area, several thousand people were at crushing densities of about 1 person per 2 square ft (.19 sq m). Both normal access and emergency access into this congested area were all but impossible, and management efforts to have people move back toward less densely occupied areas proved futile. Incidents like this one have led to the area limitations shown in 9-1.7.2, which provides for increases of occupant load in some situations.

(b) An assembly area of less concentrated use, such as a conference room, dining room, drinking establishment, exhibit room, gymnasium, or lounge — one person per 15 net sq ft (1.4 sq m).

In the 1988 *Code*, the terminology "15 sq ft (1.4 sq m) per person" was changed to read "one person per 15 net sq ft (1.4 sq m)." The intent of the Committee was to clarify the meaning of the *Code*. The intent is that one person is assumed for each 15 sq ft (1.4 sq m) that is available to be used by occupants.

Figure 9-2.   Festival Seating at a Rock Music Concert Held in a Stadium.

The 15-sq ft (1.4-sq m) occupant load factor is based on a use that has a certain amount of space occupied by furniture or a use requiring a large amount of space per person to accomplish the use. Examples of these typical uses are spaces involving the use of tables and chairs as in restaurants or conference rooms. Gymnasiums are an example of a use that requires space for the occupants to perform their function (i.e., exercising or sport games).

(c) Bleachers, pews, and similar bench-type seating — one person for 18 linear in. (45.7 linear cm).

(d) *Fixed Seating.* The occupant load of an area having fixed seats shall be determined by the number of fixed seats installed. Required aisle space serving the fixed seats shall not be used to increase the occupant load.

(e) *Kitchens.* One person per 100 gross sq ft (9.3 sq m).

This will clarify calculating the total occupant load in restaurants and cafeterias where a portion of the building is used as a kitchen, whether it is a separate room or only divided from the dining area by a serving counter. Note this occupant load is calculated by using "gross sq ft (sq m)." This takes into consideration that there will be stoves, sinks, cutting boards, counters, and other culinary machinery necessary to operate a kitchen.

(f) *Libraries.* In stack areas — one person per 100 gross sq ft (9.3 sq m); in reading rooms — one person per 50 net sq ft (4.6 sq m).

The intent of the Committee is to clarify the meaning of the *Code*. In stack areas, the terminology was changed from "100 sq ft (9.3 sq m) per person" to "one person per 100 gross sq ft (9.3 sq m)." This takes into consideration that there will be bookshelves and permanent aisles. In reading areas, the terminology was changed from "50 sq ft (4.6 sq m) per person" to "one person per 50 net sq ft (4.6 sq m)." Reading rooms typically have large magazine racks, chairs, couches, and other furnishings that are arranged by librarians to make the area attractive to the user.

Exception: The authority having jurisdiction may permit occupancy by number of persons not to exceed that for which the existing means of egress are adequate, provided that measures are established to prevent occupancy by any greater number of persons than permitted by room area or by fixed seating.

A-9-1.7.1 Suggested occupant load factors for components of large airport terminal buildings are given, however the authority having jurisdiction may elect to use different occupant load factors provided exit requirements herein are satisfied.

AIRPORT TERMINAL	SQ FT (GROSS)	SQ M (GROSS)
Concourse	100	[9.3]
Waiting Areas	15	[1.4]
Baggage Claim	20	[1.9]
Baggage Handling	300	[27.9]
Other	(See table in appendix A-5-3.1.2)	

The occupant load factors of 9-1.7.1 reflect the data developed from surveys of typical occupancies.

Consideration should be given to the actual use of a room or space. A multi-use room may have several occupant loads depending upon its function on a given day. This is especially true of multipurpose rooms in schools and hotels.

Figure 9-3a illustrates a 2500-sq ft (230-sq m) room with two 46-in. (117-cm) clear width doors. If the room were to be used as a banquet room with tables and chairs, its occupant load would be based on the 15-sq ft (1.4-sq m) factor, resulting in an occupant load of 167 occupants. If, however, the room were to be used for a stand-up cocktail party with essentially no furniture, then the occupant load would be based on the 7-sq ft (0.65-sq m) factor, resulting in an occupant load of 357 occupants. Thus, the room may have two occupant loads.

The exit capacity for the room is based on two 46-in. (117-cm) doors. Using only the criterion of exit capacity, the room can accommodate 460 occupants. Since either of the occupant loads calculated is less than the exit capacity, the situation is satisfactory.

As noted above, both criteria (exit capacity and occupant load) must be considered in establishing the permissible occupant load for a room or area. For example, the exit capacity of the room in Figure 9-3b is sufficient for an occupant load of 360 people. An occupant load calculated on the basis of the room size [3,600 sq ft (330 sq m) ÷ 7] would permit 514 people. The exit capacity of 360 must govern. This is allowed because of the special exception for existing buildings; in new construction, the exit capacity would be required to increase to 514 people in accordance with Section 5-3 since exit capacity must be provided for the occupant load determined by application of the occupant load factor.

Many times there is controversy over where to use a 7-sq ft (0.65-sq m) versus a 15-sq ft (1.4-sq m) occupant load factor. It must be remembered that these factors are based on "concentrated" versus "less concentrated" use and choices are made strictly by means of judgment. Since the occupant load factor is used to establish exit capacity and subclassification (which establishes construction, alarm, and sprinkler requirements), it is usually safer to allow a larger occupant load (with related increased safety requirements) than to try, usually with great difficulty, to enforce a small occupant load limit. (*Also see 9-1.7.2.*)

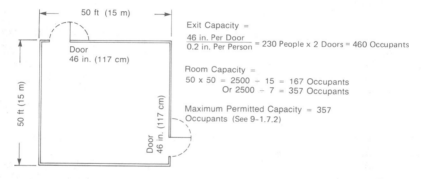

Figure 9-3a.   Determination of Maximum Permitted Occupant Load for an Existing Assembly Occupancy by Room Capacity.

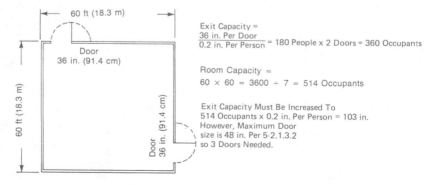

Figure 9-3b.   Determination of Occupant Load for an Existing Assembly Occupancy by Exit Capacity.   However, the Exception to 9-1.7.1 would allow the room to be restricted to an occupant load of 300.

9-1.7.2* The occupant load permitted in a building or portion thereof may be increased above that specified in 9-1.7.1 if the necessary aisles and exits are provided. To increase the occupant load, a diagram indicating placement of equipment, aisles, exits, and seating shall be provided to and approved by the authority having jurisdiction prior to any increase in occupant load. In areas not greater than 10,000 sq ft (930 sq m), the occupant load shall not exceed one person in 5 sq ft (.46 sq m); in areas greater than 10,000 sq ft (930 sq m), the occupant load shall not exceed one person in 7 sq ft (.65 sq m).

A-9-1.7.2 Existing auditorium and arena structures might not be designed for the added occupant load beyond the fixed seating. The authority having jurisdiction should consider exit access and aisles before granting additional occupant load such as festival seating, movable seating, etc. on the auditorium or arena floor area.

The accessibility of room exits is as important as the exit capacity. Therefore, where an increase is permitted over the occupant load established by 9-1.7.1, it must be demonstrated that adequate aisles and access ways leading to the room exits are provided. Spacing of tables must provide for occupied chairs plus an aisle. Consideration should be given to the probability that, when occupants leave during an emergency, they may not take time to move chairs out of the aisles. (*See 9-2.5.4.*)

Dining and drinking areas most frequently take advantage of the provision of 9-1.7.2. There have been large banquet layouts where the occupant load was successfully increased to reflect an occupant load factor of 11 sq ft (1 sq m) instead of the 15 sq ft (1.4 sq m) specified by 9-1.7.1(b). In all cases where an increase in the occupant load is permitted, the authority having jurisdiction should insist on complete fixture and furniture layouts and should strictly enforce adherence to approved layouts. As noted above, the same room may have several approved occupant loads depending on the various fixture and furniture layouts.

A major change in this paragraph from the 1985 Edition of the *Code* is a revision to the limit on the increased occupant load. This limit, which is based on an occupant load factor of 5 sq ft (0.46 sq m), was instituted for the 1985 Edition based on the Committee's concern for overcrowding, which affects the movement characteristics of the occupants.

Due to problems with festival seating (*see 9-13*), the limit was modified in this edition so as to be restricted to facilities less than or equal to 10,000 sq ft (930 sq m).

It has been shown in research at the National Research Council in Canada and by the London Transport Board that if people are crowded into a space so that each person occupies less than 7 sq ft (0.65 sq m), then movement approaches a "shuffle"; when each person occupies less than 3 sq ft (0.28 sq m), "jam point" is approached, and all movement by the occupants is effectively stopped. Thus, the maximum occupant load factor of 5 sq ft (0.46 sq m) for areas less than or equal to 10,000 sq ft

(930 sq m) was chosen by the Committee to prevent overcrowding and the attendant change in the movement characteristics of occupants.

See Figures 9-4a and 9-4b for two examples of increasing occupant load.

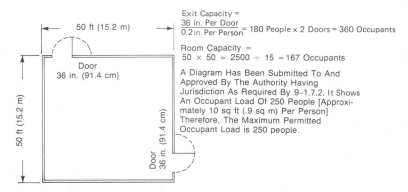

Figure 9-4a. Determination of Maximum Permitted Occupant Load for an Existing Assembly Occupancy by Room Capacity. Note that a practical upper limit for the room's population that will still ensure rapid and orderly movement to an exit may be 2,500 ÷ 5 = 500 people, based on 9-1.7.2. Since the exit capacity provides for 360 people, the authority having jurisdiction could conceivably allow a maximum permitted occupant load of 360.

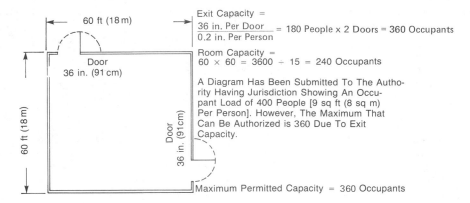

Figure 9-4b. Determination of Maximum Permitted Occupant Load for an Existing Assembly Occupancy by Exit Capacity. Note that a practical upper limit for the room's population that will still ensure rapid and orderly movement to an exit, may be 3,600 ÷ 5 = 720 people, based on 9-1.7.2. However, the exit capacity of 360 must determine the maximum permitted occupant load.

9-1.7.3 Waiting Spaces.   In theaters and other assembly occupancies where persons are admitted to the building at times when seats are not available to them, or when the permitted occupant load has been reached based on 9-1.7.1 or 9-1.7.2 and persons are allowed to wait in a lobby or similar space until seats or space are available, such use of a lobby or similar space shall not encroach upon the required clear width of exits. Such waiting shall be restricted to areas other than the required means of egress. Exits shall be provided for such waiting spaces on the basis of one person for each 3 sq ft (0.28 sq m) of waiting space area. Such exits shall be in addition to the exits specified for the main auditorium area and shall conform in construction and arrangement to the general rules for exits given in this chapter.

This is most often used for theaters, motion picture theaters, and in some restaurants. This space cannot be in or interfere with the egress routes from the rest of the assembly occupancy.

SECTION 9-2   MEANS OF EGRESS REQUIREMENTS

9-2.1 General.   All means of egress shall be in accordance with Chapter 5 and this chapter.

9-2.2 Means of Egress Components.

Many of the provisions formerly found in 9-2.11 now appear in 9-2.2. The intent of the Committee is to bring all of the components of means of egress into this section and simplify the *Code* for the user.

9-2.2.1   Components of means of egress shall be limited to the types described in 9-2.2.2 through 9-2.2.9.

Elevators and slide escapes (and revolving doors not meeting the requirements of 5-2.1.10) are not recognized as constituting required egress facilities in existing assembly occupancies. Slide escapes and elevators are not suited for rapid evacuation of the large numbers of people found in these occupancies. Further, elevators introduce other risk factors if used during a fire. (*See Section 7-4.*) It should be noted that these devices can be installed, but cannot obstruct or interfere with the required means of egress.

9-2.2.2 Doors.

9-2.2.2.1   Doors shall comply with 5-2.1.

9-2.2.2.2   Class C assembly occupancies in covered malls (*see 25-4.4.1 Exception*) may have horizontal or vertical security grilles or doors complying with 5-2.1.4.1 Exception No. 3 on the main entrance/exits.

This provision allows small restaurants in malls to use the security grilles or doors as provided in 5-2.1.4.1 Exception No. 3.

9-2.2.2.3 Panic Hardware or Fire Exit Hardware.   Any door in a required means of egress from an area having an occupant load of 100 or more persons may be provided with a latch or lock only if it is panic hardware or fire exit hardware complying with 5-2.1.7.

Exception No. 1:   In assembly occupancies having an occupant load not greater than 600, where the main exit consists of a single door or single pair of doors, locking devices complying with 5-2.1.5.1 Exception No. 2 may be used on the main exit. Any latching device on this door(s) shall be released by panic hardware.

Exception No. 1 to 9-2.2.2.3 is in recognition of provisions for locking doors contained in Chapter 5, Means of Egress. These provisions recognize the need to lock doors for security purposes and provide limits on how this can be done. These provisions also recognize, in fact, that in order for the business to function, the main door must be open. If a latching device is used in addition to the lock, panic hardware is required to release the latch.

Exception No. 2:   Special locking arrangements as permitted in 9-2.2.2.4.

9-2.2.2.4   Special locking arrangements complying with 5-2.1.6 are permitted on doors other than main entrance/exit doors.

Paragraph 9-2.2.2.4 allows delayed release hardware meeting the requirements of 5-2.1.6 to be used on all but the main exit. In addition to other requirements, 5-2.1.6 requires that the building be protected throughout by either an approved automatic sprinkler system or an approved supervised automatic fire detection system.

9-2.2.2.5   Revolving doors complying with the requirements of 5-2.1.10 for new construction are permitted.

9-2.2.2.6 Turnstiles.   No turnstiles or other devices to restrict the movement of persons shall be installed in any assembly occupancy in such a manner as to interfere in any way with required means of egress facilities.

9-2.2.3 Stairs.   Stairs shall comply with 5-2.2.

9-2.2.4 Smokeproof Enclosures.   Smokeproof enclosures shall comply with 5-2.3.

9-2.2.5 Horizontal Exits.   Horizontal exits shall comply with 5-2.4.

9-2.2.6 Ramps.   Ramps shall comply with 5-2.5.

9-2.2.7 Exit Passageways.   Exit passageways shall comply with 5-2.6.

9-2.2.8 Escalators and Moving Walks.   Escalators and moving walks complying with 5-2.7 are permitted.

9-2.2.9 Fire Escape Stairs.   Fire escape stairs complying with 5-2.8 are permitted.

9-2.3 Capacity of Means of Egress.

9-2.3.1   The capacity of means of egress shall be in accordance with Section 5-3 or, in the case of means of egress serving theater-type seating or similar seating arranged in rows, in accordance with 9-2.3.2.

9-2.3.2*   Minimum clear widths of aisles and other means of egress shall be in accordance with Table 9-2.3.2(a) or, for buildings providing smoke-protected assembly seating and for which an approved life safety evaluation is conducted, Table 9-2.3.2(b). For Table 9-2.3.2(b), the number of seats specified must be within a single assembly space and interpolation shall be permitted between the specific values shown. For both tables, the minimum clear widths shown shall be modified in accordance with all of the following:

(a) If risers exceed 7 in. (17.8 cm) in height, multiply the stair width in the tables by factor A, where

$$A = 1 + \frac{(\text{riser height - 7.0 in.})}{5}$$

(b) Stairs not having a handrail within a 30-in. (76-cm) horizontal distance shall be 25 percent wider than otherwise calculated, i.e., multiply by B = 1.25.

(c) Ramps steeper than 1 in 10 slope, used in ascent, shall have their width increased by 10 percent, i.e., multiply by factor C = 1.10.

Table 9-2.3.2(a)
For Use Without Smoke-Protected Assembly Seating

| | | Inch of Clear Width Per Seat Served | |
No. of Seats	Nominal Flow Time (sec.)	Stairs	Passageways, Ramps, and Doorways
Unlimited	200	0.300 AB	0.220 C

(1 in. = 2.54 cm)

Table 9-2.3.2(b)
For Use With Smoke-Protected Assembly Seating

| | | Inch of Clear Width Per Seat Served | |
No. of Seats	Nominal Flow Time (sec.)	Stairs	Passageways, Ramps, and Doorways
2,000	200	0.300 AB	0.220 C
5,000	260	0.200 AB	0.150 C
10,000	360	0.130 AB	0.100 C
15,000	460	0.096 AB	0.070 C
20,000	560	0.076 AB	0.056 C
25,000 or more	660	0.060 AB	0.044 C

(1 in. = 2.54 cm)

A-9-2.3.2   Tables 9-2.3.2(a) and 9-2.3.2(b) are based on a linear relationship between number of seats and nominal flow time, with a minimum of 200 seconds (3.3 minutes) for 2,000 seats plus 1 second for every additional 50 seats up to 25,000. Beyond 25,000 total seats, the nominal flow time is limited to 660 seconds (11 minutes). Nominal flow time refers to the flow time for the most-able group of patrons; some less-familiar, less-able groups might take longer to pass a point in the egress system. (Although three or more digits are noted in the tables, the resulting calculations should be assumed to provide only two significant figures of precision.)

A life safety evaluation is a written review dealing with the adequacy of life safety features relative to fire, storm, collapse, crowd behavior, and other related safety considerations. This review should be done by an approved person acceptable to the authority having jurisdiction. Such an evaluation includes, for example, a documented case that shows products of combustion in all conceivable fire scenarios will not significantly endanger occupants using means of egress in the facility (because of fire detection, automatic suppression, smoke control, large-volume space, management procedures, etc.). Moreover, means of egress facilities plus facility management capabilities should be adequate to cope with scenarios where certain egress routes are blocked for some reason.

In addition to making realistic assumptions about the capabilities of persons in the facility (e.g., an assembled crowd including many disabled persons or persons unfamiliar with the facility) the life safety evaluation should include a factor of safety of at least 2.0 in all calculations relating hazard development time and required egress time — the combination of flow time and other time needed to detect and assess an emergency condition, initiate egress, move along the egress routes, etc. This takes into account the possibility that half of the egress routes may not be used (or usable) in certain situations.

An example calculation may help describe the use of Table 9-2.3.2(b).

Within an arena providing Smoke-Protected Assembly Seating and having a total of 12,500 seats: for capacity purposes only, what should be the clear width of an aisle stair, with 8-in. (20.3-cm) risers and with a center handrail, providing means of egress for 340 seats? Interpolating between the width (0.13 and 0.096) respectively for 10,000 and 15,000 seat facilities, the required stair width, in inches, per seat served is 0.113 AB where A is 1.2 and 8 is 1.0. The aisle stair width, for capacity purposes, is the product of 340 (0.113) (1.2) (1.0) or 46.1 in. (117 cm). In this case a minimum width criterion of 48 in. (122 cm) (*see 9-2.5.6.7*) will govern its width. Previous editions of the *Code* credited this aisle stair with a capacity of only 150 persons.

> Generally 9-2.3.2 takes account of the practice, with many intermediate-size facilities, such as arenas and stadiums, to design means of egress that are intermediate between the egress capacity requirements of previous editions of the *Code* and the less-demanding egress capacity requirements that have been applied to large outdoor assembly facilities, such as those addressed by NFPA 102, *Assembly Seating, Tents, and Membrane Structures.*[3] Rather than merely giving a stamp of approval to this interpolation, the *Code* requires that extra caution be taken where reduced egress capacities are considered for a facility. In order to use the reduced egress capacities set out in Table 9-2.3.2(b), a case must first be made and accepted by the

authority having jurisdiction showing that all life safety hazards have been considered and that control measures provided to ensure that occupants evacuating the building will not be endangered by conditions developing faster than it takes for the means of egress to be cleared. This is described as a "Life Safety Evaluation," a process that should not be undertaken lightly or without special competence in a wide range of life safety issues including but not limited to firesafety.

The nominal flow time figures shown in Tables 9-2.3.2(a) and 9-2.3.2(b) are for reference and may be helpful to designers, consultants, managers, and others concerned with the expected performance of an egress system. Of course, if the facilities are to be used by groups of occupants who are unfamiliar with the facility or who are less able to move quickly and in dense groups than are younger individuals commonly found at athletic events, this will have to be taken into account, for example, when conducting the Life Safety Evaluation and in operating the facility. Alternatively, the capacity of means of egress should be increased so that a more rapid egress is possible without endangering or otherwise taxing the less able occupants. The need to consider the capabilites of occupants, in relation to circulation facility geometry, has led to the use of several correction factors in the tables' columns for clear width. In new facilities, there will be much emphasis on keeping the geometries as good as possible, and therefore, the correction factors will be 1.0 or very close to 1.0. With existing facilities, this might not be possible; however, it should be noted that handrails can be retrofitted on aisles and other means of egress to significantly improve occupant safety and comfort — an important factor in situations where efficient movement is needed. These factors are taken into account here and in other *Code* requirements for means of egress.

It should be noted that 9-2.3 addresses means of egress generally. The increased flexibility provided by Table 9-2.3.2(b) must be used with caution for proper balance between the relative capacities (and flow times) of each part of a means of egress system encountered by occupants as they leave the facility. Otherwise, with an unbalanced system, there will be queuing or waiting at some points other than the point of origin.

Attention should be given to the occupants' acceptance of the queue or the wait in their seats before proceeding out of the building; however, if a "downstream" component of the means of egress system is relatively underdesigned, even greater attention should be given to the actual and perceived conditions faced by occupants.

Figure 9-5 shows egress from a large stadium that provides egress performance that is perceived to be acceptable in terms of time and other factors. Occupants' acceptance of the longer egress flow times, permitted by the *Code* for larger assembly facilities, should be taken into account when doing a Life Safety Evaluation for the building. The photograph also shows a collection of people who can be expected to take somewhat longer to clear the building than is the case with football spectators [a reference group for the nominal flow time figures noted in Tables 9-2.3.2(a) and 9-2.3.2(b)].

Photograph Courtesy of J. L. Pauls

Figure 9-5. Crowd Egress from a Large Assembly Facility that Might be
Eligible for Egress Capacity Provisions of Table 9-2.3.2(b).

9-2.3.3 Main Entrance/Exit.   Every assembly occupancy shall be provided with a main entrance/exit. The main entrance/exit shall be of sufficient width to accommodate one-half of the total occupant load but shall be not less than the total required width of all aisles, exit passageways, and stairways leading thereto and shall be at the level of exit discharge or shall connect to a stairway or ramp leading to a street.

Exception No. 1:   A bowling establishment shall have a main entrance/exit of sufficient capacity to accommodate 50 percent of the total occupant load without regard to the number of aisles that it serves.

Exception No. 2:   In assembly occupancies where there is no well defined main entrance/exit, such as stadiums, sports arenas, and passenger stations, exits may be distributed around the perimeter of the building provided the total exit width provides 116⅔ percent of the width needed to accommodate the permitted occupant load.

The term "Main Exit" has been replaced with the term "Main Entrance/Exit." The intent of the *Code* is to require that 50 percent of the occupants will be able to exit through the same door(s) they used to enter the building. It was brought to the Committee's attention that some building owners/managers did not want to designate the "main entrance" as the "main exit" as well. Therefore, this terminology clarifies the intent of the *Code* and will require that the "main entrance" to a public assembly occupancy also be designated as the "main exit."

The usual entrance to an assembly occupancy also generally serves as its main exit. As a rule, people desire to leave a building by way of their entrance to the structure. Therefore, the main exit needs to be sized to accommodate at least 50 percent of the occupants; however, it must not be less in width than the sum of the required widths of the aisles that it serves.

Bowling establishments usually have relatively few rows of seats for spectators, but are necessarily wide to accommodate the alleys. Due to the limitation of the number of seats in a row, many more aisles are required than in other types of assembly occupancies. Exception No. 1 to 9-2.3.3 modifies what would be the excessive main exit width required to accommodate the sum of the required aisle widths served by the exit.

Exception No. 2 clarifies the intent of the *Code* to provide the same 16⅔ percent increase in exit capacity in buildings having no main exit as those with a main exit (50% + ⅔ = 16⅔%). The intent is to distribute the extra width as equally as possible among all exits. (*Also see 9-2.3.4.*)

9-2.3.4 Other Exits. Each level of an assembly occupancy shall have access to the main entrance/exit and shall be provided with additional exits of sufficient width to accommodate two-thirds of the total occupant load served by that level. Such exits shall discharge in accordance with 9-2.7. Such exits shall be located as far apart as practicable and as far from the main entrance/exit as practicable. Such exits shall be accessible from a cross aisle or a side aisle. (*See 9-2.3.3.*)

Exception No. 1: Where only two exits are required, each exit shall be of sufficient width to accommodate not less than one-half the total occupant load.

Exception No. 2: In assembly occupancies where there is no well defined main entrance/exit, such as stadiums, sports arenas, and passenger stations, exits may be distributed around the perimeter of the building provided the total exit width provides 116⅔ percent of the width needed to accommodate the permitted occupant load.

As an example of the requirements of 9-2.3.4, if an assembly occupancy had an occupant load of 900, the main exit would have to accommodate 450 people (50 percent). If there were two additional exits, together they would have to accommodate 600 people (two-thirds of the occupant load). Essentially, where more than two exits are required, the sum of the exit capacity must be at least one-sixth greater than (or 116 percent of) the total required by the occupant load. Also, 9-2.4.2 requires that, in a Class B assembly occupancy with a capacity of more than 600 people, at least three exits must be provided and no exit may be less than 44 in. (112 cm).

These requirements provide some relief from the congestion which would result if the main exit should become unusable during a fire.

9-2.4 Number of Exits. (*See also Section 5-4.*)

9-2.4.1 Every Class A assembly occupancy shall have at least four separate means of egress as remote from each other as practicable.

9-2.4.2   Every Class B assembly occupancy shall have at least two separate means of egress as remote from each other as practicable and, if of a capacity of over 600, at least three separate means of egress, each not less than 44 inches (112 cm) wide.

9-2.4.3   Every Class C assembly occupancy shall have at least two means of egress consisting of separate exits or doors leading to a corridor or other spaces giving access to two separate and independent exits in different directions.

As the concentration or number of people increases in an assembly occupancy, the chance of a simultaneous exiting by a sizable group of occupants increases. Therefore, to reduce jamming at doorways (which leads to panic and disorder), more exits at a variety of locations are needed. Paragraphs 9-2.4.1 through 9-2.4.3 provide for this design requirement.

Since 9-1.2.2 specifies that assembly areas with individual occupant loads of fewer than 50 people in buildings of occupancies other than assembly shall be classed as part of the other occupancy, no criteria are given by 9-2.4 for the number and location of exits in such an occupancy.

9-2.4.4   Balconies or mezzanines having an occupant load not greater than 50 may be served by a single means of egress and such means of egress may lead to the floor below.

The intent of the Committee was to provide relief for small balconies and mezzanines, such as choir lofts that accommodate not greater than 50 people.

9-2.4.5   Balconies or mezzanines having an occupant load greater than 50 but not greater than 100 shall have at least two remote means of egress, but both such means of egress may lead to the floor below.

These balconies might typically be found in restaurants or small theaters. The committee felt it was necessary to have two remote means of egress, but since the total number of people will be not greater than 100, it would be reasonable to let them exit onto the floor below.

9-2.4.6   Balconies or mezzanines having an occupant load greater than 100 shall have means of egress provided as for a floor.

The Committee felt than any balcony or mezzanine that could accommodate more than 100 people should be dealt with as a separate floor with regard to number of means of egress in order to avoid overloading the means of egress from the floor below and to protect people during egress from the mezzanine.

9-2.5 Arrangement of Means of Egress.   *(See also Section 5-5.)*

9-2.5.1   Exits shall be remote from each other and shall be arranged to minimize the possibility that they may be blocked by any emergency.

Exception No. 1:   A common path of travel may be permitted for the first 20 ft (6.1 m) from any point.

Exception No. 2:   As provided in 9-2.4.4.

Separation of exits as far as practicable cannot be overemphasized. Two or more exits that are located too close to each other can become unusable during the same incident. The fundamental principles of this *Code*, as expressed in Chapter 2, require remoteness of exits to the point that a single fire event will not simultaneously block both exits. This same concept applies to exit access doors. The remoteness requirements of Section 5-5 must be met.

Revolving rooftop assembly occupancies need special consideration; as the structure revolves, exit signs are often lost from view. To provide an unobstructed panoramic view, the exterior element revolves around a small stationary interior core in which the exits are often located. In many cases, the two exits are too close to each other to avoid both exits being involved in case of fire. Usually at least one stairway must transfer from its position in the stationary core to the normal location of the building stairways. This transfer, since it is a continuation of the stairway, must be made in an exit passageway possessing a fire resistance equal to that required for the stair enclosure.

9-2.5.2   Means of egress shall not be permitted through kitchens, storerooms, restrooms, closets, or hazardous areas as described in 9-3.2.

The purpose of this requirement is to make clear that exit access travel is not permitted to pass through areas subject to locking or areas possessing a hazard level higher than that normal for the occupancy.

9-2.5.3 (Reserved)

9-2.5.4 Seating.

9-2.5.4.1   The spacing of rows of chairs shall provide a space of not less than 12 in. (30.5 cm) from the back of one chair to the front of the most forward projection of the chair immediately behind it. Horizontal measurements shall be made between vertical planes. Where all chairs in a row have automatic or self-rising seats that comply with ASTM F851, *Test Method for Self-Rising Seat Mechanisms*, the measurement may be made with the seats in the up position. Where any chair in the row does not have an automatic or self-rising seat, the measurement shall be made with the seat in the down position.

The requirement for the spacing between rows of chairs is illustrated in Figure 9-6.

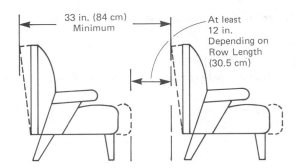

Figure 9-6.   Correct Measurement of Minimum Spacing Between Rows of Chairs
Without Self-Rising Seats.

9-2.5.4.2*   For rows of chairs served by aisles or doorways at both ends, there shall be no more than 100 seats per row, and the minimum clear width between rows of 12 in. (30.5 cm) shall be increased by 0.3 in. (0.8 cm) for every additional seat beyond 14 but need not exceed 22 in. (55.9 cm).

A-9-2.5.4.2   The system known as "continental seating" has one pair of egress doors provided for every five rows and located close to the ends of the rows. In previous editions of the *Code*, such egress doors were required to provide a minimum clear width of 66 in. (168 cm) discharging into a foyer, lobby, or to the exterior of the building. This continental seating arrangement can result in egress flow times that are approximately one-half as long as those resulting where side aisles lead to more remote doors (i.e., with nominal flow times of approximately 100 seconds rather than 200 seconds). Such superior egress flow time performance may be desirable in some situations; however, special attention should be given either to a comparably good egress capacity for other parts of the egress system or to sufficient space to accommodate queuing outside the seating space.

This is a major change in this edition of the *Code*. The new appendix note relates the expected egress flow time performance of "continental seating," as provided for in previous editions of the *Code*, to the egress flow time performance of the more flexible new requirements for egress width related to capacity. (*See 9-2.3.*) Additional design flexibility, built upon the continental seating principle of variable minimum seat row spacing and row length, is also introduced with this edition of the *Code*. The new requirement employs — as reference points for each end of the range — the previously employed requirements of 12 in. (30.5 cm) of clearance for rows up to 14 seats in length and 22 in. (55.9 cm) for rows over 45 seats in length. For example, under the new requirement, rows with 47 seats require a clearance of 21.9 in. (55.6 cm). This is calculated by subtracting 14 from 47 and multiplying the result, 33, by 0.3 in. to obtain 9.9 in., which is added to 12 in. to obtain the total required width clearance of 21.9 in. Rows with 48 to 100 seats require 22 in. (55.9 cm) of clear width.

The new flexibility, applying to all fixed seating arranged in rows, is based on the assumption that the egress time of a seating arrangement will be influenced more by the capacity of routes downstream from the rows of seating than by the rows' clear widths. Paragraph 9-2.3 provides a new standardized method for calculating the widths of those routes serving the seating space containing the seating. The combination of 9-2.3 and 9-2.5.4 offers designers of theaters, especially, much scope for laying out blocks of seating while still requiring a standard of egress flow time performance that is based on traditionally accepted egress performance (nominally about 200 seconds of flow time) resulting from very specific requirements on aisle and cross-aisle design. For example, rows longer than 14 seats are permitted, and egress door locations can be more flexibly determined than permitted under continental seating rules contained in previous *Code* editions.

Figure 9-7a shows what is possible with a theater with 630 seats in one unbroken area with 21 rows ranging uniformly from 20 to 40 seats in length. The required minimum clear width between the front row (with 20 seats) and the one behind (with 21 seats) is 14.1 in. (35.8 cm). The required minimum clear width between the back row (with 40 seats) and the one in front of it (with 39 seats) is 19.8 in. (50.3 cm). The designer has the option of making all the clear widths uniform and at least 19.8 in., or progressively increasing them from front to back, from at least 14.1 in. to at least 19.8 in., as the row lengths increase.

The theater is a Class B assembly occupancy with over 500 seats; therefore, by 9-2.4.2, it requires at least three separate means of egress, each not less than 44 in. (112 cm) in width. A main set of doors, at the back of the seating and close to the main entrance/exit, has to provide at least one-half the egress capacity. In this case, it must serve at least 315 persons. According to 9-2.3.2, the minimum total clear width of these main doorways must be 70 in. (178 cm), and thus two doorways providing 35 in. (89 cm) clear width each would suffice for *Code* capacity purposes. However, 9-2.3.3 requires that the main entrance be as wide as all aisles leading to it, so the two 47-in. (119-cm) aisles require a 94-in. (239-cm) main entrance/exit. Two additional means of egress, providing total capacity for at least 420 seats (two-thirds of the 630 seats) according to 9-2.3.4, each need to have a minimum clear width of 47 in. (119 cm) (210 times 0.22 in.) according to 9-2.3.2 and not less than 44 in. (112 cm) according to 9-2.4.2. Minimum side aisle width, connecting the front and back egress doorways, would also have to be 47 in. (119 cm). Greater widths of aisle and doorways, especially those leading to the main entrance/exit, should be considered to help improve normal convenience and other aspects that go beyond the minimum *Code* requirements for means of egress.

In the example presented in Figure 9-7a there is of course the option of doing a traditional layout with seats having no more than six intervening seats separating them from an aisle. This would require that more space be devoted to aisles and cross aisles, but this space loss could be offset by closer seat row spacings.

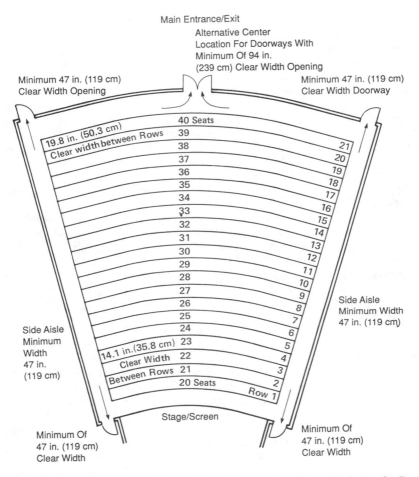

Figure 9-7a.   Minimum Means of Egress for a 630-Seat Theater Utilizing the Row Spacing and Aisle Length Provisions of 9-2.5.4.2.

9-2.5.4.3   For rows of chairs served by an aisle or doorway at one end only, the minimum clear width between rows of 12 in. (30.5 cm) shall be increased by 0.6 in. (1.5 cm) for every additional seat beyond 7, but need not exceed 22 in. (55.9 cm).

The incremental increase of 0.6 in. (1.5 cm) of required minimum clear width between rows for each additional seat to be passed to reach an aisle is the same here as in the case of the row served by aisles at each end (9-2.5.4.2).

9-2.5.4.4   For rows of chairs served by an aisle or doorway at one end only, the path of travel shall not exceed 30 ft (9.1 m) from any seat to a point where a person has a choice of two paths of travel to two exits.

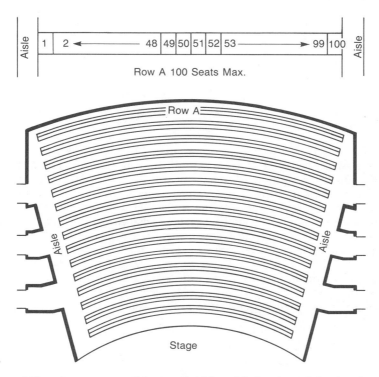

Figure 9-7b.   Arrangement of Seats and Aisles with Contintenal Seating. In prior editions of the *Code* when more than 14 seats were in a row, this arrangement was required. One hundred seats ts the maximum number for one row.

The 30-ft (9.1-m) limit effectively means that only about 18 chairs can be put into a row served by an aisle at one end only, assuming that, when one reaches the aisle, it is possible to move in either of two directions to two exits. This requirement also influences the permitted maximum length of aisles providing a common path of travel to reach the two exits.

9-2.5.4.5   Chairs without dividing arms shall have their capacity determined by allowing 18 in. (45.7 cm) per person.

The fact that the *Code* uses the traditional 18-in. (45.7-cm) figure for seat width per person for determining maximum occupant load (and egress capacity) should not necessarily be taken as an endorsement for using the 18-in. (45.7-cm) figure as a basis for ticket sales. This is especially true where events are sold out and a specific seat is assigned on each ticket. Winter events, where spectators wear bulkier clothing, are examples of those for which a more generous seat spacing should be considered in the ticket sales policy. Generally, the 18-in. (45.7-cm) figure — applied to ticket sales — makes most sense with children and younger adults, under temperate weather conditions, and with a general admission policy when a full house is not expected. Otherwise, the space to be kept clear in aisles and other means of egress might be compromised.

9-2.5.4.6   Where bleacher or grandstand seating without backs is used indoors, rows of seats shall be spaced not less than 22 in. (55.9 cm) back to back.

Exception: Folding or telescopic seating shall comply with NFPA 102, Standard for Assembly Seating, Tents, and Membrane Structures, with a limit of dead ends in vertical aisles of 16 rows.

The elimination of backs allows the entire bleacher to be a path of exit access. Assuming that they are fit and agile, plus prepared to risk a serious misstep and fall, people can simultaneously evacuate a bleacher upward or downward without using aisles. This compensates somewhat for the openness of bleacher-type structures, which can expose the entire population to a single fire either under or adjacent to the structure. The provisions of the *Code* concerning bleachers or graduated seating and folding or telescopic seating have been modified to coordinate requirements with NFPA 102, *Standard for Assembly Seating, Tents, and Membrane Structures.*[3] It should be noted that, unless certain criteria are met (as set out in NFPA 102), aisles are required for new bleachers, and such aisles must meet requirements comparable to those in the *Code*.

9-2.5.4.7*   Fixed or loose chairs, tables, and similar furnishings or equipment shall be so arranged and maintained that a path of travel to an aisle or exit is provided. The path of travel shall not exceed 10 ft. (3 m) from any point to an aisle or exit.

A-9-2.5.4.7   Figure A-9-2.5.4.7 illustrates the requirements of 9-2.5.4.7.

This provision, introduced in the 1985 Edition of the *Code*, attempts to clarify requirements for aisles in restaurants and similar assembly occupancies having tables, chairs, and other furnishings in cluster arrangements. The provision essentially establishes a cluster of tables where the travel distance from within the cluster to a well-defined and sized aisle is not to exceed 10 ft (3 m). The spacing between tables, chairs, and other furnishings within the cluster is not defined by the *Code* based on the assumption that use and service to the cluster will define adequate aisle space. When considering a restaurant with this arrangement, it is obvious that, in order to serve the tables, sufficient aisle space must be maintained for the restaurant staff. This space is considered adequate for means of egress purposes within the cluster. Note that the 10-ft (3-m) travel distance requirement within the cluster limits the occupants' exposure to these somewhat smaller aisle widths. (*See also 9-2.5.6.8 regarding aisle width.*)

9-2.5.4.8*   Rectangular banquet type tables used for drinking or dining or purposes having similar seating configurations, with the path of travel to an aisle exceeding 10 ft (3 m), shall be spaced not less than 54 in. (137 cm) apart where seating occurs back to back nor less than 36 in. (91 cm) where seating is on one side only. The path of travel to an aisle or exit shall not exceed 20 ft. (6.1 m).

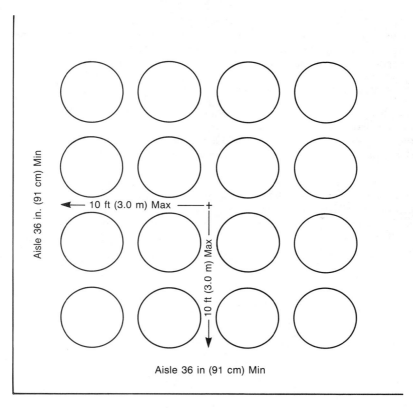

Figure A-9-2.5.4.7

A-9-2.5.4.8 Figure A-9-2.5.4.8 illustrates the requirements of 9-2.5.4.8.

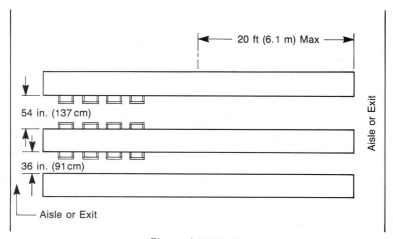

Figure A-9-2.5.4.8

Note that the provisions of 9-2.5.4.7 apply to banquet tables if they form a cluster meeting the 10-ft (3-m) travel distance to a defined aisle. Where long rows of banquet tables are used and the 10-ft (3-m) travel distance is exceeded, the table spacing provisions of 9-3.5.4.8 apply.

9-2.5.5* Tablet-Arm Chair Seating.

A-9-2.5.5   Tablet-arm chairs having a stored position have not been shown to require special regulation. Where an assembly occupancy is designed for dual purpose as instructional space and public purposes, management should require that the tablet arm be placed in the stored position when instruction is not the primary function.

The Committee carefully examined the subject of tablet-arm chairs with storing provisions and determined that these chairs present little threat to life safety. Where the tablet arm is fixed in the use position, tablet-arm chairs must be arranged to meet the aisle spacing requirements. This applies to both normal seating and continental seating. Figure 9-8 illustrates this provision.

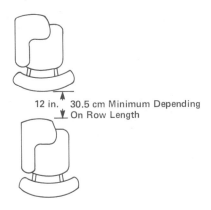

12 in.   30.5 cm Minimum Depending
On Row Length

Figure 9-8. Minimum Spacing Between Rows of Seats with Fixed Tablet Arms. Clear space between the back of a seat and the leading edge of a tablet arm in normal seating and required row spacing is set by 9-2.5.4.3, depending on row length but not less than 12 in. (30.5 cm).

9-2.5.5.1   Tablet-arm chairs shall not be permitted unless full compliance of row space requirements is provided when the tablet arm is in the usable position. Tablet-arm chairs that do not have a stored position for the tablet arm shall not be permitted unless the clearance required by 9-2.5.4 between rows of chairs is provided and maintained.

9-2.5.5.2   Where tablet-arm chairs are used, the clear width of rows of seats shall be measured with a tablet arm in the up or use position.

Exception: Tablet arms may be measured in stored position where the tablet arm automatically returns to the stored position when raised manually in one motion to a vertical position and falls to the stored position by force of gravity.

9-2.5.6 Aisles.

9-2.5.6.1 Aisle width shall provide sufficient egress capacity for the number of persons accommodated by the catchment areas served by the aisle. The catchment area served by an aisle is that portion of the total space that is naturally served by that section of the aisle. The establishment of catchment areas shall be based on a balanced use of all means of egress with the number of persons in proportion to egress capacity.

Figure 9-9 illustrates how catchment areas would be allocated in the case of a theater with four egress doorways having approximately similar egress capacity. Note that catchment areas for normal, nonemergency uses of only some of the available means of egress — especially those provided by the main entrance/exit — may be quite different from the catchment areas based on a balanced distribution of people in proportion to egress capacity of individual means of egress. Facility management procedures must take into account the difficulties of informing people about and directing them to all the available means of egress, especially when normally used, familiar routes become blocked in an emergency.

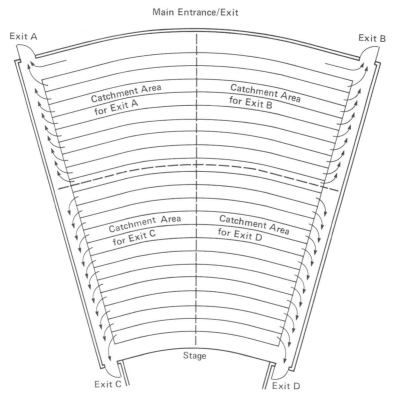

Figure 9-9. Plan of a Theater Showing how Catchment Areas for Means of Egress Are Based on a Balanced Use of All Means of Egress, in Proportion to Egress Capacity.

9-2.5.6.2   Where aisles converge to form a single path of egress travel, the required egress capacity of that path shall be not less than the combined required capacity of the converging aisles.

Note that the term "required capacity" is used here to make clear that the combined required width of the egress routes might be smaller than their combined actual widths, especially where the individual widths are made wider than required by the *Code* for egress capacity purposes. Such wider widths, beyond *Code* minimums, might be justified by considerations such as normal operating convenience.

9-2.5.6.3   Aisles shall terminate at a cross aisle, foyer, door, or vomitory giving access to an exit.

See 9-2.5.6.4 for an exception to this general rule for aisles.

9-2.5.6.4   Dead-end aisles shall not exceed 20 ft (6.1 m) in length.

Exception: A longer dead-end aisle is permitted where seats served by the dead-end aisle are not more than 24 seats from another aisle measured along a row of seats having a minimum clear width of 12 in. (30.5 cm) plus 0.6 in. (1.5 cm) for each additional seat above 7 in the row.

This exception to the traditional dead-end limit of 20 ft (6.1 m) is new in the 1988 Edition of the *Code*. The exception gives formal recognition to the inherent redundancy that exists where rows of seating are served by two or more aisles so that the blockage of any one aisle simply means that there is greater movement along rows to reach a somewhat more distant aisle. The exception recognizes that movement along rows, even with their constricted widths, provides many routes that permit faster movement to alternative aisles than would be possible with a dedicated cross aisle. As with the concept of wider clear spacings between rows where rows are longer (9-2.5.4.2), this exception gives additional credit for increased space to move along the rows to reach alternative aisles. At the row length limit of 24 seats, the required clear width spacing for use of this exception is 22.2 in. (56.4 cm). The exception may prove helpful in situations such as arenas and theaters where it is not easy to provide a cross aisle, doorway, etc., giving access to an exit, but where two or more aisles are relatively easy to reach when moving along rows.

9-2.5.6.5   In aisles where egress is possible in more than one direction, the aisles shall be uniform in required widths.

This requirement prohibits making some aisles wider at their ends (in an hourglass shape) simply because there are more people using them at their ends. A tapered aisle is acceptable and effective where there is only one direction of egress travel possible and the number of people served by the aisle increases in the direction of egress travel. In the more general case, where there are two directions of egress travel possible in the aisle, the width must be kept uniform to accommodate efficient egress travel that might have to reverse direction because of blockage at one end.

9-2.5.6.6   The width of aisles shall be sized in accordance with 9-2.3.1.

This refers to the capacity-related width requirements of 9-2.3.1. The capacity-related requirements must be considered along with other width requirements set out in 9-2.5.6.7. The final minimum width required by the *Code* is the larger of the widths established by the two sets of requirements.

9-2.5.6.7   In theater and similar type seating facilities, the minimum clear width of aisles shall be as determined by 9-2.3.2 but not less than:

(a) 42 in. (107 cm) for stairs having seating on each side.

Exception: 30 in. (76 cm) for catchment areas having not greater than 60 seats.

(b) 36 in. (91 cm) for stairs having seating on only one side.

Exception: 30 in. (76 cm) for catchment areas having not greater than 60 seats.

(c) 20 in. (51 cm) between a handrail or guardrail and seating where the aisle is subdivided by a handrail.

(d) 42 in. (107 cm) for level or ramped aisles having seating on both sides.

Exception: 30 in. (76 cm) for a catchment area of not greater than 60 seats.

(e) 36 in. (91 cm) for level or ramped aisles having seating on only one side.

Exception: 30 in. (76 cm) for catchment areas with not greater than 60 seats.

(f) 23 in. (58 cm) between a handrail and seating where aisle does not serve more than five rows on one side.

These requirements will often govern the final minimum widths of aisles especially where a relatively limited amount of egress capacity is required by 9-2.3.1. While the requirements for existing aisle widths are somewhat different from those for new facilities (as described in 8-2.5.6.7), it is useful to consider the benefits of widths similar to those required in new facilities. Figures 9-10 and 9-11 illustrate how intensively a 48-in. (122-cm) aisle stair subdivided by a center handrail can be used. Figure 9-12 shows, in overhead plan view, a large male walking down one side of a similar aisle stair, 48 in. (122 cm) wide, subdivided by a handrail. Chair seating is shown adjoining the aisle in these photographs.

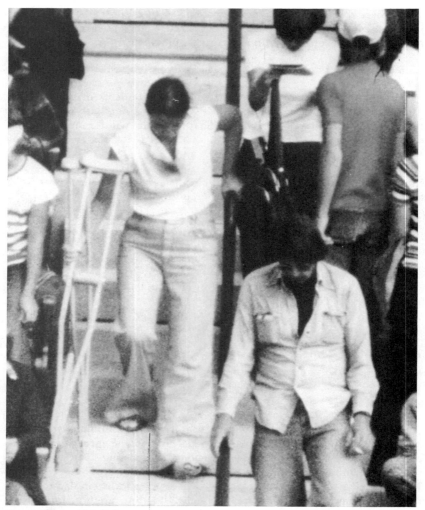

Photograph Courtesy of J. L. Pauls

Figure 9-10.   Intensive Use of Aisle Stair, 48 in. (122 cm) Wide with Central Handrail, in a Stadium.

Figure 9-11.   Intensive Use of Handrail at Center of 48-in. (122-cm) Aisle Stair
in a Stadium.   The handrail height is approximately 34 in. (86.3 cm).

Figure 9-12.   Overhead, Plan View of 48-inch (122 cm) Aisle Stair, with Center Handrail, Used by a Large Male.

Paragraph 9-2.5.6.7 (f) is based on the requirement for handrails in aisle stairs, specifically the permission to extend such handrails down the center of aisles for as much as five rows, leaving only about 23 in. (58 cm) of nominal width clear to the side of the handrail. This width is readily used by individuals moving in single or staggered file and can be used with tolerable inconvenience where people must pass by each other on the same side of the handrail. This provision of the *Code* might be helpful in cases where a short stub aisle is needed to serve rows of seating immediately beside a vomitory.

Generally, it might be noted that the effective width of aisles is often somewhat wider than is the case for egress facilities that are bounded on both sides by construction. One important exception to this generalization occurs where many people are attempting to sit on undivided benches or bleachers served by an aisle. The 18-in. (45.7-cm) spacing usually provided for each person is often too small, and there is a natural tendency for people to have their legs (sometimes several inches of hips and shoulders) occupying a significant part of the aisle width. Therefore, it is prudent when dealing with crowded, non-chair seating to increase the width of seat per person to facilitate normal circulation in the aisles.

9-2.5.6.8* In table and chair type seating facilities, the minimum clear width of aisles shall be as determined by 9-2.3.1 but not less than 36 in. (91 cm). Where loose seating occurs bordering on the aisle, the minimum aisle width is required plus an additional 19 in. (48.3 cm) for chairs on one side or an additional 38 in. (97 cm) for chairs on both sides of the aisle.

A-9-2.5.6.8

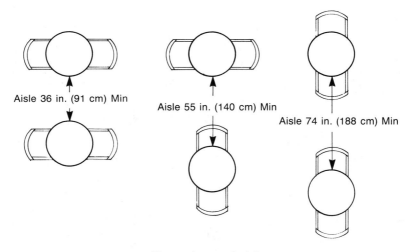

Figure A-9-2.5.6.8(a)

Figure A-9-2.5.6.8(a) illustrates the provisions of 9-2.5.6.8(a). This provides guidance on how aisles with movable chairs are to be measured, a subject that has often been questioned by enforcement officials.

Figure A-9-2.5.6.8(b) illustrates the aisle requirements for a banquet type arrangement. A reasonable space should be provided between tables for waitress or waiter access, otherwise the tables will gradually be pushed into the aisle width. This diagram illustrates aisle requirements only and would not be used to increase occupant load or approve layout, as it does not illustrate realistic layouts for servicing.

Aisle widths surrounding the clusters described in 9-2.5.4.7 and aisle widths at the end of long rows of rectangular tables as described in 9-2.5.4.8 are required to be calculated per Chapter 5, Section 5-3, and per 9-2.3.1, with a minimum width of 36 in. (91 cm). Where loose chairs are

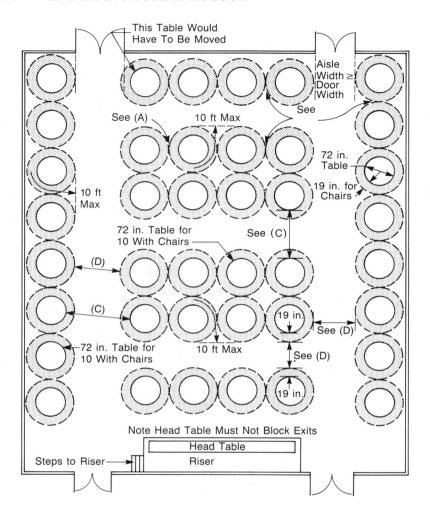

(A)   A Small Aisle Would Normally Be Provided for Waiter/Waitress Access.

(B)   No Aisle Requirement When Travel ≤ 10 ft

(C)   Distance Between Table Must Be ≥ Required Aisle Width Plus 19 in. for Chairs on One or 38 in. for Chairs on Both Sides

(D)   Aisle Must Be Sized in Accordance with 5-3.2 But Not Less Than 36 in.

Figure A-9-2.5.6.8(b)

used on aisles, the aisle width is to be increased by 19 in. (48.3 cm) for each side on which loose chairs are used, 19 in. (48.3 cm) being the most common front-to-rear measurement of chairs used for this purpose.

9-2.5.6.9 Aisle Stairs and Ramps. Every aisle with a gradient 1 in 8 or less shall consist of a ramp. Every aisle with gradient exceeding 1 in 8 shall consist of a stair having treads, risers, and handrails complying with the following requirements:

> Major changes relating to aisles were introduced in the 1985 Edition of the *Code*. The 1988 *Code* contains some minor changes that further underline the importance of design details for aisles. The changes in the previous and current editions address the need to design aisle stairs, for example, with all the attention and care required for stairs generally, supplemented by additional care because of unique design and use conditions encountered with aisles serving seating arranged in rows, especially where there are large elevation differences between the rows of seating. Paragraph 9-2.5.6.9 begins with a general requirement that divides aisles into two categories based on slope. Ideally, it would be preferable not to have to design aisles having about a 1 in 8 slope; however, sightlines might dictate such slopes in some situations. Ramps of this slope are relatively steep and problematic for people with walking difficulties. Stairs with a very small rise and long treads also present problems, notably trips and missteps because the presence of the low risers might not be evident, especially in a crowd situation. Generally, aisles also present unusual distractions for people because of their unusual lengths, the presence of other people in the aisles, and the presence of those entering the aisles from adjoining seating rows. Therefore, aisles of all slopes must be treated with considerable care and attention to human factors, both for the movement of individuals and the movement of crowds.

(a)* Tread depth shall be uniform in each aisle.

Exception to (a): In aisle stairs where a single intermediate tread is provided halfway between seating platforms, such intermediate treads may have a relatively smaller but uniform depth, but not less than 13 in. (33 cm).

> It should be noted that, for new aisles, 8-2.5.6.9(a) contains a significant change from the previous edition of the *Code*. The provision of unequal-sized treads within aisle stairs, a traditional practice once believed to be useful in facilitating access to seat rows, is no longer permitted by the *Code* for new facilities; however, an exception covering it is included for existing facilities. Even with the increased minimum tread size requirement [13 in. (33 cm)], the end result — with larger treads at the seat row entry level and smaller intermediate treads between seat row levels — is not as good, from a stair safety point of view, as consistently sized treads. This is true even for uniformly sized treads as large as about 20 in. (50.8 cm) in depth (assuming a relatively low riser height).

[Handrails, required in many cases by 9-2.5.6.9(f), help to compensate for the stretched stride length that may be needed in aisle stairs.] It is preferable to keep treads uniform so that the risk of misstepping, particularly overstepping of relatively smaller treads, is reduced.

A-9-2.5.6.9(a)   Completely uniform tread dimensions are preferred over aisle stair designs where tread depths alternate between relatively small intermediate treads between seating platforms and relatively larger treads at seating platforms. A larger tread, level with the seating platform, is not needed to facilitate easy access to and egress from a row of seating. If this arrangement is used it is important to provide a better than minimum tread depth for the intermediate tread, hence 13 in. (33.0 cm) is specified. Where nonuniformities occur due to construction tolerance, they should not exceed ³⁄₁₆ in. (0.5 cm) between adjacent treads.

Field research studies of situations where aisle step dimensions are not consistent indicate that the incidence of missteps rises significantly where tolerances of tread uniformity are not respected.

(b)* Treads shall be a minimum of 11 in. (27.9 cm).

A-9-2.5.6.9(b)   Tread depth is more important to stair safety than is riser height. Therefore, in cases where seating area gradient is less than 5 in 11, it is recommended that the tread dimension be increased beyond 11 in. (27.9 cm) rather than reducing the riser height. Where seating area gradient exceeds 8 in 11, it is recommended that the riser height be increased while maintaining a tread depth of at least 11 in. (27.9 cm).

Figure 9-13 shows a side view of an aisle stair with 11-in. (28-cm) treads used by a person with footwear measuring 12 in. (30.5 cm) in length — a condition found with about 5 percent of adults generally, and a condition that might be somewhat more common in those assembly situations attracting a higher proportion of male adults.
It should also be noted, in relation to 9-2.5.6.9(a), that there is apparently no difficulty entering or leaving the aisle or when leaving or entering the seat row with the provision of the three equal-sized, 11-in. (17.9-cm) treads at each seat row shown in the photograph.

(c) Riser heights shall be a minimum of 4 in. (10.2 cm).

At the minimum slope limit set by the *Code* for aisle stairs (for slopes exceeding 1 in 8), there is a riser height, of 4 inches (10.2 cm) where the seat platform is 32 in. (81.3 cm) deep. At such low riser heights, which present a tripping hazard if the risers are not detected by people, there is special value to the tread nosing marking requirement in 9-2.5.6.9(g).

(d) Riser heights shall not exceed 8 in. (20.3 cm).

Exception No. 1 to (d): Where the gradient of an aisle exceeds 8 in. (20.3 cm) in rise and 11 in. (27.9 cm) of run (to maintain necessary sight lines in the adjoining seating area), the rise height may exceed 8 in. (20.3 cm) but shall not exceed 11 in. (27.9 cm).

Exception No. 2 to (d): Folding and telescopic seating in accordance with NFPA 102, Standard for Assembly Seating, Tents, and Membrane Structures.

Photograph Courtesy of J. L. Pauls

Figure 9-13.   Side View of Aisle Stair, with 11-in. (17.9-cm) Treads in Stadium.

The 1988 Edition of the *Code* has reduced the maximum riser height permitted for *new* aisle stairs from 11 in. (27.9 cm) to 9 in. (22.9 cm). In addition to reducing movement safety, the unusually high risers of some aisle stairs reduce the speed and efficiency of movement, especially in the descending direction. However, to cover the situation of some existing aisles, the *Code* permits risers up to 11 in. (27.9 cm) high in existing situations. Note that in 9-2.3.2, for each additional inch of riser height above 7 in. (17.9 cm), an additional 20 percent must be added to the required capacity-related width of the aisle to satisfy *Code* requirements and achieve an acceptable egress flow time performance.

(e)* Riser heights shall be uniform within a flight.

Exception to (e): Riser height may be nonuniform but only to the extent necessary due to changes in gradient within a seating area to maintain necessary sight lines. Where nonuniformities exceed ³⁄₁₆ in. (0.5 cm) between adjacent risers, the exact location of such nonuniformities shall be indicated by a distinctive marking stripe on each tread at the nosing or leading edge adjacent to the nonuniform risers.

A-9-2.5.6.9(e)   Nonuniformities arising from construction tolerances should not exceed ³⁄₁₆ in. (0.5 cm) in adjacent risers.

A special case is made here for especially nonuniform riser heights, beyond the usual ³⁄₁₆-in. (0.5-cm) tolerance, only for situations where there is a break in the slope of a seating deck to maintain adequate sightlines. The seating deck slope may change incrementally at each row or, more commonly, there may be a large change at one or more locations. At such locations, there is often a change on the row-to-row elevation that greatly exceeds the usual ³⁄₁₆-in. (0.5-cm) tolerance. Aisle step riser heights will, as a consequence, change radically at this point. It is the special duty of the designer and owner to warn people using the aisle of this unusual change in the riser dimensions. This warning might go well beyond the usual marking of all step nosings required by 9-2.5.6.9(g). A distinctive color or other standard hazard marking is needed on the step nosings. Additional warning techniques may have to be employed in some cases to help reduce the risk of stumbles and falls.

(f) Ramped aisles having a gradient exceeding 1 in 15, and aisle stairs, shall be provided with handrails at one side or along the center line.

Where there is seating on both sides of the aisle, the handrails shall be discontinuous with gaps or breaks at intervals not exceeding five rows to facilitate access to seating and to permit crossing from one side of the aisle to the other. These gaps or breaks shall have a clear width of at least 22 in. (55.9 cm) and not greater than 36 in. (91 cm) measured horizontally, and the handrail shall have rounded terminations or bends. Where handrails are provided in the middle of aisle stairs, there shall be an additional intermediate rail located approximately 12 in. (30 cm) below the main handrail.

Exception No 1 to (f): Handrails are not required for ramped aisles having a gradient not greater than 1 in 8 and having seating on both sides.

Exception No. 2 to (f): Handrails are not required if, at the side of the aisle, there is a guardrail that complies with the graspability requirements for handrails.

Exception No. 3 to (f): Handrails are not required where risers do not exceed 7 in. (17.8 cm) in height.

This edition of the *Code* and the previous edition contain significant changes regarding provision of handrails on aisles, especially aisle stairs. It should be noted that in 8-2.5.6.9(f) there is no longer an exception permitting new aisle stairs without handrails where riser heights are less than 7 in. (17.9 cm). This is a result of growing experience with the provision and use of aisle handrails, as well as a general realization that aisles pose unique challenges to users that might go beyond those encountered on other ramps and stairs. Figures 9-10 amd 9-11 on pages 400 and 401 illustrate the variety of use conditions in aisles and the extensive use of handrails. In field research studies, aisle stair handrail use has been shown to be used about twice as often as handrails provided to meet *Code* provisions for non-aisle stairs. When one considers the unusual lengths of aisles, the unusual step geometries, and the very complex use conditions (with people entering and leaving the aisle at many rows), this high level of use is not surprising. Aside from their value in increasing the safety and comfort of people using the aisles, the handrails also help to improve egress efficiency — a benefit that is taken into account in calculation of egress capacity. (*See 9-2.3.2.*)

The required gaps between sections of center-aisle handrails are illustrated in Figure 9-12 on page 402. Spacing such gaps as frequently as every three rows is recommended where there is extensive use of aisles during events. A greater spacing, up to five rows between gaps, might be acceptable where there is little use of the aisles during events and little counterflow at any time. Gap size should be kept at the lower end of the permitted range of 22 to 36 in. (55.9 cm to 91 cm) where the aisles are unusually steep and handrail use is especially valuable in reducing the risk of falls.

Exception No.2 takes into account the proven utility of handrails that are higher than those permitted even with the increased handrail height range introduced with the 1988 Edition of the *Code*. A guardrail, 42 in. (107 cm) high, such as at the side of an aisle where there is a vomitory, can be considered a usable handrail if it offers graspability as required for handrails. (*See 5-2.2.6.5.*)

(g)* A contrasting marking stripe shall be provided on each tread at the nosing or leading edge such that the location of such tread is readily apparent, particularly when viewed in descent. Such stripes shall be at least 1 in. (2.5 cm) wide and shall not exceed 2 in. (5 cm) wide.

A-9-2.5.6.9(g)   Certain tread covering materials such as plush carpets, often used in theaters, produce an inherently well-marked tread nosing under most light conditions. On the other hand, concrete treads (with nosings having a sharp edge), especially under outdoor light conditions, are difficult to discriminate and therefore require an applied marking stripe. Slip resistance of such marking stripes should be similar to the rest of the treads and no tripping hazard should be created.

Exception to (g): The marking stripe may be omitted where tread surfaces and environmental conditions in all conditions of use are such that the location of each tread is readily apparent, particularly when viewed in descent.

Figure 9-14 suggests some of the step visibility difficulties that are commonly encountered in outdoor facilities with concrete treads. Without the helpful shadows from the handrail posts, there would be little indication of the exact location of each tread nosing. This situation requires the applied nosing markings referred to in 9-2.5.6.9(g). The distractions of the playing field and the unusually long aisle add further justification for making the steps as obvious as possible. It should be stressed that each situation needs to be carefully evaluated (with mock-ups at the design stage and with inspection of actual conditions during use) to determine whether any improvements are warranted in marking and lighting of such aisles.

Photograph Courtesy of J. L. Pauls

Figure 9-14.   View Down Aisle Stair, Provided with Center Handrail, in a Stadium.

9-2.5.6.10   Where required by the authority having jurisdiction, plans drawn to scale showing the arrangement of furnishings or equipment shall be submitted to the authority by the building owner, manager, or authorized agent to substantiate conformance with the provisions of this section and shall constitute the only acceptable arrangement until revised or additional plans are submitted and approved.

Exception: Temporary deviations from the specifics of the approved plans shall be permitted provided the occupant load is not increased and the intent of this section is maintained.

9-2.6 Travel Distance to Exits.   Exits shall be so arranged that the total length of travel from any point to reach an exit will not exceed 150 ft (45 m) in any assembly occupancy. *(See also Section 5-6.)*

Exception: The travel distance may be increased to 200 ft (60 m) in assembly occupancies protected throughout by an approved automatic sprinkler system.

Travel distance to exits from balconies or galleries that are served by unenclosed stairways must be measured to include the distance on the slope of the stair in the plane of the nosings and the distance from the bottom of the stairs to the exit. Travel distance is measured as illustrated in Figure 9-15.

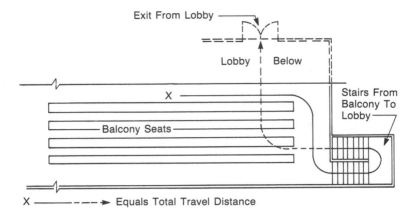

Figure 9-15. Measurement of Travel Distance to Exit Where Balconies Are Served by Unenclosed Stairs.

9-2.7 Discharge from Exits.

9-2.7.1 Exit discharge shall comply with Section 5-7.

9-2.7.2 The level of exit discharge shall be measured at the point of principal entrance to the building.

9-2.7.3 Where the principal entrance to an assembly occupancy is via a terrace, either raised or depressed, such terrace may be considered to be the level of exit discharge for the purposes of 9-1.6 if:

(a) The terrace is at least as long (measured parallel to the building) as the total width of the exit(s) it serves, but not less than 5 ft (152 cm) long, and

(b) The terrace is at least as wide (measured perpendicularly to the building) as the exit(s) it serves, but not less than 5 ft (152 cm) wide, and

(c) Required stairs leading from the terrace to grade are protected in accordance with 5-2.2.3.3 or are a minimum of 10 ft (3 m) from the building.

For existing assembly occupancies, the minimum width remains at 5 ft (152 cm). However, where the 1985 *Code* was silent on stairs, the 1988 *Code* requires stairs to be at least 10 ft (3 m) from the face of the building, unless they are protected as provided in Chapter 5.

The requirements of 9-2.7.3 are illustrated in Figure 9-16.

9-2.8 Illumination of Means of Egress. Means of egress shall be illuminated in accordance with Section 5-8.

9-2.9 Emergency Lighting. Emergency lighting shall be provided in accordance with Section 5-9.

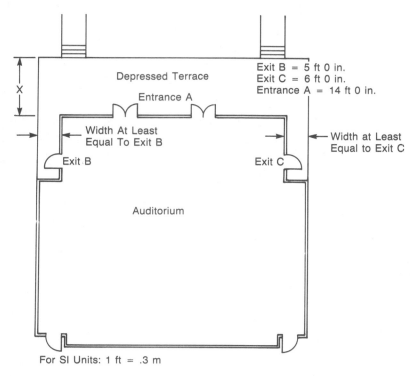

Exit B = 5 ft 0 in.
Exit C = 6 ft 0 in.
Entrance A = 14 ft 0 in.

Depressed Terrace

Entrance A

Width At Least
Equal To Exit B

Width at Least
Equal to Exit C

Exit B

Exit C

Auditorium

For SI Units: 1 ft = .3 m

Figure 9-16. Assembly Occupancy with Depressed Terrace as Principal Entrance. Assuming that each stair serves ½ of Entrance A and one of the two other exits, then x must be equal to or greater than the largest of the following: 5 ft (1.5 m) per 9-2.7.3(b); 5 ft (1.5 m) + ½ 14 ft (4.2 m) = 12 ft (3.6 m); or 6 ft (1.8 m) + ½ 14 ft (4.2 m) = 13 ft (3.9 m). Therefore, x ≥ 13 ft (3.9 m).

Exception: Class C assembly occupancies, used exclusively for a place of worship, shall not be required to have emergency lighting.

Formal Interpretation 76-72
Reference: 8-2.9, 9-2.9

Question: Where the *Code* states that all assembly occupancies and the means of egress shall be provided with emergency lighting, does this include Class C Assembly Occupancies, such as restaurants and drive-ins, that have glass almost all around the dining area?

Answer: Yes. However, the authority having jurisdiction may modify the requirements if the authority feels adequate lighting is maintained from external sources.

Issue Edition: 1976
Reference: 8-2.10
Date: September 1978

The exception to the requirement for emergency lighting is intended to apply only to Class C assembly occupancies (50 to 300 people) that are not likely to be used for any purpose except religious worship because they contain permanently fixed furnishings such as pews, pulpits, or altars.

9-2.10 Marking of Means of Egress.   Means of egress shall have signs in accordance with Section 5-10.

9-2.11 Special Features.

9-2.11.1 Railings.

(a) The fasciae of boxes, balconies, and galleries shall not rise less than 26 in. (66 cm) high above the adjacent floor or shall have substantial railings not less than 26 in. (66 cm) high above the adjacent floor.

(b) The height of the rail above footrests on the adjacent floor immediately in front of a row of seats shall be not less than 26 in. (66 cm). Railings at the ends of aisles shall be not less than 36 in. (91 cm) high for the full width of the aisle and shall be not less than 42 in. (107 cm) high for the width of the aisle where steps occur.

(c) Cross aisles shall be provided with railings not less than 26 in. (66 cm) high above the adjacent floor.

Exception No. 1:   Where the backs of seats on the front of the aisle project 24 in. (61 cm) or more above the adjacent floor of the aisle.

Exception No. 2:   Existing railings 36 in. (91 cm) high at the ends of aisles where steps occur may continue to be used.

Figure 9-17a illustrates the requirements of 9-2.11.1(a) and (b). Rail height at the fascia end of a sloping aisle must not be less than 36 in. (91 cm). However, where the aisle is not ramped but has steps, the rail height must be at least 42 in. (107 cm). There is greater danger of people tripping on steps than on a sloping surface with a maximum gradient of 1 ft (0.3 m) of rise to 8 ft (2.44 m) of run. Exception No. 2 permits continued use of existing 36-in. (91-cm) high railings. This avoids the hardship that would be placed on existing facilities if the railing had to be raised 6 in. (15.2 cm).

The *Code* requires a barrier along the downhill side of a cross aisle. [*See 9-2.11.1(c).*] The barrier may be a rail or the backs of the seats that abut the downhill side of the aisle where the backs project 24 in. (60 cm) or more above the cross aisle. The difference between the 24-in. (60-cm) back height and the required 26-in. (66-cm) railing is not sufficient to require the railing. (*See Figure 9-17b.*)

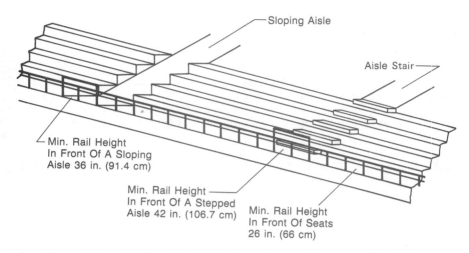

Figure 9-17a.   Railings Installed in Accordance with 9-2.11.1(a) and (b).

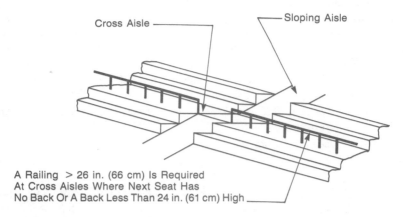

Figure 9-17b.   Barrier for Cross Aisles in Accordance with 9-2.11.1(c).   A railing [greater than 26 in. (66 cm)] is required unless the backs of seats in the row in front of the cross aisle are greater than 24 in. (60 cm) above the cross aisle.

SECTION 9-3   PROTECTION

9-3.1 Protection of Vertical Openings.   All interior stairways and other vertical openings shall be enclosed and protected as provided in Section 6-2.

Exception No. 1: Unprotected openings connecting not more than three floors may be permitted provided that they comply with 6-2.4.4.

Exception No. 2: Atriums in accordance with 6-2.4.5 are permitted.

Exception No. 3:   Stairs may be open between balconies and main assembly floors in theaters, churches, or auditoriums where the travel distance is within the allowable limits. (See 9-2.6.)

Exception No. 4:   Existing wood lath and plaster, existing ½-in. (1.3-cm) gypsum wallboard, existing installations of ¼-in. (.6-cm) thick wired glass that are, or are rendered, inoperative and fixed in the closed position, or other existing materials having similar fire resistance capabilities shall be acceptable. All such assemblies shall be in good repair and free of any condition that would diminish their original fire resistance characteristics.

Exceptions No. 1 and No. 2 permit the use of 6-2.4.4 and 6-2.4.5. *(See 6-2.4.4 and 6-2.4.5 for details. For egress requirements from off of balconies, see 9-2.4.4, 9-2.4.5 and 9-2.4.6.)*

9-3.2 Protection from Hazards.

9-3.2.1 Stages and Platforms.   *(See 9-1.3.)*

Note the new definitions for stages and platforms in 9-1.3.

Modern stages pose problems that didn't exist in the past. Scenery may be shifted horizontally, vertically, or both ways. The use of thrust stages and arena stages creates other problems.

The classic stage of the past had great height above the proscenium opening to accommodate the rigid asbestos curtain. The high void was a natural place to house combustible scenery for a performance, along with the rigging necessary for handling scene changes. This vertical storage area represented both a high fuel load and a difficult space to reach in case of a fire. Many new theaters use a flexible noncombustible curtain that does not require much height to accommodate it. Scenery on these stages is moved horizontally, thus reducing the distance necessary for storage between the top of the proscenium opening and the stage ceiling. Most combustible scenery is now stored in areas adjacent to the stage. All rigging and lighting is condensed in less vertical space.

9-3.2.1.1 Materials and Design.   (Reserved)

9-3.2.1.2 Platform Construction.   (Reserved)

9-3.2.1.3 Stage Construction.   (Reserved)

9-3.2.1.4 Accessory Rooms.   (Reserved)

9-3.2.1.5 Vents.   Legitimate stages shall be provided with one or more vents constructed of noncombustible material. Ventilators shall be located near the center and above the highest part of the stage. They shall be raised above the stage roof and shall have a total ventilation area equal to at least 5 percent of the floor area of the stage.

Regular stages exceeding 1,000 sq ft (93 sq m) in area shall be provided with vents as required for legitimate stages or shall be provided with a mechanical vent installed in an exterior wall of the stage itself. Such vent shall be automatic upon operation of the sprinkler system and shall also be capable of manual operation. The capacity of the exhaust vent shall be approximately equivalent to that which would be provided for a legitimate stage.

Vents shall open by spring action or force of gravity sufficient to overcome the effects of neglect, rust, dirt, frost, snow, or expansion by heat or warping of the framework. Glass, if used in vents, must be protected against falling onto the stage. A wire screen, if used under the glass, must be so placed that, if clogged, it cannot reduce the required vent area or interfere with the operating mechanism or obstruct the distribution of water from an automatic sprinkler. Vents shall be arranged to open automatically by the use of fusible links. The fusible links and operating cable shall hold each door closed against the minimum 30 lb (133 N) counterforce, which may be exerted by springs or counterweights. This minimum counterforce shall be exerted on each door through its entire arc of travel and for a minimum of 115 degrees. A manual control shall also be provided.

Springs, where employed to actuate doors, shall be capable of maintaining full required tension. Springs shall not be stressed more than 50 percent of their rated capacity and shall not be located directly in the air stream nor exposed to the outside.

A fusible link shall be placed in the cable control system on the underside of the vents at or above the roofline or as approved by the authority having jurisdiction and shall be so located as not to be affected by the operation of a fire sprinkler system. Remote, manual, or electrical controls shall provide for both opening and closing of the vent doors for periodic testing and shall be located at a point on the stage designated by the authority having jurisdiction. Where remote control vents are electrical, power failure shall not affect its instant operation in the event of fire. Hand winches may be employed to facilitate operation of manually controlled vents.

> Small schools typically have multipurpose classrooms and classrooms separated by folding partitions. These schools commonly have stages that are greater than 500 sq ft (46.5 sq m) but less than 1000 sq ft (93 sq m). The Committee felt the venting requirements were too restrictive for facilities with small stages. Also note the new definition of stage and platform in 9-1.3.

9-3.2.1.6 Proscenium Walls.   Where automatic sprinkler protection is not provided, the proscenium wall of every theater using movable scenery or decorations shall not have more than two openings entering the stage, exclusive of the proscenium opening. Such openings shall not exceed 21 sq ft (2.0 sq m) each and shall be fitted with self-closing fire doors.

9-3.2.1.7 Proscenium Curtain.   The proscenium opening of every legitimate stage shall be provided with a curtain constructed and mounted so as to intercept hot gases, flames, and smoke and to guard against seeing flame from a fire on the stage from the auditorium side within a five-minute period where the curtain is of asbestos. Other materials may be used if they have passed a 30-minute fire test in a small scale furnace, 3 ft (91 cm) by 3 ft (91 cm), with the sample mounted in the horizontal plane at the top of the furnace and subjected to the standard time-temperature curve.

The curtain shall be automatic-closing without the use of applied power.

Exception: In lieu of the protection required herein, all the following may be provided:

(a) A noncombustible opaque fabric curtain so arranged that it will close automatically, and

(b) An automatic fixed waterspray deluge system shall be located on the auditorium side of the proscenium opening and be so arranged that the entire face of the curtain will be wetted. The system shall be activated by combination of rate-of-rise and fixed-temperature detectors located on the ceiling of the stage. Detectors shall be spaced in accordance with their listing. The water supply shall be controlled by a deluge valve and shall be sufficient to keep the curtain completely wet for 30 minutes or until the valve is closed by fire department personnel, and

(c) The curtain shall be automatically operated in case of fire by a combination of rate-of-rise and fixed-temperature detectors that also activates the deluge spray system. Stage sprinklers and vents shall be automatically operated in case of fire by fusible elements, and

(d) Operation of the stage sprinkler system or spray deluge valve shall automatically activate the emergency ventilating system and close the curtain, and

(e) The curtain, vents, and spray deluge system valve shall also be capable of manual operation.

Substitutes for asbestos have been a concern of environmentalists, school officials, and others. It was the intent of the Committee to provide guidelines for the use of materials other than asbestos. Although not specified by the *Code* materials other than asbestos are expected to have a minimum weight of 2⅜ lbs per sq yard with a minimum warp and fill tensile strength of 400 lbs per inch, reinforced with noncorrosive wire. A small-scale furnace test was considered appropriate by the Committee for this purpose.

If, instead of the fire resistant curtain specified in 9-3.2.1.2, a flexible proscenium curtain is used, the *Code* requires an automatic water spray system with nozzles on the auditorium side of the curtain. This system must be capable of completely wetting the curtain and of maintaining wetness for at least 30 minutes or until the deluge valve is closed by the fire department. Specifications for the installation of sprinkler systems in general are found in NFPA 13, *Standard on Installation of Sprinkler Systems.*[4] Of course, for any sprinkler system to effectively minimize the hazards from fire to life safety or property, regular inspection and maintenance of the system is essential. NFPA 13A, *Recommended Practice for the Care and Maintenance of Sprinkler Systems,*[5] provides recommendations for ensuring that an extinguishing system will not fail in an emergency.

The spray nozzle system for the curtain is required to operate automatically by a combination of rate-of-rise and fixed temperature heat detectors. NFPA 72E, *Standard on Automatic Fire Detectors,*[6] and its appendix contain specifications and recommendations on the installation of heat detectors.

To complete the protection system, operation of the stage sprinklers or water spray system must also automatically close the proscenium curtain and activate the emergency ventilating system.

9-3.2.1.8 Gridirons, Fly Galleries, and Penrails.   (Reserved)

9-3.2.1.9 Fire Protection.
Every stage (legitimate, regular, or thrust) larger than 500 sq ft (46.5 sq m) in area shall have a system of automatic sprinklers at the ceiling, in usable spaces under the stage, in auxiliary spaces and dressing rooms, storerooms, and workshops. Where there is a stage gridiron, 135°F (57°C) rated sidewall sprinklers with heat-baffle plates shall be installed around the perimeter of the stage, except above the proscenium opening, at points not more than 30 in. (76 cm) below the gridiron, and with sprinklers positioned 4 to 6 in. (10.2 to 15.2 cm) below the baffle plate.

Note the new definitions of stage and platform in 9-1.3.

9-3.2.1.10 Auxiliary Stage Spaces.
Auxiliary stage spaces, such as understage areas, dressing rooms, workshops, and similar spaces associated with the functioning of a stage, shall comply with the following:

(a) No point within any auxiliary space shall be more than 50 ft (15 m) from a door providing access to an exit.

(b) There shall be at least two exits available from every auxiliary stage space, one of which shall be available within a travel distance of 75 ft (23 m). A common path of travel of 20 ft (6.1 m) shall be permitted.

(c) Auxiliary stage spaces shall be equipped with automatic sprinklers where required by 9-3.2.1.3.

(d) No workshop involving the use of combustible or flammable paints, liquids, or gases or their storage shall open directly upon a stage.

Auxiliary stage spaces are sources of serious hazards. It is therefore necessary to provide automatic fire protection and adequate exits within a short travel distance from such spaces.

9-3.2.1.11 Flame-Retardant Requirements.
Combustible scenery of cloth, film, vegetation (dry), and similar effects shall meet the requirements of NFPA 701, *Standard Methods of Fire Tests for Flame-Resistant Textiles and Films.* Foamed plastics (*see A-6-5.2.4*) may be used only by specific approval of the authority having jurisdiction. Scenery and stage properties on thrust stages shall be either noncombustible or limited-combustible materials.

It is the Committee's intent to reduce the amount of combustible material on stages. Foamed plastics as described in Chapter 6 (*see A-6-5.1.3*) have contributed to rapid fire spread in actual fire experience. Although 6-5.1.3 refers to interior finish, the Committee felt it to be an appropriate reference that could also be applied to the use of foamed plastics used on stage as props, furnishings, etc.

9-3.2.1.12 Standpipes.
Each legitimate or regular stage shall be equipped with a Class III standpipe located on each side of the stage, installed in accordance with 7-7.4.2.

There must be a standpipe located on each side of a stage to provide the stage hands and the responding fire department with a manual fire fighting capability at the area of a theater where a fire is most likely to occur. The installation of the standpipes must comply with NFPA 14, *Standard for the Installation of Standpipe and Hose Systems.*[7] NFPA 13E, *Recommendations for Fire Department Operations in Properties Protected by Sprinkler and Standpipe Systems,*[8] should also be consulted for a discussion of the necessity of a properly installed standpipe system. Standpipes are required whether or not the stage has automatic sprinkler protection.

9-3.2.2 Projection Booths.

9-3.2.2.1 Every place of assembly where an electric arc, Xenon, or other light source that generates hazardous gases, dust, or radiation is used shall have a projection room that complies with 9-3.2.2.2 from which the projection shall be made. Where cellulose nitrate film is used, the projection room shall comply with NFPA 40, *Standard for the Storage and Handling of Cellulose Nitrate Motion Picture Film. (See also Chapter 31.)*

The requirements for projection booths were developed jointly with those of NFPA 40, *Standard for the Storage and Handling of Cellulose Nitrate Motion Picture Film,*[9] and the motion picture industry at the height of movie popularity when cellulose nitrate film was still being used. Presently, only safety film is used (except at film festivals or revivals) and the risk level has been reduced. The primary function of these requirements is to build a shelter around the projection booth, eliminating it as an exposure threat to the theater audience.

The intent of 9-3.2.2.1 is to protect the audience from the dangers associated with light sources, such as electric arc or Xenon. Where incandescent light is used, projection booths are not required in assembly occupancies. Note the booth is required based on the light source, not on the projection of film.

Paragraph 31-2.8 requires that unless the construction of a projection booth complies with NFPA 40, *Standard for the Storage and Handling of Cellulose Nitrate Motion Picture Film,*[9] a conspicuous sign must be posted on the door of the projection booth and also inside the booth. The sign must state: "Safety Film Only Permitted in This Room." The intent is to ensure that cellulose nitrate film is projected only with adequate safeguards.

9-3.2.2.2 Projection Rooms for Safety Film. Projection rooms for safety film shall meet the requirements of 9-3.2.2.3 through 9-3.2.2.8.

It should be emphasized that 9-3.2.2.3 through 9-3.2.2.8 apply only to booths for the projection of cellulose acetate or other safety film. Although openings in the booth do not need to be protected, they must be provided with glass or other approved material that will completely close the opening and prevent gas, dust, or radiation from contaminating the audience or seating area.

9-3.2.2.3   Every projection room shall be of permanent construction consistent with the construction requirements for the type of building in which the projection room is located. Openings need not be protected. The room shall have a floor area of not less than 80 sq ft (7.4 sq m) for a single machine and at least 40 sq ft (3.7 sq m) for each additional machine. Each motion picture projector, floodlight, spotlight, or similar piece of equipment shall have a clear working space not less than 30 in. (76 cm) on each side and at the rear thereof, but only one such space shall be required between adjacent projectors.

The projection room and the rooms appurtenant thereto shall have a ceiling height of not less than 7 ft 6 in. (229 cm).

9-3.2.2.4   Each projection room shall have at least one out-swinging, self-closing door not less than 30 in. (76 cm) wide and 6 ft 8 in. (203 cm) high.

9-3.2.2.5   The aggregate of ports and openings for projection equipment shall not exceed 25 percent of the area of the wall between the projection room and the auditorium.

All openings shall be provided with glass or other approved material, so as to completely close the opening.

9-3.2.2.6   Projection room ventilation shall be not less than the following:

(a) *Supply Air.* Each projection room shall be provided with adequate air supply inlets so arranged to provide well distributed air throughout the room. Air inlet ducts shall provide an amount of air equivalent to the amount of air being exhausted by projection equipment. Air may be taken from the outside; from adjacent spaces within the building provided the volume and infiltration rate is sufficient; or from the building air conditioning system, provided it is so arranged as to provide sufficient air whether or not other systems are in operation.

(b) *Exhaust Air.* Projection booths may be exhausted through the lamp exhaust system. The lamp exhaust system shall be positively interconnected with the lamp so that the lamp will not operate unless there is the airflow required for the lamp. Exhaust air ducts shall terminate at the exterior of the building in such a location that the exhaust air cannot be readily recirculated into any air supply system. The projection room ventilation system may also serve appurtenant rooms, such as the generator room and the rewind room.

New projection equipment in new theaters have a console that draws air in at the floor and up through the projection machine, thus eliminating the need to provide ducts 12 in. (30.5 cm) off the floor.

The requirements for the ventilation of a projection booth are designed to effectively "isolate" the booth from the theater so that any products of combustion created by a fire in a projection booth are not circulated into the theater. This is achieved by having an independent exhaust system for the booth, making certain that the exhaust outlet on the exterior of the building is located at a point where the air intake for the theater cannot recirculate the exhausted air.

If fresh air for the projection booth's ventilation system is supplied from the general system of the building, it is essential that the combined system be arranged to ensure the required air changes in the booth even when no air is supplied to the general system of the building.

9-3.2.2.7 Each projection machine shall be provided with an exhaust duct that will draw air from each lamp and exhaust it directly to the outside of the building. The lamp exhaust may serve to exhaust air from the projection room to provide room air circulation. Such ducts shall be of rigid materials, except for a flexible connector approved for the purpose. The projection lamp and projection room exhaust systems may be combined but shall not be interconnected with any other exhaust or return air system within the buildings.

(a) *Electric Arc Projection Equipment.* The exhaust capacity shall be 200 cfm (.09 cu m/s) for each lamp connected to the lamp exhaust system, or as recommended by the equipment manufacturer. Auxiliary air may be introduced into the system through a screened opening to stabilize the arc.

(b) *Xenon Projection Equipment.* The lamp exhaust system shall exhaust not less than 300 cfm (.14 cu m/s) per lamp, or not less than that exhaust volume required or recommended by the equipment manufacturer, whichever is the greater.

The *Code* sets forth the minimum capacity for the exhaust system of a projection machine; however, a greater capacity must be provided where recommended by the manufacturer of the projection equipment. This system must be independent of any other ventilation system in the building housing the theater; however, it can be combined with projection room ventilation.

9-3.2.2.8 Miscellaneous Equipment and Storage.

(a) Each projection room shall be provided with rewind and film storage facilities.

(b) A maximum of four containers for flammable liquids not greater than 16 oz (.5 L) capacity and of a nonbreakable type may be permitted in each projection booth.

(c) Appurtenant electrical equipment, such as rheostats, transformers, and generators, may be located within the booth or in a separate room of equivalent construction.

The intent of the requirement for the storage and rewinding of film is to prevent these operations from occurring outside the projection booth at some less protected location where, if a fire occurred, the exposure to the theater would be significantly greater. All operations that relate to projection activities must be kept within the protected enclosure afforded by the projection booth.

9-3.2.3 Service Equipment, Hazardous Operations or Processes, and Storage Facilities.

9-3.2.3.1 Rooms containing high pressure boilers, refrigerating machinery of other than domestic refrigerator type, large transformers, or other service equipment subject to possible explosion shall not be located directly under or adjacent to required exits. All such rooms shall be separated by a 1-hour fire barrier from other parts of the building.

The preservation of the integrity of exits in any building is one of the principal concerns of the *Code*. Therefore, hazardous areas, even if enclosed with the required fire resistant construction, must never be located where they might directly expose a required exit to fire.

9-3.2.3.2 Opening Protection.   (Reserved)

9-3.2.3.3   Rooms or space for the storage, processing, or use of the materials specified in this section shall be protected in accordance with the following:

(a) Rooms or spaces used for the storage of combustible supplies in quantities deemed hazardous by the authority having jurisdiction, hazardous materials in quantities deemed hazardous by recognized standards, or fuel shall be separated from the remainder of the building by construction having not less than a 1-hour fire resistance rating with all openings protected by self-closing or smoke-actuated fire doors, or such rooms or spaces may be protected by an automatic extinguishing system as set forth in Section 6-4.

(b) Rooms or spaces used for processing or use of combustible supplies in quantities considered hazardous by the authority having jurisdiction, hazardous materials, or for flammable or combustible liquids in quantities deemed hazardous by recognized standards shall be separated from the remainder of the building by construction having not less than a 1-hour fire resistance rating with all openings protected by self-closing or smoke-actuated fire doors and shall also be protected by an automatic extinguishing system as set forth in Section 6-4.

(c) Boiler and furnace rooms, laundries, and maintenance shops, including woodworking and painting areas, shall be separated from the remainder of the building by construction having not less than a 1-hour fire resistance rating with all openings protected by self-closing or smoke-actuated fire doors or such rooms or spaces may be protected by an automatic extinguishing system as set forth in Section 6-4.

Exception to (c):   Rooms enclosing air-handling equipment.

(d)* Where automatic extinguishing systems are used to meet the requirements of this section, the rooms or spaces shall be separated from the remainder of the building by construction that resists the passage of smoke.

A-9-3.2.3.3(d)   It is not the intent of this provision to require a smoke barrier that meets the requirements of Section 6-3.

> The intent of the Committee is to restrict the passage of smoke through the use of glass or other non-fire-rated material. This would not permit the use of wire or louvers but would not require all the components of a standard smoke barrier.

(e) Where automatic extinguishing is used to meet the requirements of this section, the protection may be in accordance with 7-7.1.2.

> The Committee felt that the requirements identified in Chapter 7 for the use of six or fewer heads connected to the domestic system are adequate for these types of situations.

The intent of 9-3.2.3.3 is to specify the degree of protection necessary for certain hazardous areas. It has been divided into three sections based on the degree of hazard. The hazards noted in item (a) are required to be enclosed in 1-hour construction or protected by sprinklers. If the sprinkler option is chosen, an enclosure is still required; however, the enclosure need not be rated, but only form a membrane against the passage of smoke.

The hazards noted in item (b) must be enclosed in 1-hour construction and be protected by automatic sprinklers.

The hazards noted in item (c) are required to be enclosed in 1-hour construction. The 1985 Edition of the *Code* added an option for a sprinkler equivalency for the enclosure. The exception to item (c) pertains to rooms housing air-handling equipment only. If the room is used for other purposes, then the provisions of item (a) or (b) apply.

Figure 9-18 illustrates the methods of protection specified by 9-3.2.3.3.

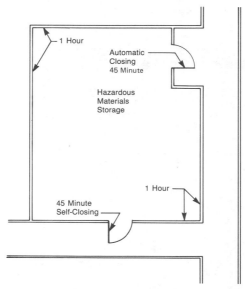

Figure 9-18(a).   Protection of Hazardous Areas. Part (a) illustrates one method of complying with 9-3.2.3.3(a). See Figure 9-18(b) for the alternate method.

The three different types of protection of hazardous areas are illustrated in these figures. Parts (a) and (b) illustrate the two options for complying with 9-3.2.3.3(a). Part (c) illustrates the requirement of 9-3.2.3.3(b) that both fire-resistive separation and automatic protection be provided. Part (d) illustrates the special provisions for boiler rooms, furnace rooms, and similar areas contained in 9-3.2.3.3(c). However, in existing buildings, boiler rooms, furnace rooms, and similar areas may use the sprinkler option as illustrated in Part (b).

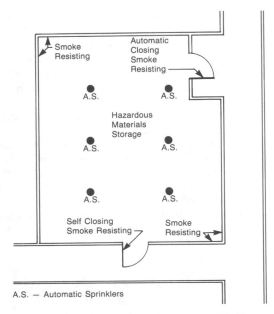

Figure 9-18(b). Protection of Hazardous Areas. Part (b) illustrates an alternate method of complying with 9-3.2.3.3(a). Part (a) illustrates another method of compliance.

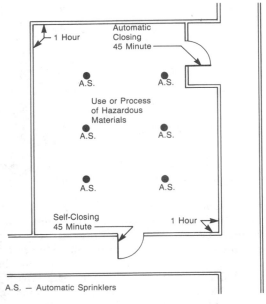

Figure 9-18(c). Protection of Hazardous Areas. Part (c) illustrates the requirements for complying with 9-3.2.3.3(b). Both one hour separation and automatic sprinkler protection is required in this case.

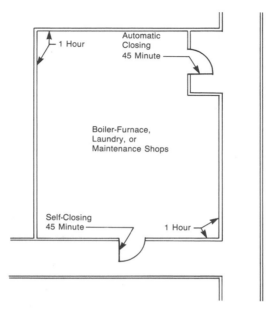

Figure 9-18(d). Protection of Hazardous Areas. Part (d) illustrates the requirements to comply with 9-3.2.3.3(c). However, in existing buildings, boiler rooms, furnace rooms and similar areas may use the sprinkler option as illustrated in Figure 9-18(b).

9-3.2.4 Special Provisions for Food Service Establishments.

9-3.2.4.1   All devices in connection with the preparation of food shall be so installed and operated as to avoid hazard to the safety of occupants.

9-3.2.4.2   All devices in connection with the preparation of food shall be of an approved type and shall be installed in an approved manner.

An "approved type" of device means that, from the standpoint of potential fire hazards, the unit is acceptable to the authority having jurisdiction. An "approved manner" of installation means installation in accordance with the requirements of the authority having jurisdiction.

9-3.2.4.3   Food preparation facilities shall be protected in accordance with 7-2.3 and are not required to have openings protected between food preparation areas and dining areas.

The intent of 9-3.2.4.3 is to provide some barrier between cooking areas and dining areas of restaurants. The intent of the barrier is to screen possible flash fires from the view of the patrons in an attempt to prevent panic. Openings in this barrier are not restricted and do not need to be protected. The *Code* is counting on the automatic extinguishing system to control any fire on the cooking surfaces, and thus no longer requires enclosure by rated construction. The degree of screening required, and thus the size of the barrier required, is left to the judgment of the authority having jurisdiction.

9-3.3 Interior Finish.

9-3.3.1 The interior finish requirements of this section shall be in accordance with Section 6-5.

9-3.3.2 Interior finish in all corridors and lobbies shall be Class A or B and, in enclosed stairways, Class A.

9-3.3.3 Interior finish in general assembly areas of Class A or Class B assembly occupancies shall be Class A or Class B. In Class C assembly occupancies, it shall be Class A, B, or C.

Exception: In any assembly occupancy, exposed portions of structural members complying with the requirements for Type IV (2HH) construction may be permitted.

9-3.3.4 Screens on which pictures are projected shall comply with requirements of Class A or Class B interior finish.

Interior finish requirements for new assembly occupancies are unequivocal and are subject to rigid interpretation. Evaluation of interior finish in existing facilities is sometimes difficult. Where flame spread characteristics cannot be readily determined using the test procedure in NFPA 255, *Method of Test of Surface Burning Characteristics of Building Materials,*[10] the questionable material should be removed or treated with approved flame retardants. Where treatment cannot reduce flame spread to required limits, automatic sprinklers may be provided to compensate for the remaining deficiency.

9-3.4 Detection, Alarm, and Communications Systems.

9-3.4.1 General. All Class A and all Class B assembly occupancies, and all theaters with more than one audience viewing room, shall be provided with an approved fire alarm system in accordance with this section.

Exception No. 1: Assembly occupancies that are a part of a mixed occupancy (see 1-4.7) may be served by a common fire alarm system provided the individual requirements of each occupancy are met.

Exception No. 2: Assembly occupancies where, in the judgement of the authority having jurisdiction, adequate alternative provisions exist or are provided for the dicovery of a fire condition and for the prompt alerting of the occupants.

Exception No. 1 can be very useful in a mixed occupancy situation, even if not a true mixed occupancy per 1-4.7. This would allow an assembly occupancy in a school, hotel, hospital, etc., to be served by the same fire alarm system as in the predominate occupancy.

The 1988 *Code* requires an approved alarm system in all Class A and Class B assembly occupancies. The Committee found no justification for the occupancy load of 2000 used in the 1985 *Code*. In Exception No.1, the Committee wanted to clarify that the intent of the alarm requirements was to meet the requirements of each occupancy in a mixed occupancy situation. This would allow an assembly occupancy in a school, hotel, hospital, mall, etc. to be served by the same fire alarm as in the predominate occupancy, provided it also met the requirements of the assembly occupancy.

Exception No. 2 to 9-3.4.1 specifically allows the authority having jurisdiction to permit continued use of fire alarm systems previously installed, provided the authority is satisfied with system arrangement.

9-3.4.2 Initiation.   Initiation of the required fire alarm system shall be by manual means in accordance with 7-6.2.1(a), which shall be provided with an emergency power source. The initiating device shall be capable of transmitting an alarm to a receiving station, located within the building, that is constantly attended when the assembly occupancy is occupied.

Exception No. 1:   Initiation may be by means of an approved automatic fire detection system, in accordance with 7-6.2.1(b), providing fire detection throughout the building.

Exception No. 2:   Initiation may be by means of an approved automatic sprinkler system, in accordance with 7-6.2.1(c), providing fire detection and protection throughout the building.

9-3.4.3 Notification.

9-3.4.3.1   The required fire alarm system shall sound an audible alarm in a constantly attended receiving station within the building for purposes of initiating emergency action.

9-3.4.3.2   Occupant notification shall be by means of either voice or prerecorded message announcement initiated by the person in the constantly attended receiving station.

9-3.4.3.3   The announcement shall be made via an approved voice communication or public address system that is audible above the ambient noise level of the assembly occupancy.

9-3.4.3.4   Where the authority having jurisdiction determines that it is impractical to have a constantly attended location in an assembly occupancy other than a theater, a fire alarm system in accordance with Section 7-6 initiated by manual stations in accordance with 7-6.2.1(a) or other approved means of initiation, that automatically provides prerecorded evacuation instructions in accordance with 7-6.3.8, may be used.

The intent of the provisions of 9-3.4 is to provide an alarm system that will not produce a panic reaction from the occupants. Editions of the *Code* prior to 1981 required no alarm system. The intent of this section is to provide a system which will permit activation of the system by pull stations as required by 7-6.2.1, but that will not sound an audible alarm in the seating or audience areas of the assembly occupancy. In lieu of the audible alarm throughout the assembly occupancy, the system must sound an alarm in a constantly attended location. (Constantly attended, in this case, means that, during the time the assembly occupancy is in use, the alarm panel must be attended.) From that constantly attended location, voice messages that instruct the occupants can be issued via a public address system. This method allows for the orderly evacuation of the occupants and permits the issuance of proper instructions on how to evacuate rather than simply sounding an evacuation alarm, which may produce panic. A change introduced in the 1985 Edition of the *Code* permits the use of prerecorded evacuation instructions that will automatically be played upon initiation of the system. With the approval of the authority having jurisdiction, this arrangement may be used in lieu of the attended station.

9-3.5 Extinguishment Requirements.   (*See 9-1.6, 9-2.6, and 9-3.2.*)

9-3.5.1 Fire Suppression Systems.   Any assembly occupancy used or capable of being used for exhibition or display purposes shall be protected throughout by an approved automatic sprinkler system in accordance with Section 7-7 where the exhibition or display area exceeds 15,000 sq ft (1400 sq m).

This requirement applies to assembly occupancies used or capable of being used for exhibition or display purposes. This would apply to many facilities over 15,000 sq ft (1,400 sq m) unless fixed seating or similar obstruction to this use is provided.

9-3.6 Corridors.   (Reserved)

9-3.6.1 Interior Corridor and Lobby Construction.   (Reserved)

SECTION 9-4   SPECIAL PROVISIONS

9-4.1 Windowless or Underground Buildings.   Windowless or underground buildings shall comply with this chapter and Section 30-7.

Many buildings that house assembly occupancies are windowless by design. In theaters, opera halls, concert halls, etc., windows are detrimental to operations. In recent years, large exhibition halls have also been constructed without windows.

Windowless buildings with an occupant load of 100 or more must be provided with a complete automatic extinguishing system, usually sprinklers. All windowless assembly occupancies must be provided with emergency lighting in accordance with Section 5-9 of the *Code*.

Subterranean assembly occupancies require special consideration. Although they are similar to windowless buildings, additional problems of access for fire fighting and rescue are created where they are located in basements or subbasements of buildings. Exits, and where possible the exit accesses, must be adequately cut off from the assembly area by construction of partitions, walls, and doors of sufficient fire resistance. Positive means must be provided to prevent smoke from contaminating the exits. Like any windowless building, a subterranean assembly occupancy requires automatic sprinkler protection, emergency lighting, and a smoke evacuation system.

9-4.2 High Rise Buildings. *(See 9-1.6.)*

9-4.3 Outdoor Assembly.

9-4.3.1 All grandstands, tents, and other places of outdoor assembly shall comply with the requirements of NFPA 102, *Standard for Assembly Seating, Tents, and Membrane Structures.*

Where an outdoor assembly occupancy is created in an enclosed court so that exits can only be provided through a surrounding building, the requirements for exits, seating, and aisles must be the same as for an indoor assembly area.

9-4.4 Special Provisions for Exhibition Halls.

Exhibition halls have problems that differ from those of theaters, restaurants, or other assembly occupancies. They are large, multi-use facilities and have high ceilings appropriate to their size. Combustible materials are frequently displayed, and the containers in which the exhibits are shipped contribute to the fuel load. Paragraph 9-3.5.1 requires most exhibition halls to be protected by automatic sprinklers.

This section has been expanded in the 1988 *Code* to provide more comprehensive guidance to the many people who are responsible for the different aspects of a trade show or exhibit. The authority having jurisdiction at the local level is often working with organizations that exhibit on a national basis and that are unaware of the local firesafety regulations. It is the Committee's intent that this *Code* provide more consistent and universal understanding of the firesafety regulations required in these occupancies and at the same time encourage more uniform enforcement practices.

The Committee learned that the trade show and exhibit hall regulations used by many jurisdictions were very similar; however, there was no nationally recognized model code that could be referenced. It was also recognized by the Committee that this lack of a model code presents a hardship as well as confusion between the local authority having jurisdiction and persons responsible for the various functions of the trade show or exhibit.

9-4.4.1   No display or exhibit shall be so installed or operated as to interfere in any way with access to any required exit or with visibility of any required exit or any required exit sign, nor shall any display block access to fire fighting equipment.

It is advisable to have prepared plans or diagrams to show the arrangement of displays or exhibits, including any that are to be suspended from the ceiling or an overhead structure. Displays or exhibits must never interfere in any way with access to any required exit, and they must not conceal exit signs. (*See Figure 9-19.*) A display should not block access to fire fighting equipment nor interfere with the normal operation of automatic extinguishing equipment or devices for smoke evacuation.

Rows of booths become exit accesses; therefore, booths and other temporary construction should be of minimal combustible construction or protected to avoid undue hazard of fire that might endanger occupants before they can reach available exits.

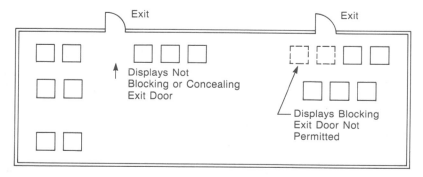

Figure 9-19.   Arrangement of Displays in an Exhibition Hall.

9-4.4.2   A storage room having an enclosure with a smoke barrier having a fire resistance rating of 1 hour and protected by an automatic fire extinguishing system shall be provided for combustible materials not on display.

Displays or exhibits of combustible material must be limited in quantity in order to reduce the fuel load to an acceptable level. Excess combustible display material and all other combustible materials that are not in use should be kept in a separate storage room until needed. A separation with a fire resistance rating of 1 hour is required between such a storage room and all other parts of the building, and the room must be protected by an automatic sprinkler system.

9-4.4.3 Exhibits.   Exhibits shall comply with the following:

(a) The travel distance within the exhibit booth or exhibit enclosure to an exit access aisle shall not be greater than 50 ft (15 m).

This requirement applies to standard exhibit booth arrangements, whether constructed of pipe and drape, or a large exhibit enclosure designed and built from other materials, which could include small booths, open displays, large board displays, etc. Also included in this requirement are exhibit enclosures that are created by the arrangement of products such as machinery or vehicles. The intent is to have a travel distance not greater than 50 ft (15 m) for occupants that are inside the enclosure, whether they are employees or patrons. Note that this is not travel distance to an exit, but only to an aisle.

(b) Exhibit booths shall be constructed of noncombustible or limited-combustible materials, pressure-treated fire retardant wood meeting the requirements of NFPA 703, *Standard for Fire Retardant Impregnated Wood and Fire Retardant Coatings for Building Materials*, or of flame-retardant materials complying with NFPA 701, *Standard Methods of Fire Tests for Flame-Resistant Textiles and Films*, both small and large scale tests. Textile wall coverings, such as carpeting having a napped, tufted, looped, or similar surface used as wall or ceiling finish, shall comply with 6-5.2.3. Plastic shall be limited to Class A or Class B interior wall and ceiling finish.

This section is intended to provide direction to manufacturers of exhibit booths as well as decorators, exhibitors, and the authority having jurisdiction. The focus of this section is on the construction components of the ceilings, walls, and floors of an exhibit booth or display area, in addition to the finish treatment. It is the intent of the Committee to also include large signs and display boards. Small signs [approximately 2 ft by 3 ft (61 cm by 91 cm) or smaller] would not normally be considered part of the wall covering. However, this section does not apply to the goods or products that are being displayed.

Plastics are limited to Class A and Class B for wall and ceiling finishes. It is the Committee's intent to prohibit the use of foamed plastics because of their inherent burning characteristics unless they meet the requirements of Section 6-5. Foamed plastics are found to be used in sign construction and display boards, and in some cases, the entire booth is constructed of foamed plastics.

(c) Curtains, drapes, and decorations shall comply with 31-1.4.

(d)* Acoustical and decorative material including, but not limited to, cotton, hay, paper, straw, moss, split bamboo, and wood chips shall be flame-retardant treated to the satisfaction of the authority having jurisdiction. Materials that cannot be treated for flame retardancy shall not be used.

A-9-4.4.3(d)   The authority having jurisdiction may use the field flame test contained in NFPA 701, *Standard Methods of Fire Tests for Flame-Resistant Textiles and Films*, as one method of determining flame retardancy.

This paragraph only addresses the materials used to decorate the booth or enhance its acoustics or aesthetics. This section does not cover products on display.

(e) Exhibit booths that are multilevel, consist of multiple rooms with ceilings, or are over 225 sq ft (20.9 sq m) with ceilings shall be protected by automatic sprinklers in buildings so protected.

Exception: Vehicles, boats, and similar exhibited products having over 100 sq ft (9.3 sq m) of roofed area shall be provided with smoke detectors acceptable to the authority having jurisdiction.

Large booths and multistory booths present special problems in exhibit halls. A fire in these booths could grow to large enough proportions to have a significant negative impact on the performance of the building's sprinkler system. It is the intent of the Committee to provide sprinkler protection in these booths by means of a temporary tap into the existing system. The Committee felt sprinklers would provide the protection necessary to extinguish a fire in its incipient stage, thus reducing the life hazard to occupants.

The Exception would exempt large vehicles, i.e., boats, mobile homes, recreational vehicles, from the sprinkler requirement but would require a smoke detector if the vehicle is greater than 100 sq ft (9.3 sq m) in area. The intent of the Committee was to provide early warning in the immediate area to allow for orderly evacuation. This provision could most probably be met by single station, battery operated smoke detectors.

(f) Open flame devices within exhibit booths shall comply with 31-2.3.

Open flame devices should be prohibited except for religious ceremonies and, where allowed, should be restricted to minimize the danger of igniting combustibles. Any use of open flames should only be allowed after approval by the authority having jurisdiction.

(g) Cooking and food warming devices in exhibit booths shall comply with 31-2.4 and the following:

1. Gas fired devices shall be installed in accordance with 7-1.1.

2. Devices shall be isolated from the public by at least 4 ft (122 cm) or a barrier between the device and the public.

3. Devices shall be limited to 288 sq in. (.19 sq m) of cooking surface area.

4. Devices shall be placed on noncombustible surface materials.

5. Devices used for cooking shall be separated from each other by a minimum distance of 2 ft (61 cm).

6. Devices shall be kept a minimum of 2 ft (61 cm) from any combustible materials.

7. Single well cooking equipment using combustible oils or solids shall have lids available for immediate use. Multi-vat cooking equipment using combustible oils or solids shall comply with 7-2.3.

8. A 20 BC fire extinguisher shall be provided within the booth for each device, or an approved automatic extinguishing system shall be provided.

The provisions of this section recognize the inherent dangers in cooking and warming devices where used in assembly occupancies that will be used for display purposes and are subject to large, transient crowds.

Item 1 requires that any gas-fired device be installed in accordance with recognized standards.

Item 2 requires distance or a barrier between the public and the device. The purpose is to minimize the possibility of accidental spills of hot greases or foods and to minimize the potential for ignition of combustibles, especially clothing worn by patrons.

Item 3: The surface area was determined to be large enough to accommodate the average-sized deep-fat fryer. It was felt by the Committee that this would allow for exhibits that display deep-fat frying and at the same time provide reasonable safeguards.

Item 4: The bottom surface of many devices could be subject to heating to temperatures that could ignite combustible surfaces..

Item 5: The minimum separation distances are necessary to minimize the danger of a fire in one device extending into another device.

Item 6: The same principle that applies to Item 5 applies to Item 6, except the exposure is combustible decorations or other products as opposed to another cooking device.

Item 7: The object of the lid is to provide to the operator a ready method of smothering the fire. Multi-vat cooking equipment must comply with NFPA 96, *Standard for the Installation of Equipment for the Removal of Smoke and Grease-Laden Vapors from Commercial Cooking Equipment.*[11]

Item 8 requires a 20-B:C extinguisher for each cooking device. The intent is to provide an extinguisher by each cooking device so the operator would be able to get to the extinguisher readily if the lid did not extinguish the fire or could not be applied. It was not the intent of the Committee to have all the extinguishers in one location.

(h) Combustible materials within exhibit booths shall be limited to a one day supply. Storage of combustible materials behind the booth is prohibited. (*See 9-4.4.2 and 31-2.6.2.*)

The intent of this section is to limit the amount of literature, brochures, boxes, give-aways and other products that are kept in the booth. The amount necessary to constitute a one-day supply is obviously going to vary; however, the authority having jurisdiction should be able to make a judgment after reviewing the activity expected by the exhibitor. Additional supplies and combustible crates (used for shipping) should be kept in a separate storage area having a fire resistance rating of one hour and protected by an automatic sprinkler system.

(i) Plans, in a form acceptable to the authority having jurisdiction, shall be submitted to the authority having jurisdiction for approval prior to the move-in of any exhibit or trade show. The plan shall show all details of the proposed exhibit or show. No exhibit or trade show shall occupy any exhibit hall without approved plans.

The intent is to provide the authority having jurisdiction with a set of plans that shows aisle widths, travel distances, exits, booth locations, display area configurations, types of displays (e.g., cooking, machinery, drapery, crafts, and arts, etc.), location of fire protection equipment (extinguishers, alarm pull stations, hose cabinets, etc.), lobby and registration area usage, etc. This is not a complete list, but it should provide some guidance in determining the plans that should be provided. The plan should also be drawn to scale. The scale used is not usually critical as long as it is indicated on the plan.

9-4.4.4 Vehicles.   Vehicles within an exhibit hall shall comply with the following:

The section on vehicles is intended to minimize the danger from both fuel and ignition sources.

(a) All fuel tank openings shall be locked and sealed in an approved manner to prevent the escape of vapors. Fuel tanks shall be not more than three-quarters nor less than one-eighth full.

It is important that the fuel tank openings are locked to prevent tampering and accessibility to fuel. It is also important that the tank openings be taped to prevent the escape of flammable vapors. When the Committee reviewed the issue of amount of allowable fuel, it was found that some jurisdictions preferred empty tanks to eliminate fuel while others preferred full tanks to prevent vapors. It was determined that most exhibitors were unaware of the regulation until they arrived at the exhibit hall. After learning the specific rule (empty or full) they proceeded to make their adjustment in the adjacent parking area or some other unsuitable area. It is also difficult for the authority having jurisdiction to determine whether a tank is absolutely full or empty. The committee felt that this fueling and defueling by exhibitors outside the hall presented a greater danger than the level of fuel in the tanks, given that they are locked, sealed, and ignition sources are eliminated from the vehicle.

(b) At least one battery cable shall be removed from each set of batteries.

It is important that at least one of the battery cables is removed from each battery. Many vehicles have more than one battery. The intent is to eliminate the possibility of a spark from the battery that might ignite fuel or surrounding combustibles. It is usually suggested that battery cable connectors be thoroughly taped after they have been removed.

(c) Fueling or defueling of vehicles shall be prohibited.

Fueling and defueling in and around the exhibit hall is extremely dangerous. [*See comments on 9-4.4.4(a).*]

(d) Vehicles shall not be moved during show hours.

The movement of vehicles inside the exhibit hall compromises exiting and access to means of egress. Vehicles should be positioned prior to the hall being accessible to the public to avoid compromising these exits. There is also a serious concern about the effects of carbon monoxide inside an exhibit hall that is occupied.

9-4.4.5 Compressed flammable gases, flammable or combustible liquids, hazardous chemicals or materials, Class II or greater lasers, blasting agents, and explosives shall be prohibited within exhibit halls.

Exception: The authority having jurisdiction may permit the limited use of any of the above items under special circumstances.

Compressed gases are subject to damage that could cause an explosion or create a serious threat to life safety under fire conditions. Flammable and combustible liquids compromise life safety by their inherent capability to contribute to rapid fire spread. Hazardous materials present a variety of hazards to life safety, from flammability to toxicity. Class II or greater lasers can cause tissue damage to humans, and blasting agents and explosives could cause a large loss of life or injury if handled improperly. Many exhibitors wish to display explosives or pesticides or a type of compressed gas container, etc.

These products can be effectively displayed by using empty containers without bringing the actual product into the hall.

The exception gives the authority having jurisdiction the discretion to permit small amounts of otherwise prohibited materials under special circumstances. For example, an exhibit or trade show for collectors of small arms ammunition or a highly supervised and closed (to the public) vocational trade show can be allowed where special controls and professional supervision are provided.

9-4.5 Special Provisions for the Handicapped.   (Reserved)

9-4.6 Special Provisions for Amusement Buildings.   (Reserved)

9-4.7 Operating Features.   *(See Chapter 31.)*

SECTION 9-5   BUILDING SERVICES

9-5.1 Utilities.   Utilities shall comply with the provisions of Section 7-1.

9-5.2 Heating, Ventilating, and Air Conditioning Equipment.   Heating, ventilating, and air conditioning equipment shall comply with the provisions of Section 7-2.

9-5.3 Elevators, Dumbwaiters, and Vertical Conveyors.   Elevators, dumbwaiters, and vertical conveyors shall comply with the provisions of Section 7-4.

9-5.4 Rubbish Chutes, Incinerators, and Laundry Chutes.   Rubbish chutes, incinerators, and laundry chutes shall comply with the provisions of Section 7-5.

REFERENCES CITED IN COMMENTARY

[1]NFPA 130, *Standard for Fixed Guideway Transit Systems*, National Fire Protection Association, Quincy, MA, 1988.

[2]NFPA 220, *Standard on Types of Building Construction*, National Fire Protection Association, Boston, MA, 1985.

[3]NFPA 102, *Standard for Assembly Seating, Tents, and Membrane Structures*, National Fire Protection Association, Boston, MA, 1986.

[4]NFPA 13, *Standard for the Installation of Sprinkler Systems*, National Fire Protection Association, Quincy, MA, 1987.

[5]NFPA 13A, *Recommended Practice for the Care and Maintenance of Sprinkler Systems*, National Fire Protection Association, Quincy, MA, 1987.

[6]NFPA 72E, *Standard on Automatic Fire Detectors*, National Fire Protection Association, Quincy, MA, 1987.

[7]NFPA 14, *Standard for the Installation of Standpipes and Hose Systems*, National Fire Protection Association, Quincy, MA, 1986.

[8]NFPA 13E, *Recommendations for Fire Department Operations in Properties Protected by Sprinkler and Standpipe Systems*, National Fire Protection Association, Quincy, MA, 1984.

[9]NFPA 40, *Standard for the Storage and Handling of Cellulose Nitrate Motion Picture Film*, National Fire Protection Association, Quincy, MA, 1982.

[10]NFPA 255, *Method of Test of Surface Burning Characteristics of Building Materials*, National Fire Protection Association, Quincy, MA, 1984.

[11]NFPA 96, *Standard for the Installation of Equipment for the Removal of Smoke- and Grease-Laden Vapors from Commercial Cooking Equipment*, National Fire Protection Association, Quincy, MA, 1987.

10 NEW EDUCATIONAL OCCUPANCIES

(See also Chapter 31.)

Educational occupancies include all buildings used for the gathering of groups of six or more people for purposes of instruction through the twelfth grade for four or more hours per day or more than twelve hours per week. Educational occupancies include:

Academies	Nursery schools
Kindergartens	Schools

Day-care facilities, for both children and adults, are provided for separately in Sections 10-7, 10-8, and 10-9.

Other occupancies associated with educational occupancies must be in accordance with the appropriate parts of this *Code.*

Operational features for educational occupancies are specified in Chapter 31, Operating Features.

SECTION 10-1   GENERAL REQUIREMENTS

10-1.1 Application.

10-1.1.1   The requirements of this chapter apply to new buildings.

Existing educational occupancies are dealt with in Chapter 11.

10-1.1.2*   Educational occupancies shall make provisions for the physically handicapped.

A-10-1.1.2   Reference is made to ANSI A117.1, *American Standard Specifications for Making Buildings and Facilities Accessible to and Usable by the Physically Handicapped.* *(See Appendix B.)*

Federal and state laws governing financial assistance for education emphasize that public educational facilities must provide equal access to education for the physically handicapped. In addition, many states specifically prohibit segregating handicapped students from other pupils, which makes it impossible to locate all physically handicapped pupils at the level of exit discharge. Unfortunately, these laws and related standards do not address the need for emergency egress of the handicapped during fires or similar events. In winning the right to equal access to educational facilities, the handicapped have placed themselves "at risk" in many buildings.

To minimize the level of risk created by interspersing the handicapped at all levels and locations within an educational building, horizontal exits permitting horizontal movement away from the area of a fire can easily be designed into new construction. This parallels the design concept in Chapter 12, New Health Care Occupancies, for the evacuation of litter-borne, bedridden, or handicapped patients from health care occupancies. Standards for the construction of elevators are discussed in Chapter 7 and in ANSI/ASME A17.1, *Safety Code for Elevators and Escalators.*[1] Standards for making buildings accessible to the handicapped are presented in ANSI A117.1, *American Standard Specifications for Making Buildings and Facilities Accessible to and Usable by the Physically Handicapped.*[2]

10-1.1.3 Educational occupancies housing classes over the twelfth grade need not comply with this chapter but shall comply with the following requirements:

(a) Instructional Building — Business Occupancy

(b) Classrooms under 50 persons — Business Occupancy

(c) Classrooms 50 persons and over — Assembly Occupancy

(d) Laboratories, Instructional — Business Occupancy

(e) Laboratories, Non-Instructional — Industrial.

The provisions of 10-1.1.3 recognize that colleges and universities do not have the same problem as elementary and high schools. Because of the maturity of the occupants, college buildings more properly resemble office occupancies. Thus, this paragraph identifies those uses and refers to other appropriate provisions of the *Code. (Also see 10-1.4.1.)*

10-1.2 Mixed Occupancies. *(See also 10-1.4.)*

10-1.2.1 Where other types of occupancy occur in the same building as an educational occupancy, the requirements of 1-4.7 of this *Code* shall be applicable.

Exception: As otherwise specified in this chapter.

Paragraph 1-4.7 of the *Code* specifies that where separate safeguards for each occupancy cannot be maintained, the most restrictive requirement of either occupancy will apply to both occupancies. Another way of stating this would be that the requirement providing the highest level of life safety would apply to both occupancies.

10-1.2.2 Assembly and Educational. Spaces subject to assembly occupancy shall comply with Chapter 8, including Special Provisions for Assembly Occupancies in Buildings of Other Occupancy, which provides that where auditorium and gymnasium exits lead through corridors or stairways also serving as exits for other parts of the building, the exit capacity shall be sufficient to permit simultaneous exit from auditorium and classroom sections.

Exception: In the case of an assembly occupancy of a type suitable only for use of the school occupant load (and therefore not subject to simultaneous occupancy), the same exit capacity may serve both sections.

The point of this requirement is that if classrooms and an assembly occupancy are likely to be occupied simultaneously, the exit capacity of the building must be designed and arranged for the combined use. For example, classrooms are often used during the evening for adult or remedial education while a school's gymnasium or auditorium is being used by another group. In such cases, the exception would not apply even though during the day the place of assembly would be used only by the school's population.

Chapter 8 has several requirements that could have a significant impact on the school if the building is not designed so that the occupancies can be treated separately. If treated as a mixed occupancy, the building will most likely have to be sprinklered throughout. (*See 8-3.6.*)

10-1.2.3 Dormitory and Classrooms. Any building used for both classroom and dormitory purposes shall comply with the applicable provisions of Chapter 16 in addition to complying with Chapter 10. Where classroom and dormitory sections are not subject to simultaneous occupancy, the same exit capacity may serve both sections.

10-1.3 Special Definitions.

Common Atmosphere. A common atmosphere exists between rooms, spaces, or areas within a building, that are not separated by an approved smoke barrier.

Flexible Plan and Open Plan Educational Buildings. Includes every building or portion of a building designed for multiple teaching stations.

(a) Flexible plan buildings have movable corridor walls and movable partitions of full-height construction with doors leading from rooms to corridors.

(b) Open plan buildings have rooms and corridors delineated by use of tables, chairs, desks, bookcases, counters, low-height 5-ft (152-cm) partitions, or similar furnishings.

Although becoming less common, flexible and open plan schools still exist. See Section 10-6 for additional requirements for these types of schools.

Interior Room. A room whose only means of egress is through an adjoining or intervening room that is not an exit.

Note that this definition of interior room does not imply a windowless room. (*See Figure 10-1.*)

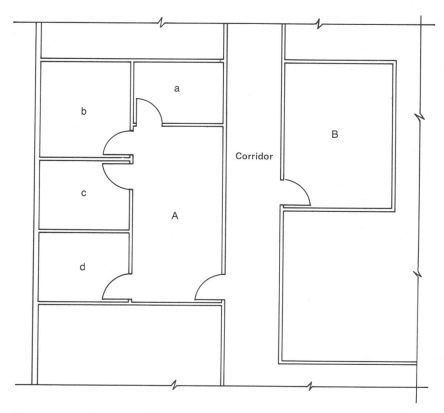

Figure 10-1.   Examples of Interior Rooms.   Rooms a, b, c, and d are interior rooms because occupants must pass through Room A before reaching the corridor. An example would be music practice rooms off a large music room. Room B, although windowless, is not an interior room as defined in Chapter 10 because the means of egress is from the room directly to the corridor.

Room.   For the purposes of this chapter, a room is a space or area bounded by any obstructions to egress that at any time enclose more than 80 percent of the perimeter of the space or area. Openings of less than 3 ft (91 cm) clear width and less than 6 ft 8 in. (203 cm) high shall not be considered in computing the unobstructed perimeter.

The intent of the last sentence in the definition of room is to prevent openings that do not qualify as a legitimate part of the means of egress from being calculated as open space. Because these small openings cannot be used for exiting, they are considered as part of the obstructed perimeter.

Separate Atmosphere.   A separate atmosphere exists between rooms, spaces, or areas that are separated by an approved smoke barrier.

Separate Means of Egress.   A means of egress separated in such a manner from other required means of egress as to provide an atmospheric separation that precludes contamination of both means of egress by the same fire. (*See Section 6-3.*)

10-1.4 Classification of Occupancy.   (*See 4-1.3.*)

10-1.4.1   Educational occupancies shall include all buildings used for educational purposes through the twelfth grade by six or more persons for four or more hours per day or more than 12 hours per week.

> This paragraph eliminates three types of schools: those dealing with small numbers of students (fewer than six), such as facilities providing private tutoring or individual lessons; those with limited operating hours, such as some sports schools or "Sunday" schools; and those educating people above the high school level, such as universities, military training, etc.
>
> The first two categories are rarely questioned, but many question the exemption for upper level education. The Committee felt that once a person leaves high school, the level of protection does not need to be greater simply because one chooses to continue one's education, while one who pursues a career in business or industry receives a different level of protection. Paragraph 10-1.1.3 provides guidance in determining how some higher education facilities would be classified.
>
> For purposes of determining occupant load, a classroom area is still an educational "use" although it may not be categorized as an educational occupancy, and the occupant load factors provided by 10-1.7 are still appropriate.
>
> Where instruction is incidental to other occupancies, the requirements for the occupancy in which the instruction occurs are applicable. Church schools that are used for instruction for a few hours during one or two days of the week are generally classed as assembly occupancies.

10-1.4.2   Educational occupancy includes part-day, nursery schools, kindergartens, and other schools whose purpose is primarily educational even though the children are of preschool age.

> The *Code* classifies part-time day-care facilities as educational occupancies if they primarily provide education in addition to care services. This parallels federal guidelines for subsidizing day-care/educational activities at both the federal and state levels. By requiring educational criteria and related activities, it was believed that a higher quality of staff will be provided for these facilities by these standards. Sections 10-7, 10-8, and 10-9 set forth special requirements for noneducational day-care facilities.

10-1.4.3   In cases where instruction is incidental to some other occupancy, the section of this *Code* governing such other occupancy shall apply.

This paragraph is not as important as it was before 10-1.4.1 removed places of higher education from Chapter 10. The following examples are uses that would nevertheless be exempted from Chapter 10 by 10-1.4.1.

In an office building or factory, a few rooms may be used for orientation or instruction in the work requirements; these rooms are subject to the *Code* requirements for offices or factories. Barber colleges and beauty schools frequently are located in commercial buildings and should be governed by the requirements of the buildings in which they occur.

10-1.4.4   Adult day-care shall include any building used for nonsleeping purposes for less than 24 hours per day to house one or more well, ambulatory or semi-ambulatory (nonbedridden) adults, none of whom requires medical injections by staff personnel. For the purposes of this definition, adults shall include those who:

(a) May require the administration of dry or liquid oral medication by staff personnel when and as prescribed by a licensed medical practitioner, and

(b) May require limited attendance, supervision, or observation, and

(c) Exhibit acceptable behavior (not harmful to self or others), and

(d) Are able to toilet self, and

(e) Are able to feed self, and

(f) Possess adequate mobility, and

(g) Are otherwise essentially homebound.

The definition of an adult day-care occupancy in this chapter is recognition of the fact that more and more senior citizens are being cared for in day-care centers resembling child day-care centers. The definition of the occupancy itself includes a definition of the type of adult who may be cared for in this occupancy. Essentially, the stated definition of an adult is to make clear that these occupancies are not nursing homes or old age homes, but are occupancies that contain persons who are capable of self-preservation, yet who need limited attendance, supervision, or observation. Adult day-care occupancies are now covered with child day-care occupancies in Sections 10-7, 10-8 and 10-9.

10-1.4.5   Other occupancies associated with educational institutions shall be in accordance with the appropriate parts of this *Code*. (*See Chapters 12, 16, 18, 20, 28, 29, and 30, and 1-4.7.*)

10-1.5 Classification of Hazard of Contents.   Contents of educational occupancies shall be classified in accordance with the provisions of Section 4-2.

In general, educational occupancies contain ordinary hazard contents. Some laboratories and storage areas may contain high hazard contents. (*See Section 5-11 for additional egress requirements for areas with high hazard.*)

10-1.6 Minumum Construction Requirements.   No Requirements.

10-1.7 Occupant Load.

10-1.7.1   The occupant load of educational buildings or any individual story or section thereof for the purpose of determining exits shall be as determined by the authority having jurisdiction but not less than one person for each 20 sq ft (1.9 sq m) of net classroom area or 50 sq ft (4.6 sq m) of net area of shops, laboratories, and similar vocational rooms. In day-care centers, the occupant load shall be not less than one person for each 35 sq ft (3.3 sq m) of net area.

> It is not the intent of this paragraph to establish a minimum number of sq ft (sq m) per child, but to assure adequate exit capacity is provided for those present. Efficient use of classroom space may result in more occupants than these occupant load factors would yield. Paragraph 10-1.7.3 clearly allows this, provided all requirements based on this higher number are met.
>
> Many states require that day-care facilities provide 35 sq ft (3.3 sq m) of net area per child. It is not the intent of this *Code* to affect such a requirement, which is provided for the welfare of the child for purposes other than life safety.

10-1.7.2   The occupant load of an area having fixed seats shall be determined by the number of fixed seats installed. Required aisle space serving the fixed seats shall not be used to increase the occupant load.

10-1.7.3   The capacity of an educational occupancy or a portion thereof may be modified from that specified above if the necessary aisles and exits are provided. An approved aisle or seating diagram shall be required by the authority having jurisdiction to substantiate such a modification.

10-1.7.4   The occupant load for determining exit requirements of individual lecture rooms, gymnasiums, or cafeterias used for assembly purposes of more than 50 persons shall be determined in accordance with 8-1.7 of this *Code*.

> The intent of this paragraph is to indicate that rooms that may be used as assembly occupancies should have their occupant loads calculated using the occupant load factors found in Chapter 8 of the *Code*. As noted for assembly occupancies, this may result in a room with more than one occupant load, depending on its use. School cafeterias are generally capable of other uses and should probably be considered as multipurpose rooms.

SECTION 10-2   MEANS OF EGRESS REQUIREMENTS

10-2.1 General.

10-2.1.1   Means of egress shall be in accordance with Chapter 5 and this section.

10-2.1.2 Rooms normally occupied by preschool, kindergarten, or first-grade pupils shall not be located above or below the level of exit discharge. Rooms normally occupied by second-grade pupils shall not be located more than one story above the level of exit discharge.

The restrictions on the location of rooms used by preschool, kindergarten, or first or second grade pupils were developed to avoid the danger of older (and larger) children overrunning the very young on stairs or ramps during a fire or other incident requiring rapid evacuation of a building. Paragraph 10-2.1.2 also recognizes that young children may need assistance or may have to be rescued.

10-2.2 Means of Egress Components.

Note that slide escapes, escalators, fire escape stairs, and revolving doors are not permitted to be credited as required egress components. Escalators and revolving doors may be installed, but cannot be considered as part of the required egress and must not obstruct or otherwise confuse required egress path.

10-2.2.1 Components of means of egress shall be limited to the types described in 10-2.2.2 through 10-2.2.7.

10-2.2.2 Doors.

10-2.2.2.1 Doors shall comply with 5-2.1.

10-2.2.2.2 Panic Hardware or Fire Exit Hardware. Any door in a required means of egress from an area having an occupant load of 100 or more persons may be provided with a latch or lock only if it is panic hardware or fire exit hardware complying with 5-2.1.7.

This paragraph is based on the total occupant load of the area served and not the required capacity of the door. For example, if an area has an occupant load of 120 persons and is served by 3 doors, each door need only have capacity for 40 persons, but since all these doors serve an area with "100 or more persons," then any latches on these doors must be released by panic hardware or fire exit hardware.

10-2.2.2.3 Special locking arrangements complying with 5-2.1.6 are permitted.

The provisions of 5-2.1.6 apply to special delayed release devices. Note that one of the requirements of 5-2.1.6 is that the building must be either fully sprinklered or fully protected by an automatic fire detection system.

10-2.2.2.4 Door Closure. Any exit door designed to normally be kept closed shall conform with 5-2.1.8.

10-2.2.2.5 Only one locking or latching device shall be permitted on a door or a leaf of a pair of doors.

10-2.2.3* Stairs.   Stairs shall comply with 5-2.2.

A-10-2.2.3   See Appendix A-5-2.2.6.5(a) Exception No. 2 regarding additional handrails on stairs that are used extensively by children 5 years or less in age.

10-2.2.4 Smokeproof Enclosures.   Smokeproof enclosures shall comply with 5-2.3.

10-2.2.5 Horizontal Exits.   Horizontal exits shall comply with 5-2.4.

10-2.2.6 Ramps.   Ramps shall comply with 5-2.5.

10-2.2.7 Exit Passageways.   Exit passageways shall comply with 5-2.7.

10-2.3 Capacity of Means of Egress.

10-2.3.1   Capacity of means of egress shall be in accordance with Section 5-3.

10-2.3.2   The same exit capacity required for any individual floor may be counted as simultaneously serving all floors above the first story or floor of exit discharge.

10-2.3.3 Minimum Corridor Width.

10-2.3.3.1   Exit access corridors shall be not less than 6 ft (183 cm) clear width.

> Note that this requirement applies regardless of the required capacity of the corridor. Larger widths may be necessary for corridors handling large numbers of students. (*See 10-2.3.1.*)
>
> This paragraph applies to exit access corridors and not to nonrequired service corridors that are provided for convenience only.
>
> "In the clear" means a 6-ft (183-cm) wide clear space with no obstructions. Paragraph 5-3.2 details how to measure the width of a portion of the means of egress.
>
> The intent of a 6-ft (183-cm) corridor is to permit two files of children with sufficient room for teachers or monitors to supervise. Extremely short corridors serving only one room may warrant consideration for some reduction in width.

10-2.3.3.2   Drinking fountains or other equipment, fixed or movable, shall not be so placed as to obstruct the required minimum 6 ft (183 cm) corridor width.

10-2.4 Number of Exits.   There shall be at least two exits available from every floor area. (*See Section 5-4.*)

10-2.5 Arrangement of Means of Egress.   (*See also Section 5-5.*)

10-2.5.1   Arrangement of means of egress shall be in accordance with Section 5-5. Dead ends shall not exceed 20 ft (6.1 m).

> This paragraph has been rewritten for the 1988 Edition. In order to simplify the *Code*, Section 5-5 provides the detail required to establish proper exiting. Paragraph 5-5.1.5 makes individual chapters responsible

for establishing dead-end limits. Twenty feet (6.1 m) has been the standard dead-end requirement for educational occupancies in the past, and the Committee felt it was still reasonable.

A school plan with outside doors or stairways at both ends of a central corridor meets the dead-end requirement. Small pockets may be created where stairways are not at the end of corridors, but at intermediate points.

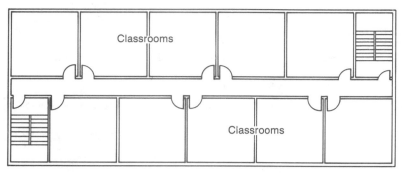

Preferred Arrangement Of Exits Without Deadends

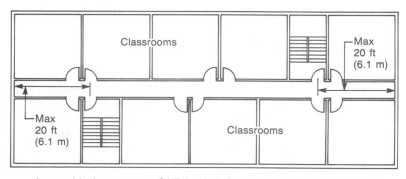

Acceptable Arrangement Of Exits With Deadends, Up To 20 ft (6.1 m)

Figure 10-2.   Stair Placement in Accordance with 10-2.5.1.

10-2.5.2   Every room or space with a capacity of more than 50 persons or more than 1,000 sq ft (93 sq m) in area shall have at least two doorways as remote from each other as practicable. Such doorways shall provide access to separate exits but, where egress is through corridors, may open upon a common corridor leading to separate exits in opposite directions.

Chapter 10 does not establish a maximum common path of travel, but instead, it sets a maximum room size with one door and then limits dead-end corridors. (See 10-2.5.1.)

See 5-2.1.4.1 for information on direction of door swing.

10-2.5.3   Doors that swing into an exit access corridor shall be recessed to prevent interference with corridor traffic; any doors not so recessed shall open 180 degrees to stop against the wall. Doors in any position shall not reduce the required corridor width by more than one half.

See 5-2.1.4.2 for more information on doors swinging into corridors.

10-2.5.4 Aisles.

10-2.5.4.1   Where there are more than 60 seats, every aisle shall be not less than 3 ft (91 cm) wide where serving seats on one side only, and not less than 3 ft 6 in. (107 cm) wide where serving seats on both sides. Where serving 60 seats or less, aisles shall not be less than 30 in. (76 cm) wide. The space between parallel rows of seats does not constitute an aisle. No more than six seats shall intervene between any seat and an aisle.

10-2.5.5*   Exterior Corridors or Balconies.

A-10-2.5.5   A corridor roofed over and enclosed on its long side and open to the atmosphere at the end may be considered an exterior corridor if either:

(a) Clear story openings for the corridor are provided on both sides of the corridor and above adjacent roofs or buildings, and such clear openings are not less than one-half the height of the corridor walls, or

(b) The corridor roof has unobstructed openings to the sky not less than 50 percent of the area of the roof.

The openings are to be equally distributed, and if louvers are installed, they are to be fixed open with a clear area based on the actual openings between louver vanes.

See Figures 10-3a and 10-3b.

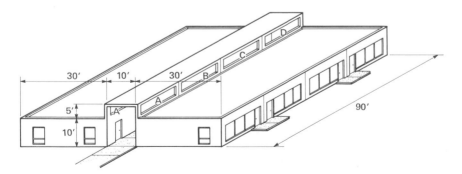

Figure 10-3a.   Exterior Corridor Using Clear Story Openings. A, B, C, and D are clear story openings. The building height is 10 ft (3 m). In order for a corridor to be considered an outside corridor, the minimum height allowable for the corridor roof must be 5 ft (1.5 m). In our example, the minimum clear story height requirements have been met.

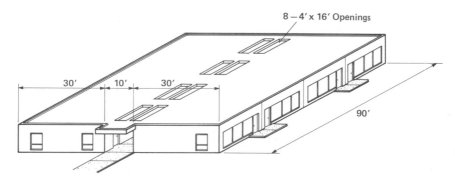

Figure 10-3b.   Exterior Corridor Using Roof Openings. The alternative to the clear story openings is that the roof have unobstructed openings to the sky that equal not less than 50 percent of the corridor roof. The example shown has eight openings. Each opening is 4 ft × 16 ft (1.2 m × 4.9 m), or 64 sq ft (5.9 sq m) each. The total square footage of the roof area equals 900 sq ft (84 sq m). The total unobstructed opening equals 512 sq ft (48 sq m) (greater than 50 percent of the total roof area). This would be an acceptable design.

10-2.5.5.1* Where exterior corridors or balconies are provided as means of egress, they shall open to the outside air except for railings or balustrades with stairs or level exits to grade not over the allowable travel distance apart and so located that an exit will be available in either direction from the door to any individual room or space, with dead ends not to exceed 20 ft (6.1 m). If balconies are enclosed by glass or in any other manner, they shall be treated as interior corridors.

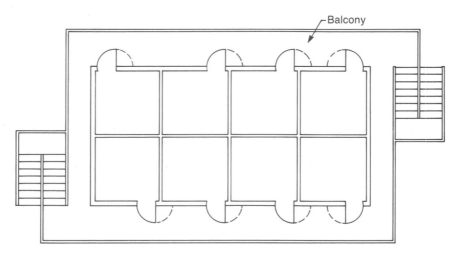

Figure 10-4.   Stair Placement, Exterior Balcony.   Distance between stairs must not be greater than the allowable travel distance would permit.

A-10-2.5.5.1 School design providing classroom exits directly to the outside or to exterior balconies open to the outside air with exterior stairways available to either direction to grade is considered preferable, from the firesafety standpoint, to the more conventional design using interior corridors, which can become untenable from the accumulation of smoke and heat.

10-2.5.5.2 The floors of balconies (exterior corridors) and stairs shall be solid, without openings, and shall comply with requirements for outside stairs as regards balustrades or railings, width and pitch of stairs, and other details, but are not required to be shielded from fire within the building by blank walls, wired glass windows or the like where the stairs are located on the side of the balcony or corridor away from the building and are separated from the building by the full required width of the balcony or corridor. Regardless of other provisions, exterior balconies and stairs may be of the same type of construction as the building that they serve.

Stairs from exterior balconies must not pass or come close to windows or other openings in stories below. Preferable stair placements complying with 10-2.5.5.1 and 10-2.5.5.2 are illustrated in Figures 10-5 and 10-6.

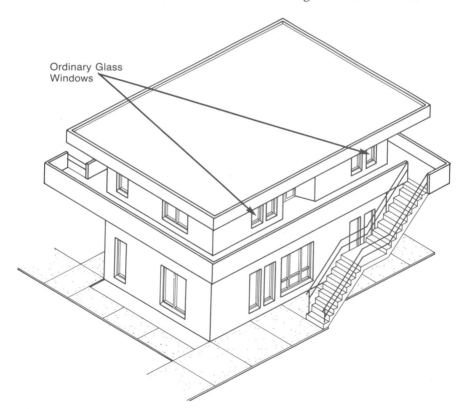

Ordinary Glass Windows

Figure 10-5. Stair Placement, Exterior Balcony. Since stairs are separated from the building by the full width of the balcony, blank walls or wired glass windows are not required near the stairs.

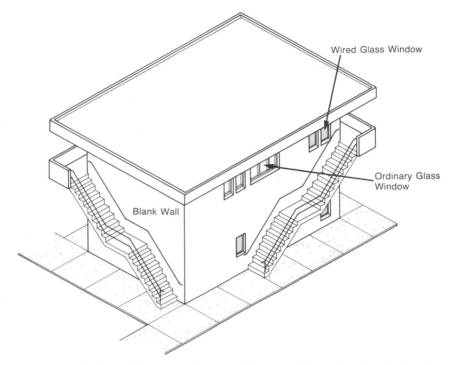

Figure 10-6. Stair Placement, Exterior Balcony. The stair placed directly against the building must not pass near unprotected openings. (*See 5-2.2 for protection requirements on outside stairs.*)

10-2.6 Travel Distance to Exits.   Travel distance to an exit shall not exceed 150 ft (45 m) from any point in a building. (*See also Section 5-6.*)

Exception: The travel distance may be increased to 200 ft (60 m) in educational occupancies protected throughout by an approved automatic sprinkler system.

10-2.7 Discharge from Exits.   Discharge from exits shall be arranged in accordance with Section 5-7.

Exception: Every classroom or room used for educational purposes or student occupancy below the floor of exit discharge shall have access to at least one exit that leads directly to the exterior at level of discharge without entering the floor above.

The basic requirements previously found in Chapter 10 are now in Chapter 5. The Exception is a slight relaxation of the requirement in Section 5-7 in that the Exception requires at least one exit to discharge directly outside, while 5-7.2 requires 50 percent to discharge directly outside. Figures 10-7 and 10-8 illustrate two types of exits that will satisfy the requirements of the Exception to 10-2.7. The enclosed stair in Figure 10-8 may serve other floors if it meets all the requirements of Chapter 5.

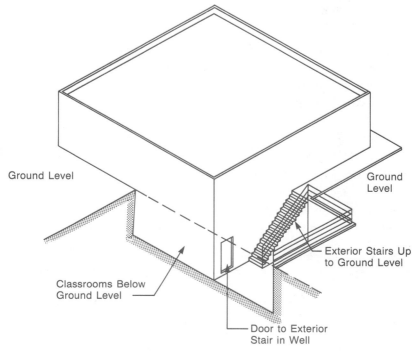

Ground Level

Ground Level

Exterior Stairs Up to Ground Level

Classrooms Below Ground Level

Door to Exterior Stair in Well

Figure 10-7.   Exit from Classroom Below Floor of Exit Discharge.

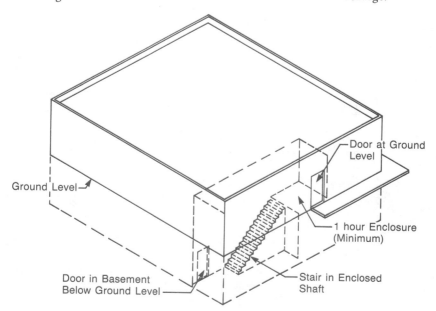

Door at Ground Level

Ground Level

1 hour Enclosure (Minimum)

Door in Basement Below Ground Level

Stair in Enclosed Shaft

Figure 10-8.   Exit from Classroom Below Floor of Exit Discharge.   The enclosed stair could be located on the outside of the building.

10-2.8 Illumination of Means of Egress. Means of egress shall be illuminated in accordance with Section 5-8.

10-2.9 Emergency Lighting. Emergency Lighting shall be provided in accordance with Section 5-9 in the following areas:

(a) In all interior stairs and corridors.

(b) In all normally occupied spaces.

Exception to (b):

1. *Administrative areas.*

2.* *General classrooms.*

3. *Mechanical rooms and storage areas.*

(c) In flexible and open plan buildings.

(d) In all portions of buildings that are interior or windowless.

A-10-2.9(b) Exception to (b)2 This does not exempt shops and laboratories.

The Exceptions to 10-2.9(b) indicate that normal classrooms, offices, and storage or mechanical spaces do not require emergency lighting. Shops, laboratories, and assembly rooms would require emergency lighting as do portions of the building that are interior or windowless.

See Figure 10-9.

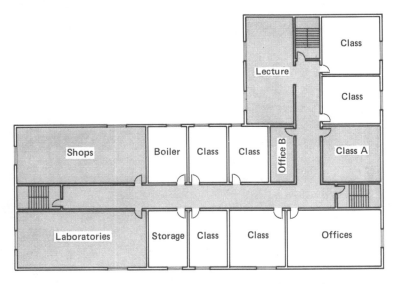

Figure 10-9. Emergency Lighting. Shaded areas indicate where emergency lighting is required. Classroom A and Office B are windowless; therefore, 10-2.9(d) overrides the Exception to 10-2.9(b). Laboratories, shops, and lecture halls do not qualify as general classrooms.

10-2.10 Marking of Means of Egress.   Means of egress shall have signs in accordance with Section 5-10.

Exception: Signs are not required in situations where location of exits is otherwise obvious and familiar to all occupants, such as in small elementary school buildings.

10-2.11 Special Features.

10-2.11.1* Windows for Rescue and Ventilation.   Every room or space used for classroom or other educational purposes or normally subject to student occupancy shall have at least one outside window for emergency rescue or ventilation. Such window shall be openable from the inside without the use of tools and provide a clear opening of not less than 20 in. (50.8 cm) in width, 24 in. (61 cm) in height, and 5.7 sq ft (.53 sq m) in area. The bottom of the opening shall be not more than 44 in. (112 cm) above the floor, and any latching device shall be capable of being operated from not more than 54 in. (137 cm) above the finished floor. In rooms located greater than three stories above grade, the openable clear height, width, and area of the window may be modified to the dimensions necessary for ventilation.

Exception No. 1: In buildings protected throughout by an approved automatic sprinkler system in accordance with Section 7-7.

Exception No. 2: Where the room or space has a door leading directly to the outside of the building.

A-10-2.11.1   It is highly desirable to have all windows of a type that can be readily opened from inside and to have them large enough and low enough for use by students, teachers, and fire fighters. Windows may serve as a supplementary means of emergency escape, particularly where ladders can be raised by fire fighters or others. Even where the location is such as to preclude the use of windows for escape purposes, they may provide air for breathing in a smoke-filled room while trapped occupants are awaiting rescue.

The dimensions specified for windows used for emergency rescue or for ventilation are based on simulations of emergency rescue conducted by the San Diego Fire Department. Windows providing clear openings of identical dimensions are also required for rescue or ventilation in one- and two-family dwellings. Figure 10-10 illustrates two configurations that achieve the required area of 5.7 sq ft (.53 sq m).

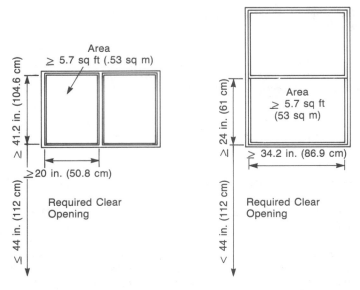

Figure 10-10.   Windows for Rescue or Ventilation, Required Dimensions.

Although the *Code* intends the fire department or others to assist students, particularly over ladders, if these windows must be used as a supplementary means of escape, the windows must permit small children in the lower grades to escape unaided. Therefore, storm sashes, screens, or devices in front of the windows must be easy to open or remove, and the sills must be low enough for children to reach.

Where the location of windows precludes their use for rescue or escape, they may still provide trapped children with air for breathing in smoke-filled rooms.

Windows may be omitted if a classroom has a door leading directly to the outside or if the building is totally sprinklered.

The Committee did not feel it was practical to expect someone to use a window above the third story as an escape window. However, it is reasonable to expect the window to be usable for ventilation during a fire.

Note that Exception No. 1 requires that the building be protected throughout by an automatic sprinkler system. One question that is often asked is: If there are only a couple of windowless classrooms can just those rooms be sprinklered? The answer is no! It must be remembered that the purpose of the window is to provide ventilation or means of escape when the interior corridor is blocked by smoke from a fire in another part of the building. Putting sprinklers only in the windowless rooms would do nothing about smoke emanating from other areas.

Formal Interpretation 73-21
Reference: 10-2.11.5 (11-2.11.5)

Question: Do doors or windows opening onto an open court satisfy the requirements?

Answer: No.

Question: Does a door opening into a horizontal exit or to an exit passageway satisfy the phrase "unless it has a door leading directly to the outside of the building"?

Answer: No.

Question: Would this section also apply to a work room partitioned off from the rest of a large classroom, library, or shop area?

Answer: Yes.

Question: Are there any other sections of the *Code* that might modify the requirements of 10-2.11.5 (11-2.11.5)?

Answer: No.

Question: The phrase "or normally subject to student occupancy" would appear to include toilet rooms. Is this correct?

Answer: No.

Issue Edition: 1973
Reference: 9-1511
Date: May 1976

In answering this formal interpretation, the Committee was probably thinking of an open court that is open to the sky but bounded on all sides, which is defined in Chapter 3 as an enclosed court.

As indicated in the formal interpretation, bathrooms are not considered spaces normally subject to student occupancy and, thus, do not require the window referred to in 10-2.11.1.

SECTION 10-3 PROTECTION

10-3.1 Protection of Vertical Openings.

10-3.1.1 Any vertical opening shall be enclosed and protected in accordance with Section 6-2.

Exception: In buildings protected throughout by an approved supervised automatic sprinkler system installed in accordance with Section 7-7, unprotected vertical openings connecting not more than three floors may be permitted in accordance with 6-2.4.4.

Chapter 6 has been changed, and under certain circumstances, would allow up to three floors to be connected without providing complete automatic sprinkler protection. The Committee felt that automatic sprinkers should be provided in educational occupancies. This is consistent with the intent of the 1985 *Code*.

10-3.1.2   Stairs shall be enclosed in accordance with Section 6-2.

Exception: Stairway enclosure will not be required for a stairway serving only one adjacent floor except a basement and not connected with stairways serving other floors and not connected to corridors.

The Exception to 10-3.1.2 is to make provisions for the so-called convenience stair. The Exception permits an unenclosed stair between two floors, provided neither floor is a basement, and provided the unenclosed stair does not expose the normally protected means of egress system of enclosed stairs and rated corridors. This may be useful, especially for libraries or offices within schools. Basements are excluded because basements usually contain hazardous areas with high fuel loads, such as storage rooms, boiler rooms, or workshops.

Figures 10-11 and 10-12 illustrate acceptable examples of the Exception to 10-3.1.2 in a multistory school.

10-3.2   Protection from Hazards.

10-3.2.1   Rooms or spaces for the storage, processing, or use of the materials specified in this section shall be protected in accordance with the following:

(a) Rooms or spaces used for the storage of combustible supplies in quantities deemed hazardous by the authority having jurisdiction, hazardous materials in quantities deemed hazardous by recognized standards, or fuel shall be separated from the remainder of the building by construction having not less than a 1-hour fire resistance rating with all openings protected by self-closing or smoke-actuated fire doors, or such rooms or spaces may be protected by an automatic extinguishing system as set forth in Section 6-4.

(b) Rooms or spaces used for processing or use of combustible supplies in quantities considered hazardous by the authority having jurisdiction, hazardous materials, or for flammable or combustible liquids in quantities deemed hazardous by recognized standards shall be separated from the remainder of the building by construction having not less than a 1-hour fire resistance rating with all openings protected by self-closing or smoke-actuated fire doors and shall also be protected by an automatic extinguishing system as set forth in Section 6-4.

(c) Boiler and furnace rooms, laundries, and maintenance shops, including woodworking and painting areas, shall be separated from the remainder of the building by construction having not less than a 1-hour fire resistance rating with all openings protected by self-closing or smoke-actuated fire doors.

Exception to (c):   Rooms enclosing air-handling equipment.

(d)* Where automatic extinguishing systems are used to meet the requirements of this section, the rooms or spaces shall be separated from the remainder of the building by construction that resists the passage of smoke.

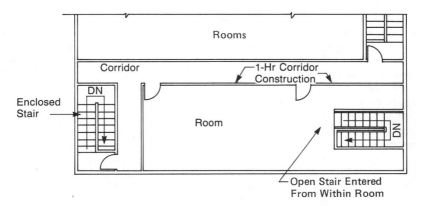

Figure 10-11.   Open Stair Complying with 10-3.1.2.

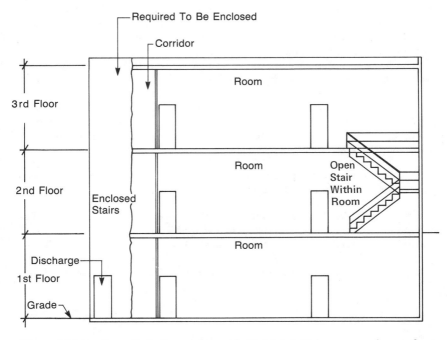

Figure 10-12.   Open Stair Complying with 10-3.1.2.   Stair serves only one floor
and is not connected to a corridor.

A-10-3.2.1(d)   It is not the intent of this provision to require a smoke barrier that
meets the requirements of Section 6-3.

The intent of 10-3.2.1 is to specify the degree of protection necessary for certain hazardous areas. It has been divided into three sections based on the degree of hazard. The hazards noted in item (a) are required to be enclosed in 1-hour construction or protected by sprinklers. If the sprinkler option is chosen, an enclosure is still required by item (d); however, the enclosure need not be rated, but only form a membrane against the passage of smoke.

The Committee felt that although sprinklers are provided and therefore fire-rated barriers may not be needed [see (a)], some barrier to control smoke migration is needed. Solid construction materials, such as glass or other non-fire-rated materials, are acceptable if they are installed in a manner that will resist smoke passing from one compartment to another. The new appendix note emphasizes that it is not the intent to require smoke barriers as provided in Section 6-3. This eliminates the more costly construction of a smoke barrier, which would require dampers and other required equipment.

Art rooms and some shops need special attention. Potentially dangerous operations involving flammable materials, specialized ovens, and ignition sources in these areas are becoming more prevalent and create increased hazards to the entire facility. It may be advisable at the high school level to include these rooms as hazardous spaces.

The hazards noted in item (b) must be enclosed in 1-hour construction and be protected by automatic sprinklers.

The hazards noted in item (c) are required to be enclosed in 1-hour construction with no option for a sprinkler equivalency for the enclosure. The Exception to item (c) pertains to rooms housing air-handling equipment only. If the room is used for other purposes, then the provisions of item (a) or (b) apply.

(e) Where automatic extinguishing is used to meet the requirements of this section, the protection may be in accordance with 7-7.1.2.

Part (e) has been added as an editorial change to highlight the fact that Chapter 7 makes these requirements available to the user of the *Code*. Paragraph 7-7.1.2 provides an economical way of providing sprinkler protection in small rooms. (*See 10-3.2.3.*)

Figure 10-13 illustrates the various protection requirements of 10-3.2.1.

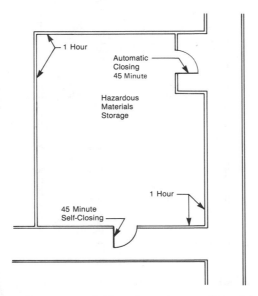

Figure 10-13(a). Protection of Hazardous Areas. Part (a) illustrates one method of complying with 10-3.2.1(a). See Figure 10-13(b) for the alternate method.

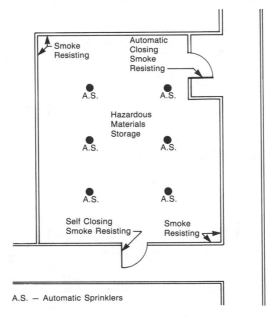

Figure 10-13(b). Protection of Hazardous Areas. Part (b) illustrates an alternate method of complying with 10-3.2.1(a). Figure 10-13(a) illustrates another method of compliance.

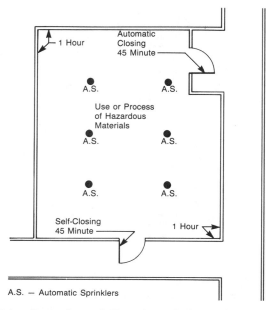

Figure 10-13(c). Protection of Hazardous Areas. Part (c) illustrates the requirements for complying with 10-3.2.1(b). Both one hour separation and automatic sprinkler protection is required in this case.

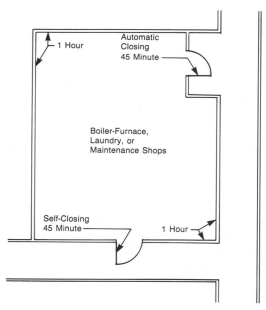

Figure 10-13(d). Protection of Hazardous Areas. Part (d) illustrates the requirements for complying with 10-3.2.1(c). Note that the automatic sprinkler option does not exist for these hazardous areas.

10-3.2.2 Food preparation facilities shall be protected in accordance with 7-2.3 and are not required to have openings protected between food preparation areas and dining areas.

> The intent of 10-3.2.2 is to provide some barrier between cooking areas and dining areas. The intent of the barrier is to screen possible flash fires from view in an attempt to prevent panic. Openings in this barrier are not restricted and do not need to be protected. The *Code* is counting on the automatic extinguishing system to control any fire on the cooking surfaces and, thus, no longer requires openings between the kitchen and dining areas to be protected. The degree of screening required, and, thus the size of the barrier required, is left to the judgment of the authority having jurisdiction.

10-3.2.3 Janitor closets shall be protected by an automatic sprinkler system, which may be in accordance with 7-7.1.2. Doors to janitor closets may have ventilating louvers.

> Where janitor closets are located off of corridors, a louvered door is usually provided for ventilation. It is necessary to provide these spaces with automatic sprinkler protection since the louvered door offers little fire resistance and permits a fire in the closet to directly affect the corridor. Paragraph 7-7.1.2 provides an economical method of providing sprinkler protection for such rooms. To accomplish this at reasonable cost, these sprinklers (not more than six in number) may be supplied from the domestic water supply to the closet if the supply is capable of providing the required quantity of water. It is advisable to provide a water-flow switch (*see Chapter 6*) to initiate an alarm when a sprinkler is opened.
>
> The minimum flow of 0.15 gpm/sq ft (6.1 L/min sq m) is based on the requirements in NFPA 13, *Standard for the Installation of Sprinkler Systems*,[3] for protecting buildings containing ordinary hazards. It is important to ensure that the domestic supply can provide the required flow and pressure at the location.

10-3.2.4 Laboratories that use chemicals shall comply with NFPA 45, *Standard on Fire Protection for Laboratories Using Chemicals*.

10-3.2.5 Stages shall be protected in accordance with Chapter 8.

10-3.3 Interior Finish.

10-3.3.1 Interior finish, in accordance with Section 6-5, shall be as follows:

(a) Exits — Class A.

(b) Other than exits — Class A or B.

Exception to (b): Fixtures and low-height partitions not over 5 ft (152 cm) high may be Class C.

Exception: The exposed portions of structural members complying with the requirements for Type IV (2HH) construction may be permitted.*

A-10-3.3.1 Exception   NFPA 220, *Standard on Types of Building Construction* (*see Appendix B*), defines Type IV (2HH) construction. (*Also see A-6-2.1.*)

Section 6-5 permits the use of fire retardant or intumescent paints and surface coatings to reduce the surface flame spread of an interior finish. These coatings will not render a finish noncombustible. They will simply delay the eventual ignition of a finish exposed to fire.

Some coatings have a short life and require frequent reapplication. Over the useful life of a building, all coatings may eventually have to be renewed. Also, some coatings will severely mar or alter the appearance of the finish. Due to these liabilities, the option of using coatings and paints may not provide the best fire protection at a reasonable cost in all cases.

Sections 31-1 and 31-3 establish limitations on decorations and student artwork on walls.

10-3.3.2 Interior Floor Finish.   No Requirements.

10-3.4 Detection, Alarm, and Communications Systems.

10-3.4.1 General.   Educational occupancies shall be provided with a fire alarm system in accordance with Section 7-6.

10-3.4.2 Initiation.

10-3.4.2.1   Initiation of the required fire alarm system shall be by manual means in accordance with 7-6.2.1(a).

Exception: In buildings where all normally occupied spaces are provided with a two-way communication system between such spaces and a constantly attended receiving station from where a general evacuation alarm can be sounded, the manual pull stations may be omitted except in locations specifically designated by the authority having jurisdiction.

The Exception to 10-3.4.2.1 is intended to give local authorities the ability to deal with the false alarm and vandalism problems present in today's schools. Where there is a two-way communication system between classrooms and a continuously attended location where a general alarm can be sounded, the need for pull stations is obviated. To qualify to use this Exception, the authority having jurisdiction must agree on which pull stations can be omitted. For the purposes of this provision, the "continuously attended" location is intended to indicate a location attended while the school building is in use as a school. This may involve providing personnel at this location during night school, when the regular school office staff is not present.

10-3.4.2.2   In buildings provided with automatic sprinkler protection, the operation of the sprinkler system shall automatically activate the fire alarm system, in addition to the initiation means required above.

10-3.4.3 Notification.

10-3.4.3.1   Occupant notification shall be by means of an audible alarm in accordance with 7-6.3.

10-3.4.3.2 Where acceptable to the authority having jurisdiction, the fire alarm system may be used to designate class change provided that the fire alarm is distinctive in signal and overrides all other use.

10-3.5 Extinguishment Requirements.

10-3.5.1 Every portion of educational buildings below the level of exit discharge shall be protected throughout by an approved automatic sprinkler system in accordance with Section 7-7.

> This provision will normally require basements of schools to be sprinklered. But since the level of exit discharge could sometimes be between two stories (e.g., one walks up from the first floor and walks down from the second floor to the level of exit discharge), the lower story would need to be sprinklered. (*See Figure 10-14*). This protection is required regardless of the use of the story. Schools that contain assembly occupancies are often required to be sprinklered due to the assembly occupancy. (*See Chapter 8.*)

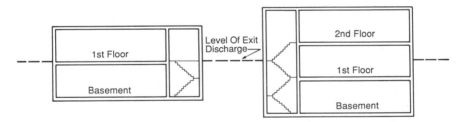

Figure 10-14. Automatic Sprinkler Protection for Levels Below the Level of Exit Discharge. The arrangement on the left illustrates a simple example where only the basement is required to be protected by sprinklers. The diagram on the right shows the case where the level of exit discharge is between floors and requires that the first floor and basement be sprinklered.

10-3.6 Interior Corridors.

10-3.6.1 Every interior corridor, including corridors in flexible plan buildings, shall be of construction having not less than a 1-hour fire resistance rating. Such corridor walls shall extend from floor slab to floor slab. All openings shall be protected with doors, frames, and hardware, including closers, that shall all have a fire protection rating of at least 20 minutes.

Exception No. 1: Such corridor protection shall not be required where all classrooms served by such corridors have at least one door directly to the outside or to an exterior balcony or corridor as in 10-2.5.5.

Exception No. 2: In buildings protected throughout by an approved supervised automatic sprinkler system installed in accordance with Section 7-7, corridor walls may be nonrated provided such walls, in conjunction with doors installed therein and ceilings at which they terminate, resist the passage of smoke.

Exception No. 2 to 10-3.6.1 is an important Exception and a significant incentive for sprinklers for two reasons. First, Chapter 6 requires that fire-rated walls extend to the roof deck or floor deck above and not terminate at ceilings unless the ceiling, by itself, is rated for 1-hr (a very rare case). This Exception allows the wall to terminate at the ceiling as long as the ceiling resists the passage of smoke. Secondly, doors in fire-rated partitions are required to be self-closing or automatic-closing, which causes significant operation and maintenance problems in schools. This Exception would allow the omission of door closers on doors other than those required to be self-closing for other reasons, such as stair doors.

It is important that this wall (non-rated) and the ceiling together resist the passage of smoke, but it is not intended that they meet all the requirements of Section 6-3 for smoke barriers.

Exception No. 3:   Where the corridor ceiling is constructed with materials that would have a 1-hour fire resistance rating when tested as a wall, the corridor may terminate at the corridor ceiling.

Exception No. 3 to 10-3.6.1 was new to the 1985 Edition of the *Code*. Its intent is to legitimize the common practice of designing a "corridor" protection system by building a tunnel, the walls and ceilings of which are constructed to meet the requirements for a 1-hour rated wall assembly.

10-3.6.2   Clothing and personal effects shall not be stored in corridors and lobbies.

Racks of clothing and personal effects create two specific problems. The first problem relates to the large amount of combustibles in the means of egress. Fires in clothing racks in corridors will seriously hamper safe evacuation from the area served by the corridor. This problem should not be underestimated. Two recent fires, one in New York (Stauffers Hotel) and one in Massachusetts (Lexington), dramatically showed the tremendous fire load presented by clothing on open coatracks. The second problem is created where the minimum acceptable width of the corridor is reduced.

Exception: Metal lockers may be installed in corridors for storage of clothing and personal effects providing the corridor width is maintained.

The first problem stated above can be corrected by providing metal lockers for storage of clothing and personal effects. This reduces accessibility of the combustibles to arsonists and also compartmentalizes the combustibles. Most fires in school lockers do not extend beyond the locker of origin. Those that do extend do not usually extend beyond the locker(s) adjacent to the locker of origin. However, the corridor must be of such width that it will allow at least the minimum required corridor width to be maintained after the lockers are installed.

10-3.7 Subdivision of Building Spaces.

10-3.7.1   School buildings shall be subdivided into compartments by smoke barriers having a 1-hour fire resistance rating and complying with Section 6-3 where:

(a) The maximum area of a compartment, including the aggregate area of all floors having a common atmosphere, exceeds 30,000 sq ft (2800 sq m); or

(b) The length or width of the building exceeds 300 ft (91 m).

The 300-ft (91-m) limit bears a direct relationship to the travel distance criteria in Chapter 10 and reflects the Committee's concern about the maximum area within an educational facility that would be immediately contaminated by products of combustion from a fire.

The Committee felt it was reasonable and prudent to require smoke barriers at maximum intervals of 300 ft (91 m) so that the products of combustion would affect a limited number of exits at one time.

The provisions of this section were changed in the 1985 Edition of the *Code* to make the provision easier to understand and enforce. Previous editions spaced smoke barriers by corridor length. By using compartment size, the intent of the provision is clear, and hopefully, confusion in enforcement is reduced.

Exception No. 1:   Where all classrooms have exterior exit access in accordance with 5-5.3.

Exception No. 2:   Buildings that consist of only one story and are protected throughout by an approved supervised automatic sprinkler system installed in accordance with Section 7-7.

A primary concern of the Committee is a corridor becoming clogged with smoke resulting in the elimination of exit access. Classrooms with exterior exit access provide the occupants a ready alternate means of escape in the event that a corridor fills with smoke.

The Committee felt that the record of automatic fire sprinklers was a good reason to reduce the compartmentation requirements. However, in multistory arrangements the Committee felt compartmentation was important to provide refuge for occupants on upper floors. This requirement is especially important for the handicapped or others who are temporarily impaired physically.

10-3.7.2   The maximum area of a smoke compartment shall not exceed 30,000 sq ft (2800 sq m) with no dimension exceeding 300 ft (91 m).

This provision applies only if 10-3.7.1 applies. If one is exempted from 10-3.7.1, then 10-3.7.3 does not apply.

SECTION 10-4   SPECIAL PROVISIONS

10-4.1 Windowless or Underground Buildings.

The provisions of this chapter pertaining to underground buildings were totally revised in the 1985 Edition of the *Code*. In recognition of the potential hazard that underground buildings present, the *Code* requires compliance with Section 30-7 and, in addition, requires compliance with the provisions of 8-4.1.3 through 8-4.1.6 if the underground building has an educational occupancy more than 30 ft (9.1 m) below the level of exit discharge, or if an educational building has a floor level more than 30 ft (9.1 m) below the level of exit discharge.

Two Exceptions to the requirements are provided for areas used only for service functions, such as boiler rooms, heater rooms, etc., and for assembly uses where there is no occupiable intervening level between the assembly occupancy and the level of exit discharge.

10-4.1.1   Windowless or underground buildings shall comply with this chapter and Section 30-7.

10-4.1.2   Underground buildings or portions of buildings having a floor level more than 30 ft (9.1 m) below the level of exit discharge shall comply with the requirements contained in 10-4.1.3 through 10-4.1.6.

Exception No. 1:   Areas within buildings used only for service to the building such as boiler/heater rooms, cable vaults, dead storage, and the like.

Exception No. 2:   Auditoriums without intervening occupiable levels complying with the requirements of Chapter 8.

10-4.1.3   Each level more than 30 ft (9.1 m) below the level of exit discharge shall be divided into not less than two smoke compartments by a smoke barrier complying with Section 6-3 and having a 1-hour fire resistance rating.

(a) Each smoke compartment shall have access to at least one exit without passing through the other required compartment. Any door connecting required compartments shall be tight-fitting, 1-hour fire doors, designed and installed to minimize passage of smoke and to close and latch automatically upon detection of smoke.

(b) Each smoke compartment shall be provided with a mechanical means of moving people vertically, such as an elevator or escalator.

(c) Each smoke compartment shall have an independent air supply and exhaust system capable of smoke control or smoke exhaust functions and providing a minimum smoke exhaust rate of six air changes per hour.

(d) Each smoke compartment shall be provided with an automatic smoke detection system throughout. The system shall be designed such that the activation of any two detectors shall cause the smoke control system to operate and the building voice alarm to sound.

10-4.1.4   The building shall be provided with emergency lighting in accordance with Section 5-9.

10-4.1.5   Any required smoke control or exhaust system shall be provided with a standby power system complying with Article 701 of NFPA 70, *National Electrical Code.*

10-4.1.6   The building shall be provided with an approved supervised voice alarm system in accordance with Section 7-6. The voice alarm system shall comply with 7-6.3.8. A prerecorded evacuation message shall be permitted.

10-4.2 High Rise Buildings.   High rise buildings shall comply with Section 30-8.

The Committee felt that an educational high rise building presents many of the same problems to the occupants and fire fighting forces that are presented by other occupancy classes in high rise buildings.

10-4.3 Flexible Plan and Open Plan Buildings.   Flexible plan and open plan buildings shall also comply with the provisions of Section 10-6.

10-4.4 Operating Features.   (*See Chapter 31.*)

SECTION 10-5   BUILDING SERVICES

10-5.1 Utilities.   Utilities shall comply with the provisions of Section 7-1.

10-5.2 Heating, Ventilating, and Air Conditioning Equipment.

10-5.2.1   Heating, ventilating, and air conditioning equipment shall comply with the provisions of Section 7-2.

10-5.2.2   Unvented fuel-fired heating equipment shall be prohibited.

The Committee did not feel that it was reasonable life safety to have unvented fuel-fired equipment in a school building with children. It was felt that the typical use of unvented equipment would jeopardize the life safety of the students, because proper venting may not be provided and potential misuse by students or injury to students, especially younger children, may occur

10-5.3 Elevators, Dumbwaiters, and Vertical Conveyors.   Elevators, dumbwaiters, and vertical conveyors shall comply with the provisions of Section 7-4.

10-5.4 Rubbish Chutes, Incinerators, and Laundry Chutes.   Rubbish chutes, incinerators, and laundry chutes shall comply with the provisions of Section 7-5.

SECTION 10-6   FLEXIBLE PLAN AND OPEN PLAN BUILDINGS

The 1985 Edition of the *Code* contained a major revision of the provisions pertaining to flexible and open plan schools. The intent of the revision was to make the *Code* easier to use while improving life safety in these special arrangements. This section requires that flexible and open plan schools comply with Sections 10-1 through 10-5, except as modified by this section.

10-6.1 General Requirements.

10-6.1.1   Flexible and open plan buildings shall comply with Sections 10-1 through 10-5, except as modified by this section.

10-6.2 Means of Egress Requirements.

10-6.2.1   Each room occupied by more than 300 persons shall have two or more means of egress entering into separate atmospheres. Where three or more means of egress are required, not more than two of them shall enter into the same atmosphere.

Rooms occupied by more than 300 persons require special treatment in flexible and open plan schools. To ensure the safety of such a large number of persons contained in one room, means of egress must be arranged so that each of the separate egress paths traverse atmospheres separate from each other. If more than two separate means of egress paths are required, no more than two shall pass through the same atmosphere. By this arrangement, one fire cannot contaminate or block all exits in an open plan or flexible plan building.

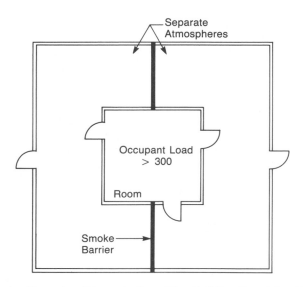

Figure 10-15.   Example of Room in Open Plan Building Requiring Two or More Means of Egress into Separate Atmospheres.

10-6.2.2   Exit access from interior rooms may pass through an adjoining or an intervening room provided that the travel distances do not exceed those set forth in 10-2.6. Foyers and lobbies constructed as required for corridors shall not be construed as intervening rooms.

10-6.2.3   Where the only means of egress from an interior room or rooms is through an adjoining or intervening room, smoke detectors shall be installed in the area of the common atmosphere through which the means of egress must pass. The detectors shall actuate alarms audible in the interior room and shall be connected to the school fire alarm system.

Exception No. 1: *Smoke detectors are not required where the aggregate occupant load is less than ten.*

Exception No. 2: *Interior rooms used exclusively for mechanical and public utility service to the buildings.*

Exception No. 3: *Where the building is protected throughout by an approved automatic sprinkler system in accordance with Section 7-7.*

If the only means of egress from a room is through an adjoining or intervening room, smoke detectors must be installed in the room through which the means of egress must pass. This is because occupants of the interior room may not be aware of a fire or smoke condition in the intervening room, the room that provides their only means of egress. Alarm-sounding smoke detectors provide the occupants with an early warning so that they can safely pass through the room. It should be noted that if a corridor does not meet the corridor construction requirements, it would be considered an intervening room. (*See the definition of interior room in 10-1.3.*)

10-6.2.4   Flexible plan schools may have walls and partitions rearranged periodically only after revised plans or diagrams have been approved by the authority having jurisdiction.

Approval of revised plans or diagrams is necessary to avoid the possibility of circuitous exit paths or other arrangements not complying with the intent of the *Code.* Also note that flexible plan buildings are required to meet the requirements for corridor protection as well as subdivision of building spaces.

10-6.2.5   Open plan schools shall have furniture, fixtures, or low-height partitions so arranged that exits will be clearly visible and unobstructed, and exit paths are direct, not circuitous. If paths or corridors are established, they shall be at least as wide as required by 10-2.3.3.

Low-height partitions are 5 ft (152 cm) or less in height.
Corridors discussed in 10-6.2.5 must not have full-height partitions in order to provide unobstructed visual surveillance of the entire open plan area by members of the faculty located at any point in the area. The requirements for corridor protection contained in 10-3.6 do not apply to open plan schools. However, the requirements of 10-3.7 on subdivision of building spaces do apply.

SECTION 10-7   DAY-CARE CENTERS

The day-care provisions are arranged to stand on their own from the rest of the chapter. The provisions of Sections 10-2 through 10-6 do not apply unless specifically referenced. The provisions include adult day care. Throughout the sections, the term "child" has been changed to "client" so that the provisions cover the entire age spectrum. Of course, in certain instances, provisions apply only to children; in those cases, the text has retained the term "child."

Formal Interpretation 76-108
Reference: 10-7 (11-7), 10-8 (11-8), 10-9 (11-9)

Question 1: Do the requirements of Sections 10-7 (11-7), 10-8 (11-8), or 10-9 (11-9) apply to church programs that provide day-care services to church members only, on a nonprofit basis?

Answer: Yes.

Question 2: Are churches also required to meet the provisions of Sections 10-7 (11-7), 10-8 (11-8), or 10-9 (11-9) in order to operate a church nursery while church services are being held?

Answer: Yes.

Question 3: Does Section 1-5 permit the city to grant an exception in these cases?

Answer: The authority having jurisdiction is given the power to grant exceptions where it is clearly evident that reasonable safety is thereby secured.

Issue Edition: 1976
Reference: 9-5.3, 9-5.4, 9-5.5
Date: March 1979

10-7.1 General Requirements.

Table 10-1 summarizes the *Code*'s requirements for the three types of day-care centers.

Table 10-1.   Minimum Requirements For Day-Care Centers

	Center		Group Home	Family Home
Number of Clients	>12		7 to 12	≤6
Number of Clients under Two Years	Any		3	2
Recommended Staff to Client Ratio	Age (yrs) <2 2-3 3-5 5-7 >7	Ratio 1:3 1:5 1:10 1:12 1:15	2:12	1:6
Building Construction (permissible height vs. age of clients)	See 10-7.1.6.1		Rec. meet applicable building codes	Rec. meet applicable building codes
Occupant Load Factor	1 person/35 sq ft*		NR	NR

*Conversion: 1 ft = .3048 m.   NR = No requirement.

Table 10-1.   Continued

	Center	Group Home	Family Home
Area of Refuge	If center above fifth floor	NR	NR
Number of Exits	2 remote (see 10-7.2.4)	2 remote (see 10-8.2.4)	2 remote (see 10-9.2.4)
Travel Distance to Exit† (ft)*	100 (from room door) 150 (from any point in a room)	150 (from any point)	150 (from any point)
Exit Discharge	To outside	At least one directly to outside	At least one directly to outside
Illumination of Means of Egress	Per Section 5-8	Per Section 5-8	Per Section 5-8
Emergency Lighting	Per 10-2.9	NR (See 31-3.5)	NR (See 31-3.5)
Door Latches (closet)	Child opens from inside	Child opens from inside	Child opens from inside
Door Locks (bathroom)	Staff unlocks	Staff unlocks	Staff unlocks
Protection of Vertical Openings	See Section 6-2	See 10-8.3.1	NR
Hazard Protection	1-hr enclosure or automatic sprinklers (see 10-7.3.2)	NR	NR
Class of Interior Finish	A (stairways, corridors, lobbies) B (other areas)	B (exits) C (all other spaces)	B (corridors, stairways, lobbies, and exits) C (all other spaces)
Class of Interior Floor Finish	I or II (corridors and exits)	NR	NR
Alarm System	Manual (direct connection to fire department if > 100 clients)	NR	NR
Smoke Detectors	See 10-7.3.4.5	See 10-8.3.4	See 10-9.3.4
Extinguishers	Standpipes if building ≥ 6 stories		
Corridor Protection	Per 10-3.6.1	NR	NR
Electric Equipment	See NFPA 70 (receptacle covers required, Chapter 7)	See NFPA 70 (receptacle covers required, Chapter 7)	See NFPA 70 (receptacle covers required, Chapter 7)
HVAC	See Chapter 7	Separated from spaces by screens/partitions	See 10-9.5.2

*Conversion: 1 ft = .3048 m.   NR = No requirement.   †50 ft increase if sprinklered.

10-7.1.1 Application.

10-7.1.1.1* The requirements detailed in Section 10-7, Day-Care Centers (more than 12 clients), are based on the minimum staff-to-client ratios that follow:

Staff Ratio	Age
1:3	0 to 2
1:5	2 to 3
1:10	3 to 5
1:12	5 to 7
1:15	7 and over

The staff-to-client ratios may be modified by the authority having jurisdiction where safeguards, in addition to those specified by this section, are provided.

A-10-7.1.1.1   It should be noted that this paragraph does not require the staff ratios indicated but only states that the requirements of this section are based on these staff ratios. If these staff ratios are not maintained, it would be the responsibility of the authority having jurisdiction to determine what additional safeguards above and beyond the requirements of this section would be necessary. Typical additional provisions may include restricting the day-care center to the level of exit discharge, requiring additional smoke detection, requiring automatic sprinkler protection, requiring better or additional means of egress and similar types of items depending upon the situation.

10-7.1.1.2*   This section establishes life safety requirements for day-care centers in which more than 12 clients receive care, maintenance, and supervision by other than their relative(s) or legal guardian(s) for less than 24 hours per day. The provisions of Sections 10-2 through 10-6 shall not apply to this section unless a specific requirement is referenced by this section.

A-10-7.1.1.2   Day-care centers do not provide for the full-time maintenance of a client. Occupancies that provide primary place of residence are dealt with in other occupancies. See Chapters 16 through 22, "Residential Occupancies."

> The intent of 10-7.1.1.2 is to differentiate between institutions where clients are in residence 24 hours a day (such as orphanages) and day-care facilities where clients who normally reside at another location are provided care. A facility supplying "total care" for each client would provide laundries, dormitories, cafeterias, and other ancillary services not found in a day-care center. The life safety requirements of such a facility would be governed by other occupancy provisions of the *Code.*

10-7.1.1.3   Centers housing children 6 years of age and older shall conform to the requirements for educational occupancies, except as noted herein.

> Centers that provide care only for children of school age are required to conform to the requirements for educational occupancies and to the special requirements for such facilities where they are located in buildings of other occupancies.

10-7.1.1.4   Where a facility houses more than one age group, the requirements for the younger shall apply unless the area housing the younger is maintained as a separate fire area.

Exception*: Staff-to-client ratios of 10-7.1.1.1 shall be based on the number of clients in each age category.

A-10-7.1.1.4 Exception   An example of this Exception is illustrated as follows: A center has 43 children

Three children age under two (1:3)	- 1 staff
Ten children age two to three (1:5)	- 2 staff

Thirty children age three to five (1:10)   - 3 staff
Total   - 6 staff

Therefore, the required staff for this center is six, not 15, which would be required for 43 children on a 1 to 3 staff ratio.

A separate fire area is usually constructed with walls that have a fire resistance rating of 2 hours. Most facilities governed by this chapter will be maintained as separate atmospheres through smoke barriers having a 1-hour fire resistance rating.

It was brought to the Committee's attention that some people were interpreting this section to apply to staff ratios. The Committee felt that to use the youngest age group to establish staff-to-client ratios for the entire group was too restrictive and did not meet the intent of the *Code* and, therefore, the Exception and appendix note were added.

10-7.1.2 Mixed Occupancies.

(a) Where centers are located in a building containing mixed occupancies, the occupancies shall be separated by 1-hour fire barriers.

Exception to (a): In assembly occupancies used primarily for worship.

(b) Centers in Apartment Buildings.

1. If the two exit accesses from the center enter the same corridor as the apartment occupancy, the exit accesses shall be separated in the corridor by a smoke barrier having not less than a 1-hour fire resistance rating. The smoke barrier shall be so located that there is an exit on each side of it.

2. The door in the smoke barrier shall be not less than 36 in. (91 cm) wide.

3. The door assembly in the smoke barrier shall have a fire protection rating of at least 20 minutes and shall be self-closing or automatic-closing in accordance with 5-2.1.8.

Where a center is located in a building housing another occupancy, the operators of the center usually have no control of the safety procedures and precautions practiced outside the center. Paragraph 10-7.1.2 requires additional protection to minimize the clients' exposure to potential hazards outside the center.

The rationale used here for protection with a 20-minute door is the same as that used in Chapters 12 and 13 for health care facilities. The fuel load of the occupancy is not considered great enough to provide a severe attack on the door. This minimum construction will provide sufficient protection against flame and a good seal against smoke spread. The 20-minute door, coupled with the 1-hour wall, provides a barrier that will either contain a fire within a space for a limited time after it has been evacuated, or will prevent a fire from entering an occupied space for a period of time.

10-7.1.3 Special Definitions.   (None.)

10-7.1.4 Classification of Occupancy.   For the purposes of this section, clients are classified in age groups as follows: clients under 6 years of age, and clients 6 years of age and older.

10-7.1.5 Classification of Hazard of Contents.   The contents shall be classified as ordinary hazard in accordance with Section 4-2.

10-7.1.6 Minimum Construction Requirements.

10-7.1.6.1   Centers shall not be located above the heights indicated for the types of construction given in Table 10-7.1.6.1. (*See 6-2.1.*)

Table 10-7.1.6.1   Height and Construction Limits

Type of Construction	Age Group	Number of Stories (Stories are counted starting at floor of exit discharge)			
		1	2	3	4 and over
I (443) I (332) II (222)	0 thru 5 6 and older	X X	X X	X X	X X
II (111) III (211) V (111)	0 thru 5 6 and older	X X	X† X	N.P. X†	N.P. N.P.
IV (2HH)	0 thru 5 6 and older	X X	X† X†	N.P. N.P.	N.P. N.P.
II (000)	0 thru 5 6 and older	X X	X† X†	N.P. N.P.	N.P. N.P.
III (200) V (000)	0 thru 5 6 and older	X† X	X† X†	N.P. N.P.	N.P. N.P.

X: Permitted construction type
N.P.: Not Permitted
X†: Permitted if entire building is protected throughout by an approved automatic sprinkler system.

10-7.1.6.2 Location.   The story below the level of exit discharge may be used in buildings of any construction type other than Type II (000), Type III (200), and Type V (000). (*See 10-7.2.4.2.*)

10-7.1.7 Occupant Load.   The occupant load for which means of egress shall be provided for any floor shall be the maximum number of persons intended to occupy that floor but not less than one person for each 35 sq ft (3.3 sq m) of net floor area used by the clients.

Where a center occupies a portion of a floor on which another occupancy exists, the occupant load for that floor is the sum of the occupant loads of the two occupancies. For example:

Net Floor Area (ft^2)		Occupant Load Factor (ft^2/person)		Occupant Load
Day-Care Center 1,750	÷	35	=	50
Assembly Occupancy 3,000	÷	7	=	429

By addition, the total occupant load for which means of egress must be provided would be 479. (*Also see commentary on 10-1.7.*)

10-7.2 Means of Egress Requirements.

10-7.2.1 General.   (None.)

10-7.2.2 Types of Exits.   (*See 10-2.2.*)

10-7.2.2.1 Stairs.   Exit stairs shall be enclosed in accordance with Chapter 5.

Paragraph 10-7.2.2.1 in conjunction with 10-7.3.1 excludes use of the provision in the Exception to 10-3.1.2 to permit an unenclosed stair between two adjacent floors when young children are on upper floors of the building. This is in recognition of the fact that young children have a low tolerance to smoke and are not capable of taking action for self-preservation on their own behalf. Thus, the *Code* attempts to protect them by enclosing all vertical openings.

10-7.2.2.2 Areas of Refuge.   In buildings over five stories above ground level, areas of refuge shall be provided for occupants of day-care centers by horizontal exits.

In all cases, where day-care centers are found on upper floors of tall buildings, areas of refuge must be designed so that the clients will survive a fire. Five stories or approximately 75 ft (23 m) is the maximum height at which the fire department can be expected to rescue the occupants of a building from outside. However, many fire departments do not have the equipment to reach this height, and in such locations, areas of refuge are necessary at lower levels.

In any event, dependence on rescue by the fire department is not prudent. The time, number of personnel, and effort involved in rescuing one person by using an extension ladder is so great that it is not possible to rescue a large number of occupants by this method.

10-7.2.3 Capacity of Means of Egress.   (*See 10-2.3.*)

10-7.2.4 Number of Exits.

10-7.2.4.1   Each floor occupied by clients shall have not less than two remote exits in accordance with Chapter 5.

10-7.2.4.2   Where the story below the level of exit discharge is occupied as a day-care center, the following apply:

(a) One means of egress shall be an outside or interior stair in accordance with 5-2.2. An interior stair, if used, shall only serve the level below the level of exit discharge. The interior stair may communicate with the level of exit discharge; however, the exit route from the level of exit discharge shall not pass through the stair enclosure.

(b) The second means of egress may be via an unenclosed stairway separated from the level of exit discharge in accordance with 6-2.4.3. The path of egress travel on the level of exit discharge shall be protected in accordance with 5-1.3.4.

The requirements for using stories below the level of exit discharge have been revised for the 1988 *Code*. The intent is to make the *Code* both easier to understand and more realistic to enforce, while providing two protected ways out. Figure 10-16 illustrates the intent of 10-7.2.4.2.

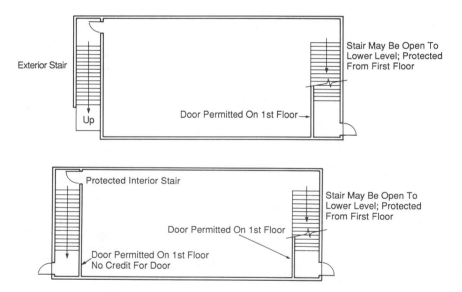

Figure 10-16. Egress for Levels Below the Level of Exit Discharge. Two methods of complying with 10-7.2.4.2 are illustrated. One stair must be a properly protected exit discharging outside, either an interior stair or outside stair. The other stair may be open to the lower level but must be separated from the first floor. This second way out either discharges directly outside or discharges through a corridor protected in accordance with 5-1.3.3.

10-7.2.5 Arrangement of Means of Egress. (*Where the story below the exit discharge is used, see also 10-7.2.4.2.*)

10-7.2.5.1 Means of egress shall be arranged in accordance with Section 5-5. Dead ends shall not exceed 20 ft (6.1 m).

Chapter 5 does not allow dead-end corridors except in accordance with the occupancy chapters. The Committee recognized that 20 ft (6.1 m) has been the accepted standard in educational occupancies and felt that it would be reasonable to retain it.

10-7.2.6 Travel Distance to Exits.

10-7.2.6.1   Travel distance shall be measured in accordance with Section 5-6.

10-7.2.6.2   Travel distance:

(a) Between any room door intended as exit access and an exit shall not exceed 100 ft (30 m);

(b) Between any point in a room and an exit shall not exceed 150 ft (45 m);

(c) Between any point in a sleeping room and an exit access door of that room shall not exceed 50 ft (15 m).

Exception: The travel distance in (a) and (b) above may be increased by 50 ft (15 m) in buildings protected throughout by an approved supervised automatic sprinkler system in accordance with Section 7-7.

Paragraph 10-7.2.6.2 is structured to state the same thing several different ways. As shown in Figure 10-17, the maximum travel distance from a room door (exit access to the corridor) to an exit door is 100 ft (30 m). The total travel distance from any point (such as in a room) to an exit is 150 ft (45 m). The maximum travel distance from a point in a sleeping room to an exit access door is 50 ft (15 m). This in-room travel distance limit may not be increased even if the building is sprinklered.

Note that the *Code* requires the sprinkler system to be supervised to take advantage of the additional travel distance.

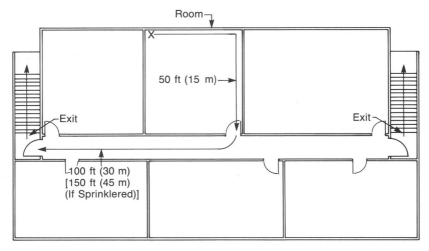

Figure 10-17.   Maximum Travel Distance to Exit, Day-Care Center.

10-7.2.7 Discharge from Exits.   All exits shall discharge directly to the outside.

Exception: As provided in 10-7.2.4.2.

10-7.2.8 Illumination of Means of Egress.   Illumination of the means of egress shall be provided in accordance with Section 5-8.

10-7.2.9 Emergency Lighting.   Emergency lighting shall be provided in accordance with 10-2.9.

10-7.2.10 Marking of Means of Egress.   Means of egress shall have signs in accordance with Section 5-10.

10-7.2.11 Special Features.

10-7.2.11.1*   Every closet door latch shall be such that children can open the door from inside the closet.

A-10-7.2.11.1   The purpose of this requirement is to prevent arrangements where a child can be trapped in a closet. It is intended that this provision be broadly interpreted by the authority having jurisdiction to include equipment like refrigerators or freezers.

10-7.2.11.2   Every bathroom door lock shall be designed to permit opening of the locked door from the outside in an emergency. The opening device shall be readily accessible to the staff.

10-7.2.11.3 Panic Hardware or Fire Exit Hardware.   Any door in a required means of egress from an area having an occupant load of 100 or more persons may be provided with a latch or lock only if it is panic hardware or fire exit hardware.

> This paragraph is based on the total occupant load of the area served and not the required capacity of the door. For example, if an area has an occupant load of 120 persons and is served by 3 doors, each door need only have capacity for 40 persons, but since all these doors serve an area with "100 or more persons," then any latches on these doors must be released by panic hardware or fire exit hardware.

10-7.2.11.4 Windows for Rescue and Ventilation.   Every room or space normally subject to client occupancy, other than bathrooms, shall have at least one outside window for emergency rescue or ventilation. Such window shall be openable from the inside without the use of tools and provide a clear opening of not less than 20 in. (50.8 cm) in width, 24 in. (61 cm) in height, and 5.7 sq ft (.53 sq m) in area. The bottom of the opening shall be not more than 44 in. (112 cm) above the floor.

In rooms located greater than three stories above grade, the openable clear height, width, and area of the window may be modified to the dimensions necessary for ventilation.

Exception No. 1:   In buildings protected throughout by an approved automatic sprinkler system in accordance with Section 7-7.

Exception No. 2:   Where the room or space has a door leading directly to the outside of the building.

The dimensions specified for windows used for emergency rescue or for ventilation are based on simulations of emergency rescue conducted by the San Diego Fire Department. Windows providing clear openings of identical dimensions are also required for rescue or ventilation in one- and two-family dwellings. Figure 10-10 (on page 454) illustrates two configurations that achieve the required area of 5.7 sq ft (.53 sq m).

Although the *Code* intends the fire department or others to assist students, particularly over ladders, if these windows must be used as a supplementary means of escape, the windows should permit small children in the lower grades to escape unaided. Therefore, storm sashes, screens, or devices in front of the windows must be easy to open or remove and the sills must be low enough for the children to reach.

Where the location of windows precludes their use for rescue or escape, they may still provide trapped children with air for breathing in smoke-filled rooms.

Windows may be omitted if a room has a door leading directly to the outside or if the building is totally sprinklered.

The Committee did not feel it was practical to expect someone to use a window above the third story as an escape window. However, it is reasonable to expect the window to be usable for ventilation during a fire.

Note that Exception No. 1 requires that the building be protected throughout by an automatic sprinkler system. One question that is often asked is: If there are only a couple of windowless rooms can we just sprinkler those rooms? The answer is no! It must be remembered that the reason for the window is the potential blockage of the interior corridor by smoke from a fire in another part of the building. Putting sprinklers only in the windowless rooms would do nothing about smoke emanating from other areas.

10-7.3 Protection.

10-7.3.1 Protection of Vertical Openings.   Any vertical opening shall be enclosed and protected in accordance with Section 6-2.

10-7.3.2 Protection from Hazards.

10-7.3.2.1   Rooms or spaces for the storage, processing, or use of the materials specified in this section shall be protected in accordance with the following:

(a) Rooms or spaces used for the storage of combustible supplies in quantities deemed hazardous by the authority having jurisdiction, hazardous materials in quantities deemed hazardous by recognized standards, or fuel shall be separated from the remainder of the building by construction having not less than a 1-hour fire resistance rating with all openings protected by self-closing or smoke-actuated fire doors, or such rooms or spaces may be protected by an automatic extinguishing system as set forth in Section 6-4.

(b) Rooms or spaces used for processing or use of combustible supplies in quantities considered hazardous by the authority having jurisdiction, hazardous materials, or for flammable or combustible liquids in quantities deemed hazardous by recognized standards shall be separated from the remainder of the building by construction having not less than a 1-hour fire resistance rating with all openings protected by self-closing or smoke-actuated fire doors and shall also be protected by an automatic extinguishing system as set forth in Section 6-4.

(c) Boiler and furnace rooms, laundries, and maintenance shops, including woodworking and painting areas, shall be separated from the remainder of the building by construction having not less than a 1-hour fire resistance rating with all openings protected by self-closing or smoke-actuated fire doors.

Exception to (c): Rooms enclosing air-handling equipment.

(d)* Where automatic extinguishing systems are used to meet the requirements of this section, the rooms or spaces shall be separated from the remainder of the building by construction that resists the passage of smoke.

A-10-7.3.2.1(d)   It is not the intent of this provision to require a smoke barrier that meets the requirements of Section 6-3.

(e) Where automatic extinguishing is used to meet the requirements of this section, the protection may be in accordance with 7-7.1.2.

Exception: Food preparation facilities protected in accordance with 7-2.3 are not required to have openings protected between food preparation areas and dining areas. Where domestic cooking equipment is used for food warming or limited cooking, protection or segregation of food preparation facilities is not required if approved by the authority having jurisdiction.

> The intent of 10-7.3.2.1 is to specify the degree of protection necessary for certain hazardous areas. It has been divided into three sections based on the degree of hazard. The hazards noted in item (a) are required to be enclosed in 1-hour construction or protected by sprinklers. If the sprinkler option is chosen, an enclosure is still required by item (d); however, the enclosure need not be rated, but only form a membrane against the passage of smoke.
>
> The Committee felt that although sprinklers are provided and therefore fire-rated barriers may not be needed [see (a)], some barriers to control smoke migration is needed. Solid construction materials, such as glass or other non-fire-rated materials are acceptable if they are installed in a manner that will resist smoke passing from one compartment to another. The new appendix note emphasizes that it is not the intent to require smoke barriers as provided in Section 6-3. This eliminates the more costly construction of a smoke barrier, which would require dampers and other required equipment.
>
> The hazards noted in item (b) must be enclosed in 1-hour construction and be protected by automatic sprinklers.
>
> The hazards noted in item (c) are required to be enclosed in 1-hour construction with no option for a sprinkler equivalency for the enclosure. The Exception to item (c) pertains to rooms housing air-handling equipment only. If the room is used for other purposes, then the provisions of item (a) or (b) apply.

Part (e) has been added as an editorial change to highlight the fact that Chapter 7 makes these requirements available to the user of the *Code*. Paragraph 7-7.1.2 provides an economical way of providing sprinkler protection in small rooms. (*See 10-3.2.3.*)

The intent of the Exception is to provide some barrier between cooking areas and dining areas. Openings in this barrier are not restricted and do not need to be protected. The *Code* is counting on the automatic extinguishing system to control any fire on the cooking surfaces and, thus, no longer requires enclosure by rated construction. The second sentence of the Exception is quite important since this limited use of cooking equipment is often found in day care centers.

Figure 10-18 illustrates the different protection requirements of 10-7.3.2.1.

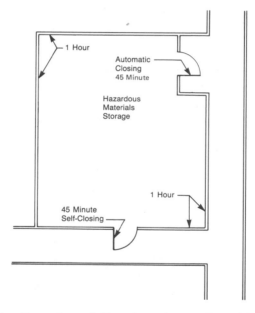

Figure 10-18(a). Protection of Hazardous Areas. Part (a) illustrates one method of complying with 10-7.3.2.1(a). See Figure 10-18(b) for the alternate method.

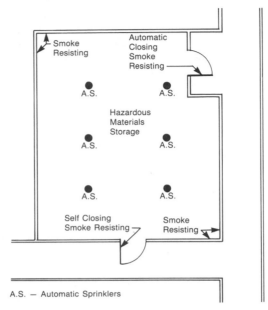

Figure 10-18(b). Protection of Hazardous Areas. Part (b) illustrates an alternate method of complying with 10-7.3.2.1(a). Figure 10-18(a) illustrates another method of compliance.

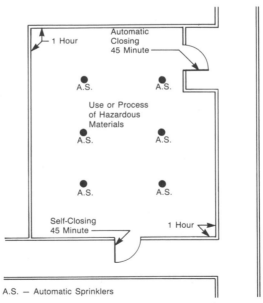

Figure 10-18(c). Protection of Hazardous Areas. Part (c) illustrates the requirements for complying with 10-7.3.2.1(b). Both one hour separation and automatic sprinkler protection is required in this case.

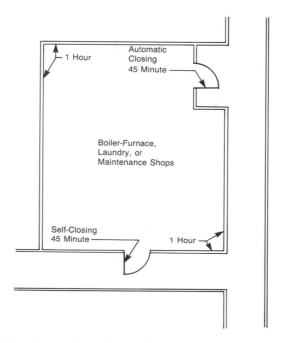

Figure 10-18(d). Protection of Hazardous Areas. Part (d) illustrates the requirements for complying with 10-7.3.2.1(c). Note that the automatic sprinkler option does not exist for these hazardous areas.

10-7.3.2.2   Janitor closets shall be protected by an automatic sprinkler system, which may be in accordance with 7-7.1.2. Doors to janitor closets may have ventilating louvers.

Where janitor closets are located off of corridors, a louvered door is usually provided for ventilation. It is necessary to provide these spaces with automatic sprinkler protection since the louvered door offers little fire resistance and permits a fire in the closet to directly affect the corridor. Paragraph 7-7.1.2 provides an economic method of providing sprinkler protection for such rooms. To accomplish this at reasonable cost, these sprinklers (not more than six in number) may be supplied from the domestic water supply to the closet if the supply is capable of providing the required quantity of water. It is advisable to provide a water-flow switch (*see Chapter* 6) to initiate an alarm when a sprinkler is opened.

The minimum flow of 0.15 gpm/sq ft (6.1 L/min/sq m) is based on the requirements in NFPA 13, *Standard for the Installation of Sprinkler Systems,*[3] for protecting buildings containing ordinary hazards. It is important to ensure that the domestic supply can provide the required flow and pressure at the location.

10-7.3.3 Interior Finish.

10-7.3.3.1   Interior finish for all walls and ceilings shall be Class A or Class B in accordance with Section 6-5. Interior finish in stairways, corridors, and lobbies shall be Class A.

10-7.3.3.2   Floor coverings within corridors and exits shall be Class I or Class II in accordance with Section 6-5.

10-7.3.4 Detection, Alarm, and Communications Systems.

10-7.3.4.1 General.   Day-care centers shall be provided with a fire alarm system in accordance with Section 7-6.

Exception No. 1: Day-care centers housed in one room.

Exception No. 2: Day-care centers with a required staff of fewer than four persons based on 10-7.1.1.1.

10-7.3.4.2 Initiation.   Initiation of the required fire alarm system shall be by manual means and by operation of any required smoke detectors. (*See 10-7.3.4.5.*)

Exception: Single station detectors.

Single station smoke detectors by definition are not connected to an alarm system and are normally installed to provide a local alarm that will alert people in the immediate area that they should exit the area.

10-7.3.4.3 Occupant Notification.   Occupant notification shall be by means of an audible alarm in accordance with 7-6.3.

10-7.3.4.4 Emergency Forces Notification.   Fire department notification shall be accomplished in accordance with 7-6.4.

Exception: Day-care centers with not more than 100 clients.

In all day-care centers, manually operated fire alarm systems should be directly connected to the fire department. The Committee felt compelled to emphasize that in centers that serve more than 100 clients, this arrangement is essential. There are fire departments that will not accept direct alarms. In such cases, positive provisions must be made for rapid notification of the fire department by remote or central station systems.

10-7.3.4.5 Detection.

(a) A smoke detection system shall be installed in accordance with Section 7-6 with placement of detectors in each story in front of doors to the stairways and at no greater than 30 ft (9.1 m) spacing in the corridors of all floors containing the center. Detectors shall also be installed in lounges, recreation areas, and sleeping rooms in the center.

(b) Single station smoke detectors powered by the house electrical service shall be provided in all rooms used for sleeping.

Exception: Centers housed in only one room.

The purpose of this requirement is obvious, but worth noting. In centers housing children younger than six, naps and sleep time are provided. The smoke detection system will provide early warning of an impending fire. An Exception is provided for centers housed in a single room where a fire will be obvious to all occupants.

10-7.3.5 Extinguishment Requirements.

10-7.3.5.1   Standpipes for fire department use shall be installed in all buildings of six stories or more housing day-care centers. (*See Section 7-7.*)

10-7.3.6 Corridors.   Exit access corridors within day-care centers shall comply with 10-3.6.1. (*See 10-7.1.2.*)

The purpose of 10-7.3.6 is to provide a minimum level of compartmentation by use of corridor separation. (*See commentary on 10-3.6.1.*)

10-7.4 Special Provisions.   (None.)

10-7.5 Building Services.

10-7.5.1 Utilities.

10-7.5.1.1   Utilities shall comply with the provisions of Section 7-1.

10-7.5.1.2   Special protective covers for all electrical receptacles shall be installed in all areas occupied by children under 6 years of age.

Children are subject to serious injury if they insert foreign objects into electrical receptacles. Protective covers must be provided and maintained in order to avoid such accidents.

10-7.5.2 Heating, Ventilating, and Air Conditioning Equipment.

10-7.5.2.1   Heating, ventilating, and air conditioning equipment shall be installed in accordance with Section 7-2.

10-7.5.2.2   Unvented fuel-fired room heaters shall not be permitted.

The Committee does not feel that reasonable life safety should allow the use of unvented fuel-fired equipment with children. (*Also see commentary on 10-5.2.2.*)

10-7.5.2.3   Any heating equipment in spaces occupied by children shall be provided with partitions, screens, or other means to protect the children from hot surfaces and open flames. If solid partitions are used to provide such protection, provisions shall be made to assure adequate air for combustion and ventilation for the heating equipment.

The Committee felt it important that safeguards be provided to protect children from the hot surfaces of heating equipment. Young children do not always know the dangers of hot surfaces. The burn injury record clearly indicates that protection be provided. The Committee also wanted to make certain that adequate air is provided for combustion of the heating equipment. Incomplete or inadequate combustion could cause serious injury or death to the occupants.

10-7.5.3 Elevators, Dumbwaiters, and Vertical Conveyors.   Elevators, dumbwaiters, and vertical conveyors shall comply with the provisions of Section 7-4.

10-7.5.4 Rubbish Chutes, Incinerators, and Laundry Chutes.   Rubbish chutes, incinerators, and laundry chutes shall comply with the provisions of Section 7-5.

SECTION 10-8   GROUP DAY-CARE HOMES

Formal Interpretation 76-108
Reference: 10-7 (11-7), 10-8 (11-8), 10-9 (11-9)

Question 1: Do the requirements of Sections 10-7 (11-7), 10-8 (11-8), or 10-9 (11-9) apply to church programs that provide day-care services to church members only, on a nonprofit basis?

Answer: Yes.

Question 2: Are churches also required to meet the provisions of Sections 10-7 (11-7), 10-8 (11-8), or 10-9 (11-9) in order to operate a church nursery while church services are being held?

Answer: Yes.

Question 3: Does Section 1-5 permit the city to grant an exception in these cases?

Answer: The authority having jurisdiction is given the power to grant exceptions where it is clearly evident that reasonable safety is thereby secured.

Issue Edition: 1976
Reference: 9-5.3, 9-5.4, 9-5.5
Date: March 1979

10-8.1 General Requirements.

10-8.1.1 Application.

10-8.1.1.1*   This section establishes life safety requirements for group day-care homes in which at least 7 but not more than 12 clients receive care, maintenance, and supervision by other than their relatives or legal guardian(s) for less than 24 hours per day (generally within a dwelling unit). The provisions of Sections 10-2 through 10-6 shall not apply to this section unless a specific requirement is referenced by this section.

A-10-8.1.1.1   Group day-care homes do not provide for the full-time maintenance of a client. Occupancies that provide a primary place of residence are dealt with in other occupancies. See Chapters 16 through 22, "Residential Occupancies."

These provisions are written keeping in mind that the typical group day-care home is usually in a residential setting.

10-8.1.1.2   The requirements detailed in Section 10-8 are based on a minimum staff-to-client ratio of two staff for up to 12 clients, with no more than three clients under age two. This staff-to-client ratio may be modified by the authority having jurisdiction where safeguards, in addition to those specified by this section, are provided.

If these staff ratios are not maintained, it would be the responsibility of the authority having jurisdiction to determine what additional safeguards above and beyond the requirements of this section would be necessary. Typical additional provisions may include restricting the group day-care home to the level of exit discharge, requiring additional smoke detection, requiring automatic sprinkler protection, requiring better or additional means of egress, and similar types of items depending upon the situation.

10-8.1.2 Mixed Occupancies.

(a) Where a group home is located in a building containing mixed occupancies, the occupancies shall be separated by 1-hour fire barriers.

Exception to (a): In assembly occupancies used primarily for worship.

(b) Homes in Apartment Buildings.

1. If the two exit accesses from the home enter the same corridor as the apartment occupancy, the exit accesses shall be separated in the corridor by a smoke barrier having not less than a 1-hour fire resistance rating. The smoke barrier shall be so located that there is an exit on each side of it.

2. The door in the smoke barrier shall be not less than 36 in. (91 cm) wide.

3. The door assembly in the smoke barrier shall have a fire protection rating of at least 20 minutes and shall be self-closing or automatic-closing in accordance with 5-2.1.8.

Group day-care homes are often found in buildings housing occupancies such as apartments, stores, or assembly occupancies. In such buildings, exit accesses usually open into a corridor. Paragraph 10-8.1.2(b) describes the requirements for safeguarding the integrity of at least one egress path from such a facility.

10-8.1.3 Special Definitions.   (None.)

10-8.1.4 Classification of Occupancy.   No Requirements.

10-8.1.5 Classification of Hazard of Contents. The contents shall be classified as ordinary hazard in accordance with Section 4-2.

10-8.1.6 Minimum Construction Requirements. (None.)

10-8.1.7 Occupant Load. No Special Requirements.

10-8.2 Means of Egress Requirements.

10-8.2.1 General. (None.)

10-8.2.2 Types of Exits. *(See 10-8.2.4.)*

10-8.2.3 Capacity of Means of Egress. *(See 10-2.3.)*

10-8.2.4 Number of Exits.

10-8.2.4.1 Each floor occupied by clients shall have not less than two remote means of escape.

> This is similar to the requirements of Chapter 22 for one- and two-family dwellings; however, 10-8.2.4.2 and 10-8.2.4.3 provide for an increase over what would normally be required for a private dwelling.

10-8.2.4.2 Where spaces on the floor above the floor of exit discharge are used by clients, at least one means of egress shall be an exit discharging directly to the outside. The second means of escape may be a window in accordance with 10-2.11.1. No room or space shall be occupied for living or sleeping purposes that is accessible only by ladder, folding stairs, or through a trap door.

> The second floor of a typical single family dwelling is served by an open stair. This would require that the second floor be served by an enclosed exit if clients are upstairs.

10-8.2.4.3 Where clients are located on a story (basement) below the level of exit discharge, at least one means of egress shall be an exit discharging directly to the outside, and the vertical travel to ground level shall not exceed 8 ft (244 cm). The second means of escape may be a window in accordance with 10-2.11.1. No facility shall be located more than one story below the ground. Any stairway to the story above shall be cut off by a fire barrier containing a door of at least a 20-minute fire protection rating, equipped with a self-closing device.

> Similar to the requirement of 10-8.2.4.2 for a second floor, this mandates that when clients are below the level of exit discharge, at least one true exit be provided. In addition, any stairway to the first floor would require at least 20-minute protection.
>
> As illustrated in Figure 10-19, there must be an exit directly from a group day-care center located in a basement to the outside, with vertical travel to ground level not exceeding 8 ft (244 cm). If a stairway to the story above were provided, it would have to be cut off from the basement by a fire barrier containing a door with a fire protection rating of at least 20 minutes.

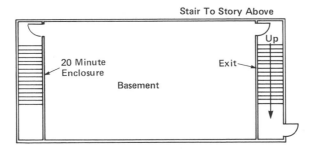

Figure 10-19.   Exit Requirements for Group Day-Care Center in Basement.

10-8.2.5 Arrangement of Means of Egress.   *(Where a story above or below the exit discharge is used, see 10-8.2.4.)*

10-8.2.5.1   Means of egress shall be arranged in accordance with Section 5-5. Dead ends shall not exceed 20 ft (6.1 m).

Chapter 5 does not allow for dead ends unless provided for by the occupancy chapters. The Committee felt that 20 ft (6.1 m) continues to be a reasonable distance for these types of occupancies.

10-8.2.6 Travel Distance to Exits.   *(See 10-2.6.)*

10-8.2.7 Discharge from Exits.   (Where the story above or below the exit discharge is used, see 10-8.2.4.)

10-8.2.8 Illumination of Means of Egress.   Illumination of the means of egress shall be provided in accordance with Section 5-8.

10-8.2.9 Emergency Lighting.   No Requirements.

10-8.2.10 Marking of Means of Egress.   No Requirements.

10-8.2.11 Special Requirements.

10-8.2.11.1*   Every closet door latch shall be such that children can open the door from the inside of the closet.

A-10-8.2.11.1   The purpose of this requirement is to prevent arrangements where a child can be trapped in a closet. It is intended that this provision be broadly interpreted by the authority having jurisdiction to include equipment like refrigerators or freezers.

10-8.2.11.2   Every bathroom door lock shall be designed to permit opening of the locked door from outside in an emergency. The opening device shall be readily accessible to the staff.

10-8.3 Protection.

10-8.3.1 Protection of Vertical Openings.   The doorway between the level of exit discharge and any floor below shall be equipped with a door assembly having a 20-minute fire protection rating. Where the floor above the floor of exit discharge is used for sleeping purposes, there shall be a door assembly having a 20-minute fire protection rating at the top or bottom of each stairway.

Also see 10-8.2.4.2 and 10-8.2.4.3.

10-8.3.2 Protection from Hazards.   No Requirements.

10-8.3.3 Interior Finish.

10-8.3.3.1   The interior finish in exits shall be Class A or B in accordance with Section 6-5.

10-8.3.3.2   Interior finish in occupied spaces in the home shall be Class A, B or C, in accordance with Section 6-5.

10-8.3.4 Detection, Alarm, and Communications Systems.

10-8.3.4.1   Within the group day-care home, smoke detectors shall be installed in accordance with 7-6.2.9.

Exception: Houses housing clients 6 years of age or older if no sleeping facilities are provided.

10-8.3.4.2   Where the group day-care home is located within a building of another occupancy, such as in apartment or office buildings, any corridors serving the group day-care home shall be provided with a smoke detection system in accordance with Section 7-6, with placement of detectors at no greater than 30 ft (9.1 m) spacing.

10-8.3.4.3   Single station smoke detectors powered by the house electrical service shall be provided in all rooms used for sleeping.

The provisions of 10-8.3.4 are two-fold: first, to provide single station smoke detectors within the group day-care home in accordance with NFPA 74, *Standard for the Installation, Maintenance, and Use of Household Fire Warning Equipment*[4]; and second, to provide a smoke detection system in the corridor serving the group day-care home where in a building of mixed occupancy. In addition, 10-8.3.4.3 requires single station smoke detectors in each sleeping room, which is not required by NFPA 74.

10-8.4 Special Provisions.   (None.)

10-8.5 Building Services.

10-8.5.1 Electrical Services.

10-8.5.1.1   Electrical wiring shall be installed in accordance with Section 7-1.

10-8.5.1.2   Special protective covers for electrical receptacles shall be installed in all areas occupied by children under 6 years of age.

10-8.5.2 Heating, Ventilating, and Air Conditioning Equipment.

10-8.5.2.1   Heating, ventilating, and air conditioning equipment shall be installed in accordance with Section 7-2.

10-8.5.2.2 Unvented fuel-fired room heaters shall not be permitted.

The Committee does not feel that reasonable life safety should allow the use of unvented fuel-fired equipment with children. (*Also see commentary on 10-5.2.2.*)

10-8.5.2.3 Any heating equipment in spaces occupied by children shall be provided with partitions, screens or other means, to protect the children from hot surfaces and open flames. If solid partitions are used to provide such protection, provisions shall be made to assure adequate air for combustion and ventilation for the heating equipment.

The Committee feels it important that safeguards be provided to protect children from the hot surfaces of heating equipment. Young children do not always know the dangers of hot surfaces. The burn injury record clearly indicates that protection be provided. The Committee also wanted to make certain that adequate air is provided for combustion of the heating equipment. Incomplete or inadequate combustion could cause serious injury or death to the occupants.

Screens that separate heating equipment from spaces occupied by children must be of closely spaced wire or expanded metal, of heavy gage, and must be securely attached to elements of the building. The purpose is to prevent children from bending the screens or inserting their fingers through the mesh.

SECTION 10-9   FAMILY DAY-CARE HOMES

Formal Interpretation 76-108
Reference: 10-7 (11-7), 10-8 (11-8), 10-9 (11-9)

Question 1: Do the requirements of Sections 10-7 (11-7), 10-8 (11-8), or 10-9 (11-9) apply to church programs that provide day-care services to church members only, on a nonprofit basis?

Answer: Yes.

Question 2: Are churches also required to meet the provisions of Sections 10-7 (11-7), 10-8 (11-8), or 10-9 (11-9) in order to operate a church nursery while church services are being held?

Answer: Yes.

Question 3: Does Section 1-5 permit the city to grant an exception in these cases?

Answer: The authority having jurisdiction is given the power to grant exceptions where it is clearly evident that reasonable safety is thereby secured.

Issue Edition: 1976
Reference: 9-5.3, 9-5.4, 9-5.5
Date: March 1979

10-9.1 General Requirements.

10-9.1.1 Application.

10-9.1.1.1* This section establishes life safety requirements for family day-care homes in which fewer than 7 clients receive care, maintenance, and supervision by other than their relatives or legal guardian(s) for less than 24 hours per day (generally within a dwelling unit). The provisions of Sections 10-2 through 10-6 shall not apply to this section unless a specific requirement is referenced by this section.

A-10-9.1.1.1 Family day-care homes do not provide for the full-time maintenance of a client. Occupancies that provide a primary place of residence are dealt with in other occupancies. See Chapters 16 through 22, "Residential Occupancies."

> Prior to the 1988 *Code*, this section dealt with "licensed" facilities.
> The Committee recognizes that licensing practices vary between jurisdictions. It was also a concern that the term "licensed family day-care home" would mean that, according to the *Code*, if a facility was not licensed, it did not have to meet the requirements of the *Code*. It is the intent of the Committee to include all family day-care centers as defined in 10-9.1.1.1, regardless of licensing.
> Family day-care homes are usually situated in single-family dwellings or in apartment houses. If they occur in apartment houses, they must also comply with the applicable requirements of 10-9.1.2.

10-9.1.1.2 The requirements detailed in Section 10-9 are based on a minimum staff-to-client ratio of one staff for up to six clients, including the caretaker's own children under age six, with no more than two children under age two.

> Many family day-care homes are located in single family residences. The Committee recognizes that in these types of situations, the caretaker's children should also be a consideration in determining staff-to-client ratios. This paragraph clarifies that distinction. The limit of two children under age two recognizes the stricter staff ratio requirements for this age group. (*For example, see staff ratio requirements for ages 0 to 2 in 10-7.1.1.1.*)

10-9.1.2 Mixed Occupancies. Where family day-care homes are located in a building containing mixed occupancies, the occupancies shall be separated by 1-hour fire barriers.

Exception: In assembly occupancies used primarily for worship.

10-9.1.3 Special Definitions. (None.)

10-9.1.4 Classification of Occupancies. No Requirements.

10-9.1.5 Classification of Hazard of Contents. (Not specifically classified.)

10-9.1.6 Minimum Construction Requirements. (None.)

10-9.1.7 Occupant Load.   No Special Requirements.

10-9.2 Means of Egress Requirements.

10-9.2.1 General.   (None.)

10-9.2.2 Types of Exits.   *(See 10-9.2.4.)*

10-9.2.3 Capacity of Means of Egress.   *(See 10-2.3.)*

10-9.2.4 Number of Exits.

10-9.2.4.1   Every room used for sleeping, living, or dining purposes shall have at least two means of escape, at least one of which shall be a door or stairway providing a means of unobstructed travel to the outside of the building at street or ground level. The second means of escape may be a window in accordance with 10-2.11.1. No room or space shall be occupied for living or sleeping purposes that is accessible only by a ladder, folding stairs, or through a trap door.

This paragraph reflects the requirements for one- and two-family dwellings. The change from means of egress to means of escape also recognizes a window of proper size as one method of escaping a fire.

10-9.2.4.2   Where clients are located on a floor (basement) below the level of exit discharge, at least one means of egress shall be an exit discharging directly to the outside, and the vertical travel to ground level shall not exceed 8 ft (244 cm). The second means of escape may be a window in accordance with 10-2.11.1. No facility shall be located more than one story below the ground.

See commentary on 10-8.2.4.3. This is the same concept.

10-9.2.5 Arrangement of Means of Egress.   *(See 10-9.2.4.)*

10-9.2.6 Travel Distance to Exits.   *(See 10-2.6.)*

10-9.2.7 Discharge from Exits.   *(See 10-9.2.4.)*

10-9.2.8 Illumination of Means of Egress.   Illumination of the means of egress shall be in accordance with Section 5-8.

10-9.2.9 Emergency Lighting.   No Requirements.

10-9.2.10 Marking of Means of Egress.   No Requirements.

10-9.2.11 Special Features.

10-9.2.11.1   Each door in a means of egress shall not be less than 28 in. (71 cm) wide.

10-9.2.11.2*   Every closet door latch shall be such that children can open the door from inside the closet.

A-10-9.2.11.2   The purpose of this requirement is to prevent arrangements where a child can be trapped in a closet. It is intended that this provision be broadly interpreted by the authority having jurisdiction to include equipment like refrigerators or freezers.

10-9.2.11.3   Every bathroom door lock shall be designed to permit the opening of the locked door from the outside in an emergency. The opening device shall be readily accessible to the staff.

10-9.3 Protection.

10-9.3.1 Protection of Vertical Openings.   (No special provisions.)

10-9.3.2 Protection from Hazards.   No Requirements.

10-9.3.3 Interior Finish.

10-9.3.3.1   The interior finish in corridors, stairways, lobbies, and exits shall be Class A or B in accordance with Section 6-5.

10-9.3.3.2   Interior finish in occupied spaces in the home shall be Class A, B, or C, in accordance with Section 6-5.

10-9.3.4 Detection, Alarm, and Communications Systems.

10-9.3.4.1   Within the family day-care home, smoke detectors shall be installed in accordance with 7-6.2.9.

Exception: Homes housing clients 6 years of age or older if no sleeping facilities are provided.

10-9.3.4.2   Where the family day-care home is located within a building of another occupancy such as in apartment or office buildings, any corridors serving the family day-care home shall be provided with a smoke detection system in accordance with Section 7-6, with placement of detectors at no greater than 30 ft (9.1 m) spacing.

10-9.3.4.3   Single station smoke detectors powered by the house electrical service shall be provided in all rooms used for sleeping.

> The provisions of 10-9.3.4 are two-fold: first, to provide single station smoke detectors within the group day-care home in accordance with NFPA 74, *Standard for the Installation, Maintenance and Use of Household Fire Warning Equipment*[4]; and second, to provide a smoke detection system in the corridor serving the group day-care home where in a building of mixed occupancy. In addition, 10-9.3.4.3 requires single station smoke detectors in each sleeping room, which is not required by NFPA 74.

10-9.4 Special Provisions.   No Requirements.

10-9.5 Building Services.

10-9.5.1 Electrical Services.

10-9.5.1.1   Electrical wiring shall be installed in accordance with Section 7-1.

10-9.5.1.2   Special protective covers for all electrical receptacles shall be installed in all areas occupied by children in homes for children under 6 years of age.

10-9.5.2 Heating, Ventilating, and Air Conditioning Equipment.

10-9.5.2.1   Heating, ventilating, and air conditioning equipment shall be installed in accordance with Section 7-2.

10-9.5.2.2   Unvented fuel-fired room heaters shall not be permitted.

> The Committee does not feel that reasonable life safety should allow the use of unvented fuel-fired equipment with children. (*Also see commentary on 10-5.2.2.*)

10-9.5.2.3   Any heating equipment in spaces occupied by children shall be provided with partitions, screens, or other means to protect the children from hot surfaces and open flames. If solid partitions are used to provide such protection, provisions shall be made to assure adequate air for combustion and ventilation for the heating equipment.

> The Committee feels it important that safeguards be provided to protect children from the hot surfaces of heating equipment. Young children do not always know the dangers of hot surfaces. The burn injury record clearly indicates that protection be provided. The Committee also wanted to make certain that adequate air is provided for combustion of the heating equipment. Incomplete or inadequate combustion could cause serious injury or death to the occupants.
>
> Screens that separate heating equipment from spaces occupied by children must be of closely spaced wire or expanded metal, of heavy gage, and must be securely attached to elements of the building. The purpose is to prevent the children from bending the screens or inserting their fingers through the mesh.

REFERENCES CITED IN COMMENTARY

[1]ANSI/ASME A17.1, *Safety Code for Elevators and Escalators*, American Society of Mechanical Engineers, 345 East 47th Street, New York, NY 10017, 1984.

[2]ANSI A117.1, *American Standard Specifications for Making Buildings and Facilities Accessible to, and Usable by, the Physically Handicapped*, American National Standards Institute, 1430 Broadway, New York, NY 10018, 1961 (reaff. 1971).

[3]NFPA 13, *Standard for the Installation of Sprinkler Systems*, National Fire Protection Association, Quincy, MA, 1987.

[4]NFPA 74, *Standard for the Installation, Maintenance, and Use of Household Fire Warning Equipment*, National Fire Protection Association, Quincy, MA, 1984.

11 EXISTING EDUCATIONAL OCCUPANCIES

(See also Chapter 31.)

Educational occupancies include all buildings used for the gathering of groups of six or more people for purposes of instruction through the twelfth grade for four or more hours per day or more than twelve hours per week. Educational occupancies include:

| Academies | Nursery schools |
| Kindergartens | Schools |

Day-care facilities, for both children and adults, are provided for separately in Sections 11-7, 11-8, and 11-9.

Other occupancies associated with educational occupancies must be in accordance with the appropriate parts of this *Code*.

Operational features for educational occupancies are specified in Chapter 31, Operating Features.

SECTION 11-1   GENERAL REQUIREMENTS

11-1.1 Application.

11-1.1.1   The requirements of this chapter apply to existing buildings.

Alterations, renovations, and modernizations to existing buildings are to be done, to the extent practical, in compliance with Chapter 8. (*See 1-4.6.*)

11-1.1.2 Reserved.

11-1.1.3   Educational occupancies housing classes over the twelfth grade need not comply with this chapter but shall comply with the following requirements:

(a) Instructional Building — Business Occupancy

(b) Classrooms under 50 persons — Business Occupancy

(c) Classrooms 50 persons and over — Assembly Occupancy

(d) Laboratories, Instructional — Business Occupancy

(e) Laboratories, Non-Instructional — Industrial.

The provisions of 11-1.1.3 recognize that colleges and universities do not have the same problems as elementary and high schools. Because of the maturity of the occupants, college buildings more properly resemble business (office) occupancies. Thus, this paragraph identifies those uses and refers to other appropriate provisions of the *Code*. (*Also see 11-1.4.1.*)

11-1.2 Mixed Occupancies.   (*See also 11-1.4.*)

11-1.2.1   Where other types of occupancy occur in the same building as an educational occupancy, the requirements of 1-4.7 of this *Code* shall be applicable.

Exception: As otherwise specified in this chapter.

Paragraph 1-4.7 of the *Code* specifies that where separate safeguards for each occupancy cannot be maintained, the most restrictive requirement of either occupancy will apply to both occupancies. Another way of stating this would be that the requirement providing the highest level of life safety would apply to both occupancies.

11-1.2.2 Assembly and Educational.   Spaces subject to assembly occupancy shall comply with Chapter 9 including Special Provisions for Assembly Occupancies in Buildings of Other Occupancy, which provides that where auditorium and gymnasium exits lead through corridors or stairways also serving as exits for other parts of the building, the exit capacity shall be sufficient to permit simultaneous exit from auditorium and classroom sections.

Exception: In the case of an assembly occupancy of a type suitable only for use of the school occupant load (and therefore not subject to simultaneous occupancy), the same exit capacity may serve both sections.

The point of this requirement is that if classrooms and an assembly occupancy are likely to be occupied simultaneously, the exit capacity of the building must be designed and arranged for the combined use. For example, classrooms are often used during the evening for adult or remedial education while a school's gymnasium or auditorium is being used by another group. In such cases, the exception would not apply even though during the day the place of assembly would be used only by the school's population.

11-1.2.3 Dormitory and Classrooms.   Any building used for both classroom and dormitory purposes shall comply with the applicable provisions of Chapter 17 in addition to complying with Chapter 11. Where classroom and dormitory sections are not subject to simultaneous occupancy, the same exit capacity may serve both sections.

11-1.3 Special Definitions.

Common Atmosphere.   A common atmosphere exists between rooms, spaces, or areas within a building that are not separated by an approved smoke barrier.

Flexible Plan and Open Plan Educational Buildings.   Includes every building or portion of a building designed for multiple teaching stations.

(a) Flexible plan buildings have movable corridor walls and movable partitions of full-height construction with doors leading from rooms to corridors.

(b) Open plan buildings have rooms and corridors delineated by use of tables, chairs, desks, bookcases, counters, low-height 5-ft (152-cm) partitions, or similar furnishings.

Although becoming less common, flexible and open plan schools still exist. See Section 11-6 for additional requirements for those types of schools.

Interior Room.   A room whose only means of egress is through an adjoining or intervening room that is not an exit.

Note that this definition of interior room does not imply a windowless room. (*See Figure 11-1.*)

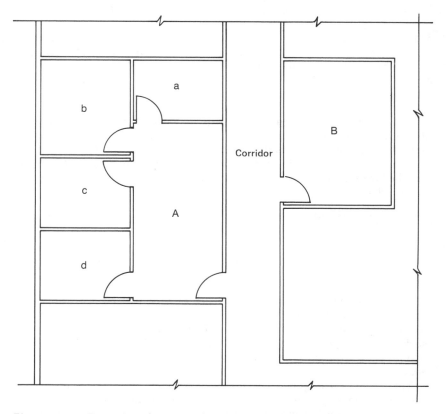

Figure 11-1. Examples of Interior Rooms. Rooms a, b, c, and d are interior rooms because occupants must pass through Room A before reaching the corridor. An example would be music practice rooms off a large music room. Room B, although windowless, is not an interior room as defined in Chapter 11 because the means of egress is from the room directly to the corridor.

Room.   For the purposes of this chapter, a room is a space or area bounded by any obstructions to egress that at any time enclose more than 80 percent of the perimeter of the space or area. Openings of less than 3 ft (91 cm) clear width and less than 6 ft 8 in. (203 cm) high shall not be considered in computing the unobstructed perimeter.

> The intent of the last sentence in the definition of room is to prevent openings that do not qualify as a legitimate part of the means of egress from being calculated as open space. Because these small openings cannot be used for exiting, they are considered as part of the obstructed perimeter.

Separate Atmosphere.   A separate atmosphere exists between rooms, spaces, or areas that are separated by an approved smoke barrier.

Separate Means of Egress.   A means of egress separated in such a manner from other required means of egress to provide an atmospheric separation that precludes contamination of both means of egress by the same fire. (*See Section 6-3.*)

Story of Exit Discharge.   The story of exit discharge is that story or stories from which the exits are primarily doors discharging directly outside essentially at grade (level of exit discharge). Where no such story exists, the story of exit discharge shall be that story that involves the fewest number of stair risers needed to reach the level of exit discharge.

> The Committee recognizes the confusion that exists in trying to determine which story should be considered the level of exit discharge where no single story is built exactly at grade level. The Committee felt this definition would help clarify the intent by designating the floor that has the fewest number of steps required to reach grade level as the story of exit discharge.

11-1.4 Classification of Occupancy.   (*See 4-1.3.*)

11-1.4.1   Educational occupancies shall include all buildings used for educational purposes through the twelfth grade by 6 or more persons for 4 or more hours per day or more than 12 hours per week.

> This paragraph eliminates three types of schools: those dealing with small numbers of students (fewer than 6), such as facilities providing private tutoring or individual lessons; those with limited operating hours, such as some sports schools or "Sunday" schools; and those educating people over the high school level, such as universities, military training, etc.
>
> The first two categories are rarely questioned but many question the exemption on upper level education. The Committee felt that once a person leaves high school, the level of protection does not need to be greater because one chooses to continue one's education, while someone who pursues a career in business or industry receives a different level of protection. Paragraph 11-1.1.3 provides guidance in determining how some higher education facilities would be classified.

For purposes of determining occupant load, a classroom area is still an educational "use" although it may not be categorized as an educational occupancy, and the occupant load factors provided by 11-1.7 are still appropriate.

Where instruction is incidental to other occupancies, the requirements for the occupancy in which the instruction occurs are applicable. Church schools that are used for instruction for a few hours during one or two days of the week are generally classed as assembly occupancies.

11-1.4.2 Educational occupancy includes part-day, nursery schools, kindergartens, and other schools whose purpose is primarily educational even though the children are of preschool age.

The *Code* classifies part-time day-care facilities as educational occupancies if they primarily provide education in addition to care services. This parallels federal guidelines for subsidizing day-care/educational activities at both the federal and state levels. By requiring educational criteria and related activities, it was believed that a higher quality of staff will be provided for these facilities by these standards. Sections 11-7, 11-8, and 11-9 set forth special requirements for noneducational day-care facilities.

11-1.4.3 In cases where instruction is incidental to some other occupancy, the section of this *Code* governing such other occupancy shall apply.

This paragraph is not as important as it was before 11-1.4.1 removed places of higher education from Chapter 11. The following examples are uses that would nevertheless be exempted from Chapter 11 by 11-1.4.1.

In an office building or factory, a few rooms may be used for orientation or instruction in the work requirements; these rooms are subject to the *Code* requirements for offices or factories. Barber colleges and beauty schools frequently are located in commercial buildings and should be governed by the requirements of the buildings in which they occur.

11-1.4.4 Adult day-care shall include any building used for nonsleeping purposes for less than 24 hours per day to house one or more well, ambulatory or semi-ambulatory (nonbedridden) adults, none of whom requires medical injections by staff personnel. For the purposes of this definition, adults shall include those who:

(a) May require the administration of dry or liquid oral medication by staff personnel when and as prescribed by a licensed medical practitioner, and

(b) May require limited attendance, supervision, or observation, and

(c) Exhibit acceptable behavior (not harmful to self or others), and

(d) Are able to toilet self, and

(e) Are able to feed self, and

(f) Possess adequate mobility, and

(g) Are otherwise essentially homebound.

The definition of an adult day-care occupancy in this chapter is recognition of the fact that more and more senior citizens are being cared for in day-care centers resembling child day-care centers. The definition of the occupancy itself includes a definition of the type of adult who may be cared for in this occupancy. Essentially, the stated definition of an adult is to make clear that these occupancies are not nursing homes or old age homes, but are occupancies that contain persons who are capable of self-preservation, yet who need limited attendance, supervision, or observation. Adult day-care occupancies are now covered with child day-care occupancies in Sections 11-7, 11-8 and 11-9.

11-1.4.5   Other occupancies associated with educational institutions shall be in accordance with the appropriate parts of this *Code.* (*See Chapters 13, 17, 19, 20, 28, 29, and 30, and 1-4.7.*)

11-1.5 Classification of Hazard of Contents.   Contents of educational occupancies shall be classified in accordance with the provisions of Section 4-2.

In general, educational occupancies contain ordinary hazard contents. Some laboratories and storage areas may contain high hazard contents. (*See Section 5-11 for additional egress requirements for areas with high hazard.*)

11-1.6 Minimum Construction Requirements.   No Requirements.

11-1.7 Occupant Load.

11-1.7.1   The occupant load of educational buildings or any individual story or section thereof for the purpose of determining exits shall be as determined by the authority having jurisdiction but not less than one person for each 20 sq ft (1.9 sq m) of net classroom area or 50 sq ft (4.6 sq m) of net area of shops, laboratories, and similar vocational rooms. In day-care centers, the occupant load shall be not less than one person for each 35 sq ft (3.3 sq m) of net area.

It is not the intent of this paragraph to establish a minimum number of sq ft (sq m) per child, but to assure adequate exit capacity is provided for those present. Efficient use of classroom space may result in more occupants than these occupant load factors would yield. Paragraph 11-1.7.3 clearly allows this, provided all requirements based on this higher number are met.

Many states require that day-care facilities provide 35 sq ft (3.3 sq m) of net area per child. It is not the intent of this *Code* to affect such a requirement, which is provided for the welfare of the child for purposes other than life safety.

11-1.7.2   The occupant load of an area having fixed seats shall be determined by the number of fixed seats installed. Required aisle space serving the fixed seats shall not be used to increase the occupant load.

11-1.7.3 The capacity of an educational occupancy or a portion thereof may be modified from that specified above if the necessary aisles and exits are provided. An approved aisle or seating diagram shall be required by the authority having jurisdiction to substantiate such a modification.

11-1.7.4 The occupant load for determining exit requirements of individual lecture rooms, gymnasiums, or cafeterias used for assembly purposes of more than 50 persons shall be determined in accordance with 9-1.7 of this *Code*.

> The intent of this paragraph is to indicate that rooms that may be used as assembly occupancies should have their occupant loads calculated using the occupant load factors found in Chapter 9 of the *Code*. As noted for assembly occupancies, this may result in a room with more than one occupant load, depending on its use. School cafeterias are generally capable of other uses and should probably be considered as multipurpose rooms.

SECTION 11-2   MEANS OF EGRESS REQUIREMENTS

11-2.1 General.

11-2.1.1 Means of egress shall be in accordance with Chapter 5 and this section.

11-2.1.2 Rooms normally occupied by preschool, kindergarten, or first-grade pupils shall not be located above or below the story of exit discharge. Rooms normally occupied by second-grade pupils shall not be located more than one story above the story of exit discharge.

> The restrictions on the location of rooms used by preschool, kindergarten, first grade or second grade pupils were developed to avoid the danger of older (and larger) children overrunning the very young on stairs or ramps during a fire or other incident requiring rapid evacuation of a building. Paragraph 11-2.1.2 also recognizes that young children may need assistance or may have to be rescued.
>
> This provision is significantly different than in Chapter 10. It is a little more flexible by using the definition of story of exit discharge introduced in this edition of the *Code* (*see 11-1.3*). What may have been a floor above or below the level of exit discharge under prior editions may qualify as the story of exit discharge under this edition. See Figure 11-2.

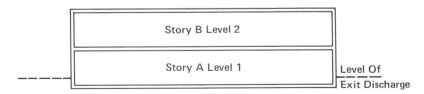

Figure 11-2 Level I Is Below the Level of Exit Discharge Under Prior Editions. Under the definition of "Story of Exit Discharge" it qualifies.

11-2.2 Means of Egress Components.

Note that slide escapes, escalators, fire escape stairs, and revolving doors are not permitted to be credited as required egress components. Escalators and revolving doors may be installed, but cannot be considered as part of required egress and must not obstruct or otherwise confuse required egress paths.

11-2.2.1   Components of means of egress shall be limited to the types described in 10-2.2.2 through 11-2.2.7.

11-2.2.2 Doors.

11-2.2.2.1   Doors shall comply with 5-2.1.

11-2.2.2.2 Panic Hardware or Fire Exit Hardware.   Any required exit door subject to use by 100 or more persons may be provided with a latch or lock only if it is panic hardware or fire exit hardware complying with 5-2.1.7.

The requirement for panic hardware in existing educational occupancies is slightly less restrictive than for new occupancies. Here panic hardware or fire exit hardware is required only on exit doors rather than egress doors; therefore, the scope of the paragraph is reduced so that it does not address exit access doors, such as corridor doors and smoke barrier doors. In addition, Chapter 8 addresses the number of people in the area served while here it addresses the required capacity of the door. Chapter 10 was made more stringent for the 1985 *Code*, but the Committee did not consider this to be of significant enough importance to require existing buildings to be retrofitted. If panic hardware or fire exit hardware is already installed in accordance with Chapter 10, it must be maintained, as removal would be an alteration, and 1-4.6 requires alterations to comply with Chapter 10.

11-2.2.2.3   Special locking arrangements complying with 5-2.1.6 are permitted.

The provisions of 5-2.1.6 apply to special delayed release devices. Note that one of the requirements of 5-2.1.6 is that the building must be either fully sprinklered or fully protected by an automatic fire detection system.

11-2.2.2.4 Door Closure.   Any exit door designed to normally be kept closed shall conform with 5-2.1.8.

11-2.2.2.5   Only one locking or latching device shall be permitted on a door or a leaf of a pair of doors.

11-2.2.3* Stairs.

A-11-2.2.3   See Appendix A-5-2.2.6.5(a) Exception No. 2 regarding additional handrails on stairs that are used extensively by children 5 years or less in age.

11-2.2.3.1   Stairs shall comply with 5-2.2.

11-2.2.3.2   Stairs shall be Class A.

Exception: Class B stairs shall be permitted where not used for student access.

11-2.2.4 Smokeproof Enclosures.   Smokeproof enclosures shall comply with 5-2.3.

11-2.2.5 Horizontal Exits.   Horizontal exits shall comply with 5-2.4.

11-2.2.6 Ramps.   Ramps shall comply with 5-2.5.

11-2.2.7 Exit Passageways.   Exit passageways shall comply with 5-2.6.

11-2.3 Capacity of Means of Egress.

11-2.3.1   Capacity of means of egress shall be in accordance with Section 5-3.

11-2.3.2   The same exit capacity required for any individual floor may be counted as simultaneously serving all floors above the first story or floor of exit discharge.

11-2.3.3 Minimum Corridor Width.

11-2.3.3.1   Exit access corridors shall be not less than 6 ft (183 cm) clear width.

Note that this requirement applies regardless of the required capacity of the corridor. Larger widths may be necessary for corridors handling large numbers of students (*See 11-2.3.1*).

This paragraph applies to exit access corridors and not to nonrequired service corridors that are provided for convenience only.

"In the clear" means a 6-ft (183-cm) wide clear space with no obstructions. Paragraph 5-3.2 details how to measure the width of a portion of the means of egress.

The intent of a 6-ft (183-cm) corridor is to permit two files of children with sufficient room for teachers or monitors to supervise. Extremely short corridors serving only one room may warrant consideration for some reduction in width.

11-2.3.3.2   Drinking fountains or other equipment, fixed or movable, shall not be so placed as to obstruct the required minimum 6 ft (183 cm) corridor width.

11-2.4 Number of Exits.   There shall be at least two exits available from every floor area. (*See Section 5-4.*)

11-2.5 Arrangement of Means of Egress.   (*See also Section 5-5.*)

11-2.5.1   Arrangement of means of egress shall be in accordance with Section 5-5. Dead ends shall not exceed 20 ft (6.1 m).

This paragraph has been rewritten for the 1988 Edition. Section 5-5 provides the detail required to establish proper exiting. Section 5-5.1.5 makes individual chapters responsible for establishing dead-end limits. Twenty feet (6.1 m) has been the standard dead-end requirement for educational occupancies in the past, and the Committee felt it was still reasonable.

A school plan with outside doors or stairways at both ends of a central corridor meets the dead-end requirement. Pockets may be created where stairways are not at the end of corridors, but at intermediate points.

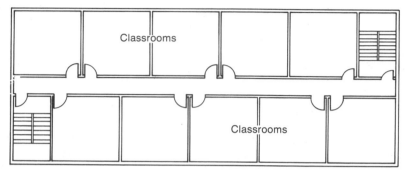

Preferred Arrangement Of Exits Without Deadends

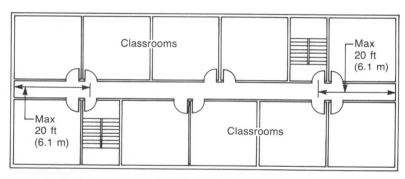

Acceptable Arrangement Of Exits With Deadends, Up To 20 ft (6.1 m)

Figure 11-3. Stair Placement in Accordance with 11-2.5.1.

11-2.5.2   Every room or space with a capacity of more than 50 persons or more than 1,000 sq ft (93 sq m) in area shall have at least two doorways as remote from each other as practicable. Such doorways shall provide access to separate exits but, where egress is through corridors, may open upon a common corridor leading to separate exits in opposite directions.

> Chapter 11 does not establish a maximum common path of travel, but instead, it sets a maximum room size with one door and then limits dead-end corridors. (*See 11-2.5.1.*)

See 5-2.1.4.1 for information on direction of door swing.

11-2.5.3   Doors that swing into an exit access corridor shall be recessed to prevent interference with corridor traffic; any doors not so recessed shall open 180 degrees to stop against the wall. Doors in any position shall not reduce the required corridor width by more than one-half.

See 5-2.1.4.2 for more information on doors swinging into corridors.

11-2.5.4 Aisles.

11-2.5.4.1   Where there are more than 60 seats, every aisle shall be not less than 3 ft (91 cm) wide where serving seats on one side only and not less than 3 ft 6 in. (107 cm) where serving seats on both sides. Where serving 60 seats or less, aisles shall not be less than 30 in. (76 cm) wide. The space between parallel rows of seats does not constitute an aisle. No more than six seats shall intervene between any seat and an aisle.

11-2.5.5* Exterior Corridors or Balconies.

A-11-2.5.5   A corridor roofed over and enclosed on its long side and open to the atmosphere at the end may be considered an exterior corridor if either:

(a) Clear story openings for the corridor are provided on both sides of the corridor and above adjacent roofs or buildings and such clear openings are not less than one-half the height of the corridor walls, or

(b) The corridor roof has unobstructed openings to the sky not less than 50 percent of the area of the roof.

The openings are to be equally distributed, and if louvers are installed, they are to be fixed open with a clear area based on the actual openings between louver vanes.

11-2.5.5.1*   Where exterior corridors or balconies are provided as means of egress, they shall open to the outside air except for railings or balustrades with stairs or level exits to grade not over the allowable travel distance apart and so located that an exit will be available in either direction from the door to any individual room or space, with dead ends not to exceed 20 ft (6.1 m). If balconies are enclosed by glass or in any other manner, they shall be treated as interior corridors.

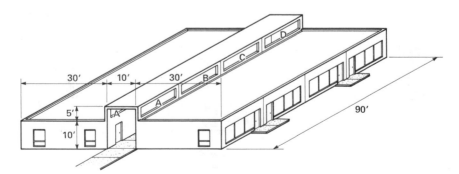

Figure 11-3a.   Exterior Corridor Using Clear Story Openings.   A, B, C, and D are clear story openings. The building height is 10 ft (3 m). The minimum height allowable for the corridor roof must be 5 ft (1.5 m). In our example, the minimum clear story height requirements have been met.

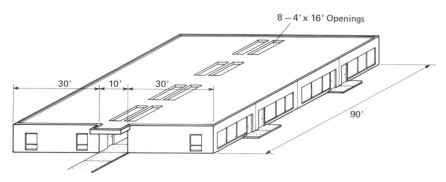

Figure 11-3b. Exterior Corridor Using Roof Openings. The alternative is that the roof have unobstructed openings to the sky that equal not less than 50 percent of the corridor roof. The example shown has eight openings. Each opening is 4 ft × 16 ft (1.2 m × 4.9 m), or 64 sq ft (5.9 sq m) each. The total square footage of the roof area equals 900 sq ft (84 sq m). The total unobstructed opening equals 512 sq ft (48 sq m) (greater than 50 percent of the total roof area). This would be an acceptable design.

A-11-2.5.5.1 School design providing classroom exits directly to the outside or to exterior balconies open to the outside air with exterior stairways available to either direction to grade is considered preferable, from the firesafety standpoint, to the more conventional design using interior corridors, which can become untenable from the accumulation of smoke and heat.

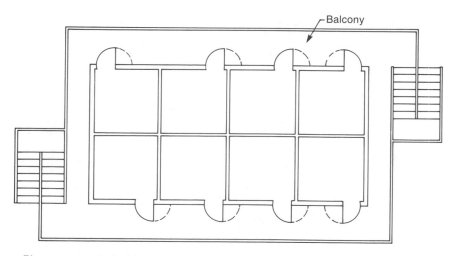

Figure 11-5. Stair Placement, Exterior Balcony. Distance between stairs must not be greater than the allowable travel distance would permit.

11-2.5.5.2   The floors of balconies (exterior corridors) and stairs shall be solid, without openings, and shall comply with requirements for outside stairs as regards balustrades or railings, width and pitch of stairs, and other details, but are not required to be shielded from fire within the building by blank walls, wired glass windows or the like where the stairs are located on the side of the balcony or corridor away from the building and are separated from the building by the full required width of the balcony or corridor. Regardless of other provisions, exterior balconies and stairs may be of the same type of construction as the building that they serve.

Stairs from exterior balconies must not pass or come close to windows or other openings in stories below. Preferable stair placements complying with 11-2.5.5.1 and 11-2.5.5.2 are illustrated in Figures 11-6 and 11-7.

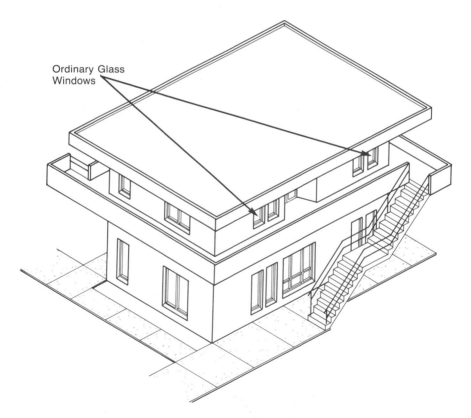

Ordinary Glass Windows

Figure 11-6.   Stair Placement, Exterior Balcony.   Since stairs are separated from the building by the full width of the balcony, blank walls or wired glass windows are not required near the stairs.

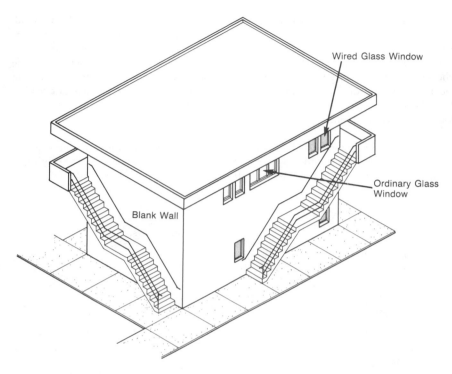

Figure 11-7. Stair Placement, Exterior Balcony. The stair placed directly against the building must not pass near unprotected openings. (*See 5-2.2 for protection requirements on outside stairs.*)

11-2.6 Travel Distance to Exits.   Travel distance to an exit shall not exceed 150 ft (45 m) from any point in a building. (*See also Section 5-6.*)

Exception No. 1: The travel distance may be increased to 200 ft (60 m) in educational occupancies protected throughout by an approved automatic sprinkler system.

Exception No. 2: Previously approved travel distances.

The Committee recognizes that there are existing educational occupancies that may have travel distances that have been previously approved by the authority having jurisdiction, and the authority having jurisdiction wants to continue to honor that approval.

11-2.7 Discharge from Exits.   Discharge from exits shall be arranged in accordance with Section 5-7.

Exception: Every classroom or room used for educational purposes or student occupancy below the floor of exit discharge shall have access to at least one exit that leads directly to the exterior at level of discharge without entering the floor above.

The basic requirements previously found in Chapter 11 are now in Chapter 5. The Exception is a slight relaxation of the requirement in Section 5-7 in that the Exception requires at least one exit to discharge directly to the outside, while 5-7.2 requires 50 percent to discharge directly outside. Figures 11-8 and 11-9 illustrate two types of exits that will satisfy the requirements of the Exception to 11-2.7. The enclosed stair in Figure 11-9 may serve other floors if it meets all the requirements of Chapter 5.

11-2.8 Illumination of Means of Egress. Means of egress shall be illuminated in accordance with Section 5-8.

11-2.9 Emergency Lighting. Emergency lighting shall be provided in accordance with Section 5-9 in the following areas:

(a) In all interior stairs and corridors.

(b) In all normally occupied spaces.

Exception to (b):

  1. Administrative areas.

  2.* General classrooms.

A-11-2.9(b) Exception to (b)2 This does not exempt shops and laboratories.

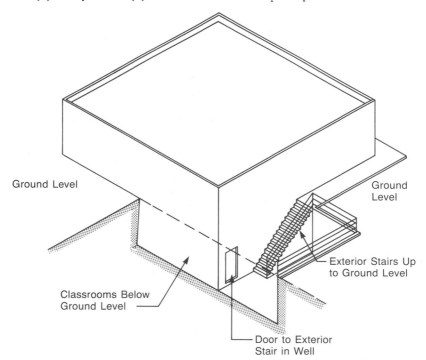

Figure 11-8.   Exit from Classroom Below Floor of Exit Discharge.

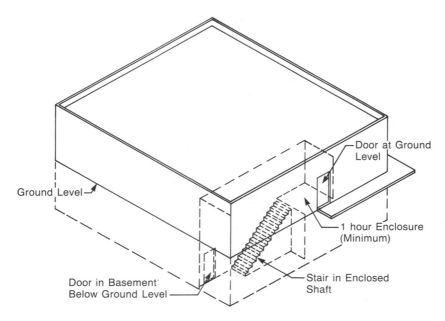

Figure 11-9.   Exit from Classroom Below Floor of Exit Discharge.   The enclosed stair could be located on the outside of the building.

3. Mechanical rooms and storage areas.

(c) In flexible and open plan buildings.

(d) In all portions of buildings that are interior or windowless.

The Exceptions to 11-2.9(b) indicate that normal classrooms, offices, and storage or mechanical spaces do not require emergency lighting. Shops, laboratories, and assembly rooms would require emergency lighting as do portions of the building that are interior or windowless. See Figure 11-10.

11-2.10 Marking of Means of Egress.   Means of egress shall have signs in accordance with Section 5-10.

Exception: Signs are not required in situations where location of exits is otherwise obvious and familiar to all occupants, such as in small elementary school buildings.

11-2.11 Special Features.

11-2.11.1* Windows for Rescue and Ventilation.   Every room or space used for classroom or other educational purposes or normally subject to student occupancy shall have at least one outside window for emergency rescue or ventilation. Such window shall be openable from the inside without the use of tools and provide a clear opening of not less than 20 in. (50.8 cm) in width, 24 in. (61 cm) in height, and 5.7 sq ft (.53 sq m) in area. The bottom of the opening shall be not more than 44 in. (112 cm) above the floor. In rooms located greater than three stories above grade, the openable clear height, width,

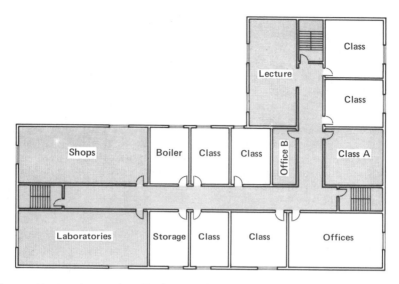

Figure 11-10. Areas that Require and do not Require Emergency Lighting. Shaded areas indicate where emergency lighting is required. Classroom A and Office B are windowless; therefore, 11-2.9(d) overrides the Exception to 11-2.9(b). Laboratories, shops, and lecture halls do not qualify as general classrooms.

and area of the window may be modified to the dimensions necessary for ventilation.

Exception No. 1: In buildings protected throughout by an approved automatic sprinkler system in accordance with Section 7-7.

Exception No. 2: Where the room or space has a door leading directly to the outside of the building.

Exception No. 3: Awning or hopper type windows that are hinged or subdivided to provide a clear opening not less than 600 sq in. (0.39 sq m) in area, nor any dimension less than 22 in. (55.9 cm) may be continued in use. Screen walls or devices in front of required windows shall not interfere with normal rescue requirements.

Exception No. 4: Where the room or space complies with the following:

(a) Doors exist that allow travel between adjacent classrooms and, when used to travel from classroom to classroom, provide direct access to exits in both directions or direct access to an exit in one direction and to a separate smoke compartment that provides access to another exit in the other direction, and

(b) the corridor is separated from the classrooms by a wall that resists the passage of smoke, and all doors between the classrooms and the corridor are self-closing or automatic-closing in accordance with 5-2.1.8, and

(c) the length of travel to exits along such paths shall not exceed 150 ft (45 m), and

(d) each communicating door shall be marked in accordance with Section 5-10, and

(e) no locking device shall be allowed on the communicating doors.

A-11-2.11.1   It is highly desirable to have all windows of a type that can be readily opened from inside and to have them large enough and low enough for use by students, teachers, and fire fighters. Windows may serve as a supplementary means of emergency escape, particularly where ladders can be raised by fire fighters or others. Even where the location is such as to preclude the use of windows for escape purposes, they may provide air for breathing in a smoke-filled room while trapped occupants are awaiting rescue.

The dimensions specified for windows used for emergency rescue or for ventilation are based on simulations of emergency rescue conducted by the San Diego Fire Department. Windows providing clear openings of identical dimensions are also required for rescue or ventilation in one- and two-family dwellings. Figure 11-11a illustrates two configurations that achieve the required area of 5.7 sq ft (.53 sq m). Figure 11-11b illustrates Exception No. 3.

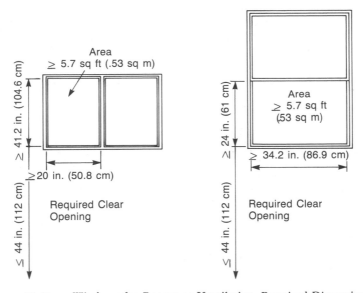

Figure 11-11a.   Windows for Rescue or Ventilation, Required Dimensions.

Although the *Code* intends the fire department or others to assist students, particularly over ladders, if these windows must be used as a supplementary means of escape, the windows should permit small children in the lower grades to escape unaided. Therefore, storm sashes, screens, or devices in front of the windows must be easy to open or remove and the sills must be low enough for children to reach.

Where the location of windows precludes their use for rescue or escape, they may still provide trapped children with air for breathing in smoke-filled rooms.

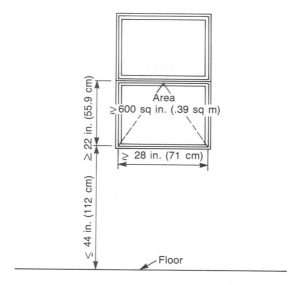

Figure 11-11b. Windows for Ventilation (Awning or Hopper-type), Recommended Dimnensions.

Windows may be omitted if a classroom has a door leading directly to the outside or if the building is totally sprinklered.

The Committee did not feel it was practical to expect someone to use a window above the third story as an escape window. However, it is reasonable to expect the window to be usable for ventilation during a fire.

Note that Exception No. 1 requires that the building be protected throughout by an automatic sprinkler system. One question that is often asked is: If there are only a couple of windowless classrooms can just those rooms be sprinklered? The answer is no! It must be remembered that the reason for the window is to provide ventilation or means of escape when the interior corridor is blocked by smoke from a fire in another part of the building. Putting sprinklers only in the windowless rooms would do nothing about smoke emanating from other areas.

Exception No. 3 is provided in recognition of a feature that was formerly recognized by the *Code*. Although the Committee felt that it should no longer be allowed in new construction, it can be continue to be permitted in existing facilities.

Exception No. 4 is new to the 1988 Edition and is allowed only in existing buildings. It recognizes a concept that had formerly been alluded to in older editions of the *Code* for the purpose of solving egress problems but was never detailed specifically in the *Code*. Figure 11-12 illustrates how Exception No. 4 can be used.

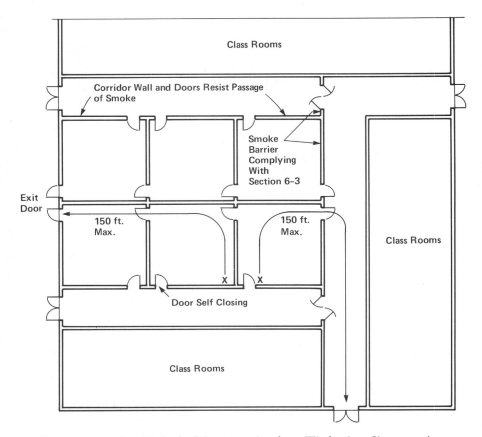

Figure 11-12. One Method of Compensating for a Windowless Classroom in an Existing Building.

Formal Interpretation 73-21
Reference: 10-2.11.5 (11-2.11.5)

Question: Do doors or windows opening onto an open court satisfy the requirements?

Answer: No.

Question: Does a door opening into a horizontal exit or to an exit passageway satisfy the phrase "unless it has a door leading directly to the outside of the building"?

Answer: No.

Question: Would this section also apply to a work room partitioned off from the rest of a large classroom, library, or shop area?

Answer: Yes.

Question: Are there any other sections of the *Code* that might modify the requirements of 10-2.11.5 (11-2.11.5)?

Answer: No.

Question: The phrase "or normally subject to student occupancy" would appear to include toilet rooms. Is this correct?

Answer: No.

Issue Edition: 1973
Reference: 9-1511
Date: May 1976

In answering this formal interpretation the Committee was probably thinking of an open court that is open to the sky but bounded on all sides, which is defined in Chapter 3 as an enclosed court.

As indicated in the formal interpretation, bathrooms are not considered spaces normally subject to student occupancy and, thus, do not require the window referred to in 11-2.11.1.

SECTION 11-3   PROTECTION

11-3.1 Protection of Vertical Openings.

11-3.1.1   Any vertical opening shall be enclosed and protected in accordance with Section 6-2.

Exception: In buildings protected throughout by an approved supervised automatic sprinkler system installed in accordance with Section 7-7, unprotected vertical openings connecting not more than three floors may be permitted in accordance with 6-2.4.4.

Chapter 6 has been changed and, under certain circumstances, would allow up to three floors to be connected without providing automatic sprinklers. The Committee felt that automatic sprinklers should be provided in educational occupancies. This is consistent with the intent of the 1985 *Code.*

11-3.1.2   Stairs shall be enclosed in accordance with Section 6-2.

Exception: Stairway enclosure will not be required for a stairway serving only one adjacent floor except a basement. Such stairway shall not be connected with stairways serving other floors nor with corridors serving other than the two floors involved.

The Exception to 11-3.1.2 would allow a two-story school building to have open stairs between the first floor and the second floor. This is not permitted by Chapter 10. Since basements usually contain hazardous areas with high fuel loads, such as storage rooms, boiler rooms, or workshops, the use of open stairs as a connection between the basement and the upper floors is prohibited. The intent is to reduce the probability of children on upper floors being exposed to the vertical spread of a fire originating in the basement of a building containing a school.

11-3.2 Protection from Hazards.

11-3.2.1 Rooms or spaces used for the storage, processing, or use of the materials specified in this section shall be protected in accordance with the following:

(a) Rooms or spaces used for the storage of combustible supplies in quantities deemed hazardous by the authority having jurisdiction, hazardous materials in quantities deemed hazardous by recognized standards, or fuel shall be separated from the remainder of the building by construction having not less than a 1-hour fire resistance rating with all openings protected by self-closing or smoke-actuated fire doors, or such rooms or spaces may be protected by an automatic extinguishing system as set forth in Section 6-4.

(b) Rooms or spaces used for processing or use of combustible supplies in quantities considered hazardous by the authority having jurisdiction, hazardous materials, or for flammable or combustible liquids in quantities deemed hazardous by recognized standards shall be separated from the remainder of the building by construction having not less than a 1-hour fire resistance rating with all openings protected by self-closing or smoke-actuated fire doors and shall also be protected by an automatic extinguishing system as set forth in Section 6-4.

(c) Boiler and furnace rooms, laundries, and maintenance shops, including woodworking and painting areas, shall be separated from the remainder of the building by construction having not less than a 1-hour fire resistance rating with all openings protected by self-closing or smoke-actuated fire doors, or such areas may be protected throughout by an approved automatic sprinkler system in accordance with Section 7-7.

Exception to (c):   Rooms enclosing air-handling equipment.

(d)* Where automatic extinguishing systems are used to meet the requirements of this section, the rooms or spaces shall be separated from the remainder of the building by construction that resists the passage of smoke.

A-11-3.2.1(d)   It is not the intent of this provision to require a smoke barrier that meets the requirements of Section 6-3.

(e) Where automatic extinguishing is used to meet the requirements of this section, the protection may be in accordance with 7-7.1.2.

The intent of 11-3.2.1 is to specify the degree of protection necessary for certain hazardous areas. It has been divided into three sections based on the degree of hazard. The hazards noted in items (a) and (c) are required to be enclosed in 1-hour construction or protected by sprinklers. If the sprinkler option is chosen, an enclosure is still required by item (d); however, the enclosure need not be rated, but only form a membrane against the passage of smoke.

The Committee felt that although sprinklers are provided and therefore fire-rated barriers may not be needed [*see (a) or (c)*], some barrier to control smoke migration is needed. Solid construction materials such as glass or other non-fire-rated materials are acceptable if they are installed in a manner that will resist smoke passing from one compartment to another. The new appendix note emphasizes that it is not the intent to require smoke barriers as provided in Section 6-3. This eliminates the more costly construction of a smoke barrier, which would require dampers and other required equipment.

Art rooms and some shops need special attention. Potentially dangerous operations involving flammable materials, specialized ovens, and ignition sources in these areas are becoming more prevalent and create increased hazards to the entire facility. It may be advisable at the high school level to include these rooms as hazardous spaces.

The hazards noted in item (b) must be enclosed in 1-hour construction and be protected by automatic sprinklers.

The Exception to item (c) pertains to rooms housing air-handling equipment only. If the room is used for other purposes, then the provisions of item (a) or (b) apply.

Part (e) has been added as an editorial change to highlight the fact that Chapter 7 makes these requirements available to the user of the *Code*. Paragraph 7-7.1.2 provides an economical way of providing sprinkler protection in small rooms. (*See 11-3.2.3.*)

Figure 11-13 illustrates the various protection requirements of 11-3.2.1.

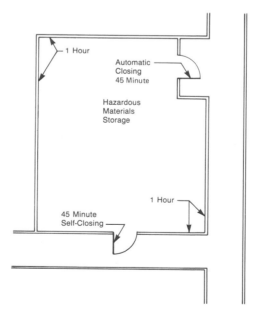

Figure 11-13 (a).   Protection of Hazardous Areas. Part (a) illustrates one method of complying with 11-3.2.1 (a). See Figure 11-13 (b) for alternate method.

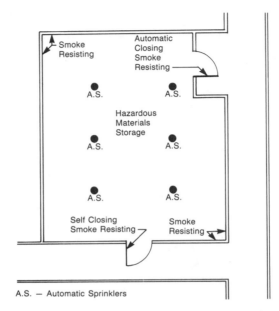

Figure 11-13 (b). Protection of Hazardous Areas. Part (b) illustrates an alternate method of complying with 11-3.2.1 (a). Figure 11-13 (a) illustrates another method of compliance.

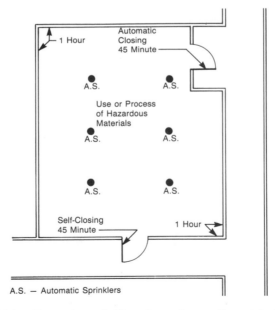

Figure 11-13 (c). Protection of Hazardous Areas. Part (c) illustrates the requirements for complying with 11-3.2.1 (b). Both one hour separation and automatic sprinkler protection is required.

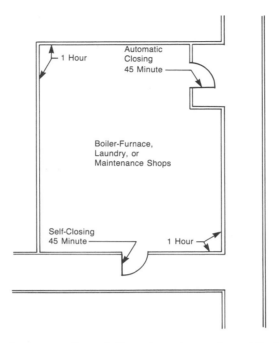

Figure 11-13(d). Protection of Hazardous Areas. Part (d) illustrates the requirements to comply with 11-3.2.1(c). However, in existing building, boiler rooms, furnace rooms and similar areas may use the sprinkler option as illustrated in Figure 11-13(b).

11-3.2.2   Food preparation facilities shall be protected in accordance with 7-2.3 and are not required to have openings protected between food preparation areas and dining areas.

The intent of 11-3.2.2 is to provide some barrier between cooking areas and dining areas. The intent of the barrier is to screen possible flash fires from view in an attempt to prevent panic. Openings in this barrier are not restricted and do not need to be protected. The *Code* is counting on the automatic extinguishing system to control any fire on the cooking surfaces, and thus no longer requires openings between the kitchen and dining areas to be protected. The degree of screening required, and thus the size of the barrier required, is left to the judgment of the authority having jurisdiction.

11-3.2.3   Janitor closets shall be protected by an automatic sprinkler system, which may be in accordance with 7-7.1.2. Doors to janitor closets may have ventilating louvers.

Where janitor closets are located off of corridors, a louvered door is usually provided for ventilation. It is necessary to provide these spaces with automatic sprinkler protection since the louvered door offers little fire resistance and permits a fire in the closet to directly affect the corridor. Paragraph 7-7.1.2 provides an economic method of providing sprinkler protection for such rooms. To accomplish this at reasonable cost, these sprinklers (not more than six in number) may be supplied from the domestic water supply to the closet if the supply is capable of providing the required quantity of water. It is advisable to provide a water-flow switch (*see Chapter 6*) to initiate an alarm when a sprinkler is opened.

The minimum flow of 0.15 gpm/sq ft (6.1 L/min/sq m) is based on the requirements in NFPA 13, *Standard for the Installation of Sprinkler Systems,*[1] for protecting buildings containing ordinary hazards. It is important to ensure that the domestic supply can provide the required flow and pressure at the location.

11-3.2.4   Laboratories that use chemicals shall comply with NFPA 45, *Standard on Fire Protection for Laboratories Using Chemicals.*

11-3.2.5   Stages shall be protected in accordance with Chapter 9.

11-3.3 Interior Finish.

11-3.3.1   Interior finish, in accordance with Section 6-5, shall be as follows:

(a) Exits — Class A

(b) Corridors and lobbies — Class A or B

Exception to (b):   Fixtures and low-height partitions not over 5 ft (152 cm) high may be Class C.

(c) All other locations — Class A, B, or C

Exception*:   The exposed portions of structural members complying with the requirements for Type IV (2HH) construction may be permitted.

A-11-3.3.1 Exception   NFPA 220, *Standard on Types of Building Construction* (*see Appendix B*), defines Type IV (2HH) construction. (*Also see A-6-2.1.*)

Section 6-5 permits the use of fire retardant or intumescent paints and surface coatings to reduce the surface flame spread of an interior finish. These coatings will not render a finish noncombustible. They will simply delay the eventual ignition of a finish exposed to fire.

Some coatings have a short life and require frequent reapplication. Over the useful life of a building, all coatings may eventually have to be renewed. Also, some coatings will severely mar or alter the appearance of the finish. Due to these liabilities, the option of using coatings and paints may not provide the best fire protection at a reasonable cost in all cases.

Sections 31-1 and 31-3 establish limitations on decorations and student artwork on walls.

11-3.3.2 Interior Floor Finish.   No Requirements.

11-3.4 Detection, Alarm, and Communications Systems.

11-3.4.1 General.   Educational occupancies shall be provided with a fire alarm system in accordance with Section 7-6.

11-3.4.2 Initiation.

11-3.4.2.1   Initiation of the required fire alarm system shall be by manual means in accordance with 7-6.2.1(a).

Exception: In buildings where all normally occupied spaces are provided with a two-way communication system between such spaces and a constantly attended receiving station from where a general evacuation alarm can be sounded, the manual pull stations may be omitted except in locations specifically designated by the authority having jurisdiction.

The Exception to 11-3.4.2.1 is intended to give local authorities the ability to deal with the false alarm and vandalism problems present in today's schools. Where there is a two-way communication system between classrooms and a continuously attended location where a general alarm can be sounded, the need for pull stations is obviated. To qualify to use this Exception, the authority having jurisdiction must agree on which pull stations can be omitted. For the purposes of this provision, the "continuously attended" location is intended to indicate a location attended while the school building is in use as a school. This may involve providing personnel at this location during night school, when the regular school office staff is not present.

11-3.4.2.2   In buildings provided with automatic sprinkler protection, the operation of the sprinkler system shall automatically activate the fire alarm system, in addition to the initiation means required above.

11-3.4.3 Notification.

11-3.4.3.1   Occupant notification shall be by means of an audible alarm in accordance with 7-6.3.

11-3.4.3.2   Where acceptable to the authority having jurisdiction, the fire alarm system may be used to designate class change provided that the fire alarm is distinctive in signal and overrides all other use.

11-3.5 Extinguishment Requirements.

11-3.5.1   Wherever student occupancy occurs below the level of exit discharge, every portion of such floor shall be protected throughout by an approved automatic sprinkler system in accordance with Section 7-7. Where student occupancy does not occur on floors below the level of exit discharge, such floors shall be separated from the rest of the building by 1-hour fire resistance rated construction or shall be protected throughout by an approved automatic sprinkler system in accordance with Section 7-7.

Levels below the level of exit discharge are not necessarily below grade. (*See Figure 11-14a and b.*) This paragraph differs from that in Chapter 10 in that it allows an option for stories not occupied by students to be separated by 1-hr fire resistance rated construction or to be sprinklered. If students occupy the floor, then it must be sprinklered. This option was first introduced in the 1985 *Code.*

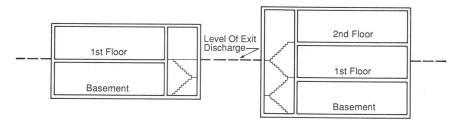

Figure 11-14.   Protection for Levels Below the Level of Exit Discharge. The arrangement on the left illustrates a simple example where only the basement is required to be sprinklered or separated. The diagram on the right shows the case where the level of exit discharge is between floors and requires that the first floor and basement be sprinklered or separated.

11-3.6 Interior Corridors.

11-3.6.1   Every interior corridor, including corridors in flexible plan buildings, shall be of smoke resistant construction having not less than a 20-minute fire resistance rating, and all openings shall be protected with doors, frames, and hardware, including closers, that shall all have a fire protection rating of at least 20 minutes.

Exception No. 1:   Such corridor protection shall not be required where all classrooms served by such corridors have at least one door directly to the outside or to an exterior balcony or corridor as in 11-2.5.5.

Exception No. 2:   Where permitted by the authority having jurisdiction, the corridor may be separated from all other areas by non-rated partitions where the building is protected throughout by an approved automatic sprinkler system with valve supervision.

Exception No. 3:   Existing doors may be 1¾-in. (4.4-cm) solid bonded wood core doors or the equivalent.

The intent of specifying 20-minute walls is to recognize that a lath and plaster wall maintained in good condition will provide approximately 20 minutes of fire resistance.

The intent of Exception No. 2 is to delete the requirement for a rated corridor wall and closers on the doors; however, a wall with doors providing a barrier against smoke is still required.

11-3.6.2   Clothing and personal effects shall not be stored in corridors and lobbies.

Racks of clothing and personal effects create two specific problems. The first problem relates to the large amount of combustibles in the means of egress. Fires in clothing racks in corridors will seriously hamper safe evacuation from the area served by the corridor. This problem should not be underestimated. Two recent fires, one in New York (Stauffers Hotel) and one in Massachusetts (Lexington), dramatically showed the tremendous fire load presented by clothing on open coatracks. The second problem is created where the minimum acceptable width of the corridor is reduced.

Exception: Metal lockers may be installed in corridors for storage of clothing and personal effects providing the corridor width is maintained.

The first problem stated above can be corrected by providing metal lockers for storage of clothing and personal effects. This reduces accessibility of the combustibles to arsonists and also compartmentalizes the combustibles. Most fires in school lockers do not extend beyond the locker of origin. Those that do extend do not usually extend beyond the locker(s) adjacent to the locker of origin. However, the corridor must be of such width that it will allow at least the minimum required corridor width to be maintained after the lockers are installed.

11-3.7 Subdivision of Building Spaces.

11-3.7.1   School buildings shall be subdivided into compartments by smoke barriers complying with Section 6-3 when:

(a) The maximum area of a compartment, including the aggregate area of all floors having a common atmosphere, exceeds 30,000 sq ft (2800 sq m); or

(b) Where the length or width of the building exceeds 300 ft (91 m).

Exception No. 1:   Where all classrooms have exterior exit access in accordance with 5-5.3.

Exception No. 2:   Buildings protected throughout by an approved automatic sprinkler system in accordance with Section 7-7.

The 300-ft (91-m) limit bears a direct relationship to the travel distance criteria in Chapter 11 and reflects the Committee's concern about the maximum area within an educational facility that would be immediately contaminated by products of combustion from a fire.

The Committee felt it was reasonable and prudent to require smoke barriers at maximum intervals of 300 ft (91 m) so that the products of combustion would affect a limited number of exits at one time.

The provisions of this section were changed in the 1985 Edition of the *Code* to make the provisions easier to understand and enforce. Previous editions spaced smoke barriers by corridor length. By using compartment size, the intent of the provision is clear, and hopefully, confusion in enforcement is reduced.

Formal Interpretation 81-31
Reference: 11-3.7.1

Question: Is it the intent of the *Code* that doors in non-fire protection rated smoke barriers, required by 11-3.7.1, be equipped with latching hardware?

Answer: Yes.

Issue Edition: 1981
Reference: 10-3.7.1, 11-3.7.1
Date: March 1983

11-3.7.2   The maximum area of a smoke compartment shall not exceed 30,000 sq ft (2800 sq m) with no dimension exceeding 300 ft (91 m).

This provision applies only if 11-3.7.1 applies. If one is exempted from 11-3.7.1, then 11-3.7.3 does not apply.

SECTION 11-4   SPECIAL PROVISIONS

11-4.1 Windowless or Underground Buildings.   Windowless buildings and underground structures shall comply with Section 30-7.

The Committee felt that Section 30-7 provides adequate provisions for existing windowless or underground buildings. Similar provisions were previously in Chapter 11. The intent is to simplify the *Code* for the user and provide better consistency between chapters within the *Code*.

11-4.2 High Rise Buildings.   (Reserved.)

11-4.3 Flexible Plan and Open Plan Buildings.   Flexible plan and open plan buildings shall also comply with the provisions of Section 11-6.

11-4.4 Operating Features.   (*See Chapter 31.*)

SECTION 11-5   BUILDING SERVICES

11-5.1 Utilities.   Utilities shall comply with the provisions of Section 7-1.

11-5.2 Heating, Ventilating, and Air Conditioning Equipment.

11-5.2.1   Heating, ventilating, and air conditioning equipment shall comply with the provisions of Section 7-2.

11-5.2.2   Unvented fuel-fired heating equipment shall be prohibited.

The Committee did not feel that it was reasonable life safety to have unvented fuel-fired equipment in a school building with children. It was felt that the typical use of unvented equipment would jeopardize the life safety of the students, because proper venting may not be provided and potential misuse by students or injury to students, especially younger children, may occur.

11-5.3 Elevators, Dumbwaiters, and Vertical Conveyors.   Elevators, dumbwaiters, and vertical conveyors shall comply with the provisions of Section 7-4.

11-5.4 Rubbish Chutes, Incinerators, and Laundry Chutes.   Rubbish chutes, incinerators, and laundry chutes shall comply with the provisions of Section 7-5.

SECTION 11-6   FLEXIBLE PLAN AND OPEN PLAN BUILDINGS

The 1985 Edition of the *Code* contained a major revision of the provisions pertaining to flexible and open plan schools. The intent of the revision was to make the *Code* easier to use while improving life safety in the special arrangements. This section requires that flexible and open plan schools comply with Sections 11-1 through 11-5, except as modified by this section.

11-6.1 General Requirements.

11-6.1.1   Flexible and open plan buildings shall comply with Sections 11-1 through 11-5 except as modified by this section.

11-6.2 Means of Egress Requirements.

11-6.2.1   Each room occupied by more than 300 persons shall have two or more means of egress entering into separate atmospheres. Where three or more means of egress are required, not more than two of them shall enter into the same atmosphere.

Rooms occupied by more than 300 persons require special treatment in flexible and open plan schools. To ensure the safety of such a large number of persons contained in one room, means of egress must be arranged so that each of the separate egress paths traverse separate atmospheres from each other. If more than two separate means of egress paths are required, no more than two shall pass through the same atmosphere. By this arrangement, one fire cannot contaminate or block all exits in an open plan or flexible plan building. See Figure 11-5.

11-6.2.2   Exit access from interior rooms may pass through an adjoining or an intervening room provided that the travel distances do not exceed those set forth in 11-2.6. Foyers and lobbies constructed as required for corridors shall not be construed as intervening rooms.

11-6.2.3   Where the only means of egress from an interior room or rooms is through an adjoining or intervening room, smoke detectors shall be installed in the area of the common atmosphere through which the means of egress must pass. The detectors shall actuate alarms audible in the interior room and shall be connected to the school fire alarm system.

Exception No. 1:   Smoke detectors are not required where the aggregate occupant load is less than ten.

Exception No. 2:   Interior rooms used exclusively for mechanical and public utility service to the buildings.

Exception No. 3:   Where the building is protected throughout by an approved automatic sprinkler system in accordance with Section 7-7.

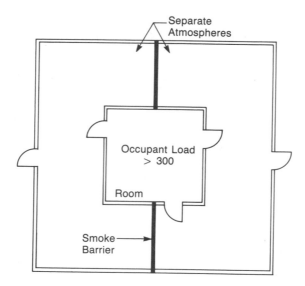

Figure 11-15.   Example of Room in Open Plan Building Requiring Two or More Means of Egress into Separate Atmospheres.

If the only means of egress from a room is through an adjoining or intervening room, smoke detectors must be installed in the room through which the means of egress must pass. This is because occupants of the interior room may not be aware of a fire or smoke condition in the intervening room, the room that provides their only means of egress. Alarm-sounding smoke detectors provide the occupants with an early warning so that they can safely pass through the room. It should be noted that if a corridor does not meet the corridor construction requirements, it would be considered an intervening space. (*See the definition of interior room in 11-1.3.*)

11-6.2.4   Flexible plan schools may have walls and partitions rearranged periodically only after revised plans or diagrams have been approved by the authority having jurisdiction.

Approval of revised plans or diagrams is necessary to avoid the possibility of circuitous exit paths or other arrangements not complying with the intent of the *Code*. Also note that flexible plan buildings are required to meet the requirements for corridor protection as well as subdivision of building spaces.

11-6.2.5   Open plan schools shall have furniture, fixtures, or low-height partitions so arranged that exits will be clearly visible and unobstructed, and exit paths are direct, not circuitous. If paths or corridors are established, they shall be at least as wide as required by 11-2.3.3.

Low-height partitions are 5 ft (152 cm) or less in height.

Corridors discussed in 11-6.2.5 must not have full-height partitions in order to provide unobstructed visual surveillance of the entire open plan area by members of the faculty located at any point in the area. The requirements for corridor protection contained in 11-3.6 do not apply to open plan schools. However, the requirements of 11-3.7 on subdivision of building spaces do apply.

11-6.2.6 Where existing flexible plan or open plan schools are remodeled and subdivided into rooms or spaces utilizing full height partitions, such schools shall comply with requirements of Section 10-1 through 10-5.

The Committee recognizes that there are many flexible or open plan schools that are being converted to standard classroom configurations. When these schools are remodeled, it is important that proper exiting, travel distances, and ventilation are provided. Sections 10-1 through 10-5 describe the specific details that must be met.

SECTION 11-7   DAY-CARE CENTERS

The day-care provisions are arranged to stand on their own from the rest of the chapter. The provisions of Sections 11-2 through 11-6 do not apply unless specifically referenced. The provisions include adult day care. Throughout the sections, the term "child" has been changed to "client" so that the provisions cover the entire age spectrum. Of course, in certain instances, provisions apply only to children; in those cases, the text has retained the term "child."

Formal Interpretation 76-108
Reference: 10-7 (11-7), 10-8 (11-8), 10-9 (11-9)

Question 1: Do the requirements of Sections 10-7 (11-7), 10-8 (11-8), or 10-9 (11-9) apply to church programs that provide day-care services to church members only, on a nonprofit basis?

Answer: Yes.

Question 2: Are churches also required to meet the provisions of Sections 10-7 (11-7), 10-8 (11-8), or 10-9 (11-9) in order to operate a church nursery while church services are being held?

Answer: Yes.

Question 3: Does Section 1-5 permit the city to grant an exception in these cases?

Answer: The authority having jurisdiction is given the power to grant exceptions where it is clearly evident that reasonable safety is thereby secured.

Issue Edition: 1976
Reference: 9-5.3, 9-5.4, 9-5.5
Date: March 1979

Table 11-1 summarizes the *Code's* requirements for the three types of day-care centers.

Table 11-1.   Minimum Requirements For Day-Care Centers

	Center	Group Home	Family Home
Number of Clients	>12	7 to 12	≤6
Number of Clients under Two Years	Any	3	2
Recommended Staff to Client Ratio	Age (yrs) Ratio <2 1:3 2-3 1:5 3-5 1:10 5-7 1:12 >7 1:15	2:12	1:6
Building Construction (permissible height vs. age of clients)	See 11-7.1.6.1	Rec. meet applicable building codes	Rec. meet applicable building codes
Occupant Load Factor	1 person/35 sq ft*	NR	NR
Area of Refuge	If center above fifth floor	NR	NR
Number of Exits	2 remote (see 11-7.2.4)	2 remote (see 11-8.2.4)	2 remote (see 11-9.2.4)
Travel Distance to Exit† (ft)*	100 (from room door) 150 (from any point in a room)	150 (from any point)	150 (from any point)
Exit Discharge	To outside	At least one directly to outside	At least one directly to outside
Illumination of Means of Egress	Per Section 5-8	Per Section 5-8	Per Section 5-8
Emergency Lighting	Per 11-2.9	NR (See 31-3.5)	NR (See 31-3.6)
Door Latches (closet)	Child opens from inside	Child opens from inside	Child opens from inside
Door Locks (bathroom)	Staff unlocks	Staff unlocks	Staff unlocks
Protection of Vertical Openings	See Section 6-2	See 11-8.3.1	NR
Hazard Protection	1-hr enclosure or automatic sprinklers (see 11-7.3.2)	NR	NR
Class of Interior Finish	B (all areas)	B (exits) C (all other spaces)	B (corridors, stairways, lobbies, and exits) C (all other spaces)
Class of Interior Floor Finish	I or II (corridors and exits)	NR	NR

*Conversion: 1 ft = .3048 m.   NR = No requirement.   †50 ft increase if sprinklered.

Table 11-1.   Continued

	Center	Group Home	Family Home
Alarm System	Manual (direct connection to fire department if > 100 clients)	NR	NR
Smoke Detectors	See 11-7.3.4.5	See 11-8.3.4	See 11-9.3.4
Extinguishers	Standpipes if building ≥ 6 stories		
Corridor Protection	Per 11-3.6.1	NR	NR
Electric Equipment	See NFPA 70 (receptacle covers required, Chapter 7)	See NFPA 70 (receptacle covers required, Chapter 7)	See NFPA 70 (receptacle covers required, Chapter 7)
HVAC	See Chapter 7	Separated from spaces by screens/partitions	See 11-9.5.2

*Conversion: 1 ft = .3048 m.   NR = No requirement.   †50 ft increase if sprinklered.

11-7.1 General Requirements.

11-7.1.1 Application.

11-7.1.1.1*   The requirements detailed in Section 11-7, Day-Care Centers (more than 12 clients), are based on the minimum staff-to-client ratios that follow:

Staff Ratio	Age
1:3	0 to 2
1:5	2 to 3
1:10	3 to 5
1:12	5 to 7
1:15	7 and over

The staff-to-client ratios may be modified by the authority having jurisdiction where safeguards, in addition to those specified by this section, are provided.

A-11-7.1.1.1   It should be noted that this paragraph does not require the staff ratios indicated but only states that the requirements of this section are based on these staff ratios. If these staff ratios are not maintained, it would be the responsibility of the authority having jurisdiction to determine what additional safeguards above and beyond the requirements of this section would be necessary. Typical additional provisions may include restricting the day-care center to the level of exit discharge, requiring additional smoke detection, requiring automatic sprinkler protection, requiring better or additional means of egress and similar types of items depending upon the situation.

11-7.1.1.2*   This section establishes life safety requirements for day-care centers in which more than 12 clients receive care, maintenance, and supervision by other than their relative(s) or legal guardian(s) for less than 24 hours per day. The provisions of Sections 11-2 through 11-6 shall not apply to this section unless a specific requirement is referenced by this section.

A-11-7.1.1.2   Day-care centers do not provide for the full-time maintenance of a client. Occupancies that provide a primary place of residence are dealt with in other occupancies. See Chapters 16 through 22, "Residential Occupancies."

The intent of 11-7.1.1.2 is to differentiate between institutions where clients are in residence 24 hours a day (such as orphanages) and day-care facilities where clients who normally reside at another location are provided care. A facility supplying "total care" for each client would provide laundries, dormitories, cafeterias, and other ancillary services not found in a day-care center. The life safety requirements of such a facility would be governed by other occupancy provisions of the *Code*.

11-7.1.1.3   Centers housing children 6 years of age and older shall conform to the requirements for educational occupancies, except as noted herein.

Centers that provide care only for children of school age are required to conform to the requirements for educational occupancies and to the special requirements for such facilities where they are located in buildings of other occupancies.

11-7.1.1.4   Where a facility houses more than one age group, the requirements for the younger shall apply, unless the area housing the younger is maintained as a separate fire area.

Exception*: Staff-to-client ratios of 11-7.1.1.1 shall be based on the number of clients in each age category.

A-11-7.1.1.4 Exception   An example of this exception is illustrated as follows: A center has 43 children

Three children age under two (1:3)	- 1 staff
Ten children age two to three (1:5)	- 2 staff
Thirty children age three to five (1:10)	- 3 staff
Total	- 6 staff

Therefore, the required staff for this center is six, not 15, which would be required for 43 children on a 1 to 3 staff ratio.

A separate fire area is usually constructed with walls that have a fire resistance rating of 2 hours. Most facilities governed by this chapter will be maintained as separate atmospheres through smoke partitions having a 1-hour fire resistance rating.

It was brought to the Committee's attention that some people were interpreting this section to apply to staff ratios. The Committee felt that to use the youngest age group to establish staff-to-client ratios for the entire group was too restrictive and did not meet the intent of the *Code* and, therefore, the Exception and appendix note were added.

11-7.1.2 Mixed Occupancies.

(a) Where centers are located in a building containing mixed occupancies, the occupancies shall be separated by 1-hour fire barriers.

Exception to (a): In assembly occupancies used primarily for worship.

(b) Centers in Apartment Buildings.

1. If the two exit accesses from the center enter the same corridor as the apartment occupancy, the exit accesses shall be separated in the corridor by a smoke barrier having not less than a 1-hour fire resistance rating. The smoke barrier shall be so located that there is an exit on each side of it.

2. The door in the smoke barrier shall be not less than 36 in. (91 cm) wide.

Exception to (b)2: Existing doors not less than 32 in. (81 cm) wide may be accepted.

3. The door assembly in the smoke barrier shall have a fire protection rating of at least 20 minutes and shall be self-closing or automatic-closing in accordance with 5-2.1.8.

Where a center is located in a building housing another occupancy, the operators of the center usually have no control of the safety procedures and precautions practiced outside the center. Paragraph 11-7.1.2 requires additional protection to minimize the clients' exposure to potential hazards outside the center.

The rationale used here for protection with a 20-minute door is the same as that used in Chapters 12 and 13 for health care facilities. The fuel load of the occupancy is not considered great enough to provide a severe attack on the door. This minimum construction will provide sufficient protection against flame and a good seal against smoke spread. The 20-minute door, coupled with the 1-hour wall, provides a barrier that will either contain a fire within a space for a limited time after it has been evacuated, or will prevent a fire from entering an occupied space for a period of time.

11-7.1.3 Special Definitions.   (None.)

11-7.1.4 Classification of Occupancy.   For the purposes of this section, clients are classified in age groups as follows: clients under 6 years of age, and clients 6 years of age and older.

11-7.1.5 Classification of Hazard of Contents.   The contents shall be classified as ordinary hazard in accordance with Section 4-2.

11-7.1.6 Minimum Construction Requirements.

11-7.1.6.1   Centers shall not be located above the heights indicated for the types of construction given in Table 11-7.1.6.1. (*See 6-2.1.*)

11-7.1.6.2 Location.   The story below the level of exit discharge may be used in buildings of any construction type other than Type II (000), Type III (200), and Type V (000). (*See 11-7.2.4.2.*)

11-7.1.7 Occupant Load.   The occupant load for which means of egress shall be provided for any floor shall be the maximum number of persons intended to occupy that floor but not less than one person for each 35 sq ft (3.3 sq m) of net floor area used by the clients.

Table 11-7.1.6.1   Height and Construction Limits

Type of Construction	Age Group	Number of Stories (Stories are counted starting at floor of exit discharge)			
		1	2	3	4 and over
I (443) I (332) II (222)	0 thru 5	X	X	X	X
	6 and older	X	X	X	X
II (111) III (211) V (111)	0 thru 5	X	X†	N.P.	N.P.
	6 and older	X	X	X†	N.P.
IV (2HH)	0 thru 5	X	X†	N.P.	N.P.
	6 and older	X	X†	N.P.	N.P.
II (000)	0 thru 5	X	X†	N.P.	N.P.
	6 and older	X	X†	N.P.	N.P.
III (200) V (000)	0 thru 5	X†	X†	N.P.	N.P.
	6 and older	X	X†	N.P.	N.P.

X: Permitted construction type
N.P.: Not Permitted
X†: Permitted if entire building is protected throughout by an approved automatic sprinkler system.

Where a center occupies a portion of a floor on which another occupancy exists, the occupant load for that floor is the sum of the occupant loads of the two occupancies. For example:

Net Floor Area (ft²)		Occupant Load Factor (ft²/person)		Occupant Load
Day-Care Center 1,750	÷	35	=	50
Assembly Occupancy 3,000	÷	7	=	429

By addition, the total occupant load for which means of egress must be provided would be 479. (*Also see commentary on 11-1.7.*)

11-7.2 Means of Egress Requirements.

11-7.2.1 General.   (None.)

11-7.2.2 Types of Exits.   (*See 11-2.2.*)

11-7.2.2.1 Stairs.   Exit stairs shall be enclosed in accordance with Chapter 5.

Paragraph 11-7.2.2.1 in conjunction with 11-7.3.1 excludes use of the provision in the Exception to 11-3.1.2 to permit an unenclosed stair between two adjacent floors when young children are on upper floors of the building. This is in recognition of the fact that young children have a low tolerance to smoke and are not capable of taking action for self-preservation on their own behalf. Thus, the *Code* attempts to protect them by enclosing all vertical openings.

11-7.2.2.2 Areas of Refuge. In buildings over five stories above ground level, areas of refuge shall be provided for occupants of day-care centers either by smokeproof enclosures or horizontal exits.

In all cases where day-care centers are found on upper floors of tall buildings, areas of refuge (smokeproof enclosures or horizontal exits) must be designed so that the clients will survive a fire. Five stories or approximately 75 ft (23 m) is the maximum height at which the fire department can be expected to rescue the occupants of a building from outside. However, many fire departments do not have the equipment to reach this height, and in such locations, areas of refuge are necessary at lower levels.

In any event, dependence on rescue by the fire department is not prudent. The time, number of personnel, and effort involved in rescuing one person by using an extension ladder is so great that it is not possible to rescue a large number of occupants by this method.

11-7.2.3 Capacity of Means of Egress. *(See 11-2.3.)*

11-7.2.4 Number of Exits.

11-7.2.4.1 Each floor occupied by clients shall have not less than two remote exits in accordance with Chapter 5.

11-7.2.4.2 Where the story below the level of exit discharge is occupied as a day-care center, the following apply:

(a) One means of egress shall be an outside or interior stair in accordance with 5-2.2. An interior stair, if used, shall only serve the level below the level of exit discharge. The interior stair may communicate with the level of exit discharge; however, the exit route from the level of exit discharge shall not pass through the stair enclosure.

(b) The second means of egress may be via an unenclosed stairway separated from the level of exit discharge in accordance with 6-2.4.3. The path of egress travel on the level of exit discharge shall be protected in accordance with 5-1.3.4.

Exception to (b): The path of travel on the level of exit discharge may be unprotected if the level of exit discharge and the level below the level of exit discharge are protected throughout by a smoke detection system or an approved automatic sprinkler system.

The requirements for using stories below the level of exit discharge have been revised for the 1988 *Code*. The intent is to make the *Code* both easier to understand and more realistic to enforce, while providing two protected ways out. Figure 11-16 illustrates the intent of 11-7.2.4.2.

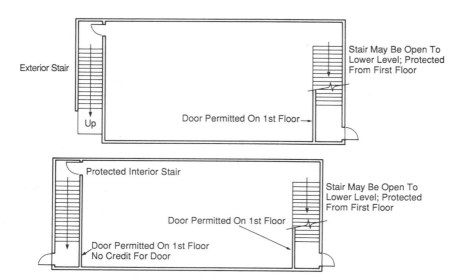

Figure 11-16. Egress for Levels Below the Level of Exit Discharge. Two methods of complying with 11-7.2.4.2 are illustrated. One stair must be a properly protected exit discharging outside, either an interior stair or outside stair. The other stair may be open to the lower level but must be separated from the first floor. This second way out either discharges directly outside or discharges through a corridor protected in accordance with 5-1.3.3. Note the Exception for corridor protection if both levels are sprinklered.

11-7.2.5 Arrangement of Means of Egress.   (Where the story below the exit discharge is used, see also 11-7.2.4.2.)

11-7.2.5.1   Means of egress shall be arranged in accordance with Section 5-5. Dead ends shall not exceed 20 ft (6.1 m).

Chapter 5 does not allow dead-end corridors except in accordance with the occupancy chapters. The Committee recognized that 20 ft (6.1 m) has been the accepted standard in educational occupancies and felt that it would be reasonable to retain it.

11-7.2.6 Travel Distance to Exits.

11-7.2.6.1   Travel distance shall be measured in accordance with Section 5-6.

11-7.2.6.2   Travel distance:

(a) Between any room door intended as exit access and an exit shall not exceed 100 ft (30 m);

(b) Between any point in a room and an exit shall not exceed 150 ft (45 m);

(c) Between any point in a sleeping room and an exit access door of that room shall not exceed 50 ft (15 m).

Exception: The travel distance in (a) and (b) above may be increased by 50 ft (15 m) in buildings protected throughout by an approved automatic sprinkler system in accordance with Section 7-7.

Paragraph 11-7.2.6.2 is structured to state the same thing several different ways. As shown in Figure 11-17, the maximum travel distance from a room door (exit access to the corridor) to an exit door is 100 ft (30 m). The total travel distance from any point (such as in a room) to an exit is 150 ft (45 m). The maximum travel distance from a point in a sleeping room to an exit access door is 50 ft (15 m). This in-room travel distance limit may not be increased even if the building is sprinklered.

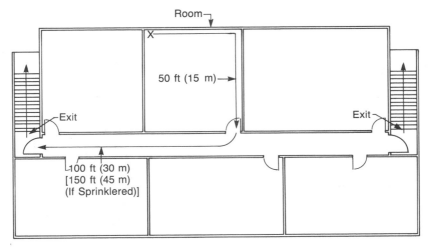

Figure 11-17. Maximum Travel Distance to Exit, Day-Care Center.

11-7.2.7 Discharge from Exits.   All exits shall discharge directly to the outside.

Exception: As provided in 11-7.2.4.2.

11-7.2.8 Illumination of Means of Egress.   Illumination of the means of egress shall be provided in accordance with Section 5-8.

11-7.2.9 Emergency Lighting.   Emergency lighting shall be provided in accordance with 11-2.9.

11-7.2.10 Marking of Means of Egress.   Means of egress shall have signs in accordance with Section 5-10.

11-7.2.11 Special Features.

11-7.2.11.1*   Every closet door latch shall be such that children can open the door from inside the closet.

A-11-7.2.11.1   The purpose of this requirement is to prevent arrangements where a child can be trapped in a closet. It is intended that this provision be broadly interpreted by the authority having jurisdiction to include equipment like refrigerators or freezers.

11-7.2.11.2   Every bathroom door lock shall be designed to permit opening of the locked door from the outside in an emergency. The opening device shall be readily accessible to the staff.

11-7.2.11.3 Panic Hardware or Fire Exit Hardware.   Any door in a required means of egress from an area having an occupant load of 100 or more persons may be provided with a latch or lock only if it is panic hardware or fire exit hardware.

This paragraph is based on the total occupant load of the area served and not the required capacity of the door. For example, if an area has an occupant load of 120 persons and is served by 3 doors, each door need only have capacity for 40 persons, but since all these doors serve an area with "100 or more persons," then any latches on these doors must be released by panic hardware or fire exit hardware.

11-7.2.11.4 Windows for Rescue and Ventilation.   Every room or space normally subject to client occupancy, other than bathrooms, shall have at least one outside window for emergency rescue or ventilation. Such window shall be openable from the inside without the use of tools and provide a clear opening of not less than 20 in. (50.8 cm) in width, 24 in. (61 cm) in height, and 5.7 sq ft (.53 sq m) in area. The bottom of the opening shall be not more than 44 in. (112 cm) above the floor.

In rooms located greater than three stories above grade, the openable clear height, width, and area of the window may be modified to the dimensions necessary for ventilation.

Exception No. 1:   In buildings protected throughout by an approved automatic sprinkler system in accordance with Section 7-7.

Exception No. 2:   Where the room or space has a door leading directly to the outside of the building.

The dimensions specified for windows used for emergency rescue or for ventilation are based on simulations of emergency rescue conducted by the San Diego Fire Department. Windows providing clear openings of identical dimensions are also required for rescue or ventilation in one- and two-family dwellings. Figure 11-11a on page 514 illustrates two configurations that achieve the required area of 5.7 sq ft (.53 sq m).

Although the *Code* intends the fire department or others to assist students, particularly over ladders, if these windows must be used as a supplementary means of escape, the windows should permit small children in the lower grades to escape unaided. Therefore, storm sashes, screens, or devices in front of the windows must be easy to open or remove and the sills must be low enough for the children to reach.

Where the location of windows precludes their use for rescue or escape, they may still provide trapped children with air for breathing in smoke-filled rooms.

Windows may be omitted if a classroom has a door leading directly to the outside or if the building is totally sprinklered.

The Committee did not feel it was practical to expect someone to use a window above the third story as an escape window. However, it is reasonable to expect the window to be usable for ventilation during a fire.

Note that Exception No. 1 requires that the building be protected throughout by an automatic sprinkler system. One question that is often asked is: If there are only a couple of windowless rooms can we just sprinkler those rooms? The answer is no! It must be remembered that the reason for the window is the potential blockage of the interior corridor by smoke from a fire in another part of the building. Putting sprinklers only in the windowless rooms would do nothing about smoke emanating from other areas.

11-7.3 Protection.

11-7.3.1 Protection of Vertical Openings.   Any vertical opening shall be enclosed and protected in accordance with Section 6-2.

11-7.3.2 Protection from Hazards.

11-7.3.2.1   Rooms or spaces for the storage, processing, or use of the materials specified in this section shall be protected in accordance with the following:

(a) Rooms or spaces used for the storage of combustible supplies in quantities deemed hazardous by the authority having jurisdiction, hazardous materials in quantities deemed hazardous by recognized standards, or fuel shall be separated from the remainder of the building by construction having not less than a 1-hour fire resistance rating with all openings protected by self-closing or smoke-actuated fire doors, or such rooms or spaces may be protected by an automatic extinguishing system as set forth in Section 6-4.

(b) Rooms or spaces used for processing or use of combustible supplies in quantities considered hazardous by the authority having jurisdiction, hazardous materials, or for flammable or combustible liquids in quantities deemed hazardous by recognized standards shall be separated from the remainder of the building by construction having not less than a 1-hour fire resistance rating with all openings protected by self-closing or smoke-actuated fire doors and shall also be protected by an automatic extinguishing system as set forth in Section 6-4.

(c) Boiler and furnace rooms, laundries, and maintenance shops, including woodworking and painting areas, shall be separated from the remainder of the building by construction having not less than a 1-hour fire resistance rating with all openings protected by self-closing or smoke-actuated fire doors, or such areas shall be protected throughout by an approved automatic extinguishing system as set forth in Section 6-4.

Exception to (c):   Rooms enclosing air-handling equipment.

(d)* Where automatic extinguishing systems are used to meet the requirements of this section, the rooms or spaces shall be separated from the remainder of the building by construction which resists the passage of smoke.

A-11-7.3.2.1(d)   It is not the intent of this provision to require a smoke barrier that meets the requirements of Section 6-3.

(e) Where automatic extinguishing is used to meet the requirements of this section, the protection may be in accordance with 7-7.1.2.

Exception: Food preparation facilities protected in accordance with 7-2.3 are not required to have openings protected between food preparation areas and dining areas. Where domestic cooking equipment is used for food warming or limited cooking, protection or segregation of food preparation facilities is not required if approved by the authority having jurisdiction.

The intent of 11-7.3.2.1 is to specify the degree of protection necessary for certain hazardous areas. It has been divided into three sections based on the degree of hazard. The hazards noted in items (a) and (c) are required to be enclosed in 1-hour construction or protected by sprinklers. If the sprinkler option is chosen, an enclosure is still required by item (d); however, the enclosure need not be rated, but only form a membrane against the passage of smoke.

The Committee felt that although sprinklers are provided and therefore fire-rated barriers may not be needed [*see (a)*], some barrier to control smoke migration is needed. Solid construction materials, such as glass or other non-fire-rated materials, are acceptable if they are installed in a manner that will resist smoke passing from one compartment to another. The new appendix note emphasizes that it is not the intent to require smoke barriers as provided in Section 6-3. This eliminates the more costly construction of a smoke barrier, which would require dampers and other required equipment.

The hazards noted in item (b) must be enclosed in 1-hour construction and be protected by automatic sprinklers.

The Exception to item (c) pertains to rooms housing air-handling equipment only. If the room is used for other purposes, then the provisions of item (a) or (b) apply.

Part (e) has been added as an editorial change to highlight the fact that Chapter 7 makes these requirements available to the user of the *Code*. Paragraph 7-7.1.2 provides an economical way of providing sprinkler protection in small rooms. (*See 11-3.2.3.*)

The intent of the Exception is to provide some barrier between cooking areas and dining areas. Openings in this barrier are not restricted and do not need to be protected. The *Code* is counting on the automatic extinguishing system to control any fire on the cooking surfaces, and, thus no longer requires enclosure by rated construction. The second sentence of the exception is quite important since this limited use of cooking equipment is often found in day care centers.

Figure 11-18 illustrates the different protection requirements of 11-7.3.2.1.

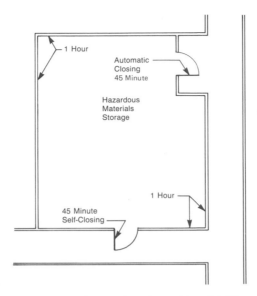

Figure 11-18 (a). Protection of Hazardous Areas. Part (a) illustrates one method of complying with 11-7.3.2.1 (a). See Figure 11-18 (b) for the alternate method.

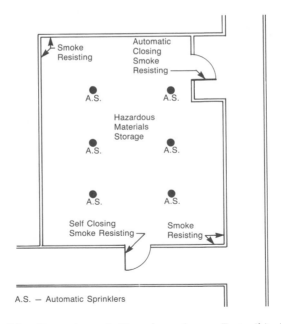

Figure 11-18 (b). Protection of Hazardous Areas. Part (b) illustrates an alternate method of complying with 11-7.3.2.1 (a). Figure 11-18 (a) illustrates another method of compliance.

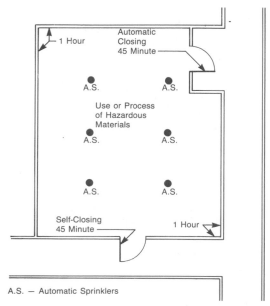

Figure 11-18(c). Protection of Hazardous Areas. Part (c) illustrates the requirements for complying with 11-7.3.2.1(b). Both one hour separation and automatic sprinkler protection is required in this case.

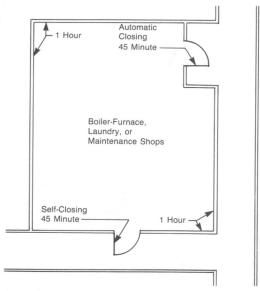

Figure 11-18(d). Protection of Hazardous Areas. Part (d) illustrates the requirements to comply with 11-7.3.2.1(c). However, in existing building, boiler rooms, furnace rooms and similar areas may use the sprinkler option as illustrated in Figure 11-18(b).

11-7.3.2.2 Janitor closets shall be protected by an automatic sprinkler system, which may be in accordance with 7-7.1.2. Doors to janitor closets may have ventilating louvers.

Where janitor closets are located off of corridors, a louvered door is usually provided for ventilation. It is necessary to provide these spaces with automatic sprinkler protection since the louvered door offers little fire resistance and permits a fire in the closet to directly affect the corridor. Paragraph 7-7.1.2 provides an economic method of providing sprinkler protection for such rooms. To accomplish this at reasonable cost, these sprinklers (not more than six in number) may be supplied from the domestic water supply to the closet if the supply is capable of providing the required quantity of water. It is advisable to provide a water-flow switch (*see Chapter 6*) to initiate an alarm when a sprinkler is opened.

The minimum flow of 0.15 gpm/sq ft (6.1 L/min/sq m) is based on the requirements in NFPA 13, *Standard for the Installation of Sprinkler Systems*, for protecting buildings containing ordinary hazards. It is important to ensure that the domestic supply can provide the required flow and pressure at the location.

11-7.3.3 Interior Finish.

11-7.3.3.1 Interior finish for all walls and ceilings shall be Class A or Class B in accordance with Section 6-5.

11-7.3.4 Detection, Alarm, and Communications Systems.

11-7.3.4.1 General. Day-care centers shall be provided with a fire alarm system in accordance with Section 7-6.

Exception No. 1: Day-care centers housed in one room.

Exception No. 2: Day-care centers with a required staff of fewer than four persons based on 11-7.1.1.1.

11-7.3.4.2 Initiation. Initiation of the required fire alarm system shall be by manual means and by operation of any required smoke detectors. (*See 11-7.3.4.5.*)

Exception: Single station detectors.

Single station smoke detectors by definition are not connected to an alarm system and are normally installed to provide a local alarm that will alert people in the immediate area that they should exit the area.

11-7.3.4.3 Occupant Notification. Occupant notification shall be by means of an audible alarm in accordance with 7-6.3.

11-7.3.4.4 Emergency Forces Notification. Fire department notification shall be accomplished in accordance with 7-6.4.

Exception: Day-care centers with not more than 100 clients.

In all day-care centers, manually operated fire alarm systems should be directly connected to the fire department. The Committee felt compelled to emphasize that in centers that serve more than 100 clients, this arrangement is essential. There are fire departments that will not accept direct alarms. In such cases, positive provisions must be made for rapid notification of the fire department by remote or central station systems.

11-7.3.4.5 Detection.

(a) A smoke detection system shall be installed in accordance with Section 7-6 with placement of detectors in each story in front of doors to the stairways and at no greater than 30 ft (9.1 m) spacing in the corridors of all floors containing the center. Detectors shall also be installed in lounges, recreation areas, and sleeping rooms in the center.

(b) Single station smoke detectors shall be provided in all rooms used for sleeping.

Exception No. 1: Centers housing clients 6 years of age or older if no sleeping facilities are provided.

Exception No. 2: Centers housed in only one room.

The purpose of this requirement is obvious, but worth noting. In centers housing children younger than six, naps and sleep time are provided. The smoke detection system will provide early warning of an impending fire. Exceptions are provided for centers housing only older clients and centers housed in a single room where a fire will be obvious to all occupants.

11-7.3.5 Extinguishment Requirements.

11-7.3.5.1   Standpipes for fire department use shall be installed in all buildings of six stories or more housing day-care centers. (*See Section 7-7.*)

11-7.3.6 Corridors.   Exit access corridors within day-care centers shall comply with 11-3.6.1. (*See 11-7.1.2.*)

The purpose of 11-7.3.6 is to provide a minimum level of compartmentation by use of corridor separation. (*See commentary on 11-3.6.1.*)

11-7.4 Special Provisions.   (None.)

11-7.5 Building Services.

11-7.5.1 Utilities.

11-7.5.1.1   Utilities shall comply with the provisions of Section 7-1.

11-7.5.1.2   Special protective covers for all electrical receptacles shall be installed in all areas occupied by children under 6 years of age.

Children are subject to serious injury if they insert foreign objects into electrical receptacles. Protective covers must be provided and maintained in order to avoid such accidents.

11-7.5.2 Heating, Ventilating, and Air Conditioning Equipment.

11-7.5.2.1   Heating, ventilating, and air conditioning equipment shall be installed in accordance with Section 7-2.

11-7.5.2.2   Unvented fuel-fired room heaters shall not be permitted.

The Committee does not feel that reasonable life safety should allow the use of unvented fuel-fired equipment with children. (*Also see commentary on 10-5.2.2.*)

11-7.5.2.3   Any heating equipment in spaces occupied by children shall be provided with partitions, screens, or other means to protect the children from hot surfaces and open flames. If solid partitions are used to provide such protection, provisions shall be made to assure adequate air for combustion and ventilation for the heating equipment.

The Committee felt it important that safeguards be provided to protect children from the hot surfaces of heating equipment. Young children do not always know the dangers of hot surfaces. The burn injury record clearly indicates that protection be provided. The Committee also wanted to make certain that adequate air is provided for combustion of the heating equipment. Incomplete or inadequate combustion could cause serious injury or death to the occupants.

11-7.5.3 Elevators, Dumbwaiters, and Vertical Conveyors.   Elevators, dumbwaiters, and vertical conveyors shall comply with the provisions of Section 7-4.

11-7.5.4 Rubbish Chutes, Incinerators, and Laundry Chutes.   Rubbish chutes, incinerators, and laundry chutes shall comply with the provisions of Section 7-5.

SECTION 11-8   GROUP DAY-CARE HOMES

Formal Interpretation 76-108
Reference: 10-7 (11-7), 10-8 (11-8), 10-9 (11-9)

Question 1: Do the requirements of Sections 10-7 (11-7), 10-8 (11-8), or 10-9 (11-9) apply to church programs that provide day-care services to church members only, on a nonprofit basis?

Answer: Yes.

Question 2: Are churches also required to meet the provisions of Sections 10-7 (11-7), 10-8 (11-8), or 10-9 (11-9) in order to operate a church nursery while church services are being held?

Answer: Yes.

Question 3: Does Section 1-5 permit the city to grant an exception in these cases?

Answer: The authority having jurisdiction is given the power to grant exceptions where it is clearly evident that reasonable safety is thereby secured.

Issue Edition: 1976
Reference: 9-5.3, 9-5.4, 9-5.5
Date: March 1979

11-8.1 General Requirements.

11-8.1.1 Application.

11-8.1.1.1* This section establishes life safety requirements for group day-care homes in which at least 7 but not more than 12 clients receive care, maintenance, and supervision by other than their relative(s) or legal guardian(s) for less than 24 hours per day (generally within a dwelling unit). The provisions of Sections 11-2 through 11-6 shall not apply to this section unless a specific requirement is referenced by this section.

A-11-8.1.1.1 Group day-care homes do not provide for the full-time maintenance of a client. Occupancies that provide a primary place of residence are dealt with in other occupancies. See Chapters 16 through 22, "Residential Occupancies."

These provisions are written keeping in mind that the typical group day-care home is usually in a residential setting.

11-8.1.1.2 The requirements detailed in Section 11-8 are based on a minimum staff-to-client ratio of two staff for up to 12 clients, with no more than three clients under age two. This staff-to-client ratio may be modified by the authority having jurisdiction where safeguards, in addition to those specified by this section, are provided.

If these staff ratios are not maintained, it would be the responsibility of the authority having jurisdiction to determine what additional safeguards above and beyond the requirements of this section would be necessary. Typical additional provisions may include restricting the group day-care home to the level of exit discharge, requiring additional smoke detection, requiring automatic sprinkler protection, requiring better or additional means of egress, and similar types of items depending upon the situation.

11-8.1.2 Mixed Occupancies.

(a) Where a group home is located in a building containing mixed occupancies, the occupancies shall be separated by 1-hour fire barriers.

Exception to (a): In assembly occupancies used primarily for worship.

(b) Homes in Apartment Buildings.

1. If the two exit accesses from the home enter the same corridor as the apartment occupancy, the exit accesses shall be separated in the corridor by a smoke barrier having not less than a 1-hour fire resistance rating. The smoke barrier shall be so located that there is an exit on each side of it.

2. The door in the smoke barrier shall be not less than 36 in. (91 cm) wide.

Exception to (b)2: Existing doors not less than 32 in. (81 cm) wide may be accepted.

3. The door assembly in the smoke barrier shall have a fire protection rating of at least 20 minutes and shall be self-closing or automatic-closing in accordance with 5-2.1.8.

Group day-care homes are often found in buildings housing occupancies such as apartments, stores, or assembly occupancies. In such buildings, exit accesses usually open into a corridor. Paragraph 11-8.1.2(b) describes the requirements for safeguarding the integrity of at least one egress path from such a facility.

11-8.1.3 Special Definitions.   (None.)

11-8.1.4 Classification of Occupancy.   No Requirements.

11-8.1.5 Classification of Hazard of Contents.   The contents shall be classified as ordinary hazard in accordance with Section 4-2.

11-8.1.6 Minimum Construction Requirements.   (None.)

11-8.1.7 Occupant Load.   No Special Requirements.

11-8.2 Means of Egress Requirements.

11-8.2.1 General.   (None.)

11-8.2.2 Types of Exits.   *(See 11-8.2.4.)*

11-8.2.3 Capacity of Means of Egress.   *(See 11-2.3.)*

11-8.2.4 Number of Exits.

11-8.2.4.1   Each floor occupied by clients shall have not less than two remote means of escape.

This is similar to the requirements of Chapter 22 for one- and two-family dwellings; however, 11-8.2.4.2 and 11-8.2.4.3 provide for an increase over what would normally be required for a private dwelling.

11-8.2.4.2   Where spaces on the floor above the floor of exit discharge are used by clients, at least one means of egress shall be an exit discharging directly to the outside. The second means of escape may be a window in accordance with 11-2.11.1. No room or space shall be occupied for living or sleeping purposes that is accessible only by ladder, folding stairs, or through a trap door.

The second floor of a typical single family dwelling is served by an open stair. This would require that the second floor be served by an enclosed exit if clients are upstairs.

11-8.2.4.3   Where clients are located on a story (basement) below the level of exit discharge, at least one means of egress shall be an exit discharging directly to the outside and the vertical travel to ground level shall not exceed 8 ft (244 cm). The second means of escape may be a window in accordance with 11-2.11.1. No facility shall be located more than one story below the ground. Any stairway to the story above shall be cut off by a fire barrier containing a door of at least a 20-minute fire protection rating, equipped with a self-closing device.

Similar to the requirement of 11-8.2.4.2 for a second floor, this mandates that when clients are below the level of exit discharge that at least one true exit be provided. In addition, any stairway to the first floor would require at least 20-minute protection.

As illustrated in Figure 11-19, there must be an exit directly from a group day-care center located in a basement to the outside, with vertical travel to ground level not exceeding 8 ft (244 cm). If a stairway to the story above were provided, it would have to be cut off from the basement by a fire barrier containing a door with a fire protection rating of at least 20 minutes.

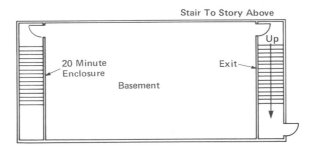

Figure 11-19.   Exit Requirements for Group Day-Care Center in Basement.

11-8.2.5 Arrangement of Means of Egress.   *(Where a story above or below the exit discharge is used, see 11-8.2.4.)*

11-8-2.5.1   Means of egress shall be arranged in accordance with Section 5-5. Dead ends shall not exceed 20 ft (6.1 m).

Chapter 5 does not allow for dead ends unless provided for by the occupancy chapters. The Committee felt that 20 ft (6.1 m) continues to be a reasonable distance for these types of occupancies.

11-8.2.6 Travel Distance to Exits.   *(See 11-2.6.)*

11-8.2.7 Discharge from Exits.   *(Where the story above or below the exit discharge is used, see 11-8.2.4.)*

11-8.2.8 Illumination of Means of Egress.   Illumination of the means of egress shall be provided in accordance with Section 5-8.

11-8.2.9 Emergency Lighting.   No Requirements.

11-8.2.10 Marking of Means of Egress.   No Requirements.

11-8.2.11 Special Requirements.

11-8.2.11.1* Every closet door latch shall be such that children can open the door from the inside of the closet.

A-11-8.2.11.1 The purpose of this requirement is to prevent arrangements where a child can be trapped in a closet. It is intended that this provision be broadly interpreted by the authority having jurisdiction to include equipment like refrigerators or freezers.

11-8.2.11.2 Every bathroom door lock shall be designed to permit opening of the locked door from outside in an emergency. The opening device shall be readily accessible to the staff.

11-8.3 Protection.

11-8.3.1 Protection of Vertical Openings.   The doorway between the level of exit discharge and any floor below shall be equipped with a door assembly having a 20-minute fire protection rating. Where the floor above the floor of exit discharge is used for sleeping purposes, there shall be a door assembly having a 20-minute fire protection rating at the top or bottom of each stairway.

Exception: Existing self-closing 1¾-in. (4.4-cm) solid bonded wood core doors without rated frames may be accepted by the authority having jurisdiction.

Also see 11-8.2.4.2 and 11-8.2.4.3.

11-8.3.2 Protection from Hazards.   No Requirements.

11-8.3.3 Interior Finish.

11-8.3.3.1 The interior finish in exits shall be Class A or B in accordance with Section 6-5.

11-8.3.3.2 Interior finish in occupied spaces in the home shall be Class A, B, or C in accordance with Section 6-5.

11-8.3.4 Detection, Alarm, and Communications Systems.

11-8.3.4.1 Within the group day-care home, smoke detectors shall be installed in accordance with 7-6.2.9.

Exception: Houses housing clients 6 years of age or older if no sleeping facilities are provided.

11-8.3.4.2 Where the group day-care home is located within a building of another occupancy, such as in apartment or office buildings, any corridors serving the group day-care home shall be provided with a smoke detection system in accordance with Section 7-6, with placement of detectors at no greater than 30 ft (9.1 m) spacing.

11-8.3.4.3 Single station smoke detectors shall be provided in all rooms used for sleeping.

The provisions of 11-8.3.4 are two-fold: first, to provide single station smoke detectors within the group day-care home in accordance with NFPA 74, *Standard for the Installation, Maintenance, and Use of Household Fire Warning Equipment*[2]; and second, to provide a smoke detection system in the corridor serving the group day-care home where in a building of mixed occupancy. In addition, 11-8.3.4.3 requires single station smoke detectors in each sleeping room, which is not required by NFPA 74.

11-8.4 Special Provisions. (None.)

11-8.5 Building Services.

11-8.5.1 Electrical Services.

11-8.5.1.1 Electrical wiring shall be installed in accordance with Section 7-1.

11-8.5.1.2 Special protective covers for electrical receptacles shall be installed in all areas occupied by children under 6 years of age.

11-8.5.2 Heating, Ventilating, and Air Conditioning Equipment.

11-8.5.2.1 Heating, ventilating, and air conditioning equipment shall be installed in accordance with Section 7-2.

11-8.5.2.2 Unvented fuel-fired room heaters shall not be permitted.

The Committee does not feel that reasonable life safety should allow the use of unvented fuel-fired equipment with children. (*Also see commentary on 10-5.2.2.*)

11-8.5.2.3 Any heating equipment in spaces occupied by children shall be provided with partitions, screens, or other means to protect the children from hot surfaces and open flames. If solid partitions are used to provide such protection, provisions shall be made to assure adequate air for combustion and ventilation for the heating equipment.

The Committee feels it important that safeguards be provided to protect children from the hot surfaces of heating equipment. Young children do not always know the dangers of hot surfaces. The burn injury record clearly indicates that protection be provided. The Committee also wanted to make certain that adequate air is provided for combustion of the heating equipment. Incomplete or inadequate combustion could cause serious injury or death to the occupants.

Screens that separate heating equipment from spaces occupied by children must be of closely spaced wire or expanded metal, of heavy gage, and must be securely attached to elements of the building. The purpose is to prevent children from bending the screens or inserting their fingers through the mesh.

SECTION 11-9   FAMILY DAY-CARE HOMES

Formal Interpretation 76-108
Reference: 10-7 (11-7), 10-8 (11-8), 10-9 (11-9)

Question 1: Do the requirements of Sections 10-7 (11-7), 10-8 (11-8), or 10-9 (11-9) apply to church programs that provide day-care services to church members only, on a nonprofit basis?

Answer: Yes.

Question 2: Are churches also required to meet the provisions of Sections 10-7 (11-7), 10-8 (11-8), or 10-9 (11-9) in order to operate a church nursery while church services are being held?

Answer: Yes.

Question 3: Does Section 1-5 permit the city to grant an exception in these cases?

Answer: The authority having jurisdiction is given the power to grant exceptions where it is clearly evident that reasonable safety is thereby secured.

Issue Edition: 1976
Reference: 9-5.3, 9-5.4, 9-5.5
Date: March 1979

11-9.1 General Requirements.

11-9.1.1 Application.

11-9.1.1.1* This section establishes life safety requirements for family day-care homes in which fewer than 7 clients receive care, maintenance, and supervision by other than their relative(s) or legal guardian(s) for less than 24 hours per day (generally within a dwelling unit). The provisions of Sections 11-2 through 11-6 shall not apply to this section unless a specific requirement is referenced by this section.

A-11-9.1.1.1 Family day-care homes do not provide for the full-time maintenance of a client. Occupancies that provide a primary place of residence are dealt with in other occupancies. See Chapters 16 through 22, "Residential Occupancies."

> Prior to the 1988 *Code*, this section dealt with "licensed" facilities.
> The Committee recognizes that licensing practices vary between jurisdictions. It was also a concern that the term "licensed family day-care home" would mean that, according to the *Code*, if a facility was not licensed, it did not have to meet the requirements of the *Code*. It is the intent of the Committee to include all family day-care centers as defined in 10-9.1.1.1, regardless of licensing.
> Family day-care homes are usually situated in single-family dwellings or in apartment houses. If they occur in apartment houses, they must also comply with the applicable requirements of 11-9.1.2.

11-9.1.1.2 The requirements detailed in Section 11-9 are based on a minimum staff-to-client ratio of one staff for up to six clients, including the caretaker's own children under age six, with no more than two children under age two.

> Many family day-care homes are located in single family residences. The Committee recognizes that in these types of situations, the caretaker's children should also be a consideration in determining staff-to-client ratios. This paragraph clarifies that distinction. The limit of two children

under age two recognizes the stricter staff ratio requirements for this age group. (For example, see staff ratio requirements for ages 0 to 2 in 11-7.1.1.1.)

11-9.1.2 Mixed Occupancies. Where family day-care homes are located in a building containing mixed occupancies, the occupancies shall be separated by 1-hour fire barriers.

Exception: In assembly occupancies used primarily for worship.

11-9.1.3 Special Definitions. (None.)

11-9.1.4 Classification of Occupancies. No Requirements.

11-9.1.5 Classification of Hazard of Contents. (Not specifically classified.)

11-9.1.6 Minimum Construction Requirements. (None.)

11-9.1.7 Occupant Load. No Special Requirements.

11-9.2 Means of Egress Requirements.

11-9.2.1 General. (None.)

11-9.2.2 Types of Exits. *(See 11-9.2.4.)*

11-9.2.3 Capacity of Means of Egress. *(See 11-2.3.)*

11-9.2.4 Number of Exits.

11-9.2.4.1 Every room used for sleeping, living, or dining purposes shall have at least two means of escape, at least one of which shall be a door or stairway providing a means of unobstructed travel to the outside of the building at street or ground level. The second means of escape may be a window in accordance with 11-2.11.1. No room or space shall be occupied for living or sleeping purposes that is accessible only by a ladder, folding stairs, or through a trap door.

This paragraph reflects the requirements for one- and two-family dwellings. The change from means of egress to means of escape also recognizes a window of proper size as one method of escaping a fire.

11-9.2.4.2 Where clients are located on a floor (basement) below the level of exit discharge, at least one means of egress shall be an exit discharging directly to the outside, and the vertical travel to ground level shall not exceed 8 ft (244 cm). The second means of escape may be a window in accordance with 11-2.11.1. No facility shall be located more than one story below the ground.

See commentary on 11-8.2.4.3. This is the same concept.

11-9.2.5 Arrangement of Means of Egress. *(See 11-9.2.4.)*

11-9.2.6 Travel Distance to Exits. *(See 11-2.6.)*

11-9.2.7 Discharge from Exits. *(See 11-9.2.4.)*

11-9.2.8 Illumination of Means of Egress. Illumination of the means of egress shall be in accordance with Section 5-8.

11-9.2.9 Emergency Lighting. No Requirements.

11-9.2.10 Marking of Means of Egress. No Requirements.

11-9.2.11 Special Features.

11-9.2.11.1 Each door in a means of egress shall not be less than 24 in. (61 cm) wide.

11-9.2.11.2* Every closet door latch shall be such that children can open the door from inside the closet.

A-11-9.2.11.2 The purpose of this requirement is to prevent arrangements where a child can be trapped in a closet. It is intended that this provision be broadly interpreted by the authority having jurisdiction to include equipment like refrigerators or freezers.

11-9.2.11.3 Every bathroom door lock shall be designed to permit the opening of the locked door from the outside in an emergency. The opening device shall be readily accessible to the staff.

11-9.3 Protection.

11-9.3.1 Protection of Vertical Openings. (No special provisions.)

11-9.3.2 Protection from Hazards. No Requirements.

11-9.3.3 Interior Finish.

11-9.3.3.1 The interior finish in corridors, stairways, lobbies, and exits shall be Class A or B in accordance with Section 6-5.

11-9.3.3.2 Interior finish in occupied spaces in the home shall be Class A, B, or C in accordance with Section 6-5.

11-9.3.4 Detection, Alarm, and Communications Systems.

11-9.3.4.1 Within the family day-care home, smoke detectors shall be installed in accordance with 7-6.2.9.

Exception: Homes housing clients 6 years of age or older if no sleeping facilities are provided.

11-9.3.4.2 Where the family day-care home is located within a building of another occupancy, such as in apartment or office buildings, any corridors serving the family day-care home shall be provided with a smoke detection system in accordance with Section 7-6, with placement of detectors at no greater than 30 ft (9.1 m) spacing.

11-9.3.4.3 Single station smoke detectors shall be provided in all rooms used for sleeping.

The provisions of 11-9.3.4 are two-fold: first, to provide single station smoke detectors within the group day-care home in accordance with NFPA 74, *Standard for the Installation, Maintenance, and Use of Household Fire Warning Equipment*[2]; and second, to provide a smoke detection system in the corridor serving the group day-care home where in a building of mixed occupancy. In addition, 11-9.3.4.3 requires single station smoke detectors in each sleeping room, which is not required by NFPA 74.

11-9.4 Special Provisions.   No Requirements.

11-9.5 Building Services.

11-9.5.1 Electrical Services.

11-9.5.1.1   Electrical wiring shall be installed in accordance with Section 7-1.

11-9.5.1.2   Special protective covers for all electrical receptacles shall be installed in all areas occupied by children in homes for children under 6 years of age.

11-9.5.2 Heating, Ventilating, and Air Conditioning Equipment.

11-9.5.2.1   Heating, ventilating, and air conditioning equipment shall be installed in accordance with Section 7-2.

11-9.5.2.2   Unvented fuel-fired room heaters shall not be permitted.

The Committee does not feel that reasonable life safety should allow the use of unvented fuel-fired equipment with children. (*Also see commentary on 10-5.2.2.*)

11-9.5.2.3   Any heating equipment in spaces occupied by children shall be provided with partitions, screens, or other means to protect the children from hot surfaces and open flames. If solid partitions are used to provide such protection, provisions shall be made to assure adequate air for combustion and ventilation for the heating equipment.

The Committee feels it important that safeguards be provided to protect children from the hot surfaces of heating equipment. Young children do not always know the dangers of hot surfaces. The burn injury record clearly indicates that protection be provided. The Committee also wanted to make certain that adequate air is provided for combustion of the heating equipment. Incomplete or inadequate combustion could cause serious injury or death to the occupants.

Screens that separate heating equipment from spaces occupied by children must be of closely spaced wire or expanded metal, of heavy gage, and must be securely attached to elements of the building. The purpose is to prevent the children from bending the screens or inserting their fingers through the mesh.

REFERENCES CITED IN COMMENTARY

[1]NFPA 13, *Standard for the Installation of Sprinkler Systems*, National Fire Protection Association, Quincy, MA, 1987.
[2]NFPA 74, *Standard for the Installation, Maintenance, and Use of Household Fire Warning Equipment*, National Fire Protection Association, Quincy, MA, 1984.

12 NEW HEALTH CARE OCCUPANCIES

(See also Chapter 31.)

This chapter covers the requirements for new health care occupancies. In editions of the *Code* prior to 1976, these occupancies were known as "Institutional Occupancies."

Detention and correctional occupancies are discussed in Chapters 14 and 15.

Health care occupancies are those used for medical or other treatment or care of four or more persons suffering from physical or mental illness, disease, or infirmity, and for the care of infants, convalescents, or infirm aged persons.

Health care occupancies addressed in this chapter include:
1. Hospitals
2. Nursing Homes
3. Limited Care Facilities
4. Ambulatory Health Care Centers.

Hospitals, nursing homes, and limited care facilities provide sleeping facilities for the occupants and are occupied by persons who are mostly incapable of self-preservation because of age, physical or mental disability, or because of security measures not under the occupants' control.

Ambulatory health care centers are significantly different from other health care occupancies in that they do not provide sleeping facilities and are, therefore, covered separately in Section 12-6.

SECTION 12-1 GENERAL REQUIREMENTS

12-1.1 Application. *(See also Section 1-4.)*

12-1.1.1 General.

12-1.1.1.1 New health care facilities shall comply with the provisions of this chapter. *(See Chapter 31 for operating features.)*

Exception*: Facilities where the authority having jurisdiction has determined equivalent safety is provided in accordance with Section 1-5.

A-12-1.1.1.1 Exception   In determining equivalancy for conversions, modernizations, renovations, or unusual design concepts of hospitals or nursing homes, the authority having jurisdiction may accept evaluations based on Chapter 3 of NFPA 101M, *Alternative Approaches to Life Safety*, utilizing the parameters for new construction.

The Exception to 12-1.1.1.1 emphasizes that Section 1-5 permits alternative designs to literal Code requirements that would still be considered in compliance with the Code. However, the authority having jurisdiction ultimately determines whether or not equivalent safety has been provided.

Paragraph 12-1.1.1.1 and accompanying Exception are not intended to limit the methods an authority having jurisdiction might use to determine equivalency. However, as noted in A-12-1.1.1.1, Chapter 3 of NFPA 101M, *Alternative Approaches to Life Safety*,[1] provides an "equivalency system" that uses numerical values to analyze the firesafety effectiveness of a building design. This system is known as the Firesafety Evaluation System (FSES). The system provides a methodology by which alternative designs can be evaluated as options to literal *Code* compliance. In providing the equivalency system, it is not the intent to limit equivalency evaluations solely to this one system. The authority having jurisdiction retains the authority to evaluate and approve alternative designs on the basis of appropriate supporting data. The FSES may be used to assist in this evaluation. This Exception in no way mandates the use of the FSES, nor does it require the authority having jurisdiction to accept the results of an evaluation using the system.

Although the FSES was developed primarily to evaluate alternative designs in existing buildings, it is particularly useful for determining equivalency for conversions, modernizations, renovations, or unusual design concepts — all of which would be considered new construction. However, the FSES is a tool to help determine equivalency, and it should not be used to circumvent *Code* requirements. In new construction, *Code* requirements must be met, or equivalent safety must be provided by alternative means approved by the authority having jurisdiction.

12-1.1.1.2   This chapter establishes life safety requirements for the design of all new hospitals, nursing homes, and limited care facilities. Where requirements vary, the specific occupancy is named in the paragraph pertaining thereto. Section 12-6 establishes life safety requirements for the design of all new ambulatory health care centers.

Chapter 13 provides the requirements for existing health care facilities and existing ambulatory health care centers.

12-1.1.1.3   Health care occupancies are those used for purposes such as medical or other treatment or care of persons suffering from physical or mental illness, disease or infirmity; for the care of infants, convalescents, or infirm aged persons.

12-1.1.1.4   Health care facilities provide sleeping accommodations for the occupants and are occupied by persons who are mostly incapable of self-preservation because of age, physical or mental disability, or because of security measures not under the occupants' control.

12-1.1.1.5   This chapter also covers ambulatory health care centers as defined in 12-1.3(d). See Section 12-6 for requirements.

Since ambulatory health care centers do not provide sleeping accommodations, they are treated separately in Section 12-6.

12-1.1.1.6   Buildings or sections of buildings that primarily house patients who are capable of judgment and appropriate physical action for self-preservation under emergency conditions in the opinion of the governing body of the facility and the governmental agency having jurisdiction may come under other chapters of the *Code* instead of Chapter 12.

12-1.1.1.7   It shall be recognized that, in buildings housing certain types of patients or having detention rooms or a security section, it may be necessary to lock doors and bar windows to confine and protect building inhabitants. In such instances, the authority having jurisdiction shall make appropriate modifications to those sections of this *Code* that would otherwise require exits to be kept unlocked.

12-1.1.1.8   Buildings or sections of buildings that house older persons and that provide activities that foster continued independence but do not include those services distinctive to health care facilities [as defined in 12-1.3(c)] may be subject to the requirements of other sections of this *Code*, such as Chapters 18 or 21.

12-1.1.1.9   Health care occupancies shall include all buildings or parts thereof with occupancy as described in this chapter under Special Definitions, 12-1.3.

12-1.1.1.10   Except for ambulatory health care centers, facilities that do not provide housing on a 24-hour basis for their occupants are classified as other occupancies and are covered by other chapters of the *Code*.

Paragraphs 12-1.1.1.3 through 12-1.1.1.10 contain explanatory material indicating some general characteristics of the occupants of health care occupancies. A few fundamental safeguards are also set forth. Formal definitions are established in 12-1.3.

As implied by the definitions of 12-1.3 and stated in 12-1.1.1.4, health care facilities, except ambulatory health care centers, are buildings that provide sleeping facilities (24-hour care) for occupants. Occupants in a health care facility may be restrained, but are housed primarily for treatment of mental or physical infirmities. Where occupants are restrained for penal or corrective purposes, the building would be classified as a detention and correctional occupancy, which is treated in Chapters 14 and 15.

If a building is used for the treatment or housing of patients, including the mentally handicapped (*see 12-1.1.1.6*) or older persons (*see 12-1.1.1.8*) where:

1. Occupants are not restrained by locked doors or other devices, and

2. The patients are ambulatory, and

3. The occupants are capable of perceiving threat and taking

appropriate action for self-preservation, then the building may be classed as an occupancy other than health care.

Occupants of health care facilities are considered to be incapable of self-preservation (*see 12-1.1.1.4*) because of age, because of physical or mental disability, or because of security measures not under the occupants' control. A significant number of occupants in health care facilities are assumed to be nonambulatory or bedridden. Other occupants, who are capable of self-movement, may have impaired judgment.

Although locking exit doors and barring windows is always undesirable from the viewpoint of life safety, the *Code* recognizes that, in some cases, it is necessary to restrain people. In these instances, provision should be made for the continuous supervision and prompt release of restrained persons. (*See 12-1.1.1.7.*) Release of occupants should be accomplished by a system capable of automatically unlocking the doors in the means of egress, or by the presence of attendants who are continuously available and equipped with keys. In any event, continuous supervision is considered essential. (*See 12-2.2.2.5.*)

12-1.1.2* Objective.   The objective of this chapter is to provide a reasonable level of safety by reducing the probability of injury and loss of life from the effects of fire with due consideration for functional requirements. This is accomplished by limiting the development and spread of a fire emergency to the room of fire origin and reducing the need for occupant evacuation, except from the room of fire origin.

A-12-1.1.2   This objective is accomplished in the context of the physical facilities, the type of activities undertaken, the provisions for the capabilities of staff, and the needs of all occupants through requirements directed at the:

(a) Prevention of ignition

(b) Detection of fire

(c) Control of fire development

(d) Confinement of the effects of fire

(e) Extinguishment of fire

(f) Provision of refuge and/or evacuation facilities

(g) Staff reaction.

It should be recognized that the well-being of an individual located in the room of fire origin can be reasonably ensured only through control of that individual's environment. That is, only through complete control of the environment, including building members, building finishes, furnishings, decorations, clothing, linens, bedding, and the like, can the individual be protected against fire. However, no code can prevent injury resulting from a person's careless actions.

Although an effort should be made to protect the individual through prevention efforts, the primary objective of the requirements of Chapter 12 is to limit fire size or to prevent fire from escaping the room of origin and thereby limit the threat to individuals outside the room of origin.

12-1.1.3 Total Concept. All health care facilities shall be so designed, constructed, maintained, and operated as to minimize the possibility of a fire emergency requiring the evacuation of occupants. Because the safety of health care occupants cannot be assured adequately by dependence on evacuation of the building, their protection from fire shall be provided by appropriate arrangement of facilities, adequate staffing, and careful development of operating and maintenance procedures composed of the following:

(a) Proper design, construction, and compartmentation; and

(b) Provision for detection, alarm, and extinguishment; and

(c) Fire prevention and the planning, training, and drilling in programs for the isolation of fire, transfer of occupants to areas of refuge, or evacuation of the building.

> Vertical movement of patients within a health care facility is an inefficient, time consuming process. In one study, it was demonstrated through the simulated evacuation of patients from a second-story ward to ground level that more than 30 minutes may be required for evacuation during a fire.
>
> The provisions of Chapter 12, therefore, are based upon a "defend in place" philosophy, which minimizes the probability of a fire necessitating vertical movement of occupants. Patients in critical care areas may be connected to life support equipment, which makes movement difficult, and, in some cases, impossible. Barriers are required to provide for the horizontal movement of patients to safe areas of refuge on a single floor level and to maintain a manageable limit on the number of occupants exposed to any single fire. Vertical means of egress (stairs or ramps) are specified by Chapter 12 as escape routes for visitors and staff and as a "last line of defense" for the movement of patients.

12-1.1.4 Additions, Conversions, Modernization, Renovation, and Construction Operations. (*See also 1-4.5 and 1-4.6.*)

12-1.1.4.1 Additions. Additions shall be separated from any existing structure not conforming to the provisions within Chapter 13 by a fire barrier having at least a 2-hour fire resistance rating constructed of materials as required for the addition.

> Paragraph 12-1.1.4.1 establishes separation criteria for additions to existing structures where existing structures do not conform to the provisions of Chapter 13. It should be emphasized that, where an existing building meets the provisions of Chapter 13, the building would be in compliance with the *Code* and the addition would not require separation.
>
> Where additions must be separated, barriers must be constructed of assemblies providing a minimum of 2-hour fire resistance. Where the structural framing of the addition or the existing buildings are of assemblies of less than 2-hour fire resistance, special provision must be made to ensure the necessary separation will be maintained for the 2-hour period.
>
> Materials used in the construction of the barrier should be "constructed to the standards of the addition." That is, if the addition is required to be

constructed of noncombustible or limited-combustible materials (construction Types I or II), then the materials used in the barrier must be limited-combustible or noncombustible as defined in NFPA 220, *Standard on Types of Building Construction.*[2] Conversely, if the addition is permitted to be constructed of combustible materials, then combustible materials may be used as a portion of the barrier.

12-1.1.4.2 Communicating openings in dividing 'fire barriers required by 12-1.1.4.1 shall occur only in corridors and shall be protected by approved self-closing fire doors. (*See also Section 6-2.*)

12-1.1.4.3 Doors in barriers required by 12-1.1.4.1 shall normally be kept closed.

Exception: Doors may be held open only if they meet the requirements of 12-2.2.2.6.

Openings in barriers separating additions from nonconforming existing structures are limited to corridors. (*See 12-1.1.4.2.*) Openings are required to be protected by 1½-hour, "B" labeled, fire door assemblies. The fire doors are required to be self-closing and to be maintained closed, or they may be held open by an automatic device in accordance with 12-2.2.2.6. (*See Figure 12-1.*)

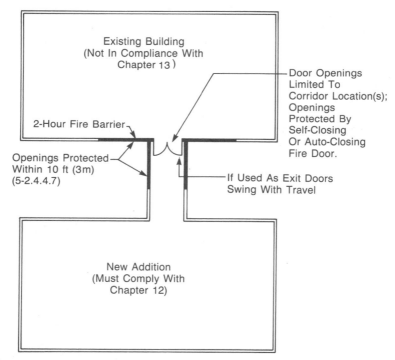

Figure 12-1. Separation of New Addition from Existing Building Not in Compliance with Chapter 13. If the addition is of fire-resistive or noncombustible (Types I or II) construction, use noncombustible or limited-combustible materials in the 2-hour fire barrier. (*See NFPA 220, Standard on Types of Building Construction.*)[2]

12-1.1.4.4 Conversions. Conversions shall comply with 1-6.4. A conversion from a hospital to a nursing home or from a nursing home to a hospital is not a change in occupancy or suboccupancy classification.

Any building converted to a health care facility from some other occupancy (dormitory, for example) must be altered to comply with the provisions of Chapter 12 for new health care facilities. The conversion of a hospital to a nursing home is sometimes questioned as to whether or not such a conversion represents a change in occupancy. Conversion of a hospital to a nursing home or vice versa would not constitute a change in occupancy. Therefore, prior to and after such a conversion, the facility must comply with the criteria of Chapter 13 for existing health care facilities.

12-1.1.4.5 Modernizations or Renovations. In modernization projects and renovations to existing facilities, only that portion of the total facility affected by the project need comply with the provisions of Chapter 12 in accordance with Section 1-4.6.

Alterations of health care facilities are regulated by 1-4.6 and 12-1.1.4.5. Alterations may not reduce the level of life safety below that which exists prior to the alterations; however, provisions in excess of the requirements for new construction are not required to be maintained. Suppose, for example, an existing hospital has a 6-ft (1.8-m) wide corridor, and a portion of the hospital is to be renovated. Even though it is an existing building, a minimum 6-ft (1.8-m) wide corridor must be maintained. Conversely, suppose a portion of an existing hospital equipped with a 10-ft (3.1-m) wide corridor is to be altered. It may be reduced to 8 ft (2.4 m), which is the requirement for new construction. If alterations require replacement of a portion of a hospital corridor wall, this portion of the wall should be increased to 1-hour fire resistance in accordance with the requirements for new construction. However, it would not be required that the corridor width be increased to 8 ft (2.4 m) unless it was practical to do so. As a minimum, in all instances, whether or not renovations or alterations are planned, existing buildings must comply with the requirements contained in Chapter 13.

Only that portion of a facility that is being renovated is required to comply with Chapter 12. For example, assume a floor of a hospital is subdivided into three sections and only one section is undergoing renovation. Only the one section being renovated would require compliance, to the extent practical, with Chapter 12.

Although an effort should always be made to satisfy the criteria for new construction during a building alteration or the installation of new equipment, the *Code* recognizes that such modifications cannot always be accomplished. Guidance for achieving "equivalency" to life safety is provided in Section 1-5. In any event, alterations or the installation of new building service equipment must be accomplished in such a manner that the level of life safety that results is equivalent or superior to that prescribed for existing buildings.

12-1.1.4.6 Construction Operations.   See 1-6.3 and Chapter 31 for life safety provisions during construction.

The introduction of "outside" workers and activities associated with the construction of an addition creates unusual risks of fire in health care occupancies. Special precautions should be taken to guard against the potential exposure created by the introduction of flammable substances or by other hazardous practices that could pose a threat to occupants. (*See 31-1.1.2.*) Temporary fire resistant barriers should be erected to separate the new construction and associated activity from the functioning areas of the existing buildings. Care should be taken to prevent blockage of means of egress for the existing building by the construction of such barriers. Special care is also necessary to ensure that all existing equipment for fire protection and all portions of the required means of egress are maintained in full working order. (*See 1-6.3.*)

Adequate escape facilities should be provided and continuously maintained for the use of construction workers. (*See 31-1.1.1 and NFPA 241, Standard for Safeguarding Building Construction and Demolition Operations.*[3])

12-1.2 Mixed Occupancies.   (*See also 1-4.7.*)

12-1.2.1*   Sections of health care facilities may be classified as other occupancies if they meet all of the following conditions:

(a) They are not intended to serve health care occupants for purposes of:

1. Housing, or

2. Treatment, or

3. Customary access by patients incapable of self-preservation.

(b) They are adequately separated from areas of health care occupancies by construction having a fire resistance rating of at least 2 hours.

A-12-1.2.1   Doctors' offices, treatment and diagnostic facilities intended solely for outpatient care and physically separated from facilities for the treatment or care of inpatients, but otherwise associated with the management of an institution, may be classified as Business Occupancy, rather than Health Care Occupancy.

12-1.2.2   Ambulatory care (*see Section 12-6*), medical clinics, and similar facilities that are contiguous to health care occupancies but are primarily intended to provide outpatient services may be classified as a business or ambulatory care occupancy, provided the facilities are separated from health care occupancies by not less than 2-hour fire-resistive construction.

Exception*:   Where a facility is intended to provide services for health care patients who are litter borne, it shall meet all requirements for health care facilities.

A-12-1.2.2 Exception   It is expected that an occasional hospital patient who may be litter-borne will enter ambulatory care, medical clinics, and similar facilities that are primarily intended to provide outpatient services and are classified as a Business or Ambulatory Care Occupancy.

Paragraphs 12-1.2.1 and 12-1.2.2 set forth criteria for classifying spaces as "other" occupancies, although they are located in buildings used primarily for health care purposes. Paragraph 12-1.2.1 would allow offices to be classified as business occupancies, cafeterias to be classified as assembly occupancies, dormitories to be classified as residential, etc., if both items (a) and (b) of 12-1.2.1 are met. Paragraph 12-1.2.1(a) notes that customary access by patients incapable of self-preservation is not permitted within the other occupancy. This paragraph is intended to allow an occasional ambulatory inpatient to visit a doctor's office — for example, in an adjacent business building — without requiring classification of the business occupancy as a health care facility. However, if either item (a) or (b) is not met, then the area would be considered "mixed occupancy," and the provisions of 1-4.7 would apply and require that the more restrictive life safety provisions apply. (*See 1-4.7.*)

Paragraph 12-1.2.2 covers a subject similar to 12-1.2.1, but specifically discusses ambulatory care centers, medical clinics, and similar areas that primarily provide outpatient services. If these facilities are separated by 2-hour fire-resistive construction, then they may be classified as ambulatory health care centers or as business occupancies, whichever applies. If, however, litter-borne inpatients are treated on any regular basis, then the facility must meet the requirements for health care occupancies. The provisions of business occupancies and ambulatory health care centers were written around the concept that most people are treated on an outpatient basis.

Note that 12-1.2.4, subject to certain qualifications, allows the means of egress from health care areas using a horizontal exit to traverse non-health care spaces.

12-1.2.3 Health care occupancies in buildings housing other occupancies shall be completely separated from them by construction having a fire resistance rating of at least 2 hours as provided for additions in 12-1.1.4.

Paragraph 12-1.2.3 requires that if a health care occupancy is located in a building of another classification (such as business, storage, mercantile, or industrial), the health care occupancy must be separated from the other occupancy by construction having a fire resistance rating of 2 hours, as detailed in 12-1.1.4. (*Also see the commentary following 12-1.1.4.1.*)

Note that 12-1.2.3 deals with occupancy classification and not with hazard of contents. Hazard of contents is treated in 12-1.2.6 and 12-1.2.7.

12-1.2.4 All means of egress from health care occupancies that traverse non-health care spaces shall conform to requirements of this *Code* for health care occupancies.

Exception: It is permissible to exit through a horizontal exit into other contiguous occupancies that do not conform to health care egress provisions but that do comply with requirements set forth in the appropriate occupancy chapter of this Code as long as the occupancy does not contain high hazard contents. The horizontal exit must comply with the requirements of 12-2.2.5.

Paragraph 12-1.2.4 specifies that the means of egress from health care occupancies that traverses non-health care spaces must conform to the requirements for health care occupancies. However, an exception is allowed where a 2-hour barrier is provided and such barrier is used as a horizontal exit. Where a 2-hour barrier serves as a horizontal exit, it is acceptable to exit into a different occupancy provided the other occupancy complies with the provisions of the *Code* that would be applicable thereto and does not contain high hazard contents. For example, if a horizontal exit is provided between a health care facility and a business occupancy, inpatients may exit into the business occupancy through a horizontal exit. In this instance, corridor width, corridor partitions, stairway details, and the like must conform to the provisions set forth within either Chapters 26 or 27, which deal with business occupancies. However, the horizontal exit must comply with all the requirements of 12-2.2.5.

12-1.2.5   Auditoriums, chapels, staff residential areas, or other occupancies provided in connection with health care facilities shall have exits provided in accordance with other applicable sections of the *Code.*

Auditoriums, chapels, and other areas separated by 2-hour construction and meeting the criteria of 12-1.2.1 and 12-1.2.2 for other occupancies are required to be designed in accordance with the appropriate occupancy chapter governing their use.

Spaces used for non-health care purpose but located within a health care facility should have means of egress features designed in accordance with the use of the space. For example, if a space located in a health care facility is used as a chapel or auditorium, occupant loads should be calculated on the basis of an assembly occupancy. Assuming an occupant load is in excess of 50, then egress features should be designed as would be appropriate for an assembly occupancy. In such circumstances, doors in the means of egress should be side-hinged swinging doors, arranged to swing in the direction of exit travel (*see 5-2.1.4.1*), and should not be equipped with a latch or lock unless such a latch or lock is operated by panic hardware. (*See 8-2.2.2.3.*)

Exit capacity should be computed on the basis of occupant characteristics. If, for example, the space is used only by staff, visitors, and others who are mobile and otherwise capable of self-preservation, then exit capacity could be computed on the basis of Chapter 8. If, on the other hand, the space is used by health care occupants, then exit capacity should be calculated in accordance with Chapter 12, even though occupant load might be calculated in accordance with Chapter 8.

12-1.2.6   Any area with a hazard of contents classified higher than that of the health care occupancy and located in the same building shall be protected as required in 12-3.2.

Paragraph 12-1.2.6 regulates spaces in a health care facility that, although comprising only a portion of the facility, contain more hazardous materials (in quantity or type) than are usually found in most other spaces.

Spaces such as rooms used for the storage of combustible materials, trash collection rooms, gift shops, and paint shops must be protected in accordance with 12-3.2.

12-1.2.7   Non-health care related occupancies classified as containing high hazard contents shall not be permitted in buildings housing health care occupancies.

Paragraph 12-1.2.7 prohibits another occupancy (such as storage) with highly hazardous contents (such as flammable liquids) from being located in a building housing health care occupancies.

This paragraph limits use based upon occupancy classification with regard to hazard of contents. For example, the paragraph is not meant to exclude laboratory operations as a portion of a health care facility. The intent is to prevent a portion of a hospital from being converted or designed for use as an educational or research facility (classed as an educational or possibly an industrial occupancy) which has laboratories using and storing sizable quantities of flammable liquids.

12-1.3 Special Definitions.

(a) *Hospital.* A building or part thereof used on a 24-hour basis for the medical, psychiatric, obstetrical, or surgical care of four or more inpatients. Hospital, wherever used in this *Code*, shall include general hospitals, psychiatric hospitals, and specialty hospitals.

(b) *Nursing Home.* A building or part thereof used on a 24-hour basis, for the housing and nursing care of four or more persons who, because of mental or physical incapacity, may be unable to provide for their own needs and safety without the assistance of another person. Nursing home, wherever used in this *Code*, shall include nursing and convalescent homes, skilled nursing facilities, intermediate care facilities, and infirmaries in homes for the aged.

(c) *Limited Care Facility.* A building or part thereof used on a 24-hour basis for the housing of four or more persons who are incapable of self-preservation because of age or physical limitation due to accident or illness or mental limitations, such as mental retardation/developmental disability, mental illness, or chemical dependency.

(d) *Ambulatory Health Care Centers.* A building or part thereof used to provide services or treatment to four or more patients at the same time and meeting either (1) or (2) below.

1. Those facilities that provide, on an outpatient basis, treatment for patients that would render them incapable of taking action for self-preservation under emergency conditions without assistance from others, such as hemodialysis units or freestanding emergency medical units.

2. Those facilities that provide, on an outpatient basis, surgical treatment requiring general anesthesia.

Paragraph 12-1.3(a) through (d) defines the characteristics of the occupancies covered by Chapter 12. Except as discussed below for ambulatory health care, a building must house four or more people incapable of self-preservation on a 24-hour basis in order to be classed as a health care occupancy.

Occupants of hospitals or nursing homes are assumed to be nonambulatory and incapable of self-preservation. In making this judgment, due consideration should be given to the use of physical restraints and tranquilizing drugs, which can render occupants immobile. Variable staffing criteria and levels of care make differentiation between hospitals and nursing homes apparent. The difference between nursing homes and limited care facilities is less clear.

Although limited care facilities house four or more occupants incapable of self-preservation, due to age or physical or mental limitations, occupants are generally considered to be ambulatory and would require only limited assistance during emergency evacuation. Buildings that house mentally handicapped occupants or persons being treated for alcohol or drug abuse who are ambulatory and may be expected to evacuate a structure with limited assistance would meet the criteria for limited care facilities. Day-care facilities that provide care for the aged, children, mentally handicapped, or others would be classified as other than health care if the care or treatment is not provided on a 24-hour basis. (*See Chapter 10.*)

Although age, in itself, is not sufficient justification to develop a separate classification for a health care occupancy, it should be recognized that the elderly present a unique problem in firesafety. Experiences in buildings where the elderly are housed reveal that the reaction of the elderly to a fire may not be directed toward self-preservation. On discovering a fire, the elderly occupant may ignore it, be transfixed by it, or seek refuge from it in his or her room and fail to notify anyone else of the fire. In some cases, the elderly have resisted efforts to remove them from the building and familiar surroundings.

Terms such as "residential," "lodging and boarding," and "custodial care," previously used in 12-1.3, have been deleted to avoid confusion with a residential occupancy classification included in Chapter 21, which was added to the 1985 Edition of the *Code*. Board and care facilities, personal care homes, halfway houses, or similar facilities house occupants who may require medication and personal care, but do not require the close supervision and services typical of the occupants in a health care facility and therefore would be classified as residential occupancies. Occupant capability must be carefully evaluated to determine whether application of health care criteria (Chapter 12) or application of lesser safeguards associated with residential occupancies (Chapter 21) is more appropriate.

Prior to the 1981 Edition of the *Code*, occupancies that offered medical services on an outpatient basis would have been regulated within the chapter dealing with business occupancies. The threat to life in an outpatient facility where four or more patients may be subject to medical procedures requiring general anesthesia, treatments such as hemodialysis, or free-standing emergency service is significantly greater than that typical of a business occupancy. Conversely, application of the requirements for health care facilities that contemplate 24-hour care would be inappropriate and would be unnecessarily restrictive. In establishing the occupancy classification of an ambulatory health care center, it was intended to develop requirements that fall between the restrictions applicable to business occupancies and health care facilities in terms of level of life safety achieved.

12-1.4 Classification of Occupancy. *(See Definitions, 12-1.3.)*

12-1.5 Classification of Hazard of Contents. The classification of hazard of contents shall be as defined in Section 4-2.

12-1.6 Minimum Construction Requirements.

12-1.6.1 For the purpose of 12-1.6, stories shall be counted starting at the primary level of exit discharge and ending at the highest occupiable level. For the purposes of this section, the primary level of exit discharge of a building shall be that floor that is level with or above finished grade of the exterior wall line for 50 percent or more of its perimeter. Building levels below the primary level shall not be counted as a story in determining the height of a building.

Formal Interpretation 81-3
Reference: 12-1.6.1

Question: Where stories are counted from an established "primary level of exit discharge," is it the intent of 12-1.6.1 that any story below not be counted regardless of the degree to which it is exposed above finished grade of exterior wall line?

Answer: See answer below.

Question: If, due to grade differences, a building has two "primary levels of exit discharge," each with the required number of exits, is it the intent of 12-1.6.1 that stories can be counted starting at the upper of the two discharge levels?

Answer: See answer below.

Question: If, due to grade differences, a building has an upper "primary level of exit discharge" and a lower level with separate independent exits to outside grade [disregarding communicating stairway(s)], is it the intent of 12-1.6.1 that stories can be counted starting at the upper "primary level of exit discharge"?

Answer: For the purpose of determining construction type and related minimum building requirements, the level of exit discharge is determined as being the lowest story having at least 50 percent of the perimeter exposed above grade. Each building can have only one primary level of exit discharge.

Issue Edition: 1981
Reference: 12-1.6.1
Date: August 1981

Allowable building construction types are determined as a function of the number of stories in a building. In determining the number of stories, the first story is considered to be the primary level of exit discharge. Only occupiable levels are counted in determining story height. For example, an unoccupied attic would not constitute a story.

Difficulties have been experienced in determining story height where a building is located on a sloping grade. Paragraph 12-1.6.1 notes that a story on a sloping site that is partially below grade should be counted as a story if the floor is level with or above grade for 50 percent or more of the perimeter of the building at the exterior wall. (*See Figure 12-2.*)

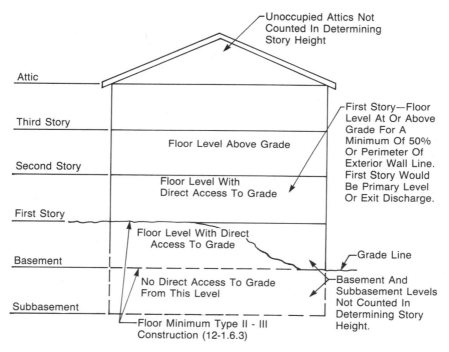

Figure 12-2. Building Section View Illustrates Application of 12-1.6.1 and 12-1.6.6.

12-1.6.2   Health care occupancies shall be limited to the following types of building construction (*see 6-2.1*):

Table 12-1.6.2

Construction Type	1 Story	2 Stories	3 Stories and <45 ft	4 or 5 Stories and <75 ft	6 or more Stores or ≥75 ft
I (443) I (332) II (222)	X	X	X†	X†	X††
II (111)	X	X††	X††	N.P.	N.P.
II (000)	X††	N.P.	N.P.	N.P.	N.P.
III (211)	X††	N.P.	N.P.	N.P.	N.P.
III (200)	N.P.	N.P.	N.P.	N.P.	N.P.
IV (2HH)	X††	N.P.	N.P.	N.P.	N.P.
V (111)	X††	N.P.	N.P.	N.P.	N.P.
V (000)	N.P.	N.P.	N.P.	N.P.	N.P.

X = Permitted type of construction
X† = Building, other than Hospitals, requires supervised automatic sprinkler protection (*see 12-3.5.1*)
X†† = Building requires supervised automatic sprinkler protection (*see 12-3.5.1*)
N.P. = Not Permitted

Exception: Any building of Type I or Type II (222 or 111) construction may include roofing systems involving combustible supports, decking, or roofing provided: (1) the roof covering meets Class A requirements in accordance with NFPA 256, Standard Methods of Fire Tests of Roof Coverings, and (2) the roof is separated from all occupied portions of the building by a noncombustible floor assembly having at least a 2-hour fire resistance rating that includes at least 2½ in. (6.4 cm) of concrete or gypsum fill. To qualify for this exception, the attic or other space so developed shall either be unoccupied or protected throughout by an approved automatic sprinkler system.

Construction types permitted in new health care facilities are indicated as a function of height in 12-1.6.2. See **NFPA 220, *Standard on Types of Building Construction*,**[2] for definitions of construction types.

Multistory, health care facilities are required to be constructed of noncombustible materials with a minimum 2-hour fire resistance rating. It is recognized that movement of patients may not be possible, and occupants of a health care facility may be required to remain in the structure for the duration of the fire. In specifying 2-hour fire resistance, it is intended that building members be adequately protected against fire effects to assure building stability for the projected fire duration.

An exception is allowed for buildings completely protected by automatic sprinklers. Type II (111) structures can be erected to a maximum of three stories where a complete system of electrically supervised automatic sprinklers is provided.

In certain areas, it has been common practice to erect a building with a flat concrete roof deck. A wood deck on wood frame peaked roof is then added for weather protection. Paragraph 12-1.6.2 contains an Exception that permits, under certain conditions, construction of such a combustible roof system on a multistory building without jeopardizing the building construction (Type I or II) classification. The Exception specifies the attic space must either be unoccupied or protected with automatic sprinklers. The term "unoccupied" is meant to disallow the presence of mechanical equipment requiring periodic maintenance, storage, or like practices, unless the space is sprinklered. (*Also see commentary following 12-3.5.1.*)

12-1.6.3 All interior walls and partitions in buildings of Type I or Type II construction shall be of noncombustible or limited-combustible materials.

NFPA 220, *Standard on Types of Building Construction*,[2] establishes restrictions relative to the use of combustible building materials within structures required to be constructed of noncombustible or limited-combustible materials. NFPA 220 should be consulted for specific limitations. The terms noncombustible and limited-combustible are defined within NFPA 220 and are repeated in Chapter 3 of the *Code* for quick reference.

12-1.6.4 Openings for the passage of pipes or conduit in walls or partitions that are required to have fire or smoke resisting capability shall be protected in accordance with 6-2.3.4.2 or 6-3.6.1.

Fire and smoke may spread across a fire-rated barrier or fire-rated wall via openings created by the passage of pipes, conduit, or other building services. Paragraph 12-1.6.4 specifies that, where such penetrations occur, suitable appliances such as metal plates, masonry fill, or other products approved for the purpose should be installed to maintain the fire and smoke resisting capability of the barrier. (*For fire and draftstopping in walls, ceilings, and attics, see 6-2.3.*)

12-1.6.5 For construction requirements of enclosures of vertical openings between floors, see 12-3.1.

12-1.6.6 All buildings with more than one level below the level of exit discharge shall have all such lower levels separated from the level of exit discharge by at least Type II (111) construction.

12-1.7 Occupant Load. The occupant load for which means of egress shall be provided for any floor shall be the maximum number of persons intended to occupy that floor but not less than one person for each 120 sq ft (11.1 sq m) gross floor area in health care sleeping departments, and not less than one person for each 240 sq ft (22.3 sq m) of gross floor area of inpatient health care treatment departments. Gross floor areas shall be measured within the exterior building walls with no deductions. (*See Chapter 3.*)

Paragraph 12-1.7 sets forth criteria for projecting occupant loads. The minimum occupant load for which exits must be provided in all buildings may not be less than that established by projections involving (1) one person for each 120 sq ft (11.1 sq m) of gross floor area in health care sleeping areas, and (2) one person for each 240 sq ft (22.3 sq m) of gross floor area in inpatient health care treatment areas. However, if by actual count, the number of persons exceeds that number projected by area calculations, then the actual number of persons present becomes the minimum population load for which exits must be provided.

The maximum number of people allowed to occupy a space is limited by available exit capacity and other functional considerations. It is not intended to limit populations based upon the area projections contained in this paragraph.

SECTION 12-2   MEANS OF EGRESS REQUIREMENTS

12-2.1 General.   Every aisle, passageway, corridor, exit discharge, exit location, and access shall be in accordance with Chapter 5.

Exception No. 1:   As modified in the following paragraphs.

Exception No. 2:   The requirements of Chapter 5 specifying net clear door width do not apply. Projections into the door opening by stops or by hinge stiles shall be permitted.

Means of egress details are to conform to the fundamental provisions in Chapter 5, except as modified in Chapter 12. (*For example, see Exception No. 2 to 12-2.1.*) Exception No. 2 would continue to allow the width of exit doors to be measured on the basis of actual door leaf width. Hinge stile and stops that project into the door opening are to be ignored in health care facilities. This is because these projections were taken into consideration when the larger widths specified in Chapter 12 were developed. In addition, these larger widths inherently meet the requirements of Chapter 5.

12-2.2* Means of Egress Components.

A-12-2.2   In planning exits, arrangements should be made to transfer patients from one section of a floor to another section of the same floor separated by a fire barrier or smoke barrier in such a manner that patients confined to their beds may be transferred in their beds. Where the building design will permit, the section of the corridor containing an entrance or elevator lobby should be separated from corridors leading from it by fire or smoke barriers. Such arrangement, where the lobby is centrally located, will, in effect, produce a smoke lock, placing a double barrier between the area to which patients may be taken and the area from which they must be evacuated because of threatening smoke and fire.

12-2.2.1   Components of the Means of Egress shall be limited to the types described in 12-2.2.2 through 12-2.2.7.

12-2.2.2 Doors.

12-2.2.2.1   Doors shall comply with 5-2.1.

12-2.2.2.2   Locks shall not be permitted on patient sleeping room doors.

Exception No. 1:   Key locking devices that restrict access to the room from the corridor and that are operable only by staff from the corridor side may be permitted. Such devices shall not restrict egress from the room.

This Exception allows rooms that are not being used to be secured by staff. However, in case someone is in the room, the *Code* requires that the lock cannot restrict egress from the room.

Exception No. 2:   Door locking arrangements are permitted in health care occupancies or portions of health care occupancies where the clinical needs of the patients require specialized security measures for their safety, provided keys are carried by staff at all times.

Some health care facilities may be required to provide resident security, but the *Code* emphasizes that staff must have immediate access to patient rooms.

12-2.2.2.3   Doors not in a required means of egress may be subject to locking.

12-2.2.2.4   Doors within a required means of egress shall not be equipped with a latch or lock that requires the use of a tool or key from the egress side.

Exception No. 1:   Door locking arrangements are permitted in mental health facilities (See 12-1.1.1.7 and 12-2.2.2.5.)

Note that 12-1.1.1.7 allows the authority having jurisdiction to make appropriate modifications to compensate for locking of egress doors.

Exception No. 2:   Special locking arrangements complying with 5-2.1.6 are permitted provided not more than one such device may be in any egress path.*

A-12-2.2.2.4 Exception No. 2   The intent of the provision is that a person following the natural path of the means of egress not encounter more than one delay release device along that path of travel to an exit. Thus, each door from the multiple floors of a building that opens into an enclosed stair may have its own delay release device, but an additional delay release device could not be present at the level of exit discharge on the door that discharges people from the enclosed stair to the outside.

Paragraph 5-2.1.6 sets minimum requirements for delayed release hardware, including the fact that the building must be protected throughout by automatic sprinklers or automatic fire detection.

In the 1985 Edition, time delay locks, in accordance with 5-2.1.6, were permitted only on exterior exit doors. In the 1988 Edition, the Exception has been changed to permit the use of time delay locks on any door. However, only one door in each means of egress for any given space may involve such a feature.

12-2.2.2.5   In buildings in which doors are locked, provisions shall be made for the rapid removal of occupants by such reliable means as the remote control of locks or by keying all locks to keys readily available to staff who are in constant attendance.

In buildings where it is necessary to lock doors, continuous supervision by staff must be provided. Provisions must be made for the prompt release of restrained persons either by equipping staff with keys or by providing remote unlocking capabilities for doors. Where staff relies on the use of keys, consideration should be given to a master key system, which would facilitate the quick release of occupants.

12-2.2.2.6*   Any door in an exit passageway, stairway enclosure, horizontal exit, smoke barrier, or hazardous area enclosure (except boiler rooms, heater rooms, and mechanical equipment rooms) may be held open only by an automatic release device that complies with 5-2.1.8. The automatic sprinkler system if provided, the required fire alarm system, and the systems required by 5-2.1.8(c) shall be arranged so as to initiate the closing action of all such doors by zone or throughout the entire facility.

A-12-2.2.2.6   It is desirable to keep doors in exit passageways, stair enclosures, horizontal exits, smoke barriers, and required enclosures around hazardous areas closed at all times to impede the travel of smoke and fire gases. Functionally, however, this involves decreased efficiency and limits patient observation by the staff of an institution. To accommodate these necessities, it is practical to presume that such doors will be kept open even to the extent of employing wood chocks and other makeshift devices. Doors in exit passageways, horizontal exits, and smoke barriers should, therefore, be equipped with automatic hold-open devices activated by the methods described regardless of whether or not the original installation of the doors was predicated on a policy of keeping them closed.

12-2.2.2.7   Where doors in a stair enclosure are held open by an automatic device as permitted in 12-2.2.2.6, initiation of a door closing action on any level shall cause all doors at all levels in the stair enclosure to close.

Where doors are held open, the automatic device must cause the doors to close upon operation of the manual fire alarm system. Further, the doors must be arranged to close automatically by actuation of either: (1) a complete smoke detection system covering the entire building; or (2) smoke detectors installed to detect smoke on either side of the door. In addition, if the facility is sprinklered, the water flow alarm shall also close the doors.
   [*See also 5-2.1.8(d) and NFPA 72E, Standard on Automatic Fire Detectors.*[4]] As a further safeguard for stairways, any action that causes a stairway door to close on one level must cause all stairway doors to close on all levels. (*See 12-2.2.2.7 and 12-3.1.2.*)

12-2.2.2.8   High rise health care occupancies shall comply with the provisions of 5-2.1.5.2. Selected doors on stairways may be equipped with hardware that prevents reentry in accordance with 5-2.1.5.2 Exception No. 1.

Paragraph 12-2.2.2.8 regulates stairway reentry in buildings having occupied floor levels more than 75 ft (23 m) above the lowest level of fire department access. In so stating the *Code* is exempting low rise health care occupancies from the requirements of 5-2.1.5.2. Stair doors must allow for reentry in accordance with Chapter 5. All stair doors must be unlocked or must be interlocked with the building fire alarm in order to unlock automatically in the event of alarm actuation. Paragraph 5-2.1.5.2 Exception No. 1 allows doors to be locked provided the following requirements are met: a minimum of two doors must be maintained unlocked; there must be a maximum of four intervening floors between operable doors; reentry must be possible at the top or next to top floor level; reentry on the top or next to top floor level must provide access to a different exit; and doors that are unlocked must be appropriately marked.

12-2.2.3 Stairs.   Stairs shall comply with 5-2.2.

12-2.2.4 Smokeproof Enclosures.   Smokeproof enclosures shall comply with 5-2.3.

12-2.2.5 Horizontal Exits.   Horizontal exits shall comply with 5-2.4, modified as follows:

(a) At least 30 net sq ft (2.8 sq m) per patient in a hospital or nursing home or 15 net sq ft (1.4 sq m) per resident in a limited care facility shall be provided within the aggregated area of corridors, patient rooms, treatment rooms, lounge or dining areas, and other low hazard areas on each side of the horizontal exit. On stories not housing bed or litter patients, at least 6 net sq ft (.56 sq m) per occupant shall be provided on each side of the horizontal exit for the total number of occupants in adjoining compartments.

(b) A single door may be used in a horizontal exit if the exit serves one direction only. Such door shall be a swinging door or a horizontal sliding door complying with 5-2.1.14. The door shall be a minimum of 44 in (112 cm) in width.

(c) A horizontal exit involving a corridor 8 ft (244 cm) or more in width serving as a means of egress from both sides of the doorway shall have the opening protected by a pair of swinging doors arranged to swing in the opposite direction from each other, with each door being at least 44 in. (112 cm) wide, or a horizontal sliding door complying with 5-2.1.14 and providing a clear opening of at least 88 in (224 cm).

(d) A horizontal exit involving a corridor 6 ft (183 cm) or more in width serving as a means of egress from both sides of the doorway shall have the opening protected by a pair of swinging doors, arranged to swing in the opposite direction from each other, with each door being at least 34 in. (86 cm) wide, or a horizontal sliding door complying with 5-2.1.14 and providing a clear opening of at least 68 in. (173 cm).

(e) An approved vision panel is required in each horizontal exit. Center mullions are prohibited.

(f) The total exit capacity of the other exits (stairs, ramps, doors leading outside the building) shall not be reduced below one-third that required for the entire area of the building.

The requirements for horizontal exits in 12-2.2.5(a) through (f) are illustrated in Figures 12-3 and 12-4.

Doors in horizontal exits are required to swing in the direction of exit travel. In the case of a fire barrier serving as a horizontal exit for two adjoining fire areas, a pair of doors arranged with each leaf to swing in a direction opposite from the other, or some other equivalent arrangement, must be used. If a fire barrier serves as a horizontal exit from just one fire area, the door opening may be protected by a single door [44 in. (112 cm) wide in hospitals and nursing homes, or 34 in. (86 cm) wide in limited care facilities] arranged to swing in the direction of exit travel.

In prohibiting center mullions, the intent is to eliminate any obstructions in the corridor that would restrict the movement of patients in beds, on litters, or in wheelchairs.

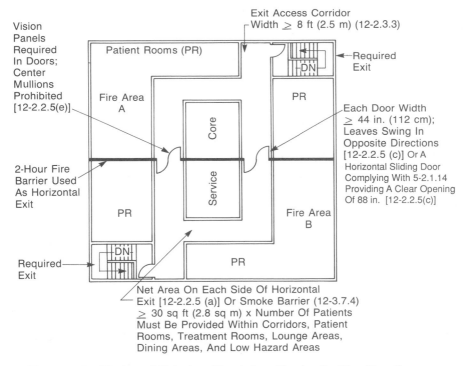

Figure 12-3. Horizontal Exits in a Hospital or Nursing Facility, New Construction. At least one exit for each fire area must be an interior stair, smokeproof enclosure, outside stair, Class A ramp, exit passageway, or door to outside (*see 12-2.4.2*). Such an exit must provide at least one-third the required exit capacity of the fire area which it serves. [*See 12-2.2.5(f).*]

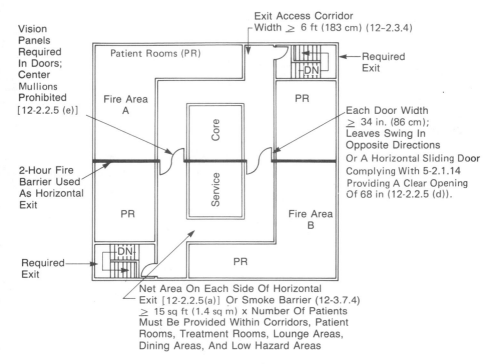

Figure 12-4.   Horizontal Exits in a Limited Care Facility, New Construction.   At least 1 exit for each fire area must be an interior stair, smokeproof enclosure, outside stair, Class A ramp, exit passageway, or door to outside (12-2.4.2). Such an exit must provide at least one-third the required exit capacity of the fire area which it serves [*See 12-2.2.5(f)*.]

Corridors in limited care facilities and psychiatric hospitals are required to be six feet wide, and therefore, it would not be practical to install a pair of 44-in. (112-cm) wide doors to protect corridor openings in a horizontal exit. In recognition of this practical consideration and because no obstructions like mullions are permitted, doors protecting openings in horizontal exits of such facilities are required to be a minimum of 34 in. (86 cm) wide.

The 1988 Edition of the *Code* recognizes the use of sliding doors complying with 5-2.1.14 for the protection of openings in horizontal exits. The use of power-operated sliding doors results in an obstruction-free opening for normal traffic while still providing adequate fire protection for openings.

Because of practical difficulties involving vertical exit travel in health care facilities, special recognition is given to horizontal travel and the use of horizontal exits. Up to two-thirds of the total required exit capacity for a given fire area may be provided by horizontal exits. [*See 12-2.2.5(f)*.] It should be noted, however, that every floor or fire section must be equipped with at least one exit consisting of a door leading directly outside the building, an interior stair, an outside stair, a smokeproof enclosure, a ramp, or an exit passageway. (*See 12-2.4.2.*) In other words, no fire area can be served only by horizontal exits. In the event a horizontal exit also serves as a smoke barrier, see commentary following 12-2.4.3 and in 12-3.7.

12-2.2.6 Ramps.

12-2.2.6.1   Ramps shall be Class A and shall comply with 5-2.5.

Exception: A Class B ramp may be used where the height of the ramp is 1 ft (30.5 cm) or less.

12-2.2.6.2   Ramps enclosed as exits shall be of sufficient width to provide exit capacity in accordance with 12-2.3.2.

Ramps are undesirable in hospitals and nursing homes because of the accident hazard in both normal and emergency traffic, except in the case of ramps of extremely gradual slope, which require so much space as to be impracticable in most situations. They are, however, the only practicable method of moving patients in beds from one story to another, except by elevators, which may not be available under fire conditions. The best plan is to provide for horizontal egress to another section of the building, minimizing the need for complete evacuation.

Ramps may be the best means for providing egress from doors two or three steps above or below the grade level, and also to compensate for minor differences in floor levels between adjoining sections of buildings. Such ramps should be in accordance with 12-2.2.6.1.

12-2.2.7 Exit Passageways.   Exit passageways shall comply with 5-2.6.

12-2.3 Capacity of Means of Egress.

12-2.3.1   The capacity of any required means of egress shall be based on its width as defined in Section 5-3.

12-2.3.2   The capacity of means of egress providing travel by means of stairs shall be 1.0 in. (2.5 cm) per person; and the capacity of means of egress providing horizontal travel (without stairs) such as doors, ramps, or horizontal exits shall be 0.7 in. (1.8 cm) per person.

Exception: The capacity of means of egress in health care occupancies protected throughout by an approved supervised automatic sprinkler system may be increased to 0.6 in. (1.5 cm) per person for travel by means of stairs and to 0.5 in. (1.3 cm) per person for horizontal travel without stairs.

The manner by which exit capacity is calculated has been changed in the 1988 Edition to recognize the concept of "effective width." (*See Chapter 2 of NFPA 101M, Manual on Alternative Approaches to Life Safety.*[1]) The new method of calculation relates the usable width of an exit and the anticipated egress flow. The new computational approach is based upon research that shows exit capacity varies with exit width, based upon a linear relationship, rather than the step function used in previous editions.

Previous editions of the *Code* calculated exit capacity based upon units of exit width [22 in. (55.9 cm)]. Increases in exit capacity were permitted only for minimum 12 in. (30.5 cm) increases (½ unit of exit width). Therefore, exit capacity for a 44 in. (112 cm) stair (2 units) was computed at 44 people (22 people per unit × 2 units). No increase in capacity was allowed for stair width increases up to an additional 11 in. (27.9 cm) [55 in. (139.7 cm) stair]. A 56 in. (142.2 cm) stair [44 in. (112 cm) plus 12 in. (30.5 cm) or 2.5 units] had a capacity of 55 persons (22 people per unit × 2.5 units).

The method prescribed by the 1988 Edition acknowledges that increasing the width of egress systems results in increasing the flow. The new arrangement computes stair egress capacity in nonsprinklered buildings on the basis of 1.0 in. (2.54 cm) per person. Therefore, a 44 in. (112 cm) stair provides adequate egress for 44 persons [44 in. (112 cm)/1.0 in. (2.54 cm) per person]. Similarly, a 50 in. (127 cm) stair would have a capacity of 50 persons.

The exit capacities in 12-2.3.2 are substantially less than for other occupancies, based upon the assumption that some of the occupants cannot leave without physical assistance and some may have to be carried or moved in beds. The increase in exit capacity for automatic sprinkler protection is based upon the assumption that sprinklers will limit fire size, thereby allowing greater time for safe egress.

Health care occupancies are the only occupancies in the *Code* that allow an increase in exit capacity due to automatic sprinkler protection. The following table readily shows the sprinkler benefit:

Capacity (Inches per person)

	Nonsprinklered	Sprinklered
Stairs	1.0	0.6
Level Travel	0.7	0.5

12-2.3.3*   Aisles, corridors, and ramps required for exit access in a hospital or nursing home shall be at least 8 ft (244 cm) in clear and unobstructed width. Where ramps are used as exits, see 12-2.2.6.

Exception: Aisles, corridors, and ramps in adjunct areas not intended for the housing, treatment, or use of inpatients may be a minimum of 44 in. (112 cm) in clear and unobstructed width.

A-12-2.3.3 Occupant characteristics are an important factor to be evaluated in setting exit criteria. Exit components in non-patient use areas, such as Administrative Office spaces, should be evaluated based upon actual use. A minimum "clear" corridor width of 44 in. (112 cm) is specified, assuming occupants in non-patient areas will be mobile and capable of evacuation without assistance.

Formal Interpretation 76-130
Reference: 12-2.3.3

Question: Is it the intent of 12-2.3.3, given a treatment suite subject to "inpatient use" that is subdivided by noncombustible partitions into individual treatment rooms without doors, that the access to these treatment rooms is required to be 8 ft (244 cm) wide?

Answer: No.

Issue Edition: 1976
Reference: 10-2.2.5.2
Date: January 1980

Exit access routes in hospitals and nursing homes are required to be 8 ft (244 cm) in clear width based on the assumption that during a fire emergency, some patients may require movement in beds, on litters, or in wheelchairs. In fact, 31-4.1.2 requires beds to be easily movable and equipped with casters. Conversely, 44-in. (112-cm) wide access routes are considered acceptable within areas not subject to use by inpatients, such as administrative office spaces where occupants are assumed to be mobile and capable of evacuation without assistance. (*See Figure 12-5.*)

Ramps enclosed and otherwise arranged and used as exits must be of sufficient width to adequately accommodate the required exit capacity on the basis of 0.7 in. (1.8 cm)/person. (*See 12-2.3.2.*) For example, if a Class A ramp is to be used as an exit for 80 persons, the ramp must be a minimum of 56 in. (142 cm) wide.

12-2.3.4* Aisles, corridors, and ramps required for exit access in a limited care facility or hospital for psychiatric care shall be at least 6 ft (183 cm) in clear and unobstructed width. Where ramps are used as exits, see 12-2.2.6.

Exception: Aisles, corridors, and ramps in adjunct areas not intended for the housing, treatment, or use of patients may be a minimum of 44 in. (112 cm) in clear and unobstructed width.

A-12-2.3.4   (*See A-12-2.3.3.*)

Occupants of limited care facilities are generally capable of movement with limited assistance. Since patients will generally not require evacuation in beds or litters, the exit access widths are set at 6 ft (183 cm). (*See Figure 12-5.*)

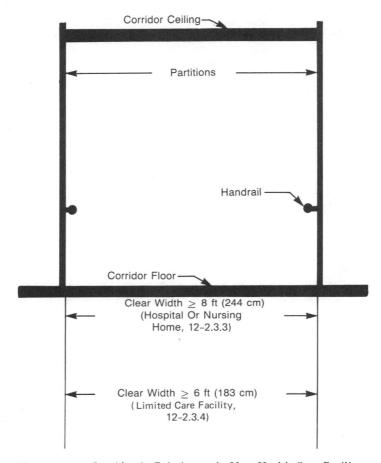

Figure 12-5. Corridor in Exit Access in New Health Care Facility.

12-2.3.5 The minimum width of doors in the means of egress from sleeping rooms; diagnostic and treatment areas, such as X-ray, surgery, or physical therapy; and nursery rooms shall be as follows:

(a) Hospitals and nursing homes: 44 in. (112 cm).

(b) Psychiatric hospitals and limited care facilities: 36 in. (91 cm).

Exception No. 1: Doors that are so located as not to be subject to use by any health care occupant may be not less than 34 in. (86 cm) wide.

Exception No. 2: Doors in exit stair enclosures shall not be less than 36 in. (91 cm) wide.

Exception No. 3: Newborn nurseries may be served by 36 in. (91 cm) doors.

Exception No. 4: A 36-in. (91-cm) door leaf may be used in conjunction with an inactive leaf of at least 8 in. (20.3 cm) with a rabbet, bevel, or astragal at the meeting edge.

The provisions of 12-2.3.5 are illustrated in Figures 12-6a through 12-6d.

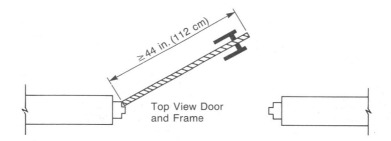

Figure 12-6a. Minimum Width of Doors in Means of Egress from Sleeping Rooms, Diagnostic, and Treatment Areas in New Hospitals and Nursing Homes. Maximum width is 48 in. (122 cm). (*See 5-2.1.3.2.*)

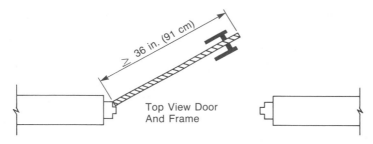

Figure 12-6b. Minimum Width of Doors in the Means of Egress from Sleeping Rooms in New Limited Care Facilities, Hospitals for Psychiatric Care, and from Nursery Rooms in Health Care Occupancies. Maximum width is 48 in. (122 cm). (*See 5-2.1.3.2.*)

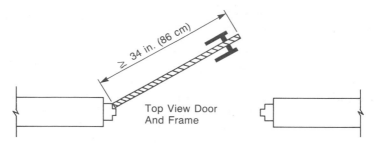

Figure 12-6c. Minimum Width of Doors in Means of Egress not Subject to Use by Health Care Occupants in New Health Care Occupancies. Maximum width is 48 in. (122 cm). (*See 5-2.1.3.2.*)

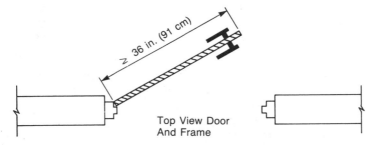

Top View Door
And Frame

Figure 12-6d. Minimum Width of Doors for Access to Exit Stair Enclosures in New Health Care Occupancies. Maximum width is 48 in. (122 cm). (*See 5-2.1.3.2.*) Doors must swing in direction of exit travel (*See 5-2.1.4.1.*)

12-2.4 Number of Exits.

12-2.4.1   At least two exits of the types described in 12-2.2.2 through 12-2.2.7, remotely located from each other, shall be provided for each floor or fire section of the building.

12-2.4.2   At least one exit from each floor or fire section shall be either:

(a) A door leading directly outside the building, or

(b) A stair, or

(c) A smokeproof enclosure, or

(d) A ramp, or

(e) An exit passageway.

Any fire section not meeting these requirements shall be considered as part of an adjoining zone. Egress shall not require return through the zone of fire origin.

12-2.4.3*   At least two exits of the types described in 12-2.2.2 through 12-2.2.7 shall be accessible from each smoke compartment. Egress may be through adjacent compartment(s), but shall not require return through the compartment of fire origin.

A-12-2.4.3   An exit is not necessary for each individual smoke compartment if there is access to an exit through other smoke compartments without passing through the smoke compartment of fire origin.

Figure 12-7 can be used to illustrate the application of 12-2.4.2 and 12-2.4.3. If both Wall I and Wall II are horizontal exits, then three fire compartments or fire sections are formed. Paragraph 12-2.4.2 would then require that Area B also be provided with an exit that must be one of the five types of exits listed. In other words, Area B must be provided with an exit other than a horizontal exit, even though two horizontal exits are already provided from Area B. If this is not done, then Area B must be considered part of one of the adjoining areas — either part of Area A, in which case no credit is given for the horizontal exit of Wall I, or part of

Area C, in which case no credit is given for the horizontal exit of Wall II. Prior to the 1985 Edition of the *Code*, this would also apply to smoke barriers. However, the *Code* now allows egress through adjoining smoke compartments. If both Wall I and Wall II were smoke barriers, the arrangement would be acceptable. If Wall I were a smoke barrier and Wall II were a horizontal exit, the arrangement comment would also be acceptable, as Areas A and B would be one fire area, with Area C being the other fire area and all requirements of 12-2.4.2 and 12-2.4.3 would be met.

For two reasons, caution should be used in determining how many smoke compartments can intervene in order to reach the ultimate exit. First, excessive moving of patients should be prevented, and second, each compartment must have sufficient area to handle all patients whom it must serve. In this example, where Wall I is a smoke barrier and Wall II is a horizontal exit, each area would have to be sufficient in size to comply with 12-2.2.5(a) for horizontal exits, or 12-3.7.4 for smoke barriers, based

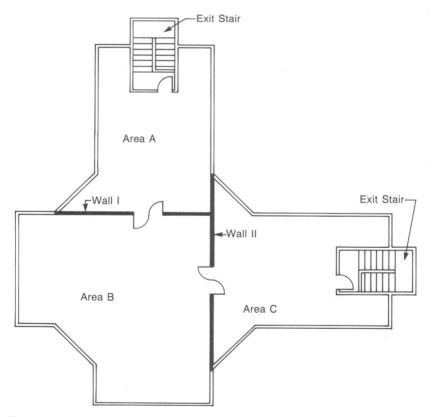

Figure 12-7.   Arrangement of Exits in a New Health Care Occupancy Involving Smoke Barriers and Horizontal Exits.   (*See commentary following 12-2.4.3 for discussion of figure.*)

on figures calculated for the entire floor, since all three areas are an integral part of the horizontal evacuation for the floor. This is easily justified considering that if a fire started near the exit for Area A, thus requiring evacuation into Area B, ultimate evacuation would be achieved only through Area C, since there is no exit from Area B. In such case, Area C would have to have sufficient area to handle patients from Areas A and B as well as those patients originally in Area C.

In order to ensure that egress does not require return through the compartment of fire origin, each compartment formed must be analyzed to ensure that a path of travel to an exit other than a horizontal exit is available. (*See Figure 12-7.*)

12-2.5 Arrangement of Means of Egress.

12-2.5.1   Every habitable room shall have an exit access door leading directly to an exit access corridor.

Exception No. 1: If there is an exit door opening directly to the outside from the room at ground level.

Exception No. 2: For patient sleeping rooms, one adjacent room, such as a sitting or anteroom, may intervene if the intervening room is not used to serve as an exit access for more than eight patient sleeping beds.

Exception No. 3: Exception No. 2 above shall apply to special nursing suites permitted in 12-2.5.3 without being limited to eight beds or basinettes.

Exception No. 4: For rooms other than patient sleeping rooms, one or more adjacent rooms, such as offices, work rooms, etc., may intervene provided that such intervening rooms are not hazardous areas as defined in 12-3.2.

The term "patient sleeping room," previously used in 12-2.5.1, has been replaced with the term "habitable room" to make clear that all occupied rooms in a health care facility must have access to a corridor leading to an exit. (*See commentary following 12-2.4.3.*)

Figures 12-8a and b illustrate the intent of 12-2.5.1. Figure 12-9 illustrates Exception No. 2 to 12-2.5.1.

Nursing suites and various treatment areas are frequently arranged with an intervening workroom located between the exit access corridor and a treatment room. Exception No. 4 to 12-2.5.1 will allow egress through spaces that are closely related in function to the treatment room and, therefore, under the immediate control of staff who, along with patients, would be forced to travel across such rooms. Where such an arrangement is used, locking hardware on doors may not restrict egress from the nursing suite or intervening room. (*See 12-2.2.2.*)

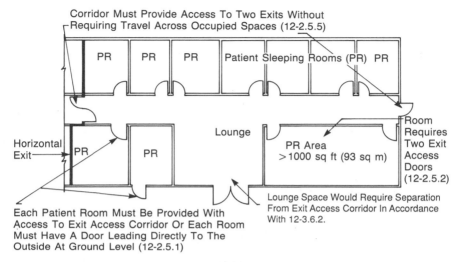

Corridor Must Provide Access To Two Exits Without
Requiring Travel Across Occupied Spaces (12-2.5.5)

PR   PR   PR   Patient Sleeping Rooms (PR) PR

Lounge

PR Area
>1000 sq ft (93 sq m)

Horizontal
Exit

PR   PR

Room
Requires
Two Exit
Access
Doors
(12-2.5.2)

Lounge Space Would Require Separation
From Exit Access Corridor In Accordance
With 12-3.6.2.

Each Patient Room Must Be Provided With
Access To Exit Access Corridor Or Each Room
Must Have A Door Leading Directly To The
Outside At Ground Level (12-2.5.1)

Figure 12-8a.   Arrangement of Exit Access in New Health Care Occupancy.   In-
correct lounge arrangement as lounge must be separated from exit access corridor.
(*See Figure 12-8b for corrected lounge arrangement.*)   Paragraph 12-2.5.1 Exception
No. 1, 12-2.5.2, and 12-2.5.5 are also illustrated.

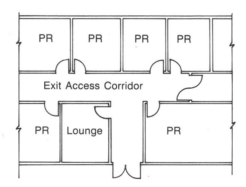

PR   PR   PR   PR

Exit Access Corridor

PR   Lounge   PR

Figure 12-8b.   Corrected Arrangement of Exit Access in New Health Care
Occupancy.   (*See Figure 12-8a.*) Lounge is separated from exit access corridor in
accordance with 12-3.6.2 as required by 12-2.5.5. (*See also 12-3.6.1 Exceptions No. 1,
2, 3 and 6, where a waiting space may be open to an exit access corridor.*)

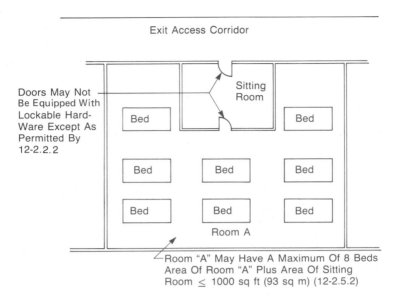

Figure 12-9. Exit Access from a Patient Sleeping Room Through an Adjacent Room in a New Health Care Occupancy. Illustration complies with 12-2.5.1 Exception No. 2 and 12-2.5.2.

12-2.5.2   Any patient sleeping room, or any suite that includes patient sleeping rooms, of more than 1,000 sq ft (93 sq m) shall have at least two exit access doors remote from each other.

Any room or any suite of rooms, other than patient sleeping rooms, of more than 2,500 sq ft (230 sq m) shall have at least two exit access doors remote from each other.

Patient sleeping rooms, or suites with sleeping rooms, greater than 1,000 sq ft (93 sq m) require two exit access doors. The doors may open onto a common corridor but are required to be as remotely located from each other as possible. Rooms or suites not used for patient sleeping purposes may be up to 2,500 sq ft (230 sq m) in area and require only one door based on the presumption that occupants are alert or ambulatory or are in most instances accompanied by staff who could assist in evacuating the space during fire or other emergency. For sleeping suites, refer to 12-2.5.3 for additional requirements. For nonsleeping suites, refer to 12-2.5.4 for additional requirements. (*Figures 12-10a and 12-10b illustrate the requirements for sleeping suites. Figures 12-11a, 12-11b, and 12-11c illustrate the requirements for nonsleeping suites.*)

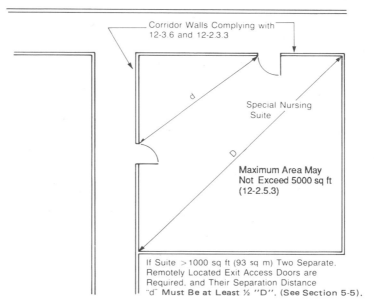

Figure 12-10a. Suites Involving Patient Sleeping Rooms in a New Health Care Occupancy. The requirements of 12-2.5.2 and 12-2.5.3 are illustrated here. The suite must comply with Figures 12-10a and 12-10b.

12-2.5.3 Any patient sleeping room that complies with the requirements previously set forth in this section may be subdivided with non-fire-rated, noncombustible or limited-combustible partitions, provided that the arrangement allows for direct and constant visual supervision by nursing personnel. Rooms that are so subdivided shall not exceed 5,000 sq ft (460 sq m).

Paragraph 12-2.5.3 makes provision for noncompartmented nursing suites, such as Intensive Care Units (ICU) or Coronary Care Units (CCU). Interior suite arrangements are not required to comply with 12-2.3.3 or 12-3.6 relative to corridor access to exits. For example, interior corridors within special nursing units are not required to be 8 ft (244 cm) wide. Doors to individual cubicles may be sliding doors. (*See Figures 12-10a and b.*)

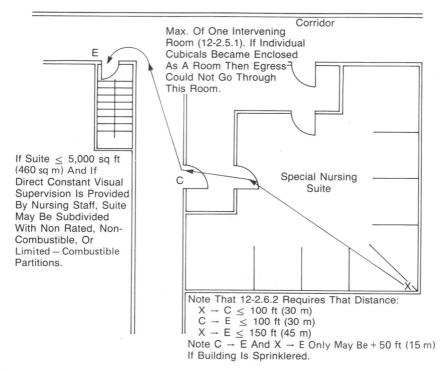

Figure 12-10b.   Suites Involving Patient Sleeping Rooms in a New Health Care Occupancy.   The requirements of 12-2.5.1, 12-2.5.2, 12-2.5.3, and 12-2.6.2 for patient sleeping suites are illustrated. The suite must comply with Figures 12-10a and b.

12-2.5.4   Any suite of rooms, other than patient sleeping rooms, that complies with the requirements previously set forth in this section may be subdivided with non-fire-rated, noncombustible, or limited-combustible partitions. Such suites shall not exceed 10,000 sq ft (930 sq m) in area and either:

(a) The maximum travel distance from any point in the suite to a corridor door shall be limited to 50 ft (15 m), or

(b) There shall be unrestricted access from patient treatment areas to a corridor with a maximum of one intervening room.

The requirements of 12-2.5.4 are illustrated in Figures 12-11a, 12-11b, and 12-11c.

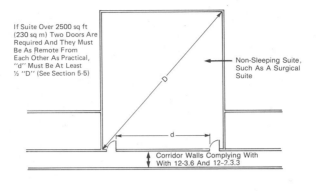

If Suite Over 2500 sq ft (230 sq m) Two Doors Are Required And They Must Be As Remote From Each Other As Practical, "d" Must Be At Least ½ "D" (See Section 5-5)

Non-Sleeping Suite, Such As A Surgical Suite

Corridor Walls Complying With With 12-3.6 And 12-2.3.3

Figure 12-11a. Suites Not Involving Patient Sleeping Rooms in a New Health Care Occupancy. This illustrates the provisions of 12-2.5.2. The suites must comply with Figures 12-11a and b or Figures 12-11b and c.

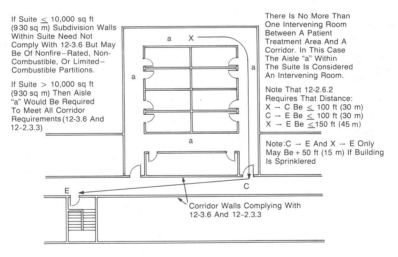

If Suite ≤ 10,000 sq ft (930 sq m) Subdivision Walls Within Suite Need Not Comply With 12-3.6 But May Be Of Nonfire−Rated, Non-Combustible, Or Limited−Combustible Partitions.

If Suite > 10,000 sq ft (930 sq m) Then Aisle "a" Would Be Required To Meet All Corridor Requirements (12-3.6 And 12-2.3.3)

There Is No More Than One Intervening Room Between A Patient Treatment Area And A Corridor. In This Case The Aisle "a" Within The Suite Is Considered An Intervening Room.

Note That 12-2.6.2 Requires That Distance: X → C Be ≤ 100 ft (30 m) C → E Be ≤ 100 ft (30 m) X → E Be ≤150 ft (45 m)

Note:C → E And X → E Only May Be + 50 ft (15 m) If Building Is Sprinklered

Corridor Walls Complying With 12-3.6 And 12-2.3.3

Figure 12-11b. Suites Not Involving Patient Sleeping Rooms in a New Health Care Occupancy. The requirements of 12-2.5.2 are illustrated in Figure 12-11a. Figures 12-11b and 12-11c illustrate the requirements of 12-2.5.4 and 12-2.6.2. The suites must comply with Figures 12-11a and b or 12-11a and c.

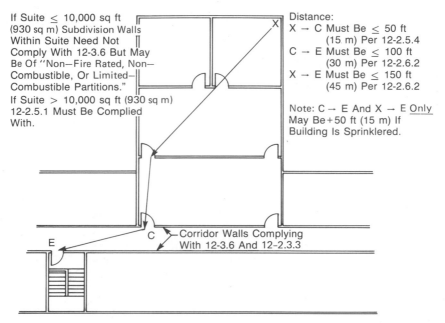

If Suite ≤ 10,000 sq ft (930 sq m) Subdivision Walls Within Suite Need Not Comply With 12-3.6 But May Be Of "Non–Fire Rated, Non–Combustible, Or Limited–Combustible Partitions."

If Suite > 10,000 sq ft (930 sq m) 12-2.5.1 Must Be Complied With.

Distance:
X → C Must Be ≤ 50 ft (15 m) Per 12-2.5.4
C → E Must Be ≤ 100 ft (30 m) Per 12-2.6.2
X → E Must Be ≤ 150 ft (45 m) Per 12-2.6.2

Note: C → E And X → E Only May Be + 50 ft (15 m) If Building Is Sprinklered.

Corridor Walls Complying With 12-3.6 And 12-2.3.3

Figure 12-11c.   Suites Not Involving Patient Sleeping Rooms in a New Health Care Occupancy. The requirements of 12-2.5.2, 12-2.5.4, and 12-2.6.2 for suites not involving patient sleeping rooms are illustrated. The suites must comply with Figures 12-11a and b or 12-11a and c.

12-2.5.5   Every corridor shall provide access to at least two approved exits in accordance with Sections 5-4 and 5-5 without passing through any intervening rooms or spaces other than corridors or lobbies.

See Figure 12-8a

12-2.5.6   Every exit or exit access shall be so arranged that no corridor, aisle, or passageway has a pocket or dead end exceeding 30 ft (9.1 m).

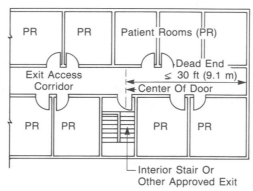

Figure 12-12.   Exit Access Corridor with Dead End Allowed by 12-2.5.6 in a New Health Care Occupancy.

12-2.6 Travel Distance to Exits.

12-2.6.1 Travel distance shall be measured in accordance with Section 5-6.

12-2.6.2 Travel distance:

(a) Between any room door required as exit access and an exit shall not exceed 100 ft (30 m);

(b) Between any point in a room and an exit shall not exceed 150 ft (45 m);

Exception: The travel distance in (a) or (b) above may be increased by 50 ft (15 m) in buildings protected throughout by an approved supervised automatic sprinkler system.

(c) Between any point in a health care sleeping room and an exit access door of that room shall not exceed 50 ft (15 m);

(d) Between any point in a suite of rooms as permitted by 12-2.5 and an exit access door of that suite shall not exceed 100 ft (30 m) and shall meet (b) above.

The requirements of 12-2.6.1 and 12-2.6.2 are illustrated in Figure 12-13. Travel distance is measured only to the closest exit, not to both exits required by 12-2.4.1. It should be noted that the 50-ft (15-m) restriction within a room applies only to sleeping rooms. (*See also 12-2.5.4 and Figures 12-10 and 12-11.*)

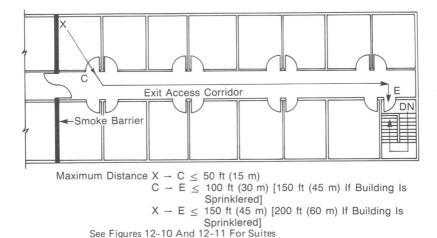

Maximum Distance X → C ≤ 50 ft (15 m)
C → E ≤ 100 ft (30 m) [150 ft (45 m) If Building Is Sprinklered]
X → E ≤ 150 ft (45 m) [200 ft (60 m) If Building Is Sprinklered]
See Figures 12–10 And 12–11 For Suites

Figure 12-13. Travel Distance in New Health Care Occupancy.

12-2.7 Discharge from Exits.

12-2.7.1 Discharge from exits shall be arranged in accordance with Section 5-7.

All exit stairs or exit ramps are required to discharge to the outside either directly or through an enclosed exit passageway. Where an exit passageway is used, the fire-resistive separation of the enclosure must be the same as required for the enclosure of a stair or ramp. Openings into the passageway must be suitably protected and limited to doors leading to spaces normally occupied. [*See 5-1.3.1(a) through (e).*] Under certain conditions, a maximum of 50 percent of the required exits may discharge to the outside through the level of exit discharge in accordance with 5-7.2.

12-2.8 Illumination of Means of Egress.

12-2.8.1   Means of egress shall be illuminated in accordance with Section 5-8.

12-2.9 Emergency Lighting.

12-2.9.1   Emergency lighting shall be provided in accordance with Section 5-9.

12-2.9.2   Buildings equipped with or in which patients require the use of life support systems (*see 12-5.1.3*) shall have emergency lighting equipment supplied by the Life Safety Branch of the electrical system as described in NFPA 99, *Standard for Health Care Facilities.*

12-2.10 Marking of Means of Egress.

12-2.10.1   Means of egress shall have signs in accordance with Section 5-10.

12-2.10.2   Buildings equipped with or in which patients require the use of life support systems (*see 12-5.1.3*) shall have illumination of the required exit and directional signs supplied by the Life Safety Branch of the electrical system as described in NFPA 99, *Standard for Health Care Facilities.*

Formal Interpretation 81-10
Reference: 12-2.10.2

Question: Is it the intent of the Committee to prohibit the use of self-luminous exit signs, as permitted by 5-10.3.3 Exception No. 2, in Health Care Facilities?

Answer: No.

Issue Edition: 1981
Reference: 12-2.10.2
Date: January 1982

Each health care facility equipped with or requiring the use of life support systems is required to have the marking of the means of egress and emergency lighting supplied by the Life Safety Branch of the electrical systems described in Chapter 3, "Electrical Systems," of NFPA 99, *Standard for Health Care Facilities.*[5]

A facility would not be required to have an emergency generator if the building is a free-standing unit in which, as a normal practice, (1) management maintains admitting and discharge policies that preclude the provision of care for any patient or resident who may need to be sustained by electrical life-support equipment, such as respirators, suction apparatus, etc., and (2) no surgical treatment requiring general anesthesia is offered, and (3) battery-operated systems or equipment are provided to maintain power to exit lights and illumination of exit corridors, stairways, medical preparation areas, and the like, for a minimum of 1½ hours. Additionally, battery power would be required to be supplied to all alarm systems. For additional information, refer to NFPA 99, *Standard for Health Care Facilities.*[5]

NFPA 99 requires that emergency power supplies be arranged and protected so as to minimize the possibility of a single incident affecting both normal and emergency power supplies simultaneously. Circuits are to be run separately. Emergency and normal circuits are "joined" at the transfer switch. Damage to the transfer switch would interrupt normal and emergency power supplies simultaneously. The transfer switch is therefore a critical item and should be separated from any potential source of fire, including the emergency generator and attendant fuel supply.

NFPA 99, *Standard for Health Care Facilities,*[5] specifies that emergency generators must be inspected at least weekly and exercised for a minimum of 30 minutes a month under load. (*Also see 31-1.3.8.*)

12-2.11 Special Features.

SECTION 12-3 PROTECTION

12-3.1 Protection of Vertical Openings.

12-3.1.1 Any stairway, ramp, elevator hoistway, light or ventilation shaft, chute, and other vertical opening between stories shall be enclosed in accordance with 6-2.4 with construction having a 2-hour fire resistance rating.

Exception No. 1: One-hour rated enclosures are permitted in buildings required to be of 1-hour construction.

Exception No. 2: Stairs that do not connect to a corridor, do not connect more than two levels, and do not serve as a means of egress need not comply with these regulations.

Exception No. 3: The fire resistance rating of enclosures connecting not more than three stories in health care occupancies protected throughout by an approved supervised automatic sprinkler system may be reduced to 1 hour.

Exception No. 4: Duct penetrations of floor assemblies that are protected in accordance with NFPA 90A, Standard for the Installation of Air Conditioning and Ventilating Systems.

Exception No. 5: Floor and ceiling openings for pipes or conduits where the opening around the pipes or conduits is sealed in an approved manner. (See 6-2.3.4.2.)

Exception No. 6: An atrium may be used in accordance with 6-2.4.5. Exception No. 1 to 6-2.4.5(g) shall not apply to patient sleeping and treatment rooms.

Paragraph 12-3.1 specifies protection levels required to maintain floor-to-floor separation in health care facilities. Two-hour enclosures are required around vertical openings in all buildings that must be of Type I or Type II (222) construction. (*See 12-1.6.2.*) One-hour enclosure of vertical openings is required in all other buildings.

Exception No. 2 to 12-3.1.1 is illustrated in Figure 12-14.

Air-handling ducts that transfer air from floor to floor should be protected as specified in NFPA 90A, *Standard for the Installation of Air Conditioning and Ventilating Systems.*[6] Note that 3-3.3.1 of NFPA 90A permits elimination of vertical shaft enclosures and allows provision of a fire damper at each point where a floor is pierced only if air-handling ducts extend through one floor only.

Exception No. 5 will allow piping and conduit to penetrate floors without requiring an enclosed shaft. Floor penetrations, however, must be adequately protected in an approved manner to maintain the required fire resistance of the floor system. The penetrations should be sealed in a fashion that will minimize the transfer of smoke.

Exception No. 6 permits atriums in health care facilities in accordance with 6-2.4.5. Special requirements for smoke barriers in atriums in health care facilities are illustrated in Figures 12-20a - d in 12-3.7. Patient sleeping and treatment rooms must be separated from the atrium by partitions complying with 12-3.6.

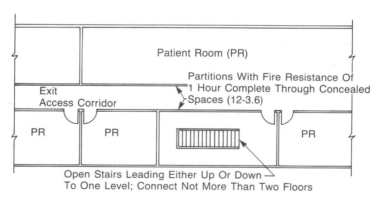

Figure 12-14.   Open Stairs in Accordance with 12-3.1.1 Exception No. 2 in New Health Care Occupancies.

Formal Interpretation 76-15
Reference: 12-3.1.1

Question: Does 12-3.1.1 intend to permit combustible materials in vertical enclosure walls unless otherwise prohibited by 12-1.6.5?

Answer: Yes.

Issue Edition: 1976
Reference: 10-2.3.1.1
Date: August 1977

Formal Interpretation 76-56
Reference: 12-3.1.1 Exception No. 2

Question: While Exception No. 2 specifies "stairs," is it the intent to include:
(a) Escalators?
Answer: Yes.

(b) Other openings?
Answer: This question cannot be answered, as this determination requires a case-by-case evaluation by the authority having jurisdiction.

Issue Edition: 1976
Reference: 10-2.3.1.1 Exception No. 2
Date: January 1978

12-3.1.2   A door in a stair enclosure shall be self-closing, shall normally be kept in a closed position, and shall be marked in accordance with Section 5-10.
Exception: Doors in stair enclosures may be held open under the conditions specified by 12-2.2.2.6 and 12-2.2.2.7.

Paragraph 12-3.1.2 requires fire doors protecting openings in stairway enclosures to be self-closing and normally maintained in a closed position. However, the Exception to 12-3.1.2 permits stairway doors with certain qualifications to be held open by an automatic closing device. Refer to the commentary following 12-2.2.2.6 and 12-2.2.2.7. Where stair doors are normally maintained in a closed position, they should be provided with a sign substantially stating "Fire Exit — Keep Door Closed."

12-3.2 Protection from Hazards.

12-3.2.1* Hazardous Areas.   Any hazardous area shall be protected in accordance with Section 6-4. The following areas listed shall be protected as indicated. The automatic extinguishing may be in accordance with 12-3.5.4. Where sprinkler protection without fire rated separation is used, the areas shall be separated from other spaces by partitions complying with 6-3.2, with doors complying with 6-3.4.

Description	Separation/Protection
Boiler and fuel-fired heater rooms	2 hrs or 1 hr and sprinklers
Employee locker rooms	1 hr or sprinklers
Gift/retail shops	See 12-3.2.5
Handicraft shops	1 hr or sprinklers
Laboratories which employ hazardous materials but such materials are in quantities less than that which would cause classification as severe hazard	1 hr or sprinklers

Description	Separation/Protection
Central/bulk laundries greater than 100 sq ft (9.3 sq m)	1 hr and sprinklers
Paint shops employing hazardous substances and materials in quantities less than that which would cause classification as severe hazard	2 hrs or 1 hr and sprinklers
Physical Plant Maintenance Shop	2 hrs or 1 hr and sprinklers
Soiled linen room	1 hr and sprinklers
Storage rooms more than 50 sq ft (4.6 sq m) in area but not more than 100 sq ft (9.3 sq m) in area storing combustible material	1 hr or sprinklers
Storage rooms more than 100 sq ft (9.3 sq m) storing combustible materials	1 hr and sprinklers
Trash collection rooms	1 hr and sprinklers

A-12-3.2.1   Rooms in clinical laboratories in which automatic processing of specimens with flammable solvents is likely to take place when the equipment is unattended present a limited hazard that may be more readily protected through use of sprinklers connected to the domestic water supply. Provisions for the enclosure of rooms used for charging linen and waste chutes or for the rooms into which chutes empty are provided in Chapter 7. In addition to the fire-resistive cutoff of rooms into which linen chutes and waste chutes discharge, automatic sprinkler protection is considered essential.

Hazardous areas are spaces with contents that, because of their basic nature (as in the case of flammable liquids) or because of the quantity of combustible materials involved, represent a significantly higher hazard than would otherwise be typical in the general areas of health care facilities.

A listing of typical hazardous areas is included in 12-3.2.1. The list is meant to be illustrative, not all inclusive. The general reference to Section 6-4 provides the authority having jurisdiction with the opportunity to regulate any space judged to represent a significantly higher hazard than most spaces. Hazardous areas must be separated from other areas by fire resistant construction, complete with approved protective devices for all openings. Where the hazard is not severe, automatic sprinkler protection may be installed as an alternative to fire resistive separation. In those instances where the hazard is judged to be severe, such as in rooms used to store soiled linen, paint shops, trash collection rooms, repair shops, large storage areas, and the like, both fire resistant separation and automatic sprinkler protection are specified. Where automatic sprinkler protection is provided and the hazard is not severe, the hazardous area must be separated from the rest of the building by nonrated barriers designed to resist the passage of smoke.

(*See commentary on 12-3.2.2 for discussion of laboratories.*)

12-3.2.2* Laboratories.   Laboratories employing quantities of flammable, combustible, or hazardous materials that are considered as severe hazard shall be protected in accordance with NFPA 99, *Standard for Health Care Facilities.*

A-12-3.2.2   The hazard level of a laboratory is considered severe if quantities of flammable, combustible or hazardous materials are present that are capable of sustaining a fire condition of sufficient magnitude to breach a 1-hour fire separation.

See NFPA *Fire Protection Handbook (see Appendix B)*, Section 7 Chapter 9, for guidance.

Laboratories that contain "ordinary" combustibles and flammable liquids in sufficient quantity to threaten a 1-hour fire separation [e.g., wood equivalent fuel loads in the range of 5 to 10 lb/sq ft (25 to 50 kg/sq m)] are considered a severe hazard. Laboratories presenting a severe hazard must be protected in accordance with Chapter 10, "Laboratories," of NFPA 99, *Standard for Health Care Facilities.*[5] Protection would include 1-hour fire resistance separation and automatic sprinkler protection.

Where fuel loads of lesser amounts are involved and quantities of flammable liquids are limited, laboratories would simply be considered hazardous areas, and would require either 1-hour separation or automatic sprinkler protection, as indicated in 12-3.2.1 and Section 6-4.

12-3.2.3 Anesthetizing Locations.   Anesthetizing locations shall be protected in accordance with NFPA 99, *Standard for Health Care Facilities.*

12-3.2.4 Medical Gas.   Medical gas storage and administration areas shall be protected in accordance with NFPA 99, *Standard for Health Care Facilities.*

12-3.2.5 Gift Shops.   Gift shops shall be protected as hazardous areas where used for the storage or display of combustibles in quantities considered hazardous. Gift shops not considered hazardous and having separately protected storage may be:

(a) Open to a lobby if the gift shop is not greater than 500 sq ft (46.5 sq m) and is protected throughout by an approved automatic sprinkler system, or

(b) Separated from a lobby with non-fire-rated walls if the gift shop is protected throughout by an approved automatic sprinkler system, or

(c) Separated from corridors by non-fire-rated walls if the gift shop is protected throughout by an approved automatic sprinkler system.

Editions of the *Code* prior to 1985 simply listed gift shops as typical hazardous areas. Many gift shops, particularly those containing combustible storage and having sizable retail areas, do present a hazard well beyond that normal to patient-occupied spaces and thus merit special protection. However, it is recognized that many small retail areas [less than 500 sq ft (46.5 sq m), for example] constitute a relatively minor hazard adequately mitigated by automatic sprinkler protection. This paragraph was added in 1985 to provide the authority having jurisdiction with guidance in judging the degree of hazard and offers the facility some flexibility in the design and operation of gift shops.

Note: to use any of the three options given, the gift shop must be judged nonhazardous, must be sprinklered and must have separately protected storage areas.

12-3.2.6 Cooking Facilities.   Cooking facilities shall be protected in accordance with 7-2.3.

Exception*: Where domestic cooking equipment is used for food warming or limited cooking, protection or segregation of food preparation facilities is not required.

A-12-3.2.6 Exception   This Exception is intended to permit small appliances used for reheating, such as microwave ovens, hot plates, toasters, and nourishment centers to be exempt from requirements of commercial cooking equipment.

Commercial cooking equipment must be installed and protected in accordance with NFPA 96, *Standard for the Installation of Equipment for the Removal of Smoke and Grease-Laden Vapors from Commercial Cooking Equipment.*[7] A regularly serviced, fixed, automatic fire extinguishing system would be required for the protection of cooking surfaces and exhaust and duct systems where cooking operations involve the potential for grease-laden vapors. Cooking operations that do not involve the release of smoke or grease-laden vapors are not subject to compliance with NFPA 96 and would not normally be treated as hazardous operations.

The Exception notes that 12-3.2.6 would not apply to a room used as a staff lounge equipped with a domestic-type range or microwave oven. Such a room would be considered similar to a treatment room and would require separation as indicated in 12-3.6.1.

12-3.3 Interior Finish.

12-3.3.1   Interior finish of walls and ceilings throughout shall be Class A in accordance with Section 6-5.

Exception No. 1: Walls and ceilings may have Class A or B interior finish in individual rooms having a capacity of not over four persons.

Exception No. 2: Corridor wall finish up to 4 ft (122 cm) in height that is restricted to the lower half of the wall may be Class A or B.

Interior finishes on walls and ceilings are limited to Class A materials, except in rooms of four or fewer persons where Class B materials are allowed.

Exception No. 2 to 12-3.3.1 allows wall finish in corridors to be of Class B materials where located 4 ft (122 cm) or less in height above the floor. This provision recognizes fire research[8] that has shown the finish on the lower half of the wall to be much less significant in its influence on early fire growth than the finish on the upper portion of the wall. In the case of textile materials on walls or ceilings, 6-5.2.3 would take precedence and require automatic sprinkler protection in conjunction with Class A materials, or such wall and ceiling materials must be proven safe by room/corner testing.

Where automatic sprinkler protection is provided, Class B materials can be used where Class A materials are normally required, and similarly, Class C materials are allowed where Class B materials would otherwise be required. (*See Section 6-5.*)

12-3.3.2* Interior floor finish in corridors and exits shall be Class I in accordance with Section 6-5.

A-12-3.3.2 It is recognized that underlayment may affect the flame spread characteristics of floor coverings. Where floor coverings involve a separate underlayment, it is suggested the underlayment/floor finish system be tested as an assembly in accordance with procedures outlined within NFPA 253, *Standard Method of Test for Critical Radiant Flux of Floor Covering Systems Using A Radiant Heat Energy Source (see Appendix B).*

Interior floor finish within corridors and exits of nonsprinklered health care facilities is required to be of Class I materials as determined in accordance with Section 6-5. Class I materials are those having a critical radiant flux of not less than 0.45 watts/sq m as determined by tests conducted in accordance with NFPA 253, *Standard Method of Test for Critical Radiant Flux of Floor Covering Systems Using a Radiant Heat Energy Source.*[9] (*See commentary on 6-5.4.*)

Regulation of interior floor finish within rooms is not considered necessary.

Where automatic sprinkler protection is provided, Class II materials can be used where Class I materials are normally specified.

12-3.4 Detection, Alarm, and Communications Systems.

12-3.4.1 General.

12-3.4.1.1 Health care occupancies shall be provided with a fire alarm system in accordance with Section 7-6.

12-3.4.1.2 All required fire alarm systems shall be electrically supervised.

12-3.4.1.3 All required fire alarm systems and detection systems shall be provided with a secondary power supply in accordance with NFPA 72A, *Standard for the Installation, Maintenance, and Use of Local Protective Signaling Systems for Guard's Tour, Fire Alarm, and Supervisory Service.*

12-3.4.2 Initiation.   Initiation of the required fire alarm systems shall be by manual means in accordance with 7-6.2 and by means of any detection devices or detection systems required.

Exception: Fire alarm pull stations in patient sleeping areas may be omitted at exits if located at all nurses' control stations or other continuously attended staff location, provided such pull stations are visible and continuously accessible and that travel distances in 7-6.2.4 are not exceeded.

Formal Interpretation 76-18
Reference: 12-3.4.2

Question: Does 12-3.4.2 intend to require a local device designed to detect smoke on either side of an opening, as referenced in 12-2.2.2.6, to be connected to the fire alarm system?

Answer: Yes. The Committee intended that, in new construction, all required fire detection devices be connected to the fire alarm system.

Issue Edition: 1976
Reference: 10-2.3.3.7
Date: August 1977

12-3.4.3 Notification.

12-3.4.3.1 Occupant Notification.   Occupant notification shall be accomplished automatically, without delay, upon operation of any fire alarm activating device by means of an internal audible alarm in accordance with 7-6.3. Presignal systems are prohibited.

12-3.4.3.2 Emergency Forces Notification.   Fire department notification shall be accomplished in accordance with 7-6.4.

Exception: Smoke detection devices or smoke detection systems equipped with reconfirmation features need not automatically notify the fire department unless the alarm condition is reconfirmed after a maximum 120 second time period.

An independent study by the National Bureau of Standards indicates a high rate of false alarms for smoke detectors installed in health care facilities.[10] The study determined 4.4 false alarms occurred per 100 smoke detectors per year. Furthermore, approximately 14 false alarms occurred for every actual alarm. Because of the high incidence of false alarms, the *Code* now permits delaying fire department notification for up to 120 seconds where smoke detectors or smoke detection systems are equipped with a reconfirmation feature.

12-3.4.4 Emergency Control.   Operation of any activating device in the required fire alarm system shall be arranged to automatically accomplish, without delay, any control functions to be performed by that device. (*See* 7-6.5.)

12-3.4.5 Detection.

12-3.4.5.1 Corridors.   An approved automatic smoke detection system shall be installed in all corridors of nursing homes and limited care facilities. Such system shall be installed in accordance with Section 7-6.

Exception: Where each patient sleeping room is protected by an approved smoke detection system, and a smoke detector is provided at smoke barriers and horizontal exits, such corridor systems will not be required on the patient sleeping room floors.

12-3.4.5.2 Spaces Open to Corridors. *(See 12-3.6.1.)*

Paragraphs 12-3.4.1 through 12-3.4.5 deal with required fire alarm equipment. Reliability is of prime importance; therefore, electrical supervision of the system and system components is specified. In the event of circuit fault, component failure, or other "trouble," continuous "trouble indication" is required and should be provided at a constantly attended location.

A manual fire alarm system is required by 12-3.4.2. Manual pull stations are normally located along the natural routes of egress and located so as to adequately cover all portions of the building. An exception to 12-3.4.2 allows pull stations, with certain qualifications, to be located at continuously attended staff positions in sleeping areas. This arrangement provides the opportunity for prompt notification of fire without requiring staff to leave their normal work station. In any case, manual pull stations should always be located so that anyone qualified to send an alarm may summon aid without having to leave the zone of his or her ordinary activities or pass out of the sight and hearing of people immediately exposed to or in direct view of a fire. In new installations, it would normally be desirable to have manual pull stations at all attended staff locations and at entrances to exits, as the additional cost of the extra pull stations would be minimal. The operation of a manual fire alarm station should automatically summon attendants who can assist in removing physically helpless occupants and in controlling mentally incompetent occupants.

The system required by 12-3.4.2 may be incorporated into an automatic system equipped to detect a fire and initiate an alarm.

Actuation of any required fire or smoke detector, activation of a required sprinkler system, or operation of a manual pull station must automatically, without delay, sound audible alarm devices within the building. Presignal systems are not permitted.

The alarm must automatically transmit to a point outside the facility. Where automatic transmission of alarms to the fire department legally committed to serve the facility is not permitted, arrangements are to be made for the prompt notification of the fire department or such other assistance as may be available in the case of fire or other emergency. Paragraph 7-6.4 lists various methods acceptable for automatically notifying the fire department. The fire department should still be called manually to verify and confirm the automatic transmission of the alarm. In larger facilities, this may be the responsibility of the facility telephone operator; in smaller facilities, it may be the responsibility of the nursing staff.

Paragraph 12-3.4.5.1 requires smoke detectors to be located in all corridors of new nursing homes and new limited care facilities. As an option to locating smoke detectors in corridors, smoke detectors may be installed in each patient's room and at smoke barriers and horizontal exits. In recognition of different staffing criteria, smoke detectors are not required in hospitals where it is presumed staff will be present to sound the alarm.

Actuation of the fire alarm must cause audible alerting devices to sound throughout the affected zone or building as appropriate. Visible alerting devices may be used but may not serve as a substitute for audible devices.

12-3.5 Extinguishment Requirements.

12-3.5.1   Where required by 12-1.6, health care facilities shall be protected throughout by an approved supervised automatic sprinkler system installed in accordance with Section 7-7.

Exception: In Types I and II construction, where approved by the authority having jurisdiction, alternative protection measures may be substituted for sprinkler protection in specified areas where the authority having jurisdiction has prohibited sprinklers, without causing a building to be classified as nonsprinklered.

Requirements for automatic sprinkler protection in new health care occupancies are contained in 12-1.6. (*See NFPA 220, Standard on Types of Building Construction,*[2] *for definitions of construction type.*) Where sprinkler protection is specified, complete building coverage, in accordance with the provisions of NFPA 13, *Standard for the Installation of Sprinkler Systems,*[11] is required. The *Code* does not exempt any area of the building from protection. (*See Section 7-7.*) However, where automatic sprinkler protection is omitted from certain spaces at the mandate of the authority having jurisdiction and the authority having jurisdiction approves alternative protective measures, the building is still considered fully protected throughout. Sprinklers may only be omitted from isolated areas in buildings of fire-rated, noncombustible construction, where the building will have sufficient structural fire resistance to outlast most fires. Use of alternative protective measures to automatic sprinklers should be carefully evaluated to assure equivalent protection. Where fixed automatic fire extinguishing systems (using halon, for example) are used as an alternative to sprinklers for specific spaces, it is suggested the spaces also be separated by fire resistant construction.

In summary, automatic sprinkler protection is required by 12-1.6.2 in any case where combustible elements are used in the construction of a health care facility. Additionally, because of the inherent risks associated with tall buildings and because of the difficulties encountered in fighting fire manually in such structures, all health care facilities having floor levels more than 75 ft (23 m) above the level of fire department vehicle access must be protected with automatic sprinklers. Health care facilities, other than hospitals, greater than two stories in height are required to be sprinklered due to the difficulty in evacuating such facilities. Hospitals are excepted in these medium height buildings due to higher staffing levels.

12-3.5.2   Where this *Code* permits exceptions for fully sprinklered health care occupancies, the sprinkler system shall be:

(a) In complete accordance with Section 7-7.

(b) Electrically connected to the fire alarm system, and

(c) Fully supervised.

The term "fully supervised" means a distinct supervisory signal must be provided to a constantly attended location in the event of any malfunction or action that would impair sprinkler performance. Supervision must be provided, for example, for water supply and sprinkler control valves, fire pump power and running conditions, water tank levels and temperatures, pressure in pressure tanks, air pressure in dry-pipe systems, building temperature, and city water pressure. (*See also Section 7-7.2.*)

Exception: In Types I and II construction, where approved by the authority having jurisdiction, alternative protection measures may be substituted for sprinkler protection in specified areas where the authority having jurisdiction has prohibited sprinklers, without causing a building to be classified as nonsprinklered.

Refer to commentary on 12-3.5.1.

12-3.5.3 The main sprinkler control valve(s) shall be electrically supervised so that at least a local alarm will sound at a constantly attended location when the valve is closed.

Also see 12-3.5.2.

12-3.5.4 Isolated hazardous areas may be protected in accordance with 7-7.1.2 if the additional requirements of this paragraph are met. An indicating shut-off valve shall be installed in an accessible location between the sprinklers and the connection to the domestic water supply. Where more than two sprinklers are installed in a single area, water flow detection shall be provided to sound the building fire alarm or notify by a signal any constantly attended location, such as PBX, security, or emergency room, whereby necessary corrective action shall be directed.

12-3.5.5 Portable fire extinguishers shall be provided in all health care occupancies in accordance with 7-7.4.l.

12-3.6 Corridors.

The provisions for corridor walls have been reorganized for the 1988 *Code* with relatively few technical changes.

Paragraph 12-3.6.1 establishes requirements to have corridor walls.

Paragraph 12-3.6.2 establishes construction requirements for such walls.

Paragraph 12-3.6.3 establishes requirements for doors in corridor walls.

Paragraph 12-3.6.4 deals with transfer grilles.

The requirements of 12-3.6.1 through 12-3.6.4 essentially stipulate that all areas that contain combustibles in sufficient quantities to produce a life-threatening fire must be separated from exit access corridors by partitions. The details of constructing such partitions depend principally on whether complete automatic sprinkler protection is or is not provided and is detailed in 12-3.6.2.

12-3.6.1*   Corridors shall be separated from all other areas by partitions complying with 12-3.6.2 through 12-3.6.4 (*also see 12-2.5.5*).

A-12-3.6.1   For the purpose of this paragraph only, the term "direct supervision" is meant to convey that the opening to the corridor from the waiting area should be visible from an occupied staff location.

Exception No. 1:   Waiting areas on a patient sleeping floor may be open to the corridor, provided:

(*a*) *The area does not exceed 250 sq ft (23.2 sq m), and*

(*b*) *The area is located to permit direct supervision by the facility staff, and*

(*c*) *The area is equipped with an electrically supervised, automatic smoke detection system installed in accordance with 12-3.4, and*

(*d*) *Not more than one such waiting area is permitted in each smoke compartment, and*

(*e*) *The area does not obstruct access to required exits.*

Exception No. 2:   Waiting areas on floors other than health care sleeping floors may be open to the corridor, provided:

(*a*) *Each area does not exceed 600 sq ft (55.7 sq m), and*

(*b*) *The area is located to permit direct supervision by the facility staff, and*

(*c*) *The area does not obstruct access to required exits, and*

(*d*) *The area is equipped with an electrically supervised, automatic smoke detection system installed in accordance with 12-3.4.*

Exception No. 3:   Buildings protected throughout by an approved supervised automatic sprinkler system may have spaces that are unlimited in size open to the corridor, provided:

(*a*) *The spaces are not used for patient sleeping rooms, treatment rooms, or hazardous areas, and*

(*b*) *Each space is located to permit direct supervision by the facility staff, and*

(*c*) *The space and corridors that the space opens onto in the same smoke compartment are protected by an electrically supervised, automatic smoke detection system installed in accordance with 12-3.4, and*

(*d*) *The space is arranged not to obstruct access to required exits.*

Exception No. 4*:   Space for nurses' stations.

A-12-3.6.1 Exception No. 4   A typical nurses' station would normally contain one or more of the following with associated furniture and furnishings.

(a) Charting area.

(b) Clerical area.

(c) Nourishment station.

(d) Storage of small amounts of medications, medical equipment and supplies, clerical supplies, and linens.

(e) Patient monitoring and communication equipment.

Exception No. 5:   Gift shops may be open to the corridor where protected in accordance with 12-3.2.5.

Exception No. 6: In a limited care facility, group meeting or multipurpose therapeutic spaces, other than hazardous areas, under continuous supervision by facility staff may be open to the corridor, provided:

(a) Each area does not exceed 1,500 sq ft (140 sq m), and

(b) The area is located to permit direct supervision by the facility staff, and

(c) The area does not obstruct any access to required exits, and

(d) The area is equipped with an electrically supervised, automatic smoke detection system installed in accordance with 12-3.4, and

(e)* Each space is protected by automatic sprinklers, or the furniture and furnishings in combination with all other combustibles within the area are of such a minimum quantity and are so arranged that a fully developed fire is unlikely to occur, and

(f) Not more than one such space is permitted per smoke compartment.

A-12-3.6.1 Exception No. 6   See A-13-3.6.1 Exception No. 2(c).

See also commentary following A-13-3.6.1 Exception No. 2(c).

Paragraph 12-3.6.1 requires that all spaces be separated from corridors by partitions. Then exceptions are provided to allow specific areas to be open to the corridor. The intent is to limit the risk of exposing the corridor to fire. Exceptions Nos. 1 through 6 to 12-3.6.1 set forth specific areas that may be open to corridors.

Waiting areas, which are subject to area limitations, may be open to the corridor under the following conditions. Each waiting area must be located to permit direct visual supervision by the staff and must be equipped with an electrically supervised automatic smoke detection system. Not more than one open waiting area is permitted in each smoke compartment on floors with rooms where patients sleep. On other floors, multiple waiting areas that comply with the preceding restrictions are permitted in each smoke compartment. In all cases, waiting spaces must be arranged so as not to obstruct access to exits. (*See Figure 12-15a.*)

Exception No. 3 to 12-3.6.1 makes provision for spaces such as recreation/lounge/waiting areas that may be open to the corridor but not subject to the area restrictions imposed on waiting spaces in previous editions of the *Code*. Exception No. 3 may be applied only within buildings fully protected by automatic sprinklers. The open space must be visually supervised by staff. The open space and interconnected corridors that are not separated from the space must be equipped with an electrically supervised smoke detection system. (*See Figure 12-15b.*)

The "direct supervision" required by Exceptions No. 1,2,3, and 6 (and assumed in Exception No. 4) is very important. It allows the staff to see, hear, or smell a developing fire or to prevent the ignition of a fire merely by their presence. The use of closed-circuit television or mirrors does not provide for all the above and should not be relied upon in new construction. Adequate supervision is not provided if the staff have to "go out of their way" or "look around the corner" to supervise the space.

Areas used for charting and communication by doctors and nurses may be open to the corridor.

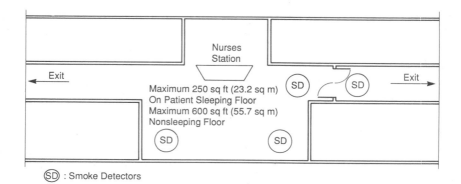

SD : Smoke Detectors

Figure 12-15a. Waiting Spaces. Waiting area complying with either 12-3.6.1, Exception No. 1 or Exception No. 2.

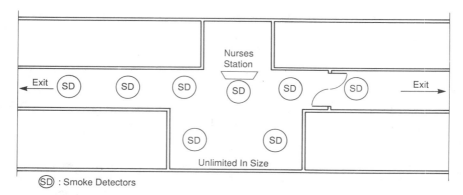

SD : Smoke Detectors

Figure 12-15b. Area Open to Corridor. Unlimited size area open to corridor in accordance with 12-3.6.1, Exception No. 3. To use this Exception, the building must be fully sprinklered.

12-3.6.2 Construction of Corridor Walls.

12-3.6.2.1 Corridor walls shall be continuous from the floor to the underside of the floor or roof deck above, through any concealed spaces, such as those above the suspended ceilings, and through interstitial structural and mechanical spaces, and shall have a fire resistance rating of at least 1 hour.

Exception No.1: In buildings protected throughout by an approved supervised automatic sprinkler system, a corridor may be separated from all other areas by non-fire-rated partitions and may be terminated at the ceiling when the ceiling is constructed to limit the transfer of smoke.

Exception No. 2: Corridor partitions may terminate at ceilings that are not an integral part of a floor construction if there exists 5 ft (152 cm) or more of space between the top of the ceiling subsystem and the bottom of the floor or roof above, provided:

(a) The ceiling shall have been tested as a part of a fire-rated assembly in accordance with NFPA 251, Standard Methods of Fire Tests of Building Construction and Materials, for a test period of 1 hour or more, and

(b) Corridor partitions form smoketight joints with the ceilings (joint filler, if used, shall be noncombustible) and,

(c) Each compartment of interstitial space that constitutes a separate smoke area is vented, in case of smoke emergency, to the outside by mechanical means having sufficient capacity to provide at least two air changes per hour, but in no case having a capacity less than 5,000 cfm (2.36 cu m/s), and

(d) The interstitial space shall not be used for storage, and

(e) The space shall not be used as a plenum for supply, exhaust or return air except as noted in (c).

12-3.6.2.2   Corridor walls shall form a barrier to limit the transfer of smoke.

12-3.6.2.3   Fixed wired glass vision panels shall be permitted in corridor walls, provided they do not exceed 1,296 sq in. (.84 sq m) in area and are mounted in steel or other approved metal frames.

Exception: There shall be no restrictions in area and fire resistance of glass and frames in buildings protected throughout by an approved supervised automatic sprinkler system installed in accordance with Section 7-7.

In nonsprinklered buildings, corridor partitions must be constructed of 1-hour fire-rated assemblies using materials selected on the basis of the construction types allowed by 12-1.6.2. All construction materials in buildings of Type I or Type II construction must satisfy the criteria for noncombustible or limited-combustible materials. (*See 12-1.6.3.*) Corridor partitions must be constructed continuously through all concealed spaces (for example, to the floor or roof deck above a suspended "lay-in" ceiling).

Openings in corridor partitions in nonsprinklered buildings must be suitably protected to maintain corridor separation. Glazing is limited to a maximum of 1,296 sq in. (.84 sq m) of wired glass set in steel or approved metal frames. Each wired glass panel must be limited to a maximum dimension of 54 in. (140 cm). The glass should be labeled, should be ¼-in. (0.6-cm) thick, and should be well embedded in putty with all exposed joints between the metal and glass struck and pointed. (*See NFPA 80, Standard for Fire Doors and Windows.*[12]) A number of wired glass panels may be used in a single partition, provided that each 1,296-sq in. (.84-sq m) section is separated from adjacent panels by a steel or other approved metal mullion. It should be recognized that the use of wired glass panels in a partition will reduce the fire resistance capability of the partition, in that there will be radiant energy transfer through the glass panel. Therefore, excessive use of wired glass panels should be avoided.

(*See Figure 12-16a.*)

Where complete automatic sprinkler protection is provided, corridor partitions need not be rated but must still be constructed to resist the passage of smoke. The materials for constructing the partitions must be selected on the basis of the construction types allowed by 12-1.6.2 and 12-1.6.3. Where suspended ceilings are provided, partitions may be terminated at the suspended ceiling without any additional special protection if the suspended ceiling will resist the passage of smoke. The ability to resist the passage of smoke must be carefully evaluated. There are no restrictions in terms of area or fire resistance for glazing used in corridor partitions in sprinklered buildings. (*See Figure 12-16b.*)

Exception No. 2 to 12-3.6.2 sets forth criteria for terminating corridor partitions at ceilings, including "lay-in" type ceilings in nonsprinklered buildings. Partitions may be terminated at a ceiling that has been tested as a portion of an assembly having a fire resistance rating of 1 hour or more. Each compartment located above such a ceiling must be equipped with an automatic mechanical smoke exhaust system capable of providing a minimum of two air changes per hour but exhausting not less than 5,000 cu ft/min (2.36 cu m/sec). (*See the additional criteria in items (a) through (e) of Exception No. 2.*) This is not a common arrangement, due to the large interstitial space needed and the energy loss resulting from the ventilation requirements.

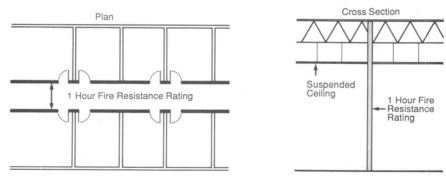

Figure 12-16a.   Corridor Wall, Nonsprinklered Buildings.   Corridor wall complying with 12-3.6.2. Note that wall must extend to floor or roof deck above unless complying with one of the Exceptions.

12-3.6.3* Corridor Doors.

12-3.6.3.1   Doors protecting corridor openings in other than required enclosures of vertical openings, exits, or hazardous areas shall be substantial doors, such as those constructed of 1¾-in. (4.4-cm) solid bonded core wood or of construction that will resist fire for at least 20 minutes.

Exception No. 1:   In buildings protected throughout by an approved supervised automatic sprinkler system installed in accordance with Section 7-7, the door construction requirements noted above are not required, but the doors shall be constructed to resist the passage of smoke.

to be "made up" from the corridor. Where a door to a sink closet, bathroom, or toilet is equipped with a grille or louver, such spaces may not be used for the storage of flammable or combustible supplies. Caution must be exercised where using this exception for sink closets, as they are often used for storage of combustibles.

Air-handling ducts penetrating corridor partitions should be adequately protected to preserve separation of exit access routes. In general, steel ducts will not require a fire damper. In any event, the possible movement of air from space to space under conditions of system operation and conditions of system shutdown should be evaluated. If there is a significant potential for the transfer of smoke from an occupied space to a corridor, consideration should be given to providing a fire damper, even though the *Code* does not explicitly require such protection.

12-3.7* Subdivision of Building Spaces.

A-12-3.7   See A-12-2.2.

12-3.7.1   Smoke barriers shall be provided, regardless of building construction type, as follows:

(a) To divide every story used by inpatients for sleeping or treatment, or any story having an occupant load of 50 or more persons, regardless of use, into at least two compartments, and

> Item (a) requires subdivision of any floor used by inpatients for sleeping or treatment, regardless of size and irrespective of the number of patients. It also requires subdivision of any other floor that has an occupant load of 50 or more persons regardless of size.

(b) To limit on any story the length and width of each smoke compartment to no more than 150 ft (45 m).

> It is not the intent of item (b) to require that the length and width be added together with the resulting sum being 150 ft (45 m) or less. It is the intent that the length be 150 ft (45 m) or less and that the width be 150 ft (45 m) or less.

Exception No. 1: Protection may be accomplished in conjunction with the provision of horizontal exits.

> In such cases, the horizontal exit would also have to be built to comply with smoke barrier requirements. (*See Section 6-3.*)

Exception No. 2: One dimension may be extended provided that the total width plus length does not exceed 300 ft (91 m) and provided that travel distance from a room to a smoke barrier door or horizontal exit is no more than 150 ft (45 m).

> Paragraph 12-3.7.1 Exception No. 2 provides the facility and the designer with some flexibility in the arrangement of smoke compartments. The application of Exception No. 2 is illustrated in Figure 12-17b. Even

with this exception, the maximum compartment size remains 22,500 sq ft (2,100 sq m) [150 ft (45 m) by 150 ft (45 m)]. However, this performance-oriented exception would allow a long narrow compartment of, for example, 250 ft by 50 ft (76 m by 15 m). In such a case, the area [12,500 sq ft (1,167 sq in)] would be considerably less than the 22,500 sq ft (2,100 sq m) otherwise permitted.

12-3.7.2 Smoke barriers shall be provided on stories that are usable but unoccupied.

12-3.7.3 Any required smoke barrier shall be constructed in accordance with Section 6-3 and shall have a fire resistance rating of at least 1 hour.

Exception: Where an atrium is used, smoke barriers may terminate at an atrium wall constructed in accordance with Exception No. 2 to 6-2.4.5(g). A minimum of two separate smoke compartments shall be provided on each floor.

See Figure 12-20a - 12-20d.

12-3.7.4 At least 30 net sq ft (2.8 sq m) per patient in a hospital or nursing home or 15 net sq ft (1.4 sq m) per resident in a limited care facility shall be provided within the aggregate area of corridors, patient rooms, treatment rooms, lounge or dining areas, and other low hazard areas on each side of the smoke barrier. On stories not housing bed or litter patients, at least 6 net sq ft (.56 sq m) per occupant shall be provided on each side of the smoke barrier for the total number of occupants in adjoining compartments.

12-3.7.5 Doors in smoke barriers shall be substantial doors, such as 1¾ in. (4.4 cm) thick, solid bonded wood core or construction that will resist fire for at least twenty minutes. Cross corridor openings in smoke barriers shall be protected by a pair of swinging doors or a horizontal sliding door complying with 5-2.1.14. Swinging doors shall be arranged so that each door will swing in a direction opposite from the other. The minimum door leaf width for swinging doors shall be as follows:

(a) hospitals and nursing homes: 44 in. (112 cm)

(b) hospitals for psychiatric care and limited care facilities: 34 in. (86 cm)

The minimum clear opening for horizontal sliding doors shall be as follows:

(a) hospitals and nursing homes: 88 in. (224 cm)

(b) hospitals for psychiatric care and limited care facilities: 68 in. (173 cm)

Formal Interpretation 76-55
Reference: 12-3.7.5

Question: Is it the intent of the *Code* to specify which door, in a pair of corridor doors, shall swing with normal travel?

Answer: No.

Issue Edition: 1976
Reference: 10-2.3.6.6.5
Date: January 1978

12-3.7.6   Doors in smoke barriers shall comply with 6-3.4 and shall be self-closing or automatic closing in accordance with 12-2.2.2.6.

Formal Interpretation 73-18A
Reference: 12-3.7.6

Question: Is it the intent of the *Code* to permit doorways to penetrate smoke barriers at places other than in corridors and public rooms?

Answer: Yes.

Question: If the answer to the first question is yes, are there any restrictions as to the number, type, etc.?

Answer: No.

Issue Edition: 1973
Reference: 10-1316
Date: August - September 1975

12-3.7.7   Vision panels of approved transparent wired glass not exceeding 1,296 sq in. (.84 sq m) in steel or other approved metal frames shall be provided in each cross corridor swinging door and at each cross corridor horizontal sliding door in a smoke barrier.

12-3.7.8   Rabbets, bevels, or astragals are required at the meeting edges, and stops are required at the head and sides of door frames in smoke barriers. Positive latching hardware is not required. Center mullions are prohibited.

The requirements of 12-3.7.1 through 12-3.7.8 for subdividing building spaces through the use smoke barriers are illustrated in Figures 12-17 through 12-21. Paragraph 12-2.2.5 discusses horizontal exits.

During a fire, the emergency evacuation of patients in a health care facility is an inefficient, time consuming process. Realistically, if patients must be moved, sizable numbers of occupants can be relocated only through horizontal travel. Smoke barriers and horizontal exits used to subdivide a building serve three purposes fundamental to the protection of inpatients in that they:

1. Limit the spread of fire and smoke,
2. Limit the number of occupants exposed to a single fire, and
3. Provide for horizontal relocation of patients by creating an area of refuge on the same floor level.

The *Code* essentially requires each story to be subdivided by a barrier into a minimum of two compartments. Although not stated in the *Code*, it would be desirable to subdivide health care facilities in such a way as to have separate banks of elevators in different smoke zones. Should evacuation of the building become necessary, patients can first be moved horizontally to a temporary area of refuge and then be removed from the building via elevators.

Openings between the meeting edges of pairs of doors and between the doors and frames must be closed to retard the transfer of smoke. Since 12-3.7.5 requires these doors to swing in opposite directions from each other, the protection at the meeting edge does not create a coordination problem and, therefore, is simple to provide.

Previous editions of the *Code* granted exceptions for doors and dampers installed in a smoke barrier where an engineered smoke control system was provided. The exceptions have been deleted in the 1988 Edition due to the absence of adequate design standards and because of unfavorable field experience with smoke control system performance.

12-3.8 Special Features.

12-3.8.1   Every patient sleeping room shall have an outside window or outside door arranged and located so that it can be opened from the inside to permit the venting of products of combustion and to permit any occupant to have direct access to fresh air in case of emergency. (*See 12-1.1.1.7 for detention screen requirements.*) The maximum allowable sill height shall not exceed 36 in. (91 cm) above the floor. Where windows require the use of tools or keys for operation, the tools or keys shall be located on the floor involved at a prominent location accessible to staff.

Exceptions and commentary to this paragraph begin on page 618.

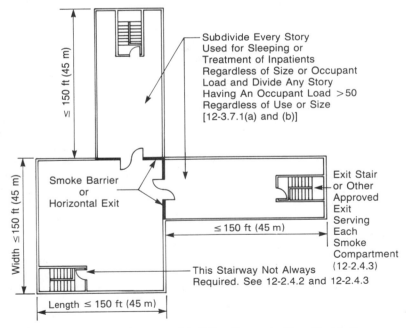

Figure 12-17.   Subdivision of Building Spaces in New Health Care Occupancies.   (*See also Figures 12-3, 12-4, and 12-7.*)

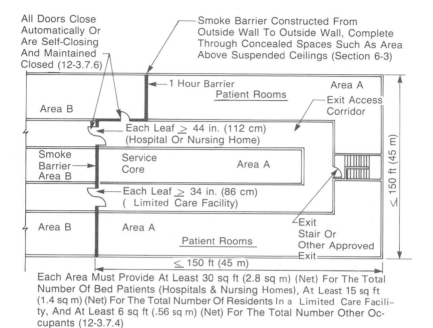

All Doors Close Automatically Or Are Self-Closing And Maintained Closed (12-3.7.6)

Smoke Barrier Constructed From Outside Wall To Outside Wall, Complete Through Concealed Spaces Such As Area Above Suspended Ceilings (Section 6-3)

1 Hour Barrier
Patient Rooms

Area A

Exit Access Corridor

Area B

Each Leaf ≥ 44 in. (112 cm)
(Hospital Or Nursing Home)

Smoke Barrier
Area B

Service Core

Area A

≤ 150 ft (45 m)

Each Leaf ≥ 34 in. (86 cm)
(Limited Care Facility)

Area B

Area A

Patient Rooms

Exit Stair Or Other Approved Exit

≤ 150 ft (45 m)

Each Area Must Provide At Least 30 sq ft (2.8 sq m) (Net) For The Total Number Of Bed Patients (Hospitals & Nursing Homes), At Least 15 sq ft (1.4 sq m) (Net) For The Total Number Of Residents In a Limited Care Facility, And At Least 6 sq ft (.56 sq m) (Net) For The Total Number Other Occupants (12-3.7.4)

Figure 12-18.   Subdivision of Building Spaces in New Health Care Occupancies.

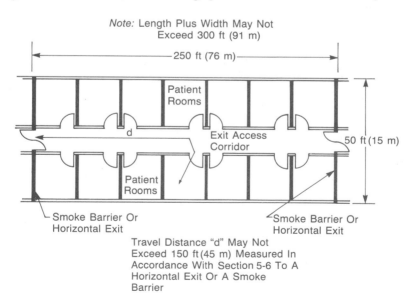

Note: Length Plus Width May Not Exceed 300 ft (91 m)

250 ft (76 m)

Patient Rooms

d

Exit Access Corridor

50 ft (15 m)

Patient Rooms

Smoke Barrier Or Horizontal Exit

Smoke Barrier Or Horizontal Exit

Travel Distance "d" May Not Exceed 150 ft (45 m) Measured In Accordance With Section 5-6 To A Horizontal Exit Or A Smoke Barrier

Figure 12-19.   Approximate Maximum Compartment Length Permitted by Exception No. 2 to 12-3.7.1.

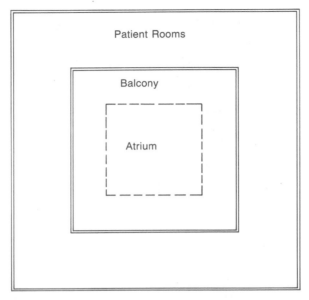

Figure 12-20a.   Illustration of a Noncomplying Atrium Arrangement in a New Health Care Occupancy. (*See Figure 12-20b for corrected arrangement. Also see Figures 12-20c and 12-20d.*)

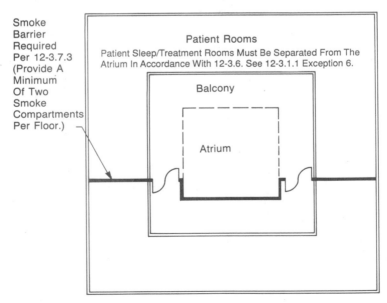

Figure 12-20b.   New Health Care Occupancy with Complying Atrium Arrangement.

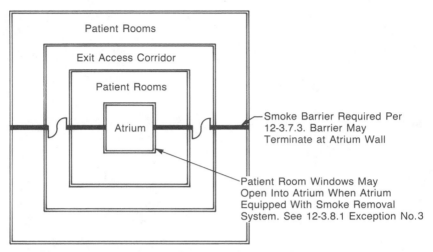

Figure 12-20c. New Health Care Occupancy with Complying Atrium Arrangement.

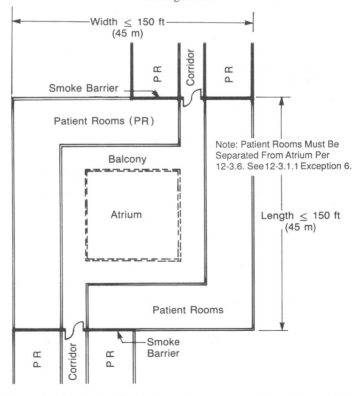

Figure 12-20d. New Health Care Occupancy with Complying Atrium Arrangement.

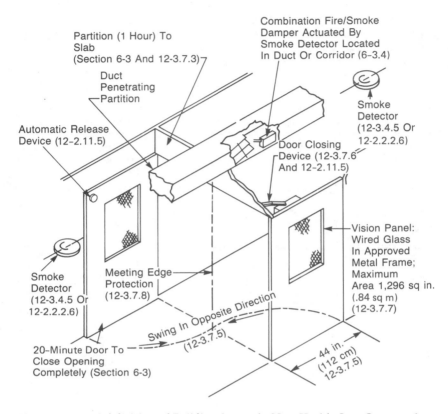

Figure 12-21.   Subdivision of Building Spaces in New Health Care Occupancies.

The following are Exceptions to 12-3.8.1, which appears on page 614.

Exception No. 1:   The window sill in special nursing care areas such as those housing ICU, CCU, hemodialysis, and neo-natal patients may be up to 60 in. (152 cm) above the floor.

Exception No. 2:   Rooms intended for occupancy of less than 24 hours, such as those housing obstetrical labor beds, recovery beds, and observation beds in the emergency department; and newborn nurseries need not comply with this requirement.

Exception No. 3:   Windows opening into atriums where the atrium has a smoke removal system are, for the purposes of this requirement, considered outside windows; such windows shall normally be closed and operable only with the use of tool or key.

Exception No. 4:   The window sill in limited care facilities may be up to 44 in. (112 cm) above the floor.

Exception No. 5:   Buildings designed with approved engineered smoke control systems in accordance with Section 7-3 need not comply with the operable features of this requirement.

Formal Interpretation 73-34
Reference: 12-3.8.1

Question: Is the requirement for operable windows contained in 12-3.8.1 obviated by compliance with 12-4.1 in every respect?

Answer: No.

Issue Edition: 1973
Reference: 10-1325
Date: January 1977

Formal Interpretation 85-3
Reference: 12-3.8.1

Question: Is it the intent that cubicles with doors, as allowed as part of a sleeping suite by 12-2.5.3, qualify as "sleeping rooms" so that each cubicle would be required to have its own outside window or door per 12-3.8.1?

Answer: No.

Issue Edition: 1985
Reference: 12-3.8.1
Date: December 1984

Paragraph 12-3.8.1 requires an outside door or outside window in each room where patients sleep. The window must be equipped with an operable section to be opened in an emergency to provide access to fresh air. The maximum allowable sill height is specified as 36 in. (91 cm), except in special nursing care areas (recovery rooms, intensive care units, coronary care units, and dialysis units) where the sill height may not be more than 60 in. (152 cm) above the floor. Limited care facilities are frequently designed similarly to residential type buildings. Sill height has been set at a maximum of 44 in. (112 cm) above the floor in such facilities, consistent with residential construction practices. Sill heights are limited to ensure access to window latches so that the operable section may be opened without special equipment.

To install windows with a latching arrangement that requires special knowledge to operate, or to place the latches at a level that requires the use of a chair or ladder for access, would not meet the intent of this section, even if the criteria for sill height were satisfied. Conversely, a window with a sill height exceeding that specified by this section, but equipped with a mechanical linkage permitting operation of the window from floor level without special tools, special knowledge, or other special equipment could satisfy the intent of this section.

It is desirable to have operable windows that have the capability of being opened without requiring a tool or a key. However, windows may be locked, provided keys are readily available. The *Code* recognizes that detention screens are sometimes necessary. Rooms so equipped should be limited in number to those where such precautions are deemed necessary. Continuous supervision should be provided for such areas. (*See 12-1.1.1.7.*)

Rooms that are occupied for less than 24 hours, such as those used for recovery, child delivery, or emergency care, or rooms used for newborn nurseries, need not be provided with a window. In excepting these rooms from the requirements for windows, the Committee felt that the high incidence of direct nursing supervision of all patients in these areas reduces the likelihood that patients will be trapped in a smoky fire. However, where it is not possible to provide windows, a conservative design should provide some added protection, such as individual sprinkler protection of enclosed areas (closets and pantries), early warning by smoke detectors, or high-volume exhaust ventilation.

For a discussion of Exception No. 3 and atrium windows, refer to the commentary on 12-3.1 and Figure 12-20c. To avoid interfering with smoke control systems, patient room windows that open into an atrium must be operated with a tool or key.

SECTION 12-4   SPECIAL PROVISIONS

12-4.1 Windowless Buildings.   See Section 30-7 for requirements for windowless buildings.

Windowless portions of health care facilities must comply with the requirements of Chapter 12 in addition to the criteria set forth for such structures in Section 30-7. Paragraph 12-4.1 does not obviate the requirements for openable patient room windows contained within 12-3.8.1.

12-4.2 High Rise Buildings.   (*See 12-1.6 and 12-2.2.2.8.*)

12-4.3 Operating Features.   (*See Chapter 31.*)

SECTION 12-5   BUILDING SERVICES

12-5.1 Utilities.

12-5.1.1   Utilities shall comply with the provisions of Section 7-1.

12-5.1.2   Alarms, emergency communication systems, and the illumination of generator set locations shall be as described in the Life Safety Branch of NFPA 99, *Standard for Health Care Facilities.*

12-5.1.3   Any health care occupancy as indicated within 12-1.1.1.2 that normally utilizes life support devices shall have electrical systems designed and installed in accordance with NFPA 99, *Standard for Health Care Facilities.*

Exception: This requirement does not apply to a facility that has life support equipment for emergency purposes only.

It is not uncommon to lose all or some power supplies during a fire emergency. Therefore, it is important that life support equipment be powered by properly designed and installed electrical systems so as not to create additional problems during the emergency.

12-5.2 Heating, Ventilating, and Air Conditioning.

12-5.2.1 Heating, ventilating, and air conditioning shall comply with the provisions of Section 7-2 and shall be installed in accordance with the manufacturer's specifications.

Exception: As modified in 12-5.2.2 following.

12-5.2.2 Any heating device other than a central heating plant shall be so designed and installed that combustible material will not be ignited by it or its appurtenances. If fuel-fired, such heating devices shall be chimney or vent connected, shall take air for combustion directly from outside, and shall be so designed and installed to provide for complete separation of the combustion system from the atmosphere of the occupied area. Any heating device shall have safety features to immediately stop the flow of fuel and shut down the equipment in case of either excessive temperatures or ignition failure.

Exception No. 1: Approved suspended unit heaters may be used in locations other than means of egress and patient sleeping areas, provided such heaters are located high enough to be out of the reach of persons using the area, and provided they are equipped with the safety features called for above.

Exception No. 2.: Fireplaces may be installed and used only in areas other than patient sleeping areas, provided that these areas are separated from patient sleeping spaces by construction having a 1-hour fire resistance rating and they comply with NFPA 211, Standard for Chimneys, Fireplaces, Vents and Solid Fuel Burning Appliances. In addition thereto, the fireplace shall be equipped with a hearth that shall be raised at least 4 in. (10.2 cm) and a fireplace enclosure guaranteed against breakage up to a temperature of 650°F (343°C) and constructed of heat tempered glass or other approved material. If, in the opinion of the authority having jurisdiction, special hazards are present, a lock on the enclosure and other safety precautions may be required.

Formal Interpretation 81-8
Reference: 12-5.2.2, 13-5.2.2

Question: Is it the intent of the Committee to permit free-standing wood burning stoves in health care facilities?

Answer: No.

Issue Edition: 1981
Reference: 12-5.2.2, 13-5.2.2
Date: January 1982

Paragraphs 12-5.2.1 and 12-5.2.2 specify safeguards for air conditioning, ventilating, heating, and other service equipment in order to minimize the possibility of such devices serving as a source of ignition. Fuel-fired heating devices, except central heating systems, must be designed to provide complete separation of the combustion system from the occupied spaces. Air for combustion must be taken directly from the outside.

A major concern of the *Code* is to prevent the ignition of clothing, bedclothes, furniture, and other furnishings by a heating device. Therefore, 31-4.7 prohibits portable heating devices in areas used by patients.

12-5.3 Elevators, Dumbwaiters, and Vertical Conveyors.   Elevators, dumbwaiters, and vertical conveyors shall comply with the provisions of Section 7-4.

Although not counted as required exits, elevators may constitute a valuable supplemental facility for evacuating patients from health care buildings. In some cases, movement of critically ill patients or patients in restraining devices may be realistically accomplished only by an elevator.

Elevators, however, have many inherent weaknesses that tend to limit reliability. Elevator access doors are designed with operating tolerances that permit smoke transfer into the shaft. Power failure during a fire could result in trapping persons on elevators that stop between floors. Elevators may, during their descent from upper floors, stop automatically at the floor where the fire is burning, allow the doors to open, and expose the occupants to the fire.

Many of these weaknesses can be minimized by providing emergency power, separating the elevator lobby from other building spaces by rated construction, designing detection and alarm equipment to prevent elevators from stopping at a floor exposed to a fire, providing an emergency smoke control system, and by pressurizing the elevator shaft and adjacent lobbies. (*See Section* 7-3.) This represents good fire protection judgment but is not the result of any requirements of this *Code*.

Through emergency planning and staff training, crowding of elevators (another potential problem) may be avoided. Emergency plans may make effective use of elevators by transferring patients through a horizontal exit, for example, to a separate fire area. Within the separate fire area, a staged evacuation program could be instituted, the elevators ultimately taking patients to the outside at ground level.

12-5.4 Rubbish Chutes, Incinerators, and Laundry Chutes.

12-5.4.1   Rubbish chutes, incinerators, and laundry chutes shall comply with the provisions of Section 7-5.

12-5.4.2   Any rubbish chute or linen chute, including pneumatic rubbish and linen systems, shall be provided with automatic extinguishing protection installed in accordance with Section 7-7. (*See Section* 7-5.)

12-5.4.3 Any trash chute shall discharge into a trash collecting room used for no other purpose and protected in accordance with Section 6-4.

12-5.4.4 An incinerator shall not be directly flue-fed nor shall any floor charging chute directly connect with the combustion chamber.

SECTION 12-6   NEW AMBULATORY HEALTH CARE CENTERS

12-6.1 General Requirements.

12-6.1.1 Application.

12-6.1.1.1 Ambulatory health care centers shall comply with the provisions of both Chapter 26 and (this) Section 12-6, as may be more stringent.

12-6.1.1.2 This section establishes life safety requirements, in addition to those required in Chapter 26, for the design of all ambulatory health care centers and outpatient surgical centers that meet the requirements of 12-1.3(d).

Ambulatory health care centers exhibit some of the occupancy characteristics of business occupancies and some of the characteristics of health care facilities. In developing Section 12-6, it was intended to prescribe a level of life safety from fire that would be greater than that typically specified for business occupancies, but less than that typically found in health care facilities. (*See commentary for 12-1.3.*)

Ambulatory health care centers are required to comply with the provisions of Chapter 26 pertaining to business occupancies, except as more restrictive provisions are established within Section 12-6.

12-6.1.2 Reserved.

12-6.1.3 Special Definitions. (*See 12-1.3*)

12-6.1.4 Classification of Occupancy. (*See 12-1.3*)

12-6.1.5 Reserved.

12-6.1.6 Minimum Construction Requirements.

12-6.1.6.1 For purposes of 12-6.1.6, stories shall be counted starting at the primary level of exit discharge and ending at the highest occupiable level. For the purposes of this section, the primary level of exit discharge of a building shall be that floor that is level with or above finished grade of this exterior wall line for 50 percent or more of its perimeter.

Allowable building construction types are determined as a function of the number of stories in a building. In determining the number of stories, the first story is considered to be the primary level of exit discharge. Only occupiable levels are counted in determining story height. For example, an unoccupied attic would not constitute a story.

Difficulties have been experienced in determining story height where a building is located on a sloping grade. Paragraph 12-6.1.6.1 notes that a story on a sloping site that is partially below grade should be counted as a story if the floor is level with or above grade for 50 percent or more of the perimeter of the building at the exterior wall. (*See Figure 12-22.*)

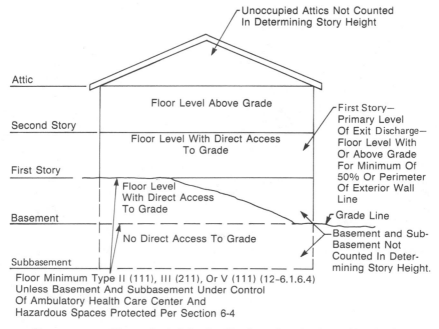

Figure 12-22.   Illustration of the Application of 12-6.1.6.1 and 12-6.1.6.4.

12-6.1.6.2   Buildings of one story in height housing ambulatory health care centers may be of Type I, II, III, IV, or V construction. (*See 6-2.1.*)

12-6.1.6.3   Buildings of two or more stories in height housing ambulatory health care centers may be of Type I (443), I (332), or II (222), Type II (111), Type III (211), Type IV (2HH), or Type V (111) construction. (*See 6-2.1.*)

Exception: Such buildings may be constructed of Type II (000), III (200), or V (000) if protected throughout by an approved automatic sprinkler system in accordance with Section 7-7.

Construction types permitted in ambulatory health care centers are summarized in Table 12-1. (*See NFPA 220, Standard on Types of Building Construction.[2]*)

Table 12-1.   Construction Types Permitted in Ambulatory
Health Care Occupancies

Construction Type	Stories	
	1	2 or more
I (443), I (332), II (222), II (111) (Fire Resistive and Protected Noncombustible)	X	X
II (000) (Unprotected Noncombustible)	X	X*
III (211) (Protected Ordinary)	X	X
III (200) (Unprotected Ordinary)	X	X*
IV (2HH) (Heavy Timber)	X	X
V (111) (Protected Wood Frame)	X	X
V (000) (Unprotected Wood Frame)	X	X*

X = Construction types allowed.
* = Automatic sprinkler protection required.

12-6.1.6.4   Any level below the level of exit discharge shall be separated from the level of exit discharge by at least Type II (111), Type III (211), or Type V (111) construction. (*See 6-2.1.*)

Exception: Such separation is not required for such levels if they are under the control of the ambulatory health care center and any hazardous spaces are protected in accordance with Section 6-4.

Refer to Figure 12-22.

12-6.1.6.5   Where new ambulatory health care centers are located in existing buildings, the authority having jurisdiction may accept construction systems of lesser fire resistance than required above if it can be demonstrated to the authority's satisfaction that in case of fire prompt evacuation of the center can be made, or that the exposing occupancies and materials of construction present no threat of either fire penetration from such occupancy into the ambulatory health care center or collapse of the structure.

This paragraph is meant to liberalize the construction requirements applicable to a new ambulatory health care center that is to be placed in an existing building. Adequate supporting data must be supplied to the authority having jurisdiction to justify such a reduction.

12-6.1.7 Occupant Load.

12-6.2 Means of Egress Requirements.

12-6.2.1 General.   Every aisle, passageway, corridor, exit discharge, exit location, and access shall be in accordance with Chapter 5.

Exception No. 1:   As modified in the following paragraphs.

Exception No. 2:   The requirements of Chapter 5 specifying net clear door width do not apply. Projections into the door opening by stops or by hinge stiles shall be permitted.

Means of egress details are to conform to the fundamental provisions expressed in Chapter 5, except as modified in Chapter 12. For example, Exception No. 2 to 12-2.1 would allow the width of exit doors to be measured on the basis of the actual door leaf width. Projections into the door opening by the hinge stile and door stops are ignored.

12-6.2.2 Means of Egress Components.

12-6.2.2.1   Components of means of egress shall be limited to the types described in 26-2.2.

12-6-2.2.2   Special locking arrangements complying with 5-2.1.6 are permitted on exterior doors.

Paragraph 5-2.1.6 establishes minimum requirements for delayed release hardware, including the requirement that the building must be protected throughout by an automatic sprinkler system or automatic fire detection system.

12-6.2.2.3   Any door in an exit passageway, horizontal exit, smoke barrier, stairway enclosure, or hazardous area enclosure may be held open only by an automatic release device that complies with 5-2.1.8. The required manual fire alarm system and the systems required by 5-2.1.8(c) shall be arranged so as to initiate the closing action of all such doors by zone or throughout the entire facility.

12-6.2.2.4   Where doors in a stair enclosure are held open by an automatic device as permitted in 12-6.2.2.3, initiation of a door closing action on any level shall cause all doors at all levels in the stair enclosure to close.

It is desirable to keep doors in exit enclosures, stair enclosures, horizontal exits, smoke barriers, and hazardous areas closed at all times to impede the spread of smoke and gases caused by a fire. However, some doors will be kept open, either for reasons of operating efficiency or comfort. Where doors in required fire or smoke barriers are to be held open, such doors must be equipped with automatic devices that are arranged to close the doors by the methods described within 12-6.2.2.3 and 5-2.1.8.

The automatic device must cause the doors to close upon operation of the manual fire alarm system. The doors must also be designed to close by actuation of a smoke detector located to detect smoke on either side of the door opening or by actuation of a complete automatic fire extinguishing or complete automatic fire detection system.

It is especially important in facilities providing health care to maintain floor-to-floor separation. Doors protecting openings in a stair enclosure may be held open by an automatic device only if arranged to close as specified above. Initiation of any action that causes a door to close at one level must cause all doors protecting openings within the stair enclosure to close and latch at all levels.

12-6.2.3 Capacity of Means of Egress.

12-6.2.3.1 The capacity of any required means of egress shall be determined in accordance with the provisions of 26-2.3 and shall be based on its width as defined in Section 5-3.

The capacity of the means of egress in ambulatory health care centers is determined on the basis of provisions in Chapter 26 dealing with business occupancies. Paragraph 26-2.3.1 refers to Section 5-3, which requires the capacity of level exit components to be computed in the basis of 0.2 in. (0.5 cm)/person, whereas stair capacity is computed using 0.3 in. (0.8 cm)/person. These capacities are much higher than would be allowed typically for a health care center and are considered permissible on the basis that the majority of occupants will be ambulatory.

12-6.2.3.2 The minimum width of any corridor or passageway required for exit access shall be 44 in. (112 cm) clear.

Corridor widths greater than 44 in. (112 cm) may be required within ambulatory health care centers. However, the minimum width for public corridors used as common exit access corridors or passageways is 44 in. (112 cm). The 44-in. (112-cm) width is stipulated on the assumption that most occupants will be ambulatory.

12-6.2.3.3 Doors in the means of egress from diagnostic or treatment areas, such as X-ray, surgical, or physical therapy shall be at least 34 in. (86 cm) wide.

In many instances, doors wider than 34 in. (86 cm) will be required. This paragraph intends to address doors used by the public or those doors that provide access to public hallways and corridors. The 34-in. (86-cm) minimum width is specified for doors on the assumption that most occupants will be ambulatory.

12-6.2.4 Number of Exits.

12-6.2.4.1 At least two exits of the types described in 26-2.2 remotely located from each other shall be provided for each floor or fire section of the building.

12-6.2.4.2 Any room and any suite of rooms of more than 1,000 sq ft (93 sq m) shall have at least two exit access doors remotely located from each other.

12-6.2.5 Arrangement of Means of Egress. *(See 26-2.5.)*

12-6.2.6 Travel Distance to Exits.

12-6.2.6.1   Travel distance shall be measured in accordance with Section 5-6.

12-6.2.6.2 Travel distance:

(a) Between any room door required as exit access and an exit shall not exceed 100 ft (30 m); and

(b) Between any point in a room and an exit shall not exceed 150 ft (45 m).

Exception: The travel distance in (a) or (b) above may be increased by 50 ft (15 m) in buildings protected throughout by an approved automatic sprinkler system.

Travel distance is measured only to the closest exit, not to both exits required by 12-6.2.4.1. The requirements of 12-6.2.6.2 are illustrated in Figure 12-23.

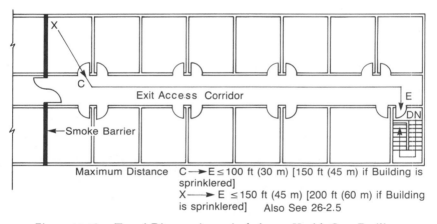

Figure 12-23.   Travel Distance in an Ambulatory Health Care Facility.

12-6.2.7 Discharge from Exits.   *(See 26-2.7.)*

12-6.2.8 Illumination of Means of Egress.   Means of egress shall be illuminated in accordance with Section 5-8.

12-6.2.9 Emergency Lighting and Essential Electrical Systems.

12-6.2.9.1   Emergency lighting shall be provided in accordance with Section 5-9.

12-6.2.9.2   Where general anesthesia or life support equipment is used, each ambulatory health care center shall be provided with an essential electrical system in accordance with NFPA 99, *Standard for Health Care Facilities.*

Exception: Where battery operated equipment is provided and acceptable to the authority having jurisdiction.

All ambulatory health care centers are required to be equipped with emergency lighting. If medical procedures requiring general anesthesia are practiced, or if life support equipment is required, ambulatory health care centers are required to be served by electrical systems meeting the criteria for essential electrical systems as detailed in Chapter 3, "Electrical Systems," of NFPA 99, *Standard for Health Care Facilities.*[5]

A facility would not be required to have an emergency generator if the building is a free-standing unit and, as a normal practice, (1) management maintains admitting and discharge policies that preclude the provision of care for any patient or resident who may need to be sustained by electrical life-support equipment, such as respirators, suction apparatus, etc., and (2) no surgical treatment requiring general anesthesia is offered, and (3) battery-operated systems or equipment are provided that would maintain power to exit lights and illumination for exit corridors, stairways, medical preparation areas, and the like, for a minimum of 1½ hours. Additionally, battery power would be required to be supplied to all alarm systems.

12-6.2.10 Marking of Means of Egress.   Means of egress shall have signs in accordance with Section 5-10.

12-6.2.11 Special Features.

12-6.3 Protection.

12-6.3.1 Protection of Vertical Openings.   *(See 26-3.1.)*

12-6.3.2 Protection from Hazards.   *(See 26-3.2.)*

12-6.3.2.1   Laboratories employing quantities of flammable, combustible, or hazardous materials that are considered as severe hazard shall be protected in accordance with NFPA 99, *Standard for Health Care Facilities.*

Laboratories that contain "ordinary" combustibles and flammable liquids in sufficient quantity to threaten a 1-hour fire separation [e.g., wood equivalent fuel loads in the range of 5 to 10 lb/sq ft (25 to 50 kg/sq m)] are considered a severe hazard. Laboratories representing a severe hazard must be protected in accordance with Chapter 10, "Laboratories," of NFPA 99, *Standard for Health Care Facilities.*[5] Protection would include 1-hour fire resistance separation and automatic sprinkler protection.

Where fuel loads of lesser amounts are involved and quantities of flammable liquids are limited, laboratories would simply be considered hazardous areas and would require either 1-hour separation or automatic sprinkler protection.

12-6.3.2.2   Anesthetizing locations shall be protected in accordance with NFPA 99, *Standard for Health Care Facilities.*

12-6.3.3 Interior Finish.   *(See 26-3.3.)*

12-6.3.4 Detection, Alarm, and Communications Systems.

12-6.3.4.1 General. Centers shall be provided with a fire alarm system in accordance with Section 7-6, except as modified below.

12-6.3.4.2 Initiation. Initiation of the required fire alarm systems shall be by manual means in accordance with 7-6.2 and by means of any detection devices or detection systems required.

12-6.3.4.3 Occupant Notification. Occupant notification shall be accomplished automatically, without delay, upon operation of any fire alarm activating device by means of an internal audible alarm in accordance with 7-6.3.

Exception: The presignal system allowed by 7-6.3.2 Exception No. 1 shall not be permitted.

12-6.3.4.4 Emergency Forces Notification. Fire department notification shall be accomplished in accordance with 7-6.4.

12-6.3.4.5 Emergency Control. Operation of any activating device in the required fire alarm system shall be arranged to automatically accomplish, without delay, any control functions required to be performed by that device. (*See 7-6.5.*)

Paragraphs 12-6.3.4.1 through 12-6.3.4.5 deal with required fire alarm equipment. Reliability is of prime importance; therefore, electrical supervision of the system and system components is specified by the standards referenced in Section 7-6. In the event of circuit fault, component failure, or other "trouble," a continuous "trouble indication" signal is required and should be provided at a constantly attended location.

A manual fire alarm system is required by 12-6.3.4.2. Manual pull stations should be located along the natural routes of egress and located so as to adequately cover all portions of the building. Manual pull stations should always be located so that anyone qualified to send an alarm may summon aid without having to leave the zone of his or her ordinary activities, or pass out of the sight and hearing of people immediately exposed to, or in direct view of, a fire. The operation of a manual fire alarm station should automatically summon attendants who can assist in removing physically helpless occupants.

The system required by 12-6.3.4.2 may be incorporated into an automatic system equipped to detect a fire and initiate an alarm.

Actuation of any required fire or smoke detector, activation of a required sprinkler system, or operation of a manual pull station must automatically, without delay, sound audible alarm devices within the building. Presignal systems are not permitted.

The alarm must automatically transmit to a point outside the facility. Where automatic transmission of alarms to the fire department legally committed to serve the facility is not permitted, arrangements are to be made for the prompt notification of the fire department or such other assistance as may be available in the case of fire or other emergency.

Paragraph 7-6.4 lists various methods acceptable for automatically notifying the fire department. The fire department should still be called manually to verify and confirm the automatic transmission of the alarm. In larger facilities, this may be the responsibility of the facility telephone operator; in smaller facilities, it may be the responsibility of the nursing staff.

Actuation of the fire alarm must cause audible alerting devices to sound throughout the affected zone or building as appropriate. Visible alerting devices may be used, but may not serve as a substitute for audible devices.

12-6.3.5 Extinguishment Requirements. (See 26-3.5.)

12-6.3.5.1 Isolated hazardous areas may be protected in accordance with 7-7.1.2 if the additional requirements of this paragraph are met. An indicating shut-off valve shall be installed in an accessible location between the sprinklers and the connection to the domestic water supply. Where more than two sprinklers are installed in a single area, water flow detection shall be provided to sound the building fire alarm or notify by a signal any constantly attended location, such as PBX, security, or emergency room, whereby necessary corrective action shall be directed.

12-6.3.5.2 Portable fire extinguishers shall be provided in ambulatory health care occupancies in accordance with 7-7.4.1.

12-6.3.6 Corridors. (See 26-3.6.)

12-6.3.7 Subdivision of Building Space.

12-6.3.7.1 Ambulatory health care occupancies shall be separated from other tenants and occupancies by walls having at least a 1-hour fire resistance rating. Such walls shall extend from the floor slab below to the floor or roof slab above. Doors shall be constructed of at least 1¾-in. (4.4-cm) solid bonded wood core or the equivalent and equipped with positive latches. These doors shall be self-closing and normally kept in the closed position except when in use. Any vision panels shall be of fixed wired glass, set in steel or other approved metal frames, and limited in size to 1,296 sq in. (.84 sq m).

Ambulatory health care centers are frequently located within buildings used for a variety of purposes. Location within buildings containing hazardous occupancies should be avoided. Where ambulatory health care centers are located within buildings of mixed use, the ambulatory health care center must be separated from adjacent tenants and occupancies by minimum 1-hour fire-rated partitions. Doors protecting openings in such partitions must be a minimum of 1¾-in. (4.5-cm) thick solid bonded wood core, or of other equivalent construction that will resist fire for a minimum of 20 minutes. The doors must be equipped with positive latching hardware of a type that cannot be held in the retracted position. These doors must be self-closing and normally maintained in the closed position, or if the doors are to be held open, an automatic device must be used as indicated in 12-6.2.2.3.

Glazing within doors and partitions is limited to a maximum of 1,296 sq in. (0.84 sq m) of wired glass, set in approved metal frames. Each wired glass panel should be limited to a maximum dimension of 54 in. (137 cm). The glass should be labeled, should be ¼ in. (0.6 cm) thick, and be well embedded in putty with all exposed joints between the metal and the glass struck and pointed. (*See NFPA 80, Standard for Fire Doors and Windows.*[12]) A number of wired glass panels may be used in a single partition provided that each 1,296-sq in. (.84-sq m) section is separated from adjacent panels by a metal mullion. The excessive use of wired glass panels should be avoided. It must be recognized that the use of wired glass panels in a partition reduces the effectiveness of the partition in that radiant energy transfer will readily occur through the glass panel.

Partitions separating ambulatory health care centers from other occupancies must extend from the floor to the floor or roof deck above, extending completely through concealed spaces above suspended ceilings, for example. The partition must form a continuous barrier. Openings around penetrations involving building services should be adequately protected to maintain the 1-hour separation. Special attention should be paid to penetrations involving air-handling ducts. In general, steel ducts will not require a fire damper. Penetrations involving nonmetallic ducts or aluminum ducts should be carefully evaluated. Fire dampers should be provided to protect duct penetrations where the projected fire exposure is judged sufficient to jeopardize the required separation because of the duct penetration. The possible movement of air from space to space under conditions of system operation and conditions of system shutdown should be evaluated for both conditions. If there is a significant potential for the transfer of smoke from an adjacent space to the ambulatory health care center or from the center to a corridor, fire dampers should be provided for duct penetrations, even though the *Code* does not specifically require such protection.

(*See Figure 12-24.*)

12-6.3.7.2 The ambulatory health care facility shall be divided into at least two smoke compartments on patient treatment floors.

Exception: Facilities of less than 2,000 sq ft (185 sq m) and protected by an approved automatic smoke detection system need not be divided.

12-6.3.7.3 Any required smoke barrier shall be constructed in accordance with Section 6-3 and shall have a fire resistance rating of at least 1 hour.

12-6.3.7.4 Vision panels in the smoke barrier shall be of fixed wired glass, set in steel or other approved metal frames, and shall be limited in size to 1,296 sq in. (.84 sq m).

12-6.3.7.5 At least 15 net sq ft (1.4 sq m) per ambulatory health care facility occupant shall be provided within the aggregate area of corridors, patient rooms, treatment rooms, lounges, and other low hazard areas on each side of the smoke compartment for the total number of occupants in adjoining compartments. The length and width of each smoke compartment shall be limited to no more than 150 ft (45 m).

Exception: One dimension may be extended provided that the total width plus length does not exceed 300 ft (91 m) and provided that travel distance from a room door to smoke barrier door or horizontal exit is not more than 150 ft (45 m).

12-6.3.7.6   Doors in smoke barriers shall be at least 1¾-in. (4.4-cm) solid bonded wood core or the equivalent and shall be self-closing. A vision panel is required.

12-6.3.7.7   Doors in smoke barriers shall normally be kept closed, or if held open, they shall be equipped with automatic devices that will release the doors upon activation of:

(a) The fire alarm system, and either

(b) A local smoke detector, or

(c) A complete automatic fire extinguishing system or complete automatic fire detection system.

The requirements of 12-6.3.7.1 through 12-6.3.7.7 for subdividing building spaces through smoke barriers are illustrated in Figures 12-24 and 12-25. Paragraph 12-2.2.5 discusses horizontal exits.

During a fire, the emergency evacuation of patients in an ambulatory health care facility could be an inefficient, time consuming process. Realistically, if nonambulatory patients must be moved, any number of occupants can be relocated only through horizontal travel. Smoke barriers and horizontal exits used to subdivide a building serve three purposes fundamental to the protection of inpatients in that they:

1. Limit the spread of fire and fire-produced contaminants,

2. Limit the number of occupants exposed to a single fire, and

3. Provide for horizontal relocation of patients by creating an area of refuge on the same floor level.

Refer to Figure 12-19 for a floor plan illustrating application of the Exception to 12-6.3.7.5.

12-6.4 Special Provisions.   *(See Section 26-4.)*

12-6.5 Building Services.

12-6.5.1 Utilities.   Utilities shall comply with the provisions of Section 7-1.

12-6.5.2 Heating, Ventilating, and Air Conditioning.

12-6.5.2.1   Heating, ventilating, and air conditioning shall comply with the provisions of Section 7-2 and shall be installed in accordance with the manufacturer's specifications.

Exception: As modified in 12-6.5.2.2 following.

12-6.5.2.2   Any heating device other than a central heating plant shall be so designed and installed that combustible material will not be ignited by it or its appurtenances. If fuel fired, such heating devices shall be chimney or vent connected, shall take air for

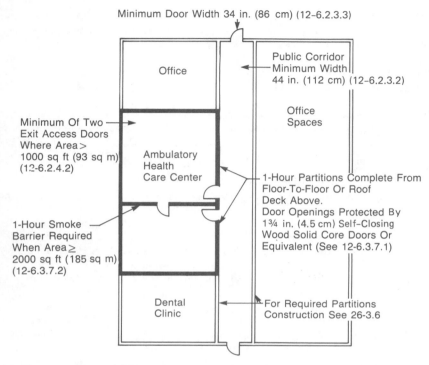

Minimum Door Width 34 in. (86 cm) (12–6.2.3.3)

Office

Public Corridor
Minimum Width
44 in. (112 cm) (12–6.2.3.2)

Office
Spaces

Minimum Of Two
Exit Access Doors
Where Area>
1000 sq ft (93 sq m)
(12–6.2.4.2)

Ambulatory
Health
Care Center

1-Hour Partitions Complete From
Floor-To-Floor Or Roof
Deck Above.
Door Openings Protected By
1¾ in. (4.5 cm) Self–Closing
Wood Solid Core Doors Or
Equivalent (See 12-6.3.7.1)

1-Hour Smoke
Barrier Required
When Area≥
2000 sq ft (185 sq m)
(12-6.3.7.2)

Dental
Clinic

For Required Partitions
Construction See 26-3.6

Figure 12-24. Subdivision Requirements for an Ambulatory Health Center.

combustion directly from the outside, and shall be so designed and installed to provide for complete separation of the combustion system from the atmosphere of the occupied area. Any heating device shall have safety features to immediately stop the flow of fuel and shut down the equipment in case of either excessive temperature or ignition failure.

Exception: Approved suspended unit heaters may be used in locations other than means of egress and patient treatment areas, provided such heaters are located high enough to be out of the reach of persons using the area and provided they are equipped with the safety features called for above.

Paragraphs 12-6.5.2.1 and 12-6.5.2.2 specify safeguards for air conditioning, ventilating, heating, and other service equipment in order to minimize the possibility of such devices serving as a source of ignition. Fuel-fired heating devices, except central heating systems, must be designed to provide complete separation of the combustion system from the occupied spaces. Air for combustion must be taken directly from the outside.

A major concern of the *Code* is to prevent the ignition of clothing, bedclothes, furniture, and other furnishings by a heating device. Therefore, 31-4.7 prohibits portable heating devices in areas used by patients.

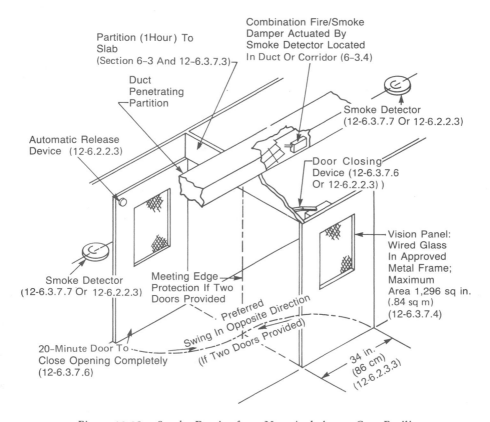

Figure 12-25.   Smoke Barrier for a New Ambulatory Care Facility.

12-6.5.3 Elevators, Dumbwaiters, and Vertical Conveyors.   Elevators, dumbwaiters, and vertical conveyors shall comply with the provisions of Section 7-4.

12-6.5.4 Rubbish Chutes, Incinerators, and Laundry Chutes.   Rubbish chutes, incinerators, and laundry chutes shall comply with the provisions of Section 7-5.

REFERENCES CITED IN COMMENTARY

[1]NFPA 101M, *Manual on Alternative Approaches to Life Safety*, National Fire Protection Association, Boston, MA, 1988.

[2]NFPA 220, *Standard on Types of Building Construction*, National Fire Protection Association, Boston, MA, 1985.

[3]NFPA 241, *Standard for Safeguarding Building Construction and Demolition Operations*, National Fire Protection Association, Boston, MA, 1986.

[4]NFPA 72E, *Standard on Automatic Fire Detectors*, National Fire Protection Association, Quincy, MA, 1987.

[5]NFPA 99, *Standard for Health Care Facilities*, National Fire Protection Association, Quincy, MA, 1987.

[6]NFPA 90A, *Standard for the Installation of Air Conditioning and Ventilating Systems*, National Fire Protection Association, Quincy, MA, 1985.

[7]NFPA 96, *Standard for the Installation of Equipment for the Removal of Smoke and Grease-Laden Vapors from Commercial Cooking Equipment*, National Fire Protection Association, Quincy, MA, 1987.

[8]Christian, W.J. and Waterman, T.E., "Flame Spread in Corridors: Effects of Location and Area of Wall Finish," *Fire Journal*, July 1971.

[9]NFPA 253, *Standard Method of Test for Critical Radiant Flux of Floor Covering Systems Using a Radiant Heat Energy Source*, National Fire Protection Association, Quincy, MA, 1984.

[10]Bukowski, R.W. and Istvan, S.M., "A Survey of Field Experience with Smoke Detectors in Health Care Facilities," NBSIR 80-2130, October 1980, Center for Fire Research, National Bureau of Standards.

[11]NFPA 13, *Standard for the Installation of Sprinkler Systems*, National Fire Protection Association, Quincy, MA, 1987.

[12]NFPA 80, *Standard for Fire Doors and Windows*, National Fire Protection Association, Quincy, MA, 1986.

13 EXISTING HEALTH CARE OCCUPANCIES

(See also Chapter 31)

This chapter covers the requirements for existing health care occupancies. In editions of the *Code* prior to 1976, these occupancies were known as "Institutional Occupancies."

Detention and correctional occupancies are covered in Chapters 14 and 15.

Health care occupancies are those used for medical or other treatment or care of four or more persons suffering from physical or mental illness, disease, or infirmity, and for the care of infants, convalescents, or aged persons.

Health care occupancies addressed in this chapter include:
1. Hospitals
2. Nursing Homes
3. Limited Care Facilities
4. Ambulatory Health Care Centers

Hospitals, nursing homes, and limited care facilities provide sleeping facilities for the occupants and are occupied by persons who are mostly incapable of self-preservation because of age, physical or mental disability, or because of security measures not under the occupants' control.

Ambulatory health care centers are significantly different from other health care occupancies in that they do not provide sleeping facilities and are, therefore, covered separately in Section 13-6.

SECTION 13-1 GENERAL REQUIREMENTS

13-1.1 Application. *(See also Section 1-4.)*

13-1.1.1 General.

13-1.1.1.1 Existing health care facilities shall comply with the provisions of this chapter. *(See Chapter 31 for operating features.)*

Exception*: Facilities where the authority having jurisdiction has determined equivalent safety is provided in accordance with Section 1-5.

A-13-1.1.1.1 Exception In determining equivalency for existing hospitals or nursing homes, the authority having jurisdiction may accept evaluations based on Chapter 3 of NFPA 101M, *Alternative Approaches to Life Safety*, utilizing the parameters for existing buildings.

Chapter 13 has been prepared for application solely to existing buildings. Prior to the 1973 Edition of the *Code*, the sections dealing with existing health care occupancies made reference to provisions contained within the section dealing with new construction. Since the 1973 Edition of the *Code*, the sections dealing with existing facilities are complete and are intended to be applied without reference to the requirements for new construction.

This section is to be applied retroactively. Due consideration has been given to the practical difficulties of making alterations in existing, functioning facilities. The specified provisions, viewed as a whole, establish minimum acceptable criteria for life safety that reasonably minimize the likelihood of a life-threatening fire.

The requirements of Chapter 13 may be modified in instances of practical difficulty or where alternate, but equal, provisions are proposed. The modifications must provide an equivalent level of protection as would be achieved by compliance with the corresponding *Code* provisions.

A Firesafety Evaluation System (FSES) has been developed and is located in Chapter 3 of NFPA 101M, *Alternative Approaches to Life Safety*.[1] The FSES uses numerical values to analyze the firesafety effectiveness of existing building arrangements or improvements proposed within existing structures. The system provides a method by which alternative improvement programs can be evaluated as options to literal *Code* compliance. In providing the equivalency system, it is not the intent to limit equivalency evaluations solely to this one system. The authority having jurisdiction retains the authority to evaluate and approve alternative improvement programs on the basis of appropriate supporting data. The FSES may be used to assist in this evaluation. This Exception in no way mandates the use of the FSES, nor does it require the authority having jurisdiction to accept the results of an evaluation using the system. The Exception to 13-1.1.1.1 emphasizes that Section 1-5 permits alternative designs to literal *Code* requirements that would still be considered in compliance with the *Code*. However, the authority having jurisdiction ultimately determines whether or not equivalent safety has been provided.

13-1.1.1.2 This chapter establishes life safety requirements for all existing hospitals, nursing homes, and limited care facilities. Where requirements vary, the specific occupancy is named in the paragraph pertaining thereto. Section 13-6 establishes life safety requirements for all existing ambulatory health care centers.

Chapter 12 provides the requirements for new health care facilities and new ambulatory health care centers, or for renovations to existing facilities.

13-1.1.1.3   Health care occupancies are those used for purposes such as medical or other treatment or care of persons suffering from physical or mental illness, disease or infirmity; for the care of infants, convalescents, or infirm aged persons.

13-1.1.1.4   Health care facilities provide sleeping accommodations for the occupants and are occupied by persons who are mostly incapable of self-preservation because of age, physical or mental disability, or because of security measures not under the occupants' control.

13-1.1.1.5   This chapter also covers ambulatory health care centers as defined in 13-1.3(d). See Section 13-6 for requirements.

   Since ambulatory health care centers do not provide sleeping accommodations, they are treated separately in Section 13-6.

13-1.1.1.6   Buildings or sections of buildings that primarily house patients who are capable of judgment and appropriate physical action for self-preservation under emergency conditions in the opinion of the governing body of the facility and the governmental agency having jurisdiction may come under other chapters of the *Code* instead of Chapter 13.

13-1.1.1.7   It shall be recognized that, in buildings housing certain types of patients or having detention rooms or a security section, it may be necessary to lock doors and bar windows to confine and protect building inhabitants. In such instances, the authority having jurisdiction shall make appropriate modifications to those sections of this *Code* that would otherwise require exits to be kept unlocked.

13-1.1.1.8   Buildings or sections of buildings that house older persons and that provide activities that foster continued independence but do not include those services distinctive to health care facilities [as defined in 13-1.3(c)] may be subject to the requirements of other sections of this *Code*, such as Chapters 19 or 21.

13-1.1.1.9   Health care occupancies shall include all buildings or parts thereof with occupancy as described in this chapter under Special Definitions, 13-1.3.

13-1.1.1.10   Except for ambulatory health care centers, facilities that do not provide housing on a 24-hour basis for their occupants are classified as other occupancies and are covered by other chapters of the *Code*.

   Paragraphs 13-1.1.1.3 through 13-1.1.1.10 contain explanatory material indicating some general characteristics of the occupants of health care occupancies. A few fundamental safeguards are also set forth. Formal definitions are established in 13-1.3.
   As implied by the definitions of 13-1.3 and stated in 13-1.1.1.4, health care facilities, except ambulatory health care centers, are buildings that provide sleeping facilities (24-hour care) for occupants. Occupants in a health care facility may be restrained, but are housed primarily for

treatment of mental or physical infirmities. Where occupants are restrained for penal or corrective purposes, the building would be classified as a detention and correctional occupancy, which is treated in Chapters 14 and 15.

If a building is used for the treatment or housing of mental patients, including the mentally handicapped (*see 13-1.1.1.6*) or older persons (*see 13-1.1.1.8*) where:

1. Occupants are not restrained by locked doors or other devices, and

2. The patients are ambulatory, and

3. The occupants are capable of perceiving threat and taking appropriate action for self-preservation, then the building may be classed as an occupancy other than health care.

Occupants of health care facilities are considered to be incapable of self-preservation (*see 13-1.1.1.4*) because of age, because of physical or mental disability, or because of security measures not under the occupants' control. A significant number of occupants in health care facilities are assumed to be nonambulatory or bedridden. Other occupants, who are capable of self-movement, may have impaired judgment.

Although locking exit doors and barring windows is always undesirable from the viewpoint of life safety, the *Code* recognizes that, in some cases, it is necessary to restrain people. In these instances, provision should be made for the continuous supervision and prompt release of restrained persons. (*See 13-1.1.1.7.*) Release of occupants should be accomplished by a system capable of automatically unlocking the doors in the means of egress, or by the presence of attendants who are continuously available and equipped with keys. In any event, continuous supervision is considered essential. (*See 13-2.2.2.5.*)

13-1.1.2* Objective.   The objective of this chapter is to provide a reasonable level of safety by reducing the probability of injury and loss of life from the effects of fire with due consideration for functional requirements. This is accomplished by limiting the development and spread of a fire emergency to the room of fire origin and reducing the need for occupant evacuation, except from the room of fire origin.

A-13-1.1.2   This objective is accomplished in the context of: the physical facilities, the type of activities undertaken, the provisions for the capabilities of staff, and the needs of all occupants through requirements directed at the:

(a) Prevention of ignition.

(b) Detection of fire.

(c) Control of fire development.

(d) Confinement of the effects of fire.

(e) Extinguishment of fire.

(f) Provision of refuge and/or evacuation facilities.

(g) Staff reaction.

It should be recognized that the well-being of an individual located in the room of fire origin can be reasonably ensured only through control of that individual's environment. That is, only through complete control of the environment, including building members, building finishes, furnishings, decorations, clothing, linens, bedding, and the like, can the individual be protected against fire. However, no code can prevent injury resulting from a person's careless actions.

Although an effort should be made to protect the individual through prevention efforts, the primary objective of the requirements of Chapter 13 is to limit fire size or to prevent fire from escaping the room of origin and thereby limit the threat posed to individuals outside the room of origin.

13-1.1.3 Total Concept. All health care facilities shall be so designed, constructed, maintained, and operated as to minimize the possibility of a fire emergency requiring the evacuation of occupants. Because the safety of health care occupants cannot be assured adequately by dependence on evacuation of the building, their protection from fire shall be provided by appropriate arrangement of facilities, adequate staffing, and careful development of operating and maintenance procedures composed of the following:

(a) Proper design, construction, and compartmentation; and

(b) Provision for detection, alarm, and extinguishment; and

(c) Fire prevention and the planning, training, and drilling in programs for the isolation of fire, transfer of occupants to areas of refuge, or evacuation of the building.

Vertical movement of patients within a health care facility is an inefficient, time consuming process. In one study, it was demonstrated through the simulated evacuation of patients from a second-story ward to ground level that more than 30 minutes may be required for evacuation during a fire.

The provisions of Chapter 13, therefore, are based upon a "defend in place" philosophy, which minimizes the probability of a fire necessitating vertical movement of occupants. Patients in critical care areas may be connected to life support equipment, which makes movement difficult, and, in some cases, impossible. Barriers are required to provide for the horizontal movement of patients to safe areas of refuge on a single floor level and to maintain a manageable limit on the number of occupants exposed to any single fire. Vertical means of egress (stairs or ramps) are specified by Chapter 13 as escape routes for visitors and staff and as a "last line of defense" for the movement of patients.

13-1.1.4 Additions, Conversions, Modernization, Renovation, and Construction Operations. *(See also 1-4.5 and 1-4.6.)*

13-1.1.4.1 Additions. Additions shall be separated from any existing structure not conforming to the provisions within Chapter 13 by a fire barrier having at least a 2-hour fire resistance rating constructed of materials as required for the addition.

Paragraph 13-1.1.4.1 establishes separation criteria for additions to existing structures where existing structures do not conform to the provisions of Chapter 13. It should be emphasized that, where an existing building meets the provisions of Chapter 13, the building would be in compliance with the *Code* and the addition would not require separation.

Where additions must be separated, barriers must be constructed of assemblies providing a minimum of 2-hour fire resistance. Where the structural framing of the addition or the existing buildings are of assemblies of less than 2-hour fire resistance, special provision must be made to ensure the necessary separation will be maintained for the 2-hour period.

Materials used in the construction of the barrier should be "constructed to the standards of the addition." That is, if the addition is required to be constructed of noncombustible or limited-combustible materials (construction Types I or II), then the materials used in the barrier must be limited-combustible or noncombustible as defined in NFPA 220, *Standard on Types of Building Construction.*[2] Conversely, if the addition is permitted to be constructed of combustible materials, then combustible materials may be used as a portion of the barrier. Any new additions must conform to the requirements of Chapter 12.

13-1.1.4.2 Communicating openings in dividing fire barriers required by 13-1.1.4.1 shall occur only in corridors and shall be protected by approved self-closing fire doors. (*See also Section 6-2.*)

13-1.1.4.3 Doors in barriers required by 13-1.1.4.1 shall normally be kept closed.

Exception: Doors may be held open only if they meet the requirements of 13-2.2.2.6.

Openings in barriers separating additions from nonconforming existing structures are limited to corridors. (*See 13-1.1.4.2.*) Openings are required to be protected by 1½-hour, "B" labeled, fire door assemblies. The fire doors are required to be self-closing and to be maintained closed, or they may be held open by an automatic device in accordance with 13-2.2.2.6. (*See Figure 13-1.*)

13-1.1.4.4 Conversions. Conversions shall comply with 1-6.4. A conversion from a hospital to a nursing home or from a nursing home to a hospital is not a change in occupancy or suboccupancy classification.

Any building converted to a health care facility from some other occupancy use (dormitory, for example) must be altered to comply with the provisions of Chapter 12 for new health care facilities. The conversion of a hospital to a nursing home is sometimes questioned as to whether or not such a conversion represents a change in occupancy. Conversion of a hospital to a nursing home or vice versa would not constitute a change in occupancy. Therefore, prior to and after such a conversion, the facility must comply with the criteria of Chapter 13 for existing health care facilities.

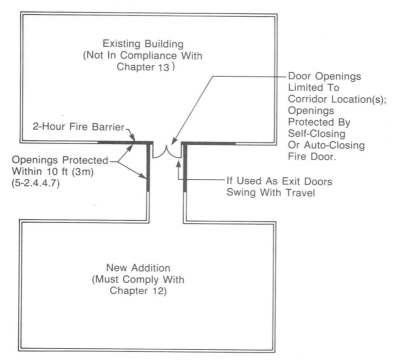

Figure 13-1. Separation of New Addition from Existing Building Not in Compliance with Chapter 13. If the addition is of fire-resistive or noncombustible (Types I or II) construction, use noncombustible or limited-combustible materials in the 2-hour barrier. (*See NFPA 220, Standard on Types of Building Construction.*[2])

13-1.1.4.5 Modernizations or Renovations.

In modernization projects and renovations to existing facilities, only that portion of the total facility affected by the project need comply with the provision of Chapter 12 in accordance with 1-4.6.

Exception: Existing health care occupancies 75 ft (23 m) or more in height shall not be required to comply with the sprinkler provision applicable to new construction when undergoing modernization or renovation provided all other applicable provisions of this Code are met.

Alterations of health care facilities are regulated by 1-4.6 and 13-1.1.4.5. Alterations may not reduce the level of life safety below that which exists prior to the alterations; however, provisions in excess of the requirements for new construction are not required to be maintained. Suppose, for example, an existing hospital has a 6-ft (1.8-m) wide corridor, and a portion of the hospital is to be renovated. Even though it is an existing building, a minimum 6-ft (1.8-m) wide corridor must be maintained. Conversely, suppose a portion of an existing hospital equipped with a 10-ft

(3.1-m) wide corridor is to be altered. It may be reduced to 8 ft (2.4 m), which is the requirement for new construction. If alterations require replacement of a portion of a hospital corridor wall, this portion of the wall should be increased to 1-hour fire resistance in accordance with the requirements for new construction. However, it would not be required that the corridor width be increased to 8 ft (2.4 m) unless it was practical to do so. As a minimum, in all instances, whether or not renovations or alterations are planned, existing buildings must comply with the requirements contained in Chapter 13.

Only that portion of a facility that is being renovated is required to comply with Chapter 12. For example, assume a floor of a hospital is subdivided into three sections and only one section is undergoing renovation. Only the one section being renovated would require compliance, to the extent practical, with Chapter 12.

Although an effort should always be made to satisfy the criteria for new construction during a building alteration or the installation of new equipment, the *Code* recognizes that such modifications cannot always be accomplished. Guidance for achieving "equivalency" to life safety is provided in Section 1-5. In any event, alterations or the installation of new building service equipment must be accomplished in such a manner that the level of life safety that results is equivalent or superior to that prescribed for existing buildings.

Existing high rise health care facilities undergoing modernization or renovation are exempted from the requirement for automatic sprinkler protection provided the facility complies with Chapter 13.

13-1.1.4.6 Construction Operations.   See 1-6.3 and Chapter 31 for life safety provisions during construction.

The introduction of "outside" workers and activities associated with construction projects creates unusual risks of fire in health care occupancies. Special precautions must be taken to guard against the potential exposure created by the introduction of flammable substances or by other hazardous practices that could pose a threat to occupants. (*See 31-1.1.2.*) Temporary fire resistant barriers should be erected to separate the new construction and associated activity from the functioning areas of the existing buildings. Care must be taken to prevent blockage of means of egress for the existing building by the construction of such barriers. Special care is also necessary to ensure that all existing equipment for fire protection and all portions of the required means of egress are maintained in full working order. (*See 1-6.3.*)

Adequate escape facilities should be provided and continuously maintained for the use of construction workers. (*See 31-1.1.1 and NFPA 241, Standard for Safeguarding Building Construction and Demolition Operations.*[3])

13-1.1.5 Modification of Retroactive Provisions.   (*See also Sections 1-4 and 1-5.*)
The requirements of this chapter may be modified if their application clearly would be impractical in the judgment of the authority having jurisdiction and if the resulting

arrangement could be considered as presenting minimum hazard to the life safety of the occupants. The requirements may be modified by the authority having jurisdiction to allow alternative arrangements that will secure as nearly equivalent safety to life from fire as practical.

In some cases, appreciable cost may be involved in bringing an existing occupancy into compliance. Where this is true, it would be appropriate for the authority having jurisdiction to prescribe a schedule, determined jointly with the owner of the facility, allowing suitable periods of time for the correction of the various deficiencies and giving due weight to the ability of the owner to secure the necessary funds. (*Also see 1-4.2, 1-4.4, Section 1-5, and 1-6.2.*)

13-1.2 Mixed Occupancies.   (*See also 1-4.7.*)

13-1.2.1*   Sections of health care facilities may be classified as other occupancies if they meet all of the following conditions:

(a) They are not intended to serve health care occupants for purposes of

1. Housing, or

2. Treatment, or

3. Customary access by patients incapable of self-preservation.

(b) They are adequately separated from areas of health care occupancies by construction having a fire resistance rating of at least 2 hours.

A-13-1.2.1   Doctors' offices, treatment and diagnostic facilities intended solely for outpatient care and physically separated from facilities for the treatment or care of inpatients, but otherwise associated with the management of an institution, may be classified as Business Occupancy rather than Health Care Occupancy.

13-1.2.2   Ambulatory care (*see Section 13-6*), medical clinics, and similar facilities that are contiguous to health care occupancies but are primarily intended to provide outpatient services may be classified as a business or ambulatory care occupancy, provided the facilities are separated from health care occupancies by not less than 2-hour fire-resistive construction.

Exception*: Where a facility is intended to provide services for health care patients who are litter borne, it shall meet all requirements for health care facilities.

A-13-1.2.2 Exception   It is expected that an occasional hospital patient who may be litter borne will enter ambulatory care, medical clinics, and similar facilities that are primarily intended to provide outpatient services and are classified as a Business or Ambulatory Care Occupancy.

Paragraphs 13-1.2.1 and 13-1.2.2 set forth criteria for classifying spaces as "other" occupancies, although they are located in buildings used primarily for health care purposes. Paragraph 13-1.2.1 would allow offices to be classified as business occupancies, cafeterias to be classified as assembly occupancies, dormitories to be classified as residential, etc., if both items (a) and (b) of 13-1.2.1 are met. Paragraph 13-1.2.1(a) notes that customary access by patients incapable of self-preservation is not permitted within the other occupancy. This paragraph is intended to allow an occasional ambulatory inpatient to visit a doctor's office — for example, in an adjacent business occupancy — without requiring classification of the business occupancy as a health care facility. However, if either item (a) or (b) is not met, then the area would be considered "mixed occupancy," and the provisions of 1-4.7 apply and require that the more restrictive life safety provisions apply. (*See 1-4.7.*)

Paragraph 13-1.2.2 covers a subject similar to 13-1.2.1, but specifically discusses ambulatory care centers, medical clinics, and similar areas that primarily provide outpatient services. If these facilities are separated by 2-hour fire-resistive construction, then they may be classified as ambulatory health care centers or as business occupancies, whichever applies. If, however, litter-borne inpatients are treated on any regular basis, then the facility must meet the requirements for health care occupancies. The provisions of business occupancies and ambulatory health care centers were written around the concept that most people are treated on an outpatient basis.

Note that 13-1.2.4, subject to certain qualifications, allows the means of egress from health care areas using a horizontal exit to traverse non-health care spaces.

13-1.2.3   Health care occupancies in buildings housing other occupancies shall be completely separated from them by construction having a fire resistance rating of at least 2 hours as provided for additions in 13-1.1.4.

Paragraph 13-1.2.3 requires that if a health care occupancy is located in a building of another classification (such as business, storage, mercantile, or industrial), the health care occupancy must be separated from the other occupancy by construction having a fire resistance rating of 2 hours, as detailed in 13-1.1.4. (*Also see the commentary following 13-1.1.4.1.*)

Note that 13-1.2.3 deals with occupancy classification and not with hazard of contents. Hazard of contents is treated in 13-1.2.6 and 13-1.2.7.

13-1.2.4   All means of egress from health care occupancies that traverse non-health care spaces shall conform to requirements of this *Code* for health care occupancies.

Exception: It is permissible to exit through a horizontal exit into other contiguous occupancies that do not conform with health care egress provisions but that do comply with requirements set forth in the appropriate occupancy chapter of this Code as long as the occupancy does not contain high hazard contents. The horizontal exit must comply with the requirements of 13-2.2.5.

Paragraph 13-1.2.4 specifies that the means of egress from health care occupancies that traverses non-health care spaces must conform to the requirements for health care occupancies. However, an exception is allowed where a 2-hour barrier is provided and such barrier is used as a horizontal exit. Where a 2-hour barrier serves as a horizontal exit, it is acceptable to exit into a different occupancy, provided the other occupancy complies with the provisions of the *Code* that would be applicable thereto and does not contain high hazard contents. For example, if a horizontal exit is provided between a health care facility and a business occupancy, inpatients may exit into the business occupancy through a horizontal exit. In this instance, corridor width, corridor partitions, stairway details, and the like must conform to the provisions set forth within either Chapters 26 or 27, which deal with business occupancies. However, the horizontal exit must comply with all the requirements of 13-2.2.5.

13-1.2.5   Auditoriums, chapels, staff residential areas, or other occupancies provided in connection with health care facilities shall have exits provided in accordance with other applicable sections of the *Code*.

Auditoriums, chapels, and other areas separated by 2-hour construction and meeting the criteria of 13-1.2.1 and 13-1.2.2 for other occupancies are required to be designed in accordance with the appropriate occupancy chapter governing their use.

Spaces used for non-health care purpose but located within a health care facility should have means of egress features designed in accordance with the use of the space. For example, if a space located in a health care facility is used as a chapel or auditorium, assuming an occupant load in excess of 50, then egress features should be designed as would be appropriate for an assembly occupancy. In such circumstances, doors in the means of egress should be side-hinged swinging doors, arranged to swing in the direction of exit travel (*see 5-2.1.4.1*), and should not be equipped with a latch or lock unless such a latch or lock is operated by panic hardware. (*See 9-2.2.2.3.*) Exit capacity should be computed on the basis of occupant characteristics. If, for example, the space is used only by staff, visitors, and others who are mobile and otherwise capable of self-preservation, then exit capacity could be computed on the basis of Chapter 9. If, on the other hand, the space is used by health care occupants, then exit capacity should be calculated in accordance with Chapter 13, even though occupant load might be calculated in accordance with Chapter 9.

13-1.2.6   Any area with a hazard of contents classified higher than that of the health care occupancy and located in the same building shall be protected as required in 13-3.2.

Paragraph 13-1.2.6 regulates spaces in a health care facility that, although comprising only a portion of the facility, contain more hazardous materials (in quantity or type) than are usually found in most other spaces.

Spaces such as rooms used for the storage of combustible materials, trash collection rooms, gift shops, and paint shops must be protected in accordance with 13-3.2.

13-1.2.7   Non-health care related occupancies classified as containing high hazard contents shall not be permitted in buildings housing health care occupancies.

Paragraph 13-1.2.7 prohibits another occupancy (such as storage) with highly hazardous contents (such as flammable liquids) from being located in a building housing health care occupancies.

This paragraph limits use based upon occupancy classification with regard to hazard of contents. For example, the paragraph is not meant to exclude laboratory operations as a portion of a health care facility. The intent is to prevent a portion of a hospital from being converted or designed for use as an educational or research facility (classed as an educational or possibly an industrial occupancy) that has laboratories using and storing sizable quantities of flammable liquids.

13-1.3 Special Definitions.

(a) *Hospital.* A building or part thereof used on a 24-hour basis for the medical, psychiatric, obstetrical, or surgical care of four or more inpatients. Hospital, wherever used in this *Code*, shall include general hospitals, psychiatric hospitals, and specialty hospitals.

(b) *Nursing Home.* A building or part thereof used on a 24-hour basis for the housing and nursing care of four or more persons who, because of mental or physical incapacity, may be unable to provide for their own needs and safety without the assistance of another person. Nursing home, wherever used in this *Code*, shall include nursing and convalescent homes, skilled nursing facilities, intermediate care facilities, and infirmaries in homes for the aged.

(c) *Limited Care Facility.* A building or part thereof used on a 24-hour basis for the housing of four or more persons who are incapable of self-preservation because of age or physical limitation due to accident or illness, or mental limitations, such as mental retardation/developmental disability, mental illness, or chemical dependency.

(d) *Ambulatory Health Care Centers.* A building or part thereof used to provide services or treatment to four or more patients at the same time and meeting either (1) or (2) below.

1. Those facilities that provide, on an outpatient basis, treatment for patients that would render them incapable of taking action for self-preservation under emergency conditions without assistance from others, such as hemodialysis units or freestanding emergency medical units.

2. Those facilities that provide, on an outpatient basis, surgical treatment requiring general anesthesia.

Paragraph 13-1.3(a) through (d) defines the characteristics of the occupancies covered by Chapter 13. Except as discussed below for ambulatory health care, a building must house four or more people incapable of self-preservation on a 24-hour basis in order to be classed as a health care occupancy.

Occupants of hospitals or nursing homes are assumed to be nonambulatory and incapable of self-preservation. In making this judgment, due consideration should be given to the use of physical restraints and tranquilizing drugs, which can render occupants immobile. Variable staffing criteria and levels of care make differentiation between hospitals and nursing homes apparent. The difference between nursing homes and limited care facilities is less clear.

Although limited care facilities house four or more occupants incapable of self-preservation due to age or physical or mental limitations, occupants are generally considered to be ambulatory and would require only limited assistance during emergency evacuation. Buildings that house mentally handicapped occupants or persons being treated for alcohol or drug abuse who are ambulatory and may be expected to evacuate a structure with limited assistance would meet the criteria for limited care facilities. Day-care facilities that provide care for the aged, children, mentally handicapped, or others would be classified as other than health care if the care or treatment is not provided on a 24-hour basis. (*See Chapter 11.*)

Although age, in itself, is not sufficient justification to develop a separate classification for a health care occupancy, it should be recognized that the elderly present a unique problem in firesafety. Experiences in buildings where the elderly are housed reveal that the reaction of the elderly to a fire may not be directed toward self-preservation. On discovering a fire, the elderly occupant may ignore it, be transfixed by it, or seek refuge from it in his or her room and fail to notify anyone else of the fire. In some cases, the elderly have resisted efforts to remove them from the building and familiar surroundings.

Terms such as "residential," "lodging and boarding," and "custodial care" previously used in 13-1.3, have been deleted to avoid confusion with a residential occupancy classification included in Chapter 21, which was added to the 1985 Edition of the *Code*. Board and care facilities, personal care homes, halfway houses, or similar facilities house occupants who may require medication and personal care but do not require the close supervision and services typical of the occupants in a health care facility and therefore would be classified as residential occupancies. Occupant capability must be carefully evaluated to determine whether application of health care criteria (Chapter 13) or application of lesser safeguards associated with residential occupancies (Chapter 21) is more appropriate.

Prior to the 1981, Edition of the *Code*, occupancies that offered medical services on an outpatient basis would have been regulated within the chapter dealing with business occupancies. The threat to life in an outpatient facility where four or more patients may be subject to medical procedures requiring general anesthesia, treatments such as hemodialysis, or free-standing emergency service is significantly greater than that typical of a business occupancy. Conversely, application of the requirements for health care facilities that contemplate 24-hour care would be inappropriate and would be unnecessarily restrictive. In establishing the occupancy classification of an ambulatory health care center, it was intended to develop requirements that fall between the restrictions applicable to business occupancies and health care facilities in terms of level of life safety achieved.

13-1.4 Classification of Occupancy. See Definitions, 13-1.3.

13-1.5 Classification of Hazard of Contents. The classification of hazard of contents shall be as defined in Section 4-2.

13-1.6 Minimum Construction Requirements.

13-1.6.1 For the purpose of 13-1.6, stories shall be counted starting at the primary level of exit discharge and ending at the highest occupiable level. For the purposes of this section, the primary level of exit discharge of a building shall be that floor that is level with or above finished grade of the exterior wall line for 50 percent or more of its perimeter. Building levels below the primary level shall not be counted as a story in determining the height of a building.

Allowable building construction types are determined as a function of the number of stories in a building. In determining the number of stories, the first story is considered to be the primary level of exit discharge. Only occupiable levels are counted in determining story height. For example, an unoccupied attic would not constitute a story.

Difficulties have been experienced in determining story height where a building is located on a sloping grade. Paragraph 13-1.6.1 notes that a story on a sloping site that is partially below grade should be counted as a story if the floor is level with or above grade for 50 percent or more of the perimeter of the building at the exterior wall. (*See Figure 13-2.*)

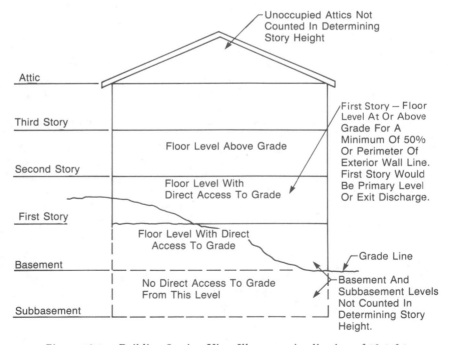

Figure 13-2.   Building Section View Illustrates Application of 13-1.6.1.

13-1.6.2   Health care occupancies shall be limited to the following types of building construction (*see 6-2.1*):

Table 13-1.6.2

Construction Type	Stories			
	1	2	3	over 3
I (443) I (332) II (222)	X	X	X	X
II (111)	X	X†	X†	N.P.
II (000)	X†	X†	N.P.	N.P.
IV (2HH)	X†	X†	N.P.	N.P.
III (211)	X†	X†	N.P.	N.P.
V (111)	X†	X†	N.P.	N.P.
III (200)	X†	N.P.	N.P.	N.P.
V (000)	X†	N.P.	N.P.	N.P.

X = Permitted type of construction
X† = Building requires automatic sprinkler protection (*See 13-3.5.1*)
N.P. = Not Permitted

Exception: Any building of Type I or Type II (222 or 111) construction may include roofing systems involving combustible supports, decking, or roofing provided: (1) the roof covering meets Class C requirements in accordance with NFPA 256, Standard Methods of Fire Tests of Roof Coverings, and (2) the roof is separated from all occupied portions of the building by a noncombustible floor assembly that includes at least 2½ in. (6.4 cm) of concrete or gypsum fill. To qualify for this exception, the attic or other space so developed shall either be unoccupied or protected throughout by an approved automatic sprinkler system.

Construction types permitted in existing health care facilities are indicated as a function of height in 13-1.6.2. See NFPA 220, *Standard on Types of Building Construction,*[2] for definitions of construction types.

Multistory, nonsprinklered health care facilities are required to be constructed of noncombustible materials with a minimum 2-hour fire resistance rating. It is recognized that movement of patients may not be possible, and occupants of a health care facility may be required to remain in the structure for the duration of the fire. In specifying 2-hour fire resistance, it is intended that building members be adequately protected against fire effects to assure building stability for the projected fire duration.

Two-story buildings, using combustible elements, are allowed where completely protected by automatic sprinklers. Type II (111) structures can be erected to three stories where a complete system of electrically supervised automatic sprinklers is provided.

In certain areas, it has been common practice to erect a building with a flat concrete roof deck. A wood deck on wood frame peaked roof is then added for weather protection. Paragraph 13-1.6.2 contains an Exception that permits, under certain conditions, construction of such a combustible roof system on a multistory building without jeopardizing the building construction (Type I or II) classification. The Exception specifies the attic space must either be unoccupied or protected with automatic sprinklers. The term "unoccupied" is meant to disallow the presence of mechanical equipment requiring periodic maintenance, storage, or like practices unless the space is sprinklered. (*Also see commentary following 13-3.5.1.*)

13-1.6.3   All interior walls and partitions in buildings of Type I or Type II construction shall be of noncombustible or limited-combustible materials.

Exception: Listed fire retardant treated wood studs may be used within non-load bearing 1-hour fire-rated partitions.

Formal Interpretation 76-79
Reference: 13-1.6.3 (Exception)

Question: Since the Committee permits the use of listed fire retardant treated wood studs in nonbearing partitions having a fire resistance rating of one hour, is it the intent of the Committee to allow the use of fire retardant treated wood studs in existing buildings having similar partitions of only 20-minute fire resistance rating?

Answer: There is a finish capacity in 1-hour fire-rated partition that would be expected to prevent the generation of smoke and gases from fire retardant treated wood studs for an extended time during fire exposure. The Committee did not intend to allow the use of fire retardant treated wood studs in partitions of only 20-minute fire resistance.

Issue Edition: 1976
Reference: 10-3.3.6.5
Date: September 1978

Formal Interpretation 76-36
Reference: 13-1.6.3 Exception

Question: Does the Exception to 13-1.6.3 intend to permit the treated wood studs in partitions of less than one hour?

Answer: No.

Issue Edition: 1976
Reference: 10-3.3.6.5 Exception
Date: August 1977

NFPA 220, *Standard on Types of Building Construction,*[2] establishes restrictions relative to the use of combustible building materials within structures required to be constructed of noncombustible or limited-combustible materials. NFPA 220 should be consulted for specific limitations. The terms noncombustible and limited-combustible are defined within NFPA 220 and are repeated in Chapter 3 of this *Code* for quick reference.

Note that the exception allows listed fire retardant treated wood studs within non-load bearing 1-hour fire-rated partitions. It does not allow them in 20-minute or 30-minute partitions since the studs would be exposed to fire sooner.

13-1.6.4 Openings for the passage of pipes or conduit in walls or partitions that are required to have fire or smoke resisting capability shall be protected in accordance with 6-2.3.4.2 or 6-3.6.1.

Fire and smoke may spread across a fire-rated barrier or fire-rated wall via openings created by the passage of pipes, conduit, or other building services. Paragraph 13-1.6.4 specifies that where such penetrations occur, suitable protection such as metal plates, masonry fill, or other products approved for the purpose should be installed to maintain the fire and smoke resisting capability of the barrier.

13-1.6.5 Firestopping. Each exterior wall of frame construction and interior stud partitions shall be firestopped so as to cut off all concealed draft openings, both horizontal and vertical, between any cellar or basement and the first floor. Such firestopping shall consist of wood at least 2 in. (5 cm) (nominal) thick or of suitable noncombustible material.

13-1.7 Occupant Load. The occupant load for which means of egress shall be provided for any floor shall be the maximum number of persons intended to occupy that floor but not less than one person for each 120 sq ft (11.1 sq m) gross floor area in health care sleeping departments, and not less than one person for each 240 sq ft (22.3 sq m) of gross floor area of inpatient health care treatment departments. Gross floor areas shall be measured within the exterior building walls with no deductions. (*See Chapter 3.*)

Paragraph 13-1.7 sets forth criteria for projecting occupant loads. The minimum occupant load for which exits must be provided in all buildings may not be less than that established by projections involving (1) one person for each 120 sq ft (11.1 sq m) of gross floor area in health care sleeping areas, and (2) one person for each 240 sq ft (22.3 sq m) of gross floor area in inpatient health care treatment areas. However, if by actual count, the number of persons exceeds that number projected by area calculations, then the actual number of persons present becomes the minimum population load for which exits must be provided.

The maximum number of people allowed to occupy a space is limited by available exit capacity and other functional considerations. It is not intended to limit populations based upon the area projections contained in this paragraph.

SECTION 13-2   MEANS OF EGRESS REQUIREMENTS

13-2.1 General.   Every aisle, passageway, corridor, exit discharge, exit location, and access shall be in accordance with Chapter 5.

Exception: As modified in the following paragraphs.

Means of egress details are to conform to the fundamental provisions expressed in Chapter 5, except as modified in Chapter 13.

13-2.2 Means of Egress Components.

In planning exits, arrangements should be made so that patients confined to their beds may be transferred from one section of a floor to another section of the same floor that is separated by a fire or smoke barrier. Where the building design will permit, the section of the corridor containing an entrance or elevator lobby should be separated from adjoining corridors by fire or smoke barriers. Where the lobby is centrally located, such an arrangement will produce a smoke lock, placing a double barrier between the area to which patients may be taken and the area from which they must be evacuated because of threatening smoke and fire. Note that this is not required by the *Code*, but is considered to be good fire protection design.

13-2.2.1   Components of the Means of Egress shall be limited to the types described in 13-2.2.2 through 13-2.2.7.

13-2.2.2 Doors.

13-2.2.2.1   Doors shall comply with 5-2.1.

13-2.2.2.2   Locks shall not be permitted on patient sleeping room doors.

Exception No. 1:   Key locking devices that restrict access to the room from the corridor and that are operable only by staff from the corridor side may be permitted. Such devices shall not restrict egress from the room.

This Exception allows rooms that are not being used to be secured by staff. However, in case someone is in the room, the *Code* requires that the lock cannot restrict egress from the room.

Exception No. 2:   Door locking arrangements are permitted in health care occupancies or portions of health care occupancies where the clinical needs of the patients require specialized security measures for their safety, provided keys are carried by staff at all times.

Some health care facilities may be required to provide resident security, but the *Code* emphasizes that staff must have immediate access to patient rooms.

13-2.2.2.3   Doors not in a required means of egress may be subject to locking.

13-2.2.2.4   Doors within a required means of egress shall not be equipped with a latch or lock that requires the use of a tool or key from the egress side.

Exception No. 1: Door locking arrangements are permitted in mental health facilities. (See 13-1.1.1.7 and 13-2.2.2.5.)

Note that 13-1.1.1.7 allows the authority having jurisdiction to make appropriate modifications to compensate for locking of egress doors.

Exception No. 2*: Special locking arrangements complying with 5-2.1.6 are permitted, provided not more than one such device may be in any egress path.

A-13-2.2.2.4 Exception No. 2   The intent of the provision is that a person following the natural path of the means of egress not encounter more than one delay release device along that path of travel to an exit. Thus, each door from the multiple floors of a building that opens into an enclosed stair may have its own delay release device, but an additional delay release device could not be present at the level of exit discharge on the door that discharges people from the enclosed stair to the outside.

Paragraph 5-2.1.6 sets minimum requirements for delayed release hardware, including the fact that the building must be protected throughout by automatic sprinklers or automatic fire detection. The 1985 Edition permitted time delay locks in accordance with 5-2.1.6 only on exterior doors. The 1988 Edition has been changed to permit the use of time delay locks on any door. However, only one door in each means of egress for any given space may involve such a feature.

13-2.2.2.5   In buildings in which doors are locked, provisions shall be made for the rapid removal of occupants by such reliable means as the remote control of locks or by keying all locks to keys readily available to staff who are in constant attendance.

In buildings where it is necessary to lock doors, continuous supervision by staff must be provided. Provisions must be made for the prompt release of restrained persons either by equipping staff with keys or by providing remote unlocking capabilities for doors. Where staff relies on the use of keys, consideration should be given to a master key system, which would facilitate the quick release of occupants.

13-2.2.2.6*   Any door in an exit passageway, stairway enclosure, horizontal exit, smoke barrier, or hazardous area enclosure may be held open only by an automatic release device that complies with 5-2.1.8. The automatic sprinkler system if provided, the required fire alarm system, and the systems required by 5-2.1.8(c) shall be arranged so as to initiate the closing action of all such doors by zone or throughout the entire facility.

A-13-2.2.2.6   It is desirable to keep doors in exit passageways, horizontal exits, smoke barriers, stair enclosures, and required enclosures around hazardous areas closed at all times to impede the travel of smoke and fire gases. Functionally, however, this involves decreased efficiency and limits patient supervision by the staff of a facility. To accommodate these necessities, it is practical to presume that such doors will be kept open even to the extent of employing wood chocks and other makeshift devices. Doors in exit passageways, horizontal exits, and smoke barriers should, therefore, be equipped with automatic hold-open devices actuated by the methods described regardless of whether or not the original installation of the doors was predicated on a policy of keeping them closed.

13-2.2.2.7   Where doors in a stair enclosure are held open by an automatic device as permitted in 13-2.2.2.6, initiation of a door closing action on any level shall cause all doors at all levels in the stair enclosure to close.

> Fire doors protecting openings in fire resistant enclosures should preferably be maintained in the closed position. Doors protecting openings in exit enclosures, stair enclosures, horizontal exits, smoke barriers, or required enclosures for hazardous areas may be held open only by a device arranged to close the door automatically. (*See 13-2.2.2.6.*) The automatic closer must cause the doors to close upon operation of the manual fire alarm system and the activation of either a local device designed to detect smoke on either side of the opening or a complete automatic smoke detection system. [*See also 5-2.1.8(d) and NFPA 72E, Standard on Automatic Fire Detectors.*[4]] In addition, if the facility is sprinklered, the water flow alarm shall also close the doors.
>
> It is especially important in health care facilities to maintain floor-to-floor separation. Doors protecting openings in a stair enclosure may be held open as permitted above. Initiation of any action that causes a door to close at one level must cause all doors at all levels in the stair enclosure to close and latch. (*See 13-2.2.2.7.*)

13-2.2.2.8*   Health care occupancies are exempted from the provisions of 5-2.1.5.2.

A-13-2.2.2.8   Doors to the enclosures of interior stair exits should be arranged to open from the stair side at least at every third floor so that it will be possible to leave the stairway at such floor should the fire render the lower part of the stair unusable during egress or should the occupants seek refuge on another floor.

13-2.2.3 Stairs.   Stairs shall comply with 5-2.2.

13-2.2.4 Smokeproof Enclosures.   Smokeproof enclosures shall comply with 5-2.3.

13-2.2.5 Horizontal Exits.   Horizontal exits shall comply with 5-2.4, modified as follows:

(a) At least 30 net sq ft (2.8 sq m) per patient in a hospital or nursing home or 15 net sq ft (1.4 sq m) per resident in a limited care facility shall be provided within the aggregated area of corridors, patient rooms, treatment rooms, lounge or dining areas, and other low hazard areas on each side of the horizontal exit. On stories not housing bed or litter patients, at least 6 net sq ft (.56 sq m) per occupant shall be provided on each side of the horizontal exit for the total number of occupants in adjoining compartments.

(b)* A door in a horizontal exit is not required to swing with exit travel as specified in 5-2.4.3.4.

(c) The total exit capacity of the other exits (stairs, ramps, doors leading outside the building) shall not be reduced below one-third that required for the entire area of the building.

(d) Door openings in horizontal exits shall be protected by a swinging door a minimum of 34 in. (86 cm) in width or a horizontal sliding door complying with 5-2.1.14 and providing a clear opening of at least 34 in. (86 cm).

A-13-2.2.5(b)   The waiver of swinging of doors in the direction of exit travel is based on the assumption that in this occupancy there will be no possibility of a panic rush that might prevent opening of doors swinging against exit travel.

A desirable arrangement, possible with corridors 8 ft (244 cm) or more in width, is to have two 42-in. (107-cm) doors, normally closed, each swinging with the exit travel (in opposite directions).

Because of practical difficulties involving vertical exit travel in health care facilities, special recognition is given to horizontal travel and the use of horizontal exits. Up to two-thirds of the total required exit capacity for a given fire area may be provided by horizontal exits. [See 13-2.2.5(c).] It should be noted, however, that every floor or fire section must be equipped with at least one exit consisting of a door leading directly outside the building, an interior stair, an outside stair, a smokeproof enclosure, a ramp, or an exit passageway. (See 13-2.4.2.) In other words, no fire area can be served only by horizontal exits. In the event a horizontal exit also serves as a smoke barrier, see the commentary of 13-2.4.3 and in 13-3.7.

Further, it is recognized that corridors in existing health care occupancies may be 4 ft (1.2 m) wide, and it is therefore impossible in many instances to install a pair of doors in a horizontal exit. However, the 4-ft (1.2-m) corridor width will permit the opening of a single door against the flow of travel with minimal difficulty. A power-operated sliding door might be used to reduce problems associated with door swing. The 1988 Edition of the *Code* permits sliding doors complying with 5-2.1.14 for the protection of openings in horizontal exits. The use of power-operated sliding doors results in an obstruction free opening for normal traffic while still providing adequate fire protection for openings.

In the case of a fire barrier serving as a horizontal exit for two adjoining fire areas and where corridor widths will permit, a pair of doors arranged with each leaf to swing in a direction opposite from the other should be used. Each leaf in the pair of doors should be a minimum of 34 in. (86.4 cm) wide.

New horizontal exits in an existing facility are considered a renovation and must be installed in accordance with Chapter 12 to the extent feasible. (*See commentary for 13-1.1.4.5 and 1-4.6.*) The requirements for horizontal exits in 13-2.2.5(a) to (d) are illustrated in Figure 13-3.

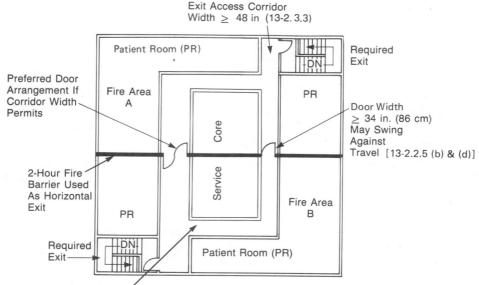

Figure 13-3. Horizontal Exits in an Existing Health Care Facility. If corridor width permits, the door arrangement as required by 12-2.2.5 should be provided.

13.2.2.6 Ramps.

13-2.2.6.1   Ramps shall comply with 5-2.5.

13-2.2.6.2   Ramps enclosed as exits shall be of sufficient width to provide exit capacity in accordance with 13-2.3.2.

Ramps are undesirable in hospitals and nursing homes due to the potential for accidents in both normal and emergency traffic, except in the case of ramps of extremely gradual slope, which require so much space as to be impracticable in most situations. They are, however, the only practicable method of moving patients in beds from one story to another, except by elevators, which may not be available under fire conditions. The best plan is to provide for horizontal egress to another section of the building, minimizing the need for complete evacuation.

Ramps may be the best means for providing egress from doors 2 or 3 steps above or below grade level (*see 5-1.5*), and may also compensate for minor differences in floor levels between adjoining sections of buildings. (*Also see 5-1.5.*) Such ramps must be constructed in accordance with 13-2.2.6.

13-2.2.7 Exit Passageways.   Exit passageways shall comply with 5-2.6.

13-2.3 Capacity of Means of Egress.

13-2.3.1   The capacity of any required means of egress shall be based on its width as defined in Section 5-3.

13-2.3.2   The capacity of means of egress providing travel by means of stairs shall be 1.0 in. (2.5 cm) per person; and the capacity of means of egress providing horizontal travel (without stairs); such as doors, ramps, or horizontal exits shall be 0.7 in. (1.8 cm) per person.

Exception: The capacity of means of egress in health care occupancies protected throughout by an approved supervised automatic sprinkler system may be increased to 0.6 in. (1.5 cm) per person for travel by means of stairs, and to 0.5 in. (1.3 cm) per person for horizontal travel without stairs.

The manner by which exit capacity is calculated has been changed in the 1988 Edition to recognize the concept of "effective width." (*See Chapter 2 of NFPA 101M, Alternative Approaches to Life Safety.*[1]) The new method of calculation relates the usable width of an exit and the anticipated egress flow. The new computational approach is based upon research that shows exit capacity varies with exit width, based upon a linear relationship, rather than the step function used in previous editions.

Previous editions of the *Code* calculated exit capacity based upon units of exit width [22 in. (55.9 cm)]. Increases in exit capacity were permitted only for minimum 12-in. (30.5-cm) increases (½ unit of exit width). Therefore, exit capacity for a 44-in. (112-cm) stair (2 units) was computed at 44 people (22 people per unit × 2 units). No increase in capacity was allowed for stair width increases up to 11 in. (27.9 cm) [55 in. (139.7 cm) stair]. A 56-in. (142.2-cm) stair [44 in. (112 cm) plus 12 in. (30.5 cm) or 2.5 units] had a capacity of 55 persons (22 people per unit × 2.5 units).

The method prescribed by the 1988 Edition acknowledges that increasing the width of egress systems results in increasing the flow. The new arrangement computes stair egress capacity in nonsprinklered buildings on the basis of 1.0 in. (2.54 cm) per person. Therefore, a 44-in. (112-cm) stair provides adequate egress for 44 persons [44 in./1.0 in. (112 cm/2.54 cm) per person]. Similarly, a 50-in. (127-cm) stair would have a capacity of 50 persons.

The exit capacities in 13-2.3.2 are substantially less than those specified in other parts of the *Code* dealing with exits for people in good health. In health care occupancies, it is assumed that some patients will not be able to escape from a fire without assistance and that others will have to be transported on beds, mattresses, litters, or in wheelchairs.

Health care occupancies are the only occupancies in the *Code* that allow an increase due to automatic sprinkler protection. The increase in exit capacity is based upon the assumption that sprinklers will limit fire size, thereby allowing greater time for safe egress.

Capacity (Inches per persons)

	Nonsprinklered	Sprinklered
Stairs	1.0	0.6
Level Travel	0.7	0.5

13-2.3.3   Any required aisle, corridor, or ramp shall be not less than 48 in. (122 cm) in clear width where serving as means of egress from patient sleeping rooms. It shall be so arranged as to avoid any obstructions to the convenient removal of nonambulatory persons carried on stretchers or on mattresses serving as stretchers.

Exception: Aisles, corridors, and ramps in adjunct areas not intended for the housing, treatment, or use of patients may be a minimum of 44 in. (112 cm) in clear and unobstructed width.

Figure 13-4 illustrates an exit access corridor that complies with 13-2.3.3. The specified minimum of 48 in. (122 cm) leaves little safety margin. Care is necessary to prevent carts, furnishings, and other materials from obstructing or interfering with potential occupant movement.

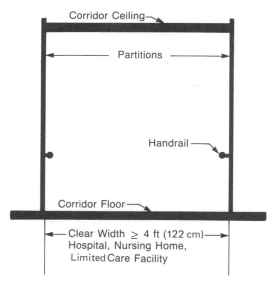

Figure 13-4.   Corridor in Exit Access in Existing Health Care Occupancy. (*See 13-2.3.3.*)

13-2.3.4   For evacuation purposes only the minimum width for doors in the means of egress from hospital, nursing home, limited care facility and psychiatric hospital sleeping rooms, diagnostic and treatment areas, such as X-ray, surgery, or physical therapy shall be at least 34 in. (86 cm) wide.

See Figure 13-5.

Formal Interpretation 76-30
Reference: 13-2.3.4

Question: Does 13-2.3.4 intend that exit doors, which are so located as not to be subject to use by health care occupants, be required to be 34 in. wide?

Answer: No. See 5-2.1.3.1.

Question: Does 13-2.3.4 intend that the 34-in. door width apply to exit stairway enclosure doors to provide a 32-in. nominal clear opening?

Answer: Yes.

Issue Edition: 1976
Reference: 10-3.2.8.3
Date: August 1977

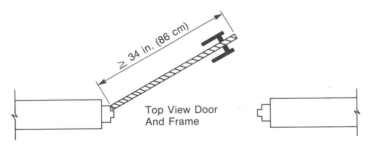

Figure 13-5.   Minimum Width of Doors in Means of Egress in Existing Health Care Facilities.

13-2.4 Number of Exits.

13-2.4.1   At least two exits of the types described in 13-2.2.2 through 13-2.2.7, remotely located from each other, shall be provided for each floor or fire section of the building.

13-2.4.2   At least one exit from each floor or fire section shall be either:

(a) A door leading directly outside the building, or

(b) A stair, or

(c) A smokeproof enclosure, or

(d) A ramp, or

(e) An exit passageway.

Any fire section not meeting these requirements shall be considered as part of an adjoining zone. Egress shall not require return through the zone of fire origin.

13-2.4.3*   At least two exits of the types described in 13-2.2.2 through 13-2.2.7 shall be accessible from each smoke compartment. Egress may be through adjacent compartment(s), but shall not require return through the compartment of fire origin.

A-13-2.4.3   An exit is not necessary for each individual smoke compartment if there is access to an exit through other smoke compartments without passing through the smoke compartment of fire origin.

Figure 13-6 can be used to illustrate the application of 13-2.4.2 and 13-2.4.3. If both Wall I and Wall II are horizontal exits, then three fire compartments or fire sections are formed. Paragraph 13-2.4.2 would then require that Area B also be provided with an exit that must be one of the five types of exits listed. In other words, Area B must be provided with an exit other than a horizontal exit, even though two horizontal exits are already provided from Area B. If this is not done, then Area B must be considered part of one of the adjoining areas — either part of Area A, in which case no credit is given for the horizontal exit of Wall I, or part of Area C, in which case no credit is given for the horizontal exit of Wall II. Prior to the 1985 Edition of the *Code*, this would also apply to smoke barriers. However, the *Code* now allows egress through adjoining smoke compartments. If both Wall I and Wall II were smoke barriers, the arrangement would be acceptable. If Wall I were a smoke barrier and Wall II were a horizontal exit, the arrangement would also be acceptable, as Areas A and B would be one fire area, with Area C being the other fire area and all requirements of 13-2.4.2 and 13-2.4.3 would be met.

For two reasons, caution should be used in determining how many smoke compartments can intervene in order to reach the ultimate exit. First, excessive moving of patients should be prevented, and second, each compartment must have sufficient area to handle all patients whom it must serve. In this example, where Wall I is a smoke barrier and Wall II is a horizontal exit, each area would have to be sufficient in size to comply with 13-2.2.5(a) for horizontal exits, or 13-3.7.4 for smoke barriers, based on figures calculated for the entire floor, since all three areas are an integral part of the horizontal evacuation for the floor. This is easily justified considering that if a fire started near the exit for Area A, thus requiring evacuation into Area B, ultimate evacuation would be achieved only through Area C, since there is no exit from Area B. In such case, Area C would have to have sufficient area to handle patients from Areas A and B as well as those patients originally in Area C.

In order to ensure that egress does not require return through the compartment of fire origin, each compartment formed must be analyzed to ensure that a path of travel to an exit other than a horizontal exit is available. (*See Figure 13-6.*)

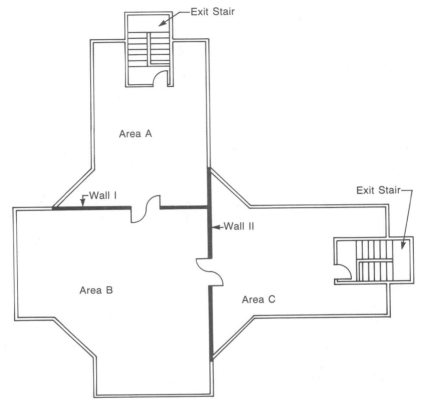

Figure 13-6. Arrangement of Exits in an Existing Health Care Occupancy Involving Smoke Barriers and Horizontal Exits. (*See commentary following 13-2.4.3 for discussion of figure.*)

13-2.5 Arrangement of Means of Egress.

13-2.5.1   Every habitable room shall have an exit access door leading directly to an exit access corridor.

The term "patient sleeping room," previously used in 13-2.5.1, has been replaced with the term "habitable room" to make clear that all occupied rooms in a health care facility must have access to a corridor leading to an exit.

Exception No. 1: If there is an exit door opening directly to the outside from the room at ground level.

Exception No. 2: For patient sleeping rooms, one adjacent room, such as a sitting or anteroom, may intervene if the intervening room is not used to serve as an exit access for more than eight patient sleeping beds.

Exception No. 3:   Exception No. 2 above shall apply to special nursing suites permitted in 13-2.5.3 without being limited to eight beds or basinettes.

Exception No. 4:   For rooms other than patient sleeping rooms, one or more adjacent rooms, such as offices, work rooms, etc., may intervene provided that such intervening rooms are not hazardous areas as defined in 13-3.2.

Figures 13-7a and b illustrate the intent of 13-2.5.1. Figure 13-8 illustrates Exception No. 2 to 13-2.5.1.

Nursing suites and various treatment areas are frequently arranged with an intervening workroom located between the exit access corridor and a treatment room. Exception No. 4 to 13-2.5.1 will allow egress through spaces that are closely related in function to the treatment room and, therefore, under the immediate control of staff who, along with patients, would be forced to travel across such rooms. Where such an arrangement is used, locking hardware on doors may not restrict egress from the nursing suite or intervening room. *(See 13-2.2.2.)*

13-2.5.2   Any patient sleeping room, or any suite that includes patient sleeping rooms, of more than 1,000 sq ft (93 sq m) shall have at least two exit access doors remote from each other.

Any room or any suite of rooms, other than patient sleeping rooms, of more than 2,500 sq ft (230 sq m) shall have at least two exit access doors remote from each other.

Patient sleeping rooms, or suites with sleeping rooms, greater than 1,000 sq ft (93 sq m) require two exit access doors. The doors may open onto a common corridor but are required to be as remotely located from

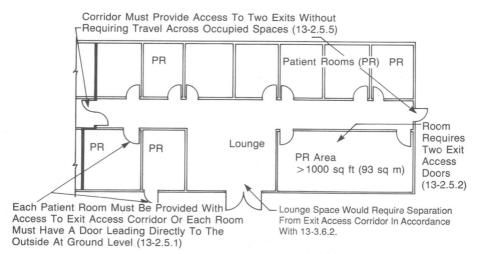

Figure 13-7a. Arrangement of Exit Access in an Existing Health Care Facility. Incorrect lounge arrangement as lounge must not interfere with exit access. *(See Figure 13-7b for corrected lounge arrangement.)* Paragraph 13-2.5.1 Exception No. 1, 13-2.5.2, and 13-2.5.5 are also illustrated.

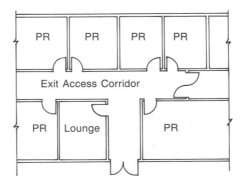

Figure 13-7b. Corrected Arrangement of Exit Access in an Existing Health Care Facility. (*See Figure 13-7a.*) Lounge is separated from exit access corridor in accordance with 13-3.6.2 as required by 13-2.5.5. (*See also 13-3.6.1 Exceptions No. 1, 2, and 5 where a waiting space may be open to an exit access corridor.*)

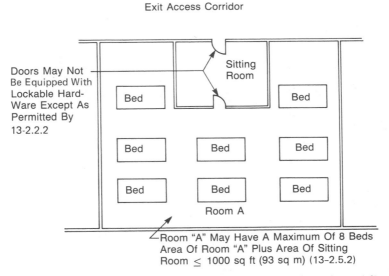

Figure 13-8. Exit Access from a Patient Sleeping Room Through an Adjacent Room in Existing Health Care Facility. This arrangement complies with 13-2.5.1 Exception No. 2 and 13-2.5.2.

each other as possible. Rooms or suites not used for patient sleeping purposes may be up to 2,500 sq ft (230 sq m) in area and require only one door based on the presumption that occupants are alert or ambulatory or are in most instances accompanied by staff who could assist in evacuating the space during fire or other emergency. For sleeping suites, refer to 13-2.5.3 for additional requirements. For nonsleeping suites, refer to 13-2.5.4 for additional requirements. Figures 13-9a and 13-9b illustrate the requirements for sleeping suites. Figure 13-10a, 13-10b, and 13-10c illustrate the requirements for nonsleeping suites.

13-2.5.3   Any patient sleeping room that complies with the requirements previously set forth in this section may be subdivided with non-fire-rated, noncombustible or limited-combustible partitions, provided that the arrangement allows for direct and constant visual supervision by nursing personnel. Rooms that are so subdivided shall not exceed 5,000 sq ft (460 sq m).

Paragraph 13-2.5.3 makes provision for noncompartmented nursing suites, such as Intensive Care Units (ICU) or Coronary Care Units (CCU). Interior suite arrangements are not required to comply with 13-2.3.3 or 13-3.6 relative to corridor access to exits. For example, interior corridors within special nursing units are not required to be 48 in. (122 cm) wide. Doors to individual cubicles may be sliding doors. (*See Figures 13-9a and b.*)

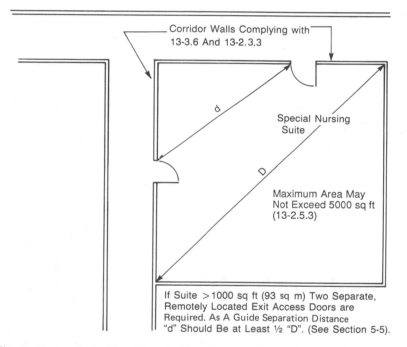

Figure 13-9a.   Suites Involving Patient Sleeping Rooms in an Existing Health Care Occupancy.   The requirements of 13-2.5.1, 13-2.5.2, and 13-2.5.3 for patient sleeping suites are illustrated here. The suite must comply with Figures 13-9a and b.

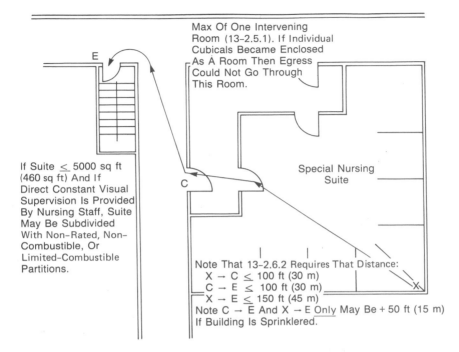

Max Of One Intervening
Room (13-2.5.1). If Individual
Cubicals Became Enclosed
As A Room Then Egress
Could Not Go Through
This Room.

E

If Suite ≤ 5000 sq ft
(460 sq ft) And If
Direct Constant Visual
Supervision Is Provided
By Nursing Staff, Suite
May Be Subdivided
With Non–Rated, Non–
Combustible, Or
Limited–Combustible
Partitions.

C

Special Nursing
Suite

Note That 13-2.6.2 Requires That Distance:
  X → C ≤ 100 ft (30 m)
  C → E ≤ 100 ft (30 m)
  X → E ≤ 150 ft (45 m)
Note C → E And X → E Only May Be + 50 ft (15 m)
If Building Is Sprinklered.

Figure 13-9b. Suites Involving Patient Sleeping Rooms in an Existing Health Care Occupancy. The requirements of 13-2.5.1, 13-2.5.2, 13-2.5.3, and 13-2.6.2 for patient sleeping suites are illustrated. The suite must comply with Figures 13-9a and 13-9b.

13-2.5.4 Any suite of rooms, other than patient sleeping rooms, that complies with the requirements previously set forth in this section may be subdivided with non-fire-rated, noncombustible, or limited-combustible partitions. Such suites shall not exceed 10,000 sq ft (930 sq m) in area and either:

(a) The maximum travel distance from any point in the suite to a corridor door shall be limited to 50 ft (15 m), or

(b) There shall be unrestricted access from patient treatment areas to a corridor with a maximum of one intervening room.

The requirements of 13-2.5.4 are illustrated in Figures 13-10a, 13-10b, and 13-10c.

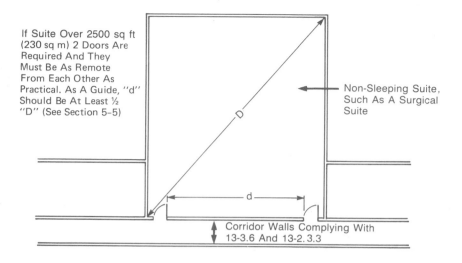

If Suite Over 2500 sq ft (230 sq m) 2 Doors Are Required And They Must Be As Remote From Each Other As Practical. As A Guide, "d" Should Be At Least ½ "D" (See Section 5–5)

Non-Sleeping Suite, Such As A Surgical Suite

Corridor Walls Complying With 13-3.6 And 13-2.3.3

Figure 13-10a. Suites Not Involving Patient Sleeping Rooms in an Existing Health Care Occupancy. This illustrates the provisions of 13-2.5.2. The suites must comply with Figures 13-10a and b or 13-10a and c.

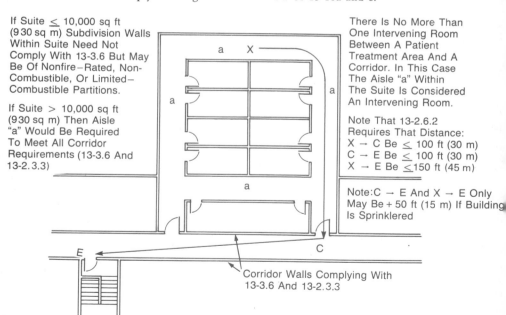

If Suite ≤ 10,000 sq ft (930 sq m) Subdivision Walls Within Suite Need Not Comply With 13-3.6 But May Be Of Nonfire–Rated, Non-Combustible, Or Limited–Combustible Partitions.

If Suite > 10,000 sq ft (930 sq m) Then Aisle "a" Would Be Required To Meet All Corridor Requirements (13-3.6 And 13-2.3.3)

There Is No More Than One Intervening Room Between A Patient Treatment Area And A Corridor. In This Case The Aisle "a" Within The Suite Is Considered An Intervening Room.

Note That 13-2.6.2 Requires That Distance:
X → C Be ≤ 100 ft (30 m)
C → E Be ≤ 100 ft (30 m)
X → E Be ≤150 ft (45 m)

Note:C → E And X → E Only May Be + 50 ft (15 m) If Building Is Sprinklered

Corridor Walls Complying With 13-3.6 And 13-2.3.3

Figure 13-10b. Suites Not Involving Patient Sleeping Rooms in an Existing Health Care Occupancy. The requirements of 13-2.5.2, 13-2.5.4, and 13-2.6.2 are illustrated. The suite must comply with 13-10a and b or 13-10a and c.

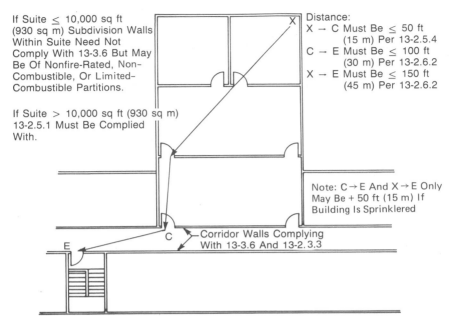

If Suite ≤ 10,000 sq ft (930 sq m) Subdivision Walls Within Suite Need Not Comply With 13-3.6 But May Be Of Nonfire-Rated, Non-Combustible, Or Limited-Combustible Partitions.

If Suite > 10,000 sq ft (930 sq m) 13-2.5.1 Must Be Complied With.

Distance:
X → C Must Be ≤ 50 ft (15 m) Per 13-2.5.4
C → E Must Be ≤ 100 ft (30 m) Per 13-2.6.2
X → E Must Be ≤ 150 ft (45 m) Per 13-2.6.2

Note: C → E And X → E Only May Be + 50 ft (15 m) If Building Is Sprinklered

Corridor Walls Complying With 13-3.6 And 13-2.3.3

Figure 13-10c. Suites Not Involving Patient Sleeping Rooms in an Existing Health Care Occupancy. The requirements of 13-2.5.2, 13-2.5.4, and 13-2.6.2 for suites not involving patient sleeping rooms are illustrated. The suite must comply with Figures 13-10a and b or 13-10a and c.

13-2.5.5* Every corridor shall provide access to at least two approved exits in accordance with Sections 5-4 and 5-5 without passing through any intervening rooms or spaces other than corridors or lobbies.

Exception: Existing dead-end corridors may be continued in use if it is not practical and feasible to alter them so that exits will be accessible in at least two different directions from all points in aisles, passageways, and corridors.

A-13-2.5.5 Every exit or exit access should be so arranged, if practical and feasible, that no corridor, passageway, or aisle has a pocket or dead end exceeding 30 ft (9.1 m). *(Also see Table A-5-6.1.)*

Exit access corridors, aisles, and passageways should preferably be arranged so that exits will be accessible in at least two different directions from all points in the corridor, aisle, or passageway. However, in many buildings, dead-end corridors exist. The *Code* intends to allow dead-end corridors of moderate length to remain without correction.

In all instances, dead-end corridors up to 30 ft (9.1 m) may remain in use without correction. For dead-end corridors in excess of 30 ft (9.1 m), considerable judgment must be exercised in determining what constitutes an excessive dead-end pocket. Where a dead-end corridor is judged excessive, corrective action should be taken either by provision of additional egress facilities or by provision of other safeguards that result in an equivalent degree of safety. Alternative approaches might involve application of additional detectors or sprinklers or provision of smoke control and the like.

13-2.6 Travel Distance to Exits.

13-2.6.1   Travel distance shall be measured in accordance with Section 5-6.

13-2.6.2 Travel distance:

(a) Between any room door required as exit access and an exit shall not exceed 100 ft (30 m);

(b) Between any point in a room and an exit shall not exceed 150 ft (45 m);

Exception: The travel distance in (a) or (b) above may be increased by 50 ft (15 m) in buildings protected throughout by an approved supervised automatic sprinkler system.

(c) Between any point in a health care sleeping room and an exit access door of that room shall not exceed 50 ft (15 m).

(d) Between any point in a suite of rooms as permitted by 13-2.5 and an exit access door of that suite shall not exceed 100 ft (30 m) and shall meet (b) above.

The requirements of 13-2.6.1 and 13-2.6.2 are illustrated in Figure 13-11. Travel distance is measured only to the closest exit. It is not measured to the second exit required by 13-2.4.1. It should be noted that the 50-ft (15-m) restriction within a room applies only to sleeping rooms. (*See also 13-2.5.4 and Figures 13-9 and 13-10.*)

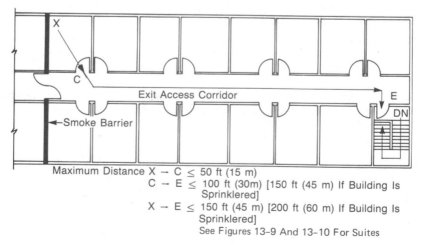

Maximum Distance X → C ≤ 50 ft (15 m)
C → E ≤ 100 ft (30m) [150 ft (45 m) If Building Is Sprinklered]
X → E ≤ 150 ft (45 m) [200 ft (60 m) If Building Is Sprinklered]
See Figures 13–9 And 13–10 For Suites

Figure 13-11.   Travel Distance in Existing Health Care Occupancies.

13-2.7 Discharge From Exits.

13-2.7.1   Discharge from exits shall be arranged in accordance with Section 5-7.

All exit stairs or exit ramps are required to discharge to the outside either directly or through an enclosed exit passageway. Where an exit passageway is used, the fire-resistive separation of the enclosure must be the same as required for the enclosure of a stair or ramp. Openings into the passageway must be suitably protected and limited to doors leading to spaces normally occupied. [*See 5-1.3.1(a) through (e).*] Under certain conditions, a maximum of 50 percent of the required exits may discharge to the outside through the level of exit discharge in accordance with 5-7.2.

13-2.8 Illumination of Means of Egress.

13-2.8.1   Means of egress shall be illuminated in accordance with Section 5-8.

13-2.9 Emergency Lighting.

13-2.9.1   Emergency lighting shall be provided in accordance with Section 5-9.

Also see 31-1.3.8.

13-2.10 Marking of Means of Egress.

13-2.10.1   Means of egress shall have signs in accordance with Section 5-10.

Exception: Where the line of exit travel is obvious, signs may be omitted in one story buildings with an occupancy of less than 30 persons.

13-2.11 Special Features.

SECTION 13-3   PROTECTION

13-3.1 Protection of Vertical Openings.

13-3.1.1   Any stairway, ramp, elevator hoistway, light or ventilation shaft, chute, and other vertical opening between stories shall be enclosed in accordance with Section 6-2.4 with construction having a 1-hour fire resistance rating.

Exception No. 1: Where a full enclosure of a stairway that is not a required exit is impracticable, the required enclosure may be limited to that necessary to prevent a fire originating in any story from spreading to any other story.

Exception No. 2: Stairs that do not connect to a corridor, do not connect more than two levels, and do not serve as a means of egress need not comply with these regulations.

Exception No. 3: Floor and ceiling openings for pipes or conduits where the opening around the pipes or conduits is sealed in an approved manner. (See 6-2.3.4.2.)

Exception No. 4: An atrium may be used in accordance with 6-2.4.5. Exception No. 1 to 6-2.4.5(g) shall not apply to patient sleeping and treatment rooms.

Paragraph 13-3.1.1 requires that vertical shafts (including stairways, ramp enclosures, elevators, light and ventilation shafts, chutes, and other vertical openings connecting stories) must be enclosed with barriers providing a minimum fire resistance of 1 hour. Openings must be protected by approved fire doors, complete with a closing device and a positive latch. Doors in stair enclosures may be held open as specified by 13-2.2.2.6 and 13-2.2.2.7.

Where a stairway is not used as a portion of the means of egress, and full enclosure is not possible, the enclosure may be limited to that necessary to prevent fire or smoke originating in any one story from spreading to another story. For example, in a two-story building, the stair might be enclosed at the first floor level and left open at the second floor level.

Exception No. 2 to 13-3.1.1 is illustrated in Figure 13-12.

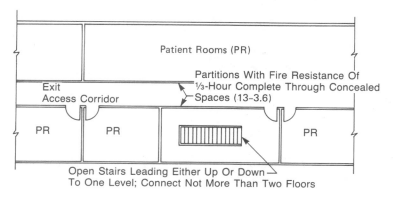

Figure 13-12. Open Stairs in Accordance with 13-3.1.1 Exception No. 2 in Existing Health Care Occupancies.

Exception No. 3 will allow piping and conduit to penetrate floors without requiring an enclosed shaft. The floor penetration, however, must be adequately protected in an approved manner to maintain the required fire resistance of the floor system. The penetration should be sealed in a fashion that will minimize the transfer of smoke.

Exception No. 4 permits atriums in existing health care facilities in accordance with 6-2.4.5. Patient sleeping and treatment rooms must be separated from the atrium by partitions complying with 13-3.6. Special requirements for smoke barriers in atriums are illustrated in Figures 13-18a - d following 13-3.7.

13-3.1.2 A door in a stair enclosure shall be self-closing, shall normally be kept in a closed position, and shall be marked in accordance with Section 5-10.

Exception: Doors in stair enclosures may be held open under the conditions specified by 13-2.2.2.6 and 13-2.2.2.7.

Refer to commentary following 13-2.2.2.7 for discussion on stairway doors.

13-3.2 Protection from Hazards.

13-3.2.1 Hazardous Areas. Any hazardous areas shall be safeguarded by a fire barrier of 1-hour fire resistance rating or provided with an automatic extinguishing system in accordance with 6-4.1. The automatic extinguishing may be in accordance with 13-3.5.4. Hazardous areas include, but are not restricted to, the following:

Boiler and fuel-fired heater rooms
Central/bulk laundries greater than 100 sq ft (9.3 sq m)
Repair shops
Handicraft shops
Employee locker rooms
Soiled linen rooms
Paint shops
Trash collection rooms

Rooms or spaces of more than 50 sq ft (4.6 sq m) including repair shops, used for storage of combustible supplies and equipment in quantities deemed hazardous by the authority having jurisdiction.

Laboratories employing quantities of flammable or combustible materials less than that which would be considered severe.

Hazardous areas are spaces with contents that, because of their basic nature (as in the case of flammable liquids) or because of the quantity of combustible materials involved, represent a significantly higher hazard than would otherwise be typical in general areas of health care facilities.

A listing of typical hazardous areas is included in 13-3.2.1. The list is meant to be illustrative, not all inclusive. The authority having jurisdiction is given the discretion to regulate any space judged to represent a hazard greater than most spaces. Hazardous areas must be separated from other areas by barriers having a 1-hour fire resistance rating, complete with approved fire doors protecting door openings; otherwise, automatic sprinkler protection must be installed. Where automatic sprinkler protection is provided, it is usually desirable to separate the hazardous area from the rest of the building by nonrated barriers designed to resist the passage of smoke, but this is not specifically required by the *Code. (See commentary under the exceptions for automatic sprinkler protection in 13-3.6.)*

Provisions for the enclosure of rooms used for charging linen and waste chutes, or for the rooms into which chutes empty, are provided in Chapter 7. In addition to the fire resistant cutoff of rooms into which linen chutes and waste chutes discharge, automatic sprinkler protection is considered essential.

Where flammable liquids are handled or stored, NFPA 30, *Flammable and Combustible Liquids Code,*[5] must be consulted to establish the minimum criteria necessary to mitigate this hazard. Rooms in clinical laboratories in which the unattended automatic processing of specimens with flammable solvents is likely to take place present a limited hazard that may be mitigated through use of sprinklers connected to the domestic water supply. Provisions for the use and storage of flammable gases and oxygen are covered in NFPA 99, *Standard for Health Care Facilities,*[6]
(See commentary on 13-3.2.2 for discussion of laboratories.)

13-3.2.2* Laboratories.   Laboratories employing quantities of flammable, combustible, or hazardous materials that are considered as severe hazard shall be protected in accordance with NFPA 99, *Standard for Health Care Facilities.*

A-13-3.2.2   The hazard level of a laboratory is considered severe if quantities of flammable, combustible, or hazardous materials are present that are capable of sustaining a fire condition of sufficient magnitude to breach a 1-hour fire separation.

See NFPA *Fire Protection Handbook* (*see Appendix B*), Section 7, Chapter 9, for guidance.

> Laboratories that contain "ordinary" combustibles and flammable liquids in sufficient quantity to threaten a 1-hour fire separation [e.g., wood equivalent fuel loads in the range of 5 to 10 lb/sq ft (25 to 50 kg/sq m)] are considered a severe hazard. Laboratories presenting a severe hazard must be protected in accordance with NFPA 99, *Standard for Health Care Facilities.*[6] Protection would include 1-hour fire resistance separation and automatic sprinkler protection.
>
> Where fuel loads of lesser amounts are involved and quantities of flammable liquids are limited, laboratories would simply be considered hazardous areas and would require either 1-hour separation or automatic sprinkler protection, as indicated in 13-3.2.1 and Section 6-4.

13-3.2.3 Anesthetizing Locations.   Anesthetizing locations shall be protected in accordance with NFPA 99, *Standard for Health Care Facilities.*

13-3.2.4 Medical Gas.   Medical gas storage and administration areas shall be protected in accordance with NFPA 99, *Standard for Health Care Facilities.*

13-3.2.5 Gift Shops.   Gift shops shall be protected as hazardous areas where used for the storage or display of combustibles in quantities considered hazardous. Gift shops not considered hazardous and having separately protected storage may be:

(a) Open to a lobby if the gift shop is not greater than 500 sq ft (46.5 sq m) and is protected throughout by an approved automatic sprinkler system, or

(b) Separated from a lobby with non-fire-rated walls if the gift shop is protected throughout by an approved automatic sprinkler system, or

(c) Separated from corridors by non-fire-rated walls if the gift shop is protected throughout by an approved automatic sprinkler system.

> Editions of the *Code* prior to 1985 have simply listed gift shops as typical hazardous areas. Many gift shops, particularly those containing combustible storage and having sizable retail areas, do present a hazard well beyond that normal to patient-occupied spaces and thus merit special protection. However, it is recognized that many small retail areas [less than 500 sq ft (46.5 sq m), for example] constitute a relatively minor hazard adequately mitigated by automatic sprinkler protection. This paragraph was added in 1985 to provide the authority having jurisdiction

with guidance in judging the degree of hazard and offers the facility some flexibility in the design and operation of gift shops.

Note: to use any of the three options given, the gift shop must be judged nonhazardous, must be sprinklered, and must have separately protected storage areas.

13-3.2.6 Cooking Facilities.   Cooking facilities shall be protected in accordance with 7-2.3.

Exception*: Where domestic cooking equipment is used for food warming or limited cooking, protection or segregation of food preparation facilities is not required.

A-13-3.2.6 Exception   This Exception is intended to permit small appliances used for reheating, such as microwave ovens, hot plates, toasters, and nourishment centers, to be exempt from requirements of commercial cooking equipment.

Commercial cooking equipment must be installed and protected in accordance with NFPA 96, *Standard for the Installation of Equipment for the Removal of Smoke and Grease-Laden Vapors from Commercial Cooking Equipment.*[7] A regularly serviced, fixed, automatic fire extinguishing system would be required for the protection of cooking surfaces and exhaust and duct systems where cooking operations involve the potential for grease-laden vapors. Cooking operations that do not involve the release of smoke or grease-laden vapors are not subject to compliance with NFPA 96 and would not normally be treated as hazardous operations.

The Exception notes that 13-3.2.6 would not apply to a room used as a staff lounge equipped with a domestic-type range or microwave oven. Such a room would be considered similar to a treatment room and would require separation as indicated in 13-3.6.1.

13-3.3* Interior Finish.

A-13-3.3   Section 6-5 provides for the application of approved flame-retardant coatings to correct excessive flame spread characteristics of certain types of existing interior finish.

13-3.3.1   Interior finish on walls and ceilings throughout shall be Class A or Class B, in accordance with Section 6-5.

Exception: In buildings protected throughout by an approved supervised automatic sprinkler system, Class C interior finish may be continued in use on all walls and ceilings within rooms separated from the exit access corridors in accordance with 13-3.6.

Existing interior finishes on walls and ceilings are limited solely on the basis of flame spread. Paragraph 6-5.3.2 exempts existing interior finishes from the limitations based upon smoke development.

Paragraph 6-5.6.1 makes provision for application of approved flame-retardant coatings to reduce flame spread characteristics of certain types of existing interior finish materials to an acceptable level. Refer to the commentary on 6-5.6.1 for additional guidance.

Where rooms are separated from corridors by barriers designed to retard the transfer of smoke and the building is completely protected by an automatic sprinkler system, Class C interior finish materials may be continued in use on walls and ceilings within the rooms so separated and protected.

13-3.3.2 Newly installed interior floor finish in corridors and exits shall be Class I in accordance with Section 6-5. No restrictions shall apply to existing interior floor finish.

Any new interior floor finish to be installed in corridors and exits within existing nonsprinklered health care facilities is required to meet the criteria for Class I materials as indicated within 6-5.4.2. However, existing floor finish materials that have been previously evaluated and judged acceptable may continue to be used.

13-3.4 Detection, Alarm, and Communications Systems.

13-3.4.1 General.   Health care occupancies shall be provided with a fire alarm system in accordance with Section 7-6.

13-3.4.2 Initiation.   Initiation of the required fire alarm systems shall be by manual means in accordance with 7-6.2 and by means of any detection devices or detection systems required.

Exception No. 1:   Fire alarm pull stations in patient sleeping areas may be omitted at exits if located at all nurses' control stations or other continuously attended staff location, provided such pull stations are visible and continuously accessible and that travel distances in 7-6.2.4 are not exceeded.

Exception No. 2:   Fixed extinguishing systems protecting commercial cooking equipment in kitchens that are protected by a complete automatic sprinkler system need not initiate the fire alarm system.

Formal Interpretation 76-19
Reference: 13-3.4.2

Question: Does 13-3.4.2 intend to require local devices designed to detect smoke on either side of an opening as referenced in 13-2.2.2.6 to be connected to the fire alarm system?

Answer: In existing buildings, it is the intent of the Committee that required fire detection devices be connected to the fire alarm system where practical.

Issue Edition: 1976
Reference: 10-3.3.3.6
Date: August 1977

Manual fire alarm systems are required for all existing health care facilities. Any required fire detection device must be connected to the fire alarm system to sound the alarm when activated. The reference to Section 7-6 would require alarm systems to be installed and maintained in accordance with appropriate NFPA standards and would specify alarm circuits be electrically supervised and that emergency power be provided.

The Exception to 13-3.4.2 allows pull stations, with certain qualifications, to be located at continuously attended staff positions in sleeping areas. This arrangement provides the opportunity for prompt notification of fire without requiring staff to leave their normal work stations. Manual pull stations should always be located so that anyone qualified to send an alarm may summon aid without having to leave the zone of their ordinary activities, or pass out of sight and hearing of people immediately exposed to, or in direct view of, a fire.

13-3.4.3 Notification.

13-3.4.3.1 Occupant Notification. Occupant notification shall be accomplished automatically, without delay, upon operation of any fire alarm activating device by means of an internal audible alarm in accordance with 7-6.3. Presignal systems are prohibited.

Exception: Where visual devices have been installed in patient sleeping areas, in place of the audible alarm, they may be accepted by the authority having jurisdiction.

Internal, audible alarm devices are required by 13-3.4.3.1, but visual alarm devices may continue to be used in areas where the patients sleep, subject to the approval of the authority having jurisdiction. This exception assumes adequate continuous supervision by the staff to ensure that the alarm is recognized. The use of visual devices places heavy reliance upon the staff to sound the alert.

13-3.4.3.2 Emergency Forces Notification. Fire department notification shall be accomplished in accordance with 7-6.4.

Exception: Smoke detection devices or smoke detection systems equipped with reconfirmation features need not automatically notify the fire department unless the alarm condition is reconfirmed after a maximum 120 second time period.

The alarm must automatically transmit to a point outside the facility. Where automatic transmission of alarms to the fire department legally committed to serve the facility is not permitted, arrangements are to be made for the prompt notification of the fire department or such other assistance as may be available in the case of fire or other emergency. Paragraph 7-6.4 lists various methods acceptable for automatic notification of the fire department. The fire department should still be notified manually to verify and confirm the automatic transmission of the alarm. In larger facilities, this may be the responsibility of the facility telephone operator; in smaller facilities, it may be the responsibility of the nursing staff.

An independent study by the National Bureau of Standards indicates a high rate of false alarms for smoke detectors installed in health care facilities.[8] The study determined 4.4 false alarms occurred per 100 smoke detectors per year. Furthermore, approximately 14 false alarms occurred for every actual alarm. Because of the high incidence of false alarms, the *Code* now permits delaying fire department notification for up to 120 seconds where smoke detectors or smoke detector systems are equipped with a reconfirmation feature.

13-3.4.4 Emergency Control. Operation of any activating device in the required fire alarm system shall be arranged to automatically accomplish, without delay, any control functions to be performed by that device. (*See 7-6.5.*)

13-3.4.5 Detection.

13-3.4.5.1 Corridors. An approved automatic smoke detection system shall be installed in all corridors of limited care facilities. Such systems shall be installed in accordance with Section 7-6.

Exception No. 1: Where each patient sleeping room is protected by an approved smoke detection system, and a smoke detector is provided at smoke barriers and horizontal exits, such corridor systems will not be required on the patient sleeping room floors.

Exception No. 2: Buildings protected throughout by an approved supervised automatic sprinkler system installed in accordance with Section 7-7.

Paragraph 13-3.4.5.1 requires smoke detectors in limited care facilities. Staffing levels in hospitals and nursing homes reasonably ensure discovery of a fire at an early stage. In existing hospitals and nursing homes, it is considered reasonable to place reliance on staff to sound the alert.

13-3.4.5.2 Spaces Open to Corridors. (*See 13-3.6.1.*)

13-3.5 Extinguishment Requirements.

13-3.5.1 Where required by 13-1.6, health care facilities shall be protected throughout by an approved automatic sprinkler system in accordance with Section 7-7.

Exception: In Types I and II construction, where approved by the authority having jurisdiction, alternative protection measures may be substituted for sprinkler protection in specified areas where the authority having jurisdiction has prohibited sprinklers, without causing a building to be classified as nonsprinklered.

In summary, automatic sprinkler protection is required by 13-1.6 in any case where combustible elements are used in the construction of a building.

Where sprinkler protection is specified, complete building coverage, in accordance with the provisions of NFPA 13, *Standard for the Installation of Sprinkler Systems,*[9] is required. The *Code* does not exempt any area of the building from protection. (*See Section 7-7.*) However, where automatic sprinkler protection is omitted from certain spaces at the mandate of the authority having jurisdiction and the authority having jurisdiction approves alternative protective measures, the building is still considered fully protected throughout. Sprinklers may only be omitted from isolated areas in buildings of fire-rated, noncombustible construction where the building will have sufficient structural fire resistance to outlast most fires. Use of alternative protective measures to automatic sprinklers should be carefully evaluated to assure equivalent protection is achieved. Where fixed automatic fire extinguishing systems (using Halon, for example) are used as an alternative to sprinklers for specific spaces, it is suggested the spaces also be separated by fire resistant construction.

13-3.5.2 Where this *Code* permits exceptions for fully sprinklered health care occupancies, the sprinkler system shall be:

(a) In complete accordance with Section 7-7.

(b) Electrically connected to the fire alarm system, and

(c) Fully supervised.

Exception: In Types I and II construction, where approved by the authority having jurisdiction, alternative protection measures may be substituted for sprinkler protection in specified areas where the authority having jurisdiction has prohibited sprinklers, without causing a building to be classified as nonsprinklered.

The term "fully supervised" means a distinct supervisory signal must be provided to a constantly attended location in the event of any malfunction or action that would impair sprinkler performance. Supervision must be provided, for example, for water supply and sprinkler control valves, fire pump power and running conditions, water tank levels and temperatures, pressure in pressure tanks, air pressure in dry-pipe systems, building temperature, and city water pressure. (*See also Section 7-7.2 and commentary for 13-3.5.1.*)

13-3.5.3 The main sprinkler control valve(s) shall be electrically supervised so that at least a local alarm will sound at a constantly attended location when the valve is closed.

Also see 13-3.5.2.

13-3.5.4 Isolated hazardous areas may be protected in accordance with 7-7.1.2 if the additional requirements of this paragraph are met. An indicating shut-off valve shall be installed in an accessible location between the sprinklers and the connection to the domestic water supply. For new installations in existing buildings, where more than two sprinklers are installed in a single area, water flow detection shall be provided to sound the building fire alarm or notify by a signal any constantly attended location, such as PBX, security, or emergency room, whereby necessary corrective action shall be directed.

13-3.5.5 Portable fire extinguishers shall be provided in all health care occupancies in accordance with 7-7.4.1.

13-3.6 Corridors.

The provisions for corridor walls have been reorganized for the 1988 *Code* with relatively few technical changes.

Paragraph 13-3.6.1 establishes requirements to have corridor walls.

Paragraph 13-3.6.2 establishes construction requirements for such walls.

Paragraph 13-3.6.3 establishes requirements for doors in corridor walls.

Paragraph 13-3.6.4 deals with transfer grilles.

The requirements of 13-3.6.1 to 13-3.6.4 essentially stipulate that all areas containing combustibles in sufficient quantity to produce a life-threatening fire must be separated from exit access corridors by partitions designed to resist the passage of smoke. The details of construction for such partitions vary depending upon whether or not automatic sprinkler protection is provided.

13-3.6.1*   Corridors shall be separated from all other areas by partitions complying with 13-3.6.2 through 13-3.6.4 (*also see 13-2.5.5*).

A-13-3.6.1   For the purpose of this paragraph only, the term "direct supervision" is meant to convey that the opening to the corridor from the waiting area should be visible from an occupied staff location.

Exception No. 1: Waiting areas may be open to the corridor, provided:

(a) Each area does not exceed 600 sq ft (55.7 sq m), and

(b) The area is located to permit direct supervision by the facility staff, and

(c) The area does not obstruct any access to required exits, and

(d) The area is equipped with an electrically supervised, automatic smoke detection system installed in accordance with 13-3.4.

Exception No. 2: Spaces other than patient sleeping rooms, treatment rooms, and hazardous areas may be open to the corridor and may be unlimited in area provided:

(a) Each space is located to permit direct supervision by the facility staff, and

(b) The space and corridors that the space opens onto in the same smoke compartment are protected by an electrically supervised, automatic smoke detection system installed in accordance with 13-3.4, and

(c)* Each space is protected by automatic sprinklers or the furnishings and furniture in combination with all other combustibles within the area are of such a minimum quantity and are so arranged that a fully developed fire is unlikely to occur, and

A-13-3.6.1 Exception No. 2(c)   A fully developed fire (flashover) occurs if the rate of heat release of the burning materials exceeds the capability of the space to absorb or vent that heat. The ability of common lining (wall, ceiling, and floor) materials to absorb heat is approximately 0.75 Btu (0.79 kJ) per sq ft of lining. The venting capability of open doors or windows is in excess of 20 Btu (21 kJ) per sq ft of opening. In a fire that has not reached flashover conditions, fire will spread from one furniture item to another only if the burning item is close to another furniture item. For example, if individual furniture items have heat release rates of 500 Btu per second (525 kw) and are separated by 12 in. (30.5 cm) separation or more, the fire is not expected to spread from item to item and flashover is unlikely to occur. Also see the NFPA *Fire Protection Handbook*, Section 21.

(d) The space does not obstruct access to required exits.

Exception No. 3*: Spaces for nurses' stations.

A-13-3.6.1 Exception No. 3   A typical nurses' station would normally contain one or more of the following with associated furniture and furnishings.

(a) Charting area.

(b) Clerical area.

(c) Nourishment station.

(d) Storage of small amounts of medications, medical equipment and supplies, clerical supplies, and linens.

(e) Patient monitoring and communication equipment.

Exception No. 4:   Gift shops may be open to the corridor where protected in accordance with 13-3.2.5.

Exception No. 5:   In a limited care facility, group meeting or multipurpose therapeutic spaces, other than hazardous areas, under continuous supervision by facility staff may be open to the corridor provided:

(a) Each area does not exceed 1,500 sq ft (140 sq m), and

(b) The area is located to permit direct supervision by the facility staff, and

(c) The area does not obstruct any access to required exits, and

(d) The area is equipped with an electrically supervised, automatic smoke detection system installed in accordance with 13-3.4, and

(e) Not more than one such space is permitted per smoke compartment.

Paragraph 13-3.6.1 requires that all spaces be separated from corridors by partitions. Then exceptions allow specific areas to be open to the corridor. The intent is to limit the risk of exposing the corridor to fire. Exceptions No. 1 through 5 to 13-3.6.1 set forth specific areas that may be open to corridors. (*See Figures 13-13a and b.*) However, patient sleeping rooms, treatment rooms, and hazardous areas must be separated by partitions.

For example, Exception No. 2 states that waiting spaces, lounges, and other similar spaces may be open to corridors on floors with rooms where patients sleep, or on floors used for other purposes. Each waiting space must be located to permit direct supervision by staff. A waiting space must also be located and arranged so that its furnishing will not interfere with or obstruct access to any required exits. The number of waiting areas open to the corridor in each smoke compartment is not limited. The spaces and the corridor within each smoke compartment to which the spaces open must be equipped with an electrically supervised automatic smoke detection system. The area of the open space is not limited. However, each space must be provided with automatic sprinkler protection, or the furnishings and furniture in combination with all other available fuels (combustibles) must be adequately restricted so a fire will be self-limiting. In making use of the fuel limiting technique, combustibles must be of a minimum quantity and adequately separated so that a fire will remain confined to the object of origin. Combustibles must be arranged and limited to a type to prevent full room involvement. (*See Figure 13-13b.*)

The "direct supervision" required by Exceptions No. 1, 2, and 5 (and assumed in Exception No. 3) is very important. It allows the staff to see, hear, or smell a developing fire or to prevent the ignition of a fire merely by their presence. The use of closed-circuit television or mirrors does not provide for all the above and is discouraged in existing facilities. However, the use of these devices may be the most reasonable remedy to an existing installation if approved by the authority having jurisdiction.

Areas used for charting and communication by doctors and nurses may be open to the corridor.

It is important to note that the installation of new corridor walls is considered a renovation, and such walls must comply with Chapter 12 to the extent feasible. (*See 1-4.6.*)

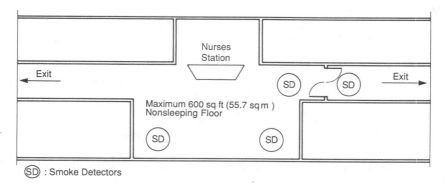

Figure 13-13a. Waiting Spaces. Waiting area complying with 13-3.6.1 Exception No. 1.

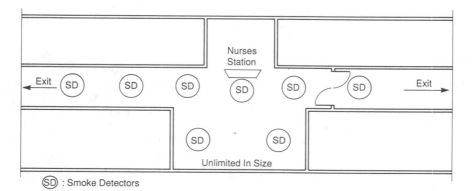

Figure 13-13b. Areas Open to Corridor. Unlimited size area open to corridor in accordance with 13-3.6.1 Exception No. 2.

13-3.6.2 Construction of Corridor Walls.

13-3.6.2.1* Corridor walls shall be continuous from the floor to the underside of the floor or roof deck above, through any concealed spaces, such as those above the suspended ceilings, and through interstitial structural and mechanical spaces, and shall have a fire resistance rating of at least 20 minutes.

Exception No. 1: In health care occupancies protected throughout by an approved supervised automatic sprinkler system, a corridor may be separated from all other areas by non-fire-rated partitions and may be terminated at the ceiling when the ceiling is constructed to limit the transfer of smoke.

Exception No. 2: Corridor partitions may terminate at ceilings that are not an integral part of a floor construction if there exists 5 ft (152 cm) or more of space between the top of the ceiling subsystem and the bottom of the floor or roof above, provided:

(a) The ceiling shall have been tested as a part of a fire-rated assembly in accordance with NFPA 251, Standard Methods of Fire Tests of Building Construction and Materials, for a test period of 1 hour or more, and

(b) Corridor partitions form smoketight joints with the ceilings (joint filler, if used, shall be noncombustible), and

(c) Each compartment of interstitial space that constitutes a separate smoke area is vented, in case of smoke emergency, to the outside by mechanical means having sufficient capacity to provide at least two air changes per hour, but in no case having a capacity less than 5,000 cfm (2.36 cu m/s), and

(d) The interstitial space shall not be used for storage, and

(e) The space shall not be used as a plenum for supply, exhaust or return air except as noted in (c).

Exception No. 3*: Corridor partitions may terminate at monolithic ceilings that resist the passage of smoke where there is a smoketight joint between the top of the partition and the bottom of the ceiling.

A-13-3.6.2.1 The intent of the 20-minute fire resistance rating for corridor partitions is to require a nominal fire rating, particularly where the fire rating of existing partitions cannot be documented. Examples of acceptable partition assemblies would include, but are not limited to, ½-in. (1.3-cm) gypsum board, wood lath and plaster, gypsum lath or metal lath and plaster.

A-13-3.6.2.1 Exception No. 3 Monolithic ceilings are continuous horizontal membranes composed of noncombustible or limited combustible materials, such as plaster or gypsum board, with seams or cracks permanently sealed.

13-3.6.2.2 Corridor walls shall form a barrier to limit the transfer of smoke.

13-3.6.2.3 Fixed wired glass vision panels shall be permitted in corridor walls, provided they do not exceed 1,296 sq in. (.84 sq m) in area and are mounted in steel or other approved metal frames.

Exception: There shall be no restrictions in area and fire resistance of glass and frames in buildings protected throughout by an approved supervised automatic sprinkler system installed in accordance with Section 7-7.

In nonsprinklered buildings, corridor partitions must be constructed of assemblies having a minimum fire resistance rating of 20 minutes. In setting the requirements for 20-minute partitions, it was intended to accept the separation provided by existing partitions of any substantial construction that are capable of serving as a barrier for a short period of time without requiring documentation of a specific fire rating. The 20-minute rating is intended to permit partitions of wood lath and plaster, ½ in. (1.27 cm) gypsum board and the like. Ordinary glass would not be permitted in nonsprinklered buildings. Materials used in the construction of partitions are limited on the basis of the construction types allowed by 13-1.6.2 and 13-1.6.3. All material used in the construction of Type I and Type II buildings must satisfy the criteria for noncombustible or limited-combustible materials. (*See 13-1.6.3.*)

Corridor partitions must be constructed continuously through all concealed spaces (e.g., through to the floor or roof deck above a suspended "lay-in" ceiling). (*See Figure 13-14a.*) Where a monolithic ceiling is provided that is composed of noncombustible materials, such as plaster or gypsum board having seams or cracks permanently sealed, thus forming a continuous horizontal membrane, it is intended to allow partitions to be terminated at the underside of the ceiling.

Openings in corridor partitions in nonsprinklered buildings must be suitably protected to maintain corridor separation. Glazing is limited to a maximum of 1,296-sq in. (0.84-sq m) of wired glass set in approved metal frames. It is preferable, but not required, that each wired glass panel be limited to a maximum dimension of 54 in. (140 cm). The glass should be labeled, should be ¼ in. (0.6 cm) thick, and should be well embedded in putty with all exposed joints between the metal and the glass struck and pointed. (*See NFPA 80, Standard for Fire Doors and Windows.*[10]) A number of wired glass panels may be used in a single partition, provided that each 1,296-sq in. (0.84-sq m) section is separated from adjacent panels by a steel or other approved metal mullion. It should be recognized that the use of wired glass panels in a partition will reduce the fire resistance capability of the partition, in that there will be radiant energy transfer through the glass panel. The excessive use of wired glass panels, therefore, should be avoided.

Where complete automatic sprinkler protection is provided, corridor partitions need not be rated but must still be constructed to resist the passage of smoke. The materials for constructing the partitions must be selected on the basis of the construction types allowed by 13-1.6.2 and 13-1.6.3. Where suspended ceilings are provided, partitions may be terminated at the suspended ceiling without any additional special protection if the suspended ceiling will resist the passage of smoke. The ability to resist the passage of smoke must be carefully evaluated. (*See Figure 13-14b.*) There are no restrictions in terms of area or fire resistance for glazing used in corridor partitions in sprinklered buildings.

Exception No. 2 to 13-3.6.2.1 sets forth criteria for terminating corridor partitions at ceilings, including "lay-in" type ceilings in nonsprinklered buildings. Partitions may be terminated at a ceiling that has been tested as a portion of an assembly having a fire resistance rating of 1 hour or more. Each compartment located above such a ceiling must be equipped with an automatic mechanical smoke exhaust system capable of providing a minimum of two air changes per hour but exhausting not less than 5,000 cu ft/min (2.36 cu m/sec). (*See the additional criteria in items (a) through (e) of Exception No. 2.*) This is not a common arrangement, due to the large interstitial space needed and the energy loss resulting from the ventilation requirements.

It is important to note that the installation of new corridor walls is considered a renovation, and such walls must comply with Chapter 12 to the extent feasible. (*See 1-4.6.*)

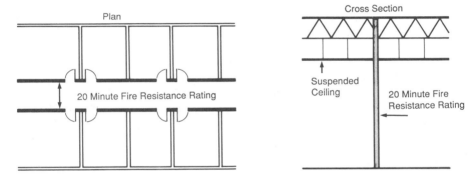

Figure 13-14a. Corridor Walls, Nonsprinklered Buildings. Corridor wall complying with 13-3.6.2. Note that wall must extend to the floor or roof deck above unless complying with one of the Exceptions.

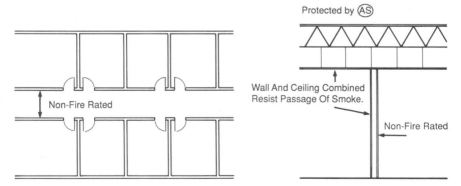

Figure 13-14b. Corridor Walls, Sprinklered Buildings. In buildings protected throughout by an approved automatic sprinkler system, walls may terminate at ceilings provided the wall and ceiling together resist the passage of smoke (*See 13-3.6.2.1 Exception No. 1.*).

13-3.6.3 Corridor Doors.

13-3.6.3.1 Doors protecting corridor openings in other than required enclosures of vertical openings, exits, or hazardous areas shall be substantial doors, such as those constructed of 1¾-in. (4.4-cm) solid bonded core wood or of construction that will resist fire for at least 20 minutes.

Exception No. 1: In buildings protected throughout by an approved supervised automatic sprinkler system in accordance with Section 7-7, the door construction requirements noted above are not required but the doors shall be constructed to resist the passage of smoke.

Exception No. 2: Doors to toilet rooms, bathrooms, shower rooms, sink closets, and similar auxiliary spaces that do not contain flammable or combustible materials.

13-3.6.3.2* Doors shall be provided with means suitable for keeping the door closed and acceptable to the authority having jurisdiction.

Exception: Doors to toilet rooms, bathrooms, shower rooms, sink closets, and similar auxiliary spaces that do not contain flammable or combustible materials.

A-13-3.6.3.2 While it is recognized that closed doors serve to maintain tenable conditions in a corridor and adjacent patient rooms, such doors, which under normal or fire conditions are self-closing, may create a special hazard for the personal safety of a room occupant. These closed doors may present a problem of delay in discovery, confining fire products beyond tenable conditions.

Since it is critical for responding staff members to be able to immediately identify the specific room involved, it is suggested that rooms having doors equipped with closing devices be protected by approved automatic smoke detection that is interconnected with the building fire alarm be considered for rooms having doors equipped with closing devices. Such detection may be located at any approved point within the room. When activated, the detector must provide warning that indicates the specific room of involvement by activation of fire alarm annunciator, nurse call system, or any other device acceptable to the authority having jurisdiction.

In existing buildings, a number of options exist to reasonably assure that patient room doors will be closed and remain closed during a fire:

(1) Doors may have positive latches, coupled with a suitable training program for staff to close the doors in an emergency.

(2) Similarly, roller latches maintained and acceptable to the authority having jurisdiction, coupled with adequate staff training, might be used.

(3) Doors protecting openings to patient sleeping or treatment rooms, or spaces having a similar combustible loading might be held closed using a closer exerting a minimum closing force of 5 lb (22 N) on the door latch stile.

13-3.6.3.3 Door frames shall be labeled, or shall be of steel construction, or shall be of other materials complying with the requirements of NFPA 252, *Standard Methods of Fire Tests of Door Assemblies*.

Exception: Door frames in buildings protected throughout by an approved supervised automatic sprinkler system installed in accordance with Section 7-7.

13-3.6.3.4   Door-closing devices are not required on doors in corridor wall openings other than those serving required enclosures of vertical openings, exits, or hazardous areas.

13-3.6.3.5   Fixed view panels of wired glass, in steel or other approved metal frames, limited to 1,296 sq in. (.84 sq m) in area, may be installed in these doors.

Exception: There shall be no restrictions in area and fire resistance of glass and frames in buildings protected throughout by an approved supervised automatic sprinkler system installed in accordance with Section 7-7.

13-3.6.3.6   Dutch doors may be used where they conform to 13-3.6.3, and in addition, both upper leaf and lower leaf shall be equipped with a latching device, and the meeting edges of the upper and lower leaves shall be equipped with an astragal, rabbet, or bevel.

Dutch doors protecting openings in enclosures around hazardous areas shall comply with NFPA 80, *Standard for Fire Doors and Windows.*

Doors in corridor partitions are required to resist the penetration of fire for at least 20 minutes, to be constructed of 1¾-in. (4.5-cm) thick solid bonded wood core, or be of equivalent construction. Doors must be capable of being closed and maintained closed during a fire. Where positive latches are used, doors must be equipped with a latch that cannot be held in the retracted position. The latch should be capable of holding the door in a closed position when subjected to stresses imposed by exposure to fire. (*See also A-13-3.6.3.2.*) Such doors are required to be installed in approved metal or "heavy wood" frames. Fixed wired glass vision panels installed in these doors may not exceed an area of 1,296 sq in. (.84 sq m) [maximum dimension of 54 in. (140 cm)] and must be set in approved metal frames. Labeled door frames and closing devices are not required except on doors protecting openings in exit enclosures, vertical openings, or required enclosures of hazardous areas.

Where complete automatic sprinkler protection is provided, doors protecting openings in corridor partitions must be installed to resist the passage of smoke, but are not required to have a fire protection rating. There are no restrictions in terms of area or fire resistance for glazing used in corridor doors in sprinklered buildings.

13-3.6.4 Transfer Grilles.   Transfer grilles, whether or not protected by fusible link operated dampers, shall not be used in these walls or doors.

Exception: Doors to toilet rooms, bathrooms, shower rooms, sink closets, and similar auxiliary spaces that do not contain flammable or combustible materials may have ventilating louvers or may be undercut.

The use of exit access corridors as an exhaust, supply, or return air plenum for a building's air-handling system is prohibited. Corridor doors may not be undercut to facilitate transfer of air, nor are transfer grilles allowed in corridor partitions (*see 13-3.6.4*) or corridor doors. (*See also 2-2.2 of NFPA 90A, Standard for the Installation of Air Conditioning and Ventilating Systems.*[11]) However, sink closets, bathrooms, and toilets may have doors equipped with a fixed grille or louver to provide make-up air from the corridor for room exhaust systems. Where the door is equipped with a grille or louver, such spaces may not be used for the storage of flammable or combustible supplies. Caution must be exercised where using this exception for sink closets, as they are often used for storage of combustibles.

Air-handling ducts penetrating corridor partitions should be adequately protected to preserve the 20-minute separation of exit access routes. Any space existing around ducts at the point of penetration of corridor partitions should be tightly sealed with a noncombustible material.

13-3.7 Subdivision of Building Spaces.

13-3.7.1   Smoke barriers shall be provided, regardless of building construction type, to divide every story used for sleeping rooms for more than 30 patients into at least two smoke compartments. The maximum area of any such smoke compartment shall not exceed 22,500 sq ft (2,100 sq m), of which both length and width shall be no more than 150 ft (45 m).

Exception No. 1:   Protection may be accomplished in conjunction with the provision of horizontal exits.

Exception No. 2:   One dimension may be extended provided that the total width plus length does not exceed 300 ft (91 m) and provided that travel distance from a room to a smoke barrier door or horizontal exit is no more than 150 ft (45 m).

It is not the intent of 13-3.7.1 to require that the length and width be added together with the resulting sum being 150 ft (45 m) or less. It is the intent that the length be 150 ft (45 m) or less and that the width be 150 ft (45 m) or less.

Paragraph 13-3.7.1 Exception No. 2 provides the facility and the designer with some flexibility in the arrangement of smoke compartments. The application of Exception No. 2 is illustrated in Figure 13-17. Even with this Exception, the maximum compartment size remains 22,500 sq ft (2,100 sq m) [150 ft by 150 ft (45 m by 45 m)]. However, this performance-oriented Exception would allow a long narrow compartment of, for example, 250 ft by 50 ft (76 m by 15 m). In such a case, the area [12,500 sq ft (1,167 sq m)] would be considerably less than the 22,500 sq ft (2,100 sq m) otherwise permitted.

13-3.7.2   For purposes of this section, the number of health care occupants shall be determined by actual count of patient bed capacity.

13-3.7.3   Any required smoke barrier shall be constructed in accordance with Section 6-3 and shall have a fire resistance rating of at least ½ hour.

Exception: Where an atrium is used, smoke barriers may terminate at an atrium wall constructed in accordance with Exception No. 2 to 6-2.4.5(g). A minimum of two separate smoke compartments shall be provided on each floor.

See Figure 13-18a - d.

13-3.7.4   At least 30 net sq ft (2.8 sq m) per patient in a hospital or nursing home or 15 net sq ft (1.4 sq m) per resident in a limited care facility shall be provided within the aggregate area of corridors, patient rooms, treatment rooms, lounge or dining areas, and other low hazard areas on each side of the smoke barrier. On stories not housing bed or litter patients, at least 6 net sq ft (.56 sq m) per occupant shall be provided on each side of the smoke barrier for the total number of occupants in adjoining compartments.

13-3.7.5   Openings in smoke barriers shall be protected by wired glass panels in steel frames, by doors of 20-minute fire protection rating, or by 1¾-in. (4.4-cm) solid bonded wood core doors as a minimum.

Exception: Doors may have wired glass vision panels, installed in steel or other approved metal frames, not exceeding 1,296 sq in. (.84 sq m).

13-3.7.6   Doors in smoke barriers shall comply with Section 6-3 and shall be self-closing. Such doors in smoke barriers shall not be required to swing with exit travel. Positive latching hardware is not required.

Exception: Doors may be held open only if they meet the requirements of 13-2.2.2.6.

13-3.7.7   Door openings in smoke barriers shall be protected by a swinging door, a minimum of 34 in. (86 cm) in width, or by a horizontal sliding door complying with 5-2.1.14 and providing a clear opening of at least 34 in. (86 cm).

The requirements of 13-3.7.1 through 13-3.7.7 for subdividing building spaces through smoke barriers are illustrated in Figures 13-15 through 13-19. Paragraph 13-2.2.5 discusses horizontal exits.

During a fire, the emergency evacuation of patients in a health care facility, is an inefficient, time consuming process. Realistically, if patients must be moved, sizable numbers of occupants can be relocated only through horizontal travel. Smoke barriers and horizontal exits used to subdivide a building serve three purposes fundamental to the protection of inpatients in that they:

1. Limit the spread of fire and fire-produced contaminants,

2. Limit the number of occupants exposed to a single fire, and

3. Provide for horizontal relocation of patients by creating an area of refuge on the same floor level.

Note that the combination fire/smoke dampers required in 6-3.5 may be omitted in engineered smoke control systems.

Several noteworthy differences exist between the requirements of 12-3.7 and 13-3.7. In existing health care occupancies:

1. Each story with sleeping accommodations for more than 30 health care occupants must be divided into at least two compartments by a smoke barrier. For application of 13-3.7.1, the number of occupants is determined by actual count of bed capacity. (*See 13-3.7.2.*)

2. Each story having more than 30 sleeping occupants must be subdivided by a smoke barrier into areas of not more than 22,500 sq ft (2,100 sq m), both the length and the width not exceeding 150 ft (45 m).

3. Smoke barriers must be constructed of assemblies providing a fire resistance rating of at least ½ hour, constructed continuously from outside wall to outside wall through concealed spaces (for example, above suspended ceilings).

4. Doors protecting openings in smoke barriers must, as a minimum, have a 20-minute fire protection rating, or be of 1¾-in. (4.5-cm) thick solid bonded wood core construction. Latching hardware is not required.

5. Openings in smoke barriers may be protected by fixed wired glass panels set in metal frames. Such panels may not exceed a maximum of 1,296 sq in. (0.84 sq m).

6. Doors in smoke barriers are required to be self-closing, but may be held open if the criteria of 13-2.2.2.6 are satisfied. Doors in smoke barriers are not required to swing in the direction of exit travel, although this is desirable.

7. Vision panels are not required in existing smoke barrier doors. However, if provided, they must be of wired glass in approved metal frames.

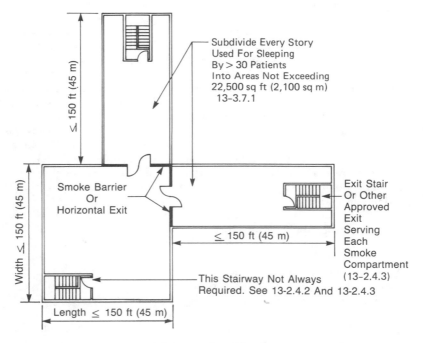

Figure 13-15.   Subdivision of Building Spaces in Existing Health Care Occupancies.

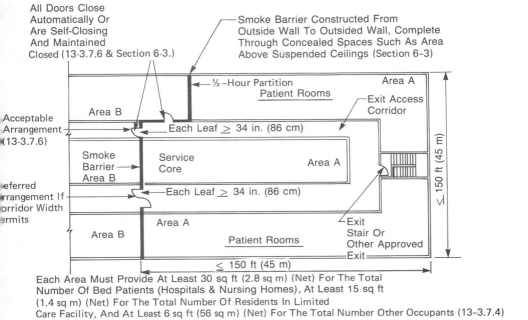

All Doors Close Automatically Or Are Self-Closing And Maintained Closed (13-3.7.6 & Section 6-3.)

Smoke Barrier Constructed From Outside Wall To Outsided Wall, Complete Through Concealed Spaces Such As Area Above Suspended Ceilings (Section 6-3)

½ –Hour Partition
Patient Rooms

Area A

Exit Access Corridor

Area B

Acceptable Arrangement (13-3.7.6)

Each Leaf ≥ 34 in. (86 cm)

Smoke Barrier
Area B

Service Core

Area A

150 ft (45 m)

eferred rrangement If orridor Width ermits

Each Leaf ≥ 34 in. (86 cm)

Area A

Area B

Patient Rooms

Exit Stair Or Other Approved Exit

≤ 150 ft (45 m)

Each Area Must Provide At Least 30 sq ft (2.8 sq m) (Net) For The Total Number Of Bed Patients (Hospitals & Nursing Homes), At Least 15 sq ft (1.4 sq m) (Net) For The Total Number Of Residents In Limited Care Facility, And At Least 6 sq ft (56 sq m) (Net) For The Total Number Other Occupants (13-3.7.4)

Figure 13-16.   Subdivision of Building Spaces in Existing Health Care Occupancies.

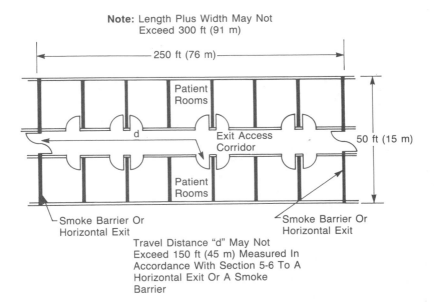

Note: Length Plus Width May Not Exceed 300 ft (91 m)

250 ft (76 m)

Patient Rooms

d

Exit Access Corridor

50 ft (15 m)

Patient Rooms

Smoke Barrier Or Horizontal Exit

Smoke Barrier Or Horizontal Exit

Travel Distance "d" May Not Exceed 150 ft (45 m) Measured In Accordance With Section 5-6 To A Horizontal Exit Or A Smoke Barrier

Figure 13-17.   Approximate Maximum Compartment Length Permitted by Exception No. 2 to 13-3.7.1.

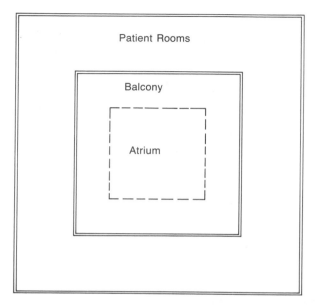

Figure 13-18a. Illustration of a Noncomplying Atrium Arrangement in an Existing Health Care Occupancy. (*See Figure 13-18b for corrected arrangement.*)

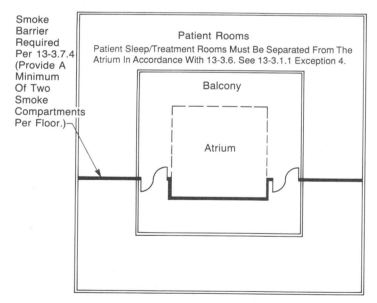

Figure 13-18b. Illustration of Complying Atrium Arrangement in Existing Health Care Occupancies. (*Also see Figures 13-18c and d.*)

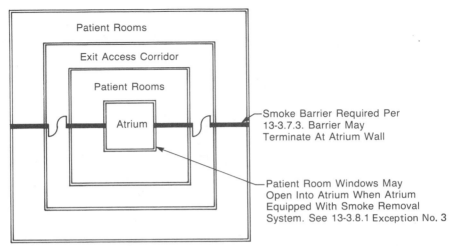

Figure 13-18c. Existing Health Care Occupancy with Complying Atrium Arrangement.

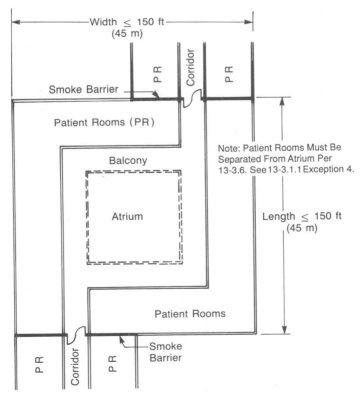

Figure 13-18d. Illustration of Complying Atrium Arrangement in Existing Health Care Occupancies. (*Also see Figures 13-18b and c.*)

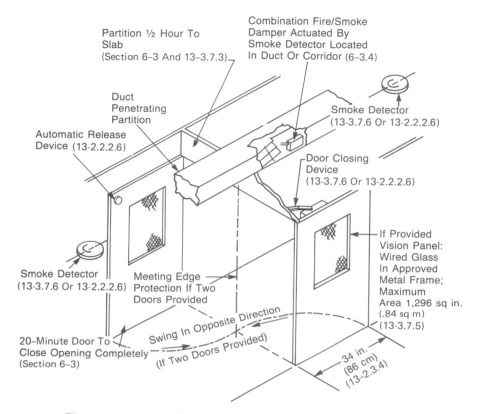

Figure 13-19.   Smoke Barrier for Existing Health Care Occupancy.

13-3.8 Special Features.

13-3.8.1   Every patient sleeping room shall have an outside window or outside door with light. The maximum allowable sill height shall not exceed 44 in. (112 cm) above the floor.

Exception No. 1:   The window sill in special nursing care areas such as those housing ICU, CCU, hemodialysis, and neo-natal patients may be up to 60 in. (152 cm) above the floor.

Exception No. 2:   Rooms intended for occupancy of less than 24 hours, such as those housing obstetrical labor beds, recovery beds, and observation beds in the emergency department; and newborn nurseries, need not comply with this requirement.

Exception No. 3:   Windows opening into atriums where the atrium has a smoke removal system are, for the purposes of this requirement, considered outside windows.

Although 13-3.8.1 requires each patient sleeping room to have an outside window or door with glazing, the window may have a fixed sash. Security glazing should be avoided. Glazing should be of a type that can be broken out should such action become necessary in a fire emergency.

Glazing should be limited to a type that, if broken out, will not develop sharp edges posing a threat to occupants outside the building at grade.

For a discussion of Exception No. 3 and atrium windows, refer to the commentary on 13-3.1 and to Figures 13-18a through d.

SECTION 13-4   SPECIAL PROVISIONS

13-4.1 Windowless Buildings.   See Section 30-7 for requirements for windowless buildings.

Windowless portions of health care facilities must comply with the requirements of Chapter 13 in addition to the criteria set forth for such structures in Section 30-7. Paragraph 13-4.1 does not obviate the requirements for patient room windows contained within 13-3.8.1.

13-4.2 High Rise Buildings.   (Reserved)

13-4.3 Operating Features.   *(See Chapter 31.)*

SECTION 13-5   BUILDING SERVICES

13-5.1 Utilities.   Utilities shall comply with the provisions of Section 7-1.

13-5.2 Heating, Ventilating, and Air Conditioning.

13-5.2.1   Heating, ventilating, and air conditioning shall comply with the provisions of Section 7-2 and shall be installed in accordance with the manufacturer's specifications.

Exception: As modified in 13-5.2.2 following.

13-5.2.2   Any heating device other than a central heating plant shall be so designed and installed that combustible material will not be ignited by it or its appurtenances. If fuel fired, such heating devices shall be chimney or vent connected, shall take air for combustion directly from the outside, and shall be so designed and installed to provide for complete separation of the combustion system from the atmosphere of the occupied area. Any heating device shall have safety features to immediately stop the flow of fuel and shut down the equipment in case of either excessive temperature or ignition failure.

Exception No. 1: Approved suspended unit heaters may be used in locations other than means of egress and patient sleeping areas, provided such heaters are located high enough to be out of the reach of persons using the area, and provided they are equipped with the safety features called for above.

Exception No. 2: Fireplaces may be installed and used only in areas other than patient sleeping areas, provided that these areas are separated from patient sleeping spaces by construction having a 1-hour fire resistance rating and they comply with NFPA 211, Standard for Chimneys, Fireplaces, Vents, and Solid Fuel Burning Appliances. In addition thereto, the fireplace shall be equipped with a fireplace enclosure guaranteed against breakage up to a temperature of 650°F (343°C) and constructed of heat tempered glass or other approved material. If, in the opinion of the authority having jurisdiction, special hazards are present, a lock on the enclosure and other safety precautions may be required.

Formal Interpretation 81-8
Reference: 12-5.2.2, 13-5.2.2

Question: Is it the intent of the Committee to permit free-standing wood burning stoves in health care facilities?

Answer: No.

Issue Edition: 1981
Reference: 12-5.2.2, 13-5.2.2
Date: January 1982

Paragraphs 13-5.2.1 and 13-5.2.2 specify safeguards for air conditioning, ventilating, heating, and other service equipment in order to minimize the possibility of such devices serving as a source of ignition. Fuel-fired heating devices, except central heating systems, must be designed to provide complete separation of the combustion system from the occupied spaces. Air for combustion must be taken directly from the outside.

A major concern of the *Code* is to prevent the ignition of clothing, bedclothes, furniture, and other furnishings by a heating device. Therefore, 31-4.7 prohibits portable heating devices in areas used by patients.

13-5.3 Elevators, Dumbwaiters, and Vertical Conveyors.   Elevators, dumbwaiters, and vertical conveyors shall comply with the provisions of Section 7-4.

Although not counted as required exits, elevators may constitute a valuable supplemental facility for evacuating patients from health care buildings. In some cases, movement of critically ill patients or patients in restraining devices may be realistically accomplished only by an elevator.

Elevators, however, have many inherent weaknesses that tend to limit reliability. Elevator access doors are designed with operating tolerances that permit smoke transfer into the shaft. Power failure during a fire could result in trapping persons on elevators that stop between floors. Elevators may, during their descent from upper floors, stop automatically at the floor where the fire is burning, allow the doors to open, and expose the occupants to the fire.

Many of these weaknesses can be minimized by providing emergency power, separating the elevator lobby from other building spaces by rated construction, designing detection and alarm equipment to prevent elevators from stopping at a floor exposed to a fire, providing an emergency smoke control system, and by pressurizing the elevator shaft and adjacent lobbies. (*See Section 7-3.*) This represents good fire protection judgment but is not the result of any requirements of this *Code*.

Through emergency planning and staff training, crowding of elevators (another potential problem) may be avoided. Emergency plans may make effective use of elevators by transferring patients through a horizontal exit, for example, to a separate fire area. Within the separate fire area, a staged evacuation program could be instituted, the elevators ultimately taking patients to the outside at ground level.

13-5.4   Rubbish Chutes, Incinerators, and Laundry Chutes.

13-5.4.1   Any existing linen and trash chute, including pneumatic rubbish and linen systems, that opens directly onto any corridor shall be sealed by fire-resistive construction to prevent further use or shall be provided with a fire door assembly suitable for a Class B location and having a fire protection rating of 1½ hours. All new chutes shall comply with Section 7-5.

13-5.4.2   Any rubbish chute or linen chute, including pneumatic rubbish and linen systems, shall be provided with automatic extinguishing protection installed in accordance with Section 7-7. (*See Section 7-5.*)

13-5.4.3   Any trash chute shall discharge into a trash collecting room used for no other purpose and protected in accordance with Section 6-4.

13-5.4.4   Existing flue-fed incinerators shall be sealed by fire-resistive construction to prevent further use.

SECTION 13-6   EXISTING AMBULATORY HEALTH CARE CENTERS

13-6.1 General Requirements.

13-6.1.1 Application.

13-6.1.1.1   Existing ambulatory health care centers shall comply with the provisions of both Chapter 27 and (this) Section 13-6, as may be more stringent.

13-6.1.1.2   This section establishes life safety requirements, in addition to those required in Chapter 27, for all ambulatory health care centers and outpatient surgical centers that meet the requirements of 13-1.3(d).

Ambulatory health care centers exhibit some of the occupancy characteristics of business occupancies and some of the characteristics of health care facilities. In developing Section 13-6, it was intended to prescribe a level of life safety from fire that would be greater than that typically specified for business occupancies, but less than that typically found in health care facilities. (*See commentary for 13-1.3.*)

Ambulatory health care centers are required to comply with the provisions of Chapter 27 pertaining to business occupancies, except as more restrictive provisions are established within Section 13-6.

13-6.1.1.3 Modification of Retroactive Provisions.   The requirements of this section may be modified if their application clearly would be impractical in the judgment of the authority having jurisdiction and if the resulting arrangement could be considered as presenting minimum hazard to the life safety of the occupants. The requirements may be modified by the authority having jurisdiction to allow alternative arrangements that will secure as nearly equivalent safety to life from fire as practical.

This section is to be applied retroactively. Due consideration has been given to the practical difficulties of making alterations in existing, functioning facilities. The specified provisions, viewed as a whole, establish minimum acceptable criteria for life safety that reasonably minimizes the likelihood of a life-threatening fire.

The requirements of Chapter 13 may be modified in instances of practical difficulty or where alternate, but equal, provisions are proposed. The modifications must provide an equivalent level of protection as would be achieved by compliance with the corresponding *Code* provisions.

In some cases, appreciable cost may be involved in bringing an existing occupancy into compliance with Section 13-1. Where this is true, it would be appropriate for the authority having jurisdiction to formulate a schedule, determined jointly with the owner of the facility, that allows suitable periods of time for correcting various deficiencies and that gives due consideration to the ability of the owner to secure the necessary funds. (*Also see 1-4.2, 1-4.4, Section 1-5, and 1-6.2.*)

13-6.1.2 Reserved.

13-6.1.3 Special Definitions.   (*See 13-1.3.*)

13-6.1.4 Classification of Occupancy.   (*See 13-1.3.*)

13-6.1.5 Reserved.

13-6.1.6 Minimum Construction Requirements.

13-6.1.6.1   For purposes of 13-6.1.6, stories shall be counted starting at the primary level of exit discharge and ending at the highest occupiable level. For the purposes of this section, the primary level of exit discharge of a building shall be that floor that is level with or above finished grade of this exterior wall line for 50 percent or more of its perimeter.

Allowable building construction types are determined as a function of the number of stories in a building. In determining the number of stories, the first story is considered to be the primary level of exit discharge. Only occupiable levels are counted in determining story height. For example, an unoccupied attic would not constitute a story.

Difficulties have been experienced in determining story height where a building is located on a sloping grade. Paragraph 13-6.1.6.1 notes that a story on a sloping site that is partially below grade should be counted as a story if the floor is level with or above grade for 50 percent or more of the perimeter of the building at the exterior wall. (*See Figure 13-20.*)

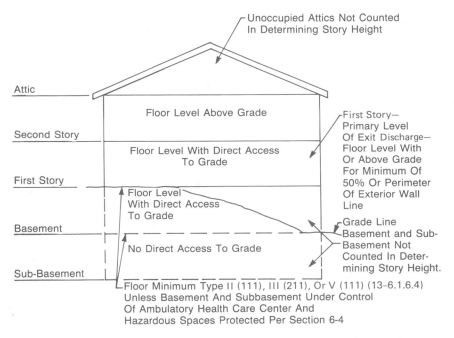

Figure 13-20.   Illustration of the Application of 13-6.1.6.1 and 13-6.1.6.4.

13-6.1.6.2   Buildings of one story in height housing ambulatory health care centers may be of Type I, II, III, IV, or V construction. (*See 6-2.1.*)

13-6.1.6.3   Buildings of two or more stories in height housing ambulatory health care centers may be of Type I (443), I (332), or II (222), Type II (111), Type III (211), Type IV (2HH), or Type V (111) construction. (*See 6-2.1.*)

Exception: Such buildings may be constructed of Type II (000), III (200), or V (000) if protected throughout by an approved automatic sprinkler system in accordance with Section 7-7.

Construction types permitted in ambulatory health care centers are summarized in Table 13-1. See NFPA 220, *Standard on Types of Building Construction.*[2]

Table 13-1.   Construction Types Permitted in Ambulatory
Health Care Occupancies

Construction Type	Stories	
	1	2 or more
I (443), I (332), II (222), II (111) (Fire Resistive and Protected Noncombustible)	X	X
II (000) (Unprotected Noncombustible)	X	X*
III (211) (Protected Ordinary)	X	X
III (200) (Unprotected Ordinary)	X	X*
IV (2HH) (Heavy Timber)	X	X
V (111) (Protected Wood Frame)	X	X
V (000) (Unprotected Wood Frame)	X	X*

X = Construction types allowed.
* = Automatic sprinkler protection required.

13-6.1.6.4   Any level below the level of exit discharge shall be separated from the level of exit discharge by at least Type II (111), Type III (211), or Type V (111) construction. (*See 6-2.1.*)

Exception: Such separation is not required for such levels if they are under the control of the ambulatory health care center and any hazardous spaces are protected in accordance with Section 6-4.

13-6.1.6.5   In existing buildings, the authority having jurisdiction may accept construction systems of lesser fire resistance than required above if it can be demonstrated to the authority's satisfaction that in case of fire prompt evacuation of the center can be made, or that the exposing occupancies and materials of construction present no threat of either fire penetration from such occupancy into the ambulatory health care center or collapse of the structure.

This paragraph allows the authority having jurisdiction to accept lesser construction types than those specified above, provided it can be demonstrated that the occupants of the ambulatory health care center are capable of evacuating the building promptly. If lesser construction types are to be accepted, potential exposures from adjacent occupancies or tenants must be provided with appropriate safeguards such as sprinklers, fire detectors, or fire-resistive separation. Structural stability must be maintained for the time required to evacuate the building, plus an additional period of time as a safety margin.

13-6.1.7 Occupant Load.

13-6.2 Means of Egress Requirements.

13-6.2.1 General. Every aisle, passageway, corridor, exit discharge, exit location, and access shall be in accordance with Chapter 5.

Exception: As modified in the following paragraphs.

Means of egress details are to conform to the fundamental provisions expressed in Chapter 5, except as modified in Chapter 27 and Chapter 13.

13-6.2.2 Means of Egress Components.

13-6.2.2.1 Components of means of egress shall be limited to the types described in 27-2.2.

13-6.2.2.2 Special locking arrangements complying with 5-2.1.6 are permitted on exterior doors.

Paragraph 5-2.1.6 establishes minimum requirements for delayed release hardware, including the requirement that the building must be protected throughout by an automatic sprinkler system or automatic fire detection system.

13-6.2.2.3 Any door in an exit passageway, horizontal exit, smoke barrier, stairway enclosure, or hazardous area enclosure may be held open only by an automatic release device that complies with 5-2.1.8. The required manual fire alarm system and the systems required by 5-2.1.8(c) shall be arranged so as to initiate the closing action of all such doors by zone or throughout the entire facility.

13-6.2.2.4 Where doors in a stair enclosure are held open by an automatic device as permitted in 13-6.2.2.3, initiation of a door closing action on any level shall cause all doors at all levels in the stair enclosure to close.

It is desirable to keep doors in exit enclosures, stair enclosures, horizontal exits, smoke barriers, and hazardous areas closed at all times to impede the spread of smoke and gases caused by a fire. However, some doors will be kept open, either for reasons of operating efficiency or comfort. Where doors in required fire or smoke barriers are to be held open, such doors must be equipped with automatic devices that are arranged to close the doors by the methods described within 13-6.2.2.3 and 5-2.1.8.

The automatic device must cause the doors to close upon operation of the manual fire alarm system. The doors must also be designed to close by actuation of a smoke detector located to detect smoke on either side of the door opening or by actuation of a complete automatic fire extinguishing or complete automatic fire detection system.

It is especially important in facilities providing health care to maintain floor-to-floor separation. Doors protecting openings in a stair enclosure may be held open by an automatic device only if arranged to close as specified above. Initiation of any action that causes a door to close at one level must cause all doors protecting openings within the stair enclosure to close and latch at all levels.

13-6.2.3 Capacity of Means of Egress.

13-6.2.3.1   The capacity of any required means of egress shall be determined in accordance with the provisions of 27-2.3 and shall be based on its width as defined in Section 5-3.

The capacity of the means of egress in ambulatory health care centers is determined on the basis of provisions in Chapter 27 dealing with business occupancies. Paragraph 27-2.3.1 refers to Section 5-3, which requires the capacity of level exit components to be computed on the basis of 0.2 in. (0.5 cm)/person, whereas stair capacity is computed using 0.3 in. (0.8 cm)/person. These capacities are much higher than would be allowed typically for a health care center and are considered permissible on the basis that the majority of occupants will be ambulatory.

13-6.2.3.2   The minimum width of any corridor or passageway required for exit access shall be 44 in. (112 cm) clear.

Corridor widths greater than 44 in. (112 cm) may be required within ambulatory health care centers. However, the minimum width for public corridors used as common exit access corridors or passageways is 44 in. (112 cm). The 44-in. (112-cm) width is stipulated on the assumption that most occupants will be ambulatory.

13-6.2.3.3   Doors in the means of egress from diagnostic or treatment areas, such as X-ray, surgical, or physical therapy shall be at least 34 in. (86 cm) wide.

In many instances, doors wider than 34 in. (86 cm) will be needed to efficiently operate. This paragraph intends to address doors used by the public or those doors that provide access to public hallways and corridors. The 34-in. (86-cm) minimum width is specified for doors on the assumption that most occupants will be ambulatory.

13-6.2.4 Number of Exits.

13-6.2.4.1   At least two exits of the types described in 27-2.2 remotely located from each other shall be provided for each floor or fire section of the building.

13-6.2.4.2   Any room and any suite of rooms of more than 1,000 sq ft (93 sq m) shall have at least two exit access doors remotely located from each other.

13-6.2.5 Arrangement of Means of Egress.   *(See 27-2.5.)*

13-6.2.6 Travel Distance to Exits.

13-6.2.6.1   Travel distance shall be measured in accordance with Section 5-6.

13-6.2.6.2 Travel distance:

(a) Between any room door required as exit access and an exit shall not exceed 100 ft (30 m); and

(b) Between any point in a room and an exit shall not exceed 150 ft (45 m).

Exception: The travel distance in (a) or (b) above may be increased by 50 ft (15 m) in buildings protected throughout by an approved automatic sprinkler system.

Travel distance is measured only to the closest exit, not to both exits required by 13-6.2.4.1. The requirements of 13-6.2.6.2 are illustrated in Figure 13-21.

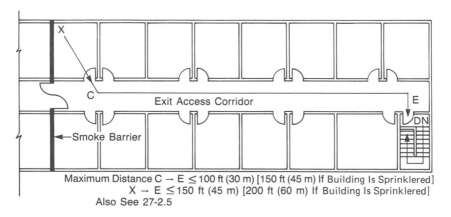

Maximum Distance C → E ≤ 100 ft (30 m) [150 ft (45 m) If Building Is Sprinklered]
X → E ≤ 150 ft (45 m) [200 ft (60 m) If Building Is Sprinklered]
Also See 27-2.5

Figure 13-21.   Travel Distance in an Existing Ambulatory Care Facility.

13-6.2.7 Discharge from Exits.   *(See 27-2.7.)*

13-6.2.8 Illumination of Means of Egress.   Means of egress shall be illuminated in accordance with Section 5-8.

13-6.2.9 Emergency Lighting and Essential Electrical Systems.

13-6.2.9.1   Emergency lighting shall be provided in accordance with Section 5-9.

13-6.2.9.2   Where general anesthesia or life support equipment is used, each ambulatory health care center shall be provided with an essential electrical system in accordance with NFPA 99, *Standard for Health Care Facilities.*

Exception: Where battery operated equipment is provided and acceptable to the authority having jurisdiction.

All ambulatory health care centers are required to be equipped with emergency lighting. If medical procedures requiring general anesthesia are practiced, or if life support equipment is required, ambulatory health care centers are required to be served by electrical systems meeting the criteria for essential electrical systems as detailed in Chapter 3, "Electrical

Systems," of NFPA 99, *Standard for Health Care Facilities.*[6]

A facility would not be required to have an emergency generator if the building is a free-standing unit and, as a normal practice, (1) management maintains admitting and discharge policies that preclude the provision of care for any patient or resident who may need to be sustained by electrical life-support equipment, such as respirators, suction apparatus, etc., and (2) no surgical treatment requiring general anesthesia is offered, and (3) battery-operated systems or equipment are provided that would maintain power to exit lights and illumination for exit corridors, stairways, medical preparation areas, and the like, for a minimum of 1½ hours. Additionally, battery power would be required to be supplied to all alarm systems.

13-6.2.10 Marking of Means of Egress.   Means of egress shall have signs in accordance with Section 5-10.

13-6.2.11 Special Features.

13-6.3 Protection.

13-6.3.1 Protection of Vertical Openings.   (*See 27-3.1.*)

13-6.3.2 Protection from Hazards.   (*See 27-3.2.*)

13-6.3.2.1   Laboratories employing quantities of flammable, combustible, or hazardous materials that are considered as severe hazard shall be protected in accordance with NFPA 99, *Standard for Health Care Facilities.*

Laboratories that contain "ordinary" combustibles and flammable liquids in sufficient quantity to threaten a 1-hour fire separation [e.g., wood equivalent fuel loads in the range of 5 to 10 lb/sq ft (25 to 50 kg/sq m)] are considered a severe hazard. Laboratories representing a severe hazard must be protected in accordance with NFPA 99, *Standard for Health Care Facilities.*[6] Protection would include 1-hour fire resistance separation and automatic sprinkler protection.

Where fuel loads of lesser amounts are involved and quantities of flammable liquids are limited, laboratories would simply be considered hazardous areas and would require either 1-hour separation or automatic sprinkler protection as indicated within 27-3.2 and Section 6-4.

13-6.3.2.2   Anesthetizing locations shall be protected in accordance with NFPA 99, *Standard for Health Care Facilities.*

13-6.3.3 Interior Finish.   (*See 27-3.3.*)

13-6.3.4 Detection, Alarm, and Communications Systems.

13-6.3.4.1 General.   Centers shall be provided with a fire alarm system in accordance with Section 7-6, except as modified below.

13-6.3.4.2 Initiation.   Initiation of the required fire alarm systems shall be by manual means in accordance with 7-6.2 and by means of any detection devices or detection systems required.

13-6.3.4.3 Occupant Notification.   Occupant notification shall be accomplished automatically, without delay, upon operation of any fire alarm activating device by means of an internal audible alarm in accordance with 7-6.3.

Exception: The presignal system allowed by 7-6.3.2 Exception No. 2 shall not be permitted.

13-6.3.4.4 Emergency Forces Notification.   Fire department notification shall be accomplished in accordance with 7-6.4.

13-6.3.4.5 Emergency Control.   Operation of any activating device in the required fire alarm system shall be arranged to automatically accomplish, without delay, any control functions required to be performed by that device. (*See 7-6.5.*)

Paragraphs 13-6.3.4.1 through 13-6.3.4.5 deal with required fire alarm equipment. Reliability is of prime importance; therefore, electrical supervision of the system and system components is specified by the standards referenced in Section 7-6. In the event of circuit fault, component failure, or other "trouble," a continuous "trouble indication" signal is required and should be provided at a constantly attended location.

A manual fire alarm system is required by 13-6.3.4.2. Manual pull stations should be located along the natural routes of egress and located so as to adequately cover all portions of the building. Manual pull stations should always be located so that anyone qualified to send an alarm may summon aid without having to leave the zone of his or her ordinary activities, or pass out of the sight and hearing of people immediately exposed to, or in direct view of, a fire. The operation of a manual fire alarm station should automatically summon attendants who can assist in removing physically helpless occupants.

The system required by 13-6.3.4.2 may be incorporated into an automatic system equipped to detect a fire and initiate an alarm.

Actuation of any required fire or smoke detector, activation of a required sprinkler system, or operation of a manual pull station must automatically, without delay, sound audible alarm devices within the building. Presignal systems are not permitted.

The alarm must automatically transmit to a point outside the facility. Where automatic transmission of alarms to the fire department legally committed to serve the facility is not permitted, arrangements are to be made for the prompt notification of the fire department or such other assistance as may be available in the case of fire or other emergency. Paragraph 7-6.4 lists various methods acceptable for automatically notifying the fire department. The fire department should still be notified manually to verify and confirm the automatic transmission of the alarm. In larger facilities, this may be the responsibility of the facility telephone operator; in smaller facilities, it may be the responsibility of the nursing staff.

Actuation of the fire alarm must cause audible alerting devices to sound throughout the affected zone or building as appropriate. Visible alerting devices may be used, but may not serve as a substitute for audible devices.

13-6.3.5 Extinguishment Requirements.   *(See 27-3.5.)*

13-6.3.5.1   Isolated hazardous areas may be protected in accordance with 7-7.1.2 if the additional requirements of this paragraph are met. An indicating shut-off valve shall be installed in an accessible location between the sprinklers and the connection to the domestic water supply. For new installations in existing buildings where more than two sprinklers are installed in a single area, water flow detection shall be provided to sound the building fire alarm, or notify by a signal any constantly attended location, such as PBX, security, or emergency room, whereby necessary corrective action shall be directed.

13-6.3.5.2   Portable fire extinguishers shall be provided in ambulatory health care occupancies in accordance with 7-7.4.1.

13-6.3.6 Corridors.

13-6.3.7 Subdivision of Building Space.

13-6.3.7.1   Ambulatory health care occupancies shall be separated from other tenants and occupancies by walls having at least a 1-hour fire resistance rating. Such walls shall extend from the floor slab below to the floor or roof slab above. Doors shall be constructed of at least 1¾-in. (4.4-cm) solid bonded wood core or the equivalent and equipped with positive latches. These doors shall be self-closing and normally kept in the closed position except when in use. Any vision panels shall be of fixed wired glass, set in steel or other approved metal frames, and limited in size to 1,296 sq in. (.84 sq m).

Ambulatory health care centers are frequently located within buildings used for a variety of purposes. Location within buildings containing hazardous occupancies should be avoided. Where ambulatory health care centers are located within buildings of mixed use, the ambulatory health care center must be separated from adjacent tenants and occupancies by minimum 1-hour fire-rated partitions. Doors protecting openings in such partitions must be a minimum of 1¾-in. (4.5-cm) thick solid bonded wood core, or of other equivalent construction that will resist fire for a minimum of 20 minutes. The doors must be equipped with positive latching hardware of a type that cannot be held in the retracted position. These doors must be self-closing and normally maintained in the closed position, or if the doors are to be held open, an automatic device must be used as indicated in 13-6.2.2.3.

Glazing within doors and partitions is limited to a maximum of 1,296 sq in. (0.84 sq m) of wired glass, set in approved metal frames. Each wired glass panel should be limited to a maximum dimension of 54 in. (137 cm). The glass should be labeled, should be ¼ in. (0.6 cm) thick, and be well embedded in putty with all exposed joints between the metal and the glass struck and pointed. (*See NFPA 80, Standard for Fire Doors and Windows.*[10]) A number of wired glass panels may be used in a single partition provided that each 1,296-sq in. (0.84-sq m) section is separated from adjacent panels by a metal mullion. The excessive use of wired glass panels should be avoided. It must be recognized that the use of wired glass panels in a partition reduces the effectiveness of the partition in that radiant energy transfer will readily occur through the glass panel.

Partitions separating ambulatory health care centers from other occupancies must extend from the floor to the floor or roof deck above, extending completely through concealed spaces above suspended ceilings, for example. The partition must form a continuous barrier. Openings around penetrations involving building services must be adequately protected to maintain the 1-hour separation. Special attention must be paid to penetrations involving air-handling ducts. In general, steel ducts will not require a fire damper. Penetrations involving nonmetallic ducts or aluminum ducts should be carefully evaluated. Fire dampers should be provided to protect duct penetrations where the projected fire exposure is judged sufficient to jeopardize the required separation because of the duct penetration. The possible movement of air from space to space under conditions of system operation and conditions of system shutdown should be evaluated for both conditions. If there is a significant potential for the transfer of smoke from an adjacent space to the ambulatory health care center or from the center to a corridor, fire dampers should be provided for duct penetrations, even though the *Code* does not specifically require such protection.

(*See Figure 13-22.*)

13-6.3.7.2 The ambulatory health care facility shall be divided into at least two smoke compartments.

Exception: Facilities of less than 2,000 sq ft (185 sq m) and protected by an approved automatic smoke detection system need not be divided.

13-6.3.7.3 Any required smoke barrier shall be constructed in accordance with Section 6-3 and shall have a fire resistance rating of at least 1 hour.

13-6.3.7.4 Vision panels in the smoke barrier shall be of fixed wired glass, set in steel or other approved metal frames, and shall be limited in size to 1,296 sq in. (.84 sq m).

13-6.3.7.5 Reserved.

13-6.3.7.6 Doors in smoke barriers shall be constructed of at least 1¾-in. (4.4-cm) solid bonded wood core or the equivalent and shall be self-closing. A vision panel is required.

13-6.3.7.7 Doors in smoke barriers shall normally be kept closed, or if held open, they shall be equipped with automatic devices that will release the doors upon activation of:

(a) The fire alarm system, and either

(b) A local smoke detector, or

(c) A complete automatic fire extinguishing system or complete automatic fire detection system.

The requirements of 13-6.3.7.1 through 13-6.3.7.7 for subdividing building spaces through smoke barriers are illustrated in Figures 13-22 and 13-23. Paragraph 13-2.2.5 discusses horizontal exits.

During a fire, the emergency evacuation of patients in an ambulatory health care facility could be an inefficient, time consuming process. Realistically, if nonambulatory patients must be moved, any number of occupants can be relocated only through horizontal travel. Smoke barriers and horizontal exits used to subdivide a building serve three purposes fundamental to the protection of inpatients in that they:

   1. Limit the spread of fire and fire-produced contaminants,

   2. Limit the number of occupants exposed to a single fire, and

   3. Provide for horizontal relocation of patients by creating an area of refuge on the same floor level.

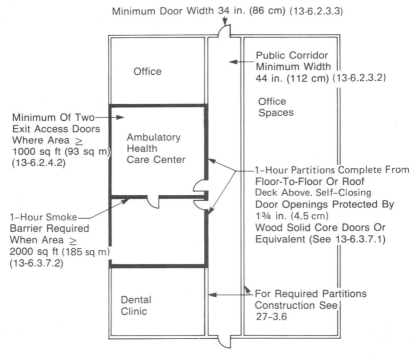

Figure 13-22.   Building Subdivision in Existing Ambulatory Health Care Center.

13-6.4 Special Provisions.   *(See Section 27-4.)*

13-6.5 Building Services.

13-6.5.1 Utilities.   Utilities shall comply with the provisions of Section 7-1.

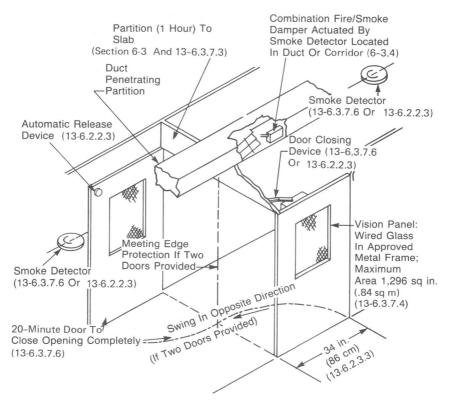

Figure 13-23. Smoke Barrier for Existing Ambulatory Health Care Occupancy Installed in Accordance with 13-6.3.7.

13-6.5.2 Heating, Ventilating, and Air Conditioning.

13-6.5.2.1 Heating, ventilating, and air conditioning shall comply with the provisions of Section 7-2 and shall be installed in accordance with the manufacturer's specifications.

Exception: As modified in 13-6.5.2.2 following.

13-6.5.2.2 Any heating device other than a central heating plant shall be so designed and installed that combustible material will not be ignited by it or its appurtenances. If fuel fired, such heating devices shall be chimney or vent connected, shall take air for combustion directly from the outside, and shall be so designed and installed to provide for complete separation of the combustion system from the atmosphere of the occupied area. Any heating device shall have safety features to immediately stop the flow of fuel and shut down the equipment in case of either excessive temperature or ignition failure.

Exception: Approved suspended unit heaters may be used in locations other than means of egress and patient treatment areas, provided such heaters are located high enough to be out of the reach of persons using the area and provided they are equipped with the safety features called for above.

Paragraphs 13-6.5.2.1 and 13-6.5.2.2 specify safeguards for air conditioning, ventilating, heating, and other service equipment in order to minimize the possibility of such devices serving as a source of ignition. Fuel-fired heating devices, except central heating systems, must be designed to provide complete separation of the combustion system from the occupied spaces. Air for combustion must be taken directly from the outside.

A major concern of the *Code* is to prevent the ignition of clothing, bedclothes, furniture, and other furnishings by a heating device. Therefore, 31-4.7 prohibits portable heating devices in areas used by patients.

13-6.5.3 Elevators, Dumbwaiters, and Vertical Conveyors. Elevators, dumbwaiters, and vertical conveyors shall comply with the provisions of Section 7-4.

13-6.5.4 Rubbish Chutes, Incinerators, and Laundry Chutes. Rubbish chutes, incinerators, and laundry chutes shall comply with the provisions of Section 7-5.

REFERENCES CITED IN COMMENTARY

[1]NFPA 101M, *Alternative Approaches to Life Safety*, National Fire Protection Association, Quincy, MA, 1988

[2]NFPA 220, *Standard on Types of Building Construction*, National Fire Protection Association, Quincy, MA, 1985.

[3]NFPA 241, *Standard for Safeguarding Building Construction and Demolition Operations*, National Fire Protection Association, Quincy, MA, 1986.

[4]NFPA 72E, *Standard on Automatic Fire Detectors*, National Fire Protection Association, Quincy, MA, 1987.

[5]NFPA 30, *Flammable and Combustible Liquids Code*, National Fire Protection Association, Quincy, MA, 1987.

[6]NFPA 99, *Standard for Health Care Facilities*, National Fire Protection Association, Quincy, MA, 1987.

[7]NFPA 96, *Standard for the Installation of Equipment for the Removal of Smoke and Grease-Laden Vapors from Commercial Cooking Equipment*, National Fire Protection Association, Quincy, MA, 1987.

[8]Bukowski, R.W. and Istvan, S.M., "A Survey of Field Experience with Smoke Detectors in Health Care Facilities," NBSIR 80-2130, October 1980, Center for Fire Research, National Bureau of Standards.

[9]NFPA 13, *Standard for the Installation of Sprinkler Systems*, National Fire Protection Association Quincy, MA 1987.

[10]NFPA 80, *Standard for Fire Doors and Windows*, National Fire Protection Association, Quincy, MA, 1986.

[11]NFPA 90A, *Standard for the Installation of Air Conditioning and Ventilating Systems*, National Fire Protection Association, Quincy, MA, 1985.

14

NEW DETENTION AND CORRECTIONAL OCCUPANCIES

(See also Chapter 31.)

SECTION 14-1 GENERAL REQUIREMENTS

The 1981 Edition of the *Life Safety Code* was the first edition to include separate chapters on detention and correctional occupancies. In previous editions, these occupancies were briefly addressed in the chapter on institutional occupancies, later renamed health care occupancies.

In 1974 the Committee on Safety to Life decided to establish a Sectional Committee on Penal Occupancies. It was, however, too late to prepare a report for the 1976 Edition of the *Code*, and in 1977 the Committee on Safety to Life was reorganized as a Technical Committee with subcommittees. The Subcommittee on Penal Occupancies was appointed, with its first working meeting taking place in January of 1978. It was soon renamed the Subcommittee on Detention and Correctional Occupancies. During this period, there were several major detention and correctional occupancy fires that underscored the need for the Subcommittee and provided information for its use. These fires included:

October 1974	Youth Correctional Center Cranston, RI	2 dead[1]
June 1975	Seminole County Jail Sanford, FL	11 dead[1]
November 1975	Lycoming County Jail Williamsport, PA	3 dead[1]
June 1976	Marion State Prison Marion, NC	9 dead[1]
June 1977	Maury County Jail Columbia, IN	42 dead[1]
June 1977	St. John City Detention Center St. John, NB, Canada	21 dead[1]
July 1977	Federal Correctional Institution Danbury, CT	5 dead[1]
December 1979	Lancaster County Jail Lancaster, SC	11 dead[2]

Another major multiple-death fire, which was reviewed during preparation of the 1985 Edition of the *Code*, occurred on November 8, 1982, in a jail in Biloxi, Mississippi, killing 29 people[3].

14-1.1 Application.

14-1.1.1 New detention and correctional facilities shall comply with the provisions of this chapter. They shall also comply with the applicable requirements of Chapter 31.

Provisions for existing detention and correctional occupancies are contained in Chapter 15.

Chapter 31, Operating Features, especially Section 31-5, sets day-to-day operating requirements, such as 24-hour staffing, ability of residents to notify staff of an emergency, preparation and maintenance of evacuation plans, staff training in the use of portable fire extinguishers, storage of combustible personal property, presence of heat-producing appliances, control of flammability of draperies and curtains, and visual and tactile identification of keys necessary for unlocking doors within the means of egress. Given that the locking of doors, which is necessary for the intended function of the facility, goes against the basic Code tenet that the means of egress system be under the control of building occupants, the presence of properly trained staff is paramount in the provision of a package of life safety equivalent to that provided in other occupancies. Chapter 31 requires the necessary staffing and training that, where combined with the *Code* requirements of Chapters 1 through 7 and 14, achieves the necessary level of life safety.

14-1.1.2 This chapter establishes life safety requirements for the design of all new detention and correctional facilities.

Exception No. 1: Use Condition I requirements are those stated in the applicable requirements of Chapters 16, 18, or 20.

See 14-1.4 for definition of Use Condition.

Exception No. 2*: Facilities determined to have equivalent safety provided in accordance with Section 1-5.

A-14-1.1.2 Exception No. 2 In determining equivalency for conversions, moderniza- tions, renovations, or unusual design concepts of detention and correctional facilities, the authority having jurisdiction may accept evaluations based on Chapter 4 of NFPA 101M, *Alternative Approaches to Life Safety*, utilizing the parameters for new construction.

The alternative approach is an equivalent system in which the user assigns numerical values to various building parameters. The individual values are totaled and compared with established values. The system provides a methodology by which alternative designs can be evaluated as options to literal *Code* compliance. The *Code* does not intend to limit acceptable equivalency evaluations solely to those based on this one system. The authority having jurisdiction retains the discretion, as expressed within Section 1-5, to evaluate and approve alternative designs on the basis of appropriate supporting data. NFPA 101M, *Alternative Approaches to Life Safety*,[4] Chapter 4, may be used to assist in this evaluation.

14-1.1.3   Detention and correctional occupancies are those used for purposes such as jails, detention centers, correctional institutions, reformatories, houses of correction, pre-release centers, and other residential-restrained care facilities where occupants are confined or housed under some degree of restraint or security.

14-1.1.4   Detention and correctional occupancies provide sleeping facilities for four or more residents and are occupied by persons who are generally prevented from taking self-preservation action because of security measures not under the occupants' control.

Residents of detention and correctional occupancies and patients in health care occupancies are judged to be incapable of self-preservation under a fire emergency. In the case of the health care occupancy patient, the incapability is due to physical or mental illness or infirmity. The detention and correctional occupancy resident, although most likely ambulatory or able-bodied, is incapable because of security measures imposed and not under the resident's control. In both cases, the occupants must await staff action before moving to either an exit or an area of refuge. Impediments to adequate egress are further compounded in detention and correctional occupancies by the resistance of staff to unlock doors leading to the outside. Thus, horizontal movement within the facility to an area of refuge may be the only means of egress system that the resident is allowed to use in a fire emergency, regardless of how many exit doors to the outside are installed. Because of this, the Total Concept described in 14-1.1.5 is important.

14-1.1.5 Total Concept.   All detention and correctional facilities shall be so designed, constructed, maintained, and operated as to minimize the possibility of a fire emergency.

Because the safety of all occupants in detention and correctional facilities cannot be adequately assured solely by a dependence on evacuation of the building, their protection from fire shall be provided by appropriate arrangement of facilities, adequate trained staff, and careful development of operating, security, and maintenance procedures composed of the following:

(a) Proper design, construction, and compartmentation,

(b) Provision for detection, alarm, and extinguishment,

(c) Fire prevention and planning, training, and drilling in programs for the isolation of fire and transfer of occupants to areas of refuge or evacuation of the building, or protection of the occupants in place,

(d) Provision of security to the degree necessary for the safety of the public and the occupants of the facility.

The Total Concept establishes a protect-in-place or defend-in-place strategy. That strategy mandates requirements aimed at minimizing the need for building evacuation by limiting the development and spread of a fire emergency to the room of fire origin since safety is not assured by relying on a means of egress system utilizing evacuation due to the fact that locks either cannot or will not be unlocked in a timely manner. The requirements (e.g., Section 31-5 Operating Features) first try to prevent ignition and, given that fires will occur, set out to detect the fire (e.g., detectors per 14-3.4.4). Other requirements aim to control how quickly the fire will develop (e.g., interior finish per 14-3.3) while still others attempt to confine the effects (e.g., compartmentation and protection of vertical openings). Extinguishment of the fire is facilitated via sprinkler, standpipe, and portable extinguisher requirements. Provisions are made for refuge areas in the promotion of horizontal exits and the requirement of smoke barriers. Lastly, heavy reliance is placed on staff reaction. All these requirements fit together so as to minimize the need for evacuation. This is the Total Concept.

14-1.1.6 Additions.   Additions shall be separated from any existing structure not conforming with the provisions within Chapter 15 by a fire barrier having at least a 2-hour fire resistance rating constructed to the standards of the addition. Doors in these partitions shall normally be kept closed.

Exception: Doors may be held open if they meet the requirements of the Exception to 5-2.1.8.

Buildings that *do* comply with the requirements for existing detention and correctional occupancies per Chapter 15 do not require separation from new additions.

Note that the positioning of doors in the separating fire barriers is not restricted to corridors only. Doors must be kept closed unless they meet the requirements for automatic closing in the Exception to 5-2.1.8.

Figure 14-1 illustrates the requirements of 14-1.1.6.

14-1.2* Mixed Occupancies.

A-14-1.2   Detention and correctional facilities are a complex of structures, each serving a definite and usually different purpose. For instance, in all probability there will be represented in many institutions an example of all, or almost all, the occupancy-type classifications found in this *Code*. Exits and other features shall be governed by the type of occupancy classification and the hazard of occupancy unless specific exceptions are made.

All buildings and structures are to be classified using this chapter and Section 4-1 as a guide, subject to the ruling of the authority having jurisdiction in case of question as to the proper classification of any individual building or structure.

Use Condition classification of the institution, as well as individual areas within the complex, are always to be considered by the authority having jurisdiction.

14-1.2.1   Egress provisions for areas of detention and correctional facilities that correspond to other occupancies shall meet the corresponding requirements of this *Code* for such occupancies. Where security operations necessitate the locking of required means of egress, necessary staff shall be provided for the supervised release of occupants during all times of use.

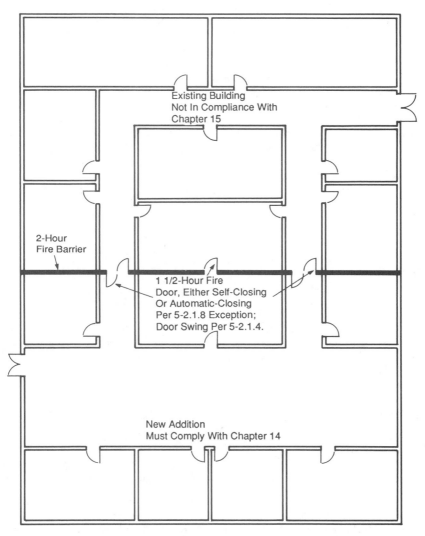

Figure 14-1. Separation of New Addition from Existing Building *Not* in Compliance with Chapter 15. (*See 14-1.1.6.*)

The requirements of Chapter 14 apply mainly to the residential portions, i.e., the sleeping and living areas, of the detention and correctional facility. For example, although the work areas might look much like a typical industrial occupancy, the requirements of Chapter 28, Industrial Occupancies, cannot be used alone because doors within the required means of egress will be locked for security. Without using the actual requirements of Chapter 14 to protect the locked industrial work areas, the concepts of Chapter 14 should be employed so as to assure that necessary trained staff with control over the locks is present to allow for immediate supervised release of occupants during all times of use should fire or similar emergency occur.

Similarly, some areas of a large facility may correspond to another occupancy classification. For example, a gymnasium would be considered an assembly occupancy (Chapter 8). If locked doors are required, prompt unlocking and release are critical.

Release of occupants may be accomplished by a remotely activated system capable of unlocking all doors in the means of egress or by a sufficient number of attendants who are continuously on duty in the immediate area of the exit doors, and who are provided with keys. Continuous supervision is essential.

14-1.2.2   Sections of detention and correctional facilities may be classified as other occupancies if they meet all of the following conditions:

(a) They are not intended to serve residents for purpose of housing, customary access, or means of egress.

(b) They are adequately separated from areas of detention or correctional occupancies by construction having a fire resistance rating of at least 2 hours.

> For example, administrative offices, maintenance areas, etc., that are not customarily used by the residents, are not part of the egress system from the residential areas, and are separated by 2-hour fire resistance rated construction, may be classified as another occupancy, such as business or industrial. In many cases, "trustees" may be employed in these areas. Their presence in these areas would not be considered a violation of item (a), provided they had freedom of egress as in a normal unlocked environment.

14-1.2.3   Detention and correctional occupancies in buildings housing other occupancies shall be completely separated from the other occupancies by construction having a fire resistance rating of at least 2 hours, as provided for additions in 14-1.1.6.

> Paragraph 14-1.2.3 requires that if a detention or correctional occupancy is located in a building of another classification (such as business or assembly), the detention or correctional occupancy must be separated from the other occupancy by construction having a fire resistance rating of 2 hours, as detailed in 14-1.1.6. The requirement addresses the common situation of a small detention lockup facility (at least 4 residents, per 14-1.1.4) located in a combination county courthouse/office/police building. Per 31-5.1.1, staffing of the detention area must be provided 24 hours per day. The remainder of the building, especially office areas, may not be occupied at night. A fire that originates and develops in an unoccupied area will not threaten the occupants of the detention facility as readily because of the 2-hour fire resistance rated barrier separating the different occupancies.
>
> Note that 14-1.2.3 deals with occupancy classification only, not with hazard of contents. Hazard of contents is addressed in 14-1.2.5.

14-1.2.4   All means of egress from detention and correctional occupancies that traverse other use areas shall, as a minimum, conform to requirements of this *Code* for detention and correctional occupancies.

Exception: It is permissible to exit through a horizontal exit into other contiguous occupancies that do not conform to detention and correctional occupancy egress provisions but that do comply with requirements set forth in the appropriate occupancy chapter of this Code, as long as the occupancy does not have high hazard contents. The horizontal exit shall comply with the requirements of 14-2.2.5.

The means of egress from detention and correctional occupancies that traverse nondetention and noncorrectional spaces must conform to the requirements for detention and correctional occupancies. However, if a 2-hour fire barrier between a detention or correctional occupancy and a business occupancy (offices) and its opening protectives (fire doors) qualify as a horizontal exit, then the means of egress system in the business occupancy need only conform to the appropriate requirements set forth in Chapter 26 for new — or Chapter 27 for existing — business occupancies.

14-1.2.5   Any area with a hazard of contents classified higher than that of the detention or correctional occupancy and located in the same building shall be protected, as required in 14-3.2.

This paragraph regulates those spaces in a detention and correctional occupancy that contain more hazardous materials (in quantity or type) than are usually found in this occupancy. Spaces, such as rooms used for the storage of highly combustible materials, trash collection rooms, and paint shops, must be protected in accordance with 14-3.2.

14-1.2.6   Non-detention or non-correctional related occupancies classified as containing high hazard contents shall not be permitted in buildings housing detention or correctional occupancies.

This paragraph prohibits another occupancy with highly hazardous contents (such as flammable liquids storage) from being located in a building housing detention and correctional occupancies. This paragraph is not meant to exclude the storage of linens in a detention and correctional occupancy. The intent is to prevent a portion of a detention and correctional facility from being converted to a warehouse and having a larger quantity or more hazardous type of combustibles than would be expected in a detention and correctional occupancy. This principally refers to residential areas. For example, industrial areas that are part of the overall detention and correctional facility, but located in a nonresidential-use building, may have flammable liquids as part of the industrial process.

14-1.3 Special Definitions.

(a) *Direct exit.*   A direct exit is an exit that serves only one area or level, and the direct exit has no openings to *other* areas or levels.

The term "direct exit" is defined here so that its particular meaning can be utilized in 14-3.7.1 Exception No. 2 dealing with subdivision of building spaces via smoke barriers.

(b) *Fire Barrier.* See Chapter 6.

(c) *Fire Compartment.* See Chapter 6.

(d) *Residential Housing Area.* Includes sleeping areas and any contiguous day room, group activity space, or other common spaces for customary access of residents.

(e) *Sallyport (Security Vestibule).* A compartment provided with two or more doors where the intended purpose is to prevent the continuous and unobstructed passage by allowing the release of only one door at a time.

See 14-2.5.4

(f) *Smoke Barrier.* See Chapter 6.

(g) *Smoke Compartment.* See Chapter 6.

14-1.4 Classification of Occupancy.

14-1.4.1*   Users and occupants of detention and correctional facilities at various times can be expected to include staff, visitors, and residents. The extent and nature of facility utilization by members of each of these groups will vary according to type of facility, its function, and programs. For applications of the life safety requirements that follow, the resident user category is divided into five groups:

Use Condition I — Free Egress

Free movement is allowed from sleeping areas, and other spaces where access or occupancy is permitted, to the exterior via means of egress meeting the requirements of the *Code.*

> In Use Condition I, there are no physical restrictions, such as locks, on the means of egress. The occupants are capable of self-preservation. An example might be a work release center where the doors are not locked. (*See Figure A-14-1.4.1.*) Because no locking of the means of egress system occurs, the occupant is as free to escape a fire emergency as an occupant of any other residential type of occupancy. It reasonably follows that Use Condition I detention and correctional occupancies are exempted from the Chapter 14 requirements by 14-1.4.3 and are charged with meeting the requirements of some other occupancy chapter, such as Chapter 16 for new hotels and dormitories. (*See 14-1.4.3.*)

Use Condition II — Zoned Egress

Free movement is allowed from sleeping areas and any other occupied smoke compartment to one or more other smoke compartments.

> The occupants have the freeeedom to move within the building, including the freedom to move from their rooms and across the smoke barrier. Doors to the outside are manually locked. (*See Figure A-14-1.4.1.*)

Use Condition III — Zoned Impeded Egress

Free movement is allowed within individual smoke compartments, such as within a residential unit comprised of individual sleeping rooms and group activity space, with egress impeded by remote control release of means of egress from such smoke compartment to another smoke compartment.

> The occupants are free to move out of their rooms but are locked within the smoke compartment.
> The locked smoke barrier door can be unlocked by a remote means. Doors to the outside are manually locked. (*See Figure A-14-1.4.1.*)

Use Condition IV — Impeded Egress

Free movement is restricted from an occupied space. Remote controlled release is provided to permit movement from all sleeping rooms, activity spaces, and other occupied areas within the smoke compartment to other smoke compartment(s).

> In Use Condition IV, occupants are locked in their cells. However, both the cell doors and the smoke barrier door can be unlocked by a remote means. Doors to the outside are manually locked. (*See Figure A-14.1.4.1.*)

Use Condition V — Contained

Free movement is restricted from an occupied space. Staff controlled manual release at each door is provided to permit movement from all sleeping rooms, activity spaces, and other occupied areas within the smoke compartment to other smoke compartment(s).

> All locks are manually locked and unlocked at the individual door. (*See Figure A-14-1.4.1.*) This places a heavy demand on staff to open the doors in an emergency. As might reasonably be expected, the most stringent requirements of Chapter 14 are called into play for Use Condition V facilities.

A-14-1.4.1   Free movement to (1) a public way, (2) a building separated from the fire area by 2-hour fire-resistive construction or 50 ft (15 m) of open space, or (3) an outside secure area having a holding space at least 50 ft (15 m) from the zone of fire origin that provides 15 sq ft (1.4 sq m) or more of refuge area per person (resident, staff, visitors, etc.) that may be present at time of fire, also fulfills the requirement of a smoke compartment.

Figure A-14-1.4.1 illustrates the five Use Conditions.

> As part of the definitions of Use Condition II through Use Condition V, reference is made to smoke compartments and the degree of locking (none, remote release, or manual operation) used for smoke barrier doors. A facility without a smoke barrier can still qualify as meeting one of those Use Conditions by allowing, in lieu of the smoke barrier, for movement to a place judged to be equivalent to another smoke compartment, such as (1) a public way, (2) a building separated from the space in question by either adequate fire resistance rated construction or

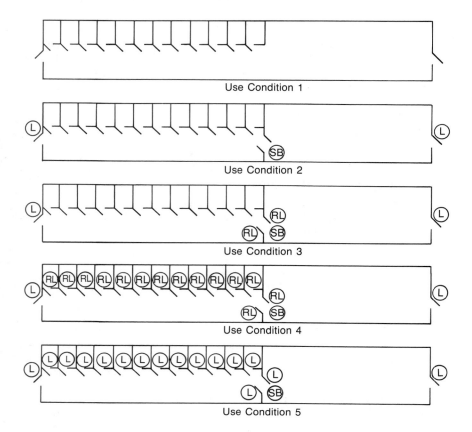

Use Condition 1

Use Condition 2

Use Condition 3

Use Condition 4

Use Condition 5

Detention and Correctional Use Conditions

Ⓛ Locked

⑧ⓁⓇ Locked—Remote Release or Equivalent

⑧ⓈⒷ Smoke Barrier or Horizontal Exit

Figure A-14-1.4.1

distance, or (3) an adequately sized outside holding area positioned a safe distance away. The locking operation of the door to this alternate place cannot be more severe than that allowed for the smoke barrier door of that particular Use Condition (i.e., no locking for Use Condition II, remote release for III and IV, and manual operation for V). (*Also see 14-3.7 and Figure 14-13.*)

Note that in Figure A-14-1.4.1 the "Locked" (L) designation means *manual* unlocking operation at the door.

14-1.4.2*   To classify as Use Condition III or IV, the arrangement, accessibility, and security of the release mechanism(s) used for emergency egress shall be such that the minimum available staff, at any time, can promptly release the locks.

A-14-1.4.2   Prompt operation is intended to be accomplished in the period of time between detection of fire by either the smoke detector(s) required by 14-3.4 or by other means (whichever comes first), and the advent of intolerable conditions forcing emergency evacuation. Fire tests have indicated that the time available is a function of the volume and height of the space involved and the rate of fire development. In traditional single-story corridor arrangements, the time between detection by smoke detectors and the advent of lethal conditions down to head height can be as short as approximately 3 minutes. In addition, it should be expected that approximately 1 minute will be required to evacuate all the occupants of a threatened smoke compartment once the locks are released. In this example, a prompt release time would be 2 minutes.

The major requirement noted in this section is that the area must be under continuous supervision and that a sufficient number of staff must be present and have the necessary keys readily available to release the locks.

14-1.4.3   Areas housing occupancies corresponding to Use Condition I — Free Egress shall conform to the requirements of residential occupancies under this *Code*.

Detention and correctional occupancies in which the occupants are not locked in at any time shall be classified as residential and shall meet the requirements of Chapters 16, 18, or 20 as appropriate. Those buildings that provide free egress, even though used as correctional occupancies, should not be classified as detention and correctional occupancies under this *Code*. Although such devices are not normally used, a facility with locking devices present on its doors should not be classified as Use Condition I because of the potential for future use of the locks. Rather, depending on the mode of operation (remote or manual), the corresponding Use Condition should be assigned, and the requirements of Chapter 14 followed. The facility could be classified as Use Condition I only if the locking devices were physically removed.

14-1.5 Classification of Hazard of Contents.   The classification of hazard of contents shall be as defined in Section 4-2.

14-1.6 Minimum Construction Requirements.

14-1.6.1   For the purpose of 14-1.6, stories shall be counted starting at the primary level of exit discharge. For the purposes of this section, the primary level of exit discharge of a building shall be that floor that is level with or above finished grade on the exterior wall line for 50 percent or more of its perimeter. Building levels below the primary level shall not be counted as a story in determining the height of the building.

See Figure 14-2 for method of counting stories.

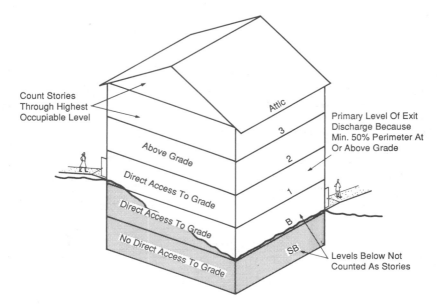

Figure 14-2. Method of Counting Stories, per 14-1.6.1, for Use in 14-1.6.3. If attic were determined to be occupiable, the figure would depict a 4-story building.

14-1.6.2 A residential housing area complying with 14-3.1.2 shall be considered as a one story building for purposes of applying 14-1.6.3.

The provisions of 14-3.1.2 address multilevel housing areas for which the vertical separation between the lowest floor level and the uppermost floor level does not exceed 13 ft (4.0 m), but the paragraph does not limit the number of levels. [*See Figure A-14-3.1.2(c).*] A multilevel housing area meeting all the requirements of 14-3.1.2 is treated as a single story in determining required building construction type per 14-1.6.3.

14-1.6.3 Detention and correctional occupancies shall be limited to the following types of building construction (*see 6-2.1*):

Table 14-1.6.3

Type of Construction	1 story with Basement	1 story without Basement	2 story	3 story	4 story and Higher
I (443) I (332) II (222)	X	X	X	X	X
II (111)	X††	X	X††	N.P.	N.P.
III (211) IV (2HH) V (111)	X††	X††	X††	N.P.	N.P.
II (000) III (200) V (000)	X†	X†	X†	N.P.	N.P.

X: Permitted types of construction

X†: Permitted if the entire building is protected throughout by an approved automatic sprinkler system in accordance with Section 7-7.

X††: X† applies in buildings where Use Condition V is used.

N.P.: Not Permitted

Recognizing that locked doors to the outside will either be reluctantly and slowly unlocked or not unlocked at all, the *Code* relies on the defend-in-place or protect-in-place strategy discussed in the commentary to 14-1.1.5. Paragraph 14-1.6.3 establishes minimum construction requirements to help assure the structural integrity of the building for the time necessary to either release residents to the outside or hold them in a safe area of refuge.

The table contained in 14-1.6.3 establishes minimum construction types for detention and correctional occupancies. Under some conditions, certain construction types are prohibited even if protected by automatic sprinklers. It should be noted that the automatic sprinkler requirements contained in this table are based on construction type. Automatic sprinkler protection may also be required by other sections of this *Code*.

See NFPA 220, *Standard on Types of Building Construction*,[5] for definitions of types of construction. (*Also see 6-2.1.*)

14-1.6.4 All interior walls and partitions in Type I or Type II construction shall be of noncombustible or limited-combustible construction.

Again, given the incapability for self-preservation of the detention and correctional facility residents due to imposed security, the integrity of building construction, under fire conditions, needs to be maintained. Thus, although NFPA 220 would not regulate the combustibility of interior walls and partitions, this *Code* provision gives credit for Type I or Type II construction, in *new* detention and correctional occupancies, only if such interior wall and partitions are of either noncombustible or limited-combustible construction.

Chapter 15, for existing detention and correctional occupancies, does not have a similar requirement.

14-1.7 Occupant Load. The occupant load for which means of egress shall be provided for any floor shall be the maximum number of persons intended to occupy that floor, but not less than one person for each 120 sq ft (11.1 sq m) gross floor area.

This paragraph establishes an occupant load factor from which an occupant load may be projected. The means of egress system must be sized to handle the *larger* of either the actual count of persons intended to occupy the space or the number of persons based on the calculation using the occupant load factor.

The *Code* intends that the occupant load factor be used only for sizing the means of egress, not for limiting the number of persons within a space. If the means of egress can handle an occupant load larger than the load calculated using the occupant load factor of 14-1.7, the *Code* would not prohibit such a load. Plumbing and sanitary codes and common sense will dictate maximum safe loading from a sociological and humanitarian standpoint in a facility with excess means of egress capacity.

SECTION 14-2 MEANS OF EGRESS REQUIREMENTS

14-2.1 General. Means of egress shall comply with Chapter 5.

Exception: As otherwise provided or modified in this section.

14-2.2 Means of Egress Components.

14-2.2.1 Components of means of egress shall be limited to the types described in 14-2.2.2 through 14-2.2.7.

14-2.2.2 Doors. Doors shall comply with 5-2.1.

Exception: As provided in 14-2.11.

14-2.2.3 Stairs.

14-2.2.3.1 Stairs shall comply with 5-2.2.

Exception: The provisions of 5-2.2.6.5(f) and 5-2.2.6.6(c) do not apply.

These two paragraphs in Chapter 5 require intermediate rails on handrails and guardrails so that a 6-in. (15.2-cm) diameter sphere will not pass through the rails. Since only adults or older juveniles use these facilities and these intermediate railings may interfere with visual observation, they are not required.

14-2.2.3.2 Spiral stairs complying with 5-2.2.2.7 are permitted for access to and between staff locations.

Paragraph 14-2.2.3.2 permits spiral stairs conforming to 5-2.2.2.7 for staff use only. Note that Chapter 5 restricts the use of spiral stairs to areas having an occupant load of five or fewer persons. Spiral stairs are not permitted for access by the residents.

14-2.2.4 Smokeproof Enclosures.   Smokeproof enclosures shall comply with 5-2.3.

14-2.2.5 Horizontal Exits.   Horizontal exits shall comply with 5-2.4, modified as follows:

(a) At least 6 sq ft (.56 sq m) of accessible space per occupant shall be provided on each side of the horizontal exit for the total number of people in adjoining compartments.

> Section 5-2.4 requires at least 3 sq ft (0.28 sq m) per occupant of accumulation space on each side of the horizontal exit. This section requires 6 sq ft (0.56 sq m) per occupant due to several factors, including personalities of the residents, their expected duration in the refuge area, and the fact that horizontal exits may comprise 100 percent of required exits.

(b) Horizontal exits may comprise 100 percent of the exits required provided that an exit, other than a horizontal exit, is accessible in some other (not necessarily adjacent) fire compartment without requiring return through the compartment of fire origin.

> This permits horizontal exits to comprise 100 percent of the exits from any fire compartment as long as the compartment is not left "dead-ended" so as to require travel through the compartment of fire origin in order to reach a door to the outside.
>
> In Figure 14-3, all compartments but F satisfy the above rule. Fire compartment F would require a door to the outside so as to preclude having to travel through compartment E, which could be the area of fire origin, to get to the outside of the building.

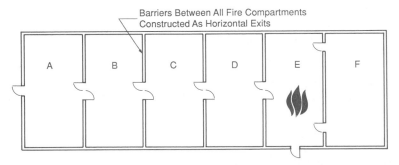

Figure 14-3.   Horizontal Exits Correctly Comprise 100 Percent of Total Exits from Fire Compartments B, C, and D.   Compartment F would require the addition of an exit door directly to the outside so as not to require travel through fire compartment E to get to the outside of the building. Compartments A and E are *Code*-complying with one horizontal exit and one exit door directly to the exterior of the building.

Because of practical difficulties involving vertical exit travel to the outside in detention and correctional occupancies, special recognition is given to horizontal travel and the use of horizontal exits. One hundred percent of the total required exit capacity for a given fire area may be provided by horizontal exits as explained above. In the event a horizontal exit also serves as a smoke barrier, see 14-2.4 and 14-3.7.

14-2.2.6 Ramps.   Ramps shall comply with 5-2.5.

14-2.2.7 Exit Passageways.   Exit passageways shall comply with 5-2.6.

14-2.3 Capacity of Means of Egress.

14-2.3.1   The capacity of any required means of egress shall be in accordance with Section 5-3.

14-2.3.2   Aisles, corridors, and ramps required for access or exit shall be at least 4 ft (122 cm) in width.

14-2.3.3   For residents' sleeping room door widths, see 14-2.11.3.

14-2.4 Number of Exits.   *(See also Section 5-4.)*

14-2.4.1   At least two exits of the types permitted in 14-2.2, remotely located from each other, shall be provided for each occupied story of the building.

14-2.4.2   At least two exits of the types permitted in 14-2.2, remotely located from each other, shall be accessible from each fire or smoke compartment.

14-2.4.3*   At least one approved exit shall be accessible from each fire compartment and each required smoke compartment into which residents may be moved in a fire emergency with the exits so arranged that egress shall not require return through the zone of fire origin.

A-14-2.4.3   An exit is not necessary for each individual fire compartment or smoke compartment if there is access to an exit through other fire compartments or smoke compartments without passing through the fire compartment or smoke compartment of origin.

See commentary following 14-2.2.5(b) and Figure 14-3.

14-2.5 Arrangement of Means of Egress.   *(See also Section 5-5.)*

14-2.5.1   Every sleeping room shall have a door leading directly to an exit access corridor.

Exception No. 1: If there is an exit door opening directly to the outside from the room at the ground level.

Exception No. 2: One adjacent room, such as a dayroom, group activity space, or other common spaces may intervene. Where individual occupant sleeping rooms adjoin a dayroom or group activity space that is utilized for access to an exitway, such sleeping rooms may open directly to the dayroom or space and may be separated in elevation by a one-half or full-story height (see 14-3.1.2).

Figure 14-4 illustrates the requirements of Exception No. 2.

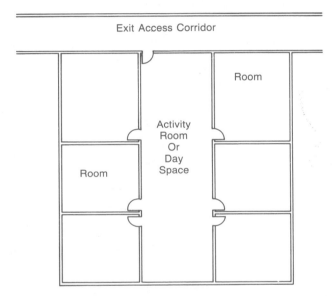

Figure 14-4.   One Adjacent Room May Intervene Between Sleeping Room and Exit Access Corridor.   Sleeping rooms may be separated in elevation by ½ to 1 story. (*See 14-2.5.1 Exception No. 2.*)

14-2.5.2   No exit or exit access shall contain a corridor, hallway, or aisle having a pocket or dead end exceeding 50 ft (15 m) for Use Conditions II, III, or IV and 20 ft (6.1 m) for Use Condition V.

Figure 14-5 illustrates the requirements of 14-2.5.2.

14-2.5.3   No common path of travel shall exceed 50 ft (15 m).

Exception: A common path of travel may be permitted for the first 100 ft (30 m) in a building protected throughout by an approved automatic sprinkler system in accordance with Section 7-7.

The limitation on common path of travel for detention and correctional occupancies is new to the 1988 Edition of the *Code*. In view of the

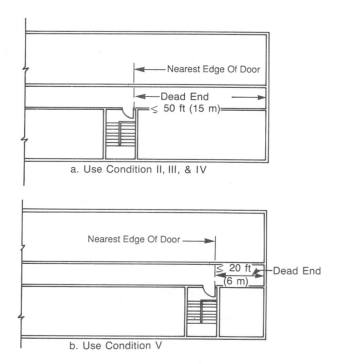

Figure 14-5. Dead-End Corridor Requirements. (*See 14-2.5.2.*)

popularity of multilevel residential housing areas (*see 14-3.1.2*) in which the individual levels do not constitute floors, the common path of travel limitation will dictate where a second exit access from any given level is necessary. (*See Figure 14-6.*)

14-2.5.4   A sallyport may be permitted in a means of egress where there are provisions for continuous and unobstructed passage through the sallyport during an emergency exit condition.

A sallyport or security vestibule, under normal day-to-day and nonfire emergency conditions, is designed to maintain the door at one end of the vestibule securely locked at any time the door at the other end is open. A door is opened; a person or persons enter the vestibule; the door through which they entered is closed and locked; the door at the opposite end is unlocked and opened; the people leave the vestibule. The sallyport is thus a security device that keeps a continuous flow of people from "storming" the exits. Under fire conditions, it would severely restrict the exit flow of occupants and not allow hose lines to be run through the openings. Thus,

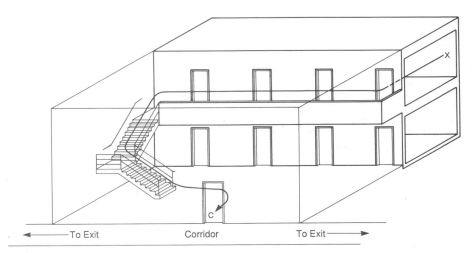

Figure 14-6.   Common Path of Travel Limitation.   If distance x to c exceeds 50 ft (15 m) [100 ft (30 m) if building is sprinklered], second exit access required for upper level. If multilevel housing area is large, common path of travel limitation could require a remote, second exit access door to corridor.

if a sallyport is to receive credit as part of the required means of egress, 14-2.5.4 requires that the door controls be overridden so as to allow continuous and unobstructed passage.

Figure 14-7 illustrates the requirements of 14-2.5.4.

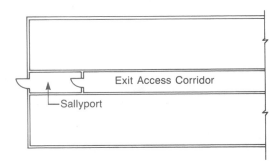

Figure 14-7.   Requirements for Sallyport or Security Vestibule. If sallyport is part of required means of egress, both doors of sallyport must be capable of being opened at the same time to provide unobstructed egress. (*See 14-2.5.4.*)

14-2.6 Travel Distance to Exits.

14-2.6.1 Travel distance:

(a) Between any room door required as exit access and an exit shall not exceed 100 ft (30 m);

(b) Between any point in a room and an exit shall not exceed 150 ft (45 m); and

(c) Between any point in a sleeping room to the door of that room shall not exceed 50 ft (15 m).

Exception No. 1: The travel distance in (a) or (b) above may be increased by 50 ft (15 m) in buildings protected throughout by an approved automatic sprinkler system or smoke control system.

Exception No. 2: The travel distance in (c) above may be increased to 100 ft (30 m) in open dormitories where the enclosing walls of the dormitory space are at least of smoketight construction. Where travel distance to the exit access door from any point within the dormitory exceeds 50 ft (15 m), at least two exit access doors remotely located from each other shall be provided.

Travel distance is measured to the closest exit, not to both exits required by 14-2.4. Figure 14-8 illustrates the requirements of 14-2.6.1.

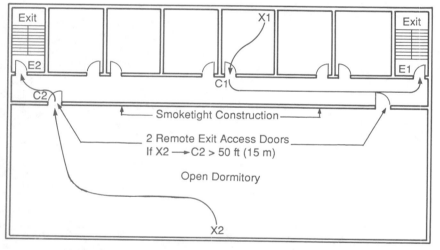

X1 → C1	≤ 50 ft (15m)
X2 → C2	≤ 100 ft (30 m)
C1 → E1 ⎫ C2 → E2 ⎭	≤ 100 ft (30 m) [150 ft (45 m) If Sprinklered Or Equipped With Smoke Control]
X1 → E1	≤ 150 ft (45 m) [200 ft (60 m) If Sprinklered Or Equipped With Smoke Control]
X2 → E2	≤ 200 ft (60 m) [250 ft (76 m) If Sprinklered Or Equipped With Smoke Control]

Figure 14-8. Maximum Travel Distance to Exits in New Detention and Correctional Occupancies. (*See 14-2.6.1.*) The travel distance is measured along the natural path of travel. (*See 5-6.2.*) "Sprinklered" means that the entire building is protected by a complete approved automatic extinguishing system. "Smoke Control" means that the entire building or fire area is equipped with a system to control the movement of smoke in accordance with Section 7-3.

14-2.7 Discharge from Exits.

14-2.7.1   Exits may discharge into a fenced or walled courtyard, provided that not more than two walls of the courtyard are the building walls from which exit is being made. Enclosed yards or courts shall be of sufficient size to accommodate all occupants at a minimum distance of 50 ft (15 m) from the building with a net area of 15 sq ft (1.4 sq m) per person.

Figures 14-9a and b illustrate 14-2.7.1.

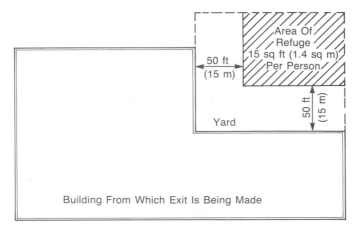

Figure 14-9a.   Exit Discharge into a Fenced Yard. (*See 14-2.7.1.*)

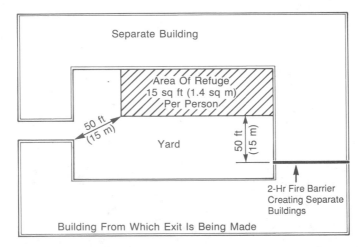

Figure 14-9b.   Exit Discharge into an Enclosed Yard. (*See 14-2.7.1.*)

14-2.7.2   All exits may discharge through the level of exit discharge. The requirements of 5-7.2 may be waived provided that not more than 50 percent of the exits discharge into a single fire compartment.

The provisions of 5-7.2 establish criteria under which up to 50 percent of the required exits, either in number or capacity, may discharge back through the level of exit discharge with the other 50 percent required to discharge directly outside. Because of the security concerns and the belief that doors to the exterior will not be readily unlocked in detention and correctional occupancies, 14-2.7.2 allows 100 percent of the exits to discharge through the level of exit discharge. In order to do this, 14-2.7.2 requires that a fire separation be provided on the level of exit discharge, which creates at least two fire compartments. Not more than one-half of the exits (in number and capacity) may discharge into any one fire compartment. This paragraph intends that the fire separation have at minimum a one-hour fire resistance rating.

14-2.8 Illumination of Means of Egress.   Illumination shall be in accordance with Section 5-8.

14-2.9 Emergency Lighting.   Emergency lighting shall be in accordance with Section 5-9.

14-2.10 Marking of Means of Egress.   Exit marking shall be provided in areas accessible to the public in accordance with Section 5-10.

Exception: Exit signs may be omitted in sleeping room areas.

The exemption of exit signs in sleeping areas of detention and correctional occupancies recognizes that the persons occupying such areas are familiar with that portion of the facility and, given that doors are unlocked, know where the exits are. Other portions of the facility may not be as familiar to residents and visitors and thus must have proper exit marking per the base requirement of 14-2.10.

14-2.11 Special Features.

14-2.11.1   Doors within means of egress shall be as required in Chapter 5.

Exception: As provided in 14-2.11.2 through 14-2.11.10.

14-2.11.2   Doors may be locked in accordance with the applicable Use Condition.

This provision overrides the basic Chapter 5 requirement that all doors within the required means of egress be unlocked from the side from which egress is to be made. It recognizes that, in order to function as intended, a detention and correctional occupancy relies on various means of locking. Rather than allowing any and all doors to be locked, 14-2.11.2 allows only the means of locking recognized by the Use Condition. Thus, a Use Condition II facility, which has a more lenient package of life safety requirements than a Use Condition V facility, cannot have sleeping rooms individually key locked. A Use Condition V facility, on the other hand, because it must comply with a more stringent set of requirements than a Use Condition II facility, can have individual doors manually key locked.

14-2.11.3* Doors to resident sleeping rooms shall be at least 28 in. (71 cm) in clear width.

A-14-2.11.3 It may be necessary to provide a certain number of resident sleeping rooms with doors providing a minimum clear width of 32 in. (81 cm) (*see 5-2.1.2.1*) in order to comply with the requirements for the physically handicapped. Such sleeping rooms should be located where there is a direct accessible access to the exterior or to an area of safe refuge (*see 14-3.7*).

14-2.11.4 Doors in a means of egress may be of the horizontal sliding type, provided the force to slide the door to its fully open position does not exceed 50 lb (222 N) with a perpendicular force against the door of 50 lb (222 N).

Paragraph 5-2.1.4.1 requires that all doors in a means of egress be side-hinged and swinging. This paragraph allows the use of sliding doors if they meet the specified requirements.

14-2.11.5 Doors from areas of refuge to the exterior may be locked with key lock in lieu of locking methods described in 14-2.11.6. The keys to unlock such doors shall be maintained and available at the facility at all times, and the locks shall be operable from the outside.

This paragraph requires that the keys be maintained and available. "Available" means readily accessible to staff for use at any time to evacuate occupants. The important points are that (1) the keys required to evacuate occupants are accessible at all times, (2) the staff is trained in the location and use of keys, and (3) staff has authorization and standing orders to unlock doors from areas of refuge to the exterior immediately under fire emergency conditions to prevent hesitation to unlock doors pending authorization from higher authorities within the facility's administration.

14-2.11.6* Any remote release used in a means of egress shall be provided with reliable means of operation, remote from the resident living areas, to release locks on all doors.

Exception: Provisions for remote locking and unlocking of occupied rooms in Use Condition IV may be waived provided not more than ten locks are necessary to be unlocked in order to move all occupants from one smoke compartment to an area of refuge as promptly as required for remote unlocking. The opening of all necessary locks shall be accomplished with no more than two separate keys. (See 14-3.7.6 for smoke barrier doors.)

A-14-2.11.6   A remote position is generally a control point where a number of doors can be unlocked simultaneously, either mechanically or electrically. In areas where there are a number of sleeping rooms, it is not practical for attendants to unlock doors individually. Doors in an exit should be unlocked prior to unlocking sleeping room doors.

This section of the *Code* does not intend to prohibit Use Condition V facilities, nor does it intend to limit Use Condition V facilities to 10 manually released locks.

"Remote" means outside the area where the occupants are restrained. It is not necessary to have the remote unlocking mechanism in a separate fire area, although this may be beneficial. Doors in the exit should be unlocked prior to unlocking sleeping room doors to prevent jamming of the exit door due to the pressure of several persons pushing on the door.

The Exception to 14-2.11.6 is to be used in conjunction with the Use Condition definitions in 14-1.4.1, primarily Use Conditions III and IV. Where remote locking is called for by the Use Condition, it must be provided, except as addressed by the Exception. The Exception permits the manual unlocking of up to ten locks to remove occupants to an area of refuge and still allow the facility to qualify as providing remote release. In other words, the manual locks do not force a Use Condition V classification. This may involve more than ten doors if multiple doors are secured with a single locking mechanism, or fewer than ten doors if a door is secured with more than one lock. Figures 14-10a and b illustrate two typical arrangements for the ten-lock Exception.

It must be recognized that the speed with which the doors can be unlocked and the occupants removed to a safe location is critical. If the ten locks cannot be rapidly released by manual unlocking due to staffing restrictions or for any other reasons, then remote unlocking must be used. If doors are equipped with locking devices, it is assumed that the locks will be used, and they must be counted in the total number of locks.

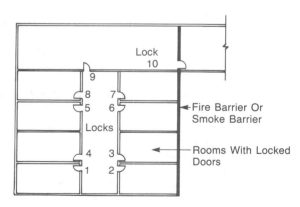

Figure 14-10a.   Maximum of Ten Manually Unlocked Doors with Each Door Equipped with a Single Key-Operated Lock.   (*See 14-2.11.6 Exception.*)

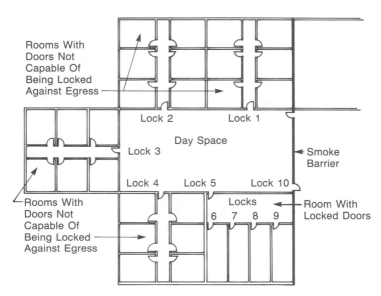

Figure 14-10b.   Maximum of Ten Manually Unlocked Locks with Areas Served by More Than One Door, Secured with a Single Manually Unlocked Door.   (*See 14-2.11.6 Exception.*)

14-2.11.7   All remote release operated doors shall be provided with a redundant means of operation as follows:

(a) Power-operated sliding doors or power-operated locks shall be so constructed that in the event of power failure, a manual mechanical means to release and open the doors is provided at each door, and either emergency power in accordance with 5-9.2.3 is provided for the power operation, or a remote manual mechanical release is provided.

(b) Mechanically operated sliding doors or mechanically operated locks shall be provided with a manual mechanical means at each door to release and open the door.

14-2.11.8   Doors remotely unlocked under emergency conditions shall not automatically relock when closed unless specific action is taken at the remote location to enable doors to relock.

> Paragraph 14-2.11.8 requires that, once doors are unlocked remotely under emergency conditions, they cannot automatically relock should they reclose unless specific action is taken to lock them. This specific action can be taken at the individual door or at the remote location.

14-2.11.9   Standby emergency power shall be provided for all electrically power-operated sliding doors and power-operated locks. Power shall be arranged to automatically operate within ten seconds upon failure of normal power and to maintain the necessary power source for at least 1½ hours.

Exception: This provision is not applicable for facilities with ten locks or less complying with the exception in 14-2.11.6.

14-2.11.10   The provisions of 5-2.1.5.2 for stairway reentry do not apply.

SECTION 14-3   PROTECTION

14-3.1 Protection of Vertical Openings.

This subsection specifies the protection required to maintain floor-to-floor separation, which helps to prevent vertical movement of the products of combustion through the building.

14-3.1.1   Any stairway, ramp, elevator, hoistway, light or ventilation shaft, chute or other vertical opening between stories shall be enclosed in accordance with Section 6-2.

Exception No. 1:   Stairs that do not connect a corridor, do not connect more than two levels, and do not serve as a means of egress need not comply with these regulations.

The convenience stair addressed by Exception No. 1 is illustrated in Figures 14-11a and b.

Exception No. 2:   Multilevel residential housing areas in accordance with 14-3.1.2.

Exception No. 3:   In residential housing areas protected throughout by an approved automatic sprinkler system, unprotected vertical openings are permitted in accordance with the conditions of 6-2.4.4, provided that the height between the lowest and highest finished floor levels does not exceed 23 ft (7.0 m). The number of levels is not restricted.

The provisions of 6-2.4.4, had they not been modified by Exception No. 3, would have limited the vertical opening to communication among a maximum of three floor levels. Given the typical multilevel housing areas, utilizing staggered partial levels as depicted in Figure 14-12, the three-floor restriction was replaced with a 23-ft (7-m) height between the lowest and highest finished floor levels so as to allow greater flexibility of use for detention and correctional occupancies. Additionally, the Exception can be used only in facilities where the residential housing areas are protected throughout by automatic sprinklers.

Exception No. 4:   Atriums in accordance with 6-2.4.5 are permitted.

14-3.1.2   Multilevel residential housing areas are permitted without enclosure protection between levels, provided all the following conditions are met:

(a)* The entire normally occupied area, including all communicating floor levels, is sufficiently open and unobstructed so that it may be assumed that a fire or other dangerous condition in any part will be readily obvious to the occupants or supervisory personnel in the area.

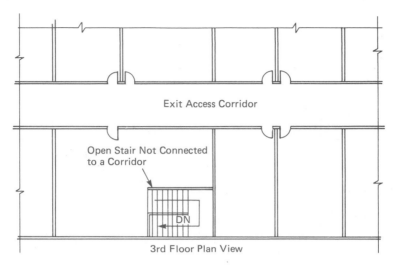

Figure 14-11a.   Plan View of Convenience Stair Allowed by 14-3.1.1 Exception No. 1.

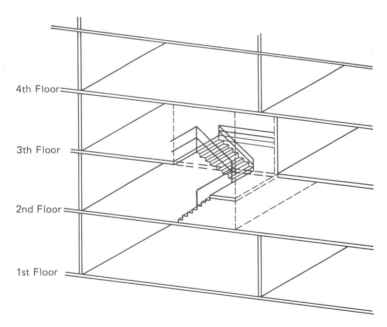

Figure 14-11b.   Open Convenience Stair as Allowed by 14-3.1.1 Exception No. 1.

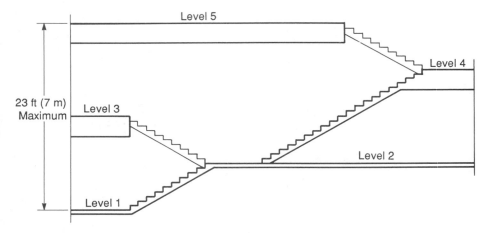

Figure 14-12.   Unprotected Vertical Openings in Sprinklered Housing Area Allowed by 14-3.1.1 Exception No. 3.

(b) Exit capacity is sufficient to provide simultaneously for all the occupants of all communicating levels and areas, with all communicating levels in the same fire area being considered as a single floor area for purposes of determination of required exit capacity.

(c)* The height between the highest and lowest finished floor levels does not exceed 13 ft (4.0 m). The number of levels is not restricted.

A-14-3.1.2(a)   It is not the intent of this requirement to restrict room face separations, which restrict visibility from the common space into individual sleeping rooms.

A-14-3.1.2(c)   The maximum vertical separation between the lowest floor level and the uppermost floor level is restricted to 13 ft (4.0 m). Figure A-14-3.1.2(c) illustrates how the height is to be determined.

> Whereas 14-3.1.1 Exception No. 3 allowed multilevel housing areas with maximum 23-ft (7-m) height between lowest and highest finished floor levels if the housing areas were fully sprinklered, 14-3.1.2 allows similar multilevel housing areas without requiring sprinklering but limits height to 13 ft (4 m).

14-3.2 Protection from Hazards.

14-3.2.1*   An area used for general storage, boiler or furnace rooms, fuel storage, janitor's closets, maintenance shops including woodworking and painting areas, laundries, and kitchens shall be separated from other parts of the building with construction having not less than a 1-hour fire resistance rating, and all openings shall be protected with self-closing fire doors, or such area shall be provided with automatic sprinkler protection. Where the hazard is severe, both the 1-hour fire resistance rated separation and automatic sprinklers shall be provided. The automatic extinguishing may be in accordance with 7-7.1.2.

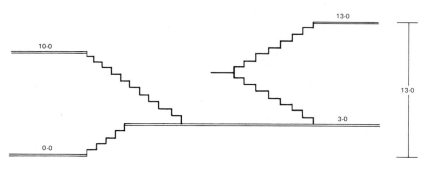

Figure A-14-3.1.2(c)

Exception No. 1: Where cooking facilities are protected per 7-2.3, kitchens need not be provided with room-wide protection.

Exception No. 2: When, in the opinion of the authority having jurisdiction, such areas are no longer incidental to residents' housing, they shall be separated by 2-hour fire barriers in conjunction with automatic sprinkler protection.

Hazardous areas are spaces with contents that, because of their basic nature (as in the case of flammable liquids) or because of the quantity of combustible materials involved, represent a significantly higher hazard than would otherwise be typical of detention and correctional occupancies.

Hazardous areas must be separated from other areas by 1-hour fire resistance rated construction complete with approved fire doors protecting door openings, or the areas may be protected by automatic sprinklers. In those instances where the hazard is judged to be severe by the authority having jurisdiction, both the fire resistance rated separation and automatic sprinkler protection are required. Where automatic sprinkler protection is provided and the hazard is not severe, the hazardous area may be separated by nonrated barriers designed to resist the passage of smoke.

Where flammable liquids are handled or stored, NFPA 30, *Flammable and Combustible Liquids Code,*[6] should be consulted to establish the minimum criteria necessary to mitigate this hazard.

A-14-3.2.1   Furnishings are usually the first items ignited in the detention and correctional environment. The type, quantity, and arrangement of furniture and other combustibles are important factors in determining how fast the fire will develop. Furnishings including upholstered items and wood items, such as wardrobes, desks, and bookshelves may provide sufficient fuel to result in room flashover. (Flashover refers to full fire involvement of all combustibles within a room once sufficient heat has been built up within the room.)

Combustible loading in any room opening onto a residential housing area should be limited to reduce the potential for room flashover. Rooms in which fuel loads are not controlled, thereby creating a potential for flashover, should be considered hazardous areas. If the separation option of 14-3.2.1 is selected, doors to such rooms, including sleeping rooms, should be self-closing.

The appendix note warns the *Code* user that even typical housing area furnishings can provide the combustible loading that will allow for fire room flashover to occur. The potential for flashover should be considered in particular for the nonsprinklered multilevel housing areas allowed by 14-3.1.2. Flashover on a lower level could rapidly deteriorate the tenability of conditions on upper levels, as the products of combustion bank down from the ceiling of the housing area, overcoming residents of the upper levels before they can make use of the means of egress system. Thus, consideration of flashover potential may lead to classification of a housing area as a hazardous area. Either sprinklering or separation, per the options of 14-3.2.1, would then be required.

14-3.2.2* Padded cells are severe hazard areas.   Doors to padded cells shall be ¾-hour self-closing and self-latching fire door assemblies.

A-14-3.2.2   It is strongly recommended that padded cells not be used due to their fire record. However, recognizing that they will be used in some cases, provisions for the protection of padded cells are provided. It is recognized that the ¾-hour fire door will be violated with the "plant on" of the padding, but a ¾-hour fire door should be the base of the assembly.

Padded cells are considered severe hazard areas due to high heat release, the speed of combustion, and the quantity of smoke produced by the padding materials. Due to this high hazard potential, padded cells must be protected by automatic sprinklers and separated by 1-hour construction. Many of the recent multiple-death fires in detention and correctional occupancies have started in padded cells.

14-3.2.3   Cooking facilities shall be protected in accordance with 7-2.3.

14-3.3 Interior Finish.

14-3.3.1   Interior wall and ceiling finish in corridors, exits, and any space not separated from corridors and exits by a partition capable of retarding the passage of smoke shall be Class A. In all other areas, interior wall and ceiling finish shall be Class A, B, or C in accordance with Section 6-5.

Paragraph 14-3.3.1 requires only that the separating partition be capable of retarding the passage of smoke. The partition must be of substantial construction, but is not required to have a fire resistance rating. (*See Chapter 6 for definition of smoke barrier.*)

14-3.3.2   Interior floor finish material in corridors and exits shall be Class I in accordance with Section 6-5.

14-3.4 Detection, Alarm, and Communications Systems.

14-3.4.1 General.

14-3.4.1.1   Detention and correctional occupancies shall be provided with a fire alarm system in accordance with Section 7-6, except as modified below.

14-3.4.1.2   All required fire alarm systems shall be electrically supervised.

14-3.4.1.3   All fire alarm systems and detection systems required in this section shall be provided with a secondary power supply, and the installation shall be in accordance with NFPA 72A, *Standard for the Installation, Maintenance, and Use of Local Protective Signaling Systems for Guard's Tour, Fire Alarm, and Supervisory Service.*

14-3.4.2 Initiation.   Initiation of the required fire alarm system shall be by manual means, in accordance with 7-6.2, and by means of any detection devices or detection systems required.

Exception No. 1:   Manual fire alarm boxes may be locked provided that staff is present within the subject area when occupied and have keys readily available to unlock the boxes.

Exception No. 2:   Manual fire alarm boxes may be located in a staff location, provided that the staff location is manned when the building is occupied and has direct supervision of the sleeping area.

14-3.4.3 Notification.

14-3.4.3.1 Occupant Notification.   Occupant notification shall be accomplished automatically, without delay, upon operation of any fire alarm initiating device in accordance with 7-6.3. Presignal systems are prohibited.

Exception*:   Any smoke detectors required by this chapter may be arranged to alarm at a constantly attended location only and are not required to accomplish general alarm indication.

A-14-3.4.3.1 Exception   The staff at the constantly attended location should have the capability to promptly initiate the general alarm function and contact the fire department or have direct communication with a control room or other location that can initiate the general alarm function and contact the fire department.

Presignal systems are prohibited by 14-3.4.3.1 since this paragraph requires that notification be provided "without delay." However, the Exception does exempt smoke detectors from sounding a general alarm.

14-3.4.3.2 Emergency Forces Notification.   Fire department notification shall be accomplished in accordance with 7-6.4.

Exception: Any smoke detectors required by this chapter are not required to transmit an alarm to the fire department.

Where the fire department is not equipped to receive such alarms or direct transmission to the fire department is not permitted, arrangements are to be made for the prompt notification of the fire department. The next best option is notification by an approved central station alarm system. Paragraph 7-6.4 provides several options for notifying the fire department automatically. Where smoke detectors are provided, they are not required to sound the fire alarm or to transmit a signal to the fire department, but are required to sound an alarm at a constantly attended location, unless specifically noted otherwise.

14-3.4.4 Detection. An approved automatic smoke detection system shall be installed, in accordance with Section 7-6, throughout all resident housing areas.

Exception No. 1: Smoke detectors may be omitted from sleeping rooms with four or fewer occupants in Use Condition II or III.

Exception No. 2: In buildings protected throughout by an approved automatic sprinkler system installed in accordance with Section 7-7, smoke detectors may be omitted from all but corridors, common spaces, and sleeping rooms with more than four occupants.

Exception No. 3: Other arrangements and positioning of smoke detectors may be used to prevent damage or tampering, or for other purposes, provided the function of detecting any fire is fulfilled and the siting of detectors is such that the speed of detection will be equivalent to that provided by the spacing and arrangements described in Section 7-6. This may include the location of detectors in exhaust ducts from cells, behind grilles, or in other locations. The equivalent performance of the design, however, must be acceptable to the authority having jurisdiction in accordance with the equivalency concepts specified in Section 1-5 of this Code.

14-3.5 Extinguishment Requirements.

14-3.5.1* High rise buildings shall comply with the automatic sprinkler requirements of 30-8.2.

A-14-3.5.1 For purposes of providing control valves and water flow devices, multilevel residential housing areas complying with 14-3.1.2 are considered to be a single floor.

Paragraph 14-3.5.1 recognizes and mandatorily implements the portion of the new Section 30-8 high rise building provisions applicable to sprinklering, namely 30-8.2. Those provisions require that a sprinkler control valve and water flow device be provided for each floor. Appendix note 14-3.5.1 clarifies that the levels of a multilevel housing area complying with 14-3.1.2 do not constitute multiple floors and thus are not required to be provided with individual control valves and water flow devices on each level.

14-3.5.2 Where required by 14-1.6, facilities shall be protected throughout by an approved supervised automatic sprinkler system in accordance with Section 7-7.

14-3.5.3 Where this *Code* permits exceptions for fully sprinklered detention and correctional occupancies, the sprinkler system shall be:

(a) In complete accordance with Section 7-7,

(b) Electrically connected to the fire alarm system, and

(c) Fully supervised.

Paragraphs 14-3.5.2 and 14-3.5.3 indicate that, where automatic sprinklers are installed to comply with the *Code*, the system shall be a complete approved automatic sprinkler system installed in accordance with NFPA 13, *Standard for the Installation of Sprinkler Systems.*[7] The use of manually operated sprinklers is not recognized by the *Code*. Informal surveys conducted by the Committee have indicated no significant problems in installing automatic sprinklers in detention and correctional facilities. The system must also be supervised in order to be credited as complying with the *Code*.

14-3.5.4 Portable fire extinguishers shall be provided in accordance with 7-7.4.1.

Exception No. 1*: Access to portable fire extinguishers may be locked.

Exception No. 2: Portable fire extinguishers may be located at staff locations only.

A-14-3.5.4 Exception No. 1 Where access to portable fire extinguishers is locked, staff should be present on a 24-hour basis and have keys readily available to unlock access to the extinguishers. Where supervision of sleeping areas is from a 24-hour manned staff location, portable fire extinguishers may be provided at the staff location in lieu of other areas.

Exception No. 1 to 14-3.5.4 permits locking of the fire extinguishers. Time is of the essence in using extinguishers; therefore, keys must be carried by the staff or be readily accessible.

14-3.5.5 Standpipe and hose systems shall be provided in accordance with 7-7.4.2 as follows:

(a) Class I standpipe systems shall be provided for any building over two stories in height, and

(b) Class III standpipe and hose systems shall be provided for all unsprinklered buildings over two stories in height.

Exception No. 1: One-inch (2.5-cm) diameter formed hose on hose reels may be used to provide Class II service.

Exception No. 2: Separate Class I and Class II systems may be used in lieu of Class III.

The standpipe requirements intend that 2½-inch (6.2-cm) hose connections be available for fire department use in any detention and correctional occupancy more than two stories in height. Additionally, if such buildings are unsprinklered, there should also be 1½-inch (3.8-cm) connections and hose for occupant (i.e., staff and resident) use.

Exception No. 1 permits the use of 1-in. (2.5-cm) formed rubber hose in place of fabric-jacket rubber-lined hose normally required in standpipe systems. The rubber hose is normally stored on reels and is somewhat easier to use.

14-3.6 Corridors. [*See 14-3.8, Special Features (Subdivision of Resident Housing Spaces).*]

14-3.7 Subdivision of Building Spaces.

14-3.7.1 Smoke barriers shall be provided, regardless of building construction type, so as to divide every story used by residents for sleeping or any other story having an occupant load of 50 or more persons, into at least two compartments.

Exception No. 1: Protection may be accomplished with horizontal exits (see 5-2.4).

Exception No. 2*:   Spaces having direct exit to (a) a public way, (b) a building separated from the resident housing area by a two-hour fire resistance rating or 50 ft (15 m) of open space, or (c) a secured open area having a holding space 50 ft (15 m) from the housing area that provides 15 sq ft (1.4 sq m) or more of refuge area per person (resident, staff, visitors) that may be present at the time of the fire fulfills the requirements for subdivision of such spaces, provided the locking arrangement of doors involved meets the requirements for doors at the compartment barrier for the use condition involved.

A-14-3.7.1 Exception No. 2   A door to the outside, by itself, does not meet the intent of the exception if emergency operating procedures do not provide for the door to be unlocked when needed. In cases where use of the door is not assured, a true smoke barrier per the base requirement of 14-3.7.1 would be needed.

14-3.7.2   Where smoke barriers are required by 14-3.7.1, smoke barriers shall be provided so as:

(a) to limit the housing to a maximum of 200 residents in any smoke compartment, and

(b) to limit the travel distance to a door in a smoke barrier:

    1. From any room door required as exit access to 100 ft (30 m),

    2. From any point in a room to 150 ft (45 m).

Exception to (b):   The travel distance may be increased by 50 ft (15 m) in buildings protected throughout by an approved automatic sprinkler system or smoke control system.

Smoke barriers and horizontal exits used to subdivide a building serve three purposes fundamental to the protection of occupants in that they:
    1. Limit the spread of fire and fire-produced contaminants,
    2. Limit the number of occupants exposed to a single fire, and
    3. Provide for horizontal relocation of occupants by creating an area of refuge on the same floor.

The requirements of 14-3.7.1 and 14-3.7.2 for subdividing building spaces are illustrated in Figure 14-13.

Figure 14-14 illustrates the requirements of Exception No. 2 to 14-3.7.1.

14-3.7.3*   Any required smoke barrier shall be constructed in accordance with Section 6-3. Barriers shall be of substantial construction and shall have structural fire resistance. Fixed wire glass or minimum 45-minute fire rated glazing vision panels shall be permitted in such barriers, provided they do not individually exceed 1,296 sq in. (.84 sq m) in area and are mounted in approved steel frames. There is no restriction on the total number of such vision panels in any barrier (e.g., a smoke barrier may consist of wire glass or minimum 45-minute fire rated glazing panels mounted in a security grille arrangement).

A-14-3.7.3   Structural fire resistance is defined as the ability of the assembly to stay in place and maintain structural integrity without consideration of heat transmission. Twelve gage steel plate suitably framed and stiffened meets this requirement.

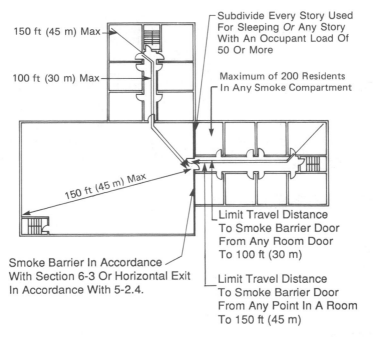

150 ft (45 m) Max

100 ft (30 m) Max

Subdivide Every Story Used For Sleeping *Or* Any Story With An Occupant Load Of 50 Or More

Maximum of 200 Residents In Any Smoke Compartment

150 ft (45 m) Max

Limit Travel Distance To Smoke Barrier Door From Any Room Door To 100 ft (30 m)

Smoke Barrier In Accordance With Section 6-3 Or Horizontal Exit In Accordance With 5-2.4.

Limit Travel Distance To Smoke Barrier Door From Any Point In A Room To 150 ft (45 m)

Figure 14-13.   Subdivision of Building Spaces in New Detention and Correctional Occupancies.

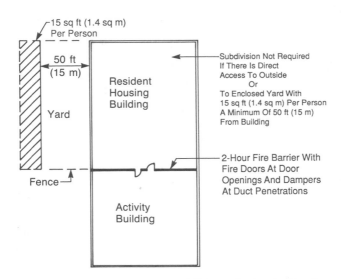

15 sq ft (1.4 sq m) Per Person

50 ft (15 m)

Yard

Resident Housing Building

Fence

Activity Building

Subdivision Not Required If There Is Direct Access To Outside Or To Enclosed Yard With 15 sq ft (1.4 sq m) Per Person A Minimum Of 50 ft (15 m) From Building

2-Hour Fire Barrier With Fire Doors At Door Openings And Dampers At Duct Penetrations

Figure 14-14.   Alternatives to Subdivision by Smoke Barriers.

Paragraph 14-3.7.3 requires smoke barriers to have structural fire resistance. However, the specific fire resistance in hours is omitted. The intent is to eliminate the use of highly combustible or flimsy materials, such as plastic sheeting, which could possibly limit smoke movement but which have little structural integrity. This paragraph does permit the entire smoke barrier to be constructed of wired glass panels not exceeding 1,296 sq in. (0.84 sq m) each in steel frame.

14-3.7.4   At least 6 net sq ft (.56 sq m) per occupant shall be provided on each side of the smoke barrier for the total number of occupants in adjoining compartments. This space shall be readily available whenever the occupants are moved across the smoke barrier in a fire emergency.

14-3.7.5   Doors in smoke barriers shall be self-closing or automatic-closing as required in 5-2.1.8 and shall provide resistance to the passage of smoke. Swinging doors shall be self-latching.

14-3.7.6   Doors in smoke barriers shall conform with the requirements for doors in means of egress as specified in Section 14-2 and shall have locking and release arrangements according to the Use Condition. The provisions of the Exception to 14-2.11.6 shall not be used for smoke barrier doors serving a smoke compartment containing more than 20 persons.

The provisions of the Exception to 14-2.11.6 allow up to ten locks to be arranged so as to require manual unlocking in a timely fashion and still be considered as providing remote unlocking. However, 14-3.7.6 does not allow for the locks on smoke barrier doors to be part of the maximum ten manually unlocked locks where the smoke compartment houses more than 20 persons.

14-3.7.7   Vision panels of approved transparent wire glass or minimum 45-minute fire rated glazing, in steel frames, and not exceeding 1,296 sq in. (.84 sq m) in area shall be provided in each door in a smoke barrier.

14-3.7.8   Smoke dampers shall be provided in accordance with 6-3.4.

Exception: Other arrangements and positioning of smoke detectors may be used to prevent damage or tampering or may be used for other purposes, provided the function of detecting any fire is fulfilled, and the siting of detectors is such that the speed of detection will be equivalent to that provided by the required spacing and arrangement.

14-3.8 Special Features.   (Subdivision of Resident Housing Spaces.)

14-3.8.1*   Subdivision of facility spaces shall comply with Table 14-3.8.1.

A-14-3.8.1   Requirements in Table 14-3.8.1 for smoketight and fire rated separations include the necessary precautions to restrict the spread of smoke through the air handling system. This, however, does not mean that smoke dampers must be provided for each opening. Smoke dampers would be one acceptable method; however, other techniques such as allowing the fans to continue to run with 100 percent supply and 100 percent exhaust would be acceptable.

Table 14-3.8.1

USE CONDITION	II		III		IV		V	
Feature	NS	AS	NS	AS	NS	AS	NS	AS
Room to Room Separation	NR	NR	NR	NR	ST	NR	FR(½)	ST
Room Face to Corridor Separation	ST	NR	ST	NR	ST	NR	FR	ST
Room Face to Common Space Separation	NR	NR	NR <50 ft* (15 m) / ST >50 ft* (15 m)	NR <50 ft* (15 m) / ST >50 ft* (15 m)	ST	NR <50 ft* (15 m) / ST >50 ft* (15 m)	FR	ST
Common Space to Corridor Separation	FR	NR	FR	NR	FR	NR	FR	ST
Total Openings in Solid Room Face	120 sq in. (.08 sq m)		120 sq in. (.08 sq m)		120 sq in. (.08 sq m)		120 sq in. (.08 sq m) Closable from inside or 120 sq in. (.08 sq m) w/smoke control	

AS — Protected by automatic sprinklers
NS — Not protected by automatic sprinklers
NR — No requirement

ST — Smoketight
FR — Fire Rated — 1 hour
FR(½) — Fire Rated — ½ hour

*This is the travel distance through the common space to the exit access corridor.

NOTE 1: Doors in openings in partitions required to be fire resistive by this chart in other than required enclosures of exits or hazardous areas shall be substantial doors, of construction that will resist fire for at least 20 minutes. Wire glass or minimum 45-minute fire rated glazing vision panels are permitted. Latches and door closers are not required on cell doors.

NOTE 2: Doors in openings in partitions required to be smoketight by the chart shall be substantial doors, of construction that will resist the passage of smoke. Latches and door closers are not required on cell doors.

NOTE 3: "Total Openings in Solid Room Face" includes all openings (undercuts, food passes, grilles, etc.), the total of which will not exceed 120 sq in. (.08 sq m). All openings shall be 36 in. (91 cm) or less above the floor.

NOTE 4: Under Use Condition II, III, or IV, a space housing not more than 16 persons and subdivided by open construction (any combination of grating doors and grating walls or solid walls) may be considered one room. The perimeter walls of such space shall be of smoketight construction. Smoke detection shall be provided in such space. Under Use Condition IV, common walls between sleeping areas within the space shall be smoketight and grating doors and fronts may be used.

Paragraph 14-3.8.1 provides for the separation of areas where residents are housed. This separation serves two basic needs: (1) it keeps the fire and its products confined to the area of origin, and (2) it protects those outside the area of origin. Table 14-3.8.1 establishes different requirements based on the Use Condition involved. Within each Use Condition, different provisions are required depending upon whether automatic sprinkler protection is or is not provided. Where a common wall is used for different purposes, such as "room face to corridor" and "common space to corridor," the most restrictive requirement shall apply to the entire wall. Table 14-3.8.1, with the notes and asterisked items, in addition to the locking options previously mentioned, provides a wide variety of options. Note 4 to the Table also provides an additional method that, in combination with the locking options previously stated, can be quite useful.

Formal Interpretation 81-18
Reference: Table 14-3.8.1

Question: Is it the intent of Table 14-3.8.1 that a room sidewall that faces a corridor in the arrangement shown by wall segment "Room-Corr" of the accompanying figure have the same separation requirements with respect to fire resistance rating or smoketightness as the adjacent common space to corridor separation wall (segment "Comm-Corr" on sketch)?

Answer: Yes. For example, in unsprinklered Use Condition III, both wall segments should be 1-hour fire resistance rated construction.

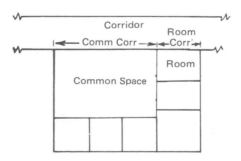

Issue Edition: 1981
Reference: Table 14-3.8.1
Date: March 1982

Formal Interpretation 81-41
Reference: 14-3.8.1, Note 4,
              15-3.8.1, Note 4

Question: Is it the intent of the Committee that Note 4 to Table 14-3.8.1 (15-3.8.1) restrict the number of occupants in an open, undivided dormitory to a maximum of 16 persons?

Answer: No.

Issue Edition: 1981
Reference: 14-3.8.1, Note 4
             15-3.8.1, Note 4
Date: April 1984

SECTION 14-4   SPECIAL PROVISIONS

14-4.1 Windowless Areas.

14-4.1.1* For the purposes of this chapter, a windowless area is a smoke compartment that does not contain operable windows or fixed windows that can be readily broken by impact.

A-14-4.1.1 Windows that are intended to be breakable should be capable of being broken with materials readily available to the facility staff.

14-4.1.2 Windowless areas shall be provided with vent openings, smoke shafts, or an engineered smoke control system to provide ventilation (mechanical or natural).

Paragraph 14-4.1.2 does not require venting or smoke control for those areas (smoke compartments) that are provided with operable windows or fixed windows that can be broken by impact.

14-4.2 Underground Buildings.

14-4.2.1 See Chapter 30 for requirements for underground buildings.

14-4.3 High Rise Buildings.   *(See 14-3.5.1.)*

14-4.4 Operating Features.   *(See Chapter 31.)*

SECTION 14-5   BUILDING SERVICES

14-5.1 Utilities.

14-5.1.1 Utilities shall comply with the provisions of Section 7-1.

14-5.1.2 Alarms, emergency communication systems, and the illumination of generator set locations shall be provided with emergency power in accordance with NFPA 70, *National Electrical Code.*

14-5.2 Heating, Ventilating, and Air Conditioning.

14-5.2.1 Heating, ventilating, and air conditioning equipment shall comply with the provisions of Section 7-2 and shall be installed in accordance with manufacturer's specifications.

Exception: As modified in 14-5.2.2 following.

14-5.2.2 Portable space heating devices are prohibited. Any heating device other than a central heating plant shall be so designed and installed that combustible material will not be ignited by it or its appurtenances. If fuel-fired, such heating devices shall be chimney or vent connected, shall take air for combustion directly from outside, and shall be so designed and installed to provide for complete separation of the combustion system from the atmosphere of the occupied area. The heating system shall have safety devices to immediately stop the flow of fuel and shut down the equipment in case of either excessive temperatures or ignition failure.

Exception: Approved suspended unit heaters may be used in locations other than means of egress and sleeping areas, provided such heaters are located high enough to be out of the reach of persons using the area, and provided they are vent connected and equipped with the safety devices called for above.

14-5.2.3 Combustion and ventilation air for boiler, incinerator, or heater rooms shall be taken directly from and discharged directly to the outside air.

14-5.3 Elevators, Dumbwaiters, and Vertical Conveyors. Elevators, dumbwaiters, and vertical conveyors shall comply with the provisions of Section 7-4.

14-5.4 Rubbish Chutes, Incinerators, and Laundry Chutes.

14-5.4.1 Rubbish chutes, incinerators, and laundry chutes shall comply with the provisions of Section 7-5.

14-5.4.2 Any rubbish chute or linen chute, including pneumatic rubbish and linen systems, shall be provided with automatic extinguishing protection installed in accordance with Section 7-7.

14-5.4.3 Any trash chute shall discharge into a trash collecting room used for no other purpose and protected in accordance with Section 6-4.

14-5.4.4 Any incinerator shall not be directly flue-fed, nor shall any floor chute directly connect with the combustion chamber.

REFERENCES CITED IN COMMENTARY

[1]"A Study of Penal Institution Fires," NFPA FR 78-1.

[2]James Bell, "Eleven Die in Jail Fire," *Fire Journal*, Vol. 74, No. 4, July 1980, pp. 23-25, 90.

[3]_____, "Twenty-Nine Die in Biloxi, Mississippi Jail Fire, *Fire Journal*, Vol. 77, No. 6, November 1983, pp. 44-49, 52-55.

[4]NFPA 101M, *Alternative Approaches to Life Safety*, National Fire Protection Association, Quincy, MA, 1988.

[5]NFPA 220, *Standard on Types of Building Construction*, National Fire Protection Association, Quincy, MA, 1985.

[6]NFPA 30, *Flammable and Combustible Liquids Code*, National Fire Protection Association, Quincy, MA, 1987.

[7]NFPA 13, *Standard for the Installation of Sprinkler Systems*, National Fire Protection Association, Quincy, MA, 1987.

15 EXISTING DETENTION AND CORRECTIONAL OCCUPANCIES

(See also Chapter 31.)

SECTION 15-1 GENERAL REQUIREMENTS

The 1981 Edition of the *Life Safety Code* was the first edition to include separate chapters on detention and correctional occupancies. In previous editions, these occupancies were briefly addressed in the chapter on institutional occupancies, later renamed health care occupancies.

In 1974 the Committee on Safety to Life decided to establish a Sectional Committee on Penal Occupancies. It was, however, too late to prepare a report for the 1976 Edition of the *Code*, and in 1977 the Committee on Safety to Life was reorganized as a Technical Committee with subcommittees. The Subcommittee on Penal Occupancies was appointed, with its first working meeting taking place in January of 1978. It was soon renamed the Subcommittee on Detention and Correctional Occupancies. During this period, there were several major detention and correctional occupancy fires that underscored the need for the Subcommittee and provided information for its use. These fires included:

October 1974	Youth Correctional Center Cranston, RI	2 dead[1]
June 1975	Seminole County Jail Sanford, FL	11 dead[1]
November 1975	Lycoming County Jail Williamsport, PA	3 dead[1]
June 1976	Marion State Prison Marion, NC	9 dead[1]
June 1977	Maury County Jail Columbia, IN	42 dead[1]
June 1977	St. John City Detention Center St. John, NB, Canada	21 dead[1]
July 1977	Federal Correctional Institution Danbury, CT	5 dead[1]
December 1979	Lancaster County Jail Lancaster, SC	11 dead[2]

Another major multiple-death fire, which was reviewed during preparation of the 1985 Edition of the *Code*, occurred on November 8, 1982 in a jail in Biloxi, Mississippi, killing 29 people[3].

15-1.1 Application.

15-1.1.1   Existing detention and correctional facilities shall comply with the provisions of this chapter. Provisions of Chapter 14 do not apply to existing detention and correctional facilities. Existing facilities shall also comply with the applicable requirements of Chapter 31.

> Chapter 31, Operating Features, especially Section 31-5, sets day-to-day operating requirements, such as 24-hour staffing, ability of residents to notify staff of an emergency, preparation and maintenance of evacuation plans, staff training in the use of portable fire extinguishers, storage of combustible personal property, presence of heat-producing appliances, control of flammability of draperies and curtains, and visual and tactile identification of keys necessary for unlocking doors within the means of egress. Given that the locking of doors, which is necessary for the intended function of the facility, goes against the basic *Code* tenet that the means of egress system be under the control of building occupants, the presence of properly trained staff is paramount in the provision of a package of life safety equivalent to that provided in other occupancies. Chapter 31 requires the necessary staffing and training that, where combined with the *Code* requirements of Chapters 1 through 7 and 15, achieves the necessary level of life safety.

15-1.1.2   This chapter establishes life safety requirements for all existing detention and correctional facilities.

Exception No. 1: Use Condition I requirements are those stated in the applicable requirements for existing buildings of Chapters 17, 19, or 20.

> See 15-1.4.1 for definition of Use Condition.

Exception No. 2*: Facilities determined to have equivalent safety provided in accordance with Section 1-5.

A-15-1.1.2 Exception No. 2   In determining equivalency for existing detention and correctional facilities, the authority having jurisdiction may accept evaluations based on Chapter 4 of NFPA 101M, *Alternative Approaches to Life Safety*, utilizing the parameters for existing buildings.

> Chapter 15 has been prepared for application solely to existing buildings.
> This section is to be applied retroactively. Due consideration has been given to the practical difficulties of making alterations in existing, functioning facilities. The specified provisions, viewed as a whole, establish *minimum* acceptable criteria for life safety that reasonably minimize the likelihood of a life-threatening fire.
> The requirements of Chapter 15 may be modified in instances of practical difficulty or where alternate, but equal, provisions are proposed. The modifications must provide an equivalent level of protection as would be achieved by compliance with the corresponding *Code* provisions.

The equivalency system contained in Chapter 4 of NFPA 101M, *Alternative Approaches to Life Safety,*[4] uses numerical values to analyze the firesafety effectiveness of existing building arrangements or improvements proposed within existing structures. The system provides a methodology by which alternative improvement programs can be evaluated as options to literal *Code* compliance. In providing the equivalency system, it is not intended to limit acceptable equivalency evaluations solely to those based on this one system. The authority having jurisdiction retains the discretion, as expressed within Section 1-5, to evaluate and approve alternative improvement programs on the basis of appropriate supporting data. Chapter 4 of NFPA 101M may be used to assist in this evaluation.

15-1.1.3 Detention and correctional occupancies are those used for purposes such as jails, detention centers, correctional institutions, reformatories, houses of correction, pre-release centers, and other residential-restrained care facilities where occupants are confined or housed under some degree of restraint or security.

15-1.1.4 Detention and correctional occupancies provide sleeping facilities for four or more residents and are occupied by persons who are generally prevented from taking self-preservation action because of security measures not under the occupants' control.

Residents of detention and correctional occupancies and patients in health care occupancies are judged to be incapable of self-preservation under a fire emergency. In the case of the health care occupancy patient, the incapability is due to physical or mental illness or infirmity. The detention and correctional occupancy resident, although most likely ambulatory or able-bodied, is incapable because of security measures imposed and not under the resident's control. In both cases, the occupants must await staff action before moving to either an exit or an area of refuge. Impediments to adequate egress are further compounded in detention and correctional occupancies by the resistance of staff to unlock doors leading to the outside. Thus, horizontal movement within the facility to an area of refuge may be the only means of egress system that the resident is allowed to use in a fire emergency, regardless of how many exit doors to the outside are installed. Because of this, the Total Concept described in 15-1.1.5 is important.

15-1.1.5 Total Concept. All detention and correctional facilities shall be so designed, constructed, maintained, and operated as to minimize the possibility of a fire emergency.

Because the safety of all occupants in detention and correctional facilities cannot be adequately assured solely by a dependence on evacuation of the building, their protection from fire shall be provided by appropriate arrangement of facilities, adequate trained staff, and careful development of operating, security, and maintenance procedures composed of the following:

(a) Proper design, construction, and compartmentation,

(b) Provision for detection, alarm, and extinguishment,

(c) Fire prevention and planning, training, and drilling in programs for the isolation of fire and transfer of occupants to areas of refuge or evacuation of the building, or protection of the occupants in place,

(d) Provision of security to the degree necessary for the safety of the public and the occupants of the facility.

> The Total Concept establishes a protect-in-place or defend-in-place strategy. That strategy mandates requirements aimed at minimizing the need for building evacuation by limiting the development and spread of a fire emergency to the room of fire origin, since safety is not assured by relying on a means of egress system utilizing evacuation due to the fact that locks either cannot or will not be unlocked in a timely manner. The requirements (e.g., Section 31-5 Operating Features) first try to prevent ignition and, given that fires will occur, set out to detect the fire (e.g., detectors per 15-3.4.4). Other requirements aim to control how quickly the fire will develop (e.g., interior finish per 15-3.3) while still others attempt to confine the effects (e.g., compartmentation and protection of vertical openings). Extinguishment of the fire is facilitated via sprinkler, standpipe, and portable extinguisher requirements. Provisions are made for refuge areas in the promotion of horizontal exits and the requirement of smoke barriers. Lastly, heavy reliance is placed on staff reaction. All these requirements fit together so as to minimize the need for evacuation. This is the Total Concept.

15-1.1.6 Additions.   Additions shall be separated from any existing structure not conforming with the provisions within Chapter 15 by a fire barrier having at least a 2-hour fire resistance rating constructed to the standards of the addition. Doors in these partitions shall normally be kept closed.

Exception: Doors may be held open if they meet the requirements of the Exception to 5-2.1.8.

> Additions must comply with the provisions of Chapter 14. This paragraph, 15-1.1.6, makes provisions for the separation of the new construction from the existing occupancy where the existing occupancy does not comply with Chapter 15.
>
> Note that the positioning of doors in the separating fire barriers is not restricted to corridors only. Doors must be kept closed unless they meet the requirements for automatic closing in the Exception to 5-2.1.8.
>
> Figure 15-1 illustrates the requirements of 15-1.1.6.

15-1.2* Mixed Occupancies.

A-15-1.2   Detention and correctional facilities are a complex of structures, each serving a definite and usually different purpose. For instance, in all probability there will be represented in many institutions an example of all, or almost all, of the occupancy-type classifications found in this *Code*. Exits and other features shall be governed by the type of occupancy classification and the hazard of occupancy unless specific exceptions are made.

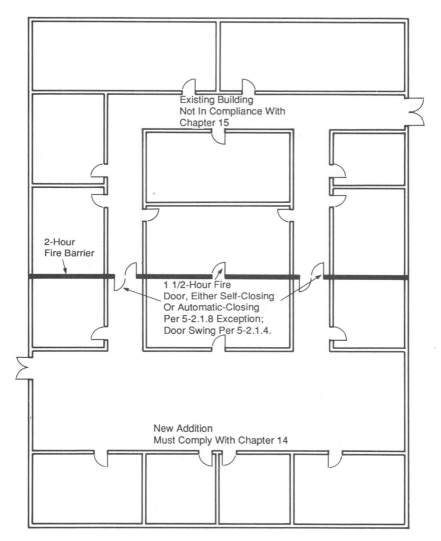

Figure 15-1. Separation of New Addition from Existing Building *Not* in Compliance with Chapter 15. *(See 15-1.1.6.)*

All buildings and structures are to be classified using this chapter and Section 4-1 as a guide, subject to the ruling of the authority having jurisdiction in case of question as to the proper classification of any individual building or structure.

Use Condition classification of the institution, as well as individual areas within the complex, are always to be considered by the authority having jurisdiction.

15-1.2.1   Egress provisions for areas of detention and correctional facilities that correspond to other occupancies shall meet the corresponding requirements of this *Code* for such occupancies. Where security operations necessitate the locking of required means of egress, necessary staff shall be provided for the supervised release of occupants during all times of use.

> The requirements of Chapter 15 apply mainly to the residential portions, i.e., the sleeping and living areas, of the detention and correctional facility. For example, although the work areas might look much like a typical industrial occupancy, the requirements of Chapter 28, Industrial Occupancies, cannot be used alone because doors within the required means of egress will be locked for security. Without using the actual requirements of Chapter 15 to protect the locked industrial work areas, the concepts of Chapter 15 should be employed so as to assure that necessary trained staff with control over the locks is present to allow for immediate supervised release of occupants during all times of use should fire or similar emergency occur.
>
> Similarly, some areas of a large facility may correspond to another occupancy classification. For example, a gymnasium would be considered an assembly occupancy (Chapter 9). If locked doors are required, prompt unlocking and release are critical.
>
> Release of occupants may be accomplished by a remotely activated system capable of unlocking all doors in the means of egress or by a sufficient number of attendants who are continuously on duty in the immediate area of the exit doors, and who are provided with keys. Continuous supervision is essential.

15-1.2.2 Sections of detention and correctional facilities may be classified as other occupancies if they meet all of the following conditions:

(a) They are not intended to serve residents for purpose of housing, customary access, or means of egress.

(b) They are adequately separated from areas of detention or correctional occupancies by construction having a fire resistance rating of at least 2 hours.

> For example, administrative offices, maintenance areas, etc., that are not customarily used by the residents, are not part of the egress system from the residential areas, and are separated by 2-hour fire resistance rated construction may be classified as another occupancy, such as business or industrial. In many cases, "trustees" may be employed in these areas. Their presence in these areas would not be considered a violation of item (a), provided they had freedom of egress as in a normal unlocked environment.

15-1.2.3 Detention and correctional occupancies in buildings housing other occupancies shall be completely separated from the other occupancies by construction having a fire resistance rating of at least 2 hours as provided for additions in 15-1.1.6.

> Paragraph 15-1.2.3 requires that if a detention or correctional occupancy is located in a building of another classification (such as business or assembly), the detention or correctional occupancy must be

separated from the other occupancy by construction having a fire resistance rating of 2 hours, as detailed in 15-1.1.6. The requirement addresses the common situation of a small detention lockup facility (at least 4 residents, per 15-1.1.4) located in a combination county courthouse/office/police building. Per 31-5.1.1, staffing of the detention area must be provided 24 hours per day. The remainder of the building, especially office areas, may not be occupied at night. A fire that originates and develops in an unoccupied area will not threaten the occupants of the detention facility as readily because of the 2-hour fire resistance rated barrier separating the different occupancies.

Note that 15-1.2.3 deals with occupancy classification only, not with hazard of contents. Hazard of contents is addressed in 15-1.2.5.

15-1.2.4 All means of egress from detention and correctional occupancies that traverse other use areas shall, as a minimum, conform to requirements of this *Code* for detention and correctional occupancies.

Exception: It is permissible to exit through a horizontal exit into other contiguous occupancies that do not conform to detention and correctional occupancy egress provisions but that do comply with requirements set forth in the appropriate occupancy chapter of this Code, as long as the occupancy does not have high hazard contents. The horizontal exit shall comply with the requirements of 15-2.2.5.

The means of egress from detention and correctional occupancies that traverse nondetention and noncorrectional spaces must conform to the requirements for detention and correctional occupancies. However, if a 2-hour fire barrier between a detention or correctional occupancy and a business occupancy (offices) and its opening protectives (fire doors) qualify as a horizontal exit, then the means of egress system in the business occupancy need only conform to the appropriate requirements set forth in Chapter 27 for existing business occupancies.

15-1.2.5 Any area with a hazard of contents classified higher than that of the detention or correctional occupancy and located in the same building shall be protected, as required in 15-3.2.

This paragraph regulates those spaces in a detention and correctional occupancy that contain more hazardous materials (in quantity or type) than are usually found in this occupancy. Spaces, such as rooms used for the storage of highly combustible materials, trash collection rooms, and paint shops, must be protected in accordance with 15-3.2.

15-1.2.6 Non-detention or non-correctional related occupancies classified as containing high hazard contents shall not be permitted in buildings housing detention or correctional occupancies.

This paragraph prohibits another occupancy with highly hazardous contents (such as flammable liquids storage) from being located in a building housing detention and correctional occupancies. This paragraph is not meant to exclude the storage of linens in a detention and correctional occupancy. The intent is to prevent a portion of a detention and correctional facility from being converted to a warehouse and having a larger quantity or more hazardous type of combustibles than would be expected in a detention and correctional occupancy. This principally refers to residential areas. For example, industrial areas that are part of the overall detention and correctional facility, but located in a nonresidential-use building, may have flammable liquids as part of the industrial process.

15-1.3 Special Definitions.

(a) *Direct exit.*   A direct exit is an exit that serves only one area or level, and the direct exit has no openings to *other* areas or levels.

The term "direct exit" is defined here so that its particular meaning can be utilized in 15-3.7.1 Exception No. 2 dealing with subdivision of building spaces via smoke barriers.

(b) *Fire Barrier.*   See Chapter 6.

(c) *Fire Compartment.*   See Chapter 6.

(d) *Residential Housing Area.*   Includes sleeping areas and any contiguous day room, group activity space, or other common spaces for customary access of residents.

(e) *Sallyport (Security Vestibule).*   A compartment provided with two or more doors where the intended purpose is to prevent the continuous and unobstructed passage by allowing the release of only one door at a time.

See 15-2.5.4.

(f) *Smoke Barrier.*   See Chapter 6.

(g) *Smoke Compartment.*   See Chapter 6.

15-1.4 Classification of Occupancy.

15-1.4.1*   Users and occupants of detention and correctional facilities at various times can be expected to include staff, visitors, and residents. The extent and nature of facility utilization by members of each of these groups will vary according to type of facility, its function, and programs. For applications of the life safety requirements that follow, the resident user category is divided into five groups:

Use Condition I — Free Egress

Free movement is allowed from sleeping areas, and other spaces where access or occupancy is permitted, to the exterior via means of egress meeting the requirements of the *Code.*

In Use Condition I, there are no physical restrictions, such as locks, on the means of egress. The occupants are capable of self-preservation. An example might be a work release center where the doors are not locked.

(*See Figure A-15-1.4.1.*) Because no locking of the means of egress system occurs, the occupant is as free to escape a fire emergency as an occupant of any other residential type of occupancy. It reasonably follows that Use Condition I detention and correctional occupancies are exempted from the Chapter 15 requirements by 15-1.4.3 and are charged with meeting the requirements of some other occupancy chapter, such as Chapter 17 for existing hotels and dormitories. (*See 15-1.4.3.*)

Use Condition II — Zoned Egress

Free movement is allowed from sleeping areas and any other occupied smoke compartment to one or more other smoke compartments.

The occupants have freedom to move within the building, including the freedom to move from their rooms and across the smoke barrier. Doors to the outside are manually locked. (*See Figure A-15-1.4.1.*)

Use Condition III — Zoned Impeded Egress

Free movement is allowed within individual smoke compartments, such as within a residential unit comprised of individual sleeping rooms and group activity space, with egress impeded by remote control release of means of egress from such smoke compartment to another smoke compartment.

The occupants are free to move out of their rooms but are locked in the smoke compartment.
The locked smoke barrier door can be unlocked by a remote means. Doors to the outside are manually locked. (See Figure A-15-1.4.1.)

Use Condition IV — Impeded Egress

Free movement is restricted from an occupied space. Remote controlled release is provided to permit movement from all sleeping rooms, activity spaces, and other occupied areas within the smoke compartment to other smoke compartment(s).

In Use Condition IV, occupants are locked in their cells. However, both the cell doors and the smoke barrier door can be unlocked by a remote means. Doors to the outside are manually locked. (*See Figure A-15.1.4.1.*)

Use Condition V — Contained

Free movement is restricted from an occupied space. Staff controlled manual release at each door is provided to permit movement from all sleeping rooms, activity spaces, and other occupied areas within the smoke compartment to other smoke compartment(s).

All locks are manually locked and unlocked at the individual door. (*See Figure A-15-1.4.1.*) This places a heavy demand on staff to open the doors in an emergency. As might reasonably be expected, the most stringent requirements of Chapter 15 are called into play for Use Condition V facilities.

A-15-1.4.1   Free movement to (1) a public way, (2) a building separated from the fire area by two-hour fire-resistive construction or 50 ft (15 m) of open space, or (3) an outside secure area having a holding space at least 50 ft (15 m) from the zone of fire origin that provides 15 sq ft (1.4 sq m) or more of refuge area per person (resident, staff, visitors, etc.) that may be present at time of fire, also fulfills the requirement of a smoke compartment.

Figure A-15-1.4.1 illustrates the five Use Conditions.

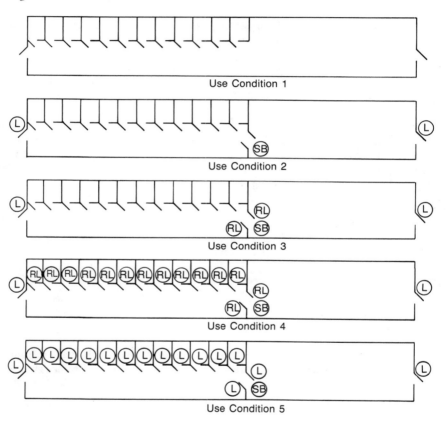

Figure A-15-1.4.1

Note that in Figure A-15-1.4.1 the "Locked" (L) designation means *manual* unlocking operation at the door.

As part of the definitions of Use Condition II through Use Condition V reference is made to smoke compartments and the degree of locking (none, remote release, or manual operation) used for smoke barrier doors. A facility without a smoke barrier can still qualify as meeting one of those Use Conditions by allowing, in lieu of the smoke barrier, for movement to a place judged to be equivalent to another smoke compartment, such as (1) a public way, (2) a building separated from the space in question by either adequate fire resistance rated construction or distance, or (3) an adequately sized outside holding area positioned a safe distance away. The locking operation of the door to this alternate place cannot be more severe than that allowed for the smoke barrier door of that particular Use Condition (i.e., no locking for Use Condition II, remote release for III and IV, and manual operation for V). (*Also see 15-3.7 and Figure 15-11.*)

15-1.4.2* To classify as Use Condition III or IV, the arrangement, accessibility, and security of the release mechanism(s) used for emergency egress shall be such that the minimum available staff, at any time, can promptly release the locks.

A-15-1.4.2 Prompt operation is intended to be accomplished in the period of time between detection of fire by either the smoke detector(s) required by 15-3.4 or by other means (whichever comes first) and the advent of intolerable conditions forcing emergency evacuation. Fire tests have indicated that the time available is a function of the volume and height of the space involved and the rate of fire development. In traditional single-story corridor arrangements, the time between detection by smoke detectors and the advent of lethal conditions down to head height can be as short as approximately 3 minutes. In addition, it should be expected that approximately 1 minute will be required to evacuate all the occupants of a threatened smoke compartment once the locks are released. In this example, a prompt release time would be 2 minutes.

The major requirement noted in this paragraph is that the area must be under continuous supervision and that a sufficient number of staff must be present and have the necessary keys readily available to release the locks.

15-1.4.3 Areas housing occupancies corresponding to Use Condition I Free Egress shall conform to the requirements of residential occupancies under this *Code*.

Detention and correctional occupancies in which the occupants are not locked in at any time shall be classified as residential and shall meet the requirements of Chapters 17, 19, or 20 as appropriate. Those buildings that provide free egress, even though used as correctional occupancies, should not be classified as detention and correctional occupancies under this *Code*. Although such devices are not normally used, a facility with locking devices present on its doors should not be classified as Use

Condition I because of the potential for future use of the locks. Rather, depending on the mode of operation (remote or manual), the corresponding Use Condition should be assigned, and the requirements of Chapter 15 followed. The facility could be classified as Use Condition I only if the locking devices were physically removed.

15-1.5 Classification of Hazard of Contents.   The classification of hazard of contents shall be as defined in Section 4-2.

15-1.6 Minimum Construction Requirement.

15-1.6.1   For the purpose of 15-1.6, stories shall be counted starting at the primary level of exit discharge. For the purposes of this section, the primary level of exit discharge of a building shall be that floor that is level with or above finished grade on the exterior wall line for 50 percent or more of its perimeter. Building levels below the primary level shall not be counted as a story in determining the height of the building.

See Figure 15-2 for method of counting stories.

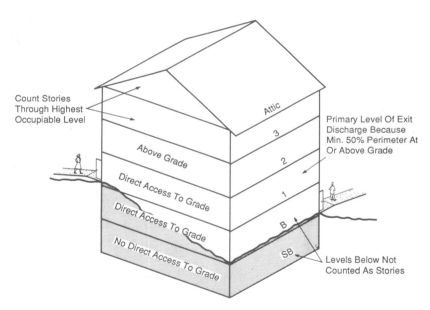

Figure 15-2.   Method of Counting Stories, per 15-1.6.1, for Use in 15-1.6.3.   If the attic were determined to be occupiable, the figure would depict a 4-story building.

15-1.6.2   A residential housing area complying with 15-3.1.2 shall be considered as a one story building for purposes of applying 15-1.6.3

The provisions of 15-3.1.2 address multilevel housing areas for which the vertical separation between the lowest floor level and the uppermost floor level does not exceed 13 ft (4.0 m), but the paragraph does not limit the number of levels. (*See Figure A-15-3.1.2(c).*) A multilevel housing area meeting all the requirements of 15-3.1.2 is treated as a single story in determining required building construction type per 15-1.6.3.

15-1.6.3 Detention and correctional occupancies shall be limited to the following types of building construction. (*See 6-2.1.*)

Table 15-1.6.3

Type of Construction	1 story with Basement	1 story without Basement	2 story	3 story	4 story and Higher
I (443) I (332) II (222)	X	X	X	X	X
II (111)	X††	X	X††	X†	X†
III (211) IV (2HH) V (111)	X††	X	X††	X†	X†
II (000) III (200) V (000)	X††	X††	X†	X†	X†

X: Permitted types of construction
X†: Permitted if the entire building is protected throughout by an approved automatic sprinkler system in accordance with Section 7-7.
X††: X† applies in buildings where Use Condition V is used.

Exception No. 1: Any building of Type I or Type II (222 or 111) construction may include roofing systems involving combustible or steel supports, decking or roofing provided:

(a) The roof covering at least meets Class C requirements in accordance with NFPA 256, Standard Methods of Fire Tests of Roof Coverings, and

(b) The roof is separated from all occupied portions of the building by a noncombustible floor assembly that includes at least 2½ in. (6.4 cm) of concrete or gypsum fill. To qualify for this exception, the attic or other space so developed shall either be unoccupied or protected throughout by an approved automatic sprinkler system.

Exception No. 2: In determining building construction type, exposed steel roof members located 16 ft (4.9 m) or more above the floor of the highest cell may be disregarded.

Recognizing that locked doors to the outside will either be reluctantly and slowly unlocked or not unlocked at all, the *Code* relies on the defend-in-place or protect-in-place strategy discussed in the commentary to 15-1.1.5. Paragraph 15-1.6.3 establishes minimum construction require-ments to help assure the structural integrity of the building for the time necessary to either release residents to the outside or hold them in a safe area of refuge.

The table contained in 15-1.6.3 establishes minimum construction types for detention and correctional occupancies. Certain construction types require automatic sprinkler protection no matter what their Use Condition. Others only require such protection where Use Condition V is involved. It should be noted that the automatic sprinkler requirements contained in this table are determined on construction type. Automatic sprinkler protection may also be required by other sections of this *Code*.

See NFPA 220, *Standard on Types of Building Construction*,[5] for definition of types of construction. (*Also see 6-2.1.*)

15-1.7 Occupant Load.   The occupant load for which means of egress shall be provided for any floor shall be the maximum number of persons intended to occupy that floor, but not less than one person for each 120 sq ft (11.1 sq m) gross floor area.

This paragraph establishes an occupant load factor from which an occupant load may be projected. The means of egress system must be sized to handle the *larger* of either the actual count of persons intended to occupy the space or the number of persons based on the calculation using the occupant load factor.

The *Code* intends that the occupant load factor be used only for sizing the means of egress, not for limiting the number of persons within a space. If the means of egress can handle an occupant load larger than the load calculated using the occupant load factor of 15-1.7, the *Code* would not prohibit such a load. Plumbing and sanitary codes and common sense will dictate maximum safe loading from a sociological and humanitarian standpoint in a facility with excess means of egress capacity.

SECTION 15-2   MEANS OF EGRESS REQUIREMENTS

15-2.1 General.   Means of egress shall comply with Chapter 5.
Exception: As otherwise provided or modified in this section.

15-2.2 Means of Egress Components.

15-2.2.1   Components of means of egress shall be limited to the types described in 15-2.2.2 through 15-2.2.8.

15-2.2.2 Doors.   Doors shall comply with 5-2.1.
Exception: As provided in 15-2.11.

15-2.2.3 Stairs.

15-2.2.3.1   Stairs shall comply with 5-2.2.
Exception: The provisions of 5-2.2.6.5(f) and 5-2.2.6.6(c) do not apply.

These two paragraphs in Chapter 5 require intermediate rails on handrails and guardrails so that a 6-in. (15.2-cm) diameter sphere will not pass through the rails. Since only adults or older juveniles use these facilities and these intermediate railings may interfere with visual observation, they are not required.

15-2.2.3.2   Spiral stairs complying with 5-2.2.2.7 are permitted for access to and between staff locations.

Paragraph 15-2.2.3.2 permits spiral stairs conforming to 5-2.2.2.7 for staff use only. Note that Chapter 5 restricts the use of spiral stairs to areas having an occupant load of five or fewer persons. Spiral stairs are not permitted for access by the residents.

15-2.2.4 Smokeproof Enclosures.   Smokeproof enclosures shall comply with 5-2.3.

15-2.2.5* Horizontal Exits.   Horizontal exits shall comply with 5-2.4, modified as follows:

(a) At least 6 sq ft (.56 sq m) of accessible space per occupant shall be provided on each side of the horizontal exit for the total number of people in adjoining compartments.

Paragraph 5-2.4 requires at least 3 sq ft (0.28 sq m) per occupant of accumulation space on each side of the horizontal exit. This section requires 6 sq ft (0.56 sq m) per occupant due to several factors, including personalities of the residents, their expected duration in the refuge area, and the fact that horizontal exits may comprise 100 percent of required exits.

(b) Horizontal exits may comprise 100 percent of the exits required provided that an exit, other than a horizontal exit, is accessible in some other (not necessarily adjacent) fire compartment without requiring return through the compartment of fire origin.

This permits horizontal exits to comprise 100 percent of the exits from any fire compartment as long as the compartment is not left "dead-ended" so as to require travel through the compartment of fire origin in order to reach a door to the outside.

In Figure 15-3, all compartments but F satisfy the above rule. Fire compartment F would require a door to the outside so as to preclude having to travel through compartment E, which could be the area of fire origin, to get to the outside of the building.

Because of practical difficulties involving vertical exit travel to the outside in detention and correctional occupancies, special recognition is given to horizontal travel and the use of horizontal exits. One hundred percent of the total required exit capacity for a given fire area may be provided by horizontal exits as explained above. In the event a horizontal exit also serves as a smoke barrier, see 15-2.4 and 15-3.7.

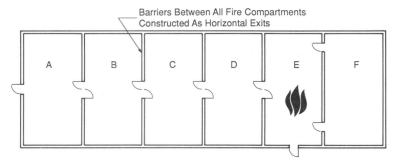

Figure 15-3. Horizontal Exits Correctly Comprise 100 Percent of Total Exits from Fire Compartments B, C, and D. Compartment F would require the addition of an exit door directly to the outside so as not to require travel through fire compartment E to get to the outside of the building. Compartments A and E are *Code*-complying with one horizontal exit and one exit door directly to the exterior of the building.

(c) A door in a horizontal exit is not required to swing with travel as specified in 5-2.4.3.4.

Although doors in existing horizontal exits are not required to swing in the direction of egress travel, it is considered good practice to do so where possible.

A-15-2.2.5 An exit is not necessary from each individual fire compartment if there is access to an exit through other fire compartments without passing through the fire compartment of origin.

See commentary following 15-2.2.5(b).

15-2.2.6 Ramps. Ramps shall comply with 5-2.5.

15-2.2.7 Exit Passageways. Exit passageways shall comply with 5-2.6.

15-2.2.8 Fire Escape Stairs. Fire escape stairs complying with 5-2.8 are permitted.

15-2.3 Capacity of Means of Egress.

15-2.3.1 The capacity of any required means of egress shall be in accordance with Section 5-3.

15-2.3.2 Aisles, corridors, and ramps required for access or exit shall be at least 3 ft (91 cm) wide.

Note that Chapter 14 for new detention and correctional occupancies requires a minimum 4-ft (122-cm) width.

15-2.3.3 For residents' sleeping room door widths, see 15-2.11.3.

15-2.4 Number of Exits. *(See also Section 5-4.)*

15-2.4.1 At least two exits of the types permitted in 15-2.2, remotely located from each other, shall be provided for each occupied story of the building.

15-2.4.2 At least two exits of the types permitted in 15-2.2, remotely located from each other, shall be accessible from each fire or smoke compartment.

15-2.4.3* At least one approved exit shall be accessible from each fire compartment and each required smoke compartment into which residents may be moved in a fire emergency with the exits so arranged that egress shall not require return through the zone of fire origin.

A-15-2.4.3 An exit is not necessary from each individual fire compartment and smoke compartment if there is access to an exit through other fire sections or smoke compartments without passing through the fire section or smoke compartment of origin.

See commentary following 15-2.2.5(b) and Figure 15-3.

15-2.5 Arrangement of Means of Egress. *(See also Section 5-5.)*

15-2.5.1 Every sleeping room shall have a door leading directly to an exit access corridor.

Exception No. 1: If there is an exit door opening directly to the outside from the room at the ground level.

Exception No. 2: One adjacent room, such as a dayroom, group activity space, or other common spaces may intervene. Where individual occupant sleeping rooms adjoin a dayroom or group activity space that is utilized for access to an exitway, such sleeping room may open directly to the dayroom or space and may be separated in elevation by a one-half or full-story height (also see 15-3.1.2).

Figure 15-4 illustrates the requirements of Exception No. 2.

15-2.5.2* Existing dead-end corridors are undesirable and shall be altered wherever possible so that exits will be accessible in at least two different directions from all points in aisles, passageways, and corridors.

A-15-2.5.2 Every exit or exit access should be so arranged, if feasible, that no corridor or aisle has a pocket or dead end exceeding 50 ft (15 m) for Use Conditions II, III, and IV and 20 ft (6.1 m) for Use Condition V.

See commentary following 14-2.5.2 and Figure 14-5.

15-2.5.3 No common path of travel shall exceed 50 ft (15 m).

Exception No. 1: A common path of travel may be permitted for the first 100 ft (30 m) in a building protected throughout by an approved automatic sprinkler system in accordance with Section 7-7.

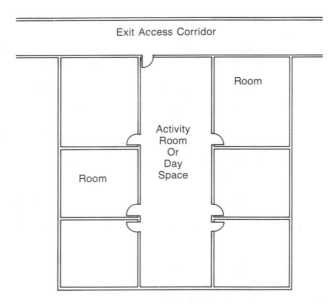

Figure 15-4.   One Adjacent Room May Intervene Between Sleeping Room and Exit Access Corridor.   Sleeping rooms may be separated in elevation by ½ to 1 story. (*See 15-2.5.1 Exception No. 2.*)

Exception No. 2:   Multilevel residential housing units in which each floor level, considered separately, has at least one-half of its individual required exit capacity accessible by exit access leading directly out of that level without traversing another communicating floor level.

Exception No. 3:   Existing excessive common paths of travel may be continued in use subject to the approval of the authority having jurisdiction and the travel distance requirements of 15-2.6.

15-2.5.4   A sallyport may be permitted in a means of egress where there are provisions for continuous and unobstructed travel through the sallyport during an emergency exit condition.

A sallyport or security vestibule, under normal day-to-day and nonfire emergency conditions, is designed to maintain the door at one end of the vestibule securely locked at any time the door at the other end is open. A door is opened; a person or persons enter the vestibule; the door through which they entered is closed and locked; the door at the opposite end is unlocked and opened; the people leave the vestibule. The sallyport is thus a security device that keeps a continuous flow of people from "storming" the exits. Under fire conditions, it would severely restrict the exit flow of occupants and not allow hose lines to be run through the openings. Thus, if a sallyport is to receive credit as part of the required means of egress, 15-2.5.4 requires that the door controls be overridden so as to allow continuous and unobstructed passage.

Figure 15-5 illustrates the requirements of 15-2.5.4.

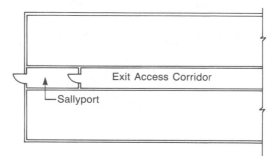

Figure 15-5. Requirements for Sallyport or Security Vestibule. If sallyport is part of required means of egress both doors of sallyport must be capable of being opened at the same time to provide unobstructed egress. (*See 15-2.5.4.*)

15-2.6 Travel Distance to Exits.

15-2.6.1 Travel distance:

(a) Between any room door required as exit access and an exit or smoke barrier shall not exceed 100 ft (30 m);

(b) Between any point in a room and an exit or smoke barrier shall not exceed 150 ft (45 m); and

(c) Between any point in a sleeping room to the door of that room shall not exceed 50 ft (15 m).

Exception No. 1: The travel distance in (a) or (b) above may be increased by 50 ft (15 m) in buildings protected throughout by an approved automatic sprinkler system or smoke control system.

Exception No. 2: The travel distance in (c) above may be increased to 100 ft (30 m) in open dormitories where the enclosing walls of the dormitory space are at least of smoketight construction. Where travel distance to the exit access door from any point within the dormitory exceeds 50 ft (15 m), at least two exit access doors remotely located from each other shall be provided.

Travel distance is measured to the closest exit, not to both exits required by 15-2.4. Figure 15-6 illustrates the requirements of 15-2.6.1.

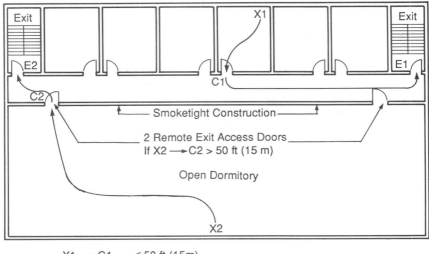

$$X1 \longrightarrow C1 \quad \leq 50 \text{ ft (15m)}$$
$$X2 \longrightarrow C2 \quad \leq 100 \text{ ft (30 m)}$$
$$\left.\begin{array}{l} C1 \longrightarrow E1 \\ C2 \longrightarrow E2 \end{array}\right\} \quad \leq 100 \text{ ft (30 m) [150 ft (45 m) If Sprinklered Or Equipped With Smoke Control]}$$
$$X1 \longrightarrow E1 \quad \leq 150 \text{ ft (45 m) [200 ft (60 m) If Sprinklered Or Equipped With Smoke Control]}$$
$$X2 \longrightarrow E2 \quad \leq 200 \text{ ft (60 m) [250 ft (76 m) If Sprinklered Or Equipped With Smoke Control]}$$

Figure 15-6. Maximum Travel Distance to Exits in Existing Detention and Correctional Occupancies. (*See 15-2.6.1.*) The travel distance is measured along the natural path of travel. (*See 5-6.2.*) "Sprinklered" means that the entire building is protected by a complete approved automatic extinguishing system. "Smoke Control" means that the entire building or fire area is equipped with a system to control the movement of smoke in accordance with Section 7-3.

15-2.7 Discharge from Exits.

15-2.7.1   Exits may discharge into a fenced or walled courtyard, provided that not more than two walls of the courtyard are the building walls from which exit is being made. Enclosed yards or courts shall be of sufficient size to accommodate all occupants at a minimum distance of 50 ft (15 m) from the building with a net area of 15 sq ft (1.4 sq m) per person.

Figures 15-7a and b illustrate 15-2.7.1.

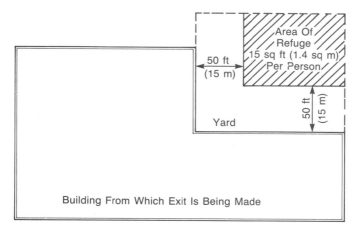

Figure 15-7a.   Exit Discharge into a Fenced Yard. (*See 15-2.7.1.*)

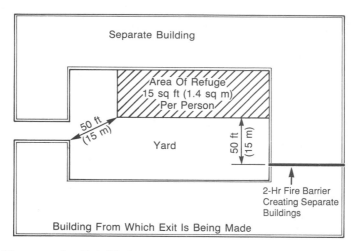

Figure 15-7b.   Exit Discharge into an Enclosed Yard. (*See 15-2.7.1.*)

15-2.7.2   All exits may discharge through the level of exit discharge. The requirements of 5-7.2 may be waived provided that not more than 50 percent of the exits discharge into a single fire compartment.

Exception: Where all exits discharge through areas on the level of discharge, a smoke barrier shall be provided to divide that level into at least two compartments with at least one exit discharging into each compartment, and each smoke compartment shall have an exit discharge to the building exterior. The level of discharge shall be provided with automatic sprinkler protection, and any other portion of the level of discharge area with access to the discharge area shall be provided with automatic sprinkler protection or separated from it in accordance with the requirements for the enclosure of exits (see 5-1.3.1).

The provisions of 5-7.2 establish criteria under which up to 50 percent of the required exits, either in number or capacity, may discharge back through the level of exit discharge with the other 50 percent required to discharge directly outside. Because of the security concerns and the belief that doors to the exterior will not be readily unlocked in detention and correctional occupancies, 15-2.7.2 allows 100 percent of the exits to discharge through the level of exit discharge. In order to do this, 15-2.7.2 requires that a fire separation be provided on the level of exit discharge, which creates at least two fire compartments. Not more than one-half of the exits (in number and capacity) may discharge into any one fire compartment. This paragraph intends that the fire separation have at minimum a one-hour fire resistance rating.

The Exception to 15-2.7.2 allows for a smoke barrier to substitute for the fire barrier if the travel route along the level of exit discharge is sprinklered.

15-2.8 Illumination of Means of Egress.   Illumination shall be in accordance with Section 5-8.

15-2.9 Emergency Lighting.   Emergency lighting shall be in accordance with Section 5-9.

Exception: Emergency lighting of at least 1-hour duration may be provided.

15-2.10 Marking of Means of Egress.   Exit marking shall be provided in areas accessible to the public in accordance with Section 5-10.

Exception: Exit signs may be omitted in sleeping areas.

The exemption of exit signs in sleeping areas of detention and correctional occupancies recognizes that the persons occupying such areas are familiar with that portion of the facility and, given that doors are unlocked, know where the exits are. Other portions of the facility may not be as familiar to residents and visitors and thus must have proper exit marking per the base requirement of 15-2.10.

15-2.11 Special Features.

15-2.11.1   Doors within means of egress shall be as required in Chapter 5.

Exception: As noted in 15-2.11.2 through 15-2.11.8.

15-2.11.2   Doors may be locked in accordance with the applicable Use Condition.

This provision overrides the basic Chapter 5 requirement that all doors within the required means of egress be unlocked from the side from which egress is to be made. It recognizes that, in order to function as intended, a detention and correctional occupancy relies on various means of locking. Rather than allowing any and all doors to be locked, 15-2.11.2 allows only the means of locking recognized by the Use Condition. Thus, a Use Condition II facility, which has a more lenient package of life safety requirements than a Use Condition V facility, cannot have sleeping rooms individually key locked. A Use Condition V facility, on the other hand, because it must comply with a more stringent set of requirements than a Use Condition II facility, can have individual doors manually key locked.

15-2.11.3* Doors to resident sleeping rooms shall be at least 28 in. (71 cm) in clear width.

Exception: Existing doors to resident sleeping rooms housing four or less residents may be 19 in. (48.3 cm) in clear width.

A-15-2.11.3 It may be necessary to provide a certain number of resident sleeping rooms with doors providing a minimum clear width of 32 in. (81 cm) (*see 5-2.1.2.1*) in order to comply with the requirements for the physically handicapped. Such sleeping rooms should be located where there is a direct accessible access to the exterior or to an area of safe refuge. (*See 15-3.7.*)

15-2.11.4 Doors in a means of egress may be of the horizontal sliding type, provided the force to slide the door to its fully open position does not exceed 50 lb (222 N) with a perpendicular force against the door of 50 lb (222 N).

Paragraph 5-2.1.4.1 requires that all doors in a means of egress be side-hinged and swinging. This exception allows the use of sliding doors if they meet the specified requirements.

15-2.11.5 Doors from areas of refuge to the exterior may be locked with key lock in lieu of locking methods described in 15-2.11.6. The keys to unlock such doors shall be maintained and available at the facility at all times, and the locks shall be operable from the outside.

This paragraph requires that the keys be maintained and available. "Available" means readily accessible to staff for use at any time to evacuate occupants. The important points are that (1) the keys required to evacuate occupants are accessible at all times, (2) the staff is trained in the location and use of keys, and (3) staff has authorization and standing orders to unlock doors from areas of refuge to the exterior immediately under fire emergency conditions to prevent hesitation to unlock doors pending authorization from higher authorities within the facility's administration.

15-2.11.6* Any remote release used in means of egress shall be provided with a reliable means of operation, remote from the resident living area, to release locks on all doors.

Exception: Provisions for remote locking and unlocking of occupied rooms in Use Condition IV may be waived provided not more than ten locks are necessary to be unlocked in order to move all occupants from one smoke compartment to an area of refuge as promptly as required for remote unlocking. The opening of all necessary locks shall be accomplished with no more than two separate keys. (See 15-3.7.6 for smoke barrier doors.)

A-15-2.11.6   A remote position is generally a control point where a number of doors can be unlocked simultaneously, either mechanically or electrically. In areas where there are a number of sleeping rooms, it is not practical for attendants to unlock doors individually. Doors in an exit should be unlocked prior to unlocking sleeping room doors.

This section of the *Code* does not intend to prohibit Use Condition V facilities, nor does it intend to limit Use Condition V facilities to 10 manually released locks.

"Remote" means outside the area where the occupants are restrained. It is not necessary to have the remote unlocking mechanism in a separate fire area, although this may be beneficial. Doors in the exit should be unlocked prior to unlocking sleeping room doors to prevent jamming of the exit door due to the pressure of several persons pushing on the door.

The Exception to 15-2.11.6 is to be used in conjunction with the Use Condition definitions in 15-1.4.1, primarily Use Conditions III and IV. Where remote locking is called for by the Use Condition, it must be provided, except as addressed by the Exception. The Exception permits the manual unlocking of up to ten locks to remove occupants to an area of refuge and still allow the facility to qualify as providing remote release. In other words, the manual locks do not force a Use Condition V classification. This may involve more than ten doors if multiple doors are secured with a single locking mechanism, or fewer than ten doors if a door is secured with more than one lock. Figures 15-8a and b illustrate two typical arrangements for the ten-lock exception.

It must be recognized that the speed with which the doors can be unlocked and the occupants removed to a safe location is critical. If the ten locks cannot be rapidly released by manual unlocking due to staffing restrictions or for any other reasons, then remote unlocking must be used. If doors are equipped with locking devices, it is assumed that the locks will be used, and they must be counted in the total number of locks.

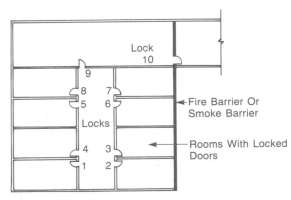

Figure 15-8a.   Maximum of Ten Manually Unlocked Doors with Each Door Equipped with a Single Key-Operated Lock.   (*See 15-2.11.6 Exception.*)

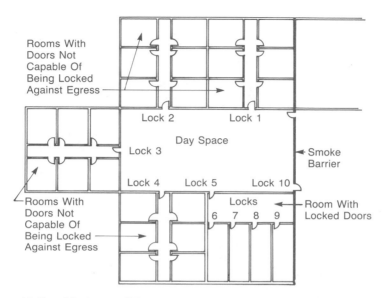

Figure 15-8b. Maximum of Ten Manually Unlocked Locks with Areas Served by More Than One Door, Secured with a Single Manually Unlocked Door. *(See 15-2.11.6 Exception.)*

15-2.11.7 All remote release operated doors shall be provided with a redundant means of operation as follows:

(a) Power-operated sliding doors or power-operated locks shall be so constructed that in the event of power failure, a manual mechanical means to release and open the doors is provided at each door, and either emergency power in accordance with 5-9.2.3 is provided for the power operation, or a remote manual mechanical release is provided.

(b) Mechanically operated sliding doors or mechanically operated locks shall be provided with a manual mechanical means at each door to release and open the door.

15-2.11.8 The provisions of 5-2.1.5.2 for stairway reentry do not apply.

SECTION 15-3   PROTECTION

15-3.1 Protection of Vertical Openings.

This subsection specifies the protection required to maintain floor-to-floor separation, which helps to prevent vertical movement of the products of combustion through the building.

15-3.1.1 Any stairway, ramp, elevator, hoistway, light or ventilation shaft, chute or other vertical opening between stories shall be enclosed in accordance with Section 6-2.

Exception No. 1: Stairs that do not connect a corridor, do not connect more than two levels, and do not serve as a means of egress need not comply with these regulations.

The convenience stair addressed by Exception No. 1 is illustrated in Figures 15-9a and b.

Exception No. 2: Multilevel residential housing areas in accordance with 15-3.1.2.

Exception No. 3: In residential housing areas protected thoughout by an approved automatic sprinkler system, unprotected vertical openings are permitted in accordance with the conditions of 6-2.4.4, provided that the height between the lowest and highest finished floor levels does not exceed 23 ft (7.0 m). The number of levels is not restricted.

The provisions of 6-2.4.4, had they not been modified by Exception No. 3, would have limited the vertical opening to communication among a maximum of three floor levels. Given the typical multilevel housing areas, utilizing staggered partial levels as depicted in Figure 15-10, the three-floor restriction was replaced with a 23-ft (7-m) height between the lowest and highest finished floor levels so as to allow greater flexibility of use for detention and correctional occupancies. Additionally, the Exception can be used only in facilities where the residential housing areas are protected throughout by automatic sprinklers.

Exception No. 4: Atriums in accordance with 6-2.4.5 are permitted.

Exception No. 5: Where full enclosure is impractical, the required enclosure may be limited to that necessary to prevent a fire originating in any story from spreading to any other story.

Exception No. 6: The fire resistance rating of enclosures in detention and correctional occupancies protected throughout by an approved automatic sprinkler system may be reduced to one hour.

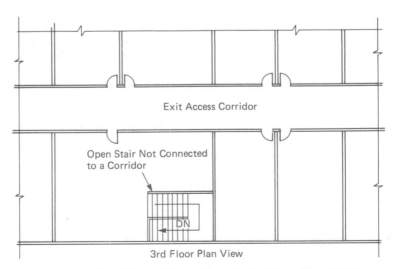

Figure 15-9a.   Plan View of Convenience Stair Allowed by 15-3.1.1
Exception No. 1.

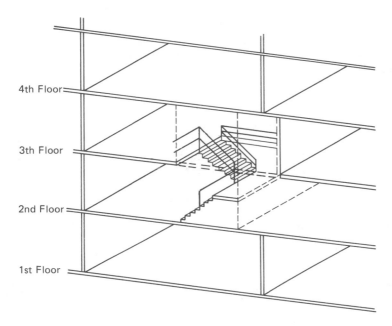

Figure 15-9b. Open Convenience Stair as Allowed by 15-3.1.1 Exception No. 1.

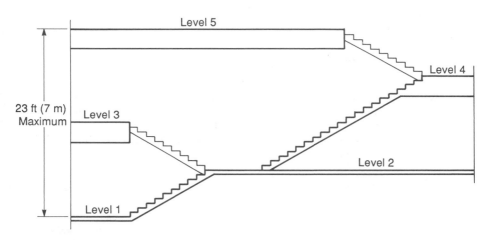

Figure 15-10. Unprotected Vertical Openings in Sprinklered Housing Area
Allowed by 15-3.1.1 Exception No. 3.

15-3.1.2 Multilevel residential housing areas are permitted without enclosure
protection between levels, provided all the following conditions are met:

(a)* The entire normally occupied area, including all communicating floor levels, is
sufficiently open and unobstructed so that it may be assumed that a fire or other

dangerous condition in any part will be readily obvious to the occupants or supervisory personnel in the area.

(b) Exit capacity is sufficient to provide simultaneously for all the occupants of all communicating levels and areas, with all communicating levels in the same fire area being considered as a single floor area for purposes of determination of required exit capacity.

(c)* The height between the highest and lowest finished floor levels does not exceed 13 ft (4.0 m). The number of levels is not restricted.

A-15-3.1.2(a)   It is not the intent of this requirement to restrict room face separations, which restrict visibility from the common space into individual sleeping rooms.

A-15-3.1.2(c)   The maximum vertical separation between the lowest floor level and the uppermost floor level is restricted to 13 ft (4.0 m). Figure A-15-3.1.2(c) illustrates how the height is to be determined.

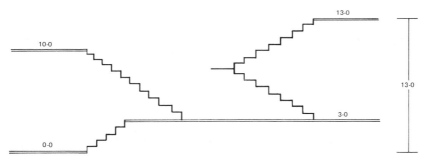

Figure A-15-3.1.2(c)

Whereas 15-3.1.1 Exception No. 3 allowed multilevel housing areas with maximum 23-ft (7-m) height between lowest and highest finished floor levels if the housing areas were fully sprinklered, 15-3.1.2 allows similar multilevel housing areas without requiring sprinklering but limits height to 13 ft (4 m).

15-3.1.3*   A multitiered open cell block may be considered as a single-story building provided that either:

1. A smoke control system is provided (*see recommended design criteria in A-15-3.1.3*) to maintain the level of smoke filling from potential cell fires at least 5 ft (152 cm) above the floor level of any occupied tier involving space that is:

(a) Use Condition IV or V.

(b) Use Condition III unless all persons housed in such space can pass through a free access smoke barrier or freely pass below the calculated smoke level with not more than 50 ft (15 m) of travel from their cell, or

2. The entire building, including cells, is provided with complete automatic sprinkler protection in accordance with 15-3.5.

A-15-3.1.3   A Recommended Method of Calculating Expected Level of Smoke in a Smoke Removal Equipped Cell Block.

This method for calculating the expected level of smoke has been developed from data experimentally produced in full-scale burnouts of test cells. The test cells were sized, loaded with fuel, and constructed to represent severe conditions of heavily fuel loaded [approximately 6 lb/sq ft (29 kg/sq m)] cells as found in prison locations. The filling rate and temperature of the effluent gas and smoke have been calculated using the data from these tests and established formulae from plume dynamics.

The application of the method described in A-15-3.1.3 should be limited to situations where there is at least 10 ft (3 m) from the floor level to the lowest acceptable level of smoke accumulation (Z); the reservoir above the lowest acceptable level for Z is at least 20 percent of the Z dimension, the length of the cell block is at least equal to Z, and the fan is at least 10 ft (3 m) higher than the floor of the highest cell.

The determination of smoke removal requirements is based on the dimensions of the cell opening. Where more than one cell opening is involved, the larger size on the level being calculated should be used.

The fan size, temperature rating, and operations means may be determined by the following procedure:

1. Acceptable smoke level.   Determine the lowest acceptable level of smoke accumulation in accordance with 15-3.1.3. The vertical distance between that level and the floor level of the lowest open cell is the value of Z to be used in connection with Figure A-15-3.1.3(a).

2. Characteristic cell opening.   Determine the opening of the cell face. Where there is more than one size of cell opening, use the largest. Match the actual opening to those shown in Figure A-15-3.1.3(b), and use the corresponding curve on Figure A-15-3.1.3(a). If there is no match between the size and shape of opening and Figure A-15-3.1.3(a), then interpolate between the curves. If the opening exceeds 6 ft (183 cm) by 6 ft (183 cm), use the curve for a 6 ft (183 cm) by 6 ft (183 cm) opening. This curve is considered to represent the maximum burning situation, and increasing the size of the opening will not increase the actual burning rate.

3. Exhaust fan rate.   Determine the exhaust fan capacity needed to extract smoke at a rate that will maintain the smoke level at a point higher than Z. This is the rate shown on the baseline of Figure A-15-3.1.3(a) corresponding to the level of Z on the vertical axis for the solid line (ventilation rate) curve appropriate to the cell door size. This exhaust capability must be provided at a point higher than Z.

4. Intake air.   Provide intake air openings that are either present or automatically provided at times of emergency smoke removal. These are to be located at or near the baseline of the cell block to allow for intake air at the rate to be vented by the fan. The openings provided shall be sufficient to avoid a friction load that can reduce the exhaust efficiency. Standard air handling design criteria are used in making this calculation.

5. Fan temperature rating.   Determine the potential temperature of gases that the fan may be required to handle. To do this, determine the distance from the floor of the highest cell to the centerline of the fan (or fan ports if the fan is in a duct or similar arrangement). Determine the intersection of this new "Z" value with the appropriate ventilation rate curve (solid line) on Figure A-15-3.1.3(a). Estimate the temperature rise by interpolating along the appropriate ventilation rate curve and between the constant

temperature rise curves (dashed lines) on Figure A-15-3.1.3(a). Provide all elements of the exhaust system that are to be above the acceptable smoke level with the capability to effectively operate with the indicated increase in temperature.

6. Operation of exhaust system. The emergency exhaust system should be arranged to initiate automatically on detection of smoke, operation of a manual fire alarm system, or direct manual operation. The capability to manually start the automatic exhaust system should be provided in a guard post in the cell block and/or at another control location. When appropriate, the emergency exhaust fans may be used for comfort ventilation as well as serving their emergency purposes.

15-3.2 Protection from Hazards.

15-3.2.1 An area used for general storage, boiler or furnace rooms, fuel storage, janitor's closets, maintenance shops including woodworking and painting areas, laundries and kitchens shall be separated from other parts of the building with construction having not less than a 1-hour fire resistance rating, and all openings shall be protected with self-closing fire doors, or such area shall be provided with automatic sprinkler protection. Where the hazard is severe, both the 1-hour fire resistance rated separation and automatic sprinklers shall be provided. The automatic extinguishing may be in accordance with 7-7.1.2.

Exception No. 1: Where cooking facilities are protected per 7-2.3, kitchens need not be provided with room-wide protection.

Exception No. 2: When, in the opinion of the authority having jurisdiction, such areas are no longer incidental to residents' housing, they shall be separated by 2-hour fire barriers in conjunction with automatic sprinkler protection.

Hazardous areas are spaces with contents that, because of their basic nature (as in the case of flammable liquids) or because of the quantity of combustible materials involved, represent a significantly higher hazard than would otherwise be typical of detention and correctional occupancies.

Hazardous areas must be separated from other areas by 1-hour fire resistance rated construction complete with approved fire doors protecting door openings, or the areas may be protected by automatic sprinklers. In those instances where the hazard is judged to be severe by the authority having jurisdiction, both the fire resistance rated separation and automatic sprinkler protection are required. Where automatic sprinkler protection is provided and the hazard is not severe, the hazardous areas may be separated by nonrated barriers designed to resist the passage of smoke.

Where flammable liquids are handled or stored, NFPA 30, *Flammable and Combustible Liquids Code,*[6] should be consulted to establish the minimum criteria necessary to mitigate this hazard.

15-3.2.2* Padded cells are severe hazard areas. Doors to padded cells shall be ¾-hour self-closing and self-latching fire door assemblies.

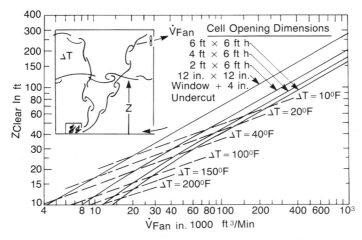

ΔT—Temperature of Upper Layer Gases Above Ambient
—Ventilation Rate Curves
– –Constant Temperature Rise Curves
$\dot{V}_{Fan}$ — Fan Discharge Capacity (As Installed)
Z_{Clear} — Distance From Cell Floor to Smoke Layer

Conversion: (ft) × .3048 = (m); (cu ft/min) × .00047 = (cu m/s); (°F-32) ÷ 1.8 = °C.

Figure A-15-3.1.3(a)   Cell Block Smoke Control Ventilation Curves.

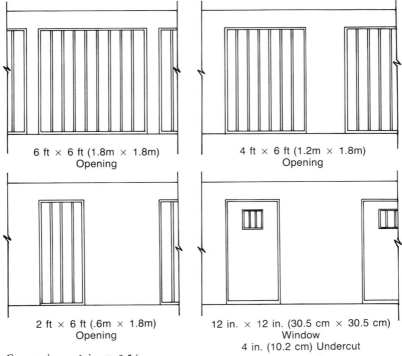

6 ft × 6 ft (1.8m × 1.8m)
Opening

4 ft × 6 ft (1.2m × 1.8m)
Opening

2 ft × 6 ft (.6m × 1.8m)
Opening

12 in. × 12 in. (30.5 cm × 30.5 cm)
Window
4 in. (10.2 cm) Undercut

Conversion: 1 in. = 2.54 cm.

Figure A-15-3.1.3(b)   Typical Cell Openings.

A-15-3.2.2   It is strongly recommended that padded cells not be used due to their fire record. However, recognizing that they will be used in some cases, provisions for the protection of padded cells are provided. It is recognized that the ¾-hour fire door will be violated with the "plant on" of the padding, but a ¾-hour fire door should be the base of the assembly.

Padded cells are considered severe hazard areas due to high heat release, the speed of combustion, and the quantity of smoke produced by the padding materials. Due to this high hazard potential, padded cells must be protected by automatic sprinklers and separated by 1-hour construction. Many of the recent multiple-death fires in detention and correctional occupancies have started in padded cells.

15-3.2.3   Cooking facilities shall be protected in accordance with 7-2.3.

15-3.3 Interior Finish.

15-3.3.1   Interior wall and ceiling finish in corridors and exits and any space not separated from the corridors and exits by a partition capable of retarding the passage of smoke shall be Class A or B. In all other areas, interior wall and ceiling finish shall be Class A, B, or C in accordance with Section 6-5.

Paragraph 15-3.3.1 requires only that the separating partition be capable of retarding the passage of smoke. The partition must be of substantial construction, but is not required to have a fire resistance rating. (*See Chapter 6 for definition of smoke barrier.*)

15-3.3.2   Interior floor finish material in corridors and exits shall be Class II in accordance with Section 6-5.

Exception: Existing floor finish material of Class A or B in nonsprinklered buildings and Class A, B, or C in sprinklered buildings, may be continued in use provided that they have been evaluated based upon tests in accordance with 6-5.3.1.

Prior to the 1981 Edition of the *Code*, floor finish was tested in accordance with NFPA 255, *Method of Test of Surface Burning Characteristics of Building Materials.*[7] This Exception allows material that was tested and approved by this method to remain in use.

15-3.4 Detection, Alarm, and Communications Systems.

15-3.4.1 General.

15-3.4.1.1   Detention and correctional occupancies shall be provided with a fire alarm system in accordance with Section 7-6, except as modified below.

15-3.4.1.2   All required fire alarm systems shall be electrically supervised.

Exception: Existing nonelectrically supervised systems may be allowed in buildings protected by a complete automatic extinguishing system.

15-3.4.1.3   All fire alarm systems and detection systems required in this section shall be provided with a secondary power supply, and the installation shall be in accordance with NFPA 72A, *Standard for the Installation, Maintenance, and Use of Local Protective Signaling Systems for Guard's Tour, Fire Alarm, and Supervisory Service.*

15-3.4.2 Initiation.   Initiation of the required fire alarm system shall be by manual means, in accordance with 7-6.2, and by means of any detection devices or detection systems required.

Exception No. 1:   Manual fire alarm boxes may be locked provided that staff is present within the subject area when occupied and have keys readily available to unlock the boxes.

Exception No. 2:   Manual fire alarm boxes may be located in a staff location, provided that the staff location is manned when the building is occupied and has direct supervision of the sleeping area.

15-3.4.3 Notification.

15-3.4.3.1 Occupant Notification.   Occupant notification shall be accomplished automatically, without delay, upon operation of any fire alarm initiating device in accordance with 7-6.3. Presignal systems are prohibited.

Exception*:   Any smoke detectors required by this chapter may be arranged to alarm at a constantly attended location only and are not required to accomplish general alarm indication.

A-15-3.4.3.1 Exception   The staff at the constantly attended location should have the capability to promptly initiate the general alarm function and contact the fire department or have direct communication with a control room or other location that can initiate the general alarm function and contact the fire department.

Presignal systems are prohibited by 15-3.4.3.1 since this paragraph requires that notification be provided "without delay." However, the Exception does exempt smoke detectors from sounding a general alarm.

15-3.4.3.2 Emergency Forces Notification.   Fire department notification shall be accomplished in accordance with 7-6.4.

Exception: Any smoke detectors required by this chapter are not required to transmit an alarm to the fire department.

Where the fire department is not equipped to receive such alarms or direct transmission to the fire department is not permitted, arrangements are to be made for the prompt notification of the fire department. The next best option is notification by an approved central station alarm system. Paragraph 7-6.4 provides several options for notifying the fire department automatically. Where smoke detectors are provided, they are not required to sound the fire alarm or to transmit a signal to the fire department, but are required to sound an alarm at a constantly attended location, unless specifically noted otherwise.

15-3.4.4 Detection.   An approved automatic smoke detection system shall be installed, in accordance with Section 7-6, throughout all resident housing areas.

Exception No. 1: Smoke detectors may be omitted from sleeping rooms with 4 or fewer occupants in Use Condition II or III.

Exception No. 2: In buildings protected throughout by an approved automatic sprinkler system installed in accordance with Section 7-7, smoke detectors may be omitted from all but corridors, common spaces, and sleeping rooms with more than four occupants.

Exception No. 3: Other arrangements and positioning of smoke detectors may be used to prevent damage or tampering, or for other purposes, provided the function of detecting any fire is fulfilled and the siting of detectors is such that the speed of detection will be equivalent to that provided by the spacing and arrangements described in Section 7-6. This may include the location of detectors in exhaust ducts from cells, behind grilles, or in other locations. The equivalent performance of the design, however, must be acceptable to the authority having jurisdiction in accordance with the equivalency concepts specified in Section 1-5 of this Code.

15-3.5 Extinguishment Requirements.

15-3.5.1 Reserved.

15-3.5.2*   Where required by 15-1.6, facilities shall be protected throughout by an approved supervised automatic sprinkler system in accordance with Section 7-7.

A-15-3.5.2   Where the openings in ceilings or partitions are ¼ in. (.6 cm) or larger in the least dimension, where the thickness or depth of the material does not exceed the least dimension of the openings, and where such openings constitute at least 70 percent of the area of the ceiling or partition material, the disruption of sprinkler spray patterns may be disregarded.

15-3.5.3   Where this *Code* permits exceptions for fully sprinklered detention and correctional occupancies, the sprinkler system shall be:

   (a) In complete accordance with Section 7-7,

   (b) Electrically connected to the fire alarm system, and

   (c) Fully supervised.

Paragraphs 15-3.5.2 and 15-3.5.3 indicate that, where automatic sprinklers are installed to comply with the *Code*, the system shall be a complete approved automatic sprinkler system installed in accordance with NFPA 13, *Standard for the Installation of Sprinkler Systems.*[8] The use of manually operated sprinklers is not recognized by the *Code*. Informal surveys conducted by the Committee have indicated no significant problems in installing automatic sprinklers in detention and correctional facilities. The system must also be supervised in order to be credited as complying with the *Code*.

15-3.5.4   Portable fire extinguishers shall be provided in accordance with 7-7.4.1.

Exception No. 1*: Access to portable fire extinguishers may be locked.

Exception No. 2: Portable fire extinguishers may be located at staff locations only.

A-15-3.5.4 Exception No. 1 Where access to portable fire extinguishers is locked, staff should be present on a 24-hour basis and have keys readily available to unlock access to the extinguishers. Where supervision of sleeping areas is from a 24-hour manned staff location, portable fire extinguishers may be provided at the staff location in lieu of within the sleeping area.

> Exception No.1 to 15-3.5.4 permits locking of the fire extinguishers. Time is of the essence in using extinguishers; therefore, keys must be carried by the staff or be readily accessible.

15-3.5.5 Standpipe and hose systems shall be provided in accordance with 7-7.4.2 as follows:

(a) Class I standpipe systems shall be provided for any building over two stories in height, and

(b) Class III standpipe and hose systems shall be provided for all unsprinklered buildings over two stories in height.

Exception No. 1: One-inch (2.5-cm) diameter formed hose on hose reels may be used to provide Class II service.

Exception No. 2: Separate Class I and Class II systems may be used in lieu of Class III.

> The standpipe requirements intend that 2½-inch (6.2-cm) hose connections be available for fire department use in any detention and correctional occupancy more than two stories in height. Additionally, if such buildings are unsprinklered, there should also be 1½-inch (3.8-cm) connections and hose for occupant (i.e., staff and resident) use.
>
> Exception No. 1 permits the use of 1-in. (2.5-cm) formed rubber hose in place of fabric-jacket rubber-lined hose normally required in standpipe systems. The rubber hose is normally stored on reels and is somewhat easier to use.

15-3.6 Corridors. [*See 15-3.8, Special Features (Subdivision of Resident Housing Spaces).*]

15-3.7 Subdivision of Building Spaces.

15-3.7.1* Smoke barriers shall be provided, regardless of building construction type, so as to divide every story used by residents for sleeping by ten or more persons, or any other story having an occupant load of 50 or more persons, into at least two compartments.

Exception No. 1: Protection may be accomplished with horizontal exits (see 5-2.4).

Exception No. 2: Spaces having direct exit to (a) a public way, (b) a building separated from the resident housing area by a 2-hour fire resistance rating or 50 ft (15 m) of open space, or (c) a secured open area having a holding space 50 ft (15 m) from the housing area that provides 15 sq ft (1.4 sq m) or more of refuge area per person (resident, staff, visitors) that may be present at the time of the fire fulfills the requirements for subdivision of such spaces, provided the locking arrangement of doors involved meets the requirements for doors at the compartment barrier for the use condition involved.

A-15-3.7.1 Consideration can be given for large open areas which may function as smoke sinks as an alternative to the installation of more than one smoke barrier as required by this section. Vertical movement downward to an area of refuge may be accepted by the authority having jurisdiction in lieu of horizontal movement.

15-3.7.2   Where smoke barriers are required by 15-3.7.1, smoke barriers shall be provided so as:

(a) to limit the housing to a maximum of 200 residents in any smoke compartment, and

(b)* to limit the travel distance to a door in a smoke barrier:

1. From any room door required as exit access to 100 ft (30 m),

2. From any point in a room to 150 ft (45 m).

Exception to (b): The travel distance may be increased by 50 ft (15 m) in buildings protected throughout by an approved automatic sprinkler or smoke control system.

A-15-3.7.2(b)   Consideration should be given to increasing the travel distance to a smoke barrier to coincide with existing range lengths and exits.

Smoke barriers and horizontal exits used to subdivide a building serve three purposes fundamental to the protection of occupants in that they:
1. Limit the spread of fire and fire-produced contaminants,
2. Limit the number of occupants exposed to a single fire, and
3. Provide for horizontal relocation of occupants by creating an area of refuge on the same floor.
The requirements of 15-3.7.1 and 15-3.7.2 for subdividing building spaces are illustrated in Figures 15-11 and 15-12.

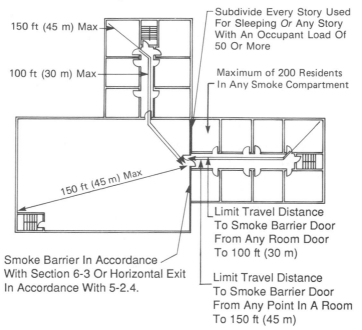

Figure 15-11. Subdivision of Building Spaces in Existing Detention and Correctional Occupancies.

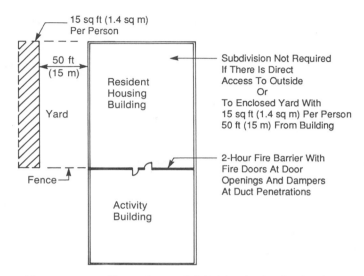

Figure 15-12.   Alternatives to Subdivision by Smoke Barriers.

15-3.7.3* Any required smoke barrier shall be constructed in accordance with Section 6-3. Barriers shall be of substantial construction and shall have a structural fire resistance. Fixed wire glass or minimum 45-minute fire rated glazing vision panels shall be permitted in such barriers, provided they do not individually exceed 1,296 sq in. (.84 sq m) in area and are mounted in approved steel frames. There is no restriction on the total number of such vision panels in any barrier (e.g., a smoke barrier may consist of wire glass or minimum 45-minute fire rated glazing panels mounted in a security grille arrangement).

A-15-3.7.3 Structural fire resistance is defined as the ability of the assembly to stay in place and maintain structural integrity without consideration of heat transmission. Twelve gage steel plate suitably framed and stiffened meets this requirement.

Paragraph 15-3.7.3 requires smoke barriers to have structural fire resistance. However, the specific fire resistance in hours is omitted. The intent is to eliminate the use of highly combustible or flimsy materials, such as plastic sheeting, which could possibly limit smoke movement but which have little structural integrity. This paragraph does permit the entire smoke barrier to be constructed of wired glass panels not exceeding 1,296 sq in (0.84 sq m) each in steel frame.

15-3.7.4 At least 6 net sq ft (.56 sq m) per occupant shall be provided on each side of the smoke barrier for the total number of occupants in adjoining compartments. This space shall be readily available whenever the occupants are moved across the smoke barrier in a fire emergency.

15-3.7.5 Doors in smoke barriers shall be self-closing or automatic-closing as required in 5-2.1.8 and shall provide resistance to the passage of smoke. Swinging doors shall be self-latching. Such doors are not required to swing with exit travel.

15-3.7.6 Doors in smoke barriers shall conform with the requirements for doors in means of egress as specified in Section 15-2 and shall have locking and release arrangements according to the Use Condition. The provisions of the Exception to 15-2.11.6 shall not be used for smoke barrier doors serving a smoke compartment containing more than 20 persons.

The provisions of the Exception to 15-2.11.6 allow up to ten locks to be arranged so as to require manual unlocking in a timely fashion and still be considered as providing remote unlocking. However, 15-3.7.6 does not allow for the locks on smoke barrier doors to be part of the maximum ten manually unlocked locks where the smoke compartment houses more than 20 persons.

15-3.7.7 Vision panels of approved transparent wire glass or minimum 45-minute fire rated glazing, or other material approved by the authority having jurisdiction, in steel frames, and not exceeding 1,296 sq in. (.84 sq m) in area shall be provided in each door in a smoke barrier.

15-3.7.8 Smoke dampers shall be provided in accordance with 6-3.5.

Exception: Other arrangements and positioning of smoke detectors may be used to prevent damage or tampering or may be used for other purposes, provided the function of detecting any fire is fulfilled, and the siting of detectors is such that the speed of detection will be equivalent to that provided by the required spacing and arrangement.

15-3.8 Special Features. (Subdivision of Resident Housing Spaces.)

15-3.8.1* Subdivision of facility spaces shall comply with Table 15-3.8.1.

A-15-3.8.1 Requirements in Table 15-3.8.1 for smoketight and fire rated separations include taking the necessary precautions to restrict the spread of smoke through the air handling system. This, however, does not mean that smoke dampers must be provided for each opening. Smoke dampers would be one acceptable method; however, other techniques such as allowing the fans to continue to run with 100 percent supply and 100 percent exhaust would be acceptable.

Paragraph 15-3.8.1 provides for the separation of areas where residents are housed. This separation serves two basic needs: (1) it keeps the fire and its products confined to the area of origin, and (2) it protects those outside the area of origin. Table 15-3.8.1 establishes different requirements based on the Use Condition involved. Within each Use Condition, different provisions are required depending upon whether automatic sprinkler protection is or is not provided. Where a common wall is used for different purposes, such as "room face to corridor" and "common space to corridor," the most restrictive requirement shall apply to the entire wall. Table 15-3.8.1, with the notes and asterisked items, in addition to the locking options previously mentioned, provides a wide variety of options. Note 4 to the table also provides an additional method that, in combination with the locking options previously stated, can be quite useful.

Table 15-3.8.1

USE CONDITION	II		III		IV		V	
Feature	NS	AS	NS	AS	NS	AS	NS	AS
Room to Room Separation	NR	NR	NR	NR	ST	NR	ST	ST**
Room Face to Corridor Separation	NR	NR	ST***	NR	ST***	NR	FR***	ST**
Room Face to Common Space Separation	NR	NR	NR <50 ft* (15 m) ST*** >50 ft* (15 m)	NR <50 ft* (15 m) ST** >50 ft* (15 m)	ST***	NR <50 ft* (15 m) ST** >50 ft* (15 m)	ST***	ST**
Common Space to Corridor Separation	ST	NR	ST	NR	ST	NR	FR	ST**
Total Openings in Solid Room Face	120 sq in. (.08 sq m)		120 sq in. (.08 sq m)		120 sq in. (.08 sq m)		120 sq in. (.08 sq m) Closable from inside or 120 sq in. (.08 sq m) w/smoke control	

AS — Protected by automatic sprinklers
NS — Not protected by automatic sprinklers
NR — No requirement

ST — Smoketight
FR — Fire Rated — 1 hour

*This is the travel distance through the common space to the exit access corridor.

**May be NR where there is either

(a) an approved automatic smoke detection system installed in all corridors and common spaces, or,

(b) multi-tiered cell blocks meeting the requirements of 15-3.1.3.

***May be NR in multi-tiered open cell blocks meeting the requirements of 15-3.1.3.

NOTE 1: Doors in openings in partitions required to be fire resistive by this chart in other than required enclosures of exits or hazardous areas shall be substantial doors, of construction that will resist fire for at least 20 minutes. Wire glass or minimum 45-minute fire rated glazing vision panels are permitted. Latches and door closers are not required on cell doors.

NOTE 2: Doors in openings in partitions required to be smoketight by the chart shall be substantial doors, of construction that will resist the passage of smoke. Latches and door closers are not required on cell doors.

NOTE 3: "Total Openings in Solid Room Face" includes all openings (undercuts, food passes, grilles, etc.), the total of which will not exceed 120 sq in. (.08 sq m). Under Use Condition II, III, IV, a space housing not more than 16 persons and subdivided by open construction (any combination of grating doors and grating walls or solid walls) may be considered one room. The perimeter walls of such space shall be of smoketight construction. Smoke detection shall be provided in such space. Under Use Condition IV, common walls between sleeping areas within the space shall be smoketight and grating doors and fronts may be used.

Formal Interpretation 81-41
Reference: 14-3.8.1, Note 4
                    15-3.8.1, Note 4

Question: Is it the intent of the committee that Note 4 to 14-3.8.1 (15-3.8.1) restrict the number of occupants in an open, undivided dormitory to a maximum of 16 persons?

Answer: No.

Issue Edition: 1981
Reference: 14-3.8.1, Note 4,
                    15-3.8.1, Note 4
Date: April 1984

SECTION 15-4   SPECIAL PROVISIONS

15-4.1 Windowless Areas.

15-4.1.1*   For purposes of this chapter, a windowless area is a smoke compartment that does not contain operable windows or fixed windows that can be readily broken by impact.

A-15-4.1.1   Windows that are intended to be breakable should be capable of being broken with materials readily available to the facility staff.

15-4.1.2   Windowless areas shall be provided with vent openings, smoke shafts, or an engineered smoke control system to provide ventilation (mechanical or natural).

Paragraph 15-4.1.2 does not require venting or smoke control for those areas (smoke compartments) that are provided with operable windows or fixed windows that can be broken by impact.

15-4.2 Underground Buildings.

15-4.2.1   See Chapter 30 for requirements for underground buildings.

15-4.3 High Rise Buildings.   (Reserved).

15-4.4 Operating Features.   (*See Chapter 31.*)

SECTION 15-5   BUILDING SERVICES

15-5.1 Utilities.

15-5.1.1   Utilities shall comply with the provisions of Section 7-1.

15-5.1.2 Alarms, emergency communication systems, and the illumination of generator set installations shall be provided with emergency power in accordance with NFPA 70, *National Electrical Code.*

Exception: Systems complying with earlier editions of NFPA 70 and not presenting a life safety hazard may be continued in use.

15-5.2 Heating, Ventilating, and Air Conditioning.

15-5.2.1 Heating, ventilating, and air conditioning equipment shall comply with the provisions of Section 7-2 and shall be installed in accordance with the manufacturer's specifications.

Exception No. 1: As modified in 15-5.2.2 following.

Exception No. 2: Systems complying with earlier editions of the applicable codes and not presenting a life safety hazard may be continued in use.

15-5.2.2 Portable space heating devices are prohibited. Any heating device other than a central heating plant shall be so designed and installed that combustible material will not be ignited by it or its appurtenances. If fuel-fired, such heating devices shall be chimney or vent connected, shall take air for combustion directly from outside, and shall be so designed and installed to provide for complete separation of the combustion system from the atmosphere of the occupied area. The heating system shall have safety devices to immediately stop the flow of fuel and shut down the equipment in case of either excessive temperatures or ignition failure.

Exception: Approved suspended unit heaters may be used in locations other than means of egress and sleeping areas, provided such heaters are located high enough to be out of reach of persons using the area, and provided they are vent connected and equipped with the safety devices called for above.

15-5.2.3 Combustion and ventilation air for boiler, incinerator, or heater rooms shall be taken directly from and discharged directly to the outside air.

15-5.3 Elevators, Dumbwaiters, and Vertical Conveyors.   Elevators, dumbwaiters, and vertical conveyors shall comply with the provisions of Section 7-4.

15-5.4 Rubbish Chutes, Incinerators, and Laundry Chutes.

15-5.4.1 Rubbish chutes, incinerators, and laundry chutes shall comply with the provisions of Section 7-5.

15-5.4.2 Any rubbish chute or linen chute, including pneumatic rubbish and linen systems, shall be provided with automatic extinguishing protection installed in accordance with Section 7-7.

15-5.4.3 Any trash chute shall discharge into a trash collecting room used for no other purpose and protected in accordance with Section 6-4.

15-5.4.4 Any incinerator shall not be directly flue-fed, nor shall any floor chute directly connect with the combustion chamber.

References Cited in Commentary

[1] "A Study of Penal Institution Fires," NFPA FR 78-1.

[2] James Bell, "Eleven Die in Jail Fire," *Fire Journal*, Vol. 74, No. 4, July 1980, pp. 23-25, 90.

[3] James Bell, "Twenty-Nine Die in Biloxi, Mississippi Jail Fire, *Fire Journal*, Vol. 77, No. 6, November 1983, pp. 44-49, 52-55.

[4] NFPA 101M, *Alternative Approaches to Life Safety*, National Fire Protection Association, Quincy, MA 1988.

[5] NFPA 220, *Standard on Types of Building Construction*, National Fire Protection Association, Quincy, MA, 1985.

[6] NFPA 30, *Flammable and Combustible Liquids Code*, National Fire Protection Association, Quincy, MA, 1987.

[7] NFPA 255, *Method of Test of Surface Burning Characteristics of Building Materials*, National Fire Protection Association, Quincy, MA, 1984.

[8] NFPA 13, *Standard for the Installation of Sprinkler Systems*, National Fire Protection Association, Quincy, MA, 1987.

16

NEW HOTELS AND DORMITORIES

(See also Chapter 31.)

Prior to the 1981 Edition of the *Code*, all residential occupancies were treated in one chapter. In the 1981 Edition they were split into several chapters in order to simplify and clarify the *Code*, resulting in a document that is easier to use.

Residential occupancies are those in which sleeping accommodations are provided for normal residential purposes, and include all buildings designed to provide sleeping accommodations. They are treated separately in the *Code* in the following groups:

Hotels, motels, dormitories (Chapters 16 and 17)

Apartment buildings (Chapters 18 and 19)

Lodging or rooming houses (Chapter 20)

Board and care facilities (Chapter 21)

One- and two-family dwellings (Chapter 22)

Exceptions to the groups listed above are health care occupancies, which are covered in Chapters 12 and 13, and detention and correctional occupancies, which are covered in Chapters 14 and 15. In earlier editions of the *Code*, they were classified as "institutional occupancies."

A review of 4-1.6 underscores a common principle of life safety with which the *Code* is concerned as applied to all the residential occupancies considered by Chapters 16 through 23. Paragraph 4-1.6 states: "Residential occupancies are those occupancies in which sleeping accommodations are provided for normal residential purposes and include all buildings designed to provide sleeping accommodations." This use of residential occupancies is central to the *Code's* provisions in Chapters 16 through 23, because people who are asleep will be unaware of a rapidly developing fire and, when alerted, may be somewhat confused due to being awakened suddenly. Other factors on which the provisions of Chapters 16 through 23 were based are the presence of hazards (such as cooking and heating equipment) in residential occupancies and the degree of familiarity of the occupant with his or her living space (ranging from transients with little or no familiarity, as in hotels, to total familiarity in single-family dwellings).

SECTION 16-1 GENERAL REQUIREMENTS

16-1.1 Application.

16-1.1.1 This chapter establishes life safety requirements for all new hotels and for modified buildings according to the provisions of Section 1-4. (*See Chapter 31 for operating features.*)

Hotels and dormitories are defined in 16-1.3.1. It should be noted that lodging or rooming houses that contain more than 16 people are considered hotels and must comply with Chapter 16. Existing hotels are covered in Chapter 17.

16-1.1.2 New dormitories shall comply with the requirements for new hotels.

Exception: Any dormitory divided into suites of rooms, with one or more bedrooms opening into a living room or study that has a door opening into a common corridor serving a number of suites, shall be classified as an apartment building.

The Exception to 16-1.1.2 recognizes that the now popular dormitory design of a group of bedrooms clustered around a living room duplicates a typical apartment design of several bedrooms clustered around a living room (or a kitchen). Since the design and the risk of fire are the same, the *Code* treats this arrangement the same as that of an apartment building. (*See Figure 16-1.*)

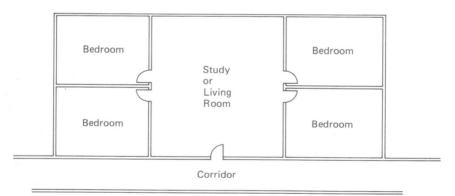

Figure 16-1. Arrangement of Dormitory Suite Treated as an Apartment Under the Exception to 16-1.1.2. More than one bedroom opens into a study or living room that has a door opening into a corridor. The corridor serves a number of suites.

16-1.2 Mixed Occupancies.

16-1.2.1 Where another type of occupancy occurs in the same building as a residential occupancy, the requirements of 1-4.7 of this *Code* shall be applicable.

16-1.2.2 For requirements on mixed mercantile and residential occupancies, see 24-1.2.

16-1.2.3 Any ballroom, assembly or exhibition hall, and other space used for purposes of public assembly shall be in accordance with Chapter 8. Any dining area having a capacity of 50 or more persons shall be treated as an assembly occupancy.

Most of the larger hotels consist of several occupancies — Hotel, Assembly (ballrooms, restaurants, lounges), Business (large administrative areas), and Mercantile (large shopping areas), among others. Unless these areas are adequately separated and protected, the complex is a mixed occupancy and the most stringent provisions of the various occupancies must be applied. Note that small administrative areas and small gift shops or newsstands do not justify invoking mixed occupancy requirements. This can be very important with regard to the construction and sprinkler requirements for assembly occupancies and with regard to sprinkler requirements for mercantile occupancies. (*See discussion following 16-1.6, 16-3.2, and 16-3.5.*)

16-1.3 Definitions.

16-1.3.1 Terms applicable to this chapter are defined in Chapter 3 of this *Code*; where necessary, other terms will be defined in the text as they may occur.

Dormitories. Includes buildings or spaces in buildings where group sleeping accommodations are provided for more than 16 persons not members of the same family group in one room or in a series of closely associated rooms under joint occupancy and single management, as in college dormitories, fraternity houses, military barracks; with or without meals, but without individual cooking facilities.

In 16-1.3.1, the phrase "without individual cooking facilities" refers to the absence of cooking equipment in any room or unit of a dormitory. If this equipment is present throughout a facility, the occupancy should be classed as an apartment building. The phrase "with or without meals" connotes the *Code's* acceptance of a central cafeteria used to serve meals for the occupants of a dormitory.

Hotels. Includes buildings or groups of buildings under the same management in which there are more than 16 sleeping accommodations for hire, primarily used by transients who are lodged with or without meals, whether designated as a hotel, inn, club, motel, or by any other name. So-called apartment hotels shall be classified as hotels because they are potentially subject to transient occupancy like that of hotels.

Lodging or rooming houses containing more than 16 people are treated as hotels. Where units have individual cooking facilities, the *Code* would classify the occupancy as an apartment building. (*See 18-1.3.*) However, where the authority believes that the hazards of both a hotel (people unfamiliar with surroundings) and an apartment building (higher fuel load, greater ignition sources, and travel through multiple rooms) are present, it may be appropriate to classify the building as a mixed occupancy (Hotel and Apartment).

16-1.4 Classification of Occupancy. (*See 16-1.3.*)

16-1.5 Classification of Hazard of Contents.

16-1.5.1   The contents of residential occupancies shall be classified as ordinary hazard in accordance with Section 4-2. For the design of automatic sprinkler systems, the classification of contents in NFPA 13, *Standard for the Installation of Sprinkler Systems*, shall apply.

> NFPA 13, *Standard for the Installation of Sprinkler Systems*,[1] would classify the contents as "light" for the purpose of designing extinguishing systems. The difference in classification is based on the threat to life or life safety (ordinary) versus the threat to the extinguishing capability of the automatic sprinkler system (light).

16-1.6 Minimum Construction Requirements.   No Special Requirements.

> Although this chapter does not establish minimum construction requirements, if the hotel contains an assembly occupancy, Chapter 8 does establish minimum construction requirements based on the location of the assembly occupancy.

16-1.7 Occupant Load.

16-1.7.1*   The occupant load in numbers of persons for whom exits are to be provided shall be determined on the basis of one person per 200 sq ft (18.6 sq m) gross floor area, or the maximum probable population of any room or section under consideration, whichever is greater. The occupant load of any open mezzanine or balcony shall be added to the occupant load of the floor below for the purpose of determining exit capacity.

A-16-1.7.1   Dormitory-type occupancy, particularly where 2- or 3-tier bunks are used with close spacing, may produce an occupant load substantially greater than one person per 200 sq ft (18.6 sq m) gross floor area. However, even though sleeping areas are densely populated, the building as a whole may not necessarily exceed one person per 200 sq ft (18.6 sq m) gross area, owing to the space taken for toilet facilities, halls, closets, and living rooms not used for sleeping purposes.

> This discussion does not preclude the need for providing exit capability from concentrated sleeping areas (bunk rooms) based on the "maximum probable population" rather than on the design figure. If the actual population of a bunk room exceeds one person per 200 sq ft (18.6 sq m), the exit capacity (door widths, etc.) will have to be designed based on the actual population load. See 5-3.1 for further details on the use of occupant load for determining capacity of the means of egress.
>
> The occupant loads for areas of hotels used for nonresidential purposes are based on the use of the area. Occupant loads for assembly areas are calculated in accordance with 8-1.7, and those for mercantile areas are calculated in accordance with 24-1.7, etc.

SECTION 16-2 MEANS OF EGRESS REQUIREMENTS

16-2.1 General.

16-2.1.1 All means of egress shall be in accordance with Chapter 5 and this chapter.

Rather than repeat many of the provisions of Chapter 5, a general reference to Chapter 5 is made. Many of the requirements that follow in Section 16-2 pick up provisions from Chapter 5 that are options for the occupancy chapters, such as the Exception to 16-2.2.2.2, which allows the use of special locking arrangements per 5-2.1.6; or that prohibit the use of an item if it is not listed (note that alternating tread devices are not listed in 16-2.2); or that establish limits based on criteria provided in Chapter 5, such as corridor dead-end limits in 16-2.5.3.

16-2.2 Means of Egress Components.

16-2.2.1 General.

16-2.2.1.1 Components of means of egress shall be limited to the types described in 16-2.2.2 through 16-2.2.7.

16-2.2.1.2 In buildings protected throughout by an approved supervised automatic sprinkler system installed in accordance with 16-3.5.1, exit enclosures may have a fire resistance rating of not less than one hour, and the fire protection rating of doors may be one hour.

In recognition of the relatively low fuel loads in hotels, the fire resistance rating for exit enclosures, as well as other vertical openings (*see 16-3.1.1 Exception No. 4*), need not exceed one hour; however, as a safeguard, this is permitted only in buildings protected throughout by automatic sprinklers. This is not permitted for assembly occupancies or business occupancies and, therefore, cannot be utilized where mixed occupancies are involved; nor can it be used for stairways or vertical openings involving or passing through other occupancies.

In facilities where occupancies are adequately separated and treated independently, it could be feasible to have a 1-hour enclosure in the hotel portion and a 2-hour enclosure elsewhere. (*See Figure 16-2.*)

16-2.2.2 Doors.

16-2.2.2.1 Doors shall comply with 5-2.1.

16-2.2.2.2* No door in any means of egress shall be locked against egress when the building is occupied.

Exception: Special locking arrangements complying with 5-2.1.6 are permitted.

A-16-2.2.2.2 It is the intent of this requirement that security measures, where installed, should not prevent egress.

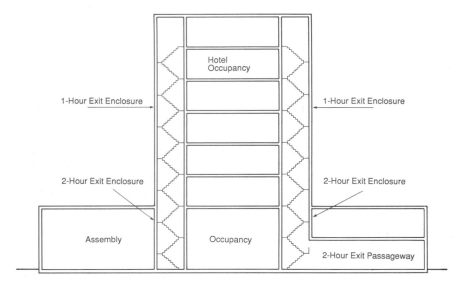

Figure 16-2.   Protection of Exit Enclosures and Other Vertical Openings in a Fully Sprinklered Hotel.   The Exception for the two-hour enclosure does not apply to other occupancies in a hotel complex nor to mixed occupancies.

Paragraph 16-2.2.2.2 prohibits a hotel from having any door locked "against egress" while the building is occupied. This requirement permits a door to have a locking device that allows the door to be opened from within the building for the purpose of egress, but does not allow the door to be opened from outside the building. Ordinary double cylinder locks and chain locks would not meet these provisions. Several tragic multiple-death fires have occurred where a key could not be found to unlock these devices.

The language of 5-2.1.5.1 is clear. "Locks, if provided, shall not require the use of a key, tool, special knowledge, or effort for operation from the inside of the building." This eliminates double cylinder locks and chain locks that require a key to operate from the inside. Paragraph 5-2.1.5.3 calls for a simple operation to open a door; the presence of a two-handed knob operation, and the like, is specifically prohibited.

Chapter 5 now specifically recognizes the need for security chains or rods on hotel room doors and allows one additional releasing device. The typical hotel room door has three devices: the latch, the lock, and the security chain or rod. However, the *Code* allows only two releasing actions for new installations. This requirement is met by using a latch and lock set that has a lock bolt that automatically retracts when the latch handle is turned from the inside; thus, only one releasing action is needed for the two devices. The second action is the release of the security chain or rod. In neither case, however, can the devices require the use of a key, tool, special knowledge, or effort.

The Exception to 16-2.2.2.2 recognizes the use of the delay release lock provided for in 5-2.1.6. This requires that the building either be protected throughout by automatic sprinklers or equipped throughout with a fire detection system. The 15- or 30-second delay permitted by 5-2.1.6 does not affect the immediate release of the lock upon activation of the sprinklers or detectors, or upon loss of power to the lock. This device helps the hotel provide the security needed for seldom used doors or stairs, while at the same time it keeps the door available for use, which chains and padlocks are unable to do.

16-2.2.2.3*   Every stairwell door shall allow reentry from the stairwell to the interior of the building, or an automatic release shall be provided to unlock all stairwell doors to allow reentry. Such automatic release shall be actuated with the initiation of the building fire alarm system. Also, stairwell doors shall unlock upon loss of power controlling the lock or locking mechanism.

A-16-2.2.2.3   This arrangement makes it possible to leave the stairway at any floor should the fire render the lower part of the stair unusable during egress or should the occupants seek refuge on another floor.

The provisions of 16-2.2.2.3 are more stringent than those of Chapter 5 in that the provisions of Exception No. 1 to 5-2.1.5.2 are not allowed in hotels. The Committee felt that hotels do not encounter the circumstances that business occupancies do where tenants lease an entire floor with no public corridor arrangement, and therefore, the Exception was unwarranted. If hotels wish to restrict normal movement in stairs, the automatic release system can be used. Numerous fatalities occurred in stairways at the MGM Grand Hotel in Las Vegas in 1980 where people were in smoke filled stairways and were locked out of floors.[2]

16-2.2.2.4   Revolving doors complying with 5-2.1.10 are permitted.

16-2.2.3 Stairs.   Stairs shall comply with 5-2.2.

16-2.2.4 Smokeproof Enclosures.   Smokeproof enclosures shall comply with 5-2.3.

16-2.2.5 Horizontal Exits.   Horizontal exits shall comply with 5-2.4.

16-2.2.6 Ramps.   Ramps shall comply with 5-2.5.

16-2.2.7 Exit Passageways.   Exit passageways shall comply with 5-2.6.

16-2.3 Capacity of Means of Egress.

16-2.3.1   The capacity of means of egress shall be in accordance with Section 5-3.

16-2.3.2   Street floor exits shall be sufficient for the occupant load of the street floor plus the required capacity of stairs and ramps discharging onto the street floor.

Paragraph 16-2.3.2 requires street-floor exit designs that have sufficient width to provide for the intermingling of exits from the street floor with those exits discharging down from the upper floors and discharging up from the lower floors. This is the traditional grand lobby design found in many hotels and in many sizable mercantile occupancies where stairs and street-floor exits converge at one or two exterior door locations. Paragraph 5-7.2 restricts the number and arrangement of stairs that discharge through the street floor.

Figure 16-3 shows a typical arrangement of multiple exits discharging on the street floor.

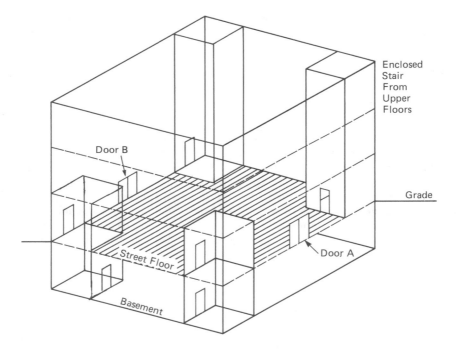

Figure 16-3. Capacity of Means of Egress in Accordance with 16-2.3.2. Required widths of Doors A and B are based on the number of people expected to use them. Assuming that the street floor has an occupant load of 500, and each upper floor has an occupant load of 200, and the basement 100, then required exit capacity for the street floor would be calculated as follows:

500 (Street floor) + 200/2 (upper floor max 50% per 5-7.2) +
100/2 (basement max 50% per 5-7.2) = 650 total using
exits on street floor × 0.2 in. (0.5 cm) of door per person = 130 in. (325 cm) ÷
2 exits = 65 in. (163 cm) at A and at B.

16-2.3.3 The minimum corridor width shall be sufficient to accommodate the required occupant load, but not less than 44 in. (112 cm).

Exception:* *Corridors within individual guest rooms or individual guest suites.*

A-16-2.3.3 Exception   This provision applies to corridors within an individual room or suite and does not apply where a suite can be subdivided and rented separately.

16-2.4 Number of Exits.   *(See also Section 5-4.)*

16-2.4.1   Not less than two exits shall be accessible from every floor, including floors below the level of exit discharge and occupied for public purposes.

> Paragraph 5-4.1.2 will require greater number of exits for floors with more than 500 people. This will probably have little effect on hotels, since floors large enough to have more than 500 people would probably need additional exits to meet travel distance limitations.

16-2.5 Arrangement of Exits.

16-2.5.1   Access to all required exits shall be in accordance with Section 5-5.

16-2.5.2   No common path of travel shall exceed 35 ft (10.7 m). Travel within a guest room or suite shall not be included when calculating common path of travel.

Exception: In buildings protected throughout by an approved supervised automatic sprinkler system, common path of travel shall not exceed 50 ft (15 m).

16-2.5.3   No dead-end corridor shall exceed 35 ft (10.7 m).

Exception: In buildings protected throughout by an approved supervised automatic sprinkler system, dead-end corridors shall not exceed 50 ft (15 m).

> Common path of travel is normally measured from the most remote point subject to occupancy *(see **5-5.1.2** and the definition of Common Path of Travel in 3-2)*; therefore, this is a modified common path of travel, as measurement does not extend into the guest room or suite. Common path of travel within the suite is, in essence, regulated by 16-2.5.4, which limits single exit access to suites under 2,000 sq ft (185 sq m).
>
> Since the dead-end limits of 16-2.5.3 are the same, it is difficult to envision an excessive, modified common path of travel that is not also a violation of the dead-end provision. *(See Figure 16-4.)*

16-2.5.4   Any room, or any suite of rooms, in excess of 2,000 sq ft (185 sq m) shall be provided with at least two exit access doors remote from each other.

16-2.6 Travel Distance to Exits.

16-2.6.1   Any exit as indicated in 16-2.4.1 shall be such that it will not be necessary to travel more than 100 ft (30 m) from the door of any room to reach the nearest exit. Travel distance to exits shall be measured in accordance with Section 5-6.

Exception No. 1:   Travel distance to exits may be increased to 200 ft (60 m) for exterior ways of exit access arranged in accordance with 5-5.3.

Exception No. 2:   Travel distance to exits may be increased to 200 ft (60 m) if the exit access and any portion of the building that is tributary to the exit access are protected throughout by an approved supervised automatic sprinkler system in accordance with 16-3.5.1. In addition, the portion of the building in which the 200-ft (60-m) travel distance is permitted shall be

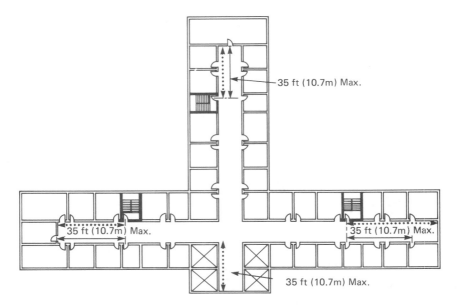

Figure 16-4 Common path of Travel (Modified) and Dead-End Limitations in a Nonsprinklered Hotel. Modified common paths of travel are indicated by ←⟶ and dead ends are indicated by ◄····► . Note that it is possible to have a dead end that is not a common path of travel, but with the modified common path of travel it is difficult to envision a realistic situation that is not also a dead end.

separated from the remainder of the building by construction having a fire resistance rating of not less than 1 hour for buildings not more than three stories in height, and 2 hours for buildings more than three stories in height.

See Figure 16-5.

16-2.6.2 Travel distance within a room or suite to a corridor door shall not exceed 75 ft (23 m).

Exception: One hundred twenty-five ft (38-m) travel distance is allowed in buildings protected by an approved supervised automatic sprinkler system in accordance with 16-3.5.1.

Due to revisions in Section 5-6, travel distance is now measured from the most remote point - subject to occupancy (the former provision exempting rooms with 6 or less people with 50 ft (15 m) or less travel distance has been deleted). To be consistent with Section 5-6, the Committee has revised the method of measuring travel distance in hotels. The distance within the room or suite has been increased by 25 ft (7.5 m) as compensation. Should the travel distance within a room or suite be excessive, another remote door to the corridor would need to be added. (*Also see 16-2.5.4.*) (*See Figure 16-5.*)

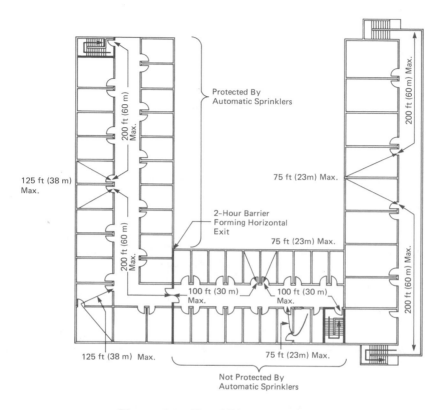

Figure 16-5.   Travel Distance in Hotels.

16-2.7 Discharge from Exits.

16-2.7.1   Exit discharge shall comply with Section 5-7.

16-2.7.2*   Any required exit stair that is so located that it is necessary to pass through the lobby or other open space to reach the outside of the building shall be continuously enclosed down to a level of exit discharge, or to a mezzanine within a lobby at a level of exit discharge.

A-16-2.7.2   Where open stairways are permitted, they are considered as exit access to exits rather than as exits, and requirements for distance to exits include the travel on such stairs. (*See 5-6.4.*)

16-2.7.3   The distance of travel from the termination of the exit enclosure to an exterior door leading to a public way shall not exceed 100 ft (30 m).

Section 5-7 does allow a maximum of 50 percent of the number and capacity of exits to discharge through the street floor under limited conditions. (*See* 5-7.2.) This is slightly liberalized by 16-2.7.2 by including a mezzanine within the lobby. In other words, 50 percent of the exits could discharge onto a mezzanine with occupants then traveling across the mezzanine, downstairs to the lobby level, and outside. However, 16-2.7.3 adds a provision not found in 5-7.2 by restricting the distance from the termination of the exit enclosure to the exterior door to a maximum of 100 ft (30.5 m).

(*See Figures 16-6 and 16-7.*) (*Also see commentary on 5-7.2.*)

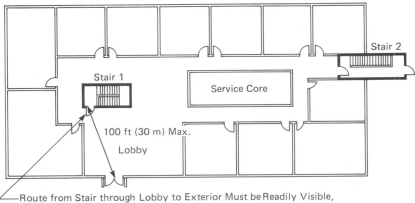

Figure 16-6.   Arrangement of Means of Egress in Accordance with 16-2.7. (*See Section* 5-7.)   Stair 1 (50 percent of the total number and capacity of exits) discharges through the first floor. Stair 2 discharges directly to the exterior (it may discharge through an exit passageway to the exterior). Since other areas on the first floor (the level of exit discharge) are not separated from the path that a person leaving Stair 1 must follow to exit through the lobby, the entire first floor must be completely sprinklered. If the rest of the floor were separated (to the extent required for the stair enclosure), only the path to the exit discharge would have to be sprinklered.

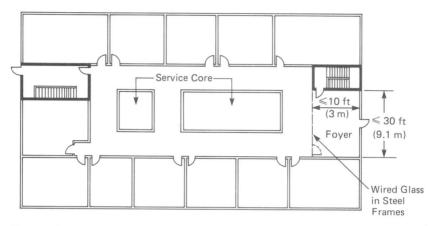

Figure 16-7. Foyer Constructed in Compliance with 16-2.7. (*See* 5-7.2.) The foyer must serve only as a means of egress.

16-2.8 Illumination of Means of Egress.

16-2.8.1   Means of egress shall be illuminated in accordance with Section 5-8.

16-2.9 Emergency Lighting.

16-2.9.1   Emergency lighting in accordance with Section 5-9 shall be provided in all buildings with more than 25 rooms.

Exception: Where each guest room has a direct exit to the outside of the building at grade level (as in motels).

The Exception to 16-2.9.1 does not apply to motels with exterior balconies and stairs, but only to those with doors directly to grade.

16-2.10 Marking of Means of Egress.

16-2.10.1   Means of egress shall have signs in accordance with Section 5-10.

16-2.10.2   An approved luminescent or self luminous exit sign shall be placed on each door to an exit stair from an interior corridor. Such sign shall have appropriate wording in plainly legible letters not less than 4½ in. (11.4 cm) nor more than 6 in. (15.2 cm) high with the principal strokes of letters not less than ¾ in. (1.9 cm) wide. The bottom of the sign shall be not less than 6 in. (15.2 cm) nor more than 8 in. (20.3 cm) above the floor.

Over the last five years, the Committee has received numerous requests to add requirements for exit signs at lower heights, especially in hotels. In the 1985 Edition to the *Code*, provisions were made in Chapter 5 for exit signs at lower heights (*see 5-10.1.4*); however, the *Code* contained no requirements for installing such signs. The Subcommittee on Residential

Occupancies studied the problem and believed that there would be a benefit in having a sign *on* the door to stairways. This sign does not have to be illuminated but must be either luminesent or self-luminous. The installation of the sign must be such as not to destroy the fire protection rating of the door on which it is installed.

16-2.11 Special Features.

SECTION 16-3   PROTECTION

16-3.1 Protection of Vertical Openings.

16-3.1.1   Every stairway, elevator shaft, and other vertical opening shall be enclosed or protected in accordance with 6-2.4.

Exception No. 1: Unprotected vertical openings connecting not more than three floors may be permitted in accordance with the conditions of 6-2.4.4.

Exception No. 2: An atrium may be utilized in accordance with 6-2.4.5.

Exception No. 3: Stairway enclosures shall not be required where a one-story stair connects two levels within a single dwelling unit, guest room, or suite.

With regard to Exception No. 1 to 16-3.1.1, it should be noted that 6-2.4.4 requires automatic sprinkler protection for ordinary hazard occupancies. The requirements for atriums in 6-2.4.5 also mandate total automatic sprinkler protection. Therefore, unless complying with Exception No. 3, automatic sprinkler protection must be provided in buildings with unprotected vertical openings.

Exception No. 4: In buildings protected throughout by an approved supervised automatic sprinkler system installed in accordance with 16-3.5.1, fire resistance of walls may be one hour and fire protection rating of doors may be one hour.

See commentary following 16-2.2.1.2.

16-3.1.2   No floor below the level of exit discharge used only for storage, heating equipment, or purposes other than residential occupancy shall have unprotected openings to floors used for residential purposes.

16-3.2 Protection from Hazards.

16-3.2.1   Any room containing high-pressure boilers, refrigerating machinery, transformers, or other service equipment subject to possible explosion shall not be located directly under or directly adjacent to exits. All such rooms shall be effectively cut off from other parts of the building as specified in Section 6-4.

16-3.2.2   Every hazardous area shall be separated from other parts of the building by construction having a fire resistance rating of at least 1 hour, and communicating openings shall be protected by approved self-closing fire doors, or such area shall be equipped with an automatic fire extinguishing system. Hazardous areas include, but are not limited to:

Boiler and heater rooms

Laundries

Repair shops

Rooms or spaces used for storage of combustible supplies and equipment in quantities deemed hazardous by the authority having jurisdiction.

The list in 16-3.2.2 is not all-inclusive. It is the responsibility of the authority having jurisdiction to determine which areas are hazardous.

16-3.3 Interior Finish.

16-3.3.1   Interior finish on walls and ceilings, in accordance with Section 6-5, shall be as follows:

(a) Exit enclosures — Class A.

(b) Corridors and lobbies — Class A or B.

(c) All other spaces — Class A, B, or C.

16-3.3.2   Interior floor finish in corridors and exits shall be Class I or Class II in accordance with Section 6-5.

The provisions for interior finish in 16-3.3 were rewritten for the 1976 Edition of the *Code* to reflect the elimination of the Class D and E categories of interior finish and to provide more specific guidance on where these requirements apply in hotels. In the 1981 Edition, the interior floor finish requirements were modified to reflect critical radiant flux requirements. Section 6-5 contains strict limitations on the use of textile or carpetlike materials on walls or ceilings.

16-3.4 Detection, Alarm, and Communications Systems.

16-3.4.1 General.   A fire alarm system in accordance with Section 7-6 shall be provided.

An exception for hotels of three or fewer stories with exterior exit access, which was provided in earlier editions of the *Code*, no longer applies in new construction.

16-3.4.2 Initiation.   Initiation of the required fire alarm system shall be by:

(a) Manual means in accordance with 7-6.2, and

(b) A manual fire alarm station located at the hotel desk or other convenient central control point under continuous supervision by responsible employees, and

(c) Any automatic sprinkler system, and

(d) Any required automatic detection system.

Exception to (d): Sleeping room smoke detectors are not required to initiate the building fire alarm system.

Here the *Code* requires that, in addition to the normal distribution of manual fire alarm stations (7-6.2), the front desk or telephone operator's location or similar location must also have a manual pull station. The intent is to have a pull station at the location guests would call in an emergency.

The *Code* exempts sleeping room smoke detectors from activating the building fire alarm system. Technically, the detectors usually installed in sleeping rooms are single station or multiple station detectors and are not a part of a "required automatic detection *system*" (emphasis added) and, therefore, are automatically exempted. The Exception emphasizes this, but also clarifies that if they are part of a system (*see 16-3.4.4.2 Exception*), they are not required to initiate the building fire alarm system. The *Code* does *not* prohibit room detectors from activating the system; however, this is discouraged to prevent numerous activations, which could occur in large hotels in particular. The purpose of the detector in the room is to warn the occupants of that room. Detectors are available that annunciate at a central point, alert the occupants of the room, and notify management that something is wrong in that room without sounding an alarm throughout the facility. (*Also see commentary following 16-3.4.4.2.*)

16-3.4.3 Notification.

16-3.4.3.1   Occupant notification shall be provided automatically, without delay, by internal audible alarm in accordance with 7-6.3.

Exception: A presignal system (see 7-6.3.2 Exception No. 1) may be used only in buildings protected throughout by an approved automatic sprinkler system and then only where permitted by the authority having jurisdiction.

Distribution of audible alarm devices in hotels must be thoroughly reviewed. In most new construction, corridor walls are of such character (soundproofed) that a sounding device would be required in each room to provide adequate alarm sound levels; otherwise, the sound level in the corridor would have to approach dangerous decibel levels in order to provide levels adequate to awaken guests in their rooms.

Presignal systems have repeatedly been involved in delay of alarms in multiple-death fires. The problem of false alarms in hotels, however, is very real. Therefore, due to the excellent life loss record in sprinklered hotels, the *Code* allows presignal systems in sprinklered hotels, but the authority having jurisdiction can establish how such a system is to be arranged.

16-3.4.3.2   An annunciator panel connected with the fire alarm system shall be provided. The location of the annunciator shall be approved by the authority having jurisdiction.

Exception: Buildings not greater than two stories in height and with not more than 50 rooms.

16-3.4.3.3   In high rise buildings, occupant notification shall be provided by an approved means of voice communication in accordance with 7-6.3.

16-3.4.3.4* Provisions shall be made for the immediate notification of the public fire department by either telephone or other means in case of fire. Where there is no public fire department, this notification shall go to the private fire brigade.

A-16-3.4.3.4 The provision for immediate notification of the public fire department is intended to include, but not be limited to, all of the arrangements listed in 7-6.4, Emergency Forces Notification. Other arrangements that depend on a clerk or other member of the staff to notify the fire department may also be acceptable. In such case, however, it is essential that a trained staff member and an immediately available means of calling the fire department are continuously available. If a telephone is to be used, it should not be of any type or arrangement that requires a coin or the unlocking of a device to contact the fire department.

This paragraph does not require a direct fire alarm connection to the fire department; however, this would be the best method by which to comply with 16-3.4.3.4. The telephone required would have to be equipped for direct outside dial without going through a switchboard and could not be a pay phone.

16-3.4.4 Detection.

16-3.4.4.1 A corridor smoke detection system in accordance with Section 7-6 shall be provided.

Exception: Buildings protected throughout by an approved automatic sprinkler system installed in accordance with 16-3.5.1.

16-3.4.4.2 Each sleeping room shall be provided with an approved single station smoke detector, in accordance with 7-6.2.9, powered from the building electrical service.

Exception: Single station smoke detection shall not be required when sleeping rooms contain smoke detectors connected to a central alarm system which also alarm locally.

This requirement was new to the 1985 Edition of the *Code*. It provides for house powered, single station smoke detectors in each sleeping room or suite. The purpose of these detectors is to alert the occupant of the room to the presence of a fire originating in that room or suite. These detectors would not normally be tied into the building fire alarm. [*See 16-3.4.2(d) Exception.*] Upon leaving the room, the door would shut behind the occupant (*see 16-3.6.3*), and the occupant would pull a manual alarm station. Failure to sound the alarm manually would be compensated for by corridor smoke detectors or by automatic sprinklers. [*See 16-3.4.4.1. Also see commentary following 16-3.4.2(d).*]

16-3.5 Extinguishment Requirements.

16-3.5.1* Where an automatic sprinkler system is installed, either for total or partial building coverage, the system shall be installed in accordance with Section 7-7.

Exception: In guest rooms and in guest room suites, sprinkler installations may be omitted in closets not over 24 sq ft (2.2 sq m) and bathrooms not over 55 sq ft (5.1 sq m).

A-16-3.5.1   Although not required by the *Code*, the use of residential sprinklers or quick response sprinklers is encouraged for new installations of sprinkler systems within dwelling units, apartments, and guest rooms. Caution must be used, as the system must be designed for the sprinkler being used.

This paragraph does not require sprinklers but sets requirements for where they are installed. The *Code* provides significant incentive to install sprinklers with regard to: travel distance (16-2.6.1 and 16-2.6.2); exit discharge (16-2.7); vertical openings (16-3.1); interior finish (16-3.3); corridor smoke detection (16-3.4.4.1); corridor walls (16-3.6.1); smoke barriers (16-3.7.1); and operable windows (16-4.1). The *Code* mandates that all new high rise hotels be sprinklered. (*See 16-3.5.2. Also see commentary on 16-1.2.*)

The purpose is to provide a sprinkler system that will aid in the detection and control of residential fires and thus provide improved protection against injury and life loss. A sprinkler system installed in accordance with this standard is expected to prevent flashover (total involvement) in the room of fire origin when sprinklered and to improve the chance of occupants to escape or be evacuated. It is not designed nor intended to protect property.

16-3.5.2   All high rise buildings shall be protected throughout by an approved supervised automatic sprinkler system installed in accordance with 16-3.5.1.

The problems of fighting fires in high rise buildings and the resulting life safety problems are well documented. Prior to the 1988 Edition of the *Code*, automatic sprinkler protection for high rise buildings was not mandated, but numerous other items were required to compensate for buildings lacking automatic sprinkler protection. As this list grew, it reached the point of being impractical, and therefore, the *Code* now mandates sprinkler protection in all new high rise hotels. (*See the definition of high rise in Section 3-2.*)

16-3.5.3   Open air parking structures complying with NFPA 88A, *Standard for Parking Structures*, need not be sprinklered under this *Code*.

Since many hotels contain open air parking structures, the Committee felt that for *Life Safety Code* purposes *only*, an exemption for these structures was warranted. However, should sprinkler protection be required by other codes or by the *Life Safety Code* for reasons other than those found in 16-3.5, then sprinkler protection must be provided in these structures.

16-3.5.4   Portable fire extinguishers shall be provided in hazardous areas. Where provided, portable fire extinguishers shall be installed and maintained in accordance with 7-7.4.1.

16-3.6 Minimum Fire Resistance Requirements for Protection of Guest Rooms (Corridors).

16-3.6.1 Interior corridor walls shall consist of fire barriers having at least a 1-hour fire resistance rating.

Exception: In buildings protected throughout by an approved supervised automatic sprinkler system installed in accordance with 16-3.5.1, corridor walls shall have at least a ½-hour fire resistance rating.

The criteria in 16-3.6 reflect the Committee's concern for providing safety for the occupant in his or her room during a fire. The focus of this concern is the presence of occupants on a 24-hour-a-day basis with sleeping accommodations. This minimum corridor wall construction will either block fire movement from the corridor into a room or block fire in a room from entering the corridor.

Although in truly new construction the reduction to ½-hour fire resistance would have little benefit, it can play a major role in rehabilitation, renovations, or conversions of existing structures that are required to meet the provisions for new construction. (*See 1-4.6.*) Most existing lath and plaster walls provide 20- to 30-minute fire resistance ratings and, by providing automatic sprinkler protection throughout the building, the walls would not have to be replaced.

16-3.6.2 Each guest room door that opens onto an interior corridor shall have a fire protection rating of at least 20 minutes. Openings shall resist the passage of smoke.

The door required by 16-3.6.2 provides a level of protection commensurate with the expected fuel load in the room and the fire resistance of the corridor wall construction. The purpose is to box a fire out of a room, or to box it within the room by means of corridor wall and door construction. (*See 16-3.6.3.*) It has been shown in fuel load studies conducted by the National Bureau of Standards that residential occupancies will have fuel loads in the 20- to 30-minute range.

16-3.6.3 Each guest room door that opens onto an interior corridor shall be self-closing and shall meet the requirements of 16-3.6.2.

Since 16-3.6.2 requires guest room doors to have a 20-minute fire protection rating, then NFPA 80, *Standard for Fire Doors and Windows,*[3] requires the door to be self closing; however, the Committee feels that this is such an important point that it repeats the requirement in 16-3.6.3 rather than rely totally on the reference document. Numerous hotel fires have resulted in multiple fatalities due to the lack of, or poor maintenance of, door closers.

16-3.6.4 Unprotected openings shall be prohibited in partitions of corridors serving as exit access from guest rooms.

16-3.6.5   No transom or transfer grille shall be installed in partitions separating the corridors from guest rooms.

Paragraph 2-2.2 of **NFPA 90A,** *Standard for the Installation of Air Conditioning and Ventilating Systems,*[4] prohibits public corridors from being used as a portion of the supply, return, or exhaust air system.

Transoms have been prohibited in hotels for many years due to tragic fires that resulted where their presence led to the transmission of fire and smoke through corridors and directly into occupied rooms, causing multiple deaths.

Figure 16-8 illustrates the requirements of 16-3.6.

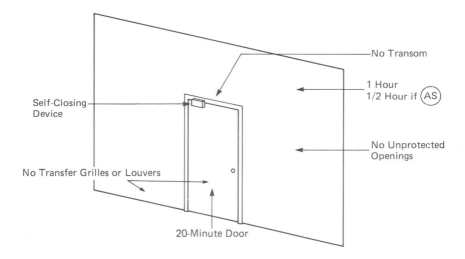

Figure 16-8.   Provisions for the Protection of Guest Rooms (Corridors) in New Hotels.   The need for the self-closing 20-minute fire-rated door cannot be overemphasized. There are no exceptions or options to the self-closing door.

16-3.7 Subdivision of Building Spaces.

16-3.7.1   Every guest room floor shall be divided into at least two smoke compartments of approximately the same size, with smoke barriers in accordance with Section 6-3. Smoke dampers are not required.

Additional smoke barriers shall be provided such that the maximum travel distance from a guest room corridor door to a smoke barrier shall not exceed 150 ft (45 m).

Exception No. 1:   Buildings protected throughout by an approved supervised automatic sprinkler system installed in accordance with 16-3.5.1.

Exception No. 2:   Where each guest room is provided with exterior ways of exit access arranged in accordance with 5-5.3.

Exception No. 3:   Smoke barriers are not required where the aggregate corridor length on each floor is not more than 150 ft (45 m).

This requirement was new to the 1985 Edition of the *Code*. It requires all but relatively small floors to be subdivided into two smoke compartments. This provides for horizontal movement of people and limits the number of rooms — and therefore people — exposed to a single fire that may be blocking a corridor. Since no fire rating is required for the barrier and smoke dampers are not required, the requirement is not overly burdensome in typical hotel or dormitory construction. The exception for automatic sprinklers again reflects the excellent life loss record of buildings so equipped.

A horizontal exit may be used to comply with 16-3.7.1 and thereby serve more than one function.

16-3.8 Special Features.

SECTION 16-4   SPECIAL PROVISIONS

16-4.1* Operable Windows.   Each guest room shall be provided with at least one outside window. Such windows shall be openable from the inside, without the use of tools, and provide a clear opening of not less than 20 in. (50.8 cm) in width, 24 in. (61 cm) in height, and 5.7 sq ft (.53 sq m) in area. The bottom of the opening shall not be more than 44 in. (112 cm) above the floor. In rooms located greater than six stories above grade, the openable clear height, width, and area of the window may be modified to the dimensions necessary for ventilation.

Exception No. 1: Buildings protected throughout by an approved supervised automatic sprinkler system installed in accordance with 16-3.5.1.

Exception No. 2: Where a guest room has a door leading directly to the outside of building.

Exception No. 3: Buildings provided with an approved engineered smoke control system in accordance with Section 7-3.

A-16-4.1   Windows may serve as a means of emergency escape, particularly where ladders can be raised by fire fighters or others. Even where the location is such as to preclude the use of windows for escape purposes, they may provide air for breathing in a smoke-filled room while trapped occupants are awaiting rescue. Windows should have sills not too high above the floor; windows lower than 44 in. (112 cm) above the floor are preferable.

Where awning- or hopper-type windows are used, they should be so hinged or subdivided as to provide a clear opening of at least 5.7 sq ft (.53 sq m). Where storm windows, screens, or burglar guards are used, these should be provided with quick-opening devices so that they may be readily opened from the inside for emergency egress.

Several recent multiple-death hotel fires have graphically illustrated the problem of guest rooms equipped with nonoperable windows, both in low rise and high rise buildings. An operable window can allow an occupant access to fresh air and/or rescue. If a window is opened and smoke is drawn into a room, an operable window can be shut, but a fixed window that has been broken cannot.

The windows specified here are the same as those specified for other residential occupancies and schools.

The door described in Exception No. 2 does not have to be an exit access door but can be a door to a balcony, as this serves the same function as a window. In most hotels there is a reluctance, due to security, to have operable windows; therefore, Exception No. 1 will often be used. Use of Exception No. 3 is not practical in most hotels due to the design of typical hotel HVAC systems.

Since high rise buildings are now required to be sprinklered, Exception No. 1 will eliminate the need for operable windows in high rise buildings.

16-4.2 High Rise Buildings.   (*See 16-3.5.2.*)

16-4.3 Operating Features.   (*See Chapter 31.*)

SECTION 16-5   BUILDING SERVICES

16-5.1 Utilities.   Utilities shall comply with the provisions of Section 7-1.

16-5.2 Heating, Ventilating, and Air Conditioning.   Heating, ventilating, and air conditioning equipment shall comply with the provisions of Section 7-2, except as otherwise required in this chapter.

16-5.3* Elevators, Dumbwaiters, and Vertical Conveyors.   Elevators, dumbwaiters, and vertical conveyors shall comply with the provisions of Section 7-4. In high rise buildings, one elevator shall be provided with a protected power supply and be available for use by the fire department in case of emergency.

A-16-5.3   "Protected Power Supply" means a source of electrical energy of sufficient capacity to permit proper operation of the elevator and its associated control and communications systems and whose point of origin, system of distribution, type and size of over-current protection, degree of isolation from other portions of the building electrical system, and degree of mechanical protection are such that it is unlikely that the supply would be disrupted at any but the advance stages of building fire-involvement or by structural collapse.

A "Protected Power Supply" should provide at least the level of reliability associated with, and may consist of, an electrical distribution system whose service equipment is located and installed in accordance with Sections 230-72(b) and 230-82, Exception No. 5 of NFPA 70, *National Electrical Code (see Appendix B)*, and that has no other connection to the "normal" building electrical distribution system. A "Protected Power Supply" need not incorporate two sources of energy or automatic transfer capability from a "normal" to an "emergency" source, e.g., an alternate set of service conductors.

The number and type of elevators to be connected to a "Protected Power Supply" should be limited, or the characteristics of the "Protected Power Supply" should be selected, so as to ensure conformance with Section 230-95 of NFPA 70, *National Electrical Code (see Appendix B)*, without the provision of ground fault protection for the supply.

An elevator installation supplied by a "Protected Power Supply" should comply with Article 620 of NFPA 70, *National Electrical Code (see Appendix B)*, except that the "energy absorption means" required by Section 620-91 should always be connected on the load-side of the disconnecting means and should not consist of loads likely to become inoperative or disconnected under the conditions assumed to exist where the elevator is under the control of fire department personnel, e.g., light and power loads external to the elevator equipment room.

16-5.4 Rubbish Chutes, Incinerators, and Laundry Chutes.   Rubbish chutes, incinerators, and laundry chutes shall comply with the provisions of Section 7-5.

The 1985 Edition of the *Code* eliminated the special section on dormitories. Dormitories are now covered as hotels due to several changes to hotel requirements regarding windows, alarms, and building subdivisions, which made special requirements for dormitories unnecessary.

REFERENCES CITED IN COMMENTARY

[1] NFPA 13, *Standard for the Installation of Sprinkler Systems*, National Fire Protection Association, Quincy, MA, 1987.

[2] Best, Richard and Demers, David P., Investigation Report on the MGM Grand Hotel Fire, Las Vegas, Nevada, National Fire Protection Association, Quincy, MA, NFPA No. LS-4, 1982.

[3] NFPA 80, *Standard for Fire Doors and Windows*, National Fire Protection Association, Quincy, MA, 1986.

[4] NFPA 90A, *Standard for the Installation of Air Conditioning and Ventilating Systems*, National Fire Protection Association, Quincy, MA, 1985.

17

EXISTING HOTELS AND DORMITORIES

(See also Chapter 31.)

Prior to the 1981 Edition of the *Code*, all residential occupancies were treated in one chapter. In the 1981 Edition they were split into several chapters in order to simplify and clarify the *Code*, resulting in a document that is easier to use.

Residential occupancies are those in which sleeping accommodations are provided for normal residential purposes and include all buildings designed to provide sleeping accommodations. They are treated separately in the *Code* in the following groups:

Hotels, motels, dormitories (Chapters 16 and 17)
Apartment buildings (Chapters 18 and 19)
Lodging or rooming houses (Chapter 20)
Board and care facilities (Chapter 21)
One- and two-family dwellings (Chapter 22)

Exceptions to the groups listed above are health care occupancies, which are covered in Chapters 12 and 13, and detention and correctional occupancies, which are covered in Chapters 14 and 15. In earlier editions of the *Code*, they were classified as "institutional occupancies."

A review of 4-1.6 underscores a common principle of life safety with which the *Code* is concerned as applied to all the residential occupancies considered by Chapters 16 through 23. Paragraph 4-1.6 states: "Residential occupancies are those occupancies in which sleeping accommodations are provided for normal residential purposes and include all buildings designed to provide sleeping accommodations." This use of residential occupancies is central to the *Code's* provisions in Chapters 16 through 23, because people who are asleep will be unaware of a rapidly developing fire and, when alerted, may be somewhat confused due to being awakened suddenly. Other factors on which the provisions of Chapters 16 through 23 were based are the presence of hazards (such as cooking and heating equipment) in residential occupancies and the degree of familiarity of the occupant with his or her living space (ranging from transients with little or no familiarity, as in hotels, to total familiarity in single-family dwellings).

SECTION 17-1   GENERAL REQUIREMENTS

17-1.1 Application.

17-1.1.1   This chapter establishes life safety requirements for all existing hotels. (*See Chapter 31 for operating features.*)

Hotels and dormitories are defined in 17-1.3.1. It should be noted that lodging or rooming houses that contain more than 16 people are considered hotels and must comply with Chapter 17. New hotels are covered in Chapter 16.

Renovations, modernizations, and similar work must comply with 1-4.7, which states that such work must comply with Chapter 16 to the extent practical.

17-1.1.2   Existing dormitories shall comply with the requirements for existing hotels.

Exception: Any dormitory divided into suites of rooms, with one or more bedrooms opening into a living room or study that has a door opening into a common corridor serving a number of suites, shall be classified as an apartment building.

The Exception to 17-1.1.2 recognizes that the now popular dormitory design of a group of bedrooms clustered around a living room duplicates a typical apartment design of several bedrooms clustered around a living room (or a kitchen). Since the design and the risk of fire are the same, the *Code* treats this arrangement the same as that of an apartment building. (*See Figure 17-1.*)

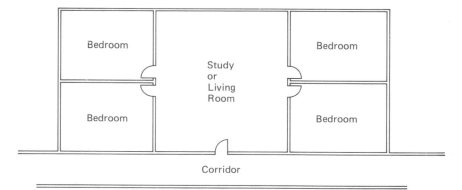

Figure 17-1.   Arrangement of Dormitory Suite Treated as an Apartment Under the Exception to 17-1.1.2.   More than one bedroom opens into a study or living room that has a door opening into a corridor. The corridor serves a number of suites.

17-1.2 Mixed Occupancies.

17-1.2.1   Where another type of occupancy occurs in the same building as a residential occupancy, the requirements of 1-4.7 of this *Code* shall be applicable.

17-1.2.2   For requirements on mixed mercantile and residential occupancies, see 25-1.2.

17-1.2.3   Any ballroom, assembly or exhibition hall, and other space used for purposes of public assembly shall be in accordance with Chapter 9. Any dining area having a capacity of 50 or more persons shall be treated as an assembly occupancy.

Most of the larger hotels consist of several occupancies — Hotel, Assembly (ballrooms, restaurants, lounges), Business (large administrative areas), and Mercantile (large shopping areas), among others. Unless these areas are adequately separated and protected, the complex is a mixed occupancy and the most stringent provisions of the various occupancies must be applied. Note that small administrative areas and small gift shops or newsstands do not justify invoking mixed occupancy requirements. This can be very important with regard to the construction and sprinkler requirements for assembly occupancies and with regard to sprinkler requirements for mercantile occupancies. (*See discussion following 17-1.6, 17-3.2, and 17-3.5.*)

17-1.3 Definitions.

17-1.3.1   Terms applicable to this chapter are defined in Chapter 3 of this *Code*; where necessary, other terms will be defined in the text as they may occur.

Dormitories.   Includes buildings or spaces in buildings where group sleeping accommodations are provided for more than 16 persons not members of the same family group in one room or in a series of closely associated rooms under joint occupancy and single management, as in college dormitories, fraternity houses, military barracks; with or without meals, but without individual cooking facilities.

In 17-1.3.1, the phrase "without individual cooking facilities" refers to the absence of cooking equipment in any room or unit of a dormitory. If this equipment is present throughout a facility, the occupancy should be classed as an apartment building. The phrase "with or without meals" connotes the *Code*'s acceptance of a central cafeteria used to serve meals for the occupants of a dormitory.

Hotels.   Includes buildings or groups of buildings under the same management in which there are more than 16 sleeping accommodations for hire, primarily used by transients who are lodged with or without meals, whether designated as a hotel, inn, club, motel, or by any other name. So-called apartment hotels shall be classified as hotels because they are potentially subject to transient occupancy like that of hotels.

Lodging or rooming houses containing more than 16 people are treated as hotels. Where units have individual cooking facilities, the *Code* would classify the occupancy as an apartment building. (*See 19-1.3.*) However, where the authority believes that the hazards of both a hotel (people unfamiliar with surroundings) and an apartment building (higher fuel load, greater ignition sources, and travel through multiple rooms) are present, it may be appropriate to classify the building as a mixed occupancy (Hotel and Apartment).

17-1.4 Classification of Occupancy.   *(See 17-1.3.)*

17-1.5 Classification of Hazard of Contents.

17-1.5.1   The contents of residential occupancies shall be classified as ordinary hazard in accordance with Section 4-2. For the design of automatic sprinkler systems, the classification of contents in NFPA 13, *Standard for the Installation of Sprinkler Systems*, shall apply.

> NFPA 13, *Standard for the Installation of Sprinkler Systems*,[1] would classify the contents as "light" for the purpose of designing extinguishing systems. The difference in classification is based on the threat to life or life safety (ordinary) versus the threat to the extinguishing capability of the automatic sprinkler system (light).

17-1.6 Minimum Construction Requirements.   No Special Requirements.

> Although this chapter does not establish minimum construction requirements, if the hotel contains an assembly occupancy, Chapter 9 does establish minimum construction requirements based on the location of the assembly occupancy.

17-1.7 Occupant Load.

17-1.7.1*   The occupant load in numbers of persons for whom exits are to be provided shall be determined on the basis of one person per 200 sq ft (18.6 sq m) gross floor area, or the maximum probable population of any room or section under consideration, whichever is greater. The occupant load of any open mezzanine or balcony shall be added to the occupant load of the floor below for the purpose of determining exit capacity.

A-17-1.7.1   Dormitory-type occupancy, particularly where 2- or 3-tier bunks are used with close spacing, may produce an occupant load substantially greater than one person per 200 sq ft (18.6 sq m) gross floor area. However, even though sleeping areas are densely populated, the building as a whole may not necessarily exceed one person per 200 sq ft (18.6 sq m) gross area, owing to the space taken for toilet facilities, halls, closets, and living rooms not used for sleeping purposes.

> This discussion does not preclude the need for providing exit capability from concentrated sleeping areas (bunk rooms) based on the "maximum probable population" rather than on the design figure. If the actual population of a bunk room exceeds one person per 200 sq ft (18.6 sq m), the exit capacity (door widths, etc.) will have to be designed based on the actual population load. See 5-3.1 for further details on the use of occupant load for determining capacity of the means of egress.
>
> The occupant loads for areas of hotels used for nonresidential purposes are based on the use of the area. Occupant loads for assembly areas are calculated in accordance with 9-1.7, and those for mercantile areas are calculated in accordance with 25-1.7, etc.

SECTION 17-2   MEANS OF EGRESS REQUIREMENTS

17-2.1 General.

17-2.1.1   All means of egress shall be in accordance with Chapter 5 and this chapter.

Rather than repeat many of the provisions of Chapter 5, a general reference to Chapter 5 is made. Many of the requirements that follow in Section 17-2 pick up provisions from Chapter 5 that are options for the occupancy chapters, such as the Exception to 17-2.2.2.2, which allows the use of special locking arrangements per 5-2.1.6; or that prohibit the use of an item if it is not listed (note that alternating tread devices are not listed in 17-2.2); or that establish limits based on criteria provided in Chapter 5, such as corridor dead-end limits in 17-2.5.3.

17-2.2 Means of Egress Components.

17-2.2.1 General.

17-2.2.1.1   Components of means of egress shall be limited to the types described in 17-2.2.2 through 17-2.2.9.

17-2.2.1.2   In buildings protected throughout by an approved automatic sprinkler system installed in accordance with 17-3.5.1, exit enclosures may have a fire resistance rating of not less than one hour, and the fire protection rating of doors may be one hour.

In recognition of the relatively low fuel loads in hotels, the fire resistance rating for exit enclosures, as well as other vertical openings (*see 17-3.1.1 Exception No. 4*), need not exceed one hour; however, as a safeguard, this is permitted only in buildings protected throughout by automatic sprinklers. This is not permitted for assembly occupancies or business occupancies and, therefore, cannot be utilized where mixed occupancies are involved; nor can it be used for stairways or vertical openings involving or passing through other occupancies.

In facilities where occupancies are adequately separated and treated independently, it could be feasible to have a 1-hour enclosure in the hotel portion and 2-hour enclosure elsewhere. (*See Figure 17-2.*)

17-2.2.2 Doors.

17-2.2.2.1   Doors shall comply with 5-2.1.

17-2.2.2.2*   No door in any means of egress shall be locked against egress when the building is occupied.

Exception: Special locking arrangements complying with 5-2.1.6 are permitted.

A-17-2.2.2.2   It is the intent of this requirement that security measures, where installed, should not prevent egress.

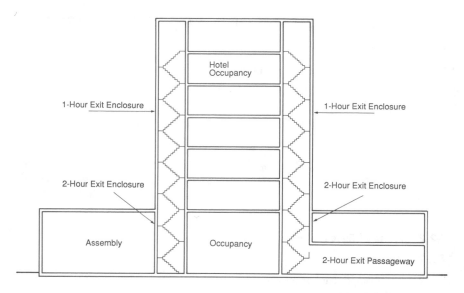

Figure 17-2.   Protection of Exit Enclosures and Other Vertical Openings in a Fully Sprinklered Hotel.   The Exception for the two-hour enclosure does not apply to other occupancies in a hotel complex nor to mixed occupancies.

Paragraph 17-2.2.2.2 prohibits a hotel from having any door locked "against egress" while the building is occupied. This requirement permits a door to have a locking device that allows the door to be opened from within the building for the purpose of egress, but does not allow the door to be opened from outside the building. Ordinary double cylinder locks and chain locks would not meet these provisions. Several tragic multiple-death fires have occurred where a key could not be found to unlock these devices.

The language of 5-2.1.5.1 is clear. "Locks, if provided, shall not require the use of a key, tool, special knowledge, or effort for operation from the inside of the building." This eliminates double cylinder locks and chain locks that require a key to operate from the inside. Paragraph 5-2.1.5.3 calls for a simple operation to open a door; the presence of a two-handed knob operation, and the like, is specifically prohibited.

Chapter 5 now specifically recognizes the need for security chains or rods as well as locks on hotel room doors and allows two additional releasing devices for existing installations. The typical hotel room door has three devices: the latch, the lock, and the security chain or rod. The *Code* prefers only two releasing actions (*see commentary following 16-2.2.2.2*) but recognizes the existence of thousands of installations that require the use of three actions. Where new installations are being made in an existing hotel, the *Code* requires (*see 1-4.6*) that the installation comply with Chapter 16.

The Exception to 17-2.2.2.2 recognizes the use of the delay release lock provided for in 5-2.1.6. This requires that the building either be protected throughout by automatic sprinklers or equipped throughout with a fire detection system. The 15- or 30-second delay permitted by 5-2.1.6 does not affect the immediate release of the lock upon activation of the sprinklers or detectors, or upon loss of power to the lock. This device helps the hotel provide the security needed for seldom used doors or stairs, while at the same time it keeps the door available for use, which chains and padlocks are unable to do.

17-2.2.2.3* Every stairwell door shall allow reentry from the stairwell to the interior of the building, or an automatic release shall be provided to unlock all stairwell doors to allow reentry. Such automatic release shall be actuated with the initiation of the building fire alarm system. Also, stairwell doors shall unlock upon loss of power controlling the lock or locking mechanism.

A-17-2.2.2.3 This arrangement makes it possible to leave the stairway at any floor should the fire render the lower part of the stair unusable during egress or should the occupants seek refuge on another floor.

The provisions of 17-2.2.2.3 are more stringent than those of Chapter 5 in that the provisions of Exception No. 1 to 5-2.1.5.2 are not allowed in hotels. The Committee felt that hotels do not encounter the circumstances that business occupancies do where tenants lease an entire floor with no public corridor arrangement, and therefore, the Exception was unwarranted. If hotels wish to restrict normal movement in stairs, the automatic release system can be used. Numerous fatalities occurred in stairways at the MGM Grand Hotel in Las Vegas in 1980 where people were in smoke filled stairways and were locked out of floors.[2]

17-2.2.2.4 Revolving doors complying with 5-2.1.10 are permitted.

17-2.2.3 Stairs. Stairs shall comply with 5-2.2.

17-2.2.4 Smokeproof Enclosures. Smokeproof enclosures shall comply with 5-2.3.

17-2.2.5 Horizontal Exits. Horizontal exits shall comply with 5-2.4.

17-2.2.6 Ramps. Ramps shall comply with 5-2.5.

17-2.2.7 Exit Passageways. Exit passageways shall comply with 5-2.6.

17-2.2.8* Escalators. Escalators previously approved as a component in the means of egress may continue to be given credit.

A-17-2.2.8 Due to the nature of escalators, they are no longer acceptable as a component in the means of egress. However, since many escalators have been used for exit access and exit discharge in the past, credit may be continued. Very few escalators have ever been installed in a manner to qualify as an exit. For information on escalator protection and requirements, the reader is referred to previous editions of the *Code*.

17-2.2.9 Fire Escape Stairs.   Fire escape stairs complying with 5-2.8 are permitted.

17-2.3 Capacity of Means of Egress.

17-2.3.1   The capacity of means of egress shall be in accordance with Section 5-3.

17-2.3.2   Street floor exits shall be sufficient for the occupant load of the street floor plus the required capacity of stairs and ramps discharging onto the street floor.

> Paragraph 17-2.3.2 requires street-floor exit designs that have sufficient width to provide for the intermingling of exits from the street floor with exits discharging down from the upper floors and discharging up from the lower floors. This is the traditional grand lobby design found in many hotels and in many sizable mercantile occupancies where stairs and street-floor exits converge at one or two exterior door locations.
>
> Paragraph 5-7.2 restricts the number and arrangement of stairs that discharge through the street floor.
>
> Figure 17-3 shows a typical arrangement of multiple exits discharging on the street floor.

17-2.4 Number of Exits.   *(See also Section 5-4.)*

17-2.4.1   Not less than two exits shall be accessible from every floor, including floors below the level of exit discharge and occupied for public purposes.

> Paragraph 5-4.1.2 will require greater number of exits for floors with more than 500 people. This will probably have little effect on hotels, since floors large enough to have more than 500 people would probably need additional exits to meet travel distance limitations.

17-2.5 Arrangement of Exits.

17-2.5.1   Access to all required exits shall be in accordance with Section 5-5.

17-2.5.2   No common path of travel shall exceed 35 ft (10.7 m). Travel within a guest room or suite shall not be included when calculating common path of travel.
Exception: In buildings protected throughout by an approved supervised automatic sprinkler system in accordance with 17-3.5.1, common path of travel shall not exceed 50 ft (15 m).

> Common path of travel is normally measured from the most remote point subject to occupancy (*see 5-5.1.2 and the definition of Common Path of Travel in Section 3-2*); therefore, this is a modified common path of travel, as measurement does not extend into the guest room or suite. Since the limits for common path and dead end are different for existing buildings, the arrangement shown in Figure 17-4 is possible without violating either provision.

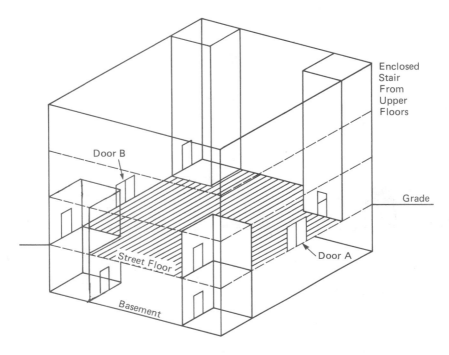

Figure 17-3. Capacity of Means of Egress in Accordance with 17-2.3.2. Required widths of Doors A and B are based on the number of people expected to use them. Assuming that the street floor has an occupant load of 500, and each upper floor has an occupant load of 200, and the basement 100, then required exit capacity for the street floor would be calculated as follows:

500 (street floor) + 200/2 (upper floor max 50% per 5-7.2) +
100/2 (basement max 50% per 5-7.2) = 650 total using
exits on street floor × 0.2 in. (0.5 cm) of door per person = 130 in. (325 cm) ÷
2 exits = 65 in. (163 cm) at A and at B.

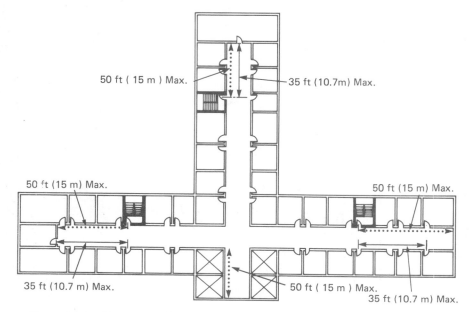

Figure 17-4.   Common Path of Travel (Modified) and Dead-End Limitations in a Nonsprinklered Hotel. Modified common paths of travel are indicated by ←——→ and dead ends are indicated by ◄·····► .

17-2.5.3   No dead-end corridor shall exceed 50 ft (15 m).

17-2.6 Travel Distance to Exits.

17-2.6.1   Any exit as indicated in 17-2.4.1 shall be such that it will not be necessary to travel more than 100 ft (30 m) from the door of any room to reach the nearest exit. Travel distance to exits shall be measured in accordance with Section 5-6.

Exception No. 1:   Travel distance to exits may be increased to 200 ft (60 m) for exterior ways of exit access arranged in accordance with 5-5.3.

Exception No. 2:   Travel distance to exits may be increased to 200 ft (60 m) if the exit access and any portion of the building that is tributary to the exit access are protected throughout by an approved automatic sprinkler system in accordance with 17-3.5.1. In addition, the portion of the building in which the 200-ft (60-m) travel distance is permitted shall be separated from the remainder of the building by construction having a fire resistance rating of not less than 1 hour for buildings not more than three stories in height, and 2 hours for buildings more than three stories in height.

See Figure 17-5.

17-2.6.2   Travel distance within a room or suite to a corridor door shall not exceed 75 ft (23 m).

Exception: One hundred twenty-five ft (38-m) travel distance is allowed in buildings protected by an automatic sprinkler system in accordance with 17-3.5.1.

Due to revisions in Section 5-6, travel distance is now measured from the most remote point subject to occupancy (the former provision exempting rooms with 6 or less people with 50 ft (15 m) or less travel distance has been deleted). To be consistent with Section 5-6, the Committee has revised the method of measuring travel distance in hotels. The distance within the room or suite has been increased by 25 ft (7.5 m) as compensation. Should the travel distance within a room or suite be excessive, another remote door to the corridor would need to be added. (*See Figure 17-5.*)

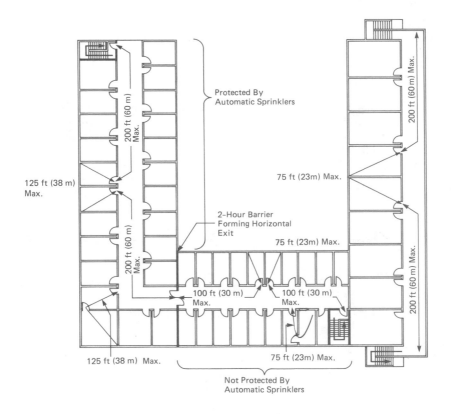

Figure 17-5.   Travel Distance in Hotels.

17-2.7 Discharge from Exits.

17-2.7.1   Exit discharge shall comply with Section 5-7.

17-2.7.2* Any required exit stair that is so located that it is necessary to pass through the lobby or other open space to reach the outside of the building shall be continuously enclosed down to a level of exit discharge or to a mezzanine within a lobby at a level of exit discharge.

A-17-2.7.2 Where open stairways or escalators are permitted, they are considered as exit access to exits rather than as exits, and requirements for distance to exits include the travel on such stairs. (*See* 5-6.4.)

17-2.7.3 The distance of travel from the termination of the exit enclosure to an exterior door leading to a public way shall not exceed 150 ft (45 m) in buildings protected throughout by an approved automatic sprinkler system and shall not exceed 100 ft (30 m) in all other buildings.

Section 5-7 does allow a maximum of 50 percent of the number and capacity of exits to discharge through the street floor under limited conditions. (*See* 5-7.2.) This is slightly liberalized by 17-2.7.2 by including a mezzanine within the lobby. In other words, 50 percent of the exits could discharge onto a mezzanine with occupants then traveling across the mezzanine, downstairs to the lobby level, and outside. However, 17-2.7.3 adds a provision not found in 5-7.2 by restricting the distance from the termination of the exit enclosure to the exterior door to a maximum of 100 ft (30.5 m) in nonsprinklered buildings and 150 ft (45 m) in buildings fully sprinklered.

See Figures 17-6 and 17-7. (*Also see commentary on* 5-7.2.)

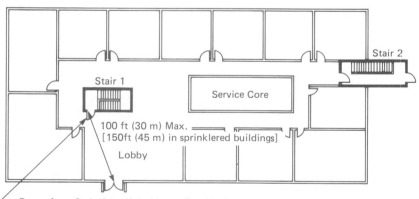

Route from Stair through Lobby to Exterior Must be Readily Visible, Identified, Clear, and Unobstructed.

Figure 17-6. Arrangement of Means of Egress in Accordance with 17-2.7. (*See Section* 5-7.2.) Stair 1 (50 percent of the total number and capacity of exits) discharges through the first floor. Stair 2 discharges directly to the exterior (it may discharge through an exit passageway to the exterior). Since other areas on the first floor (the level of exit discharge) are not separated from the path that a person leaving Stair 1 must follow to exit through the lobby, the entire first floor must be completely sprinklered. If the rest of the floor were separated (to the extent required for the stair enclosure), only the path to the exit discharge would have to be sprinklered.

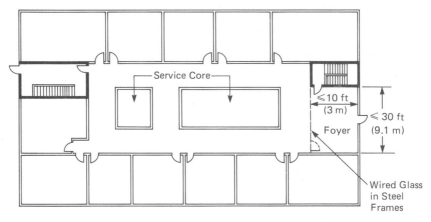

Figure 17-7.   Foyer Constructed in Compliance with 17-2.7. (*See* 5-7.2.)   The foyer must serve only as a means of egress.

17-2.8 Illumination of Means of Egress.

17-2.8.1   Means of egress shall be illuminated in accordance with Section 5-8.

17-2.9 Emergency Lighting.

17-2.9.1   Emergency lighting in accordance with Section 5-9 shall be provided in all buildings with more than 25 rooms.

Exception: Where each guest room has a direct exit to the outside of the building at grade level (as in motels).

The Exception to 17-2.9.1 does not apply to motels with exterior balconies and stairs, but only to those with doors directly to grade.

17-2.10 Marking of Means of Egress.

17-2.10.1   Means of egress shall have signs in accordance with Section 5-10.

17-2.11 Special Features.

SECTION 17-3   PROTECTION

17-3.1 Protection of Vertical Openings.

17-3.1.1   Every stairway, elevator shaft, and other vertical opening shall be enclosed or protected in accordance with 6-2.4 or provide means of satisfying the requirements of Section 2-9.

Exception No. 1: Unprotected vertical openings connecting not more than three floors may be permitted in accordance with the conditions of 6-2.4.4.

Exception No. 2: An atrium may be utilized in accordance with 6-2.4.5.

Exception No. 3:   Stairway enclosures shall not be required where a one-story stair connects two levels within a single dwelling unit, guest room, or suite.

Exception No. 4:   In any building protected throughout by an approved automatic sprinkler system in accordance with 17-3.5.1, and where exits and required ways of travel thereto are adequately safeguarded against fire and smoke within the building or where every individual room has direct access to an exterior exit without passing through any public corridor, the protection of vertical openings not part of required exits may be waived by the authority having jurisdiction to such extent as such openings do not endanger required means of egress.

Exception No. 5:   In existing buildings not more than two stories in height, unprotected openings may be permitted by the authority having jurisdiction if the building is protected throughout by an approved automatic sprinkler system in accordance with Section 7-7.

Paragraph 17-3.1.1 provides for the enclosure of vertical openings in existing hotels by means of a performance approach, i.e., either enclose them per 6-2.2 or satisfy the objectives of Section 2-9.

With regard to Exception No. 1 to 17-3.1.1, it should be noted that 6-2.4.4 requires automatic sprinkler protection for ordinary hazard occupancies, which includes hotels. Paragraph 6-2.4.5 requires buildings with atriums to be protected throughout by automatic sprinklers.

Exception No. 4 allows unprotected openings under the following conditions:

1. Subject to the approval of the authority having jurisdiction;
2. The building is totally sprinklered;
3. Exits and exit accesses are adequately separated from the remainder of the building;
4. In lieu of the preceding condition (No. 3), every room has direct access to an exterior exit without going through a public corridor; and
5. Shafts enclosing required exit stairs are protected.

Exception No. 5 allows unprotected vertical openings under the following conditions:

1. Subject to the approval of the authority having jurisdiction;
2. Two-story building;
3. The building is totally sprinklered.

Therefore, unless the unprotected vertical opening complies with Exception No. 3, the building that contains the opening is required to be either fully sprinklered or at least partially sprinklered. (*See* 6-2.4.4.)

17-3.1.2   No floor below the level of exit discharge used only for storage, heating equipment, or purposes other than residential occupancy shall have unprotected openings to floors used for residential purposes.

17-3.2 Protection from Hazards.

17-3.2.1   Any room containing high pressure boilers, refrigerating machinery, transformers, or other service equipment subject to possible explosion shall not be located directly under or directly adjacent to exits. All such rooms shall be effectively cut off from other parts of the building as specified in Section 6-4.

17-3.2.2 Every hazardous area shall be separated from other parts of the building by construction having a fire resistance rating of at least 1 hour, and communicating openings shall be protected by approved self-closing fire doors, or such area shall be equipped with an automatic fire extinguishing system. Hazardous areas include, but are not limited to:

Boiler and heater rooms
Laundries
Repair shops

Rooms or spaces used for storage of combustible supplies and equipment in quantities deemed hazardous by the authority having jurisdiction.

> The list in 17-3.2.2 is not all-inclusive. It is the responsibility of the authority having jurisdiction to determine which areas are hazardous.

17-3.3 Interior Finish.

17-3.3.1 Interior finish on walls and ceilings, in accordance with Section 6-5, shall be as follows:

(a) Exit enclosures — Class A or B.

(b) Corridors and lobbies that are part of an exit access — Class A or B.

(c) All other spaces — Class A, B, or C.

17-3.3.2 Interior floor finish in corridors and exits shall be Class I or Class II in accordance with Section 6-5.

Exception: Previously installed floor coverings may be continued in use, subject to the approval of the authority having jurisdiction.

> The provisions for interior finish in 17-3.3 were rewritten for the 1976 Edition of the *Code* to reflect the elimination of the Class D and E categories of interior finish and to provide more specific guidance on where these requirements apply in hotels. In the 1981 Edition, the interior floor finish requirements were modified to reflect critical radiant flux requirements.
>
> Section 6-5 contains strict limitations on the use of textile or carpetlike materials on walls or ceilings.

17-3.4 Detection, Alarm, and Communications Systems.

17-3.4.1 General. A fire alarm system in accordance with Section 7-6, except as modified below, shall be provided.

Exception: Buildings where each guest room has exterior exit access in accordance with 5-5.3 and the building is not greater than 3 stories in height.

17-3.4.2 Initiation. Initiation of the required fire alarm system shall be by:

(a) Manual means in accordance with 7-6.2, and

Exception to (a): Manual means as specified in 7-6.2, in excess of the alarm station at the hotel desk per (b) below, may be waived where there are other effective means (such as complete automatic sprinkler or automatic detection systems) for notification of fire as required.

(b) A manual fire alarm station located at the hotel desk or other convenient central control point under continuous supervision by responsible employees, and

(c) Any required automatic sprinkler system, and

(d) Any required detection system.

Exception to (d): Sleeping room smoke detectors are not required to initiate the building fire alarm system.

Here the *Code* requires that, in addition to the normal distribution of manual fire alarm stations (7-6.2), the front desk or telephone operator's location or similar location must also have a manual pull station. The intent is to have a pull station at the location guests would call in an emergency.

Paragraph 17-3.4.2 eliminates the requirements for fire alarm boxes located so that all portions of a building are within 200 ft (60 m) of a box (*see Section* 7-6) if an automatic sprinkler system or an automatic detection system is provided throughout the building. This does not eliminate the need for the alarm system; it only deletes the requirement for additional manual fire alarm stations.

The *Code* exempts sleeping room smoke detectors from activating the building fire alarm system. Technically, the detectors usually installed in sleeping rooms are single station or multiple station detectors and are not a part of a "required automatic detection *system*" (emphasis added) and, therefore, are automatically exempted. The Exception emphasizes this, but also clarifies that if they are part of a system, they are not required to initiate the building fire alarm system. The *Code* does *not* prohibit room detectors from activating the system; however, this is discouraged to prevent numerous activations, which could occur in large hotels in particular. The purpose of the detector in the room is to warn the occupants of that room. Detectors are available that annunciate at a central point, alert the occupants of the room, and notify management that something is wrong in that room without sounding an alarm throughout the facility. (*Also see commentary following* 17-3.4.4.)

17-3.4.3 Notification.

17-3.4.3.1   Occupant notification shall be provided automatically, without delay, by internal audible alarm in accordance with 7-6.3.

Exception: A presignal system (see 7-6.3.2 Exception No. 1) may be used only where permitted by the authority having jurisdiction.

Distribution of audible alarm devices in hotels must be thoroughly reviewed. Often alarm devices in corridors cannot be heard in rooms, or if heard, are not loud enough to waken guests. Survivors of several recent multiple-death hotel fires have reported either not hearing alarms or mistaking the alarm for a neighbor's alarm clock.

Presignal systems have repeatedly been involved in delay of alarms in multiple-death fires. The problem of false alarms in hotels, however, is very real. Therefore, the *Code* allows presignal systems in hotels, but the authority having jurisdiction can establish how such a system is to be arranged.

17-3.4.3.2* Provisions shall be made for the immediate notification of the public fire department by either telephone or other means in case of fire. Where there is no public fire department, this notification shall go to the private fire brigade.

A-17-3.4.3.2 The provision for immediate notification of the public fire department is intended to include, but not be limited to, all of the arrangements listed in 7-6.4, Emergency Forces Notification. Other arrangements that depend on a clerk or other member of the staff to notify the fire department may also be acceptable. In such case, however, it is essential that a trained staff member and an immediately available means of calling the fire department are continuously available. If a telephone is to be used, it should not be of any type or arrangement that requires a coin or the unlocking of a device to contact the fire department.

This paragraph does not require a direct fire alarm connection to the fire department; however, that would be the best method by which to comply with 17-3.4.3.2. The telephone required would have to be equipped for direct outside dial without going through a switchboard and it could not be a pay phone.

17-3.4.4 Detection. Each sleeping room shall be provided with an approved single station smoke detector, in accordance with 7-6.2.9, powered from the building electrical service.

Exception: Buildings having an existing corridor smoke detection system in accordance with Section 7-6, connected to the building fire alarm system.

Prior to the 1985 Edition of the *Code*, neither corridor nor room smoke detectors were required in existing hotels (in the 1981 Edition, existing dormitories were required to have one or the other). However, new hotels were required to have corridor smoke detectors. New hotels are required to have both corridor and room detectors. (*See 16-3.4.4.*) For existing hotels, the *Code* requires that either corridor detectors be provided or room detectors be provided. By allowing either method, the Committee is not saying that both perform a similar function, but is simply recognizing that many hotels were provided with corridor detectors based on prior editions of the *Code*. The *Code* does not permit corridor smoke detectors to be installed instead of room smoke detectors, but says that if a corridor smoke detection system has already been installed, then room detectors need not be added at this time. It would not be unreasonable to consider that both may be required for existing nonsprinklered hotels in the future, and hotel and dormitory owners may wish to consider this when doing renovations.

17-3.5 Extinguishment Requirements.

17-3.5.1* Where an automatic sprinkler system is installed, either for total or partial building coverage, the system shall be installed in accordance with Section 7-7.

Exception: In guest rooms and in guest room suites, sprinkler installations may be omitted in closets not over 24 sq ft (2.2 sq m) and bathrooms not over 55 sq ft (5.1 sq m).

A-17-3.5.1 Although not required by the *Code*, the use of residential sprinklers or quick response sprinklers is encouraged for new installations of sprinkler systems within dwelling units, apartments, and guest rooms. Caution must be used, as the system must be designed for the sprinkler being used.

This paragraph does not require sprinklers but sets requirements for where they are installed. The *Code* provides significant incentive to install sprinklers with regard to: travel distance (17-2.6.1 and 17-2.6.2); exit discharge (17-2.7); vertical openings (17-3.1); interior finish (17-3.3); corridor walls (17-3.6.1); and smoke barriers (17-3.7.1). (*Also see commentary following 17-1.2.*) It should also be noted by those considering renovations to hotels and dormitories that the Subcommittee on Residential Occupancies has gone on record and has made a commitment to study additional sprinkler requirements for hotels and dormitories during the next *Code* revision cycle.

17-3.5.2 Portable fire extinguishers shall be provided in hazardous areas. Where provided, portable fire extinguishers shall be installed and maintained in accordance with 7-7.4.1.

17-3.6 Minimum Fire Resistance Requirements for Protection of Guest Rooms (Corridors).

17-3.6.1 Interior corridor walls shall consist of fire barriers having at least a 30-minute fire resistance rating.

Exception No. 1: In buildings protected throughout by an approved automatic sprinkler system in accordance with 17-3.5.1, no fire resistance rating shall be required, but the walls and all openings therein shall resist the passage of smoke.

Exception No. 2: Where interior corridor walls have openings from transfer grilles, see 17-3.6.6.

The criteria in 17-3.6 reflect the Committee's concern for providing safety for the occupant in his or her room during a fire. The focus of this concern is the presence of occupants on a 24-hour-a-day basis with sleeping accommodations. This minimum corridor wall construction will either block fire movement from the corridor into a room or block fire in a room from entering the corridor. Corridor partitions in both sprinklered and nonsprinklered facilities are intended to be constructed to resist the passage of smoke.

The intent of the 30-minute fire-resistive rating for corridor partitions is to require a nominal fire rating, particularly where the fire rating of existing partitions cannot be documented. Examples of acceptable partition assemblies would include, but are not limited to, ½-in. (1.3-cm) gypsum board, wood lath and plaster, gypsum lath, or metal lath and plaster.

17-3.6.2 Each guest room door that opens onto an interior corridor shall have a fire protection rating of at least 20 minutes.

Exception No. 1: Previously approved 1¾-in. (4.4-cm) solid bonded wood core doors may remain in use.

Exception No. 2: Where automatic sprinkler protection is provided in the corridor in accordance with 19-3.5.2 through 19-3.5.4, doors shall not be required to have a fire protection rating but shall resist the passage of smoke. Doors shall be equipped with latches for keeping doors tightly closed.

Formal Interpretation 81-16
Reference: 17-3.6.2

Question: Is it the intent of 17-3.6.2, Exception No. 1 that 1¾-in. thick solid bonded wood core doors with ornate carvings (for aesthetic reasons) on either one or both sides, that reduce the effective thickness of the door to less than 1¾ inches qualify as 1¾-in. thick doors and thus meet the exception?

Answer: No.

Issue Edition: 1981
Reference: 17-3.6.2
Date: April 1982

The door required by 17-3.6.2 provides a level of protection commensurate with the expected fuel load in the room and the fire resistance of the corridor wall construction. The purpose is to box a fire out of a room, or to box it within the room by means of corridor wall and door construction. (*See 17-3.6.3.*) It has been shown in fuel load studies conducted by the National Bureau of Standards that residential occupancies will have fuel loads in the 20- to 30-minute range.

Exception No. 2 would allow a non-rated door that resists the passage of smoke in buildings that are fully sprinklered or that have sprinklers installed in accordance with Option 3 for apartment buildings. (*See 19-3.5.2 and the commentary following 19-3.5.2 for information on Option 3 sprinkler requirements.*)

17-3.6.3 Each guest room door that opens onto an interior corridor shall be self-closing and shall meet the requirements of 17-3.6.2.

Since 16-3.6.2 requires guest room doors to have a 20-minute fire protection rating, then NFPA 80, Standard for Fire Doors and Windows,[3] requires the door to be self closing; however, the Committee feels that this is such an important point that it repeats the requirement in 17-3.6.3

rather than rely totally on the reference document. Numerous hotel fires have resulted in multiple fatalities due to the lack of, or poor maintenance of, door closers.

17-3.6.4   Unprotected openings shall be prohibited in partitions of interior corridors serving as exit access from guest rooms.

17-3.6.5   Existing transoms installed in corridor partitions of sleeping rooms shall be fixed in the closed position and shall be covered or otherwise protected to provide a fire resistance rating at least equivalent to that of the wall in which they are installed.

Transoms have been prohibited in hotels for many years due to tragic fires that resulted where their presence led to the transmission of fire and smoke through corridors and directly into occupied rooms, thus causing multiple deaths.

17-3.6.6   Transfer grilles, whether protected by fusible link operated dampers or not, shall not be used in these walls or doors.

Exception No. 1:   Where a corridor smoke detection system is provided that, when sensing smoke, will sound the building alarm and shut down return or exhaust fans that draw air into the corridor from the guest rooms. The grilles shall be located in the lower one-third of the wall or door height.

Exception No. 2:   Where automatic sprinkler protection is provided in the corridor in accordance with 19-3.5.2 through 19-3.5.4, and where the transfer grille is located in the lower one-third of the wall or door height.

Paragraph 2-2.2 of **NFPA 90A**, *Standard for the Installation of Air Conditioning and Ventilating Systems*,[4] prohibits public corridors from being used as a portion of the supply return or exhaust air system. However, very old hotels (prior to 1950) often use corridors for supply or return air. The *Code* recognizes this and sets criteria for their continued existence under limited conditions.

Exception No. 2 is based on the Option 3 corridor sprinkler system for apartment buildings.

Figure 17-8 illustrates the requirements of 17-3.6.

17-3.7 Subdivision of Building Spaces.

17-3.7.1   Every guest room floor shall be divided into at least two smoke compartments of approximately the same size with smoke barriers in accordance with Section 6-3. Smoke dampers are not required.

Additional smoke barriers shall be provided such that the maximum travel distance from a guest room corridor door to a smoke barrier shall not exceed 150 ft (45 m).

Exception No. 1:   Buildings protected throughout by an approved automatic sprinkler system installed in accordance with 17-3.5.1 or a sprinkler system conforming to 19-3.5.1 through 19-3.5.3.

Exception No. 2:   Where each guest room is provided with exterior ways of exit access arranged in accordance with 5-5.3.

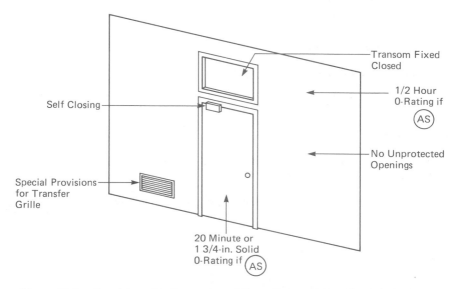

Figure 17-8.   Provisions for Protection of Guest Rooms (Corridors) in Existing Hotels.   The need for the self-closing door cannot be overemphasized. There are no exceptions or options for the self-closing device. Although no rating is required where sprinkler protection is provided, the wall shall be substantial and shall resist the passage of smoke.

Exception No. 3:   Smoke barriers are not required where the aggregate corridor length on each floor is not more than 150 ft (45 m).

This requirement was new to the 1985 Editon of the *Code*. It requires all but relatively small floors to be subdivided into two smoke compartments. This provides for horizontal movement of people and limits the number of rooms — and therefore people — exposed to a single fire that may be blocking a corridor. Since no fire rating is required for the barrier and smoke dampers are not required, the requirement is not overly burden-some in typical hotel or dormitory construction. The exception for automatic sprinklers again reflects the excellent life loss record of buildings so equipped.

A horizontal exit may be used to comply with 17-3.7.1 and thereby serve more than one function.

17-3.8 Special Features.

SECTION 17-4   SPECIAL PROVISIONS

17-4.1 Operating Features.   *(See Chapter 31.)*

17-4.2 High Rise Buildings.   (Reserved.)

SECTION 17-5   BUILDING SERVICES

17-5.1 Utilities.   Utilities shall comply with the provisions of Section 7-1.

17-5.2 Heating, Ventilating, and Air Conditioning.

17-5.2.1   Heating, ventilating, and air conditioning equipment shall comply with the provisions of Section 7-2, except as otherwise required in this chapter.

17-5.2.2   Unvented fuel-fired heaters shall not be used.

17-5.3 Elevators, Dumbwaiters, and Vertical Conveyors.   Elevators, dumbwaiters, and vertical conveyors shall comply with the provisions of Section 7-4.

17-5.4 Rubbish Chutes, Incinerators, and Laundry Chutes.   Rubbish chutes, incinerators, and laundry chutes shall comply with the provisions of Section 7-5.

The 1985 Edition of the *Code* eliminated the special section on dormitories. Dormitories are now covered as hotels due to several changes to hotel requirements regarding windows, alarms, and building subdivisions, which made special requirements for dormitories unnecessary.

REFERENCES CITED IN COMMENTARY

[1]NFPA 13, *Standard for the Installation of Sprinkler Systems*, National Fire Protection Association, Quincy, MA, 1987.
[2]Best, Richard and Demers, David P., Investigation Report on the MGM Grand Hotel Fire, Las Vegas, Nevada, National Fire Protection Association, Quincy, MA, NFPA No. LS-4, 1982.
[3]NFPA 80, *Standard for Fire Doors and Windows*, National Fire Protection Association, Quincy, MA, 1986.
[4]NFPA 90A, *Standard for the Installation of Air Conditioning and Ventilating Systems*, National Fire Protection Association, Quincy, MA, 1985.

18

NEW APARTMENT BUILDINGS

(See also Chapter 31.)

Prior to the 1981 Edition of the *Code*, all residential occupancies were treated in one chapter. In that edition, they were split into several chapters in order to simplify and clarify the *Code*, resulting in a document that is easier to use.

Residential occupancies are those in which sleeping accommodations are provided for normal residential purposes and include all buildings designed to provide sleeping accommodations. They are treated separately in the *Code* in the following groups:

Hotels, motels, dormitories (Chapters 16 and 17)
Apartment buildings (Chapters 18 and 19)
Lodging or rooming houses (Chapter 20)
Board and care facilities (Chapter 21)
One- and two-family dwellings (Chapter 22)

Exceptions to the groups listed above are health care occupancies, which are covered in Chapters 12 and 13, and detention and correctional occupancies, which are covered in Chapters 14 and 15. In earlier editions of the *Code*, they were classified as "institutional occupancies."

A review of 4-1.6 underscores a common principle of life safety with which the *Code* is concerned as applied to all the residential occupancies considered by Chapters 16 through 23. Paragraph 4-1.6 states: "Residential occupancies are those occupancies in which sleeping accommodations are provided for normal residential purposes and include all buildings designed to provide sleeping accommodations." This use of residential occupancies is central to the *Code's* provisions in Chapters 16 through 23, because people who are asleep will be unaware of a rapidly developing fire and, when alerted, may be somewhat confused due to being awakened suddenly. Other factors on which the provisions of Chapters 16 through 23 were based are the presence of hazards (such as cooking and heating equipment) and the degree of familiarity of the occupant with his or her living space (ranging from transients with little or no familiarity, as in hotels, to total familiarity in single-family dwellings).

SECTION 18-1   GENERAL REQUIREMENTS

18-1.1 Application.

18-1.1.1   All new buildings classified as apartment buildings by 18-1.3.1 shall conform to the provisions of this chapter and shall meet the requirements of one of the following options (*see Table 18-1*):

Option 1:   Buildings without fire suppression or detection systems;

Single station smoke detectors in each unit are required per 18-3.4.4.1.

Option 2:   Buildings provided with a complete automatic fire detection and notification system;

Option 3:   Buildings provided with automatic sprinkler protection in selected areas;

Option 4:   Buildings protected throughout by an approved automatic sprinkler system.

18-1.1.2 High Rise Buildings.   High rise buildings shall comply with Option 4.

Paragraph 18-1.1.1 identifies four different ways of arranging apartment buildings for life safety that are acceptable to the *Code*. These four systems are:

1. Buildings without fire suppression or detection systems;
2. Buildings with an automatic fire detection system;
3. Buildings provided with an automatic sprinkler system in corridors only; and
4. Buildings protected by a total automatic sprinkler system.

In the 1976 Edition of the *Code*, Section 11-3 covered both new and existing apartment buildings, with 11-3.1 to 11-3.4 providing general requirements for all apartment buildings, and 11-3.5 through 11-3.8 each covering one of the four options. In that edition, every apartment building was required to meet the provisions of 11-3.1 through 11-3.4 and any one of the requirements of 11-3.5 through 11-3.8. This arrangement resulted in a considerable amount of cross-referencing not only in Section 11-3, but also in Sections 11-1, 11-2, and Chapter 6; sometimes a very confusing text resulted. Since the 1981 Edition was undergoing extensive editorial revision to provide separate chapters for new and existing buildings and to split up the residential chapter, it was decided to reorganize the apartment chapters to make them easier to use and eliminate cross-referencing where possible. As a result of this restructuring, all sections of Chapter 18 then applied to all new apartment buildings. This application continues in the 1988 Edition. There are various paragraphs and parts of paragraphs that apply to different options. Every apartment building must meet one of the four options.

The Committee, recognizing the equivalency provisions found in Section 1-5 of the *Code*, saw a need to establish in advance four equivalent *Code* complying schemes to provide a high degree of design flexibility. The equivalencies developed were based on the Committee's professional judgment, the results of full-scale fire tests conducted at the National Bureau of Standards, and a review of the most recent fire experiences. These options are considered to be equivalent to each other in providing a minimum level of life safety for apartments. Because some systems have additional protective capability (detectors, automatic sprinklers, etc.), greater building heights and larger building areas are permitted. Where the design provides only the minimum level of safety called for in the *Code*, lower building heights and smaller building areas are specified.

This overall approach provides one of the first "system" design attempts to be codified. Whereas a total system would have many design approaches, this is a more limited, or bounded, system in that only four different approaches are available. Yet, a designer can identify an appropriate design from the four approaches based on the building's size, height, and arrangement. This provides the designer an opportunity to put together a safety approach that best fits the building, rather than fitting a building to a single codified design criterion. However, this system works only where the designer and the authority having jurisidiction agree on the plan selected at the earliest design phase.

High rise buildings are now required to be protected throughout by an approved supervised automatic sprinkler system and, therefore, must comply with Option 1. (*See 18-3.5.*)

In the 1988 *Code*, although Option 3 still exists, no alternatives are allowed for Option 3 in new construction.

18-1.1.3   Every individual living unit covered by this chapter shall comply with the minimum provisions of Section 22-2 for one- and two-family dwellings.

This paragraph requires that every living unit (apartment) comply with Section 22-2 of Chapter 22 on one- and two-family dwellings. This is important for several reasons. First, it establishes two means of escape from every bedroom and living area of a living unit (apartment) having two rooms or more (this exempts efficiency-type apartments). Paragraph 22-2.1.2 establishes several different types of "second means of escape" that can be provided, the most common of which is the operable window; however, Chapter 22 also sets certain requirements regarding that operable window in addition to those for minimum size and arrangement. The window must be within 20 ft (6.1 m) of grade or be accessible by fire department rescue apparatus or open onto a balcony. If this requirement cannot be met, a second means of escape complying with one of the other three types listed in 22-2.1.2 must be provided. A second means of escape is exempted if the dwelling unit is protected by an automatic sprinkler system in accordance with either NFPA 13, *Standard for the Installation of Sprinkler Systems,*[1] or NFPA 13D, *Standard for the Installation of Sprinkler Systems in One- and Two-Family Dwellings and Mobile Homes.*[2] Note that this would not require that the entire apartment building be sprinklered, but only the living unit that does not comply with the secondary means of escape.

Another important provision of Section 22-2 reduces the minimum widths of doors within the dwelling unit to 28 in. (71 cm) in width rather than the 32 in. (81 cm) in width specified by Chapter 5. It also allows the use of sliding doors, the use of stairs that do not meet the requirements for new stairs in Chapter 5, and the use of winders and spiral stairs within the living unit. (*See commentary on Chapter 22 for additional information on means of escape from living units.*)

18-1.2 Mixed Occupancies.

18-1.2.1   Where another type of occupancy occurs in the same building as a residential occupancy, the requirements of 1-4.7 of this *Code* shall be applicable.

18-1.2.2   For requirements on mixed mercantile and residential occupancies, see 24-1.2.

18-1.3 Definitions.

18-1.3.1   Terms applicable to this chapter are defined in Chapter 3 of this *Code*; where necessary, other terms will be defined in the text as they may occur.

Apartment Buildings.   Includes buildings containing three or more living units with independent cooking and bathroom facilities, whether designated as apartment house, tenement, garden apartment, or by any other name.

18-1.4 Classification of Occupancy.   (*See 18-1.3.1.*)

18-1.5 Classification of Hazard of Contents.

18-1.5.1   The contents of residential occupancies shall be classified as ordinary hazard in accordance with Section 4-2.

NFPA 13, *Standard for the Installation of Sprinkler Systems*,[1] would classify the contents as "light" for the purpose of designing extinguishing systems. The difference in classification is based on the threat to life or life safety (ordinary) versus the threat to the extinguishing capability of the automatic sprinkler system (light).

18-1.6 Minimum Construction Requirements.   No Special Requirements.

18-1.7 Occupant Load.

18-1.7.1*   The occupant load in numbers of persons for whom exits are to be provided shall be determined on the basis of one person per 200 sq ft (18.6 sq m) gross floor area, or the maximum probable population of any room or section under consideration, whichever is greater. The occupant load of any open mezzanine or balcony shall be added to the occupant load of the floor below for the purpose of determining exit capacity.

A-18-1.7.1   Dormitory-type occupancy, particularly where 2- or 3-tier bunks are used with close spacing, may produce an occupant load substantially greater than one person per 200 sq ft (18.6 sq m) gross floor area. However, even though sleeping areas are densely populated, the building as a whole may not necessarily exceed one person per 200 sq ft (18.6 sq m) gross area, owing to the space taken for toilet facilities, halls, closets, and living rooms not used for sleeping purposes.

See 5-3.1 for further details on the use of occupant load for determining capacity of the means of egress.

SECTION 18-2   MEANS OF EGRESS REQUIREMENTS

18-2.1 General.

18-2.1.1   All means of egress shall be in accordance with Chapter 5 and this chapter.

Rather than repeat many of the provisions of Chapter 5, a general reference to Chapter 5 is made. Many of the requirements that follow in Section 18-2 pick up provisions from Chapter 5 that are options for the occupancy chapters, such as Exception No. 1 to 18-2.2.2.2, which allows the use of special locking arrangements per 5-2.1.6; or that prohibit the use of an item if it is not listed (note that alternating tread devices are not listed in 18-2.2); or that establish limits based on criteria provided in Chapter 5, such as corridor dead-end limits in 18-2.5.3.

18-2.2 Means of Egress Components.

18-2.2.1 General.

18-2.2.1.1   Components of means of egress shall be limited to the types described in 18-2.2.2 through 18-2.2.7.

18-2.2.1.2   In buildings utilizing Option 4, exit enclosures shall have a fire resistance rating of not less than one hour with a fire protection rating of doors of one hour.

In recognition of the relatively low fuel loads in apartment buildings, the fire resistance rating for exit enclosures, as well as other vertical openings (*see 18-3.1.1 Exception No. 3*), need not exceed one hour; however, as a safeguard, this is permitted only in buildings protected throughout by automatic sprinklers (Option 4). This is not permitted for assembly occupancies or business occupancies and, therefore, cannot be utilized where mixed occupancies are involved; nor can it be used for stairways or vertical openings involving or passing through other occupancies.

In facilities where occupancies are adequately separated and treated independently, it could be feasible to have a 1-hour enclosure in the apartment portion and a 2-hour enclosure elsewhere.

18-2.2.2 Doors.

18-2.2.2.1   Doors shall comply with 5-2.1.

18-2.2.2.2*   No door in any means of egress shall be locked against egress when the building is occupied.

Exception No. 1:   Special locking arrangements complying with 5-2.1.6 are permitted.

Exception No. 2:   Doors serving a single dwelling unit may be provided with a lock complying with 5-2.1.5.1 Exception No. 3.

A-18-2.2.2.2   It is the intent of this requirement that security measures, when installed, should not prevent egress.

Paragraph 18-2.2.2.2 prohibits an apartment building from having any door locked "against egress" while the building is occupied. This requirement permits a door to have a locking device that allows the door to be opened from within the building for the purpose of egress, but does not allow the door to be opened from outside the building. Ordinary double cylinder locks and chain locks would not meet these provisions. Several tragic multiple-death fires have occurred where a key could not be found to unlock these devices.

The language of 5-2.1.5.1 is clear: "Locks, if provided, shall not require the use of a key, tool, special knowledge, or effort for operation from the inside of the building." This eliminates double cylinder locks and chain locks that require a key to operate from the inside. Paragraph 5-2.1.5.3 calls for a simple operation to open a door; a two-handed knob operation, and the like, is specifically prohibited by 5-2.1.5.3.

Chapter 5 now specifically recognizes the need for security chains or rods on apartment doors and allows one additional releasing device. The typical apartment door has three devices: the latch, the lock, and the security chain or rod. However, the *Code* allows only two releasing actions for new installations. This requirement is met by using a latch and lock set that has a lock bolt that automatically retracts when the latch handle is turned from the inside; thus, only one releasing action is needed for the two devices. The second action is the release of the security chain or rod. In neither case, however, can the devices require the use of a key, tool, special knowledge, or effort.

Exception No. 1 to 18-2.2.2.2 recognizes the use of the delay release lock provided for in 5-2.1.6. This requires that the building either be protected throughout by automatic sprinklers or equipped throughout with a fire detection system. The 15- or 30-second delay permitted by 5-2.1.6 does not affect the immediate release of the lock upon activation of the sprinklers or detectors, or upon loss of power to the lock. This device helps the apartment building provide the security needed for seldom used doors or stairs, while at the same time it keeps the door available for use, which chains and padlocks are unable to do.

The second Exception allows the use of a "captive key" type lock on individual apartment doors. (*See Chapter 5 for details.*)

18-2.2.2.3   Revolving doors complying with 5-2.1.10 are permitted.

18-2.2.3 Stairs.

18-2.2.3.1   Stairs shall comply with 5-2.2.

18-2.2.3.2 Within any individual living unit, stairs more than one story above or below the entrance floor level of the living unit shall not be permitted.

This paragraph requires that no level of an apartment be more than one story away from an entrance. This would normally restrict an apartment from having more than three stories, one up and one down. However, if an apartment has entrances at more than one level, then more than three levels could be utilized. However, 18-3.1.1 would allow only two levels to be open to each other; the third level would need to be protected.

18-2.2.3.3 Spiral stairs complying with 5-2.2.2.7 are permitted within a single living unit.

18-2.2.3.4 Winders complying with 5-2.2.2.8 are permitted within a single living unit.

18-2.2.4 Smokeproof Enclosures. Smokeproof enclosures shall comply with 5-2.3.

18-2.2.5 Horizontal Exits. Horizontal exits shall comply with 5-2.4.

18-2.2.6 Ramps. Ramps shall comply with 5-2.5.

18-2.2.7 Exit Passageways. Exit passageways shall comply with 5-2.6.

18-2.3 Capacity of Means of Egress.

18-2.3.1 The capacity of means of egress shall be in accordance with Section 5-3.

18-2.3.2 Street floor exits shall be sufficient for the occupant load of the street floor plus the required capacity of stairs and ramps discharging onto the street floor.

Paragraph 18-2.3.2 requires street-floor exit designs that have sufficient width to provide for the intermingling of exits from the street floor with those exits discharging down from the upper floors and discharging up from the lower floors. This is the traditional grand lobby design where stairs and street-floor exits converge at one or two exterior door locations. Similar discussion on this matter is found in Chapter 16. Paragraph 5-7.2 restricts the number and arrangement of stairs that discharge through the street floor.

Figure 18-1 shows a typical arrangement of multiple exits discharging on the street floor.

18-2.3.3 The minimum corridor width shall be sufficient to accommodate the required occupant load, but not less than 44 in. (112 cm).

Exception: Corridors with a required capacity not greater than 50, as defined in Section 5-3, shall be not less than 36 in. (91 cm) in width.

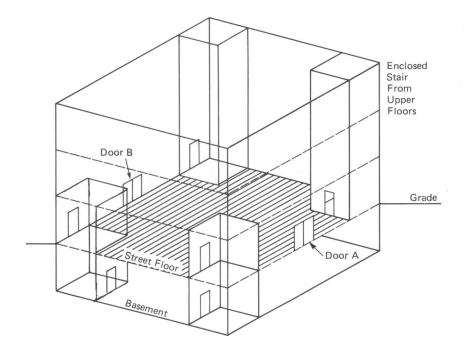

Figure 18-1. Capacity of Means of Egress in Accordance with 18-2.3.2. Required widths of Doors A and B are based on the number of people expected to use them. Assuming that the street floor has an occupant load of 500, and each upper floor has an occupant load of 200, and the basement 100, then required exit capacity for the street floor would be calculated as follows:

500 (street floor) + 200/2 (upper floor max 50% per 5-7.2) + 100/2 (basement max 50% per 5-7.2) = 650 total using exits on street floor X 0.2 in. (0.5 cm) of door per person = 130 in. (325 cm) ÷ 2 exits = 65 in. (163 cm) at A and at B.

18-2.4 Number of Exits.   *(See also Section 5-4.)*

18-2.4.1   Every living unit shall have access to at least two separate exits remote from each other as required by 5-5.1.

Exception No. 1: Any living unit may have a single exit provided:

(a) That living unit has an exit door directly to the street or yard at ground level, or

(b) That living unit has direct access to an outside stair complying with 5-2.2, serving a maximum of two units both located on the same floor, or

(c) That living unit has direct access to an interior stair serving that unit only and separated from all other portions of the building with fire barriers having a one-hour fire resistance rating with no opening therein.

Exception No. 1 provides for a single exit under three different potential arrangements. The first arrangement is where the living unit has an exit direct to the street or to the yard at ground level. This is common in a townhouse or row house arrangement. This would permit the front door to be the only required exit, and therefore, there would be no requirements for a rear door. If a rear door were provided, it would not have to meet the requirements of the *Code*; more importantly, in this case, it would not have to meet the swing requirements or the locking requirements of the *Code*. The second arrangement is where an apartment has direct access to an outside stair. The third arrangement allowed by Exception No. 1 permits an apartment to be served by a single exit if that single exit is separated from all *other* portions of the building by barriers having a 1-hour fire resistance rating with no openings therein. This would be a private stairway. Conditions (b) and (c) of Exception No. 1 are illustrated in Figure 18-2.

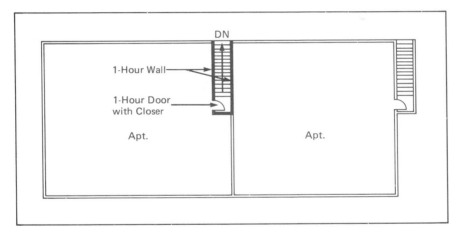

Figure 18-2. Two Methods of Complying with 18-2.4.1 Exception No. 1 for a Single Exit. The enclosed stair is no longer required to be separated from the unit it serves as long as it is separated from all other spaces.

Exception No. 2: *Any building of three stories or less with not more than 4 living units per floor may have a single exit under the following conditions:*

(a) The stairway is completely enclosed by barriers having a fire resistance rating of at least 1 hour with self-closing 1-hour fire protection rated doors protecting all openings between the stairway enclosure and the building.

(b) The stairway does not serve more than ½ story below the level of exit discharge.

(c) All corridors serving as access to exits have at least a 1-hour fire resistance rating.

(d) There is not more than 35 ft (10.7 m) of travel distance from the entrance door of any living unit to an exit.

(e) Three-quarter hour fire rated horizontal and vertical separation between living units is provided.

Exception No. 2 to 18-2.4.1 provides the basic design approach used for "garden" apartments where the apartment entrances open onto a single enclosed stair. Often, the stair is open to the exterior or is glass-enclosed on the front of the building. The Exception allows a single exit under this arrangement. Note that the stairway must be separated from the building by construction of at least a 1-hour fire resistance rating, and the doors must be 1-hour rated and self-closing. A frequent violation of this Exception is the construction of the door and the lack of a door closer.

These two exceptions apply to any of the four options.

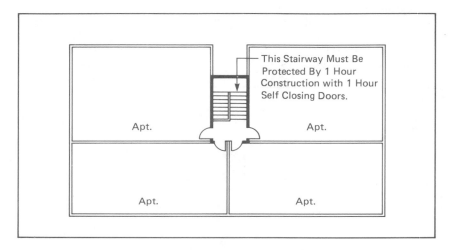

This Stairway Must Be Protected By 1 Hour Construction with 1 Hour Self Closing Doors.

Apt.   Apt.

Apt.   Apt.

Figure 18-3.   One Method of Complying with 18-2.4.1 Exception No. 2.

18-2.5 Arrangement of Exits.

18-2.5.1   Access to all required exits shall be in accordance with Section 5-5.

18-2.5.2   No common path of travel shall exceed 35 ft (10.7 m). Travel within a dwelling unit shall not be included when calculating common path of travel.

Exception: In buildings protected throughout by an approved supervised automatic sprinkler system, common path of travel shall not exceed 50 ft (15 m).

Common path of travel is normally measured from the most remote point subject to occupancy (*see 5-5.1.2 and the definition of common path of travel in Section 3-2*); therefore, this is a modified common path of travel, as measurement does not extend into the guest room or suite.

Since the dead-end limits of 18-2.5.3 are the same as those of 18-2.5.2, it is difficult to envision an excessive, modified common path of travel that is not also a violation of the dead-end provision. (*See Figure 18-4.*)

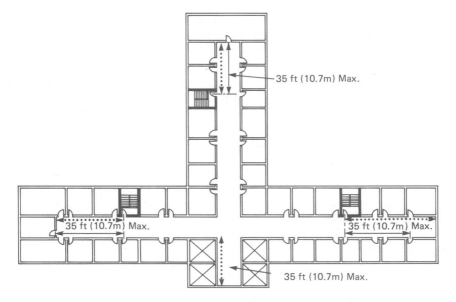

Figure 18-4. Common Path of Travel (Modified) and Dead-End Limitations in a Nonsprinklered Apartment Building. Modified common paths of travel are indicated by ◄——► and dead ends are indicated by ◄····► . Note that it is possible to have a dead end that is not a common path of travel, but with the modified common path of travel, it is difficult to envision a realistic situation that is not also a dead end.

18-2.5.3   No dead-end corridor shall exceed 35 ft (10.7 m).

Exception: In buildings protected throughout by an approved supervised automatic sprinkler system, dead-end corridors shall not exceed 50 ft (15 m).

18-2.6 Travel Distance to Exits.

18-2.6.1   Travel distance within a living unit (apartment) to a corridor door shall not exceed the following limits:

(a) For buildings using Options 1, 2, or 3 — 75 ft (23 m).

(b) For buildings using Option 4 — 125 ft (38 m).

Due to revisions in Section 5-6, travel distance is now measured from the most remote point subject to occupancy [the former provision exempting rooms with 6 or fewer people, with 50 ft (15 m) or less travel distance has been deleted]. To be consistent with Section 5-6, the Committee has revised the method of measuring travel distance in apartment buildings. The distances within the unit have been increased as compensation. Should the travel distance within a unit be excessive, another remote door to the corridor would need to be added.

18-2.6.2 The travel distance from a living unit (apartment) entrance door to the nearest exit shall not exceed the following limits:

(a) For buildings using Option 1, 2, or 3 — 100 ft (30 m).

(b) For buildings using Option 4 — 200 ft (60 m).

Exception: Travel distance to exits may be increased to 200 ft (60 m) for exterior ways of exit access arranged in accordance with 5-5.3.

18-2.7 Discharge from Exits.

18-2.7.1 Exit discharge shall comply with Section 5-7.

Section 5-7 does allow a maximum of 50 percent of the number and capacity of exits to discharge through the level of exit discharge (street floor) under limited conditions. Two permitted arrangements are illustrated in Figures 18-5 and 18-6.

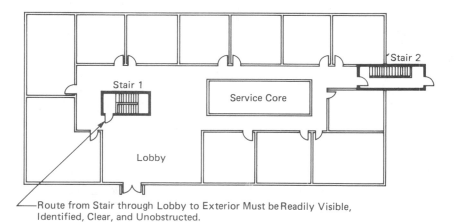

Route from Stair through Lobby to Exterior Must be Readily Visible, Identified, Clear, and Unobstructed.

Figure 18-5. Arrangement of Means of Egress in Accordance with 5-7.2. Stair 1 (50 percent of the total number and capacity of exits) discharges through the first floor. Stair 2 discharges directly to the exterior (it may discharge through an exit passageway to the exterior). Since other areas on the first floor (the level of exit discharge) are not separated from the path that a person leaving Stair 1 must follow to exit through the lobby, the entire first floor must be completely sprinklered. If the rest of the floor were separated (to the extent required for the stair enclosure), only the path to the exit discharge would have to be sprinklered.

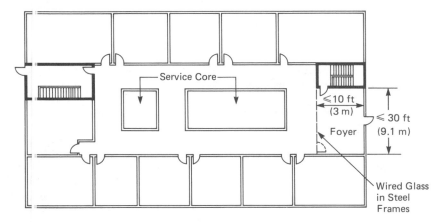

Figure 18-6. Foyer Constructed in Compliance with 5-7.2. The foyer must serve only as a means of egress.

18-2.8 Illumination of Means of Egress.

18-2.8.1 Means of egress shall be illuminated in accordance with Section 5-8.

18-2.9 Emergency Lighting.

18-2.9.1 Emergency lighting in accordance with Section 5-9 shall be provided in all buildings with greater than 12 living units or greater than three stories in height.

Exception: Where every living unit has a direct exit to the outside of the building at grade level.

This Exception does not apply to all buildings with exterior exit access, but only to those where each unit has direct exit to grade.

18-2.10 Marking of Means of Egress.

18-2.10.1 Means of egress shall have signs in accordance with Section 5-10 in all buildings requiring more than one exit.

18-2.11 Special Features.

SECTION 18-3 PROTECTION

18-3.1 Protection of Vertical Openings.

18-3.1.1 Every stairway, elevator shaft, and other vertical opening shall be enclosed or protected in accordance with 6-2.4.

Exception No. 1: Stairway enclosures shall not be required where a one-story stair connects two levels within a single dwelling unit, guest room, or suite.

See 18-2.2.3.2.

Exception No. 2:   An atrium may be utilized in accordance with 6-2.4.5.

Since 6-2.4.5 requires total automatic sprinkler protection, atriums can only be used in buildings using Option 4.

Exception No. 3:   In buildings using Option 4, fire resistance of walls may be 1 hour and fire protection rating of doors may be 1 hour.

In recognition of the relatively low fuel loads in apartment buildings, the fire protection rating of required enclosure of vertical openings need not exceed 1 hour. Similar provisions are made for exit enclosures. (*See 18-2.2.1.2.*) However, as a safeguard, this is permitted only in buildings protected throughout by automatic sprinklers (Option 4). (*Also see commentary following 18-2.2.1.2.*)

Exception No. 4:   There shall be no unprotected vertical opening in any building or fire section with only one exit.

18-3.1.2   No floor below the level of exit discharge used only for storage, heating equipment, or purposes other than residential occupancy open to the public shall have unprotected openings to floors used for residential purposes.

18-3.2 Protection from Hazards.

18-3.2.1   In buildings using Option 1, 2, or 3, every hazardous area shall be separated from other parts of the building by construction having a fire resistance rating of at least 1 hour, and communicating openings shall be protected by approved smoke-actuated automatic, or self-closing fire doors with a fire protection rating of ¾ hour, or such area shall be equipped with an automatic extinguishing system. Hazardous areas include, but are not limited to:

Boiler and heater rooms
Laundries
Repair shops
Rooms or spaces used for storage of combustible supplies and equipment in quantities deemed hazardous by the authority having jurisdiction.

Formal Interpretation 81-38
Reference: 18-3.2.1

Question: Is it the intent of the committee that the requirements of 18-3.2.1 be applied to residential-type heating appliances, such as domestic hot water heaters, domestic furnaces, or domestic boilers, where installed within a dwelling unit in an apartment building? [NOTE: NFPA 97M, *Standard Glossary of Terms Relating to Chimneys, Vents, and Heat Producing Appliances,* defines a residential-type heating appliance as a fuel burning or electric heating appliance, except high pressure steam boilers, for heating building spaces having a volume not more than 25,000 cu ft (708 cm).]

An wer: No.

Issue Edition: 1981
Refer :nce: 18-3.2.1
Date: January 1984

18-3.2.2 In buildings using Option 4, the enclosure for hazardous areas shall be of smoke-resisting construction with or without a fire resistance rating.

18-3.3 Interior Finish.

18-3.3.1 Interior finish on walls and ceilings, in accordance with Section 6-5, shall be as follows:

(a) Exit enclosures — Class A

(b) Lobbies and corridors — Class A or B

(c) All other spaces — Class A, B, or C

18-3.3.2 Interior Floor Finish. In buildings using Option 1 or 2, interior floor finish in corridors and exits shall be Class I or Class II in accordance with Section 6-5.

See commentary in Section 6-5, especially the discussion on interior floor finish. Paragraph 6-5.2.3 establishes stringent requirements regarding the use of textile or carpetlike material on walls and ceilings. The interior finish for walls and ceilings, other than textile or carpetlike material, can be lowered one class (A to B, B to C) in Option 4 buildings and in corridors of Option 3 buildings. (*See 6-5.7.*)

18-3.4 Detection, Alarm, and Communications Systems.

18-3.4.1 General. Apartment buildings with more than three stories or with more than 11 living units shall be provided with a fire alarm system in accordance with Section 7-6.

Exception: Where each living unit is separated from other contiguous living units by fire barriers (see Section 6-2) having a fire resistance rating not less than ¾ hour and where each living unit has either its own independent exit or its own independent stairway or ramp discharging at grade.

The intent of this Exception is to eliminate the requirement for a fire alarm system in a "townhouse" type apartment building.

18-3.4.2 Initiation.

18-3.4.2.1 Initiation of the required fire alarm system shall be by manual means in accordance with 7-6.2.

18-3.4.2.2 In buildings using Option 2, the required fire alarm system shall be initiated by the automatic fire detection system, in addition to the manual initiation means of 18-3.4.2.1.

18-3.4.2.3 In buildings using Option 3, the required fire alarm system shall be initiated upon operation of the automatic sprinkler system, in addition to the manual initiation means of 18-3.4.2.1.

18-3.4.2.4 In buildings using Option 4, the required fire alarm system shall be initiated upon operation of the automatic sprinkler system, in addition to the manual initiation means of 18-3.4.2.1.

18-3.4.3 Notification.

18-3.4.3.1 An annunciator panel connected with the required fire alarm system shall be provided. The location of the annunciator panel shall be approved by the authority having jurisdiction.

Exception: Buildings not greater than two stories in height and with not more than 50 living units.

18-3.4.3.2 Occupant notification shall be accomplished automatically, without delay, by an internal audible alarm signal in accordance with 7-6.3. Presignal systems are prohibited.

18-3.4.4 Detection.

18-3.4.4.1* Approved single station or multiple station smoke detectors continuously powered by house electrical service shall be installed in accordance with 7-6.2.9 in every living unit within the apartment building regardless of the number of stories or number of apartments. When activated, the detector shall initiate an alarm that is audible in the sleeping rooms of that unit. This individual unit detector shall be in addition to any sprinkler system or other detection system that may be installed in the building.

A-18-3.4.4.1 Previous editions of the *Code* allowed the single station smoke detector required by this section to be omitted from each apartment where a total automatic smoke detection system was installed throughout the building. With such a system, when one detector is activated, an alarm is sounded throughout the building. Experience with complete systems in apartment buildings has shown that numerous false alarms are likely to occur. Where there is a problem with frequent false alarms, occupants either ignore the alarm, or the system is either disconnected or otherwise rendered inoperative.

The detector(s) required by 18-3.4.4.1 should usually be located in the hall area(s) giving access to rooms used for sleeping. In multilevel living units, the upper level detector should usually be located at the top of the stairs. The detector(s) should be mounted on the ceiling or on the wall within 12 in. (30.5 cm) of, but no closer than 6 in. (15.2 cm) to, the ceiling. The detector should be remotely located from the cooking area. Where unusual factors such as room configuration, air movement, or stagnant air pockets require consideration, the authority having jurisdiction and the designer should determine the placement of the detectors. (*See NFPA 74, Standard for the Installation, Maintenance, and Use of Household Fire Warning Equipment,*[3] *for additional details.*)

Note that the detector must be powered by "house current," either through direct wiring of the detector or by using plug-in type detectors. Battery-powered units will not meet the provision of 18-3.4.4.1.

It is not the intent of the paragraph to prohibit interconnecting detectors (multiple-station vs. single-station) within a single apartment if the apartment needs more than one detector; in fact, this is required by the second sentence.

Also note that this requirement is in addition to any other detection or suppression system required.

18-3.4.4.2   In buildings using Option 2, a total automatic fire detection system is required. An automatic fire detection system is one that is designed to give complete coverage with fire detectors in accordance with the spacings and layouts given in NFPA 72E, *Standard on Automatic Fire Detectors*, and laboratory test data, and is one in which the detectors are tied together to initiate the alarm and other automatic fire protection devices.

In buildings utilizing Option 2, a total automatic fire detection system is required, and this system must be interconnected with the building fire alarm system in accordance with 18-3.4.2.2. Note that this paragraph does not require smoke detectors but would allow the use of either heat detectors or smoke detectors. This system is required in addition to the single-station or multiple-station smoke detectors required by 18-3.4.4.1. Heat detectors are allowed by this paragraph since they would be used in addition to the smoke detectors as stated above. The feeling of the Committee here is that the single-station or multiple-station smoke detectors would alert the occupants within the apartment of a fire originating within that unit. Upon evacuation of the apartment, the door would close (*see 18-3.6.2*), and the occupants would activate a manual fire alarm station required by 18-3.4.2.1. If the occupants failed to activate a manual fire alarm station and the fire continued to develop in the apartment, the heat detectors would activate and sound the building fire alarm system prior to the fire becoming a threat to other apartment units. This system has proved very effective where used. In addition, since the system is required to be tied into the building fire alarm system, it would eliminate many false alarms that might occur if the entire building were protected by automatic smoke detection.

18-3.5 Extinguishment Requirements.

18-3.5.1*   Where an automatic sprinkler system is installed, either for total or partial building coverage, the system shall be installed in accordance with Section 7-7.

Exception: In individual living units, sprinkler installation may be omitted in closets not over 12 sq ft (1.1 sq m) and bathrooms not over 55 sq ft (5.1 sq m). Closets that contain equipment such as washers, dryers, furnaces, or water heaters shall be sprinklered regardless of size.

A-18-3.5.1   Although not required by the *Code*, the use of residential sprinklers or quick response sprinklers is encouraged for new installations of sprinkler systems within dwelling units, apartments, and guest rooms. Caution must be used, as the system must be designed for the sprinkler being used.

This paragraph does not mandate the installation of sprinklers, but sets provisions for their installation where required. The *Code* provides numerous incentives to install sprinklers and does mandate that all new high rise apartment buildings be protected throughout with automatic sprinklers. New to the 1988 *Code* is an appendix note to encourage that sprinklers within dwelling units be approved residential or quick response sprinklers. The intent is to get the quick response provided by these sprinklers as well as high spray pattern provided by residential sprinklers. Designers of sprinkler systems must be cautious, as these sprinklers cannot always be put on a system designed for standard sprinklers. There are also situations where residential fast response sprinklers have not currently been listed for such uses as vaulted ceilings. In such cases, the designer needs to provide the best alternative sprinkler.

The Exception has been carefully reworded for the 1988 *Code*. First, the closet size has been reduced due to the potential fuel load in large closets within an apartment building (as compared to a normal load in a hotel). Secondly, the spaces exempted are limited to those *within* a living unit; public areas are not exempted. Finally, the last sentence has been added to clarify that the intent of this Exception is for regular closets and bathrooms, not for closets that contain equipment.

18-3.5.2   In buildings using Option 3, automatic sprinklers shall be installed in corridors along the corridor ceiling, and one sprinkler head shall be opposite the center of and inside any living unit door opening onto the corridor.

Figure 18-7 illustrates typical sprinkler location as required by 18-3.5.2.

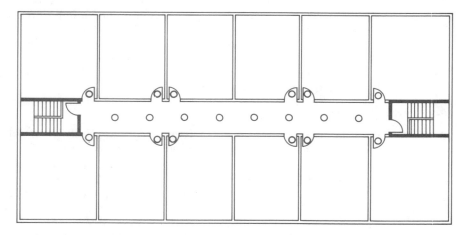

Figure 18-7.   Typical Sprinkler Locations that Comply with the Sprinkler Location Requirements of Option 3.

18-3.5.3 The sprinkler installation required in 18-3.5.2 shall meet the requirements of Section 7-7 in terms of workmanship and materials.

18-3.5.4 The installation of the corridor sprinklers required by 18-3.5.2 shall meet the spacing and protection area requirements of Section 7-7.

18-3.5.5 Buildings using Option 4 shall be protected throughout by an approved supervised automatic sprinkler system complying with 18-3.5.1.

18-3.5.6 Portable fire extinguishers shall be provided in hazardous areas. Where provided, portable fire extinguishers shall be installed and maintained as specified 7-7.4.1.

18-3.5.7 All high rise buildings shall comply with Option 4 (total automatic sprinkler protection).

The problems of fighting fires in high rise buildings and the resulting life safety problems are well documented. Prior to the 1988 Edition of the *Code*, automatic sprinkler protection for high rise buildings was not mandated, but numerous other items were required to compensate for buildings lacking automatic sprinkler protection. As this list grew, it reached the point of impracticality, and therefore, the *Code* now mandates sprinkler protection in all new high rise apartment buildings. (*See the definition of high rise in Section 3-2.*)

18-3.5.8 Open air parking structures complying with NFPA 88A, *Standard for Parking Structures*, need not be sprinklered under this *Code*.

Since many apartment buildings contain open air parking structures, the Committee felt that for *Life Safety Code* purposes *only*, an exemption for these structures was warranted. However, should sprinkler protection be required by other codes or by the *Life Safety Code* for reasons other than those found in 16-3.5, then sprinkler protection must be provided in these structures.

18-3.6 Corridors.

18-3.6.1 Exit access corridors shall be protected as follows:

(a) In buildings using Option 1 or 2, corridor walls shall have a fire resistance rating of not less than 1 hour.

(b) In buildings using Option 3, corridor walls shall have a fire resistance rating of not less than ¾ hour.

(c) In buildings using Option 4, corridor walls shall have a fire resistance rating of not less than ½ hour.

The criteria in 18-3.6 reflect the Committee's concern for providing safety for the occupant in his or her apartment during a fire. The focus of this concern is the presence of occupants on a 24-hour-a-day basis with sleeping accommodations. This minimum corridor wall construction will either block fire movement from the corridor into an apartment or block fire in an apartment from entering the corridor. (*Also see 18-5.2.*)

Although in truly new construction the reduction to ¾-hour or ½-hour fire resistance would have little benefit, it can play a major role in rehabilitation, renovations, or conversions of existing structures that are required to meet the provisions for new construction. (*See 1-4.6.*) Most existing lath and plaster walls provide 20- to 30-minute fire resistance ratings, and by providing automatic sprinkler protection throughout the building, the walls would not have to be replaced.

18-3.6.2   Doors between apartments and corridors shall be self-closing.

Requiring self-closing doors between apartments and corridors may lead to a significant reduction in fatalities caused by fire in apartment buildings. Studies of typical apartment fires have shown that the cause of fire spreading beyond the apartment or room of origin was due to the door being left open as the occupant fled the fire.

In other cases, a person suspecting a fire died after opening the door to a room fully involved with fire, or after causing full involvement of the room by introducing oxygen through the open door. Spring-loaded hinges or a closer would have caused these doors to close, preventing smoke or fire from spreading down the corridor and exposing other occupants.

18-3.6.3*   The fire protection rating of doors from living units to corridors shall be not less than 20 minutes.

A-18-3.6.3   Longer ratings may be required where doors are provided for property protection as well as life safety.

This does not require a listed or labeled assembly, but addresses only the door.

The door required by 18-3.6.3 provides a level of protection commensurate with the expected fuel load in the room and the fire resistance of the corridor wall construction. The purpose is to box a fire out of a room, or to box it within the room by means of corridor wall and door construction criteria. It has been shown in fuel load studies conducted by the National Bureau of Standards that residential occupancies will have fuel loads in the 20- to 30-minute range.

Figure 18-8 illustrates the requirements of 18-3.6.

18-3.7 Subdivisions of Building Spaces.

18-3.7.1 Horizontal Exits.   Sufficient horizontal exits are required to limit the maximum gross area per story between horizontal exits to that specified below:

(a) The gross area per story between horizontal exits shall not be limited for the purposes of this *Code* for buildings not greater than three stories in height.

(b) In buildings using Option 1 or 2, the gross area per story between horizontal exits shall be a maximum of 20,000 sq ft (1900 sq m).

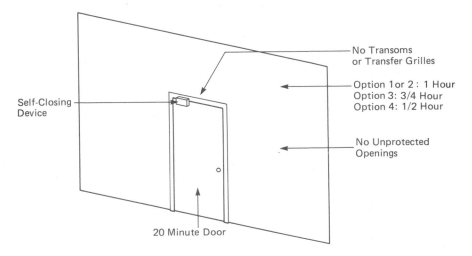

Figure 18-8. The Corridor Wall and Door Provisions of 18-3.6.

Note that the area limitation is for maximum gross area between horizontal exits. Its purpose is to establish the maximum potential area that would be directly exposed to a fire, thus limiting the number of occupants that would be directly exposed. This parallels the philosophy codified in Chapter 12, which also limits the area of exposure for patients to 22,500 sq ft (2,100 sq m) between smoke barriers. Chapter 18 is similar to Chapter 12 in that both deal with sleeping occupants. Also note that, as the fire protection features become more substantial, the area limit is increased.

It must be remembered that Chapter 5 requires each fire compartment formed by a horizontal exit to have an exit other than a horizontal exit. Since high rise buildings must comply with Option 4, this provision covers buildings lower than high rise, but greater than three stories in height.

18-3.7.2 Smoke Barriers.   Smoke barriers in accordance with Section 6-3 shall be provided in exit access corridors to establish at least two compartments approximately equal in size. The maximum length of each smoke compartment measured along the corridor shall not exceed 200 ft (60 m). Smoke dampers are not required.

Exception No. 1: Buildings using Option 4.

Exception No. 2: Exterior exit access in accordance with 5-5.3 that provides access to two exits.

Exception No. 3: Buildings allowed to comply with 18-2.4.1 Exceptions No. 1 or 2.

Exception No. 4: Buildings with exits not more than 50 ft (15 m) apart.

Exception No. 5: Where each dwelling unit has direct access to the exterior at grade.

Smoke barriers are required to isolate a fire and to prevent its products of combustion from contaminating all access to stairs.

The smoke barriers required by 18-3.7.2 are relatively easy to provide since no fire resistance rating is required and smoke dampers are exempted. In most cases, installing a set of cross corridor doors with smoke actuated automatic closers will accomplish the goal of the requirement. This can be accomplished in conjunction with the horizontal exits required by 18-3.7.1. Sprinklered buildings are exempt (Exception No. 1), as are buildings with a single exit (Exception No. 3) and buildings that do not utilize corridors as required exit access (Exceptions No. 2 and 5).

It should be noted that Exception No. 4 does not require smoke barriers every 50 ft (15 m), but only exempts a smoke barrier where the stair spacing is less than 50 ft (15 m) apart.

18-3.8 Special Features.

SECTION 18-4   SPECIAL PROVISIONS

18-4.1 Windows for Rescue and Ventilation.   *(See 18-1.1.3.)*
Exception: Buildings using Option 4.

18-4.2 High Rise Buildings.   *(See 18-1.1.1, 18-3.5.7.)*

18-4.3 Operating Features.   *(See Chapter 31.)*

SECTION 18-5   BUILDING SERVICES

18-5.1 Utilities.   Utilities shall comply with the provisions of Section 7-1.

18-5.2 Heating, Ventilating, and Air Conditioning.   Heating, ventilating, and air conditioning equipment shall comply with the provisions of Section 7-2.

Paragraph 2-2.2 of NFPA 90A, *Standard for the Installation of Air Conditioning and Ventilating Systems,*[4] prohibits the use of public corridors in residential occupancies as part of the supply, return, or exhaust air system.

18-5.3 Elevators, Dumbwaiters, and Vertical Conveyors.   Elevators, dumbwaiters, and vertical conveyors shall comply with the provisions of Section 7-4.

18-5.4 Rubbish Chutes, Incinerators, and Laundry Chutes.   Rubbish chutes, incinerators, and laundry chutes shall comply with the provisions of Section 7-5.

Table 18-1 summarizes the various requirements based on the four different options.

The following are two examples of how to use Table 18-1.

Example 1:   What are the interior finish requirements in exit enclosures for a five-story apartment building equipped with an automatic detection system?

Answer: Enter the table under the column heading "Total Automatic Detection Option No. 2." In the section "Exits — Vertical," find the heading "Flame Spread (Walls and Ceilings)." The requirement for this building is Class A interior finish for the exits.

Example 2:   What is the maximum dead-end distance permitted in an apartment building equipped with sprinklers located only in corridors and inside the doors leading into each living unit?

Answer: Enter the table under the column heading "Sprinkler Protection in Selected Areas Option No. 3." In the section "Exit Access," across the row headed "Maximum Dead End," you will find 35 ft (10.7 m) as the answer.

**Table 18-1   Alternate Requirements for
New Apartment Buildings According to Protection Provided**
(*See actual Code provisions for details*)

	No Suppression or Detection System Option No. 1	Total Automatic Detection Option No. 2	Sprink. Prot. in Select. Areas Option No. 3	Auto Ext. NFPA 13 (with exceptions) Option No. 4
Max. Gross Area per Story Between Horizontal Exits				
1-3 Stories	NR	NR	NR	NR
≥4 Stories <HR	20,000 sq ft (1,900 sq m)	20,000 sq ft (1,900 sq m)	NR	NR
HR	NP	NP	NP	NR
Exit Access				
Travel Distance	100 ft (30 m)	100 ft (30 m)	100 ft (30 m)	200 ft (60 m)
Smoke Barrier Req. (*See 18-3.7.2.*)	Req.	Req.	Req.	NR
Max. Common Path of Travel (Mod)	35 ft (10.7 m)	35 ft (10.7 m)	35 ft (10.7 m)	50 ft (15 m)
Max. Dead End	35 ft (10.7 m)	35 ft (10.7 m)	35 ft (10.7 m)	50 ft (15 m)
Fire Resistance				
Walls	1 hr	1 hr	¾ hr	½ hr
Doors (Fire Protection Rating)	20 min	20 min	20 min	20 min
Flame Spread				
Walls & Ceilings	A or B	A or B	A or B	A, B, or C
Floors	I or II	I or II	NR	NR
Exits—Vertical				
Fire Resistance Walls				
1-3 Stories	1 hr	1 hr	1 hr	1 hr
>3 Stories	2 hr	2 hr	2 hr	1 hr
Smokeproof Enclosures				
≥1 Story <HR	NR	NR	NR	NR
HR	NP	NP	NP	NR
Doors				
1-3 Stories	1 hr	1 hr	1 hr	1 hr
>3 Stories	1½ hr	1½ hr	1½ hr	1 hr
Flame Spread				
Walls & Ceilings	A	A	A	A or B
Floors	I or II	I or II	NR	NR

Req.=Required (*See Code for details and Exceptions.*)
NR=No Requirements
NA=Not Applicable
NP=Option Not Permitted For High Rise Buildings
HR=High Rise Buildings

Table 18-1 (Continued)

	No Suppression or Detection System Option No. 1	Total Automatic Smoke Detection Option No. 2	Sprink. Prot. in Select. Areas Option No. 3	Auto Ext. NFPA 13 (with exceptions) Option No. 4
Exits—Horizontal				
Fire Resistance				
Walls	2 hr	2 hr	2 hr	NA
Doors	1½ hr	1½ hr	1½ hr	NA
Habitable Spaces				
Max. Distance to Corridor	75 ft	75 ft	75 ft	125 ft
Door	(23 m)	(23 m)	(23 m)	(38 m)
Flamespread Walls &				
Ceilings	A, B, or C	A, B, or C	A, B, or C	A, B, or C
Smoke Detector in Unit	Req.	Req.	Req.	Req.
Door to Corridor Self-				
Closing	Req.	Req.	Req.	Req.
Bedroom Windows, per				
Section 22-2				
(See 18-1.1.2.)	Req.	Req.	Req.	NR
Alarm System				
>3 Stories or >11 Units	manual	manual & auto	manual & auto	manual & auto
>2 Stories or >50 Units	annunciator	annunciator	annunciator	annunciator
	panel	panel	panel	panel
HR	NP	NP	NP	
HVAC				
HR; Pressurized Corridor,				
0.01 in. Water (2.5 Pa),				
min.	NP	NP	NP	NR
Elevator				
ANSI	A17.1	A17.1	A17.1	A17.1

Req.=Required (See Code for details and Exceptions.)
NR=No Requirements
NA=Not Applicable
NP=Option Not Permitted For High Rise Buildings
HR=High Rise Buildings

References Cited in Commentary

[1]NFPA 13, *Standard for the Installation of Sprinkler Systems*, National Fire Protection Association, Quincy, MA, 1987.

[2]NFPA 13D, *Standard for the Installation of Sprinkler Systems in One- and Two-Family Dwellings and Mobile Homes*, National Fire Protection Association, Quincy, MA, 1984.

[3] NFPA 74, *Standard for the Installation, Maintenance, and Use of Household Fire Warning Equipment*, National Fire Protection Association, Quincy, MA, 1984.

[4]NFPA 90A, *Standard for the Installation of Air Conditioning and Ventilating Systems*, National Fire Protection Association, Quincy, MA, 1985.

19

EXISTING APARTMENT BUILDINGS

(See also Chapter 31.)

Prior to the 1981 Edition of the *Code*, all residential occupancies were treated in one chapter. In that edition, they were split into several chapters in order to simplify and clarify the *Code*, resulting in a document that is easier to use.

Residential occupancies are those in which sleeping accommodations are provided for normal residential purposes and include all buildings designed to provide sleeping accommodations. They are treated separately in the *Code* in the following groups:

Hotels, motels, dormitories (Chapters 16 and 17)
Apartment buildings (Chapters 18 and 19)
Lodging or rooming houses (Chapter 20)
Board and care facilities (Chapter 21)
One- and two-family dwellings (Chapter 22)

Exceptions to the groups listed above are health care occupancies, which are covered in Chapters 12 and 13, and detention and correctional occupancies, which are covered in Chapters 14 and 15. In earlier editions of the *Code*, they were classified as "institutional occupancies."

A review of 4-1.6 underscores a common principle of life safety with which the *Code* is concerned as applied to all the residential occupancies considered by Chapters 16 through 23. Paragraph 4-1.6 states: "Residential occupancies are those occupancies in which sleeping accommodations are provided for normal residential purposes and include all buildings designed to provide sleeping accommodations." This use of residential occupancies is central to the *Code's* provisions in Chapters 16 through 23, because people who are asleep will be unaware of a rapidly developing fire and, when alerted, may be somewhat confused due to being awakened suddenly. Other factors on which the provisions of Chapters 16 through 23 were based are the presence of hazards (such as cooking and heating equipment) and the degree of familiarity of the occupant with his or her living space (ranging from transients with little or no familiarity, as in hotels, to total familiarity in single-family dwellings).

SECTION 19-1   GENERAL REQUIREMENTS

19-1.1 Application.

19-1.1.1   All existing buildings classified as apartment buildings by 19-1.3 shall conform to the provisions of this chapter and shall meet the requirements of one of the following options:

Option 1: Buildings without fire suppression or detection systems;

Single station smoke detectors in each unit are required per 19-3.4.4.1.

Option 2: Buildings provided with a complete automatic fire detection and notification system;

Option 3: Buildings provided with automatic sprinkler protection in selected areas;

Option 4: Buildings protected throughout by an approved automatic sprinkler system.

Paragraph 19-1.1.1 identifies four different ways of arranging apartment buildings for life safety that are acceptable to the *Code*. These four systems are:

1. Buildings without fire suppression or detection systems;
2. Buildings with an automatic fire detection system;
3. Buildings provided with an automatic sprinkler system in corridors only; and
4. Buildings protected by a total automatic sprinkler system.

In the 1976 Edition of the *Code*, Section 11-3 covered both new and existing apartment buildings, with 11-3.1 to 11-3.4 providing general requirements for all apartment buildings, and 11-3.5 through 11-3.8 each covering one of the four options. In that edition, every apartment building was required to meet the provisions of 11-3.1 through 11-3.4, and any one of the requirements of 11-3.5 through 11-3.8. This arrangement resulted in a considerable amount of cross-referencing not only in Section 11-3, but also in Sections 11-1, 11-2, and Chapter 6; sometimes a very confusing text resulted. Since the 1981 Edition was undergoing extensive editorial revision to provide separate chapters for new and existing buildings and to split up the residential chapter, it was decided to reorganize the apartment chapters to make them easier to use and eliminate cross-referencing where possible. As a result of this restructuring, all sections of Chapter 19 then applied to all existing apartment buildings. This application continues in the 1988 Edition. There are various paragraphs and parts of paragraphs that apply to different options. Every apartment building must meet one of the four options.

The Committee, recognizing the equivalency provisions found in Section 1-5 of the *Code*, saw a need to establish in advance four equivalent *Code* complying schemes to provide a high degree of flexibility. The equivalencies developed were based on the Committee's professional judgment, the results of full-scale fire tests conducted at the National

Bureau of Standards, and a review of the most recent fire experiences. These options are considered to be equivalent to each other in providing a minimum level of life safety for apartments. Because some systems have additional protective capability (detectors, automatic sprinklers, etc.), greater building heights and larger building areas are permitted. Where the building provides only the minimum level of safety called for in the *Code*, lower building heights and smaller building areas are specified.

This overall approach provides one of the first "system" design attempts to be codified. Whereas a total system would have many approaches, this is a more limited, or bounded, system in that only four different approaches are available. Yet, an owner can identify an appropriate option from the four approaches based on the building's size, height, and arrangement. This provides the owner an opportunity to put together a safety approach that best fits the building, rather than fitting a building to a single codified criterion. However, this system works only where the owner and the authority having jurisdiction agree on the plan selected at the earliest possible time.

19-1.1.2 Reserved.

19-1.1.3 Every individual living unit covered by this chapter shall comply with the minimum provisions of Section 22-2 for one- and two-family dwellings.

This paragraph requires that every living unit (apartment) comply with Section 22-2 of Chapter 22 on one- and two-family dwellings. This is important for several reasons. First, it establishes two means of escape from every bedroom and living area of a living unit (apartment) having two rooms or more (this exempts efficiency-type apartments). Paragraph 22-2.1.2 establishes several different types of "second means of escape" that can be provided, the most common of which is the operable window; however, Chapter 22 also sets certain requirements regarding that operable window in addition to those for minimum size and arrangement. The window must be within 20 ft (6.1 m) of grade or be accessible by fire department rescue apparatus or open onto a balcony. If this requirement cannot be met, a second means of escape complying with one of the other three types listed in 22-2.1.2 must be provided. A second means of escape is exempted if the dwelling unit is protected by an automatic sprinkler system in accordance with either NFPA 13, *Standard for the Installation of Sprinkler Systems,*[1] or NFPA 13D, *Standard for the Installation of Sprinkler Systems in One- and Two-Family Dwellings and Mobile Homes.*[2] Note that this would not require that the entire apartment building be sprinklered, but only the living unit that does not comply with the secondary means of escape.

Another important provision of Section 22-2 reduces the minimum widths of doors within the dwelling unit to 28 in. (71 cm) in width rather than the 32 in. (81 cm) in width specified by Chapter 5. It also allows the use of sliding doors, the use of stairs that do not meet the requirements for new stairs in Chapter 5, and the use of winders and spiral stairs within the living unit. (*See commentary on Chapter 22 for additional information on means of escape from living units.*)

19-1.2 Mixed Occupancies.

19-1.2.1   Where another type of occupancy occurs in the same building as a residential occupancy, the requirements of 1-4.7 of this *Code* shall be applicable.

19-1.2.2   For requirements on mixed mercantile and residential occupancies, see 25-1.2.

19-1.3 Definitions.

19-1.3.1   Terms applicable to this chapter are defined in Chapter 3 of this *Code*; where necessary, other terms will be defined in the text as they may occur.

Apartment Buildings.   Includes buildings containing three or more living units with independent cooking and bathroom facilities, whether designated as apartment house, tenement, garden apartment, or by any other name.

19-1.4 Classification of Occupancy.   *(See 19-1.3.1.)*

19-1.5 Classification of Hazard of Contents.

19-1.5.1   The contents of residential occupancies shall be classified as ordinary hazard in accordance with Section 4-2.

> NFPA 13, *Standard for the Installation of Sprinkler Systems*,[1] would classify the contents as "light" for the purpose of designing extinguishing systems. The difference in classification is based on the threat to life or life safety (ordinary) versus the threat to the extinguishing capability of the automatic sprinkler system (light).

19-1.6 Minimum Construction Requirements.   No Special Requirements.

19-1.7 Occupant Load.

19-1.7.1*   The occupant load in numbers of persons for whom exits are to be provided shall be determined on the basis of one person per 200 sq ft (18.6 sq m) gross floor area, or the maximum probable population of any room or section under consideration, whichever is greater. The occupant load of any open mezzanine or balcony shall be added to the occupant load of the floor below for the purpose of determining exit capacity.

A-19-1.7.1   Dormitory-type occupancy, particularly where 2- or 3-tier bunks are used with close spacing, may produce an occupant load substantially greater than one person per 200 sq ft (18.6 sq m) gross floor area. However, even though sleeping areas are densely populated, the building as a whole may not necessarily exceed one person per 200 sq ft (18.6 sq m) gross area, owing to the space taken for toilet facilities, halls, closets, and living rooms not used for sleeping purposes.

> See 5-3.1 for further details on the use of occupant load for determining capacity of the means of egress.

SECTION 19-2   MEANS OF EGRESS REQUIREMENTS

19-2.1 General.

19-2.1.1   All means of egress shall be in accordance with Chapter 5 and this chapter.

Rather than repeat many of the provisions of Chapter 5, a general reference to Chapter 5 is made. Many of the requirements that follow in Section 19-2 pick up provisions from Chapter 5 that are options for the occupancy chapters, such as Exception No. 1 to 19-2.2.2.2, which allows the use of special locking arrangements per 5-2.1.6; or that prohibit the use of an item if it is not listed (note that alternating tread devices are not listed in 19-2.2); or that establish limits based on criteria provided in Chapter 5, such as corridor dead-end limits in 19-2.5.3.

19-2.2 Means of Egress Components.

19-2.2.1 General.

19-2.2.1.1   Components of means of egress shall be limited to the types described in 19-2.2.2 through 19-2.2.9.

19-2.2.1.2   In buildings utilizing Option 4, exit enclosures shall have a fire resistance rating of not less than one hour with a fire protection rating of doors of one hour.

In recognition of the relatively low fuel loads in apartment buildings, the fire resistance rating for exit enclosures, as well as other vertical openings (*see 19-3.1.1 Exception No. 3*), need not exceed one hour; however, as a safeguard, this is permitted only in buildings protected throughout by automatic sprinklers (Option 4). This is not permitted for assembly occupancies or business occupancies and, therefore, cannot be utilized where mixed occupancies are involved; nor can it be used for stairways or vertical openings involving or passing through other occupancies.

In facilities where occupancies are adequately separated and treated independently, it could be feasible to have a 1-hour enclosure in the apartment portion and 2-hour enclosure elsewhere.

19-2.2.2 Doors.

19-2.2.2.1   Doors shall comply with 5-2.1.

19-2.2.2.2*   No door in any means of egress shall be locked against egress when the building is occupied.

Exception No. 1: Special locking arrangements complying with 5-2.1.6 are permitted.

Exception No. 2: Doors serving a single dwelling unit may be provided with a lock complying with 5-2.1.5.1 Exception No. 3.

A-19-2.2.2.2   It is the intent of this requirement that security measures, when installed, should not prevent egress.

Paragraph 19-2.2.2.2 prohibits an apartment building from having any door locked "against egress" while the building is occupied. This requirement permits a door to have a locking device that allows the door to be opened from within the building for the purpose of egress, but does not allow the door to be opened from outside the building. Ordinary double cylinder locks and chain locks would not meet these provisions. Several tragic multiple-death fires have occurred where a key could not be found to unlock these devices.

The language of 5-2.1.5.1 is clear: "Locks, if provided, shall not require the use of a key, tool, special knowledge, or effort for operation from the inside of the building." This eliminates double cylinder locks and chain locks that require a key to operate from the inside. Paragraph 5-2.1.5.3 calls for a simple operation to open a door; a two-handed knob operation, and the like, is specifically prohibited by 5-2.1.5.3.

Chapter 5 now specifically recognizes the need for security chains or rods on apartment doors as well as a lock, and allows two additional releasing devices. The typical apartment door has three devices: the latch, the lock, and the security chain or rod. The *Code* prefers only two releasing actions (*see commentary following 18-2.2.2.2*); however, it recognizes the existence of thousands of installations that require the use of three actions. Where new installations are being made in an existing apartment building, the *Code* requires (*see 1-4.6*) the installation to comply with Chapter 18.

Exception No. 1 to 19-2.2.2.2 recognizes the use of the delay release lock provided for in 5-2.1.6. This requires that the building either be protected throughout by automatic sprinklers or equipped throughout with a fire detection system. The 15- or 30-second delay permitted by 5-2.1.6 does not affect the immediate release of the lock upon activation of the sprinklers or detectors, or upon loss of power to the lock. This device helps the apartment building provide the security needed for seldom used doors or stairs, while at the same time it keeps the door available for use, which chains and padlocks are unable to do.

The second Exception allows the use of a "captive key" type lock on individual apartment doors. (*See Chapter 5 for details.*)

19-2.2.2.3   Revolving doors complying with 5-2.1.10 are permitted.

19-2.2.3 Stairs.

19-2.2.3.1   Stairs shall comply with 5-2.2.

19-2.2.3.2   Within any individual living unit, stairs more than one story above or below the entrance floor level of the living unit shall not be permitted.

This paragraph requires that no level of an apartment be more than one story away from an entrance. This would normally restrict an apartment from having more than three stories, one up and one down. However, if an apartment has entrances at more than one level, then more than three levels could be utilized. However, 19-3.1.1 would allow only two levels to be open to each other; the third level would need to be protected.

19-2.2.3.3   Spiral stairs complying with 5-2.2.2.7 are permitted within a single living unit.

19-2.2.3.4   Winders complying with 5-2.2.2.8 are permitted.

19-2.2.4 Smokeproof Enclosures.   Smokeproof enclosures shall comply with 5-2.3. (*See also 19-2.11.1.*)

19-2.2.5 Horizontal Exits.   Horizontal exits shall comply with 5-2.4.

19-2.2.6 Ramps.   Ramps shall comply with 5-2.5.

19-2.2.7 Exit Passageways.   Exit passageways shall comply with 5-2.6.

19-2.2.8* Escalators.   Escalators previously approved as a component in the means of egress may continue to be given credit.

A-19-2.2.8   Due to the nature of escalators, they are no longer acceptable as a component in the means of egress. However, since many escalators have been used for exit access and exit discharge in the past, credit may be continued. Very few escalators have ever been installed in a manner to qualify as an exit. For information on escalator protection and requirements, the reader is referred to previous editions of the *Code*.

19-2.2.9 Fire Escape Stairs.   Fire escape stairs complying with 5-2.8 are permitted.

19-2.3 Capacity of Means of Egress.

19-2.3.1   The capacity of means of egress shall be in accordance with Section 5-3.

19-2.3.2   Street floor exits shall be sufficient for the occupant load of the street floor plus the required capacity of stairs and ramps discharging onto the street floor.

> Paragraph 19-2.3.2 requires street-floor exit designs that have sufficient width to provide for the intermingling of exits from the street floor with those exits discharging down from the upper floors and discharging up from the lower floors. This is the traditional grand lobby design where stairs and street-floor exits converge at one or two exterior door locations. Similar discussion on this matter is found in Chapter 17. Paragraph 5-7.2 restricts the number and arrangement of stairs that discharge through the street floor.
>
> Figure 19-1 shows a typical arrangement of multiple exits discharging on the street floor.

19-2.4 Number of Exits.   (*See also Section 5-4.*)

19-2.4.1   Every living unit shall have access to at least two separate exits remote from each other as required by 5-5.1.

Exception No. 1:   Any living unit may have a single exit provided:

(a) That living unit has an exit door directly to the street or yard at ground level, or

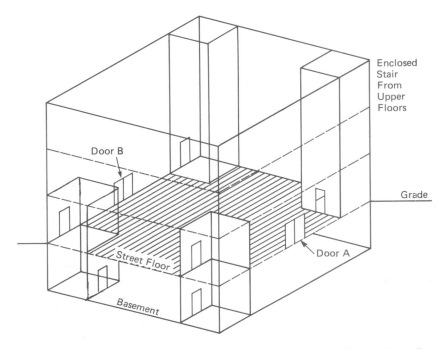

Figure 19-1. Capacity of Means of Egress in Accordance with 19-2.3.2. Required widths of Doors A and B are based on the number of people expected to
use them. Assuming that the street floor has an occupant load of 500, and each
upper floor has an occupant load of 200, and the basement 100, then required exit
capacity for the street floor would be calculated as follows:

500 (street floor) + 200/2 (upper floor max 50% per 5-7.2) +

100/2 (basement max 50% per 5-7.2) = 650 total using

exits on street floor × 0.2 in. (0.5 cm) of door per person = 130 in. (325 cm) ÷
2 exits = 65 in. (163 cm) at A and at B.

*(b) That living unit has direct access to an outside stair complying with 5-2.2, serving a
maximum of two units both located on the same floor, or*

*(c) That living unit has direct access to an interior stair serving that unit only and
separated from all other portions of the building with fire barriers having a 1-hour fire
resistance rating with no opening therein.*

Exception No. 1 provides for a single exit under three different
potential arrangements. The first arrangement is where the living unit has
an exit direct to the street or to the yard at ground level. This is common
in a townhouse or row house arrangement. This would permit the front
door to be the only required exit, and therefore, there would be no
requirements for a rear door. If a rear door were provided, it would not
have to meet the requirements of the *Code*; more importantly, in this case,

it would not have to meet the swing requirements or the locking requirements of the *Code*. The second arrangement is where an apartment has direct access to an outside stair. The third arrangement allowed by Exception No. 1 permits an apartment to be served by a single exit if that single exit is a 1-hour enclosed stairway serving that apartment only. This would be a private stairway. Conditions (b) and (c) of Exception No. 1 are illustrated in Figure 19-2.

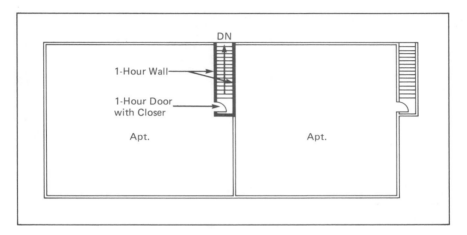

DN

1-Hour Wall

1-Hour Door
with Closer

Apt.

Apt.

Figure 19-2. Two Methods of Complying with 19-2.4.1 Exception No. 1 for a Single Exit. Although not specifically addressed by the *Code*, it would appear to be reasonable to allow the enclosed stairway to be open to the unit it serves.

Exception No. 2: *Any building of three stories or less may have a single exit under the following conditions:*

(a) The stairway is completely enclosed by barriers having a fire resistance rating of at least 1 hour with self-closing 1-hour fire protection rated doors protecting all openings between the stairway enclosure and the building.

(b) The stairway does not serve more than one-half story below the level of exit discharge.

(c) All corridors serving as access to exits have at least a 1-hour fire resistance rating.

(d) There is not more than 35 ft (10.7 m) of travel distance from the entrance door of any living unit to an exit.

(e) Three-quarter hour fire rated horizontal and vertical separation between living units is provided.

Exception No. 2 to 19-2.4.1 provides the basic design approach used for "garden" apartments where the apartment entrances open onto a single enclosed stair. Often, the stair is open to the exterior or is glass-enclosed on the front of the building. The Exception allows a single exit under this arrangement. Note that the stairway must be separated from the building by construction of at least a 1-hour fire resistance rating, and the doors must be 1-hour rated and self-closing. A frequent violation of this Exception is the construction of the door and the lack of a door closer. Figure 19-3 illustrates one potential method for using Exception No. 2.

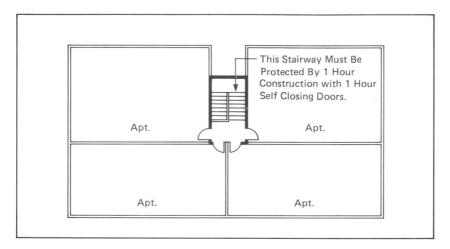

This Stairway Must Be Protected By 1 Hour Construction with 1 Hour Self Closing Doors.

Apt.   Apt.

Apt.   Apt.

Figure 19-3.   One Method of Complying with 19-2.4.1 Exception No. 2.

Exception No. 3:   A building of any height with not more than four living units per floor, with a smokeproof enclosure or outside stair in accordance with the requirements of 5-2.3 as the exit, immediately accessible to all living units served thereby, may have a single exit. ["Immediately accessible" means there is not more than 20 ft (6.1 m) of travel distance from the entrance door of any living unit to an exit.]

Exception No. 3 is not a common arrangement. Note that there are no height limitations, but only four units per floor are permitted. Apartments must have immediate access to a smokeproof enclosure or an outside stair that meets the requirements of a smokeproof enclosure. The exemptions contained under the requirements for outside stairs in Chapter 5 for unprotected openings exposing a stair would not be able to be used in this case, as the *Code* specifically refers to 5-2.3 on smokeproof enclosures, which does not permit unprotected openings exposing the stair.

These three exceptions apply to any of the four options.

19-2.5 Arrangement of Exits.

19-2.5.1   Access to all required exits shall be in accordance with Section 5-5.

19-2.5.2   No common path of travel shall exceed 35 ft (10.7 m). Travel within a dwelling unit shall not be included when calculating common path of travel.

Exception: In buildings protected throughout by an approved supervised automatic sprinkler system, common path of travel shall not exceed 50 ft (15 m).

Common path of travel is normally measured from the most remote point subject to occupancy (*see 5-5.1.2 and the definition of common path of travel in Section 3-2*); therefore, this is a modified common path of travel, as measurement does not extend into the guest room or suite. Since the limits for common path and dead end are different for existing buildings, the arrangement shown in Figure 19-4 is possible without violating either provision.

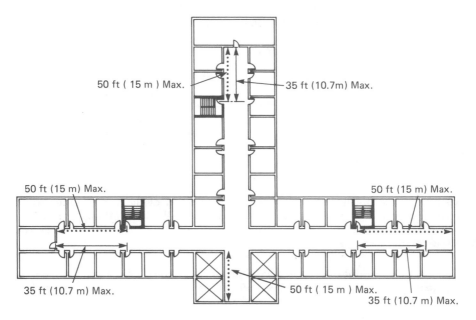

Figure 19-4.   Common Path of Travel (Modified) and Dead-End Limitations in a Nonsprinklered Apartment Building.   Modified common paths of travel are indicated by ←——→ and dead ends are indicated by ◄· · · ·► .

19-2.5.3   No dead-end corridor shall exceed 50 ft (15 m).

19-2.6 Travel Distance to Exits.

19-2.6.1   Travel distance within a living unit (apartment) to a corridor door shall not exceed the following limits:

(a) For buildings using Option 1 or 3 — 75 ft (23 m).

(b) For buildings using Option 2 or 4 — 125 ft (38 m).

Due to revisions in Section 5-6, travel distance is now measured from the most remote point subject to occupancy (the former provision exempting rooms with 6 or fewer people, with 50 ft (15 m) or less travel distance has been deleted). To be consistent with Section 5-6, the Committee has revised the method of measuring travel distance in apartment buildings. The distances within the unit have been increased as compensation. Should the travel distance within a unit be excessive, another remote door to the corridor would need to be added.

19-2.6.2   The travel distance from a living unit (apartment) entrance door to the nearest exit shall not exceed the following limits:

(a) For buildings using Option 1 — 100 ft (30 m).

(b) For buildings using Option 2 or 3 — 150 ft (45 m).

(c) For buildings using Option 4 — 200 ft (60 m).

Exception: Travel distance to exits may be increased to 200 ft (60 m) for exterior ways of exit access arranged in accordance with 5-5.3.

19-2.7 Discharge from Exits.

19-2.7.1   Exit discharge shall comply with Section 5-7.

19-2.7.2   Any required exit stair that is located so that it is necessary to pass through the lobby or other open space to reach the outside of the building shall be continuously enclosed down to a level of exit discharge or to a mezzanine within a lobby at a level of exit discharge.

19-2.7.3   The distance of travel from the termination of the exit enclosure to an exterior door leading to a public way shall not exceed 150 ft (45 m) in buildings protected throughout by an approved automatic sprinkler system and shall not exceed 100 ft (30 m) in all other buildings.

Section 5-7 does allow a maximum of 50 percent of the number and capacity of exits to discharge through the street floor under limited conditions. (*See* 5-7.2.) This is slightly liberalized by 19-2.7.2 by including a mezzanine within the lobby. In other words, 50 percent of the exits could discharge onto a mezzanine with occupants then traveling across the mezzanine, downstairs to the lobby level and outside. However, 19-2.7.3 adds a provision not found in 5-7.2 by restricting the distance from the termination of the exit enclosure to the exterior door to a maximum of 100 ft (30.5 m) in nonsprinklered buildings and 150 ft (45 m) in buildings fully sprinklered.

See Figures 19-5 and 19-6. (*Also see discussion of 5-7.2.*)

19-2.8 Illumination of Means of Egress.

19-2.8.1   Means of egress shall be illuminated in accordance with Section 5-8.

19-2.9 Emergency Lighting.

19-2.9.1   Emergency lighting in accordance with Section 5-9 shall be provided in all buildings with greater than 12 living units or greater than three stories in height.

Exception: Where every living unit has a direct exit to the outside of the building at grade level.

This Exception does not apply to all buildings with exterior exit access, but only to those where each unit has direct exit to grade.

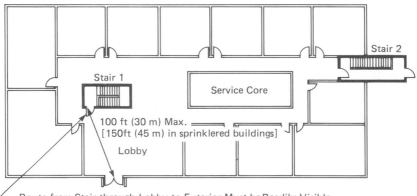

Route from Stair through Lobby to Exterior Must be Readily Visible, Identified, Clear, and Unobstructed.

Figure 19-5.   Arrangement of Means of Egress in Accordance with 5-7.2.   Stair 1 (50 percent of the total number and capacity of exits) discharges through the first floor. Stair 2 discharges directly to the exterior (it may discharge through an exit passageway to the exterior). Since other areas on the first floor (the level of exit discharge) are not separated from the path that a person leaving Stair 1 must follow to exit through the lobby, the entire first floor must be completely sprinklered. If the rest of the floor were separated (to the extent required for the stair enclosure), only the path to the exit discharge would have to be sprinklered.

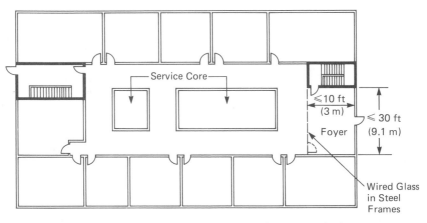

Figure 19-6.   Foyer Constructed in Compliance with 5-7.2.   The foyer must serve only as a means of egress.

19-2.10 Marking of Means of Egress.

19-2.10.1   Means of egress shall have signs in accordance with Section 5-10 in all buildings requiring more than one exit.

19-2.11 Special Features.

19-2.11.1*   In high rise buildings using Option 1, 2, or 3, smokeproof enclosures shall be provided in accordance with 5-2.3.

A-19-2.11.1   The Committee recognizes the need to provide smoke control in existing buildings. Smokeproof enclosures can be accomplished without the use of a vestibule in accordance with 5-2.3.

> This paragraph is very significant for nonsprinklered high rise apartment buildings. If smokeproof enclosures are not already provided, it may be much more realistic to add sprinkler protection than to modify stairs into smokeproof enclosures.

SECTION 19-3   PROTECTION

19-3.1 Protection of Vertical Openings.

19-3.1.1   Every stairway, elevator shaft, and other vertical opening shall be enclosed or protected in accordance with 6-2.4 or provide means of satisfying the requirements of Section 2-9.

Exception No. 1:   Stairway enclosures shall not be required where a one-story stair connects two levels within a single dwelling unit, guest room, or suite.

> See also 19-2.2.3.2.

Exception No. 2:   An atrium may be utilized in accordance with 6-2.4.5.

> Since 6-2.4.5 requires total automatic sprinkler protection, atriums can only be used in buildings using Option 4.

Exception No. 3:   In buildings using Option 4, fire resistance of walls may be ¾ hour for buildings of one to three stories, and 1 hour for buildings greater than three stories; and fire protection rating of doors may be ¾ hour for buildings up to three stories and 1 hour for buildings greater than three stories.

> In recognition of the relatively low fuel loads in apartment buildings, the fire protection rating of required enclosure of vertical openings need not exceed 1 hour. Similar provisions are made for exit enclosures. (*See 19-2.2.1.2.*) However, as a safeguard, this is permitted only in buildings protected throughout by automatic sprinklers (Option 4). (*Also see commentary following 19-2.2.1.2.*)

Exception No. 4:   Unprotected vertical openings connecting not more than three floors may be permitted in accordance with the conditions of 6-2.4.4.

Since 6-2.4.4 requires automatic sprinkler protection, the Exception will most likely be used only in buildings using Option 4.

Exception No. 5: In any building protected throughout by an approved automatic sprinkler system in accordance with Section 7-7, and where exits and required ways of travel thereto are adequately safeguarded against fire and smoke within the building, or where every individual room has direct access to an exterior exit without passing through any public corridor, the protection of vertical openings not part of required exits may be waived by the authority having jurisdiction to such extent as such openings do not endanger required means of egress.

19-3.1.2 No floor below the level of exit discharge used only for storage, heating equipment, or purpose other than residential occupancy open to the public shall have unprotected openings to floors used for residential purposes.

19-3.2 Protection from Hazards.

19-3.2.1 In buildings using Option 1, 2, or 3, every hazardous area shall be separated from other parts of the building by construction having a fire resistance rating of at least 1 hour, and communicating openings shall be protected by approved smoke-actuated automatic, or self-closing fire doors with a fire protection rating of ¾ hour, or such area shall be equipped with an automatic extinguishing system. Hazardous areas include, but are not limited to:

Boiler and heater rooms
Laundries
Repair shops
Rooms or spaces used for storage of combustible supplies and equipment in quantities deemed hazardous by the authority having jurisdiction.

19-3.2.2 In buildings using Option 4, the enclosure for hazardous areas shall be of smoke-resisting construction with or without a fire resistance rating.

19-3.3 Interior Finish.

19-3.3.1 Interior finish on walls and ceilings, in accordance with Section 6-5, shall be as follows:

(a) Exit enclosures — Class A or B

(b) Lobbies and corridors — Class A or B

(c) All other spaces — Class A, B, or C

19-3.3.2 Interior Floor Finish. In buildings using Option 1 or 2, interior floor finish in corridors and exits shall be Class I or Class II in accordance with Section 6-5.

Exception: Previously installed floor coverings may be continued in use, subject to the approval of the authority having jurisdiction.

See commentary in Section 6-5, especially the discussion on interior floor finish. Paragraph 6-5.2.3 establishes stringent requirements regarding the use of textile or carpetlike material on walls and ceilings. The interior finish for walls and ceilings, other than textile or carpetlike material, can be lowered one class (A to B, B to C) in Option 4 buildings and in corridors of Option 3 buildings. (*See 6-5.7.*)

19-3.4 Detection, Alarm, and Communication Systems.

19-3.4.1 General.   Apartment buildings with more than three stories or with more than 11 living units shall be provided with a fire alarm system in accordance with Section 7-6.

Exception: Where each living unit is separated from other contiguous living units by fire barriers (see Section 6-2) having a fire resistance rating not less than ¾ hour, and where each living unit has either its own independent exit or its own independent stairway or ramp discharging at grade.

The intent of this Exception is to eliminate the requirement for a fire alarm system in a "townhouse" type apartment building.

19-3.4.2 Initiation.

19-3.4.2.1   Initiation of the required fire alarm system shall be by manual means in accordance with 7-6.2.

19-3.4.2.2   In buildings using Option 2, the required fire alarm system shall be initiated by the automatic fire detection system, in addition to the manual initiation means of 19-3.4.2.1.

19-3.4.2.3   In buildings using Option 3, the required fire alarm system shall be initiated upon operation of the automatic sprinkler system, in addition to the manual initiation means of 19-3.4.2.1.

19-3.4.2.4   In buildings using Option 4, the required fire alarm system shall be initiated upon operation of the automatic sprinkler system, in addition to the manual initiation means of 19-3.4.2.1.

19-3.4.3 Notification.

19-3.4.3.1   An annunciator panel connected with the required fire alarm system shall be provided. The location of the annunciator panel shall be approved by the authority having jurisdiction.

Exception: Buildings not greater than two stories in height and with not more than 50 living units.

19-3.4.3.2   Occupant notification shall be by an internal audible alarm signal in accordance with 7-6.3.

19-3.4.4 Detection.

19-3.4.4.1   Approved single station or multiple station smoke detectors, continuously powered by the house electrical service, shall be installed in accordance with 7-6.2.9 in every living unit within the apartment building regardless of the number of stories or number of apartments. When activated, the detector shall initiate an alarm that is audible in the sleeping rooms of that unit. This individual unit detector shall be in addition to any sprinkler system or other detection system that may be installed in the building.

Exception: The single station smoke detector is not required where the building is equipped with a total automatic smoke detection system throughout.

The detector(s) required by 19-3.4.4.1 should usually be located in the hall area(s) giving access to rooms used for sleeping. In multilevel living units, the upper level detector should usually be located at the top of the stairs. The detector(s) should be mounted on the ceiling or on the wall within 12 in. (30.5 cm) of, but no closer than 6 in. (15.2 cm) to, the ceiling. The detector should be remotely located from the cooking area. Where unusual factors such as room configuration, air movement, or stagnant air pockets require consideration, the authority having jurisdiction and the designer should determine the placement of the detectors. (*See NFPA 74, Standard for the Installation, Maintenance, and use of Household Fire Warning Equipment,*[3] *for additional details.*)

Note that the detector must be powered by "house current," either through direct wiring of the detector or by using plug-in type detectors. Battery-powered units will not meet the provision of 19-3.4.4.1.

It is not the intent of the paragraph to prohibit interconnecting detectors (multiple-station vs. single-station) within a single apartment if the apartment needs more than one detector; in fact, this is required by the second sentence.

Also note that this requirement is in addition to any other detection or suppression system required.

19-3.4.4.2   In buildings using Option 2, a total automatic fire detection system is required. An automatic fire detection system is one that is designed to give complete coverage with fire detectors in accordance with the spacings and layouts given in NFPA 72E, *Standard on Automatic Fire Detectors,* and laboratory test data, and is one in which the detectors are tied together to initiate the alarm and other automatic fire protection devices.

In buildings utilizing Option 2, a total automatic fire detection system is required, and this system must be interconnected with the building fire alarm system in accordance with 19-3.4.2.2. Note that this paragraph does not require smoke detectors but would allow the use of either heat detectors or smoke detectors. This system is required in addition to the single-station or multiple-station smoke detectors required by 19-3.4.4.1. Heat detectors are allowed by this paragraph since they would be used in addition to the smoke detectors as stated above. The feeling of the Committee here is that the single-station or multiple-station smoke detectors would alert the occupants within the apartment of a fire originating within that unit. Upon evacuation of the apartment, the door would close (*see 19-3.6.2*), and the occupants would activate a manual pull station required by 19-3.4.2.1. If the occupants failed to activate a manual pull station and the fire continued to develop in the apartment, the heat detectors would activate and sound the building fire alarm system prior to the fire becoming a threat to other apartment units. This system has proved very effective where used. In addition, since the system is required to be tied into the building fire alarm system, it would eliminate many false alarms that might occur if the entire building were protected by automatic smoke detection.

19-3.5 Extinguishment Requirements.

19-3.5.1* Where an automatic sprinkler system is installed, either for total or partial building coverage, the system shall be installed in accordance with Section 7-7.

Exception: In individual living units, sprinkler installations may be omitted in closets not over 24 sq ft (2.2 sq m) and bathrooms not over 55 sq ft (5.1 sq m). Closets that contain equipment such as washers, dryers, furnaces, or water heaters shall be sprinklered regardless of size.

A-19-3.5.1   Although not required by the *Code* the use of residential sprinklers or quick response sprinklers is encouraged for new installations of sprinkler systems within dwelling units, apartments, and guest rooms. Caution must be used as the system must be designed for the sprinkler being used.

This paragraph does not mandate the installation of sprinklers, but sets provisions for their installation where required. The *Code* provides numerous incentives to install sprinklers. Some of the more significant incentives for existing buildings include 19-2.11.1, 19-3.6.1 and 19-3.7.1. New to the 1988 *Code* is the nonmandatory Appendix note to encourage that sprinklers within dwelling units be approved residential or quick response sprinklers. The intent is to get the quick response provided by these sprinklers as well as high spray pattern provided by residential sprinklers. Designers of sprinkler systems must be cautious, as these sprinklers cannot always be put on a system designed for standard sprinklers. There are also situations where residential fast response sprinklers have not currently been listed for such uses as vaulted ceilings. In such cases, the designer could provide the best alternative sprinkler.

The Exception has been carefully reworded for the 1988 *Code*. The spaces exempted are limited to those *within* a living unit; public areas are not exempted. The last sentence has been added to clarify that the intent of this Exception is for regular closets and bathrooms, not for closets that contain equipment.

19-3.5.2   In buildings using Option 3, automatic sprinklers shall be installed in corridors along the corridor ceiling, and one sprinkler head shall be opposite the center of and inside any living unit door opening into the corridor.

Exception: The sprinkler head inside living units may be omitted if the door to the living unit has a fire protection rating of at least 20 minutes and is self-closing.

Figure 19-7 illustrates typical sprinkler location as required by 19-3.5.2.

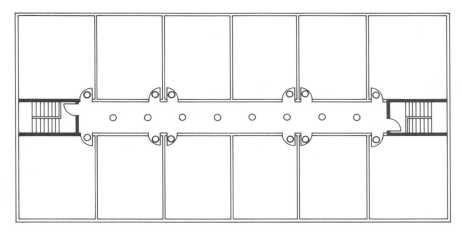

Figure 19-7. Typical Sprinkler Locations that Comply with the Sprinkler Location Requirements of Option 3.

19-3.5.3 The sprinkler installation required in 19-3.5.2 shall meet the requirements of Section 7-7 in terms of workmanship and materials.

19-3.5.4 The installation of the corridor sprinklers required in 19-3.5.2 shall not exceed the maximum spacing and protection area requirements of Section 7-7.

19-3.5.5 Buildings using Option 4 shall be protected throughout by an approved automatic sprinkler system complying with 19-3.5.1. The automatic sprinkler system shall meet the requirements of Section 7-7 for supervision for buildings greater than six stories in height.

19-3.5.6 Portable fire extinguishers shall be provided in hazardous areas. Where provided, portable fire extinguishers shall be installed and maintained as specified in 7-7.4.1.

19-3.6 Corridors.

19-3.6.1* Exit access corridors shall be protected as follows:

(a) In buildings using Option 1 or 2, corridor walls shall have a fire resistance rating of not less than 30 minutes.

(b) In buildings using Option 3 or 4, corridor walls shall have a fire resistance rating of not less than ½ hour.

A-19-3.6.1 The intent of the Committee is to recognize that existing partitions of sound wood-lath and plaster, wire-lath and plaster, or gypsum lath and plaster construction have demonstrated the ability to contain most room fires. Recent data on archaic construction methods has established the fire resistance "rating" of such construction at about 20 minutes. Such construction meets the intent of this section.

The criteria in 19-3.6.1 reflect the Committee's concern for providing safety for the occupant in his or her apartment during a fire. The focus of this concern is the presence of occupants on a 24-hour-a-day basis with sleeping accommodations. This minimum corridor wall construction will either block fire movement from the corridor into an apartment or block fire in an apartment from entering the corridor.

19-3.6.2   Doors between living units and corridors shall be self-closing. Doors shall be equipped with latches for keeping doors tightly closed.

Requiring self-closing doors between apartments and corridors may lead to a significant reduction in fatalities caused by fire in apartment buildings. Studies of typical apartment fires have shown that the cause of fire spreading beyond the apartment or room of origin was due to the door being left open as the occupant fled the fire.

In other cases, a person suspecting a fire died after opening the door to a room fully involved with fire, or after causing full involvement of the room by introducing oxygen through the open door. Spring-loaded hinges or a closer would have caused these doors to close, preventing smoke or fire from spreading down the corridor and exposing other occupants.

19-3.6.3*   The fire protection rating of doors from living units to corridors shall be not less than 20 minutes.

Exception No. 1:   Previously approved 1¾-in. (4.4-cm) solid bonded wood core doors may continue in use.

Exception No. 2:   In buildings using Option 3 or 4, doors shall be so constructed as to resist the passage of smoke.

A-19-3.6.3   This does not require a listed or labeled assembly, but addresses only the door.

The door required by 19-3.6.3 provides a level of protection commensurate with the expected fuel load in the room and the fire resistance of the corridor wall construction. The purpose is to box a fire out of a room or to box it within the room by means of corridor wall and door construction. It has been shown in fuel load studies conducted by the National Bureau of Standards that residential occupancies will have fuel loads in the 20- to 30-minute range.

19-3.6.4   Transfer grilles, whether protected by fusible link operated dampers or not, shall not be permitted in these walls or doors.

Paragraph 2-2.2 of NFPA 90A, *Standard for the Installation of Air Conditioning and Ventilating Systems*,[4] prohibits the use of public corridors in residential occupancies as part of the supply, return, or exhaust air system.

Figure 19-8 illustrates the requirements of 19-3.6.

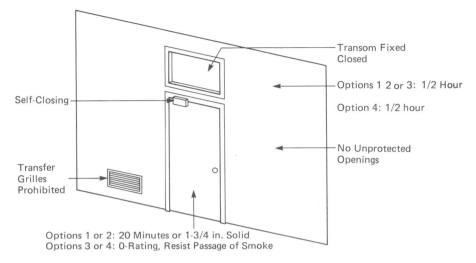

Figure 19-8.   The Corridor Wall and Door Provisions of 19-3.6.

19-3.7 Subdivision of Building Spaces.

19-3.7.1 Smoke Barriers.   Smoke barriers in accordance with Section 6-3 shall be provided in exit access corridors to establish at least two compartments approximately equal in size. The maximum length of each smoke compartment measured along the corridor shall not exceed 200 ft (60 m). Smoke dampers are not required.

Exception No. 1:   Buildings using Option 4.

Exception No. 2:   Exterior exit access in accordance with 5-5.3 that provides access to two exits.

Exception No. 3:   Buildings allowed to comply with 19-2.4.1 Exceptions No. 1, 2, or 3.

Exception No. 4:   Buildings with exits not more than 50 ft (15 m) apart.

Exception No. 5:   Where each dwelling unit has direct access to the exterior at grade.

The smoke barriers required by 19-3.7.1 are relatively easy to provide since no fire resistance rating is required and smoke dampers are exempted. In most cases, installing a set of cross corridor doors with smoke actuated automatic closers will accomplish the goal of the requirement. This can be accomplished in conjunction with horizontal exits. Sprinklered buildings are exempt (Exception No. 1), as are buildings with a single exit (Exception No. 3) and buildings that do not utilize corridors as required exit access (Exceptions No. 2 and 5).

It should be noted that Exception No. 4 does not require smoke barriers every 50 ft (15 m), but only exempts a smoke barrier where the stair spacing is less than 50 ft (15 m) apart.

19-3.8 Special Features.

SECTION 19-4   SPECIAL PROVISIONS

19-4.1 Windows for Rescue and Ventilation.   *(See 19-1.1.3.)*
Exception: Buildings using Option 4.

19-4.2 High Rise Buildings.   *(See 19-2.11.1.)*

19-4.3 Operating Features.   *(See Chapter 31.)*

SECTION 19-5   BUILDING SERVICES

19-5.1 Utilities.   Utilities shall comply with the provisions of Section 7-1.

19-5.2 Heating, Ventilating, and Air Conditioning.

Paragraph 2-2.2 of NFPA 90A, *Standard for the Installation of Air Conditioning and Ventilating Systems*,[4] prohibits the use of public corridors in residential occupancies as part of the supply, return, or exhaust air system.

19-5.2.1   Heating, ventilating, and air conditioning equipment shall comply with the provisions of Section 7-2.

19-5.2.2   Unvented fuel-fired heaters shall not be used.

19-5.3 Elevators, Dumbwaiters, and Vertical Conveyors.   Elevators, dumbwaiters, and vertical conveyors shall comply with the provisions of Section 7-4.

19-5.4 Rubbish Chutes, Incinerators, and Laundry Chutes.   Rubbish chutes, incinerators, and laundry chutes shall comply with the provisions of Section 7-5.

Table 19-1 summarizes the various requirements based on the four different options.

The following are two examples of how to use Table 19-1.

Example 1:   What are the interior finish requirements in an exit stairway for a five-story apartment building equipped with an automatic detection system?

Answer: Enter the table under the column heading "Total Automatic Detection Option No. 2." In the section "Exits — Vertical," find the heading "Flame Spread (Walls and Ceilings)." The requirement for this building is Class A or B interior finish for the exits.

Example 2:   What is the maximum dead-end distance permitted in an existing apartment building equipped with sprinklers located only in corridors and inside the doors leading into each living unit?

Answer: Enter the table under the column heading "Sprinkler Protection in Selected Areas Option No. 3." In the section "Exit Access," across from the row headed "Dead End," you will find 35 ft (10.7 m) as the answer.

Table 19-1 Alternate Requirements for
Existing Apartment Buildings According to Protection Provided
(*See actual Code provisions for details*)

	No Suppression or Detection System Option No. 1	Total Automatic Detection Option No. 2	Sprink. Prot. in Select. Areas Option No. 3	Auto Ext. NFPA 13 (with exceptions) Option No. 4
Max. Gross Area per Story Between Horizontal Exits				
1-3 Stories	NR	NR	NR	NR
≥4 Stories <HR	NR	NR	NR	NR
HR	NR	NR	NR	NR
Exit Access				
Travel Distance	100 ft (30 m)	150 ft (45 m)	150 ft (45 m)	200 ft (60 m)
Smoke Barrier Req. (*See 19-3.7.1.*)	Req.	Req.	Req.	NR
Max. Common Path of Travel (Mod)	35 ft (10.7 m)	35 ft (10.7 m)	35 ft (10.7 m)	50 ft (15 m)
Max. Dead End	50 ft (15 m)	50 ft (15 m)	50 ft (15 m)	50 ft (15 m)
Fire Resistance				
Walls	½ hr	½ hr	½ hr	½ hr
Doors (Fire Protection Rating)	20 min	20 min	N/A	N/A
Flame Spread				
Walls & Ceilings	A or B	A or B	A or B	A, B, or C
Floors	I or II	I or II	NR	NR
Exits—Vertical				
Fire Resistance Walls				
1-3 Stories	1 hr	1 hr	1 hr	¾ hr
>3 Stories	2 hr	2 hr	2 hr	1 hr
Smokeproof Enclosures				
≥1 Story <HR	NR	NR	NR	NR
HR	Req.	Req.	Req.	NR
Doors				
1-3 Stories	1 hr	1 hr	1 hr	¾ hr
>3 Stories	1½ hr	1½ hr	1½ hr	1 hr
Flame Spread				
Walls & Ceilings	A or B	A or B	A or B	A, B, or C
Floors	I or II	I or II	NR	NR
Exits—Horizontal				
Fire Resistance				
Walls	2 hr	2 hr	2 hr	NA
Doors	1½ hr	1½ hr	1½ hr	NA

Req.=Required (*See Code for details and Exceptions.*)
NR=No Requirements
NA=Not Applicable
HR=High Rise Buildings

Table 19-1 (Continued)

	No Suppression or Detection System Option No. 1	Total Automatic Detection Option No. 2	Sprink. Prot. in Select. Areas Option No. 3	Auto Ext. NFPA 13 (with exceptions) Option No. 4
Habitable Spaces				
Max. Distance to Corridor Door	75 ft (23 m)	125 ft (38 m)	75 ft (23 m)	125 ft (38 m)
Flame Spread Walls & Ceilings	A, B, or C	A, B, or C	A, B, or C	A, B, or C
Smoke Detector in Unit	Req.	Req.	Req.	Req.
Door to Corridor Self-Closing	Req.	Req.	Req.	Req.
Bedroom Windows, per Section 22-2 (See 19-1.1.2.)	Req.	Req.	Req.	NR
Alarm System				
>3 Stories or >11 Units	manual	manual & auto	manual & auto	manual & auto
>2 Stories or >50 Units	annunciator panel	annunciator panel	annunciator panel	annunciator panel
HVAC				
HR; Pressurized Corridor, 0.01 in. Water (2.5 Pa), min.	NR	NR	NR	NR
Elevator				
ANSI	A17.1	A17.1	A17.1	A17.1

Req.=Required (See Code for details and Exceptions.)
NR=No Requirements
NA=Not Applicable
HR=High Rise Buildings

REFERENCES CITED IN COMMENTARY

[1]NFPA 13, *Standard for the Installation of Sprinkler Systems*, National Fire Protection Association, Quincy, MA, 1987.

[2]NFPA 13D, *Standard for the Installation of Sprinkler Systems in One- and Two-Family Dwellings and Mobile Homes*, National Fire Protection Association, Quincy, MA, 1984.

[3]NFPA 74, *Standard for the Installation, Maintenance, and use of Household Fire Warning Equipment*, National Fire Protection Association, Quincy, MA, 1984.

[4]NFPA 90A, *Standard for the Installation of Air Conditioning and Ventilating Systems*, National Fire Protection Association, Quincy, MA, 1985.

20 LODGING OR ROOMING HOUSES

SECTION 20-1 GENERAL REQUIREMENTS

Residential occupancies are those in which sleeping accommodations are provided for normal residential purposes and include all buildings designed to provide sleeping accommodations. They are treated separately in the *Code* in the following groups:

Hotels, motels, dormitories (Chapters 16 and 17)
Apartment buildings (Chapters 18 and 19)
Lodging or rooming houses (Chapter 20)
Board and care facilities (Chapter 21)
One- and two-family dwellings (Chapter 22).

Exceptions to the groups listed above are health care occupancies, which are covered in Chapters 12 and 13, and detention and correctional occupancies, which are covered in Chapters 14 and 15. In earlier editions of the *Code*, they were classified as "institutional occupancies."

A review of 4-1.6 underscores a common principle of life safety with which the *Code* is concerned as applied to all the residential occupancies considered by Chapters 16 through 23. Paragraph 4-1.6 states: "Residential occupancies are those occupancies in which sleeping accommodations are provided for normal residential purposes and include all buildings designed to provide sleeping accommodations." This use of residential occupancies is central to the *Code's* provisions in Chapters 16 through 23, because people who are asleep will be unaware of a rapidly developing fire and, when alerted, may be somewhat confused due to being awakened suddenly. Other factors on which the provisions of Chapters 16 through 23, were based are the presence of hazards (such as cooking and heating equipment) in residential occupancies and the degree of familiarity of the occupant with his or her living space (ranging from transients with little or no familiarity, as in hotels, to total familiarity in single-family dwellings).

20-1.1 Application.

20-1.1.1 This chapter applies only to lodging or rooming houses providing sleeping accommodations for 16 or fewer persons. Lodging or rooming houses include buildings in which separate sleeping rooms are rented providing sleeping accommodations for a total of 16 or fewer persons on either a transient or permanent basis, with or without meals but without separate cooking facilities for individual occupants, except as provided in Chapter 22.

If sleeping accommodations for more than 16 people are provided, the occupancy should be classified as a hotel. The Chapter 22 reference concerns the allowance for room rental to a maximum of three "outsiders" in one- and two-family dwellings.

20-1.1.2   The requirements of this chapter are applicable to new buildings, and to existing or modified buildings according to the provisions of Section 1-4 of this *Code*.

In the 1981 Edition of the *Code*, there was an additional paragraph that stated, "In addition to the following provisions, every lodging or rooming house shall comply with the minimum requirements for one- and two-family dwellings." This paragraph was removed in the 1985 Edition of the *Code*. The requirements of Chapter 22 are either repeated in Chapter 20 or, as in 20-2.1.2, a specific reference has replaced this more general reference.

20-1.2 Mixed Occupancies.

20-1.2.1   Where another type of occupancy occurs in the same building as a residential occupancy, the requirements of 1-4.7 of this *Code* shall be applicable.

20-1.2.2   For requirements on mixed mercantile and residential occupancies, see 24-1.2 or 25-1.2.

20-1.3 Definitions.

20-1.3.1   Terms applicable to this chapter are defined in Chapter 3 of this *Code*; where necessary, other terms will be defined in the text as they may occur.

20-1.4 Classification of Occupancy.   *(See 20-1.1.1.)*

20-1.5 Classification of Hazard of Contents.

20-1.5.1*   The contents of residential occupancies shall be classified as ordinary hazard in accordance with Section 4-2.

A-20-1.5.1   The *Code* recognizes the potential application of NFPA 13D, *Standard for the Installation of Sprinkler Systems in One- and Two-Family Dwellings and Mobile Homes*, to lodging and rooming houses inasmuch as these occupancies can usually be considered similar in character to one- and two-family dwellings.

NFPA 13, *Standard for the Installation of Sprinkler Systems*,[1] would classify the contents as "light" for the purpose of designing extinguishing systems. The difference in classification is based on the threat to life or life safety (ordinary) versus the threat to the extinguishing capability of the automatic sprinkler system (light).

20-1.6 Minimum Construction Requirements. No Special Requirements.

20-1.7 Occupant Load. *(See 20-1.1.1.)*

SECTION 20-2   MEANS OF ESCAPE

20-2.1 Number and Means of Escape.

20-2.1.1 Every sleeping room shall have access to a primary means of escape so located as to provide a safe path of travel to the outside of the building without traversing any corridor or space exposed to an unprotected vertical opening. Where the sleeping room is above or below the level of exit discharge, the primary means shall be an enclosed interior stair, an exterior stair, a horizontal exit, or an existing fire escape stair.

> In 20-2.1.1, the phrase "means of escape" is separate and distinct from means of egress and indicates the Committee's acceptance of slightly less than a *Code*-conforming means of egress for evacuating a lodging or rooming house during a fire. Note that the *Code* requires at least one means of escape from levels above or below the level of exit discharge to be an enclosed interior stairway, an exterior stairway, or a horizontal exit (or an existing fire escape). The Committee intended at least one means of escape to be of a high degree of quality, but was reluctant to tie the criteria directly to the *Code*, because most rooming or lodging houses are converted homes where a *Code*-conforming exit arrangement is seldom found. However, the Committee recognized the aspect of public liability involved in lodging guests and intended a level of escape quality higher than that normally found in a single-family home.
>
> It is 20-2.1.1 in conjunction with 20-2.2 and 20-3.1.1 that provides the major difference between a one- or two-family dwelling and a lodging or rooming house: the protection of vertical openings. By eliminating exposure to unprotected vertical openings (normally found in single-family dwellings), the *Code* requires a quality of exit arrangement that is a level above that normally found in a single-family dwelling. Figures 20-1, 20-2, and 20-3 illustrate three possible methods of complying with 20-2.1.1.

20-2.1.2 In addition to the primary route each sleeping room and living area shall have a second means of escape in accordance with 22-2.1.2.

Exception: If the sleeping room or living area has a door leading directly outside the building with access to grade or to a stairway that meets the requirements for exterior stairs in 20-2.1.1, that exit shall be considered as meeting all of the exit requirements for that sleeping room or living area.

> Editions of the *Code* prior to 1985 required two means of escape but did not specify what was acceptable for the secondary escapes (other than windows for the level of exit discharge). In order to clarify its

Second Floor

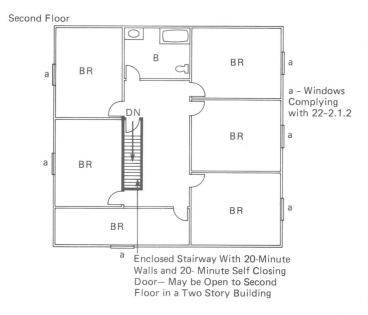

a – Windows Complying with 22-2.1.2

^a Enclosed Stairway With 20-Minute Walls and 20- Minute Self Closing Door— May be Open to Second Floor in a Two Story Building

First Floor

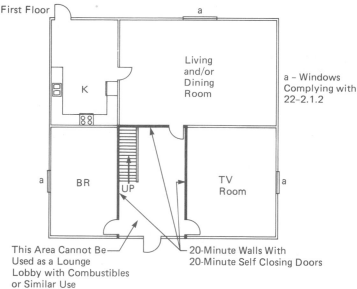

a – Windows Complying with 22–2.1.2

This Area Cannot Be Used as a Lounge Lobby with Combustibles or Similar Use

20-Minute Walls With 20-Minute Self Closing Doors

Figure 20-1. Means of Escape—Lodging and Rooming House—Example 1. This example illustrates an enclosed interior stair discharging directly outside. Access to the interior stair is via an interior corridor that is not exposed to an unprotected vertical opening. The second means of escape could be windows acceptable to the authority having jurisdiction per 20-2.1.2. The enclosure at the bottom of the stair can be done several ways; this is only one example.

requirements, the *Code* specifies that the secondary escape must comply with 22-2.1.2. It should be noted that 22-2.1.2 exempts a secondary escape if the building is sprinklered in accordance with either NFPA 13, *Standard for the Installation of Sprinkler Systems,*[1] or NFPA 13D, *Standard for the Installation of Sprinkler Systems in One- and Two-Family Dwellings and Mobile Homes.*[2] In conjunction with 20-2.1.3 Exception, 20-3.1.1 Exception, 20-3.3.2 Exception No. 2, and 20-3.4 Exception, this exemption makes sprinklering a lodging or rooming house a very viable alternative.

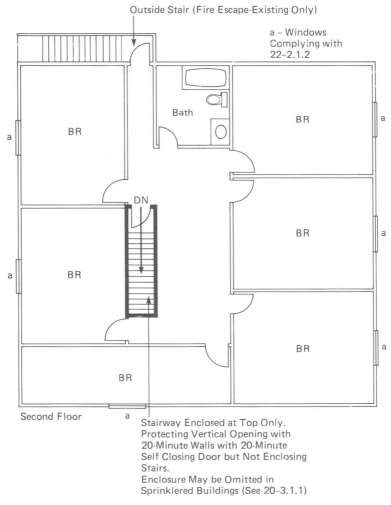

Figure 20-2. Means of Escape—Lodging and Rooming House—Example 2. This example illustrates an exterior stair complying with 5-2.5. (*See 20-2.1.1.*) The exterior stair is accessed via the interior corridor, which is not exposed to an unprotected vertical opening. The second means of escape is via windows complying with 22-2.1.2.

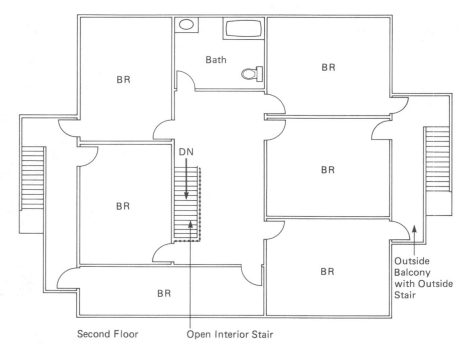

Second Floor   Open Interior Stair

Figure 20-3. Means of Escape—Lodging and Rooming House—Example 3. This example illustrates an outside stair with exterior exit access complying with 5-2.5. (*See 20-2.1.1.*) Access is not through the interior corridor, which is exposed by the open stair. The second means of escape is via the open interior stair.

20-2.1.3   Every story of every lodging or rooming house that is greater than 2,000 sq ft (185 sq m) or where the travel distance to the primary means of escape is greater than 75 ft (23 m) shall be provided with two primary means of escape remote from each other.

Exception No. 1: Existing buildings.

Exception No. 2: Buildings protected throughout by an approved supervised automatic sprinkler system in accordance with 20-3.5.

20-2.2   Interior stairways shall be enclosed with 20-minute fire barriers with all openings protected with smoke-actuated automatic or self-closing doors having a fire resistance comparable to that required for the enclosure. The stairway shall comply with 5-2.2.3.5.

Also see 20-2.1.1 and 20-3.1.1.

Exception No. 1: Stairs connecting two levels only may be open to other than the street floor.

Exception No. 2: Stairways may be unprotected in accordance with the Exception to 20-3.1.1.

Figure 20-4 illustrates the use of Exception No. 1.

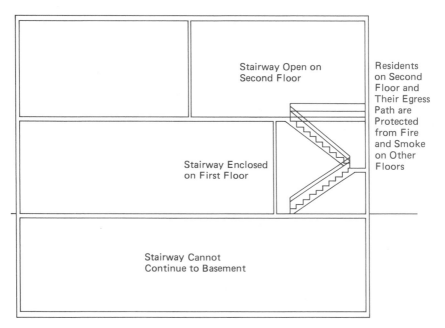

Figure 20-4. A Stairway That Connects Two Levels May Be Open to a Floor Other Than the Street Floor. (*Also see Figure 20-2.*)

20-2.3 No door or path of travel to a means of egress shall be less than 28 in. (71 cm) wide.

Exception: Bathroom doors may be 24 in. (61 cm) wide.

20-2.4 Every closet door latch shall be such that it can be readily opened from the inside in case of emergency.

20-2.5 Every bathroom door shall be designed to permit the opening of the locked door from the outside in an emergency.

20-2.6 Winders in accordance with 5-2.2.2.8 are permitted.

20-2.7* No door in any means of egress shall be locked against egress when the building is occupied.

Exception: Special locking arrangements complying with 5-2.1.6 are permitted.

A-20-2.7 It is the intent of this requirement that security measures, where installed, should not prevent egress.

Paragraph 20-2.7 prohibits a lodging or rooming house from having any door locked "against egress" while the building is occupied. This requirement permits a door to have a locking device that allows the door to be opened from within the building for the purpose of egress, but does not allow the door to be opened from outside the building. Ordinary double cylinder locks and chain locks would not meet these provisions. Several tragic multiple-death fires have occurred where a key could not be found to unlock these devices.

The language of 5-2.1.5.1 is clear. "Locks, if provided, shall not require the use of a key, tool, special knowledge, or effort for operation from the inside of the building." This eliminates double cylinder locks and chain locks that require a key to operate from the inside. Paragraph 5-2.1.5.3 calls for a simple operation to open a door; the presence of a two-handed knob operation, and the like, is specifically prohibited.

Chapter 5 now specifically recognizes the need for security chains or rods on guest room doors and allows one additional releasing device. The typical guest room door has three devices: the latch, the lock, and the security chain or rod. However, the *Code* allows only two releasing actions for new installations. This requirement is met by using a latch and lock set that has a lock bolt that automatically retracts when the latch handle is turned from the inside; thus, only one releasing action is needed for the two devices. The second action is the release of the security chain or rod. In neither case, however, can the devices require the use of a key, tool, special knowledge, or effort. For existing installations, three actions are permitted; the latch, the lock, and the security device.

The Exception to 20-2.7 recognizes the use of the delay release lock provided for in 5-2.1.6. This requires that the building either be protected throughout by automatic sprinklers or equipped throughout with a fire detection system. The 15- or 30-second delay permitted by 5-2.1.6 does not affect the immediate release of the lock upon activation of the sprinklers or detectors, or upon loss of power to the lock. This device helps the facility provide the security needed for seldom used doors or stairs, while at the same time it keeps the door available for use, which chains and padlocks are unable to do.

20-2.8 Doors serving a single dwelling unit may be provided with a lock in accordance with 5-2.1.5.1 Exception No. 3.

SECTION 20-3   PROTECTION

20-3.1 Protection of Vertical Openings.

20-3.1.1   Vertical openings shall be protected so that no primary exit route is exposed to an unprotected vertical opening. The vertical opening is considered protected if the opening is cut off and enclosed in a manner that provides a smoke and fire resisting capability of not less than 20 minutes. Any doors or openings shall have fire and smoke resisting capability equivalent to the enclosure and shall be automatic-closing on detection of smoke or shall be self-closing.

Exception: In buildings three stories or less in height, protected throughout by an approved automatic sprinkler system installed in accordance with Section 20-3.5.1, unprotected vertical openings are permitted. However, in such case, there shall still remain a primary means of exit from each sleeping area that does not require occupants to pass through a portion of a lower floor, unless that route is separated from all spaces on that floor by construction having a 20-minute fire resistance rating.

This provision coordinates with 20-2.1.1. (*See commentary following 20-2.1.1.*)

20-3.1.2 Exterior stairs shall be reasonably protected against blockage by a fire that would simultaneously expose both the interior and exterior means of escape. This may be accomplished by physical separation distance, arrangement of the stairs, protection of the openings exposing the stairs, or other means acceptable to the authority having jurisdiction.

20-3.2 Interior Finish. Interior finish on walls and ceilings of occupied spaces shall be Class A, B, or C as defined in Section 6-5. There are no requirements for interior floor finish.

20-3.3 Detection, Alarm, and Communications Systems.

20-3.3.1 General. Lodging and rooming houses shall be provided with a fire alarm system in accordance with Section 7-6.

Exception: Buildings that have a smoke detection system meeting or exceeding the requirements of 20-3.3.4 and have that detection system include at least one manual fire alarm station per floor arranged to initiate the smoke detection alarm.

This Exception allows a multiple station smoke detector "system" with manual pull stations to substitute for a "standard" NFPA 72A, *Standard for the Installation, Maintenance, and Use of Local Protective Signaling Systems,*[3] fire alarm system.

20-3.3.2 Initiation. Initiation of the required fire alarm system shall be by manual means in accordance with 7-6.2.

Exception: Buildings protected throughout by an approved automatic sprinkler system installed in accordance with 20-3.5.1, with alarm initiation in accordance with 7-6.2.1(c).

20-3.3.3 Notification. Occupant notification shall be provided automatically, without delay, by internal audible alarm in accordance with 7-6.3. Presignal systems are prohibited.

20-3.3.4 Detection. Approved smoke detectors meeting the requirements of 7-6.2.9 shall be provided.

Exception: Existing battery powered detectors, rather than house electric service powered detectors, shall be accepted when, in the opinion of the authority having jurisdiction, the facility has demonstrated testing, maintenance, and battery replacement programs that ensure power reliability to the detectors.

20-3.4 Separation of Sleeping Rooms.   All sleeping rooms shall be separated from escape route corridors by walls and doors that are smoke resistant. There shall be no louvers or operable transoms or other air passages penetrating the wall except properly installed heating and utility installations other than transfer grilles. Transfer grilles are prohibited. Doors shall be provided with latches or other mechanisms suitable for keeping the doors closed. No doors shall be arranged so as to prevent the occupant from closing the door. Doors shall be self-closing or automatic-closing upon detection of smoke.

Exception: Door closing devices are not required in buildings protected throughout by an approved automatic sprinkler system installed in accordance with 20-3.5.1.

> This provision was new to the 1985 Edition of the *Code*. The requirement is similar to the corridor requirements of hotels and apartment buildings, but no fire resistance rating is required. Unlike hotels and apartment buildings, door closers are exempted in sprinklered lodging or rooming houses.

20-3.5 Extinguishment Requirements.

20-3.5.1*   Where an automatic sprinkler system is required or is used as an alternative method of protection, either for total or partial building coverage, the system shall be installed in accordance with Section 7-7 and shall activate the fire alarm system in accordance with Section 7-6.

Exception No. 1: Sprinkler installations may be omitted in closets not over 12 sq ft (1.1 sq m) and bathrooms not over 55 sq ft (5.1 sq m).

Exception No. 2: In existing lodging and rooming houses, sprinkler installation may be omitted in closets not over 24 sq ft (2.2 sq m) and bathrooms not over 55 sq ft (5.1 sq m).

A-20-3.5.1   Although not required by the *Code* the use of residential sprinklers or quick response sprinklers is encouraged for new installations of sprinkler systems within dwelling units, apartments and guest rooms. Caution must be used as the system must be designed for the sprinkler being used.

SECTION 20-4   SPECIAL PROVISIONS

20-4.1 Operating Features.   *(See Chapter 31.)*

SECTION 20-5   BUILDING SERVICES

20-5.1 Utilities.   Utilities shall comply with the provisions of Section 7-1.

20-5.2 Heating, Ventilating, and Air Conditioning.

20-5.2.1 Heating, ventilating, and air conditioning equipment shall comply with the provisions of Sections 7-2.1 and 7-2.2.

20-5.2.2 No stove or combustion heater shall be so located as to block escape in case of fire arising from malfunction of the stove or heater.

20-5.2.3 Unvented fuel-fired heaters shall not be used.

REFERENCES CITED IN COMMENTARY

[1]NFPA 13, *Standard for the Installation of Sprinkler Systems*, National Fire Protection Association, Quincy, MA, 1987.

[2]NFPA 13D, *Standard for the Installation of Sprinkler Systems in One- and Two-Family Dwellings and Mobile Homes*, National Fire Protection Association, Quincy, MA, 1984.

[3]NFPA 72A, *Standard for the Installation, Maintenance, and Use of Local Protective Signaling Systems*, National Fire Protection Association, Quincy, MA, 1987.

21 RESIDENTIAL BOARD AND CARE OCCUPANCIES

SECTION 21-1   GENERAL REQUIREMENTS

21-1.1 Application.

It is intended that this chapter be applied to all residential board and care facilities. However, such facilities will rarely be called such names as XYZ Residential Board and Care Facility. They will operate under a variety of names and they may house a variety of different kinds of populations. Therefore, it is important to understand what distinguishes this occupancy from others that provide sleeping accommodations, such as lodging houses, hotels, nursing homes, and hospitals. The definitions in 21-1.3 will be helpful in making this distinction. Additional help in recognizing types of facilities that are intended to be covered by this chapter can be found in A-21-1.3. The list is not all-inclusive.

The fire death problem in buildings of this occupancy classification is well documented.[1] In the past nine years, it has not been uncommon to find a multiple-death board and care fire reported in *Fire Journal*®. The following is extracted from a memo to state fire marshals, state training directors, and provincial fire marshals from NFPA regarding boarding house firesafety, dated July 10, 1984.

> Boarding homes are known by a variety of names: board and care homes, halfway houses, retirement homes, rooming houses, or community living facilities. Regardless of what the facilities are called, an estimated 300,000 boarding homes house 2,000,000 people in the U.S.[2] The facilities range from specially designed and constructed buildings to converted single-family homes and dormitories.
>
> The residents of boarding homes are often unable to meet the demands of independent living and are at a greater risk from fire than the general population. Typically, the victims of boarding home fires are the elderly or former mental health patients who have been released from various institutions. These residents may not require daily medical care but nonetheless may have disabilities that reduce their ability to save themselves in a fire.
>
> The policy of deinstitutionalizing chronic mental patients began in the mid-1950s. The nation's mental hospital population from a

peak of over half a million in the mid-1950s, dropped to roughly half that number by the mid-1960s, and roughly one fourth the peak figure by 1980. The National Institute of Mental Health estimated in 1980 that 800,000 chronic mental patients were both deinstitutionalized and living in sorely lacking conditions.[3] The chronic mental patients released in the late 1970s also included a higher percentage of physically handicapped individuals, and these patients have been less likely to maintain outpatient follow-up care.

Since 1978, multiple-death boarding home fires (those that kill three or more persons) have resulted in 296 deaths. Compared to the estimated boarding home population, this indicates that the risk of dying in a multiple-death fire is roughly five times as high in a boarding home than in all other residential occupancies combined. Many multiple-death boarding home fires kill at least half the tenants of the properties involved.

An analysis of recent fatal boarding home fires reveals the lack of basic fire protection provisions in these buildings, including: inadequate means of egress, combustible interior finishes, unenclosed stairways, lack of automatic detection or sprinkler systems, or lack of emergency training for staff and residents. Many of the facilities were either licensed for an occupancy other than a boarding home (such as a hotel) or were unlicensed, underground "boarding homes." None of the facilities were provided with automatic sprinkler protection.

There is no particular mystery about how to reduce the number of fatal boarding home fires. Provision of enclosed stairs, provision of two means of egress, avoidance of the use of combustible interior finishes, compartmentation, provision of automatic detection and sprinkler systems, and instruction of staff and residents in emergency procedures would greatly reduce the number of fatalities.

A partial list of multiple-death board and care fires since 1979 appears on the following page:

21-1.1.1*   All facilities classified as residential board and care occupancies shall conform to the requirements of this chapter. This chapter is divided into four sections as follows:

(a) Section 21-1 — General Requirements.

(b) Section 21-2 — Small Facilities (i.e., Sleeping accommodations for not more than 16 residents).

(c) Section 21-3 — Large Facilities (i.e., Sleeping accommodations for more than 16 residents).

(d) Section 21-4 — Suitability of an Apartment Building to House a Board and Care Occupancy.

Date	Occupancy	Civilians Killed	Civilians Injured
4/2/79	Wayside Inn Boarding House Farmington, MO	25	9
4/11/79	1715 Lamont Street Washington, DC	10	4
11/11/79	Coats Boarding Home Pioneer, OH	14	0
7/26/80	Brinley Inn Boarding Home* Bradley Beach, NJ	24	4
8/16/80	Boarding Home Honolulu, HI	3	0
11/30/80	Donahue Foster Home Detroit, MI	5	0
1/9/81	Beachview Rest Home* Keansburg, NJ	31	10
10/28/82	Perrys' Domiciliary Care Home* Pittsburgh, PA	5	1
2/7/83	Silver Leaves Group Home* Eau Claire, WI	6	0
3/13/83	Shannons Foster Care Home* Gladstone, MI	5	3
4/19/83	Central Community Home* Worcester, MA	7	2
8/31/83	Anandale Village* Lawrenceville, GA	8	0

*These are incidents in which NFPA has evidence that elderly occupants or former mental health patients were tenants.

A-21-1.1.1   The requirements in this chapter are designed to accommodate typical changes in the capabilities of the residents, such as those due to accidents, temporary illness, cyclical variations in capabilities, and gradual aging. This is based on the assumption that the capabilities of the residents will be evaluated at least annually, and for residents with geriatric problems or degenerative diseases, at least every six months. Also, residents should be reevaluated after each accident or illness that requires hospitalization.

The requirements of this chapter are based on two main concepts:
(a) Larger buildings, which are more difficult to evacuate, require more built-in fire protection than smaller buildings.
(b) People who are more difficult to evacuate require more built-in building fire protection than people who are easier to evacuate.

It is also anticipated that a small facility will typically be located in a structure that has the appearance of and operates similar to a dwelling. The operation and size of the small facility also requires unique considerations with respect to the protection features provided. Certain protection features that are appropriate for large facilities, such as smoke barriers, may not be appropriate and may not provide adequate protection in small facilities. For this reason, an Exception that appeared in the 1985 *Code* and that permitted small facilities to comply with the requirements for large facilities has been modified. As stated in 21-2.1.3, Exception No. 2, a small facility that has previously been approved based on the requirements for a large facility may continue to be evaluated in this manner. However, any other small facility shall meet the provisions for a small facility and may not use the provisions for a large facility as an alternative.

The chapter follows the same outline as the other occupancy chapters within the *Code*. However, due to the four major sections (21-1, 21-2, 21-3, and 21-4) the standard chapter outline begins with the next number in Sections 21-2, 21-3, and 21-4. For example, the 3.1 subsection of each occupancy chapter (e.g., 18-3.1) usually contains the requirements for vertical opening protection. In Chapter 21, 21-2.3.1 and 21-3.3.1 contain the vertical opening provisions.

21-1.2 Mixed Occupancies.

21-1.2.1   Where another type of occupancy occurs in the same building as a residential board and care occupancy, the requirements of 1-4.7 of this *Code* shall apply.

Exception No. 1:   Occupancies that are completely separated from all portions of the building used for a residential board and care facility and its exit system by construction having a fire resistance rating of at least 2 hours.

Exception No. 1 specifically requires that the residential board and care facility and its exit system be separated from the other occupancy. Therefore, if the residential board and care facility is located on the second floor and Exception No. 1 is to be applied, the exit stair would need to have a 2-hour fire-rated enclosure even though 6-2.4 would permit a 1-hour fire-rated enclosure. If the residential board and care facility is located on the same floor as the other occupancy, the occupancy separation could also serve as a horizontal exit, provided the provisions of 5-2.4 are met, and Exception No. 1 may be applied.

Exception No. 2:   Apartment buildings housing residential board and care occupancies in conformance with Section 21-4. In such facilities, any safeguards required by Section 21-4 that are more restrictive than those for other housed occupancies apply only to the extent prescribed by Section 21-4.

21-1.3 Definitions.

A number of key issues are addressed in the definitions, perhaps the most important of which are the introduction of the concepts of "personal care," "evacuation capability," and "point of safety."

Residential Board and Care Occupancy.* A building or part thereof used to provide lodging, boarding, and personal care services for four or more residents unrelated by blood or marriage to its owners or operators.

A-21-1.3 Residential Board and Care Occupancy. Following are examples of facilities that may be classified as residential board and care occupancies.

(a) A group housing arrangement for physically or mentally handicapped persons who normally may attend school in the community, attend church in the community, or otherwise use community facilities.

(b) A group housing arrangement for physically or mentally handicapped persons who are undergoing training in preparation for independent living, for paid employment or for other normal community activities.

(c) A group housing arrangement for the elderly that provides personal care services but that does not provide nursing care.

(d) Facilities for social rehabilitation, alcoholism, drug abuse, or mental health problems that contain a group housing arrangement and that provide personal care services but do not provide acute care.

(e) Other group housing arrangements that provide personal care services but not nursing care.

Personal Care. "Personal care" means protective care of a resident who does not require chronic or convalescent medical or nursing care. Personal care involves responsibility for the safety of the resident when in the building. Protective care may include a daily awareness by the management of the resident's functioning and his or her whereabouts, the arrangement of appointments and reminders of appointments for a resident, the ability and readiness to intervene if a crisis arises for a resident, supervision in areas of nutrition and medication, and actual provision of transient medical care.

Personal care is a significant concept because the occupants of a board and care facility are persons who need care. This is not care in the medical sense, as might be provided in a hospital or nursing home, but rather a form of assistance in meeting the demands of daily life. The reference to "transient medical care" means the kind of medical care that is normally provided in the home by one family member for another, not skilled nursing or acute medical care.

Evacuation Capability.* Evacuation capability is the ability of the occupants, residents, and staff as a group to either evacuate the building or relocate from the point of occupancy to a point of safety. Following are the levels of evacuation capability covered by this chapter:

(a) *Prompt.* Evacuation capability equivalent to the capability of the general population where applying the requirements for residential occupancies covered by Chapters 16, 17, 18, 19, 20, and 22.

(b) *Slow.* Evacuation capability of the group to move to a point of safety in a timely manner, with some of the residents requiring assistance from the staff.

(c) *Impractical.* A group, even with staff assistance, that cannot reliably move to a point of safety in a timely manner.

A-21-1.3 Evacuation Capability. The evacuation capability of the residents and staff is a function of both the ability of the residents to evacuate and the assistance provided by the staff. It is intended that the evacuation capability be determined by a procedure acceptable to the authority having jurisdiction. It is also intended that the timing of drills, the rating of residents, and similar actions related to determining the evacuation capability be performed by persons approved by or acceptable to the authority having jurisdiction. The evacuation capability can be determined by the use of the definitions in 21-1.3, the application of NFPA 101M, *Alternative Approaches to Life Safety*, Chapter 5, or a program of drills (timed).

Where drills are used, in determining evacuation capability, it is suggested that the facility conduct and record fire drills 12 times per year (4 times per year on each shift), and that the facility conduct the drills in consultation with the authority having jurisdiction. Records should indicate the time to evacuate, date and time of day, location of simulated fire origin, the escape paths used, along with comments relating to residents who resisted or failed to participate in the drills.

Translation of drill times to evacuation capability may be determined as: (a) 3 minutes or less, Prompt; (b) over 3 minutes, but not in excess of 13 minutes, Slow; and (c) more than 13 minutes, Impractical.

Evacuation capability in all cases is based on the time of day or night when evacuation of the facility would be most difficult (i.e., sleeping residents or fewer staff present).

Where the facility management does not furnish an evacuation capability determination acceptable to the authority having jurisdiction, the evacuation capability should be classed as "slow," providing the following conditions are met; otherwise the evacuation capability should be considered "impractical to evacuate."

(a) All residents are able to travel to centralized dining facilities without continuous staff assistance, and

(b) There is continuous staffing whenever there are residents in the facility.

> Evacuation capability is a factor in all the *Code* chapters. However, in most chapters, the *Code* makes the silent assumption that the building occupants have similar evacuation capabilities, and the requirements are based on the ability to reach safety by means of exits. In the "institutional occupancy" chapters, the *Code* assumes that many of the building occupants will be completely incapable of evacuating the building, and the protection of life from fire is achieved by the "defend in place" method. In large residential buildings (hotels and apartment buildings), where evacuation capability may be poor due to the large size of the building, considerable built-in fire protection is required.
>
> In this chapter, evacuation capability is not assumed. All residential board and care facilities do not have the same evacuation capability. This should be obvious because of the numerous and diverse types of facilities that are included in this occupancy type. In an orphanage, a shelter for battered women, a group home for high-functioning mentally handicapped persons, a halfway house for prison parolees, etc., the occupants may have normal evacuation capability. In facilities housing elderly, physically impaired persons, occupants may be slow-moving or may need

assistance in recognizing that evacuation is needed. In some facilities, evacuation of the building may not be practical at all.

Evacuation capability for an entire facility is not determined on the basis of the least capable resident. A facility that houses one impaired resident may have excellent evacuation capability if the on-duty staff or a resident "buddy" is able to provide the assistance needed to effect a prompt evacuation of the entire group, without jeopardizing the safety of the other residents. It should also be noted that evacuation capability is based on the ability to relocate to a point of safety that is not necessarily a public way. (*See the definition of Point of Safety.*)

The protection features required by this chapter are intended to parallel the evacuation capability of the occupants. As such, the fire endurance of the structure, interior finish materials, types and arrangement of means of escape and exits, as well as corridor enclosure provisions, vary based on whether a facility houses occupants who are prompt, slow, or impractical to evacuate. Facilities that are impractical to evacuate utilize the "defend in place" concept. In small facilities, this is achieved by improving the protection of vertical openings and by mandating the installation of automatic sprinkler systems. In large facilities, this is achieved by referencing the provisions of Chapters 12 and 13.

Guidance in determining the evacuation capability of a specific facility is provided in A-21-1.3.

Hazardous Area. A hazardous area is any space that contains storage or other activity having fuel conditions exceeding that of a one- or two-family dwelling and possessing the potential for a fully involved fire. Hazardous areas include, but are not limited to, areas for cartoned storage, food or household maintenance items in wholesale or institutional-type quantities and concentrations, or massed storage of residents' belongings. Areas containing approved, properly installed and maintained furnaces and heating equipment, and furnace rooms, cooking, and laundry facilities are not classed as hazardous areas solely on the basis of such equipment.

Hazardous areas are spaces with contents that, because of their basic nature (as in the case of flammable liquids) or because of the quantity of combustible materials involved, represent a significantly greater fire hazard than would otherwise be typical of residential board and care occupancies. The mere presence of heat producing appliances, such as furnaces, cooking equipment, or dryers, does not constitute a hazardous area. To be considered a hazardous area, the contents should be such that a fire or explosion could develop and present a danger of propagating to adjacent spaces where a fire barrier or automatic sprinkler system is not provided.

Point of Safety. A point of safety is a location that meets one of the following conditions:

(a) It is exterior to and away from the building.

(b) It is within a building of any construction protected throughout by an approved automatic sprinkler system and is either:

1. Within an exit enclosure meeting the requirements of this *Code*, or

2. Within another portion of the building that is separated by smoke barriers in accordance with Section 6-3 having a fire resistance rating of at least 20 minutes and that has access to a means of escape or exit that does not require return to the area of fire involvement and that conforms to the requirements of this *Code*.

(c) It is within a building of Type I, Type II (222) or (111), Type III (211), Type IV, or Type V (111) construction (*see 6-2.1*) and is either:

1. Within an exit enclosure meeting the requirements of this *Code*, or

2. Within another portion of the building that is separated by smoke barriers in accordance with Section 6-3 having a fire resistance rating of at least 20 minutes and that has access to a means of escape or exit that does not require return to the area of fire involvement and that conforms to the requirements of this *Code*.

> "Point of safety" is another concept that is not new in the *Code*, but this chapter defines it. It is well known that there are many buildings from which evacuation of all occupants to the outdoors cannot be achieved within a reasonable amount of time, even with the most capable of occupants. This chapter establishes the criteria for a point of safety within the building. This is basically the point at which the residents can remain in safety until the fire is extinguished or until outside assistance can arrive to complete the evacuation to the exterior.

Resident.   A person who is receiving personal care and resides in a residential board and care facility.

Staff.   A person who provides personal care services, supervision, or assistance to residents.

21-1.4 Acceptability of Means of Egress or Escape.   No means of escape or means of egress shall be considered as complying with the minimum criteria for acceptance unless emergency evacuation drills are regularly conducted using that route in accordance with the requirements of 31-7.3.

> Exits are worthless unless the residents are familiar with them and feel comfortable using them. An exit that is never used in drills will probably not be used in an emergency evacuation.

SECTION 21-2   SMALL FACILITIES

See Table 21-1 on page 909 for a summary of the major requirements.

21-2.1 General.

21-2.1.1 Scope.   This section applies to residential board and care occupancies providing sleeping accommodations for not more than 16 residents. Where there are

Table 21-1.   Summary of Major Requirements for Small Facilities

Parameter	Evacuation Capability		
	Prompt	Slow	Impractical
1. Construction 21-2.1.4	No Requirements	20-Minute Fire Resistant or Sprinklered	1-Hour Fire-Rated or Sprinklered
2. Means of Escape 21-2.2	1 Primary and 1 Emergency Route	2 Remote Routes	2 Remote Routes
3. Vertical Openings 21-2.3.1	20-Minute Fire Resistant	20-Minute Fire Resistant	20-Minute Fire Resistant
4. Protection of Hazardous Areas 21-2.3.2	Defines 2 Levels	Defines 2 Levels	Defines 2 Levels
5. Interior Finish 21-2.3.3	Class A,B,C No Req. for Floor Finish	Class A and B No Req. for Floor Finish	Class A and B No Req. For Floor Finish
6. Manual F.A. 21-2.3.4	Section 7-6 Local	Section 7-6 Local	Section 7-6 Local
7. Smoke Detection 21-2.3.5	1 Each Level + Each Living and Day Room	1 Each Level + Each Living and Day Room	1 Each Level + Each Living and Day Room
8. Sprinklers 21-2.3.6	Not Required	Not Required	Required
9. Separation of Sleeping Rooms 21-2.3.7	Smoke-Resisting Self-Closing Door	20-Minute Fire Resistant and Self-Closing Door	20-Minute Fire Resistant and Self-Closing Door

This table summarizes major items. See specific requirements for additional details and exceptions.

sleeping accommodations for more than 16 residents, the occupancy will be classed as a large facility. The requirements for large facilities are in Section 21-3.

21-2.1.2   The requirements of this section are applicable to new construction and existing buildings according to the provisions of Section 1-4 of this *Code*.

21-2.1.3 Requirements Based on Evacuation Capability.

21-2.1.3.1   Small facilities shall comply with the requirements of Section 21-2 as indicated for the appropriate evacuation capability.

Exception No. 1*: Facilities where the authority having jurisdiction has determined equivalent safety is provided in accordance with Section 1-5.

Exception No. 2:   Facilities that were previously approved as complying with the requirements for a large facility with the same evacuation capability.

A-21-2.1.3.1 Exception No. 1   In determining equivalency for existing buildings, conversions, modernizations, renovations, or unusual design concepts, the authority having jurisdiction may accept evaluations based on NFPA 101M, *Alternative Approaches to Life Safety*, Chapter 6.

An Exception that appeared in the 1985 *Code* and permitted small facilities to comply with the requirements for large facilities has been restricted to apply to previously approved facilities only (Exception No. 2). The protection features applicable to large facilities may not necessarily provide protection for small facilities. In the case of "prompt" and "slow" facilities, the requirements are such that the use of the Exception would provide no benefit to the user of the *Code*.

21-2.1.4 Minimum Construction Requirements.

21-2.1.4.1 Prompt.   No Special Requirements.

21-2.1.4.2 Slow.   The facility shall be housed in a building where the interior is fully sheathed with lath and plaster or material with a 15-minute finish rating, including all portions of the bearing walls, bearing partitions, floor constructions, and roofs. All columns, beams, girders, and trusses are similarly encased, or otherwise treated to provide a minimum of at least a 20-minute fire resistance rating.

Exception No. 1:   Buildings with the only exposed steel or wood serving as columns and support beams (but not joists) located in the basement area are considered as fully sheathed.

Exception No. 2:   Buildings of Type I, Type II (111), Type III (211), Type IV, or Type V (111) construction. (See 6-2.1.)

Exception No. 3:   Buildings where all portions not sheathed are protected by an approved automatic sprinkler system in accordance with 21-2.3.5.

Exception No. 4:   Unfinished, unused, and essentially inaccessible loft, attic, or crawl spaces.

Exception No. 5:   Where the facility can demonstrate to the authority having jurisdiction that the group is capable of evacuating the building in eight minutes or less or achieves an E-Score of three or less using NFPA 101M, Alternative Approaches to Life Safety, Chapter 5.

See Figure 21-1 for examples of some acceptable construction types.

Exception No. 5 is intended to allow unsheathed, unsprinklered wood frame construction in facilities that house groups capable of evacuation to a point of safety within eight minutes. For such groups, the additional evacuation time provided by fire resistant sheathing is not an absolute necessity.

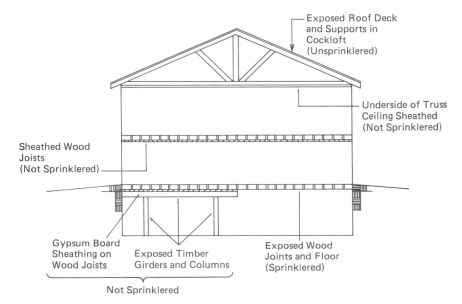

Figure 21-1. A Few Permissible Types of Construction. They may be mixed within a single building.

21-2.1.4.3 Impractical.   Buildings may be of any type construction in accordance with 6-2.1 other than Type II (000), Type III (200), or Type V (000). (*Also see 21-2.3.5.2.*)

Exception: Buildings protected throughout by an approved supervised automatic sprinkler system in accordance with 21-2.3.5 may be of Type II (000), Type III (200), or Type V (000) construction.

Paragraph 21-2.3.5.2 mandates that all small residential board and care facilities that are impractical to evacuate be protected with a supervised automatic sprinkler system. In order for the Exception to apply, the entire building and not just the residential board and care facilities must be protected with a supervised automatic sprinkler system.

21-2.2 Means of Escape.

21-2.2.1 Number of Means of Escape.   Every facility shall have at least two remotely located means of escape that do not involve windows from each normally occupied story. At least one of these means of escape shall comply with 21-2.2.2.

Exception No. 1:   In prompt facilities, one means of escape may involve windows complying with 21-2.2.3(c).

Exception No. 2:   A second means of escape from each story is not required where the entire building is protected throughout by an approved automatic sprinkler system complying with 21-2.3.5, and the facility has two means of escape.

Paragraph 21-2.2.1 as well as 21-2.2.2 and 21-2.2.3 establish the criteria for acceptable means of escape in small facilities. This paragraph mandates that each story of the facility be provided with at least two means of escape. If the entire building housing the residential board and care facility is protected throughout by an automatic sprinkler system in accordance with 21-2.3.5 and the facility itself has at least two means of escape, each story need have only one means of escape. In this instance, the single means of escape shall meet the criteria for a primary means of escape. (*See 21-2.2.2.*)

The paragraph only permits the use of windows as a means of escape in prompt facilities. Where a window is considered in means of escape, the window shall meet the criteria established in 21-2.2.3. Windows are not permitted to be considered as a primary means of escape.

21-2.2.2 Primary Means of Escape.   Every sleeping room and living area shall have access to a primary means of escape so located as to provide a safe path of travel to the outside of the building without traversing any corridor or other space exposed to unprotected vertical openings. Where sleeping rooms or living areas are above or below the level of exit discharge, the primary means of escape shall be an enclosed interior stair, exterior stair, horizontal exit, or an existing fire escape stair. Also, in slow and impractical facilities, the primary means of escape for each sleeping room shall not be exposed to common living spaces such as living rooms and kitchens.

This paragraph requires at least one means of escape from every sleeping room and living area to be protected from vertical openings. As such, the primary means of escape provides some degree of quality and reliability but may not meet the criteria of an exit. If the level is other than the level of exit discharge, the primary means of escape will need to be an enclosed stairway, an exterior stairway, or possibly a horizontal exit.

In slow and impractical facilities, the primary means of escape is further restricted in that it cannot be exposed to common living spaces. As such, the primary means of escape from a sleeping room may not include travel through a day room, common use space, or space that is open to a common living space. The objective of this requirement is to reduce the probability that smoke and heat from a fire in a common use area will affect the primary means of escape. This provision is based in part on historical fire experience, which indicates that fires in residential board and care facilities frequently originate in common living spaces.

(*For additional discussion see commentary following 20-2.2.1.*)

21-2.2.3 Secondary Means of Escape.   In addition to the primary route, each sleeping room shall have a second means of escape or alternate protection that consists of one of the following:

(a) A door, stairway, passage, or hall providing a means of unobstructed travel to the outside of the dwelling at street or ground level that is independent of and remote from the primary means of escape.

(b) A passage through adjacent nonlockable space, independent of and remote from the primary means of escape to any approved means of escape.

(c) An outside window or door operable from the inside without the use of tools and providing a clear opening of not less than 20 in. (50.8 cm) in width, 24 in. (61 cm) in height, and 5.7 sq ft (.53 sq m) in area. The bottom of the opening shall not be more than 44 in. (112 cm) off the floor. Such means of escape shall be acceptable if:

(1) the window is within 20 ft (6.1 m) of grade or,

(2) the window is directly accessible to fire department rescue apparatus as approved by the authority having jurisdiction, or

(3) the window or door opens onto an exterior balcony.

(d) The sleeping room shall be separated from all other parts of the facility by construction having a fire resistance rating of at least 20 minutes and shall be equipped with a door that resists passage of fire for at least 20 minutes and is designed and installed to minimize smoke leakage. A means of providing smoke venting and fresh air to the occupants shall be provided.

Exception No. 1: If the sleeping room has a door leading directly to the outside of the building with access to grade, or to a stairway that meets the requirements for exterior stairs in 21-2.3.1.2, that means of escape shall be considered as meeting all the escape requirements for the sleeping room.

Exception No. 2: A second means of escape or alternate protection from each sleeping room is not required where the facility is protected throughout by an approved automatic sprinkler system complying with 21-2.3.5.

Exception No. 3: Existing approved means of escape may be ..tinued in service.

The provisions of 21-2.2.3 require that every sleeping room be provided with a second means of escape in addition to the primary means of escape required by 21-2.2.2. The only two exceptions to the requirement for the second means of escape are (1) if the sleeping room has a door leading directly to the outside of the building; or (2) where the residential board and care facility is protected throughout with an automatic sprinkler system in accordance with 21-2.3.5. Although either case is an acceptable alternative, Exception No. 2 may be the more practical method to use to avoid having to provide the second means of escape. For example, if the facility is housed in an apartment building that does not have windows complying with item (c), an automatic sprinkler system could be installed within the facility in lieu of retrofitting complying windows for the sleeping rooms.

The primary purpose for the second means of escape is to allow the occupants to have some reasonable escape mechanism when a fire or smoke blocks the primary means of escape. Paragraph 21-2.2.3(a) through (d) of the *Code* provides four acceptable methods for providing a second means of escape.

(1) It is the intent of item (a) that the door, stairway, passage, or hall be independent of and remote from the primary means of escape required in 21-2.2.2. If the sleeping room has a second door that leads to the same hallway as the door serving as a primary means of escape, little additional protection is provided, since a fire or smoke could affect both of the doors at approximately the same time. If the corridor within the facility into

which a sleeping room door opens is separated from all common living spaces (as required by 21-2.2.2 for slow and impractical facilities), it may be determined that the arrangement is acceptable provided the corridor does in fact lead to two separate, independent, and remote means of escape. Such an arrangement is similar to that permitted in other occupancies in which protected corridors are provided. In such a case, little if any additional safety would be provided by requiring two doors from the sleeping room to the corridor.

(2) Figure 21-2 illustrates an example of how the second means of escape may pass through an adjacent space, such as another sleeping room, provided the occupant has free and unobstructed access to the space in accordance with item (b).

(3) The use of an operable window of the minimum dimensions specified in item (c) is permitted only in prompt facilities by 21-2.2.1 but is permitted as the secondary means of escape for each sleeping room in all facilities. Figure 21-3 illustrates the minimum dimensions required for escape windows. Note that it is not possible to use the minimum dimensions for width and height and still comply with minimum area dimension. In addition to the minimum size of the window, the utility of the window must be assured by one of three methods.

First, the window must be within 20 ft of grade so that jumping is possible, if necessary. The second method would permit fire department rescue of the occupant from the window. The authority having jurisdiction must determine the acceptable means of fire department rescue (e.g., aerial ladder apparatus, ground ladders, etc.) and the additional needs required to accept the method, such as fire department vehicle accessibility. The third method allows the occupant to reach an exterior balcony to breathe fresh air while awaiting either rescue or fire extinguishment.

(4) Item (d) is, in fact, another alternative to providing the second means of escape. In lieu of the second means of escape, the sleeping room must be completely separated from all other parts of the building (not just the corridor). In addition, a means of smoke venting and access to fresh air must be provided. A window to the outside that does not comply with item (c) may be an acceptable means of providing smoke venting and fresh air, provided the window is of substantial enough size to serve as a reasonable vent.

(*For additional information, see commentary following 22-2.1.2.*)

21-2.2.4 Enclosed Interior Stairs.   Interior stairways shall be enclosed with 20-minute fire barriers with all openings protected with smoke actuated automatic or self-closing doors having a fire resistance comparable to that required for the enclosure. Stairways shall comply with 5-2.2.3.5.

Also see 21-2.2.1 and 21-2.2.2.

Exception No. 1:   Stairs connecting two levels only may be open to other than the street floor.

Exception No. 2:   In prompt and slow facilities, stairways may be unprotected in accordance with the Exception to 21-2.3.1.1.

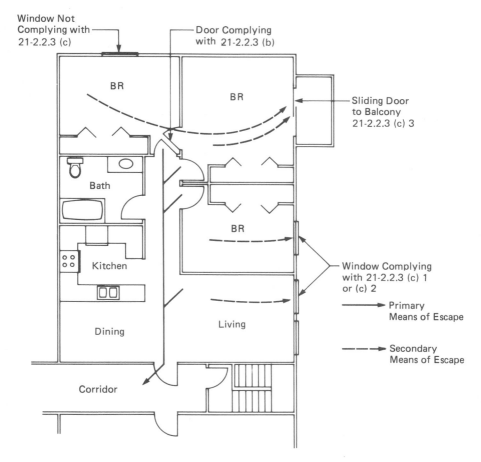

Figure 21-2.   Figure 21-2 Illustrates One Use of 21-2.2.3(b).   An example of a board and care facility within an apartment building in which a sleeping room has a window that does not comply with 21-2.2.3(c) and in which there is no door to the corridor. The balcony door in the upper right bedroom would not be needed if the facility were sprinklered in accordance with NFPA 13, *Standard for the Installation of Sprinkler Systems,*[4] or NFPA 13D, *Standard for the Installation of Sprinkler Systems in One- and Two-Family Dwellings and Mobil Homes*[5] or if the sleeping room in question were protected in accordance with 21-2.2.3(d).

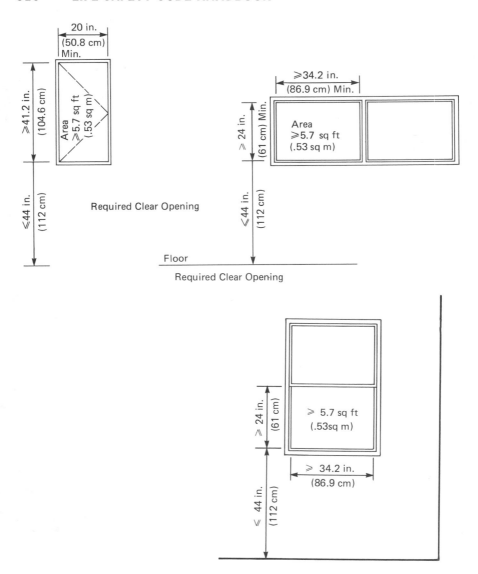

Figure 21-3.   Minimum Size and Dimensions of Outside Windows Used as a Second Means of Escape per 21-2.2.3(c).

Figure 21-4 illustrates the use of Exception No. 1 to 21-2.2.4.

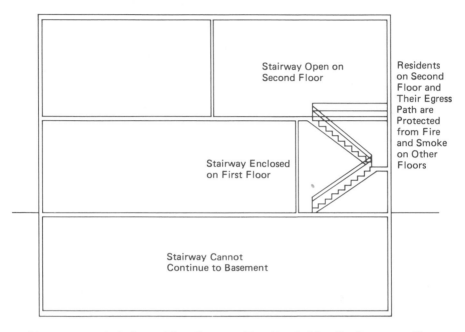

Figure 21-4.   A Stairway That Connects Two Levels May Be Open to a Floor Other Than the Street Floor.

21-2.2.5 Doors.

21-2.2.5.1   No door or path of travel to a means of egress shall be less than 32 in. (81 cm) wide.

Exception No. 1:   In existing buildings and in conversions, 28-in. (71-cm) doors may be continued in use.

Exception No. 2:   Bathroom doors may be 24 in. (61 cm) wide.

21-2.2.5.2   Every closet door latch shall be such that it can be readily opened from the inside in case of emergency.

21-2.2.5.3   Every bathroom door shall be designed to permit the opening of the locked door from the outside in an emergency.

21-2.2.5.4   No door in any means of egress shall be locked against egress when the building is occupied.

Paragraph 21-2.2.5.4 prohibits a residential board and care facility from having any door in the means of egress locked against egress while the building is occupied. This requirement permits a door to have a locking device that allows the door to be opened from within the facility for the purpose of egress, but does not allow the door to be open from outside the facility. Ordinary double cylinder locks and chain locks would not meet these provisions.

The language of 5-2.1.5.1 is clear: "Locks, if provided, shall not require the use of a key, tool, special knowledge, or effort for operation from the inside of the building." This eliminates double cylinder locks and chain locks that require a key to be operated from the inside. Paragraph 5-2.1.5.3 calls for a simple operation to open a door; the presence of a two-handed knob operation, and the like, is specifically prohibited.

21-2.2.6   The width, risers, and treads of every stair shall comply with the minimum requirements for Class B stairs as described in 5-2.2.

Exception: Existing noncomplying stairs may be continued in use subject to the approval of the authority having jurisdiction.

Note this allows the use of Class B stairs even in new construction.

21-2.2.7   Winders in accordance with 5-2.2.2.8 are permitted.

21-2.3 Protection.

21-2.3.1 Protection of Vertical Openings.

21-2.3.1.1   Vertical openings shall be protected so that no primary exit route is exposed to an unprotected vertical opening. The vertical opening is considered protected if the opening is cut off and enclosed in a manner that provides a fire resisting capability of not less than 20 minutes and resists the passage of smoke. Any doors or openings shall have fire and smoke resisting capability equivalent to the enclosure and shall be self-closing or automatic-closing in accordance with 5-2.1.8.

Exception: In buildings three or fewer stories in height, housing prompt and slow facilities protected throughout by an approved automatic sprinkler system in accordance with 21-2.3.5, unprotected vertical openings are permitted. However, in such case, there shall still remain a primary means of exit from each sleeping area that does not require occupants to pass through a portion of a lower floor, unless that route is separated from all spaces on that floor by construction having a 20-minute fire resistance rating.

This provision coordinates with 21-2.2.2. The lack of vertical opening protection has been identified as a contributing factor in many of the multiple-death fires in residential board and care facilities.

21-2.3.1.2   Exterior stairs shall be reasonably protected from blockage by a fire that would simultaneously expose both the interior and exterior means of escape. This may be accomplished by physical separation distance, arrangement of the stairs, protection of the openings exposing the stairs, or other means acceptable to the authority having jurisdiction.

This paragraph does not mandate compliance with the provisions of Chapter 5 for an exterior stair. However, if the exterior stair is to be considered a primary means of escape, consideration must be given to protecting the stair to reduce the likelihood that a fire within the facility will render the stair useless. Whereas the provision applies to small facilities, it should be noted that 5-2.2.3.2 does exempt outside stairs serving a two-story building from the protection requirements of that section if a remote second exit is provided. In this case, a remote second means of escape may eliminate the need to protect the exterior stair.

21-2.3.2 Hazardous Areas. Any hazardous area shall be protected in accordance with the following:

(a) If a hazardous area is on the same floor as, and is in or abuts a primary means of escape or a sleeping room, the hazardous area shall be protected by either:

1. An enclosure with a fire resistance rating of at least 1 hour with a self-closing or automatic-closing fire door in accordance with 5-2.1.8 having a fire protection rating of at least ¾ hour, or

2. Automatic sprinkler protection, in accordance with 21-2.3.5, of the hazardous area and a separation that will resist the passage of smoke between the hazardous area and the exposed sleeping area or primary exit route. Any doors in such separation shall be self-closing or automatic-closing in accordance with 5-2.1.8.

(b) Other hazardous areas shall be protected by either:

1. An enclosure with a fire resistance rating of at least 20 minutes with a self-closing or automatic-closing door in accordance with 5-2.1.8 at least equivalent to a 1¾-in. (4.4-cm) solid bonded wood core construction, or

2. Automatic sprinkler protection, in accordance with 21-2.3.5, of the hazardous area regardless of enclosure.

The protection of hazardous areas is based on the potential impact of a fire in the area on a primary means of escape or sleeping rooms. If the hazardous area is on the same floor as sleeping rooms or a primary means of escape, and the rooms or means of escape is exposed to the hazardous area, the construction shall be capable of containing a fire, or automatic sprinkler protection shall be provided to control a fire, and the construction shall be capable of resisting smoke spread outside the area. If the hazardous area is on a different floor or does not abut a primary means of escape or sleeping rooms, the construction shall be capable of containing a fire for a limited time, or automatic sprinkler protection shall be provided to control a fire.

For example, a basement in a wood frame residence is used for the storage of combustible materials. The basement is not a required means of escape. If the basement storage area does not abut a sleeping area on the same floor, sheathing the ceiling to provide fire resistance is not required if the basement is sprinklered.

21-2.3.3 Interior Finish. Interior wall and ceiling finish shall be Class A or Class B in accordance with Section 6-5. There are no requirements for interior floor finish.

Exception: Class C interior wall and ceiling finish is permitted in prompt facilities.

The 1985 Edition contained an Exception for structural elements of heavy timber. The Exception has been eliminated from Chapter 21 since similar language is now incorporated in 6-5.3.4.

21-2.3.4 Detection, Alarm, and Communication Systems.

21-2.3.4.1 Fire Alarm Systems.   A manual fire alarm system shall be provided in accordance with Section 7-6.

Exception No. 1:   If there are interconnected smoke detectors meeting the requirements of 21-2.3.4.2, and there is at least one manual fire alarm station per floor arranged to continuously sound the smoke detector alarms.

Exception No. 2:   Other manually activated continuously sounding alarms acceptable to the authority having jurisdiction.

A means of manually activating a fire alarm signal is required. If there is a "system" of interconnected multiple-station smoke detectors, the manual fire alarm requirement can be met by providing a manual station on each floor that is integrated with the smoke detectors. However, Exception No. 2 recognizes that, in a small building, a sophisticated manual fire alarm system, using components "listed" for use in fire alarm systems, may not be necessary. The requirements can be satisfied by the installation of electric bells activated by a clearly identified switch on each floor when approved by the authority having jurisdiction.

21-2.3.4.2 Smoke Detectors.   Approved smoke detectors shall be installed in accordance with 7-6.2.9. These shall be powered by the house electrical service and, when activated, shall initiate an alarm that is audible in all sleeping areas. Detectors shall be installed on all levels, including basements, but excluding crawl spaces and unfinished attics. Additional detectors shall be installed for living rooms, dens, day rooms, and similar spaces.

Exception: Detectors may be omitted in buildings protected throughout by an approved automatic sprinkler system in accordance with 21-2.3.5 using quick response or residential sprinklers.

This paragraph does not specifically require a "system" of smoke detectors in a small facility. If the building is small enough, single station detectors may be able to meet the criterion of audibility in all sleeping areas. However, if the building is of significant size or consists of multiple levels, interconnected multiple-station detectors will probably be needed. Additional detectors are required in the living rooms and day rooms because fire statistics show that most of multiple-death fires in board and care homes have started in such rooms. In order to eliminate the detectors as permitted by the Exception, the entire building must be protected with an automatic sprinkler system in accordance with 21-2.3.6.

21-2.3.5 Automatic Extinguishing Systems.

21-2.3.5.1   Where an automatic sprinkler system is installed, either for total or partial building coverage, the system shall be in accordance with Section 7-7 and shall activate the fire alarm system in accordance with Section 7-6.

This paragraph does not require the installation of automatic sprinklers. The purpose of this section is to establish the criteria to be followed if the facility chooses to use the sprinkler alternatives provided in this chapter.

Exception No. 1:   In impractical facilities, a sprinkler system complying with NFPA 13D, Standard for the Installation of Sprinkler Systems in One- and Two-Family Dwellings and Mobile Homes, with a 30-minute water supply, may be used provided all habitable areas and closets are sprinklered. Automatic sprinklers may be omitted in bathrooms not over 55 sq ft (5.1 sq m), provided such spaces are finished with lath and plaster, or material with a 15-minute finish rating.

Exception No. 2:   In prompt and slow facilities, a sprinkler system complying with NFPA 13D, Standard for the Installation of Sprinkler Systems in One- and Two-Family Dwellings and Mobile Homes, may be used. Automatic sprinklers may be omitted in small compartmented areas, such as closets not over 24 sq ft (2.2 sq m) and bathrooms not over 55 sq ft (5.1 sq m), provided such spaces are finished with lath and plaster, or materials with a 15-minute finish rating.

Exception No. 1 recognizes the "defend in place" concept utilized in impractical facilities by increasing the duration of the water supply and by mandating sprinklers in all habitable areas, including closets. As such, the areas in which NFPA 13D does not require sprinklers is greatly reduced.

The omission of sprinklers in bathrooms and closets as permitted in Exception No. 2 is intended to reinforce the exemption for sprinklers in these areas. It is intended that all the exceptions for sprinkler coverage permitted by NFPA 13D are applicable.

21-2.3.5.2 Impractical.   All impractical facilities shall be protected throughout by an approved supervised automatic sprinkler system in accordance with 21-2.3.5.1.

This paragraph requires that all small facilities housing occupants classed as impractical to evacuate be fully sprinklered. All Exceptions for sprinklers other than the allowance for unprotected vertical openings described in the Exception to 21-2.3.1.1 may be used.

21-2.3.5.3   Sprinkler piping serving not more than six sprinklers for any isolated hazardous area may be installed in accordance with 7-7.1.2.

Paragraph 7-7.1.2 provides a sprinkler design criteria of 0.15 gal per minute per sq ft for systems using six sprinklers or less to protect an isolated area. The paragraph does not specify the intended duration of the water supply. In areas where the connection to the domestic water supply would result in an unlimited duration due to the presence of public water, this is not an issue. However, facilities that utilize a private water system (well) are not as fortunate. The duration should therefore be acceptable to the authority having jurisdiction based on the hazard. In determining the acceptable duration, the criteria of 21-2.3.5.1 should also be considered.

21-2.3.6 Construction of Corridor Walls.

21-2.3.6.1   The separation walls of sleeping rooms shall be capable of resisting fire for at least 20 minutes. This is considered achieved if the partitioning is finished on both sides with lath and plaster, or material with a 15-minute finish rating. Sleeping room doors shall be substantial doors, such as those of 1¾-in. (4.4-cm) solid bonded wood core construction, or of other construction of equal or greater stability and fire integrity. Any vision panels shall be of wired glass, not exceeding 1,296 sq in. (0.84 sq m) in area each, installed in approved frames.

Exception No. 1: In prompt facilities, all sleeping rooms may be separated from the escape route by walls and doors that are smoke resistant.

Exception No. 2: Where the facility can demonstrate to the authority having jurisdiction that the group is capable of evacuating the building in eight minutes or less, or achieves an E-score of three or less using NFPA 101M, Alternative Approaches to Life Safety, Chapter 5, sleeping rooms may be separated from escape routes by walls and doors that are smoke resistant.

In facilities housing occupants capable of evacuating to a point of safety within eight minutes, the additional evacuation time provided by substantial corridor wall construction is not an absolute necessity.

Exception No. 3: Corridor walls and doors that are capable of resisting the passage of smoke and that are protected by automatic sprinklers in accordance with 21-2.3.5 on both sides of the wall and door. In such instances, there is no limitation on the type or size of glass panels.

In essence, the Exception means that the fire resistance requirements shall not apply where sprinkler protection is provided on both sides of the wall and door.

Exception No. 4: Sleeping arrangements not in bedrooms may be provided for nonresident staff members provided the audibility of the alarm in the sleeping area is sufficient to waken the staff that might be asleep.

It is recognized that there are many board and care homes that employ "sleep-in" staff. The Exception is intended to allow staff members to sleep in locations that are not separated from the corridors by construction meeting the minimum requirements for construction of corridor walls. The existence of a staff cot in the supervisor's station or in the living room, etc., is not intended to cause the room to be reclassified as a sleeping room.

21-2.3.6.2   There shall be no louvers or operable transoms or other air passages penetrating the wall except properly installed heating and utility installations other than transfer grilles. Transfer grilles are prohibited.

21-2.3.6.3   Doors shall be provided with latches or other mechanisms suitable for keeping the doors closed. No doors shall be arranged so as to prevent the occupant from closing the door.

21-2.3.6.4   Doors shall be self-closing or automatic-closing in accordance with 5-2.1.8.

Exception: Door closing devices are not required in buildings protected throughout by an approved automatic sprinkler system in accordance with Section 7-7.

The Exception is not the same as Exception No. 3 to 21-2.3.6.1. In order for the door closing device to be eliminated, the entire building must be protected throughout by an approved automatic sprinkler system.

21-2.4 Operating Features.   *(See Chapter 31.)*

21-2.5 Building services.

21-2.5.1 Utilities.   Utilities shall comply with Section 7-1.

21-2.5.2 Heating, Ventilating, and Air Conditioning Equipment.

21-2.5.2.1   Heating, ventilating, and air conditioning equipment shall comply with the provisions of 7-2.1 and 7-2.2 except as otherwise required in this chapter.

21-2.5.2.2   No stove or combustion heater shall be so located as to block escape in case of fire arising from malfunctioning of the stove or heater.

21-2.5.2.3   Unvented fuel-fired heaters shall not be used in any room used for sleeping purposes.

SECTION 21-3   LARGE FACILITIES

See Table 21-2 on page 924 for summary of major requirements.

21-3.1 General.

21-3.1.1 Scope.   This section applies to residential board and care occupancies providing sleeping accommodations for more than 16 residents. Facilities having sleeping accommodations for not more than 16 residents shall be evaluated in accordance with Section 21-2, Small Facilities. However, existing facilities meeting the requirements of this section are considered to meet the requirements of Section 21-2 for prompt evacuation capability or slow evacuation capability.

21-3.1.2   The requirements of this section are applicable to new construction and existing buildings according to the provisions of Section 1-4 of this *Code.*

21-3.1.3 Requirements Based on Evacuation Capability.

21-3.1.3.1 Prompt and Slow.   Large facilities shall comply with the requirements of Section 21-3 as indicated for the appropriate evacuation capability.

Exception No. 1*: Facilities where the authority having jurisdiction has determined equivalent safety is provided in accordance with Section 1-5.

Exception No. 2: Facilities that were previously approved as complying with 21-3.1.3.2.

Table 21-2. Summary of Major Requirements for Large Facilities

Parameter	Evacuation Capability		
	Prompt	Slow	Impractical
1. Construction 21-3.1.4	See Table 21-3	See Table 21-3	12-1.6 or 13-1.6
2. Means of Egress 21-3.2	2 Exits per Floor	2 Exits per Floor	Section 12-2 or 13-2
3. Vertical Openings 21-3.3.1	6-2.4	6-2.4	12-3.1 or 13-3.1
4. Protection of Hazardous Areas 21-3.3.2	1 hour enclosure or sprinklers	1 hour enclosure or sprinklers	12-3.2 or 13-3.2
5. Interior Finish 21-3.3.3	Class A and B Class I and II Corr. and Exit Floor	Class A and B Class I and II Corr. and Exit Floor	12-3.3 or 13-3.3
6. Manual F.A. 21-3.3.4	Local	Local	12-3.4 or 13-3.4
7. Smoke Detection 21-3.3.4.7 21-3.3.4.8	Sleeping Rooms—Single Station Corridors and Common Areas per NFPA 72E	Sleeping Rooms—Single Station Corridors and Common Areas per NFPA 72E	12-3.4 or 13-3.4
8. Sprinklers 21-3.3.5	Not Required (*Also see Table 21-3*)	Not Required (*Also see Table 21-3*)	Required Except Certain Type I and II (222) Bldgs.
9. Separation of Sleeping Rooms 2-3.3.6.2	New—1 Hour Existing—20 minutes	New—1 Hour Existing—20 minutes	12-3.6 or 13-3.6
10. Smoke Control 21-3.3.7	Smoke Barrier	Smoke Barrier	12-3.7 or 13-3.7

A-21-3.1.3.1 Exception No. 1 In determining equivalency for existing buildings, conversions, modernizations, renovations, or unusual design concepts, the authority having jurisdiction may accept evaluations based on NFPA 101M, *Alternative Approaches to Life Safety*, Chapter 6.

Exception No. 2 has been restricted to facilities that were previously approved as having complied with the criteria for impractical facilities. It is anticipated that the staffing level in prompt and slow facilities is not the same as that which is typically found in health care facilities or impractical facilities.

21-3.1.3.2 Impractical.   Facilities housing groups of persons classed as impractical to evacuate shall meet the requirements for limited care facilities, Chapter 12 or 13, as appropriate.

Exception*: Facilities where the authority having jurisdiction has determined equivalent safety is provided in accordance with Section 1-5.

A-21-3.1.3.2 Exception   In determining equivalency for existing buildings, conversions, modernizations, renovations, or unusual design concepts, the authority having jurisdiction may accept evaluations based on NFPA 101M, *Alternative Approaches to Life Safety*, Chapter 3, using the following mandatory safety requirements:

	CONTAIN-MENT S_a		EXTINGUISH-MENT S_b		PEOPLE MOVEMENT S_c	
ZONE LOCATION	New	Exist.	New	Exist.	New	Exist.
FIRST FLOOR	9	5	6	6	6	3
ABOVE OR BELOW FIRST FLOOR	14	9	8	8	9	5
OVER 75 ft (23 m) in HEIGHT	14	9	18	8	10	5

The difficulty in evacuating this type of facility is comparable to that of a health care facility. Therefore, the user is referred to the *Code* chapters dealing with that occupancy.

21-3.1.4 Minimum Construction Requirements.

21-3.1.4.1   Construction requirements for large facilities shall be as required by this section. Where noted as "fully sheathed," the interior shall be covered with lath and plaster, or materials with a 15-minute finish rating.

21-3.1.4.2   For the purpose of construction requirements, stories shall be counted starting at the primary level of exit discharge and ending at the highest occupied level. For the purposes of this section, the primary level of exit discharge of a building shall be that floor that is level with or above finished grade of the exterior wall line for 50 percent or more of its perimeter. Building levels below the primary level shall not be counted as a story in determining the height of a building.

21-3.1.4.3   The minimum construction requirements (*see 6-2.1*), based on the highest story normally used by board and care residents, are:

(a) *One- or Two-Story Facilities.*   Any construction type that meets the requirements for 1-hour or greater fire resistance rating, or is Type IV (2HH), or is fully sheathed, or is protected throughout by an approved automatic sprinkler system in accordance with 21-3.3.5.

Exception to (a):   One-story facilities having 30 or fewer residents, housing groups capable of prompt evacuation, may be of any construction.

(b) *Three- to Six-Story Facilities.*   Type I, II, or III construction that meets the requirements for 1-hour or greater fire resistance rating, and Type IV construction that is protected throughout by an automatic sprinkler system in accordance with 21-3.3.5, or any other type of construction that is both sheathed and protected throughout by an approved automatic sprinkler system in accordance with 21-3.3.5, other than Type V (000).

Exception to (b):   Three- or four-story facilities of Type V (000) construction that are both sheathed and protected throughout by an approved automatic sprinkler system in accordance with 21-3.3.5.

(c) *Facilities More Than Six Stories High.*   Any Type I or Type II (222) construction. Any Type II (111), Type III (211), or Type IV (2HH) construction that is protected throughout by an approved automatic sprinkler system in accordance with 21-3.3.5.

Exception to (a), (b), and (c):   Any building of Type I or Type II (222 or 111) construction may include roofing systems involving combustible supports, decking, or roofing provided: (1) the roof covering meets Class A requirements in accordance with NFPA 256, Standard Methods of Fire Tests of Roof Coverings, and (2) the roof is separated from all occupied portions of the building by a noncombustible floor assembly having at least a 2-hour fire resistance rating that includes at least 2½ in. (6.4 cm) of concrete or gypsum fill. To qualify for this Exception, the attic or other space so developed shall either be unused or protected throughout by an approved automatic sprinkler system in accordance with 21-3.3.5.

Minimum construction requirements are necessary since this chapter requires evacuation only to a "point of safety," and therefore, the residents of a large facility will frequently remain inside the building during a fire emergency. Therefore, the stability of the building must be maintained either by the use of fire resistant construction or by suppression of a fire automatically before it can threaten the stability of the building. (*See Table 21-3 for a summary of permissible construction types*). Note that in the Exception to item (a), buildings from which there is a reasonable expectation of prompt evacuation to the exterior of the building are exempted from the minimum construction requirements.

21-3.1.5 Occupant Load.   The occupant load in numbers of persons for whom exits are to be provided shall be determined on the basis of one person per 200 sq ft (18.6 sq m) gross floor area, or the maximum probable population of any room or section under consideration, whichever is greater. The occupant load of any open mezzanine or balcony shall be added to the occupant load of the floor below for the purpose of determining exit capability.

Table 21-3. Minimum Construction Standards for
Large Facilities with Prompt and Slow Evacuation Capability

Construction Type	Number of Stories						
	1	2	3	4	5	6	7+
Type I	X	X	X	X	X	X	X
Type II (222)	X	X	X	X	X	X	X
Type II (111)	X	X	X	X	X	X	(AS)
Type II (000)†	$^*/$(AS)	$^*/$(AS)	*(AS)	*(AS)	*(AS)	*(AS)	NP
Type III (211)	X	X	X	X	X	X	(AS)
Type III (200)†	$^*/$(AS)	$^*/$(AS)	*(AS)	*(AS)	*(AS)	*(AS)	NP
Type IV (2HH)	X	X	(AS)	(AS)	(AS)	(AS)	(AS)
Type V (111)	X	X	*(AS)	*(AS)	*(AS)	*(AS)	NP
Type V (000)†	$^*/$(AS)	$^*/$(AS)	*(AS)	*(AS)	NP	NP	NP

X = Permitted
NP = Not permitted
(AS) = Permitted if sprinklered
*(AS) = Permitted if sheathed *and* sprinklered
$^*/$(AS) = Permitted if sheathed *or* sprinklered
† = Permitted up to 1 story high, unsheathed and unsprinklered if housing 30 or fewer residents with prompt evacuation capability

If the actual occupant load of the facility exceeds one person per 200 sq ft (18.6 sq m), the exit capacity must be designed to meet the anticipated occupant load. The determination of actual occupant load should be based on the number of residents, staff, and visitors. However, the minimum exit capacity must not be less than that required for a density of one person per 200 sq ft (18.6 sq m).

Since mezzanines need not have their own exits, the occupant load of the mezzanine must be included with the occupant load of the floor below.

21-3.2 Means of Egress.

21-3.2.1   All means of egress shall be in accordance with Chapter 5.

21-3.2.2 Means of Egress Components.

21-3.2.2.1   Components of means of egress shall be limited to the types described in 21-3.2.2.2 through 21-3.2.2.7.

21-3.2.2.2 Doors.

(a) Doors shall comply with 5-2.1.

(b) No door in any means of egress shall be locked against egress when the building is occupied.

Exception: Special locking requirements complying with 5-2.1.6 are permitted.

Paragraph 21-3.2.2.2(b) prohibits a facility from having any door locked "against egress" while the building is occupied. The requirement permits a door to have a locking device that allows the door to be opened from within the building for the purpose of egress, but does not allow the door to be opened from outside the building. Ordinary double cylinder locks and chain locks would not meet these provisions.

The language of 5-2.1.5.1 is clear: "Locks, if provided, shall not require the use of a key, tool, special knowledge, or effort for operation from the inside of the building." This eliminates double cylinder locks and chain locks that require a key to be operated from the inside. Paragraph 5-2.1.5.3 calls for a simple operation to open the door; the presence of a two-handed knob operation, and the like, is specifically prohibited.

It is important to remember that the resident sleeping room doors are doors in the means of egress. However, 5-2.1.5.3 permits the sleeping room doors to have additional releasing actions. (*See 5-2.1.5.3 for details.*)

The Exception does permit the use of special locking arrangements that comply with 5-2.1.6.

(c) Every stairwell door shall allow reentry from the stairwell to the interior of the building or an automatic release shall be provided to unlock all stairwell doors to allow reentry. Such automatic release shall be activated with the initiation of the building fire alarm system. Also, they shall unlock upon loss of the power controlling the lock or locking mechanism.

(d) Revolving doors complying with 5-2.1.10 are permitted.

21-3.2.2.3 Stairs. Stairs shall comply with 5-2.2.

21-3.2.2.4 Smokeproof Enclosures. Smokeproof enclosures shall comply with 5-2.3.

21-3.2.2.5 Horizontal Exits. Horizontal exits shall comply with 5-2.4.

21-3.2.2.6 Ramps. Ramps shall comply with 5-2.5.

21-3.2.2.7 Exit Passageways. Exit passageways shall comply with 5-2.6.

21-3.2.3 Capacity of Means of Egress.

21-3.2.3.1 The capacity of means of egress shall be in accordance with Section 5-3.

21-3.2.3.2 Street floor exits shall be sufficient for the occupant load of the street floor plus the required capacity of stairs and ramps discharging on the street floor.

Paragraph 21-3.2.3.2 requires that street floor exit designs have sufficient width to provide for the intermingling of exits from the street floor with those exits discharging down from the upper floors and discharging up from the lower floors. Section 5-7 restricts the number and arrangement of stairs that discharge through the street floor.

Figure 21-5 shows an arrangement of multiple exits discharging on the street floor.

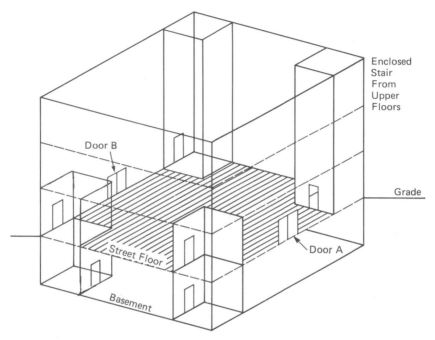

Figure 21-5. Capacity of Means of Egress in Accordance with 21-3.2.3.2. Required widths of Doors A and B are based on the number of people expected to use them: 0.2 inches (0.5 cm) per person on the street floor and for every person traveling down from the upper floors and up from the lower floors that must traverse the street floor to exit.

21-3.2.3.3 The width of corridors shall be sufficient for the occupant load served, but not less than 44 in. (112 cm).

Exception: Corridors serving an occupant load of less than 50 may be 36 in. (91 cm) in width.

21-3.2.4 Number of Exits. Not less than two exits shall be accessible from every floor, including floors below the level of exit discharge and occupied for public purposes. (*See also Section 5-4.*)

Similar to provisions for hotels, there are no exceptions to permit a single exit building.

21-3.2.5 Arrangement of Exits.

21-3.2.5.1   Access to all required exits shall be in accordance with Section 5-5.

21-3.2.5.2   Exits shall be so arranged that, from any corridor room door, exits will be accessible in at least two different directions.

Exception: Up to the first 35 ft (10.7 m) of exit travel from a corridor room door may be along a corridor with exit access in one direction only.

Note that this Exception actually describes a modified dead end or modified common path of travel. It is not always measured as a true dead end since the room door may not be at the end of the corridor; yet, it is not truly a common path of travel, since the distance is measured from the room door and not the most remote point. Figure 21-6 illustrates the method of measuring per 21-3.2.5.2 Exception.

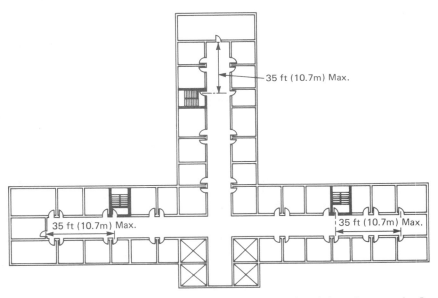

Figure 21-6.   The "Modified" Dead End Used in Board and Care Occupancies Is Illustrated by this Figure. Note that where a room door is not located at the end of the corridor, the actual dead end is longer. Since the elevator lobby has no room doors, it has no "modified" dead end.

21-3.2.5.3   Any room, or any suite of rooms, in excess of 2,000 sq ft (185 sq m) shall be provided with at least two exit access doors remote from each other.

Exception: Existing buildings.

21-3.2.6 Travel Distance to Exits.

21-3.2.6.1   Any exit as indicated in 21-3.2.4 shall be such that it will not be necessary to travel more than 100 ft (30 m) from the door of any room to reach the nearest exit. Travel distance to exits shall be measured in accordance with Section 5-6.

Exception No. 1:   Travel distance to exits may be increased to 200 ft (60 m) for exterior ways of exit access arranged in accordance with 5-5.3.

Exception No. 2:   Travel distance to exits may be increased to 200 ft (60 m) if the exit access and any portion of the building that is tributary to the exit access are protected throughout by an approved automatic sprinkler system. In addition, the portion of the building in which the 200 ft (60 m) travel distance is permitted shall be separated from the remainder of the building by construction having a fire resistance rating of not less than 1 hour for buildings not greater than three stories in height, and 2 hours for buildings greater than three stories in height.

See Figure 21-7.

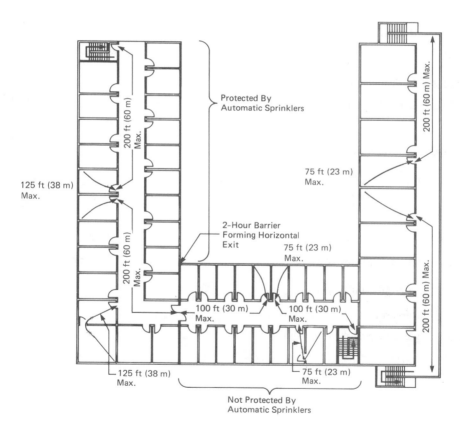

Figure 21-7.   Travel Distance in Large Facilities.

21-3.2.6.2   Travel within a room or suite or living unit to a corridor door shall not exceed 75 ft (23 m).

Exception: 125 ft (38 m) travel distance is allowed in buildings protected throughout by an approved automatic sprinkler system in accordance with 21-3.3.5.

Paragraph 21-3.2.6.2 limits the travel distance permitted within a room or suite. Note that the travel distance may be increased by 50 ft (15 m) in buildings protected throughout by an automatic sprinkler system.

21-3.2.7 Discharge from Exits.

21-3.2.7.1   Exit discharge shall comply with Section 5-7.

21-3.2.8 Illumination of Means of Egress.

21-3.2.8.1   Means of egress shall be illuminated in accordance with Section 5-8.

21-3.2.9 Emergency Lighting.

21-3.2.9.1   Emergency lighting in accordance with Section 5-9 shall be provided in all buildings with more than 25 rooms.

Exception: Where each guest room has a direct exit to the outside of the building at ground level, no emergency lighting shall be required.

The Exception to 21-3.2.9.1 does not apply to facilities with exterior balconies and stairs, but only to those with doors opening directly to grade.

21-3.2.10 Marking of Means of Egress.

21-3.2.10.1   Means of egress shall be marked in accordance with Section 5-10.

21-3.2.11 Special Features.

21-3.3 Protection.

21-3.3.1 Protection of Vertical Openings.

21-3.3.1.1   Every stairway, elevator shaft, and other vertical opening shall be enclosed or protected in accordance with 6-2.4.

Exception No. 1:   Unprotected vertical openings connecting not more than three floors may be permitted in accordance with the conditions of 6-2.4.4.

Exception No. 2:   An atrium may be utilized in accordance with 6-2.4.5.

Exception No. 3:   In existing buildings protected throughout by an approved automatic sprinkler system in accordance with 21-3.3.5, and where exits and required ways of travel thereto are adequately safeguarded against fire and smoke within the building, or where every individual room has direct access to an exterior exit without passing through any public corridor, the protection of vertical openings not part of required exits may be waived by the authority having jurisdiction to such extent as such openings do not endanger required means of egress.

Exception No. 4: In existing buildings not more than two stories in height, unprotected vertical openings may be permitted by the authority having jurisdiction if the building is protected throughout by an approved automatic sprinkler system in accordance with 21-3.3.5.

Exception No. 1 is the only condition under which an unprotected vertical opening may be permitted without automatic sprinkler protection throughout the building. However, 6-2.4.4 does require automatic sprinkler protection in a communicating space with ordinary hazard contents, and the space must be separated from the remainder of the building by a 1-hour fire barrier.

21-3.3.1.2   No floor below the level of exit discharge used only for storage, heating equipment, or purposes other than residential occupancy shall have unprotected openings to floors used for residential occupancy.

21-3.3.2 Protection from Hazards.

21-3.3.2.1   Any room containing high-pressure boilers, refrigerating machinery, transformers, or other service equipment subject to possible explosion shall not be located directly under or directly adjacent to exits. All such rooms shall be effectively cut off from other parts of the building as specified in Section 6-4.

21-3.3.2.2   Every hazardous area shall be separated from other parts of the building by construction having a fire resistance rating of at least 1 hour, and communicating openings shall be protected by approved self-closing fire doors, or such area shall be equipped with automatic fire extinguishing systems. Hazardous areas include, but are not limited to:

Boiler and heater rooms
Laundries
Repair shops

Rooms or spaces used for storage of combustible supplies and equipment in quantities deemed hazardous by the authority having jurisdiction.

The list in 21-3.3.2.2 is not all-inclusive. It is the responsibility of the authority having jurisdiction to determine which areas are hazardous. Hazardous areas are spaces with contents that, because of their basic nature or because of the quantity of combustible materials involved, represent a significantly higher hazard than would otherwise be typical in residential board and care facilities.

21-3.3.3 Interior Finish.   Interior wall and ceiling finish within exit enclosures in new buildings shall be Class A. In all other areas and in existing buildings, interior wall and ceiling finish shall be Class A or Class B in accordance with Section 6-5. Interior floor finish shall be Class I or Class II in corridors and exits.

Exception: Previously installed floor covering, subject to the approval of the authority having jurisdiction.

21-3.3.4 Detection, Alarm, and Communications Systems.

21-3.3.4.1 General.   A fire alarm system in accordance with Section 7-6 shall be provided.

Exception: Existing board and care facilities where each sleeping room has exterior exit access in accordance with 5-5.3, and the building is not greater than 3 stories in height.

21-3.3.4.2 Initiation.   Initiation of the required fire alarm system shall be by:

(a) Manual means in accordance with 7-6.2, and

Exception to (a): In existing board and care facilities, a manual means, as specified in 7-6.2, in excess of the alarm station at a constantly attended location per (b) below, may be waived where there are other effective means (such as complete automatic sprinkler or automatic detection systems) for notification of fire as required.

(b) A manual fire alarm station located at a convenient central control point under continuous supervision by responsible employees, and

(c) Any automatic sprinkler system, and

Exception to (c): In existing buildings, automatic sprinkler systems that are not required by another section of this Code need not initiate the fire alarm system.

(d) Any required detection system.

Exception to (d): Sleeping room smoke detectors are not required to initiate the building fire alarm system.

> Paragraph 21-3.3.4.2(b) requires that, in addition to the normal distribution of manual pull stations (*see* 7-6.2), a location such as that of the telephone operator must also have a manual pull station. The intent is to have a pull station at the location residents would call in an emergency.

21-3.3.4.3 Annunciator Panel.   An annunciator panel connected with the fire alarm system shall be provided. The location of the annunciator shall be approved by the authority having jurisdiction.

Exception No. 1: Buildings not greater than two stories in height and with not more than 50 sleeping rooms.

Exception No. 2: Existing Buildings.

21-3.3.4.4 Occupant Notification.   Occupant notification shall be provided automatically, without delay, by internal audible alarm in accordance with 7-6.3.

> Distribution of audible alarm devices in residential board and care facilities must be thoroughly reviewed. In most new construction, corridor walls are of such character (soundproofed) that a sounding device would be required in each room to provide adequate alarm sound levels; otherwise, the sound level in the corridor would have to approach dangerous decibel levels in order to provide levels adequate to awaken residents in their rooms.

21-3.3.4.5   High rise buildings shall be provided with an approved means of voice communication in accordance with 7-6.3.

Exception No. 1: Buildings equipped with a public address system.

Exception No. 2: Existing board and care facilities.

21-3.3.4.6* Fire Department Notification. Provisions shall be made for the immediate notification of the public fire department by either telephone or other means in case of fire. Where there is no public fire department, this notification shall go to the private fire brigade.

A-21-3.3.4.6 *(See A-16-3.4.3.4.)*

This paragraph does not require a direct fire alarm connection to the fire department. If a telephone is provided, the telephone would have to be equipped for direct outside dial without going through a switchboard and could not be a pay phone.

21-3.3.4.7 Smoke Detectors. Each sleeping room shall be provided with an approved single station smoke detector in accordance with 7-6.2.9, powered from the building electrical service.

Exception No. 1: Existing battery powered detectors, rather than house electric service powered detectors, shall be accepted where, in the opinion of the authority having jurisdiction, the facility has demonstrated testing, maintenance, and battery replacement programs that insure power reliability to the detectors.

Exception No. 2: Existing board and care facilities having an existing corridor smoke detection system in accordance with Section 7-6, connected to the building fire alarm system.

The purpose of the room detectors is to alert the occupants of a sleeping room to the presence of a fire originating in that room. The detectors would not normally be tied into the building fire alarm. [*See 21-3.3.4.2(d) Exception.*] Upon leaving the room, the door would shut behind the occupant (*see 21-3.3.6.6*), and the occupant would pull a manual alarm station. Failure to sound the alarm manually would be somewhat compensated for by corridor smoke detectors or by automatic sprinklers. (*See 21-3.3.4.8, 21-3.3.5.*)

Exception No. 1 applies to existing battery-powered detectors only, and not to all existing facilities. Battery-powered detectors are to be permitted only if they already exist and the facility can document that the detectors are properly maintained and tested so as to increase the reliability of the detectors.

Exception No. 2 recognizes that this was the previous requirement of the *Code.* Note that the installation of a corridor smoke detection system does not eliminate the need for single station smoke detectors in each room, but if a building already has a corridor smoke detection system, then single station smoke detectors do not have to be added.

21-3.3.4.8 Smoke Detection System. All corridors and common spaces shall be provided with smoke detectors in accordance with NFPA 72E, *Standard on Automatic Fire Detectors,* arranged to initiate an alarm that is audible in all sleeping areas.

Exception No. 1: Detectors may be omitted from common spaces in facilities protected throughout by an approved automatic sprinkler system in accordance with 21-3.3.5.

Exception No. 2: Unenclosed corridors, passageways, balconies, colonnades, or other arrangements where one or more sides along the long dimension is fully or extensively open to the exterior at all times.

A system of smoke detectors is required in the corridors and in any common spaces of any facility that is not fully sprinklered. Note that the sprinkler Exception does not apply to 21-3.3.4.7. The Committee has specifically emphasized in its discussion of this issue that it is not equating sprinklers and smoke detectors, but that it does feel that a *fully* sprinklered building is an adequate alternative to smoke detectors in *common spaces.* If the facility is built "motel style," using exterior access corridors, smoke detection is not required in the exterior corridors.

21-3.3.5 Extinguishment Requirements.

21-3.3.5.1* Automatic Extinguishment Systems.   Where an automatic sprinkler system is installed either for total or partial building coverage, the system shall be installed in accordance with Section 7-7 and shall activate the fire alarm system in accordance with Section 7-6.

Exception: Automatic sprinklers may be omitted in small compartmented areas such as closets not over 24 sq ft (2.2 sq m) and bathrooms not over 55 sq ft (5.1 sq m), provided such spaces are finished with lath and plaster, or materials with a 15-minute finish rating.

A-21-3.3.5.1   This type of building is outside the scope of NFPA 13D, *Standard for the Installation of Sprinkler Systems in One- and Two-Family Dwellings and Mobile Homes.* In any case, where the features of an NFPA 13D system are desirable to such a facility, which may be considered comparable to a one- and two-family dwelling, the authority having jurisdiction may be contacted under Section 1-5 of the *Code.*

This paragraph does not require the installation of automatic sprinklers. The purpose of the paragraph is to establish the criteria to be followed if the facility chooses to use the sprinkler alternatives provided in this chapter. The *Code* does provide significant incentives to install sprinklers with regard to: building construction (21-3.1.4.3); travel distance (21-3.2.6.1 and 21-3.2.6.2); exit discharge (21-3.2.7); vertical openings (21-3.3.1); hazardous areas (21-3.3.2.2); interior finish (21-3.3.3); corridor smoke detection (21-3.3.4.8); corridor walls (21-3.3.6.1); door closers (21-3.3.6.6); smoke barriers (21-3.3.7.1); and operable windows (21-3.4.1).

21-3.3.5.2   All new high rise buildings shall be protected throughout by an approved supervised automatic sprinkler system in accordance with 21-3.3.5.

21-3.3.5.3 Portable Fire Extinguishers.   Portable fire extinguishers in accordance with 7-7.4.1 shall be provided near hazardous areas.

21-3.3.6 Corridors and Separation of Sleeping Rooms.

21-3.3.6.1   Access shall be provided from every resident use area to at least one means of egress that is separated from all other rooms or spaces by fire barriers complying with 21-3.3.6.3 through 21-3.3.6.6.

Exception No. 1: Rooms or spaces, other than sleeping rooms, if those rooms or spaces are protected throughout by an approved automatic sprinkler system installed in accordance with 21-3.3.5.

Exception No. 2: Rooms or spaces, other than sleeping rooms, if those rooms or spaces are provided with a smoke detection and alarm system connected to activate the building evacuation alarm. Furnishings, finishes, and furniture, in combination with all other combustibles within the space, are of such minimum quantity and are so arranged that a fully developed fire is unlikely to occur.

Exception No. 3: Facilities housing groups capable of prompt evacuation in buildings not over two stories in height that have at least two remotely located means of escape that do not involve windows. The arrangement shall be such that there is at least one such means of escape from each sleeping room that provides a path of travel to the outside without traversing any corridor or other spaces exposed to unprotected vertical openings or common living spaces, such as living rooms and kitchens.

It is permissible, under some circumstances, to have access to an exit through a sitting room, TV room, living room, or other common use space. However, because such rooms have been the location of origin of numerous multiple-death fires, this paragraph is intended to preclude having all exit access paths exposed to a fire in such a space. Exceptions are provided so that all egress paths may be exposed to the common use space if that space is furnished and finished with materials that will not result in flashover in the room and if early warning smoke detection is provided, or if the space is sprinklered. (*See Figure 21-8 for examples.*)

21-3.3.6.2   Sleeping rooms shall be separated from corridors and other common spaces by fire barriers complying with 21-3.3.6.3 through 21-3.3.6.6.

21-3.3.6.3   Fire barriers required by 21-3.3.6.1 or 21-3.3.6.2 shall have a fire resistance rating of not less than 1 hour.

Exception No. 1: In existing buildings and conversions such fire barriers shall have a fire resistance rating of not less than 20 minutes.

Exception No. 2: In buildings protected throughout by an approved automatic sprinkler system installed in accordance with 21-3.3.5, such barriers shall have a fire resistance rating of not less than 30 minutes in new construction and in existing buildings, no fire resistance rating is required.

Exception No. 3: In buildings not greater than two stories in height, housing groups capable of prompt evacuation, with a maximum of 30 residents, such barriers shall have a fire resistance rating of not less than 30 minutes in new construction, and in existing facilities, no fire resistance rating is required.

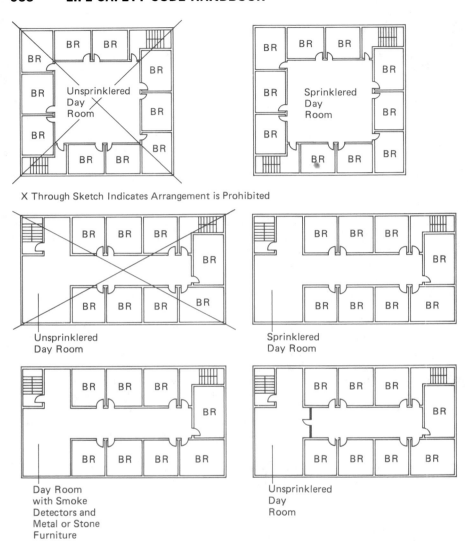

X Through Sketch Indicates Arrangement is Prohibited

Examples of Permitted and Prohibited Arrangements

Figure 21-8.   Examples of Permitted and Prohibited Arrangements.

In general, sleeping rooms in new facilities must be separated from corridors by construction having a fire resistance rating of at least 1 hour. If the building is protected throughout by an automatic sprinkler system or if it is a moderately sized prompt facility (Exception No. 3), the corridor walls may have a 30-minute fire resistance rating.

In existing board and care facilities and in buildings being converted to a board and care facility, the sleeping rooms must be separated from corridors by construction having a fire resistance rating of at least 20 minutes. Therefore, existing hotels and health care facilities can be converted to a board and care facility without requiring replacement of corridor walls, provided the hotel or health care facility has complied with the applicable provisions of the *Code*. If such existing building is protected throughout by an automatic sprinkler system or if it is a moderately sized prompt facility (Exception No. 3), the corridor walls need not have a fire resistance rating but shall be capable of resisting the passage of smoke.

21-3.3.6.4   Doors in fire barriers required by 21-3.3.6.1 or 21-3.3.6.2 shall have a fire protection rating of not less than 20 minutes.

Exception No. 1:   Existing 1¾-in. (4.4-cm) solid bonded wood core doors.

Exception No. 2:   In buildings protected throughout by an approved automatic sprinkler system installed in accordance with 21-3.3.5, existing doors in renovations and conversions, and doors in existing buildings that are nonrated may be continued in use.

Exception No. 3:   Walls that are required to only resist the passage of smoke, without a fire resistance rating, may have doors that resist the passage of smoke without a fire protection rating.

The intent of Exception No. 2 is to minimize the impact of converting from a health care facility or hotel to a board and care facility.

21-3.3.6.5   Walls and doors required by 21-3.3.6.1 and 21-3.3.6.2 shall be constructed to resist the passage of smoke. There shall be no louvers, transfer grilles, operable transoms, or other air passages penetrating such walls or doors except properly installed heating and utility installations.

21-3.3.6.6   Doors in walls required by 21-3.3.6.1 and 21-3.3.6.2 shall be self-closing or automatic-closing in accordance with 5-2.1.8. Doors in walls separating sleeping rooms from corridors shall be automatic closing in accordance with 5-2.1.8.

Exception No. 1:   Doors to sleeping rooms that have occupant control locks such that access is normally restricted to the occupants or staff personnel may be self-closing.

Exception No. 2:   In buildings protected throughout by an approved automatic sprinkler system installed in accordance with 21-3.3.5, doors, other than doors to hazardous areas, vertical openings, and exit enclosures are not required to be self-closing or automatic-closing.

A reliable means of closing sleeping room doors during a fire is required unless the building is sprinklered. Generally, automatic, smoke-activated closers will be required. In facilities in which the residents control the privacy lock on their own sleeping room doors, a simple self-closer (e.g., spring hinges or a hydraulic door check) is acceptable, because, in practice, such doors are usually kept closed. Therefore, the likelihood that the door will be chocked or blocked open is minimized.

21-3.3.7 Subdivision of Building Spaces.

21-3.3.7.1 Every sleeping room floor shall be divided into at least two smoke compartments of approximately the same size, with smoke barriers in accordance with Section 6-3. Smoke dampers are not required.

Additional smoke barriers shall be provided such that the maximum travel distance from a sleeping room corridor door to a smoke barrier shall not exceed 150 ft (45 m).

Exception No. 1: Buildings protected throughout by an approved automatic sprinkler system in accordance with 21-3.3.5.

Exception No. 2: Where each sleeping room is provided with exterior ways of exit access arranged in accordance with 5-5.3.

Exception No. 3: Smoke barriers are not required where the aggregate corridor length on each floor is not more than 150 ft (45 m).

The smoke barrier provides for horizontal movement of people and limits the number of rooms — and therefore people — exposed to a single fire that may be blocking a corridor. Since no fire rating is required for the barrier and smoke dampers are not required, the provision of smoke barriers is not overly burdensome. The exception for automatic sprinklers again reflects the excellent life loss record of buildings so equipped.

A horizontal exit may be used to comply with 21-3.3.7 and thereby serve more than one function. Also, if the smoke barrier has at least a 20-minute fire resistance rating, protection is provided throughout the building by an automatic sprinkler system, and the smoke compartment has access to an exit that does not require return to the fire area, the smoke compartment may be considered a point of safety. (*See definition for "point of safety."*)

21-3.4 Special Provisions.

21-3.4.1* Operable Windows. Each guest room shall be provided with at least one outside window. Such windows shall be openable from the inside, without the use of tools, and provide a clear opening of not less than 20 in. (50.8 cm) in width, 24 in. (61 cm) in height, and 5.7 sq ft (.53 sq m) in area. The bottom of the opening shall not be more than 44 in. (112 cm) above the floor. In rooms located greater than six stories above grade, the openable clear height, width, and area of the window may be modified to the dimensions necessary for ventilation.

Exception No. 1: Buildings protected throughout by an approved automatic sprinkler system in accordance with 21-3.3.5.

Exception No. 2: Where a guest room has a door leading directly to the outside of the building.

Exception No. 3: Buildings provided with an approved engineered smoke control system in accordance with Section 7-3.

Exception No. 4: Existing Buildings.

A-21-3.4.1 Windows may serve as a means of emergency escape, particularly where ladders can be raised by fire fighters or others. Even where the location is such as to preclude the use of windows for escape purposes, they may provide air for breathing in a smoke-filled room while trapped occupants are awaiting rescue. Windows should have sills not too high above the floor; windows lower than 44 in. (112 cm) above the floor are preferable.

Where awning- or hopper-type windows are used, they should be so hinged or subdivided as to provide a clear opening of at least 5.7 sq ft (.53 sq m). Where storm windows, screens, or burglar guards are used, these should be provided with quick-opening devices so that they may be readily opened from the inside for emergency egress.

> An operable window can allow an occupant access to fresh air and/or rescue. If a window is opened and smoke is drawn into the room, an operable window can be closed, but a fixed window that has been broken cannot be closed. The windows specified herein are the same as those in other residential occupancies and in schools. The door described in Exception No. 2 does not have to be an exit access door but can be a door to a balcony, as this would serve the same purpose as a window.

21-3.4.2 Operating Features.   *(See Chapter 31.)*

21-3.5 Building Services.

21-3.5.1 Utilities.   Utilities shall comply with the provisions of Section 7-1.

21-3.5.2 Heating, Ventilation, and Air Conditioning.

21-3.5.2.1   Heating, ventilating, and air conditioning equipment shall comply with the provisions of Section 7-2.

21-3.5.2.2   No stove or combustion heater shall be so located as to block escape in case of fire arising from malfunctioning of the stove or heater.

21-3.5.2.3   Unvented fuel-fired heaters shall not be used in any room used for sleeping purposes.

21-3.5.3 Elevators, Dumbwaiters, and Vertical Conveyors.

21-3.5.3.1   Elevators, dumbwaiters, and vertical conveyors shall comply with the provisions of Section 7-4.

21-3.5.3.2*   In new high rise buildings, one elevator shall be provided with a protected power supply and be available for use by the fire department in case of emergency.

A-21-3.5.3.2   *(See A-16-5.3.)*

21-3.5.4 Rubbish Chutes, Incinerators, and Laundry Chutes.   Rubbish chutes, incinerators, and laundry chutes shall comply with the provisions of Section 7-5.

SECTION 21-4   SUITABILITY OF AN APARTMENT BUILDING TO HOUSE A BOARD AND CARE OCCUPANCY

Board and care occupancies in apartment buildings will usually be small facilities housing 16 or fewer residents. It is intended that the board and care occupancy be made to conform to the requirements of Section 21-2 for small board and care facilities. In the unusual case where an apartment houses a large board and care facility, it would be reasonable for the authority having jurisdiction, using 1-4.3, to apply the provisions of Section 21-3 to the apartment. In addition, the apartment building in which the facility is housed is required to comply with the requirements for apartment buildings in Chapters 18 or 19 and the additional criteria presented in this section.

21-4.1 General.

21-4.1.1 Scope.   This section applies to apartment buildings that have one or more individual apartments used as a board and care occupancy. This section determines the suitability of such buildings to house a residential board and care facility. The suitability of such buildings for apartments not used for board and care occupancies is covered in Chapter 18 or 19, as appropriate.

21-4.1.2   Requirements for individual apartments used as a residential board and care occupancy are specified in Section 21-2, Small Facilities. Egress from the apartment into the common building corridor shall be considered acceptable egress from the board and care facility.

See commentary following the section title.

21-4.1.3 Requirements Based on Evacuation Capability.

21-4.1.3.1   Apartment buildings housing board and care facilities shall comply with requirements of 21-4.

Exception*: Facilities where the authority having jurisdiction has determined that equivalent safety for housing a residential board and care facility is provided in accordance with Section 1-5.

A-21-4.1.3.1 Exception   In determining equivalency for existing buildings, conversions, modernizations, renovations, or unusual design concepts, the authority having jurisdiction may accept evaluations based on NFPA 101M, *Alternative Approaches to Life Safety*, Chapter 6.

21-4.1.3.2   All facilities shall meet the requirements of Chapter 18 or 19, as appropriate, and the additional requirements of 21-4.

21-4.1.4 Minimum Construction Requirements.   In addition to the requirements in Chapter 18 or 19, as appropriate, apartment buildings housing residential board and care facilities housing groups classed as prompt or slow shall meet the construction requirements of 21-3.1.4, and those housing groups classed as impractical to evacuate shall meet the construction requirements of 12-1.6 or 13-1.6 as appropriate. In applying the construction requirements, the height shall be determined by the height of the residential board and care facility above the primary level of exit discharge.

21-4.2 Means of Egress.   The requirements of Section 18-2 or 19-2, as appropriate, apply only to parts of the means of egress serving the apartment(s) used as residential board and care occupancy.

21-4.3 Protection.

21-4.3.1 Interior Finish.   The requirements of 18-3.3 or 19-3.3, as appropriate, apply only to parts of the means of egress serving the apartment(s) used as a residential board and care occupancy.

21-4.3.2 Construction of Corridor Walls.   The requirements of 18-3.6 or 19-3.6, as appropriate, apply only to corridors serving the residential board and care facility including that portion of the corridor wall separating the residential board and care facility from the common corridor.

21-4.3.3 Subdivision of Building Spaces.   The requirements of 18-3.7 or 19-3.7, as appropriate, apply to those stories with an apartment(s) used as a residential board and care occupancy.

21-4.4 Operating Features.   (*See Chapter 31.*)

REFERENCES CITED IN COMMENTARY

[1]*Fire Safety in Boarding Homes,* NFPA SPP-76, Quincy, MA, 1982.

[2]*Boarding Home Fires: New Jersey,* Hearing before the Select Committee on Aging, House of Representatives, Ninety-seventh Congress, Comm. Pub. No. 97-304, March 9, 1981.

[3]*Toward a National Plan for the Chronically Mentally Ill,* Bethesda, MD, National Institute of Mental Health, 1980.

[4]NFPA 13, *Standard for The Installation of Sprinkler Systems,* National Fire Protection Association, Quincy, MA, 1987.

[5]NFPA 13D, *Standard for the Installation of Sprinkler Systems in One- and Two-Family Dwellings and Mobile Homes,* National Fire Protection Association, Quincy, MA, 1984.

22 ONE- AND TWO-FAMILY DWELLINGS

The requirements of Chapter 22 are important even if they are not enforced in one- and two-family dwellings. Both Chapters 18 and 19 require that all living units (apartments) comply with Section 22-2. In addition, Chapters 16 and 17 require windows complying with 22-2.1.2 for hotels and dormitories as does Chapter 20 for lodging and rooming houses and Chapter 21 for board and care facilities.

SECTION 22-1   GENERAL REQUIREMENTS

22-1.1 Application.

22-1.1.1   This chapter establishes life safety requirements for all one- and two-family dwellings. One- and two-family dwellings include buildings containing not more than two dwelling units in which each living unit is occupied by members of a single family with no more than three outsiders, if any, accommodated in rented rooms.

If more than three outsiders are accommodated, the requirements of Chapter 20 apply.

Formal Interpretation 76-138
Reference: 22-1.1.1

Question 1: Is it to be interpreted that "occupied by members of a single family" literally means all the people living in the same house; household?

Answer 1: See response below.

Question 2: Is it the intent of the Committee that "occupied by members of a single family" be literally interpreted as a social unit consisting of parents and children that they rear; the children of the same parents; and one's husband (or wife) and children?

Answer 2: See response below.

Question 3: Is it the intent of the Committee that "occupied by members of a single family" be literally interpreted as a group of people related by ancestry or marriage; relatives?

Answer 3: See response below.

Question 4: Is it the intent of the Committee that "occupied by members of a single family" be literally interpreted as all those claiming descent from a common ancestor; tribe or clan; lineage?

Answer 4: See response below.

Question 5: Was it the intent of the Committee when publishing NFPA *101, Life Safety Code,* 22-1.1.1, to include as a member of a single family a person who is: a longtime friend, not of blood or marriage relationship, not paying rent, but who contributes or has contributed monies to the owner of the house, thus subsidizing house operation expenses?

Answer 5: See response below.

Response: It is the intent of the Committee that "occupied by members of a single family" be literally interpreted as a social unit consisting of parents and children that they rear, the children of the same parents, and one's husband (or wife) and including children they adopt. It should be noted, however, that 22-1.1.1 does allow for up to three outsiders to be accommodated.

Issue Edition: 1976
Reference: 11-1.3.1(e)
Date: September 1980

22-1.1.2   The requirements of this chapter are applicable to new buildings and to existing or modified buildings according to the provisions of Section 1-4 of this *Code.*

22-1.2 Mixed Occupancies.

22-1.2.1   Where another type of occupancy occurs in the same building as a residential occupancy, the requirements of 1-4.7 of this *Code* shall be applicable.

22-1.2.2   For requirements on mixed mercantile and residential occupancies, see 24-1.2 or 25-1.2.

22-1.3 Definitions.

22-1.3.1   Terms applicable to this chapter are defined in Chapter 3 of this *Code;* where necessary, other terms will be defined in the text as they may occur.

22-1.4 Classification of Occupancy.   *(See 22-1.1.1.)*

22-1.5 Classification of Hazard of Contents.

22-1.5.1   The contents of residential occupancies shall be classified as ordinary hazard in accordance with 4-2.1.

NFPA 13, *Standard for the Installation of Sprinkler Systems,*[1] would classify the contents as "light" for the purpose of designing of extinguishing systems. The difference in classification is based on the threat to life or life safety (ordinary) versus the threat to the extinguishing capability of the automatic sprinkler system (light).

It is not the intent of this paragraph to prohibit the use of NFPA 13D, *Standard for the Installation of Sprinkler Systems in One- and Two-Family Dwellings and Mobile Homes.*[2]

22-1.6 Minimum Construction Requirements.   No Special Requirements.

22-1.7 Occupant Load.   No Requirements.

SECTION 22-2*   MEANS OF ESCAPE REQUIREMENTS

A-22-2   The Committee has adopted the phrase "means of escape" to indicate a way out of a residential unit that does not conform to the strict definition of means of egress but does meet the intent of the definition by providing an alternative way out of a building. (*See A-5-1.1.1.*)

22-2.1 Number of Means of Escape.

22-2.1.1 Primary Means of Escape.   In any dwelling or living unit of two rooms or more, every bedroom and living area shall have at least two means of escape or alternate protection, at least one of which shall be a door or stairway providing a means of unobstructed travel to the outside of the dwelling at street or ground level. No bedroom or living area shall be accessible by only a ladder or folding stairs or through a trap door.

> The Committee, recognizing that it is rare to find a *Code*-complying exit (or an enclosed vertical opening) in a single-family dwelling, called for the quality of egress that is normally found in dwelling design. Note that a "door or stairway providing a means of unobstructed travel to the outside" covers nearly every egress arrangement found in a dwelling today.
>
> Paragraph 22-2.1.1 prohibits the addition of a bedroom or den in an attic if the space is accessible only by a trap door or folding ladder. Direct stair access is required.

22-2.1.2* Second Means of Escape.   The second means of escape or alternate protection shall be one of the following:

(a) A door, stairway, passage, or hall providing a way of unobstructed travel to the outside of the dwelling at street or ground level that is independent of and remote from the primary means of escape.

(b) A passage through adjacent nonlockable spaces independent of and remote from the primary means of escape to any approved means of escape.

(c) An outside window or door operable from the inside without the use of tools and providing a clear opening of not less than 20 in. (50.8 cm) in width, 24 in. (61 cm) in height, and 5.7 sq ft (.53 sq m) in area. The bottom of the opening shall not be more than 44 in. (112 cm) off the floor. Such means of escape shall be acceptable if:

1. The window is within 20 ft (6.1 m) of grade, or

2. The window is directly accessible to fire department rescue apparatus as approved by the authority having jurisdiction, or

3. The window or door opens onto an exterior balcony.

(d) The bedroom or living area shall be separated from all other parts of the living unit by construction having a fire resistance rating of at least 20 minutes and shall be equipped with a door that resists passage of fire for at least 20 minutes and is designed and installed to minimize smoke leakage. A means of providing smoke venting and fresh air to the occupants shall be provided.

Exception No. 1: *A second means of escape or alternate protection is not required:*

(a) If the bedroom or living area has a door leading directly to the outside of the building, at or to grade level; or

(b) If the dwelling unit is protected throughout by an approved automatic sprinkler system in accordance with NFPA 13, Standard for the Installation of Sprinkler Systems, or NFPA 13D, Standard for the Installation of Sprinkler Systems in One- and Two-Family Dwellings and Mobile Homes, as applicable.

Exception No. 2: Existing approved means of escape may be continued in use.

A-22-2.1.2 For use of emergency escape devices, refer to A-5-1.1.1.

The provisions of 22-2.1.2 require that every bedroom and every living area (living room, family room, den, etc.) be provided with a second means of escape above and beyond that provided for compliance with 22-2.1.1.

There are only two exceptions to the requirement for a second means of escape from each bedroom or living area. These are: (1) if the bedroom or living area has a door opening directly to the outside of the building (this is not a very common arrangement, but it may occur); or (2) where the dwelling unit is protected throughout by an approved automatic sprinkler system in accordance with NFPA 13, *Standard for the Installation of Sprinkler Systems,*[1] or NFPA 13D, *Standard for the Installation of Sprinkler Systems in One- and Two-Family Dwellings and Mobile Homes.*[2] The latter exception would probably be the most practical and common way to avoid having to provide the second means of escape; for instance, in an underground dwelling without windows or a dwelling with nonconforming windows, or in an apartment building containing an apartment unit(s) that does not have windows complying with item (c). These types of dwellings could be protected in accordance with NFPA 13,[1] which allows the use of NFPA 13D[2] within the apartment. Note that this does not require the entire apartment building to be sprinklered, but only the apartment unit that does not have the conforming windows.

The primary purpose of the second means of escape is to allow a person to have an alternate escape route when a fire and/or smoke blocks the normal way out of the dwelling unit. Paragraph 22-2.1.2 (a) through (d) of the *Code* provides for four different types of second means of escape.

(1) It is the intent of item (a) that this door, stairway, passage, or hall be independent of and remote from the primary means of escape required in 22-2.1.1. If a room has a second door that leads to the same hallway as

the first door, little, if any, additional safety is provided, since a fire in the living room or other common space of the dwelling unit would block egress from both these doors at approximately the same time. If the corridor within the dwelling unit is separated from all living spaces and leads to two separate ways out of the dwelling unit, it may be judged that it does, in fact, lead to two separate, independent, and remote means of escape. Although two doors leading out of a sleeping room may not be practical or effective in a single-family dwelling, Figure 22-1 illustrates a method that may utilize this provision within an apartment building. (*See Figures 22-1 and 22-2.*)

(2) Item (b) was new to the 1985 Edition of the *Code*; however, it could be interpreted as having been allowed as a subpart of item (a) in previous editions. Figure 22-3 illustrates an example of how this provision may be used.

(3) The use of an operable window of the minimum dimensions specified in item (c) has been allowed in prior editions of the *Code* and continues to be allowed in the 1988 Edition. Figure 22-5 illustrates the minimum dimensions allowed for escape windows. Note that it is not possible to use the two minimum dimensions and still comply with the minimum area dimension. The 1985 Edition of the *Code* added restrictions to the use of the outside window. These restrictions will have relatively little impact on the typical one- and two-family dwelling but will have significant impact on apartment buildings. The outside window must comply with one of the following three methods. The first method makes it possible to jump from the window [the window must be within 20 ft (6.1 m) of grade]. The second method allows the fire department to rescue an occupant from a window. This can be achieved by either aerial ladder apparatus or ground ladders or by other means acceptable to the authority having jurisdiction. Depending on fire department vehicle access and equipment available to the fire department, a low rise apartment building could utilize standard operable windows as a secondary means of escape from apartment unit bedrooms and living areas. The third method allows an occupant to reach an exterior balcony to breathe fresh air while awaiting either rescue or fire extinguishment. This method could be utilized either in low rise or high rise apartment buildings. (*See Figures 22-1, 22-3, and 22-4.*)

Exception No. 2 to 22-2.1.2 allows an existing means of escape, approved by the authority having jurisdiction, to continue to be used. With the exception of those instances where the means of escape is of extremely poor quality, this would limit the impact on existing buildings when they are required to comply with 22-2.1.2.

(4) Item (d) was a new provision in the 1985 *Code* and is, in fact, a second means of alternate protection rather than a second means of escape. This provision could be utilized either in underground dwellings or in dwelling units of apartment buildings that cannot comply with 22-2.1.2(a), (b), or (c) and that are not exempted from the second means of escape or alternate protection. Note that a means of supplying smoke venting and fresh air must be provided. This would probably be achieved by provision of a window in the bedroom or living area, which need not

comply with item (c) but from which a reasonable level of smoke venting and amount of fresh air can be provided. (*See Figure 22-4.*)

High rise apartment buildings that are not provided with exterior balconies accessible from every living area or bedroom do not comply with item (c); therefore, unless they comply with items (a), (b), or (d), these buildings would have to comply with one of the two exceptions for the second means of escape. Since item (a) of Exception No. 1 would be impractical in a high rise apartment building, the apartment units involved would have to be sprinklered under item (b) of Exception No. 1. If this is done, it would be most practical to sprinkler the entire building and use the appropriate exceptions provided for sprinklered buildings in Chapters 18 or 19.

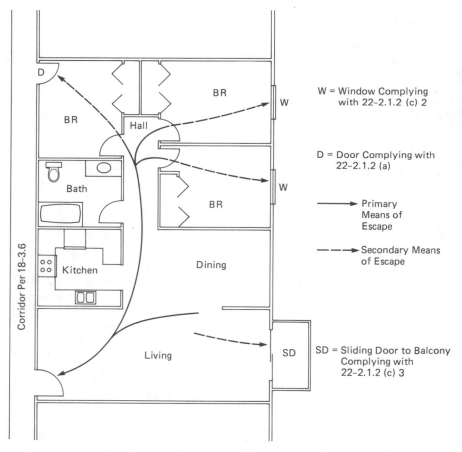

Figure 22-1.   Illustrates the Use of 22-2.1.2(a).   An example of an apartment that has a bedroom (*see upper left corner*) without a window or where the window does not comply with 22-2.1.2(c). The second means of escape from the other bedrooms and living room in this apartment comply with 22-2.1.2(c).

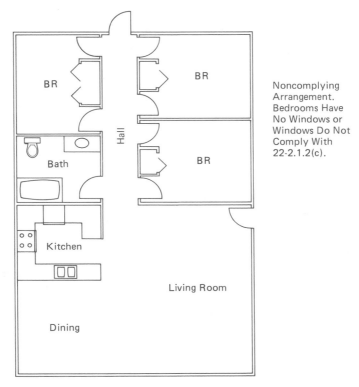

Figure 22-2.   Figure 22-2 Illustrates a Noncomplying Arrangement.   Although each bedroom has two doors, both doors lead to the same hall, which would be affected by a single fire in the living room, dining room, or kitchen. The second door from each bedroom adds little, if any, life safety. This arrangement, which may be found in an underground dwelling, would require sprinkler protection in accordance with NFPA 13, *Standard for the Installation of Sprinkler Systems,*[1] or NFPA 13D, *Standard for the Installation of Sprinkler Systems in One- and Two-Family Dwellings and Mobile Homes.*[2]

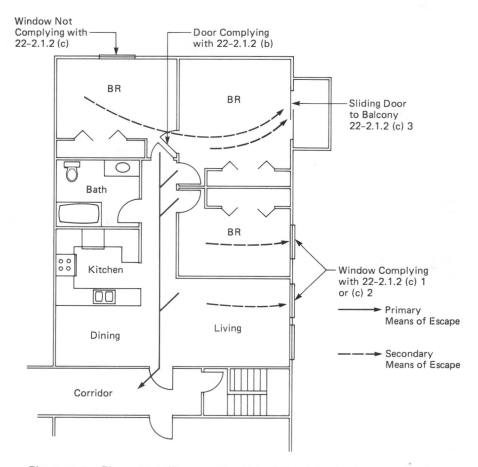

Figure 22-3.   Figure 22-3 Illustrates One Use of 22-2.1.2(b).   An example of an apartment unit in which the bedroom has a window that does not comply with 22-2.1.2(c) and in which there is no door to the corridor (as in Figure 22-1).   The balcony door in the upper right bedroom would not be needed if the apartment were sprinklered in accordance with NFPA 13, *Standard for the Installation of Sprinkler Systems*,[1] or NFPA 13D, *Standard for the Installation of Sprinkler Systems in One- and Two-Family Dwellings and Mobile Homes*[2] or if the bedroom in question were protected in accordance with 22-2.1.2(d).

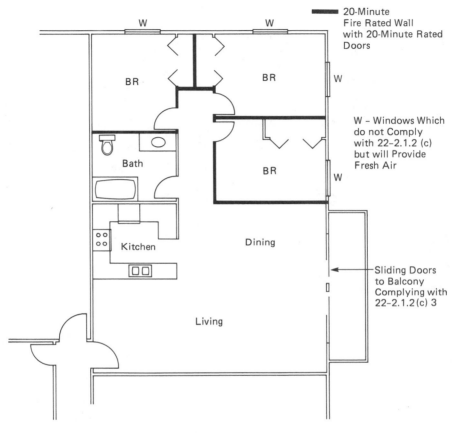

Figure 22-4.   Figure 22-4 Illustrates the Use of 22-2.1.2(d).   The bedrooms have windows that do not comply with 22-2.1.2(c), but the bedrooms are separated from each other and the rest of the living unit by 20-minute fire-rated construction. The 20-minute construction would not be required if the unit were sprinklered in accordance with NFPA 13, *Standard for the Installation of Sprinkler Systems,*[1] or NFPA 13D, *Standard for the Installation of Sprinkler Systems in One- and Two-Family Dwellings and Mobile Homes.*[2]

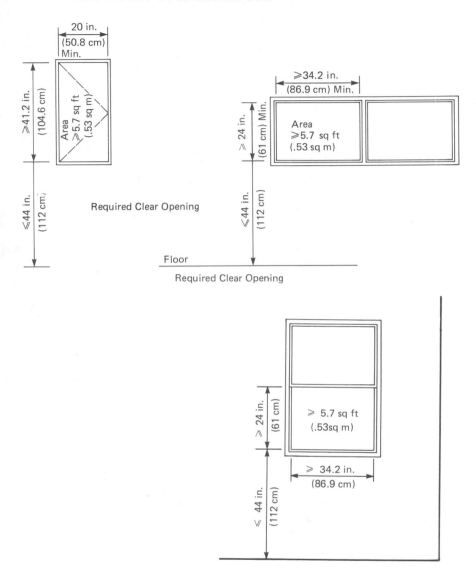

Figure 22-5. Minimum Size and Dimensions of Outside Windows Used as a Second Means of Escape per 22-2.1.2(c).

22-2.1.3 Every story of every dwelling or living unit that is greater than 2,000 sq ft (185 sq m) or that has a travel distance to the primary means of escape greater than 75 ft (23 m) shall be provided with two primary means of escape remote from each other.

Exception No. 1: Existing buildings.

Exception No. 2: Buildings protected throughout by an approved supervised automatic sprinkler system in accordance with Section 7-7.

22-2.2 Arrangement of Means of Escape.

22-2.2.1 No required path of travel from any room to the outside shall be through another room or apartment not under the immediate control of the occupant of the first room or through a bathroom or other space subject to locking.

Paragraph 22-2.2.1 was drafted to reflect the fact that one- and two-family dwellings may have up to three rooms rented to outsiders, or may be arranged so that a second family must egress through the living space of the other family. (This is often found in older homes not originally built as duplexes, but later converted to this design.) In either case, egress for the tenants or for the second family must be independent of any other family's living space.

22-2.3 Doors.

22-2.3.1 No door in the path of travel of a means of escape shall be less than 28 in. (71 cm) wide.

Exception: Bathroom doors may be 24 in. (61 cm) wide.

Although Chapter 5 requires 32-in. (81-cm) wide doors in new construction and 28-in. (71-cm) wide doors in existing buildings, 22-2.3.1 allows the use of 28-in. (71-cm) wide doors [24 in. (61 cm) for bathrooms] in both new and existing buildings. (*See Figure 22-6.*) This applies to doors in one- and two-family dwellings and those within apartments (dwelling units).

The 28-in. (71-cm) wide doors specified in 22-2.3.1 are found in dwelling designs, but ease of access and the need to move furniture and appliances usually dictate a larger size, reflecting prudent architectural design.

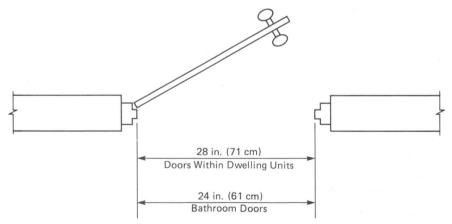

28 in. (71 cm)
Doors Within Dwelling Units

24 in. (61 cm)
Bathroom Doors

Figure 22-6. Minimum Width of Doors Within a Dwelling Unit per 22-2.3.1. Note that bathroom doors may be 4 in. (10.2 cm) smaller than the specified minimum. Closet doors that are not normally part of the means of escape are not regulated.

22-2.3.2   Every closet door latch shall be such that children can open the door from inside the closet.

22-2.3.3   Every bathroom door lock shall be designed to permit the opening of the locked door from the outside in an emergency.

Paragraphs 22-2.3.2 and 22-2.3.3 reflect the fact that during a fire young children will often seek refuge in bathrooms or closets (or under beds). Provisions for unlocking bathroom and closet doors permit ease of rescue by the fire department or by parents.

22-2.3.4   Doors may be swinging or sliding and are exempt from the requirements of 5-2.1.4.1.

22-2.3.5*   No door in any means of escape shall be locked against egress when the building is occupied. All locking devices that impede or prohibit egress or that cannot be easily disengaged shall be prohibited.

A-22-2.3.5   It is the intent of this requirement that security measures, where installed, should not prevent egress.

Paragraph 22-2.3.5 prohibits a one- or two-family dwelling (or a dwelling unit) from having any door locked against egress while the building is occupied. This requirement permits a door to have a locking device that allows the door to be opened from within the building for the purpose of egress, but does not allow the door to be opened from outside the building. Ordinary double cylinder locks and chain locks would not meet these provisions. Several tragic multiple-death fires have occurred where a key could not be found to unlock these devices.

The language of 5-2.1.5.1 is clear: "Locks, if provided, shall not require the use of a key, tool, special knowledge, or effort for operation from the inside of the building." This eliminates double cylinder locks and chain locks that require a key to be operated from the inside. Paragraph 5-2.1.5.1 calls for a simple operation to open a door; the presence of a two-handed knob operation, and the like, is specifically prohibited. *(See 5-2.1.5.3 Exception for additional information on latches and locks.)*

This applies only to doors or windows that are part of the required escape system. Often the rear door of a dwelling is not part of the required escape system and therefore could be equipped with a double cylinder lock.

22-2.4 Vertical Means of Escape, Stairs.

22-2.4.1   The width, risers, and treads of every stair shall comply with the minimum requirements for Class B stairs, as described in 5-2.2. Winders and spiral stairs in accordance with Chapter 5 are permitted within a single living unit.

Note that this allows the use of Class B stairs within the dwelling unit, even in new construction.

SECTION 22-3   PROTECTION

22-3.1 Protection of Vertical Openings.   No Requirements.

22-3.2 Interior Finish.

22-3.2.1   Interior finish on walls and ceilings of occupied spaces shall be Class A, B, or C as defined in Section 6-5.

Note that Class D interior finish (flame spread 200-500) is no longer permitted in one- or two-family dwellings. It was the intent of the Committee that this reduction in combustible finishes would increase the level of life safety from fire in dwellings. The use of high flame spread interior decorative paneling has been a factor in many fatal residential fires.

22-3.2.2 Interior Floor Finish.   No Requirements.

22-3.3 Detection, Alarm, and Communications Systems.

22-3.3.1 Detection.   Approved single station or multiple station smoke detectors continuously powered by the house electrical service shall be installed in accordance with 7-6.2.9.

Exception No. 1:   Dwelling units protected by an approved smoke detection system installed in accordance with Section 7-6, having an approved means of occupant notification.

Exception No. 2:   In existing construction, approved smoke detectors powered by batteries may be used.

Note that directly wired or plug-in type detectors are required in lieu of battery units. However, existing dwellings are permitted to use battery-powered units.

The detector(s) should usually be located in the hall area(s) giving access to rooms used for sleeping. In multilevel living units, the upper level detector should usually be located at the top of the stairs. The detector(s) should be mounted on the ceiling or on the wall within 12 in. (30.5 cm) of, but not closer than 6 in. (15.2 cm) to, the ceiling. The detector should be remotely located from the cooking area. Where unusual factors, such as room configuration, air movement, stagnant air pockets, etc., require consideration, the authority having jurisdiction and the designer should determine the placement of the detectors. See NFPA 74, *Standard for the Installation, Maintenance, and Use of Household Fire Warning Equipment.*[3]

SECTION 22-4 (RESERVED)

SECTION 22-5 BUILDING SERVICES

22-5.1 Heating Equipment. No stove or combustion heater shall be so located as to block escape in case of fire arising from malfunctioning of the stove or heater.

This requirement takes on added meaning in light of today's high energy costs, which have resulted in the use of alternative fuels in the home.

Formal Interpretation 81-32
Reference: 22-5

Question 1: Is it the intent of the Committee to allow wall-mounted natural gas or LP-Gas fueled heating units that are vented to the exterior in a hallway that is the primary means of egress?

Answer: No.

Question 2: If the answer to Question 1 above is no, is it the intent of the Committee to allow central heating units that use natural gas or LP-Gas fuel, that are properly vented to the exterior and have combustion air, in separate enclosed closets in a hallway that is a primary means of egress?

Answer: Yes.

Issue Edition: 1981
Reference: 22-5
Date: April 1984

REFERENCES CITED IN COMMENTARY

[1]NFPA 13, *Standard for the Installation of Sprinkler Systems*, National Fire Protection Association, Quincy, MA, 1987.
[2]NFPA 13D, *Standard for the Installation of Sprinkler Systems in One- and Two-Family Dwellings and Mobile Homes*, National Fire Protection Association, Quincy, MA, 1984.
[3]NFPA 74, *Standard for the Installation, Maintenance, and Use of Household Fire Warning Equipment*, National Fire Protection Association, Quincy, MA, 1984.

CHAPTER 23 (RESERVED)

The Committee on Safety to Life has reserved this chapter for future use.

24 NEW MERCANTILE OCCUPANCIES

(See also Chapter 31.)

Mercantile occupancies include stores, markets, and other rooms, buildings, or structures used for the display and sale of merchandise. Included in this occupancy group are:

Supermarkets
Department stores
Drugstores
Auction rooms
Shopping centers

Minor merchandising operations in buildings consisting predominantly of other occupancies, such as a newsstand in an office building, must meet the *Life Safety Code* requirements of the predominant occupancy.

SECTION 24-1   GENERAL REQUIREMENTS

24-1.1 Application.

24-1.1.1   New mercantile occupancies shall comply with the provisions of Chapter 24. *(See Chapter 31 for operating features.)*

Existing mercantile occupancies must comply with Chapter 25 of the *Code.*

24-1.1.2   This chapter establishes life safety requirements for all new mercantile buildings. Specific requirements for suboccupancy groups, such as Class A, B, and C stores and covered malls, are contained in paragraphs pertaining thereto.

For the definitions of Class A, B, and C stores, see 24-1.4.2.

24-1.1.3   Additions to existing buildings shall conform to the requirements for new construction. Existing portions of the structure need not be modified, provided that the new construction has not diminished the fire safety features of the facility.

Exception: Existing portions shall be upgraded if the addition results in a change of mercantile subclassification (see 24-1.4.2).

Paragraph 24-1.1.3 and its Exception are intended to indicate that additions to existing mercantile occupancies must conform to the requirements for new occupancies; the existing portion of the occupancy may generally continue in use as long as it complies with the provisions for existing mercantile occupancies contained in Chapter 25 of the *Code*. If, however, the addition results in a change in the mercantile occupancy classification, such as a change from a Class C mercantile to a Class B mercantile or from a Class B mercantile to a Class A mercantile, then the existing occupancy, as well as the new construction, must be upgraded to meet the provisions for new occupancies.

24-1.2 Mixed Occupancies.

24-1.2.1   Mixed occupancies shall comply with 1-4.7.

24-1.2.2   Combined Mercantile and Residential Occupancies.

24-1.2.2.1   No dwelling unit shall have its sole means of egress through any mercantile occupancy in the same building.

24-1.2.2.2   No multiple dwelling occupancy shall be located above a mercantile occupancy.

Exception No. 1:   Where the dwelling occupancy and exits therefrom are separated from the mercantile occupancy by construction having a fire resistance rating of at least 1 hour.

Exception No. 2:   Where the mercantile occupancy is protected throughout by an approved automatic sprinkler system in accordance with Section 7-7.

The requirements for mixed occupancies were developed to address a once common (but now slowly disappearing) occupancy arrangement: the corner tavern, grocery store, or retail store that has a dwelling on the upper floors. The *Code* divides this type of combined occupancy into two classes.

Where there is a single dwelling above or adjacent to the mercantile operation, the *Code* prohibits (*see 24-1.2.2.1*) the dwelling occupancy from having its sole means of egress pass through the mercantile occupancy. If the dwelling has an exit through the mercantile occupancy, it must have a second exit that is independent of and does not pass through the mercantile occupancy.

The *Code* prohibits a multiple dwelling occupancy to be located above a mercantile occupancy unless one of the following conditions is met:

1. The dwellings and their exits are separated from the mercantile occupancy by construction with a fire resistance rating of at least 1 hour, or

2. The mercantile occupancy is protected by an automatic sprinkler system. Sprinkler systems have proven to be an excellent alternative to 1-hour construction under these circumstances. (*See Section 7-7 of the Code, NFPA 13, Standard for the Installation of Sprinkler Systems,*[1] *and NFPA 13A, Recommended Practice for the Inspection, Testing, and Maintenance of Sprinkler Systems.*[2])

The *Code* established these requirements because of the long historical record of deaths and injuries that have occurred where fire originated in mercantile occupancies and spread to unsuspecting occupants of the dwelling units above the mercantile occupancies.

24-1.3 Special Definitions.

(a) *Anchor Store.* A department store or major merchandising center having direct access to the covered mall but having all required means of egress independent of the covered mall.

From a merchandising point of view, a shopping mall developer or operator may refer to any of the major tenants with vast expanses of floor space and instant name recognition, often positioned at the ends and corners of the covered mall building, as anchor stores. However, the *Code* reserves the use of the term for those stores having means of egress independent from the covered mall. (*See Figure 24-1.*)

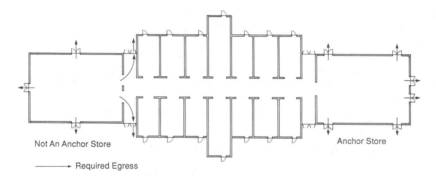

Not An Anchor Store

Anchor Store

⎯⎯⎯▶ Required Egress

Figure 24-1. Anchor Store. Illustration of the difference between a store that is an anchor store and a store that, although large, is not an anchor store. Note that required egress from an anchor store cannot pass through the mall.

(b) *Class A Stores.* [*See 24-1.4.2.1(a).*]

(c) *Class B Stores.* [*See 24-1.4.2.1(b).*]

(d) *Class C Stores.* [*See 24-1.4.2.1(c).*]

(e) *Covered Mall.* A covered or roofed interior area used as a pedestrian way and connected to a building(s) or portions of a building housing single or multiple tenants.

A covered mall can be considered as such even if it is open to the outside elements at one or more points.

(f) *Covered Mall Building.* A building, including the covered mall, enclosing a number of tenants and occupancies, such as retail stores, drinking and dining establishments, entertainment and amusement facilities, offices, and other similar uses, wherein two or more tenants have a main entrance into the covered mall.

The definition of "covered mall building" is differentiated from that of "covered mall" so that certain requirements can be applied only to the covered pedestrian way, i.e., the covered mall, while other requirements can be applied to the entire building, including all tenant spaces and common areas, i.e., the covered mall building. For example, the provisions of 24-4.4 require automatic sprinkler protection throughout the entire covered mall building but require smoke control only within the covered mall.

(g) *Gross Leasable Area.*   The total floor area designated for tenant occupancy and exclusive use, expressed in square feet (square meters), measured from centerlines of adjoining partitions and exteriors of outside walls.

(h) *Open-Air Mercantile Operations.*   Operations conducted outside of all structures with the operations area devoid of all walls and roofs except for small, individual, weather canopies.

24-1.4 Classification of Occupancy.

24-1.4.1   Mercantile occupancies shall include all buildings and structures or parts thereof with occupancy as described in 4-1.7.

It is important to review again the *Code*'s definition (*see 4-1.7*) of a mercantile occupancy. Note that this definition does not include "minor merchandising operations in buildings predominantly of other occupancies, such as a newsstand in an office building…" Paragraph 4-1.7 requires that such occupancies be subject to the exit requirements of the predominant (major) occupancy.

24-1.4.2 Subclassification of Occupancy.

24-1.4.2.1   Mercantile occupancies shall be subclassified as follows:

(a) *Class A.*   All stores having aggregate gross area of more than 30,000 sq ft (2,800 sq m) or utilizing more than three levels, excluding mezzanines, for sales purposes.

(b) *Class B.*   All stores of more than 3,000 sq ft (280 sq m) but not more than 30,000 sq ft (2,800 sq m) aggregate gross area, or utilizing floors above or below the street floor level for sales purposes. (Mezzanines permitted, see 24-1.4 2.3.)

Exception to (b):   If more than three floors, excluding mezzanines, are utilized, the store shall be Class A, regardless of area.

(c) *Class C.*   All stores of not more than 3,000 sq ft (280 sq m) gross area used for sales purposes on one story only, excluding mezzanines.

The mezzanines allowed by the one-third area rule of 24-1.4.2.3 do not constitute either a floor or a level and, therefore, are not a factor in determining mercantile occupancy subclassification based on number of floors used for sales purposes. The area of such mezzanines used for sales purposes (*see 24-1.4.2.2*) is, however, a factor with respect to the occupancy subclassification cut-off points based on floor area. For example, a store with a 2,100-sq ft (195-sq m) main sales floor and a 700-sq ft (65-sq m) sales mezzanine is a Class C mercantile occupancy, whereas a store with a 2,400-sq ft (225-sq m) main sales floor and a 800-sq ft (75-sq m) sales mezzanine is a Class B mercantile occupancy. In each case the mezzanine meets the maximum one-third area rule and is not counted as a floor or level. In the second case, the area of the 800-sq ft (75-sq m) sales mezzanine, when added to the 2,400-sq ft (225-sq m) main sales floor, exceeds the maximum 3,000 sq ft (280-sq m) sales area size for Class C mercantile occupancies and results in a Class B mercantile occupancy classification.

Mezzanines in excess of the maximum one-third area rule of 24-1.4.2.3 constitute floors and thus, sales levels, and need to be considered as such in determining mercantile occupancy subclassification. For example, a set of plans might show a proposed store with three floor levels, each 8,000 sq ft (740 sq m) in area, used for sales purposes, and a single 4,000-sq ft (370-sq m) sales "mezzanine." The store actually will use four floor levels for sales purposes because the so-called "mezzanine" is not a mezzanine based on the maximum one-third area rule of 24-1.4.2.3. Although the 30,000-sq ft (2,800-sq m) sales area limitation associated with Class A mercantile occupancies is not exceeded, the four floor levels used for sales purposes result in a Class A mercantile occupancy subclassification.

The following table summarizes the requirements of 24-1.4.2.1 for qualifying a store as Class A, B, or C. This classification process is important because it leads to specific life safety criteria that apply to each class of store. The criteria vary in degree of stringency dependent upon a store's classification.

Table 24–1. Subclassification of Mercantile Occupancies

Store Class	By Height		By Aggregate Gross Area† (sq ft)
A	>3 Floors‡	or	>30,000
B	≤3 Floors‡	and	>3,000 and ≤30,000
C	One Floor Only§	and	≤3,000

†Sections of floors not used for sales are not counted in the area classification.
‡Floors not used for sales above or below a sales floor are not counted in the height classification.
§A mezzanine < ⅓ the area of the floor below is permitted.

24-1.4.2.2 For the purpose of the classification in 24-1.4.2.1, the aggregate gross area shall be the total gross area of all floors used for mercantile purposes and, where a store is divided into sections, regardless of fire separation, shall include the area of all sections used for sales purposes. Areas of floors not used for sales purposes, such as an area used only for storage and not open to the public, shall not be counted for the purposes of the above classifications, but exits shall be provided for such nonsales areas in accordance with their occupancy, as specified by other chapters of this *Code*.

Some mercantile occupancies have their sales and storage areas together, e.g., furniture warehouse sales areas. In these cases, the occupancy should be classified using all aggregate gross area open to public use.

24-1.4.2.3 The floor area of a mezzanine or the aggregate floor area of multiple mezzanines shall not exceed one third of the floor area of the room or story in which the mezzanines are located. A mezzanine or aggregated mezzanines in excess of the one-third area limitation shall be treated as a story or stories.

Examples of mezzanine arrangements to which the maximum one-third area rule of 24-1.4.2.3 can be applied are illustrated in Figures 24-2 (a) through (f). For purpose of illustration, accept as a given that all mezzanines as well as the entire main floor level are used for sales purposes. In Figures (a), (b), (c), and (d), only a single story, or single floor level, with mezzanine exists because the aggregate areas of the mezzanines, i.e., 3,000 sq ft (280 sq m), do not exceed one-third of the floor area, i.e., 10,000 sq ft (930 sq m), of the room or story in which the mezzanine is located.

In Figure (e), the single so-called "mezzanine" with 4,000 sq ft (370 sq m) of floor area exceeds the one-third area rule and thus is not a mezzanine but rather a floor level in and of itself. Figure (e), therefore, depicts a two-story mercantile occupancy.

In Figure (f), one of the 3,000-sq ft (280-sq m) mezzanines fits within the maximum one-third area allowance and can be called a mezzanine without constituting a floor level. The other mezzanine, although of the same size and thus by itself not exceeding the one-third area rule, does create a floor level because the sum of the areas of the two mezzanines, i.e., 6,000 sq ft (560 sq m), exceeds one-third of the 10,000-sq ft (930-sq m) lower floor level. Thus, the figure shows a two-story mercantile occupancy with a mezzanine.

Although the mezzanines in Figures (a) through (d) do not establish separate floor levels, their areas, because they are used for sales, are included in the total gross sales area against which the Class A, B, and C mercantile occupancy subclassification definitions of 24-1.4.2.1 are applied. Figures (a) through (d) each show 13,000 sq ft (1,200 sq m) of sales area.

24-1.4.2.4 Where a number of stores under different management are located in the same building or adjoining buildings, the aggregate gross area of all such stores shall be used in determining classification per 24-1.4.2.1.

Exception No. 1: Where individual stores are separated by fire barriers with a 2-hour fire resistance rating.

Exception No. 2: Covered mall buildings. (See 24-4.4.)

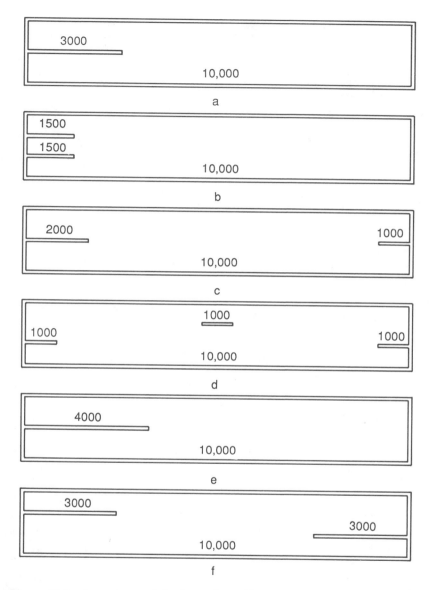

Figure 24-2a, b, c, d, e and f. Examples of Mercantile Occupancy Mezzanine Arrangement Elevation Views. (*See commentary associated with 24-1.4.2.3.*) All values are expressed in square feet. For metric values, 1 sq ft = 0.093 sq m.

Paragraphs 24-1.4.2.1 through 24-1.4.2.4 further clarify the classification of stores as Class A, B, or C. Most of these provisions are included in the footnotes to Table 24-1. The following should be noted for emphasis:

1. The aggregate gross area is the sum of the gross areas of all floors used for mercantile (sales) purposes.

2. If the store is divided into sections, only the sales sections should be included in the aggregate gross area.

3. If there are sections or floors used for sales that are considered as separate "stores" (because they are under different management), without minimum 2-hour fire resistance rated separation (fire walls or fire barriers) between each "store," the aggregate gross area of all such "stores" is to be used in classifying the occupancy as Class A, B, or C, except as provided for covered mall buildings. (*See* 24-4.4.)

24-1.5 Classification of Hazard of Contents. Mercantile occupancies' contents shall be classed as ordinary hazard in accordance with Section 4-2.

Exception: Mercantile occupancies shall be classified as high hazard if high hazard commodities are displayed or handled without protective wrappings or containers, in which case the following additional provisions shall apply:

(a) Exits shall be located so that not more than 75 ft (23 m) of travel from any point is required to reach the nearest exit.

(b) From every point there shall be at least two exits accessible by travel in different directions (no common path of travel).

(c) All vertical openings shall be enclosed.

Rather than simply referring the user to Section 4-2 for classification of hazard of contents, as most other occupancy chapters do, the requirement of 24-1.5 stresses that, unless an extraordinarily hazardous situation exists, the contents of mercantile occupancies shall be classed as ordinary hazard. Such wording is meant to keep the user from classifying the hazard of contents as high hazard unless a situation equivalent to the dispensing of explosives in bulk is present. Given that the package of life safety afforded by the chapter's requirements, taken as a whole, anticipates significant quantities of combustibles on display, the requirements should provide an acceptable level of safety without classifying the typical mercantile occupancy environment as highly hazardous. In other words, the chapter's requirements should be adequate without imposing the stringent high hazard contents requirements of the Exception to 24-1.5 on all but the most hazardous of mercantile occupancies.

Some procedures that would require classifying a mercantile occupancy as highly hazardous are: dispensing gunpowder or other explosives in bulk; selling polyurethane foam; or dispensing gasoline or flammable solvents by pouring them into open containers. The sales of such flammable liquids as camp stove fuel, rubbing alcohol, etc., should be controlled by NFPA 30, *Flammable and Combustible Liquids Code,*[3] as to display configuration, total amounts, and separations from ignition sources. Figure 24-3 illustrates an arrangement of exits from a high hazard area in a mercantile occupancy.

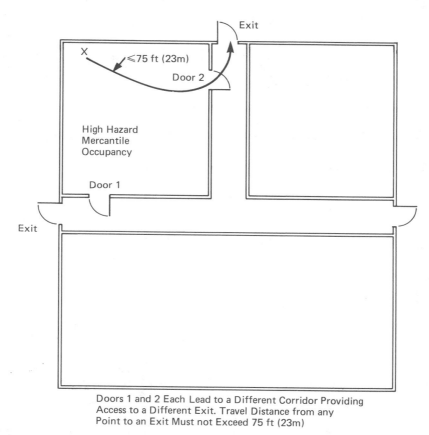

Doors 1 and 2 Each Lead to a Different Corridor Providing
Access to a Different Exit. Travel Distance from any
Point to an Exit Must not Exceed 75 ft (23m)

Figure 24-3.   Exit Arrangement from an Area of a Mercantile Occupancy Defined
as Highly Hazardous by 24-1.5.

24-1.6 Minimum Construction Requirements.   No Special Requirements.

The phrase "minimum construction" is used in the *Code* to describe the construction of the building housing the occupancy. Some occupancy chapters, such as Chapters 12 and 13, which address the life safety needs of nonambulatory occupants, require a certain minimum building construction type to help assure building structural integrity for the time period needed for a lengthy evacuation or for safe refuge within the building. Because mercantile occupancies characteristically have ambulatory customers and employees and do not provide sleeping accommodations, there are no minimum construction requirements imposed. Since there are no special requirements, the provisions of a local or state building code, if applicable, would apply.

24-1.7 Occupant Load.

24-1.7.1* For purposes of determining required exits, the occupant load of mercantile buildings or parts of buildings used for mercantile purposes shall be not less than the following:

(a) Street floor: one person for each 30 sq ft (2.8 sq m) gross floor area of sales space. In stores with no street floor, as defined in Chapter 3, but with access directly from the street by stairs or escalators, the principal floor at the point of entrance to the store shall be considered the street floor.

Exception to (a): In stores where, due to differences in grade of streets on different sides, there are two or more floors directly accessible from streets (not including alleys or similar back streets), for the purpose of determining occupant load, each such floor shall be considered a street floor. The occupant load factor shall be one person for each 40 sq ft (3.7 sq m) gross floor area of sales space.

(b) Sales floors below the street floor: same as street floor.

(c) Upper floors used for sales: one person for each 60 sq ft (5.6 sq m) gross floor area of sales space.

(d) Floors or portions of floors used only for offices: one person for each 100 sq ft (9.3 sq m) gross floor area of office space.

(e) Floors or portions of floors used only for storage, receiving, shipping, and not open to the general public: one person per each 300 sq ft (27.9 sq m) gross area of storage, receiving, or shipping space.

(f) Floors or portions of floors used for assembly purposes: occupant load determined in accordance with Chapter 8 for such assembly occupancies.

(g)* Covered mall buildings: determined in accordance with 24-1.7.1(a) through (f).

Exception: The covered mall, where considered a pedestrian way (see Exception to 24-4.4.1), shall not be assessed an occupant load. However, means of egress from the covered mall shall be provided for an occupant load determined by dividing the gross leasable area (not including anchor stores) by the appropriate occupant load factor listed below:

Gross Leasable Area [See 24-1.3(g).] (sq ft)	Occupant Load Factor (sq ft) (sq m)	
Less than 150,000 (14,000 sq m)	30	*(2.79)*
Over 150,000 (14,000 sq m) but less than 200,000 (18,500 sq m)	35	*(3.25)*
Over 200,000 (18,500 sq m) but less than 250,000 (23,000 sq m)	40	*(3.72)*
Over 250,000 (23,000 sq m) but less than 300,000 (28,000 sq m)	45	*(4.18)*
Over 300,000 (28,000 sq m) but less than 400,000 (37,000 sq m)	50	*(4.65)*
Over 400,000 (37,000 sq m)	55	*(5.11)*

Each individual tenant space shall have means of egress to the outside or to the covered mall based on occupant loads figured utilizing 24-1.7.1 (a) through (f).

Each individual anchor store shall have means of egress independent of the covered mall.

A-24-1.7.1 These figures were established on the basis of counts of the population of typical store buildings during periods of maximum occupancy, such as before Christmas or during special sales. In some cases, the actual occupancy may be more dense than indicated by these figures, but it may reasonably be assumed that in any large mercantile building, all areas will not be similarly crowded at the same time, and the average occupant load should seldom exceed these figures.

In some types of stores, the occupant load will normally be much less than indicated: for example, in furniture stores. However, the character of mercantile operations is subject to such rapid changes that it is not prudent in designing exit facilities to assume that any store will never be crowded, and for this reason, the same load figures are used for all types of stores.

A-24-1.7.1(g) The table used in determining the occupancy load for covered mall shopping centers of varying sizes is arrived at empirically in surveying over 270 covered mall shopping centers, in the study of mercantile occupancy parking requirements, and in observing the number of occupants per vehicle during peak seasons.

These studies show that with an increase in shopping center size, there is a decrease in the number of occupants per square foot of gross leasable area.

This phenomenon is explained when one considers that above a certain shopping center gross leasable area [approx. 600,000 sq ft (56,000 sq m)], a multiplicity of the same types of stores starts to occur: the purpose is to increase the choices available to a customer for any given type of merchandise. Therefore, when shopping center size increases, the occupant load increases as well, but at a declining rate. In using the table, the occupant load factor is applied to only the gross leasable area utilizing the covered mall as a means of egress.

The values show that, during normal use of a mercantile occupancy, the public will congregate, for the most part, on the street floor or in a basement "sales" area.

To differentiate between street floors and other sales floors, the street floor is any floor that has an entrance/exit directly accessible from the street. If differences in the ground level on different sides of a store create several floors of this nature, the *Code* treats them all as street floors; however, a slightly different occupant load factor is used per the Exception to (a). It is important to note that, if access to a store from the street is only by means of stairs or escalators, the principal floor at the point of entrance to the store must be considered the street floor. In assigning a higher occupant load to the street floor, the *Code* recognizes merchandising techniques, since these floors sell merchandise conducive to high traffic and customers are often forced to walk through portions of the street floor to reach escalators, elevators, and stairs to other floors. Thus, larger numbers of occupants are expected to be present on the street floor.

Given that the terms "covered mall" and "covered mall building" have different meanings [*see commentary following 24-1.3(f)*], the intent of 24-1.7.1(g) and its Exception is that the egress capacity of the overall covered mall building be sized to handle a number of occupants calculated in two steps. First, the occupant load is calculated for all stores and tenant spaces using the occupant load factors of 24-1.7.1(a) through (f). Second, the required egress capacity for the covered mall itself, meaning the covered pedestrian way, is calculated using values from the table of the Exception to 24-1.7.1(g). Each store or tenant space must have sufficient egress capacity for its occupant load. The covered mall must have egress capacity based on 24-1.7.1(g).

For example, consider a covered mall building with 21 tenant stores, all on the "street floor," each having 6,000 sq ft (560 sq m) of sales area, but 7,500 sq ft (700 sq m) of gross leasable area [assume that the other 1,500 sq ft (140 sq m) is storage]. Using an occupant load factor of 30 sq ft (2.8 sq m) per person for the sales areas and 300 sq ft (28 sq m) for the storage areas, each store must size its means of egress system to handle 205 persons (6,000/30 + 1,500/300 = 200 + 5 = 205). People can be sent back through the covered mall as part of the required means of egress from the stores. The covered mall, based on the 21 tenant stores, each with 7,500 sq ft (700 sq m) of gross leasable area (i.e., 21 × 7,500 = 157,500 sq ft of gross leasable area) must provide a means of egress system for 157,500 ÷ 35 = 4,500 persons.

24-1.7.2   Where mezzanines open to the floor below or other unprotected vertical openings between floors as permitted by the Exceptions to 24-3.1, the occupant load (or area) of the mezzanine or other subsidiary floor level shall be added to that of the street floor for the purpose of determining required exits, provided, however, that in no case shall the total exit capacity be less than would be required if all vertical openings were enclosed.

Figures 24-4 and 24-5 illustrate the requirements of 24-1.7.2. Figure 24-4 illustrates the case where a mezzanine is open to the street floor (which by the definition in Chapter 3 contains the main exit to the exterior or public way). The exits from the street floor must accommodate the people expected to occupy the street floor and the mezzanine, as well as the required capacity provided by the stairs from the upper floors discharging through the street floor.

In Figure 24-5, where the mezzanine is not open to the street floor, the capacity of the exits on the street floor must be able to accommodate the people expected to occupy the street floor and the capacity of the stairs from the upper floors discharging through the street floor. The enforcing official should note that the calculations required for the arrangement in Figure 24-5 will establish the minimum exit width that the *Code* will allow where exits from upper floors discharge into a street floor, whether or not the mezzanine is open to the street floor.

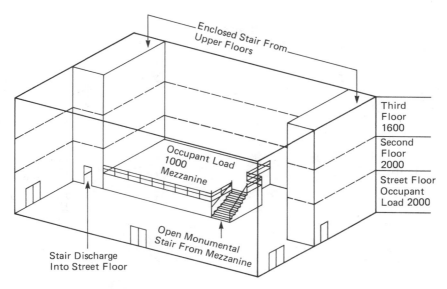

Figure 24-4. Mercantile Occupancy with a Mezzanine Open to the Street Floor. To determine the exit capacity for the street floor, the occupant load of the mezzanine (1,000) is added to the occupant load of the street floor (2,000). In addition, since one-half of the exits from the upper floors discharge through the street floor, the exit capacity of the street floor must be able to accommodate the capacity of the stair exits discharging through it. The maximum occupant load on any upper floor is 2,000 (second floor) and 24-2.7 permits at maximum one-half of the exits or exit capacity to discharge through the street floor, provided that the building is sprinklered. Therefore, the street floor must be provided with egress capacity for 4,000 persons or 800 in. (2,030 cm) of exit width using the factor of 0.2 in. (0.5 cm) per person for level exit components found in 5-3.3.1 (2,000 for street floor + 1,000 for mezzanine + 1,000 for upper floors = 4,000).

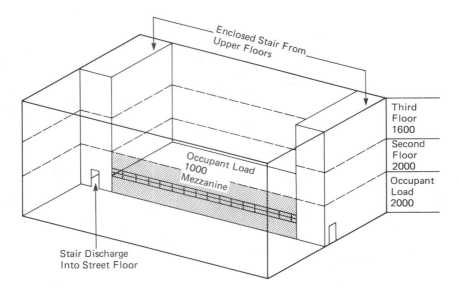

Figure 24-5. Mercantile Occupancy with a Mezzanine Not Open to the Street Floor. The street floor requires egress capacity for 3,000 persons (2,000 for the street floor + 1,000 for stairs discharging through the street floor).

SECTION 24-2   MEANS OF EGRESS REQUIREMENTS

24-2.1 General.

24-2.1.1   All means of egress shall be in accordance with Chapter 5 and this chapter.

24-2.1.2   No inside open stairway or ramp may serve as a component of the required means of egress system for more than one floor.

> This provision prohibits the use of open stairways or ramps as an egress facility for more than one floor; it does not establish permission for the open stairway or ramp to exist. See 24-3.1, under the subject of protection of vertical openings, to determine if the open stairway or ramp is permitted.

24-2.1.3   Where there are two or more floors below the street floor, the same stair or other exit may serve all floors, but all required exits from such areas shall be independent of any open stairways between the street floor and the floor below it.

24-2.1.4   Where a level, outside exit from upper floors is possible owing to hills, such outside exits may serve instead of horizontal exits. If, however, such outside exits from the upper floor also serve as an entrance from a principal street, the upper floor shall be classed as a street floor in accordance with the definition in Chapter 3 and is subject to the requirements of this section for street floors.

Paragraph 24-2.1.4 reconfirms the requirements of 24-1.7.1(a) for classification of floors as street floors. Figure 24-6 illustrates a case where two floors qualify as street floors because each has one side at a ground level. Note, however, that each has its other sides either above or below the building's other ground level. As a result, these floors must have their exits arranged to allow horizontal travel to the exterior at one end of the floor and vertical travel (either up or down to ground level) at the other end of the floor. This means that the exit capacity to the exterior must be able to accommodate, in the case of Floor 1, people from the upper floors who may need to travel down to and through the exits to the exterior from Floor 1. The reverse is true for Floor 2, which must size its exterior exit capacity to accommodate occupants who may travel up from Floor 1 as well as occupants who may have to travel down to and through the exterior exits on Floor 2. Paragraphs 5-3.1.4, 24-1.7.2, and 24-2.3.2 demonstrate how to add exit capacity based on expected occupant use from floors above the street floor. This method is equally valid for adding exit capacity based on expected occupant use from floors below the street floor. Figure 24-8 provides an example of how to calculate exit capacity for a street floor such as Floor 2 in Figure 24-6.

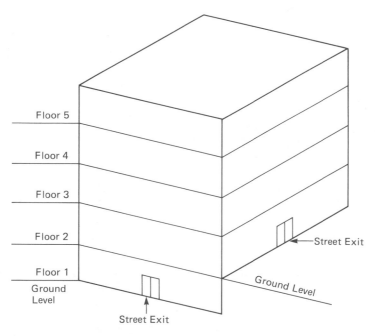

Figure 24-6. Mercantile Occupancy with Two Street Floors. The exit capacity of each street floor would have to comply with 24-2.3.2. (*Also see Figure 24-8.*)

24-2.1.5 For special considerations with contents of high hazard, see 24-1.5.

24-2.2 Means of Egress Components.

24-2.2.1 Components of means of egress shall be limited to the types described in 24-2.2.2 through 24-2.2.8.

24-2.2.2 Doors.

24-2.2.2.1 Doors shall comply with 5-2.1.

24-2.2.2.2* Locks complying with 5-2.1.5.1 Exception No. 2 shall be permitted only on principal entrance/exit doors.

A-24-2.2.2.2 The term "principal entrance/exit doors" is intended to imply doors that the authority having jurisdiction can be reasonably assured will be unlocked in order for the facility to do business.

This provision permits doors to be equipped with a key-operated lock in accordance with the provisions of Chapter 5. (*See Figure 24-7.*)

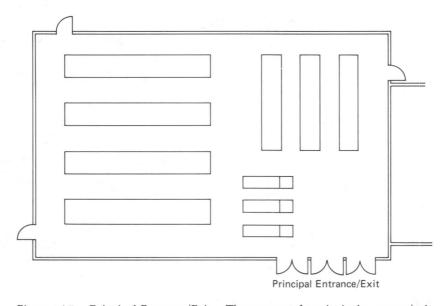

Principal Entrance/Exit

Figure 24-7. Principal Entrance/Exit. The concept of a principal entrance/exit as used in 24-2.2.2.2 is illustrated here.

24-2.2.2.3 Selected doors on stairwells may be equipped with hardware that prevents reentry in accordance with 5-2.1.5.2 Exception No. 1.

Had use of Exception No. 1 to 5-2.1.5.2 not been specifically recognized by this occupancy chapter, the basic requirements of 5-2.1.5.2 would have applied. That would have required either reentry from the stairwell back onto all floors at all times or similar reentry following automatic release of locking devices as a result of initiation of the building fire alarm system. Exception No. 1 to 5-2.1.5.2 allows for some stairwell doors to remain locked from the stairwell side of the door, while other doors must allow reentry, in recognition of building security needs. The location and numbers of resulting reentry points provide the same overall level of life safety for this occupancy as that intended by the base provisions of 5-2.1.5.2.

24-2.2.2.4   Special locking arrangements in accordance with 5-2.1.6 are permitted.

In recognition of the security needs of a mercantile occupancy, use of the delay release device covered by 5-2.1.6 is allowed on any door. In effect, the allowable 15- or 30- second delay will be experienced only under nonfire conditions or very early in a fire's growth, given that the door must be immediately usable upon sprinkler operation or smoke or heat detection and upon loss of power controlling the locking mechanism. The building must be protected throughout by an approved automatic sprinkler system or automatic fire detection system.

24-2.2.2.5   Where horizontal or vertical security grilles or doors are used as a part of the required means of egress from a tenant space, such grilles or doors shall comply with 5-2.1.4.1 Exception No. 3.

24-2.2.2.6   All doors at the foot of stairs from upper floors or at the head of stairs leading to floors below the street floor shall swing with the exit travel.

This provision requires doors that would not otherwise have to swing in the direction of egress travel under any of the three conditions of 5-2.1.4.1 to do so, based on their location. This is because of the queuing and accumulation of people that tend to occur at doors in such locations, which makes it difficult to step back to allow the door to swing.

24-2.2.2.7   Revolving doors shall comply with 5-2.1.10.

The requirements of 5-2.1.10 specify that the presence of a revolving door, whether or not it receives credit as part of the means of egress, mandates that a conforming side-hinged swinging door be positioned and usable within the same wall as and within 10 ft (3 m) of the revolving door. This helps to assure that once people are drawn toward the door, if the collapsibility and other safety features of the door should fail and leave it unusable, egress from that vicinity would still be possible without having to retrace steps and perhaps move back toward the fire.

24-2.2.3 Stairs.

24-2.2.3.1   Stairs shall comply with 5-2.2.

24-2.2.3.2   Spiral stairs complying with 5-2.2.2.7 are permitted.

Note that 5-2.2.2.7 only permits spiral stairs to serve an occupant load of five or fewer. They may be effectively used in storage areas having a small occupant load.

24-2.2.4 Smokeproof Enclosures. Smokeproof enclosures shall comply with 5-2.3.

24-2.2.5 Horizontal Exits. Horizontal exits shall comply with 5-2.4.

24-2.2.6 Ramps. Ramps shall comply with 5-2.5.

24-2.2.7 Exit Passageways. Exit passageways shall comply with 5-2.6.

24-2.2.8 Alternating Tread Devices. Alternating tread devices complying with 5-2.11 are permitted.

The provisions of 5-2.11 in effect limit the use of alternating tread devices to locations where the *Code* recognizes the use of fire escape ladders. (*See 5-2.9.*)

24-2.3 Capacity of Means of Egress.

24-2.3.1 The capacity of means of egress shall be in accordance with Section 5-3.

24-2.3.2 In Class A and Class B stores, street floor exits shall be sufficient for the occupant load of the street floor plus the required capacity of stairs and ramps discharging through the street floor.

In 24-2.3.2, the *Code* requires that the exits for the street floor of a Class A or B store have sufficient capacity to handle the people who, in exiting the building during an emergency, must travel up from the basement sales area or down from the upper sales floors and mix with the customers already on the street floor.

Since people move more quickly in the horizontal direction than in the vertical direction, it is permissible to provide less door width than stair width. For example, per the egress capacity factors of 5-3.3.1, in mercantile occupancies, level components and ramps require only 0.2 in. (0.5 cm) of width per person, whereas stairs require 0.3 in. (0.8 cm) of width per person. Figure 24-8 provides an example of how to calculate the required exit capacity for the street floor.

24-2.4 Number of Exits. (*See also Section 5-4.*)

24-2.4.1 At least two separate exits shall be accessible from every part of every floor, including floors below the street floor.

Exception: A single means of egress shall be permitted in a Class C mercantile occupancy where travel distance to the exit or covered mall, where it is considered as a pedestrian way, is not more than 75 ft (23 m) or more than 100 ft (30 m) where the story on which the occupancy is located is protected throughout by an approved automatic sprinkler system in accordance with Section 7-7.

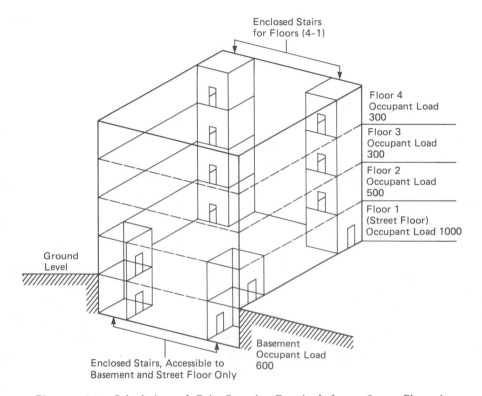

Figure 24-8. Calculation of Exit Capacity Required for a Street Floor in Accordance with 24-2.3.2.

Street floor occupant load alone, plus	1,000
maximum upper floor occupant load discharging back through street floor (500 ÷ 2), plus	250
basement occupant load discharging back through street floor (600 ÷ 2)	300

1,550 persons x 0.2 in. (0.5 cm) per person for level exit components per 5-3.3.1 = 310 in. (787 cm) of exit width required from the street floor exit system.

The *Code* allows this Exception to the basic requirement for the presence of at least two remote exits from an occupancy in the instance of very small Class C mercantile stores, such as tobacco shops, shoe shine stands, and newsstands. If the travel distance from any point in such a store to an exit is 75 ft (23 m) or less, the probability that a fire might surprise and overcome the customers before they could escape is low. (*See*

Figure 24-9.) Further, by allowing up to 100 ft (30 m) of travel distance with a single exit, the Exception intends to provide additional exiting flexibility to those small stores that provide a high degree of "self-protection" by means of automatic sprinkler installations.

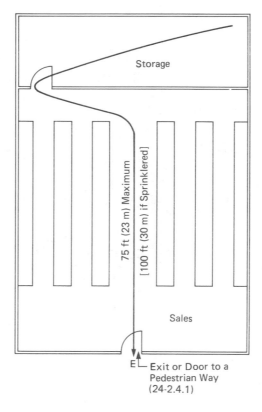

Figure 24-9.   Single Exit. A Class C mercantile occupancy may be provided with a single exit if X → E ≤ 75 ft (23 m) or, if story is sprinklered, 100 ft (30 m).

24-2.5 Arrangement of Means of Egress.

24-2.5.1   Exits shall be arranged in accordance with Section 5-5.

24-2.5.2*   No dead-end corridor shall exceed 20 ft (6.1 m).

Exception: In buildings protected throughout by an approved supervised automatic sprinkler system, dead-end corridors shall not exceed 50 ft (15 m).

A-24-2.5.2   The purpose of this paragraph is to avoid pockets or dead ends of such size that they pose an undue danger of persons becoming trapped in case of fire.

The Exception to 24-2.5.2 recognizes the additional level of safety to life that a complete automatic sprinkler system provides, and allows added flexibility when designing the location of corridors and exits in buildings where approved sprinkler systems are installed.

24-2.5.3*   No common path of travel shall exceed 75 ft (23 m).

Exception: A common path of travel may be permitted for the first 100 ft (30 m) in a building protected throughout by an approved supervised automatic sprinkler system in accordance with Section 7-7.

The maximum common path of travel allowed in mercantile occupancies by the previous edition of the *Code* was 50 ft (15 m) [75 ft (23 m) if sprinklered]. Based on the deletion from this edition of the previous Chapter 5 provisions that applied to the point where measurement of travel distance and common path begins for small rooms [i.e., distance within room was not counted if there was a maximum six-person occupant load and a maximum 50-ft (15-m) of travel within the room], the allowable common path has been increased without either reducing the level of safety to life or imposing a hardship on designers.

(*See commentary following 5-5.1.5 for discussion on common path of travel.*)

A-24-2.5.3   The common path of travel requirement permits small areas such as rooms or alcoves with only one way out where the distance is small enough so that there is little likelihood that a fire might develop to such proportions as to block escape before the occupants become aware of the fire and make their way out.

24-2.5.4   Aisles leading to each exit are required. The aggregate width of such aisles shall be equal to at least the required width of the exit.

24-2.5.5   In no case shall any required aisle be less than 36 in. (91 cm) in clear width.

24-2.5.6   In Class A stores, at least one aisle of 5 ft (152 cm) minimum width shall lead directly to an exit.

The intent of 24-2.5.4 through 24-2.5.6 is to ensure that the interior arrangement of counters, racks, and displays of merchandise does not block or obscure accesses to an exit. Figure 24-10 illustrates an arrangement that meets the requirements for a Class A store. Essentially, the width of the exit determines the minimum width of the aisle, except that one of the aisles must be at least 5 ft (152 cm) wide.

24-2.5.7   If the only means of customer entrance is through one exterior wall of the building, two-thirds of the required exit width shall be located in this wall.

In establishing 24-2.5.7, the *Code* is concerned about the arrangement of many discount and variety stores, which have one large main exit/entrance located in the front of the store, and the other exits (which cannot be used as entrances) situated at points unfamiliar to the public. In these cases, the wall containing the main exit/entrance must be sized to handle two-thirds of the required exit capacity of the store because most of the customers will instinctively try to use this exit during a fire. Such an arrangement is shown in Figure 24-10.

24-2.5.8   At least one-half of the required exits shall be so located as to be reached without going through checkout stands. In no case shall checkout stands or associated railings or barriers obstruct exits, required aisles, or approaches thereto.

This is one of the most frequently violated provisions of Chapter 24. Many supermarkets and discount and variety stores are arranged so that it is necessary to pass through checkout counters, around shopping carts, and through turnstiles in order to exit the facility. Obviously, this causes congestion or blockage during an emergency. The *Code* requires at least one-half of all exits to be located so that people can avoid having to pass through or around these impediments to egress.

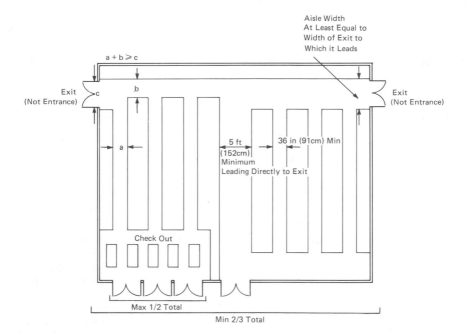

Figure 24-10.   Means of Egress Arrangement in a Mercantile Occupancy.   The conditions described and the resulting requirements of 24-2.5.4 through 24-2.5.8 are illustrated here.

24-2.5.9* Where wheeled carts or buggies are used by customers, adequate provision shall be made for the transit and parking of such carts to minimize the possibility that they may obstruct means of egress.

A-24-2.5.9 In order to eliminate the obstruction to the means of egress of the interior exit access and the exterior exit discharge, it is the intent to provide adequate area for transit and parking of wheeled carts or buggies used by customers. This includes corral areas adjacent to exits that are constructed to restrict the movement of wheeled carts or buggies therefrom.

In states where returnable beverage bottle legislation has recently been enacted, stores and markets have had to find space for the collection of empty bottles and the refund of deposit charges. The area most commonly used is near the entrance/exit where wheeled shopping carts were formerly stored clear of the path of egress travel. The carts are now often stored so as to obstruct the means of egress. This illustrates a situation where a planned complying means of egress is compromised overnight by changing conditions.

24-2.5.10* Exit access in all Class C stores and exit access in Class B stores that have an occupant load not exceeding 200 and are protected throughout by an approved automatic sprinkler system may pass through storerooms provided the following conditions are met:

(a) Not more than 50 percent of exit access is provided through the storeroom.

(b) The storeroom is not subject to locking.

(c) The main aisle through the storeroom shall be not less than 44 in. (112 cm) wide.

(d) The path of travel, defined with fixed barriers, through the storeroom shall be direct and continuously maintained in an unobstructed condition.

In (a) above, the storeroom is limited to providing a maximum of 50 percent of the store's exit access, either in number of exits or exit capacity. Thus, given that two exits are required, neither of the following limits can be exceeded:

1. Only one of the two required exits can be reached by exit access travel through the storeroom, and

2. A maximum of half the store's occupant load can exit through the storeroom.

In addition to allowing exit access in all Class C stores to pass through storerooms, 24-2.5.10 allows exit access in some Class B stores to pass through storerooms where that store is protected throughout by an approved automatic sprinkler system, and recognizes the increased safety to life that a sprinkler system provides.

Figures 24-11 and 24-12 show examples of the application of 24-2.5.10.

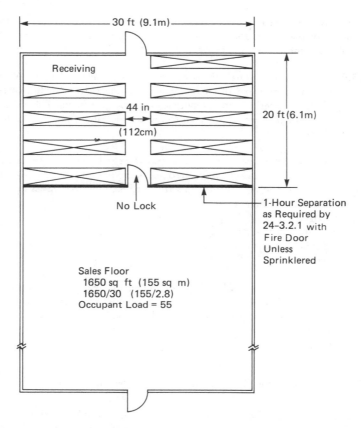

Figure 24-11. Example of Exit Access Through Storeroom as Permitted by 24-2.5.10. The aisle within the storeroom must be defined by fixed barriers, such as those formed by the ends of shelving. The aisle must be kept unobstructed.

A-24-2.5.10   It is not the intent to allow exit access through Class A mercantile occupancy storerooms.

24-2.6 Travel Distance to Exits.   Travel distance to exits, measured in accordance with Section 5-6, shall be no more than 100 ft (30 m).

Exception: An increase in the above travel distance to 200 ft (60 m) shall be permitted in a building protected throughout by an approved automatic sprinkler system in accordance with Section 7-7.

A review of 5-6.2 will show that the travel distance requirements apply to only the first (or nearest) exit from a point in the building. In other words, the 100-ft (30-m) travel distance limit means that at least one exit must be within 100 ft (30 m) of a point in the building, not that all exits must be within 100 ft (30 m) of that same point in the building.

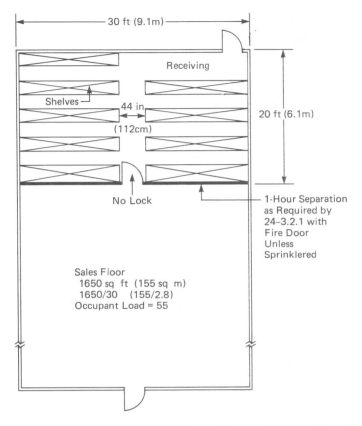

Figure 24-12. Example of Exit Access Through Storeroom That Will Be Problematic Because of Relationship to Receiving Area.

The maximum travel distance allowed in sprinklered mercantile occupancies by the previous edition of the *Code* was 150 ft (45 m). Based on the deletion in this edition of the previous Chapter 5 provisions that applied to the point where measurement of travel distance begins for small rooms [i.e., distance within room was not counted if there was a maximum six-person occupant load and a maximum 50-ft (15-m) of travel within the room], the allowable travel distance for sprinklered mercantile occupancies has been increased to 200 ft (60 m) without either reducing the level of safety to life or imposing a hardship on designers. For nonsprinklered mercantile occupancies, the maximum 100-ft (30-m) travel distance has not been similarly increased due in part to recognition of the high combustible load characteristic of mercantile occupancies and associated with merchandise on display.

24-2.7 Discharge from Exits.

24-2.7.1 Exit discharge shall comply with Section 5-7 except as modified by 24-2.7.2.

24-2.7.2* Fifty percent of the exits may discharge through the level of exit discharge in accordance with 5-7.2 where the building is protected throughout by an approved automatic sprinkler system in accordance with Section 7-7, and the distance of travel from the terminiation of the exit enclosure to an outside street door shall not exceed 50 ft (15 m).

A-24-2.7.2 The basis for the Exception to the general rule on complete enclosure of exits up to their point of discharge to the outside of the building is that, with the specified safeguards, reasonable safety is maintained.

A stairway is not considered to discharge through the street floor area if it leads to the street through a fire resistance rated enclosure (exit passageway) separating it from the main area, even though there are doors between the first floor stairway landing and the main area.

The provisions of 24-2.7.2 should not be confused with open stairways as permitted by 24-3.1 (Exception No. 1).

> Note that a limit is applied to this arrangement so that no more than 50 percent of the exits from either the entire building or from any floor can be arranged to discharge through the street floor. Further, this can only be done if the building is sprinklered throughout. Also note that the path of travel on the first floor from the stair enclosure to the outside door cannot exceed 50 ft (15 m). The remaining 50 percent of the exits must discharge directly to the exterior.
>
> This paragraph is more stringent than the comparable 5-7.2 since it mandates that the building be protected throughout by automatic sprinklers, sets a 50-ft (15-m) limit of travel on the street floor, and requires that the street floor have exit capacity to accommodate the street floor and the stairs discharging through the street floor. These requirements are not mandated by 5-7.2. The extra requirements are imposed in recognition of the high combustible load of merchandise on display, which is characteristic of mercantile occupancies.

24-2.8 Illumination of Means of Egress.   Means of egress shall be illuminated in accordance with Section 5-8.

> Note that illumination for the means of egress is not the same as emergency lighting; failure of the building power supply may cause failure of the means of egress illumination system, which is not required to have a back-up, auxiliary, or secondary power supply unless required by 24-2.9.

24-2.9 Emergency Lighting.   Class A and Class B stores shall have emergency lighting facilities in accordance with Section 5-9.

> Class C stores, due to their small size and small occupant load, are not required by the *Code* to have emergency lighting facilities.

24-2.10 Marking of Means of Egress. Means of egress shall have signs in accordance with Section 5-10.

Exception: Where an exit is immediately apparent from all portions of the sales area, the exit marking may be omitted.

The intent of the Exception to the provision for marking the means of egress is to avoid requiring exit signs in small areas where the exit is readily apparent. For example, exit signs would not be required in the office of a service station, the purchase and eating areas of a small "fast food" restaurant, or in a Class C store whose size and arrangement comply with the Exception to 24-2.4.1.

24-2.11 Special Features.

SECTION 24-3 PROTECTION

24-3.1* Protection of Vertical Openings. Each stairway, elevator shaft, escalator opening, or other vertical opening shall be enclosed or protected in accordance with Section 6-2.

Exception No 1: In Class A or Class B mercantile occupancies protected throughout by an approved supervised automatic sprinkler system in accordance with Section 7-7, unprotected vertical openings shall be permitted as follows:

(a) Between any two floors, or

(b) Between the street floor and the first adjacent floor below and the first adjacent floor (or mezzanines) above, or

(c) In accordance with 6-2.4.4.

Exception No. 2: In Class C mercantile occupancies, openings may be unprotected between the street floor and mezzanine.

Exception No. 3: Atriums in accordance with 24-4.5 are permitted.

A-24-3.1 See 24-1.7.2 for provisions on determining occupant load for exit purposes where vertical openings are unprotected.

Follow the provisions of 24-1.7 for properly assessing the occupant load to develop sufficient exit capacity for a store in which floors or mezzanines are open to the street floor. Exception No. 1 to 24-3.1 specifies under which conditions such openings are permitted in sprinklered Class A and Class B stores.

Item (a) allows any two floors, regardless of floor level within building, to have otherwise unprotected vertical openings between them.

Item (b) allows the floors immediately above and immediately below the street floor to be open to the street floor at the same time.

In lieu of item (b), item (c) allows a store that is fully sprinklered to have three contiguous levels open to each other under the provisions of 6-2.4.4. A fully sprinklered building is a requirement in excess of 6-2.4.4, which requires only the open or communicating spaces to be sprinklered.

Exception No. 2 to 24-3.1 recognizes the limited size and probable small population of Class C stores. For these reasons, any Class C store may have unprotected openings to a mezzanine.

Note that 24-4.5 has provisions that differ from 6-2.4.5.

24-3.2 Protection from Hazards.

24-3.2.1   Hazardous areas, including but not limited to areas used for general storage, boiler or furnace rooms, fuel storage, janitor closets, maintenance shops including woodworking and painting areas, and kitchens, shall:

(a) Be separated from other parts of the building by fire barriers having a fire resistance rating of not less than 1 hour with all openings therein protected by ¾-hour fire protection rated self-closing fire doors, or

(b) The area shall be protected by an automatic extinguishing system in accordance with Section 7-7.

24-3.2.2   Areas with high hazard contents as defined in Section 4-2 shall be provided with both fire-resistive separation and automatic sprinkler protection.

Paragraphs 24-3.2.1 and 24-3.2.2 reflect the intent of Section 6-4, which: (1) requires separation of a hazardous area from the rest of a building by suitable construction, or (2) mandates the installation of an automatic sprinkler system in a hazardous area, or (3) requires both where the hazard is severe.

24-3.3 Interior Finish.

24-3.3.1   Interior finish on walls and ceilings shall be Class A or B, in accordance with Section 6-5.

24-3.3.2 Interior Floor Finish.   No Requirements.

24-3.4 Detection, Alarm, and Communications Systems.

24-3.4.1 General.   Class A mercantile occupancies shall be provided with a fire alarm system in accordance with Section 7-6.

Class B and C mercantile occupancies are not required to have a fire alarm system.

24-3.4.2 Initiation.   Initiation of the required fire alarm system shall be by manual means per 7-6.2.1(a).

Exception No. 1:   Initiation may be by means of an approved automatic fire detection system, in accordance with 7-6.2.1(b), providing protection throughout the building.

Exception No. 2:   Initiation may be by means of an approved automatic sprinkler system, in accordance with 7-6.2.1(c), providing protection throughout the building.

Since all Class A stores must be sprinklered (*see 24-3.5*), it is logical that Exception No. 2 will be the most common method of activating the fire alarm system, since this allows the elimination of the manual pull stations if the sprinkler water flow activates the fire alarm system. Nuisance alarms might be reduced by eliminating the manual pull stations and satisfying the initiation requirements via water flow through the sprinkler system.

24-3.4.3 Notification.

24-3.4.3.1 At all times that the store is occupied (*see 5-2.1.1.3*), the required fire alarm system shall:

(a) Sound a general audible alarm throughout the store, or

(b) Sound an audible alarm in a continuously attended location for purposes of initiating emergency action.

Note that the *Code* provides a choice between two methods of notification. Many Class A stores do have a continuously attended location and item (b) can be used; if such a location is not provided or not considered reliable by the authority having jurisdiction, item (a) would have to be applied.

24-3.4.3.2 Occupant Notification. Occupant notification shall be by live voice public address system announcement originating from the attended location where the alarm signal is received. (*See 24-3.4.3.1.*) The system may be used for other announcements. (*See 7-6.3.9 Exception No. 2.*)

Exception: Any other occupant notification means permitted by 7-6.3 may be used in lieu of live voice public address system announcement.

This Exception would allow a system using 24-3.4.3.1(a) to use an automatic voice alarm or regular alarm sounding devices in lieu of the live voice alarm.

24-3.4.3.3 Emergency Forces Notification. Emergency forces notification shall include notifying:

(a) The fire department in accordance with 7-6.4, and

(b) The local fire brigade, if provided, via the attended location where the alarm signal is received. (*See 24-3.4.3.1.*)

Paragraph 7-6.4 allows for several different methods of automatically notifying the fire department.

24-3.5 Extinguishment Requirements.

24-3.5.1 Mercantile occupancies shall be protected throughout by an approved automatic sprinkler system in accordance with Section 7-7 as follows:

(a) In all buildings three or more stories in height.

(b) In all buildings with a story over 12,000 sq ft (1,100 sq m).

(c) In all buildings exceeding 24,000 sq ft (2,200 sq m) in gross area.

(d) Throughout stories below the level of exit discharge where such stories have an area exceeding 2,500 sq ft (230 sq m) where used for the sale, storage, or handling of combustible goods and merchandise.

For discussions of what constitutes an "approved automatic sprinkler system," see NFPA 13, *Standard for the Installation of Sprinkler Systems,*[1] NFPA 13A, *Recommended Practice for the Inspection, Testing, and Maintenance of Sprinkler Systems,*[2] and *Automatic Sprinkler and Standpipe Systems.*[4]

Item (a) requires that all buildings with three or more stories be protected with a complete automatic sprinkler system.

Under the provisions of item (b), a building with a total gross area of not more than 24,000 sq ft (2,200 sq m) (Class B or C), but with any one floor of more than 12,000 sq ft (1,100 sq m) in area, would have to be protected with a complete automatic sprinkler system. A building with a total gross area of not more than 24,000 sq ft (2,200 sq m) would not be required to be sprinklered as long as no floor exceeds 12,000 sq ft (1,100 sq m), and the building is less than three stories in height.

The intent of item (c) is to require that all buildings with a total gross area of more than 24,000 sq ft (2,200 sq m) be protected with a complete automatic sprinkler system.

Items (a), (b), and (c) require that all Class A stores and the larger Class B stores be protected by automatic sprinklers.

Item (d) ensures that all basement areas larger than 2,500 sq ft (230 sq m) (whether the space is used for sales, storage, or the handling of combustible merchandise) be sprinklered to avoid the potential threat to the occupants of the floors above. Studies have shown that there is a higher rate of fire incidence in basements than in other areas of stores. Because smoke and heat rise, a fire in a basement can quickly render exits and exit discharges located on the street floor unusable.

24-3.5.2   Automatic sprinkler systems in Class A stores shall be supervised in accordance with 7-7.2.

Although supervision of sprinkler systems is required only for Class A stores, such supervision is desirable for all automatic sprinkler systems and could be required by the authority having jurisdiction as part of his or her approval.

24-3.5.3   Portable fire extinguishers shall be provided in all mercantile occupancies in accordance with 7-7.4.1.

The provision of portable extinguishers is for use by the properly trained employees of the mercantile occupancy as required by 31-8.2.

24-3.6 Corridors.

24-3.6.1   Where access to exits is limited to corridors, such corridors shall be separated from use areas by fire barriers having a fire resistance rating of at least 1 hour.

Exception No. 1: Where exits are available from an open floor area.

Exception No. 2: Corridors need not have a fire resistance rating within a space occupied by a single tenant.

Exception No. 3: Corridors need not have a fire resistance rating within buildings protected throughout by an approved automatic sprinkler system.

Where access to exits is limited to corridors, separation requirements are spelled out. Similar requirements apply to business occupancies. (*Also see 26-3.6.1.*)

24-3.6.2 Doors and frames, each with a minimum 20-minute fire protection rating, equipped with a positive latch and closing device, shall be used to protect openings in 1-hour partitions separating the corridor from use areas.

24-3.6.3 Glass vision panels within 1-hour fire-rated partitions, or doors therein, shall be limited to fixed wired glass in approved steel frames and shall be 1,296 sq in. (.84 sq m) or less in size per panel.

24-3.7 Subdivision of Building Spaces. No Special Requirements.

24-3.8 Special Features.

SECTION 24-4 SPECIAL PROVISIONS

24-4.1 Windowless or Underground Buildings. (*See Section 30-7.*)

24-4.2 High Rise Buildings. No additional requirements.

Section 30-8, High Rise Buildings, is new to the 1988 Edition of the *Code*. It is menu-oriented in that its provisions, singly, in various combinations, or in total, must be mandated by a specific occupancy chapter requirement. For new mercantile occupancies, 24-4.2 does not require any of the provisions of Section 30-8. Rather, the sprinkler system mandated by 24-3.5.1 and the associated system supervision requirement of 24-3.5.2 help assure that high rise mercantile occupancies will be adequately protected.

24-4.3 Open-Air Mercantile Operations.

24-4.3.1 Open-air mercantile operations, such as open-air markets, gasoline filling stations, roadside stands for the sale of farm produce, and other outdoor mercantile operations shall be so arranged and conducted as to maintain free and unobstructed ways of travel at all times to permit prompt escape from any point of danger in case of fire or other emergency, with no dead ends in which persons might be trapped due to display stands, adjoining buildings, fences, vehicles, or other obstructions.

Paragraph 24-4.3.1 is virtually an open-ended provision that provides guidance for the arrangement, use, and display of merchandise for sale in open-air mercantile operations. The phrase "ways of travel" is purposely used to avoid confusion with "means of egress," which is strictly defined and whose use implies the minimum requirements of Chapter 5. "Ways of travel" is not defined and implies no specific minimum *Code* provisions.

Most open-air mercantile operations have unlimited means of entering and evacuating the areas used to display goods. For this reason, it is not necessary to provide specific *Code* requirements beyond the precautionary measures expressed in this paragraph.

24-4.3.2   If mercantile operations are conducted in roofed-over areas, they shall be treated as mercantile buildings, provided that canopies over individual small stands to protect merchandise from the weather shall not be construed to constitute buildings for the purpose of this *Code*.

The intent of 24-4.3.2 is to exempt small merchandise stands with canopies from classification as mercantile buildings. All other "roofed-over" areas should be treated as buildings, classified by area and height as Class A, B, or C mercantile occupancies, and subject to the appropriate provisions of Chapter 24.

24-4.4 Covered Mall Buildings.   The purpose of this section is to establish minimum standards of life safety for covered mall buildings having not more than three levels.

24-4.4.1   The covered mall building shall be treated as a single building for the purpose of calculation of means of egress and shall be subject to the requirements for appropriate occupancies. The covered mall shall be at least of sufficient clear width to accommodate egress requirements as set forth in other sections of this *Code*.

Exception: The covered mall may be considered to be a pedestrian way, in which case the distance of travel within a tenant space to an exit or to the covered mall shall be a maximum of 200 ft (60 m) (see Exception to 24-2.6), or shall be the maximum for the appropriate occupancy; plus an additional 200 ft (60 m) shall be permitted for travel through the covered mall space if all the following requirements are met:

(a) The covered mall shall be at least of sufficient clear width to accommodate egress requirements as set forth in other sections of this chapter, but in no case less than 20 ft (6.1 m) wide in its narrowest dimension.

(b)* On each side of the mall floor area, the covered mall shall be provided with an unobstructed exit access of not less than 10 ft (3 m) in clear width parallel to and adjacent to the mall tenant front. Such exit access shall lead to an exit having a minimum of 66 in. (168 cm) in width. (See 24-4.4.2.)

(c) The covered mall and all buildings connected thereto shall be protected throughout by an approved electrically supervised automatic sprinkler system in accordance with Section 7-7.

(d) Walls dividing stores from each other shall extend from the floor to the underside of the roof deck or floor deck above. No separation is required between a tenant space and the covered mall.

(e)* The covered mall shall be provided with a smoke control system.

A-24-4.4.1 Exception (b)   The minimum requirement for terminating mall exit access in not less than 66 in. (168 cm) width relates to the minimum requirement for at least one aisle in Class A stores [30,000 sq ft (2,800 sq m) or greater] to be 5 ft (152 cm) in width.

A-24-4.4.1 Exception (e) Smoke control systems for covered malls are necessary to maintain the covered mall reasonably free of products of combustion for at least the duration required to evacuate the building and to minimize migration of products of combustion from one tenant to another. Systems that can be engineered to accomplish this include:

(a) Separate or mechanical exhaust or control systems.

(b) Mechanical exhaust or control systems in conjunction with the heating, ventilating, and air conditioning systems.

(c) Automatically or manually released gravity roof vent devices, such as skylights, relief dampers, or smoke vents.

(d) Combinations of (a), (b), and (c) or any other engineered system designed to accomplish the purpose of this section.

Formal Interpretation 81-25
Reference: 1-4.7, 8-1.6, 24-4.4.1

Given that, per 8-1.6, a 3-story shopping mall with a food park (restaurant) on the third level is required to be of fire-resistive construction under the criteria for a Class A place of assembly above grade level.

Question 1: Is it possible to construct an anchor store of a different construction type from the mall building by separating it from the mall building by a 3-hour fire wall?

Question 2: Are 3-hour fire doors required for openings in this 3-hour wall between the mall and the anchor store?

Question 3: If the answer to Question 2 is no, is any type of opening protection required for openings between the mall and anchor store?

Answer: With only a few exceptions, the *Life Safety Code* sets no specific occupancy separation requirements. The authority having jurisdiction determines what separation is needed, if any, based on 1-4.7 and the 1.2 section of each occupancy chapter. The local building code or the model building codes may be consulted by the authority having jurisdiction in making this determination, keeping life safety rather than property protection in mind.

Issue Edition: 1981
Reference: 1-4.5, 8-1.6, 24-4.3.1
Date: October 1982

In recent years, covered mall shopping areas have increased in both number and size. Two options or approaches for dealing with the life safety aspects of these complexes were developed. The first approach (described in the base paragraph of 24-4.4.1) considers the mall and the attached stores as essentially one large Class A store subject to all the provisions of Chapter 24. Viewed this way, the covered mall would be treated as an aisle of a store.

The other approach, introduced in the 1976 Edition of the *Life Safety Code*, permits the mall to be considered as a "pedestrian way" by which occupants of the attached stores may egress during a fire. The phrase "pedestrian way" was chosen both to convey the meaning of the term "exit access" and to allow the mall to be treated as if it were an area of refuge.

The Exception to 24-4.4.1 recognizes that, if the mall and all the buildings attached to the mall were protected by automatic sprinklers, people fleeing into the mall from a fire in a store would be moving into a space whose volume, size, and arrangement affords most of the benefits provided by an enclosed stair or a horizontal exit. The Exception considers the mall as a virtual area of refuge for the buildings attached to it, even though the mall is not separated from these attached buildings by the type of construction normally provided for an exit as required by 5-1.3.1.

Where a covered mall is considered as a pedestrian way, the maximum travel distance to an exit or to the mall from any point within a store attached to the mall is 200 ft (60 m). This reflects the judgment that using the mall for egress is as acceptable (or as safe) as using an exit. An additional travel distance of up to 200 ft (60 m) is permitted within the mall [in addition to the 200 ft (60 m) already allowed within the store] if all of the following conditions are met:

1. The covered mall building, meaning the covered mall and all buildings attached to it, must be sprinklered. The sprinkler system must be electrically supervised. Note that if the shopping complex were considered as one building rather than as a covered mall building with complying pedestrian way, sprinkler protection would almost always also be required under the 24,000-sq ft (2,200-sq m) gross area criterion of 24-3.5.1(c).

2. The clear width of the mall must be at least 20 ft (6.1 m), or wider if the required exit capacity demands it. Note that where the covered mall of a shopping center is considered as a pedestrian way, no occupant load is calculated for the mall. The required capacity of the means of egress for the covered mall is calculated on the basis of aggregate gross leasable area of the attached stores, excluding anchor stores. See the detailed commentary on the subject following A-24-1.7.1.

3. At least 10 ft (3 m) of clear unobstructed space must be available for exit access in front of all store fronts. This requirement is designed to prohibit displays of merchandise, kiosks, or small sales stands from being placed within 10 ft (3 m) of the store fronts and ensures that the mall will have a minimum clear width of 20 ft (6.1 m).

4. Each exit access must terminate at an exit with a minimum width of 66 in. (168 cm).

5. Walls separating stores must run continuously from the floor slab to the roof slab, but not necessarily through the roof, and need not have any specified fire resistance rating. The intent of such separation is to resist the passage of smoke. The store front need not be separated from the mall by construction.

6. The covered mall, but not the stores, must have a smoke control

system. Since the individual stores are open to the mall, this requirement is essential if the mall is to be used as a safe means of egress.

If these six conditions are not met, the mall may still be considered a pedestrian way, but the additional travel distance to an exit would not be allowed. In other words, from any point within the overall covered mall building, which includes the stores and the pedestrian way, there would be a limit of 100 ft (30 m) of travel distance [200 ft (60 m) if the store and mall were sprinklered] from any point to an exit to the exterior. In the majority of configurations, this restriction would preclude the use of the mall as an exit access.

Figure 24-13 illustrates many of the requirements necessary for a mall to be considered as a pedestrian way.

The *Fire Protection Handbook*[5] contains a comprehensive discussion of the hazards to life safety specific to covered mall shopping centers.

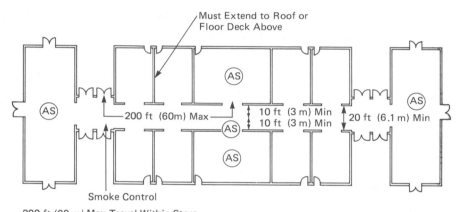

Figure 24-13. A Covered Mall Being Used as a Pedestrian Way.

24-4.4.2 Exit Details.

24-4.4.2.1 Every floor of a covered mall shall have no less than two exits remotely located from each other.

Paragraph 24-4.4.2.1 reaffirms the fundamental *Code* requirement for always providing at least two ways out.

24-4.4.2.2 No less than one-half the required exit widths for each Class A or Class B store connected to a covered mall shall lead directly outside without passage through the mall.

Note that the larger stores (Class A and B mercantile occupancies) must still have 50 percent of their exits arranged to be independent of the mall.

24-4.4.2.3* Each individual anchor store shall have means of egress independent of the covered mall.

A-24-4.4.2.3 It is not the intent of this paragraph to require that large stores be considered anchor stores. A store not considered in determining the occupant load of the mall must be arranged so that all of its means of egress will be independent of the covered mall.

24-4.4.2.4 Every covered mall shall be provided with unobstructed exit access parallel to and adjacent to the connected buildings. This exit access shall extend to each mall exit.

Paragraph 24-4.4.2.4 reiterates the provisions of item (b) of the Exception to 24-4.4.1 without mentioning that the exit access must have a clear width of at least 10 ft (3 m).

24-4.4.3 Detection, Alarm, and Communications Systems.

24-4.4.3.1 General. Covered malls shall be provided with a fire alarm system in accordance with Section 7-6.

24-4.4.3.2 Initiation. Initiation of the required fire alarm system shall be by the approved automatic sprinkler system in accordance with 7-6.2.1(c).

Note that manual pull stations are not required but that the sprinkler system must have a water flow alarm, and this must be connected to the fire alarm system.

24-4.4.3.3 Notification. At all times that the store is occupied (*see 5-2.1.1.3*), the required fire alarm system shall:

(a) Sound a general audible alarm throughout the store, or

(b) Sound an audible alarm in a continuously attended location for the purpose of initiating emergency action.

Note that the *Code* provides a choice between two methods of notification. Many large shopping malls do have a continuously attended location, and item (b) can be used; if such a location is not provided or not considered reliable by the authority having jurisdiction, item (a) would have to be applied.

24-4.4.3.4 Occupant Notification. Occupant notification shall be by live voice public address system announcement originating from the attended location where the alarm signal is received. (*See 24-4.4.3.3.*) The system may be used for other announcements. (*See 7-6.3.9 Exception No. 2.*)

Exception: Any other occupant notification means permitted by 7-6.3 may be used in lieu of live voice public address system announcement.

This Exception would allow a system using 24-4.4.3.3(a) to use an automatic voice alarm or regular alarm sounding devices in lieu of the live voice alarm.

24-4.4.3.5 Emergency Forces Notification. Emergency forces notification shall include notifying:

(a) The fire department in accordance with 7-6.4, and

(b) The local fire brigade, if provided, via the attended location where the alarm signal is received. (*See 24-4.4.3.3.*)

Paragraph 7-6.4 allows for several different methods of automatically notifying the fire department.

24-4.4.3.6 Emergency Control. The fire alarm system shall be arranged to automatically actuate smoke management or smoke control systems in accordance with 7-6.5.2(c).

24-4.5 Atriums.

24-4.5.1 Atriums are permitted provided they comply with 6-2.4.5 and 24-4.5.2 through 24-4.5.4.

Whereas the previous edition of the *Code* limited the contents within an atrium in a mercantile occupancy to low hazard contents, this edition has no similar restriction. Rather, the limitation to either low hazard or ordinary hazard contents per 6-2.4.5 applies and, in combination with the other provisions of 6-2.4.5 and the special provisions of 24-4.5.2 through 24-4.5.4, creates the necessary level of safety to life to allow the floor openings created by an atrium.

24-4.5.2 The atrium is provided with an automatic ventilation system independently operated by all of the following:

(a) Approved smoke detectors located at the top of the space and adjacent to each return air intake from the atrium, and

(b) The required automatic fire extinguishing system, and

(c) Manual controls that are readily accessible to the fire department.

The intent of 24-4.5.2 is to require a smoke control system as noted in 6-2.4.5(e) and to modify the provisions of 6-2.4.5(f) by not requiring the manual alarm to activate the smoke control system. Note that 24-4.5.3.2 does not require manual pull stations.

The reason for not requiring the manual alarm to activate the system is the possibility of a manual alarm being pulled on a floor other than the fire floor, thus possibly causing the smoke control system to function improperly.

24-4.5.3 Detection, Alarm, and Communications Systems.

24-4.5.3.1 General. Buildings housing atriums shall be provided with a fire alarm system in accordance with Section 7-6.

24-4.5.3.2 Initiation. Initiation of the required fire alarm system shall occur independently by:

(a) Activation of the smoke detection system [*see 7-6.2.1(b)*], and

(b) Activation of the automatic sprinkler system [*see 7-6.2.1(c)*].

Manual pull stations are not required.

Since an atrium is required to have a smoke detection system and protection throughout by an automatic sprinkler system, the activation of either of these systems shall initiate the fire alarm system. Note that the manual pull stations are not required; this is consistent with 24-3.4.2.

24-4.5.3.3 Notification. At all times that the store is occupied (*see 5-2.1.1.3*), the required fire alarm system shall:

(a) Sound a general audible alarm throughout the store, or

(b) Sound an audible alarm in a continuously attended location for purposes of initiating emergency action.

Note that the *Code* provides a choice between two methods of notification. Many buildings with atriums do have a continuously attended location and item (b) can be used; if such a location is not provided or not considered reliable by the authority having jurisdiction, item (a) would have to be applied.

24-4.5.3.4 Occupant Notification. Occupant notification shall be by live voice public address system announcement originating from the attended location where the alarm signal is received. (*See 24-4.5.3.3.*) The system may be used for other announcements. (*See 7-6.3.9 Exception No. 2.*)

Exception: Any other occupant notification means permitted by 7-6.3 may be used in lieu of live voice public address system announcement.

This Exception would allow a system using 24-4.5.3.3(a) to use an automatic voice alarm or regular alarm sounding devices in lieu of the live voice alarm.

24-4.5.3.5 Emergency Forces Notification. Emergency forces notification shall include notifying:

(a) The fire department in accordance with 7-6.4, and

(b) The local fire brigade, if provided.

Paragraph 7-6.4 allows for several different methods of automatically notifying the fire department.

24-4.5.3.6 Emergency Control. The fire alarm system shall be arranged to automatically actuate smoke management or smoke control systems in accordance with 7-6.5.2(c).

24-4.5.4 All electrical equipment essential for smoke control or automatic extinguishing equipment for buildings more than six stories or 75 ft (23 m) in height containing an atrium shall be provided with an emergency source of power in accordance with NFPA 70, *National Electrical Code,* Section 700-12(b), or equivalent.

Note that emergency power complying with Section 700-12(b) of NFPA 70, *National Electrical Code*,[6] requires a generator set.

24-4.6 Operating Features. *(See Chapter 31.)*

SECTION 24-5 BUILDING SERVICES

24-5.1 Utilities. Utilities shall comply with the provisions of Section 7-1.

24-5.2 Heating, Ventilating, and Air Conditioning Equipment. Heating, ventilating, and air conditioning equipment shall comply with the provisions of Section 7-2.

24-5.3 Elevators, Dumbwaiters, and Vertical Conveyors. Elevators, dumbwaiters, and vertical conveyors shall comply with the provisions of Section 7-4.

24-5.4 Rubbish Chutes, Incinerators, and Laundry Chutes. Rubbish chutes, incinerators, and laundry chutes shall comply with the provisions of Section 7-5.

REFERENCES CITED IN COMMENTARY

[1]NFPA 13, *Standard for the Installation of Sprinkler Systems*, National Fire Protection Association, Quincy, MA, 1987.

[2]NFPA 13A, *Recommended Practice for the Inspection, Testing, and Maintenance of Sprinkler Systems*, National Fire Protection Association, Quincy, MA, 1987.

[3]NFPA 30, *Flammable and Combustible Liquids Code*, National Fire Protection Association, Quincy, MA, 1987.

[4]John L. Bryan, *Automatic Sprinkler and Standpipe Systems*, National Fire Protection Association, Boston, MA, 1976.

[5]*Fire Protection Handbook*, 16th ed., National Fire Protection Association, Quincy, MA, 1986, pp. 9-57 to 9-60.

[6]NFPA 70, *National Electrical Code*, National Fire Protection Association, Quincy, MA, 1987.

25 EXISTING MERCANTILE OCCUPANCIES

(See also Chapter 31.)

Mercantile occupancies include stores, markets, and other rooms, buildings, or structures used for the display and sale of merchandise. Included in this occupancy group are:

Supermarkets
Department stores
Drugstores
Auction rooms
Shopping centers

Minor merchandising operations in buildings consisting predominantly of other occupancies, such as a newsstand in an office building, must meet the *Life Safety Code* requirements of the predominant occupancy.

SECTION 25-1 GENERAL REQUIREMENTS

25-1.1 Application.

25-1.1.1 Existing mercantile occupancies shall comply with the provisions of Chapter 25. *(See Chapter 31 for operating features.)*

In understanding the full intent and scope of 25-1.1.1, it is necessary to review it concurrently with Sections 1-4, 1-5, and 1-6. While a building code may exclude existing buildings from coverage under some form of a "grandfather clause," the *Life Safety Code*, by virtue of its very interest in safety to life, does not condone existing building arrangements that do not comply with the *Code* except under a very narrow and strict set of guidelines. These guidelines are contained in this chapter.

Because a building may be in compliance with an earlier edition of the *Code* does not mean that it is "grandfathered" so as not to have to comply with a newer edition that has been adopted as law in that jurisdiction. The Committee on Safety to Life is especially careful not to make the requirements that are applicable to existing buildings more stringent from one edition of the *Code* to the next unless the change is absolutely needed to enhance the overall package of safety to life intended by the *Code*. Thus, the old adage of "once in compliance, always in compliance" does not hold.

25-1.1.2 This chapter establishes life safety requirements for existing buildings. Specific requirements for suboccupancy groups, such as Class A, B, and C stores and covered malls, are contained in paragraphs pertaining thereto.

For the definitions of Class A, B, and C stores, see 25-1.4.2.

25-1.1.3 Additions to existing buildings shall conform to the requirements for new construction. Existing portions of the structure need not be modified, provided that the new construction has not diminished the fire safety features of the facility.

Exception: Existing portions shall be upgraded if the addition results in a change of mercantile subclassification. (See 25-1.4.2.)

Paragraph 25-1.1.3 and its Exception are intended to indicate that additions to existing mercantile occupancies must conform to the requirements for new occupancies; the existing portion of the occupancy may generally continue in use as long as it complies with the provisions for existing mercantile occupancies contained in this chapter. If, however, the addition results in a change in the mercantile occupancy classification, such as a change from a Class C mercantile to a Class B mercantile or from a Class B mercantile to a Class A mercantile, then the existing occupancy, as well as the new construction, must be upgraded to meet the provisions for new occupancies.

25-1.2 Mixed Occupancies.

25-1.2.1 Mixed occupancies shall comply with 1-4.7.

25-1.2.2 Combined Mercantile and Residential Occupancies.

25-1.2.2.1 No dwelling unit shall have its sole means of egress through any mercantile occupancy in the same building.

25-1.2.2.2 No multiple dwelling occupancy shall be located above a mercantile occupancy.

Exception No. 1: Where the dwelling occupancy and exits therefrom are separated from the mercantile occupancy by construction having a fire resistance rating of at least 1 hour.

Exception No. 2: Where the mercantile occupancy is protected throughout by an approved automatic sprinkler system in accordance with Section 7-7.

Exception No. 3: As permitted in 25-1.2.2.3.

25-1.2.2.3 A building with not more than two dwelling units above a mercantile occupancy shall be permitted, provided that the mercantile occupancy is protected by an automatic fire detection system in accordance with Section 7-6.

The requirements for mixed occupancies were developed to address a once common (but now slowly disappearing) occupancy arrangement: the corner tavern, grocery store, or retail store that has a dwelling on the upper floors. The *Code* divides this type of combined occupancy into two classes.

Where there is a single dwelling above or adjacent to the mercantile operation, the *Code* prohibits (*see 25-1.2.2.1*) the dwelling occupancy from having its sole means of egress pass through the mercantile occupancy in the same building. If the dwelling has an exit through the mercantile occupancy, it must have a second exit that is independent of and does not pass through the mercantile occupancy.

The *Code* prohibits a multiple dwelling occupancy to be located above a mercantile occupancy unless one of the following conditions is met:

1. The dwellings and their exits are separated from the mercantile occupancy by construction with a fire resistance rating of at least 1 hour, or

2. The mercantile occupancy is protected by an automatic sprinkler system. Sprinkler systems have proven to be an excellent alternative to 1-hour construction under these circumstances. (*See Section 7-7 of the Code, NFPA 13, Standard for the Installation of Sprinkler Systems,*[1] *and NFPA 13A, Recommended Practice for the Inspection, Testing, and Maintenance of Sprinkler Systems.*[2]) or

3. There are no more than two dwelling units, and the mercantile occupancy is protected by an automatic fire detection system that must be capable of sounding an alarm in the dwelling occupancies as required by Sections 2-7 and 7-6.

The *Code* established these requirements because of the long historical record of deaths and injuries that have occurred where fire originated in mercantile occupancies and spread to unsuspecting occupants of the dwelling units above the mercantile occupancies.

25-1.3 Special Definitions.

(a) *Anchor Store.* A department store or major merchandising center having direct access to the covered mall but having all required means of egress independent of the covered mall.

From a merchandising point of view, a shopping mall developer or operator may refer to any of the major tenants with vast expanses of floor space and instant name recognition, often positioned at the ends and corners of the covered mall building, as anchor stores. However, the *Code* reserves the use of the term for those stores having means of egress independent from the covered mall. (*See Figure 25-1.*)

(b) *Class A Stores.* [*See 25-1.4.2.1(a)*].

(c) *Class B Stores.* [*See 25-1.4.2.1(b)*].

(d) *Class C Stores.* [*See 25-1.4.2.1(c)*].

(e) *Covered Mall.* A covered or roofed interior area used as a pedestrian way and connected to a building(s) or portions of a building housing single or multiple tenants.

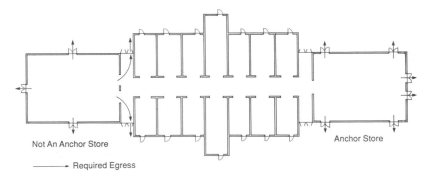

Not An Anchor Store

Anchor Store

———→ Required Egress

Figure 25-1.   Anchor Store.   Illustration of the difference between a store that is an anchor store and a store that, although large, is not an anchor store. Note that required egress from an anchor store cannot pass through the mall.

A covered mall can be considered as such even if it is open to the outside elements at one or more points.

(f) *Covered Mall Building.* A building, including the covered mall, enclosing a number of tenants and occupancies, such as retail stores, drinking and dining establishments, entertainment and amusement facilities, offices, and other similar uses, wherein two or more tenants have a main entrance into the covered mall.

The definition of "covered mall building" is differentiated from that of "covered mall" so that certain requirements can be applied only to the covered pedestrian way, i.e., the covered mall, while other requirements can be applied to the entire building, including all tenant spaces and common areas, i.e., the covered mall building. For example, the provisions of 25-4.4 require automatic sprinkler protection throughout the entire covered mall building but require smoke control only within the covered mall.

(g) *Gross Leasable Area.* The total floor area designated for tenant occupancy and exclusive use, expressed in square feet (square meters), measured from centerlines of joining partitions and exteriors of outside walls.

(h) *Open-Air Mercantile Operations.* Operations conducted outside of all structures with the operations area devoid of all walls and roofs except for small, individual, weather canopies.

25-1.4 Classification of Occupancy.

25-1.4.1   Mercantile occupancies shall include all buildings and structures or parts thereof with occupancy as described in 4-1.7.

It is important to review again the *Code*'s definition (*see 4-1.7*) of a mercantile occupancy. Note that this definition does not include "minor merchandising operations in buildings predominantly of other occupancies, such as a newsstand in an office building..." Paragraph 4-1.7 requires that such occupancies be subject to the exit requirements of the predominant (major) occupancy.

25-1.4.2 Subclassification of Occupancy.

25-1.4.2.1   Mercantile occupancies shall be subclassified as follows:

(a) *Class A.*   All stores having aggregate gross area of more than 30,000 sq ft (2,800 sq m), or utilizing more than three levels, excluding mezzanines, for sales purposes.

(b) *Class B.*   All stores of more than 3,000 sq ft (280 sq m) but not more than 30,000 sq ft (2,800 sq m) aggregate gross area, or utilizing floors above or below the street floor level for sales purposes. (Mezzanines permitted, see 25-1.4.2.3.)

Exception to (b): If more than three floors, excluding mezzanines, are utilized, the store shall be Class A, regardless of area.

(c) *Class C.*   All stores of not more than 3,000 sq ft (280 sq m) gross area used for sales purposes on one story only, excluding mezzanines.

The mezzanines allowed by the one-half area rule of 25-1.4.2.3 do not constitute either a floor or a level and, therefore, are not a factor in determining mercantile occupancy subclassification based on number of floors used for sales purposes. The area of such mezzanines used for sales purposes (*see 25-1.4.2.2*) is, however, a factor with respect to the occupancy subclassification cut-off points based on floor area. For example, a store with a 2,000-sq ft (186-sq m) main sales floor and a 1,000-sq ft (93-sq m) sales mezzanine is a Class C mercantile occupancy, whereas a store with a 2,400-sq ft (225-sq m) main sales floor and a 1,200-sq ft (112-sq m) sales mezzanine is a Class B mercantile occupancy. In each case the mezzanine meets the maximum one-half area rule and is not counted as a floor or level. In the second case, the area of the 1,200-sq ft (112-sq m) sales mezzanine, when added to the 2,400-sq ft (225-sq m) main sales floor, exceeds the maximum 3,000-sq ft (280-sq m) sales area size for Class C mercantile occupancies and results in a Class B mercantile occupancy classification.

Mezzanines in excess of the maximum one-half area rule of 25-1.4.2.3 constitute floors and thus, sales levels, and need to be considered as such in determining mercantile occupancy subclassification. For example, a set of plans might show a proposed store with three floor levels, each 8,000 sq ft (740 sq m) in area, used for sales purposes, and a single 5,000-sq ft (465-sq m) sales "mezzanine." The store actually will use four floor levels for sales purposes because the so-called "mezzanine" is not a mezzanine based on the maximum one-half area rule of 25-1.4.2.3. Although the 30,000-sq ft (2,800-sq m) sales area limitation associated with Class A mercantile occupancies is not exceeded, the four floor levels used for sales purposes result in a Class A mercantile occupancy subclassification.

The following table summarizes the requirements of 25-1.4.2.1 for qualifying a store as Class A, B, or C. This classification process is important because it leads to specific life safety criteria that apply to each class of store. The criteria vary in degree of stringency dependent upon a store's classification.

Table 25–1. Subclassification of Mercantile Occupancies

Store Class	By Height		By Aggregate Gross Area† (sq ft)
A	>3 Floors‡	or	>30,000
B	≤3 Floors‡	and	>3,000 and ≤30,000
C	One Floor Only§	and	≤3,000

†Sections of floors not used for sales are not counted in the area classification.
‡Floors not used for sales above or below a sales floor are not counted in the height classification.
§A mezzanine < ½ the area of the floor below is permitted.

25-1.4.2.2   For the purpose of the classification in 25-1.4.2.1, the aggregate gross area shall be the total gross area of all floors used for mercantile purposes and, where a store is divided into sections, regardless of fire separation, shall include the area of all sections used for sales purposes. Areas of floors not used for sales purposes, such as an area used only for storage and not open to the public, shall not be counted for the purposes of the above classifications, but exits shall be provided for such nonsales areas in accordance with their occupancy, as specified by other chapters of this *Code*.

Some mercantile occupancies have their sales and storage areas together, e.g., furniture warehouse sales areas. In these cases, the occupancy should be classified using all aggregate gross area open to public use.

25-1.4.2.3   The floor area of a mezzanine or the aggregate floor area of multiple mezzanines shall not exceed one-half of the floor area of the room or story in which the mezzanines are located. A mezzanine or aggregated mezzanines in excess of the one-half area limitation shall be treated as floors.

The mezzanine measurement provisions of 25-1.4.2.3 for existing mercantile occupancies use a "one-half" area rule, whereas the provisions of 24-1.4.2.3 for new mercantile occupancies use a "one-third" area rule. The "one-third" rule for new mercantile occupancy mezzanines coincides with the Chapter 3 definition of mezzanine. Given that the "one-half" area rule applied to mercantile occupancies long before the generalized definition of mezzanine was added to Chapter 3, it has been retained for existing (but not new) mercantile occupancies to prevent the abrupt noncompliance of existing buildings caused by an issue that by itself does not significantly lower the level of safety to life in an existing building. Therefore, mezzanines in existing mercantile occupancies continue to be judged based on the historical "one-half" area criteria.

Examples of mezzanine arrangements to which the maximum one-half area rule of 25-1.4.2.3 can be applied are illustrated in Figures 25-2(a) through (f). For purpose of illustration, accept as a given that all mezzanines as well as the entire main floor level are used for sales purposes. In Figures (a), (b), (c), and (d), only a single story, or single floor level, with mezzanine exists, because the aggregate areas of the mezzanines, i.e., 5,000 sq ft (465 sq m), do not exceed one-half of the floor area, i.e., 10,000 sq ft (930 sq m), of the room or story in which the mezzanine is located.

In Figure (e), the single so-called "mezzanine" with 6,000 sq ft (560 sq m) of floor area exceeds the one-half area rule and thus is not a mezzanine but rather a floor level in and of itself. Figure (e), therefore, depicts a two-story mercantile occupancy.

In Figure (f), one of the 4,000-sq ft (370-sq m) mezzanines fits within the maximum one-half area allowance and can be called a mezzanine without constituting a floor level. The other mezzanine, although of the same size and thus by itself not exceeding the one-half area rule, does create a floor level because the sum of the areas of the two mezzanines, i.e., 8,000 sq ft (745 sq m), exceeds one-half of the 10,000-sq ft (930-sq m) lower floor level. Thus, the figure shows a two-story mercantile occupancy with a mezzanine.

Although the mezzanines in Figures (a) through (d) do not establish separate floor levels, their areas, because they are used for sales, are included in the total gross sales area against which the Class A, B, and C mercantile occupancy subclassification definitions of 25-1.4.2.1 are applied. Figures (a) through (d) each show 15,000 sq ft (1400 sq m) of sales area.

25-1.4.2.4   Where a number of stores under different management are located in the same building or in adjoining buildings, the aggregate gross area of all such stores shall be used in determining classification per 25-1.4.2.1.

Exception No. 1:   *Where individual stores are separated by fire barriers with a 1-hour fire resistance rating.*

Note that, for new mercantile occupancies (*see 24-1.4.2.4 Exception No. 1*), the fire resistance rated separation required for exemption from aggregation of gross area is 2-hour rather than the 1-hour rating of this paragraph.

Exception No. 2:   *Covered mall buildings. (See 25-4.4.)*

Paragraphs 25-1.4.2.2 through 25-1.4.2.4 further clarify the classification of stores as Class A, B, or C. Most of these provisions are included in the footnotes to Table 25-1. The following should be noted for emphasis:

1. The aggregate gross area is the sum of the gross areas of all floors used for mercantile (sales) purposes.

2. If the store is divided into sections, only the sales sections should be included in the aggregate gross area.

3. If there are sections or floors used for sales that are considered as separate "stores" (because they are under different management), without minimum 1-hour fire resistance rated separation (fire walls or fire barriers) between each "store," the aggregate gross area of all such "stores" is to be used in classifying the occupancy as Class A, B, or C, except as provided for covered mall buildings. (*See 25-4.4.*)

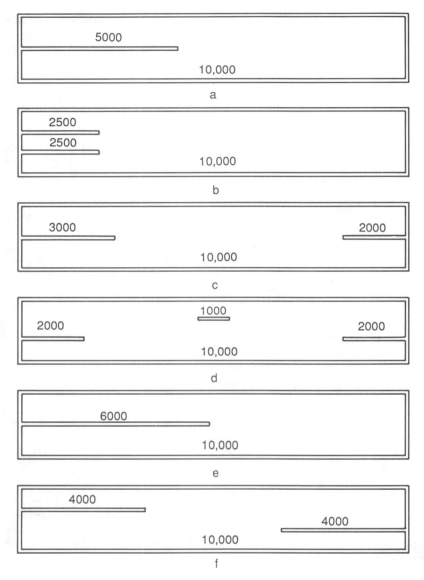

Figures 25-2(a), (b), (c), (d), (e), and (f).   Examples of Mercantile Occupancy Mezzanine Arrangement Elevation Views. (*See commentary associated with 25-1.4.2.3*).   All values are expressed in square feet. For metric values, 1 sq ft = 0.093 sq m.

25-1.5 Classification of Hazard of Contents.   Mercantile occupancies' contents shall be classed as ordinary hazard in accordance with Section 4-2.

Exception: Mercantile occupancies shall be classified as high hazard if high hazard commodities are displayed or handled without protective wrappings or containers, in which case the following additional provisions shall apply:

(a) Exits shall be located so that not more than 75 ft (23 m) of travel from any point is required to reach the nearest exit.

(b) From every point there shall be at least two exits accessible by travel in different directions (no common path of travel).

(c) All vertical openings shall be enclosed.

Rather than simply referring the user to Section 4-2 for classification of hazard of contents, as most other occupancy chapters do, the requirement of 25-1.5 stresses that, unless an extraordinarily hazardous situation exists, the contents of mercantile occupancies shall be classed as ordinary hazard. Such wording is meant to keep the user from classifying the hazard of contents as high hazard unless a situation equivalent to the dispensing of explosives in bulk is present. Given that the package of life safety afforded by the chapter's requirements, taken as a whole, anticipates significant quantities of combustibles on display, these requirements should provide an acceptable level of safety without classifying the typical mercantile occupancy environment as highly hazardous. In other words, the chapter's requirements should be adequate without imposing the stringent high hazard contents requirements of the Exception to 25-1.5 on all but the most hazardous of mercantile occupancies.

Some procedures that would require classifying a mercantile occupancy as highly hazardous are: dispensing gunpowder or other explosives in bulk; selling polyurethane foam; or dispensing gasoline or flammable solvents by pouring them into open containers. The sales of such flammable liquids as camp stove fuel, rubbing alcohol, etc., should be controlled by NFPA 30, *Flammable and Combustible Liquids Code*,[3] as to display configuration, total amounts, and separations from ignition sources. Figure 25-3 illustrates an arrangement of exits from a high hazard area in a mercantile occupancy.

25-1.6 Minimum Construction Requirements.   No Special Requirements.

The phrase "minimum construction" is used in the *Code* to describe the construction of the building housing the occupancy. Some occupancy chapters, such as Chapters 12 and 13, which address the life safety needs of nonambulatory occupants, require a certain minimum building construction type to help assure building structural integrity for the time period needed for a lengthy evacuation or for safe refuge within the building. Because mercantile occupancies characteristically have ambulatory customers and employees and do not provide sleeping accommodations, there are no minimum construction requirements imposed. Since there are no special requirements, the provisions of a local or state building code, if applicable, would apply.

25-1.7 Occupant Load.

25-1.7.1* For purposes of determining required exits, the occupant load of

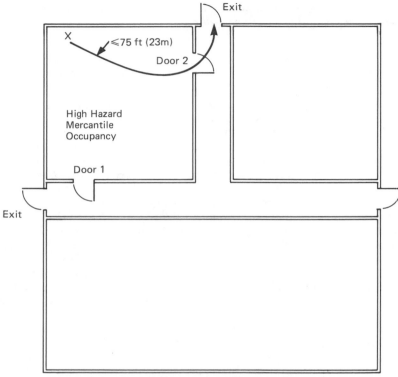

Doors 1 and 2 Each Lead to a Different Corridor Providing
Access to a Different Exit. Travel Distance from any
Point to an Exit Must not Exceed 75 ft (23m)

Figure 25-3.   Exit Arrangement from an Area of a Mercantile Occupancy Defined
as Highly Hazardous by 25-1.5.

mercantile buildings or parts of buildings used for mercantile purposes shall be not less than the following:

(a) Street floor: one person for each 30 sq ft (2.8 sq m) gross floor area of sales space. In stores with no street floor, as defined in Chapter 3, but with access directly from the street by stairs or escalators, the principal floor at the point of entrance to the store shall be considered the street floor.

Exception to (a):   In stores where, due to differences in grade of streets on different sides, there are two or more floors directly accessible from streets (not including alleys or similar back streets), for the purpose of determining occupant load, each such floor shall be considered a street floor. The occupant load factor shall be one person for each 40 sq ft (3.7 sq m) gross floor area of sales space.

(b) Sales floors below the street floor: same as street floor.

(c) Upper floors used for sales: one person for each 60 sq ft (5.6 sq m) gross floor area of sales space.

(d) Floors or portions of floors used only for offices: one person for each 100 sq ft (9.3 sq m) gross floor area of office space.

(e) Floors or portions of floors used only for storage, receiving, shipping and not open to the general public: one person per each 300 sq ft (27.9 sq m) gross area of storage, receiving, or shipping space.

(f) Floors or portions of floors used for assembly purposes: occupant load determined in accordance with Chapter 9 for such assembly occupancies.

(g)* Covered mall buildings: determined in accordance with 25-1.7.1(a) through (f).

Exception: The covered mall, where considered a pedestrian way (see Exception to 25-4.4.1), shall not be assessed an occupant load. However, means of egress from the covered mall shall be provided for an occupant load determined by dividing the gross leasable area (not including anchor stores) by the appropriate occupant load factor listed below:

Gross Leasable Area [See 25-1.3(g).] (sq ft)	Occupant Load Factor	
	(sq ft)	(sq m)
Less than 150,000 (14,000 sq m)	30	*(2.79)*
Over 150,000 (14,000 sq m) but less than 200,000 (18,500 sq m)	35	*(3.25)*
Over 200,000 (18,500 sq m) but less than 250,000 (23,000 sq m)	40	*(3.72)*
Over 250,000 (23,000 sq m) but less than 300,000 (28,000 sq m)	45	*(4.18)*
Over 300,000 (28,000 sq m) but less than 400,000 (37,000 sq m)	50	*(4.65)*
Over 400,000 (37,000 sq m)	55	*(5.11)*

Each individual tenant space shall have means of egress to the outside or to the covered mall based on occupant loads figured utilizing 25-1.7.1 (a) through (f).

Each individual anchor store shall have means of egress independent of the covered mall.

A-25-1.7.1   These figures were established on the basis of counts of the population of typical store buildings during periods of maximum occupancy, such as before Christmas or during special sales. In some cases, the actual occupancy may be more dense than indicated by these figures, but it may reasonably be assumed that in any large mercantile building, all areas will not be similarly crowded at the same time, and the average occupant load should seldom exceed these figures.

In some types of stores, the occupant load will normally be much less than indicated: for example, in furniture stores. However, the character of mercantile operations is subject to such rapid changes that it is not prudent in designing exit facilities to assume that any store will never be crowded, and for this reason, the same load figures are used for all types of stores.

A-25-1.7.1(g)   The table used in determining the occupancy load for covered mall shopping centers of varying sizes is arrived at empirically in surveying over 270 covered mall shopping centers, in studying mercantile occupancy parking requirements, and in observing the number of occupants per vehicle during peak seasons.

These studies show that with an increase in shopping center size, there is a decrease in the number of occupants per square foot of gross leasable area.

This phenomenon is explained when one considers that above a certain shopping center gross leasable area [approx. 600,000 sq ft (56,000 sq m)], a multiplicity of the same types of stores starts to occur: the purpose is to increase the choices available to a customer for any given type of merchandise. Therefore, when shopping center size increases, the occupant load increases as well, but at a declining rate. In using the table, the occupant load factor is applied to only the gross leasable area utilizing the covered mall as a means of egress.

The values show that, during normal use of a mercantile occupancy, the public will congregate, for the most part, on the street floor or in a basement "sales" area.

To differentiate between street floors and other sales floors, the street floor is any floor that has an entrance/exit directly accessible from the street. If differences in the ground level on different sides of a store create several floors of this nature, the *Code* treats them all as street floors; however, a slightly different occupant load factor is used per the Exception to (a). It is important to note that, if access to a store from the street is only by means of stairs or escalators, the principal floor at the point of entrance to the store must be considered the street floor. In assigning a higher occupant load to the street floor, the *Code* recognizes merchandising techniques, since these floors sell merchandise conducive to high traffic and customers are often forced to walk through portions of the street floor to reach escalators, elevators, and stairs to other floors. Thus, larger numbers of occupants are expected to be present on the street floor.

Given that the terms "covered mall" and "covered mall building" have different meanings [*see commentary following 25-1.3(f)*], the intent of 25-1.7.1(g) and its Exception is that the egress capacity of the overall covered mall building be sized to handle a number of occupants calculated in two steps. First, the occupant load is calculated for all stores and tenant spaces using the occupant load factors of 25-1.7.1(a) through (f). Second, the required egress capacity for the covered mall itself, meaning the covered pedestrian way, is calculated using values from the table of the Exception to 25-1.7.1(g). Each store or tenant space must have sufficient egress capacity for its occupant load. The covered mall must have egress capacity based on 24-1.7.1(g).

For example, consider a covered mall building with 21 tenant stores, all on the "street floor," each having 6,000 sq ft (560 sq m) of sales area, but 7,500 sq ft (700 sq m) of gross leasable area [assume that the other 1,500 sq ft (140 sq m) is storage]. Using an occupant load factor of 30 sq ft (2.8 sq m) per person for the sales areas and 300 sq ft (28 sq m) for the storage areas, each store must size its means of egress system to handle 205 persons (6,000/30 + 1,500/300 = 200 + 5 = 205). People can be sent back through the covered mall as part of the required means of egress from the stores. The covered mall, based on the 21 tenant stores, each with 7,500 sq ft (700 sq m) of gross leasable area (i.e., 21 × 7,500 = 157,500 sq ft of gross leasable area) must provide a means of egress system for 157,000 ÷ 35 = 4,500 persons.

25-1.7.2   Where mezzanines open to the floor below or other unprotected vertical openings between floors as permitted by the Exceptions to 25-3.1, the occupant load (or area) of the mezzanine or other subsidiary floor level shall be added to that of the street floor for the purpose of determining required exits, provided, however, that in no case shall the total exit capacity be less than would be required if all vertical openings were enclosed.

Figures 25-4 and 25-5 illustrate the requirements of 25-1.7.2. Figure 25-4 illustrates the case where a mezzanine is open to the street floor (which by the definition in Chapter 3 contains the main exit to the exterior or public way). The exits from the street floor must accommodate the people expected to occupy the street floor and the mezzanine as well as the required capacity provided by the stairs from the upper floors discharging through the street floor.

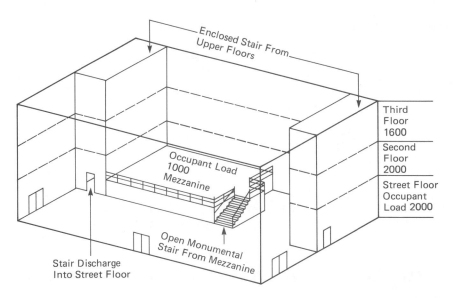

Figure 25-4.   Mercantile Occupancy with a Mezzanine Open to the Street Floor.   To determine the exit capacity for the street floor, the occupant load of the mezzanine (1,000) is added to the occupant load of the street floor (2,000). In addition, since one-half of the exits from the upper floors discharge through the street floor, the exit capacity of the street floor must be able to accommodate the capacity of the stair exits discharging through it. The maximum occupant load on any upper floor is 2,000 (second floor) and 25-2.7 permits at maximum one-half of the exits or exit capacity to discharge through the street floor, provided that the building is sprinklered. Therefore, the street floor must be provided with egress capacity for 4,000 persons or 800 in. (2030 cm) of exit width using the factor of 0.2 in. (0.5 cm) per person for level exit components found in 5-3.3.1 (2,000 for street floor + 1,000 for mezzanine + 1,000 for upper floors = 4,000).

In Figure 25-5, where the mezzanine is not open to the street floor, the capacity of the exits on the street floor must be able to accommodate the people expected to occupy the street floor and the capacity of the stairs from the upper floors discharging through the street floor. The enforcing official should note that the calculations required for the arrangement in Figure 25-5 will establish the minimum exit width that the *Code* will allow where exits from upper floors discharge into a street floor, whether or not the mezzanine is open to the street floor.

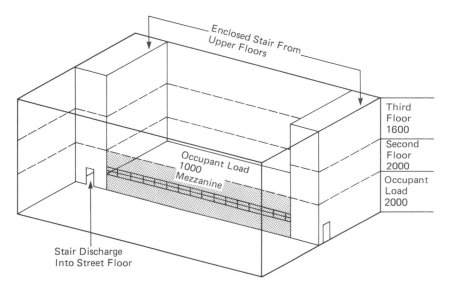

Figure 25-5. Mercantile Occupancy with a Mezzanine Not Open to the Street Floor. The street floor requires egress capacity for 3,000 persons (2,000 for the street floor + 1,000 for stairs discharging through the street floor).

SECTION 25-2   MEANS OF EGRESS REQUIREMENTS

25-2.1 General.

25-2.1.1   All means of egress shall be in accordance with Chapter 5 and this chapter.

25-2.1.2   No inside open stairway, escalator, or ramp may serve as a component of the required means of egress system for more than one floor.

This provision prohibits the use of open stairways, escalators, or ramps as an egress facility for more than one floor; it does not establish permission for the open stairway, ramp, or escalator to exist. See 25-3.1, under the subject of protection of vertical openings, to determine if the open stairway, ramp, or escalator is permitted.

25-2.1.3   Where there are two or more floors below the street floor, the same stair or other exit may serve all floors, but all required exits from such areas shall be independent of any open stairways between the street floor and the floor below it.

25-2.1.4   Where a level, outside exit from upper floors is possible owing to hills, such outside exits may serve instead of horizontal exits. If, however, such outside exits from the upper floor also serve as an entrance from a principal street, the upper floor shall be classed as a street floor in accordance with the definition of Chapter 3 and is subject to the requirements of this section for street floors.

Paragraph 25-2.1.4 reconfirms the requirements of 25-1.7.1(a) for the classification of floors as street floors. Figure 25-6 illustrates a case where two floors qualify as street floors because each has one side at a ground level. Note, however, that each has its other sides either above or below the building's other ground level. As a result, these floors must have their exits arranged to allow horizontal travel to the exterior at one end of the floor and vertical travel (either up or down to ground level) at the other end of the floor. This means that the exit capacity to the exterior must be able to accommodate, in the case of Floor 1, people from the upper floors who may need to travel down to and through the exits to the exterior from Floor 1. The reverse holds true for Floor 2, which must size its exterior exit capacity to accommodate occupants who may travel up from Floor 1 as well as occupants who may have to travel down to and through the exterior exits on Floor 2. Paragraphs 5-3.1.4, 25-1.7.2, and 25-2.3.2 demonstrate how to add exit capacity based on expected occupant use from floors above the street floor. This method is equally valid for adding exit capacity based on expected occupant use from floors below the street floor. Figure 25-8 provides an example of how to calculate exit capacity for a street floor such as Floor 2 in Figure 25-6.

25-2.1.5   For special considerations with contents of high hazard, see 25-1.5.

25-2.2 Means of Egress Components.

25-2.2.1   Components of means of egress shall be limited to the types described in 24-2.2.2 through 24-2.2.10.

25-2.2.2 Doors.

25-2.2.2.1   Doors shall comply with 5-2.1.

25-2.2.2.2*   Locks complying with 5-2.1.5.1 Exception No. 2 shall be permitted only on principal entrance/exit doors.

A-25-2.2.2.2   The term "principal entrance/exit doors" is intended to imply doors that the authority having jurisdiction can be reasonably assured will be unlocked in order for the facility to do business.

This provision permits doors to be equipped with a key-operated lock in accordance with the provisions of Chapter 5. (*See Figure 25-7.*)

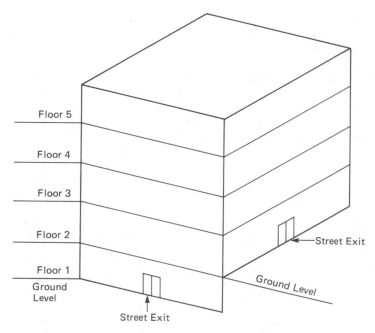

Figure 25-6.   Mercantile Occupancy with Two Street Floors.   See Figure 25-8 to determine the exit capacity of the street floors.

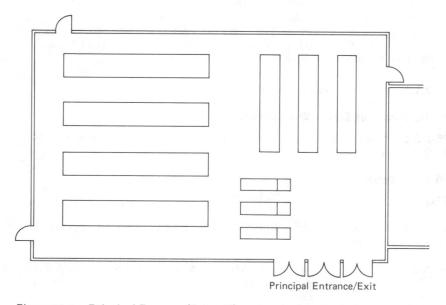

Figure 25-7.   Principal Entrance/Exit.   The concept of a principal entrance/exit as used in 25-2.2.2.2 is illustrated here.

25-2.2.2.3   The reentry provisions of 5-2.1.5.2 need not be met. (*See 5-2.1.5.2 Exception No. 3.*)

Had use of Exception No. 3 to 5-2.1.5.2 not been specifically recognized by this occupancy chapter, the basic requirements of 5-2.1.5.2 that provide for reentry from stairwells back onto all floors of the building would have applied. By this recognition of Exception No. 3, existing mercantile occupancies are exempt from the reentry provisions.

25-2.2.2.4   Special locking arrangements in accordance with 5-2.1.6 are permitted.

In recognition of the security needs of a mercantile occupancy, use of the delay release device covered by 5-2.1.6 is allowed on any door. In effect, the allowable 15- or 30-second delay will be experienced only under nonfire conditions or very early in a fire's growth, given that the door must be immediately usable upon sprinkler operation or smoke or heat detection and upon loss of power controlling the locking mechanism. The building must be protected throughout by an approved automatic sprinkler system or automatic fire detection system.

25-2.2.2.5   Where horizontal or vertical security grilles or doors are used as a part of the required means of egress from a tenant space, such grilles or doors shall comply with 5-2.1.4.1 Exception No. 3.

25-2.2.2.6   All doors at the foot of stairs from upper floors or at the head of stairs leading to floors below the street floor shall swing with the exit travel.

This provision requires doors that would not otherwise have to swing in the direction of egress travel under any of the three conditions of 5-2.1.4.1 to do so, based on their location. This is because of the queuing and accumulation of people that tend to occur at doors in such locations, which makes it difficult to step back to allow the door to swing.

25-2.2.2.7   Revolving doors shall comply with 5-2.1.10.

Existing revolving doors may continue to be used without having to meet some of the more stringent requirements applicable to new revolving doors if such exemption is approved by the authority having jurisdiction. (*See 5-2.1.10 and the commentary following 24-2.2.2.7.*)

25-2.2.2.8   In Class C mercantile occupancies, doors may swing inward where such doors serve only the street floor area.

25-2.2.3 Stairs.

25-2.2.3.1   Stairs shall comply with 5-2.2.

25-2.2.3.2   Spiral stairs complying with 5-2.2.2.7 are permitted.

Note that 5-2.2.2.7 only permits spiral stairs to serve an occupant load of five or fewer. They may be effectively used in storage areas having a small occupant load.

25-2.2.3.3   Winders complying with 5-2.2.2.8 are permitted.

25-2.2.4 Smokeproof Enclosures.   Smokeproof enclosures shall comply with 5-2.3.

25-2.2.5 Horizontal Exits.   Horizontal exits shall comply with 5-2.4.

25-2.2.6 Ramps.   Ramps shall comply with 5-2.5.

25-2.2.7 Exit Passageways.   Exit passageways shall comply with 5-2.6.

25-2.2.8 Escalators and Moving Walks.   Escalators and moving walks complying with 5-2.7 are permitted.

Note that to qualify as required exits, escalators must meet the requirements of 5-2.2.3 dealing with enclosure.

25-2.2.9 Fire Escape Stairs.   Fire escape stairs complying with 5-2.8 are permitted.

Note that 5-2.8.1 permits existing buildings to use or continue to use fire escape stairs for no more than 50 percent of the building's required exit capacity.

25-2.2.10 Alternating Tread Devices.   Alternating tread devices complying with 5-2.11 are permitted.

The provisions of 5-2.11 in effect limit the use of alternating tread devices to locations where the *Code* recognizes the use of fire escape ladders. (*See* 5-2.9.)

25-2.3 Capacity of Means of Egress.

25-2.3.1   The capacity of means of egress shall be in accordance with Section 5-3.

25-2.3.2   In Class A and Class B stores, street floor exits shall be sufficient for the occupant load of the street floor plus the required capacity of stairs, ramps, escalators and moving walks discharging through the street floor.

In 25-2.3.2, the *Code* requires that the exits for the street floor of a Class A or B store have sufficient capacity to handle the people who, in exiting the building during an emergency, must travel up from the basement sales area or down from the upper sales floors and mix with the customers already on the first or street floor.

Since people move more quickly in the horizontal direction than in the vertical direction, it is permissible to provide less door width than stair width. For example, per the egress capacity factors of 5-3.3.1, in mercantile occupancies, level components and ramps require only 0.2 in. (0.5 cm) of width per person, whereas stairs require 0.3 in. (0.8 cm) of width per person. Figure 25-8 provides an example of how to calculate the required exit capacity for the street floor.

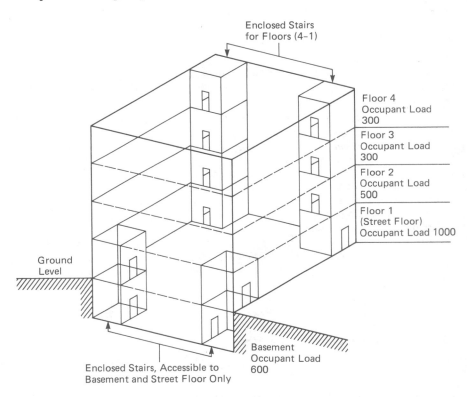

Figure 25-8. Calculation of Exit Capacity Required for a Street Floor in Accordance with 25-2.3.2.

Street floor occupant load alone, plus	1,000
maximum upper floor occupant load discharging back through street floor (500 ÷ 2), plus	250
basement occupant load discharging back through street floor (600 ÷ 2)	300

1,550 persons x 0.2 in. (0.5 cm) per person for level exit components per 5-3.3.1 = 310 in. (787 cm) of exit width required from the street floor exit system.

25-2.4 Number of Exits.

25-2.4.1   The number of exits shall be in accordance with 25-2.4.2 and 25-2.4.3. The requirements of Section 5-4 shall not apply.

25-2.4.2   In Class A and Class B stores, at least two separate exits shall be accessible from every part of every floor, including floors below the street floor.

25-2.4.3   In Class C stores, at least two separate exits shall be provided as specified by 25-2.4.2.

Exception No. 1:   Where no part of the Class C stores is more than 75 ft (23 m) from the exit or covered mall, where it is considered as a pedestrian way, a single exit shall be permitted.

Exception No. 2:   Where no part of the Class C store is more than 100 ft (30 m) from the exit or covered mall, where it is considered as a pedestrian way, and the story on which it is located is protected throughout by an approved automatic sprinkler system in accordance with Section 7-7, a single exit shall be permitted.

The *Code* allows this Exception to the basic requirement for the presence of at least two remote exits from an occupancy in the instance of very small Class C mercantile stores, such as tobacco shops, shoe shine stands, and newsstands. If the travel distance from any point in such a store to an exit is 75 ft (23 m) or less, the probability that a fire might surprise and overcome the customers before they could escape is low. Further, by allowing up to 100 ft (30 m) of travel distance with a single exit, Exception No. 2 intends to provide additional exiting flexibility to those small stores that provide a high degree of "self-protection" by means of automatic sprinkler installations. (*See Figure 25-9.*)

25-2.5 Arrangement of Means of Egress.

25-2.5.1   Exits shall be arranged in accordance with Section 5-5.

25-2.5.2*   No dead-end corridor shall exceed 50 ft (15 m).

Exception*:   Existing dead-end corridors exceeding 50 ft (15 m) may be continued in use subject to the approval of the authority having jurisdiction and the travel distance requirements of 25-2.6.

A-25-2.5.2   The purpose of this paragraph is to avoid pockets or dead ends of such size that they pose an undue danger of persons becoming trapped in case of fire.

A-25-2.5.2 Exception   It is recognized that excessive dead ends exist and, in some cases, are impractical to eliminate. The authority having jurisdiction may allow these to continue, taking into consideration any or all of the following:

Tenant arrangement.

Automatic sprinkler protection.

Smoke detection.

Exit remoteness.

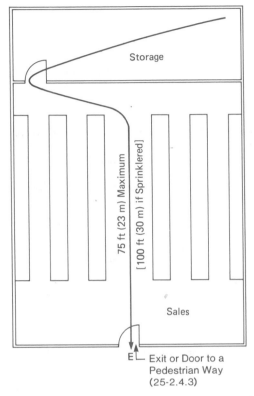

Figure 25-9. Single Exit. A Class C Mercantile Occupancy may be provided with a single exit if X → E ≤ 75 ft (23 m) or, if story is sprinklered, 100 ft (30 m).

25-2.5.3* No common path of travel shall exceed 75 ft (23 m).

Exception No. 1: A common path of travel may be permitted for the first 100 ft (30 m) on a story protected throughout by an approved automatic sprinkler system in accordance with Section 7-7.

Exception No. 2*: Existing excessive common paths of travel may be continued in use subject to the approval of the authority having jurisdiction and the travel distance requirements of 25-2.6.

The maximum common path of travel allowed in mercantile occupancies by the previous edition of the *Code* was 50 ft (15 m) [75 ft (23 m) if protected by smoke detectors or 100 ft (30 m) if sprinklered]. Based on the deletion from this edition of the previous Chapter 5 provisions that applied to the point where measurement of travel distance and common path begins for small rooms [i.e., distance within room was not counted if there was a maximum six person occupant load and a maximum 50-ft (15-m) of travel within the room], the allowable common path has been increased without either reducing the level of safety to life or imposing a hardship on designers.

(See the commentary following 5-5.1.5 for a discussion on common path of travel.)

A-25-2.5.3   The common path of travel requirement permits small areas such as rooms or alcoves with only one way out where the distance is small enough so that there is little likelihood that a fire might develop to such proportions as to block escape before the occupants become aware of the fire and make their way out.

A-25-2.5.3 Exception No. 2   It is recognized that excessive common paths of travel exist and, in some cases, are impractical to eliminate. The authority having jurisdiction may allow these to continue, taking into consideration any or all of the following:

Tenant arrangement.

Automatic sprinkler protection.

Smoke detection.

Exit remoteness.

25-2.5.4   Aisles leading to each exit are required. The aggregate width of such aisles shall be equal to at least the required width of the exit.

25-2.5.5   In no case shall any required aisle be less than 28 in. (71 cm) in clear width.

25-2.5.6   In Class A stores, at least one aisle of 5 ft (152 cm) minimum width shall lead directly to an exit.

The intent of 25-2.5.4 through 25-2.5.6 is to ensure that the interior arrangement of counters, racks, and displays of merchandise does not block or obscure accesses to an exit. Figure 25-10 illustrates an arrangement that meets the requirements for a Class A store. Essentially, the width of the exit determines the minimum width of the aisle, except that one of the aisles must be at least 5 ft (152 cm) wide.

25-2.5.7   If the only means of customer entrance is through one exterior wall of the building, two-thirds of the required exit width shall be located in this wall.

In establishing 25-2.5.7, the *Code* is concerned about the arrangement of many discount and variety stores, which have one large main exit/entrance located in the front of the store, and the other exits (which cannot be used as entrances) situated at points unfamiliar to the public. In these cases, the wall containing the main exit/entrance must be sized to handle two-thirds of the required exit capacity of the store because most of the customers will instinctively try to use this exit during a fire. Such an arrangement is shown in Figure 25-10.

25-2.5.8 At least one-half of the required exits shall be so located as to be reached without going through checkout stands. In no case shall checkout stands or associated railings or barriers obstruct exits, required aisles, or approaches thereto.

This is one of the most frequently violated provisions of Chapter 25. Many supermarkets and discount and variety stores are arranged so that it is necessary to pass through checkout counters, around shopping carts, and through turnstiles in order to exit the facility. Obviously, this causes congestion or blockage during an emergency. The *Code* requires at least one-half of all exits to be located so that people can avoid having to pass through or around these impediments to egress.

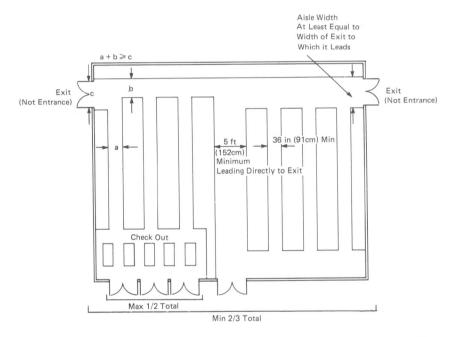

Figure 25-10. Means of Egress Arrangement in a Mercantile Occupancy. The conditions described and the resulting requirements of 25-2.5.4 through 25-2.5.8 are illustrated here.

25-2.5.9* Where wheeled carts or buggies are used by customers, adequate provision shall be made for the transit and parking of such carts to minimize the possibility that they may obstruct means of egress.

A-25-2.5.9 In order to eliminate the obstruction to the means of egress of the interior exit access and the exterior exit discharge, it is the intent to provide adequate area for transit and parking of wheeled carts or buggies used by customers. This includes corral areas adjacent to exits that are constructed to restrict the movement of wheeled carts or buggies therefrom.

In states where returnable beverage bottle legislation has recently been enacted, stores and markets have had to find space for the collection of empty bottles and the refund of deposit charges. The area most commonly used is near the entrance/exit where wheeled shopping carts were formerly stored clear of the path of egress travel. The carts are now often stored so as to obstruct the means of egress. This illustrates a situation where a planned complying means of egress is compromised overnight by changing conditions.

25-2.5.10   Exit access in Class A stores protected throughout with an approved supervised automatic sprinkler system in accordance with Section 7-7 and in all Class B or Class C stores may pass through storerooms provided the following conditions are met:

(a) Not more than 50 percent of exit access is provided through the storeroom.

(b) The storeroom is not subject to locking.

(c) The main aisle through the storeroom shall be not less than 44 in. (112 cm) wide.

(d) The path of travel, defined with fixed barriers, through the storeroom shall be direct and continuously maintained in an unobstructed condition.

In (a) above, the storeroom is limited to providing a maximum of 50 percent of the store's exit access, either in number of exits or exit capacity. Thus, given that two exits are required, neither of the following limits can be exceeded:

1. Only one of the two required exits can be reached by exit access travel through the storeroom, and

2. A maximum of half the store's occupant load can exit through the storeroom.

In addition to allowing exit access in all Class B and C stores to pass through storerooms, 25-2.5.10 allows exit access in some Class A stores to pass through storerooms where that store is protected throughout by an approved automatic sprinkler system, and recognizes the increased safety to life that a sprinkler system provides.

Figures 25-11 and 25-12 give examples of the application of the provisions of 25-2.5.10.

25-2.6 Travel Distance to Exits.   Travel distance to exits, measured in accordance with Section 5-6, shall be no more than 150 ft (45 m).

Exception: An increase in the above travel distance to 200 ft (60 m) shall be permitted in a building protected throughout by an approved automatic sprinkler system in accordance with Section 7-7.

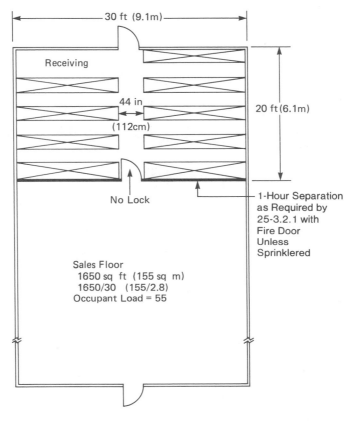

Figure 25-11. Example of Exit Access Through Storeroom as Permitted by 25-2.5.10. The aisle within the storeroom must be defined by fixed barriers, such as those formed by the ends of shelving. The aisle must be kept unobstructed.

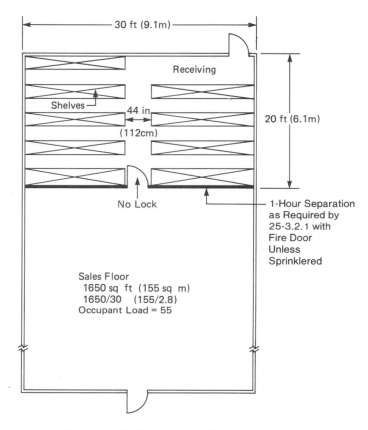

Figure 25-12. Example of Exit Access Through Storeroom That Will Be Problematic Because of Relationship to the Receiving Area.

A review of 5-6.2 will show that the travel distance requirements apply to only the first (or nearest) exit from a point in the building. In other words, the 150-ft (45-m) travel distance limit means that at least one exit must be within 150 ft (45 m) of a point in the building, not that all exits must be within 150 ft (45 m) of that same point in the building.

The maximum travel distance allowed in mercantile occupancies by the previous edition of the *Code* was 100 ft (30 m) and, if the building were sprinklered, a 50 ft (15 m) increase was allowed to 150 ft (45 m). Based on the deletion in this edition of the previous Chapter 5 provisions that applied to the point where measurement of travel distance begins for small rooms [i.e., distance within room was not counted if there was a maximum six-person occupant load and a maximum 50-ft (15-m) of travel within the room], the allowable travel distance for existing mercantile occupancies has been increased to 150 ft (45 m) and, if the building is sprinklered, 200 ft (60 m). If the allowable travel distance had not been increased, given that its measurement now always begins within the room, many existing means of egress arrangements that had made use of the "small room" exception and complied with the previous edition of the *Code* would be faced with noncompliance.

25-2.7 Discharge from Exits.

25-2.7.1   Exit discharge shall comply with Section 5-7 except as modified by 25-2.7.2.

25-2.7.2*   Fifty percent of the exits may discharge through the level of exit discharge in accordance with 5-7.2 where the building is protected throughout by an approved automatic sprinkler system in accordance with Section 7-7, and the distance of travel from the termination of the exit enclosure to an outside street door shall not exceed 50 ft (15 m).

A-25-2.7.2   The basis for the Exception to the general rule on complete enclosure of exits up to their point of discharge to the outside of the building is that, with the specified safeguards, reasonable safety is maintained.

A stairway is not considered to discharge through the street floor area if it leads to the street through a fire resistance rated enclosure (exit passageway) separating it from the main area, even though there are doors between the first floor stairway landing and the main area.

The provisions of 25-2.7.2 should not be confused with open stairways as permitted by 25-3.1 (Exception No. 1).

> Note that a limit is applied to this arrangement so that no more than 50 percent of the exits from either the entire building or from any floor can be arranged to discharge through the street floor. Further, this can only be done if the building is sprinklered throughout. Also note that the path of travel on the first floor from the stair enclosure to the outside door cannot exceed 50 ft (15 m). The remaining 50 percent of the exits must discharge directly to the exterior.
>
> Paragraph 25-2.7 is more stringent than the comparable 5-7.2 since it mandates that the building be protected throughout by automatic sprinklers; it sets a 50-ft (15-m) limit of travel on the street floor; and it requires that the street floor have exit capacity to accommodate the street floor and the stairs discharging through the street floor. These requirements are not mandated by 5-7.2. The extra requirements are imposed in recognition of the high combustible load of merchandise on display, which is characteristic of mercantile occupancies.

25-2.8 Illumination of Means of Egress.   Means of egress shall be illuminated in accordance with Section 5-8.

> Note that illumination for the means of egress is not the same as emergency lighting; failure of the building power supply may cause failure of the means of egress illumination system, which is not required to have a back-up, auxiliary, or secondary power supply unless required by 25-2.9.

25-2.9 Emergency Lighting. Class A and Class B stores shall have emergency lighting facilities in accordance with Section 5-9.

Class C stores, due to their small size and small occupant load, are not required by the *Code* to have emergency lighting facilities.

25-2.10 Marking of Means of Egress. Means of egress shall have signs in accordance with Section 5-10.

Exception: Where an exit is immediately apparent from all portions of the sales area, the exit marking may be omitted.

The intent of the Exception to the provision for marking the means of egress is to avoid requiring exit signs in small areas where the exit is readily apparent. For example, exit signs would not be required in the office of a service station, the purchase and eating areas of a small "fast food" restaurant, or in a Class C store whose size and arrangement comply with the Exceptions to 25-2.4.3.

25-2.11 Special Features.

SECTION 25-3 PROTECTION

25-3.1* Protection of Vertical Openings. Each stairway, elevator shaft, escalator opening, or other vertical opening shall be enclosed or protected in accordance with Section 6-2.

Exception No. 1: In Class A or Class B mercantile occupancies, openings may be unprotected between any two floors, such as between the street floor and the floor below, or between the street floor and mezzanine, or between the street floor and second floor.

Exception No. 2: In Class A or B mercantile occupancies protected throughout by an approved automatic sprinkler system in accordance with Section 7-7, unprotected vertical openings shall be permitted as follows:

(a) Between the street floor and floor below and to the floor above the street floor or to mezzanines above the street floor; or

(b) Between the street floor, street floor mezzanine and second floor, but not among more than three floor levels; or

(c) In accordance with 6-2.4.4; or

(d) Among all floors permitted in Class B mercantile occupancies; or

(e) One floor above those permitted may be open if such floor is not used for sales purposes.

Exception No. 3: In Class C mercantile occupancies, unprotected vertical openings shall be permitted as follows:

(a) Between the street floor and mezzanine; or

(b) Between the street floor and the floor below or the second floor if not used for sales purposes.

Exception No. 4: Atriums in accordance with 25-4.5 are permitted.

A-25-3.1 See 25-1.7.2 for provisions on determining occupant load for exit purposes where vertical openings are unprotected.

Follow the provisions of 25-1.7 for properly assessing the occupant load to develop sufficient exit capacity for a store in which floors or mezzanines are open to the street floor. Exceptions No. 1 and No. 2 to 25-3.1 specify under which conditions such openings are permitted in Class A and B stores. Exception No. 3 allows certain unprotected vertical openings in Class C stores.

Exception No. 1 allows for unprotected vertical openings between *any* two floors. Although the term "such as" is used and all the examples involve a street floor and a floor adjacent to that street floor, the 2-story unprotected vertical opening could occur, for example, between floors four and five of a multistory department store. Interpreting the Exception to require that the street floor be included as one of the levels involved in the 2-story vertical opening would leave existing mercantile occupancies without any option for a similar opening between upper floors of the building. Yet, sprinklered new mercantile occupancies are afforded the option via 24-3.1 Exception No. 1(a). The apparent inconsistency resulted from a change made to Chapter 24 during the Public Comment period of the revision cycle for which no corresponding Public Comment was received on Chapter 25. It is the intent to allow for the 2-story unprotected opening to occur anywhere within an existing mercantile occupancy without the requirement for sprinklers that is imposed on new mercantile occupancies. However, mercantile occupancies of any appreciable size must be sprinklered by the requirements of 25-3.5.

As a condition of Exception No. 2, unprotected vertical openings, mainly various forms of 3-story openings, are allowed if the mercantile occupancy is protected throughout by automatic sprinklers. Subpart (c) provides permission to use the provisions of 6-2.4.4. Subpart (e) would allow up to a 4-story unprotected vertical opening in, for example, a 4-story building in which only the first three stories are used for sales purposes.

Exception No. 3 allows for certain unprotected vertical openings in Class C mercantile occupancies, which by definition involve only a single sales floor or a sales floor and sales mezzanine, all of limited sizes. Although it is most common to locate a Class C mercantile occupancy such that its main sales floor is a street floor, the Class C mercantile might, for example, occupy space on the third floor of a covered mall building. (*See* 25-4.4.) Thus, it is not the intent to restrict the 2-story opening between the main sales floor and the mezzanine of a Class C mercantile occupancy, as addressed by 25-3.1 Exception No. 3(a), so that the main sales floor must be a street floor. Rather, taking guidance from the 2-story vertical opening allowed for Class A and B mercantile occupancies by 25-3.1 Exception No. 1 and its associated commentary, the opening can occur within a Class C mercantile occupancy located on any floor of, for example, a multistory covered mall building.

Note that 25-4.4 has provisions that differ from 6-2.2.3.5.

25-3.2 Protection from Hazards.

25-3.2.1   Hazardous areas, including but not limited to areas used for general storage, boiler or furnace rooms, fuel storage, janitor closets, maintenance shops including woodworking and painting areas, and kitchens, shall:

(a) Be separated from other parts of the building by fire barriers having a fire resistance rating of not less than 1 hour with all openings therein protected by ¾-hour fire protection rated self-closing fire doors, or

(b) The area shall be protected by an automatic extinguishing system in accordance with Section 7-7.

25-3.2.2   Areas with high hazard contents as defined in Section 4-2 shall be provided with both fire-resistive separation and automatic sprinkler protection.

> Paragraphs 25-3.2.1 and 25-3.2.2 reflect the intent of Section 6-4 which: (1) requires separation of a hazardous area from the rest of a building by suitable construction, or (2) mandates the installation of an automatic sprinkler system in a hazardous area, or (3) requires both where the hazard is severe.

25-3.3 Interior Finish.

25-3.3.1   Interior finish on walls and ceilings shall be Class A or B, in accordance with Section 6-5.

Exception: Existing Class C interior finish shall be permitted as follows:

(a) On walls.

(b) Throughout Class C stores.

> Essentially, 25-3.3.1 Exception states that in existing Class C stores only, all the interior finish (walls and ceilings) may be rated as Class C (flame spread of 0-200). All existing Class A and B stores may have Class C interior finish on the walls, but not on the ceiling.

25-3.3.2 Interior Floor Finish.   No Requirements.

25-3.4 Detection, Alarm, and Communications Systems.

25-3.4.1 General.   Class A mercantile occupancies shall be provided with a fire alarm system in accordance with Section 7-6.

25-3.4.2 Initiation.   Initiation of the required fire alarm system shall be by manual means per 7-6.2.1(a).

Exception No. 1:   Initiation may be by means of an approved automatic fire detection system, in accordance with 7-6.2.1(b), providing protection throughout the building.

Exception No. 2:   Initiation may be by means of an approved automatic sprinkler system, in accordance with 7-6.2.1(c), providing protection throughout the building.

> Since most Class A stores will be sprinklered (*see* 25-3.5), it is logical that Exception No. 2 will be the most common method of activating the fire alarm system, since this allows the elimination of the manual pull

stations if the sprinkler water flow activates the fire alarm system. Nuisance alarms might be reduced by eliminating the manual pull stations and satisfying the initiation requirements via water flow through the sprinkler system.

25-3.4.3 Notification.

25-3.4.3.1 At all times that the store is occupied (*see 5-2.1.1.3*), the required fire alarm system shall:

(a) Sound a general audible alarm throughout the store, or

(b) Sound an audible alarm in a continuously attended location for purposes of initiating emergency action.

Note that the *Code* does provide a choice between two methods of notification. Many Class A stores do have a continuously attended location, and item (b) can be used; if such a location is not provided or not considered reliable by the authority having jurisdiction, item (a) would have to be applied.

25-3.4.3.2 Occupant Notification. Occupant notification shall be by live voice public address system announcement originating from the attended location where the alarm signal is received. (*See 25-3.4.3.1.*) The system may be used for other announcements. (*See 7-6.3.9 Exception No. 2.*)

Exception: Any other occupant notification means permitted by 7-6.3 may be used in lieu of live voice public address system announcement.

This Exception would allow a system using 25-3.4.3.1(a) to have an automatic voice alarm or regular alarm sounding devices in lieu of the live voice alarm.

25-3.5 Extinguishment Requirements.

25-3.5.1 Mercantile occupancies shall be protected throughout by an approved automatic sprinkler system in accordance with Section 7-7 as follows:

(a) In all buildings with a story over 15,000 sq ft (1,400 sq m) in area.

(b) In all buildings exceeding 30,000 sq ft (2,800 sq m) in gross area.

(c) Throughout stories below the level of exit discharge where such stories have an area exceeding 2,500 sq ft (230 sq m) where used for the sale, storage, or handling of combustible goods and merchandise.

Exception: Single-story buildings that meet the requirements of a street floor.

For discussions of what constitutes an "approved automatic sprinkler system," see NFPA 13, *Standard for the Installation of Sprinkler Systems,*[1] NFPA 13A, *Recommended Practice for the Inspection, Testing, and Maintenance of Sprinkler Systems,*[2] and *Automatic Sprinkler and Standpipe Systems.*[4]

Under the provisions of item (a), a building with a total gross area of not more than 30,000 sq ft (2,800 sq m) (Class B or C), but with any one floor of more than 15,000 sq ft (1,400 sq m) in area, would have to be protected with a complete automatic sprinkler system. A building with a total gross area of not more than 30,000 sq ft (2,800 sq m) would not be required to be sprinklered as long as the area of no floor exceeds 15,000 sq ft (1,400 sq m).

The intent of item (b) is to require that all buildings with a total gross area of more than 30,000 sq ft (2,800 sq m) be protected with a complete automatic sprinkler system.

The intent of item (c) is to ensure that all basement areas larger than 2,500 sq ft (230 sq m) (whether the space is used for sales, storage, or the handling of combustible merchandise) be sprinklered to avoid the potential threat to the occupants of the floors above. Studies have shown that there is a higher rate of fire incidence in basements than in other areas of stores. Because smoke and heat rise, a fire in a basement can quickly render exits and exit discharges located on the street floor unusable.

Although supervision of the sprinkler system is not required, such supervision is desirable and could be required by the authority having jurisdiction as part of his or her approval.

The Exception appears only in Chapter 25 and thus is for existing buildings only. It is felt that in existing one-story "street floor only" buildings that comply with all the other provisions of the *Code*, including travel distance, adequate life safety is provided in an existing building so that retroactively requiring the building to be sprinklered is not needed.

25-3.5.2   Portable fire extinguishers shall be provided in all mercantile occupancies in accordance with 7-7.4.1.

The provision of portable extinguishers is for use by the properly trained employees of the mercantile occupancy as required by 31-8.2.

25-3.6 Corridors.   No Special Requirements.

There are no corridor separation requirements for existing mercantile occupancies, whereas such requirements appear in 24-3.6 for new mercantile occupancies.

25-3.7 Subdivision of Building Spaces.   No Special Requirements.

25-3.8 Special Features.

SECTION 25-4   SPECIAL PROVISIONS

25-4.1 Windowless or Underground Buildings.   *(See Section 30-7.)*

25-4.2 High Rise Buildings.   No additional requirements.

Section 30-8, High Rise Buildings, is new to the 1988 Edition of the *Code*. It is menu-oriented in that its provisions, singly, in various combinations, or in total, must be mandated by a specific occupancy chapter requirement. For existing mercantile occupancies, paragraph 25-4.2 does not require any of the provisions of Section 30-8. Rather, the sprinkler system mandated by 25-3.5.1, based on floor area, helps assure that high rise mercantile occupancies will be adequately protected.

25-4.3 Open-Air Mercantile Operations.

25-4.3.1   Open-air mercantile operations, such as open-air markets, gasoline filling stations, roadside stands for the sale of farm produce, and other outdoor mercantile operations shall be so arranged and conducted as to maintain free and unobstructed ways of travel at all times to permit prompt escape from any point of danger in case of fire or other emergency, with no dead ends in which persons might be trapped due to display stands, adjoining buildings, fences, vehicles, or other obstructions.

Paragraph 25-4.3.1 is virtually an open-ended provision that provides guidance for the arrangement, use, and display of merchandise for sale in open-air mercantile operations. The phrase "ways of travel" is purposely used to avoid confusion with "means of egress," which is strictly defined and whose use implies the minimum requirements of Chapter 5. "Ways of travel" is not defined and implies no specific minimum *Code* provisions. Most open-air mercantile operations have unlimited means of entering and evacuating the areas used to display goods. For this reason, it is not necessary to provide specific *Code* requirements beyond the precautionary measures expressed in this paragraph.

25-4.3.2   If mercantile operations are conducted in roofed-over areas, they shall be treated as mercantile buildings, provided that canopies over individual small stands to protect merchandise from the weather shall not be construed to constitute buildings for the purpose of this *Code*.

The intent of 25-4.3.2 is to exempt small merchandise stands with canopies from classification as mercantile buildings. All other "roofed-over" areas should be treated as buildings, classified by area and height as Class A, B, or C mercantile occupancies, and subject to the appropriate provisions of Chapter 25.

25-4.4 Covered Mall Buildings.

25-4.4.1   The covered mall building shall be treated as a single building for the purpose of calculation of means of egress and shall be subject to the requirements for appropriate occupancies. The covered mall shall be at least of sufficient clear width to accommodate egress requirements as set forth in other sections of this *Code*.

Exception: The covered mall may be considered to be a pedestrian way, in which case the distance of travel within a tenant space to an exit or to the covered mall shall be a maximum of 200 ft (60 m) (see Exception to 25-2.6), or shall be the maximum for the appropriate occupancy; plus, an additional 200 ft (60 m) shall be permitted for travel through the covered mall space if all the following requirements are met:

(a) The covered mall shall be at least of sufficient clear width to accommodate egress requirements as set forth in other sections of this chapter, but in no case less than 20 ft (6.1 m) wide in its narrowest dimension.

(b)* On each side of the mall floor area, the covered mall shall be provided with an unobstructed exit access of not less than 10 ft (3 m) in clear width parallel to and adjacent to the mall tenant front. Such exit access shall lead to an exit having a minimum of 66 in. (168 cm) in width. (See 25-4.4.2.)

(c) The covered mall and all buildings connected thereto shall be protected throughout by an approved electrically supervised automatic sprinkler system in accordance with Section 7-7.

(d) Walls dividing stores from each other shall extend from the floor to the underside of the roof deck or floor deck above. No separation is required between a tenant space and the covered mall.

(e)* The covered mall shall be provided with a smoke control system.

A-25-4.4.1 Exception (b)   The minimum requirement for terminating mall exit access in not less than 66 in. (168 cm) of exit width relates to the minimum requirement for at least one aisle in Class A stores [30,000 sq ft (2,800 sq m) or greater] to be 5 ft (152 cm) in width.

A-25-4.4.1 Exception (e)   Smoke control systems for covered malls are necessary to maintain the covered mall reasonably free of products of combustion for at least the duration required to evacuate the building and to minimize migration of products of combustion from one tenant to another. Systems that can be engineered to accomplish this include:

(a) Separate or mechanical exhaust or control systems.

(b) Mechanical exhaust or control systems in conjunction with the heating, ventilating, and air conditioning systems.

(c) Automatically or manually released gravity roof vent devices, such as skylights, relief dampers, or smoke vents.

(d) Combinations of (a), (b), and (c) or any other engineered system designed to accomplish the purpose of this section.

In recent years, covered mall shopping areas have increased in both number and size. Two options or approaches for dealing with the life safety aspects of these complexes were developed. The first approach (described in the base paragraph of 25-4.4.1) considers the mall and the attached stores as essentially one large Class A store subject to all the provisions of Chapter 25. Viewed this way, the covered mall would be treated as an aisle of a store.

The other approach, introduced in the 1976 Edition of the *Life Safety Code*, permits the mall to be considered as a "pedestrian way" by which occupants of the attached stores may egress during a fire. The phrase "pedestrian way" was chosen by the Committee both to convey the meaning of the term "exit access" and to allow the mall to be treated as if it were an area of refuge.

The Exception to 25-4.4.1 recognizes that if the mall and all the buildings attached to the mall were protected by automatic sprinklers, people fleeing into the mall from a fire in a store would be moving into a space whose volume, size, and arrangement afforded most of the benefits provided by an enclosed stair or a horizontal exit. The Exception considers the mall as a virtual area of refuge for the buildings attached to it, even though the mall is not separated from these attached buildings by the type of construction normally provided for an exit as required by 5-1.3.1.

Where a covered mall is considered as a pedestrian way, the maximum travel distance to an exit or to the mall from any point within a store attached to the mall is 200 ft (60 m). This reflects the judgment that using the mall for egress is as acceptable (or as safe) as using an exit. An additional travel distance of up to 200 ft (60 m) is permitted within the mall [in addition to the 200 ft (60 m) already allowed within the store] if all of the following conditions are met:

1. The covered mall building, meaning the covered mall and all buildings attached to it, must be sprinklered. The sprinkler system must be electrically supervised. Note that if the shopping complex were considered as one building rather than as a covered mall building with complying pedestrian way, sprinkler protection would almost always also be required under the 30,000-sq ft (2,800-sq m) gross area criterion of 25-3.5.1(b).

2. The clear width of the mall must be at least 20 ft (6.1 m), or wider if the required exit capacity demands it. Note that where the covered mall of a shopping center is considered as a pedestrian way, no occupant load is calculated for the mall. The required capacity of the means of egress for the covered mall is calculated on the basis of aggregate gross leasable area of the attached stores, excluding anchor stores. See the detailed commentary on this subject following A-25-1.7.1.

3. At least 10 ft (3 m) of clear unobstructed space must be available for exit access in front of all store fronts. This requirement is designed to prohibit displays of merchandise, kiosks, or small sales stands from being placed within 10 ft (3 m) of the store fronts and ensures that the mall will have a minimum clear width of 20 ft (6.1 m).

4. Each exit access must terminate at an exit with a minimum width of 66 in. (168 cm).

5. Walls separating stores must run continuously from the floor slab to the roof slab, but not necessarily through the roof, and need not have any given specified fire resistance rating. The intent of such separation is to resist the passage of smoke. The store front need not be separated from the mall by construction.

6. The covered mall, but not the stores, must have a smoke control system. Since the individual stores are open to the mall, this requirement is essential if the mall is to be used as a safe means of egress.

If these six conditions are not met, the mall may still be considered a pedestrian way, but the additional travel distance to an exit would not be allowed. In other words, from any point within the overall covered mall building, which includes the stores and the pedestrian way, there would be a limit of 150 ft (45 m) of travel distance [200 ft (60 m) if the store and mall were sprinklered] from any point to an exit to the exterior. In the majority of configurations, this restriction would preclude the use of the mall as an exit access.

Figure 25-13 illustrates many of the requirements necessary for a covered mall to be considered as a pedestrian way.

The *Fire Protection Handbook*[5] contains a comprehensive discussion of the hazards to life safety specific to covered mall shopping centers.

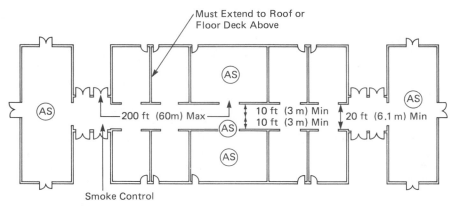

Figure 25-13.   A Covered Mall Being Used as a Pedestrian Way.

25-4.4.2 Exit Details.

25-4.4.2.1   Every floor of a covered mall shall have no less than two exits remotely located from each other.

Paragraph 25-4.4.2.1 reaffirms the fundamental *Code* requirement for always providing at least two ways out.

25-4.4.2.2   No less than one-half the required exit widths for each Class A or Class B store connected to a covered mall shall lead directly outside without passage through the mall.

Note that the larger stores (Class A and B mercantile occupancies) must still have 50 percent of their exits arranged to be independent of the mall.

25-4.4.2.3*   Each individual anchor store shall have means of egress independent of the covered mall.

A-25-4.4.2.3   It is not the intent of this paragraph to require that large stores be considered anchor stores. A store not considered in determining the occupant load of the mall must be arranged so that all of its means of egress will be independent of the covered mall.

25-4.4.2.4   Every covered mall shall be provided with unobstructed exit access parallel to and adjacent to the connected buildings. This exit access shall extend to each mall exit.

Paragraph 25-4.4.2.4 reiterates the provisions of item (b) of the Exception to 25-4.4.1 without mentioning that the exit access must have a clear width of at least 10 ft (3 m).

25-4.4.3 Detection, Alarm, and Communications Systems.

25-4.4.3.1 General. Covered malls shall be provided with a fire alarm system in accordance with Section 7-6.

25-4.4.3.2 Initiation. Initiation of the required fire alarm system shall be by the approved automatic sprinkler system in accordance with 7-6.2.1(c).

Note that manual pull stations are not required but that the sprinkler system must have a water flow alarm, and this must be connected to the fire alarm system.

25-4.4.3.3 Notification. At all times that the store is occupied (*see 5-2.1.1.3*), the required fire alarm system shall:

(a) Sound a general audible alarm throughout the store, or

(b) Sound an audible alarm in a continuously attended location for the purpose of initiating emergency action.

Note that the *Code* provides a choice between two methods of notification. Many large malls do have a continuously attended location, and item (b) can be used; if such a location is not provided or not considered reliable by the authority having jurisdiction, item (a) would have to be applied.

25-4.4.3.4 Occupant Notification. Occupant notification shall be by live voice public address system announcement originating from the attended location where the alarm signal is received. (*See 25-4.4.3.3.*) The system may be used for other announcements. (*See 7-6.3.9 Exception No. 2.*)

Exception: Any other occupant notification means permitted by 7-6.3 may be used in lieu of live voice public address system announcement.

This Exception would allow a system using 25-4.3.3.3(a) to use an automatic voice alarm or regular alarm sounding devices in lieu of the live voice alarm.

25-4.4.3.5 Emergency Forces Notification. Emergency forces notification shall include notifying:

(a) The fire department in accordance with 7-6.4, and

(b) The local fire brigade, if provided, via the attended location where the alarm signal is received. (*See 25-4.4.3.3.*)

Paragraph 7-6.4 allows for several different methods of automatically notifying the fire department.

25-4.4.3.6 Emergency Control. The fire alarm system shall be arranged to automatically actuate smoke management or smoke control systems in accordance with 7-6.5.2(c).

25-4.5 Atriums.

25-4.5.1 Atriums are permitted provided they comply with 6-2.4.5 and 25-4.5.2 through 25-4.5.4.

> Whereas the previous edition of the *Code* limited the contents within an atrium in a mercantile occupancy to low hazard contents, this edition has no similar restriction. Rather, the limitation to either low hazard or ordinary hazard contents per 6-2.4.5 applies and, in combination with the other provisions of 6-2.4.5 and the special provisions of 25-4.5.2 through 25-4.5.4, creates the necessary level of safety to life to allow the floor openings created by an atrium.

25-4.5.2 The atrium is provided with an automatic ventilation system independently operated by all of the following:

(a) Approved smoke detectors located at the top of the space and adjacent to each return air intake from the atrium, and

(b) The required automatic fire extinguishing system, and

(c) Manual controls that are readily accessible to the fire department.

> The intent of 25-4.5.2 is to require a smoke control system as noted in 6-2.4.5(e) and to modify the provisions of 6-2.4.5(f) by not requiring the manual alarm to activate the smoke control system. Note that 25-4.5.3.2 does not require manual pull stations.
>
> The reason for not requiring the manual alarm to activate the system is the possibility of a manual alarm being pulled on a floor other than the fire floor, thus possibly causing the smoke control system to function improperly.

25-4.5.3 Detection, Alarm, and Communications Systems.

25-4.5.3.1 General. Buildings housing atriums shall be provided with a fire alarm system in accordance with Section 7-6.

25-4.5.3.2 Initiation. Initiation of the required fire alarm system shall occur, independently, by:

(a) Activation of the smoke detection system [*see 7-6.2.1(b)*], and

(b) Activation of the automatic sprinkler system [*see 7-6.2.1(c)*].

Manual pull stations are not required.

25-4.5.3.3 Notification. At all times that the store is occupied (*see 5-2.1.1.3*), the required fire alarm system shall:

(a) Sound a general audible alarm throughout the store, or

(b) Sound an audible alarm in a continuously attended location for purposes of initiating emergency action.

Note that the *Code* provides a choice between two methods of notification. Many buildings with atriums do have a continuously attended location, and item (b) can be used; if such a location is not provided or not considered reliable by the authority having jurisdiction, item (a) would have to be applied.

25-4.5.3.4 Occupant Notification. Occupant notification shall be by live voice public address system announcement originating from the attended location where the alarm signal is received. (*See 25-4.5.3.3.*) The system may be used for other announcements. (*See 7-6.3.9 Exception No. 2.*)

Exception: Any other occupant notification means permitted by 7-6.3 may be used in lieu of live voice public address system announcement.

This Exception would allow a system using 25-4.5.3.3(a) to have an automatic voice alarm or regular alarm sounding devices in lieu of the live voice alarm.

25-4.5.3.5 Emergency Forces Notification. Emergency forces notification shall include notifying:

(a) The fire department in accordance with 7-6.4, and

(b) The local fire brigade, if provided.

Paragraph 7-6.4 allows for several different methods of automatically notifying the fire department.

25-4.5.3.6 Emergency Control. The fire alarm system shall be arranged to automatically actuate smoke management or smoke control systems in accordance with 7-6.5.2(c).

25-4.5.4 All electrical equipment essential for smoke control or automatic extinguishing equipment for buildings more than six stories or 75 ft (23 m) in height containing an atrium shall be provided with an emergency source of power in accordance with NFPA 70, *National Electrical Code*, Section 700-12(b), or equivalent.

Note that emergency power complying with Section 700-12(b) of NFPA 70, *National Electrical Code*,[6] requires a generator set.

25-4.6 Operating Features. (*See Chapter 31.*)

SECTION 25-5   BUILDING SERVICES

25-5.1 Utilities. Utilities shall comply with the provisions of Section 7-1.

25-5.2 Heating, Ventilating, and Air Conditioning Equipment. Heating, ventilating, and air conditioning equipment shall comply with the provisions of Section 7-2.

25-5.3 Elevators, Dumbwaiters, and Vertical Conveyors. Elevators, dumbwaiters, and vertical conveyors shall comply with the provisions of Section 7-4.

25-5.4 Rubbish Chutes, Incinerators, and Laundry Chutes.   Rubbish chutes, incinerators, and laundry chutes shall comply with the provisions of Section 7-5.

REFERENCES CITED IN COMMENTARY

[1]NFPA 13, *Standard for the Installation of Sprinkler Systems*, National Fire Protection Association, Quincy, MA, 1987.

[2]NFPA 13A, *Recommended Practice for the Inspection, Testing, and Maintenance of Sprinkler Systems*, National Fire Protection Association, Quincy, MA, 1987.

[3]NFPA 30, *Flammable and Combustible Liquids Code*, National Fire Protection Association, Quincy, MA, 1987.

[4]John L. Bryan, *Automatic Sprinkler and Standpipe Systems*, National Fire Protection Association, Boston, MA, 1976.

[5]*Fire Protection Handbook*, 16th ed., National Fire Protection Association, Quincy, MA, 1986, pp. 9-57 to 9-60.

[6]NFPA 70, *National Electrical Code*, National Fire Protection Association, Quincy, MA, 1987.

26

NEW BUSINESS OCCUPANCIES

(See also Chapter 31.)

Business occupancies are those used for the transaction of business, for the keeping of accounts and records, and similar purposes. Minor office occupancies incidental to operations in another occupancy are considered as part of the predominating occupancy and are subject to the provisions of this *Code* as they apply to the predominating occupancy. The commentary following 26-1.4 discusses classification of business occupancies in more detail.

Determination of what constitutes a "minor" or "incidental" office area cannot be based solely on percentage of business area in comparison to overall building area. For example: A 200-sq ft (19-sq m) office area in a 4,000-sq ft (370-sq m) warehouse can reasonably be judged incidental to the storage operations and result in the building being classified as a storage occupancy. A 20,000-sq ft (1860-sq m) office area in a 400,000-sq ft (37 200-sq m) distribution warehouse represents the same proportion of business use area as the 200-sq ft (19-sq m) office in the 4,000-sq ft (370-sq m) example above but cannot be judged incidental. *(See Figure 26-1.)*. The 20,000-sq ft (1860-sq m) office area probably has an occupant load of approximately 200 persons. The *Code* requirements applicable to business occupancies, which are more stringent than those applicable to storage occupancies, are needed to protect the occupants of the office area adequately. The distribution warehouse is thus a mixed occupancy; part storage occupancy and part business occupancy. If packaging operations are present, it might also be part industrial occupancy. Therefore, the requirements of 1-4.7 for mixed occupancies would apply.

SECTION 26-1   GENERAL REQUIREMENTS

26-1.1 Application.

26-1.1.1   New construction shall comply with the provisions of this chapter. *(See Chapter 31 for operating features.)*

See Section 1-4 for application provisions.

Exception*:   Facilities where the authority having jurisdiction has determined equivalent safety is provided in accordance with Section 1-5.

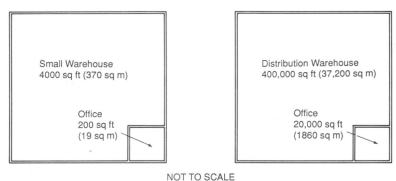

NOT TO SCALE

Figure 26-1.   Determination of "Incidental" Office Use Cannot Be Based on Percentage of Overall Building Area.   (*See commentary on previous page.*)

A-26-1.1.1 Exception   In determining equivalency for conversions, modernizations, renovations, or unusual design concepts of business occupancies, the authority having jurisdiction may use NFPA 101M, *Alternative Approaches to Life Safety*, Chapter 7 utilizing the parameters for new construction.

This Exception emphasizes that Section 1-5 permits alternative designs to literal *Code* compliance in which a building would still be considered as *Code* conforming. However, the authority having jurisdiction ultimately determines whether or not equivalent safety has been provided.

Paragraph 26-1.1.1 and accompanying Exception do not intend to limit the methods an authority having jurisdiction might use to determine equivalency. However, as noted in A-26-1.1.1, Chapter 7 of NFPA 101M, *Alternative Approaches to Life Safety,*[1] provides an "equivalency system" that uses numerical values to analyze the firesafety effectiveness of a building design. This system is known as the Firesafety Evaluation System (FSES). The system provides a methodology by which alternative designs can be evaluated as options to literal *Code* compliance. In providing the equivalency system, it is not intended to limit equivalency evaluations solely to those based on this one system. The authority having jurisdiction retains the authority to evaluate and approve alternative designs on the basis of appropriate supporting data. The FSES may be used to assist this evaluation. This Exception in no way mandates the use of the FSES nor does it require the authority having jurisdiction to accept the results of an evaluation using the system.

Although the FSES was primarily developed to evaluate alternative designs in existing buildings, it is particularly useful for determining equivalency for conversions, modernizations, renovations, or unusual design concepts — all of which would be considered new construction. However, the FSES is a tool used to help determine equivalency, and it should not be used to circumvent *Code* requirements. In new construction, *Code* requirements must be met or equivalent safety provided by alternative means approved by the authority having jurisdiction.

26-1.1.2 This chapter establishes life safety requirements for all new business buildings. Specific requirements for high rise buildings [buildings over 75 ft (23 m) in height] are contained in paragraphs pertaining thereto.

Existing buildings are discussed in Chapter 27. Section 26-4 contains additional requirements for high rise buildings.

26-1.1.3 Additions to existing buildings shall conform to the requirements for new constructon. Existing portions of the structure need not be modified, provided that the new construction has not diminished the fire safety features of the facility.

Although construction of an addition generally does not require existing portions of the building to be modified, Figure 26-2 illustrates a case where the planned new construction would diminish the firesafety features of the existing building and thus necessitate corrective action within the existing portion of the building. The placement of new room A creates an excessively long dead-end corridor B, which must be corrected.

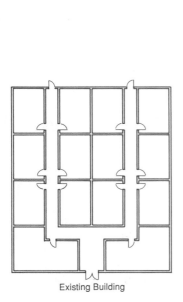
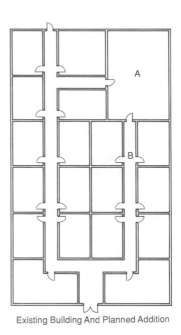

Existing Building   Existing Building And Planned Addition

Figure 26-2. The Placement of New Room A Creates an Excessively Long Dead-End Corridor B in the Existing Building, Which Must Be Corrected.

26-1.2 Mixed Occupancies. Mixed occupancies shall comply with 1-4.7.

26-1.3 Special Definitions. None.

26-1.4 Classification of Occupancy.

26-1.4.1   Business occupancies shall include all buildings and structures or parts thereof with occupancy described in 4-1.8.

In reviewing the *Code's* definition (*see 4-1.8*) of a business occupancy, note that the definition does not include types of stores that, although considered "businesses," are covered under the provisions of Chapter 24; these include, for example, supermarkets, department stores, and other occupancies that display and sell merchandise to large numbers of people. Also not included are the assembly portions of city halls, town halls, and courthouses, which are covered under Chapter 8.

The following constitute business occupancies and are covered by the provisions of Chapter 26:

1. Those occupancies used for the transaction of business (other than those classified as mercantile occupancies).

2. Those occupancies used for keeping accounts and records and for similar purposes.

Included in (1) and (2) are: doctors' offices, dentists' offices (*see Chapter 12 for ambulatory health care centers*), and general offices, as well as city halls, town halls, and courthouses, all of which have areas for keeping books and records, and transacting public business. Other occupancies included under the definition of business occupancies are service facilities common to office buildings, such as newsstands, lunch counters (serving fewer than 50 people), barber shops, and beauty parlors.

Also, by reference in Chapter 10, college classroom buildings are considered office buildings.

26-1.5 Classification of Hazard of Contents.

26-1.5.1   The contents of business occupancies shall be classified as ordinary hazard in accordance with Section 4-2.

Rather than simply referring the user to Section 4-2 for classification of hazard of contents as most other occupancy chapters do, the requirement of 26-1.5.1 stresses that unless an extraordinarily hazardous situation exists, the contents of business occupancies shall be classed as ordinary hazard. Such wording is meant to keep the user from classifying the hazard of contents as high hazard unless a combustible load far in excess of the usual, yet considerable, quantity of boxed records and paper files is present. Isolated hazardous areas within the overall ordinary hazard business occupancy, such as storage rooms, must be protected or separated per the requirements of 26-3.2.

26-1.5.2   For purposes of the design of an automatic sprinkler system, a business occupancy shall be classified as "light hazard occupancy," as identified by NFPA 13, *Standard for the Installation of Sprinkler Systems.*

The classification of hazard of contents under the definitions in Section 4-2 has no bearing on or relationship to the hazard classification in NFPA 13, *Standard for the Installation of Sprinkler Systems.*[2] Thus, an ordinary hazard business occupancy might be protected by a light hazard sprinkler system.

Paragraph 26-1.5.2 was written into the *Code* to indicate that contents classed as ordinary under the *Code* for the purpose of life safety are not classified as ordinary under NFPA 13, *Standard for the Installation of Sprinkler Systems.*[2] As indicated in 26-1.5.2, for purposes of sprinkler design, the anticipated fuel load of business occupancies in Chapter 26 is classed as "light hazard."

26-1.6 Minimum Construction Requirements. No Requirements.

The provisions of a local or state building code may apply.

Some occupancy chapters, such as Chapters 12 and 13, which address the life safety needs of nonambulatory occupants, require a certain minimum building construction type to help assure building structural integrity for the time period needed for a lengthy evacuation or for safe refuge within the building. Because business occupancies characteristically have ambulatory occupants and do not provide sleeping accommodations, there are no minimum construction requirements imposed.

26-1.7 Occupant Load.

26-1.7.1* For purposes of determining required means of egress, the occupant load of business buildings or parts of buildings used for business purposes shall be no less than one person per 100 sq ft (9.3 sq m) of gross floor area. The occupant load for parts of buildings used for other purposes shall be calculated using occupant load factors associated with the use.

A-26-1.7.1 In calculating the occupant load of a business occupancy, it is important to base the calculation on the actual uses of the various building areas. For example, given that buildings having educational uses above grade 12 are for the most part business occupancies because they are exempted from being classed as educational occupancies under Chapters 10 and 11, occupant load factors of 20 sq ft (1.9 sq m) net for classroom areas and 50 sq ft (4.6 sq m) net for instructional laboratory areas should be used. Occupant load calculations for conference rooms should be based on 7 or 15 sq ft (0.65 or 1.4 sq m) net per person. For typical office areas, the occupant load calculation should be based on the 100 sq ft (9.3 sq m) gross factor.

Since the number of people expected to occupy certain types of office buildings can be determined with a great degree of accuracy, e.g., through a company's detailed arrangement of its office space, it may prove beneficial to compare such a figure with one calculated on the basis of one person per 100 sq ft (9.3 sq m) of gross floor area. (*See 26-1.7.1.*) In concentrated office occupancies (particularly those used for government operations), the actual number of people found in a space may exceed the figure calculated by gross area. As emphasized in Section 5-3, where this is the case, the exit capacity must be designed on the basis of the actual occupant load. Note that the converse is not true; that is, if the actual occupant load is less than the gross area calculation, the *Code* still requires that the gross area calculation be used to determine the required exit capacity.

26-1.7.2   In the case of a mezzanine open to the floor below or other unprotected vertical openings between floors as permitted by 26-3.1, the occupant load of the mezzanine or other subsidiary floor level shall be added to that of the street floor for the purpose of determining required exits. However, in no case shall the total exit capacity be less than would be required if all vertical openings were enclosed.

The requirements of 26-1.7.2 are identical to those of 24-1.7.2 for mercantile occupancies. The examples in Figures 24-4 and 24-5 illustrating how to determine the exit capacity for the street floor of a mercantile occupancy apply equally well to a business occupancy. Note that 26-2.3.3 is consonant with 24-2.3.2; in both mercantile and business occupancies, the street floor needs to provide exit capacity for the required capacity of stairways discharging through the street floor.

SECTION 26-2   MEANS OF EGRESS REQUIREMENTS

26-2.1 General.

26-2.1.1   All means of egress shall be in accordance with Chapter 5 and this chapter.

26-2.1.2   If, owing to differences in grade, any street floor exits are at points above or below the street or ground level, such exits shall comply with the provisions for exits from upper floors or floors below the street floor.

Figure 24-6 illustrates a case where two street floors of a mercantile occupancy are at ground level at one side of a building, but are either above or below ground level at the other sides. Many business occupancies have a similar configuration. The two street floors must have their exits arranged to allow horizontal travel to the exterior at one end of the floor and vertical travel (either up or down to ground level) at the other end of the floor. This means that the exit capacity to the exterior must be able to accommodate, in the case of Floor 1, people from the upper floors who may need to travel down to and through the exits to the exterior on Floor 1. The reverse is true for Floor 2, which must size its exit capacity to the exterior to accommodate occupants who may travel up from Floor 1 as well as occupants who may have to travel down to and through the exits to the exterior on Floor 2. Paragraphs 5-3.1.4, 26-1.7.2, and 26-2.3.3 demonstrate how to add exit capacity based on expected occupant use from floors above the street floor. This method is equally valid for adding exit capacity based on expected occupant use from floors below the street floor. Figure 24-8 provides an example of how to calculate exit capacity for a street floor such as Floor 2 in Figure 24-6.

26-2.1.3   Where two or more floors below the street floor are occupied for business use, the same stairs or ramps may serve each.

Exception: No inside open stairway or ramp may serve as a required egress facility from more than one floor level.

It is important to remember that the width of the stair or ramp is based on the floor with the largest occupant load. This ensures that a stair or other component of a means of egress will accommodate the population of any floor it serves. Again, note the prohibition against open stairs or ramps serving more than one floor.

26-2.1.4   Floor levels below the street floor used only for storage, heating, and other service equipment, and not subject to business occupancy shall have exits in accordance with Chapter 29.

A significant reduction in the number and size of exits is allowed for floors used for the purposes specified in 26-2.1.4, since the expected population of such floors will be well below that of the typical business floor.

26-2.2 Means of Egress Components.

26-2.2.1   Components of means of egress shall be limited to the types described in 26-2.2.2 through 26-2.2.8.

26-2.2.2 Doors.

26-2.2.2.1   Doors shall comply with 5-2.1.

26-2.2.2.2*   Locks complying with 5-2.1.5.1 Exception No. 2 shall be permitted only on principal entrance/exit doors.

A-26-2.2.2.2   The term "principal entrance/exit doors" is intended to imply doors that the authority having jurisdiction can be reasonably assured will be unlocked in order for the facility to do business.

26-2.2.2.3   Selected doors on stairwells may be equipped with hardware that prevents reentry in accordance with 5-2.1.5.2 Exception No. 1.

See commentary following 5-2.1.5.2.
Had use of Exception No. 1 to 5-2.1.5.2 not been specifically recognized by this occupancy chapter, the basic requirements of 5-2.1.5.2 would have applied. That would have required either reentry from the stairwell back onto all floors at all times or similar reentry following automatic release of locking devices as a result of initiation of the building fire alarm system. Exception No. 1 to 5-2.1.5.2 allows for some stairwell doors to remain locked from the stairwell side of the door, while other doors must allow reentry, in recognition of building security needs. The location and number of resulting reentry points provides the same overall level of safety to life for this occupancy as that intended by the base provisions of 5-2.1.5.2.

26-2.2.2.4   Special locking arrangements in accordance with 5-2.1.6 are permitted.

In recognition of the security needs of a business occupancy, use of the delay release device covered by 5-2.1.6 is allowed on any door. In effect, the allowable 15- or 30-second delay will be experienced only under nonfire conditions or very early in a fire's growth, given that the door must be immediately usable upon sprinkler operation or smoke or heat detection and upon loss of power controlling the locking mechanism. The building must be protected throughout by an approved automatic sprinkler system or automatic fire detection system.

26-2.2.2.5   Where horizontal or vertical security grilles or doors are used as part of the required means of egress from a tenant space, such grilles or doors shall comply with 5-2.1.4.1 Exception No. 3.

26-2.2.2.6   Revolving doors shall comply with 5-2.1.10.

26-2.2.3 Stairs.

26-2.2.3.1   Stairs shall comply with 5-2.2.

26-2.2.3.2   Spiral stairs complying with 5-2.2.2.7 are permitted.

Note that spiral stairs can serve only an occupant load of five or fewer.

26-2.2.4 Smokeproof Enclosures.   Smokeproof enclosures shall comply with 5-2.3.

26-2.2.5 Horizontal Exits.   Horizontal exits shall comply with 5-2.4.

26-2.2.6 Ramps.   Ramps shall comply with 5-2.5.

26-2.2.7 Exit Passageways.   Exit passageways shall comply with 5-2.6.

26-2.2.8 Alternating Tread Devices.   Alternating tread devices complying with 5-2.11 are permitted.

The provisions of 5-2.11 in effect limit the use of alternating tread devices to locations where the *Code* recognizes the use of fire escape ladders. (*See* 5-2.9.)

Note that escalators are no longer a component of an acceptable means of egress. If escalators are present, they cannot be considered part of the egress system.

26-2.3 Capacity of Means of Egress.

26-2.3.1   The capacity of means of egress shall be in accordance with Section 5-3.

26-2.3.2   The minimum width of any corridor or passageway shall be 44 in. (112 cm) in the clear.

Formal Interpretation 81-34
Reference: 26-2.3.2

Question 1: Is it the intent of the Committee that 26-2.3.2 apply to noncorridor or nonpassageway areas of exit access such as the spaces between rows of desks created by office layout or low-height partitions?

Answer: No.

Question 2: Is it the intent of the Committee that 26-2.3.2 require that all corridors and passageways be at least 44 in. in width (wider if serving an occupant load greater than 200) regardless of occupant load served (i.e., small number of persons)?

Answer: Yes.

Issue Edition: 1981
Reference: 26-2.3.1
Date: January 1984

26-2.3.3   Street floor exits shall be sufficient for the occupant load of the street floor plus the required capacity of stairs and ramps discharging through the street floor.

26-2.4 Number of Exits.   (*See also Section 5-4.*) Not less than two exits shall be accessible from every part of every floor, including floor levels below the street floor occupied for business purposes or uses incidental thereto.

> Paragraph 26-2.4 would require the 310 in. (787 cm) of exit width calculated in Figure 24-8 to be divided into at least two groupings located at opposite or remote points on the street floor. If only two groupings are used, each should be approximately 150-160 in. (381-406 cm) in width. Similarly, the required stair capacity from the upper and lower floors must be separated into at least two groupings remotely located from each other.

Exception No. 1: For a room or area with a total occupant load of less than one hundred persons, having an exit that discharges directly to the outside at the level of exit discharge of the building, with a total distance of travel, including travel within the exit, from any point of not over 100 ft (30 m), a single exit may be permitted. Such travel shall be on the same floor level or, if the traversing of stairs is required, such stairs shall not be more than 15 ft (4.5 m) in height, and they shall be provided with complete enclosures to separate them from any other part of the building, with no door openings therein. A single outside stairway in accordance with 5-2.2 may serve all floors allowed within the 15 ft (4.5 m) vertical travel limitation.

Figures 26-3 and 26-4 illustrate two cases where a single exit from a room or area in a business occupancy is allowed. (*See Exception No. 1 to 26-2.4.*) In the first case, the travel distance from the area is on the same floor level as the exit. In the second case, stairs must be traversed.

The criteria for allowing the single exit are:

1. Occupant load less than 100;

2. Direct exit to a street or to an open exterior area at ground level;

3. Total distance no more than 100 ft (30 m) from anywhere in the room to the exterior. Note that this is total distance from any point to the exterior, not travel distance as measured in Section 5-6, and therefore, includes distance traveled on enclosed stair (exit);

4. Any stairs must be no more than 15 ft (4.5 m) in height; and

5. Any stairs must be completely enclosed with no door openings between the stair enclosure and the rest of the building, or stairs must be classified as an outside stair.

If any of these conditions is not met, two exits are required from the room or space in question.

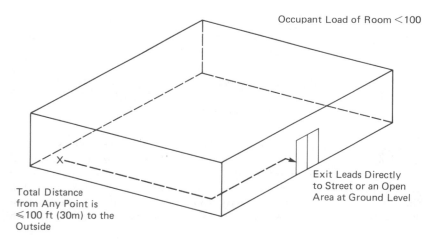

Occupant Load of Room <100

Exit Leads Directly to Street or an Open Area at Ground Level

Total Distance from Any Point is ≤100 ft (30m) to the Outside

Figure 26-3. Single Exit from an Area or Room in a Business Occupancy. Travel from area to exit is horizontal.

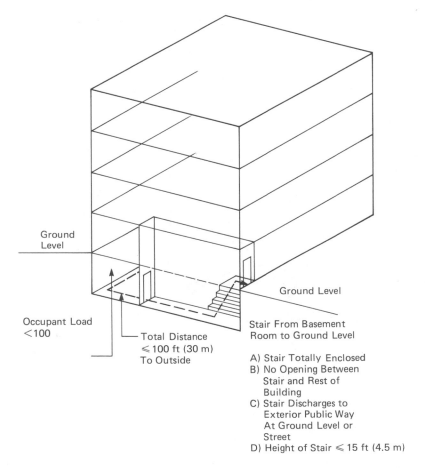

Ground
Level

Ground Level

Occupant Load
<100

Stair From Basement
Room to Ground Level

Total Distance
⩽ 100 ft (30 m)
To Outside

A) Stair Totally Enclosed
B) No Opening Between
   Stair and Rest of
   Building
C) Stair Discharges to
   Exterior Public Way
   At Ground Level or
   Street
D) Height of Stair ⩽ 15 ft (4.5 m)

Figure 26-4.   Single Exit from an Area or Room in a Business Occupancy Where
Stairs Must Be Traversed.

*Exception No. 2:   Any business occupancy not over three stories and not exceeding an occupant
load of 30 people per floor may be permitted with a single separate exit to each floor if the total
travel distance to the outside of the building does not exceed 100 ft (30 m) and if such exit is
enclosed in accordance with 5-1.3 and serves no other levels and discharges directly to the
outside. A single outside stairway in accordance with 5-2.2 may serve all floors.*

Figure 26-5 illustrates a single exit from the third floor of a business
occupancy. The criteria for allowing the single exit are:
   1. The building is not more than three stories high;
   2. Each floor has no more than 30 occupants;
   3. Total distance from any point on any floor to the exterior at
ground level is no more than 100 ft (30 m), including travel over stairs;

4. The stair is not used by, nor has an opening to, any other floor; and

5. The stair is totally enclosed or is classified as an outside stair.

If any of these conditions is not met, the floor must have two exits.

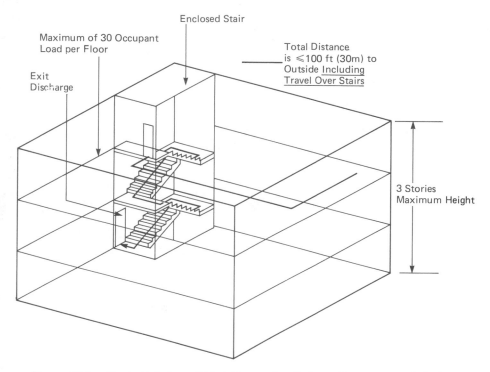

Figure 26-5.   Single Exit from Third Floor of a Business Occupancy.   Stair is totally enclosed, has opening only at third floor, and discharges directly to street with no communication at second and first floors. A similar arrangement could be provided for the second floor of the same building.

26-2.5 Arrangement of Means of Egress.

26-2.5.1   Exits shall be arranged in accordance with Section 5-5.

26-2.5.2   No dead-end corridor shall exceed 20 ft (6.1 m).

Exception: In buildings protected throughout by an approved supervised automatic sprinkler system, in accordance with Section 7-7, dead-end corridors shall not exceed 50 ft (15 m).

As they have separate and distinct requirements, the *Code* separates dead-end corridors and common path of travel into two distinct and separate paragraphs. Dead-end corridors are limited to 20 ft (6.1 m) in buildings that are not protected throughout by an approved supervised automatic sprinkler system. Buildings that are sprinklered may have 50-ft (15-m) dead-end corridors.

Three typical dead-end corridors are illustrated in Figure 26-6.

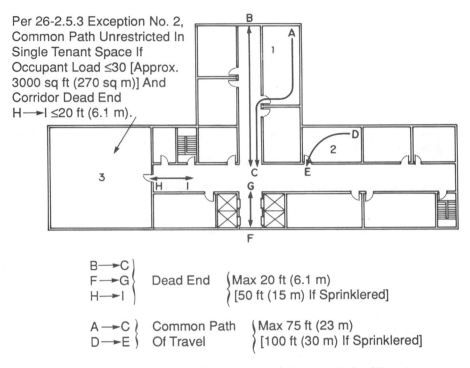

Per 26-2.5.3 Exception No. 2, Common Path Unrestricted In Single Tenant Space If Occupant Load ≤30 [Approx. 3000 sq ft (270 sq m)] And Corridor Dead End H——I ≤20 ft (6.1 m).

B——C
F——G   Dead End   Max 20 ft (6.1 m)
H——I   [50 ft (15 m) If Sprinklered]

A——C   Common Path   Max 75 ft (23 m)
D——E   Of Travel   [100 ft (30 m) If Sprinklered]

Figure 26-6.   Illustration of Dead Ends and Common Path of Travel.

26-2.5.3   No common path of travel shall exceed 75 ft (23 m).

Exception No. 1:   A common path of travel may be permitted for the first 100 ft (30 m) in a building protected throughout by an approved supervised automatic sprinkler system in accordance with Section 7-7.

The previous edition of the *Code* limited common path of travel to 50 ft (15 m) or, if the building was sprinklered, 75 ft (23 m). Based on the deletion from this edition of the previous Chapter 5 provisions that applied to the point where measurement of travel distance and common path begins for small rooms [i.e., distance within room was not counted if there was a maximum six-person occupant load and a maximum 50 ft (15 m) of travel within the room], the allowable common path has been increased without either reducing the level of safety to life or imposing a hardship on designers. *(See the commentary following 5-5.1.5 for a discussion on common path of travel.)*

Exception No. 2:   A single tenant space that does not exceed an occupant load of 30 people may have a single exit access from that tenant space, provided the corridor to which that exit access leads does not exceed a 20 ft (6.1 m) dead end.

The restriction on common path of travel is separate and distinct from the restriction on dead-end corridors. Although a common path of travel may at times involve a dead-end corridor, and dead ends may involve common path of travel, this is not always the case. For an example, see the elevator lobby illustrated in Figure 26-6, which is a dead-end corridor but not a common path of travel.

Common path of travel is measured similarly to travel distance (*see Section 5-6*), except that instead of being terminated at the entrance of an exit, common path of travel measurement is terminated at that point where the occupant has a choice of two distinct and separate paths to an exit. (*See definition of Common Path of Travel in Chapter 3.*) It should be noted that the beginning point of the measurement is the same as the beginning point of travel distance measurement. In other words, the beginning point is 1 ft (30.5 cm) from the most remote point (Rooms 1 and 2 in Figure 26-6). Figure 26-7 provides an additional illustration of common path of travel in a business occupancy. (*Also see the commentary in Section 5-5 on arrangement of means of egress.*)

Exception No. 1 allows the common path of travel to be extended to 100 ft (30 m) in buildings protected throughout by an approved supervised automatic sprinkler system. The exception recognizes the additional safety to life that a complete automatic sprinkler system provides and allows added flexibility when designing the location of corridors and exits in buildings where approved sprinkler systems are installed. In addition, Exception No. 2 exempts a single tenant space with a maximum occupant load of 30 people [normally approximately 3,000 sq ft (270 sq m)] from the common path of travel requirement, provided that the single door from that tenant space leads to a corridor that does not have a dead end in excess of 20 ft (6.1 m) (Room 3 in Figure 26-6).

A question often asked concerns the conditions under which an office space or suite requires two exit access doors. It is the common path of travel restriction that regulates when an office space needs two exit access doors. If the common path of travel is exceeded, a second door from the office space would be required. It would be positioned so that any resulting common path of travel would be within the allowable distances. In addition, the second door must be remotely located from the first door, and each door must lead to remote exits via remote paths. Therefore, in one requirement, the *Code* not only regulates the number of exit access doors required from an office area, but also the arrangement of those doors.

26-2.6 Travel Distance to Exits.   Travel distance to exits, measured in accordance with Section 5-6, shall be no more than 200 ft (60 m).

Exception: An increase in the above travel distance to 300 ft (91 m) shall be permitted in a building protected throughout by an approved automatic sprinkler system in accordance with Section 7-7.

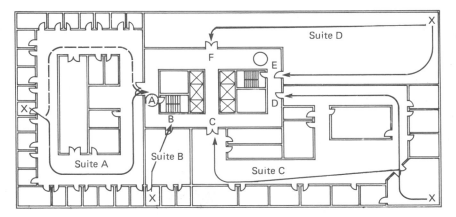

Figure 26-7. Common Path of Travel. In Suite A the travel from X → A is a common path of travel; even though there are two routes to A, they both go through the common point A. In Suite B the travel from X → B is a common path of travel but is permitted due to the suite having an occupant load not exceeding 30 persons, meaning generally that it is less than 3,000 sq ft (280 sq m) in area (26-2.5.3 Exception No. 2). It is also less than the maximum common path of travel. Although Suites C and D do not have common paths of travel, the remoteness of the exit access doors from these suites is questionable.

A review of 5-6.2 will show that the travel distance requirements apply to only the first (or nearest) exit from a point in a building. For example, the 200-ft (60-m) travel distance limit means that at least one exit must be within 200 ft (60 m) of a point in the building, not that all exits must be within 200 ft (60 m) of that point in the building.

26-2.7 Discharge from Exits.   Exit discharge shall comply with Section 5-7.

26-2.8 Illumination of Means of Egress.   Means of egress shall be illuminated in accordance with Section 5-8.

26-2.9 Emergency Lighting.

26-2.9.1   Emergency lighting shall be provided in accordance with Section 5-9 in any building where:

(a) The building is two or more stories in height above the level of exit discharge, or

(b) The occupancy is subject to 100 or more occupants above or below the level of exit discharge, or

(c) The occupancy is subject to 1,000 or more total occupants.

If any of the three conditions of 26-2.9.1 exist, emergency lighting as specified in Section 5-9 is required for the building. Note that condition (a) specifically mentions buildings having two floors above the level of exit discharge or a minimum of three floors.

26-2.9.2   Emergency lighting in accordance with Section 5-9 shall be provided for all windowless or underground structures meeting the definition of 30-1.3.

26-2.10 Marking of Means of Egress.   Means of egress shall have signs in accordance with Section 5-10.

26-2.11 Special Features.

SECTION 26-3   PROTECTION

26-3.1 Protection of Vertical Openings.

26-3.1.1   Every stairway, elevator shaft, escalator opening, and other vertical opening shall be enclosed or protected in accordance with Section 6-2.

Exception No. 1:   Unprotected vertical openings connecting not more than three floors used for business occupancy only may be permitted in accordance with the conditions of 6-2.4.4.

Note that 6-2.4.4 requires that if the communicating space (i.e., the vertical opening and all areas open to it) has ordinary hazard contents, it must be protected by automatic sprinklers. Per 26-1.5, business occupancies are considered ordinary hazard.

Exception No. 2:   A vertical opening enclosure will not be required for a vertical opening where:

(a) The vertical opening connects only two adjacent floors, neither of which is a basement, and

(b) The vertical opening is not a required means of egress, and

(c) The vertical opening is not connected with corridors or other stairways.

Exception No. 2 to 26-3.1.1 allows, for example, a two-level office or reference library in an office building. Item (a) restricts the use of this Exception to two levels only. Item (b) requires that the stairs not be part of the means of egress; therefore, the space would have to have access to exits on both levels. Item (c) requires that the areas connected by the opening be separated from corridors and other stairways.

Exception No. 3:   Atriums in accordance with 26-4.3 are permitted.

The provisions of 26-4.3 contain additional requirements that must be met where the building has an atrium.

26-3.1.2   Floors below the street floor used for storage or other than business occupancy shall have no unprotected openings to business occupancy floors.

Enforcing 26-3.1.2 prevents the possibility that a fire in a hazardous area with a high fuel load (e.g., areas used for shops, repairs, storage of maintenance supplies, files, or records) might directly expose the floor of exit discharge through an unprotected vertical opening. Studies have shown that there is a higher rate of fire incidence in basements than in other areas of business occupancies. Because smoke and heat rise, a fire in a basement can quickly cause exits and exit discharges located on the street floor to become unusable.

26-3.2 Protection from Hazards.

26-3.2.1 Hazardous areas, including but not limited to areas used for general storage, boiler or furnace rooms, fuel storage, janitor closets, maintenance shops including woodworking and painting areas, and kitchens, shall:

(a) Be separated from other parts of the building by fire barriers having a fire resistance rating of not less than 1 hour with all openings therein protected by ¾-hour fire protection rated self-closing fire doors, or

(b) The area shall be protected by an automatic extinguishing system in accordance with Section 7-7.

26-3.2.2 High hazard content areas, as defined in Section 4-2, shall be protected by both fire resistance rated construction and automatic extinguishing equipment.

Paragraphs 26-3.2.1 and 26-3.2.2 follow the general pattern of Section 6-4, which calls for either separation of the hazardous area from the remainder of the occupancy by means of construction, or minimization of the hazard by the installation of an automatic extinguishing system in the hazardous area. Where the hazard is severe, both methods of protection are required.

Section 6-4 contains two additional mandatory provisions. One is a reference to NFPA 30, *Flammable and Combustible Liquids Code*,[3] and the other is a reference to NFPA 45, *Standard on Fire Protection for Laboratories using Chemicals*.[4] (*See 6-4.3 and 6-4.4.*)

26-3.3 Interior Finish.

26-3.3.1 Interior finish on walls and ceilings of exits and of enclosed corridors furnishing access thereto or ways of travel therefrom shall be Class A or Class B in accordance with Section 6-5.

26-3.3.2 In office areas, Class A, Class B, or Class C interior finish shall be provided in accordance with Section 6-5.

26-3.3.3 Interior floor finish in corridors and exits shall be Class I or Class II in accordance with Section 6-5.

Chapter 26 for new business occupancies is among the few occupancy chapters that regulate interior floor finish. The requirement that such finish be Class I or Class II (*see Section 6-5*) applies only to exits, such as enclosed stairs, and to corridors. The intent is that the interior floor finish materials used in corridors and exits resist the spread of fire should the interior floor finish in these areas be exposed to the radiant energy from a fully developed room fire via an open door. Section 6-5 contains a provision that allows a reduction for sprinklered buildings. Since Chapter 26 specifies a Class II interior floor finish, there is no rating required for floor finish in sprinklered buildings.

26-3.4 Detection, Alarm, and Communications Systems.

26-3.4.1 General. A fire alarm system in accordance with Section 7-6 shall be provided in any business occupancy where:

(a) The building is two or more stories in height above the level of exit discharge, or

(b) The occupancy is subject to 100 or more occupants above or below the level of exit discharge, or

(c) The occupancy is subject to 1,000 or more total occupants.

A fire alarm system is required in a business occupancy under the same conditions as those under which emergency lighting is required. If any one of the three conditions listed above exists in the building, then the fire alarm system must be provided. Note that "two or more stories in height above the level of exit discharge" normally means a building with three or more stories.

26-3.4.2 Initiation. Initiation of the required fire alarm system shall be by manual means per 7-6.2.1(a).

Exception No. 1: Initiation may be by means of an approved automatic fire detection system, in accordance with 7-6.2.1(b), providing protection throughout the building.

Exception No. 2: Initiation may be by means of an approved automatic sprinkler system, in accordance with 7-6.2.1(c), providing protection throughout the building.

This paragraph clearly states that a fire alarm system is required, but the manual pull stations may be eliminated if the system is activated by either an automatic fire detection system providing protection throughout the building or an automatic sprinkler system providing protection throughout the building. This does not exempt the fire alarm system, but exempts only the manual pull stations.

26-3.4.3 Notification.

26-3.4.3.1 At all times that the building is occupied (*see 5-2.1.1.3*), the required fire alarm system shall:

(a) Sound a general audible alarm throughout the building, or

(b) Sound an audible alarm in a continuously attended location for purposes of initiating emergency action.

This paragraph requires that when the fire alarm system is actuated (*see 26-3.4.2*), the system shall either automatically sound a general alarm throughout the building, or, if a continuously attended location is provided (as is often the case in high rise buildings), the alarm may sound at that location only, with the appropriate emergency action being initiated from that location.

26-3.4.3.2 Occupant Notification. Occupant notification shall be by live voice public address system announcement originating from the attended location where the alarm signal is received. (*See 26-3.4.3.1.*) The system may be used for other announcements. (*See 7-6.3.9 Exception No. 2.*)

Exception: Any other occupant notification means permitted by 7-6.3 may be used in lieu of live voice public address system announcement.

It is preferable for a voice alarm system to be controlled from the continuously attended location referred to in 26-3.4.3.1. The Exception would be used primarily in buildings where a continuously attended location is not provided and would allow either a recorded voice system or a general audible alarm.

26-3.5 Extinguishment Systems. Portable fire extinguishers shall be provided in every business occupancy in accordance with 7-7.4.1. (*See also Section 26-4.*)

Although no requirements are stated here for automatic sprinkler systems, paragraph 26-4.2.2 requires high rise office buildings to be protected by automatic sprinklers, and 26-4.3, through its reference to Chapter 6, requires a building containing an atrium to be sprinklered. Additional incentives to install sprinklers are provided in regard to: delay release hardware (26-2.2.2.4); dead ends (26-2.5.2); common path of travel (26-2.5.3); travel distance (26-2.6); protection from hazards (26-3.2); interior finish (26-3.3 via Section 6-5); and corridors (26-3.6.1).

26-3.6 Corridors.

26-3.6.1 Where access to exits is limited to corridors, such corridors shall be separated from use areas by partitions having a fire resistance rating of at least 1 hour.

Exception No. 1: Where exits are available from an open floor area.*

Exception No. 2: Corridors need not have a fire resistance rating within a space occupied by a single tenant.*

Exception No. 3: Corridors need not have a fire resistance rating within buildings protected throughout by an approved automatic sprinkler system.

A-26-3.6.1 Exception No. 1 Where exits are available from an open floor area, such as open plan buildings, corridors need not be separated. (An example of an open plan building is one in which the work spaces and accesses to exits are delineated by the use of tables, desks, bookcases, counters, or by partitions that are less than floor to ceiling height.)

A-26-3.6.1 Exception No. 2 It is the intent of this paragraph that a single tenant be limited to an area occupied under a single management and work the same hours. The concept is that people under the same employ working the same hours would largely be familiar with their entire tenant space. It is not the intent to apply this just because tenants might be owned by the same organization. For example, in a government-owned office building, the offices of different federal agencies would be considered tenants since an employee normally works for one agency. The agencies may work various hours. Another example would be a classroom building of a university, since some classrooms may be being used at times when other classrooms are not being used.

The requirement in 26-3.6.1 is quite straightforward.

Exception No. 1 provides for the now popular "office landscape" or "open office" arrangement. If there is direct access to exits from the open area, it is not necessary to require separated corridors. This Exception recognizes that a fire in an open space is subject to more rapid observation and response than a fire in an enclosed room or office.

Exception No. 2 recognizes that, in areas occupied by a single tenant, there is a high level of familiarity with the area and the partitioned offices or spaces are frequented by the same people. The appendix note to Exception No. 2 provides further discussion on this subject.

Exception No. 3 recognizes the value of automatic sprinklers as a life safety feature.

26-3.6.2 Doors and frames, each with a minimum 20-minute fire protection rating, equipped with a positive latch and closing device, shall be used to protect openings in 1-hour partitions separating the corridor from use areas.

Note that 26-3.6.2 does require closing devices and positive latching devices on the doors. It also requires a 20-minute rating for the door frame and for the door itself.

26-3.6.3 Glass vision panels within 1-hour fire-rated partitions, or doors therein, shall be limited to fixed wired glass in approved steel frames and shall be 1,296 sq in. (.84 sq m) or less in size per panel.

Note that there is no upper limit on the number of glass vision panels that may be installed in a corridor, only a limit of 1,296 sq in. (0.84 sq m) on the area of each individual panel.

SECTION 26-4   SPECIAL PROVISIONS

26-4.1 Windowless or Underground Buildings.   *(See Section 30-7.)*

26-4.2* High Rise Buildings.

A-26-4.2   In the design of high rise buildings, special consideration should also be given to a life safety system including, among others, the following features:

Movement of occupants to safety.

Control of fire and smoke.

Psychological features.

Communications.

Elevators *(see A-7-4.1)*.

Emergency planning.

Overall system reliability.

The problems high rise buildings pose for safety to life, fire fighting, and fire protection in general are covered in *High-Rise Building Fires and Fire Safety*,[5] *Fighting High-Rise Building Fires — Tactics and Logistics*,[6] and *Fires in High-Rise Buildings*.[7] All three publications contain extensive bibliographies on the subject.

See the definition of High Rise Building in Chapter 3.

26-4.2.1 General. In addition to the requirements of this section, all high rise buildings shall comply with all other applicable provisions of this *Code*.

Where 26-4.2.1 makes reference to "all other applicable provisions of this *Code*," it is not the intent to require compliance with Section 30-8, High Rise Buildings.

Section 30-8 is new to the 1988 Edition of the *Code*. It is menu-oriented in that its provisions, singly, in various combinations, or in total, must be mandated by a specific occupancy chapter requirement. Chapter 26 for new business occupancies does not require any of the provisions of Section 30-8. Rather, in the wholly self-contained set of requirements of 26-4.2.2, 26-4.2.3, 26-4.2.4, and 26-4.2.5, many of the concepts of Section 30-8 are reworded and made mandatory.

26-4.2.2 Extinguishment Requirements. High rise buildings shall be protected throughout by an approved electrically supervised automatic sprinkler system installed in accordance with Section 7-7. A sprinkler control valve and a water flow device shall be provided for each floor.

26-4.2.3 Detection, Alarm, and Communications Systems.

26-4.2.3.1 General. Detection, alarm, and communications systems as specified by 26-4.2.3.2 and 26-4.2.3.3 shall be provided in all buildings with an occupied story 150 ft (45 m) or more in height, measured from the lowest level of fire department vehicle access.

Rather than reference Section 30-8, the alarm system requirements for high rise business occupancy buildings come from the general 26-3.4 alarm requirements and from those of 26-4.2.3.2 and 26-4.2.3.3. For example, new high rise business occupancies are required to have a fire alarm system per 26-3.4.1.

The provisions of 26-4.2.3.2 and 26-4.2.3.3 are *additional* provisions for those high rise buildings that are 150 ft (45 m) or more in height.

26-4.2.3.2 A fire alarm system utilizing voice communication shall be installed in accordance with Section 7-6.

The additional voice communication requirement of 26-4.2.3.2 applies at the 150-ft (45-m) building height rather than the 75-ft (23-m) height that applies to high rise buildings per Section 30-8. The intent is to apply this requirement to buildings of approximately 12 stories or more based upon the belief that general building evacuation can be accomplished in buildings that are 12 or fewer stories in height.

26-4.2.3.3   Two-way telephone communication service shall be provided for fire department use. This system shall be in accordance with NFPA 72F, *Standard for the Installation, Maintenance, and Use of Emergency Voice/Alarm Communication Systems*. The communication system shall operate between the central control station and every elevator car, every elevator lobby, and each floor level of exit stairs.

Exception: Where the fire department radio system is approved as an equivalent system.

With respect to two-way telephone communication requirements, the same 150-ft (45-m) height criteria has been specified because the technology of portable two-way communication units has improved greatly, and thus, equipment available to fire departments should be adequate to serve buildings that are 12 or fewer stories in height.

26-4.2.4 Standby Power.   Standby power in accordance with NFPA 70, *National Electrical Code*, Article 701 shall be provided. The standby power system shall have a capacity and rating sufficient to supply all required equipment. Selective load pickup and load shedding shall be permitted in accordance with NFPA 70, *National Electrical Code*. The standby power system shall be connected to the following:

(a) Emergency lighting system

(b) Fire alarm system

(c) Electric fire pump

(d) Central Control Station equipment and lighting

(e) At least one elevator serving all floors and be transferable to any elevator

(f) Mechanical equipment for smokeproof enclosures.

Whereas Section 30-8, if referenced, would have specifically required emergency lighting, the provisions of 26-4.2.4 on standby power do not address emergency lighting because emergency lighting is already required for new high rise building occupancies per 26-2.9.1. (*See 26-4.2.1, which reminds the user that the other requirements of this Code apply.*)

26-4.2.5* Central Control Station.   A central control station shall be provided in a location approved by the fire department. The control station shall contain:

(a) Voice fire alarm system panels and controls

(b) Fire department two-way telephone communications service panels and controls

(c) Fire detection and fire alarm system annunciation panels

(d) Elevator floor location and operation annunciators

(e) Sprinkler valve and water flow annunciators

(f) Emergency generator status indicators

(g) Controls for any automatic stairway door unlocking system

(h) Fire pump status indicators

(i) A telephone for fire department use with controlled access to the public telephone system.

A-26-4.2.5   It is not the intent of the paragraph to require any of the equipment in the list other than the telephone for fire department use, but only to provide the controls, panels, annunciators, and similar equipment at this location where the equipment is provided or required by another section of the *Code*.

26-4.3 Atriums.

26-4.3.1   Atriums are permitted provided they comply with 6-2.4.5 and 26-4.3.2 through 26-4.3.4.

> Whereas the previous edition of the *Code* limited the contents within an atrium in a business occupancy to low hazard contents, this edition has no similar restriction. Rather, the limitation to either low hazard *or* ordinary hazard contents per 6-2.4.5 applies and, in combination with the other provisions of 6-2.4.5 and the special provisions of 26-4.3.2 through 26-4.3.4, creates the necessary level of safety to life to allow the floor openings created by an atrium.

26-4.3.2   The atrium is provided with an automatic ventilation system independently operated by all of the following:

(a) Approved smoke detectors located at the top of the space and adjacent to each return air intake from the atrium, and

(b) The required automatic fire extinguishing system, and

(c) Manual controls that are readily accessible to the fire department.

> The intent of 26-4.3.2 is to require a smoke control system as noted in 6-2.4.5(e) and to modify the provisions of 6-2.4.5(f) by not requiring the manual alarm to activate the smoke control system. Note that 26-4.3.3.2 does not require manual pull stations.
>
> The reason for not requiring the manual alarm to activate the system is the possibility of a manual alarm being pulled on a floor other than the fire floor, thus possibly causing the smoke control system to function improperly.

26-4.3.3 Detection, Alarm, and Communications Systems.

26-4.3.3.1 General.   Buildings housing atriums shall be provided with a fire alarm system in accordance with Section 7-6.

> Buildings housing atriums are required to be provided with a fire alarm system regardless of 26-3.4.

26-4.3.3.2 Initiation.   Initiation of the required fire alarm system shall occur independently by:

(a) Activation of the smoke detection system [*see 7-6.2.1(b)*], and

(b) Activation of the automatic sprinkler system [see 7-6.2.1(c)].

Manual pull stations are not required.

Since an atrium is required to have a smoke detection system and be protected throughout by an automatic sprinkler system, the activation of either of these systems shall initiate the fire alarm system. Note that manual pull stations are not required; this is consistent with 26-3.4.2.

26-4.3.3.3 Notification. At all times that the building is occupied (see 5-2.1.1.3), the required fire alarm system shall:

(a) Sound a general audible alarm throughout the building, or

(b) Sound an audible alarm in a continuously attended location for purposes of initiating emergency action.

This paragraph establishes that when the fire alarm system is activated, it shall either sound a general audible alarm throughout the building or, if a continuously attended location is provided, sound at that location only.

26-4.3.3.4 Occupant Notification. Occupant notification shall be by live voice public address system announcement originating from the attended location where the alarm signal is received. (See 26-4.3.3.3.) The system may be used for other announcements. (See 7-6.3.9 Exception No. 2.)

Exception: Any other occupant notification means permitted by 7-6.3 may be used in lieu of live voice public address system announcement.

It is preferable for a voice alarm system to be controlled from the continuously attended location referred to in 26-4.3.3.3. The Exception would be used primarily in buildings where a continuously attended location is not provided and would allow either a recorded voice system or a general audible alarm.

26-4.3.3.5 Emergency Forces Notification. Emergency forces notification shall include notifying:

(a) The fire department in accordance with 7-6.4, and

(b) The local fire brigade, if provided.

Paragraph 7-6.4 allows several different methods of automatically notifying the fire department.

26-4.3.3.6 Emergency Control. The fire alarm system shall be arranged to automatically actuate smoke management or smoke control systems in accordance with 7-6.5.2(c).

26-4.3.4 All electrical equipment essential for smoke control, or automatic extinguishing equipment for buildings more than six stories or 75 ft (23 m) in height containing an atrium shall be provided with an emergency source of power in accordance with NFPA 70, *National Electrical Code*, Section 700-12(b), or equivalent.

26-4.4 Operating Features. (See Chapter 31.)

SECTION 26-5 BUILDING SERVICES

26-5.1 Utilities. Utilities shall comply with the provisions of Section 7-1.

26-5.2 Heating, Ventilating, and Air Conditioning Equipment. Heating, ventilating, and air conditioning equipment shall comply with the provisions of Section 7-2.

26-5.3 Elevators, Dumbwaiters, and Vertical Conveyors. Elevators, dumbwaiters, and vertical conveyors shall comply with the provisions of Section 7-4.

Referring to Section 7-4 and its referenced document, ANSI/ASME A17.1, *Safety Code for Elevators and Escalators*,[8] will provide design criteria and specifications for the proper arrangement of an elevator control system that will provide both automatic recall during a fire and use to the fire department that is exclusive of the normal automatic control mode of the elevator system.

26-5.4 Rubbish Chutes, Incinerators, and Laundry Chutes. Rubbish chutes, incinerators, and laundry chutes shall comply with the provisions of Section 7-5.

REFERENCES CITED IN COMMENTARY

[1]NFPA 101M, *Alternative Approaches to Life Safety*, National Fire Protection Association, Quincy, Ma, 1988.
[2]NFPA 13, *Standard for the Installation of Sprinkler Systems*, National Fire Protection Association, Quincy, MA, 1987.
[3]NFPA 30, *Flammable and Combustible Liquids Code*, National Fire Protection Association, Quincy, MA, 1987.
[4]NFPA 45, *Standard on Fire Protection for Laboratories Using Chemicals*, National Fire Protection Association, Quincy, MA, 1986.
[5]*High-Rise Building Fires and Fire Safety,* NFPA SPP-18, National Fire Protection Association, Boston, MA, 1973.
[6]Robert F. Mendes, *Fighting High-Rise Building Fires — Tactics and Logistics*, NFPA FSP-44, National Fire Protection Association, Boston, MA, 1975.
[7]*Fires in High-Rise Buildings*, NFPA SPP-25, National Fire Protection Association, Boston, MA, 1974.
[8]ANSI/ASME A17.1, *Safety Code for Elevators and Escalators*, American Society of Mechanical Engineers, 345 East 47th Street, New York, NY 10017, 1987.

27 EXISTING BUSINESS OCCUPANCIES

(See also Chapter 31.)

Business occupancies are those used for the transaction of business, for the keeping of accounts and records, and similar purposes. Minor office occupancies incidental to operations in another occupancy are considered as part of the predominating occupancy and are subject to the provisions of this *Code* as they apply to the predominating occupancy. The commentary following 27-1.4 discusses classification of business occupancies in more detail.

Determination of what constitutes a "minor" or "incidental" office area cannot be based solely on percentage of business area in comparison to overall building area. For example: A 200-sq ft (19-sq m) office area in a 4,000-sq ft (370-sq m) warehouse can reasonably be judged incidental to the storage operations and result in the building being classified as a storage occupancy. A 20,000-sq ft (1,860-sq m) office area in a 400,000-sq ft (37,200-sq m) distribution warehouse represents the same proportion of business use area as the 200-sq ft (19-sq m) office in the 4,000-sq ft (370-sq m) example above but cannot be judged incidental. *(See Figure 27-1.)* The 20,000-sq ft (1,860-sq m) office area probably has an occupant load of approximately 200 persons. The *Code* requirements applicable to business occupancies, which are more stringent than those applicable to storage occupancies, are needed to protect the occupants of the office area adequately. The distribution warehouse is thus a mixed occupancy; part storage occupancy and part business occupancy. If packaging operations are present, it might also be part industrial occupancy. Therefore, the requirements of 1-4.7 for mixed occupancies would apply.

SECTION 27-1   GENERAL REQUIREMENTS

27-1.1 Application.

27-1.1.1   Existing business occupancies shall comply with the provisions of this chapter. *(See Chapter 31 for operating features.)*

Exception*: Facilities where the authority having jurisdiction has determined equivalent safety is provided in accordance with Section 1-5.

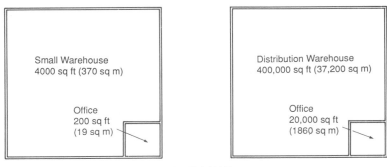

NOT TO SCALE

Figure 27-1. Determination of "Incidental" Office Use Cannot Be Based on Percentage of Overall Building Area. (*See commentary on previous page.*)

A-27-1.1.1 Exception In determining equivalency for business occupancies, the authority having jurisdiction may use NFPA 101M, *Alternative Approaches to Life Safety*, Chapter 7 utilizing the parameters for existing buildings.

In understanding the full intent and scope of 27-1.1.1, it is necessary to review it concurrently with Sections 1-4, 1-5, and 1-6. While a building code may exclude existing buildings from coverage under some form of a "grandfather clause," the *Life Safety Code*, by virtue of its very interest in safety to life, does not condone existing building arrangements that do not comply with the *Code* except under a very narrow and strict set of guidelines. These guidelines are contained in this chapter.

Because a building may be in compliance with an earlier edition of the *Code* does not mean that it is "grandfathered" so as not to have to comply with a newer edition that has been adopted as law in that jurisdiction. The Committee on Safety to Life is especially careful not to make the requirements that are applicable to existing buildings more stringent from one edition of the *Code* to the next unless the change is absolutely needed to provide the overall package of safety to life intended by the *Code*. Thus, the old adage of "once in compliance, always in compliance," does not hold.

Chapter 7 of NFPA 101M, *Alternative Approaches to Life Safety*,[1] is a new Firesafety Evaluation System (FSES) or methodology for judging the equivalency of requirements for business occupancies.

Chapter 27 has been prepared for application solely to existing buildings. In editions of the *Code* prior to 1973, the sections dealing with existing business occupancies made reference to provisions contained within the section dealing with new construction. Since the 1973 Edition of the *Code*, the sections dealing with existing facilities have been complete and are intended to be applied without reference to the requirements for new construction.

This section is to be applied retroactively. Due consideration has been given to the practical difficulties of making alterations in existing, functioning facilities. The specified provisions, viewed as a whole, establish minimum acceptable criteria for safety to life that reasonably minimize the likelihood of a life-threatening fire.

The requirements of Chapter 27 may be modified in instances of practical difficulty or where alternate, but equal, provisions are proposed. The modifications must provide a level of protection equivalent to that achieved by compliance with the corresponding *Code* provisions.

A Firesafety Evaluation System (FSES) has been developed and is located in Chapter 7 of NFPA 101M. The FSES uses numerical values to analyze the firesafety effectiveness of existing building arrangements or improvements proposed within existing structures. The system provides a method by which alternative improvement programs can be evaluated as options to literal *Code* compliance. In providing the equivalency system, it is not intended to limit equivalency evaluations solely to those based on this one system. The authority having jurisdiction retains the authority to evaluate and approve alternative improvement programs on the basis of appropriate supporting data. The FSES may be used to assist in this evaluation. This Exception in no way mandates the use of the FSES nor does it require the authority having jurisdiction to accept the results of an evaluation using the system. The Exception emphasizes that Section 1-5 permits alternative designs to literal *Code* compliance in which a building would still be considered as *Code* conforming. However, the authority having jurisdiction ultimately determines whether or not equivalent safety has been provided.

27-1.1.2 This chapter establishes life safety requirements for existing business buildings. Specific requirements for high rise buildings [buildings over 75 ft (23 m) in height] are contained in paragraphs pertaining thereto.

New buildings are discussed in Chapter 26. Section 27-4 contains additional requirements for high rise buildings.

The provisions of 26-1.1.3 affect existing buildings and warrant additional discussion. Although construction of an addition generally does not require existing portions of the building to be modified, Figure 27-2 illustrates a case where the planned new construction would diminish the firesafety features of the existing building and thus necessitate corrective action within the existing portion of the building. The placement of new room A creates an excessively long dead-end corridor B, which must be corrected.

27-1.2 Mixed Occupancies.   Mixed occupancies shall comply with 1-4.7.

27-1.3 Special Definitions.   None.

27-1.4 Classification of Occupancy.

27-1.4.1   Business occupancies shall include all buildings and structures or parts thereof with occupancy described in 4-1.8.

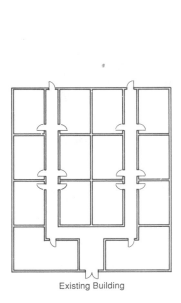
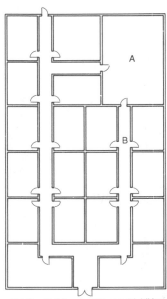

Existing Building   Existing Building And Planned Addition

Figure 27-2. The Placement of New Room A Creates an Excessively Long
Dead-End Corridor B in the Existing Building, Which Must Be Corrected.

In reviewing the *Code*'s definition (*see 4-1.8*) of a business occupancy,
note that the definition does not include types of stores that, although
considered "businesses," are covered under the provisions of Chapter 25;
these include, for example, supermarkets, department stores, and other
occupancies that display and sell merchandise to large numbers of people.
Doctors' offices and treatment and diagnostic facilities not meeting the
definition of a health care occupancy are included in business occupancies. (*See Chapter 13*). Also not included are the assembly portions of city
halls, town halls, and courthouses, which are covered under Chapter 9.

The following constitute business occupancies and are covered by the
provisions of Chapter 27:

1. Those occupancies used for the transaction of business (other than
those classified as mercantile occupancies).

2. Those occupancies used for keeping accounts and records and for
similar purposes.

Included in (1) and (2) are: doctors' offices, dentists' offices (*See
Chapter 13 for ambulatory health care centers*), and general offices as well as
city halls, town halls, and courthouses, all of which have areas for keeping
books and records, and transacting public business. Other occupancies
included under the definition of business occupancies are service facilities
common to office buildings, such as newsstands, lunch counters (serving
fewer than 50 people), barber shops, and beauty parlors.

Also, by reference in Chapter 11, college classroom buildings are
considered office buildings.

27-1.5 Classification of Hazard of Contents.

27-1.5.1   The contents of business occupancies shall be classified as ordinary hazard in accordance with Section 4-2.

Rather than simply referring the user to Section 4-2 for classification of hazard of contents as most other occupancy chapters do, the requirement of 27-1.5.1 stresses that unless an extraordinarily hazardous situation exists, the contents of business occupancies shall be classed as ordinary hazard. Such wording is meant to keep the user from classifying the hazard of contents as high hazard unless a combustible load far in excess of the usual, yet considerable, quantity of boxed records and paper files is present. Isolated hazardous areas within the overall ordinary hazard business occupancy, such as storage rooms, must be protected or separated per the requirements of 27-3.2.

27-1.5.2   For purposes of the design of an automatic sprinkler system, a business occupancy shall be classified as "light hazard occupancy," as identified by NFPA 13, *Standard for the Installation of Sprinkler Systems.*

The classification of hazard of contents under the definitions in Section 4-2 has no bearing on or relationship to the hazard classification in NFPA 13, *Standard for the Installation of Sprinkler Systems.*[2] Thus, an ordinary hazard business occupancy might be protected by a light hazard sprinkler system.

Paragraph 27-1.5.2 was written into the *Code* to indicate that contents classed as ordinary under the *Code* for the purpose of life safety are not classified as ordinary under NFPA 13, *Standard for the Installation of Sprinkler Systems.*[2] As indicated in 27-1.5.2, for purposes of sprinkler design, the anticipated fuel load of business occupancies in Chapter 27 is classed as "light hazard."

27-1.6 Minimum Construction Requirements.   No Requirements.

The provisions of a local or state building code may apply.

Some occupancy chapters, such as Chapters 12 and 13, which address the life safety needs of nonambulatory occupants, require a certain minimum building construction type to help assure building structural integrity for the time period needed for a lengthy evacuation or for safe refuge within the building. Because business occupancies characteristically have ambulatory occupants and do not provide sleeping accommodations, there are no minimum construction requirements imposed.

27-1.7 Occupant Load.

27-1.7.1*   For purposes of determining required means of egress, the occupant load of business buildings or parts of buildings used for business purposes shall be no less than one person per 100 sq ft (9.3 sq m) of gross floor area. The occupant load for parts of buildings used for other purposes shall be calculated using occupant load factors associated with the use.

A-27-1.7.1 In calculating the occupant load of a business occupancy, it is important to base the calculation on the actual uses of the various building areas. For example, given that buildings having educational uses above grade 12 are for the most part business occupancies because they are exempted from being classed as educational occupancies under Chapters 10 and 11, occupant load factors of 20 sq ft (1.9 sq m) net for classroom areas and 50 sq ft (4.6 sq m) net for instructional laboratory areas should be used. Occupant load calculations for conference rooms should be based on 7 or 15 sq ft (0.65 or 1.4 sq m) net per person. For typical office areas, the occupant load calculation should be based on the 100 sq ft (9.3 sq m) gross factor.

Since the number of people expected to occupy certain types of office buildings can be determined with a great degree of accuracy, e.g., through a company's detailed arrangement of its office space, it may prove beneficial to compare such a figure with one calculated on the basis of one person per 100 sq ft (9.3 sq m) of gross floor area. (*See* 27-1.7.1.) In concentrated office occupancies (particularly those used for government operations), the actual number of people found in a space may exceed the figure calculated by gross area. As emphasized in Section 5-3, where this is the case, the exit capacity must be designed on the basis of the actual occupant load. Note that the converse is not true; that is, if the actual occupant load is less than the gross area calculation, the *Code* still requires that the gross area calculation be used to determine the required exit capacity.

27-1.7.2 In the case of a mezzanine open to the floor below or other unprotected vertical openings between floors as permitted by 27-3.1, the occupant load of the mezzanine or other subsidiary floor level shall be added to that of the street floor for the purpose of determining required exits. However, in no case shall the total exit capacity be less than would be required if all vertical openings were enclosed.

The requirements of 27-1.7.2 are identical to those of 25-1.7.2 for mercantile occupancies. The examples in Figures 25-4 and 25-5 illustrating how to determine the exit capacity for the street floor of a mercantile occupancy apply equally well to a business occupancy. Note that 27-2.3.3 is consonant with 25-2.3.2; in both mercantile and business occupancies, the street floor needs to provide exit capacity for the required capacity of stairways discharging through the street floor.

SECTION 27-2 MEANS OF EGRESS REQUIREMENTS

27-2.1 General.

27-2.1.1 All means of egress shall be in accordance with Chapter 5 and this chapter.

27-2.1.2 If, owing to differences in grade, any street floor exits are at points above or below the street or ground level, such exits shall comply with the provisions for exits from upper floors or floors below the street floor.

Figure 25-6 illustrates a case where two street floors of a mercantile occupancy are at ground level at one side of a building, but are either above or below ground level at the other sides. Many business occupancies have a similar configuration. The two street floors must have their exits arranged to allow horizontal travel to the exterior at one end of the floor and vertical travel (either up or down to ground level) at the other end of the floor. This means that the exit capacity to the exterior must be able to accommodate, in the case of Floor 1, people from the higher floors who may need to travel down to and through the exits to the exterior on Floor 1. The reverse is true for Floor 2, which must size its exit capacity to the exterior to accommodate occupants who may travel up from Floor 1 as well as occupants who may have to travel down to and through the exits to the exterior on Floor 2. Paragraphs 5-3.1.4, 27-1.7.2, and 27-2.3.3 demonstrate how to add exit capacity based on expected occupant use from floors above the street floor. This method is equally valid for adding exit capacity based on expected occupant use from floors below the street floor. Figure 25-8 provides an example of how to calculate exit capacity for a street floor such as Floor 2 in Figure 25-6.

27-2.1.3 Where two or more floors below the street floor are occupied for business use, the same stairs, escalators, or ramps may serve each.

Exception: No inside open stairway, escalator, or ramp may serve as a required egress facility from more than one floor level.

It is important to remember that the width of the stair, escalator, or ramp is based on the floor with the largest occupant load. This ensures that a stair or other component of a means of egress will accommodate the population of any floor it serves. Again, note the prohibition against open stairs, escalators, or ramps serving more than one floor.

27-2.1.4 Floor levels below the street floor used only for storage, heating, and other service equipment, and not subject to business occupancy shall have exits in accordance with Chapter 29.

A significant reduction in the number and size of exits is allowed for floors used for the purposes specified in 27-2.1.4, since the expected population of such floors will be well below that of the typical business floor.

27-2.2 Means of Egress Components.

27-2.2.1 Components of means of egress shall be limited to the types described in 27-2.2.2 through 27-2.2.10.

27-2.2.2 Doors.

27-2.2.2.1 Doors shall comply with 5-2.1.

27-2.2.2.2*   Locks complying with 5-2.1.5.1 Exception No. 2 shall be permitted only on principal entrance/exit doors.

A-27-2.2.2.2   The term "principal entrance/exit doors" is intended to imply doors that the authority having jurisdiction can be reasonably assured will be unlocked in order for the facility to do business.

27-2.2.2.3   The reentry provisions of 5-2.1.5.2 need not be met. (*See 5-2.1.5.2 Exception No. 3.*)

Had Exception No. 3 to 5-2.1.5.2 not been specifically recognized by this occupancy chapter, the basic requirements of 5-2.1.5.2, mandating reentry capabilities from stairwells back onto all floors of the building, would have applied. By calling Exception No. 3 into play, existing business occupancies are exempt from the reentry provisions.

27-2.2.2.4   Special locking arrangements in accordance with 5-2.1.6 are permitted.

In recognition of the security needs of a business occupancy, use of the delay release device covered by 5-2.1.6 is allowed on any door. In effect, the allowable 15- or 30-second delay will be experienced only under nonfire conditions or very early in a fire's growth, given that the door must be immediately usable upon sprinkler operation or smoke or heat detection and upon loss of power controlling the locking mechanism. The building must be protected throughout by an approved automatic sprinkler system or automatic fire detection system.

27-2.2.2.5   Where horizontal or vertical security grilles or doors are used as part of the required means of egress from a tenant space, such grilles or doors shall comply with 5-2.1.4.1 Exception No. 3.

27-2.2.2.6   Revolving doors shall comply with 5-2.1.10.

Existing revolving doors may continue to be used without having to meet some of the more stringent requirements applicable to new revolving doors if such exemption is approved by the authority having jurisdiction. (*See 5-2.1.10.*)

27-2.2.3 Stairs.

27-2.2.3.1   Stairs shall comply with 5-2.2.

27-2.2.3.2   Spiral stairs complying with 5-2.2.2.7 are permitted.

Note that spiral stairs can serve only an occupant load of five or fewer.

27-2.2.3.3   Winders complying with 5-2.2.2.8 are permitted.

27-2.2.4 Smokeproof Enclosures.   Smokeproof enclosures shall comply with 5-2.3.

27-2.2.5 Horizontal Exits.   Horizontal exits shall comply with 5-2.4.

27-2.2.6 Ramps.   Ramps shall comply with 5-2.5.

27-2.2.7 Exit Passageways.   Exit passageways shall comply with 5-2.6.

27-2.2.8 Escalators and Moving Walks.   Escalators and moving walks complying with 5-2.7 are permitted.

For an escalator to count as an exit and continue to receive credit for providing exit capacity for 75 persons as allowed by earlier editions of the *Code*, it is required that the escalator be enclosed in the same manner as an interior exit stair. (*See 5-2.2.3 and Section 6-2.*) Note that escalators protected in accordance with the sprinkler-vent method, the spray nozzle method, the rolling shutter method, or the partial enclosure method do not constitute acceptable exits and cannot be used in calculating the required exit capacity.

27-2.2.9 Fire Escape Stairs.   Fire escape stairs complying with 5-2.8 are permitted.

Note that 5-2.8.1 permits existing buildings to continue to use fire escape stairs for no more than 50 percent of their required exit capacity.

27-2.2.10 Alternating Tread Devices.   Alternating tread devices complying with 5-2.11 are permitted.

The provisions of 5-2.11 in effect limit the use of alternating tread devices to those locations where the *Code* recognizes the use of fire escape ladders. (*See 5-2.9.*)

27-2.3 Capacity of Means of Egress.

27-2.3.1   The capacity of means of egress shall be in accordance with Section 5-3.

27-2.3.2   The minimum width of any corridor or passageway shall be 44 in. (112 cm) in the clear.

27-2.3.3   Street floor exits shall be sufficient for the occupant load of the street floor plus the required capacity of stairs, ramps, escalators, and moving walks discharging through the street floor.

27-2.4 Number of Exits.

27-2.4.1   The number of exits shall be in accordance with 27-2.4.2. The requirements of 5-4.1.2 shall not apply.

27-2.4.2   Not less than two exits shall be accessible from every part of every floor, including floor levels below the street floor occupied for business purposes or uses incidental thereto.

Paragraph 27-2.4.2 would require the 310 in. (787 cm) of exit width calculated in Figure 25-8 to be divided into at least two groupings located at opposite or remote points on the street floor. If only two groupings are used, each should be approximately 150-160 in. (381-406 cm) in width. Similarly, the required stair capacity from the upper and lower floors must be separated into at least two groupings remotely located from each other.

Exception No. 1:   For a room or area with a total occupant load of less than one hundred persons, having an exit that discharges directly to the outside at the level of exit discharge of the building, with a total distance of travel, including travel within the exit, from any point of not over 100 ft (30 m), a single exit may be permitted. Such travel shall be on the same floor level or, if the traversing of stairs is required, such stairs shall not be more than 15 ft (4.5 m) in height, and they shall be provided with complete enclosures to separate them from any other part of the building, with no door openings therein. A single outside stairway in accordance with 5-2.2 may serve all floors allowed within the 15 ft (4.5 m) vertical travel limitation.

Figures 27-3 and 27-4 illustrate two cases where a single exit from a room or area in a business occupancy is allowed. (*See Exception No. 1 to 27-2.4.*) In the first case, the travel distance from the area is on the same floor level as the exit. In the second case, stairs must be traversed.

The criteria for allowing the single exit are:

1. Occupant load less than 100;

2. Direct exit to a street or to an open exterior area at ground level;

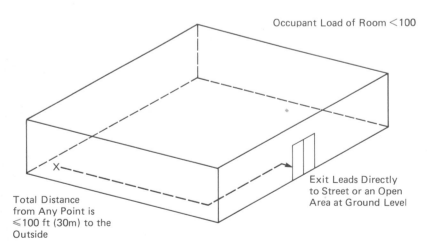

Occupant Load of Room <100

Exit Leads Directly to Street or an Open Area at Ground Level

Total Distance from Any Point is ≤100 ft (30m) to the Outside

Figure 27-3.   Single Exit from an Area or Room in a Business Occupancy. Travel from area to exit is horizontal.

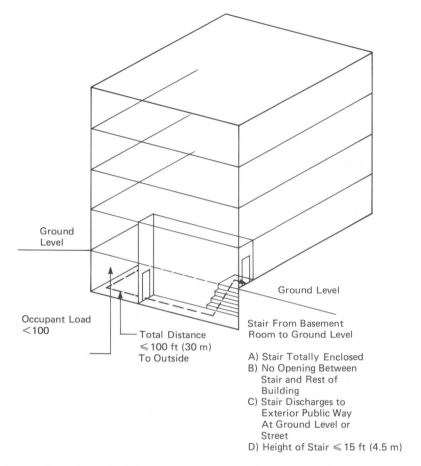

Ground
Level

Occupant Load
<100

Total Distance
≤ 100 ft (30 m)
To Outside

Ground Level

Stair From Basement
Room to Ground Level

A) Stair Totally Enclosed
B) No Opening Between
   Stair and Rest of
   Building
C) Stair Discharges to
   Exterior Public Way
   At Ground Level or
   Street
D) Height of Stair ≤ 15 ft (4.5 m)

Figure 27-4.   Single Exit from an Area or Room in a Business Occupancy Where
Stairs Must Be Traversed.

3. Total distance no more than 100 ft (30 m) from anywhere in the
room to the exterior. Note that this is total distance from any point to the
exterior, not travel distance as measured in Section 5-6, and therefore,
includes distance traveled on enclosed stair (exit);

4. Any stairs must be no more than 15 ft (4.5 m) in height; and

5. Any stairs must be completely enclosed with no door openings
between the stair enclosure and the rest of the building, or stairs must be
classified as an outside stair.

If any of these conditions is not met, two exits are required from the
room or space in question.

Exception No. 2:   Any business occupancy not over three stories and not exceeding an occupant load of 30 people per floor may be permitted with a single separate exit to each floor if the total travel distance to the outside of the building does not exceed 100 ft (30 m), and if such exit is enclosed in accordance with 5-1.3 and serves no other levels and discharges directly to the outside. A single outside stairway in accordance with 5-2.2 may serve all floors.

Figure 27-5 illustrates a single exit from the third floor of a business occupancy. The criteria for allowing a single exit are:

1. The building is not more than three stories high;

2. Each floor has no more than 30 occupants;

3. Total distance from any point on any floor to the exterior at ground level is no more than 100 ft (30 m), including travel over stairs;

4. The stair is not used by, nor does it have an opening to, any other floor; and

5. The stair is totally enclosed or is classified as an outside stair.

If any of these conditions is not met, the floor must have two exits.

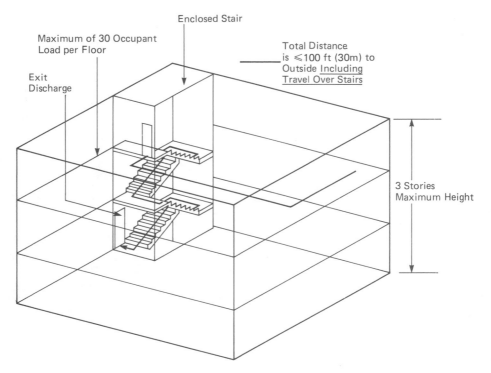

Figure 27-5.   Single Exit from Third Floor of a Business Occupancy.   Stair is totally enclosed, has opening only at third floor, and discharges directly to street with no communication at second and first floors. A similar arrangement could be provided for the second floor of the same building.

27-2.5 Arrangement of Means of Egress.

27-2.5.1   Exits shall be arranged in accordance with Section 5-5.

27-2.5.2   No dead-end corridor shall exceed 50 ft (15 m).

Exception*:   Existing dead-end corridors exceeding 50 ft (15 m) may be continued in use subject to the approval of the authority having jurisdiction and the travel distance requirements of 27-2.6.

A-27-2.5.2 Exception   It is recognized that excessive dead ends exist and in some cases are impractical to eliminate. The authority having jurisdiction may allow these to continue, taking into consideration any or all of the following:

Tenant arrangement.

Automatic sprinkler protection.

Smoke detection.

Exit remoteness.

As they have separate and distinct requirements, the *Code* separates dead-end corridors and common path of travel into two distinct and separate paragraphs. Three typical dead-end corridors are illustrated in Figure 27-6.

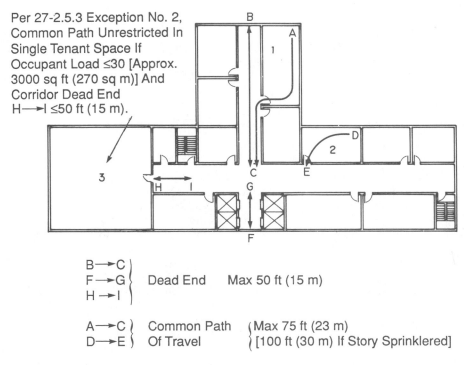

Per 27-2.5.3 Exception No. 2, Common Path Unrestricted In Single Tenant Space If Occupant Load ≤30 [Approx. 3000 sq ft (270 sq m)] And Corridor Dead End H—I ≤50 ft (15 m).

B→C
F→G   Dead End   Max 50 ft (15 m)
H→I

A→C   Common Path   Max 75 ft (23 m)
D→E   Of Travel   [100 ft (30 m) If Story Sprinklered]

Figure 27-6.   Illustration of Dead Ends and Common Path of Travel.

27-2.5.3   No common path of travel shall exceed 75 ft (23 m).

Exception No. 1:   A common path of travel may be permitted for the first 100 ft (30 m) on a story protected throughout by an approved automatic sprinkler system in accordance with Section 7-7.

The previous edition of the *Code* limited common path of travel to 50 ft (15 m) or 75 or 100 ft (23 or 30 m) under various detector and sprinkler exceptions. Based on the deletion from this edition of the previous Chapter 5 provisions that applied to the point where measurement of travel distance and common path begins for small rooms [i.e., distance within room was not counted if there was a maximum six-person occupant load and a maximum 50 ft (15 m) of travel within the room], the allowable common path has been increased without either reducing the level of safety to life or imposing a hardship on designers.

(See the commentary following 5-5.1.5 for a discussion on common path of travel.)

Exception No. 2:   A single tenant space that does not exceed an occupant load of 30 people may have a single exit access, provided the corridor to which that exit access leads does not have a dead end in excess of 50 ft (15 m).

Exception No. 3*:   Existing excessive common paths of travel may be continued in use subject to the approval of the authority having jurisdiction and the travel distance requirements of 27-2.6.

A-27-2.5.3 Exception No. 3   It is recognized that excessive common paths of travel exist and in some cases are impractical to eliminate. The authority having jurisdiction may allow these to continue, taking into consideration any or all of the following:

Tenant arrangement.

Automatic sprinkler protection.

Smoke detection.

Exit remoteness.

The restriction on common path of travel is separate and distinct from the restriction on dead-end corridors. Although a common path of travel may at times involve a dead-end corridor, and dead ends may involve common path of travel, this is not always the case. For an example, see the elevator lobby illustrated in Figure 27-6, which is a dead end corridor but not a common path of travel.

Common path of travel is measured similarly to travel distance (*see Section 5-6*), except that instead of being terminated at the entrance of an exit, common path of travel measurement is terminated at that point where the occupant has a choice of two distinct and separate paths to an exit. *(See definition of Common Path of Travel in Chapter 3.)* It should be noted that the beginning point of the measurement is the same as the beginning point of travel distance measurement. In other words, the beginning point is 1 ft (30.5 cm) from the most remote point (Rooms 1 and 2 in Figure 27-6).

Figure 27-7 provides an additional illustration of common path of travel in a business occupancy. *(Also see the commentary in Section 5-5 on arrangement of means of egress.)*

Exception No. 1 allows the common path of travel to be extended to 100 ft (30 m) on stories protected throughout by an approved supervised automatic sprinkler system. The Exception recognizes the additional safety to life that an automatic sprinkler system provides and allows added flexibility when designing the location of corridors and exits in buildings where approved sprinkler systems are installed. In addition, Exception No. 2 exempts a single tenant space with a maximum occupant load of not more than 30 people [normally approximately 3,000 sq ft (270 sq m)] from the common path of travel requirement, provided that the single door from that tenant space leads to a corridor that does not have a dead end in excess of 50 ft (15 m) (Room 3 in Figure 27-6).

A question often asked concerns the conditions under which an office space or suite requires two exit access doors. It is the common path of travel restriction that regulates when an office space needs two exit access doors. If the common path of travel is exceeded, a second door from the office space would be required. It would be positioned so that any resulting common path of travel would be within the allowable distances. In addition, the second door must be remotely located from the first door, and each door must lead to remote exits via remote paths. Therefore, in one requirement, the *Code* not only regulates the number of exit access doors required from an office area, but also the arrangement of those doors.

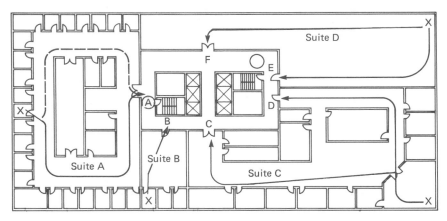

Figure 27-7. Common Path of Travel. In Suite A the travel from X → A is a common path of travel; even though there are two routes to A, they both go through the common point A. In Suite B the travel from X → B is a common path of travel but is permitted due to the suite having an occupant load not exceeding 30 persons, meaning generally that it is less then 3,000 sq ft (280 sq m) in area (27-2.5.3 Exception No. 2). It is also less than the maximum common path of travel. Although Suites C and D do not have common paths of travel, the remoteness of the exit access doors from these suites is questionable.

27-2.6 Travel Distance to Exits.   Travel distance to exits, measured in accordance with Section 5-6, shall be no more than 200 ft (60 m).

Exception: An increase in the above travel distance to 300 ft (91 m) shall be permitted in a building protected throughout by an approved automatic sprinkler system in accordance with Section 7-7.

A review of 5-6.2 will show that the travel distance requirements apply to only the first (or nearest) exit from a point in a building. For example, the 200-ft (60-m) travel distance limit means that at least one exit must be within 200 ft (60 m) of a point in the building, not that all exits must be within 200 ft (60 m) of that point in the building.

The maximum travel distance allowed in existing business occupancies was not changed even though there was a deletion in this edition of the previous Chapter 5 provisions applicable to the point where measurement of travel distance begins for small rooms [i.e., distance within room was not counted if there was a maximum six-person occupant load and a maximum 50 ft (15 m) of travel within the room].

The allowable travel distance has not been increased, and given that its measurement now always begins within the room, the current *Code* might place some existing means of egress arrangements, that had made use of the "small room" exception and complied with the previous edition of the *Code*, into noncompliance. Given the lenient travel distance allowances afforded business occupancies, it was judged that further increases could not be justified given the *Code*'s intended minimum level of safety to life.

27-2.7 Discharge from Exits.   Exit discharge shall comply with Section 5-7.

27-2.8 Illumination of Means of Egress.   Means of egress shall be illuminated in accordance with Section 5-8.

27-2.9 Emergency Lighting.

27-2.9.1   Emergency lighting shall be provided in accordance with Section 5-9 in any building where:

(a) The building is two or more stories in height above the level of exit discharge, or

(b) The occupancy is subject to 100 or more occupants above or below the level of exit discharge, or

(c) The occupancy is subject to 1,000 or more total occupants.

If any of the three conditions of 27-2.9.1 exist, emergency lighting as specified in Section 5-9 is required for the building. Note that condition (a) specifically mentions buildings having two floors above the level of exit discharge or a minimum of three floors.

27-2.9.2   Emergency lighting in accordance with Section 5-9 shall be provided for all windowless or underground structures meeting the definition of 30-1.3.

27-2.10 Marking of Means of Egress. Means of egress shall have signs in accordance with Section 5-10.

27-2.11 Special Features.

SECTION 27-3   PROTECTION

27-3.1 Protection of Vertical Openings.

27-3.1.1   Every stairway, elevator shaft, escalator opening, and other vertical opening shall be enclosed or protected in accordance with Section 6-2.

Exception No. 1:   Unprotected vertical openings connecting not more than three floors used for business occupancy only may be permitted in accordance with the conditions of 6-2.4.4.

Note that 6-2.4.4.4 requires that if the communicating space (i.e., the vertical opening and all areas open to it) has ordinary hazard contents, it must be protected by automatic sprinklers. Per 27-1.5, business occupancies are considered ordinary hazard.

Exception No. 2:   A vertical opening enclosure will not be required for a vertical opening where:

(a) The vertical opening connects only two adjacent floors, neither of which is a basement, and

(b) The vertical opening is not a required means of egress, and

(c) The vertical opening is not connected with corridors or other stairways.

Exception No. 2 to 27-3.1.1 allows, for example, a two-level office or reference library in an office building. Item (a) restricts the use of this Exception to two levels only. Item (b) requires that the stairs not be part of the means of egress; therefore, the space would have to have access to exits on both levels. Item (c) requires that the areas connected by the opening be separated from corridors and other stairways.

Exception No. 3:   Atriums in accordance with 27-4.3 are permitted.

The provisions of 27-4.3 contain additional requirements that must be met where the building has an atrium.

Exception No. 4:   In buildings protected throughout by an approved automatic sprinkler system in accordance with Section 7-7, vertical openings may be unprotected if no unprotected vertical opening serves as any part of any required exit facility and all required exits consist of smokeproof enclosures in accordance with 5-2.3, outside stairs in accordance with 5-2.2, or horizontal exits in accordance with 5-2.4.

In Exception No. 4 to 27-3.1.1, not only must the building be protected with complete automatic sprinkler protection, but all building exits must consist of either smokeproof enclosures, outside stairs, horizontal exits, or a door leading directly to the outside at ground level. Otherwise, the unprotected vertical openings must be suitably enclosed.

27-3.1.2   Floors below the street floor used for storage or other than business occupancy shall have no unprotected openings to business occupancy floors.

Enforcing 27-3.1.2 prevents the possibility that a fire in a hazardous area with a high fuel load (e.g., areas used for shops, repairs, storage of maintenance supplies, files, or records) might directly expose the floor of exit discharge through an unprotected vertical opening. Studies have shown that there is a higher rate of fire incidence in basements than in other areas of business occupancies. Because smoke and heat rise, a fire in a basement can quickly cause exits and exit discharges located on the street floor to become unusable.

27-3.2 Protection from Hazards.

27-3.2.1   Hazardous areas, including but not limited to areas used for general storage, boiler or furnace rooms, fuel storage, janitor closets, maintenance shops including woodworking and painting areas, and kitchens, shall:

(a) Be separated from other parts of the building by fire barriers having a fire resistance rating of not less than 1 hour with all openings therein protected by ¾-hour fire protection rated self-closing fire doors, or

(b) The area shall be protected by an automatic extinguishing system in accordance with Section 7-7.

27-3.2.2   High hazard content areas, as defined in Section 4-2, shall be protected by both fire resistance rated construction and automatic extinguishing equipment.

Paragraphs 27-3.2.1 and 27-3.2.2 follow the general pattern of Section 6-4, which calls for either separation of the hazardous area from the remainder of the occupancy by means of construction, or minimization of the hazard by the installation of an automatic extinguishing system in the hazardous area. Where the hazard is severe, both methods of protection are required.

Section 6-4 contains two additional mandatory provisions. One is a reference to NFPA 30, *Flammable and Combustible Liquids Code*,[3] and the other is a reference to NFPA 45, *Standard on Fire Protection for Laboratories Using Chemicals*.[4] (See 6-4.3 and 6-4.4.)

27-3.3 Interior Finish.

27-3.3.1   Interior finish on walls and ceilings of exits and of enclosed corridors furnishing access thereto or ways of travel therefrom shall be Class A or Class B in accordance with Section 6-5.

27-3.3.2   In office areas, Class A, Class B, or Class C interior finish shall be provided in accordance with Section 6-5.

27-3.3.3 Interior Floor Finish.   No Requirements.

Unlike Chapter 26 for new business occupancies, which regulates interior floor finish in corridors and exits, Chapter 27 has no interior floor finish requirements on existing installations. If floor finish materials in corridors and exits are replaced or added, paragraph 1-4.6 requires compliance with the provisions applicable to new construction, namely 26-3.3.3.

(See the commentary following 26-3.3.3.)

27-3.4 Detection, Alarm, and Communications Systems.

27-3.4.1 General.   A fire alarm system in accordance with Section 7-6 shall be provided in any business occupancy where:

(a) The building is two or more stories in height above the level of exit discharge, or

(b) The occupancy is subject to 100 or more occupants above or below the level of exit discharge, or

(c) The occupancy is subject to 1,000 or more total occupants.

A fire alarm system is required in a business occupancy under the same conditions as those under which emergency lighting is required. If any one of the three conditions listed above exists in the building, then the fire alarm system must be provided. Note that "two or more stories in height above the level of exit discharge" normally means a building with three or more stories.

27-3.4.2 Initiation.   Initiation of the required fire alarm system shall be by manual means per 7-6.2.1(a).

Exception No. 1:   Initiation may be by means of an approved automatic fire detection system, in accordance with 7-6.2.1(b), providing protection throughout the building.

Exception No. 2:   Initiation may be by means of an approved automatic sprinkler system, in accordance with 7-6.2.1(c), providing protection throughout the building.

This paragraph clearly states that a fire alarm system is required, but the manual pull stations may be eliminated if the system is activated by either an automatic fire detection system providing protection throughout the building or an automatic sprinkler system providing protection throughout the building. This does not exempt the fire alarm system, but exempts only the manual pull stations.

27-3.4.3 Notification.

27-3.4.3.1   At all times that the building is occupied *(see 5-2.1.1.3)*, the required fire alarm system shall:

(a) Sound a general audible alarm throughout the building, or

(b) Sound an audible alarm in a continuously attended location for purposes of initiating emergency action.

This paragraph requires that when the fire alarm system is actuated (*See* 27-3.4.2), the system shall either automatically sound a general alarm throughout the building, or, if a continuously attended location is provided (as is often the case in high rise buildings), the alarm may sound at that location only, with the appropriate emergency action being initiated from that location.

27-3.4.3.2 Occupant Notification.   Occupant notification shall be by live voice public address system announcement originating from the attended location where the alarm signal is received. (*See 27-3.4.3.1.*) The system may be used for other announcements. (*See 7-6.3.9 Exception No. 2.*)

Exception: Any other occupant notification means permitted by 7-6.3 may be used in lieu of live voice public address system announcement.

It is preferable for a voice alarm system to be controlled from the continuously attended location referred to in 27-3.4.3.1. The Exception would be used primarily in buildings where a continuously attended location is not provided and would allow either a recorded voice system or a general audible alarm.

27-3.5 Extinguishment Requirements.   Portable fire extinguishers shall be provided in every business occupancy in accordance with 7-7.4.1. (*See also Section 27-4.*)

Although no requirements are stated here for automatic sprinkler systems, paragraph 27-4.2.1 requires high rise office buildings to be protected by automatic sprinklers or the equivalent, and 27-4.3, through its reference to Chapter 6, requires a building containing an atrium to be sprinklered. Additional incentives to install sprinklers are provided in regard to: delay release hardware (27-2.2.2.4); dead ends (27-2.5.2); common path of travel (27-2.5.3); travel distance (27-2.6); protection from hazards (27-3.2); and interior finish (27-3.3 via Section 6-5).

27-3.6 Corridors.   Reserved.

SECTION 27-4   SPECIAL PROVISIONS

27-4.1 Windowless or Underground Buildings.   (*See Section 30-7.*)

27-4.2 High Rise Buildings.

See the definition of High Rise Building in Chapter 3.

27-4.2.1   All high rise business occupancy buildings shall be provided with a reasonable degree of safety from fire that shall be accomplished by the installation of a complete approved automatic sprinkler system in accordance with Section 7-7 or an engineered life safety system approved by the authority having jurisdiction, which may consist of a combination of any or all of the following systems:

Partial automatic sprinkler protection.

Smoke detection alarms.

Smoke control.

Compartmentation,

and/or other approved systems.

The problems high rise buildings pose for safety to life, fire fighting, and fire protection in general are covered in *High-Rise Building Fires and Fire Safety*,[5] *Fighting High-Rise Building Fires — Tactics and Logistics*,[6] and *Fires in High-Rise Buildings*.[7] All three publications contain extensive bibliographies on the subject.

27-4.2.2*   A limited but reasonable time shall be allowed for compliance with any part of this section, commensurate with the magnitude of expenditure and the disruption of services.

A-27-4.2.2   In some cases, appreciable cost may be involved in bringing an existing occupancy into compliance. Where this is true, it would be appropriate for the authority having jurisdiction to prescribe a schedule determined jointly with the facility, allowing suitable periods of time for the correction of the various deficiencies and giving due weight to the ability of the owner to secure the necessary funds.

27-4.2.3   In addition to the above requirements, all buildings, regardless of height, shall comply with all other applicable provisions of this chapter.

Paragraph 27-4.2.3 emphasizes that the provision for the installation of automatic sprinkler protection does not preclude the need for meeting the other requirements in the *Code* unless specific exceptions for the presence of automatic sprinklers are granted in the *Code*'s text.

27-4.3 Atriums.

27-4.3.1   Atriums are permitted provided they comply with 6-2.4.5 and 27-4.3.2 through 27-4.3.4.

Whereas the previous edition of the *Code* limited the contents within an atrium in a business occupancy to low hazard contents, this edition has no similar restriction. Rather, the limitation to either low hazard *or* ordinary hazard contents per 6-2.4.5 applies and, in combination with the other provisions of 6-2.4.5 and the special provisions of 27-4.3.2 through 27-4.3.4, creates the necessary level of safety to life to allow the floor openings created by an atrium.

27-4.3.2   The atrium is provided with an automatic ventilation system independently operated by all of the following:

(a) Approved smoke detectors located at the top of the space and adjacent to each return air intake from the atrium, and

(b) The required automatic fire extinguishing system, and

(c) Manual controls that are readily accessible to the fire department.

The intent of 27-4.3.2 is to require a smoke control system as noted in 6-2.2.3.5(f), and to modify the provisions of 6-2.2.3.5(g) by not requiring the manual alarm to activate the smoke control system. Note that 27-4.3.3.2 does not require manual pull stations.

The reason for not requiring the manual alarm to activate the system is the possibility of a manual alarm being pulled on a floor other than the fire floor, thus possibly causing the smoke control system to function improperly.

27-4.3.3 Detection, Alarm, and Communications Systems.

27-4.3.3.1 General.   Buildings housing atriums shall be provided with a fire alarm system in accordance with Section 7-6.

Buildings housing atriums are required to be provided with a fire alarm system regardless of 27-3.4.

27-4.3.3.2 Initiation.   Initiation of the required fire alarm system shall occur independently by:

(a) Activation of the smoke detection system [*see 7-6.2.1(b)*], and

(b) Activation of the automatic sprinkler system [*see 7-6.2.1(c)*].

Manual pull stations are not required.

Since an atrium is required to have a smoke detection system and be protected throughout by an automatic sprinkler system, the activation of either of these systems shall initiate the fire alarm system. Note that manual pull stations are not required; this is consistent with 27-3.4.2.

27-4.3.3.3 Notification.   At all times that the building is occupied (*see 5-2.1.1.3*), the required fire alarm system shall:

(a) Sound a general audible alarm throughout the building, or

(b) Sound an audible alarm in a continuously attended location for purposes of initiating emergency action.

This paragraph establishes that when the fire alarm system is activated, it shall either sound a general audible alarm throughout the building or, if a continuously attended location is provided, sound at that location only.

27-4.3.3.4 Occupant Notification.   Occupant notification shall be by live voice public address system announcement originating from the attended location where the alarm signal is received. (*See 27-4.3.3.3.*) The system may be used for other announcements. (*See 7-6.3.9 Exception No. 2.*)

Exception: Any other occupant notification means permitted by 7-6.3 may be used in lieu of live voice public address system announcement.

It is preferable for a voice alarm system to be controlled from the continuously attended location referred to in 27-4.3.3.3. The Exception would be used primarily in buildings where a continuously attended location is not provided and would allow either a recorded voice system or a general audible alarm.

27-4.3.3.5 Emergency Forces Notification. Emergency forces notification shall include notifying:

(a) The fire department in accordance with 7-6.4, and

(b) The local fire brigade, if provided.

Paragraph 7-6.4 allows several different methods of automatically notifying the fire department.

27-4.3.3.6 Emergency Control. The fire alarm system shall be arranged to automatically actuate smoke management or smoke control systems in accordance with 7-6.5.2(c).

27-4.3.4 All electrical equipment essential for smoke control, or automatic extinguishing equipment for buildings more than six stories or 75 ft (23 m) in height containing an atrium shall be provided with an emergency source of power in accordance with NFPA 70, *National Electrical Code*, Section 700-12(b), or equivalent.

27-4.4 Operating Features. *(See Chapter 31.)*

SECTION 27-5 BUILDING SERVICES

27-5.1 Utilities. Utilities shall comply with the provisions of Section 7-1.

27-5.2 Heating, Ventilating, and Air Conditioning Equipment. Heating, ventilating, and air conditioning equipment shall comply with the provisions of Section 7-2.

27-5.3 Elevators, Dumbwaiters, and Vertical Conveyors. Elevators, dumbwaiters, and vertical conveyors shall comply with the provisions of Section 7-4.

Referring to Section 7-4 and its referenced document, ANSI/ASME A17.3, *Safety Code for Existing Elevators and Escalators*,[8] will provide design criteria and specifications for the proper arrangement of an elevator control system that will provide both automatic recall during a fire and use to the fire department that is exclusive of the normal automatic control mode of the elevator system.

27-5.4 Rubbish Chutes, Incinerators, and Laundry Chutes. Rubbish chutes, incinerators, and laundry chutes shall comply with the provisions of Section 7-5.

REFERENCES CITED IN COMMENTARY

[1]NFPA 101M, *Alternative Approaches to Life Safety*, National Fire Protection Association, Quincy, Ma, 1988.

[2]NFPA 13, *Standard for the Installation of Sprinkler Systems*, National Fire Protection Association, Quincy, MA, 1987.

[3]NFPA 30, *Flammable and Combustible Liquids Code*, National Fire Protection Association, Quincy, MA, 1987.

[4]NFPA 45, *Standard on Fire Protection for Laboratories Using Chemicals*, National Fire Protection Association, Quincy, MA, 1986.

[5]*High-Rise Building Fires and Fire Safety,* NFPA SPP-18, National Fire Protection Association, Boston, MA, 1973.

[6]Robert F. Mendes, *Fighting High-Rise Building Fires — Tactics and Logistics*, NFPA FSP-44, National Fire Protection Association, Boston, MA, 1975.

[7]*Fires in High-Rise Buildings*, NFPA SPP-25, National Fire Protection Association, Boston, MA, 1974.

[8]ANSI/ASME A17.3, *Safety Code for Existing Elevators and Escalators*, American Society of Mechanical Engineers, 345 East 47th Street, New York, NY 10017, 1987.

28 INDUSTRIAL OCCUPANCIES

(See also Chapter 31.)

Industrial occupancies is a broad classification. The following are examples of industrial occupancies:

Factories of all kinds	Creameries
Laboratories	Gas plants
Drycleaning plants	Refineries
Power plants	Sawmills
Pumping stations	Smokehouses
Laundries	

Formal Interpretation 81-7
Reference: Chapter 28

Question 1: Is it the intent of the Committee to generically classify power plants, including generator rooms, turbine rooms, and boiler rooms, as "special purpose" industrial occupancies?

Answer: Yes.

Question 2: Is it the intent of the Committee to generically classify coal preparation buildings as "high hazard" industrial occupancies?

Answer: Yes.

Question 3: Is it the intent of the Committee that "special purpose" industrial occupancies comply with all the requirements of Chapter 28, unless specifically exempted in the *Code*?

Answer: Yes; however, the authority having jurisdiction may approve alternate provisions based on an engineering study of the specific circumstances involved. The resulting arrangement must provide a level of life safety equivalent to that provided by the *Code*. (*See Section 1-5.*)

Issue Edition: 1981
Reference: Chapter 28
Date: April 1982

SECTION 28-1   GENERAL REQUIREMENTS

28-1.1 Application.   The requirements of this chapter apply to both new and existing Industrial Occupancies. Industrial occupancies include factories making products of all kinds and properties used for operations such as processing, assembling, mixing, packaging, finishing or decorating, repairing, and similar operations.

Unlike most other occupancies covered in the *Code*, both new and existing industrial occupancies are covered in one chapter. Where the requirements vary, it is common for exceptions for existing industrial occupancies to appear or for additional requirements that are limited to new industrial occupancies to be included.

The potential for loss of life from fire in an industrial occupancy is directly related to the hazard of the industrial operation or process. Records show that the majority of multiple-death industrial fires are the result of flash fires in highly combustible material, or of explosions involving combustible dusts, flammable liquids, or gases.

Although industrial fire losses constitute a high percentage of the annual fire loss in property, such fires have not, as a general rule, resulted in extensive loss of life. A number of operating features common to industrial occupancies have contributed to this favorable record. Continued emphasis on proper exit design and maintenance and day-to-day attention to industrial safety and training programs can help to perpetuate this trend.

One of the major elements to be considered in the design of an industrial building's life safety system is the widespread utilization of automatic sprinkler protection. Originally developed for industrial property protection, the automatic sprinkler has also been largely responsible for an excellent life safety record in industrial occupancies. This record has been recognized by fire protection engineers and other authorities, as evidenced by the widespread use of automatic sprinkler systems for life safety protection in buildings with significant hazards to life. Automatic sprinkler protection in industrial occupancies has been a principal factor in ensuring safety to life through the control of "fire spread." Limiting the size of a fire by the operation of sprinklers provides sufficient time for the safe evacuation of people exposed to a fire. The contribution of the automatic sprinkler to safety to life can be fully appreciated only when the wide range of fire risks related to the variety of processes used in an industrial facility is recognized.

Employees and other occupants of industrial buildings are generally ambulatory and capable of quick response to fires and are also able to exit rapidly once properly alerted. To capitalize on this employee capability, many industrial facilities include life safety measures in their emergency preplanning. A well-conceived plan provides a valuable tool in preventing loss of life. Provisions that should be included in the emergency preplan include measures for alerting employees, identification and posting of exit access routes, establishment of group assembly areas for evacuees outside the building, plus procedures for determining if all employees have safely exited. Responsibilities are usually established and assigned in the preplan to ensure that the tasks necessary to facilitate safe evacuation of the building are performed. The preplan should routinely be evaluated through simulated fire exercises and fire drills. Only through the execution of such drills can weaknesses in the preplan be recognized and the plan modified.

Although the life safety record in industry has been relatively good, a major problem may be emerging in the trend toward constructing large industrial plants housing hazardous operations. The introduction of new materials, such as extensive quantities of plastics, has increased the need for additional measures to help ensure the safety to life of employees from fire. Compared with industrial buildings of the early twentieth century, the modern industrial complex has placed a larger number of employees in a more complex and increasingly hazardous environment. This trend has increased the need for industrial management to concentrate on life safety principles, not only during the design stage but also during day-to-day plant operations.

In their employee training programs most industrial firms include an orientation in the use of first aid fire fighting equipment, such as in-plant standpipes, hose, and fire extinguishers. Industrial training of this type, where fully utilized, has resulted in a major reduction in property loss and loss of life. Although first aid fire fighting measures are primarily a property protection measure, there is also a significant life safety benefit. In any situation where the spread of a fire is checked through effective employee action, employee life safety is also provided. If fire spread is restricted to the incipient stages, there is no significant threat to life safety.

28-1.2 Mixed Occupancies.   In any building occupied for both industrial and other purposes, exits shall comply with 1-4.7.

In addition to having exits comply with the 1-4.7 requirements for mixed occupancies, the intent of this paragraph is that the entire means of egress system and other life safety safeguards addressed by the *Code* comply with 1-4.7.

28-1.3 Special Definitions.   None.

Although no special definitions reside in the 28-1.3 section, industrial occupancies are subclassified by the definitions of 28-1.4.1 (a), (b), and (c) using the labels, "general," "special purpose," and "high hazard" industrial occupancy.

28-1.4 Classification of Occupancy.   (*See 4-1.9.*)

The method for determining the degree of hazard to life safety posed by an industrial occupancy is at best a result of personal judgment and not an exact science. The authority having jurisdiction must use judgment based on past experience, a review of reference materials, and full discussion with third parties to evaluate the life safety measures in an industrial occupancy. The *Code* establishes broad categories of occupancy classification so that the relative risks to life safety posed by various types of buildings can be assessed.

One mistake common to occupancy hazard classification in industrial buildings is the use of risk categories for automatic sprinklers per NFPA 13, *Standard for the Installation of Sprinkler Systems,*[1] in determining the hazard to life safety. While the guidelines in NFPA 13 may not differ greatly from those of the *Code* when considering classification of high hazard occupancies, the remaining NFPA 13 categories are usually not suitable for the general industrial occupancy classification of the *Code.* This is particularly true when considering classification of low hazard occupancies, which are classified differently by NFPA 13 (i.e., light hazard) than by the *Code.* The difference is that a life safety classification is concerned with determining the overall hazard to occupants in a manufacturing building in order to implement an adequate means of egress system, while the NFPA 13 classification system is concerned with defining the hazard so that a sprinkler system can be designed to meet the challenge of the hazard.

To examine the conflicts between life safety occupancy classification and classifications in other fire codes, consider a metalworking plant using a flammable solvent in a dip tank coating operation. The normally low hazard classification of the metalworking plant, from a life safety standpoint, should not be changed to high hazard solely because of a dip tank coater located in the plant. Adequate means of safe egress leading away from the coater is needed to ensure the safety of the occupants, but additional exits and a reduction in travel distance to an exit, as specified for a high hazard occupancy, are not required. However, should the coater be the principal piece of equipment in a separately enclosed area, then that area should be considered as a high hazard industrial occupancy.

When determining the life safety hazard classification for an industrial occupancy, the authority having jurisdiction should carefully analyze the nature of an industrial operation to ensure the correct interpretation of the hazard to occupants. A number of resources are available as aids in correctly determining the degree of risk to life safety. One useful aid that should not be overlooked is the expertise of the industrial plant operator. The operator has available a wealth of hazard information. However, the information may be treated as confidential material to prevent competitors from learning the details of an industrial process. An enforcing authority should work to build the trust of the operator by carefully handling such material. It is vital that process data be kept confidential since once an enforcing authority is known to be a source of data on industrial secrets, further cooperation will be difficult to obtain.

Another resource is the engineering department of the company responsible for a facility's insurance coverage. Also, discussions with officials in jurisdictions with similar facilities and a review of NFPA literature will lead to further information on the process and its associated hazards.

To assess the risk to life safety in an industrial occupancy, a number of factors should be considered.

It should be determined if the manufacturing process includes the handling of flammable, reactive, or explosive materials in quantities that could expose most of the occupants to an initial fire or explosion. If so, the occupancy is a strong candidate for a high hazard classification.

It should also be determined if the manufacturing process requires many people, or if it is basically a large collection of machines or equipment occasionally attended by operators. In some instances, the operators will even be clustered in one location, such as a control room. If a building is predominantly occupied by machinery or equipment and has few employees, the building can be classified as a special purpose industrial occupancy. [*See 28-1.4.1(b).*]

If an industrial building is used mostly for storage of materials (such as preparatory stock for assembly or finished goods), then it meets the requirements for a storage occupancy. (*See Chapter 29.*)

Occupancy classification is dependent on the burning and explosive characteristics of the materials in a building, not on the quantity of combustibles. For example, there would be no reason to change the life safety classification of a building to high hazard simply because a manufacturing process included extensive quantities of ordinary combustible materials distributed in such a manner that the process would be considered a "high combustible load."

The classification of an industrial occupancy for life safety purposes does not depend on the type of structure housing the industrial process. The basic purpose of the hazard classification in Chapter 4 is to evaluate the risk of contents. (*See Section 4-2.*) The classification is determined by an evaluation of the contents and other factors of a fire's development that control the time available to evacuate the occupants safely. Once employees are evacuated to a safe location, the extent of fire spread in the structure becomes a problem of property protection. As long as life safety measures are met, the fact that a building can be heavily damaged by fire is beyond the scope of this *Code*. (*Also see commentary following 28-1.4.1(b) and 28-1.4.1(c).*)

28-1.4.1 Subclassification of Industrial Occupancies. Each industrial occupancy shall be subclassified according to its use as follows:

(a) *General Industrial Occupancy.* Ordinary and low hazard manufacturing operations conducted in buildings of conventional design suitable for various types of manufacture. Included are multistory buildings where floors are rented to different tenants, or buildings suitable for such occupancy and, therefore, subject to possible use for types of manufacturing with a high density of employee population.

(b) *Special Purpose Industrial Occupancy.* Includes ordinary and low hazard manufacturing operations in buildings designed for and suitable only for particular types of operations, characterized by a relatively low density of employee population, with much of the area occupied by machinery or equipment.

It can be difficult to determine if a building is a special purpose industrial occupancy. For example, a structure is often erected to protect a large machine or equipment from weather. Once constructed, authorities may try to impose exit requirements applicable to a general industrial occupancy, even though there is to be only a handful of personnel in the building. Steel mills, paper plants, generating plants, telephone switch buildings, and other operations with large machines are examples of the types of industrial occupancies requiring massive structures for process control and weather protection. Often, these structures represent minimum hazards to life safety and should be classed as special purpose industrial occupancies. In many of the more modern operations, all process control is conducted from a control room by remote control, which further reduces the number of occupants likely to be exposed to a fire.

On the other hand, the special purpose industrial occupancy classification cannot be applied to a building simply to reduce exit requirements. Economic considerations, or staffing limitations resulting in fewer occupants than usual, cannot be used as justification for reducing life safety features; the full number and arrangement of exits required for a general industrial occupancy should be maintained. A reduction in aisles, exit doors, stairways, and other components of the means of egress cannot be justified by the temporary classification of a building as a special purpose industrial occupancy.

(c)* *High Hazard Industrial Occupancy.* Includes those buildings having high hazard materials, processes, or contents. Incidental high hazard operations in low or ordinary occupancies and protected in accordance with Section 4-2 and 28-3.2 shall not be the basis for overall occupancy classification.

A-28-1.4.1(c)   High hazard occupancy may include occupancies where gasoline and other flammable liquids are handled, used, or are stored under such conditions as to involve possible release of flammable vapors; where grain dust, wood flour or plastic dusts, aluminum or magnesium dust, or other explosive dusts may be produced; where hazardous chemicals or explosives are manufactured, stored, or handled; where cotton or other combustible fibers are processed or handled under conditions such as to produce flammable flyings, and other situations of similar hazard.

Chapter 28, Industrial Occupancies, and Chapter 29, Storage Occupancies, include detailed provisions on high hazard occupancy.

A high hazard occupancy classification is limited to those industrial buildings housing extremely hazardous operations. Incidental use of restricted quantities of flammable liquids in a building does not constitute a high hazard occupancy, although some extra life safety precautions may be required during the limited period of use. Refer to NFPA 30, *Flammable and Combustible Liquids Code*,[2] for guidance. Storage of flammable liquids, such as paint, in sealed containers would not require a high hazard occupancy classification unless the operation included mixing or blending operations requiring the containers to be opened. Mixing and blending of flammable liquids could be conducted in a separate room with a fire barrier between the storage and mixing areas. In such an operation, the mixing and blending room would be a high hazard industrial occupancy, while the adjacent, fire-separated storage area would be considered a general purpose industrial occupancy, or possibly a storage occupancy subject to the requirements of Chapter 29.

Combustible dusts released from an industrial or manufacturing process constitute a significant life safety problem and often require a high hazard classification. Major loss of life has occurred in industrial occupancies that release extensive quantities of combustible dusts. Every opportunity for the quick escape of employees working in operations releasing combustible dust should be provided to prevent injury or loss of life should a dust explosion occur. In high hazard occupancies with an explosion potential, the provisions of 28-3.2 require special consideration of techniques for explosion suppression or venting to ensure the life safety of a building's occupants. Full utilization of fire protection engineering techniques should be employed in such occupancies to minimize the potential risk to life safety.

The industrial occupancy most obviously requiring classification as a high hazard occupancy is one associated with the production of explosives or highly reactive chemicals. In some especially hazardous operations, extra exits will be necessary to ensure rapid occupant egress in order to prevent loss of life should an explosion or fire occur. Where installation of the preventive or protective measures specified in 28-3.2 is not possible due to the nature of the industrial operation, consideration should be given to operating procedures that restrict access to a limited number of people during the hazardous portion of the operation. The procedure would limit life safety exposure to those trained personnel who are fully aware of the extent of the hazard. Procedures should also include a record of personnel who have signed in or out to ensure prompt determination of the number of personnel exposed to a hazardous operation and, thus, the number who may require rescue.

28-1.5 Classification of Hazard of Contents.   Classification of hazard of contents shall be as defined in Section 4-2.

28-1.6 Minimum Construction Standards.   No occupancy requirement.

Some occupancy chapters, such as Chapters 12 and 13, which address the life safety needs of nonambulatory occupants, require a certain minimum building construction type to help assure building structural integrity for the time period needed for a lengthy evacuation or for safe refuge within the building. Because industrial occupancies characteristically have ambulatory occupants and do not provide sleeping accommodations, there are no minimum construction requirements imposed.

28-1.7* Occupant Load. The occupant load of industrial occupancies for determination of means of egress shall be one person per 100 sq ft (9.3 sq m) of gross floor area.

Exception: In a special purpose industrial occupancy, the occupant load shall be the maximum number of persons to occupy the area under any probable conditions.

A-28-1.7 In most cases, the requirements for maximum travel distance to exits will be the determining factor rather than numbers of occupants, as exits provided to satisfy travel distance requirements will be sufficient to provide exit capacity for all occupants, except in cases of unusual arrangement of buildings or high occupant load of a general manufacturing occupancy.

The occupant load of an industrial building is based on an average of 100 sq ft (9.3 sq m) of gross floor area per occupant. Many industrial users of the *Code* confuse this concept with the actual number of employees. The usual complaint is that the number of potential employees determined for exit purposes by the 100-sq ft (9.3-sq m) criterion far exceeds the anticipated or actual number of employees. Many industrial managers argue that using the larger number as a basis for exit design requires more exits, wider doors, and more passageways than are needed for exit purposes, reducing productive work space and resulting in increased cost.

The concept of determining occupant load is not actually related to the number of anticipated or actual employees, but is a means of calculating the minimum exit requirements based on the needs of an average industrial occupancy. While actual conditions may vary in an individual location, the amount of exit width determined by the occupant load calculation will normally provide the necessary, adequate, and required exits for a typical industrial building with little or no penalty to the building's owner/operator.

See Figure 28-1 for examples of occupant load determination using the occupant load factor for a general industrial occupancy and actual probable number of occupants for special purpose industrial occupancies.

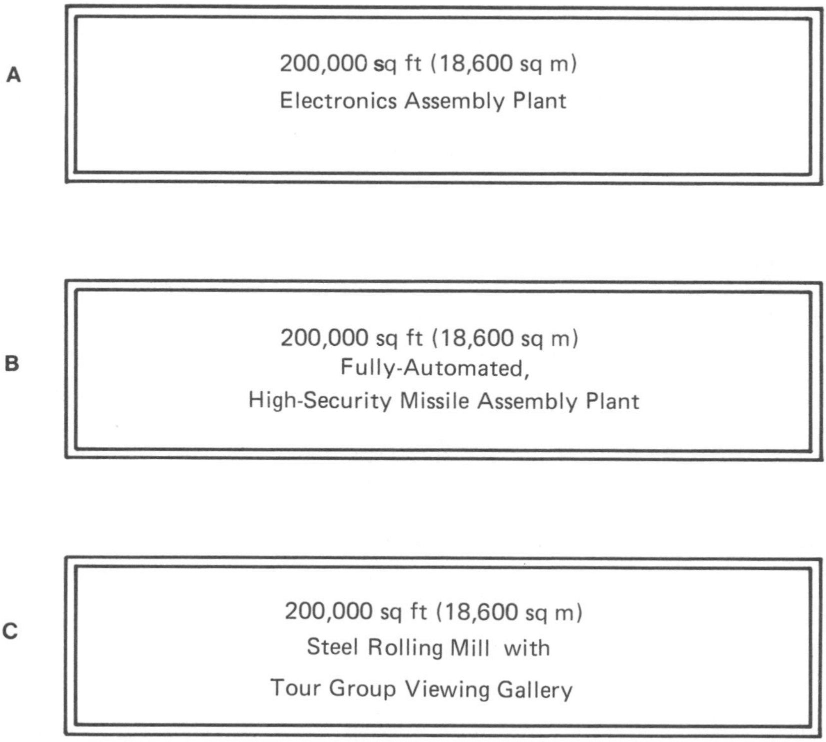

A

```
200,000 sq ft (18,600 sq m)

Electronics Assembly Plant
```

B

```
200,000 sq ft (18,600 sq m)
Fully-Automated,
High-Security Missile Assembly Plant
```

C

```
200,000 sq ft (18,600 sq m)
Steel Rolling Mill with
Tour Group Viewing Gallery
```

Figure 28-1.   Determination of Occupant Load of Industrial Occupancies.

In A, the general industrial occupancy must provide a means of egress for at least 2,000 persons based on use of an occupant load factor of one person per 100 sq ft (9.3 sq m).

In B, a special purpose industrial occupancy can size its means of egress for the maximum 20 persons who are apt to occupy the facility under any probable condition.

In C, the 200-person tour groups that visit this special purpose industrial occupancy on the first Monday of each month must be added to the 45 employees who are normally present, for a total occupant load of 245 persons.

SECTION 28-2   MEANS OF EGRESS REQUIREMENTS

28-2.1 General.

28-2.1.1   Each required means of egress shall be in accordance with the applicable portions of Chapter 5.

28-2.2 Means of Egress Components.

Formal Interpretation 81-1
Reference: 28-2.2

Question: Is it the intent of the *Code* to permit grating-type floors as a means of egress in "Special Purpose Industrial Occupancies" where such flooring is not required to provide vertical fire separation?

Answer: Yes.

Issue Edition: 1981
Reference: 28-2.2
Date: December 1980

Formal Interpretation 81-2
Reference: 28-2.2

Question: Is it the intent of 28-2.2 to require that all new interior and exterior exit stairs for "Special Purpose Industrial Occupancies" be provided with solid treads and landing? (*See 5-2.2.4.5.*)

Answer: Yes.

Issue Edition: 1981
Reference: 28-2.2
Date: January 1981

28-2.2.1   Components of means of egress shall be limited to the types described in 28-2.2.2 through 28-2.2.12.

28-2.2.2 Doors.

28-2.2.2.1   Doors shall comply with 5-2.1.

Given that doors are required to comply with 5-2.1 and that Exception Nos. 1 and 3 to 5-2.1.5.2, which provide exemptions from the stairwell door reentry requirements, are not specifically recognized by Chapter 28, the basic reentry provisions of 5-2.1.5.2 apply to both new and existing industrial occupancies. That paragraph requires that every stairwell door must either allow reentry from the stairwell to the interior of the building (meaning no stairwell doors are permitted to be locked from stair side) or locked doors must automatically unlock upon initiation of the building fire alarm system so as to allow reentry. (*See 5-2.1.5.2.*)

28-2.2.2.2   Special locking arrangements complying with 5-2.1.6 are permitted.

In recognition of the security needs of some industrial occupancies, use of the delay release device covered by 5-2.1.6 is allowed on any door. In effect, the allowable 15- or 30-second delay will be experienced only under nonfire conditions or very early in a fire's growth, given that the door must be immediately usable upon sprinkler operation or smoke or heat detection and upon loss of power controlling the locking mechanism. The building must be protected throughout by an approved automatic sprinkler system or automatic fire detection system.

28-2.2.2.3 In low and ordinary hazard industrial occupancies, horizontal sliding doors may be used in a means of egress serving an occupant load of not more than fifty in accordance with 5-2.1.4.1 Exception No. 6.

28-2.2.2.4 In low and ordinary hazard industrial occupancies, horizontal sliding doors may be used in horizontal exits and smoke barriers in accordance with 5-2.1.4.1 Exception No. 7. (*See 28-2.2.5.2.*)

Both 28-2.2.2.3 and 28-2.2.2.4 recognize limited use of horizontal sliding doors in other than high hazard industrial occupancies where the *Code* would normally require a side-hinged swinging door. Both Exception Nos. 6 and 7 to 5-2.1.4.1 address horizontal sliding doors that meet all the special requirements of 5-2.1.14. (*See 5-2.1.14.*)

28-2.2.3 Stairs.

28-2.2.3.1 Stairs shall comply with 5-2.2.

28-2.2.3.2 Spiral stairs complying with 5-2.2.2.7 are permitted.

Note that, per Chapter 5, spiral stairs can serve only an occupant load of five or fewer.

28-2.2.3.3 In existing buildings, winders complying with 5-2.2.2.8 are permitted.

28-2.2.4 Smokeproof Enclosures. Smokeproof enclosures shall comply with 5-2.3.

28-2.2.5 Horizontal Exits.

28-2.2.5.1 Horizontal exits shall comply with 5-2.4.

28-2.2.5.2* In horizontal exits where the doorway is protected by a fire door on each side of the wall in which it is located, one fire door shall be of the swinging type as provided in 5-2.4.3.3, and the other may be an automatic sliding fire door that shall be kept open whenever the building is occupied.

A-28-2.2.5.2 The customary building code requirement for fire doors on both sides of an opening in a fire wall may be met by having an automatic sliding fire door on one side, and self-closing fire door swinging out from the other side of the wall. This arrangement qualifies only as a horizontal exit from the side of the sliding door. (*For further information, see A-5-2.4.3.3.*)

The intent of 28-2.2.5.2 is to recognize the common practice of combining a horizontal exit used for life safety with a fire barrier of significant fire resistance rating used for property protection. Opening protectives for such a fire barrier can require the use of a series of two doors in order to achieve the required number of hours of fire protection rating. Both doors cannot swing in the same direction without interfering with each other. Operation of two doors that swing in opposite directions is cumbersome for daily or common usage. One swinging and one sliding door, as shown in Figure 28-2, provide an acceptable arrangement for day-to-day functioning of the building. The "open" sliding door does not compromise life safety because, by the time its fusible link mechanism releases the door and allows it to close, temperatures in the vicinity of the door opening would render use of the door impractical.

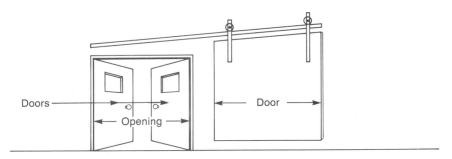

Figure 28-2.   Example of Combination Swinging and Sliding Doors Allowed by 28-2.2.5.2.

28-2.2.6 Ramps.   Ramps shall comply with 5-2.5.

28-2.2.7 Exit Passageways.   Exit passageways shall comply with 5-2.6.

28-2.2.8 Escalators and Moving Walks.   In existing buildings, previously approved escalators and moving walks complying with 5-2.7 may be continued in use.

28-2.2.9 Fire Escape Stairs.   Existing fire escape stairs complying with 5-2.8 are permitted.

28-2.2.10 Fire Escape Ladders.   Fire escape ladders complying with 5-2.9 are permitted.

28-2.2.11 Slide Escapes.   Approved slide escapes complying with 5-2.10 may be used as required exits for both new and existing high hazard industrial occupancies. Slide escapes shall be counted as exits only when regularly used in drills or for normal exit so that occupants are, through practice, familiar with their use.

The intent of 28-2.2.11 is to allow the use of slide escapes, which are a common means of egress from areas housing explosives or other highly hazardous materials in chemical industry buildings. The provision allows consideration of slide escapes as the required exit from high hazard industrial occupancies and modifies the limitations in Chapter 5; in 5-2.10.2 only 25 percent of the required exits may be provided by slide escapes. In many high hazard industrial occupancies, slide escapes are the only practical means of ensuring safe egress prior to an explosion or flash fire. To restrict the use of slide escapes to only 25 percent of the required exits would create an unsafe condition and possibly result in injury or loss of life.

28-2.2.12 Alternating Tread Devices.   Alternating tread devices complying with 5-2.11 are permitted.

The provisions of 5-2.11 in effect limit the use of alternating tread devices to those locations where the *Code* recognizes the use of fire escape ladders. (*See* 5-2.9.)

28-2.3 Capacity of Means of Egress.

28-2.3.1   The capacity of means of egress shall be in accordance with Section 5-3.

Exception: In special purpose industrial occupancies, means of egress shall be provided at least for the persons actually employed; spaces not subject to human occupancy because of the presence of machinery or equipment may be excluded from consideration.

The Exception to 28-2.3.1 places practical limits on the number of required exits and on the arrangement of the means of egress in a special purpose industrial occupancy. There is no life safety purpose served by providing exits from the center of a large machine or equipment installation where there are no occupants under normal operating conditions. A number of industries provide weather shelter for large processes and equipment. Typical examples include steel rolling mills, paper extruders, and metalworking machines, all of which occupy a majority of the floor space in the sheltered building. In many of the more sophisticated operations, full process control is conducted from a remotely located control room. Personnel are normally in the building only for maintenance and adjustment purposes, and then only on a limited basis. To provide exits from such special purpose industrial occupancies would serve no useful purpose and would unjustly impose a severe economic penalty in the name of safety.

The large areas normally enclosed by special purpose structures would require excessive exit width if the occupant load were calculated on the basis of 100 sq ft (9.3 sq m) per person. If provisions for the capacity of the means of egress in a special purpose industrial occupancy were based on the requirements specified for general industrial occupancies, the result would be extensive egress facilities for nonexistent occupants. Such arrangements might actually result in the requirement of exits from the interior of machinery and equipment, which would be incompatible with the equipment's design. In many cases these exits would be from locations that, even under normal operating conditions, would be considered dangerous for humans. Poorly conceived exit facilities serve no life safety purpose and detract from an otherwise well-designed exit system.

28-2.3.2   The minimum width of any corridor or passageway serving as a required exit, exit access, or exit discharge shall be 44 in. (112 cm) in the clear.

It is not the intent of 28-2.3.2 to limit the width of a corridor or passageway to 44 in. (112 cm). Where a corridor serves more than 220 persons (i.e., 0.2 in. (0.5 cm) × 220 = 44 in. (112 cm) per 5-3.3.1), a corridor width greater than 44 in. (112 cm) is required. The width of a corridor must be at least as wide as the required width of the exit to which it leads.

28-2.4 Number of Exits.   *(See also Section 5-4.)*

28-2.4.1   No less than two exits shall be provided for every story or section, including stories below the floor of exit discharge used for general industrial purposes or for uses incidental thereto.

Exception: In low and ordinary hazard industrial occupancies, a single means of egress shall be permitted from any story or section, provided that the exit can be reached within the distance allowed as common path of travel. (See 28-2.5.1 Exception.)

This Exception recognizes that there are small floors or areas in low and ordinary hazard industrial occupancies that, with access to only a single exit, are no less safe than larger areas of the building that have access to two exits after first traveling through the maximum allowable common path. In the case of the single exit, upon traveling the 50 ft (15 m) of common path allowed by 28-2.5.1 Exception, the occupant enters an exit *(see Figure 28-3)* and is judged to have reached a point of safety. In the larger building area, which has a minimum of two exits, once the occupant has traveled the allowable 50 ft (15 m) of common path and reached a point where travel to the exits is possible in different directions, an additional 150 ft (45 m) [200 ft (60 m) if building is sprinklered] of exit access travel is be allowed before the safety of an exit is reached.

28-2.4.2   Floors or portions thereof with an occupant load of more than 500 shall have the minimum number of separate and remote means of egress specified by 5-4.1.2.

Exception: Existing buildings.

Prior editions of the *Code* required more than two exits based on occupant load in the case of assembly occupancies only. Third, fourth, and subsequent exits were provided in industrial occupancies in order to meet travel distance requirements or as convenient extras for day-to-day nonemergency use. New paragraph 5-4.1.2 extends the concept of requiring three or four exits based on occupant load. The Exception to 28-2.4.2 exempts existing buildings from the new requirement so as not to force existing, previously complying means of egress systems into noncompliance.

28-2.4.3   There shall be at least two separate means of egress from every high hazard area regardless of size.

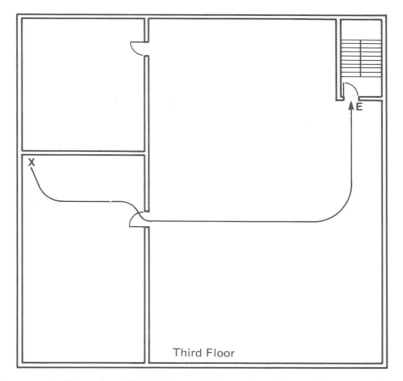

Figure 28-3. Example of Single Means of Egress from Story of Low or Ordinary Hazard Industrial Occupancy, Which Is Permitted Provided Distance to Exit (X to E) Does Not Exceed Allowable Common Path of Travel [i.e., 50 ft (15 m) per 28-2.5.1 Exception].

The provision of 28-2.4.3 is vital to life safety in high hazard occupancies. The requirement for two means of egress for all high hazard occupancies recognizes that there is always the possibility that a fire or explosion could occur that could block or destroy one of the two exits. Two separate and equal means of egress from high hazard areas provide a necessary redundancy to ensure the evacuation of occupants under fire or explosion conditions and to minimize the potential for injury or loss of life. It is not the intent of this paragraph to require two means of egress from very small high hazard areas, such as a paint spray booth, if the single path of travel does not pass through or lead towards the hazardous operation.

28-2.5 Arrangement of Means of Egress. *(See also Section 5-5.)*

28-2.5.1* Where two or more exits are required, they shall be so arranged as to be reached by different paths of travel in different directions.

Exception: A common path of travel may be permitted for the first 50 ft (15 m) from any point in low and ordinary hazard occupancies.

A-28-2.5.1   Unless exits are suitably located, this requirement may interfere with the practice in multiple tenant manufacturing buildings of renting a wing or large section to a single tenant who closes the corridor with a door subject to locking and treats the corridor inside the door as part of his manufacturing space. No required exit may be blocked by a door subject to locking against the exit travel.

The requirements of 28-2.5.1 must be considered by designers, inspectors, and authorities having jurisdiction, particularly where sections of a building are occupied by more than a single tenant. Obviously, uncontrolled access between areas of different ownership is not desirable from a tenant's point of view. However, security provisions between separate facilities must never be allowed to restrict the use of a required means of egress. Where multiple tenants occupy the same building and use common exit facilities, careful consideration is required to ensure continued use of the means of egress over the life of a building. Often a tenant will close off an exit corridor with a door subject to locking and treat the corridor on that side of the door as part of the manufacturing space. If such a practice eliminates another tenant's access to an exit, alternate exits must be provided.

28-2.5.2   No dead end may be more than 50 ft (15 m) deep. Dead ends are not permitted in high hazard occupancies.

See the discussion of dead ends and common path of travel in Chapter 5. A common path of travel cannot be tolerated in high hazard occupancies. See commentary in Chapters 26 and 27 for a discussion on dead ends and common path of travel in office areas. See definition of common path of travel in Chapter 3.

28-2.6 Travel Distance to Exits.

28-2.6.1   Travel distance limitations shall be in accordance with 5-6.5.

Exception No. 1:   As permitted by 28-2.6.2.

Exception No. 2:   As permitted by 28-2.6.3.

Exception No. 3:   Travel distance to exits in high hazard industrial occupancies shall not exceed 75 ft (23 m).

Prior to this edition of the *Code*, Section 5-6 on measurement of travel distance explained the concept of travel distance and established the rules with respect to measurement, but did not set travel distance limitations. Rather, each occupancy chapter was left to prescribe the allowable travel distance limits. New paragraph 5-6.5 establishes travel distance limitations of 200 ft (60 m) in buildings not sprinklered and 250 ft (76 m) in sprinklered buildings, and uses its Exception No. 1 to allow the occupancies to set different limits as necessary.

Paragraph 28-2.6.1 recognizes the travel distance limitations of 5-6.5 and then establishes additional allowances via Exception Nos. 1 through 3.

28-2.6.2 In low or ordinary hazard general industrial occupancies, travel distance may be increased to 400 ft (122 m) if the following additional provisions are met in full:

(a) Shall limit application to one-story buildings.

(b)* Shall provide smoke and heat venting by engineered means or by building configuration to insure that occupants shall not be overtaken by spread of fire or smoke within 6 ft (183 cm) of floor level before they have time to reach exits.

(c) Shall provide automatic sprinkler or other automatic fire extinguishing systems in accordance with Section 7-7. The extinguishing system shall be supervised.

A-28-2.6.2(b) Smoke and heating venting should be in accordance with NFPA 204M, *Guide for Smoke and Heat Venting (see Appendix B).*

The provisions of 28-2.6.2 are meant to provide flexibility for determining layout of exits in an industrial building with a large floor area housing low or ordinary hazard general industrial occupancies.

The construction of tunnels and elevated means of egress from the center of an industrial building with an extensive floor area is rarely attempted. Only a handful of buildings have ever been provided with such an exit facility, and most were World War II airframe manufacturing buildings of massive size. In most industrial buildings it is not practicable or economical to construct exit tunnels or overhead passageways. These special types of means of egress are not easily altered if modifications are necessary to adjust to changes in an industrial facility's layout. Additionally, the construction costs for tunnels and elevated passageways are high due to the special design features required to make them safe, including fire resistance rated supports for the elevated passageways and waterproofing and other features necessary to maintain the integrity of the underground tunnels. Another negative factor in constructing such facilities is the confining nature of a tunnel or elevated passage, which will tend to divert employees away from such means of egress.

The use of horizontal exits through firewalls is common in many industrial occupancies. Full consideration of the provisions in Chapter 5 is required to ensure the safe use of these types of exits. A common violation of those provisions is the failure to provide the proper type of door in a fire wall. The roll-up type of fire door cannot be considered as an acceptable element of a means of egress. Since a horizontal exit may be used from both sides of a fire wall, careful consideration of the direction of door swing is required so that credit can be given for the horizontal exit from both sides of the fire wall. In many instances, two doors swinging in opposite directions will be required so that the exit may be used as a means of egress from both sides of the fire wall. (*See 5-2.4.2.3 and 28-2.2.*)

A common example of travel distance to an exit in a general purpose industrial occupancy that is classified as a low or ordinary hazard is 400 ft (122 m), per the requirements of items (a) through (c) in 28-2.6.2.

Item (a) limits use of the increased travel distance provisions to one-story buildings to utilize horizontal movement of the occupants through the means of egress. Any stairs or other impediments to the rapid movement of people would result in slower evacuation of the building and increase the possibility of exposure to smoke or fire.

To satisfy the intent of item (b), a great deal of judgment must be exercised in the design of systems for smoke and heat venting. The provisions in the *Code* recommending utitilization of the guidelines of NFPA 204M, *Guide for Smoke and Heat Venting*,[3] should be, in most instances, sufficient. The limitation on the accumulation of smoke is a key factor in the design of the smoke removal system. The average evacuation speed of a person walking is normally considered to be 250 ft (76 m) per minute or a little over 4 ft (122 cm) per second. Where applied to the 400-ft (122-m) travel distance allowed by the *Code*, the maximum time to reach an exit should not exceed 2 minutes. It is an extremely rare situation where the smoke that accumulates in an industrial building will be so extensive that it fills the structure and descends to less than 6 ft (183 cm) above the floor level in 2 minutes. With the added benefit of a properly designed system for smoke and heat venting, there will be little chance that the means of egress will be blocked by smoke.

Use of available computer-run smoke-filling and evacuation time models has recently provided the documentation that allowed a designer to meet the smoke and heat venting requirements by having only a high ceiling and no mechanical smoke removal equipment.

Installation of a complete automatic extinguishing system as required by item (c) is intended to ensure control and extinguishment of incipient fires, thus minimizing the exposure of the occupants to a fire. It is not the intent of this paragraph to require automatic sprinkler protection since a number of equally effective extinguishing agents and systems may be utilized for specific fire hazards. What is important in this provision is the necessity for automatic initiation of the fire control and extinguishing system to minimize the extent of the occupants' exposure to fire. The installed system is required to be fully supervised to ensure that it will operate when a fire occurs. Adequate procedures must be provided by the building's owner or tenant to ensure the prompt correction of any impairments to the extinguishing systems. In some facilities, the degree of fire risk during the impairment period may require limitations on hazardous operations and the number of occupants so that the level of safety to life will be equivalent to that provided when the extinguishing system is operational.

28-2.6.3   In low or ordinary hazard special purpose industrial occupancies, travel distance may be increased to 300 ft (91 m), or if the building is protected throughout by an automatic sprinkler system in accordance with Section 7-7, travel distance may be increased to 400 ft (122 m).

Low and ordinary hazard special purpose industrial occupancies, which are characterized by large, specialized equipment and low occupant load, are allowed an increase in travel distance over that allowed low and ordinary general industrial occupancies. Paragraph 28-2.6.3 permits an increase to 300 ft (91 m) if nonsprinklered and 400 ft (122 m) if sprinklered, without having to meet the additional requirements of 28-2.6.2.

For a summary of the various travel distance allowances for industrial occupancies, see Figure 28-4.

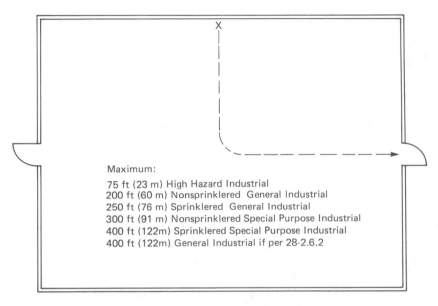

Figure 28-4.   Summary of Travel Distance Options Allowed by 28-2.6.1 through 28-2.6.3.

28-2.7 Discharge from Exits.   Discharge from exits shall be in accordance with Section 5-7.

The purpose of 5-7.2 is to control the arrangement of exits from upper stories that discharge to the outside through a lower floor level. The basis for this Exception to the general rule for complete enclosure of exits up to their point of discharge to the outside of the building is that with the safeguards specified in 5-7.2 (especially automatic sprinkler protection for the level of discharge), reasonable safety is maintained. In evaluating the arrangement of exits, a stairway is not considered as discharging through the level of discharge if it leads to the outside through an exit passageway, even though there are doors between the stairway landing and the level of discharge.

28-2.8 Illumination of Means of Egress.

28-2.8.1   Illumination of means of egress shall be provided in accordance with Section 5-8.

Exception: Means of egress illumination may be eliminated in structures occupied only during daylight hours, with skylights or windows arranged to provide, during these hours, the required level of illumination on all portions of the means of egress.

Paragraph 28-2.8.1 is not meant to require the installation of extensive and unneeded illumination systems in industrial occupancy buildings. Illumination is required for the exit access, which is limited to designated aisles, corridors, and passageways leading to an exit. There is no requirement to provide illumination throughout the entire building, which in many industrial occupancies would involve lighting an extensive floor area. The purpose of the lighting system is to ensure that people are able to see the means of egress and not to illuminate the operation of production facilities.

The *Code* also does not require illumination of the means of egress if the building is occupied only during the daylight hours. To meet the requirements of the Exception to 28-2.8.1, the building, including stairways, must have sufficient windows and skylights to ensure natural illumination. The authority having jurisdiction should make certain that the building is not occupied during the night.

28-2.9 Emergency Lighting.

28-2.9.1   All industrial occupancies shall have emergency lighting in accordance with Section 5-9.

Exception No. 1: Special purpose industrial occupancies do not require emergency lighting where routine human habitation is not the case.

Exception No. 2: Emergency lighting may be eliminated in structures occupied only during daylight hours with skylights or windows arranged to provide, during those hours, the required level of illumination on all portions of the means of egress.

Exceptions to the requirement for emergency lighting are included in the *Code* for the same reasons that illumination of the means of egress is not required. (*See 28-2.8.1.*) An additional exception has been made for special purpose industrial occupancies, which do not routinely have human habitation, since there is no need to install an extensive and costly emergency lighting system where there are no occupants.

28-2.10 Marking of Means of Egress.

28-2.10.1   Signs designating exits or ways of travel thereto shall be provided in accordance with Section 5-10.

28-2.11 Special Features.

SECTION 28-3   PROTECTION

28-3.1 Protection of Vertical Openings.

28-3.1.1   Every stairway, elevator shaft, escalator opening, and other vertical opening shall be enclosed or protected in accordance with Chapter 5 and Section 6-2.

Exception No. 1: Unprotected vertical openings connecting not more than three floors may be permitted in accordance with the conditions of 6-2.4.4.

Exception No. 2: An atrium may be utilized in accordance with 6-2.4.5.

Exceptions No. 1 and No. 2 to 28-3.1.1 recognize the provisions of Chapter 6 for limited vertical openings and atriums as adequate for industrial occupancies.

Exception No. 3: In special purpose and high hazard occupancies where unprotected vertical openings are in new or existing buildings and necessary to manufacturing operations, they may be permitted beyond the specified limits, provided every floor level has direct access to one or more enclosed stairways or other exits protected against obstruction by any fire or smoke in the open areas connected by the unprotected vertical openings.

Exception No. 3 to 28-3.1.1 strictly limits the use of unprotected vertical openings in high hazard and special purpose industrial occupancies. Direct access to one or more enclosed stairways or to other exits is required from any areas connected by unprotected vertical openings. This provision recognizes that many high hazard and special purpose industrial occupancies require openings between floor levels to accommodate piping, conveyors, and other devices and equipment essential to the orderly operation of the facility. In most of these situations, full enclosure is not practical or feasible. In high hazard occupancies, the provision of two means of egress will, in most situations, be sufficient to comply with this Exception. In special purpose occupancies, additional exits or other special arrangements will normally be required to comply with the provision that stairways and exits be protected against obstruction from fire and smoke in the open areas connected by the unprotected vertical openings.

Exception No. 4: Existing open stairways, existing open ramps, and existing escalators may be unenclosed or unprotected where connecting only two floor levels.

Exception No. 4 to 28-3.1.1 limits existing open stairways, existing open ramps, and existing escalators that are unenclosed or unprotected by allowing them to connect only two floors. An existing open stairway connecting three floors would have to be enclosed, protected, or allowed by another of the Exceptions to 28-3.1.1.

Exception No. 5: In existing buildings with low or ordinary hazard contents and protected throughout by an approved automatic sprinkler system in accordance with Section 7-7, vertical openings may be unprotected provided the vertical opening does not serve as a required exit. All required exits under such conditions shall consist of smokeproof enclosures in accordance with 5-2.3, outside stairs in accordance with 5-2.2, or horizontal exits in accordance with 5-2.4.

Exception No. 5 to 28-3.1.1 recognizes that an existing industrial occupancy may contain unprotected vertical openings and still provide a reasonable level of safety to life if the building contains only low or ordinary hazards and is protected by a complete automatic sprinkler system. Smokeproof enclosures and outside stairways (the only types of vertical exits allowed by this Exception) must be fully enclosed or protected against vertical fire spread and meet the requirements of Chapter 5. The unenclosed vertical openings may not serve as part of the means of egress, although they can remain as convenience openings and stairways for normal operations.

While the major reason for allowing this provision is economic, due to the high cost of enclosing all vertical openings in existing buildings, there is actually little effect on the life safety of occupants where the building houses low or ordinary hazards. However, there will be some problems in fire control since unprotected vertical openings can contribute to fire spread in buildings and result in extensive property damage; thus, the requirement for a complete automatic sprinkler system.

28-3.2* Protection from Hazards. Every high hazard industrial occupancy, operation, or process shall have automatic extinguishing systems or such other protection as may be appropriate to the particular hazard, such as explosion venting or suppression for any area subject to an explosion hazard, designed to minimize danger to occupants in case of fire or other emergency before they have time to utilize exits to escape.

A-28-3.2 Emergency lighting should be considered where operations require lighting to perform orderly manual emergency operation or shutdown, maintain critical services, or provide safe start-up after a power failure.

The intent of 28-3.2 is to provide for the life safety of the occupants of industrial buildings through control of the risk associated with hazardous operations. The alternatives in the paragraph are not meant to be inclusive, and a proper fire protection engineering solution might not incorporate the listed provisions. The *Code* is intended to allow for engineering judgment in a wide range of potentially hazardous situations, some where protection may be limited. The intent of the paragraph is also broad in application since in many highly hazardous operations, an explosion may be immediately preceded by a fire or other emergency, such as an overheated reactor vessel, an exothermic reaction, or increased pressure. Since such conditions may be initiators of an explosion, depending on the process and arrangement of the equipment, immediate egress from the facility may be necessary. If fire or other emergencies are likely to proceed rapidly to an explosion, adequate precautions will be necessary for life safety.

In many modern facilities, provisions that will prove adequate for the life safety of a building's occupants may already be included for process control and property protection, and any additional measures will not increase the life safety of operators to an appreciable degree.

Section 12, Chapter 11, of the NFPA *Fire Protection Handbook*[4] discusses the basic principles of explosion prevention, venting, and suppression. This section also contains an extensive bibliography on the subject.

Recommendations for the design and utilization of vents to limit pressures developed by explosions are contained in NFPA 68, *Guide for Venting of Deflagrations.*[5] Standards for explosion prevention systems are found in NFPA 69, *Standard on Explosion Prevention Systems.*[6] Also see the NFPA *Industrial Fire Hazards Handbook.*[7]

28-3.3 Interior Finish.

28-3.3.1   Interior wall and ceiling finish shall be Class A, B, or C in accordance with Section 6-5 in operating areas, and shall be as required by 5-1.4 in exit enclosures.

28-3.3.2 Interior Floor Finish.   No occupancy requirements.

28-3.4 Detection, Alarm, and Communications Systems.

28-3.4.1 General.   Industrial occupancies shall be provided with a fire alarm system in accordance with Section 7-6.

Exception: If the total capacity of the building is under 100 persons and fewer than 25 persons are above or below the level of exit discharge.

28-3.4.2 Initiation.   Initiation of the required fire alarm system shall be by either manual or automatic means in accordance with 7-6.2.

28-3.4.3 Notification.

28-3.4.3.1   The required fire alarm system shall sound an audible alarm in a continuously attended location for purposes of initiating emergency action.

28-3.4.3.2   In high hazard industrial occupancies (*see 28-1.4*), the required fire alarm system shall automatically initiate an occupant evacuation alarm signal per 7-6.3.

The requirements of 28-3.4.3 contain two separate and distinct provisions for audible alarms activated from fire alarm systems. In low and ordinary hazard occupancies, the system is not required to activate an evacuation alarm but is required to sound an alarm in a continuously attended location to initiate emergency action. The intent of this provision is to allow an interface between the alarm system and the plant's emergency organization. The alarm system may be controlled from a central security console or a similar location. The key factor is that the location from which the alarm sounds must be continuously staffed. This requirement need not be interpreted as mandating installation of supervisory service, such as to a central station, but the location must be fully attended during all periods when the building is occupied. In high hazard occupancies, the alarm must be arranged to sound an evacuation signal, since the safety of the occupants of these areas depends on their being immediately notified of a fire.

28-3.5 Extinguishing Requirements.   None.

28-3.6 Corridors.   The provisions of 5-1.3.4 shall not apply.

Had 28-3.6 not provided an exemption to the provisions of 5-1.3.4, all new industrial occupancy corridors serving more than 30 persons would have been required to have a 1-hour fire resistance rating with openings protected by 20-minute fire protection rated door assemblies. Given the ambulatory nature of the occupants of the industrial occupancy and the operational need for openings even where corridors are provided, the exemption to 5-1.3.4 was adopted.

SECTION 28-4   SPECIAL PROVISIONS

28-4.1 Operating Features.   (*See Chapter 31.*)

28-4.2 High Rise Buildings.   No requirements.

SECTION 28-5   BUILDING SERVICES

28-5.1 Utilities.   Utilities shall comply with the provisions of Section 7-1.

28-5.2 Heating, Ventilating, and Air Conditioning Equipment.   Heating, ventilating, and air conditioning equipment shall comply with the provisions of Section 7-2.

28-5.3 Elevators, Dumbwaiters, and Vertical Conveyors.   Elevators, dumbwaiters, and vertical conveyors shall comply with the provisions of Section 7-4.

28-5.4 Rubbish Chutes, Incinerators, and Laundry Chutes.   Rubbish chutes, incinerators, and laundry chutes shall comply with the provisions of Section 7-5.

REFERENCES CITED IN COMMENTARY

[1]NFPA 13, *Standard for the Installation of Sprinkler Systems*, National Fire Protection Association, Quincy, MA, 1987.
[2]NFPA 30, *Flammable and Combustible Liquids Code*, National Fire Protection Association, Quincy, MA, 1987
[3]NFPA 204M, *Guide for Smoke and Heat Venting*, National Fire Protection Association, Quincy, MA, 1985.
[4]NFPA *Fire Protection Handbook*, 16th ed., National Fire Protection Association, Quincy, MA, 1986, pp. 12-75 to 12-91.
[5]NFPA 68, *Guide for Venting of Deflagrations*, National Fire Protection Association, Quincy, MA, 1988.
[6]NFPA 69, *Standard on Explosion Prevention Systems*, National Fire Protection Association, Quincy, MA, 1986.
[7]*Industrial Fire Hazards Handbook*, 2nd ed., National Fire Protection Association, Quincy, MA, 1984.

29 STORAGE OCCUPANCIES

(See also Chapter 31.)

Storage occupancies include all buildings or structures utilized primarily for the storage or sheltering of goods, merchandise, products, vehicles, or animals. Included in this occupancy group are:

Barns	Hangars
Bulk oil storage	Parking garages
Cold storage	Stables
Freight terminals	Truck and marine terminals
Grain elevators	Warehouses

Minor storage incidental to another occupancy is treated as part of the other occupancy.

SECTION 29-1 GENERAL REQUIREMENTS

29-1.1 Application. The requirements of this chapter apply to both new and existing storage occupancies. Storage occupancies include all buildings or structures used primarily for the storage or sheltering of goods, merchandise, products, vehicles, or animals.

Note that this chapter applies to both new and existing facilities. Where the requirements vary, it is common for exceptions for existing storage occupancies to appear or for additional requirements to be presented that are limited in application to new storage occupancies.

29-1.2 Mixed Occupancies. *(See 1-4.7 and 29-1.4.)*

29-1.3 Special Definitions. None.

29-1.4 Classification of Occupancy. Storage occupancies shall include all occupancies defined in 4-1.10. Incidental storage in another occupancy shall not be the basis for overall occupancy classification.

Exception: Storage occupancies or areas of storage occupancies that are used for the purpose of packaging, labeling, sorting, special handling, or other operations requiring an occupant load greater than that normally contemplated for storage shall be classified as industrial occupancies. (See Chapter 28.)

Life safety provisions for storage locations are not extensive since the number of occupants is generally low and many of those who occupy such a structure are present for only a short duration. Further, occupants of storage occupancies do not normally remain in one location; instead, their assignments require that they move about and perform activities of a temporary nature.

Fire records indicate a minimum of life safety problems in storage occupancies. A study by the NFPA Fire Records Department found that during a four-year period, 123 deaths occurred in storage occupancies, which is 1.4 percent of the total number of fatalities from fires recorded during the same period. This number is not conclusive since the data does not distinguish between those deaths due to fire-associated injuries and those due to lack of proper exit facilities.

Due to the special characteristics of storage occupancies, a number of provisions have been included in the *Code* to modify, as required, provisions normally applicable to occupancies with larger populations.

The purpose of the Exception to 29-1.4 is to provide suitable exit facilities for storage occupancies or portions of storage occupancies where a storage building has a population greater than normally expected. It is sometimes common practice to place large numbers of people in a storage building to conduct an industrial type of operation, such as labeling, sorting, or packaging; this will require extra exit facilities in accordance with the provisions for an industrial occupancy as contained in Chapter 28.

29-1.5 Classification of Hazard of Contents.   Contents of storage occupancies shall be classified as high hazard, ordinary hazard, or low hazard in accordance with Section 4-2, depending upon the character of the materials stored, their packaging, and other factors.

In the past few years, a great deal of fire protection literature has concentrated on the risk associated with rack storage facilities. Although NFPA 231C, *Standard for Rack Storage of Materials*,[1] was developed because of the increased awareness of the fire potential inherent in rack storage methods, there is no basis for comparison between the hazard categories in NFPA 231C and those of the *Code*. NFPA 231C hazard categories are established for the design of automatic sprinkler systems. In determining hazards to life safety, all commodity classifications in NFPA 231C, can be considered as low or ordinary hazards. Particular attention should be paid to the scope (Section 1-1) of NFPA 231C, which excludes commodities that could be classified as highly hazardous materials.

There is a great temptation to use the potential for rapid fire growth inherent in high-piled or racked storage as justification for establishing strict life safety provisions. However, the typical arrangement of buildings with this type of storage is adequate to allow safe and rapid egress at the first notification or discovery of fire. Should a building not be protected by automatic sprinklers, the *Code* then contains adequate provisions (such as those for travel distance to an exit) to help ensure the survival of the occupants.

29-1.6 Minimum Construction Standards.   No occupancy requirements.

Some occupancy chapters such as Chapters 12 and 13, which address the life safety needs of nonambulatory occupants, require a certain minimum building construction type to help assure building structural integrity for the time period needed for a lengthy evacuation or for safe refuge within the building. Because storage occupancies characteristically have few occupants and those few occupants are ambulatory, there are no minimum construction requirements imposed.

29-1.7 Occupant Load.   No Requirements.

Although no occupant load factor is established for use in calculating a minimum occupant load for which the means of egress system must be sized, a storage occupancy does have an occupant load. The occupant load is established as the maximum number of persons apt to occupy the storage occupancy under any foreseeable mode of facility operation. Because of the low occupant load characteristic of a storage occupancy, compliance with other *Code* provisions, such as (1) minimum door and corridor or passageway widths, (2) minimum number of exits, and (3) travel distance allowances, generally provides a means of egress system capable of handling the actual occupant load without having to consider the occupant load specifically when designing the means of egress.

SECTION 29-2   MEANS OF EGRESS REQUIREMENTS

29-2.1 General.   Every required means of egress shall be in accordance with the applicable portions of Chapter 5.

29-2.2 Means of Egress Components.

29-2.2.1   Components of means of egress shall be limited to the types described in 29-2.2.2 through 29-2.2.11.

29-2.2.2 Doors.

29-2.2.2.1   Doors shall comply with 5-2.1.

29-2.2.2.2   Special locking arrangements complying with 5-2.1.6 are permitted.

This permits the time delay lock described in 5-2.1.6 which requires that the building be protected either by a complete automatic sprinkler system or an automatic fire detection system.

29-2.2.2.3   Horizontal sliding doors may be used in a means of egress serving an occupant load of not more than 50 in accordance with 5-2.1.4.1 Exception No. 6.

For a discussion of what constitutes the occupant load of a storage occupancy, see the commentary following 29-1.7.

29-2.2.2.4   Horizontal sliding doors may be used in horizontal exits and smoke barriers in accordance with 5-2.1.4.1 Exception No. 7. (*See 29-2.2.5.2.*)

Both 29-2.2.2.3 and 29-2.2.2.4 recognize limited use of horizontal sliding doors in storage occupancies where the *Code* would normally require a side-hinged swinging door. Exception Nos. 6 and 7 to 5-2.1.4.1 address horizontal sliding doors that meet all the special requirements of 5-2.1.14. (*See 5-2.1.14.*)

29-2.2.3 Stairs.

29-2.2.3.1   Stairs shall comply with 5-2.2.

29-2.2.3.2   Spiral stairs complying with 5-2.2.2.7 are permitted.

Note that, per Chapter 5, spiral stairs can serve only an occupant load of five or fewer.

29-2.2.3.3   In existing buildings, winders complying with 5-2.2.2.8 are permitted.

29-2.2.4 Smokeproof Enclosures.   Smokeproof enclosures shall comply with 5-2.3.

29-2.2.5 Horizontal Exits.

29-2.2.5.1   Horizontal exits shall comply with 5-2.4.

29-2.2.5.2*   In horizontal exits where the doorway is protected by a fire door on each side of the wall in which it exists, one fire door shall be of the swinging type as provided in 5-2.4.3.3, and the other may be an automatic sliding fire door that shall be kept open whenever the building is occupied.

A-29-2.2.5.2   The customary requirement of building codes for fire doors on both sides of an opening in a fire wall may be met by having an automatic-sliding fire door on one side, and a self-closing fire door swinging out from the other side of the wall. This arrangement qualifies only as a horizontal exit from the side of the sliding door. (*For further information, see A-5-2.4.3.3.*)

The intent of 29-2.2.5.2 and its Appendix item is to recognize the common practice of combining a horizontal exit used for life safety with a fire barrier of significant fire resistance rating used for property protection. Opening protectives for such a fire barrier can require the use of a series of two doors in order to achieve the required number of hours of fire protection rating. Both doors cannot swing in the same direction without interfering with each other. Operation of two doors that swing in opposite directions is cumbersome for daily or common usage. One swinging and one sliding door provide an acceptable arrangement for day-to-day functioning of the building as shown in Figure 29-1. The "open" sliding door does not compromise life safety because, by the time its fusible link mechanism releases the door and allows it to close, temperatures in the vicinity of the door opening render use of the door impractical.

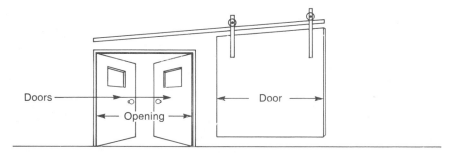

Figure 29-1. Example of Combination Swinging and Sliding Doors Allowed by 29-2.2.5.2.

29-2.2.6 Ramps. Ramps shall comply with 5-2.5.

29-2.2.7 Exit Passageways. Exit passageways shall comply with 5-2.6.

29-2.2.8 Fire Escape Stairs. Existing fire escape stairs complying with 5-2.8 are permitted.

29-2.2.9 Fire Escape Ladders. Fire escape ladders complying with 5-2.9 are permitted.

29-2.2.10 Slide Escapes. Existing slide escapes complying with 5-2.10 are permitted.

29-2.2.11 Alternating Tread Devices. Alternating tread devices complying with 5-2.11 are permitted.

The provisions of 5-2.11 in effect limit the use of alternating tread devices to those locations where the *Code* recognizes the use of fire escape ladders. (*See 5-2.9.*)

29-2.3 Capacity of Means of Egress.

29-2.3.1 The capacity of a means of egress shall be in accordance with Section 5-3.

See commentary following 29-1.7.

29-2.3.2 The minimum width of any corridor or passageway serving as a required exit or means of travel to or from a required exit shall be 44 in. (112 cm) in the clear.

29-2.4 Number of Means of Egress. (*See also Section 5-4.*)

29-2.4.1 Every building or structure used for storage and every section thereof considered separately shall have at least two separate means of egress as remote from each other as practicable.

Exception No. 1: In low hazard storage occupancies, a single means of egress shall be permitted from any story or section.

Exception No. 2: In ordinary hazard storage occupancies, a single means of egress shall be permitted from any story or section, provided that the exit can be reached within the distance allowed as common path of travel. (See 29-2.5.1 Exception No. 3.)

Based in part on the small number of people typically found in a storage occupancy and the exemplary life safety fire record of such facilities, this 1988 Edition of the *Code* relaxes, via Exception Nos. 1 and 2, the basic rule for the provision of two, separate, remote means of egress. Exception No. 1 recognizes that a low hazard storage occupancy is not subject to a self-propagating fire and thus can tolerate a single means of egress. Exception No. 2 allows a single means of egress in an ordinary hazard storage occupancy if the total travel distance to the single exit does not exceed the 50-ft (15-m) or 100-ft (30-m) common path of travel allowance for nonsprinklered and sprinklered buildings, respectively. (*See 29-2.5.1 Exception No. 3.*) This allowance is made because such a single exit arrangement is as good as or better than a two-exit arrangement that makes use of the maximum common path of travel allowance. (*See Figures 29-2a and b.*)

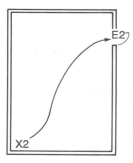

X1-C1 Common Path Of Travel
X1-E1 Total Travel Distance
X2-E2 Total Travel To Single Exit
        Within Allowable Common Path

Figure 29-2a

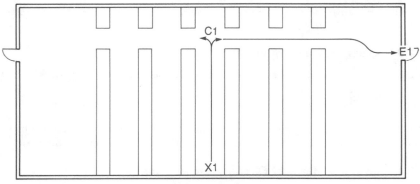

Figure 29-2b

Figures 29-2a and b. A single exit as shown in Figure 29-2a, located within the distance allowed as common path, as addressed by 29-2.4.1 Exception No. 2 for ordinary hazard storage occupancies, creates a situation no worse than the common path of travel shown as X1-C1 in Figure 29-2b.

29-2.4.2   Floors or portions thereof with an occupant load of more than 500 shall have the minimum number of separate and remote means of egress specified by 5-4.1.2.

Exception: Existing buildings.

29-2.5 Arrangement of Means of Egress.   *(See also Section 5-5.)*

29-2.5.1   Where two or more means of egress are required, they shall be arranged so as to be reached by different paths of travel in different directions.

Exception No. 1:   Existing buildings.

Exception No. 2:   Low hazard storage occupancies.

See 29-2.4.1 Exception No. 1.

Exception No. 3:   Common paths of travel and dead ends shall be allowed in ordinary hazard storage occupancies, provided that they do not exceed 50 ft (15 m) in an unsprinklered building and 100 ft (30 m) in a building protected throughout by an approved automatic sprinkler system in accordance with Section 7-7.

Even in a storage occupancy, with its characteristically low occupant load, an occupant should not be forced to travel in one direction only for more than 50 ft (15 m) [100 ft (30 m) in a sprinklered building] without an option to branch off and head toward another remote exit. Thus, both common path of travel and dead-end corridor limitations are established by Exception No. 3.

29-2.5.2   Travel from all locations in a storage occupancy of high hazard contents shall be via at least two separate routes to exits remote from each other.

29-2.5.3   No dead ends are permitted in high hazard occupancies.

29-2.6 Travel Distance to Exits.   *(See also Section 5-6.)*

29-2.6.1*   Travel to exits shall not exceed 200 ft (60 m) from any point to reach the nearest exit.

Exception No. 1:   In a building protected throughout by an approved automatic sprinkler system in accordance with Section 7-7, travel distance may be increased to 400 ft (122 m).

Exception No. 2:   There shall be no limitations on travel to exits for low hazard storage occupancy.

Exception No. 3:   Every area used for the storage of high hazard commodities shall have an exit within 75 ft (23 m) of any point in the area where persons may be present. Travel distance shall be measured in accordance with 5-6.

Exception No. 4:   In areas used for the storage of high hazard commodities and protected throughout by an approved automatic sprinkler system in accordance with Section 7-7, distances to an exit shall be within 100 ft (30 m) of any point in the area where persons may be present.

A-29-2.6.1   The travel distance to exits specified contemplate a low population density. Consideration should be given to locating areas that have a relatively high population, such as lunchrooms, meeting rooms, packaging areas, and offices near the outside wall of the building, to keep the travel distance to a minimum.

Paragraph 29-2.6.1 and its Exceptions establish the limitations on travel distance for storage occupancies. Note that the provisions make a direct relationship between the hazard of contents and the life safety requirements for a building. Thus, in low hazard storage occupancies, there is no limitation on travel distance. As the hazard of contents increases, travel limitations are required. Storage buildings housing ordinary hazards and lacking protection are limited to 200 ft (60 m) of travel distance to an exit. A distance of 400 ft (122 m) is permissible if complete automatic sprinkler protection is provided. In high hazard storage occupancies, travel distance is restricted to a maximum of 75 ft (23 m) if unsprinklered and 100 ft (30 m) if the building is equipped with a complete automatic sprinkler system.

The elimination of travel distance restrictions for low hazard storage occupancies is realistic since the small fire risk represented by such materials, coupled with the low occupant population, provides a minimal risk to life safety. Imposing restrictive provisions would not be consistent with good fire protection and reasonable life safety requirements since the possibility of fire is very low and little difficulty is expected to be experienced by occupants exiting the building. (*See Section 4-2 for the definition of low hazard contents.*)

29-2.7 Discharge from Exits.   Discharge from exits shall be in accordance with Section 5-7.

29-2.8 Illumination of Means of Egress.

29-2.8.1   Illumination of means of egress shall be provided in accordance with Section 5-8.

Exception: In structures occupied only during daylight hours with windows arranged to provide, during daylight hours, the required level of illumination of all portions of the means of egress, illumination may be eliminated by special permission of the authority having jurisdiction.

The provisions of 29-2.8.1 are not intended to require the installation of extensive and unneeded exit illumination systems in storage occupancies. Illumination is required for the exit and for the exit access, which is limited to designated aisles, corridors, and passageways leading to an exit. Limiting the extent of the lighting system to a building's egress areas eliminates the necessity for placing specialized lighting systems throughout storage areas, a practice that would be extremely costly with little or no return in safety to life.

The Exception allows a waiver of the requirement for installing illumination systems if a building, including stairways, is sufficiently lighted during periods of occupancy by means of natural lighting. The term "windows," as used in the text of the Exception, should not be interpreted literally. The term is meant to include skylights, open wall sections, and similar means of illumination by natural sources. Provisions are based on the fact that there is no need for a lighting system if the building is unoccupied during non-daylight hours.

29-2.9 Emergency Lighting.

29-2.9.1 All storage occupancies shall have emergency lighting in accordance with Section 5-9.

Exception No. 1: Storage occupancies do not require emergency lighting when not normally occupied.

Exception No. 2: In structures occupied only during daylight hours with skylights or windows arranged to provide, during these hours, the required level of illumination of all portions of the means of egress, emergency lighting may be eliminated.

Exceptions to the requirement for the installation of emergency lighting are included for the reasons stated in 29-2.8.1. Exception No. 1 allows circuit arrangements that disconnect power from emergency lighting systems when the building is unoccupied. In many warehouses, power is turned off during periods when the building is unoccupied. The power disconnection serves fire prevention, energy conservation, and security purposes.

29-2.10 Marking of Means of Egress. Signs designating exits or ways of travel thereto shall be provided in accordance with Section 5-10.

29-2.11 Special Features.

SECTION 29-3 PROTECTION

29-3.1 Protection of Vertical Openings.

29-3.1.1 Every stairway, elevator shaft, escalator opening, manlift opening, and other vertical opening shall be enclosed or protected in accordance with Section 6-2.

Exception No. 1: Unprotected vertical openings connecting not more than three floors may be permitted in accordance with the conditions of 6-2.4.4.

Exception No. 2: An atrium may be utilized in accordance with 6-2.4.5.

Exception No. 3: In existing buildings with low or ordinary hazard contents and protected throughout by an approved automatic sprinkler system in accordance with Section 7-7, vertical openings may be unprotected where they do not serve as required exits. All required exits under such conditions shall consist of smokeproof enclosures in accordance with 5-2.3, outside stairs in accordance with 5-2.2, or horizontal exits in accordance with 5-2.4.

Exception No. 3 to 29-3.1.1 recognizes that an existing storage occupancy may contain unprotected vertical openings and still provide a reasonable level of safety to life if the building houses only low or ordinary hazard contents and is protected by a complete automatic sprinkler system. Smokeproof towers and outside stairways (the only types of vertical exits allowed by this Exception) must be fully enclosed or protected against vertical fire spread and meet the requirements of Chapter 5. The unenclosed vertical openings must not be used in any way as a means of egress, although they can remain as convenience stairways for normal operations.

While the major reason for allowing this provision is economic, due to the high cost of enclosing all vertical openings in existing buildings, there is actually little effect on the life safety of occupants where the building houses low or ordinary hazard contents. However, there will be some problems in fire control since unprotected vertical openings can contribute to fire spread in buildings and result in extensive property damage; thus, the requirement for a complete automatic sprinkler system.

29-3.2 Protection from Hazards.   No occupancy requirements.

29-3.3 Interior Finish.

29-3.3.1   Interior wall and ceiling finish shall be Class A, B, or C in accordance with Section 6-5 in the storage areas and shall be as required by 5-1.4 in exit enclosures.

29-3.3.2 Interior Floor Finish.   No occupancy requirements.

29-3.4 Detection, Alarm, and Communications Systems.

29-3.4.1 General.   Storage occupancies shall be provided with a fire alarm system in accordance with Section 7-6.

Exception No. 1: Storage occupancies limited to low hazard contents.

Exception No. 2: Storage occupancies with ordinary or high hazard contents not exceeding an aggregate floor area of 100,000 sq ft (9,300 sq m).

Exception No. 3: Storage occupancies with complete automatic extinguishment protection.

29-3.4.2 Initiation.   Initiation of the required fire alarm system shall be by either manual or automatic means in accordance with 7-6.2.

29-3.4.3 Notification.   The required fire alarm system shall sound an audible alarm in a continuously attended location for purposes of initiating emergency action.

Subsection 29-3.4 requires the installation of a fire alarm system in unsprinklered storage occupancies with an aggregate floor area of over 100,000 sq ft (9,300 sq m). An alarm system is not required in a storage occupancy limited to low hazard contents regardless of size, nor is it required in a sprinklered storage occupancy regardless of size. Visibility is limited in buildings with large floor areas due to the placement of storage, and personnel working in the storage areas could be unaware of a fire for a long period of time. If the fire spreads, which is a good possibility in an unprotected storage building, means of exit access could be blocked. The alarm system will provide a means of alerting all occupants to the presence of the fire and allow for timely exit. The alarm is required to sound in a continuously attended location as a precaution in case it is necessary to alert additional fire fighting personnel or initiate search and rescue procedures. The *Code* does not specify an alarm system as a property protection requirement, although the probability of property loss is reduced in any occupancy where an alarm system is installed. In buildings provided with an automatic sprinkler system, it is anticipated that an alarm will sound in a continuously attended location upon operation of the sprinkler system.

29-3.5 Extinguishing Requirements. None.

29-3.6 Corridors. The provisions of 5-1.3.4 shall not apply.

The provisions of 5-1.3.4, had they not been specifically exempted, would have required 1-hour fire resistance rated corridors if the corridor served more than 30 persons. The exemplary life safety fire record of storage occupancies and the functional need served by open floor areas makes separation of corridors unnecessary.

SECTION 29-4   SPECIAL PROVISIONS

29-4.1 Operating Features. *(See Chapter 31.)*

29-4.2 High Rise Buildings. No Requirements.

SECTION 29-5   BUILDING SERVICES

29-5.1 Utilities. Utilities shall comply with the provisions of Section 7-1.

29-5.2 Heating, Ventilating, and Air Conditioning Equipment. Heating, ventilating, and air conditioning equipment shall comply with the provisions of Section 7-2.

29-5.3 Elevators, Dumbwaiters, and Vertical Conveyors. Elevators, dumbwaiters, and vertical conveyors shall comply with the provisions of Section 7-4.

29-5.4 Rubbish Chutes, Incinerators, and Laundry Chutes. Rubbish chutes, incinerators, and laundry chutes shall comply with the provisions of Section 7-5.

SECTION 29-6*   SPECIAL PROVISIONS FOR AIRCRAFT HANGARS

A-29-6 For further information on aircraft hangars, see NFPA 409, *Standard on Aircraft Hangars* (*see Appendix B*).

29-6.1 The requirements of Sections 29-1, through 29-5 shall be met, except as modified by 29-6.2 through 29-6.4.

29-6.2   Exits from aircraft storage or servicing areas shall be provided at intervals of not more than 150 ft (45 m) on all exterior walls. There shall be a minimum of two exits serving each aircraft storage or servicing area. Horizontal exits through interior fire walls shall be provided at intervals of not more than 100 ft (30 m) along the wall.

Exception: Dwarf or "smash" doors in doors accommodating aircraft may be used to comply with these requirements.

> Paragraph 29-6.2 provides two alternate methods of providing exit from aircraft hangars. Where exit is possible through the outside wall, a spacing of 150 ft (45 m) between exit doors is adequate. In larger hangars, the servicing bay may be provided with offices and shops along one or more sides, with the wall construction having a fire resistance rating. In cases where the wall has a fire resistance rating, exit spacing of up to 100 ft (30 m) is specified. Should the wall be nonrated, then access to the outside is required. During poor weather, large hangar doors cannot be left open to ensure a means of egress, so it is common procedure to provide small personnel access doors in the larger aircraft hangar door. The small door can be considered a normal means of egress from an aircraft hangar. If possible, the door should swing in the direction of egress; however, this may not be possible due to the design of the aircraft door. (*For further information on aircraft hangars, see NFPA 409, Standard on Aircraft Hangars.*[2])

29-6.3   Exits from mezzanine floors in aircraft storage or servicing areas shall be so arranged that the maximum travel distance to reach the nearest exit from any point on the mezzanine shall not exceed 75 ft (23 m). Such exits shall lead directly to a properly enclosed stairwell discharging directly to the exterior, to a suitable cutoff area, or to outside stairs.

29-6.4   No dead end may be more than 50 ft (15 m) deep.

Exception: No dead end shall be allowed for high hazard areas.

SECTION 29-7* SPECIAL PROVISIONS FOR GRAIN OR OTHER BULK STORAGE ELEVATORS

A-29-7   For further information, see NFPA 61B, *Standard for the Prevention of Fires and Explosions in Grain Elevators and Facilities Handling Bulk Raw Agricultural Commodities (see Appendix B)*. The exit requirements for storage elevators are based upon the possibility of fire and are not based upon the possibility of grain dust explosions.

29-7.1   The requirements of Sections 29-1 through 29-5 shall be met, except as modified in 29-7.2 through 29-7.4.

29-7.2   There shall be at least two means of egress from all working levels of the head house. One of these means of egress shall be a stair to the level of exit discharge that is enclosed by a dust-resistant 1-hour fire resistance rated enclosure in accordance with 5-1.3. The second means of egress may be either:

(a) An exterior stair or basket ladder-type fire escape accessible from all working levels of the head house that provides a passage to ground level, or

(b) An exterior stair or basket ladder-type fire escape accessible from all working levels of the head house that provides access to the top of adjoining structures that provide a continuous path to the means of egress described in 29-7.3.

Exception: Stair enclosures in existing structures may have non-fire-rated dust-resistant enclosures.

It is not the intent of 29-7.2 to require a fully dust-tight shaft since the door will allow passage of limited amounts of dust during the normal course of day-to-day operations. The shaft should, however, be separated from the operating areas by fire resistance rated construction and be as free of dust as possible.

29-7.3   There shall be an exterior stair or basket ladder-type fire escape that provides passage to ground level from the top of the end of the adjoining structure, such as a silo, conveyor, gallery, or gantry, etc.

29-7.4 Underground Spaces.

29-7.4.1   Underground spaces shall have at least two means of egress, one of which may be a means of escape. The means of escape shall be arranged to eliminate dead ends.

29-7.4.2   Travel distance to means of escape or exit shall not exceed 200 ft (60 m).

Exception No. 1:   Existing facilities.

Exception No. 2:   In a building protected throughout by an approved automatic sprinkler system in accordance with Section 7-7, travel distance may be increased to 400 ft (122 m).

Section 29-7 provides three basic requirements:

1. Two means of egress from all working levels of the head house.

2. A means of egress at the end of all galleries, etc., thereby eliminating dead ends.

3. A means of escape provided to eliminate dead ends in underground areas.

Paragraph 29-7.2 requires that one means of egress from the head house shall be an enclosed stair. The alternate means of egress can be either an outside stair or basket ladder-type fire escape connecting all working levels and leading to either the ground or the top of an adjoining structure that complies with 29-7.3.

The principal hazard of elevator storage structures that handle combustible materials is a dust explosion. A dust explosion can be violent enough to damage or destroy the primary means of egress required in 29-7.2.

SECTION 29-8 SPECIAL PROVISIONS FOR PARKING GARAGES

29-8.1 General Requirements.

29-8.1.1* Application.   The following provisions apply to parking garages of closed or open type, above or below ground, but not to mechanical or exclusively attendant parking facilities, which are not occupied by customers and thus require a minimum of exits.

A-29-8.1.1   For further information on garages, including a definition of "open garage," see NFPA 88A, *Standard for Parking Structures (see Appendix B).*

The intent of the special provisions for garages is to provide adequate life safety for the patrons of parking facilities, who will probably be unfamiliar with the garage and its arrangement. Where parking attendants are the only occupants that enter the parking area, the *Code's* intent is to provide exits in accordance with the previous sections of Chapter 29. In such instances, the provisions for ordinary hazard occupancies apply.

(*For further information on garages, see NFPA 88A, Standard for Parking Structures.*[3])

29-8.1.2 Mixed Occupancies.

29-8.1.2.1   Where both parking and repair operations are conducted in the same building, the entire building shall comply with Chapter 28.

Exception: If the parking and repair sections are separated by 1-hour fire-rated construction, the parking and repair sections may be treated separately.

The Exception to 29-8.1.2.1 allows a building to house parking and repair operations simultaneously if they are separated by 1-hour fire resistance rated construction. The repair operation would be governed by the provisions of Chapter 28 and the parking facilities by those of Chapter 29. Guidelines for the rating of construction assemblies can be found in NFPA 220, *Standard on Types of Building Construction.*[4] Special requirements for repair garages can be found in NFPA 88B, *Standard for Repair Garages.*[5]

29-8.1.2.2   In areas where repair operations are conducted, the exits shall comply with Chapter 28, Industrial Occupancies.

29-8.1.3 Special Definitions.

Open-Air Parking Structure.   Buildings, structures, or portions thereof used for parking motor vehicles and having not less than 25 percent of the total wall area open to atmosphere at each level, utilizing at least two sides of the structure.

29-8.1.4 Classification of Occupancy.   Incidental vehicle parking in another occupancy shall not be the basis for overall occupancy classification.

29-8.1.5 Classification of Hazard of Contents.   Garages used only for the storage of vehicles shall be classified as ordinary hazard in accordance with Section 4-2.

Paragraph 29-8.1.5 appropriately classifies the hazard of contents as ordinary hazard for garages used only for the storage of vehicles. With the increased use of plastic materials in vehicle bodies and interiors, a garage presents a hazard greater than that of low hazard contents.

29-8.1.6 Minimum Construction Requirements.   No Special Requirements.

29-8.1.7 Occupant Load.   No Requirements.

See commentary following 29-1.7.

29-8.2 Means of Egress Requirements.

29-8.2.1 General.   Required means of egress shall be in accordance with the applicable portions of Chapter 5.

29-8.2.2 Means of Egress Components.

29-8.2.2.1   Components of means of egress shall be limited to the types described in 29-8.2.2.2 through 29-8.2.2.8.

29-8.2.2.2 Doors.

(a) Doors shall comply with 5-2.1.

(b) Special locking arrangements complying with 5-2.1.6 are permitted.

This item permits the time delay lock described in 5-2.1.6, which requires that the building be protected throughout by automatic sprinklers or a complete fire detection system.

(c) Horizontal sliding doors may be used in a means of egress serving an occupant load of not more than fifty in accordance with 5-2.1.4.1 Exception No. 6.

See commentary following 29-2.2.2.3.

(d) Horizontal sliding doors may be used in horizontal exits and smoke barriers in accordance with 5-2.1.4.1 Exception No. 7.

See commentary following 29-2.2.2.4.

(e) An opening for the passage of automobiles may serve as an exit from a street floor, provided no door or shutter is installed therein.

29-8.2.2.3 Stairs.

(a) Stairs shall comply with 5-2.2.

(b) In existing buildings, winders in accordance with 5-2.2.2.8 are permitted.

29-8.2.2.4 Smokeproof Enclosures. Smokeproof enclosures shall comply with 5-2.3.

29-8.2.2.5 Horizontal Exits. Horizontal exits shall comply with 5-2.4.

29-8.2.2.6 Ramps. Ramps shall comply with 5-2.5 and shall not be subject to normal vehicular traffic where used as an exit.

Exception No. 1: In a ramp-type open garage with open vehicle ramps not subject to closure, the ramp may serve in lieu of the second exit from floors above the level of exit discharge, provided the ramp discharges directly outside of the street level.

Exception No. 2: For garages extending only one floor level below the level of exit discharge, a vehicle ramp leading directly to the outside may serve in lieu of the second exit, provided no door or shutter is installed therein.

The Exceptions to 29-8.2.2.6 allow the designer to take advantage of the garage ramps as part of the means of egress. Properly arranged ramps can facilitate safe egress to a degree well in excess of that required for the given number of occupants.

Exception No. 1 allows consideration of ramps as an alternate secondary means of egress from floors above the street level where arranged so that discharge to the street level is clear and unobstructed. Ramps from floors above the street level are required to be open and must not be subject to closure by walls or some other means that will confine smoke and heat in the ramp structure. Under Exception No. 1, it is possible to use a ramp as part of the exit design only if a parking garage is an open-type structure. Ramps in closed garages cannot be considered as part of the exit system, and normal means of egress (listed in 29-8.2.2) should be installed.

Exception No. 2 allows a ramp to be used as an alternate secondary means of egress in a closed or open garage that extends not more than one floor level below the level of exit discharge. The ramp must not have a door or a shutter and must lead directly outside.

29-8.2.2.7 Exit Passageways. Exit passageways shall comply with 5-2.6.

29-8.2.2.8 Fire Escape Stairs. Fire escape stairs complying with 5-2.8 are permitted for existing garages only.

29-8.2.3 Capacity of Means of Egress. *(Also see 29-8.2.4, Number of Exits, and 29-8.2.5, Arrangement of Means of Egress.)*

See commentary following 29-1.7.

29-8.2.3.1 The minimum width of any corridor or passageway serving as a required exit or means of travel to or from a required exit shall be 44 in. (112 cm) in the clear.

29-8.2.4 Number of Exits. *(See also Section 5-4.)*

29-8.2.4.1 Every floor of every garage shall have access to at least two separate exits.

Note that there is no exception to the two-exit rule for parking garages.

29-8.2.4.2   Floors or portions thereof with an occupant load of more than 500 shall have the minimum number of separate and remote means of egress specified by 5-4.1.2.

Exception: Existing buildings.

29-8.2.5 Arrangement of Means of Egress.   *(See also Section 5-5.)*

29-8.2.5.1   Exits shall be so arranged that from any point in the garage the paths of travel to the two exits will be in different directions.

Exception: A common path of travel may be permitted for the first 50 ft (15 m) from any point.

29-8.2.5.2   No dead end may be more than 50 ft (15 m) deep.

29-8.2.5.3   If any gasoline pumps are located within any closed parking garage, exits shall be arranged and located to meet the following:

(a) Travel away from the gasoline pump in any direction will lead to an exit, with no dead end in which occupants might be trapped by fire or explosion at any gasoline pump.

(b) Such exit shall lead to the outside of the building on the same level or to stairs; no upward travel shall be permitted unless direct outside exits are available from that floor.

(c) Any story below that story at which gasoline is being dispensed shall have exits leading direct to the outside via outside stairs or doors at ground level.

Paragraph 29-8.2.5.3 specifies the special conditions necessary to protect the occupants of closed parking garages from fires that may be caused by gasoline-dispensing operations located inside the building. Item (c) requires that direct access to the outside be provided from floors below a story on which gasoline is dispensed. This eliminates the possibility of gasoline vapors, which are heavier than air, accumulating in enclosed portions of a means of egress, such as inside exit stairways.

The hazards associated with dispensing gasoline inside buildings are avoided by outdoor dispensing, such as occurs in ordinary gasoline filling stations. (*See NFPA 30A, Automotive and Marine Service Station Code,[6] for requirements on indoor dispensing of gasoline.*)

29-8.2.6 Travel Distance to Exits.   Exits in garages shall be so arranged that no point in the area will be more than 150 ft (45 m) (measured in accordance with Section 5-6) from the nearest complying permissible exit.

Exception No. 1: Travel distance may be increased to 200 ft (60 m) for open floors of unsprinklered, open-air garages and 300 ft (91 m) in open-air garages protected throughout by an approved automatic sprinkler system.

Exception No. 2: Travel distance may be increased to 200 ft (60 m) for enclosed parking garages protected throughout by an approved automatic sprinkler system in accordance with Section 7-7.

Exception No. 3: For new garages with vehicle ramps serving in lieu of the second exit per 29-8.2.2.6 Exception No. 1, travel distance shall be measured to the exit discharge.

Exception No. 4: For existing garages with vehicle ramps serving in lieu of the second exit per 29-8.2.2.6 Exception No. 1, no travel distance requirements apply.

29-8.2.7 Discharge from Exits.   No special occupancy provisions.

29-8.2.8 Illumination of Means of Egress.   Every public space, hall, stair enclosure, and other means of egress shall have illumination in accordance with Section 5-8.

Exception: In structures occupied only during daylight hours with windows arranged to provide, during daylight hours, the required level of illumination of all portions of the means of egress, illumination may be eliminated by special permission of the authority having jurisdiction.

29-8.2.9 Emergency Lighting.   Every public space, hall, stair enclosure, and other means of egress shall have emergency lighting in accordance with Section 5-9.

Exception: In structures occupied only during daylight hours with skylights or windows arranged to provide, during these hours, the required level of illumination of all portions of the means of egress, emergency lighting may be eliminated.

29-8.2.10 Marking of Means of Egress.   Signs designating exits or ways of travel thereto shall be provided in accordance with Section 5-10.

29-8.2.11 Special Features.

29-8.3 Protection.

29-8.3.1 Protection of Vertical Openings.   No Requirements.

29-8.3.2 Protection from Hazards.   No Requirements. *(See 29-8.1.2.1.)*

29-8.3.3 Interior Finish.

29-8.3.3.1 Interior Wall and Ceiling Finish.   Interior wall and ceiling finish shall be Class A, B, or C in accordance with Section 6-5 in garages, and shall be as required by 5-1.4 in exit enclosures.

29-8.3.3.2 Interior Floor Finish.   No Requirements.

29-8.3.4 Detection, Alarm, and Communications Systems.

29-8.3.4.1 General.   Garages exceeding an aggregate floor area of 100,000 sq ft (9,300 sq m) shall be provided with a fire alarm system in accordance with Section 7-6.

Exception No. 1: Open-air parking structures.

Exception No. 2: Garages protected throughout by an approved automatic sprinkler system in accordance with Section 7-7.

29-8.3.4.2 Initiation. Initiation of the required fire alarm system shall be by either manual or automatic means in accordance with 7-6.2.

29-8.3.4.3 Notification. The required fire alarm system shall sound an audible alarm in a continuously attended location for purposes of initiating emergency action.

29-8.3.5 Extinguishing Requirements. None.

29-8.3.6 Corridors. The provisions of 5-1.3.4 shall not apply.

See commentary following 29-3.6.

29-8.4 Special Provisions.

29-8.4.1 High Rise Buildings. No Requirements.

REFERENCES CITED IN COMMENTARY

[1]NFPA 231C, *Standard for Rack Storage of Materials*, National Fire Protection Association, Quincy, MA, 1986.
[2]NFPA 409, *Standard on Aircraft Hangars*, National Fire Protection Association, Quincy, MA, 1985.
[3]NFPA 88A, *Standard for Parking Structures*, National Fire Protection Association, Quincy, MA, 1985.
[4]NFPA 220, *Standard on Types of Building Construction*, National Fire Protection Association, Quincy, MA, 1985.
[5]NFPA 88B, *Standard for Repair Garages*, National Fire Protection Association, Quincy, MA, 1985.
[6]NFPA 30A, *Automotive and Marine Service Station Code*, National Fire Protection Association, Quincy, MA, 1987.

30

SPECIAL STRUCTURES AND HIGH RISE BUILDINGS

(See also Chapter 31.)

A "usual" occupancy might be present in an "unusual" or special structure; for example, a large convention center (Class A assembly occupancy) located on a pier so that the facility is surrounded by water on three sides, or a moderate size restaurant (Class C assembly occupancy) located on an upper level of an air-traffic control tower. An authority having jurisdiction should ensure that any engineered solutions to the special structure's inherent egress deficiencies provide an overall level of safety to life equivalent to that specified by the requirements of the occupancy chapter applicable to the use.

Occupancies in unusual or special structures also include any building or structure that cannot be properly classified in any of the other occupancy groups, either by reason of some function not covered by the provisions of those groups or some unusual combination of functions necessary to the purpose of the building or structure. Such miscellaneous buildings and structures must conform to the fundamental principles stated in Chapter 2 as well as to the provisions of this chapter.

SECTION 30-1   GENERAL REQUIREMENTS

30-1.1 Application.   The requirements of this chapter apply to both new and existing occupancies in special structures and to those occupancies regulated by Chapters 8 through 29 that are in a special structure or building.

Exception: Any building, tower, or vessel surrounded by water and under the jurisdiction of the US Coast Guard, such as a lighthouse, offshore oil platform, or vessel mooring point, and designed and arranged in accordance with Coast Guard regulations is exempt from the requirements of this chapter.

Occupancies in unusual structures present a special challenge to life safety. Many of the structures covered by the provisions of Chapter 30 are also governed by provisions in other chapters of the *Code*. As a basic requirement, the provisions for specific occupancies in Chapters 8 through 29 take precedence over the provisions in Chapter 30. However, all occupancies in windowless and underground buildings must comply with the additional provisions of 30-7 for complete automatic sprinkler protection, emergency lighting, and smoke venting.

Although the *Code* is essentially complete, providing adequate means of egress from many special structures will require unique solutions. Obviously, engineered solutions in many instances will exceed the minimum provisions of Chapter 30. Still, the uniqueness of a structure should not become an excuse for reducing safety to life. The *Code* user is cautioned to exercise judgment where determining the exit requirements for unusual structures not included in the scope of Chapter 30.

30-1.2 Mixed Occupancies.   (*See 1-4.7.*)

30-1.3 Special Definitions.

30-1.3.1 Tower.   Independent structure or portion of a building occupied for observation, signaling, or similar limited use and not open to general use.

Formal Interpretation 81-35
Reference: 30-1.3.1, 30-2.4

Question: Is it the intent of the Committee on Safety to Life that the definition of "Tower" in 30-1.3.1 apply to a multistory building housing (1) an observation deck on the top level with a typical occupant load of 4 to 5 persons engaged in aircraft direction and control, and (2) other floors with kitchens, training areas, conference rooms, offices, and mechanical and support areas, some with an occupant load of more than 15 persons?

Answer: No.

Issue Edition: 1981
Reference: 30-1.3.1, 30-2.4
Date: October 1983

30-1.3.2 Vehicle.   Any trailer, railroad car, street car, bus, or similar conveyance that is not mobile or is attached to a building or is permanently fixed to a foundation.

30-1.3.3 Vessel.   Any ship, barge, or other vessel permanently fixed to a foundation or mooring or unable to get under way under its own power and occupied for purposes other than navigation.

30-1.3.4* Underground Structure.   A structure or portions of a structure in which the story is below the level of exit discharge.

Exception: A structure or portions of a structure shall not be considered an underground structure if:

(a) The story is provided on at least two sides with at least 20 sq ft (1.9 sq m) of opening entirely above the adjoining grade level in each 50 lineal ft (15 m) of exterior enclosing wall area, and

(b) The openings have minimum dimensions of not less than 22 in. (55.9 cm) in width and 24 in. (61 cm) in height and are unobstructed to allow for ventilation and rescue operations from the exterior, and

(c) The bottom of the openings are not more than 44 in. (112 cm) above the floor, and

(d) The openings are readily identifiable from both the exterior and interior of the story, and

(e) The openings are readily openable from both the exterior and interior of the story.

A-30-1.3.4 In determining openings in exterior walls, doors or access panels may be included. Windows may also be included if they are openable or provide a breakable glazed area.

The Exception to the definition of underground structures establishes the criteria by which the provision of openings for ventilation and rescue exempts stories below the level of exit discharge from classification as underground. The basement in Figure 30-1 is not considered underground if:

1. Openings are provided on at least two sides, and
2. Openings are entirely above adjoining grade level, and
3. Openings comprise a minimum of 20 sq ft (1.9 sq m) of area per 50 lineal ft (15 m) of walls, and
4. X = a minimum width of 22 in. (55.9 cm) of unobstructed opening
   Y = a minimum height of 24 in. (60 cm) of unobstructed opening
   Z = a maximum of 44 in. (112 cm) from floor to bottom of opening, and
5. Openings are readily identified, and
6. Openings are readily openable.

The openings can take the form of a window or an access panel.

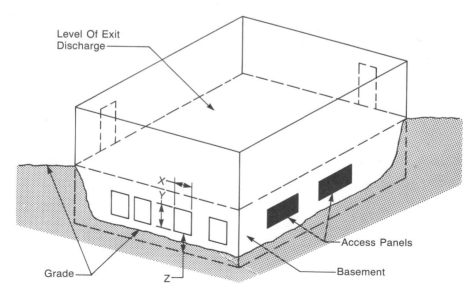

Figure 30-1. If the conditions of the Exception to the definition of underground structures (*see* 30-1.3.4) are met, the basement would not be considered underground.

30-1.3.5 Windowless Structure.   A structure or portions of a structure lacking means for direct access to the outside from the enclosing walls, or outside openings for ventilation or rescue through windows.

Exception No. 1:   A one-story structure or portion thereof shall not be considered a windowless structure if:

(a) The story is provided with grade level doors, access panels, or windows, on two sides of the building, spaced not more than 125 ft (38 m) apart in the exterior walls, and

(b) The access panels or windows have a minimum dimension of not less than 22 in. (55.9 cm) in width and 24 in. (61 cm) in height and are unobstructed to allow for ventilation and rescue operations, and

(c) The bottom of the openings are not more than 44 in. (112 cm) above the floor, and

(d) The openings are readily identifiable from both the exterior and interior of the story, and

(e) The openings are readily openable from both the exterior and interior of the story.

Exception No. 2:   A structure or portion thereof more than one story in height shall not be considered a windowless structure if:

(a) Access openings are provided for the first story as required in Exception No. 1 above, and

(b) Every story above the first floor is provided with access openings or windows on two sides of the building, spaced not more than 30 ft (9.1 m) apart, and

(c) The openings have minimum dimensions of not less than 22 in. (55.9 cm) in width and 24 in. (61 cm) in height and are unobstructed to allow for ventilation and rescue operations, and

(d) The bottoms of the openings are not more than 44 in. (112 cm) above the floor, and

(e) The openings are readily identifiable from both the exterior and interior of the story, and

(f) The openings are readily openable from both the exterior and interior of the story.

In connection with the above discussion on underground structures, note that a structure is not considered windowless if certain provisions are made for openings for ventilation and rescue. The provisions are more stringent for multistory structures than for single-story structures.

30-1.3.6 Water Surrounded Structure.   A structure fully surrounded by water.

30-1.3.7 Open Structure.   Operations and equipment conducted in open air and not enclosed within buildings, such as found in oil refining and chemical processing plants. Roofs or canopies providing shelter without enclosing walls may be provided and shall not be considered an enclosure.

Subsection 30-1.3 defines the special structures considered in Chapter 30. If an occupancy in one of these structures is regulated by Chapters 8 through 29, then the provisions of the appropriate chapter also apply. One frequently confusing arrangement is an assembly occupancy, such as a restaurant or sightseeing lookout point, located on a tower structure. A number of towers have been constructed for promotional purposes in cities and amusement centers, many reaching heights of 500 ft (150 m). Despite such unusual arrangements, the placement of an assembly occupancy on a tower requires consideration of the provisions in Chapters 8 and 9 in addition to the requirements of Chapter 30. (*See 30-1.4.*) However, towers serving special purposes, such as fire observation, radio or television transmission, or some other similar purpose, need meet only the requirements of Chapter 30.

30-1.4 Classification of Occupancy. Occupancies regulated by Chapters 8 through 29 that are in special structures or buildings shall meet the requirements of those chapters, except as modified by Chapter 30.

30-1.5 Classification of hazard of contents shall be as defined in Section 4-2.

30-1.6 Minimum Construction Standard. No special occupancy provisions.

30-1.7 Occupant Load. The occupant load of special structures shall be as determined by the maximum actual design occupant load.

Exception: Any special structure or part of a special structure utilized for an occupancy regulated by Chapters 8 through 29, in which case the requirements of the appropriate chapter shall apply.

SECTION 30-2   MEANS OF EGRESS REQUIREMENTS

30-2.1 General. Each required means of egress shall be in accordance with the applicable portions of Chapter 5.

30-2.2* Means of Egress Components.

A-30-2.2 Escape chutes, controlled descent devices, and elevators may provide escape routes in special structures; however, they should not be substituted for the provisions of this *Code*.

30-2.2.1 Components of means of egress shall be limited to the types described in 30-2.2.2 through 30-2.2.11.

Special structures containing occupancies regulated by Chapters 8 through 30 must also meet the requirements of Chapters 8 through 30 as discussed above. Therefore, the acceptable components will often be further restricted by the occupancy chapter.

30-2.2.2 Doors.

30-2.2.2.1 Doors shall comply with 5-2.1.

30-2.2.2.2 Horizontal sliding doors may be used in a means of egress serving an occupant load of not more than fifty in accordance with 5-2.1.4.1 Exception No. 6.

30-2.2.2.3 Horizontal sliding doors may be used in horizontal exits and smoke barriers in accordance with 5-2.1.4.1 Exception No. 7.

Both 30-2.2.2.2 and 30-2.2.2.3 recognize limited use of horizontal sliding doors in special structures where the *Code* would normally require a side-hinged swinging door. Before allowing use of horizontal sliding doors for a usual occupancy in an unusual structure, the *Code* user should check the appropriate occupancy chapter to see if use of 5-2.1.4.1 Exception No. 6 or No. 7 is permitted for that occupancy. (*See commentary following 30-1.3.7.*) Exceptions No. 6 and No. 7 to 5-2.1.4.1 address horizontal sliding doors that meet all the special requirements of 5-2.1.14. (*See 5-2.1.14.*)

30-2.2.3 Stairs.

30-2.2.3.1   Stairs shall comply with 5-2.2.

30-2.2.3.2   Spiral stairs complying with 5-2.2.2.7 are permitted.

30-2.2.3.3   In existing buildings, winders complying with 5-2.2.2.8 are permitted.

30-2.2.4 Smokeproof Enclosures.   Smokeproof enclosures shall comply with 5-2.3.

30-2.2.5 Horizontal Exits.   Horizontal exits shall comply with 5-2.4.

30-2.2.6 Ramps.   Ramps shall comply with 5-2.5.

30-2.2.7 Exit Passageways.   Exit passageways shall comply with 5-2.6.

30-2.2.8 Escalators and Moving Walks.   In existing buildings, previously approved escalators and moving walks complying with 5-2.7 may be continued in use.

30-2.2.9 Fire Escape Stairs.   Fire escape stairs complying with 5-2.8 are permitted for existing buildings.

30-2.2.10 Fire Escape Ladders.

30-2.2.10.1   Fire escape ladders complying with 5-2.9 are permitted.

30-2.2.10.2   Towers and open structures, such as a forest fire observation or railroad signal tower, designed for occupancy by not more than three persons employed therein may be served by ladder instead of stairs.

30-2.2.11 Alternating Tread Devices.   Alternating tread devices complying with 5-2.11 are permitted.

The provisions of 5-2.11 in effect limit the use of alternating tread devices to those locations where the *Code* recognizes the use of fire escape ladders. (*See 5-2.9.*)

30-2.3 Capacity of Means of Egress.

30-2.3.1   The width and capacity of a means of egress shall be in accordance with Chapter 5.

Exception No. 1: *The means of egress for towers shall be provided for the persons expected to occupy the space.*

Exception No. 2: *Open structures.*

Exception No. 3: *Spaces not subject to human occupancy because of machinery or equipment may be excluded from consideration.*

Exception No. 2 to 30-2.3.1 recognizes the multiple means of egress possible from open structures, such as those found in petrochemical and process industries. An open structure is actually an access platform to the equipment that it surrounds or supports. Normal occupancy is very limited and occasional in nature. If a fire should block one means of egress, a number of alternate means of egress still remain accessible. In addition to escape via the fixed means of egress, rescue is possible from any portion of the structure by use of the emergency procedures of fire fighting personnel. Potential exposure of portions of the structure not involved in a fire is minimal since in open platforms, flames, heat, and smoke are safely dispersed directly to the atmosphere and not into the uninvolved portions of the structure.

30-2.3.2 The minimum width of any corridor or passageway serving as a required exit or means of travel to or from a required exit shall be 44 in. (112 cm) in the clear.

Exception: *Where ladders are permitted by 30-2.2.*

30-2.3.3 Required means of egress for multistoried special structures may serve floors other than the level where required. However, for purposes of designing means of egress, an interior egress facility shall serve only one floor.

Exception No. 1: *No inside open stairway, escalator, or ramp may serve as a required egress facility from more than one floor level.*

Exception No. 2: *Open structures.*

30-2.4 Number of Exits. *(See also Section 5-4.)*

30-2.4.1 No less than two exits shall be provided for every story or section, including stories below the floor of exit discharge.

Exception No. 1: *Piers used exclusively to moor cargo vessels and to store materials, where provided with proper exit facilities from structures thereon to the pier and a single means of access to the mainland as appropriate with the pier's arrangement.*

Exception No. 2: *The grade level of open structures which by their very nature contain an infinite number of exits.*

Exception No. 3*: *Towers may be provided with a single exit if the following conditions are met:*

(a) The tower is subject to less than twenty-five persons on any one floor level.

(b) The tower is not used for living or sleeping purposes and is subject to occupancy by only able-bodied persons.

(c) The tower is of Type I, II, or IV construction. (See 6-2.1.)

(d) The tower interior finish is Class A or B.

(e) The tower has no combustible materials in, under, or in the immediate vicinity, except necessary furniture.

(f) There are no high hazard occupancies in the tower or immediate vicinity.

Exception No. 4: Open structures occupied by not more than three people with travel distance to exit not more than 200 ft (60 m).

A-30-2.4.1 Exception No. 3   The Washington Monument, Washington, D.C., is an example of a tower where it would not be practicable to provide a second stairway.

Formal Interpretation 81-35
Reference: 30-1.3.1, 30-2.4

Question: Is it the intent of the Committee on Safety to Life that the definition of "Tower" in 30-1.3.1 apply to a multistory building housing (1) an observation deck on the top level with a typical occupant load of 4 to 5 persons engaged in aircraft direction and control, and (2) other floors with kitchens, training areas, conference rooms, offices, and mechanical and support areas, some with an occupant load of more than 15 persons?

Answer: No.

Issue Edition: 1981
Reference: 30-1.3.1, 30-2.4
Date: October 1983

The intent of Exception No. 1 to 30-2.4.1 is to recognize the open nature of a pier and to equate a pier with a public way for purposes of exit arrangement. Note that the Exception applies mainly to cargo and storage piers, which are occupied by a limited number of people, most of whom are accustomed to a pier's arrangement. Under these conditions, the risk to life safety is considered minimal, and one exit is acceptable.

Exception No. 3 to 30-2.4.1 restricts the provisions for a single means of egress from a tower. Calculation of the number of people [fewer than 25 — see item (a) of this Exception] should be based on the actual number expected to occupy the facility. This method of determination is valid since the facility is not subject to the provisions for calculating occupant load specified in Chapters 8 through 29. Limitations on the combustibility and interior finish of the structure are established so that the potential exposure of the tower occupants to fire is minimal. Types I, II, and IV construction [*see item (c) of Exception No. 3*] are defined in NFPA 220, *Standard on Types of Building Construction.*[1]

One of the difficult aspects of the requirements for exits from towers is determination of the exposure of the tower to combustible materials under or in the immediate vicinity of the structure. Judgment should be used by the authority having jurisdiction and other users of the *Code* to ensure that arbitrary limitations are not established that restrict the use of the tower too severely. As an example, a forest fire tower is usually placed in a clearing in a large forest. The proximity of trees to the tower could be interpreted as constituting combustible materials in the "immediate" vicinity of the tower. Reasonable clearances [such as a clear space of 50 ft (15 m) to 100 ft (30 m) between the tower and forest] could be considered adequate separation for the life safety of the tower's occupants. Similar judgment will be needed where evaluating the clearance between high hazard occupancies and towers.

30-2.4.2   Floors or portions thereof with an occupant load of more than 500 shall have the minimum number of separate and remote means of egress specified by 5-4.1.2.

Exception: Existing buildings.

30-2.5 Arrangement of Means of Egress.   *(See also Section 5-5.)*

30-2.5.1   Where two or more exits are required, they shall be arranged so as to be reached by different paths of travel in different directions.

Exception: A common path of travel may be permitted for the first 50 ft (15 m) from any point.

30-2.5.2   No dead end may be more than 50 ft (15 m) deep.

30-2.5.3* Piers.

A-30-2.5.3   For further information on pier fire protection, see NFPA 307, *Standard for the Construction and Fire Protection of Marine Terminals, Piers, and Wharves (see Appendix B).*

30-2.5.3.1   Piers not meeting requirements of 30-2.4.1 Exception No. 1 and occupied for other than cargo handling and storage shall have exits arranged in accordance with Chapters 8 through 29. *(See 30-1.4.)* In addition, one of the following measures shall be provided on piers extending over 150 ft (45 m) from shore to minimize the possibility that fire under or on the pier may block escape of occupants to shore.

30-2.5.3.2   The pier shall be arranged to provide two separate ways of travel to shore, such as by two well separated walkways or independent structures.

30-2.5.3.3   The pier deck shall be open and fire resistive, set on noncombustible supports.

30-2.5.3.4   The pier shall be open and unobstructed and shall be 50 ft (15 m) or more in width if less than 500 ft (150 m) long, or its width shall be not less than ten percent of its length if over 500 ft (150 m) long.

30-2.5.3.5   The pier deck shall be provided with automatic sprinkler protection for combustible substructure and all superstructures, if any.

The provisions of 30-2.5.3.1 through 30-2.5.3.5 apply to all pier structures except those structures controlled by Exception No. 1 to 30-2.4.1. Note that these provisions are in addition to those contained in

Chapters 8 through 29 for those piers exceeding 150 ft (45 m) in length. The provisions of 30-2.5.3.2 through 30-2.5.3.5 are not required to be applied in total; in other words, the pier need comply with only one of the four paragraphs.

30-2.6 Travel Distance to Exits.   Travel to exits, where not regulated by Chapters 8 through 29, shall not exceed 100 ft (30 m).

Exception No. 1:   In a building or structure protected throughout by an approved automatic sprinkler system in accordance with Section 7-7, travel distance may be increased to 150 ft (45 m).

Exception No. 2:   Where ladders are permitted in 30-2.2.10.2.

Exception No. 3:   Open structures.

30-2.7 Discharge from Exits.   Discharge from exits shall be in accordance with Section 5-7.

Exception: Towers or other structures provided with one exit, as permitted by 30-2.4 and arranged in accordance with 30-2.5, may have 100 percent of the exit discharge through areas on the level of discharge.

30-2.8 Illumination of Means of Egress.   Illumination of means of egress shall be provided in accordance with Section 5-8.

Exception No. 1:   Open structures.

Exception No. 2:   Towers with ladders for exits as permitted by 30-2.2.10.2.

30-2.9 Emergency Lighting.   Emergency lighting shall be provided in accordance with Section 5-9.

Exception No. 1:   Open structures.

Exception No. 2:   Towers with ladders for exits as permitted by 30-2.2.10.2.

Exception No. 3:   Locations not routinely inhabited by humans.

Exception No. 4:   Structures occupied only during daylight hours with windows arranged to provide, during daylight hours, the required level of illumination of all portions of the means of egress, upon special approval of the authority having jurisdiction.

30-2.10 Marking of Means of Egress.   Signs designating exits or ways of travel thereto shall be provided in accordance with Section 5-10.

Exception No. 1:   Towers with ladders for exits as permitted by 30-2.2.10.2.

Exception No. 2:   Open structures.

Exception No. 3:   Locations where routine human habitation is not provided.

30-2.11 Special Features.

SECTION 30-3   PROTECTION

30-3.1 Protection of Vertical Openings.   Every stairway, elevator shaft, escalator opening, and other vertical opening shall be enclosed or protected in accordance with Chapter 5 and Section 6-2.

Exception No. 1: In towers where there is no occupancy below the top floor level, stairs may be open with no enclosure required, or fire escape stairs may be used where the structure is entirely open.

Exception No. 2: Towers with ladders for exits as permitted by 30-2.2.10.2.

Exception No. 3: Open structures.

30-3.2 Protection from Hazards. Every special structure shall have automatic, manual, or such other protection as may be appropriate to the particular hazard designed to minimize danger to occupants in case of fire or other emergency before they have time to utilize exits to escape.

Exception: Special structures, such as open structures, with only occasional occupancy.

The provisions of 30-3.2 require careful analysis by *Code* users to ensure that fire protection required for life safety is provided. The key element of the requirement is that the protection be adequate to safeguard occupants during the time required to reach exits. Fire protection systems that may be needed for property protection or to control fire losses in a process or occupancy will, in many cases, be excessive for the life safety of occupants, and are beyond the scope of this *Code*.

30-3.3 Interior Finish.

30-3.3.1 Interior wall and ceiling finish shall be Class A, B, or C, in accordance with Section 6-5, and as required by 5-1.4 in exit enclosures.

30-3.3.2 Interior Floor Finish. No special occupancy requirements.

30-3.4 Detection, Alarm, and Communications Systems.

30-3.4.1 General. A fire alarm system shall be provided in accordance with Section 7-6.

Exception No. 1: Towers designed for occupancy by not more than three persons.

Exception No. 2: Open structures.

30-3.4.2 Initiation. Initiation of the required fire alarm system shall be by either manual or automatic means in accordance with 7-6.2.

30-3.4.3 Notification. The required fire alarm system shall sound an audible alarm in a continuously attended location for purposes of initiating emergency action.

30-3.5 Extinguishing Requirements. None.

30-3.6 Corridors. The corridor provisions for the occupancy involved within the special structure shall apply.

SECTION 30-4 SPECIAL PROVISIONS

30-4.1 Operating Features. *(See Chapter 31.)*

30-4.2 High Rise Buildings.   The high rise building provisions for the occupancy involved within the special structure shall apply. (*See Chapters 8 through 29.*)

Exception: Existing buildings.

SECTION 30-5   BUILDING SERVICES

30-5.1 Utilities.   Utilities shall comply with the provisions of Section 7-1.

30-5.2 Heating, Ventilating, and Air Conditioning Equipment.   Heating, ventilating, and air conditioning equipment shall comply with the provisions of Section 7-2.

30-5.3 Elevators, Dumbwaiters, and Vertical Conveyors.   Elevators, dumbwaiters, and vertical conveyors shall comply with the provisions of Section 7-4.

30-5.4 Rubbish Chutes, Incinerators, and Laundry Chutes.   Rubbish chutes, incinerators, and laundry chutes shall comply with the provisions of Section 7-5.

SECTION 30-6*   SPECIAL PROVISIONS FOR VEHICLES AND VESSELS

A-30-6   Firesafety information for manufactured home parks will be found in NFPA 501A, *Standard for Firesafety Criteria for Manufactured Home Installations, Sites, and Communities* (*see Appendix B*).

30-6.1   Any vehicle as defined by 30-1.3.2 that is subject to human occupancy shall comply with the requirements of this *Code* that are appropriate to buildings of similar occupancy. (*See 30-1.4.*)

30-6.2   Any ship, barge, or other vessel permanently fixed to a foundation or mooring, or unable to get under way under its own power, and occupied for purposes other than navigation shall be subject to the requirements of this *Code* applicable to buildings of similar occupancy.

SECTION 30-7 SPECIAL PROVISIONS FOR UNDERGROUND STRUCTURES AND WINDOWLESS BUILDINGS

See the definitions of underground structures and windowless structures in 30-1.3.

30-7.1 General.

30-7.1.1   In addition to meeting the applicable requirements of this section, occupancies in underground structures and windowless buildings meeting the purposes regulated by Chapters 8 through 29 shall meet the requirements of those chapters. (*See 30-1.4.*)

30-7.1.2   Windowless or underground structures with an occupant load of more than 50 persons shall be protected throughout by an approved automatic sprinkler system in accordance with Section 7-7.

Exception: Existing structures with an occupant load not greater than 100.

30-7.1.3   Windlowless or underground structures shall be provided with emergency lighting in accordance with Section 5-9.

Exception: One- and two-family dwellings.

30-7.2 Underground Structures.

30-7.2.1   Exits from underground structures having an occupant load greater than 50 shall be cut off from the level of exit discharge per Section 5-1 and shall be provided with outside smoke venting facilities or other means to prevent the exits from becoming charged with smoke from any fire in the area served by the exits.

Exception No. 1:   Existing structures with an occupant load not greater than 100.

Exception No. 2:   As modified by Chapters 8 through 29.

30-7.2.2   Underground structures with an occupant load greater than 100 having combustible contents, interior finish, or construction shall have automatic smoke venting facilities in accordance with Chapter 7 in addition to automatic sprinkler protection.

Exception: Existing structures.

The provisions contained in 30-7.1.1 through 30-7.2.2 for control of life safety deficiencies in windowless or underground buildings are minimal and are considered to be in addition to those contained in Chapters 8 through 29. It is not the intent of these paragraphs to provide a means of circumventing the life safety provisions contained in other chapters of the *Code.* If the building under consideration is windowless or underground and, due to its occupancy classification, subject to stricter requirements than those contained in Chapter 30, then those stricter provisions of the *Code* must be followed.

Windowless and underground structures pose special risks to life safety since the buildings cannot be easily vented of products of combustion. In an area from which there is no direct access to the outside and where there are no windows to permit outside fire department rescue operations and ventilation, any fire or smoke may tend to produce panic. Therefore, additional corrective measures, such as complete automatic sprinkler protection and automatic smoke venting systems, must be provided where necessary to ensure an adequate level of safety to life.

"Fire Hazards of Windowless Buildings"[2] discusses the life safety problems encountered in windowless buildings; "Underground Buildings"[3] contains a detailed review of the fire experience in underground structures.

SECTION 30-8   HIGH RISE BUILDINGS

Section 30-8 is new to the 1988 Edition of the *Code* and does not require, by itself, that any special provisions be applied to high rise buildings. Rather, it is intended to serve as a menu of high rise building options that can be wholly or partially mandated by other *Code* sections. For example,

Chapter 10 for new educational occupancies requires that new construction be provided with the entire package of requirements of Section 30-8.

30-8.1 General.

30-8.1.1   Where required by Chapters 8 through 30, the provisions of this section shall apply to high rise buildings as defined in Chapter 3.

Exception: As modified by Chapters 8 through 30.

30-8.1.2   In addition to the requirements of this section, all other applicable provisions of this *Code* shall be complied with.

30-8.2 Extinguishment Requirements.

30-8.2.1*   High rise buildings shall be protected throughout by an electrically supervised, approved, automatic sprinkler system installed in accordance with Section 7-7. A sprinkler control valve and a water flow device shall be provided for each floor.

A-30-8.2.1   Where an occupancy chapter permits the omission of sprinklers in specific spaces, such as small bathrooms and closets in residential occupancies, the building is still considered to be "protected throughout" for the purposes of this section.

30-8.3 Detection, Alarm, and Communication Systems.

30-8.3.1*   A fire alarm system utilizing voice communication shall be installed in accordance with Section 7-6.

A-30-8.3.1   The need for voice communication can be based on a decision regarding staged or partial evacuation vs total evacuation of all floors. The determination of need is a function of occupancy classification and building height.

30-8.3.2   Two-way telephone communication service shall be provided for fire department use. This system shall be in accordance with NFPA 72F, *Standard for the Installation, Maintenance, and Use of Emergency Voice/Alarm Communication Systems.* The communication system shall operate between the central control station and every elevator car, every elevator lobby, and each floor level of exit stairs.

Exception: Where the fire department radio system is approved as an equivalent system.

30-8.4 Emergency Lighting and Standby Power.

30-8.4.1   Emergency lighting in accordance with Section 5-9 shall be provided.

30-8.4.2   Standby power in accordance with NFPA 70, *National Electrical Code,* and NFPA 110, *Emergency and Standby Power Systems,* Class I, Type 60 shall be provided. The standby power system shall have a capacity and rating sufficient to supply all required equipment. Selective load pickup and load shedding shall be permitted in accordance with NFPA 70, *National Electrical Code.* The standby power system shall be connected to the following:

(a) Emergency lighting system.

(b) Fire alarm system.

(c) Electric fire pump.

(d) Central control station equipment and lighting.

(e) At least one elevator serving all floors and shall be transferable to any elevator.

(f) Mechanical equipment for smokeproof enclosures.

30-8.5 Central Control Station.

30-8.5.1*   A central control station shall be provided in a location approved by the fire department. The control station shall contain:

(a) Voice fire alarm system panels and controls.

(b) Fire department two-way telephone communications service panels and controls.

(c) Fire detection and fire alarm system annunciation panels.

(d) Elevator floor location and operation annunciators.

(e) Sprinkler valve and water flow annunciators.

(f) Emergency generator status indicators.

(g) Controls for any automatic stairway door unlocking system.

(h) Fire pump status indicators.

(i) A telephone for fire department use with controlled access to the public telephone system.

A-30-8.5.1   It is not the intent of the paragraph to require any of the equipment in the list, other than the telephone for fire department use, but only to provide the controls, panels, annunciators, and similar equipment at this location where the equipment is provided or required by another section of the *Code*.

REFERENCES CITED IN COMMENTARY

[1]NFPA 220, *Standard on Types of Building Construction*, National Fire Protection Association, Quincy, MA 1985.

[2]E. E. Juillerat, "Fire Hazards of Windowless Buildings," NFPA *Quarterly*, Vol. 58, No. 1, July 1964, pp. 22-30.

[3]Horatio Bond, "Underground Buildings," *Fire Journal*, Vol. 59, No. 4, July 1965, pp. 52-55.

31 OPERATING FEATURES

(See also Section 31-2 through 31-9 for special occupancy requirements.)

Chapter 31 serves a unique purpose in the *Life Safety Code*. It specifies activities that complement the structural features mandated by the *Code* in order to ensure a minimum acceptable level of safety to life. Usually, codes and standards confine themselves to the subject of proper building arrangements, with no emphasis or advice on such areas as maintenance, inspections, drills, or the contents (furniture or furnishings) of a structure.

These items are germane to the scope and content of the *Code* because, as stated in Section 2-1, "the design of exits and other safeguards shall be such that reliance for safety to life in case of fire or other emergency will not depend solely on any single safeguard; additional safeguards shall be provided for life safety in case any single safeguard is ineffective due to some human or mechanical failure."

Prevention of "human or mechanical failure" involves the *Code* in the areas of care, operation, maintenance, and inspection of equipment. Further, since life safety depends upon proper action by humans at the time of an emergency, drills and checklists of emergency procedures become critical. Because the protection safeguards built into a structure may be defeated by the introduction of hazardous material, it is necessary to address those aspects of a building's contents (such as their arrangement, flammability, or toxicity under combustion) that have a bearing on safety to life.

In Chapter 31, these factors are covered for all occupancies in general, and are then reinforced for each specific occupancy. Most of Section 31-1 applies to all occupancies. Some individual provisions, such as 31-1.4.1, which addresses compliance for draperies per NFPA 701, *Standard Methods of Fire Tests for Flame-Resistant Textiles and Films,*[1] apply only where specifically required by a provision of Sections 31-2 through 31-9, which cover individual occupancies.

Finally, Chapter 31 focuses on how people (occupants, owners, tenants, and maintenance personnel) can augment the *Code* with respect to life safety. This allows people to be involved in providing for their own safety and security. If such involvement is properly addressed in the public sector, the enthusiasm generated could conceivably ensure total, or near total, compliance with all *Code* requirements.

SECTION 31-1   GENERAL REQUIREMENTS

31-1.1 Construction, Repair, Improvement Operations.

31-1.1.1   In buildings under construction, adequate escape facilities shall be maintained at all times for the use of construction workers. Escape facilities shall consist of doors, walkways, stairs, ramps, fire escapes, ladders, or other approved means or devices arranged in accordance with the general principles of the *Code* insofar as they can reasonably be applied to buildings under construction. See also NFPA 241, *Standard for Safeguarding Construction, Alteration, and Demolition Operations.*

31-1.1.2   Flammable or explosive substances or equipment for repairs or alterations may be introduced in a building of normally low or ordinary hazard classification while the building is occupied only if the condition of use and safeguards provided are such as not to create any additional danger or handicap to egress beyond the normally permissible conditions in the building.

31-1.2 Means of Egress Reliability.

31-1.2.1   Every required exit, exit access, or exit discharge shall be continuously maintained free of all obstructions or impediments to full instant use in the case of fire or other emergency.

> Paragraph 31-1.2.1 does not specify who will be responsible for keeping exits free and clear. The person responsible for each facility, whether manager, owner, or operator, must make certain that required exit components are maintained in usable condition. The authority having jurisdiction has the power to ensure that this is being done.

31-1.2.2 Furnishings and Decorations in Means of Egress.

31-1.2.2.1   No furnishings, decorations, or other objects shall be so placed as to obstruct exits, access thereto, egress therefrom, or visibility thereof.

31-1.2.2.2   Hangings or draperies shall not be placed over exit doors or otherwise located as to conceal or obscure any exit. Mirrors shall not be placed on exit doors. Mirrors shall not be placed in or adjacent to any exit in such a manner as to confuse the direction of exit.

> Paragraphs 31-1.2.2.1 and 31-1.2.2.2 provide guidance for the interior decoration and maintenance of such places as restaurants and theaters where excessive decoration used to establish a "style" or "theme" often totally obscures, and in some cases obstructs, exits. In such a case, the authority having jurisdiction must take care to ensure that normal access to a free and unobstructed exit is not lost in the pursuit of period or style authenticity.

31-1.2.2.3   There shall be no obstruction by railings, barriers, or gates that divide the open space into sections appurtenant to individual rooms, apartments, or other uses. Where the authority having jurisdiction finds the required path of travel to be obstructed by furniture or other movable objects, the authority may require that they be fastened out of the way or may require that railings or other permanent barriers be installed to protect the path of travel against encroachment.

Paragraph 31-1.2.2.3 relates to the arrangement of furniture, as well as railings, gates, or barriers, found in lobbies, foyers, waiting spaces, or staging areas of businesses, hospitals, health care clinics, hotels, and apartments. Because these large spaces are often subdivided by furniture (chairs, tables, and plants) or by railings and gates, steps must be taken to prevent furnishings from blocking the access to exits. This paragraph suggests fastening furnishings clear of access to exits or placing railings around them to ensure that they will be held in a fixed position and cannot be easily moved or rearranged, to cause obstruction of an access to an exit.

31-1.3 Equipment Maintenance and Testing.

31-1.3.1   Whenever or wherever any device, equipment, system, condition, arrangement, level of protection, or any other feature is required for compliance with the provisions of this *Code*, such device, equipment, system, condition, arrangement, level of protection, or other feature shall thereafter be permanently maintained unless the *Code* exempts such maintenance.

Given that the *Code* requires the specific device or system, such equipment is necessary to provide the minimum level of safety to life mandated by the *Code* and, therefore, must be maintained in usable condition. Without such maintenance, the overall level of safety to life would fall below *Code* standards.

31-1.3.2   Every required automatic sprinkler system, fire detection and alarm system, smoke control system, exit lighting, fire door, and other item of equipment required by this *Code* shall be continuously in proper operating condition.

31-1.3.3   Any equipment requiring test or periodic operation to assure its maintenance shall be tested or operated as specified elsewhere in this *Code* or as directed by the authority having jurisdiction.

31-1.3.4   Systems shall be under the supervision of a responsible person who shall cause proper tests to be made at specified intervals and have general charge of all alterations and additions.

31-1.3.5   Systems shall be tested at intervals required by the appropriate standards listed in Chapter 32.

31-1.3.6* Automatic Sprinkler Systems.   All automatic sprinkler systems required by this *Code* shall be continuously maintained in reliable operating condition at all times, and such periodic inspections and tests shall be made as are necessary to assure proper maintenance.

A-31-1.3.6 NFPA 13A, *Recommended Practice for the Inspection, Testing, and Maintenance of Sprinkler Systems* (*see Appendix B*), gives detailed information on maintenance procedures.

31-1.3.7* Alarm and Fire Detection Systems. Fire alarm signaling equipment shall be restored to service as promptly as possible after each test or alarm and shall be kept in normal condition for operation. Equipment requiring rewinding or replenishing shall be rewound or replenished as promptly as possible after each test or alarm.

A-31-1.3.7 NFPA 72H, *Guide for Testing Procedures for Local, Auxiliary, Remote Station, and Proprietary Protective Signaling Systems*, gives detailed information on testing procedures.

31-1.3.8 Periodic Testing of Emergency Lighting Equipment. A functional test shall be conducted on every required emergency lighting system at 30-day intervals for a minimum of 30 seconds. An annual test shall be conducted for the 1½-hour duration. Equipment shall be fully operational for the duration of the test. Written records of testing shall be kept by the owner for inspection by the authority having jurisdiction.

31-1.3.9 Smokeproof Enclosures and Pressurized Stairs. Before mechanical equipment is accepted by the authority having jurisdiction, it shall be tested to confirm that such equipment is operating in compliance with the *Code*. All operating parts of the system shall be tested semiannually by approved personnel, and a log shall be kept of the results.

Paragraphs 31-1.3.1 through 31-1.3.9 emphasize that any system or mechanical device installed to ensure life safety must be maintained in working condition. Maintenance should be performed according to a set schedule established either by code (this *Code* or other referenced codes and standards) or by the authority having jurisdiction. If this maintenance is not performed, failure of these systems is a possibility. Thus, failure to provide maintenance results in a non-*Code*-complying facility, particularly if the system that has not been maintained is required by the *Code* or has been installed to provide an equivalency to the *Code*'s requirements.

31-1.4 Furnishings, Decorations, and Treated Finishes. (*See also 31-1.2.2.*)

31-1.4.1* Draperies, curtains, and other similar furnishings and decorations shall be flame resistant where required by the applicable provisions of this chapter. These materials required herein to be tested in accordance with NFPA 701, *Standard Methods of Fire Tests for Flame-Resistant Textiles and Films*, shall comply with both the small- and large-scale tests.

A-31-1.4.1 For details of flame-retardant treatments and tests thereof, see NFPA 701, *Standard Methods of Fire Tests for Flame-Resistant Textiles and Films* (*see Appendix B*). Furnishings and decorations tested in accordance with this standard should comply with both the small- and large-scale tests.

NFPA 701, *Standard Methods of Fire Tests for Flame-Resistant Textiles and Films*,[1] does an adequate job of measuring the level of hazard presented by draperies and other loosely hanging fabrics and films.

In 1983, two new test methods for the assessment of upholstered furniture were approved by NFPA: NFPA 260A, *Standard Methods of Tests and Classification System for Cigarette Ignition Resistance of Components of Upholstered Furniture*,[2] and NFPA 260B, *Standard Method of Test for Determining Resistance of Mock-Up Upholstered Furniture Material Assemblies to Ignition by Smoldering Cigarettes*.[3] Paragraph 31-4.5.5 makes use of NFPA 260B test results to regulate newly introduced upholstered furniture in nonsprinklered health care occupancies. Paragraph A-31-6.6.1 recommends the use of NFPA 260B test results in the selection of new upholstered furniture for use in nonsprinklered hotels, dormitories, and apartment buildings in areas not separated from corridors.

31-1.4.2* Furnishings or decorations of an explosive or highly flammable character shall not be used.

A-31-1.4.2 Christmas trees not effectively flame-retardant treated, ordinary crepe paper decorations, and pyroxylin plastic decorations may be classed as highly flammable.

The *Code* relies on the authority having jurisdiction to exercise judgment in enforcing 31-1.4.2.

31-1.4.3 Fire retardant coatings shall be maintained so as to retain the effectiveness of the treatment under service conditions encountered in actual use.

See NFPA 703, *Standard for Fire Retardant Impregnated Wood and Fire Retardant Coatings for Building Materials*.[4]

31-1.5* Fire Exit Drills.

A-31-1.5 The term "fire exit drill" is used to avoid confusion between drills held for the purpose of rapid evacuation of buildings and drills of fire fighting practice that from a technical viewpoint are correctly designated as "fire drills," although this term is by common usage applied to egress drills in schools, etc.

The purpose of fire exit drills is to ensure the efficient and safe use of the exit facilities available. Proper drills ensure orderly exit under control and prevent the panic that has been responsible for the greater part of the loss of life in the major fire disasters of history. Order and control are the primary purposes of the drill. Speed in emptying buildings, while desirable, is not in itself an object, and should be made secondary to the maintenance of proper order and discipline.

The usefulness of a fire exit drill and the extent to which it can be carried depends upon the character of the occupancy, it being most effective in occupancies where the occupant load of the building is under discipline and subject to habitual control. For example, schools offer possibilities of more highly developed and valuable fire exit drills than other types of occupancy.

In buildings where the occupant load is of a changing character and not under discipline, such as hotels or department stores, no regularly organized fire exit drill, such as that which may be conducted in schools, is possible. In such cases, the fire exit drills must be limited to the regular employees, who can, however, be thoroughly schooled in the proper procedure and can be trained to properly direct other occupants of the building in case of fire. In occupancies such as hospitals, regular employees can be rehearsed in the proper procedure in case of fire; such training always is advisable in all occupancies whether or not regular fire exit drills can be held.

> Paragraphs 31-1.5.1 through 31-1.5.6 serve as a primer on how to conduct a fire exit drill. Sections 31-2 through 31-9 provide specific details that correlate a drill directly with the characteristics of the occupancy in question.

31-1.5.1 Fire exit drills conforming to the provisions of this chapter of the *Code* shall be regularly conducted in occupancies where specified by the provisions of this chapter, or by appropriate action of the authority having jurisdiction. Drills shall be designed in cooperation with the local authorities.

31-1.5.2 Fire exit drills, where required by the authority having jurisdiction, shall be held with sufficient frequency to familiarize all occupants with the drill procedure and to have the conduct of the drill a matter of established routine.

31-1.5.3 Responsibility for the planning and conduct of drills shall be assigned only to competent persons qualified to exercise leadership.

31-1.5.4 In the conduct of drills, emphasis shall be placed upon orderly evacuation under proper discipline rather than upon speed.

31-1.5.5* Drills shall include suitable procedures to make sure that all persons in the building, or all persons subject to the drill, actually participate.

A-31-1.5.5 If a fire exit drill is considered merely as a routine exercise from which some persons may be excused, there is a grave danger that in an actual fire the drill will fail in its intended purpose.

31-1.5.6* Drills shall be held at unexpected times and under varying conditions to simulate the unusual conditions that occur in the case of fire.

A-31-1.5.6 Fire is always unexpected. If the drill is always held in the same way at the same time it loses much of its value, and when for some reason in actual fire it is not possible to follow the usual routine of the fire exit drill to which occupants have become accustomed, confusion and panic may ensue. Drills should be carefully planned to simulate actual fire conditions. Not only should they be held at varying times, but different means of exit should be used based upon an assumption that, for example, some given stairway is unavailable by reason of fire or smoke, and all the occupants must be led out by some other route. Fire exit drills should be designed to familiarize the occupants with all available means of exits, particularly emergency exits that are not habitually used during the normal occupancy of the building.

31-1.6 Flammable Liquids.   Flammable liquids shall be stored and handled in accordance with NFPA 30, *Flammable and Combustible Liquids Code.*

31-1.7   Laboratories that use chemicals shall comply with NFPA 45, *Standard on Fire Protection for Laboratories Using Chemicals,* unless otherwise modified by other provisions of this *Code.*

31-1.8 Maintenance.   Whenever or wherever any device, equipment, system, condition, arrangement, level of protection, or any other feature is required for compliance with the provisions of this *Code,* such device, equipment, system, condition, arrangement, level of protection, or other feature shall thereafter be permanently maintained unless the *Code* exempts such maintenance.

See commentary following 31-1.3.1.

SECTION 31-2   ASSEMBLY OCCUPANCIES

31-2.1* Drills.   The employees or attendants of places of public assembly shall be schooled and drilled in the duties they are to perform in case of fire, panic, or other emergency in order to be of greatest service in effecting orderly exit of assemblages.

A-31-2.1   Attention is directed to the importance of having an adequate number of competent attendants on duty at all times when the assembly occupancy is occupied.

31-2.1.1   Employees or attendants of assembly occupancies shall be instructed in the proper use of portable fire extinguishers and other manual fire suppression equipment if provided.

The *Code* does not require fire extinguishers for life safety in an assembly occupancy. However, the Committee feels that, if fire extinguishers are provided, the staff must be trained in their use to prevent a false sense of security and possible injury. The extent of this training, e.g., instruction only, instruction and hands-on use, etc., is determined by the authority having jurisdiction.

31-2.2*   In theaters, motion picture theaters, auditoriums, and other similar Class A and B assembly occupancies where there are noncontinuous programs, an audible announcement shall be made prior to the start of each program to notify occupants of the location of the exits to be used in case of a fire or other emergency.

Exception: Assembly occupancies in schools when used for nonpublic events.

A-31-2.2   It is not the intent of this provision to require an announcement in bowling alleys, cocktail lounges, restaurants, or places of worship.

This is a relatively simple requirement that can make a significant difference during an emergency. Notice that it does not apply to assembly occupancies where the flow of people is constantly changing, such as in a restaurant.

31-2.3 Open Flame Devices.   No open flame devices shall be used in any assembly occupancy.

Exception No. 1*: When necessary for ceremonial, religious, or demonstration purpose, the authority having jurisdiction may permit open flame devices under such restrictions as are necessary to avoid danger of ignition of combustible materials or injury to occupants.

Exception No. 2: Open flame devices may be used on stages when a necessary part of theatrical performances, provided adequate precautions satisfactory to the authority having jurisdiction are taken to prevent ignition of any combustible materials.

Exception No. 3: Gas lights may be permitted provided adequate precautions satisfactory to the authority having jurisdiction are taken to prevent ignition of any combustible materials.

Exception No. 4: Candles may be used on tables if securely supported on substantial noncombustible bases so located as to avoid danger of ignition of combustible materials and only if approved by the authority having jurisdiction. Candle flames shall be protected.

Exception No. 5: As permitted in 31-2.4.

A-31-2.3 Exception No. 1   Securely supported altar candles in churches, well separated from any combustible material, may be permitted. On the other hand, lighted candles carried by children wearing cotton robes present a hazard too great to be permitted even for the most worthy cause. There are many other situations of intermediate hazard where the authority having jurisdiction will have to exercise judgment.

31-2.4 Special Food Service Devices.   Portable cooking equipment, not flue-connected, shall be permitted only as follows:

(a) Equipment fueled by small heat sources that can be readily extinguished by water, such as candles or alcohol-burning equipment (including "solid alcohol"), may be used provided adequate precautions satisfactory to the authority having jurisdiction are taken to prevent ignition of any combustible materials.

(b) Candles may be used on tables used for food service if securely supported on substantial noncombustible bases so located as to avoid danger of ignition of combustible materials and only if approved by the authority having jurisdiction. Candle flames shall be protected.

(c) "Flaming Sword" or other equipment involving open flames and flamed dishes, such as cherries jubilee, crepes suzette, etc., may be permitted provided that necessary precautions are taken and subject to the approval of the authority having jurisdiction.

The list of tragic fires in assembly occupancies caused by "friendly" fire (alcohol or solid alcohol fires in restaurants, flames used for dramatic effects in theaters, etc.) is well-documented. Paragraph 31-2.3 and its Exceptions provide a fundamental exercise in fire prevention, whereby the use of these open flame devices is tightly controlled. The first step in fire prevention is prevention of ignition, which is addressed by 31-2.3 and 31-2.4.

31-2.5 Smoking.

31-2.5.1   Smoking in assembly occupancies shall be regulated by the authority having jurisdiction.

31-2.5.2 In rooms or areas where smoking is prohibited, plainly visible "NO SMOKING" signs shall be posted.

31-2.5.3 No person shall smoke in prohibited areas that are so posted.

Exception: The authority having jurisdiction may permit smoking on a stage only when it is a necessary and rehearsed part of a performance and only by a regular performing member of the cast.

31-2.5.4 Where smoking is permitted, suitable ashtrays or receptacles shall be provided in convenient locations.

31-2.6 Furnishings, Decorations, and Stage Scenery.

31-2.6.1 Draperies, curtains, and other similar furnishings, decorations, and stage settings shall be in accordance with the provisions of 31-1.4.

31-2.6.2 The authority having jurisdiction shall impose controls on the amount and arrangement of combustible contents, including decorations, in assembly occupancies to provide an adequate level of safety to life from fire.

31-2.6.3 There shall be no exposed foamed plastics.

The scenery found stored in the fly sections of a stage, plus that used in a stage production, represents a sizable (and usually highly combustible) fuel load. Classic theater fires (for example, the Iroquois Theater, Chicago, 1903) involve the ignition of the scenery on stage and subsequent exposure to the audience caused by this sizable amount of burning fuel. Chapters 8 and 9 provide for a curtain of noncombustible material to drop, thus separating the fuel from the audience, and for the installation of extinguishing systems (both automatic and manual) on or around the stage. In 31-2.6.1 through 31-2.6.3, the *Code* controls the hazard level of fuel stored or placed outside the proscenium arch and attempts to limit the flammability of all the scenery, thus minimizing the level of exposure (hazard) to the audience. Ignition sources are controlled by 31-2.3.

31-2.7 Seating.

31-2.7.1 Seats in assembly occupancies accommodating more than 200 persons shall be securely fastened to the floor except where fastened together in groups of not less than three nor more than seven and as permitted by 31-2.7.2. All seats in balconies and galleries shall be securely fastened to the floor, except in places of worship.

31-2.7.2 Seats not secured to the floor may be permitted in restaurants, night clubs, and other occupancies where the fastening of seats to the floor may be impracticable, provided that in the area used for seating (excluding dance floor, stage, etc.), there shall be not more than one seat for each 15 sq ft (1.4 sq m) of net floor area and adequate aisles to reach exits shall be maintained at all times.

Exception: Seating diagrams shall be submitted for approval of the authority having jurisdiction to allow increase in occupant load per 8-1.7.2 and 9-1.7.2.

The function of 31-2.7.1 and 31-2.7.2 is to prevent the movement of seats so that aisles, rows, and access to the exits do not become blocked in an assembly occupancy during the jostling that occurs when people flee from a fire.

31-2.7.3   Every room constituting an assembly occupancy and not having fixed seats shall have the occupant load of the room posted in a conspicuous place, near the main exit from the room. Approved signs shall be maintained in a legible manner by the owner or his authorized agent. Signs shall be durable and shall indicate the number of occupants permitted for each room use.

31-2.8 Projection Room.   Unless the projection room is constructed in accordance with NFPA 40, *Standard for the Storage and Handling of Cellulose Nitrate Motion Picture Film*, there shall be posted on the outside of each projection room door, and within the projection room proper, a conspicuous sign with 1-in. (2.5-cm) block letters stating: "Safety Film Only Permitted in This Room."

31-2.9 Coat Racks.   Clothing and personal effects shall not be stored in corridors and lobbies.

Clothing hung on hooks along corridor walls or on racks in lobbies greatly increases the combustible load and will generally allow flame to spread quickly. Given that Chapters 8 and 9 regulate corridor and lobby interior wall finish, surfaces covered by combustible clothing should not be created that would allow flame to spread more quickly than is allowed for wall surfaces.

SECTION 31-3   EDUCATIONAL OCCUPANCIES

Firesafety, including an approved fire evacuation plan, should be included in the curriculum of all educational occupancies. This part of the curriculum should be approved by the authority having jurisdiction. The NFPA Learn Not to Burn Curriculum[®][5] is a proven system of firesafety education in schools.

31-3.1 Drills.

31-3.1.1*   Fire exit drills shall be conducted regularly in accordance with the applicable provisions of the following paragraphs.

A-31-3.1.1   The requirements are of necessity general in scope, as it is appreciated that they must apply to all types of schools as well as conditions of occupancies, such as truant schools, schools for mentally handicapped, the vision impaired, hearing and speech impaired, and public schools. It is fully recognized that no one code can meet all the conditions of the various buildings involved, and it will be necessary for some school authorities to issue supplements to these requirements, but all supplements should be consistent with these requirements.

Drills for educational occupancies, particularly at the grade school level, are essential to ensure an orderly response during a fire. Unfortunately, the predictability of such drills often leads to their becoming self-defeating. When an alarm bell sounds and a fire department monitor is seen in a corridor, some teachers ignore the bell, assuming that it is a false alarm; if the bell sounds and a fire department monitor is *not* seen, teachers opt for either a "we all go" or "we all stay" posture, which is decided upon in the hallway. While the bell continues to ring, the students remain in class. Therefore, when a bell sounds, primary emphasis should be placed on evacuation, regardless of who is or is not present in the hallways, or whether or not fire equipment is parked in front of the school. Essentially, the fire department and the school should vary the timing and arrangement of the drills, but not vary the required response, which is orderly evacuation. (*Also see 31-1.5.*)

31-3.1.2* There shall be at least two fire exit drills held during the first two weeks of a school term and eight additional fire exit drills during the year. In climates where the weather is severe during the winter months, at least six drills should be held at the beginning of the school term and four drills held after the winter months to complete the ten required drills.

A-31-3.1.2 "Practice drills" may be held during inclement weather. Such drills would be held at the regular dismissal time, when the pupils are fully clothed, by using the exit drill alarm signal. With such drills there would be no necessity of a return signal.

31-3.1.3* Drills shall be executed at different hours of the day or evening; during the changing of classes; when the school is at assembly; during the recess or gymnastic periods; etc., so as to avoid distinction between drills and actual fires. If a drill is called when pupils are going up and down the stairways, as during the time classes are changing, the pupils shall be instructed to form in file and immediately proceed to the nearest available exit in an orderly manner.

A-31-3.1.3 Cards of instruction should be conspicuously posted describing the procedure of the drills.

31-3.1.4* Every fire exit drill shall be an exercise in school management for principal and teachers, with the chief purpose of every drill being the complete control of the class so that the teacher will form its ranks quickly and silently, may halt it, turn it, or direct it as desired. Great stress shall be laid upon the execution of each drill in a brisk, quiet, and orderly manner. Running shall be prohibited. In case there are pupils incapable of holding their places in a line moving at a reasonable speed, provisions shall be made to have them taken care of by the more sturdy pupils, who will keep them from moving independently from the regular line of march.

A-31-3.1.4 If for any reason a line becomes blocked, some of the pupils should be countermarched to another exit in order to prevent panic conditions arising as a result of inactivity.

31-3.1.5   Monitors shall be appointed from the more mature pupils to assist in the proper execution of all drills. They shall be instructed to hold doors open in the line of march or to close doors where necessary to prevent spread of fire or smoke per 5-2.1.8. There shall be at least two substitutes for each appointment so as to provide for proper performance in case of absence of the regular monitors. The searching of toilet or other rooms shall be the duty of the teachers or other members of the staff. If the teachers are to search, it should be done after they have joined their classes to the preceeding lines.

31-3.1.6   As all drills simulate an actual fire condition, pupils shall not be allowed to obtain clothing after the alarm is sounded, even when in home rooms, on account of the confusion that would result in forming the lines and the danger of tripping over dragging apparel.

31-3.1.7   Each class or group shall proceed to a predetermined point outside the building and remain there while a check is made to see that all are accounted for, leaving only when a recall signal is given to return to the building, or when dismissed. Such points shall be sufficiently far away from the building and from each other as to avoid danger from any fire in the building, interference with fire department operations, or confusion between different classes or groups.

31-3.1.8*   Where necessary for drill lines to cross roadways, signs reading "STOP! SCHOOL FIRE DRILL," or equivalent, shall be carried by monitors to the traffic intersecting points in order to stop traffic during the period of the drill.

A-31-3.1.8   Wherever possible, drill lines should not cross a street or highway, especially where the traffic is heavy. It is recommended that, where drill lines must cross roadways, a police officer, school janitor, or a teacher acting as a traffic officer be on duty to control traffic during drills.

31-3.1.9*   Fire exit drills in schools shall not include any fire extinguishing operations.

A-31-3.1.9   Instructors and employees should be trained in the function and use of such equipment to meet an emergency.

As indicated in the Appendix note, instructors and employees should be trained in the function and use of fire extinguishing equipment for the purpose of meeting an emergency; however, their primary responsibility is to lead students to safety.

31-3.2 Signals.

31-3.2.1   All fire exit drill alarms shall be sounded on the fire alarm system.

31-3.2.2   Whenever any of the school authorities determine that an actual fire exists, they shall immediately call the local fire department using the public fire alarm system or such other facilities as are available.

31-3.2.3 In order to prevent pupils from being returned to a building that is burning, the recall signal shall be one that is separate and distinct from, and cannot be mistaken for, any other signals. Such signals may be given by distinctive colored flags or banners. If the recall signal is electrical, the push buttons or other controls shall be kept under lock, the key for which shall be in the possession of the principal or some other designated person in order to prevent a recall at a time when there is a fire. Regardless of the method of recall, the means of giving the signal shall be kept under a lock.

31-3.3 Inspection.

31-3.3.1* It shall be the duty of principals and teachers to inspect all exit facilities daily in order to make sure that all stairways, doors, and other exits are in proper condition.

A-31-3.3.1 Particular attention should be given to keeping all doors unlocked, having doors closed that serve to protect the safety of paths of egress, such as doors on stairway enclosures, closed and under no conditions blocked open, keeping outside stairs and fire escape stairs free from all obstructions and clear of snow and ice, and allowing no accumulation of snow or ice or materials of any kind outside exit doors that might prevent the opening of the door or interfere with rapid escape from the building.

Any condition likely to interfere with safe exit should be immediately corrected if possible or otherwise should be reported at once to the appropriate authorities.

31-3.3.2 Open-plan buildings require extra surveillance to ensure that exit paths are maintained clear of obstruction and are obvious.

31-3.4 Day-Care Centers.

31-3.4.1 Fire prevention inspections shall be conducted monthly by a trained senior member of the staff. A copy of the latest inspection form shall be posted in a conspicuous place in the day-care facility.

Paragraph 31-3.4.1 does not intend to eliminate inspections by the personnel of fire prevention bureaus where they exist, but rather means to supplement such inspections. Where no fire department inspections are made or where they are made infrequently, monthly inspections must be made by a senior member of the staff who has been trained to make such inspections by the authority having jurisdiction.

31-3.4.2* An approved fire evacuation plan shall be executed not less than once per month.

A-31-3.4.2 It is recommended that firesafety be a part of the educational program of the center.

Firesafety, including an approved fire evacuation plan, should be included in the curriculum of all day-care centers, group day-care homes, and family day-care homes. This part of the curriculum should be approved by the authority having jurisdiction. The NFPA Learn Not to Burn Curriculum[5] is a proven system of firesafety education in schools.

31-3.4.3 Flammable and combustible liquids shall be stored in areas accessible only to designated individuals and as required in 31-1.6.

To ensure that only designated individuals have access to flammable or combustible liquids, such materials should be kept in locked areas.

31-3.4.4 Wastebaskets and other waste containers shall be made of noncombustible materials.

31-3.5 Group Day-Care Homes. At least one operable flashlight shall be provided for each staff member in a location accessible to the staff for use in the event of a power failure.

31-3.6 Family Day-Care Homes. At least one operable flashlight shall be provided in a location accessible to the staff for use in the event of a power failure.

31-3.7 Day-Care Staff. Adequate adult staff shall be on duty, alert, awake, and in the facility at all times when clients are present.

31-3.8 Furnishings and Decorations.

31-3.8.1 Draperies, curtains, and other similar furnishings and decorations in educational occupancies shall be in accordance with the provisions of 31-1.4.

31-3.8.2 Clothing and personal effects shall not be stored in corridors and lobbies.

Exception: Metal lockers may be installed in corridors for storage of clothing and personal effects provided the corridor width is maintained.

See commentary following 31-2.9.

31-3.9 Child-prepared artwork and teaching materials may be attached directly to the walls and shall not exceed 20 percent of the wall area.

It is not only necessary to limit the quantity of child-prepared materials displayed, but also to avoid placing these materials near the exit access doors in a room. Where possible, such materials should be fastened to the wall at the top and bottom of displays.

31-3.10 Unvented Fuel-Fired Heating Equipment. Unvented fuel-fired heating equipment shall be prohibited in educational occupancies and in all categories of day-care facilities.

SECTION 31-4* HEALTH CARE OCCUPANCIES

A-31-4 Health care occupants have, in large part, varied degrees of physical disability, and their removal to the outside or even disturbance by moving is inexpedient or impractical in many cases, except as a last resort. Similarly recognizing that there may be an operating necessity for the restraint of the mentally ill, often by use of barred windows and locked doors, exit drills are usually extremely disturbing, detrimental, and frequently impracticable.

In most cases, fire and exit drills as ordinarily practiced in other occupancies cannot be conducted in health care occupancies. Fundamentally, superior construction, early discovery and extinguishment of incipient fires, and prompt notification must be relied upon to reduce the occasion for evacuation of buildings of this class to a minimum.

31-4.1 Attendants, Evacuation Plan, Fire Exit Drills.

31-4.1.1 The administration of every hospital, nursing home, and limited care facility shall have in effect and available to all supervisory personnel, written copies of a plan for the protection of all persons in the event of fire and for their evacuation to areas of refuge and for evacuation from the building when necessary. All employees shall be periodically instructed and kept informed with respect to their duties under the plan. A copy of the plan shall be readily available at all times in the telephone operator's position or at the security center.

The provisions of 31-4.1.3 to 31-4.2.3 inclusive shall apply.

31-4.1.2 Every bed intended for use by health care occupants shall be easily movable under conditions of evacuation and shall be equipped with the type and size casters to allow easy mobility, especially over elements of the structure such as expansion plates and elevator thresholds. The authority having jurisdiction may make exceptions in the equipping of beds intended for use in areas limited to patients such as convalescent, self-care, or mental health patients.

> Although the function of 31-4.1.2 is to provide for the horizontal movement of patients in their beds, normal hospital practice is to move patients through the hospital on narrow carts or in wheelchairs. Thus, hospitals have little or no practice in moving patients in large beds. In addition, the furniture (chairs, nightstand, food tray/table) in a room must be moved out of the way to allow a bed to be turned and moved out. This requires extra time that is usually unavailable to the staff during a fire. Emphasis should be placed on moving patients who are in the room of fire origin as well as others who are directly exposed to the fire. It is also important to confine to their rooms those patients who are not immediately threatened during the fire.

31-4.1.3* Fire exit drills in health care occupancies shall include the transmission of a fire alarm signal and simulation of emergency fire conditions except that the movement of infirm or bedridden patients to safe areas or to the exterior of the building is not required. Drills shall be conducted quarterly on each shift to familiarize facility personnel (nurses, interns, maintenance engineers, and administrative staff) with signals and emergency action required under varied conditions. At least twelve drills shall be held every year. When drills are conducted between 9:00 p.m. (2100 hours) and 6:00 a.m. (0600 hours), a coded announcement may be used instead of audible alarms.

A-31-4.1.3 Many hospitals conduct fire exit drills without disturbing patients by advance planning in the choice of location of the simulated emergency and by closing doors to patients' rooms or wards in the vicinity prior to the initiation of the drill. The purpose of a fire drill is to test the efficiency, knowledge, and response of institutional personnel. Its purpose is not to disturb or excite patients.

Convalescent patients should be removed from involved zones lest their curiosity or anxiety hamper fire brigade activity or cause themselves injury. All sections should be assured of a necessary complement of doctors, nurses, attendants, and other employees in reserve in readiness to assist in the transfer of bed patients to less exposed areas or sections.

Formal Interpretation 73-38
Reference: 31-4.1.3

Question: In a multibuilding hospital complex, is it a requirement to conduct a fire exit drill quarterly on each shift in each hospital building that houses or is frequented by patients?

Answer: Yes.

Question: In a multibuilding hospital complex, is it a requirement to conduct a fire exit drill quarterly on each shift in each hospital building that houses patients?

Answer: Yes.

Question: In a multibuilding hospital complex, is it a requirement to conduct a fire exit drill quarterly on each shift in only one of the patient-occupied buildings?

Answer: No.

Issue Edition: 1973
Reference: 17-4113
Date: May 1977

   Also see 31-1.5.

31-4.1.4   Employees of health care facilities shall be instructed in life safety procedures and devices.

31-4.2 Procedure in Case of Fire.

31-4.2.1*   For health care occupancies, the proper protection of patients requires the prompt and effective actions of health care personnel. The basic actions required of staff shall include the removal of all occupants directly involved with the fire emergency, transmission of an appropriate fire alarm signal to warn other building occupants, confinement of the effects of the fire by closing doors to isolate the fire area, and the execution of those evacuation duties as detailed in the Facility Firesafety Plan. See Appendix A for a more detailed suggested emergency plan.

A-31-4.2.1   Each facility has specific characteristics that may vary from other facilities sufficiently to prevent the specification of a universal emergency procedure. The following recommendations, however, contain many of the elements that should be considered and adapted as appropriate to the individual facility.

Upon discovery of fire, personnel should immediately take the following action:

(a) If any person is involved in the fire, the discoverer should go to the aid of that person, calling aloud an established code phrase. The use of a code provides for both the immediate aid of any endangered person and the transmission of an alarm. Any person in the area, upon hearing the code called aloud, should activate the building fire alarm using the nearest manual alarm station.

(b) If a person is not involved in the fire, the discoverer should activate the building fire alarm using the nearest manual alarm station.

(c) Personnel, upon hearing the alarm signal, should immediately execute their duties as outlined in the facility firesafety plan.

(d) The telephone operator should determine the location of the fire as indicated by the audible signal. In a building equipped with an uncoded alarm system, a person on the floor of fire origin should be responsible for promptly notifying the facility telephone operator of the fire location.

(e) If the telephone operator receives a telephone alarm reporting a fire from a floor, the operator should regard that alarm in the same fashion as an alarm received over the fire alarm system. The operator should immediately notify the fire department and alert all facility personnel of the place of fire and its origin.

(f) If the building fire alarm system is out of order, any person discovering a fire should immediately notify the telephone operator by telephone. The operator should then transmit this information to the fire department and alert the building occupants.

31-4.2.2 A written facility firesafety plan shall provide for:

(a) Use of alarms

(b) Transmission of alarm to fire department

(c) Response to alarms

(d) Isolation of fire

(e) Evacuation of area

(f) Preparation of building for evacuation

(g) Extinguishment of fire.

31-4.2.3 All facility personnel shall be instructed in the use of, and response to, fire alarms; and, in addition, they shall be instructed in the use of the code phrase to ensure transmission of an alarm under the following conditions:

(a) When the discoverer of a fire must immediately go to the aid of an endangered person.

(b) During a malfunction of the building fire alarm system.

Personnel hearing the code announced shall first activate the building fire alarm using the nearest manual alarm station and shall then immediately execute their duties as outlined in the firesafety plan.

In addition to the requirements of 31-4.2, evacuation plans should stress that the doors of as many patient rooms as possible be closed in order to shut out smoke spreading from a fire and, if possible, to confine the fire in a room. This single action taken by the staff in manually closing the doors achieves the *Code*-mandated level of safety to life found in Chapters 12 and 13. In studies of fires in health care institutions in which the staff closed doors, the fire spread was readily confined and there was either no loss of life or life loss was low.

In many recent serious loss-of-life fires in health care facilities, staff either did not close doors or they reopened them. The fire spread was sizable, and the life loss was high. Emphasis must be placed on training staff to sound an alarm and to rescue patients (as needed), and then to close all doors. The last step has the most significant effect on limiting the spread of fire and smoke.

31-4.3 Maintenance of Exits.   Proper maintenance shall be provided to ensure the dependability of the method of evacuation selected. Facilities that find it necessary to lock exits shall at all times maintain an adequate staff qualified to release and conduct occupants from the immediate danger area to a place of safety in case of fire or other emergency.

31-4.4* Smoking.   Smoking regulations shall be adopted and shall include the following minimal provisions:

(a) Smoking shall be prohibited in any room, ward, or compartment where flammable liquids, combustible gases, or oxygen are used or stored and in any other hazardous location. Such areas shall be posted with "NO SMOKING" signs.

(b) Smoking by patients classified as not responsible shall be prohibited.

Exception to (b): When the patient is under direct supervision.

(c) Ashtrays of noncombustible material and safe design shall be provided in all areas where smoking is permitted.

(d) Metal containers with self-closing cover devices into which ashtrays may be emptied shall be readily available to all areas where smoking is permitted.

A-31-4.4   The most rigid discipline with regard to prohibition of smoking may not be nearly so effective in reducing incipient fires from surreptitious smoking as the open recognition of smoking, with provision of suitable facilities for smoking. Proper education and training of the staff and attendants in the ordinary fire hazards and their abatement is unquestionably essential. The problem is a broad one, variable with different types and arrangement of buildings; the effectiveness of rules of procedure, necessarily flexible, depends in large part upon the management.

Smoking in bed or discarding smoking materials into ordinary waste containers not designed for holding them leads the list of causes of fires in health care occupancies. The requirements of 31-4.4 must be met in order to minimize the chance of ignition.

31-4.5 Bedding, Furnishings, and Decorations.

31-4.5.1   Draperies, curtains, including cubicle curtains, and other similar furnishings and decorations in health care occupancies shall be in accordance with the provisions of 31-1.4.

Formal Interpretation 81-40
Reference: 31-4.5.1

Question: Is it the Committee's intent that shower curtains in health care facilities fall under the requirements of 31-4.5.1?

Answer: No.

Issue Edition: 1981
Reference: 31-4.5
Date: February 1984
Also see commentary following A-31-1.4.1.

31-4.5.2* Bedding, furnishings, and decorations in health care occupancies shall be in accordance with the provisions of 31-1.4.

A-31-4.5.2 Furniture, including mattresses, is recognized as providing combustibles for the support of fire, and, as such, appropriate measures should be taken to protect the facility and occupants from immediate danger. Calculations have shown a 1- to 2-megawatt fire could produce flashover within a 12 ft × 15 ft × 9 ft (3.7 m × 4.5 m × 2.7 m) room with the door in the fully opened position. Limiting the maximum instantaneous net heat release of furnishings to 500 kw or less in nonsprinklered buildings would effectively limit fire size and minimize the potential for flashover.

31-4.5.3* Combustible decorations are prohibited in any health care occupancy unless flame-retardant.

Exception: Combustible decorations of such limited quantities that a hazard of fire development or spread is not present, such as photographs and paintings.

A-31-4.5.3 Decorations meeting the requirements of this paragraph should pass both the large- and small-scale tests of NFPA 701, *Standard Methods of Fire Tests for Flame-Resistant Textiles and Films (see Appendix B).*

31-4.5.4 Wastebaskets and other waste containers shall be of noncombustible or other approved materials.

Formal Interpretation 88-1 (supersedes 85-4)
Reference: 31-4.5.4.

Question No. 1: Is it the intent of 31-4.5.4 to regulate clean-linen carts for fire retardancy?

Answer: No.

Question No. 2: Is it the intent of 31-4.5.4 to regulate soiled-linen carts for fire retardancy?

Answer: No.

Question No. 3: Is it the intent of 31-4.5.4 to regulate trash carts for fire retardancy?

Answer: Yes.

Question No. 4: Is it a literal interpretation of the *Code* that 31-4.5.4 regulates mobile trash carts?

Answer: Yes.

Issue Edition: 1988
Reference: 31-4.5.4
Date: January 1988

The purpose of 31-4.5.4 is to try to contain any fire that may start in a waste container. A combustible container or container that collapses during fire exposure will help spread the fire. If the trash container is adjacent to a bed, there is a high probability that the bed linens will ignite regardless of whether or not the container is approved. This fire spread scenerio is very common in health care facilities.

31-4.5.5   Newly introduced upholstered furniture within health care occupancies shall be shown to resist ignition by cigarettes as determined by tests conducted in accordance with NFPA 260B, *Standard Method of Test for Determining Resistance of Mock-Up Upholstered Furniture Material Assemblies to Ignition by Smoldering Cigarettes,* and shall have a char length not exceeding 1.5 in. (3.8 cm).

Exception: Health Care Occupancies protected throughout with an approved automatic sprinkler system in accordance with Section 7-7.

This requirement, which applies to newly introduced upholstered furniture in nonsprinklered health care occupancies, regulates on the basis of test results from NFPA 260B, *Standard Method of Test for Determining Resistance of Mock-Up Upholstered Furniture Material Assemblies to Ignition by Smoldering Cigarettes.*[3] NFPA 260B provides no pass/fail criteria, and thus, the maximum 1.5-in. (3.8-cm) char length allowance was specified as the "best judgment" of the *Code* authors.

31-4.6   Where engineered smoke control systems are provided in accordance with Chapter 12, such systems shall be tested to verify proper operation in accordance with design criteria prior to occupancy.

31-4.7 Portable Space Heating Devices.   Portable space heating devices are prohibited in all health care and ambulatory health care occupancies.

Exception: Portable space heating devices shall be permitted to be used in nonsleeping staff and employee areas when the heating elements of such devices are limited to not more than 212°F (100°C).

31-4.8 Construction, Repair, and Improvement Operations.

31-4.8.1   Construction, repair, and improvement operations shall comply with 31-1.1.

31-4.8.2   The means of egress in any area undergoing construction, repair, or improvements shall be inspected daily. (*See 31-1.2.1.*)

SECTION 31-5   DETENTION AND CORRECTIONAL OCCUPANCIES

31-5.1 Attendants, Evacuation Plan, Fire Exit Drills.

31-5.1.1   Detention and correctional facilities, or those portions of facilities having such occupancy, must be provided with 24-hour staffing. Staff must be within three floors or 300 ft (91 m) horizontal distance of the access door of each resident housing area.

In addition, for Use Conditions III, IV, and V, the arrangement shall be such that the staff involved can start release of locks necessary for emergency evacuation or rescue and initiate other necessary emergency actions within two minutes of alarm.

31-5.1.2*   Provisions shall be made so that residents in Use Conditions III, IV, and V can readily notify staff of an emergency.

A-31-5.1.2   This can be met by electronic or oral monitoring systems, visual monitoring, call signals, or other means.

Use Conditions III, IV, and V rely on staff action to protect residents; therefore, the staff needs to be made aware of conditions immediately, as residents may discover a fire before automatic detection devices react.

31-5.1.3*   The administration of every detention or correctional facility shall have in effect and provided to all supervisory personnel, written copies of a plan for the protection of all persons in the event of fire and for their evacuation to areas of refuge and for evacuation from the building when necessary. All employees shall be instructed and drilled with respect to their duties under the plan. The plan shall be coordinated with and reviewed by the fire department legally committed to serve the facility.

A-31-5.1.3   There should be periodic coordinated training involving detention/correctional facility personnel and personnel of the fire department legally committed to serving the facility.

A properly designed and well-tested plan is of great importance, especially in a detention and correctional occupancy where residents depend heavily on staff performance in order to survive a fire.

31-5.1.4   Employees of detention and correctional occupancies shall be instructed in the proper use of portable fire extinguishers and other manual fire suppression equipment that they may be called upon to use. With respect to new staff, such training shall be provided promptly upon commencement of duty. With respect to existing staff, refresher training shall be provided at least annually.

31-5.2   Books, clothing, and other combustible personal property allowed in sleeping rooms shall be stored in closable metal lockers or a fire resistant container.

31-5.3   The amount of heat-producing appliances, such as toasters, hot plates, etc., and the overall use of electrical power within a sleeping room shall be controlled by facility administration.

31-5.4 Furnishings and Decorations.

31-5.4.1   Draperies, curtains, including privacy curtains, and other similar furnishings and decorations in detention and correctional occupancies shall be in accordance with the provisions of 31-1.4.

31-5.4.2*   Combustible decorations are prohibited in any detention or correctional occupancy unless flame-retardant.

A-31-5.4.2   Decorations meeting the requirements of this paragraph should pass both the large- and small-scale tests of NFPA 701, *Standard Methods of Fire Tests for Flame-Resistant Textiles and Films* (*see Appendix B*).

31-5.4.3   Wastebaskets and other waste containers shall be of noncombustible or other approved materials.

31-5.4.4   Furnishings, such as mattresses and upholstered or cushioned furniture, shall not be of a highly flammable character.

31-5.5 Keys.   All keys necessary for unlocking doors installed in means of egress shall be individually identified by both touch and sight.

> **Loss of keys, broken keys, incorrect keys, etc., have played a major role in several multiple-death detention and correctional occupancy fires.**

31-5.6 Portable Space Heating Devices.   Portable space heating devices are prohibited.

SECTION 31-6   RESIDENTIAL OCCUPANCIES

31-6.1 Hotel Emergency Organization.

31-6.1.1*   All employees of hotels shall be instructed and drilled in the duties they are to perform in the event of fire, panic, or other emergency.

A-31-6.1.1   The exact nature of this emergency organization must of necessity be governed by such factors as the number of available employees, the structural conditions, the degree of compliance with this *Code*, and other elements pertinent to the individual situation.

In order to be efficient, any such organization must depend upon:

(a) A definite working plan.

(b) Competent leadership.

(c) Rigid discipline.

(d) Maintenance of necessary apparatus.

(e) A schedule of sufficient training under discipline with such apparatus.

It will be found advisable to secure the cooperation of local fire department officials in developing and training such an organization of employees.

31-6.1.2* Drills of the emergency organization shall be held at monthly intervals, covering such points as the operation and maintenance of the available first aid fire appliances, the testing of guest alerting devices, and a study of instructions for emergency duties.

A-31-6.1.2 It is recommended that emergencies be assumed to have arisen at various locations in the occupancy in order to train employees in logical procedures.

31-6.2 Emergency Duties.

31-6.2.1 Upon discovery of fire, some or all of these duties will become immediately imperative, the number and sequence depending upon the exact situation encountered:

Alarms

Notify office.

Notify public fire department.

Notify private fire brigade.

Guests

Warn guests or others who are or may become endangered.

Assist occupants to safety, with special attention to aged, infirm, or otherwise incapacitated persons.

Search rooms to be sure all occupants have escaped.

Man all elevators, including those of automatic type, with competent operators.

Extinguishment

Extinguish or control the fire using available first aid equipment.

Send messenger to meet public fire department upon arrival in order to direct latter to exact location of fire. (The public fire department is in full command upon arrival.)

Special Equipment

Fire Pumps — stand by for instant operation.

Ventilating Equipment — in case of dense smoke, stand by, operate under proper instructions to clear area affected.

Refrigerating Equipment — if machines are definitely endangered, shut them down and blow refrigerant to sewer or atmosphere to prevent explosion.

Generators and Motors — protect against water damage with tarpaulins — shut down motors not needed — keep generators operating to furnish lights, elevator power, etc.

Boilers — if necessary to abandon boiler room, extinguish or dump fire and lower steam pressure by blowing to sewer or atmosphere to prevent possible explosion.

31-6.3 Dormitories.

31-6.3.1 Drills. Fire exit drills shall be regularly conducted in accordance with 31-1.5.

31-6.4 Emergency Instructions for Residents or Guests.

31-6.4.1* A floor diagram reflecting the actual floor arrangement, exit locations, and room identification shall be posted in a location and manner acceptable to the authority having jurisdiction on or immediately adjacent to every guest room door in hotels and in every resident room in dormitories.

A-31-6.4.1 Floor diagrams should reflect the actual floor arrangement and should be oriented with the actual direction to the exits.

Note that the manner in which the information is to be posted and the nature of its contents are at the discretion of the authority having jurisdiction. This will vary depending on the building, its layout, the protection provided, etc.

31-6.4.2* Fire safety information shall be provided to allow guests to make a decision to either: evacuate to the outside; evacuate to an area of refuge; remain in place; or any combination of the three.

A-31-6.4.2 Factors for developing the firesafety information include construction type, suppression systems, alarm and detection systems, building layout, and building HVAC systems, etc.

31-6.5 Emergency Instructions for Residents of Apartment Buildings.

31-6.5.1 Emergency instructions shall be provided to each living unit on a yearly basis indicating the location of alarms, exiting paths, and actions to be taken, both in response to a fire in the living unit and in response to the sounding of the alarm system.

31-6.6 Furnishings and Decorations.

31-6.6.1* New draperies, curtains, and other similar furnishings and decorations in hotels and dormitories shall be in accordance with the provisions of 31-1.4.

A-31-6.6.1 In nonsprinklered hotels, dormitories, or apartment buildings, new upholstered furniture located in areas not separated from corridors by corridor walls as specified in the *Code* should be tested in accordance with NFPA 260B, *Standard Method of Test for Determining Resistance of Mock-up Upholstered Furniture Material Assemblies to Ignition by Smoldering Cigarettes*, with a char-length not exceeding 1.5 in. (3.8 cm) and should be labeled indicating such compliance.

See commentary following 31-4.5.5 Exception.

31-6.7 Unvented fuel-fired heaters shall not be used in residential occupancies.

Exception: Listed and approved unvented fuel-fired heaters in one- and two-family dwellings.

SECTION 31-7   BOARD AND CARE HOMES

31-7.1 Emergency Plan.   The administration of every residential board and care facility shall have in effect and available to all supervisory personnel written copies of a plan for the protection of all persons in the event of fire and for their remaining in place, for their evacuation to areas of refuge and from the building when necessary. The plan shall include special staff actions including fire protection procedures needed to ensure the safety of any resident and shall be amended or revised upon admission to the home of any resident with unusual needs. All employees shall be periodically instructed and kept informed with respect to their duties and responsibilities under the plan. Such instruction shall be reviewed by the staff at least every two months. A copy of the plan shall be readily available at all times within the facility.

31-7.2 Resident Training.   All residents participating in the emergency plan shall be trained in the proper actions to take in the event of fire. This training shall include actions to take if the primary escape route is blocked. If the resident is given rehabilitation or habilitation training, training in fire prevention and actions to take in the event of a fire shall be a part of the rehabilitation training program. Residents shall be trained to assist each other in case of fire to the extent their physical and mental abilities permit them to do so without additional personal risk.

31-7.3 Fire Exit Drills.   Fire exit drills shall be conducted at least twelve times per year, four times a year on each shift. The drills may be announced in advance to the residents. The drills shall involve the actual evacuation of all residents to an assembly point as specified in the emergency plan and shall provide residents with experience in exiting through all exits required by the *Code*. Exits not used in any fire drill shall not be credited in meeting the requirements of this *Code* for board and care homes.

Exception No. 1:   Actual exiting from windows shall not be required to meet the requirements of this section; opening the window and signaling for help shall be an acceptable alternative.

Exception No. 2:   If the board and care home has an evacuation capability rating of "Impractical," those residents who cannot meaningfully assist in their own evacuation or who have special health problems need not actively participate in the drill. Section 31-4 applies in such instances.

Also see 31-1.5.

31-7.4 Smoking.

31-7.4.1   Where smoking is permitted, noncombustible safety-type ashtrays or receptacles shall be provided in convenient locations.

SECTION 31-8   MERCANTILE OCCUPANCIES

31-8.1 Drills.   In every Class A or B store, employees shall be regularly trained in fire exit drill procedures in general conformance with 31-1.5.

31-8.2   Employees of mercantile occupancies shall be instructed in the proper use of portable fire extinguishers.

The extent of this training, e.g., instruction only, instruction and hands-on use, etc., is determined by the authority having jurisdiction.

SECTION 31-9   BUSINESS OCCUPANCIES

31-9.1 Drills.   In any building subject to occupancy by more than 500 persons or more than 100 above or below the street level, employees and supervisory personnel shall be instructed in fire exit drill procedures in accordance with 31-1.5 and shall hold practice drills periodically where practicable.

31-9.2   Employees of business occupancies shall be instructed in the proper use of portable fire extinguishers.

The extent of this training, e.g., instruction only, instruction and hands-on use, etc., is determined by the authority having jurisdiction.

REFERENCES CITED IN COMMENTARY

[1]NFPA 701, *Standard Methods of Fire Tests for Flame-Resistant Textiles and Films*, National Fire Protection Association, Quincy, MA 1977.

[2]NFPA 260A, *Standard Methods of Tests and Classification System for Cigarette Ignition Resistance of Components of Upholstered Furniture*, National Fire Protection Association, Quincy, MA, 1986.

[3]NFPA 260B, *Standard Method of Test for Determining Resistance of Mock-Up Upholstered Furniture Material Assemblies to Ignition by Smoldering Cigarettes*, National Fire Protection Association, Quincy, MA, 1983.

[4]NFPA 703, *Standard for Fire Retardant Impregnated Wood and Fire Retardant Coatings for Building Materials*, National Fire Protection Association, Quincy, MA, 1985.

[5]NFPA Learn Not to Burn Curriculum, Firesafety Program for Grades Kindergarten Through Eight, National Fire Protection Association, Quincy, MA, 1981.

32 REFERENCED PUBLICATIONS

This chapter contains the mandatory referenced publications that, prior to the 1985 Edition of the *Code*, were found in Appendix B-1 of the *Code*. Appendix B now contains only nonmandatory referenced publications.

(See Appendix B for other referenced publications that are advisory and thus do not constitute part of the requirements of this Code.)

32-1 The following documents or portions thereof are referenced within this *Code* and shall be considered part of the requirements of this *Code* to the extent called for by the *Code*. The edition indicated for each reference is current as of the date of the NFPA issuance of this document. These references are listed separately to facilitate updating to the latest edition by the user.

The numbers in parentheses represent the paragraph numbers from chapters of this *Code* that reference, in a mandatory way, the given publication.

The Committee on Safety to Life recognizes that it is sometimes not practical to continually upgrade existing buildings or installations to comply with all the requirements of the following referenced publications. Existing buildings or installations that do not comply with the provisions of the following referenced publications may be continued in service, subject to approval by the authority having jurisdiction and provided the lack of conformity with these standards does not present a serious hazard to the occupants.

There are two important points to be made regarding Section 32-1. First, the listed documents are mandatory only to the extent called for in the *Code*. For example, although NFPA 13, *Standard for the Installation of Sprinkler Systems*, is listed here, this does not mean all buildings have to be sprinklered, but rather that, where the *Code* requires them to be sprinklered, NFPA 13 is to be used for sprinkler installation. Second, the Committee recognizes that existing installations need not be continuously upgraded as new editions of the referenced standards are adopted, provided the authority having jurisdiction agrees that no serious life safety hazard is present.

32-1.1 NFPA Publications. The following publications are available from the National Fire Protection Association, Batterymarch Park, Quincy, MA 02269.

NFPA 10-1988, *Standard for Portable Fire Extinguishers* (7-7.4.1, 31-1.3.5)

NFPA 11-1988, *Standard for Low Expansion Foam and Combined Agent Systems* (7-7.3, 31-1.3.5)

NFPA 11A-1988, *Standard for Medium and High Expansion Foam Systems* (7-7.3, 31-1.3.5)

NFPA 12-1985, *Standard on Carbon Dioxide Extinguishing Systems* (7-7.3, 31-1.3.5)

NFPA 12A-1987, *Standard on Halon 1301 Fire Extinguishing Systems* (7-7.3, 31-1.3.5)

NFPA 12B-1985, *Standard on Halon 1211 Fire Extinguishing Systems* (7-7.3, 31-1.3.5)

NFPA 13-1987, *Standard for the Installation of Sprinkler Systems* (6-2.4.7, 7-7.1.1, 16-1.5.1, 17-1.5.1, 22-2.1.2, 26-1.5.2, 27-1.5.2, 31-1.3.5)

NFPA 13D-1984, *Standard for the Installation of Sprinkler Systems in One- and Two-Family Dwellings and Mobile Homes* (7-7.1.1, 21-2.3.5.1, 22-2.1.2, 31-1.3.5)

NFPA 14-1986, *Standard for the Installation of Standpipe and Hose Systems* (7-7.4.2, 31-1.3.5)

NFPA 15-1985, *Standard for Water Spray Fixed Systems for Fire Protection* (7-7.3, 31-1.3.5)

NFPA 16-1986, *Standard on Deluge Foam-Water Sprinkler and Foam-Water Spray Systems* (7-7.3, 31-1.3.5)

NFPA 17-1985, *Standard for Dry Chemical Extinguishing Systems* (7-7.3, 31-1.3.5)

NFPA 17A-1986, *Standard for Wet Chemical Extinguishing Systems* (7-7.3, 31-1.3.5)

NFPA 20-1987, *Standard for the Installation of Centrifugal Fire Pumps* (7-7.3, 31-1.3.5)

NFPA 22-1987, *Standard for Water Tanks for Private Fire Protection* (31-1.3.5)

NFPA 30-1987, *Flammable and Combustible Liquids Code* (6-4.3, 31-1.6)

NFPA 31-1987, *Standard for the Installation of Oil Burning Equipment* (7-2.2)

NFPA 40-1988, *Standard for the Storage and Handling of Cellulose Nitrate Motion Picture Film* (8-3.2.2.1, 9-3.2.2.1, 31-2.8)

NFPA 45-1986, *Standard on Fire Protection for Laboratories Using Chemicals* (6-4.4, 10-3.2.4, 11-3.2.4, 31-1.7)

NFPA 54-1988, *National Fuel Gas Code* (7-1.1, 7-2.2)

NFPA 58-1986, *Standard for the Storage and Handling of Liquefied Petroleum Gases* (7-1.1)

NFPA 70-1987, *National Electrical Code* (5-9.2.2, 6-2.4.7, 7-1.2, 7-2.2, 7-6.1.3, 8-4.1.4, 10-4.1.5, 14-5.1.2, 15-5.1.2, 24-4.5.4, 25-4.5.4., 26-4.2.4, 26-4.3.4, 27-4.3.4, 30-8.4.2)

NFPA 71-1987, *Standard for the Installation, Maintenance, and Use of Signaling Systems for Central Station Service* (7-6.1.3, 7-6.4, 31-1.3.5)

NFPA 72A-1987, *Standard for the Installation, Maintenance, and Use of Local Protective Signaling Systems for Guard's Tour, Fire Alarm, and Supervisory Service* (7-6.1.3, 7-6.3.3, 12-3.4.1.3, 14-3.4.1.3, 15-3.4.1.3, 31-1.3.5)

NFPA 72B-1986, *Standard for the Installation, Maintenance, and Use of Auxiliary Protective Signaling Systems for Fire Alarm Service* (7-6.1.3, 7-6.4, 31-1.3.5)

NFPA 72C-1986, *Standard for the Installation, Maintenance, and Use of Remote Station Protective Signaling Systems* (7-6.1.3, 7-6.4, 31-1.3.5)

NFPA 72D-1986, *Standard for the Installation, Maintenance, and Use of Proprietary Protective Signaling Systems* (7-6.1.3, 7-6.4, 31-1.3.5)

NFPA 72E-1987, *Standard on Automatic Fire Detectors* (5-2.1.8, 6-3.5.2, 6-3.5.3, 7-6.1.3, 7-6.2.7, 7-6.2.8, 18-3.4.4.2, 19-3.4.4.2, 21-3.3.4.8, 31-1.3.5)

NFPA 72F-1985, *Standard for the Installation, Maintenance, and Use of Emergency Voice/Alarm Communication Systems* (7-6.1.3, 26-4.2.3.3, 30-8.3.2)

NFPA 74-1984, *Standard for the Installation, Maintenance, and Use of Household Fire Warning Equipment* (7-6.1.3, 7-6.2.9, 31-1.3.5)

NFPA 80-1986, *Standard for Fire Doors and Windows* (5-2.1.14.1, 6-2.3.6, 12-3.6.3.6, 13-3.6.3.6, 31-1.3.5)

NFPA 82-1983, *Standard on Incinerators, Waste and Linen Handling Systems and Equipment* (7-5.2)

NFPA 88A-1985, *Standard for Parking Structures* (16-3.5.3, 18-3.5.8)

NFPA 90A-1985, *Standard for the Installation of Air Conditioning and Ventilating Systems* (6-2.5.1, 7-2.1, 12-3.1.1)

NFPA 90B-1984, *Standard for the Installation of Warm Air Heating and Air Conditioning Systems* (7-2.1)

NFPA 91-1983, *Standard for the Installation of Blower and Exhaust Systems for Dust, Stock, and Vapor Removal or Conveying* (7-2.2)

NFPA 96-1987, *Standard for the Installation of Equipment for the Removal of Smoke and Grease-Laden Vapors from Commercial Cooking Equipment* (7-2.3, 31-1.3.5)

NFPA 99-1987, *Standard for Health Care Facilities* (6-4.4, 12-2.9.2, 12-2.10.2, 12-3.2.2, 12-3.2.3, 12-3.2.4, 12-5.1.2, 12-5.1.3, 12-6.2.9.2, 12-6.3.2.1, 12-6.3.2.2, 13-3.2.2, 13-3.2.3, 13-3.2.4, 13-6.2.9.2, 13-6.3.2.1, 13-6.3.2.2, 31-1.3.5)

NFPA 101M-1988, *Manual on Alternative Approaches to Life Safety* (21-2.1.4.2, 21-2.3.6.1)

NFPA 102-1986, *Standard for Assembly Seating, Tents, and Membrane Structures* (8-2.5.4.6, 8-2.5.6.9, 8-4.3.1, 9-2.5.4.6, 9-2.5.6.9, 9-4.3.1)

NFPA 110-1988, *Standard for Emergency and Standby Power Systems* (30-8.4.2)

NFPA 211-1988, *Standard for Chimneys, Fireplaces, Vents, and Solid Fuel Burning Appliances* (7-2.2, 12-5.2.2, 13-5.2.2)

NFPA 220-1985, *Standard on Types of Building Construction* (6-2.1, 6-5.3.4)

NFPA 241-1986, *Standard for Safeguarding Construction, Alteration, and Demolition Operations* (31-1.1.1)

NFPA 251-1985, *Standard Methods of Fire Tests of Building Construction and Materials* (Section 3-2, 6-2.3.5, 12-3.6.2.1, 13-3.6.2.1)

NFPA 252-1984, *Standard Methods of Fire Tests of Door Assemblies* (5-1.3.4, 6-2.3.2, 6-2.3.6, 12-3.6.3.3, 13-3.6.3.3)

NFPA 253-1984, *Standard Method of Test for Critical Radiant Flux of Floor Covering Systems Using a Radiant Heat Energy Source* (Section 3-2, 6-5.4.1)

NFPA 255-1984, *Standard Method of Test of Surface Burning Characteristics of Building Materials* (6-5.3.1)

NFPA 256-1987, *Standard Methods of Fire Tests of Roof Coverings* (12-1.6.2, 13-1.6.2, 15-1.6.3, 21-3.1.4.3)

NFPA 257-1985, *Standard for Fire Tests of Window Assemblies* (Section 3-2, 6-2.3.6)

NFPA 260B-1983, *Standard Method of Test for Determining Resistance of Mock-Up Upholstered Furniture Material Assemblies to Ignition by Smoldering Cigarettes* (31-4.5.5)

NFPA 701-1977, *Standard Methods of Fire Tests for Flame-Resistant Textiles and Films* (8-3.2.1.11, 8-4.4.3, 9-3.2.1.11, 9-4.4.3, 31-1.4.1)

NFPA 703-1985, *Standard for Fire Retardant Impregnated Wood and Fire Retardant Coatings for Building Materials* (6-5.6.1, 8-4.4.3, 9-4.4.3)

NFPA 1221-1988, *Standard for the Installation, Maintenance, and Use of Public Fire Service Communication Systems* (7-6.1.3, 31-1.3.5)

32-1.2 Other Publications.

ANSI A14.3-1984, *Safety Code for Fixed Ladders*, American National Standards Institute, 1430 Broadway, New York, NY 10018 (5-2.9.2)

ANSI/ASME A17.1-1987, *Safety Code for Elevators and Escalators*, American Society of Mechanical Engineers, 345 East 47th Street, New York, NY 10017 (7-4.2, 7-4.4)

ANSI/ASME A17.3-1986, *Safety Code for Existing Elevators and Escalators*, American Society of Mechanical Engineers, 345 East 47th Street, New York, NY 10017 (7-4.3)

ASTM E136-1982, *Standard Test Method for Behavior of Materials in a Vertical Tube Furnace at 750°F*, American Society for Testing and Materials, 1916 Race Street, Philadelphia, PA 19103 (Section 3-2)

ASTM F851-1983, *Standard Test Method for Self-Rising Seat Mechanisms*, American Society for Testing and Materials, 1916 Race Street, Philadelphia, PA 19103 (8-2.5.4.1, 9-2.5.4.1)

APPENDIX A

Appendix A is not a part of the requirements of this NFPA Code, but is included for information purposes only.

The material contained in Appendix A of the 1988 *Life Safety Code* is included within this *Handbook*, and therefore Appendix A is not repeated here.

APPENDIX B

Referenced Publications

B-1 The following documents or portions thereof are referenced within this *Code* for informational purposes only and thus are not considered part of the requirements of this *Code*. The edition indicated for each reference is the current edition as of the date of the NFPA issuance of this document.

The numbers in parentheses represent the paragraph numbers from the Appendices of this *Code* that reference, in an advisory manner, the given publication.

Note that the mandatory referenced publications are now listed in Chapter 32. Many of the documents listed here are also listed in Chapter 32 and, although not mandatory here, are so in Chapter 32.

B-1.1 NFPA Publications. National Fire Protection Association, Batterymarch Park, Quincy, MA 02269.

NFPA 10-1988, *Standard for Portable Fire Extinguishers* (A-7-7.4.1)

NFPA 11-1988, *Standard for Low Expansion Foam and Combined Agent Systems* (A-7-7.3)

NFPA 12-1985, *Standard on Carbon Dioxide Extinguishing Systems* (A-7-7.3)

NFPA 12A-1987, *Standard on Halon 1301 Fire Extinguishing Systems* (A-7-7.3)

NFPA 12B-1985, *Standard on Halon 1211 Fire Extinguishing Systems* (A-7-7.3)

NFPA 13-1987, *Standard for the Installation of Sprinkler Systems* (A-4-2.2.1)

NFPA 13A-1987, *Recommended Practice for the Inspection, Testing, and Maintenance of Sprinkler Systems* (A-31-1.3.6)

NFPA 13D-1984, *Standard for the Installation of Sprinkler Systems in One- and Two-Family Dwellings and Mobile Homes* (A-20-1.5.1, A-21-3.3.5.1)

NFPA 15-1985, *Standard for Water Spray Fixed Systems for Fire Protection* (A-7-7.3)

NFPA 17-1985, *Standard for Dry Chemical Extinguishing Systems* (A-7-7.3)

NFPA 61B-1980, *Standard for the Prevention of Fires and Explosions in Grain Elevators and Facilities Handling Bulk Raw Agricultural Commodities* (A-29-7)

NFPA 68-1988, *Guide for Explosion Venting of Deflagrations* (A-6-4.2)

NFPA 70-1987, *National Electrical Code* (A-5-9.2.2, A-5-9.2.3, A-16-5.3)

NFPA 71-1987, *Standard for the Installation, Maintenance, and Use of Signaling Systems for Central Station Service* (A-7-7.2.1)

NFPA 72A-1987, *Standard for the Installation, Maintenance, and Use of Local Protective Signaling Systems for Guard's Tour, Fire Alarm, and Supervisory Service* (A-7-6.1.2, A-7-7.2.1)

NFPA 72B-1986, *Standard for the Installation, Maintenance, and Use of Auxiliary Protective Signaling Systems for Fire Alarm Service* (A-7-7.2.1)

NFPA 72C-1986, *Standard for the Installation, Maintenance, and Use of Remote Station Protective Signaling Systems* (A-7-7.2.1)

NFPA 72D-1986, *Standard for the Installation, Maintenance, and Use of Proprietary Protective Signaling Systems* (A-7-7.2.1)

NFPA 72G-1985, *Guide for the Installation, Maintenance, and Use of Notification Appliances for Protective Signaling Systems* (A-7-6.1.3)

NFPA 72H-1988, *Guide for Testing Procedures for Local, Auxiliary, Remote Station, and Proprietary Protective Signaling Systems* (A-7-6.1.3, A-31-1.3.7)

NFPA 80-1986, *Standard for Fire Doors and Windows* (A-5-1.3.4, A-6-2.3.2)

NFPA 88A-1985, *Standard for Parking Structures* (A-29-8.1.1)

NFPA 90A-1985, *Standard for the Installation of Air Conditioning and Ventilating Systems* (A-6-2.3.4.2, A-7-3.1)

NFPA 99-1987, *Standard for Health Care Facilities* (A-12-3.2.1)

NFPA 101M-1988, *Manual on Alternative Approaches to Life Safety* (A-12-1.1.1.1, A-13-1.1.1.1, A-14-1.1.2, A-15-1.1.2, A-21-1.3, A-21-2.1.3.1, A-21-3.1.3.1, A-21-4.1.3.1, A-26-1.1.1, A-27-1.1.1)

NFPA 105-1985, *Recommended Practice for the Installation of Smoke- and Draft-Control Door Assemblies* (A-5-1.3.4, A-5-2.3.2, A-5-2.4.3.5, A-6-3.4.1)

NFPA 204M-1985, *Guide for Smoke and Heat Venting* [A-28-2.6.2(b)]

NFPA 220-1985, *Standard on Types of Building Construction* (A-3-2, A-6-2.1, A-10-3.3.1, A-11-3.3.1)

NFPA 253-1984, *Standard Method of Test for Critical Radiant Flux of Floor Covering Systems Using a Radiant Heat Energy Source* (A-12-3.3.2)

NFPA 255-1984, *Standard Method of Test of Surface Burning Characteristics of Building Materials* (A-6-5.2.3, A-6-5.3.1, A-6-5.3.2)

NFPA 259-1987, *Standard Test Method for Potential Heat of Building Materials* (A-3-2)

NFPA 260B-1983, *Standard Method of Test for Determining Resistance of Mock-Up Upholstered Furniture Material Assemblies to Ignition by Smoldering Cigarettes* (A-31-6.6.1)

NFPA 307-1985, *Standard for the Construction and Fire Protection of Marine Terminals, Piers, and Wharves* (A-30-2.5.3)

NFPA 409-1985, *Standard on Aircraft Hangars* (A-29-6)

NFPA 501A-1987, *Standard for Firesafety Criteria for Manufactured Home Installations, Sites, and Communities* (A-30-6)

NFPA 701-1977, *Standard Methods of Fire Tests for Flame-Resistant Textiles and Films* (A-6-5.3.1, A-8-4.4.3, A-9-4.4.3, A-31-1.4.1, A-31-4.5.3, A-31-5.4.2)

NFPA 1221-1988, *Standard for the Installation, Maintenance, and Use of Public Fire Service Communication Systems* (A-7-7.2.1)

NFPA FPH1686, *NFPA Fire Protection Handbook*, 16th Edition, 1986 (A-7-3.1, A-7-7.1.1, A-12-3.2.2, A-13-3.6.1)

NFPA SPP-53, Butcher and Parnell, *Smoke Control in Fire Safety Design* [A-6-2.6.4.5(f), A-7-3.1]

B-1.2 Other Publications.

ASHRAE *Handbook and Product Directory — 1985 Fundamentals*, American Society of Heating, Refrigerating, and Air Conditioning Engineers, 1791 Tullie Circle, N.E., Atlanta, GA 30329 (A-5-2.3.2, A-7-3.1)

ANSI/ASME A17.1-1987, *Safety Code for Elevators and Escalators*, American Society of Mechanical Engineers, 345 East 47th St., New York, NY 10017 (A-7-4.1)

ANSI/ASME A17.3-1986, *Safety Code for Existing Elevators and Escalators*, American Society of Mechanical Engineers, 345 East 47th Street, New York, NY 10017 (A-7-4.1)

ANSI A117.1-1986, *Specifications for Making Buildings and Facilities Accessible to, and Usable by, the Physically Handicapped*, American National Standards Institute, 1430 Broadway, New York, NY 10018 (A-2-10, A-5-2.2.4.4, A-8-4.5, A-10-1.1.3)

Templer, J., Mullet, G., Archea, J., and Margulis, S., *An Analysis of the Behavior of Stair Users*, National Bureau of Standards NBS BSS 120. Available from National Technical Information Service (NTIS), Springfield, VA 22151 (A-5-2.2.4.4)

Klote and Fothergill, *Design of Smoke Control Systems for Buildings*, ASHRAE, 345 East 47th Street, New York, NY 10017 (A-5-2.3.2, A-7-3.1)

FF1-70, *Standard for the Surface Flammability of Carpets and Rugs* (Pill Test) (A-6-5.4.1)

Fisher, F., MacCracken, B., and Williamson, R. Brady, *Room Fire Experiments of Textile Wall Coverings*, ES-7853 for American Textile Manufacturers Institute, University of California Fire Research Laboratory, Berkeley, CA 94720, March, 1986 (A-6-5.2.3)

1985	1988
CHAPTER 1	
1-1	1-1
1-!.1	1-1.1
1-2	1-2
1-2.1	1-2.1
1-2.2	1-2.2
1-3	1-3
1-3.1	1-3.1
1-3.2	1-3.2
1-3.3	1-3.3
1-3.4	1-3.4
1-3.5	1-3.5
1-3.6	1-3.6
1-3.7	1-3.7
1-4	1-4
1-4.1	1-4.1
1-4.2	1-4.2
1-4.3	1-4.3
1-4.4	1-4.4
1-4.5	1-4.5
1-4.6	1-4.6
1-4.7	1-4.7
1-4.8	1-4.8
1-4.9	1-4.9
1-5	1-5
1-5.1	1-5.1
1-5.2	1-5.2
1-5.3	1-5.3
1-6	1-6
1-6.1	1-6.1
1-6.2	1-6.2
1-6.3	1-6.3
1-6.4	1-6.4
CHAPTER 2	
2-1	2-1
2-2	2-2
2-3	2-3
2-4	2-4
2-5	2-5
2-6	2-6
2-7	2-7
2-8	2-8
2-9	2-9
2-10	2-10
CHAPTER 3	
3-1	3-1
3-1.1	3-1.1
3-1.2	3-1.2
3-1.3	3-1.3
3-2	3-2
CHAPTER 4	
4-1	4-1
4-1.1	4-1.1
4-1.2	4-1.2
4-1.3	4-1.3
4-1.4	4-1.4
4-1.5	4-1.5

1985	1988
4-1.6	4-1.6
4-1.7	4-1.7
4-1.8	4-1.8
4-1.9	4-1.9
4-1.10	4-1.10
4-1.11	4-1.11
4-1.12	4-1.12
4-2	4-2
4-2.1	4-2.1
4-2.1.1	4-2.1.1
4-2.1.2	4-2.1.2
4-2.1.3	4-2.1.3
4-2.2	4-2.2
4-2.2.1	4-2.2.1
4-2.2.2	4-2.2.2
4-2.2.3	4-2.2.3
4-2.2.4	4-2.2.4
CHAPTER 5	
5-1.1	5-1.1
5-1.1.1	5-1.1.1
5-1.1.2	5-1.1.2
5-1.2	5-1.2
5-1.2.1	5-1.2.1
5-1.2.2	5-1.2.2
5-1.2.3	5-1.2.3
5-1.2.4	5-1.2.4
5-1.2.5	5-1.2.5
--	5-1.2.6
5-1.2.6	5-1.2.7
5-1.3	5-1.3
5-1.3.1	5-1.3.1
6-2.2.9	5-1.3.2
5-1.3.2	5-1.3.3
5-1.3.3	5-1.3.4
5-1.4	5-1.4
5-1.5	5-1.5
5-1.6	5-1.6
--	5-1.6.1
--	5-1.6.2
5-1.7	5-1.7
5-1.7.1	5-1.7.1
5-1.7.2	5-1.7.2
5-1.7.3	5-1.7.3
5-2	5-2
5-2.1	5-2.1
5-2.1.1	5-2.1.1
5-2.1.1.1	5-2.1.1.1
5-2.1.1.2	5-2.1.1.3
5-2.1.2	5-2.1.2
5-2.1.2.1	5-2.1.2.1
5-2.1.2.2	--
5-2.1.3	5-2.1.3
5-2.1.3.1	5-2.1.3.1
5-2.1.3.2	5-2.1.3.2
5-2.1.3.3	5-2.1.3.3
5-2.1.4	5-2.1.4
5-2.1.4.1	5-2.1.4.1
5-2.1.4.2	5-2.1.4.2
5-2.1.4.3	5-2.1.4.3

1985	1988
5-2.1.4.4	5-2.1.4.4
5-2.1.5	5-2.1.5
5-2.1.5.1	5-2.1.5.1
5-2.1.5.2	5-2.1.5.2
5-2.1.5.3	5-2.1.5.3
5-2.1.5.4	5-2.1.5.4
5-2.1.6	5-2.1.6
5-2.1.6.1	5-2.1.6.1
5-2.1.6.2	5-2.1.6.2
5-2.1.6.3	5-2.1.6.3
5-2.1.7	5-2.1.7
5-2.1.7.1	5-2.1.7.1
5-2.1.7.2	5-2.1.7.2
5-2.1.7.3	5-2.1.7.3
5-2.1.7.4	5-2.1.7.4
5-2.1.8	5-2.1.8
5-2.1.9	5-2.1.9
5-2.1.10	5-2.1.10
5-2.1.10.1	5-2.1.10.1
5-2.1.10.2	5-2.1.10.2
5-2.1.10.3	5-2.1.10.3
5-2.1.11	5-2.1.11
5-2.1.11.1	5-2.1.11.1
5-2.1.11.2	5-2.1.11.2
5-2.1.12	5-2.1.12
5-2.1.13	5-2.1.13
--	5-2.1.14
5-2.2	5-2.2
5-2.2.1	5-2.2.1
5-2.2.2	5-2.2.2
5-2.2.2.1	5-2.2.2.1
--	5-2.2.2.2
--	5-2.2.2.3
5-2.2.2.2	5-2.2.2.5
5-2.2.2.3	5-2.2.2.6
5-2.2.2.4	5-2.2.2.7
5-2.2.2.5	5-2.2.2.8
5-2.2.3	5-2.2.3
5-2.2.3.1	5-2.2.3.1 +
	5-2.2.3.6
--	5-2.2.3.2
5-2.2.3.2	5-2.2.3.3
5-2.2.3.3	5-2.2.3.4
5-2.2.3.4	5-2.2.3.5
5-2.2.3.5	5-2.2.5.2
5-2.2.4	5-2.2.4
5-2.2.4.1	5-2.2.4.1
5-2.2.4.2	5-2.2.4.2
5-2.2.4.3	5-2.2.4.3
5-2.2.4.4	5-2.2.4.4
5-2.2.4.5	5-1.6
5-2.2.4.6	5-2.2.4.5
5-2.2.4.7	5-2.2.5.3
5-2.2.4.8	5-2.2.2.3
5-2.2.4.9	5-2.2.4.6
5-2.2.4.10	5-2.2.4.7
5-2.2.5	5-2.2.5
5-2.2.5.1	5-2.2.5.1
5-2.2.5.2	--
5-2.2.5.3	--

1985	1988	1985	1988	1985	1988
5-2.2.5.4	--	--	5-2.5.4.6	5-3.1.1	5-3.1.1
5-2.2.6	5-2.2.6	5-2.5.5	5-2.5.5	5-3.1.2	5-3.1.2
5-2.2.6.1	5-2.2.6.1 +	5-2.5.5.1	5-2.5.5.1	5-3.1.3	5-3.1.3
	5-2.2.6.2	5-2.5.5.2	--	5-3.1.4	5-3.1.4
5-2.2.6.2	5-2.2.6.3	5-2.5.5.3	--	5-3.1.5	5-3.1.5
5-2.2.6.3	5-2.2.6.4	5-2.5.5.4	--	5-3.2	5-3.2
5-2.2.6.4	5-2.2.6.5	5-2.6	5-2.6	5-3.2.1	--
5-2.2.6.5	5-2.2.6.6	5-2.6.1	5-2.6.1	5-3.2.2	5-3.2
5-2.3	5-2.3	5-2.6.2	5-2.6.2	5-3.3	5-3.3
5-2.3.1	5-2.3.1	5-2.6.3	5-2.6.3		5-3.3.1
5-2.3.2	5-2.3.2	5-2.6.4	5-2.6.4		5-3.3.2
5-2.3.3	5-2.3.3	5-2.7	5-2.7	5-3.4	5-3.4
5-2.3.4	5-2.3.4	5-2.7.1	5-2.7.1	5-3.4.1	5-3.4.1
5-2.3.5	5-2.3.5	5-2.8	5-2.8	5-3.4.2	5-3.4.2
5-2.3.6	5-2.3.6	5-2.8.1	5-2.8.1	5-4	5-4
5-2.3.7	5-2.3.7	5-2.8.1.1	5-2.8.1.1	5-4.1	5-4.1
5-2.3.8	5-2.3.8	5-2.8.1.2	5-2.8.1.2	5-4.1.1	5-4.1.1
5-2.3.9	5-2.3.9	5-2.8.1.3	5-2.8.1.3	--	5-4.1.2
	5-2.3.9.1	5-2.8.1.4	5-2.8.1.4	--	5-4.1.3
--	5-2.3.9.2	5-2.8.1.5	5-2.8.1.5	5-5	5-5
5-2.3.10	5-2.3.10	5-2.8.1.6	5-2.8.1.6	5-5.1	5-5.1
5-2.3.10.1	5-2.3.10.1	5-2.8.1.7	5-2.8.1.7	5-5.1.1	5-5.1.1
5-2.3.10.2	5-2.3.10.2	5-2.8.2	5-2.8.2	5-5.1.2	5-5.1.2
5-2.3.11	5-2.3.11	5-2.8.2.1	5-2.8.2	5-5.1.3	5-5.1.3
5-2.3.12	5-2.3.12	5-2.8.3	5-2.8.3	--	5-5.1.4
5-2.3.13	5-2.3.13	5-2.8.3.1	5-2.8.3.1	5-5.1.4	5-5.1.5
5-2.4	5-2.4	5-2.8.3.2	5-2.8.3.2	5-5.1.5	5-5.1.6
5-2.4.1	5-2.4.1	5-2.8.3.3	5-2.8.3.3	5-5.1.6	5-5.1.7
5-2.4.2	5-2.4.2	5-2.8.4	5-2.8.4	5-5.2	5-5.2
5-2.4.2.1	5-2.4.2.1	5-2.8.5	5-2.8.5	5-5.2.1	5-5.2.1
5-2.4.2.2	5-2.4.2.2	5-2.8.5.1	5-2.8.5.1	5-5.2.2	5-5.2.2
5-2.4.2.3	5-2.4.2.3	5-2.8.5.2	5-2.8.5.2	5-5.3	5-5.3
5-2.4.2.4	5-2.4.2.4	5-2.8.6	5-2.8.6	5-5.3.1	5-5.3.1
5-2.4.3	5-2.4.3	5-2.8.6.1	5-2.8.6.1	5-5.3.2	5-5.3.2
5-2.4.3.1	5-2.4.3.1	5-2.8.6.2	--	5-5.3.3	5-5.3.3
5-2.4.3.2	5-2.4.3.2	5-2.8.6.3	5-2.8.6.2	5-5.3.4	5-5.3.4
5-2.4.3.3	5-2.4.3.4 +	5-2.8.7	5-2.8.7	5-5.3.5	5-5.3.5
	5-2.4.3.5	5-2.8.7.1	5-2.8.7.1	5-5.3.6	5-5.3.6
--	5-2.4.3.6	5-2.8.7.2	5-2.8.7.2	5-5.3.7	5-5.3.7
5-2.4.3.4	5-2.4.3.3	5-2.8.7.3	5-2.8.7.3	5-5.3.8	5-5.3.8
5-2.4.4	5-2.4.4	5-2.8.7.4	5-2.8.7.4	5-5.3.9	5-5.3.9
5-2.4.4.1	5-2.4.4.1	5-2.8.7.5	5-2.8.7.5	5-6	5-6
5-2.4.4.2	5-2.4.4.2	5-2.8.7.6	5-2.8.7.6	5-6.1	5-6.1
5-2.4.4.3	5-2.4.4.3	5-2.8.7.7	5-2.8.7.7	5-6.2	5-6.2
5-2.4.4.4	5-2.4.4.4	5-2.8.7.8	5-2.8.7.8	5-6.3	5-6.3
5-2.4.4.5	5-2.4.4.5	5-2.8.7.9	5-2.8.7.9	5-6.4	--
5-2.4.4.6	5-2.4.4.6	5-2.8.8	5-2.8.8	5-6.5	5-6.4
5-2.4.4.7	--	5-2.8.8.1	5-2.8.8.1	--	5-6.5
5-2.4.4.8	5-2.4.4.7	5-2.8.8.2	5-2.8.8.2	5-6.6	5-6.6
5-2.5	5-2.5	5-2.9	5-2.9	5-7	5-7
5-2.5.1	5-2.5.1	5-2.9.1	5-2.9.1	5-7.1	5-7.1
5-2.5.2	5-2.5.2	5-2.9.2	5-2.9.2	5-7.2	5-7.2
5-2.5.3	5-2.5.3	5-2.10	5-2.10	5-7.3	5-7.3
5-2.5.3.1	5-2.5.3.1	5-2.10.1	5-2.10.1	5-7.4	5-7.4
5-2.5.3.2	5-2.5.3.2	5-2.10.1.1	5-2.10.1.1	5-7.5	5-7.5
5-2.5.3.3	5-2.5.3.3	5-2.10.1.2	5-2.10.1.2	5-8	5-8
5-2.5.3.4	5-2.5.3.4	5-2.10.1.3	5-2.10.1.3	5-8.1	5-8.1
5-2.5.3.5	5-2.5.3.5	5-2.10.2	5-2.10.2	5-8.1.1	5-8.1.1
5-2.5.4	5-2.5.4	5-2.10.2.1	5-2.10.2.1	5-8.1.2	5-8.1.2
5-2.5.4.1	5-2.5.4.1	5-2.10.2.2	5-2.10.2.2	5-8.1.3	5-8.1.3
5-2.5.4.2	5-2.5.4.2	--	5-2.11	5-8.1.4	5-8.1.4
5-2.5.4.3	--	--	5-2.11.1	5-8.1.5	5-8.1.5
5-2.5.4.4	5-2.5.4.3	--	5-2.11.2	5-8.2	5-8.2
5-2.5.4.5	5-2.5.4.4	5-3	5-3	5-8.2.1	5-8.2.1
5-2.5.4.6	5-2.5.4.5	5-3.1	5-3.1	5-8.2.2	5-8.2.2

1985	1988
5-9	5-9
5-9.1	5-9.1
5-9.1.1	5-9.1.1
5-9.1.2	5-9.1.2
5-9.2	5-9.2
5-9.2.1	5-9.2.1
5-9.2.2	5-9.2.2
5-9.2.3	5-9.2.3
5-9.2.4	5-9.2.4
5-9.3	5-9.3
5-10	5-10
5-10.1	5-10.1
5-10.1.1	5-10.1.1 +
	5-10.1.2
5-10.1.2	5-10.1.3
5-10.1.3	5-10.1.4
5-10.1.4	5-10.1.5
5-10.2	5-10.2
5-10.3	5-10.3
5-10.3.1	5-10.3.1
5-10.3.2	5-10.3.2
5-10.3.3	5-10.3.3
5-10.3.4	5-10.3.4
5-10.3.5	5-10.3.5
5-10.3.6	5-10.3.6
5-10.4	--
5-10.4.1	5-10.4.1
5-10.4.1.1	5-10.4.1.1
5-10.4.1.2	A-5-10.4.1.1
--	5-10.4.1.2
5-10.4.2	5-10.4.2
5-10.4.2.1	5-10.4.2
5-11	5-11
5-11.1	5-11.1
5-11.2	5-11.2
5-11.3	5-11.3
5-11.4	5-11.4

CHAPTER 6

1985	1988
6-1	6-1
6-1.1	6-1.1
6-1.1.1	6-1.1.1
6-2	6-2
6-2.1	6-2.1
6-2.2	6-2.2
6-2.2.1	6-2.2.1
6-2.2.2	6-2.2.2
--	6-2.3
6-2.2.3	6-2.4
6-2.2.3.1	6-2.4.1
6-2.2.3.2	6-2.4.2
6-2.2.3.3	6-2.4.3
6-2.2.3.4	6-2.4.4
6-2.2.3.5	6-2.4.5
6-2.2.3.6	6-2.4.6
6-2.2.3.7	6-2.4.7
6-2.2.4	6-2.3.1
6-2.2.5	6-2.3.2
6-2.2.6	6-2.3.3
--	6-2.3.4
6-2.2.7	6-2.3.4.1
6-2.2.8	6-2.3.4.2
6-2.2.9	5-1.3.2
6-2.2.10	6-2.3.5
6-2.2.11	6-2.3.6

1985	1988
6-2.3	6-2.5
6-2.3.1	6-2.5.1
6-2.3.2	6-2.5.2
6-3	6-3
6-3.1	6-3.1
6-3.2	6-3.2
--	6-3.3
6-3.3	6-3.4
6-3.3.1	6-3.4.1
6-3.3.2	6-3.4.2
6-3.3.3	6-3.4.3
6-3.4	6-3.5
6-3.4.1	6-3.5.1
6-3.4.2	6-3.5.2
6-3.4.3	6-3.5.3
6-3.5	6-3.6
6-3.5.1	6-3.6.1
6-3.5.2	6-3.6.2
6-4	6-4
6-4.1	6-4.1
6-4.2	6-4.2
6-4.3	6-4.3
--	6-4.4
6-5	6-5
6-5.1	6-5.1
--	6-5.1.1
6-5.1.1	6-5.1.2 +
	6-5.2.5
6-5.1.2	6-5.1.3 +
	6-5.2.2
6-5.1.3	6-5.2.4
6-5.1.4	6-5.3.4
6-5.2	6-5.3
6-5.2.1	6-5.3.2
6-5.2.2	6-5.3.1
6-5.2.3	--
6-5.2.4	6-5.1.4
6-5.3	6-5.4
6-5.3.1	6-5.4.2
6-5.3.2	6-5.4.1
6-5.4	6-5.6
6-5.4.1	6-5.6.1
6-5.4.2	6-5.6.2
6-5.5	6-5.7
6-5.5.1	6-5.7.1
6-5.5.2	6-5.7.2
6-5.6	6-5.5
6-5.7	6-5.2
6-5.7.1	6-5.3.3 +
	6-5.4.3
6-5.7.2	6-5.2.3

CHAPTER 7

1985	1988
7-1	7-1
7-1.1	7-1.1
7-1.2	7-1.2
7-2	7-2
7-2.1	7-2.1
7-2.2	7-2.2
7-2.3	7-2.3
7-3	7-3
7-3.1	7-3.1
7-4	7-4
7-4.1	7-4.1
7-4.2	7-4.2

1985	1988
7-4.3	7-4.3
7-4.4	7-4.4
7-4.5	7-4.5
7-5	7-5
7-5.1	7-5.1
7-5.2	7-5.2
7-5.3	7-5.3
7-6	7-6
7-6.1	7-6.1
7-6.1.1	7-6.1.1
7-6.1.2	7-6.1.2
7-6.1.3	7-6.1.3
7-6.1.4	7-6.1.4
7-6.1.5	7-6.1.7
7-6.1.6	7-6.1.5
--	7-6.1.6
7-6.2	7-6.2
7-6.2.1	7-6.2.1
7-6.2.2	7-6.2.2
7-6.2.3	7-6.2.3
7-6.2.4	7-6.2.4
7-6.2.5	7-6.2.5
7-6.2.6	7-6.2.6
--	7-6.2.7
--	7-6.2.8
7-6.2.7	7-6.2.9
7-6.3	7-6.3
7-6.3.1	7-6.3.1
7-6.3.2	7-6.3.2
7-6.3.3	7-6.3.3
7-6.3.4	7-6.3.4
7-6.3.5	7-6.3.5
7-6.3.6	7-6.3.6
7-6.3.7	7-6.3.7
7-6.3.8	7-6.3.8
7-6.3.9	7-6.3.9
7-6.3.10	7-6.3.10
7-6.4	7-6.4
7-6.5	7-6.5
7-6.5.1	7-6.5.1
7-6.5.2	7-6.5.2
7-6.5.3	7-6.5.3
7-6.5.4	7-6.5.4
7-6.5.5	7-6.5.5
7-6.6	7-6.6
7-6.6.1	7-6.6.1
7-6.6.2	--
7-7	7-7
7-7.1	7-7.1
7-7.1.1	7-7.1.1
7-7.1.2	7-7.1.2
7-7.1.3	7-7.1.3
7-7.1.4	--
7-7.2	7-7.2
7-7.2.1	7-7.2.1
7-7.2.2	7-7.2.2
7-7.2.3	7-7.2.3
7-7.3	7-7.3
7-7.4	
7-7.4.1	
7-7.4.2	

CHAPTER 8

1985	1988
8-1	8-1
8-1.1	8-1.1

1985	1988
8-1.2	8-1.2
8-1.2.1	8-1.2.1
8-1.2.2	8-1.2.2
8-1.2.3	8-1.2.3
8-1.2.4	8-1.2.4
8-1.3	8-1.3
8-1.4	8-1.4
8-1.4.1	8-1.4.1
8-1.5	8-1.5
8-1.6	8-1.6
8-1.7	8-1.7
8-1.7.1	8-1.7.1
8-1.7.2	8-1.7.2
8-1.7.3	8-1.7.3
8-2	8-2
8-2.1	8-2.1
8-2.2	8-2.2
8-2.2.1	8-2.2.1 through
	8-2.2.7
8-2.2.2	8-2.2.2.6
8-2.3	8-2.3
8-2.3.1	8-2.3.1
--	8-2.3.2
8-2.3.2	8-2.3.3
8-2.3.3	8-2.3.4
8-2.4	8-2.4
8-2.4.1	8-2.4.1
8-2.4.2	8-2.4.2
8-2.4.3	8-2.4.3
--	8-2.4.4
--	8-2.4.5
--	8-2.4.6
8-2.5	8-2.5
8-2.5.1	8-2.5.1
8-2.5.2	8-2.5.2
--	8-2.5.3
8-2.5.3	8-2.5.4
8-2.5.3(a)	8-2.5.4.1
8-2.5.3(b)	8-2.5.4.2
8-2.5.3(c)	8-2.5.4.3 +
	8-2.5.4.4
8-2.5.3(d)	8-2.5.4.5
8-2.5.3(e)	8-2.5.4.6
8-2.5.3(f)	8-2.5.4.2
8-2.5.4	8-2.5.5
8-2.5.5	8-2.5.6
8-2.5.5.1	--
8-2.5.5.2	8-2.5.6.6
8-2.5.5.3	8-2.5.6.3
8-2.5.5.4	8-2.5.6.4
8-2.5.5.5	--
8-2.5.5.6	--
8-2.5.5.7	8-2.5.4.7
8-2.5.5.8	8-2.5.4.8
8-2.5.5.9	8-2.5.6.8
8-2.5.5.10	8-2.5.6.9
8-2.5.5.11	8-2.5.6.10
8-2.6	8-2.6
8-2.7	8-2.7
8-2.7.1	8-2.7.1
8-2.7.2	--
8-2.7.3	8-2.7.2
8-2.7.4	8-2.7.3
8-2.8	8-2.8
8-2.8.1	8-2.8

1985	1988
8-2.8.2	5-8.1.3
8-2.9	8-2.9
8-2.10	8-2.10
8-2.11	8-2.11
8-2.11.1	8-2.2.2.3
8-2.11.2	8-2.2.2.2
8-2.11.3	8-2.11.1
8-3	8-3
8-3.1	8-3.1
8-3.2	8-3.2
8-3.2.1	8-3.2.1
8-3.2.1.1	8-3.2.1.1
8-3.2.1.2	8-3.2.1.2
8-3.2.1.3	8-3.2.1.3
8-3.2.1.4	8-3.2.1.4
8-3.2.1.5	8-3.2.1.5
8-3.2.1.6	8-3.2.1.6
8-3.2.1.7	8-3.2.1.7
8-3.2.1.8	8-3.2.1.8
8-3.2.1.9	8-3.2.1.9
8-3.2.1.10	8-3.2.1.10
8-3.2.1.11	8-3.2.1.11
8-3.2.2	8-3.2.2
8-3.2.2.1	8-3.2.2.1
8-3.2.2.2	8-3.2.2.2
8-3.2.2.3	8-3.2.2.3
8-3.2.2.4	8-3.2.2.4
8-3.2.2.5	8-3.2.2.5
8-3.2.2.6	8-3.2.2.6
8-3.2.2.7	8-3.2.2.7
8-3.2.2.8	8-3.2.2.8
8-3.2.3	8-3.2.3
8-3.2.3.1	8-3.2.3.1
8-3.2.3.2	8-3.2.3.2
8-3.2.3.3	8-3.2.3.3
8-3.2.4	8-3.2.4
8-3.2.4.1	8-3.2.4.1
8-3.2.4.2	8-3.2.4.2
8-3.2.4.3	8-3.2.4.3
8-3.3	8-3.3
8-3.3.1	8-3.3.1
8-3.3.2	8-3.3.2
8-3.3.3	8-3.3.3
8-3.3.4	8-3.3.4
8-3.4	8-3.4
8-3.4.1	8-3.4.1
8-3.4.2	8-3.4.2
8-3.4.3	8-3.4.3
8-3.4.3.1	8-3.4.3.1
8-3.4.3.2	8-3.4.3.2
8-3.4.3.3	8-3.4.3.3
8-3.4.3.4	8-3.4.3.4
8-3.5	8-3.5
8-3.5.1	8-3.5.1
--	8-3.6
--	8-3.6.1
8-4	8-4
8-4.1	8-4.1
8-4.1.1	8-4.1.1
8-4.1.2	8-4.1.2
8-4.1.3	8-4.1.3
8-4.1.4	--
8-4.1.5	8-4.1.4
8-4.1.6	8-4.1.5
--	8-4.2

1985	1988
8-4.2	8-4.3
8-4.2.1	8-4.3.1
8-4.3	8-4.4
8-4.3.1	8-4.4.1
8-4.3.2	8-4.4.3
8-4.3.3	8-4.4.2
8-4.4	8-4.5
--	8-4.6
8-4.5	8-4.7
8-5	8-5
8-5.1	8-5.1
8-5.2	8-5.2
8-5.3	8-5.3
8-5.4	8-5.4

CHAPTER 9

1985	1988
9-1	9-1
9-1.1	9-1.1
9-1.1.1	9-1.1.1
9-1.1.2	9-1.1.2
9-1.1.3	9-1.1.3
9-1.2	9-1.2
9-1.2.1	9-1.2.1
9-1.2.2	9-1.2.2
9-1.2.3	9-1.2.3
9-1.2.4	9-1.2.4
9-1.3	9-1.3
9-1.4	9-1.4
9-1.4.1	9-1.4.1
9-1.5	9-1.5
9-1.6	9-1.6
9-1.7	9-1.7
9-1.7.1	9-1.7.1
9-1.7.2	9-1.7.2
9-1.7.3	9-1.7.3
9-2	9-2
9-2.1	9-2.1
9-2.2	9-2.2
9-2.2.1	9-2.2.1 through
	9-2.2.9
9-2.2.2	9-2.2.2.6
9-2.3	9-2.3
9-2.3.1	9-2.3.1
--	9-2.3.2
9-2.3.2	9-2.3.3
9-2.3.1	9-2.3.1
--	9-2.3.2
9-2.3.2	9-2.3.3
9-2.3.3	9-2.3.4
9-2.4	9-2.4
9-2.4.1	9-2.4.1
9-2.4.2	9-2.4.2
9-2.4.3	9-2.4.3
--	9-2.4.4
--	9-2.4.5
--	9-2.4.6
9-2.5	9-2.5
9-2.5.1	9-2.5.1
9-2.5.2	9-2.5.2
--	9-2.5.3
9-2.5.3	9-2.5.4
9-2.5.3(a)	9-2.5.4.1
9-2.5.3(b)	9-2.5.4.2
9-2.5.3(c)	9-2.5.4.3 +
	9-2.5.4.4

1985	1988	1985	1988	1985	1988
9-2.5.3(d)	9-2.5.4.5	9-3.3.2	9-3.3.2	10-2.3.3.1	10-2.3.3.1
9-2.5.3(e)	9-2.5.4.6	9-3.3.3	9-3.3.3	10-2.3.3.2	10-2.3.3.2
9-2.5.3(f)	9-2.5.4.2	9-3.3.4	9-3.3.4	10-2.4	10-2.4
9-2.5.4	9-2.5.5	9-3.4	9-3.4	10-2.4.1	10-2.4
9-2.5.5	9-2.5.6	9-3.4.1	9-3.4.1	10-2.5	10-2.5
9-2.5.5.1	--	9-3.4.2	9-3.4.2	10-2.5.1	10-2.5.1
9-2.5.5.2	9-2.5.6.6	9-3.4.3	9-3.4.3	10-2.5.2	10-2.5.2
9-2.5.5.3	9-2.5.6.3	9-3.4.3.1	9-3.4.3.1	10-2.5.3	10-2.5.3
9-2.5.5.4	9-2.5.6.4	9-3.4.3.2	9-3.4.3.2	10-2.5.4	10-2.5.4
9-2.5.5.5	--	9-3.4.3.3	9-3.4.3.3	10-2.5.4.1	10-2.5.4.1
9-2.5.5.6	--	9-3.4.3.4	9-3.4.3.4	10-2.5.5	10-2.5.5
9-2.5.5.7	9-2.5.4.7	9-3.5	9-3.5	10-2.5.5.1	10-2.5.5.1
9-2.5.5.8	9-2.5.4.8	9-3.5.1	9-3.5.1	10-2.5.5.2	10-2.5.5.2
9-2.5.5.9	9-2.5.6.8	--	9-3.6	10-2.6	10-2.6
9-2.5.5.10	9-2.5.6.9	--	9-3.6.1	10-2.7	10-2.7
9-2.5.5.11	9-2.5.6.10	9-4	9-4	10-2.8	10-2.8
9-2.6	9-2.6	9-4.1	9-4.1	10-2.9	10-2.9
9-2.7	9-2.7	--	9-4.2	10-2.10	10-2.10
9-2.7.1	9-2.7.1	9-4.2	9-4.3	10-2.11	10-2.11
9-2.7.2	--	9-4.2.1	9-4.3.1	10-2.11.1	10-2.2.2.4
9-2.7.3	9-2.7.2	9-4.3	9-4.4	10-2.11.2	10-2.2.2.5
9-2.7.4	9-2.7.3	9-4.3.1	9-4.4.1	10-2.11.3	10-2.2.2.2
9-2.8	9-2.8	9-4.3.2	9-4.4.3	10-2.11.4	10-2.2.2.3
9-2.8.1	9-2.8	9-4.3.3	9-4.4.2	10-2.11.5	10-2.11.1
9-2.8.2	5-8.1.3	--	9-4.5	10-3	10-3
9-2.9	9-2.9	--	9-4.5	10-3.1	10-3.1
9-2.10	9-2.10	--	9-4.6	10-3.1.1	10-3.1.1
9-2.11	9-2.11	9-4.5	9-4.7	10-3.1.2	10-3.1.2
9-2.11.1	9-2.2.2.3	9-5	9-5	10-3.2	10-3.2
9-2.11.2	9-2.2.2.2	9-5.1	9-5.1	10-3.2.1	10-3.2.1
9-2.11.3	9-2.11.1	9-5.2	9-5.2	10-3.2.2	10-3.2.2
9-3	9-3	9-5.3	9-5.3	10-3.2.3	10-3.2.3
9-3.1	9-3.1	9-5.4	9-5.4	10-3.2.4	10-3.2.4
9-3.2	9-3.2			10-3.2.5	10-3.2.5
9-3.2.1	9-3.2.1	**CHAPTER 10**		10-3.3	10-3.3
--	9-3.2.1.1	10-1	10-1	10-3.3.1	10-3.3.1
--	9-3.2.1.2	10-1.1	10-1.1	10-3.3.2	10-3.3.2
--	9-3.2.1.3	10-1.1.1	10-1.1.1	10-3.4	10-3.4
--	9-3.2.1.4	10-1.1.2	10-2.1.2	10-3.4.1	10-3.4.1
9-3.2.1.1	9-3.2.1.5	10-1.1.3	10-1.1.2	10-3.4.2	10-3.4.2
9-3.2.1.2	9-3.2.1.7	10-1.1.4	10-1.1.3	10-3.4.2.1	10-3.4.2.1
--	9-3.2.1.8	10-1.2	10-1.2	10-3.4.2.2	10-3.4.2.2
9-3.2.1.3	9-3.2.1.9	10-1.2.1	10-1.2.1	10-3.4.3	10-3.4.3
9-3.2.1.4	9-3.2.1.10	10-1.2.2	10-1.2.2	10-3.4.3.1	10-3.4.3.1
9-3.2.1.5	9-3.2.1.6	10-1.3	10-1.3	10-3.4.3.2	10-3.4.3.2
9-3.2.1.6	9-3.2.1.12	10-1.4	10-1.4	10-3.5	10-3.5
9-3.2.2	9-3.2.2	10-1.4.1	10-1.4.1	10-3.5.1	10-3.5.1
9-3.2.2.1	9-3.2.2.1	10-1.4.2	10-1.4.2	10-3.6	10-3.6
9-3.2.2.2	9-3.2.2.2	10-1.4.3	10-1.4.3	10-3.6.1	10-3.6.1
9-3.2.2.3	9-3.2.2.3	10-1.4.4	10-1.4.4	--	10-3.6.2
9-3.2.2.4	9-3.2.2.4	10-1.4.5	10-1.4.5	10-3.7	10-3.7
9-3.2.2.5	9-3.2.2.5	10-1.5	10-1.5	10-3.7.1	10-3.7.1
9-3.2.2.6	9-3.2.2.6	10-1.6	10-1.6	10-3.7.2	10-3.7.2
9-3.2.2.7	9-3.2.2.7	10-1.7	10-1.7	10-4	10-4
9-3.2.2.8	9-3.2.2.8	10-1.7.1	10-1.7.1	10-4.1	10-4.1
9-3.2.3	9-3.2.3	10-1.7.2	10-1.7.2	10-4.1.1	10-4.1.1
9-3.2.3.1	9-3.2.3.1	10-1.7.3	10-1.7.3	10-4.1.2	10-4.1.2
--	9-3.2.3.2	10-1.7.4	10-1.7.4	10-4.1.3	10-4.1.3
9-3.2.3.2	9-3.2.3.3	10-2.1	10-2.1 +	10-4.1.4	10-4.1.4
9-3.2.4	9-3.2.4		10-2.1.1	10-4.1.5	10-4.1.5
9-3.2.4.1	9-3.2.4.1	10-2.2	10-2.2	10-4.1.6	10-4.1.6
9-3.2.4.2	9-3.2.4.2	10-2.3	10-2.3	10-4.2	10-4.3
9-3.2.4.3	9-3.2.4.3	10-2.3.1	10-2.3.1	10-4.3	10-4.4
9-3.3	9-3.3	10-2.3.2	10-2.3.2	10-5	10-5
9-3.3.1	9-3.3.1	10-2.3.3	10-2.3.3	10-5.1	10-5.1

1985	1988	1985	1988	1985	1988
10-5.2	10-5.2 +	10-7.3.5.1	10-7.3.5.1	10-9.1.7	10-9.1.7
	10-5.2.1	10-7.3.6	10-7.3.6	10-9.2	10-9.2
10-5.3	10-5.3	10-7.4	10-7.4	10-9.2.1	10-9.2.1
10-5.4	10-5.4	10-7.5	10-7.5	10-9.2.2	10-9.2.2
10-6	10-6	10-7.5.1	10-7.5.1	10-9.2.3	10-9.2.3
10-6.1	10-6.1	10-7.5.1.1	10-7.5.1.1	10-9.2.4	10-9.2.4
10-6.1.1	10-6.1.1	10-7.5.1.2	10-7.5.1.2	10-9.2.4.1	10-9.2.4.1
10-6.2	10-6.2	10-7.5.2	10-7.5.2	10-9.2.4.2	10-9.2.4.2
10-6.2.1	--	10-7.5.3	10-7.5.3	10-9.2.4.3	--
10-6.2.1.1	10-6.2.1	10-7.5.4	10-7.5.4	10-9.2.5	10-9.2.5
10-6.2.1.2	10-6.2.2	10-8	10-8	10-9.2.6	10-9.2.6
10-6.2.1.3	10-6.2.3	10-8.1	10-8.1	10-9.2.7	10-9.2.7
10-6.2.1.4	10-6.2.4	10-8.1.1	10-8.1.1	10-9.2.8	10-9.2.8
10-6.2.1.5	10-6.2.5	10-8.1.1.1	10-8.1.1.1	10-9.2.9	10-9.2.9
10-7	10-7	10-8.1.2	10-8.1.2	10-9.2.10	10-9.2.10
10-7.1	10-7.1	10-8.1.3	10-8.1.3	10-9.2.11	10-9.2.11
10-7.1.1	10-7.1.1	10-8.1.4	10-8.1.4	10-9.2.11.1	10-9.2.11.1
10-7.1.1.1	10-7.1.1.1	10-8.1.5	10-8.1.5	10-9.2.11.2	10-9.2.11.2
10-7.1.1.2	10-7.1.1.2	10-8.1.6	10-8.1.6	10-9.2.11.3	10-9.2.11.3
10-7.1.1.3	10-7.1.1.3	10-8.1.7	10-8.1.7	10-9.3	10-9.3
10-7.1.1.4	10-7.1.1.4	10-8.2	10-8.2	10-9.3.1	10-9.3.1
10-7.1.2	10-7.1.2	10-8.2.1	10-8.2.1	10-9.3.2	10-9.3.2
10-7.1.3	10-7.1.3	10-8.2.2	10-8.2.2	10-9.3.3	10-9.3.3
10-7.1.4	10-7.1.4	10-8.2.3	10-8.2.3	10-9.3.3.1	10-9.3.3.1
10-7.1.5	10-7.1.5	10-8.2.4	10-8.2.4	10-9.3.3.2	10-9.3.3.2
10-7.1.6	10-7.1.6	10-8.2.4.1	10-8.2.4.1	10-9.3.4	10-9.3.4
10-7.1.6.1	10-7.1.6.1	10-8.2.4.2	10-8.2.4.2	10-9.3.4.1	10-9.3.4.1
10-7.1.6.2	10-7.1.6.2	10-8.2.4.3	10-8.2.4.3	10-9.3.4.2	10-9.3.4.2
10-7.1.7	10-7.1.7	10-8.2.5	10-8.2.5	--	10-9.3.4.3
10-7.2	10-7.2	10-8.2.6	10-8.2.6	10-9.3.4.3	--
10-7.2.1	10-7.2.1	10-8.2.7	10-8.2.7	10-9.4	10-9.4
10-7.2.2	10-7.2.2	10-8.2.8	10-8.2.8	10-9.5	10-9.5
10-7.2.2.1	10-7.2.2.1	10-8.2.9	10-8.2.9	10-9.5.1	10-9.5.1
10-7.2.2.2	10-7.2.2.2	10-8.2.10	10-8.2.10	10-9.5.1.1	10-9.5.1.1
10-7.2.3	10-7.2.3	10-8.2.11	10-8.2.11	10-9.5.1.2	10-9.5.1.2
10-7.2.4	10-7.2.4	10-8.2.11.1	10-8.2.11.1	10-9.5.2	10-9.5.2
10-7.2.4.1	10-7.2.4.1	10-8.2.11.2	10-8.2.11.2	10-9.5.2.1	10-9.5.2.1
10-7.2.4.2	10-7.2.4.2	10-8.3	10-8.3		
10-7.2.5	10-7.2.5	10-8.3.1	10-8.3.1	CHAPTER 11	
10-7.2.6	10-7.2.6	10-8.3.2	10-8.3.2	11-1	11-1
10-7.2.6.1	10-7.2.6.1	10-8.3.3	10-8.3.3	11-1.1	11-1.1
10-7.2.6.2	10-7.2.6.2	10-8.3.3.1	10-8.3.3.1	11-1.1.1	11-1.1.1
10-7.2.7	10-7.2.7	10-8.3.3.2	10-8.3.3.2	11-1.1.2	11-2.1.2
10-7.2.8	10-7.2.8	10-8.3.4	10-8.3.4	11-1.1.3	11-1.1.3
10-7.2.9	10-7.2.9	10-8.3.4.1	10-8.3.4.1	11-1.2	11.1.2
10-7.2.10	10-7.2.10	10-8.3.4.2	10-8.3.4.2	11-1.2.1	11-1.2.1
10-7.2.11	10-7.2.11	10-8.3.4.3	10-8.3.4.3	11-1.2.2	11-1.2.2
10-7.2.11.1	10-7.2.11.1	10-8.4	10-8.4	11-1.3	11-1.3
10-7.2.11.2	10-7.2.11.2	10-8.5	10-8.5	11-1.4	11-1.4
--	10-7.2.11.3	10-8.5.1	10-8.5.1	11-1.4.1	11-1.4.1
--	10-7.2.11.4	10-8.5.1.1	10-8.5.1.1	11-1.4.2	11-1.4.2
10-7.3	10-7.3	10-8.5.1.2	10-8.5.1.2	11-1.4.3	11-1.4.3
10-7.3.1	10-7.3.1	10-8.5.2	10-8.5.2	11-1.4.4	11-1.4.4
10-7.3.2	10-7.3.2 +	10-8.5.2.1	10-8.5.2.1	11-1.4.5	11-1.4.5
	10-7.3.2.1	10-8.5.2.2	10-8.5.2.1	11-1.5	11-1.5
10-7.3.3	10-7.3.3	10-9	10-9	11-1.6	11-1.6
10-7.3.3.1	10-7.3.3.1	10-9.1	10-9.1	11-1.7	11-1.7
10-7.3.3.2	10-7.3.3.2	10-9.1.1	10-9.1.1	11-1.7.1	11-1.7.1
10-7.3.4	10-7.3.4	10-9.1.1.1	10-9.1.1.1	11-1.7.2	11-1.7.2
10-7.3.4.1	10-7.3.4.1	--	10-9.1.1.2	11-1.7.3	11-1.7.3
10-7.3.4.2	10-7.3.4.2	10-9.1.2	10-9.1.2	11-1.7.4	11-1.7.4
10-7.3.4.3	10-7.3.4.3	10-9.1.3	10-9.1.3	11-2.1	11-2.1 +
10-7.3.4.4	10-7.3.4.4	10-9.1.4	10-9.1.4		11-2.1.1
10-7.3.4.5	10-7.3.4.5	10-9.1.5	10-9.1.5	11-2.2	11-2.2
10-7.3.5	10-7.3.5	10-9.1.6	10-9.1.6	11-2.3	11-2.3

1985	1988
11-2.3.1	11-2.3.1
11-2.3.2	11-2.3.2
11-2.3.3	11-2.3.3
11-2.3.3.1	11-2.3.3.1
11-2.3.3.2	11-2.3.3.2
11-2.4	11-2.4
11-2.4.1	11-2.4
11-2.5	11-2.5
11-2.5.1	11-2.5.1
11-2.5.2	11-2.5.2
11-2.5.3	11-2.5.3
11-2.5.4	11-2.5.4
11-2.5.4.1	11-2.5.4.1
11-2.5.5	11-2.5.5
11-2.5.5.1	11-2.5.5.1
11-2.5.5.2	11-2.5.5.2
11-2.6	11-2.6
11-2.7	11-2.7
11-2.8	11-2.8
11-2.9	11-2.9
11-2.10	11-2.10
11-2.11	11-2.11
11-2.11.1	11-2.2.2.4
11-2.11.2	11-2.2.2.5
11-2.11.3	11-2.2.2.2
11-2.11.4	11-2.2.2.3
11-2.11.5	11-2.11.1
11-3	11-3
11-3.1	11-3.1
11-3.1.1	11-3.1.1
11-3.1.2	11-3.1.2
11-3.2	11-3.2
11-3.2.1	11-3.2.1
11-3.2.2	11-3.2.2
11-3.2.3	11-3.2.3
11-3.2.4	11-3.2.4
11-3.2.5	11-3.2.5
11-3.3	11-3.3
11-3.3.1	11-3.3.1
11-3.3.2	11-3.3.2
11-3.4	11-3.4
11-3.4.1	11-3.4.1
11-3.4.2	11-3.4.2
11-3.4.2.1	11-3.4.2.1
11-3.4.2.2	11-3.4.2.2
11-3.4.3	11-3.4.3
11-3.4.3.1	11-3.4.3.1
11-3.4.3.2	11-3.4.3.2
11-3.5	11-3.5
11-3.5.1	11-3.5.1
11-3.6	11-3.6
11-3.6.1	11-3.6.1
--	11-3.6.2
11-3.7	11-3.7
11-3.7.1	11-3.7.1
11-3.7.2	11-3.7.2
11-4	11-4
11-4.1	11-4.1
11-4.2	11-4.3
11-4.3	11-4.4
11-5	11-5
11-5.1	11-5.1
11-5.2	11-5.2 +
	11-5.2.1
11-5.3	11-5.3

1985	1988
11-5.4	11-5.4
11-6	11-6
11-6.1	11-6.1
11-6.1.1	11-6.1.1
11-6.2	11-6.2
11-6.2.1	--
11-6.2.1.1	11-6.2.1
11-6.2.1.2	11-6.2.2
11-6.2.1.3	11-6.2.3
11-6.2.1.4	11-6.2.4
11-6.2.1.5	11-6.2.5
11-7	11-7
11-7.1	11-7.1
11-7.1.1	11-7.1.1
11-7.1.1.1	11-7.1.1.1
11-7.1.1.2	11-7.1.1.2
11-7.1.1.3	11-7.1.1.3
11-7.1.1.4	11-7.1.1.4
11-7.1.2	11-7.1.2
11-7.1.3	11-7.1.3
11-7.1.4	11-7.1.4
11-7.1.5	11-7.1.5
11-7.1.6	11-7.1.6
11-7.1.6.1	11-7.1.6.1
11-7.1.6.2	11-7.1.6.2
11-7.1.7	11-7.1.7
11-7.2	11-7.2
11-7.2.1	11-7.2.1
11-7.2.2	11-7.2.2
11-7.2.2.1	11-7.2.2.1
11-7.2.2.2	11-7.2.2.2
11-7.2.3	11-7.2.3
11-7.2.4	11-7.2.4
11-7.2.4.1	11-7.2.4.1
11-7.2.4.2	11-7.2.4.2
11-7.2.5	11-7.2.5
11-7.2.6	11-7.2.6
11-7.2.6.1	11-7.2.6.1
11-7.2.6.2	11-7.2.6.2
11-7.2.7	11-7.2.7
11-7.2.8	11-7.2.8
11-7.2.9	11-7.2.9
11-7.2.10	11-7.2.10
11-7.2.11	11-7.2.11
11-7.2.11.1	11-7.2.11.1
11-7.2.11.2	11-7.2.11.2
--	11-7.2.11.3
--	11-7.2.11.4
11-7.3	11-7.3
11-7.3.1	11-7.3.1
11-7.3.2	11-7.3.2 +
	11-7.3.2.1
11-7.3.3	11-7.3.3
11-7.3.3.1	11-7.3.3.1
11-7.3.4	11-7.3.4
11-7.3.4.1	11-7.3.4.1
11-7.3.4.2	11-7.3.4.2
11-7.3.4.3	11-7.3.4.3
11-7.3.4.4	11-7.3.4.4
11-7.3.4.5	11-7.3.4.5
11-7.3.5	11-7.3.5
11-7.3.5.1	11-7.3.5.1
11-7.3.6	11-7.3.6
11-7.4	11-7.4
11-7.5	11-7.5

1985	1988
11-7.5.1	11-7.5.1
11-7.5.1.1	11-7.5.1.1
11-7.5.1.2	11-7.5.1.2
11-7.5.2	11-7.5.2
11-7.5.3	11-7.5.3
11-7.5.4	11-7.5.4
11-8	11-8
11-8.1	11-8.1
11-8.1.1	11-8.1.1
11-8.1.1.1	11-8.1.1.1
11-8.1.2	11-8.1.2
11-8.1.3	11-8.1.3
11-8.1.4	11-8.1.4
11-8.1.5	11-8.1.5
11-8.1.6	11-8.1.6
11-8.1.7	11-8.1.7
11-8.2	11-8.2
11-8.2.1	11-8.2.1
11-8.2.2	11-8.2.2
11-8.2.3	11-8.2.3
11-8.2.4	11-8.2.4
11-8.2.4.1	11-8.2.4.1
11-8.2.4.2	11-8.2.4.2
11-8.2.4.3	11-8.2.4.3
11-8.2.5	11-8.2.5
11-8.2.6	11-8.2.6
11-8.2.7	11-8.2.7
11-8.2.8	11-8.2.8
11-8.2.9	11-8.2.9
11-8.2.10	11-8.2.10
11-8.2.11	11-8.2.11
11-8.2.11.1	11-8.2.11.1
11-8.2.11.2	11-8.2.11.2
11-8.3	11-8.3
11-8.3.1	11-8.3.1
11-8.3.2	11-8.3.2
11-8.3.3	11-8.3.3
11-8.3.3.1	11-8.3.3.1
11-8.3.3.2	11-8.3.3.2
11-8.3.4	11-8.3.4
11-8.3.4.1	11-8.3.4.1
11-8.3.4.2	11-8.3.4.2
11-8.3.4.3	11-8.3.4.3
11-8.4	11-8.4
11-8.5-	11-8.5
11-8.5.1	11-8.5.1
11-8.5.1.1	11-8.5.1.1
11-8.5.1.2	11-8.5.1.2
11-8.5.2	11-8.5.2
11-8.5.2.1	11-8.5.2.1
11-8.5.2.2	11-8.5.2.1
11-9	11-9
11-9.1	11-9.1
11-9.1.1	11-9.1.1
11-9.1.1.1	11-9.1.1.1
11-9.1.2	11-9.1.2
11-9.1.3	11-9.1.3
11-9.1.4	11-9.1.4
11-9.1.5	11-9.1.5
11-9.1.6	11-9.1.6
11-9.1.7	11-9.1.7
11-9.2	11-9.2
11-9.2.1	11-9.2.1
11-9.2.2	11-9.2.2
11-9.2.3	11-9.2.3

1985	1988
11-9.2.4	11-9.2.4
11-9.2.4.1	11-9.2.4.1
11-9.2.4.2	11-9.2.4.2
11-9.2.4.3	--
11-9.2.5	11-9.2.5
11-9.2.6	11-9.2.6
11-9.2.7	11-9.2.7
11-9.2.8	11-9.2.8
11-9.2.9	11-9.2.9
11-9.2.10	11-9.2.10
11-9.2.11	11-9.2.11
11-9.2.11.1	11-9.2.11.1
11-9.2.11.2	11-9.2.11.2
11-9.2.11.3	11-9.2.11.3
11-9.3	11-9.3
11-9.3.1	11-9.3.1
11-9.3.2	11-9.3.2
11-9.3.3	11-9.3.3
11-9.3.3.1	11-9.3.3.1
11-9.3.3.2	11-9.3.3.2
11-9.3.4	11-9.3.4
11-9.3.4.1	11-9.3.4.1
11-9.3.4.2	11-9.3.4.2
--	11-9.3.4.3
11-9.3.4.3	--
11-9.4	11-9.4
11-9.5	11-9.5
11-9.5.1	11-9.5.1
11-9.5.1.1	11-9.5.1.1
11-9.5.1.2	11-9.5.1.2
11-9.5.2	11-9.5.2
11-9.5.2.1	11-9.5.2.1

CHAPTER 12

1985	1988
12-1	12-1
12-1.1	12-1.1
12-1.1.1	12-1.1.1
12-1.1.1.1	12-1.1.1.1
12-1.1.1.2	12-1.1.1.2
12-1.1.1.3	12-1.1.1.3
12-1.1.1.4	12-1.1.1.4
12-1.1.1.5	12-1.1.1.5
12-1.1.1.6	12-1.1.1.6
12-1.1.1.7	12-1.1.1.7
12-1.1.1.8	--
12-1.1.1.9	12-1.1.1.8
12-1.1.1.10	12-1.1.1.9
--	12-1.1.1.10
12-1.1.2	12-1.1.2
12-1.1.3	12-1.1.3
12-1.1.4	12-1.1.4
12-1.1.4.1	12-1.1.4.1
12-1.1.4.2	12-1.1.4.2
12-1.1.4.3	12-1.1.4.3
12-1.1.4.4	12-1.1.4.4
--	12-1.1.4.5
12-1.1.4.5	12-1.1.4.6
12-1.2	12-1.2
12-1.2.1	12-1.2.1
12-1.2.2	12-1.2.2
12-1.2.3	12-1.2.3
12-1.2.4	12-1.2.4
12-1.2.5	12-1.2.5
12-1.2.6	12-1.2.6
12-1.2.7	12-1.2.7

1985	1988
12-1.3	12-1.3
12-1.4	12-1.4
12-1.5	12-1.5
12-1.6	12-1.6
12-1.6.1	12-1.6.1
12-1.6.2	12-1.6.2
12-1.6.3	12-1.6.6
12-1.6.4	12-1.6.5
12-1.6.5	12-1.6.3
12-1.6.6	12-1.6.4
12-1.7	12-1.7
12-2	12-2
12-2.1	12-2.1
12-2.2	12-2.2.1
12-2.2.1	12-2.2.2
12-2.2.2	12-2.2.3
12-2.2.3	12-2.2.4
12-2.2.4	12-2.2.5
12-2.2.5	12-2.2.6
12-2.2.6	12-2.2.7
12-2.3	12-2.3
12-2.3.1	12-2.3.1
12-2.3.2	12-2.3.2
12-2.3.3	12-2.3.3
12-2.3.4	12-2.3.4
12-2.3.5	--
12-2.3.6	12-2.3.5
12-2.3.7	12-2.3.5
12-2.4	12-2.4
12-2.4.1	12-2.4.1
12-2.4.2	12-2.4.2
12-2.4.3	12-2.4.3
12-2.5	12-2.5
12-2.5.1	12-2.5.1
12-2.5.2	12-2.5.2
12-2.5.3	12-2.5.3
12-2.5.4	12-2.5.4
12-2.5.5	12-2.5.5
12-2.5.6	12-2.5.6
12-2.6	12-2.6
12-2.6.1	12-2.6.1
12-2.6.2	12-2.6.2
12-2.7	12-2.7
12-2.7.1	12-2.7.1
12-2.8	12-2.8
12-2.8.1	12-2.8.1
12-2.8.2	--
12-2.9	12-2.9
12-2.9.1	12-2.9.1
12-2.9.2	12-2.9.2
12-2.10	12-2.10
12-2.10.1	12-2.10.1
12-2.10.2	12-2.10.2
12-2.11	12-2.11
12-2.11.1	12-2.2.2.2
12-2.11.2	12-2.2.2.3
12-2.11.3	12-2.2.2.4
12-2.11.4	12-2.2.2.5
12-2.11.5	12-2.2.2.6
12-2.11.6	12-2.2.2.7
12-2.11.7	12-2.2.2.8
12-3	12-3
12-3.1	12-3.1
12-3.1.1	12-3.1.1
12-3.1.2	12-3.1.2

1985	1988
12-3.2	12-3.2
12-3.2.1	12-3.2.1
12-3.2.2	12-3.2.2
--	12-3.2.3
--	12-3.2.4
12-3.2.3	12-3.2.5
12-3.2.4	12-3.2.6
12-3.3	12-3.3
12-3.3.1	12-3.3.1
12-3.3.2	12-3.3.2
12-3.4	12-3.4
12-3.4.1	12-3.4.1
12-3.4.1.1	12-3.4.1.1
12-3.4.1.2	12-3.4.1.2
12-3.4.1.3	12-3.4.1.3
12-3.4.2	12-3.4.2
12-3.4.3	12-3.4.3
12-3.4.3.1	12-3.4.3.1
12-3.4.3.2	12-3.4.3.2
12-3.4.4	12-3.4.4
12-3.4.5	12-3.4.5
12-3.5	12-3.5
12-3.5.1	12-3.5.1
12-3.5.2	12-3.5.2
12-3.5.3	12-3.5.3
12-3.5.4	12-3.5.4
12-3.5.5	12-3.5.5
12-3.6	12-3.6
12-3.6.1	12-3.6.1 +
	12-3.6.2
12-3.6.2	12-3.6.2.3
12-3.6.3	12-3.6.3
12-3.6.4	12-3.6.3.6
12-3.6.5	12-3.6.4
12-3.7	12-3.7
12-3.7.1	12-3.7.1
12-3.7.2	12-3.7.2
12-3.7.3	12-3.7.3
12-3.7.4	12-3.7.4
12-3.7.5	12-3.7.5
12-3.7.6	12-3.7.6
12-3.7.7	12-3.7.7
12-3.7.8	12-3.7.8
12-3.8	12-3.8
12-3.8.1	12-3.8.1
12-4	12-4
12-4.1	12-4.1
12-4.2	12-4.2
12-5	12-5
12-5.1	12-5.1
12-5.1.1	12-5.1.1
12-5.1.2	12-5.1.2
12-5.1.3	12-5.1.3
12-5.2	12-5.2
12-5.2.1	12-5.2.1
12-5.2.2	12-5.2.2 +
	31-4.7
12-5.3	12-5.3
12-5.4	12-5.4
12-5.4.1	12-5.4.1
12-5.4.2	12-5.4.2
12-5.4.3	12-5.4.3
12-5.4.4	12-5.4.4
12-6	12-6
12-6.1	12-6.1

1985	1988
12-6.1.1	12-6.1.1
12-6.1.1.1	12-6.1.1.1
12-6.1.1.2	12-6.1.1.2
12-6.1.2	12-6.1.2
12-6.1.3	12-6.1.3
12-6.1.4	12-6.1.4
12-6.1.5	12-6.1.5
12-6.1.6	12-6.1.6
12-6.1.6.1	12-6.1.6.1
12-6.1.6.2	12-6.1.6.2
12-6.1.6.3	12-6.1.6.3
12-6.1.6.4	12-6.1.6.4
12-6.1.6.5	12-6.1.6.5
12-6.1.7	12-6.1.7
12-6.2	12-6.2
12-6.2.1	12-6.2.1
12-6.2.2	12-6.2.2.1
12-6.2.3	12-6.2.3
12-6.2.3.1	12-6.2.3.1
12-6.2.3.2	12-6.2.3.2
12-6.2.3.3	12-6.2.3.3
12-6.2.4	12-6.2.4
12-6.2.4.1	12-6.2.4.1
12-6.2.4.2	12-6.2.4.2
12-6.2.5	12-6.2.5
12-6.2.6	12-6.2.6
12-6.2.6.1	12-6.2.6.1
12-6.2.6.2	12-6.2.6.2
12-6.2.7	12-6.2.7
12-6.2.8	12-6.2.8
12-6.2.9	12-6.2.9
12-6.2.9.1	12-6.2.9.1
12-6.2.9.2	12-6.2.9.2
12-6.2.10	12-6.2.10
12-6.2.11	12-6.2.11
12-6.2.11.1	12-6.2.2.2
12-6.2.11.2	12-6.2.2.3
12-6.2.11.3	12-6.2.2.4
12-6.3	12-6.3
12-6.3.1	12-6.3.1
12-6.3.2	12-6.3.2
12-6.3.2.1	12-6.3.2.1
12-6.3.2.2	12-6.3.2.2
12-6.3.3	12-6.3.3
12-6.3.4	12-6.3.4
12-6.3.4.1	12-6.3.4.1
12-6.3.4.2	12-6.3.4.2
12-6.3.4.3	12-6.3.4.3
12-6.3.4.4	12-6.3.4.4
12-6.3.4.5	12-6.3.4.5
12-6.3.5	12-6.3.5
12-6.3.5.1	12-6.3.5.1
12-6.3.5.2	12-6.3.5.2
12-6.3.6	12-6.3.6
12-6.3.7	12-6.3.7
12-6.3.7.1	12-6.3.7.1
12-6.3.7.2	12-6.3.7.2
12-6.3.7.3	12-6.3.7.3
12-6.3.7.4	12-6.3.7.4
12-6.3.7.5	12-6.3.7.5
12-6.3.7.6	12-6.3.7.6
12-6.3.7.7	12-6.3.7.7
12-6.4	12-6.4
12-6.5	12-6.5
12-6.5.1	12-6.5.1

1985	1988
12-6.5.2	12-6.5.2
12-6.5.2.1	12-6.5.2.1
12-6.5.2.2	12-6.5.2.2 +
	31-4.7
12-6.5.3	12-6.5.3
12-6.5.4	12-6.5.4

CHAPTER 13

1985	1988
13-1	13-1
13-1.1	13-1.1
13-1.1.1	13-1.1.1
13-1.1.1.1	13-1.1.1.1
13-1.1.1.2	13-1.1.1.2
13-1.1.1.3	13-1.1.1.3
13-1.1.1.4	13-1.1.1.4
13-1.1.1.5	13-1.1.1.5
13-1.1.1.6	13-1.1.1.6
13-1.1.1.7	13-1.1.1.7
13-1.1.1.8	--
13-1.1.1.9	13-1.1.1.8
13-1.1.1.10	13-1.1.1.9
--	13-1.1.1.10
13-1.1.2	13-1.1.2
13-1.1.3	13-1.1.3
13-1.1.4	13-1.1.4
13-1.1.4.1	13-1.1.4.1
13-1.1.4.2	13-1.1.4.2
13-1.1.4.3	13-1.1.4.3
13-1.1.4.4	13-1.1.4.4
--	13-1.1.4.5
13-1.1.4.5	13-1.1.4.6
13-1.1.5	13-1.1.5
13-1.1.5.1	13-1.1.5
13-1.2	13-1.2
13-1.2.1	13-1.2.1
13-1.2.2	13-1.2.2
13-1.2.3	13-1.2.3
13-1.2.4	13-1.2.4
13-1.2.5	13-1.2.5
13-1.2.6	13-1.2.6
13-1.2.7	13-1.2.7
13-1.3	13-1.3
13-1.4	13-1.4
13-1.5	13-1.5
13-1.6	13-1.6
13-1.6.1	13-1.6.1
13-1.6.2	13-1.6.2
13-1.6.3	13-1.6.3
13-1.6.4	13-1.6.4
13-1.6.5	13-1.6.5
13-1.7	13-1.7
13-2	13-2
13-2.1	13-2.1
13-2.2	13-2.2.1
13-2.2.1	13-2.2.2
13-2.2.2	13-2.2.3
13-2.2.3	13-2.2.4
13-2.2.4	13-2.2.5
13-2.2.5	13-2.2.6
13-2.2.6	13-2.2.7
13-2.3	13-2.3
13-2.3.1	13-2.3.1
13-2.3.2	13-2.3.2
13-2.3.3	13-2.3.3
13-2.3.4	13-2.3.4

1985	1988
13-2.4	13-2.4
13-2.4.1	13-2.4.1
13-2.4.2	13-2.4.2
13-2.4.3	13-2.4.3
13-2.5	13-2.5
13-2.5.1	13-2.5.1
13-2.5.2	13-2.5.2
13-2.5.3	13-2.5.3
13-2.5.4	13-2.5.4
13-2.5.5	13-2.5.5
13-2.6	13-2.6
13-2.6.1	13-2.6.1
13-2.6.2	13-2.6.2
13-2.7	13-2.7
13-2.7.1	13-2.7.1
13-2.7.2	--
13-2.8	13-2.8
13-2.8.1	13-2.8.1
13-2.9	13-2.9
13-2.9.1	13-2.9.1
13-2.10	13-2.10
13-2.10.1	13-2.10.1
13-2.11	13-2.11
13-2.11.1	13-2.2.2.2
13-2.11.2	13-2.2.2.3
13-2.11.3	13-2.2.2.4
13-2.11.4	13-2.2.2.5
13-2.11.5	13-2.2.2.6
13-2.11.6	13-2.2.2.7
13-2.11.7	13-2.2.2.8
13-3	13-3
13-3.1	13-3.1
13-3.1.1	13-3.1.1
13-3.1.2	13-3.1.2
13-3.2	13-3.2
13-3.2.1	13-3.2.1
13-3.2.2	13-3.2.2
--	13-3.2.3
--	13-3.2.4
13-3.2.3	13-3.2.5
13-3.2.4	13-3.2.6
13-3.3	13-3.3
13-3.3.1	13-3.3.1
13-3.3.2	13-3.3.2
13-3.4	13-3.4
13-3.4.1	13-3.4.1
13-3.4.2	13-3.4.2
13-3.4.3	13-3.4.3
13-3.4.3.1	13-3.4.3.1
13-3.4.3.2	13-3.4.3.2
13-3.4.4	13-3.4.4
13-3.4.5	13-3.4.5.1
13-3.5	13-3.5
13-3.5.1	13-3.5.1
13-3.5.2	13-3.5.2
13-3.5.3	13-3.5.3
13-3.5.4	13-3.5.4
13-3.5.5	13-3.5.5
13-3.5.6	13-3.6
13-3.6.1	13-3.6.1 +
	13-3.6.2
13-3.6.2	13-3.6.2.3
13-3.6.3	13-3.6.3
13-3.6.4	13-3.6.3.6
13-3.6.5	13-3.6.4

1985	1988	1985	1988	1985	1988
13-3.7	13-3.7	13-6.2.11.1	13-6.2.2.2	14-2.1	14-2.1
13-3.7.1	13-3.7.1	13-6.2.11.2	13-6.2.2.3	14-2.2	14-2.2
13-3.7.2	--	13-6.2.11.3	13-6.2.2.4	14-2.2.1	14-2.2.1
13-3.7.3	13-3.7.3	13-6.3	13-6.3	14-2.3	14-2.3
13-3.7.4	13-3.7.4	13-6.3.1	13-6.3.1	14-2.3.1	14-2.3.1
13-3.7.5	13-3.7.2	13-6.3.2	13-6.3.2	14-2.3.2	14-2.3.2
13-3.7.6	13-3.7.5	13-6.3.2.1	13-6.3.2.1	14-2.3.3	14-2.3.3
13-3.7.7	13-3.7.6	13-6.3.2.2	13-6.3.2.2	14-2.4	14-2.4
--	13-3.7.7	13-6.3.3	13-6.3.3	14-2.4.1	14-2.4.1
13-3.8	13-3.8	13-6.3.4	13-6.3.4	14-2.4.2	14-2.4.2
13-3.8.1	13-3.8.1	13-6.3.4.1	13-6.3.4.1	14-2.4.3	14-2.4.3
13-4	13-4	13-6.3.4.2	13-6.3.4.2	14-2.5	14-2.5
13-4.1	13-4.1	13-6.3.4.3	13-6.3.4.3	14-2.5.1	14-2.5.1
13-4.2	13-4.2	13-6.3.4.4	13-6.3.4.4	14-2.5.2	14-2.5.2
13-5	13-5	13-6.3.4.5	13-6.3.4.5	--	14-2.5.3
13-5.1	13-5.1	13-6.3.5	13-6.3.5	14-2.5.3	14-2.5.4
13-5.2	13-5.2	13-6.3.5.1	13-6.3.5.1	14-2.6	14-2.6
13-5.2.1	13-5.2.1	13-6.3.5.2	13-6.3.5.2	14-2.6.1	14-2.6.1
13-5.2.2	13-5.2.2 +	13-6.3.6	13-6.3.6	14-2.7	14-2.7
	31-4.7	13-6.3.7	13-6.3.7	14-2.7.1	14-2.7.1
13-5.3	13-5.3	13-6.3.7.1	13-6.3.7.1	14-2.7.2	14-2.7.2
13-5.4	13-5.4	13-6.3.7.2	13-6.3.7.2	14-2.8	14-2.8
13-5.4.1	13-5.4.1	13-6.3.7.3	13-6.3.7.3	14-2.9	14-2.9
13-5.4.2	13-5.4.2	13-6.3.7.4	13-6.3.7.4	14-2.10	14-2.10
13-5.4.3	13-5.4.3	13-6.3.7.5	13-6.3.7.6	14-2.11	14-2.11
13-5.4.4	13-5.4.4	13-6.3.7.6	13-6.3.7.7	14-2.11.1	14-2.11.1
13-6	13-6	13-6.4	13-6.4	14-2.11.2	14-2.11.2
13-6.1	13-6.1	13-6.5	13-6.5	14-2.11.3	14-2.11.3
13-6.1.1	13-6.1.1	13-6.5.1	13-6.5.1	14-2.11.4	14-2.11.4
13-6.1.1.1	13-6.1.1.1	13-6.5.2	13-6.5.2	14-2.11.5	14-2.11.5
13-6.1.1.2	13-6.1.1.2	13-6.5.2.1	13-6.5.2.1	14-2.11.6	14-2.11.6
13-6.1.1.3	13-6.1.1.3	13-6.5.2.2	13-6.5.2.2 +	14-2.11.7	14-2.11.7
13-6.1.1.3.1	13-6.1.1.3		31-4.7	14-2.11.8	14-2.11.8
13-6.1.2	13-6.1.2	13-6.5.3	13-6.5.3	14-2.11.9	14-2.11.9
13-6.1.3	13-6.1.3	13-6.5.4	13-6.5.4	14-2.11.10	14-2.11.10
13-6.1.4	13-6.1.4			14-2.11.11	14-2.2.3.2
13-6.1.5	13-6.1.5	**CHAPTER 14**		14-3	14-3
13-6.1.6	13-6.1.6	14-1	14-1	14-3.1	14-3.1
13-6.1.6.1	13-6.1.6.1	14-1.1	14-1.1	14-3.1.1	14-3.1.1
13-6.1.6.2	13-6.1.6.2	14-1.1.1	14-1.1.1	14-3.1.2	14-3.1.2
13-6.1.6.3	13-6.1.6.3	14-1.1.2	14-1.1.2	14-3.2	14-3.2
13-6.1.6.4	13-6.1.6.4	14-1.1.3	14-1.1.3	14-3.2.1	14-3.2.1
13-6.1.6.5	13-6.1.6.5	14-1.1.4	14-1.1.4	14-3.2.2	14-3.2.2
13-6.1.7	13-6.1.7	14-1.1.5	14-1.1.5	14-3.2.3	14-3.2.3
13-6.2	13-6.2	14-1.1.6	14-1.1.6	14-3.3	14-3.3
13-6.2.1	13-6.2.1	14-1.2	14-1.2	14-3.3.1	14-3.3.1
13-6.2.2	13-6.2.2	14-1.2.1	14-1.2.1	14-3.3.2	14-3.3.2
13-6.2.3	13-6.2.3	14-1.2.2	14-1.2.2	14-3.4	14-3.4
13-6.2.3.1	13-6.2.3.1	14-1.2.3	14-1.2.3	14-3.4.1	14-3.4.1
13-6.2.3.2	13-6.2.3.2	14-1.2.4	14-1.2.4	14-3.4.1.1	14-3.4.1.1
13-6.2.3.3	13-6.2.3.3	14-1.2.5	14-1.2.5	14-3.4.1.2	14-3.4.1.2
13-6.2.4	13-6.2.4	14-1.2.6	14-1.2.6	14-3.4.1.3	14-3.4.1.3
13-6.2.4.1	13-6.2.4.1	14-1.3	14-1.3	14-3.4.2	14-3.4.2
13-6.2.4.2	13-6.2.4.2	14-1.4	14-1.4	14-3.4.3	14-3.4.3
13-6.2.5	13-6.2.5	14-1.4.1	14-1.4.1	14-3.4.3.1	14-3.4.3.1
13-6.2.6	13-6.2.6	14-1.4.2	14-1.4.2	14-3.4.3.2	14-3.4.3.2
13-6.2.6.1	13-6.2.6.1	14-1.4.3	14-1.4.3	14-3.4.4	14-3.4.4
13-6.2.6.2	13-6.2.6.2	14-1.5	14-1.5	14-3.5	14-3.5
13-6.2.7	13-6.2.7	14-1.6	14-1.6	--	14-3.5.1
13-6.2.8	13-6.2.8	14-1.6.1	14-1.6.1	14-3.5.1	14-3.5.2
13-6.2.9	13-6.2.9	--	14-1.6.2	14-3.5.2	14-3.5.3
13-6.2.9.1	13-6.2.9.1	14-1.6.2	14-1.6.3	14-3.5.3	14-3.2.1
13-6.2.9.2	13-6.2.9.2	14-1.6.3	14-1.6.4	14-3.5.4	14-3.5.4
13-6.2.10	13-6.2.10	14-1.7	14-1.7	14-3.5.5	14-3.5.5
13-6.2.11	13-6.2.11	14-2	14-2	14-3.6	14-3.6

1985	1988
14-3.7	14-3.7
14-3.7.1	14-3.7.1 +
	14-3.7.2
14-3.7.2	14-3.7.3
14-3.7.3	14-3.7.4
14-3.7.4	14-3.7.5
14-3.7.5	14-3.7.6
14-3.7.6	14-3.7.7
14-3.7.7	14-3.7.8
14-3.8	14-3.8
14-3.8.1	14-3.8.1
14-4	14-4
14-4.1	14-4.1
14-4.1.1	14-4.1.1
14-4.1.2	14-4.1.2
14-4.2	14-4.2
14-4.2.1	14-4.2.1
--	14-4.6.3
14-4.3	14-4.4
14-5	14-5
14-5.1	14-5.1
14-5.1.1	14-5.1.1
14-5.1.2	14-5.1.2
14-5.2	14-5.2
14-5.2.1	14-5.2.1
14-5.2.2	14-5.2.2
14-5.2.3	14-5.2.3
14-5.3	14-5.3
14-5.4	14-5.4
14-5.4.1	14-5.4.1
14-5.4.2	14-5.4.2
14-5.4.3	14-5.4.3
14-5.4.4	14-5.4.4

CHAPTER 15

1985	1988
15-1	15-1
15-1.1	15-1.1
15-1.1.1	15-1.1.1
15-1.1.2	15-1.1.2
15-1.1.3	15-1.1.3
15-1.1.4	15-1.1.4
15-1.1.5	15-1.1.5
15-1.1.6	15-1.1.6
15-1.2	15-1.2
15-1.2.1	15-1.2.1
15-1.2.2	15-1.2.2
15-1.2.3	15-1.2.3
15-1.2.4	15-1.2.4
15-1.2.5	15-1.2.5
15-1.2.6	15-1.2.6
15-1.3	15-1.3
15-1.4	15-1.4
15-1.4.1	15-1.4.1
15-1.4.2	15-1.4.2
15-1.4.3	15-1.4.3
15-1.5	15-1.5
15-1.6	15-1.6
15-1.6.1	15-1.6.1
--	15-1.6.2
15-1.6.2	15-1.6.3
15-1.7	15-1.7
15-2	15-2
15-2.1	15-2.1
15-2.2	15-2.2
15-2.2.1	15-2.2.1

1985	1988
15-2.3	15-2.3
15-2.3.1	15-2.3.1
15-2.3.2	15-2.3.2
15-2.3.3	15-2.3.3
15-2.4	15-2.4
15-2.4.1	15-2.4.1
15-2.4.2	15-2.4.2
15-2.4.3	15-2.4.3
15-2.5	15-2.5
15-2.5.1	15-2.5.1
15-2.5.2	15-2.5.2
--	15-2.5.3
15-2.5.3	15-2.5.4
15-2.6	15-2.6
15-2.6.1	15-2.6.1
15-2.7	15-2.7
15-2.7.1	15-2.7.1
15-2.7.2	15-2.7.2
15-2.8	15-2.8
15-2.9	15-2.9
15-2.10	15-2.10
15-2.11	15-2.11
15-2.11.1	15-2.11.1
15-2.11.2	15-2.11.2
15-2.11.3	15-2.11.3
15-2.11.4	15-2.11.4
15-2.11.5	15-2.11.5
15-2.11.6	15-2.11.6
15-2.11.7	15-2.11.7
15-2.11.8	15-2.11.8
15-2.11.9	--
15-3	15-3
15-3.1	15-3.1
15-3.1.1	15-3.1.1
15-3.1.2	15-3.1.2
15-3.1.3	15-3.1.3
15-3.2	15-3.2
15-3.2.1	15-3.2.1
15-3.2.2	15-3.2.2
15-3.2.3	15-3.2.3
15-3.3	15-3.3
15-3.3.1	15-3.3.1
15-3.3.2	15-3.3.2
15-3.4	15-3.4
15-3.4.1	15-3.4.1
15-3.4.1.1	15-3.4.1.1
15-3.4.1.2	15-3.4.1.2
15-3.4.1.3	15-3.4.1.3
15-3.4.2	15-3.4.2
15-3.4.3	15-3.4.3
15-3.4.3.1	15-3.4.3.1
15-3.4.3.2	15-3.4.3.2
15-3.4.4	15-3.4.4
15-3.5	15-3.5
--	15-3.5.1
15-3.5.1	15-3.5.2
15-3.5.2	15-3.5.3
15-3.5.3	15-3.2.1
15-3.5.4	15-3.5.4
15-3.5.5	15-3.5.5
15-3.6	15-3.6
15-3.7	15-3.7
15-3.7.1	15-3.7.1 +
	15-3.7.2
15-3.7.2	15-3.7.3

1985	1988
15-3.7.3	15-3.7.4
15-3.7.4	15-3.7.5
15-3.7.5	15-3.7.6
15-3.7.6	15-3.7.7
15-3.8	15-3.8
15-3.8.1	15-3.8.1
15-4	15-4
15-4.1	15-4.1
15-4.1.1	15-4.1.1
15-4.1.2	15-4.1.2
15-4.2	15-4.2
15-4.2.1	15-4.2.1
--	15-4.3
15-4.3	15-4.4
15-5	15-5
15-5.1	15-5.1
15-5.1.1	15-5.1.1
15-5.1.2	15-5.1.2
15-5.2	15-5.2
15-5.2.1	15-5.2.1
15-5.2.2	15-5.2.2
15-5.2.3	15-5.2.3
15-5.3	15-5.3
15-5.4	15-5.4
15-5.4.1	15-5.4.1
15-5.4.2	15-5.4.2
15-5.4.3	15-5.4.3
15-5.4.4	15-5.4.4

CHAPTER 16

1985	1988
16-1	16-1
16-1.1	16-1.1
16-1.1.1	16-1.1.1
16-1.1.2	16-1.1.2
16-1.2	16-1.2
16-1.2.1	16-1.2.1
16-1.2.2	16-1.2.2
16-1.2.3	16-1.2.3
16-1.3	16-1.3
16-1.3.1	16-1.3.1
16-1.4	16-1.4
16-1.5	16-1.5
16-1.5.1	16-1.5.1
16-1.6	16-1.6
16-1.7	16-1.7
16-1.7.1	16-1.7.1
16-2	16-2
16-2.1	16-2.1
16-2.1.1	--
16-2.1.2	--
16-2.1.3	--
16-2.2	16-2.2
16-2.2.1	16-2.2.1
16-2.3	16-2.3
16-2.3.1	16-2.3.1
16-2.3.2	16-2.3.2
16-2.3.3	16-2.3.2
16-2.3.4	16-2.3.2
--	16-2.3.3
16-2.4	16-2.4
16-2.4.1	16-2.4.1
16-2.5	16-2.5
16-2.5.1	16-2.5.1
16-2.5.2	16-2.5.2 +
	16-2.5.3

1985	1988	1985	1988	1985	1988
16-2.5.3	16-2.5.4	17-1.1	17-1.1	17-3.4.3.2	17-3.4.3.2
16-2.6	16-2.6	17-1.1.1	17-1.1.1	17-3.4.4	17-3.4.4
16-2.6.1	16-2.6.1	17-1.1.2	17-1.1.2	17-3.5	17-3.5
16-2.6.2	16-2.6.2	17-1.2	17-1.2	17-3.5.1	17-3.5.1
16-2.7	16-2.7	17-1.2.1	17-1.2.1	17-3.5.2	17-3.5.2
16-2.7.1	16-2.7.1	17-1.2.2	17-1.2.2	17-3.6	17-3.6
16-2.7.2	16-2.7.1	17-1.2.3	17-1.2.3	17-3.6.1	17-3.6.1
16-2.8	16-2.8	17-1.3	17-1.3	17-3.6.2	17-3.6.2
16-2.8.1	16-2.8.1	17-1.3.1	17-1.3.1	17-3.6.3	17-3.6.3
16-2.9	16-2.9	17-1.4	17-1.4	17-3.6.4	17-3.6.5
16-2.9.1	16-2.9.1	17-1.5	17-1.5	17-3.6.5	17-3.6.5
16-2.10	16-2.10	17-1.5.1	17-1.5.1	17-3.6:6	17-3.6.6
16-2.10.1	16-2.10.1	17-1.6	17-1.6	17-3.7	17-3.7
--	16-2.10.2	17-1.7	17-1.7	17-3.7.1	17-3.7.1
16-2.11	16-2.11	17-1.7.1	17-1.7.1	17-3.8	17-3.8
16-2.11.1	16-2.2.2.2	17-2	17-2	17-3.8.1	--
16-2.11.2	16-2.2.2.3	17-2.1	17-2.1	17-4	17-4
16-3	16-3	17-2.1.1	--	17-4.1	17-4.1
16-3.1	16-3.1	17-2.1.2	--	17-5	17-5
16-3.1.1	16-3.1.1	17-2.1.3	--	17-5.1	17-5.1
16-3.1.2	16-2.7.2	17-2.2	17-2.2	17-5.2	17-5.2
16-3.1.3	16-3.1.2	17-2.2.1	17-2.2.1	17-5.3	17-5.3
16-3.2	16-3.2	17-2.2.2	17-2.2.8	17-5.4	17-5.4
16-3.2.1	16-3.2.1	17-2.3	17-2.3		
16-3.2.2	16-3.2.2	17-2.3.1	17-2.3.1	**CHAPTER 18**	
16-3.3	16-3.3	17-2.3.2	17-2.3.2	18-1	18-1
16-3.3.1	16-3.3.1	17-2.3.3	17-2.3.2	18-1.1	18-1.1
16-3.3.2	16-3.3.2	17-2.3.4	17-2.3.2	18-1.1.1	18-1.1.1
16-3.4	16-3.4	17-2.4	17-2.4	18-1.1.2	18-1.1.2
16-3.4.1	16-3.4.1	17-2.4.1	17-2.4.1	18-1.2	18-1.2
16-3.4.2	16-3.4.2	17-2.5	17-2.5	18-1.2.1	18-1.2.1
16-3.4.3	16-3.4.3	17-2.5.1	17-2.5.1	18-1.2.2	18-1.2.2
16-3.4.3.1	16-3.4.3.2	17-2.5.2	17-2.5.2 +	18-1.3	18-1.3
16-3.4.3.2	16-3.4.3.1		17-2.5.3	18-1.3.1	18-1.3.1
16-3.4.3.3	16-3.4.3.3			18-1.4	18-1.4
16-3.4.3.4	16-3.4.3.4	17-2.6	17-2.6	18-1.5	18-1.5
16-3.4.4	16-3.4.4	17-2.6.1	17-2.6.1	18-1.5.1	18-1.5.1
16-3.4.4.1	16-3.4.4.1	17-2.6.2	17-2.6.2	18-1.6	18-1.6
16-3.4.4.2	16-3.4.4.2	17-2.7	17-2.7	18-1.7	18-1.7
16-3.5	16-3.5	17-2.7.1	17-2.7.1	18-1.7.1	18-1.7.1
16-3.5.1	16-3.5.1	17-2.7.2	17-2.7.1	18-2	18-2
--	16-3.5.2	17-2.8	17-2.8	18-2.1	18-2.1
--	16-3.5.3	17-2.8.1	17-2.8.1	18-2.2	18-2.2
16-3.5.2	16-3.5.4	17-2.9	17-2.9	18-2.2.1	18-2.2.1
16-3.6	16-3.6	17-2.9.1	17-2.9.1	18-2.3	18-2.3
16-3.6.1	16-3.6.1	17-2.10	17-2.10	18-2.3.1	18-2.3.1
16-3.6.2	16-3.6.2	17-2.10.1	17-2.10.1	18-2.3.2	18-2.3.2
16-3.6.3	16-3.6.3	17-2.11	17-2.11	18-2.3.3	--
16-3.6.4	16-3.6.5	17-2.11.1	17-2.2.2.2	18-2.3.4	--
16-3.6.5	16-3.6.5	17-2.11.2	17-2.2.2.3	18-2.4	18-2.4
16-3.7	16-3.7	17-3	17-3	18-2.4.1	18-2.4.1
16-3.7.1	16-3.7.1	17-3.1	17-3.1	18-2.5	18-2.5
16-3.8	16-3.8	17-3.1.1	17-3.1.1	18-2.5.1	18-2.5.1
16-3.8.1	--	17-3.1.2	17-2.7.2	18-2.6	18-2.6
16-4	16-4	17-3.1.3	17-3.1.2	18-2.6.1	18-2.6.1
16-4.1	16-4.1	17-3.2	17-3.2	18-2.6.2	18-2.6.2
16-4.2	16-4.2	17-3.2.1	17-3.2.1	18-2.6.3	18-2.5.2
16-5	16-5	17-3.2.2	17-3.2.2	18-2.7	18-2.7
16-5.1	16-5.1	17-3.3	17-3.3	18-2.7.1	18-2.7.1
16-5.2	16-5.2	17-3.3.1	17-3.3.1	18-2.7.2	18-2.7.1
16-5.3	16-5.3	17-3.3.2	17-3.3.2	18-2.8	18-2.8
16-5.4	16-5.4	17-3.4	17-3.4	18-2.8.1	18-2.8.1
		17-3.4.1	17-3.4.1	18-2.9	18-2.9
CHAPTER 17		17-3.4.2	17-3.4.2	18-2.9.1	18-2.9.1
17-1	17-1	17-3.4.3	17-3.4.3	18-2.10	18-2.10
		17-3.4.3.1	17-3.4.3.1		

1985	1988	1985	1988	1985	1988
18-2.10.1	18-2.10.1	19-1.3.1	19-1.3.1	19-3.5.1	19-3.5.2
18-2.11	18-2.11	19-1.4	19-1.4	19-3.5.2	19-3.5.3
18-2.11.1	18-2.2.3.2	19-1.5	19-1.5	19-3.5.3	19-3.5.4
18-2.11.2	--	19-1.5.1	19-1.5.1	19-3.5.4	19-3.5.5
18-2.11.3	18-2.2.2.2	19-1.6	19-1.6	19-3.5.5	19-3.5.6
18-2.11.4	18-2.2.3.3	19-1.7	19-1.7	19-3.6	19-3.6
18-2.11.5	18-2.2.3.4	19-1.7.1	19-1.7.1	19-3.6.1	19-3.6.1
18-3	18-3	19-2	19-2	19-3.6.2	19-3.6.2
18-3.1	18-3.1	19-2.1	19-2.1	19-3.6.3	19-3.6.3
18-3.1.1	18-3.1.1	19-2.2	19-2.2	19-3.6.4	19-3.6.4
18-3.1.2	--	19-2.2.1	19-2.2.1	19-3.7	19-3.7
18-3.1.3	--	19-2.2.2	19-2.2.8	19-3.7.1	19-3.7.1
18-3.1.4	18-3.1.2	19-2.3	19-2.3	19-4	19-4
18-3.2	18-3.2	19-2.3.1	19-2.3.1	19-4.1	19-4.2
18-3.2.1	18-3.2.1	19-2.3.2	19-2.3.2	19-5	19-5
18-3.2.2	18-3.2.2	19-2.3.3	--	19-5.1	19-5.1
18-3.3	18-3.3	19-2.3.4	--	19-5.2	19-5.2.1
18-3.3.1	18-3.3.1	19-2.4	19-2.4	19-5.3	19-5.3
18-3.3.2	18-3.3.2	19-2.4.1	19-2.4.1	19-5.4	19-5.4
18-3.4	18-3.4	19-2.5	19-2.5		
18-3.4.1	18-3.4.1	19-2.5.1	19-2.5.1	**CHAPTER 20**	
18-3.4.2	18-3.4.2	19-2.6	19-2.6	20-1	20-1
18-3.4.2.1	18-3.4.2.1	19-2.6.1	19-2.6.1	20-1.1	20-1.1
18-3.4.2.2	18-3.4.2.2	19-2.6.2	19-2.6.2	20-1.1.1	20-1.1.1
18-3.4.2.3	18-3.4.2.3	19-2.6.3	19-2.5.2	20-1.1.2	10-1.1.2
18-3.4.2.4	18-3.4.2.4	19-2.7	19-2.7	20-1.2	20-1.2
18-3.4.3	18-3.4.3	19-2.7.1	19-2.7.1	20-1.2.1	20-1.2.1
18-3.4.3.1	18-3.4.3.1	19-2.7.2	19-2.7.1	20-1.2.2	20-1.2.2
18-3.4.3.2	18-3.4.3.2	19-2.8	19-2.8	20-1.3	20-1.3
18-3.4.3.3	--	19-2.8.1	19-2.8.1	20-1.3.1	20-1.3.1
18-3.4.4	18-3.4.4	19-2.9	19-2.9	20-1.4	20-1.4
18-3.4.4.1	18-3.4.4.1	19-2.9.1	19-2.9.1	20-1.5	20-1.5
18-3.4.4.2	18-3.4.4.2	19-2.10	19-2.10	20-1.5.1	20-1.5.1
18-3.5	18-3.5	19-2.10.1	19-2.10.1	20-1.6	20-1.6
18-3.5.1	18-3.5.2	19-2.11	19-2.11	20-1.7	20-1.7
18-3.5.2	18-3.5.3	19-2.11.1	19-2.2.3.2	20-2	20-2
18-3.5.3	18-3.5.4	19-2.11.2	19-2.11.1	20-2.1	20-2.1
18-3.5.4	18-3.5.5	19-2.11.3	19-2.2.2.2	20-2.1.1	20-2.1.1
18-3.5.5	18-3.5.6	19-2.11.4	19-2.2.3.3	20-2.1.2	20-2.1.2
18-3.6	18-3.6	19-2.11.5	19-2.2.3.4	20-2.2	20-2.2
18-3.6.1	18-3.6.1	19-3	19-3	20-2.3	20-2.3
18-3.6.2	18-3.6.2	19-3.1	19-3.1	20-2.4	20-2.4
18-3.6.3	18-3.6.3	19-3.1.1	--	20-2.5	20-2.5
18-3.7	18-3.7	19-3.1.2	19-2.7.2	20-2.6	20-2.6
18-3.7.1	18-3.7.1	19-3.1.3	19-3.1.2	20-2.7	20-2.7
18-3.7.2	18-3.7.2	19-3.2	19-3.2	20-3	20-3
18-3.8	18-3.8	19-3.2.1	19-3.2.1	20-3.1	20-3.1
18-3.8.1	--	19-3.2.2	19-3.2.2	20-3.1.1	20-3.1.1
18-4	18-4	19-3.3	19-3.3	20-3.1.2	20-3.1.2
18-4.1	18-4.2	19-3.3.1	19-3.3.1	20-3.2	20-3.2
18-5	18-5	19-3.3.2	19-3.3.2	20-3.3	20-3.3
18-5.1	18-5.1	19-3.4	19-3.4	20-3.3.1	20-3.3.1
18-5.2	18-5.2	19-3.4.1	19-3.4.1	20-3.3.2	20-3.3.2
18-5.3	18-5.3	19-3.4.2	19-3.4.2	20-3.3.3	20-3.3.3
18-5.4	18-5.4	19-3.4.2.1	19-3.4.2.1	20-3.3.4	20-3.3.4
		19-3.4.2.2	19-3.4.2.2	20-3.4	20-3.4
CHAPTER 19		19-3.4.2.3	19-3.4.2.3	20-4	20-4
19-1	19-1	19-3.4.2.4	19-3.4.2.4	20-4.1	20-4.1
19-1.1	19-1.1	19-3.4.3	19-3.4.3	20-5	20-5
19-1.1.1	19-1.1.1	19-3.4.3.1	19-3.4.3.1		
19-1.1.2	19-1.1.2	19-3.4.3.2	19-3.4.3.2	**CHAPTER 21**	
19-1.2	19-1.2	19-3.4.4	19-3.4.4	21-1	21-1
19-1.2.1	19-1.2.1	19-3.4.4.1	19-3.4.4.1	21-1.1	21-1.1
19-1.2.2	19-1.2.2	19-3.4.4.2	19-3.4.4.2	21-1.1.1	21-1.1.1
19-1.3	19-1.3	19-3.5	19-3.5	21-1.2	21-1.2

1985	1988
21-1.2.1	21-1.2.1
21-1.3	21-1.3
21-1.4	21-1.4
21-2	21-2
21-2.1	21-2.1
21-2.1.1	21-2.1.1
21-2.1.2	21-2.1.2
21-2.2	21-2.1.3
21-2.2.1	21-2.1.3.1
21-2.2.2	21-2.1.3
21-2.2.2.1	--
21-2.2.2.2	21-2.3.2
21-2.2.2.3	21-2.3.4.1
21-2.2.2.4	21-2.3.4.2
21-2.2.2.5	21-2.3.5.1
21-2.2.3	21-2.1.3
21-2.2.3.1	--
21-2.2.3.2	21-2.1.4.2
21-2.2.3.3	21-2.2.1 +
	21-2.2.2
21-2.2.3.4	21-2.3.3
21-2.2.3.5	21-2.3.5.1
21-2.2.3.6	21-2.3.6
21-2.2.4	21-2.1.3
21-2.2.4.1	--
21-2.2.4.2	21-2.1.4.3
21-2.2.4.3	21-2.3.1.1
21-2.2.4.4	21-2.3.5.2
21-2.2.4.5	21-2.3.5.1
21-3	21-3
21-3.1	21-3.1
21-3.1.1	21-3.1.1
21-3.1.2	21-3.1.2
21-3.2	21-3.1.3
21-3.2.1	21-3.1.3.1
21-3.2.2	21-3.1.3.1
21-3.2.2.1	--
21-3.2.2.2	21-3.1.4
21-3.2.2.3	21-3.3.6.1
21-3.2.2.4	21-3.3.3
21-3.2.2.5	21-3.3.4.8
21-3.2.2.6	21-3.3.5.1
21-3.2.2.7	21-3.3.5.3
21-3.2.2.8	21-3.3.6.2
21-3.2.3	21-3.1.3.2
21-3.2.3.1	21-3.1.3.2
21-4	21-4
21-4.1	21-4.1
21-4.1.1	21-4.1.1
21-4.1.2	21-4.1.2
21-4.2	21-4.1.3
21-4.2.1	21-4.1.3.1
21-4.2.2	21-4.1.3.2
21-4.2.3	21-4.1.4
21-4.2.4	21-4.2
21-4.2.5	21-4.3.1
21-4.2.6	21-4.3.2
21-4.2.7	21-4.3.3
21-5	21-4.4

CHAPTER 22

1985	1988
22-1	22-1
22-1.1	22-1.1
22-1.1.1	22-1.1.1
22-1.1.2	22-1.1.2
22-1.2	22-1.2
22-1.2.1	22-1.2.1
22-1.2.2	22-1.2.2
22-1.3	22-1.3
22-1.3.1	22-1.3.1
22-1.4	22-1.4
22-1.5	22-1.5
22-1.5.1	22-1.5.1
22-1.6	22-1.6
22-1.7	22-1.7
22-2	22-2
22-2.1	22-2.1
22-2.1.1	22-2.1.1
22-2.1.2	22-2.1.2
22-2.2	22-2.2
22-2.2.1	22-2.2.1
22-2.3	22-2.3
22-2.3.1	22-2.3.1
22-2.3.2	22-2.3.2
22-2.3.3	22-2.3.3
22-2.3.4	22-2.3.4
22-2.3.5	22-2.3.5
22-2.4	22-2.4
22-2.4.1	22-2.4.1
22-3	22-3
22-3.1	22-3.1
22-3.2	22-3.2
22-3.2.1	22-3.2.1
22-3.2.2	22-3.2.2
22-3.3	22-3.3
22-3.3.1	22-3.3.1
22-4	22-4
22-5	22-5
22-5.1	22-5.1

CHAPTER 24

1985	1988
24-1	24-1
24-1.1	24-1.1
24-1.1.1	24-1.1.1
24-1.1.2	24-1.1.2
24-1.1.3	24-1.1.3
24-1.2	24-1.2
24-1.2.1	24-1.2.2
24-1.2.1.1	24-1.2.2.1
24-1.2.1.2	24-1.2.2.2
24-1.3	24-1.3
24-1.4	24-1.4
24-1.4.1	24-1.4.1
24-1.4.2	24-1.4.2
24-1.4.2.1	24-1.4.2.1
24-1.4.2.2	24-1.4.2.2
24-1.4.2.3	24-1.4.2.3
24-1.4.2.4	24-1.4.2.4
24-1.5	24-1.5
24-1.6	24-1.6
24-1.7	24-1.7
24-1.7.1	24-1.7.1
24-1.7.2	24-1.7.2
24-2	24-2
24-2.1	24-2.1
24-2.1.1	24-2.1.1
24-2.1.2	24-2.1.2
24-2.1.3	24-2.1.3
24-2.1.4	24-2.1.4
24-2.1.5	24-2.1.5

1985	1988
24-2.2	24-2.2
24-2.2.1	24-2.2.1
24-2.3	24-2.3
24-2.3.1	24-2.3.1
24-2.3.2	24-2.3.2
24-2.4	24-2.4
24-2.4.1	24-2.4.1
24-2.4.2	24-2.4.2
24-2.5	24-2.5
24-2.5.1	24-2.5.1
24-2.5.2	24-2.5.2
24-2.5.3	24-2.5.3
24-2.5.4	24-2.5.4
24-2.5.5	24-2.5.5
24-2.5.6	24-2.5.6
24-2.5.7	24-2.5.7
24-2.5.8	24-2.5.8
24-2.5.9	24-2.5.9
24-2.5.10	24-2.5.10
24-2.6	24-2.6
24-2.7	24-2.7
24-2.8	24-2.8
24-2.9	24-2.9
24-2.10	24-2.10
24-2.11	24-2.11
24-2.11.1	24-2.2.2.6
24-2.11.2	24-2.2.2.2
24-2.11.3	24-2.2.2.4
24-2.11.4	24-2.2.2.3
24-2.11.5	24-2.2.2.5
24-2.11.6	24-2.2.3.2
24-3	24-3
24-3.1	24-3.1
24-3.2	24-3.2
24-3.2.1	24-3.2.1
24-3.2.2	7-7.1.2
24-3.2.3	24-3.2.2
24-3.3	24-3.3
24-3.3.1	24-3.3.1
24-3.3.2	24-3.3.2
24-3.4	24-3.4
24-3.4.1	24-3.4.1
24-3.4.2	24-3.4.2
24-3.4.3	24-3.4.3
24-3.4.3.1	24-3.4.3.1
24-3.4.3.2	24-3.4.3.2
24-3.4.3.3	24-3.4.3.3
24-3.5	24-3.5
24-3.5.1	24-3.5.1
24-3.5.2	24-3.5.2
24-3.5.3	24-3.5.3
24-3.6	24-3.6
24-3.6.1	24-3.6.1
24-3.6.2	24-3.6.2
24-3.6.3	24-3.6.3
24-3.7	24-3.7
24-3.8	24-3.8
24-4	24-4
24-4.1	24-4.1
24-4.2	24-4.3
24-4.2.1	24-4.3.1
24-4.2.2	24-4.3.2
24-4.3	24-4.4
24-4.3.1	24-4.4.1
24-4.3.2	24-4.4.2

1985	1988		1985	1988		1985	1988
24-4.3.2.1	24-4.4.2.1		25-2.3.1	25-2.3.1		25-4.3.3.2	25-4.4.3.2
24-4.3.2.2	24-4.4.2.2		25-2.3.2	25-2.3.2		25-4.3.3.3	25-4.4.3.3
24-4.3.2.3	24-4.4.2.3		25-2.4	25-2.4		25-4.3.3.4	25-4.4.3.4
24-4.3.2.4	24-4.4.2.4		25-2.4.1	25-2.4.2		25-4.3.3.5	25-4.4.3.5
24-4.3.3	24-4.4.3		25-2.4.2	25-2.4.3		25-4.3.3.6	25-4.4.3.6
24-4.3.3.1	24-4.4.3.1		25-2.5	25-2.5		25-4.4	25-4.5
24-4.3.3.2	24-4.4.3.2		25-2.5.1	25-2.5.1		25-4.4.1	25-4.5.1
24-4.3.3.3	24-4.4.3.3		25-2.5.2	25-2.5.2		25-4.4.2	--
24-4.3.3.4	24-4.4.3.4		25-2.5.3	25-2.5.3		25-4.4.3	--
24-4.3.3.5	24-4.4.3.5		25-2.5.4	25-2.5.4		25-4.4.4	25-4.5.2
24-4.3.3.6	24-4.4.3.6		25-2.5.5	25-2.5.5		25-4.4.5	25-4.5.3
24-4.4	24-4.5		25-2.5.6	25-2.5.6		25-4.4.5.1	25-4.5.3.1
24-4.4.1	24-4.5.1		25-2.5.7	25-2.5.7		25-4.4.5.2	25-4.5.3.2
24-4.4.2	--		25-2.5.8	25-2.5.8		25-4.4.5.3	25-4.5.3.3
24-4.4.3	--		25-2.5.9	25-2.5.9		25-4.4.5.4	25-4.5.3.4
24-4.4.4	24-4.5.2		25-2.5.10	25-2.5.10		25-4.4.5.5	25-4.5.3.5
24-4.4.5	24-4.5.3		25-2.6	25-2.6		25-4.4.5.6	25-4.5.3.6
24-4.4.5.1	24-4.5.3.1		25-2.7	25-2.7		25-4.4.6	25-4.5.4
24-4.4.5.2	24-4.5.3.2		25-2.8	25-2.8		25-4.5	25-4.6
24-4.4.5.3	24-4.5.3.3		25-2.9	25-2.9		25-5	25-5
24-4.4.5.4	24-4.5.3.4		25-2.10	25-2.10		25-5.1	25-5.1
24-4.4.5.5	24-4.5.3.5		25-2.11	25-2.11		25-5.2	25-5.2
24-4.4.5.6	24-4.5.3.6		25-2.11.1	25-2.2.2.6		25-5.3	25-5.3
24-4.4.6	24-4.5.4		25-2.11.2	25-2.2.2.2		25-5.4	25-5.4
24-4.5	24-4.6		25-2.11.3	25-2.2.2.4			
24-5	24-5		25-2.11.4	25-2.2.2.3		**CHAPTER 26**	
24-5.1	24-5.1		25-2.11.5	25-2.2.2.5		26-1	26-1
24-5.2	24-5.2		25-2.11.6	25-2.2.3.2		26-1.1	26-1.1
24-5.3	24-5.3		25-2.11.7	25-2.2.3.3		26-1.1.1	26-1.1.1
24-5.4	24-5.4		25-2.11.8	25-2.2.2.8		26-1.1.2	26-1.1.2
			25-3	25-3		26-1.1.3	26-1.1.3
CHAPTER 25			25-3.1	25-3.1		26-1.2	26-1.2
25-1	25-1		25-3.2	25-3.2		26-1.2.1	--
25-1.1	25-1.1		25-3.2.1	25-3.2.1		26-1.2.1.1	--
25-1.1.1	25-1.1.1		25-3.2.2	7-7.1.2		26-1.3	26-1.3
25-1.1.2	25-1.1.2		25-3.2.3	25-3.2.2		26-1.4	26-1.4
25-1.1.3	25-1.1.3		25-3.3	25-3.3		26-1.4.1	26-1.4.1
25-1.2	25-1.2		25-3.3.1	25-3.3.1		26-1.5	26-1.5
25-1.2.1	25-1.2.2		25-3.3.2	25-3.3.2		26-1.5.1	26-1.5.1
25-1.2.1.1	25-1.2.2.1		25-3.4	25-3.4		26-1.5.2	26-1.5.2
25-1.2.1.2	25-1.2.2.2		25-3.4.1	25-3.4.1		26-1.6	26-1.6
25-1.2.1.3	25-1.2.2.3		25-3.4.2	25-3.4.2		26-1.7	26-1.7
25-1.3	25-1.3		25-3.4.3	25-3.4.3		26-1.7.1	26-1.7.1
25-1.4	25-1.4		25-3.4.3.1	25-3.4.3.1		26-1.7.2	26-1.7.2
25-1.4.1	25-1.4.1		25-3.4.3.2	25-3.4.3.2		26-2	26-2
25-1.4.2	25-1.4.2		25-3.5	25-3.5		26-2.1	26-2.1
25-1.4.2.1	25-1.4.2.1		25-3.5.1	25-3.5.1		26-2.1.1	26-2.1.1
25-1.4.2.2	25-1.4.2.2		25-3.5.2	25-3.5.2		26-2.1.2	26-2.1.2
25-1.4.2.3	25-1.4.2.3		25-3.6	25-3.6		26-2.1.3	--
25-1.4.2.4	25-1.4.2.4		25-3.7	25-3.7		26-2.1.4	26-2.1.3
25-1.5	25-1.5		25-3.8	25-3.8		26-2.1.5	26-2.1.4
25-1.6	25-1.6		25-4	25-4		26-2.2	26-2.2
25-1.7	25-1.7		25-4.1	25-4.1		26-2.2.1	26-2.2.1
25-1.7.1	25-1.7.1		25-4.2	25-4.3		26-2.3	26-2.3
25-1.7.2	25-1.7.2		25-4.2.1	25-4.3.1		26-2.3.1	26-2.3.1
25-2	25-2		25-4.2.2	25-4.3.2		26-2.3.2	26-2.3.2
25-2.1	25-2.1		25-4.3	25-4.4		26-2.3.3	26-2.3.3
25-2.1.1	25-2.1.1		25-4.3.1	25-4.4.1		26-2.4	26-2.4
25-2.1.2	25-2.1.2		25-4.3.2	25-4.4.2		26-2.5	26-2.5
25-2.1.3	25-2.1.3		25-4.3.2.1	25-4.4.2.1		26-2.5.1	26-2.5.1
25-2.1.4	25-2.1.4		25-4.3.2.2	25-4.4.2.2		26-2.5.2	26-2.5.2
25-2.1.5	25-2.1.5		25-4.3.2.3	25-4.4.2.3		26-2.5.3	26-2.5.3
25-2.2	25-2.2		25-4.3.2.4	25-4.4.2.4		26-2.6	26-2.6
25-2.2.1	25-2.2.1		25-4.3.3	25-4.4.3		26-2.7	26-2.7
25-2.3	25-2.3		25-4.3.3.1	25-4.4.3.1		26-2.7.1	26-2.7

1985	1988
26-2.7.2	26-2.7
26-2.8	26-2.8
26-2.9	26-2.9
26-2.9.1	26-2.9.1
26-2.9.2	26-2.9.2
26-2.10	26-2.10
26-2.11	26-2.11
26-2.11.1	26-2.2.2.2
26-2.11.2	26-2.2.2.3
26-2.11.3	26-2.2.2.4
26-2.11.4	26-2.2.2.5
26-2.11.5	26-2.2.3.2
26-3	26-3
26-3.1	26-3.1
26-3.1.1	26-3.1.1
26-3.1.2	26-3.1.2
26-3.2	26-3.2
26-3.2.1	26-3.2.1
26-3.2.2	7-7.1.2
26-3.2.3	26-3.2.2
26-3.3	26-3.3
26-3.3.1	26-3.3.1
26-3.3.2	26-3.3.2
26-3.3.3	26-3.3.3
26-3.4	26-3.4
26-3.4.1	26-3.4.1
26-3.4.2	26-3.4.2
26-3.4.3	26-3.4.3
26-3.4.3.1	26-3.4.3.1
26-3.4.3.2	26-3.4.3.2
26-3.5	26-3.5
26-3.6	26-3.6
26-3.6.1	26-3.6.1
26-3.6.2	26-3.6.2
26-3.6.3	26-3.6.3
26-4	26-4
26-4.1	26-4.1
26-4.2	26-4.2
26-4.2.1	26-4.2.2
26-4.2.2	26-4.2.1
26-4.3	26-4.3
26-4.3.1	26-4.3.1
26-4.3.2	--
26-4.3.3	--
26-4.3.4	26-4.3.2
26-4.3.5	26-4.3.3
26-4.3.5.1	26-4.3.3.1
26-4.3.5.2	26-4.3.3.2
26-4.3.5.3	26-4.3.3.3
26-4.3.5.4	26-4.3.3.4
26-4.3.5.5	26-4.3.3.5
26-4.3.5.6	26-4.3.3.6
26-4.3.6	26-4.3.4
26-4.4	26-4.4
26-5	26-5
26-5.1	26-5.1
26-5.2	26-5.2
26-5.3	26-5.3
26-5.4	26-5.4

CHAPTER 27

1985	1988
27-1	27-1
27-1.1	27-1.1
27-1.1.1	27-1.1.1
27-1.1.2	27-1.1.2
27-1.2	27-1.2
27-1.2.1	--
27-1.2.1.1	--
27-1.3	27-1.3
27-1.4	27-1.4
27-1.4.1	27-1.4.1
27-1.5	27-1.5
27-1.5.1	27-1.5.1
27-1.5.2	27-1.5.2
27-1.6	27-1.6
27-1.7	27-1.7
27-1.7.1	27-1.7.1
27-1.7.2	27-1.7.2
27-2	27-2
27-2.1	27-2.1
27-2.1.1	27-2.1.1
27-2.1.2	27-2.1.2
27-2.1.3	--
27-2.1.4	27-2.1.3
27-2.1.5	27-2.1.4
27-2.2	27-2.2
27-2.2.1	27-2.2.1
27-2.3	27-2.3
27-2.3.1	27-2.3.1
27-2.3.2	27-2.3.2
27-2.3.3	27-2.3.3
27-2.4	27-2.4
27-2.5	27-2.5
27-2.5.1	27-2.5.1
27-2.5.2	27-2.5.2
27-2.5.3	27-2.5.3
27-2.6	27-2.6
27-2.7	27-2.7
27-2.7.1	27-2.7
27-2.7.2	27-2.7
27-2.8	27-2.8
27-2.9	27-2.9
27-2.9.1	27-2.9.1
27-2.9.2	27-2.9.2
27-2.10	27-2.10
27-2.11	27-2.11
27-2.11.1	27-2.2.2.2
27-2.11.2	27-2.2.2.3
27-2.11.3	27-2.2.2.4
27-2.11.4	27-2.2.2.5
27-2.11.5	27-2.2.3.2
27-2.11.6	27-2.2.3.3
27-3	27-3
27-3.1	27-3.1
27-3.1.1	27-3.1.1
27-3.1.2	27-3.1.2
27-3.2	27-3.2
27-3.2.1	27-3.2.1
27-3.2.2	7-7.1.2
27-3.2.3	27-3.2.2
27-3.3	27-3.3
27-3.3.1	27-3.3.1
27-3.3.2	27-3.3.2
27-3.3.3	27-3.3.3
27-3.4	27-3.4
27-3.4.1	27-3.4.1
27-3.4.2	27-3.4.2
27-3.4.3	27-3.4.3
27-3.4.3.1	27-3.4.3.1
27-3.4.3.2	27-3.4.3.2
27-3.5	27-3.5
27-4	27-4
27-4.1	27-4.1
27-4.2	27-4.2
27-4.2.1	27-4.2.1
27-4.2.2	27-4.2.2
27-4.2.3	27-4.2.3
27-4.3	27-4.3
27-4.3.1	27-4.3.1
27-4.3.2	--
27-4.3.3	--
27-4.3.4	27-4.3.2
27-4.3.5	27-4.3.3
27-4.3.5.1	27-4.3.3.1
27-4.3.5.2	27-4.3.3.2
27-4.3.5.3	27-4.3.3.3
27-4.3.5.4	27-4.3.3.4
27-4.3.5.5	27-4.3.3.5
27-4.3.5.6	27-4.3.3.6
27-4.3.6	27-4.3.4
27-4.4	27-4.4
27-5	27-5
27-5.1	27-5.1
27-5.2	27-5.2
27-5.3	27-5.3
27-5.4	27-5.4

CHAPTER 28

1985	1988
28-1	28-1
28-1.1	28-1.1
28-1.2	28-1.2
28-1.3	28-1-3
28-1.4	28-1.4
28-1.4.1	28-1.4.1
28-1.4.2	28-1.4.1
28-1.4.3	28-1.4.1
28-1.5	28-1.5
28-1.6	28-1.6
28-1.7	28-1.7
28-2	28-2
28-2.1	28-2.1
28-2.1.1	28-2.1.1
28-2.2	28-2.2
28-2.3	28-2.3
28-2.3.1	28-2.3.1
28-2.3.2	28-2.3.2
28-2.4	28-2.4
28-2.4.1	28-2.4.1
28-2.4.2	28-2.4.3
28-2.5	28-2.5
28-2.5.1	28-2.5.1
28-2.5.2	28-2.5.2
28-2.6	28-2.6
28-2.6.1	28-2.6.1
28-2.6.2	28-2.6.2
28-2.7	28-2.7
28-2.8	28-2.8
28-2.8.1	28-2.8.1
28-2.9	28-2.9
28-2.9.1	28-2.9.1
28-2.10	28-2.10
28-2.10.1	28-2.10.1
28-2.11	28-2.11
28-2.11.1	28-2.2.2.2
28-2.11.2	28-2.2.3.2

1985	1988	1985	1988	1985	1988
28-2.11.3	28-2.2.3.3	29-4	29-4	30-1.3.1	30-1.3.1
28-3	28-3	29-4.1	29-4.1	30-1.3.2	30-1.3.2
28-3.1	28-3.1	29-5	29-5	30-1.3.3	30-1.3.3
28-3.1.1	28-3.1.1	29-6	29-6	30-1.3.4	30-1.3.4
28-3.2	28-3.2	29-6.1	29-6.1	30-1.3.5	30-1.3.5
28-3.3	28-3.3	29-6.2	29-6.2	30-1.3.6	30-1.3.6
28-3.3.1	28-3.3.1	29-6.3	29-6.3	30-1.3.7	30-1.3.7
28-3.3.2	28-3.3.2	29-6.4	29-6.4	30-1.4	30-1.4
28-3.4	28-3.4	29-7	29-7	30-1.5	30-1.5
28-3.4.1	28-3.4.1	29-7.1	29-7.1	30-1.6	30-1.6
28-3.4.2	28-3.4.2	29-7.2	29-7.2	30-1.7	30-1.7
28-3.4.3	28-3.4.3	29-7.3	29-7.3	30-2	30-2
28-3.4.3.1	28-3.4.3.1	29-7.4	29-7.4	30-2.1	30-2.1
28-3.4.3.2	28-3.4.3.2	29-7.4.1	29-7.4.1	30-2.2	30-2.2
28-4	28-4	29-7.4.2	29-7.4.2	30-2.3	30-2.3
28-4.1	28-4.1	29-8	29-8	30-2.3.1	30-2.3.1
		29-8.1	29-8.1	30-2.3.2	30-2.3.2
CHAPTER 29		29-8.1.1	29-8.1.1	30-2.3.3	30-2.3.3
29-1	29-1	29-8.1.2	29-8.1.2	30-2.4	30-2.4.1
29-1.1	29-1.1	29-8.1.2.1	29-8.1.2.1	30-2.5	30-2.5
29-1.2	29-1.2	29-8.1.2.2	29-8.1.2.2	30-2.5.1	30-2.5.1
29-1.3	29-1.3	29-8.1.3	29-8.1.3	30-2.5.2	30-2.5.2
29-1.4	29-1.4	29-8.1.4	29-8.1.4	30-2.5.3	30-2.5.3
29-1.5	29-1.5	29-8.1.5	29-8.1.5	30-2.5.3.1	30-2.5.3.1
29-1.6	29-1.6	29-8.1.6	29-8.1.6	30-2.5.3.2	30-2.5.3.2
29-1.7	29-1.7	29-8.1.7	29-8.1.7	30-2.5.3.3	30-2.5.3.3
29-2	29-2	29-8.2	29-8.2	30-2.5.3.4	30-2.5.3.4
29-2.1	29-2.1	29-8.2.1	29-8.2.1	30-2.5.3.5	30-2.5.3.5
29-2.2	29-2.2	29-8.2.2	29-8.2.2	30-2.6	30-2.6
29-2.3	29-2.3	29-8.2.3	29-8.2.3	30-2.7	30-2.7
29-2.3.1	29-2.3.1	29-8.2.3.1	29-8.2.3.1	30-2.8	30-2.8
29-2.3.2	29-2.3.2	29-8.2.4	29-8.2.4	30-2.9	30-2.9
29-2.4	29-2.4	29-8.2.5	29-8.2.5	30-2.10	30-2.10
29-2.4.1	29-2.4.1	29-8.2.5.1	29-8.2.5.1	30-2.11	30-2.11
29-2.5	29-2.5	29-8.2.5.2	29-8.2.5.2	30-2.11.1	30-2.2.3.2
29-2.5.1	29-2.5.1	29-8.2.5.3	29-8.2.5.3	30-2.11.2	30-2.2.3.3
29-2.5.2	29-2.5.3	29-8.2.6	29-8.2.6	30-3	30-3
29-2.6	29-2.6	29-8.2.7	29-8.2.7	30-3.1	30-3.1
29-2.6.1	29-2.6.1	29-8.2.8	29-8.2.8	30-3.2	30-3.2
29-2.7	29-2.7	29-8.2.9	29-8.2.9	30-3.3	30-3.3
29-2.8	29-2.8	29-8.2.10	29-8.2.10	30-3.3.1	30-3.3.1
29-2.8.1	29-2.8.1	29-8.2.11	29-8.2.11	30-3.3.2	30-3.3.2
29-2.9	29-2.9	29-8.2.11.1	29-8.2.2.2(b)	30-3.4	30-3.4
29-2.9.1	29-2.9.1	29-8.2.11.2	29-8.2.2.3(b)	30-3.4.1	30-3.4.1
29-2.10	29-2.10	29-8.3	29-8.3	30-3.4.2	30-3.4.2
29-2.11	29-2.11	29-8.3.1	29-8.3.1	30-3.4.3	30-3.4.3
29-2.11.1	29-2.2.2.2	29-8.3.2	29-8.3.2	30-4	30-4
29-2.11.2	29-2.2.3.2	29-8.3.3	29-8.3.3	30-4.1	30-4.1
29-2.11.3	29-2.2.3.3	29-8.3.3.1	29-8.3.3.1	30-5	30-5
29-3	29-3	29-8.3.3.2	29-8.3.3.2	30-6	30-6
29-3.1	29-3.1	29-8.3.4	29-8.3.4	30-6.1	30-6.1
29-3.1.1	29-3.1.1	29-8.3.4.1	29-8.3.4.1	30-6.2	30-6.2
29-3.2	29-3.2	29-8.3.4.2	29-8.3.4.2	30-7	30-7
29-3.3	29-3.3	29-8.3.4.3	29-8.3.4.3	30-7.1	30-7.1
29-3.3.1	29-3.3.1			30-7.1.1	30-7.1.1
29-3.3.2	29-3.3.2	**CHAPTER 30**		30-7.1.2	30-7.1.2
29-3.4	29-3.4	30-1	30-1	30-7.1.3	30-7.1.3
29-3.4.1	29-3.4.1	30-1.1	30-1.1	30-7.2	30-7.2
29-3.4.2	29-3.4.2	30-1.2	30-1.2	30-7.2.1	30-7.2.1
29-3.4.3	29-3.4.3	30-1.3	30-1.3	30-7.2.2	30-7.2.2

Index

-A-

Additions .... 1-4.5; see also under specific occupancies
Definition 3-2
Air conditioning ..... 7-2; see also Building services under specific occupancies
Aircraft hangars 29-6, A-29-6
Aisles .... see under specific occupancies
Alarm systems .... 7-6, A-7-6; see also under specific occupancies
Audible alarm indicating appliances ..... 7-6.3.6 thru 7-6.3.9
Auxiliary fire alarm relay 7-6.5.5, A-7-6.5.5
Devices for doors 5-1.7.2, 5-2.1.5, A-5-2.1.5
Fundamental requirements 2-7, 7-6.1
Initiating protective signaling system 7-6.2
Maintenance and testing of 7-6.1.3, 7-6.1.6, 31-1.3.2, 31-1.3.7, A-7-6.1.3, A-7.6.1.6
Manual stations .... 7-6.2.2 thru 7-6.2.5
Signal initiation 7-6.2, 31-3.2
Alterations, building 1-4.6, 31-1.1.2, A-1-4.6
Alternating tread device ... 5-2.11, A-5-2.11
Ambulatory health care centers .. 12-6, 13-6
Alarm systems in 12-6.3.4, 13-6.3.4
Application of requirements for 12-6.1.1, 13-6.1.1
Modification of retroactive provisions 13-6.1.1.3
Building construction for 12-6.1.6, 13-6.1.6
Building services 12-6.5, 13-6.5
Air conditioning 12-6.5.2.1, 13-6.5.2.1
Elevators 12-6.5.3, 13-6.5.3
Heating 12-6.5.2, 13-6.5.2
Incinerators 12-6.5.4, 13-6.5.4
Laundry chutes ... 12-6.5.4, 13-6.5.4
Rubbish chutes ... 12-6.5.4, 13-6.5.4
Utilities 12-6.5.1, 13-6.5.1
Ventilation 12-6.5.2, 13-6.5.2
Building spaces, subdivision of 12-6.3.7, 13-6.3.7
Classification of 4-1.4, 12-1.2.2, 12-6.1.4, 13-1.2.2, 13-6.1.4, A-12-1.2.2, A-13-1.2.2
Communication systems in 12-6.3.4, 13-6.3.4
Corridors 12-6.3.6, 13-6.3.6
Minimum width 12-6.2.3.2, 13-6.2.3.2
Definition .... 12-1.3(d), 13-1.3(d)
Detection systems in ... 12-6.3.4, 13-6.3.4
Doors
Automatic 12-6.2.2.3, 12-6.2.2.4, 13-6.2.2.3, 13-6.2.2.4
In smoke barriers 12-6.3.7.6, 12-6.3.7.7, 13-6.3.7.6, 13-6.3.7.7
Treatment areas 12-6.2.3.3, 13-6.2.3.3
Emergency lighting in 12-6.2.9, 13-6.2.9
Existing buildings 13-6
Exits
Discharge from ... 12-6.2.7, 13-6.2.7
Number of 12-6.2.4, 13-6.2.4
Travel distance to 12-6.2.6, 13-6.2.6
Extinguishing requirements for 12-6.3.5, 13-6.3.5
General requirements for .. 12-6.1, 13-6.1
Interior finish in 12-6.3.3, 13-6.3.3
Locks in 12-1.1.1.7, 12-6.2.2.2, 13-1.1.1.7, 13-6.2.2.2
Means of egress 12-6.2, 13-6.2
Arrangement of ... 12-6.2.5, 13-6.2.5
Capacity of 12-6.2.3, 13-6.2.3
Components of ... 12-6.2.2, 13-6.2.2
Illumination of ... 12-6.2.8, 13-6.2.8
Marking of 12-6.2.10, 13-6.2.10
New buildings 12-6
Occupant load in 12-6.1.7, 13-6.1.7
Notification of occupants and emergency forces 12-6.3.4.3, 13-6.3.4.3
Protection 12-6.3, 13-6.3
From hazards 12-6.3.2, 13-6.3.2
Of vertical openings 12-6.3.1, 13-6.3.1
Amusement buildings .... 8-4.6, 9-4.6, A-8.4.6, A-9-4.6; see also Assembly occupancies
Definition 8-1.3, 9-1.3
Anesthetizing locations 12-3.2.3, 12-6.2.9.2, 12-6.3.2.2, 13-3.2.3, 13-6.2.9.2, 13-6.3.2.2
Apartment buildings ..... Chaps. 18 and 19

Chapters 1-7 and 31 reference general requirements. Chapters 8, 10, 12, 14, 16, 18, 24 and 26 reference requirements for new occupancies. Chapters 9, 11, 13, 15, 17, 19, 25 and 27 reference requirements for existing occupancies. Chapters 20, 21, 22, 28, 29 and 30 reference requirements for both new and existing occupancies.

Alarm systems in 18-3.4, 19-3.4
Application of requirements
  for 18-1.1, 19-1.1
Atriums in 18-3.1, 19-3.1
Board and care occupancies in 21-4
Building services in 18-5, 19-5
  Air conditioning 18-5.2, 19-5.2
  Elevators 18-5.3, 19-5.3
  Heating 18-5.2, 19-5.2
  Incinerators 18-5.4, 19-5.4
  Laundry chutes 18-5.4, 19-5.4
  Rubbish chutes 18-5.4, 19-5.4
  Utilities 18-5.1, 19-5.1
  Ventilation 18-4.1, 18-5.2,
                  19-4.1, 19-5.2
Classification of 18-1.4, 19-1.4
Communication systems in 18-3.4,
                  19-3.4
Contents of, hazard
  classification 18-1.5, 19-1.5
Corridors
  Construction of 18-3.6, 19-3.6
  Dead end 18-2.5.3, 19-2.5.3
  Minimum width .. 18-2.3.3, 19-2.3.3
Day care centers in .... 10-7.1.2(b),
                  11-7.1.2(b)
Definition 18-1.3.1, 19-1.3.1
Detection systems in ... 18-3.4.4, 19-3.4.4,
              A-18-3.4.4, A-19-3.4.4
Doors in 18-2.2.2, 18-3.6.2,
  19-2.2.2, 19-3.6.2, A-18-2.2.2, A-19-2.2.2
  Fire protection rating 18-3.6.3,
    19-3.6.3, A-18-3.6.3, A-19-3.6.3
Emergency instructions for
  residents 31-6.4, 31-6.5
Emergency lighting in 18-2.9, 19-2.9
Existing buildings .... Chap. 19
Exits
  Discharge from 18-2.7, 19-2.7
  Horizontal 18-3.7.1, 19-3.7.1
  Number of 18-2.4, 19-2.4
  Passageways 18-2.2.7, 19-2.2.7
  Travel distance to .. 18-2.5.2, 18-2.6,
                  19-2.5.2, 19-2.6
Extinguishment requirements
  for 18-3.5, 19-3.5
Furnishings and decorations
  in 31-6.6, A-31-6.6
General requirements for 18-1, 19-1
Group day care homes in .... 10-8.1.2(b),
                  11-8.1.2(b)
Interior finish in 18-3.3, 19-3.3
Locks in 18-2.2.2.2, 18-2.11,
  19-2.2.2.2, 19-2.11, A-18-2.2.2.2,
                  A-19-2.2.2.2
Means of egress 18-2, 19-2
  Arrangement of 18-2.5, 19-2.5
  Capacity of 18-2.3, 19-2.3
  Illumination of 18-2.8, 19-2.8
  Marking of 18-2.10, 19-2.10
Mixed occupancies of 18-1.2, 19-1.2
New buildings .... Chap. 18
Notification system 18-3.4.3, 19-3.4.3
Occupant load of 18-1.7, 19-1.7,
              A-18-1.7, A-19-1.7
Protection 18-3, 19-3

From hazards 18-3.2, 19-3.2
  Of vertical openings .. 18-3.1, 19-3.1
  Smoke control in 18-3.7.2, 19-3.7.2
  Special provisions for 18-4, 19-4
  Stairs in 18-2.2.3, 19-2.2.3
  Windows in 18-4.1, 19-4.1
Application of code 1-4, A-1-4
Area of refuge 5-2.4.2, 10-7.2.2.2,
              11-7.2.2.2, A-2-1
Areas .... see Floor area;
    Hazardous areas; High hazard areas
Arena stage
  Definition 3-2
Assembly occupancies ...... Chaps. 8 and 9
  Accessory rooms 8-3.1.4, 9-3.2.1.4
  Additions to 9-1.1.2
  Aisles in 8-2.3.2, 8-2.5.6, 9-2.3.2,
        9-2.5.6, A-8-2.3.2, A-8-2.5.6,
              A-9-2.3.2, A-9-2.5.6
    Width of 8-2.5.6.7, 8-2.5.6.8,
          9-2.5.6.7, 9-2.5.6.8,
          A-8-2.5.6.8, A-9-2.5.6.8
  Alarm systems in 8-3.4, 9-3.4,
              A-8-3.4, A-9-3.4
  Amusement buildings 8-4.6, 9-4.6,
              A-8-4.6, A-9-4.6
  Application of requirements
    for 8-1.1, 9-1.1
  Atriums in 8-3.1, 9-3.1
  Balconies in .... 8-2.4.4 thru 8-2.4.6,
              9-2.4.4 thru 9-2.4.6
  Building construction for 5-1.3.4,
              8-1.6, 9-1.6
  Building services in .... 8-3.2.3.3(c),
        8-5, 9-3.2.3.3(c), 9-5
    Air conditioning 8-5.2, 9-5.2
    Elevators 8-5.3, 9-5.3
    Heating 8-5.2, 9-5.2
    Incinerators 8-5.4, 9-5.4
    Laundry chutes 8-5.4, 9-5.4
    Rubbish chutes 8-5.4, 9-5.4
    Utilities 8-5.1, 9-5.1
    Ventilation 8-3.2.1.5, 8-3.2.6.6,
        8-5.2, 9-3.2.1.5, 9-3.2.6.6, 9-5.2
  Projection rooms 8-3.2.2.6,
        8-3.2.2.7, 9-3.2.2.6, 9-3.2.2.7
  Building spaces, subdivision of . 8-3.2.1.6,
        8-4.1.3, 9-3.2.1.6, 9-4.1.3
  Classification of 4-1.2, 8-1.4.1,
              9-1.4.1, A-4-1.2
  Communication systems in .. 8-3.4, 9-3.4
  Contents of, hazard
    classification 8-1.5, 9-1.5
  Corridors, construction
    of 5-1.3.4, A-5-1.3.4
  Definitions 8-1.3, 9-1.3,
              A-8-1.3, A-9-1.3
  Detection systems in 8-3.4, 9-3.4
  Doors in .... 8-2.2.1 thru 8-2.2.7,
              9-2.2.1 thru 9-2.2.7
  Drills for 31-2.1, A-31-2.1
  Emergency lighting in 8-2.9, 9-2.9
  Equipment and storage 8-3.2.2.8,
        8-3.2.3, 9-3.2.2.8, 9-3.2.3
  Exhibition halls and exhibits 8-4.4,
              9-4.4

Existing buildings . . . . Chap. 9
Exits 8-2.3.4, 9-2.3.4
    Discharge from 8-2.7, 9-2.7
    Main 8-2.3.3, 9-2.3.3
    Number of 8-2.4, 9-2.4
    Special 8-3.2.1.10, 9-3.2.1.10
    Travel distance to 8-2.6, 9-2.6
Extinguishment requirements
    for 8-3.5, 9-3.5
Flame retardant requirements
    for 8-3.2.1.11, 9-3.2.1.11
Fly galleries 8-3.2.1.8, 9-3.2.1.8
    Definition 8-3.1, 9-3.1
Food service in . . . 8-3.2.4, 9-3.2.4, 31-2.4
Furnishings and decorations
    in 8-3.2.1.7, 9-3.2.1.7, 31-2.6
General requirements for . . 8-1, 9-1, 31-2
Gridirons 8-3.2.1.8, 9-3.2.1.8
    Definition 8-1.3, 9-1.3
Hazardous operations or processes
    in 8-3.2.3, 9-3.2.3
High rise buildings 8-4.2, 9-4.2
Hotel occupancies with . . . 16-1.2, 17-1.2
Interior finish in 8-3.3, 9-3.3
Locks in 8-2.2.3, 9-2.2.3
Means of egress in 8-2, 9-2
    Arrangement of 8-2.5, 9-2.5
    Capacity of 8-2.3, 9-2.3
    Components of 8-2.2, 9-2.2
    Illumination of 8-2.8, 9-2.8
    Marking of 8-2.10, 9-2.10
Mixed occupancies of 8-1.2, 9-1.2,
    16-1.2.3, 17-1.2.3, A-8-1.2, A-9-1.2
New buildings . . . . Chap. 8
Notification system 8-3.4.3, 9-3.4.3
Occupant load of 8-1.7, 9-1.7
    Posting of notice 31-2.7.3
Open flame devices in . . . 8-4.4.3, 9-4.4.3,
    31-2.3, A-31-2.3
Outdoor 8-4.3, 9-4.3
Panic hardware in 8-2.2.2.3
Pinrails 8-3.2.1.8, 9-3.2.1.8
    Definition 8-1.3, 9-1.3
Projection booths in 8-3.2.2, 9-3.2.2
Projection rooms in 8-3.2.2, 9-3.2.2
Proscenium curtain in   8-3.2.1.7, 9-3.2.1.7
Proscenium walls in . . 8-3.2.1.6, 9-3.2.1.6
    Definition 8-1.3, 9-1.3
Protection 8-3, 9-3
    From hazards 8-3.2, 9-3.2
    Of food service
        establishments . . 8-3.2.4, 9-3.2.4
    Of projection booths 8-3.2.2,
        9-3.2.2
    Of service equipment 8-3.2.3,
        9-3.2.3
    Of stages and platforms 8-3.2.1,
        9-3.2.1
    Of storage facilities 8-3.2.3,
        9-3.2.3
    Of vertical openings 8-3.1, 9-3.1

Railings in 8-2.11, 9-2.11
Ramps in 8-2.2.6, 8-2.5.6.9,
    9-2.2.6, 9-2.5.6.9
Seating for 8-2.5.4, 8-2.5.5.4,
    9-2.5.4, 9-2.5.5.4
    Definitions 8-1.3, 9-1.3,
        A-8-1.3, A-9-1.3
    Table-arm 8-2.5.5, 9-2.5.5,
        A-8-2.5.5, A-9-2.5.5
Smoke control 8-4.1.3, 8-4.1.4,
    9-4.1.3, 9-4.1.4
Smoking in 31-2.5
Special provisions for 8-4, 9-4
    Handicapped 8-4.5, 9-4.5,
        A-8-4.5, A-9-4.5
    Vehicles 8-4.4.4, 9-4.4.4
Stage scenery in 31-2.6
    Definition 8-1.3, 9-1.3
Stages and platforms 8-3.2.1, 9-3.2.1
    Construction of 8-3.2.1.2,
        8-3.2.1.3, 9-3.2.1.2,
        9-3.2.1.3
    Definitions 8-1.3, 9-1.3,
        A-8-1.3, A-9-1.3
    Materials and design 8-3.2.11,
        9-3.2.11
    Stairs 8-2.2.3, 8-2.5.6.9,
        8-3.1 Ex.3, 9-2.2.3,
        9-2.5.6.9, 9-3.1 Ex.3
    Aisle 8-2.5.6.9, 9-2.5.6.9
    Storage facilities in 8-3.2.2.8,
        8-3.3.2.3, 9-3.2.2.8, 9-3.3.2.3
    Underground buildings 8-4.1, 9-4.1
    Waiting spaces in 8-1.7.3, 9-1.7.3
    Windowless buildings 8-4.1, 9-4.1
Atriums 6-2.4.5, A-6-2.4.5;
        see also under
        specific occupancies
    Definition 3-2
Attendants
    Detention and correctional
        occupancies 14-1.1.5,
            15-1.1.5, 31-4.1
    Health care occupancies 12-1.1.3,
            13-1.1.3, 31-5.1
Auditoriums 12-1.2.5, 13-1.2.5;
        see also Assembly occupancies
Authority having jurisdiction
    Definition 3-2
    Modifications of Code by 1-5.2
Automatic
    Definition 3-2
**Automatic detection, of protective
    signaling systems** 7-6.2
Automatic sprinklers 7-6.2.6, 7-7.1,
        A-7-7.1; see also Extinguishment
        systems under specific occupancies
    Interior finish and 6-5.7
    Maintenance of 31-1.3.2, 31-1.3.6,
            31-3.5, A-31-1.3.6
    Supervision of 7-7.2, A-7-7.2

Chapters 1-7 and 31 reference general requirements. Chapters 8, 10, 12, 14, 16, 18, 24 and 26 reference requirements for new occupancies. Chapters 9, 11, 13, 15, 17, 19, 25 and 27 reference requirements for existing occupancies. Chapters 20, 21, 22, 28, 29 and 30 reference requirements for both new and existing occupancies.

-B-

Balconies
As corridors 10-2.5.5, 11-2.5.5,
    A-10-2.5.5, A-11-2.5.5
Assembly occupancies ...... 8-2.4.4 thru
    8-2.4.6, 9-2.4.4 thru 9-2.4.6
As exit access 5-5.3.2
Mercantile occupancies 24-1.7.2,
    25-1.7.2
With horizontal exits 5-2.4.4
With outside stairs 5-2.2.5.1
Barriers .... see Fire barriers;
    Smoke barriers
Board and care occupancies .... see
    Residential board and
    care occupancies
Bridges, with horizontal exits 5-2.4.4
Building services .... see also under
    specific occupancies
Air conditioning 7-2
Dumbwaiters 7-4
Elevators 7-4, A-7-4
Heating 7-2
Incinerators 7-5
Laundry chutes 7-5
Maintenance of equipment 31-1.3
Rubbish chutes 7-5
Utilities 7-1
Ventilation 7-2
Vertical conveyors 7-4
Building spaces, subdivision of .... see
    Compartmentation; Fire barriers;
    Smoke barriers; under specific occupancies
Buildings
Alterations to 1-4.6, A-1-4.6
Apartment ..... see Apartment buildings
Covered malls
    Definition .... 24-1.3(f), 25-1.3(f)
Definition 3-2
Existing 1-4.1, 1-4.4, A-1-4.4;
    see also specific occupancies
    Definition 3-2
    Occupancy of .... 1-6.1 thru
    1-6.3, A-1-6.3
Flexible plan, educational
    occupancies 10-6
    Definition 10-1.3, 11-1.3
    Means of egress
    requirements 10-6.2, 11-6.2
High-rise 8-4.2, 26-4.2, 27-4.2,
    A-26-4.2, A-27-4.2
Occupancy of 1-6, A-1-6
Open plan, educational occupan-
    cies 10-4.3, 11-4.3
    Definition 10-1.3, 11-1.3
    Means of egress
    requirements 10-6.2, 11-6.2
Service equipment of .... Chap. 7
Under construction 31-1.1.1
Underground 30-7.2
    Definition 30-1.3.4, A-30-1.3.4
Windowless .... 30-7; see also
    under specific occupancies
Bulk storage elevators 29-7, A-29-7
Business occupancies .... Chaps. 26 and 27

Additions to 26-1.1.3
Alarm systems in 26-3.4, 26-4.2.3,
    26-4.3.3, 27-3.4, 27-4.2.3, 27-4.3.3
Application of requirements
    for 26-1.1, 27-1.1
Atriums in 26-3.1.1 Ex.3, 26-4.3,
    27-3.1.1 Ex.3, 27-4.3
Building construction for .. 26-1.6, 27-1.6
Building services in 26-5, 27-5
    Air conditioning 26-5.4, 27-5.4
    Elevators 26-5.3, 27-5.3
    Heating 26-5.2, 27-5.2
    Incinerators 26-5.4, 27-5.4
    Laundry chutes 26-5.4, 27-5.4
    Rubbish chutes 26-5.4, 27-5.4
    Utilities 26-5.1, 27-5.1
    Ventilation 26-4.3.2, 26-5.2,
    27-4.3.2, 27-5.2
Classification of 4-1.8, 26-1.4,
    27-1.4,A-4-1.8
Combined with mercantile
    occupancy 26-1.2.1, 27-1.2.1
Communications systems 26-3.4, 26-4.2.3,
    26-4.3.3, 27-3.4, 27-4.2.3, 27-4.3.3
Contents of, hazard
    classification 26-1.5, 27-1.5
Corridors
    Construction of 26-3.6, A-26-3.6
    Dead-end 26-2.5.2, 27-2.5.2
    Minimum width of 26-2.3.2,
    27-2.3.2
Definition of 4-1.8
Detection systems in 26-3.4, 26-4.2.3,
    26-4.3.3, 27-3.4, 27-4.2.3, 27-4.3.3
Doors in 31-9.1
Drills in 31-9.1
Emergency lighting in 26-2.9, 27-2.9
Existing buildings .... Chap. 27
Exits
    Discharge from 26-2.7, 27-2.7
    Travel distance to 26-2.6, 27-2.6
    Number of 26-2.4, 27-2.4
Extinguishment requirements in .. 26-3.5,
    26-4.2.2, 27-3.5, 27-4.2.2
General requirements of 26-1,
    27-1, 31-9
High rise buildings 26-4.2, 27-4.2,
    A-26-4.2, A-27-4.2
Interior finish in 26-3.3, 27-3.3
Locks in 26-2.2.2, 27-2.2.2,
    A-26-2.2.2, A-27-2.2.2
Means of egress 26-2.2, 27-2.2
    Arrangement of 26-2.5, 27-2.5
    Capacity of 26-2.3, 27-2.3
    Components of 26-2.2, 27-2.2
    Illumination of 26-2.8, 27-2.8
    Marking of 26-2.10, 27-2.10
Mixed occupancies of 26-1.2, 27-1.2
New buildings .... Chap. 28
Notification 26-3.4.3, 26-4.3.3.3,
    27-3.4.3, 27-4.3.3.3
    Emergency forces 26-4.3.3.5,
    27-4.3.3.5
    Occupants 26-4.3.3.2,
    26-4.3.3.4, 27-3.4.3.2,
    27-4.3.3.4

Occupant load of 26-1.7,
            27-1.7, A-26-1.7, A-27-1.7
Protection 26-3, 27-3
  From hazards 26-3.2, 27-3.2
  Of vertical openings .. 26-3.1, 27-3.1
  Smoke control in 26-4.3.4, 27-4.3.4
  Special provisions for 26-4, 27-4
  Underground buildings 26-4.1, 27-4.1
  Windowless buildings 26-4.1, 27-4.1

                    -C-

Cellular or foamed plastic
  materials 6-5.2.4, A-6-5.2.4
Chutes .... see also Building services
              under specific occupancies
  Enclosures for 7-5
  Escape A-30-2.2
  Laundry 7-5
  Rubbish 7-5
Classifications, of
  Assembly occupancies ... 8-1.4.1, 9-1.4.1
  Hazard of contents 4-2.2, A-4-2.2
  Interior finish 6-5.3.2, A-6-5.3.2
  Interior floor finish 6-5.4.2
  Occupancy 4-1
  Ramps 5-2.5.2
  Stairs 5-2.2.2
  Stores 24-1.4.2, 25-1.4.2
Classrooms
  Classifications of 10-1.1.3, 10-1.2.3,
              11-1.1.3, 11-1.2.3
  Dormitories and 10-1.2.3, 11-1.2.3
Coatings, fire retardant 6-5.6
Combustible
  Definition 3-2
Combustion
  Definition 3-2
Common atmosphere
  Definition 10-1.3, 11-1.3
Common path of travel .... see also
              Exits; Means of egress
  Concept of A-5-5.1.6
  Definition 3-2, 5-1.2.6
Communicating space 6-2.4.4
Communications systems 7-6, A-7-6;
              see also Alarm systems;
              Protective signaling systems;
              Communication systems under
              specific occupancies
  Voice 7-6.3.9
Compartmentation 6-2.2, A-6-2.2;
      see also Building spaces, subdivisions of,
              under specific occupancies
Concealed spaces, fire protection
  of 6-2.5, A-6-2.5
Construction .... see also Building
      construction under specific occupancies
  Escape facilities during ... 31-1.1, 31-4.8
  Exit access corridors ... 5-1.3.4, A-5-1.3.4
  Fire escape ladders 5-2.9.2

Fire protection requirements for ... 6-2.1,
      A-6.2.1; see also specific occupancies
New, requirements for 1-4.1, 1-4.6,
                      A-1-4.6
Operations, requirements for 31-1.1
Contents see also under specific occupancies
  Hazard of 4-2, A-4-2
    Classification of 4-2.2, A-4-2.2
    Definition 4-2.1.1
  High hazard 5-11, A-5-11
Conveyors, vertical 7-4
Cooking equipment
  Commercial 7-2.3
  Domestic 10-7.3.2.2, 11-7.3.2.2,
      12-3.2.6 13-3.2.6, A-12-3.2.6, A-13-3.2.6
  Portable 31-2.4
Cooking facilities .... see Food
              preparation facilities
Corridors .... see also under
              specific occupancies
  Capacity, for egress 5-3.3.2
  Exit access 5-1.3.4, A-5-1.3.4
  Exterior 10-2.5.5, 11-2.5.5,
              A-10-2.5.5, A-11-2.5.5
  Interior 10-3.6, 11-3.6
Court
  Definition 3-2
  Enclosed
    Definition 3-2
Covered malls 24-4.3, 25-4.3
  Definition .... 24-1.3(d), 25-1.3(d)
Critical radiant flux
  Definition 3-2
  Interior floor finish 6-5.4, A-6-5.4

                    -D-

Day care centers 10-7, 11-7
Adult
  Definition 10-1.4.4, 11-1.4.4
  Alarm systems in 10-7.3.4,
                      11-7.3.4
  Apartment buildings
    as ..... 10-7.1.2(b), 11-7.1.2(b)
  Application of requirements
    for 10-7.1.1, 11-7.1.1,
              A-10-7.1.1, A-11-7.1.1
  Areas of refuge in 10-7.2.2.2,
                      11-7.2.2.2
  Building construction for 10-7.1.6,
                      11-7.1.6
  Building services in 10-7.5, 11-7.5
    Air conditioning .. 10-7.5.2, 11-7.5.2
    Elevators 10-7.5.3, 11-7.5.3
    Heating 10-7.5.2, 11-7.5.2
    Incinerators 10-7.5.4, 11-7.5.4
    Laundry chutes ... 10-7.5.4, 11-7.5.4
    Rubbish chutes ... 10-7.5.4, 11-7.5.4
    Utilities 10-7.5.1, 11-7.5.1
    Ventilation 10-7.2.11.4, 10-7.5.2,
              11-7.2.11.4, 11-7.5.2

Building spaces, subdivision
of .... 10-7.1.2(b),
10-7.3.2.1, 11-7.1.2(b), 11-7.3.2.1
Classification of occupancy 10-7.1.4,
11-7.1.4
Communications systems 10-7.3.4,
11-7.3.4
Contents of, hazard
classification 10-7.1.5, 11-7.1.5
Corridors 10-7.3.6, 11-7.3.6
Detection systems in ... 10-7.3.4, 11-7.3.4
Doors in .... 10-7.1.2(b), 11-7.1.2(b)
Emergency lighting in 10-7.2.9,
11-7.2.9
Evacuation plan for 31-3.4.2,
A-31-3.4.2
Existing buildings 11-7
Exits
Discharge from ... 10-7.2.7, 11-7.2.7
Number of 10-7.2.4, 11-7.2.4
Travel distance to 10-7.2.6,
11-7.2.6
Extinguishment requirements
in .... 10-7.3.2.1(d), 10-7.3.5,
11-7.3.2.1(d), 11-7.3.5,
A-10-7.3.2.1(d), A-11-7.3.2.1(d)
General requirements 10-7.1,
11-7.1, 31-3.4
Group .... see Group day-care homes
Interior finish in 10-7.3.3, 11-7.3.3
Location of 10-7.1.6.1, 10-7.1.6.2,
11-7.1.6.1, 11-7.1.6.2
Locks in 10-7.2.11, 11-7.2.11,
A-10-7.2.11, A-11-7.2.11
Means of egress in 10-7.2, 11-7.2
Arrangement of ... 10-7.2.5, 10-7.4.2,
11-7.2.5, 11-7.4.2
Illumination of ... 10-7.2.8, 11-7.2.8
Marking of 10-7.2.10, 11-7.2.10
Mixed occupancies of .. 10-7.1.2, 11-7.1.2
New buildings 10-7
Notification
Of emergency forces 10-7.3.4.4,
11-7.3.4.4
Of occupants .. 10-7.3.4.3, 11-7.3.4.3
Occupant load of 10-7.1.7, 11-7.1.7
Panic hardware in 10-7.2.11.3,
11-7.2.11.3
Protection 10-7.3, 11-7.3
From hazards 10-7.3.2, 11-7.3.2
Of storage areas 10-7.3.2.1,
11-7.3.2.1
Of vertical openings 10-7.3.1,
11-7.3.1
Smoke control in .... 10-7.1.2(b),
10-7.3.2.1(d), 11-7.1.2(b), 11-7.3.2.1(d),
A-10-7.3.2.1(d), A-11-7.3.2.1(d)
Staff in 10-7.1.1.1, 11-7.1.1.1,
31-3.4.1, 31-3.7, A-10-7.1.1.1, A-11-7.1.1.1
Stairs in 10-7.2.2.1, 11-7.2.2.1
Windows in 10-7.2.11.4, 11-7.2.11.4
Dead ends A-5-6.1;
see also Corridors; Exits
Concept of A-5-5.1.6
Decorations .... see Furnishings
and decorations

Delayed release locks 5-2.1.6,
A-5-2.1.6; see also Locks under specific
occupancies
Detection systems, smoke 7-6, A-7-6;
see also under specific occupancies
Maintenance of 31-1.3.2, 31-1.3.7,
A-31-1.3.7
Partial systems 7-6.2.8
Signal initiation 7-6.2
Detectors, smoke 7-6.2.9, 7-6.3.2;
see also Detection systems
Definition 3-2
Detention and correctional
occupancies .... Chaps. 14 and 15
Additions to 14-1.1.6, 15-1.1.6
Alarm systems in 14-3.4, 15-3.4
Application of requirements
for 14-1.1, 15-1.1
Attendants in 31-5.1, A-31-5.1
Building construction for .. 14-1.6, 15-1.6
Building services in 14-5, 15-5
Air conditioning 14-5.2, 15-5.2
Elevators 14-5.3, 15-5.3
Heating 14-5.2, 15-5.2
Incinerators 14-5.4, 15-5.4
Laundry chutes 14-5.4, 15-5.4
Rubbish chutes 14-5.4, 15-5.4
Utilities 14-5.1, 15-5.1
Ventilation 14-5.2, 15-5.2
Building spaces, subdivision of ... 14-3.7,
14-3.8, 15-3.7, 15-3.8, A-14-3.7,
A-14-3.8, A-15-3.7, A-15-3.8
Classification of 4-1.5, 14-1.2.2,
14-1.4, 15-1.2.2, 15-1.4,
A-14-1.4, A-15-1.4
Use conditions ... 14-1.4.1, 15-1.4.1,
A-14-1.4.1, A-15-1.4.1
Communications systems in 14-3.4,
15-3.4
Contents of, hazard
classification 14-1.2.5, 14-1.5,
15-1.2.5, 15-1.5
Corridors
Construction of 14-3.8, 15-3.8
Dead end 14-2.5.2,
15-2.5.2, A-15-2.5.2
Minimum width of 14-2.3.2,
15-2.3.2
Definitions 14-1.1.3, 15-1.1.3
Detection systems in 14-3.4.4,
14-3.7.8, 15-3.4.4, 15-3.7.8
Doors in 14-2.11, 15-2.11,
A-14-2.11, A-15-2.11
In smoke barriers ..... 14-3.7.5 thru
14-3.7.7, 15-3.7.5 thru 15-3.7.7
Drills in 31-5.1, A-31-5.1
Emergency lighting in 14-2.9, 15-2.9
Evacuation plan for 31-5.1, A-31-5.1
Existing buildings .... Chap. 15
Exits
Direct, definition .... 14-1.3(a),
15-1.3(a)
Discharge from 14-2.7, 15-2.7
Horizontal 14-2.2.5, 15-2.2.5
Number of 14-2.4, 15-2.4,
A-14-2.4, A-15-2.4

Travel distance to 14-2.6, 15-2.6
Extinguishment requirements 14-3.5,
15-3.5, 31-5.1.4, A-14-3.5, A-15-3.5
Furnishings and decorations
in 31-5.4, A-31-5.4
General requirements of 14-1,
15-1, 31-5
High rise buildings 14-4.3, 15-4.3
Interior finish in 14-3.3, 15-3.3
Locks for 14-1.2.1, 14-2.11, 15-1.2.1,
15-2.11, 31-5.5, A-14-2.11, A-15-2.11
Means of egress 14-1.2.4, 14-2,
15-1.2.4, 15-2
Arrangement of 14-2.5, 15-2.5
Capacity of 14-2.3, 15-2.3
Components of 14-2.2, 15-2.2
Illumination of 14-2.8, 15-2.8
Marking of 14-2.10, 15-2.10
Mixed occupancies of 14-1.2, 15-1.2,
A-14-1.2, A-15-1.2
New buildings .... Chap. 14
Notification 14-3.4.3, 15-3.4.3
Emergency forces 14-3.4.3.2,
15-3.4.3.2
Occupants 14-3.4.3.1,
15-3.4.3.1, A-14-3.4.3.1, A-15-3.4.3.1
Occupant load of 14-1.7, 15-1.7
Protection 14-3, 15-3
From hazards 14-3.2, 15-3.2,
A-14-3.2, A-15-3.2
Of vertical openings 14-3.1,
15-3.1, A-14-3.1, A-15-3.1
Smoke control in 14-3.7.8, 15-3.7.8
Special provisions for 14-4, 15-4
Stairs in 14-2.2.3, 15-2.2.3
Total concept of 14-1.1.5, 15-1.1.5
Underground buildings 14-4.2, 15-4.2
Windowless areas 14-4.1, 15-4.1,
A-14-4.1, A-15-4.1
Discharge from exits .... see Exits,
discharge from
Door closure 5-2.1.8
Doors .... 5-2.1; see also
under specific occupancies
Alarm devices for 5-1.7.2,
5-2.1.5, A-5-2.1.5
Balanced 5-2.1.13
Dutch 12-3.6.3.6, 13-3.6.3.6
Folding partitions 5-2.1.12
Fire 5-2.1.7.1, 5-2.4.3.4, 5-2.4.3.6
Fire barrier 6-2.3.6
Force to open 5-2.1.4,
5-2.1.9, A-5-2.1.4
Horizontal exit 5-2.4.3.3, 5-2.4.3.5,
5-2.4.3.6, A-5-2.4.3.3, A-5-2.4.3.5
Latches and locks for 5-2.1.2.1,
5-2.1.5, A-5-2.1.5; see also Locks
Pairs of 5-2.1.5.4
Panic hardware for 5-2.1.7
Power-operated 5-2.1.9
Revolving 5-2.1.10

Screen 5-2.1.4.4
Self-closing devices for .. 5-2.1.8, 5-2.3.11
Sliding 5-2.1.4.1, 5-2.1.14
Smoke barrier 6-3.4, A-6-3.4
Special locking arrangements 5-2.1.6
Stairwell 5-2.1.5.2, A-5-2.1.5.2
Storm.................... 5-2.1.4.4
Swinging and swing of 5-2.1.4,
5-2.1.9, 5-2.1.10(e), A-5-2.1.4
Dormitories .... 10-1.2.3; see also
Hotels and dormitories
Definition 16-1.3.1, 17-1.3.1
Drills in 31-6.3
Draft stop 6-2.5, A-6-2.5
Definition 3-2
Draperies .... 31-1.4; see also
Furnishings and decorations
Drills 31-1.5, A-31-1.5;
see also under specific occupancies
Ducts, smoke dampers in 6-3.5
Dumbwaiters .... 7-4; see also
Building services under specific
occupancies

-E-

Educational occupancies .. Chaps. 10 and 11
Aisles in 10-1.7.2, 10-1.7.3,
10-2.5.4, 11-1.7.2, 11-1.7.3, 11-2.5.4
Alarm systems in 10-3.4, 10-4.1.6,
11-3.4, 11-4.1.6, 31-3.2
Application of requirements
for 10-1.1, 11-1.1
Assembly requirements
in 10-1.2.2, 11-1.2.2
Balconies in 10-2.5.5, 11-2.5.5,
A-10-2.5.5, A-11-2.5.5
Building services in 10-5, 11-5
Air conditioning 10-5.2, 11-5.2
Elevators 10-5.3, 11-5.3
Heating 10-5.2, 11-5.2, 31-3.10
Incinerators 10-5.4, 11-5.4
Laundry chutes 10-5.4, 11-5.4
Rubbish chutes 10-5.4, 11-5.4
Utilities 10-5.1, 11-5.1
Ventilation 10-5.2, 11-5.2
Building spaces, subdivision
of 10-3.7, 10-4.1.3, 11-3.7
Classification of 4-1.3, 10-1.4,
11-1.4, A-4-1.3
Classrooms in 10-1.1.3, 10-1.2.3,
11-1.1.3, 11-1.2.3
Common atmosphere
Definition 10-1.3, 11-1.3
Communications systems .. 10-3.4, 11-3.4
Contents of, hazard
classification 10-1.5, 11-1.5
Corridors
Exterior 10-2.5.5, 11-2.5.5,
A-10-2.5.5 A-11-2.5.5
Interior 10-3.6, 11-3.6

Minimum width .. 10-2.3.3, 11-2.3.3
Day care centers ... see Day care centers
Definitions 10-1.3, 11-1.3
Detection systems 10-3.4, 11-3.4
Doors in 10-2.2.2.2, 10-2.5.3,
10-2.11, 11-2.2.2.2,
11-2.5.3, 11-2.11
Dormitories in 10-1.2.3, 11-1.2.3
Drills in 31-3.1, 31-3.2.1,
A-31-3.1
Emergency lighting in 10-2.9,
10-4.1.4, 11-2.9, 11-4.1.4
Existing buildings .... Chap. 11
Exits
Discharge from 10-2.7, 11-2.7
Number of 10-2.4, 11-2.4
Travel distance to 10-2.6, 11-2.6
Extinguishment requirements 10-3.5,
11-3.5
Family day care homes .... see
Family day care homes
Flexible plan .. 10-4.3, 10-6, 11-4.3, 11-6
Definition 10-3.1, 11-3.1
Food preparation facilities 10-3.2.2,
11-3.2.2
Furnishings and decorations 31-3.8
General requirements of 10-1,
11-1, 31-3
Group day care homes .... see
Group day care homes
Inspection of 31-3.3, A-31-3.3
Interior finish in 10-3.3, 11-3.3
Laboratories in 10-1.1.3,
10-3.2.4, 11-1.1.3, 11-3.2.4
Locks in 10-2.2.2.3, 10-2.11,
11-2.2.2.3, 11-2.11
Means of egress 10-2, 11-2
Arrangement of 10-2.5,
10-6.2.1, 11-2.5, 11-6.2.1
Capacity of 10-2.3, 11-2.3
Components of 10-2.2, 11-2.2
Illumination of 10-2.8, 11-2.8
Marking of 10-2.10, 11-2.10
Mixed occupancies of 10-1.2, 11-1.2
New buildings .... Chap. 10
Notification of occupants 10-3.4.3,
11-3.4.3
Occupant load of 10-1.7, 11-1.7
Open plan 10-4.3, 10-6, 11-4.3, 11-6
Definition 10-1.3, 11-1.3
Panic hardware in 10-2.2.2.2,
11-2.2.2.2
Protection 10-3, 11-3
From hazards 10-3.2, 11-3.2,
A-10-3.2, A-11-3.2
Separate atmosphere
Definition 10-1.3, 11-1.3
Smoke control in .. 10-4.1.5, 11-4.1.5
Special provisions for 10-4, 11-4
Stairs in 10-2.2.3, 10-2.5.5.2,
10-3.1.2, 11-2.2.3, 11-2.5.5.2,
11-3.1.2, A-10-2.2.3, A-11-2.2.3
Underground buildings 10-4.1,
11-4.1
Windowless buildings 10-4.1,
11-4.1

Windows in 10-2.11.1, 11-2.11.1,
A-10-2.11.1, A-11-2.11.1
Egress .... see Means of egress
Electrical services .... 7-1.2; see also
Building services under
specific occupancies
Elevation, changes in 5-1.6
Elevators .... 7-4, A-7-4; see also
Building services under
specific occupancies
Grain and bulk storage 29-7, A-29-7
Emergency control system 7-6.5
Emergency lighting 5-9, 5-10.3.6,
A-5-9; see also under
specific occupancies
Maintenance and testing of 31-1.3.8
Performance of system for 5-9.2,
A-5-9.2
Requirements for 5-9.1
Stairs, smokeproof enclosures ... 5-2.3.14
Enclosures 5-1.3.1
Atriums .... 6-2.4.5(g)
Chutes 7-5
Exit passageways 5-2.6.2,
6-2.4.6, 6-2.4.7
Exits 5-1.3.1
Floor openings 6-2.4.3, A-6-2.4.3
Ramps 5-2.5.3
Stairs 5-2.2.3, A-5-2.2.3
Smokeproof 5-2.3, A-5-2.3
Equipment, building service .... see
Building services
Equipment maintenance, requirements
for 31-1.3
Equivalency concepts in Life Safety
Code 1-5, A-1-5
Escalators 7-4.2, 7-4.3
Enclosure and protection
of 6-2.4.6, 6-2.4.7
Means of egress .. 5-2.7, 6-2.4.6, 28-2.2.8
Escape chutes A-30-2.2
Escapes, slide .... see Slide escapes
Evacuation plans 31-4.1, 31-5.1,
31-7.1; see also under
specific occupancies
Evacuation signaling systems 7-6.3.3
thru 7-6.3.5, 7-6.3.8
Exhaust system ..... see Ventilating system
Exhibition halls 8-4.4, 9-4.4
Vehicles in 8-4.4.4, 9-4.4.4
Exhibits 8-4.4.3, 9-4.4.3,
A-8-4.4.3, A-9-4.4.3
Existing
Buildings 1-4.1, 1-4.4,
A-1-4.4; see also
specific occupancies
Definition 3-2
Exit access
Corridors 5-1.3.4, A-5-1.3.4
Definition 3-2, 5-1.2.2
Exterior ways of 5-5.3
Marking of 5-10.1.3
Width of 5-3.4.1, 5-3.4.2
Exit discharge 5-7, A-5-7;
see also specific occupancies
Definition 3-2, 5-1.2.4

Exit passageways 5-2.6, A-5-2.6
Enclosures for 5-2.6.2
Floors for 5-2.6.4
Requirements for 5-2.6.1, 5-2.7.1
Width of 5-2.6.3
Exit signs .... see Signs, exit
Exits .... see also Means of egress;
   Exits under specific occupancies
Definition 3-2, 5-1.2.3, A-5-1.2.3
Discharge from 5-7, A-5-7
Enclosure of 5-1.3.1
Fundamental requirements 2-1,
     2-3, 2-4, 2-5, A-2-1
Horizontal 5-2.4, A-5-2.4
 Application of 5-2.4.1, A-5-2.4.1
 Balconies and bridges with ... 5-2.4.4
 Definition 5-1.2.5, A-5-1.2.5
 Doors in 5-2.4.3.3, 5-2.4.3.5,
    A-5-2.4.3.3, A-5-2.4.3.5
 Egress by, from area of
  refuge 5-2.4.2
 Walls for 5-2.4.3, A-5-2.4.3
Interior finish in 5-1.4
Main, assembly occupancy 8-2.3.3,
       9-2.3.3
Marking 2-5, 5-10
Number of .... see Means of egress
Travel distance to 5-6, A-5-6
Units of width of 5-3.2, A-5-3.2
Explosion suppression system 6-4.2,
       A-6-4.2
Extinguishers, portable fire 7-7.4.1,
       A-7-7.4.1
Extinguishing equipment 7-7, A-7-7
Automatic 7-7.3, A-7-7.3
Automatic sprinklers 7-7.1, A-7-7.1
Manual 7-7.4, A-7-7.4
Extinguishment requirements .... see
    under specific occupancies

     -F-

Factories .... see Industrial occupancies
Family day care homes 10-9, 11-9;
   see also Day care centers
Alarm systems in 10-9.3.4, 11-9.3.4
Application of requirements
 for 10-9.1.1, 11-9.1.1,
   A-10-9.1.1, A-11-9.1.1
Building services in 10-9.5, 11-9.5
 Electrical 10-9.5.1, 11-9.5.1
 Heating 10-9.5.2, 11-9.5.2
Communication systems
 in 10-9.3.4, 11-9.3.4
Detection systems in ... 10-9.3.4, 11-9.3.4
Doors in 10-9.2.11, 11-9.2.11
Existing buildings 11-9
Exits, number of 10-9.2.4, 11-9.2.4
General requirements for 10-9.1,
     11-9.1, 31-3.6
Interior finish in 10-9.3.3, 11-9.3.3

Locks in 10-9.2.11, 11-9.2.11
Means of egress 10-9.2, 11-9.2
 Illumination of ... 10-9.2.8, 11-9.2.8
Mixed occupancies of .. 10-9.1.2, 11-9.1.2
New buildings 10-9
Protection 10-9.3, 11-9.3
Fire alarm systems ..... see Alarm systems
Fire barriers 6-2.2.2, 6-2.3,
    A-6-2.2.2, A-6-2.3
Definition 3-2
Doors and windows in 6-2.3.6
Fire resistance classification 6-2.3.1
Floor-ceiling assemblies as 6-2.3.5
Horizontal exits 5-2.4.3.1, 5-2.4.3.2
Openings in 5 2.4.3.2, 6-2.3.2,
    6-2.3.4, A-6-2.3.2,
     A-6-2.3.4
Fire compartments 6-2.2, A-6-2.2
Definition 3-2
Fire departments, notification
 of 7-6.4, A-7-6.4
Fire detection systems .... see
    Detection systems
Fire escape ladders 5-2.9
Construction and installation 5-2.9.2
Fire escape stairs 5-2.8
Access to 5-2.8.3
Details for .... 5-2.8.4, Tables
    5-2.8.4 (A and B)
Guards and handrails for 5-2.8.5,
     5-2.8.7.5
Intervening spaces 5-2.8.8
Materials and strength 5-2.8.6
Protection of openings of 5-2.8.2
Swinging stairs 5-2.8.7, A-5-2.8.7
Visual enclosure of 5-2.8.5.2
Fire exit drills 31-1.5, A-31-1.5
Fire exit hardware 5-2.1.7
Fire protection .... see also
   under specific occupancies
Equipment 7-1.1
 Automatic sprinklers 7-7.1,
     A-7-7.1
 Detection, alarm, and commu-
  nicating systems 7-6, A-7-6
 Extinguishing equipment 7-7.3,
   7-7.4, A-7-7.3, A-7-7.4
 Smoke control systems 7-3.1,
     A-7-3.1
Features of .... Chap. 6
Compartmentation 6-2.2, A-6-2.2
Concealed spaces 6-2.5, A-6-2.5
Construction 6-2.1, A-6-2.1
Fire barriers 6-2.3, A-6-2.3
Interior finish 6-5, A-6-5
Smoke barriers 6-3, A-6-3
Special hazards 6-4, A-6-4
Vertical openings 2-9, 6-2.4, A-6-2.4
Fire resistance rating
Construction 6-2.1, A-6-2.1
Definition 3-2

Enclosure of floor openings 6-2.4.3,
A-6-2.4.3
Fire barriers 6-2.3.1
Requirements 31-1.4, A-31-1.4
Fire retardant coatings
Maintenance of 31-1.4.3
Protection of interior finish 6-5.6
Fireplaces 12-5.2.2 Ex.2, 13-5.2.2 Ex.2
Firestopping 6-2.5, A-6-2.5
Fire windows
Definition 3-2
**Flame retardant requirements, assem-
bly occupancies** .. 8-3.2.1.11, 9-3.2.1.11
Flame spread
Definition 3-2
Interior finish classification 6-5.3.2,
A-6-5.3.2
Flammable and combustible liquids
Laboratories with 12-3.2.2, 12-3.2.4,
12-6.3.2.1, 13-3.2.2, 13-3.2.4, 13-6.3.2.1
Storage of 31-1.6, 31-3.4.3
Flexible plan buildings ...... see Buildings,
flexible plan
Floor area
Either side of horizontal exits .. 5-2.4.2.4
Gross
Definition 3-2
Net
Definition 3-2
Floor finish ...... see Interior finish, floors
Floor level, of doors 5-2.1.3.3
**Floor openings, fire protection
of** 6-3.6.1, 6-3.6.2
Enclosed 6-2.4.2, 6-2.4.3,
A-6-2.4.2, A-6-2.4.3
Unenclosed, communicating
space 6-2.4.4
Floors
Exit passageways 5-2.6.4
Street
Definition 3-2
Folding partitions .... see Partitions, folding
Food preparation facilities
Assembly occupancies 8-3.2.4.3,
9-3.2.4.3
Day care centers .... 10-7.3.2.1(e),
11-7.3.2.1(e)
Educational occupancies 10-3.2.2,
11-3.2.2
Food service devices 8-4.4.3,
9-4.4.3, 31-2.4
Food service establishments 8-3.2.4,
9-3.2.4
Fundamental requirements .... Chap 2, A-2
Furnishings and decorations .... see
also under specific occupancies
In means of egress 31-1.2.2
Maintenance and testing of 31-1.4
Requirements 31-1.4, A-31-1.4
Furniture, upholstered 31-4.5.5

-G-

Garages, parking .... 29-8; see
also Storage occupancies
Alarm systems in 29-8.3.4

Application of requirements
for 29-8.1.1, A-29-8.1.1
Classification of 29-8.1.4
Communications systems in 29-8.3.4
Contents of, hazard classification 29-8.1.5
Corridors 29-8.3.6
Minimum width 29-8.2.3.1
Definitions 29-8.1.3
Detection systems in 29-8.3.4
Doors in 29-8.2.2.2,
29-8.2.11.3, 29-8.2.11.4
Emergency lighting in 29-8.2.9
Exits
Number of 29-8.2.4
Travel distance to 29-8.2.6
Types of 29-8.2.2
Gasoline pumps in 29-8.2.5.3
General requirements 29-8.1
Interior finish in 29-8.3.3
Locks in 29-8.2.11.1
Means of egress 29-8.2
Arrangement of 29-8.2.5
Capacity of 29-8.2.3
Components of 29-8.2.2
Illumination of 29-8.2.8
Marking of 29-8.2.10
Mixed occupancies of 29-8.1.2
Notification 29-8.3.4.3
Open-air structures 16-3.5.3,
17-3.5.3, 29-8.3.4.1
Definition 29-8.1.3
Protection 29-8.3
Ramps in 29-8.2.2.6, 29-8.2.6
Repair operations in 29-8.1.2
Stairs in 29-8.2.2.3
General industrial occupancy ..... 28-1.4(a)
Gift shops 12-3.2.5, 13-3.2.5
Grain or bulk storage elevators 29-7,
A-29-7
Group day care homes 10-8, 11-8
Alarm systems in 10-8.3.4, 11-8.3.4
Apartment buildings with ... 10-8.1.2(b),
11-8.1.2(b)
Application of requirements for . 10-8.11,
11-8.11, A-10-8.11, A-11-8.11
Building services in 10-8.5, 11-8.5
Electrical 10-8.5.1, 11-8.5.1
Heating 10-8.5.2, 11-8.5.2
Classification of 10-8.1.4, 11-8.1.4
Communications systems
in 10-8.3.4, 11-8.3.4
Contents of, hazard
classification 10-8.1.5,
11-8.1.5
Detection systems in ... 10-8.3.4, 11-8.3.4
Doors in .... 10-8.1.2(b), 10-8.2.4.3,
11-8.1.2(b), 11-8.2.4.3
Existing buildings 11-8
Exits
Discharge from ... 10-8.2.7, 11-8.2.7
Number of 10-8.2.4, 11-8.2.4
General requirements of 10-8.1,
11-8.1, 31-8.5
Interior finish in 10-8.3.3, 11-8.3.3
Locks in 10-8.2.11, 11-8.2.11,
A-10-8.2.11, A-11-8.2.11

Means of egress 10-8.2, 11-8.2
   Arrangement of 10-8.2.5
   Illumination of ... 10-8.2.8, 11-8.2.8
New buildings 10-8
Protection 10-8.3, 11-8.3
   Of vertical openings 10-8.3.1,
                      11-8.3.1
Guards 5-2.2.6, A-5-2.2.6
   Definition 3-2
   Details for 5-2.2.6.6
   Fire escape stairs 5-2.8.5
Guest rooms, in hotels 16-3.6, 17-3.6

-H-

Halls, exhibition 8-4.4, 9-4.4
Handicapped, provisions for 8-4.5,
      9-4.5, 10-1.1.2, A-2-10,
      A-8-4.5, A-9-4.5, A-10-1.1.2
Handrails
   Definition 3-2
   Details for 5-2.6.6.5, A-5-2.2.6.5
   Stairs 5-2.2.6, A-5-2.2.6
   Fire escape stairs .. 5-2.8.5, 5-2.8.7.5
Hangars, aircraft 29-6, A-29-6
Hardware, door 5-2.1.7
Hazard of contents .... 4-2, A-4-2; see
   also Contents under specific occupancies
   Classification of 4-2.2, A-4-2.2
   Definition 4-2.1.1
   General 4-2.1, A-4-2.1
Hazardous areas 6-4, A-6-4
   Definition 3-2, 21-1.3
   Means of egress 5-11, A-5-11
Hazards, protection from 6-4, A-6-4;
   see also under specific occupancies
Headroom requirements 5-1.5,
             5-2.2.1, A-5-1.5
Health care occupancies .. Chaps. 12 and 13
   Additions to 12-1.1.4, 13-1.1.4
   Aisles in 12-2.3.3, 13-2.3.3,
           A-12-2.3.3, A-13-2.3.3
   Alarm systems in 12-3.4, 13-3.4,
           31-4.1.3, A-31-4.1.3
   Ambulatory care 12-1.2.2, 13-1.2.2,
           A-12-1.2.2, A-13-1.2.2;
   see also Ambulatory health care centers
   Application of requirements
     for 12-1.1, 13-1.1,
            A-12-1.1, A-13-1.1
   Atriums in 12-3.1.1, 12-3.7.3,
           13-3.1.1, 13-3.7.3
   Attendants in 31-4.1, 31-4.2.3,
           A-31-4.1
   Building construction for 12-1.1.4,
        12-1.6, 13-1.1.4, 13-1.6
   Building services in 12-5, 13-5
     Air conditioning 12-5.2, 13-5.2
     Elevators 12-5.3, 13-5.3
     Heating 12-5.2, 13-5.2, 31-4.7
     Incinerators 12-5.4, 13-5.4

     Laundry chutes 12-5.4, 13-5.4
     Rubbish chutes 12-5.4, 13-5.4
     Utilities 12-5.1, 13-5.1
     Ventilation 12-5.2, 13-5.2
   Building spaces, subdivision
     of 12-3.7,
                 13-3.7
   Classification of 4-1.4, 12-1.4, 13-1.4
   Communication systems in 12-3.4,
                13-3.4
   Contents of, hazard
     classification 12-1.2.6,
       12-1.5, 13-1.2.6, 13-1.5
   Conversions of 12-1.1.4.4, 13-1.1.4.4
   Corridors in 12-3.6, 13-3.6
     Doors in 12-3.6.3, 13-3.6.3,
        A-12-3.6.3, A-13-3.6.3
     Protection of 12-3.4.5, 13-3.4.5
     Separation from other
       areas 12-3.6.1,
        13-3.6.1. A-12-3.6.1,
        A-13-3.6.1
   Corridors
     Wall construction
       of 12-3.6.2, 13-3.6.2
     Width of 12-2.3.3, 12-2.3.4,
       13-2.3.3, 13-2.3.4, A-12-2.3.3,
       A-12-2.3.4, A-13-2.3.3, A-13-2.3.4
   Definitions 12-1.3, 13-1.3
   Detection systems in 12-3.4, 13-3.4
   Doors in 12-2.2.2, 13-2.2.2
     Barriers 12-1.1.4.3,
       12-3.7.5 thru 12-3.7.8,
      13-1.1.4.3, 13-3.7.5 thru 13-3.7.8
     Corridors .... see Corridors, doors in
     Minimum width .. 12-2.3.5, 13-2.3.5
     Stair enclosures ... 12-3.1.2, 13-3.1.2
   Drills in 31-4.1, A-31-4.1
   Emergency lighting in 12-2.9, 13-2.9
   Evacuation plan in 31-4.1, 31-4.2,
           A-31-4.1, A-31-4.2
   Existing buildings .... Chap. 13
   Exits
     Discharge from 12-2.7, 13-2.7
     Horizontal 12-1.2.4,
       12-2.2.5, 13-1.2.4, 13-2.2.5
     Maintenance of 31-4.3
     Number of 12-2.4, 13-2.4,
        A-12-2.4, A-13-2.4
     Travel distance to 12-2.6, 13-2.6
   Extinguishment requirements
     in 12-3.5, 13-3.5
   Furnishings, decorations and
     bedding in 31-4.5, A-31-4.5
   General requirements of 12-1,
          13-1, 31-4, A-31-4
   Gift shops in 12-3.2.5, 13-3.2.5
   Hospitals
     Definition ...... 12-1.3(a), 13-1.3(a)
   Interior finish in 12-3.3, 13-3.3,
        A-12-3.3, A-13-3.3

Chapters 1-7 and 31 reference general requirements. Chapters 8, 10, 12, 14, 16, 18, 24 and 26 reference requirements for new occupancies. Chapters 9, 11, 13, 15, 17, 19, 25 and 27 reference requirements for existing occupancies. Chapters 20, 21, 22, 28, 29 and 30 reference requirements for both new and existing occupancies.

Limited care facility
    Definition .... 12-1.3(c), 13-1.3(c)
    Locks in 12-2.2.2, 12-2.11,
      13-2.2.2, 13-2.11, A-12-2.2.2, A-13-2.2.2
    Means of egress 12-1.2.4, 12-2,
      13-1.2.4, 13-2, 31-4.8.2
      Arrangement of 12-2.5, 13-2.5
      Capacity of 12-2.3, 13-2.3,
        A-12-2.3, A-13-2.3
      Components of 12-2.2, 13-2.2,
        A-12-2.2, A-13-2.2
      Illumination of 12-2.8, 13-2.8
      Marking of 12-2.10, 13-2.10
    Mixed occupancies of 12-1.2, 13-1.2,
      A-12-1.2, A-13-1.2
    Modernization (or renovation)
      of 12-1.1.4, 13-1.1.4
    New buildings .... Chap. 12
    Notification of occupants and emer-
      gency forces 12-3.4.3, 13-3.4.3
    Nursing homes
      Definition ...... 12-1.3(b), 13-1.3(b)
      Occupant load of 12-1.7, 13-1.7
    Procedures in case of fire 31-4.2,
      A-31-4.2
    Protection 12-3, 13-3
      From hazards 12-3.2, 13-3.2,
        A-12-3.2, A-13-3.2
      Of vertical openings .. 12-3.1, 13-3.1
    Ramps in 12-2.3.3, 12-2.3.4,
      13-2.3.3, 13-2.3.4, A-12-2.3.3, A-12-2.3.4,
      A-13-2.3.3, A-13-2.3.4
    Smoke control in 12-3.7, 12-3.8,
      13-3.7, 13-3.8, 31-4.6
    Smoking in 31-4.4, A-31-4.4
    Special provisions for 12-4, 13-4
    Stairs in 12-2.2.3, 13-2.2.3
    Total concept in 12-1.1.3, 13-1.1.3
    Windowless buildings 12-4.1, 13-4.1
    Windows in 12-3.8.1, 13-3.8.1
Heaters, unit .... see Building services,
    heating, under specific occupancies
Heating systems ..... 7-2; see also Building
    services under specific
    occupancies
High hazard areas
    Definition 3-2
High hazard contents 4-2.2, 5-11,
    A-4-2.2.4, A-5-11
High hazard industrial
    occupancies .... 28-1.4(c),
    A-28-1.4(c)
High rise buildings
    Central control station .. 30-8.5, A-30-8.5
    Definition 3-2, A-3-2
    Detection, alarm, and
      communication systems 30-8.3,
      30-8.5, A-30-8.3, A-30-8.5
    Emergency lighting and standby
      power 30-8.4
    Extinguishment
      requirements 30-8.2, A-30-8.2
    General requirements 30-8.1
Homes .... see Family day
    care homes; Group day care homes
Horizontal exits ...... see Exits, horizontal

Hospitals .... see also Health
    care occupancies
    Definition .... 12-1.3(a), 13-1.3(a)
Hotels and dormitories ... Chaps. 16 and 17
    Alarm systems in 16-3.4, 17-3.4
    Application of requirements
      for 16-1.1, 17-1 1
    Atriums in 16-3.1, 17-3.1
    Building services for 16-5, 17-5
      Air conditioning 16-5.2, 17-5.2
      Elevators 16-5.3, 17-5.3
      Emergency situations 31-6.2
      Heating 16-5.2, 17-5.2, 31-6.7
      Incinerators 16-5.4, 17-5.4
      Laundry chutes 16-5.4, 17-5.4
      Rubbish chutes 16-5.4, 17-5.4
      Utilities 16-5.1, 17-5.1
      Ventilation 16-5.2, 17-5.2
    Building spaces, subdivision
      of 16-3.7, 17-3.7
    Classification of 16-1.3, 17-1.3
    Communications systems in 16-3.4,
      17-3.4
    Contents of, hazard
      classification 16-1.5,
      17-1.5
    Corridors
      Construction of 16-3.6, 17-3.6
      Dead ends in 16-2.5.3, 17-2.5.3
      Minimum width .. 16-2.3.3, 17-2.3.3
    Definitions 16-1.3, 17-1.3
    Detection systems in ... 16-3.4.4, 17-3.4.4
    Doors in 16-2.2.2, 16-3.6.3,
      17-2.2.2, 17-3.6.3
    Drills in 31-6.1, 31-6.3, A-31-6.1
    Emergency lighting in 16-2.9, 17-2.9
    Emergency organization in 31-6.1,
      31-6.4, A-31-6.1, A-31-6.4
    Existing buildings .... Chap. 17
    Exits
      Arrangement of 16-2.5, 17-2.5
      Discharge from 16-2.7, 17-2.7
      Number of 16-2.4, 17-2.4
      Travel distance to 16-2.6,
      16-2.7.2, 17-2.6, 17-2.7.2
    Extinguishment requirements in .. 16-3.5,
      17-3.5, A-16-3.5, A-17-3.5
    Furnishings and decorations 16-6.6,
      A-31-6.6
    General requirements of 16-1,
      17-1, 31-6
    Guest rooms in 16-3.6, 17-3.6
    Interior finish in 16-3.3, 17-3.3
    Locks in 16-2.11, 17-2.11,
      A-16-2.11, A-17-2.11
    Means of egress 16-2, 17-2
      Arrangement of 16-2.5, 17-2.5
      Capacity of 16-2.3, 17-2.3
      Components of 16-2.2, 17-2.2
      Illumination of 16-2.8, 17-2.8
      Marking of 16-2.10, 17-2.10
    Mixed occupancies of 16-1.2, 17-1.2
    New buildings .... Chap. 16
    Notification 16-3.4.3, 17-3.4.3, 31-6.2
      Of fire department 16-3.4.3.4,
      17-3.4.3.4, A-16-3.4.3.4, A-17-3.4.3.4

Of occupants .. 16-3.4.3.1, 17-3.4.3.1
Occupant load of 16-1.7, 17-1.7,
A-16-1.7, A-17-1.7
Protection 16-3, 17-3
From hazards 16-3.2, 17-3.2
Of vertical openings .. 16-3.1, 17-3.1
Smoke control in 16-3.7, 17-3.7
Special provisions for 16-4, A-16-4
Windows in 16-4.1, A-16-4.1

-I-

Illumination
Emergency lighting 5-9,
5-10.3.6, A-5-9
Means of egress 5-8, A-5-8
Signs, exit 5-10.3, A-5-10.3
**Improvement operations, requirements
for** 31-1.1
Incinerators .... 7-5; see also Building
services under specific occupancies
Industrial occupancies .... Chap. 28
Alarm systems in 28-3.4
Application of requirements for .. 28-1.1
Atriums in 28-3.1.1 Ex.2
Building services in 28-5
Air conditioning 28-5.2
Elevators 28-5.3
Heating 28-5.2
Incinerators 28-5.4
Laundry chutes 28-5.4
Rubbish chutes 28-5.4
Utilities 28-5.1
Ventilation 28-5.2
Classifications of 4-1.9, 28-1.4
General .... 28-1.4(a)
High hazard .... 28-1.4(c),
A-28-1.4(c)
Special purpose .... 28-1.4(b)
Common path of travel in 28-2.5.1
Communications systems in 28-3.4
Corridors 28-3.6
Dead end 28-2.5.2
Minimum width of 28-2.3.2
Detection systems in 28-3.4
Doors in 28-2.2.2, 28-2.11
Emergency lighting in .. 28-2.9, A-28-2.9
Exits
Horizontal 28-2.2.5, A-28-2.2.5
Number of 28-2.4
Slide escapes as 28-2.2.11
Travel distance to .. 28-2.6, A-28-2.6
Types of 28-2.2, A-28-2.2
Extinguishing requirements .. 28-2.6.2(c),
28-3.5
General requirements of 28-1
Interior finish in 28-3.3
Locks in 28-2.2.2, 28-2.11
Means of egress 28-2
Arrangement of .. 28-2.5, A-28-2.5
Capacity of 28-2.3

Components of 28-2.2
Illumination of 28-2.8
Marking of 28-2.10
Mixed occupancies of 28-1.2
Notification 28-3.4.3
Occupant load of 28-1.7, A-28-1.7
Protection 28-3
From hazards 28-3.2, A-28-3.2
Of vertical openings 28-3.1
Special provisions for 28-4
Stairs in 28-2.2.3, 28-2.11.2
**Inspection, of educational
occupancies** 31-3.3,
A-31-3.3; see also Maintenance
Interior finish 6-5, A-6-5;
see also under specific occupancies
Automatic sprinklers and 6-5.7
Definition 6-5
Exit enclosures 5-1.4
Fire retardant coatings 6-5.6
Flame spread of 5-1.4
Hazard of 6-5.1.4
Interior floor finish 6-5.1.1,
6-5.1.3, 6-5.2.2, A-6-5.1.1, A-6-5.2.2
Classifications 6-5.4, A-6-5.4
Interior walls and ceilings 6-5.1.1,
6-5.1.2, 6-5.2.1, A-6-5.1.1
Classifications 6-5.3, A-6-5.3
Trim and incidental finish 6-5.5
Use of materials .. 6-5.2, 6-5.3.4, A-6-5.2
Interior rooms, educational occupancies
Definition 10-1.3, 11-1.3

-L-

Laboratories
Classifications of 10-1.1.3, 11-1.1.3
Protection of ... 6-4.4, 10-3.2.4, 11-3.2.4,
12-3.2.2, 12-6.3.2.1, 13-3.2.2,
13-6.3.2.1, A-12-3.2.2, A-13-3.2.2
Ladders, fire escape 5-2.9
Latches, for doors 5-2.1.5, A-5-2.1.5
Laundry chutes ...... 7-5; see also Building
services under specific occupancies
Life Safety Code
Application of 1-4
Additions 1-4.5
Existing buildings 1-4.1,
1-4.2, 1-4.4, 1-6.2, A-1-4.4
Governing requirements 1-4.8,
A-1-4.8
Mixed occupancies 1-4.7
Modernization and
renovation 1-4.6, A-1-4.6
Provisions in excess of Code
requirements 1-4.9
Changes of occupancy in .. 1-6.4, A-1-6.4
Equivalency concepts in 1-5, A-1-5
Fundamental requirements of ... Chap. 2
Maintenance under 1-7
Modification of requirements 1-5.2

Chapters 1-7 and 31 reference general requirements. Chapters 8, 10, 12, 14, 16, 18, 24 and 26 reference requirements for new occupancies. Chapters 9, 11, 13, 15, 17, 19, 25 and 27 reference requirements for existing occupancies. Chapters 20, 21, 22, 28, 29 and 30 reference requirements for both new and existing occupancies.

Occupancy requirements in ... 1-6, A-1-6
Purpose of 1-2
Scope of 1-3, A-1-3
Life Safety Evaluation
Definition 8-1.3
Life support devices 12-5.1.3,
12-6.2.9.2, 13-5.1.3, 13-6.2.9.2
Lighting, emergency .... see
Emergency lighting
Limited care facility
Definition .... 12-1.3(c), 13-1.3(c)
Limited-combustible
Definition 3-2
Living units, travel distance
within 18-2.6.1, 19-2.6.1
Loads
Live
Definition 3-2
Occupant .... see Occupant load
Locks ... see also under specific occupancies
Delayed release 5-2.1.6, A-5-2.1.6
Doors 5-2.1.5, A-5-2.1.5
Fundamental requirements 2-4
Lodging or rooming houses ...... Chap. 20
Alarm systems in 20-3.3
Application of requirements for .. 20-1.1
Building services 20-5
Air conditioning 20-5.2
Heating 20-5.2, 31-6.7
Utilities 20-5.1
Ventilation 20-5.2
Building spaces, subdivision of ... 20-3.4
Classification of 20-1.1.1, 20-1.4
Communications systems in 20-3.3
Contents of, hazard
classification 20-1.5,
A-20-1.5
Corridors, construction of 20-3.4
Definition of 20-1.1.1
Detection systems in 20-3.3.4
Doors in .... 20-2.3 thru 20-2.8,
20-3.4, A-20-2
Extinguishment requirements 20-3.5,
A-20-3.5
General requirements of 20-1
Interior finish in 20-3.2
Locks in .... 20-2.5 thru 20-2.8, A-20-2.7
Means of escape 20-2
Interior stairways 20-2.2
Number of 20-2.1
Mixed occupancies of 20-1.2.1
Notification of occupants 20-3.3.3
Protection of vertical openings ... 20-3.1
Smoke control in 20-3.4
Special provisions for 20-4
Stairs in 20-2.2, 20-3.1.2

-M-

Main exit .... see Exits, main
Maintenance
Exits, in health care
occupancies 31-4.3
General
requirements 1-7,
31-1.3, 31-1.7

Protective signaling systems 7-6.1.6,
A-7-6.1.6
Means of egress reliability 31-1.2,
31-3.3, 31-4.3
Means of egress ... Chap. 5; see also Exits;
Means of egress under
specific occupancies
Alternating tread devices 5-2.11, A-5-2.11
Application of 5-1.1, A-5-1.1
Arrangement of 5-5, A-5-5
Capacity of 5-3, 5-7.2, A-5-3
Measurement of 5-3.2, A-5-3.2
Occupant load and ... 5-3.1, A-5-3.1
Per unit width 5-3.3
Components of 5-2
Definition 5-1.2.1
Doors 5-2.1, A-5-2.1
During building
construction 31-1.1.1,
31-4.8
Emergency lighting of 5-9, A-5-9
Escalators 5-2.7
Exit passageways 5-2.6, A-5-2.6
Fire escape ladders 5-2.9
Fire escape stairs 5-2.8
Floor level in 5-2.1.3
Changes in 5-1.6
Handicapped access
requirements 5-2.1.3.1
Hazardous areas 5-11, A-5-11
Headroom in 5-1.5
Horizontal exits 5-2.4, A-5-2.4
Illumination of 2-6, 5-8, A-5-8
Impediments or obstructions to 5-1.7,
5-2.1.5, 5-5.2, 31-1.2, A-5-1.7, A-5-5.2
Maintenance of 31-1.2, 31-3.3
Marking of .... 5-2.1.4.1 Ex.3(b),
5-10, A-5-10
Illumination of signs 5-10.3,
A-5-10.3
Size of signs 5-10.2, A-5-10.2
Specific requirements 5-10.4
Moving walks 5-2.7
Number of exits for 2-8, 5-4, A-5-4
Ramps 5-2.5, A-5-2.5
Reliability of 31-1.2
Separate
Definition 10-1.3, 11-1.3
Separation of 5-1.3, 6-2
Slide escapes 5-2.10
Smokeproof enclosures 5-2.3, A-5-2.3
Stairs 5-2.2, A-5-2.2
Turnstiles 5-2.1.11
Width of 5-2.1.2, 5-3.2,
5-3.4, A-5-2.1.2, A-5-3.2
Workmanship in 5-1.7, A-5-1.7
Means of escape
Definition 3-2
Group day care homes 10-8.3.4,
11-8.3.4
Lodging and rooming houses 20-2
One- and two-family dwellings 22-2,
A-22-2
Second 5-2.1.4.1 Ex.3, 22-2.1.2
Mercantile occupancies .. Chaps. 24 and 25
Additions to 24-1.1.3, 25-1.1.3

Aisles in .... 24-2.5.4 thru
24-2.5.6, 24-2.5.10(c),
25-2.5.4 thru 25-2.5.6, 25-2.5.10(c)
Alarm systems in 24-3.4,
24-4.3.3.3, 24-4.4.5, 24-4.5.3,
25-3.4, 25-4.3.3.3, 25-4.4.5, 25-4.5.3
Anchor store
Definition ...... 24-1.3(g), 25-1.3(g)
Application of requirements for .. 24-1.1,
25-1.1
Atriums in 24-4.5, 25-4.5
Building services for 24-5, 25-5
Air conditioning 24-5.2, 25-5.2
Elevators 24-5.3, 25-5.3
Heating 24-5.2, 25-5.2
Incinerators 24-5.4, 25-5.4
Laundry chutes 24-5.4, 25-5.4
Rubbish chutes 24-5.4, 25-5.4
Utilities 24-5.1, 25-5.1
Ventilation 24-4.4.2, 24-5.2,
25-4.4.2, 25-5.2
Building spaces, subdivision
of 24-3.7, 25-3.7
Classification of
Occupancy 4-1.7, 24-1.4, 25-1.4
Stores 24-1.3, 24-1.4.2,
25-1.3, 25-1.4.2
Subclassification of
occupancy ... 24-1.4.2, 25-1.4.2
Combined business
occupancies 26-1.2.1, 27-1.2.1
Combined mercantile and
residential 24-1.2.1, 25-1.2.1
Common path of travel
in 24-2.5.3, 25-2.5.3
Communications systems
in 24-3.4, 24-4.3.3,
24-4.4.3, 25-3.4, 25-4.3.3, 25-4.4.3
Contents of, hazard
classification 24-1.5, 24-2.1.5,
25-1.5, 25-2.1.5
Corridors 24-3.6, 25-3.6
Dead-end 24-2.5.2, 25-2.5.2,
A-24-2.5.2, A-25-2.5.2
Covered mall buildings ... 24-4.4, 25-4.4,
A-24-4.4, A-25-4.4
Definition .... 24-1.3(f), 25-1.3(f)
Covered malls 24-4.3, 25-4.3,
A-24-4.3.1, A-25-4.3.1
Definition ...... 24-1.3(e), 25-1.3(e)
Definitions 4-1.7, 24-1.3
Detection systems in ... 24-3.4, 24-4.3.3.3,
24-4.4.3, 25-3.4, 25-4.3.3.3, 25-4.4.3
Doors in 24-2.2.2, 24-3.6.2,
25-2.2.2, 25-3.6.2
Drills in 31-8.1
Emergency lighting in 24-2.9, 25-2.9
Existing buildings .... Chap. 25
Exits
Covered malls 24-4.3.2,
25-4.3.2, A-24-4.3.2, A-25-4.3.2

Details 24-4.4.2,
25-4.4.2, A-24-4.4.2, A-25-4.4.2
Discharge from 24-2.7,
25-2.7, A-24-2.7, A-25-2.7
Number of 24-2.4, 25-2.4
Travel distance to .... 24-1.5(a),
24-2.6, 25-1.5(a), 25-2.6
Extinguishment requirements
for 24-3.5, 25-3.5
General requirements of 24-1,
25-1, 31-8
Gross leasable area
Definition .... 24-1.3(f), 25-1.3(f)
Interior finish in 24-3.3, 25-3.3
Locks in 24-2.2.2, 25-2.2.2,
A-24-2.2.2, A-25-2.2.2
Means of egress 24-2, 25-2
Arrangement of 24-2.5,
25-2.5, A-24-2.5, A-25-2.5
Capacity of 24-2.3, 25-2.3
Components of 24-2.2, 25-2.2
Marking of 24-2.10, 25-2.10
Mezzanines 24-1.4.2.3,
24-1.7.2, 25-1.4.2.3, 25-1.7.2
Mixed occupancies of 24-1.2, 25-1.2
New buildings .... Chap. 26
Notification 24-3.4.3, 25-3.4.3
Emergency forces 24-3.4.3.3,
24-4.4.3.5, 24-4.5.3.5, 25-3.4.3.3,
25-4.4.3.5, 25-4.5.3.5
Occupants ... 24-3.4.3.2, 24-4.4.3.4,
24-4.5.3.4, 25-4.4.3.4, 25-4.5.3.4
Occupant load of 24-1.7,
25-1.7, A-24-1.7, A-25-1.7
Open-air operations 24-4.3, 25-4.3
Definition ...... 24-1.3(h), 25-1.3(h)
Protection 24-3, 25-3
From hazards 24-3.2, 25-3.2
Of vertical openings 24-3.1,
25-3.1, A-24-3.1, A-25-3.1
Smoke control in .... 24-4.3.1 Ex.(e),
24-4.4.3.6, 24-4.5.3.6, 25-4.3.1 Ex.(e),
25-4.4.3.6, 25-4.5.3.6, 25-4.3.1 Ex.(e),
A-25-4.3.1 Ex.(e)
Special provisions for 24-4, 25-4
Stairs in 24-2.2.3,
24-2.11.6, 25-2.2.3, 25-2.11.6
Underground buildings 24-4.1, 25-4.1
Windowless buildings 24-4.1, 25-4.1
Mezzanines
Definition 3-2
Mixed occupancies .... 1-4.7; see
also Residential occupancies; Mixed
occupancies under specific occupancies
Mobile structures 1-3.5
Modernization 1-4.6, A-1-4.6
Monumental stairs 5-2.2.2.5
Moving walks 7-4.2, 7-4.3
Enclosure and protection
of 6-2.4.6, 6-2.4.7
Means of egress 5-2.7, 6-2.4.6

-N-

Noncombustible
Definition 3-2
Notification . . . . see also under
specific occupancies
Fire departmentmergency
forces 7-6.4, A-7-6.4
Occupants . . . . . 7-6.1.7(b), 7-6.3, A-7-6.3
Nursing homes . . . . see also Health
care occupancies
Definition . . . . 12-1.3(b), 13-1.3(b)

-O-

Occupancies, specific
Ambulatory health care centers 12-6, 13-6
Apartment buildings . . . Chaps. 18 and 19
Assembly occupancies . . . Chaps. 8 and 9
Board and care occupancies . . . . see
Residential board and care occupancies
Business occupancies . . Chaps. 26 and 27
Day care centers 10-7, 11-7
Detention and correctional occupan-
cies . . . . Chaps. 14 and 15
Dormitories . . see Hotels and dormitories
Educational
occupancies . . . . . . Chaps. 10 and 11
Family day care homes 10-9, 11-9
Garages, parking 29-8
Group day care homes 10-8, 11-8
Health care occupancies . . . . . Chaps. 12
and 13
Hotels and dormitories . . . . Chaps. 16
and 17
Industrial occupancies . . . . Chap. 28
Lodging or rooming houses . . . . Chap. 20
Mercantile occupancies . . . . . . Chaps. 24
and 25
One- and two-family
dwellings . . . . Chap. 22
Residential board and care
occupancies . . . . Chap. 21
Residential occupancies . . . . Chaps. 16-22
Rooming houses . . . . see Lodging or
rooming houses
Storage occupancies . . . . Chap. 29
Unusual structures . . . . Chap. 30
Occupancy 1-6, A-1-6
Building 1-6, A-1-6
Classification of . . . . 4-1, 31-2 thru 31-9,
A-4-1; see also under
specific occupancies
Changes in 1-6.4, A-1-6.4
Definition 3-2, 5-2.1.1.3
Mixed 1-4.7
Occupant load . . . . see also under
specific occupancies
Definition 3-2
Means of egress and 5-3.1,
5-4.1.2, A-5-3.1
Occupants, notification of . . . . 7-6.1.7(b),
7-6.3, A-7-6.3; see also under specific
occupancies
Occupiable story
Definition 3-2

One- and two-family dwellings . . . . Chap. 22
Alarm systems in 22-3.3
Application of requirements for . . 22-1.1
Building services in 22-5
Heating equipment . . . 22-5.1, 31-6.7
Building spaces, subdivision
of . . . . 22-2.1.2(d)
Classification of 22-1.4
Contents of, hazard
classification 22-1.5
Detection systems in 22-3.3
Doors in 22-2.3, A-22-2.3
Extinguishment systems
in . . . . 22-2.1.2(d) Ex.1
General requirements of 22-1
Interior finish in 22-3.2
Locks in . . . 22-2.3.3, 22-2.3.5, A-22-2.3.5
Means of escape, requirements
for 22-2, A-22-2
Arrangement of 22-2.2
Number of 22-2.1
Primary 22-2.1.1
Second 22-2.1.2, A-22-2.1.2
Mixed occupancies with 22-1.2
Protection of 22-3
Smoke control in . . . . 22-2.1.2(d)
Stairs in 22-2.4
Windows in . . . . 22-2.1.2(c)
Open-air mercantile operations 24-4.3,
25-4.3
Definition . . . . 24-1.3(h), 25-1.3(h)
Open flame devices, assembly
occupancies 8-4.4.3, 9-4.3.3,
31-2.3, A-31-2.3
Open plan buildings . . . . see Buildings,
open plan
Openings . . . . see Floor openings;
Vertical openings; Wall openings
Operating features, requirements
for . . . . Chap. 31
Alarm systems 31-1.3.6, A-31-1.3.6
Automatic sprinkler
systems 31-1.3.5, A-31-1.3.5
Construction 31-1.1
Equipment maintenance 31-1.3
Fire detection systems 31-1.3.6,
A-31-1.3.6
Fire exit drills 31-1.5
Furnishings and decorations 31-1.2.2
General 31-1
Improvement operations 31-1.1
Maintenance 31-1.3
Means of egress reliability 31-1.2
Repairs 31-1.1
Testing 31-1.3
Outdoor assembly 8-4.3, 9-4.3
Outside ramps . . . . see Ramps
Outside stairs . . . . see Stairs

-P-

Paints, fire retardant 6-5.6
Panic A-1-3.1
Panic hardware 5-2.1.7
Parking garages . . . . . see Garages, parking
Partitions . . . . see also Smoke barriers

Folding, doors in 5-2.1.1
Passageways, exit . . . . see Exit passageways
Platforms 8-3.2.1, 9-3.2.1
Definition . 8-1.3, 9-1.3, A-8-1.3, A-9-1.3
Plenums 6-2.5.1, A-6-2.5.1
Definition 3-2
Point of safety
Definition 21-1.3
Pressurized stairs . . . . see Stairs
Procedure in case of fire, health care
occupancies 31-4.2, A-31-4.2
Projection booths 8-3.2.2, 9-3.2.2
Projection equipment 8-3.2.2.7
a and b), 9-3.2.2.7(a and b)
Projection rooms . . . 8-3.2.2, 9-3.2.2, 31-2.8
Proscenium wall
Definition 8-1.3
Protection . . . . see Fire protection;
Protection under specific occupancies
Protective signaling systems 7-6, A-7-6;
see also Alarm systems
Emergency control 7-6.5, A-7-6.5
Emergency forces notification 7-6.4,
A-7-6.4
General requirements 7-6.1, A-7-6.1
Location of controls 7-6.6
Maintenance of 31-1.3
Occupant notification 7-6.3, A-7-6.3
Signal initiation . . 7-6.1.7, 7-6.2, A-7-6.2
Public way
Definition 3-2
Purpose of code 1-2

-R-

Railings, assembly occupancies 8-2.11.1
Ramps
Classifications of 5-2.5.2, 5-3.3.1
Definition 3-2, 5-1.2.7, 5-2.5
Details for 5-2.5.4
Enclosure and protection
of 5-2.5.3, A-5-2.5.3
Outside
Separation and protection
of 5-2.5.3.3
Special provisions for 5-2.5.5
Visual protection of 5-2.5.3.5,
A-5-2.5.3.5
Separated exit 5-1.3.1
Renovation 1-4.6, A-1-4.6
Repair operations, requirements for . . 31-1.2
Resident
Definition 21-1.3
Residential board and care
occupancies . . . . Chap. 21
Alarm systems in 21-2.3.4, 21-3.3.4
Apartment buildings, requirements
for 21-1.1.1, 21-4
Apartments, individual,
requirements for 21-2,
21-4.1.1, 21-4.1.2

Application of general requirements
for 21-1.1, A-21-1.1
Building construction for 21-2.1.4,
21-3.1.4, 21-4.1.4
Building services in
Air conditioning . . 21-2.5.2, 21-3.5.2
Elevators 21-3.5.3
Heating 21-2.5.2, 21-3.5.2
Incinerators 21-3.5.4
Large facilities 21-3.5
Laundry chutes 21-3.5.4
Rubbish chutes 21-3.5.4
Small facilities 21-2.5
Utilities 21-2.5.1, 21-3.5.1
Ventilation 21-2.5.2, 21-3.5.2
Building spaces, subdivision
of 21-3.3.2.2,
21-3.3.6, 21-3.3.7, 21-4.3.3
Communications systems in 21-3.3.4
Corridors
Access 21-3.3.6
Construction of . . . 21-2.3.7, 21-4.3.2
Width of 21-3.2.3.3
Definitions 21-1.3, A-21-1.3
Detection systems 21-3.3.4
Detectors, smoke 21-2.3.5, 21-3.3.4.7
Doors in
Large facilities 21-3.2.2.2,
21-3.3.6.4 thru 21-3.3.6.6
Small facilities 21-2.2.5,
21-2.3.7.3, 21-2.3.7.4
Drills for 31-7.2, 31-7.3
Emergency lighting in 21-3.2.9
Emergency plan for 31-7.1
Evacuation capability 31-7.3
Apartment buildings 21-4.1.3,
A-21-4.1.3
Definition 21-1.3, A-21-1.3
Large facilities 21-3.1.3,
A-21-3.1.3
Small facilities 21-2.1.3,
A-21-2.1.3
Exits
Arrangement of 21-3.2.5
Discharge from 21-3.2.7
Number of 21-3.2.4
Travel distance to 21-3.2.6
Extinguishment systems/requirements
Large facilities . . . 21-2.3.2, 21-2.3.6
Small facilities . 21-3.3.5, A-21-3.3.5
Furnishings and decorations in . . 31-7.5.2
General requirements 21-1, 31-7
Hazardous areas in 21-2.3.2
Definition 21-1.3
High rise buildings 21-3.3.4.5,
21-3.3.5.2, 21-3.5.3.2
Interior finish in 21-2.3.3,
21-3.3.3, 21-4.3.1
Large facilities, requirements
for 21-1.1.1, 21-3
Locks in . . 21-2.2.5, 21-3.2.2.2, A-21-2.2.5

Means of egress ... 21-2.2, 21-3.2, 21-4.2
    Acceptability of 21-1.4, 31-7.3
    Capacity of 21-3.2.3
    Components of 21-3.2.2
    Illumination of 21-3.2.8
    Large facilities 21-3.2
    Marking of 21-3.2.10
Means of escape
    Acceptability of 21-1.4
    Arrangement of 21-2.2.2,
                   21-3.3.6.1 Ex.3
    Number of 21-2.2.1
    Primary 21-2.2.2
    Secondary 21-2.2.3
    Small facilities 21-2.2
Mixed occupancies of 21-1.2
Notification
    Fire department 21-3.3.4.6,
                   A-21-3.3.4.6
    Occupants 21-3.3.4.4
Occupant load of 21-3.1.5
Personal care
    Definition 21-1.3
Point of safety
    Definition 21-1.3
Protection 21-2.3, 21-3.3, 21-4.3
    Of hazardous areas 21-2.3.2,
                   21-3.3.2
    Of vertical openings 21-2.3.1,
                   21-3.3.1
Resident
    Definition 21-1.3
Small facilities, requirements
    for 21-1.1.1, 21-2
Smoke control in .... 21-2.2.3(d)
Smoking in 31-7.4
Special provisions for 21-3.4
Staff
    Definition 21-1.3
Stairs in 21-2.3.1.2, 21-3.2.3.3
    Enclosed interior 21-2.2.4
    Exterior 21-2.3.1.2
Windows in 21-3.4.1, A-21-3.4.1
Residential occupancies 4-1.6,
                   Chaps. 16-22
Combined mercantile
    and 24-1.2.1, 25-1.2.1
Emergency duties in 31-6.2
Emergency instructions for
    occupants 31-6.4
Emergency organization
    in hotels 31-6.1
General requirements for 31-6
Residential housing area
    Definition .... 14-1.3(d), 15-1.3(d)
Revolving doors 5-2.1.10
Rooming houses .... see Lodging or
                 rooming houses
Rooms
    Accessory, assembly
      occupancies 8-3.2.1.4,
                 9-3.2.1.4
    Definitions, educational
      occupancies 10-1.3, 11-1.3
    Interior, educational occupancies
      Definition 10-1.3, 11-1.3

Rubbish chutes ...... 7-5; see also Building
    services under specific occupancies

-S-

Safety film, storage of .. 8-3.2.2.2, 9-3.2.2.2
Sallyport
    Definition .... 14-1.3(e), 15-1.3(e)
Schools ...... see Educational occupancies
Scope of code 1-3, A-1-3
Screen doors 5-2.1.4.4
Seating .... see Assembly
               occupancies, seating
Seats
    Not secured to the floor 31-2.7.2
    Secured to the floor 31-2.7.1
Self-closing
    Definition 3-2
    Devices for doors 5-2.1.8, 5-2.3.11
Separate atmosphere, educational
   occupancies
    Definition 10-1.3, 11-1.3
Separate means of egress
    Definition 10-1.3, 11-1.3
Separated exit stair 5-1.3.1
Shopping centers .... see Mercantile
               occupancies
Signs
    Directional 5-10.4.1, A-5-10.4.1
    Exit 5-10, A-5-10
    Illumination of 5-10.3, A-5-10.3
    Low level 5-10.1.4, A-5-10.1.4
    Occupant load 31-2.7.3
    Projection room 31-2.8
    Size of 5-10.2, A-5-10.2
    Special 5-10.4.2, A-5-10.4.2
Slide escapes 5-2.10
    Capacity of 5-2.10.2
    Requirements for 5-2.10.1
Smoke barriers 6-2.4.1, 6-3, A-6-3
    Definition 3-2, 10-1.3, 11-1.3
    Doors in 6-3.4, A-6-3.4
    Fire barriers as 6-3.3
    Penetrations and openings in 6-3.6
    Smoke dampers 6-3.5
Smoke compartments 6-3
    Definition 3-2, A-3-2
Smoke control systems 7-3, A-7-3
    Maintenance of 31-1.3.2
Smoke detection systems .... see
    Detection systems; Detection systems
        under specific occupancies
Smoke detectors
    Definition 3-2
Smokeproof enclosures, for
   stairs 5-2.3, A-5-2.3
    Maintenance and testing of 31-1.3.9
Smoking
    Assembly occupancies 31-2.5
    Board and care occupancies 31-7.4
    Health care occupancies 31-4.4, A-31-4.4
Special purpose industrial
   occupancies .... 28-1.4(b)
Special structures .... 4-1.11; see also
           Unusual structures
Sprinklers .... see Automatic sprinklers

Stage scenery, assembly
  occupancies 31-2.6
Definition 8-1.3, 9-1.3
Smokeproof enclosures for 5-2.3,
                                    A-5-2.3
Spiral 5-2.2.2.7
Swinging 5-2.8.7, A-5-2.8.7
Treads for 5-2.2.4.4,
                      5-2.2.4.5, A-5-2.2.4.4
  Depth 5-2.2.2.3, A-5-2.2.2.3
  Slope 5-2.2.2.2, A-5-2.2.2.2
  Types of 5-2.2.2, A-5-2.2.2
  Vertical means of escape 22-2.4
  Winders in 5-2.2.2.8
Stages 8-3.2.1, 9-3.2.1
Arena
  Definition 3-2
Definition 8-1.3, 9-1.3
Thrust
  Definition 8-1.3, 9-1.3
Stairs 5-2.2, A-5-2.2;
    see also under specific occupancies
Construction of 5-2.2.4.1, 5-2.2.4.2
Curved 5-2.2.2.6
Details for 5-2.2.4, A-5-2.2.4
Dimensional criteria 5-2.2.2.1,
                              A-5-2.2.2.1
Enclosures and protection
  of 5-2.2.3, A-5-2.2.3
Fire escape .... see Fire escape stairs
Guards and handrails
  for 5-2.2.6, A-5-2.2.6
Landings 5-2.2.4.3
Marking of 5-2.2.3.6
Monumental 5-2.2.2.5
Outside 5-2.2.2.5, 5-2.2.5.3
  Definition 3-2
  Protection and separation
    of 5-2.2.3.3,
              5-2.2.3.4, A-5-2.2.3.3
  Special provisions
    for 5-2.2.5, A-5-2.2.5
Pressurized 5-2.3.9, 5-2.3.10.1
  Maintenance and testing ... 31-1.3.9
Riser height of ... 5-2.2.2.3, A-5-2.2.2.3
Separated exit 5-1.3.1
Contents of, hazard
  classification 29-1.5
Corridors, minimum width 29-2.3.2
Detection systems in 29-3.4
Doors in 29-2.2.2
Emergency lighting in 29-2.9
Exits
  Aircraft hangars 29-6.2, 29-6.3
  Horizontal 29-2.2.5,
                    29-6.2, A-29-2.2.5
  Number of 29-2.4
  Travel distance to .. 29-2.6, A-29-2.6
Extinguishment systems in ... 29-2.6 Ex.4
General requirements of 29-1.1
Grain or bulk storage

elevators 29-7, A-29-7
Interior finish in 29-3.3
Locks in 29-2.2.2.2, 29-2.11.1
Means of egress 29-2
  Aircraft hangars 29-6.2, 29-6.3
  Arrangement of 29-2.5
  Capacity of 29-2.3
  Components of 29-2.2
  Grain or bulk storage
    elevators .... 29-7.2 thru 29-7.4
  Illumination of 29-2.8
  Marking of 29-2.10
  Parking garages ...... see Garages,
                                    parking
Mixed occupancies of 29-1.2, 29-1.4
Notification 29-3.4.3
Parking garages ... see Garages, parking
Protection 29-3
  Of vertical openings 29-3.1
Special provisions for 29-4
  Aircraft hangars 29-6, A-29-6
  Grain or bulk storage
    elevators 29-7, A-29-7
  Parking garages 29-8, A-29-8
Stairs in 29-2.2.3, 29-7.2, 29-7.3
Underground spaces 29-7.4
Standpipe and hose system 7-7.4.2
Storage occupancies .... Chap. 29
Aircraft hangars 29-6, A-29-6
Alarm systems in 29-3.4
Application of requirements for .. 29-1.1
Building services 29-5
  Air conditioning 29-5.2
  Elevators 29-5.3
  Heating 29-5.2
  Incinerators 29-5.4
  Laundry chutes 29-5.4
  Rubbish chutes 29-5.4
  Utilities 29-5.1
  Ventilation 29-5.2
Classification of 4-1.10,
                        29-1.4, A-4-1.10
Communications systems in 29-3.4
Stores .... see also Mercantile occupancies
Classifications of 24-1.3,
              24-1.4.2.1, 25-1.3, 25-1.4.2.1
Definition 24-1, 25-1
Storm doors 5-2.1.4.4
Story 14-1.6.1, 15-1.6.1
Definition 3-2
Occupiable
  Definition 3-2
Street
Definition 3-2
Street floor
Definition 3-2
Structures
Definition 3-2
Mobile 1-3.5
Special, classification of 4-1.11;
              see also Unusual structures

Chapters 1-7 and 31 reference general requirements. Chapters 8, 10, 12, 14, 16, 18, 24 and 26 reference requirements for new occupancies. Chapters 9, 11, 13, 15, 17, 19, 25 and 27 reference requirements for existing occupancies. Chapters 20, 21, 22, 28, 29 and 30 reference requirements for both new and existing occupancies.

Underground .... 30-7.2; see
     also under specific occupancies
Subterranean buildings .... see
          Underground structures
Supervision, of automatic
     sprinklers 7-7.2, A-7-7.2
Swinging doors 5-2.1.4, 5-2.1.9,
          5-2.1.10(e), 5-2.4.3.4, A-5-2.1.4
Swinging stairs 5-2.8.7, A-5-2.8.7

-T-

Terminals .... see Storage occupancies
Terrace, entrance to assembly
     occupancy 8-2.7.3, 9-2.7.3
Testing, equipment .... 31-1.3; see also
                    Maintenance
Textile materials, interior
     finish 6-5.2.3, A-6-5.2.3
Theaters .... see Assembly occupancies
Thrust stage
     Definition 8-1.3, 9-1.3
Towers
     Definition 30-1.3.1
     Means of egress
          requirements 30-2.2.10.2,
          30-2.4.1 Ex.3, 30-2.7, A-30-2.4.1 Ex.3
     Protection of 30-3.1 Ex.1
Treated finishes, requirements for ... 31-1.4
Turnstiles 5-2.1.11

-U-

Underground structures .... 30-7.2; see
     also under specific occupancies
     Definition 30-1.3.4, A-30-1.3.4
Unusual structures .... Chap. 30
     Alarm systems in 30-3.4
     Application of requirements for .. 30-1.1
     Building services 30-5
          Air conditioning 30-5.2
          Elevators 30-5.3
          Heating 30-5.2
          Incinerators 30-5.4
          Laundry chutes 30-5.4
          Rubbish chutes 30-5.4
          Utilities 30-5.1
          Ventilation 30-5.2
     Classification of 30-1.4
     Communications systems in 30-3.4
     Corridors 30-3.6
          Minimum width 30-2.3.2
     Definitions 30-1.3
     Doors in 30-2.2.2
          Horizontal sliding 30-2.2.2.2,
                         30-2.2.2.3
     Detection systems in 30-3.4
     Emergency lighting in 30-2.9
     Escalators and moving walks
          in 30-2.2.8
     Exits
          Discharge from 30-2.7
          Number of 30-2.4
          Travel distance to 30-2.6
          Types of 30-2.2
     General requirements for 30-1

High rise buildings 30-4.2, 30-8
     Interior finish in 30-3.3
     Means of egress 30-2
          Arrangement of 30-2.5
          Capacity of 30-2.3
          Components of 30-2.2, A-30-2.2
          Illumination of 30-2.8
          Marking of 30-2.10
          Multi-storied structures 30-2.3.3
          Notification 30-3.4.3
          Occupant load of 30-1.7
          Open structures 30-2.2.10.2,
                         30-2.4.1 Ex.4
          Definition 30-1.3.7
          Piers 30-2.4.1 Ex.1, 30-2.5.3,
                         A-30-2.5.3
          Protection 30-3
               From hazards 30-3.2
               Of vertical openings 30-3.1
          Special provisions for 30-4
          Stairs in 30-2.2.3
          Towers .... see also Towers
          Definition 30-1.3.1
          Underground structures 30-7
          Definition 30-1.3.4, A-30-1.3.4
          Vehicles 30-6, A-30-6
          Definition 30-1.3.2
          Vessels 30-6, A-30-6
          Definition 30-1.3.3
          Water surrounded structures 30-1.1
          Definition 30-1.3.6
          Windowless structures 30-7
          Definition 30-1.3.5
Upholstered furniture 31-4.5.5
Utilities .... 7-1; see also Building
          services under specific occupancies

-V-

Vehicles 1-3.5, 30-6, A-30-6
     Definition 30-1.3.2
     Inside assembly
          occupancies 8-4.4.4, 9-4.4.4
Ventilation systems .... 7-2; see also
          Building services under
                    specific occupancies
     Smokeproof enclosures, stairs ... 5-2.3.7,
          5-2.3.8, 5-2.3.10, 5-2.3.12
Vertical conveyers 7-4
Vertical openings 6-2.4, A-6-2.4
     Definition 3-2
     Protection of .... see Protection,
                    vertical openings
Vessels 1-3.5, 30-6, A-30-6
     Definition 30-1.3.3
Visual protection
     Outside ramps 5-2.5.3.5, A-5-2.5.3.5
     Outside stairs 5-2.2.5.2, A-5-2.2.5.2

-W-

Waiting spaces, assembly
     occupancies 8-1.7.3, 9-1.7.3
Wall openings, protection of 5-2.4.4.7
Walls
     Corridor 5-1.3.4

Horizontal exits 5-2.4.3, A-5-2.4.3
Proscenium
    Definition 8-1.3
Warehouses .... see Storage occupancies
Water surrounded structures 30-1.1
Definition 30-1.3.6
Way, public
Definition 3-2
**Windowless areas, detention and
    correctional occupancies** 14-4.1,
                                       15-4.1
Windowless buildings .... 30-7; see also
                under specific occupancies

Windowless structures
Definition 30-1.3.5
Windows .... see also under
                        specific occupancies
Fire
    Definition 3-2
Fire barriers with 6-2.3.6
Workmanship, in means of egress 5-1.7

-Y-

Yard
Definition 3-2